*Literature
and the
Writing Process*

Literature and the Writing Process

ELIZABETH McMAHAN
ILLINOIS STATE UNIVERSITY

SUSAN DAY
ILLINOIS STATE UNIVERSITY

ROBERT FUNK
EASTERN ILLINOIS UNIVERSITY

MACMILLAN PUBLISHING COMPANY
NEW YORK

PRINTED IN THE UNITED STATES OF AMERICA

Macmillan Publishing Company
866 Third Avenue, New York, New York 10022

Collier Macmillan Canada, Inc.

LIBRARY OF CONGRESS CATALOGING-IN-PUBLICATION DATA

McMahan, Elizabeth.
   Literature and the writing process.

   Includes index.
   1. College readers.   2. English language—Rhetoric.
3. Literature—Collections.   I. Day, Susan.   II. Funk,
Robert.   III. Title.
PE1417.M45   1986   808′.0427   85–15602
ISBN 0-02-379740-1

Printing: 2   3   4   5   6   7   8   Year: 6   7   8   9   0   1   2   3   4   5

ACKNOWLEDGMENTS

Atheneum Publishers, Inc. W. S. MERWIN, "For the Anniversary of My Death" from *The
Lice.* Copyright © 1967 W. S. Merwin. Reprinted with the permission of Atheneum
Publishers, Inc.
Robert Bly. ROBERT BLY, "Driving to Town Late to Mail a Letter" © 1962. Reprinted by
permission of Robert Bly.
Jonathan Cape Ltd. HENRY REED, "Naming of Parts" from *A Map of Verona.* Reprinted by
permission of Jonathan Cape Ltd.
Corinth Books. IMAMU AMIRI BARAKA, "In Memory of Radio." Reprinted with the permission
of Corinth Books.
Jonathan Clowes Limited. DORIS LESSING, "A Woman on a Roof." Copyright © 1963 Doris
Lessing. Reprinted by permission of Jonathan Clowes Ltd., London, on behalf of Doris
Lessing.
Don Congdon Associates, Inc. RAY BRADBURY, "The Pedestrian." Copyright © 1966 by Ray
Bradbury and renewed in 1984 by Ray Bradbury. Reprinted by permission of Don Cong-
don Associates.
Dodd, Mead & Company, Inc. ARNA BONTEMPS, "A Summer Tragedy." Reprinted by permis-
sion of Dodd, Mead & Company, Inc. from *The Old South* by Arna Bontemps. Copyright
renewed 1961 by Arna Bontemps. Copyright © 1973 by Alberta Bontemps, Executrix.
Doubleday & Co., Inc. JAMES BALDWIN, "Sonny's Blues" from the book *Going to Meet the
Man* by James Baldwin. Copyright © 1948, 1951, 1957, 1958, 1960, 1965 by James Baldwin.
A Dial Press Book. Reprinted by permission of Doubleday & Co., Inc. THEODORE ROETHKE,

ISBN   0-02-379740-1

"My Papa's Waltz" by Theodore Roethke. Copyright 1942 by Hearst Magazines, Inc. From the book *The Collected Poems of Theodore Roethke.* Reprinted by permission of Doubleday & Co., Inc. "I Knew a Woman" by Theodore Roethke. Copyright 1954 by Theodore Roethke. From *The Collected Poems of Theodore Roethke.* Reprinted by permission of Doubleday & Co., Inc. "Elegy for Jane," copyright 1950 by Theodore Roethke from the book *The Collected Poems of Theodore Roethke* by Theodore Roethke. Reprinted by permission of Doubleday & Company, Inc. BASHO, "The Sudden Chillness" by Basho from *An Introduction of Haiku* translated by Harold Henderson. Copyright © 1958 by Harold G. Henderson. Reprinted by permission of Doubleday & Company, Inc.

Norma Millay Ellis. EDNA ST. VINCENT MILLAY, "Love is not all" from *Collected Poems,* Harper & Row. Copyright 1931, 1958 by Edna St. Vincent Millay and Norma Millay Ellis. "First Fig" from *Collected Poems,* Harper & Row. Copyright 1922, 1950 by Edna St. Vincent Millay.

Faber and Faber Ltd. T. S. ELIOT. "The Hollow Men" and "The Love Song of J. Alfred Prufrock." Reprinted by permission of Faber and Faber Ltd from *Collected Poems 1909–1962* by T. S. Eliot.

Farrar, Straus & Giroux, Inc. JOHN BERRYMAN, "Dream Song #14" from *77 Dream Songs* by John Berryman. Copyright © 1959, 1962, 1963, 1964 by John Berryman. RANDALL JARRELL, "Death of the Ball Turret Gunner" from *The Complete Poems* by Randall Jarrell. Copyright 1945, © 1969 by Mrs. Randall Jarrell. Copyright renewed © 1973 by Mrs. Randall Jarrell. SHIRLEY JACKSON, "The Lottery" from *The Lottery* by Shirley Jackson. Copyright 1948, 1949 by Shirley Jackson. Copyright renewed © 1976, 1977 by Laurence Hyman, Barry Hyman, Mrs. Sarah Webster, and Mrs. Joanne Schnurer. "The Lottery" appeared originally in *The New Yorker.* Reprinted by permission of Farrar, Straus and Giroux, Inc. ROBERT LOWELL, "Skunk Hour" from *Life Studies* by Robert Lowell. Copyright © 1956, 1959 by Robert Lowell. Reprinted by permission of Farrar, Straus and Giroux, Inc. ALBERT MORAVIA, "The Chase" © 1962. Reprinted by permission of Farrar, Straus & Giroux.

Ellis J. Freedman. ISHMAEL REED, "Beware: Do Not Read This Poem." Copyright © 1972, Ishmael Reed. Reprinted by permission.

Grove Press, Inc. H. D., "Heat" from *Selected Poems by H. D.* Reprinted by permission of Grove Press, Inc. HAROLD PINTER, *The Dumb Waiter.* Reprinted by permission of Grove Press, Inc. Copyright © 1960 by Harold Pinter. FERNANDO ARRABAL, *Picnic on the Battlefield.* Reprinted by permission of Grove Press, Inc. Copyright © 1967 by Calder and Boyars Ltd., London.

Donald Hall. DONALD HALL, "My Son, My Executioner" from *The Alligator Bride: Poems New and Selected.* Reprinted with permission of the author.

G. K. Hall & Co. CLAUDE MCKAY, "America" from *The Selected Poems of Claude McKay.* Copyright 1981 and reprinted with the permission of Twayne Publishers, a division of G. K. Hall & Co., Boston.

Harcourt Brace Jovanovich, Inc. KATHERINE ANNE PORTER, "The Jilting of Granny Weatherall." Copyright 1930, 1958 by Katherine Anne Porter. Reprinted from her volume *Flowering Judas and Other Stories* by permission of Harcourt Brace Jovanovich, Inc. EUDORA WELTY, "A Worn Path." Copyright 1941, 1969 By Eudora Welty. Reprinted from her volume *A Curtain of Green and Other Stories* by permission of Harcourt Brace Jovanovich, Inc. T. S. ELIOT, "The Love Song of J. Alfred Prufrock" and "The Hollow Men" from *Collected Poems 1909–1962* by T. S. Eliot, copyright 1936 by Harcourt Brace Jovanovich, Inc.; copyright © 1963, 1964 by T. S. Eliot. Reprinted by permission of the publisher. FLANNERY O'CONNOR, "Good Country People" from *A Good Man Is Hard to Find and Other Stories,* copyright © 1955 by Flannery O'Connor; renewed 1983 by Regina O'Connor. Reprinted by permission of Harcourt Brace Jovanovich, Inc. E. E. CUMMINGS, "anyone lived in a pretty how town." Copyright 1940 by E. E. Cummings; renewed 1968 by Marion Morehouse Cummings. Reprinted from *Complete Poems 1913–1962* E. E. Cummings by permission of Harcourt Brace Jovanovich, Inc. "pity this busy monster, manunkind." Copyright 1944 by E. E. Cummings; renewed 1972 by Nancy T. Andrews. Reprinted from *Complete Poems 1913–1962* by E. E. Cummings by permission of Harcourt Brace Jovanovich, Inc. CARL SANDBURG, "Fog" from *Chicago Poems* by Carl Sandburg, copyright 1916 by Holt, Rinehart and Winston, Inc.; renewed 1944 by Carl Sandburg. Reprinted by permission of Harcourt Brace Jovanovich, Inc. "Grass" from *Cornhuskers* by Carl Sandburg, copyright 1918 by Holt, Rinehart and Winston, Inc.; renewed 1946 by Carl Sandburg. Reprinted by permission of Harcourt Brace Jovanovich, Inc. SOPHOCLES, from *The Antigone of Sophocles:* An English Version by Dudley Fitts and Robert Fitzgerald, copyright 1939 by Harcourt Brace Jovanovich, Inc.; renewed 1967 by Dudley Fitts and Robert Fitzgerald. Reprinted by permission of the publisher. *Caution:* All rights, including professional, amateur, motion picture, recitation, lecturing, performance, public reading, radio broadcasting, and television are strictly reserved. Inquiries on all rights should be addressed to Harcourt Brace Jovanovich, Inc., 111 Fifth Avenue, New York, NY 10003. RICHARD WILBUR, "First Snow in Alsace" from *The Beautiful Changes and Other Poems,* copyright 1947, 1975 by Richard Wilbur. Reprinted by permission of Harcourt Brace Jovanovich, Inc.

Harper & Row, Publishers, Inc. SYLVIA PLATH, "The Rival." Copyright © 1962 by Ted Hughes. "Daddy." Copyright © 1963 by Ted Hughes from *The Collected Poems of Sylvia Plath* by Sylvia Plath. Reprinted by permission of Harper & Row, Publishers, Inc. GWENDOLYN BROOKS, "A Song in the Front Yard" and "Kitchenette Building." Copyright 1944 by Gwendolyn Brooks. Reprinted by permission of Harper & Row, Publishers, Inc. "We Real Cool"—The Pool Players. Seven at the Golden Shovel. Copyright © 1959 by Gwendolyn Brooks from *The World of Gwendolyn Brooks* by Gwendolyn Brooks. COUNTEE CULLEN, "Incident" from *On These I Stand* by Countee Cullen. Copyright 1925 by Harper & Row, Publishers, Inc. Renewed 1953 by Ida M. Cullen. Reprinted by permission of Harper & Row, Publishers, Inc. ALLEN GINSBERG, "A Supermarket in California" from *Collected Poems 1947–1980* by Allen Ginsberg (1984) Copyright © 1955 by Allen Ginsberg. By permission of Harper & Row, Publishers, Inc.

Harvard University Press. EMILY DICKINSON, "It was not death, for I stood up," "She rose to his requirement," "Because I could not stop for death," "The Soul selects her own society," "I heard a fly buzz—when I died," "Much madness is divinest sense," "She dealt her pretty words like blades," "He put the belt around my life." Reprinted by permission of the publishers and the Trustees of Amherst College from *The Poems of Emily Dickinson,* edited by Thomas H. Johnson, Cambridge, Mass. The Belknap Press of Harvard University Press, Copyright 1951, © 1955, 1979, 1983 by The President and Fellows of Harvard College.

David Higham Associates Limited. DYLAN THOMAS, "Do not go gentle into that good night," "The hand that signed the paper," and "The force that through the green fuse drives the flower" from *Collected Poems,* published by Dent. Reprinted by permission of David Higham Associated Limited, London.

Holt, Rinehart and Winston, A. E. HOUSMAN, "Loveliest of trees, the cherry now," "To an Athlete Dying Young," and "When I was One- and Twenty" from "A Shropshire Lad"— authorized edition—from *The Collected Poems of A. E. Housman.* Copyright 1939, 1940, © 1965 by Holt, Rinehart and Winston. Copyright © 1967, 1968 by Robert E. Symons. Reprinted by permission of Holt, Rinehart and Winston, Publishers. "Eight O'Clock" from *The Collected Poems of A. E. Housman.* Copyright 1922 by Holt, Rinehart and Winston. Copyright 1950 by Barclays Bank Ltd. Reprinted by permission of Holt, Rinehart and Winston, Publishers. ROBERT FROST, "Design," "Fire and Ice," "Neither Out Far Nor In Deep," "Mending Wall," "Desert Places," "Birches," and "The Silken Tent" from *The Poetry of Robert Frost* edited by Edward Connery Lathem. Copyright 1916, 1923, 1930, 1939, © 1969 by Holt, Rinehart and Winston. Copyright 1936, 1942, 1944, 1951, © 1958 by Robert Frost. Copyright © 1964, 1967, 1970 by Lesley Frost Ballantine. Reprinted by permission of Holt, Rinehart and Winston, Publishers.

Houghton Mifflin Company. ARCHIBALD MACLEISH, "Ars Poetica" from *New and Collected Poems 1917–1976* by Archibald MacLeish. Copyright © 1976 by Archibald MacLeish. Reprinted by permission of Houghton Mifflin Company. ANNE SEXTON, "You All Know the Story of the Other Woman" from *Love Poems* by Anne Sexton. Copyright © 1967, 1968, 1969 by Anne Sexton. Reprinted by permission of Houghton Mifflin Company.

Olwyn Hughes. SYLVIA PLATH, Canadian rights for "The Rival" and "Daddy," from *Ariel* by Sylvia Plath, published by Faber & Faber, London, copyright Ted Hughes 1965.

Ursula K. Le Guin. URSULA K. LE GUIN, "The Ones Who Walk Away from Omelas." Copyright © 1973, 1975 by Ursula K. Le Guin; reprinted by permission of the author and the author's agent, Virginia Kidd.

Little, Brown and Company. OGDEN NASH, "The Parent," "The Cow," and "Reflections on Ingenuity" from *Verses from 1929 On* by Ogden Nash. Copyright 1930, 1931, 1933 by Ogden Nash. By permission of Little, Brown and Company. "Grandpa is ashamed" from *There's Always Another Rainbow* by Ogden Nash. Copyright © 1966 by Ogden Nash. By permission of Little, Brown and Company. "Common Sense" from *The Face Is Familiar* by Ogden

Nash. Copyright 1931 by Ogden Nash. By permission of Little, Brown and Company. EMILY DICKINSON, "Poem #479" from *The Complete Poems of Emily Dickinson.* Edited by Thomas H. Johnson. Copyright 1929 by Martha Dickinson Bianchi; copyright © renewed 1957 by Mary L. Hampson.

Liveright Publishing Corporation. E. E. CUMMINGS, "O sweet spontaneous." Reprinted from *Tulips & Chimneys* by E. E. Cummings by permission of Liveright Publishing Corporation. Copyright 1923, 1925 and renewed 1951, 1953 by E. E. Cummings. Copyright © 1973, 1976 by The Trustees for the E. E. Cummings Trust. Copyright © 1973, 1976 by George James Firmage. "next to of course god america i" and "since feeling is first." Reprinted from *IS 5* poems by E. E. Cummings by permission of Liveright Publishing Corporation. Copyright © 1985 by E. E. Cummings Trust. Copyright 1926 by Horace Liveright. Copyright © 1954 by E. E. Cummings. Copyright © 1985 by George James Firmage. JEAN TOOMER. "Reapers" is reprinted from *Cane* by Jean Toomer, by permission of Liveright Publishing Corporation. Copyright 1923 by Boni & Liveright. Copyright renewed 1951 by Jean Toomer.

Louisiana State University Press. KATE CHOPIN, "The Storm" from *The Complete Works of Kate Chopin,* edited by Per Seyersted. By permission of Louisiana State University Press.

Macmillan Publishing Company, Inc. W. B. YEATS, "Sailing to Byzantium." Reprinted with permission of Macmillan Publishing Company from *The Poems* by W. B. Yeats, edited by Richard J. Finneran. Copyright 1928 by Macmillan Publishing Company, renewed 1956. "The Second Coming." Reprinted by permission of Macmillan Publishing Company from *The Poems* by W. B. Yeats, edited by Richard J. Finneran. Copyright 1924 by Macmillan Publishing Company, renewed 1952 by Bertha Georgie Yeats. "The Wild Swans at Coole." Reprinted with permission of Macmillan Publishing Company from *The Poems* by W. B. Yeats, edited by Richard J. Finneran. Copyright 1919 by Macmillan Publishing Company, renewed 1947 by Bertha Georgie Yeats. MARIANNE MOORE, "Poetry." Reprinted with permission of Macmillan Publishing Company from *Collected Poems* by Marianne Moore. Copyright 1935 by Marianne Moore, renewed 1963 by Marianne Moore and T. S. Eliot. EDWIN ARLINGTON ROBINSON, "Eros Turannos." Reprinted with permission of Macmillan Publishing Company from *Collected Poems* by Edwin Arlington Robinson. Copyright 1916 by Edwin Arlington Robinson, renewed 1944 by Ruth Nivison. THOMAS HARDY, "The Darkling Thrush," "The Ruined Maid," and "Channel Firing" from *The Complete Poems of Thomas Hardy,* edited by James Gibson (New York: Macmillan, 1978). Courtesy of Macmillan Publishing Company.

The Marvell Press. PHILIP LARKIN. "Poetry of Departures" by Philip Larkin is reprinted from *The Less Deceived* by permission of The Marvell Press, England.

Mnemosyne Publishing Inc. PAUL LAWRENCE DUNBAR, "We Wear the Mask" from *Lyrics of Lowly Life.* Reprinted by permission of Mnemosyne Publishing Inc.

William Morrow & Company, Inc. NIKKI GIOVANNI, "Dreams" from *Black Feeling, Black Talk, Black Judgment* by Nikki Giovanni. Copyright © 1968, 1970 by Nikki Giovanni. By permission of William Morrow & Company. "Woman Poem" from *Black Feeling, Black Talk, Black Judgment* by Nikki Giovanni. Copyright © 1968, 1970 by Nikki Giovanni. By permission of William Morrow & Company.

John Murray (Publishers) Ltd. JOHN BETJEMAN, "In Westminster Abbey." Reprinted by permission of John Murray (Publishers) Ltd.

Howard Nemerov. HOWARD NEMEROV, "The Town Dump" from *The Collected Poems of Howard Nemerov.* The University of Chicago Press, 1977. Reprinted by permission of the author.

New Directions Publishing Corporation. DENISE LEVERTOV, "The Ache of Marriage." Denise Levertov, *Poems 1960–1967.* Copyright © 1964 by Denise Levertov Goodman. YUKIO MISHIMA, "Patriotism." Yukio Mishima, *Death in Midsummer.* Copyright © 1966 by New Directions Publishing Corporation. GARY SNYDER, "Running Water Music." Gary Snyder, *Regarding Wave.* Copyright © 1970 by Gary Snyder. DYLAN THOMAS, "Do not go gentle . . . ," "The Hand that Signed the Paper," and "The Force That Through. . . ." Dylan Thomas, *The Poems of Dylan Thomas.* Copyright 1939 by New Directions Publishing Corporation; copyright 1952 by Dylan Thomas. WILFRED OWEN, "Dulce et Decorum Est." Wilfred Owen, *The Collected Poems of Wilfred Owen.* Copyright © 1963 by Chatto and Windus Ltd. EZRA POUND, "The River Merchant's Wife" and "In a Station of the Metro." Ezra Pound, *Personae.* Copyright 1926 by Ezra Pound. STEVIE SMITH, "Not Waving But Drowning." Stevie Smith, *Collected Poems.* Copyright © 1972 by Stevie Smith. WILLIAM CARLOS WILLIAMS, "Dance Russe" and "The Red Wheelbarrow." William Carlos Williams,

The Collected Earlier Poems. Copyright 1938 by New Directions Publishing Corporation. Reprinted by permission of New Directions Publishing Corporation.

W. W. Norton & Company, Inc. ADRIENNE RICH, "Living in Sin," "Aunt Jennifer's Tigers," and "The Middle-Aged." Reprinted from *The Fact of a Doorframe, Poems Selected and New, 1950–1974*, by Adrienne Rich, by permission of W. W. Norton & Company, Inc. Copyright © 1984 by Adrienne Rich. Copyright © 1975, 1978 by W. W. Norton & Company, Inc. Copyright © 1981 by Adrienne Rich.

Oxford University Press, Inc. RICHARD EBERHART, "The Fury of Aerial Bombardment" from *Collected Poems 1930–1976* by Richard Eberhart. Copyright © 1960, 1976 by Richard Eberhart. Reprinted by permission of Oxford University Press, Inc. ANTON CHEKHOV, "The Marriage Proposal." © Ronald Hingley 1968. Reprinted from *The Oxford Chekhov:* vol. 1 *Short Plays*, translated and edited by Ronald Hingley (1968) by permission of Oxford University Press. REED WHITTEMORE, "Clamming," "The Fall of the House of Usher" © 1965, 1970. Reprinted by permission of Oxford University Press.

Dudley Randall. DUDLEY RANDALL, "Ballad of Birmingham" from *Poem Counterpoem*, copyright 1966, and "To the Mercy Killers," copyright 1966 by *Negro Digest*. Reprinted by permission of the author.

Random House, Inc. Alfred A. Knopf. W. H. AUDEN, "The Unknown Citizen" "Lullaby" and "Musee des Beaux Arts." Copyright 1940 and renewed 1968 by W. H. Auden. Reprinted from *W. H. Auden: Collected Poems*, edited by Edwin Mendelson, by permission of Random House, Inc. PAUL GOODMAN, "Haiku poem," by permission of Random House, Inc. STEPHEN SPENDER, "An Elementary School Classroom in a Slum." Copyright 1942 and renewed 1970 by Stephen Spender. Reprinted from *Collected Poems 1928–1953*, by Stephen Spender, by permission of Random House, Inc. KATHERINE MANSFIELD, "Bliss." Copyright 1920 by Alfred A. Knopf, Inc. and renewed 1948 by John Middleton Murray. Reprinted from *The Short Stories of Katherine Mansfield*, by permission of the publisher. TENNESSEE WILLIAMS, "The Glass Menagerie." From *The Glass Menagerie*, by Tennessee Williams. Copyright 1945 by Tennessee Williams and Edwina Williams and renewed 1973 by Tennessee Williams. Reprinted by permission of Random House, Inc. WILLIAM FAULKNER, "A Rose for Emily." Copyright 1930 and renewed 1958 by William Faulkner. Reprinted from *Collected Stories of William Faulkner*, by permission of Random House, Inc. KARL SHAPIRO, "Auto Wreck." Copyright 1942 and renewed 1970 by Karl Shapiro. Reprinted from *Collected Poems 1940–1978*, by Karl Shapiro, by permission of Random House, Inc. ROBINSON JEFFERS, "November Surf" and "Hurt Hawks." Copyright 1928, 1932 and renewed 1956, 1960 by Robinson Jeffers. Reprinted from *Selected Poems*, by Robinson Jeffers, by permission of Random House, Inc. JOHN UPDIKE, "A & P." Copyright © 1962 by John Updike. Reprinted from *Pigeon Feathers and Other Stories*, by John Updike, by permission of Alfred A. Knopf, Inc. Originally appeared in *The New Yorker*. WALLACE STEVENS, "The Snow Man," "The Emperor of Ice-Cream," and "Anecdote of the Jar." Copyright 1923 and renewed 1951 by Wallace Stevens. Reprinted from *The Collected Poems of Wallace Stevens*, by permission of Alfred A. Knopf, Inc. LANGSTON HUGHES, "Harlem (Dream Deferred)" and "Puzzled (Here on the Edge of Hell)." Copyright 1951 by Langston Hughes. Copyright 1948 by Alfred A. Knopf, Inc. Reprinted from *The Panther and the Lash: Poems of Our Times*, by Langston Hughes, by permission of Alfred A. Knopf, Inc. JOHN CROWE RANSOM, "Bells for John Whiteside's Daughter." Copyright 1924 by Alfred A. Knopf, Inc. and renewed 1952 by John Crowe Ransom. Reprinted from *Selected Poems*, Third Edition, Revised and Enlarged, by John Crowe Ransom, by permission of the publisher. W. D. SNODGRASS, "April Inventory." Copyright © 1957 by W. D. Snodgrass. Reprinted from *Heart's Needle*, by W. D. Snodgrass, by permission of Alfred A. Knopf, Inc.

Schocken Books Inc. FRANZ KAFKA, "A Hunger Artist." Reprinted by permission of Schocken Books Inc. from *The Penal Colony* by Franz Kafka, trans. Willa and Edwin Muir. Copyright © 1948, 1976 by Schocken Books Inc.

Scott, Foresman and Company. DAVID BEVINGTON, "footnotes only to accompany *Othello* from *The Complete Works of Shakespeare*. Copyright © 1980, 1973 by Scott, Foresman and Company. Reprinted by permission.

Charles Scribner's Sons. RING LARDNER, "Haircut" from *The Love Nest and Other Stories*. Copyright 1925 Ellis Lardner; copyright renewed 1953. Reprinted with the permission of Charles Scribner's Sons. ERNEST HEMINGWAY, "Hills Like White Elephants" from *The Short Stories of Ernest Hemingway*. Copyright 1938 Ernest Hemingway; copyright renewed © 1966 Mary Hemingway. Reprinted with the permission of Charles Scribner's Sons. ROBERT CREELEY, "A Marriage" from *For Love: Poems 1950–1960*. Copyright © 1962 Robert Creeley. Reprinted with the permission of Charles Scribner's Sons. CAROLYN WELLS, "There was a young fellow named Tate" courtesy Charles Scribner's Sons. HENRIK IBSEN, "Hedda Gabler" courtesy Charles Scribner's Sons. EDWIN ARLINGTON ROBINSON, "Reuben Bright" from *The Children of the Night* by Edwin Arlington Robinson. Reprinted with the permission of Charles Scribner's Sons.

Simon & Schuster. DORIS LESSING, "A Woman on a Roof" from *A Man and Two Women* by Doris Lessing. © 1958, 1962, 1963 by Doris Lessing. Reprinted by permission of Simon & Schuster.

Helen W. Thurber and Rosemary T. Sauers. JAMES THURBER, "The Secret Life of Walter Mitty." Copr. © 1942 James Thurber. Copr. © 1970 Helen W. Thurber and Rosemary T. Sauers. From *My World—And Welcome to It*, published by Harcourt Brace Jovanovich.

The Vanguard Press. JOYCE CAROL OATES, "Where Are You Going, Where Have You Been?" from *The Wheel of Love and Other Stories* by Joyce Carol Oates. Copyright 1967, 1970 by Joyce Carol Oates. Reprinted by permission of Vanguard Press.

Viking Penguin Inc. JAMES JOYCE, "Araby" and "Eveline" from *Dubliners* by James Joyce. Copyright 1916 by B. W. Huebsch. Definitive text copyright © 1967 by the Estate of James Joyce. Reprinted by permission of Viking Penguin Inc. JOHN STEINBECK, "The Chrysanthemums" from *The Long Valley* by John Steinbeck. Copyright 1937, renewed © 1965 by John Steinbeck. Reprinted by permission of Viking Penguin Inc. SHERWOOD ANDERSON, "Nobody Knows" from *Winesburg, Ohio* by Sherwood Anderson. Copyright 1919 by B. W. Heubsch, copyright renewed 1947 by Eleanor Copenhaven Anderson. Reprinted by permission of Viking Penguin Inc. D. H. LAWRENCE, "The Rocking Horse Winner" from *The Complete Short Stories of D. H. Lawrence*. Copyright 1933 by the Estate of D. H. Lawrence. Copyright renewed 1961 by Angelo Ravagli and C. Montague Weekley, Executors of the Estate of Frieda Lawrence Ravagli. Reprinted by permission of Viking Penguin Inc. "Snake" and "Piano" from *The Complete Poems of D. H. Lawrence*, Collected and edited by Vivian de Sola Pinto and F. Warren Roberts. Copyright © 1964, 1971 by Angelo Ravagli and C. M. Weekley, Executors of the Estate of Frieda Lawrence Ravagli. Reprinted by permission of Viking Penguin Inc. DOROTHY PARKER, "One Perfect Rose" from *The Portable Dorothy Parker*. Copyright 1926, renewed © 1954 by Dorothy Parker. Reprinted by permission of Viking Penguin Inc. MAXINE KUMIN, "Woodchucks" from *Our Ground Time Here Will Be Brief* by Maxine Kumin. Copyright © 1971 by Maxine Kumin. Reprinted by permission of Viking Penguin Inc. ARTHUR MILLER, *Death of a Salesman* by Arthur Miller. Copyright 1939, renewed © 1977 by Arthur Miller. Reprinted by permission of Viking Penguin Inc.

A. P. Watt Ltd. ROBERT GRAVES, "The Cool Web" from *Collected Poems 1975*. Reprinted by permission of Robert Graves.

Wesleyan University Press. JAMES WRIGHT, "A Blessing." Copyright © 1961 by James Wright. Reprinted from *Collected Poems* by permission of Wesleyan University Press.

Preface

This text grew out of our long-standing interest in the possibilities of integrating the studies of literature and composition. Many of our students have learned to write thoughtfully and correctly using literature as their material. Great literature is always thought-provoking, always new: why not mobilize it in the pursuit of a valuable skill? Toward that end, we have combined an introduction to literature with concurrent instruction in writing.

Literature and the Writing Process presents literary selections as material for the students to read and write about, not as models for them to emulate. The text is designed to guide the students step by step through the allied processes of critical reading and critical writing. The writing instruction, concurrent with the literary study, follows a well-established order beginning with larger questions of organization and proceeding to particular issues like word choice and manuscript form. The writing assignments also follow a clearly defined arrangement beginning with descriptive writing and ending with argumentation and the research paper.

Part One of the text provides an overview of the composition process—prewriting, writing, and rewriting—using James Joyce's short story "Eveline" as subject matter for writing exercises and short papers. Parts Two, Three, and Four provide chapters offering specific advice about analyzing short fiction, poetry, and drama, plus instruction for composing essays about this literature. Each of these parts begins with a set of questions for students to apply to that type of literature and concludes with an anthology of the genre it covers. The drama section has a chapter on researched writing about literature—advice on doing bibliographical work, note taking, integrating sources, using MLA documentation, and avoiding plagiarism. Realizing that previous writing courses may not have completely eradicated sentence-level problems, we have included at the book's end a concise handbook for correcting errors. This handbook will serve as a reference, as will the glossary of literary and rhetorical terms which follows it.

The composition theory integrated into this book has been informed by the valuable work of James Moffett, James Kinneavy, Janet Emig, Nancy Sommers, and Linda Flower. The approach to literature is basically formalist, which we feel applies most directly to traditional rhetoric, with some added spice from reader response theory. Throughout the process of writing we have been helped by our reviewers, Brian S. Best, Brigham Young University; Robert P. Burke, Joliet Junior College; Peggy Cole, Arapahoe Community College; Paul B. Davis, University of New Mexico; Paul D. Farkas, Metropolitan State College; Michael C. Flanigan, University of Oklahoma; Elaine Ginsberg, West Virginia University; Phillip A. Holcomb, Angelo State University; Robert M. Holland, University of Akron; Stanley J. Kozikowski, Bryant College; Jack Matthews, Ohio University; Russell J. Meyer, University of Missouri—Columbia; Robin C. Mitchell, Brookfield Academy; George Miller, University of Delaware; John J. Ruszkiewicz, University of Texas at Austin; Katherine Speyer, Macmillan Publishing Company; A. D. Van Nostrand, Georgia Institute of Technology; Elizabeth Wahlquist, Brigham Young University. And for supporting us in ways from the most practical to the most subtle, our warm gratitude goes to Mark Silverstein, Cynthia Brophy, Mark Tappmeyer, Tim Bidle, Bryan Dahldorf, Dan LeSeure, Dave Isenberg, Margaret Scarry, Robert Freese, for his excellent design, and our incomparable editors, Pat Cabeza and Tony English.

Elizabeth McMahan
Susan Day
Robert Funk

Contents

PART TWO *Writing about Short Fiction* 43

Anthology of Short Fiction   *119*

PART THREE *Writing about Poetry* 381

Anthology of Poetry   *429*

PART FOUR *Writing about Drama*   *555*

## *Anthology of Drama*									*679*

## PART FIVE *The Editing Process*					*959*

## *A Handbook for Correcting Errors*					*961*

PART ONE

Composing: An Overview

This text serves a dual purpose: to enable you to enjoy, understand, and learn from imaginative literature; and to help you to write clearly, intelligently, and correctly about what you have learned. For most people, the most difficult part of the writing process is getting started. We will provide help at this stage and then show you how to follow through to the completion of a finished paper you can be proud of.

1

The Prewriting Process

Your study of writing, as we approach it in this book, will focus on the composing process: prewriting, writing, rewriting, and editing. The first section of the text takes you through each stage, explaining one way of putting together a paper on James Joyce's "Eveline." The following sections, which include more short stories, plus poems and plays, offer further advice for understanding and writing about these various kinds of literature.

We realize, of course, that our chronological, linear (step-by-step) explanations of the writing process are not entirely true to experience; most of us juggle at least two of the steps at a time when we write. We put down half a sentence, go back and revise it, make notes of some details to include later in the essay, and then finish the sentence, perhaps crossing out and correcting a misspelled word—a combination of prewriting, writing, rewriting, and editing. We have of necessity adopted the linear, step-by-step presentation because it allows us to explain this complicated process.

Reading for Writing

To prepare yourself for our discussion of the stages of writing an essay about a literary topic, find a comfortable spot and read the following short story.

James Joyce *1882–1941*

EVELINE

She sat at the window watching the evening invade the avenue. Her head was leaned against the window curtains and in her nostrils was the odour of dusty cretonne. She was tired.

Few people passed. The man out of the last house passed on his way home; she heard his footsteps clacking along the concrete pavement and afterwards crunching on the cinder path before the new red houses. One time there used to be a field there in which they used to play every evening with other people's children. Then a man from Belfast bought the field and built houses in it—not like their little brown houses but bright brick houses with shining roofs. The children of the avenue used to play together in that field—the Devines, the Waters, the Dunns, little Keogh the cripple, she and her brothers and sisters. Ernest, however, never played: he was too grown up. Her father used often to hunt them in out of the field with his blackthorn stick; but usually little Keogh used to keep *nix* and call out when he saw her father coming. Still they seemed to have been rather happy then. Her father was not so bad then; and besides, her mother was alive. That was a long time ago; she and her brothers and sisters were all grown up; her mother was dead. Tizzie Dunn was dead, too, and the Waters had gone back to England. Everything changes. Now she was going to go away like the others, to leave her home.

Home! She looked round the room, reviewing all its familiar objects which she had dusted once a week for so many years, wondering where on earth all the dust came from. Perhaps she would never see again those familiar objects from which she had never dreamed of being divided. And yet during all those years she had never found out the name of the priest whose yellowing photograph hung on the wall above the broken harmonium beside the coloured print of the promises made to Blessed Margaret Mary Alacoque. He had been a school friend of her father. Whenever he showed the photograph to a visitor her father used to pass it with a casual word:

"He is in Melbourne now."

She had consented to go away, to leave her home. Was that wise? She tried to weigh each side of the question. In her home anyway she had shelter and food; she had those whom she had known all her life about her. Of course she had to work hard, both in the house and at business. What would they say of her in the Stores when they found out that she had run away with a fellow? Say she was a fool, perhaps; and her place would be filled up by advertisement. Miss Gavan would be glad. She had always had an edge on her, especially whenever there were people listening.

"Miss Hill, don't you see these ladies are waiting?"

"Look lively, Miss Hill, please."

She would not cry many tears at leaving the Stores.

But in her new home, in a distant unknown country, it would not be like that. Then she would be married—she, Eveline. People would treat her with respect then. She would not be treated as her mother had been. Even now, though she was over nineteen, she sometimes felt herself in danger of her father's violence. She knew it was that that had given her the palpitations. When they were growing up he had never gone for her, like he used to go for Harry and Ernest, because she was a girl; but latterly he had begun to threaten her and say what he would do to her only for her dead mother's sake. And now she had nobody to protect her. Ernest was dead and Harry, who was in the church decorating business, was nearly always down somewhere in the country. Besides, the invariable squabble for money on Saturday nights had begun to weary her unspeakably. She always gave her entire wages—seven shillings—and Harry always sent up what he could but the trouble was to get any money from her father. He said she used to squander the money, that she had no head, that he wasn't going to give her his hard-earned money to throw about the streets, and much more, for he was usually fairly bad on Saturday night. In the end he would give her the money and ask her had she any intention of buying Sunday's dinner. Then she had to rush out as quickly as she could and do her marketing, holding her black leather purse tightly in her hand as she elbowed her way through the crowds and returning home late under her load of provisions. She had hard work to keep the house together and to see that the two young children who had been left to her charge went to school regularly and got their meals regularly. It was hard work—a hard life—but now that she was about to leave it she did not find it a wholly undesirable life.

She was about to explore another life with Frank. Frank was very kind, manly, open-hearted. She was to go away with him by the night-boat to be his wife and to live with him in Buenos Ayres where he had a home waiting for her. How well she remembered the first time she had seen him; he was lodging in a house on the main road where she used to visit. It seemed a few weeks ago. He was standing at the gate, his peaked cap pushed back on his head and his hair tumbled forward over a face of bronze. Then they had come to know each other. He used to meet her outside the Stores every evening and see her home. He took her to see *The Bohemian Girl* and she felt elated as she sat in an unaccustomed part of the theatre with him. He was awfully fond of music and sang a little. People knew that they were courting and, when he sang about the lass that loves a sailor, she always felt pleasantly confused. He used to call her Poppens out of fun. First of all it had been an excitement for her to have a fellow and then she had begun to like him. He had tales of distant countries. He had started as a deck boy at a pound a month on a ship of the Allan Line going out to Canada. He told her the names of the ships he had been on and the names of the different services. He had sailed through the Straits of Magellan and he told her stories of the terrible Patagonians. He had fallen on his feet in Buenos Ayres, he said, and had come over to the old country just for a holiday. Of course, her father had found out the affair and had forbidden her to have anything to say to him.

"I know these sailor chaps," he said.

One day he had quarrelled with Frank and after that she had to meet her lover secretly.

The evening deepened in the avenue. The white of two letters in her lap grew indistinct. One was to Harry; the other was to her father. Ernest had been her favourite but she liked Harry too. Her father was becoming old lately, she noticed; he would miss her. Sometimes he could be very nice. Not long before, when she had been laid up for a day, he had read her out a ghost story and made toast for her at the fire. Another day, when their mother was alive, they had all gone for a picnic to the Hill of Howth. She remembered her father putting on her mother's bonnet to make the children laugh.

Her time was running out but she continued to sit by the window, leaning her head against the window curtain, inhaling the odour of dusty cretonne. Down far in the avenue she could hear a street organ playing. She knew the air. Strange that it should come that very night to remind her of the promise to her mother, her promise to keep the home together as long as she could. She remembered the last night of her mother's illness; she was again in the close dark room at the other side of the hall and outside she heard a melancholy air of Italy. The organ-player had been ordered to go away and given sixpence. She remembered her father strutting back into the sickroom saying:

"Damned Italians! coming over here!"

As she mused the pitiful vision of her mother's life laid its spell on the very quick of her being—that life of commonplace sacrifices closing in final craziness. She trembled as she heard again her mother's voice saying constantly with foolish insistence:

"Derevaun Seraun! Derevaun Seraun!"[1]

She stood up in a sudden impulse of terror. Escape! She must escape! Frank would save her. He would give her life, perhaps love, too. But she wanted to live. Why should she be unhappy? She had a right to happiness. Frank would take her in his arms, fold her in his arms. He would save her.

She stood among the swaying crowd in the station at the North Wall. He held her hand and she knew that he was speaking to her, saying something about the passage over and over again. The station was full of soldiers with brown baggages. Through the wide doors of the sheds she caught a glimpse of the black mass of the boat, lying in beside the quay wall, with illumined portholes. She answered nothing. She felt her cheek pale and cold and, out of a maze of distress, she prayed to God to direct her, to show her what was her duty. The boat blew a long mournful whistle into the mist. If she went, tomorrow she would be on the sea with Frank, steaming towards Buenos Ayres. This passage had been booked. Could she still draw back after all he had done for her? Her distress awoke a nausea in her body and she kept moving her lips in silent fervent prayer.

A bell clanged upon her heart. She felt him seize her hand:

"Come!"

All the seas of the world tumbled about her heart. He was drawing her into them: he would drown her. She gripped with both hands at the iron railing.

---

[1] "The end of pleasure is pain!"

"Come!"

No! No! No! It was impossible. Her hands clutched the iron in frenzy. Amid the seas she sent a cry of anguish.

"Eveline! Evvy!"

He rushed beyond the barrier and called to her to follow. He was shouted at to go on but he still called to her. She set her white face to him, passive, like a helpless animal. Her eyes gave him no sign of love or farewell or recognition.

(1914)

Now that your reading of Joyce's story has given you material to mull over, you should consider some things that good writers think about as they prepare to write. Granted, experienced writers might go over some of these prewriting matters almost unconsciously—and perhaps *as* they write instead of before. But in order to explain how to get the process going for you, we will present these considerations one by one.

Who Are My Readers?

Unless you are writing a journal or a diary for your own satisfaction, your writing always has an audience—the person or group of people who will read it. You need to keep this audience in mind as you plan what to say and as you choose the best way to express your ideas.

ANALYZE THE AUDIENCE

No doubt you already have considerable audience awareness. You would never write a job application letter using the latest in-group slang, nor would you normally correspond with your dear Aunt Minnie in impersonal formal English. Writing for diverse groups about whom you know little is more difficult than writing for a specific audience whom you know well. In this class, for instance, you will be writing for your fellow students and for your instructor, a mixed group often thrown together by a computer. Although they are diverse, they do share some characteristics. For one thing, when you begin to write a paper about "Eveline," you know that your audience has read the story; thus you need not summarize the plot. Also, the people in your audience are college-educated (or becoming so); therefore, you need not avoid difficult words like *epitome, eclectic* or *protean* if they are the appropriate choices. Other shared qualities will become apparent as you get to know your classmates and your instructor.

PREWRITING ACTIVITIES

Compose a brief letter persuading Eveline that she should (or should not) leave Frank. Your argumentative tactics, your attitude, and even your word choice must be affected by what you know about Eveline from reading the story—her essential timidity, her self-doubt, her capacity for self-deception.

Then, write briefly to her bullying father explaining to him why his dutiful daughter has deserted him.

Finally, write Frank a short letter explaining why Eveline will not be going away with him.

Be prepared to discuss with the class specific ways in which your letters are different when you change your audience.

Why Am I Writing?

Every kind of writing, even a grocery list, has a purpose. You seldom sit down to write without some aim in mind, and this purpose affects your whole approach to writing. The immediate response to the question, "Why am I writing?" may be that your teacher or your employer asked you to. But that answer will not help you understand the reasons that make writing worth doing—and worth reading.

REASONS FOR WRITING

Sometimes you may write in order *to express* your own feelings, as in a diary or a love letter. More frequently, though, you will be writing for several other people, and the response you want from these prospective readers will determine your purpose. If, for instance, you want your audience to be amused by your writing (as with an informal essay or friendly letter), your purpose is *to entertain.* If you want your readers to gain some knowledge from your writing (say, how to get to your house from the airport), then you are writing *to inform.* If you want your readers to agree with an opinion or to accept an idea (as in a letter to the editor or an advertisement), then you are writing *to persuade.* Of course, these aims overlap—as do most things in the writing process—but usually one purpose predominates.

Most of your writing in this course, as in real life, will attempt to persuade in one way or another. Your purpose is often to convince your reader to agree with the points you are making. Logical ideas set down in clear, interesting writing should prove convincing and keep your readers reading.

PREWRITING ACTIVITIES

In writing the three letters to various characters, you have already noticed how audience and purpose can change the way you think and write about "Eveline." After studying the four writing suggestions which follow, reread the story. You may discover that you have more ideas and feelings about it than you first imagined. Thinking about prospective readers and determining your purpose will help you to understand your own views and reactions better.

1. If your purpose is *to express* your personal response:
   Write down your feelings about Eveline in a journal entry or in a brief note to a close friend. Do you sympathize with Eveline? Pity her? Does she irritate you or make you angry? Be as forthright as you can.
2. If your purpose is *to inform* someone else:
   Write a brief summary (less than one hundred words) of "Eveline" for a fellow student who wants to know if the story is worth reading.
   Write a slightly longer summary for your instructor (or someone else who has read the story) who wants to know if you have grasped its important points.
   Which summary was easier to write? What purposes besides providing information were involved in each summary?
3. If your purpose is *to entertain* yourself or your readers:
   How would you rewrite the ending of "Eveline" to make it more positive or romantic—to make it appeal to a wider audience? Would such an ending be consistent with the earlier parts of the story? Would it be true to human experience?
4. If your purpose is *to persuade* your readers:
   The author tells us that Eveline held two letters in her lap, but we do not know their contents. Write your version of one of them. Try to construe from evidence in the story what Eveline would have said to convince her father or her brother that she had good reasons for going away with Frank. How would she persuade them to forgive her? Consider also what other purposes Eveline would try to achieve in each of these letters.

What Ideas Should I Use?

Understanding literature involves learning what questions to ask yourself as you examine a literary work. To sharpen your comprehension of the story and develop ideas for writing, you may want to use one of the following three methods of discovering ideas, all of which involve questioning. This whole process of deciding what ideas to use in writing is called *invention*.

SELF-QUESTIONING

These are the kinds of questions you might ask yourself when studying a work of literature: questions about characters, their circumstances, their motives and conflicts, their fears and expectations, their relations with other characters; questions about the setting in which the story takes place; questions about any repeated details that seem significant; questions about the meaning and value of actions and events. Write out your responses to these questions about "Eveline" and keep them handy when you begin your essay.

1. What is Eveline's home life like?
2. How does she expect her new life to be different?
3. Do you think this expectation is realistic?
4. Why is the word *dust* mentioned so often?
5. List all the concrete details you can find that describe Eveline's home.
6. How old is Eveline? Is her age important for any reason?
7. What sort of person is her father? What kind of "bad way" is he in on Saturday nights?
8. How does Eveline feel about her father?
9. What sort of person was Eveline's mother? What happened to her? Does Eveline identify with her mother in any way?
10. How does Eveline feel about her dead mother?
11. What do you think her mother meant when she kept repeating "the end of pleasure is pain"? Why would she say this? Was she really crazy?
12. What does Eveline's father mean when he tells her, "I know these sailor chaps"? What possible reasons could he have for trying to break up Eveline's romance?
13. What sort of person is Frank? What does Eveline actually know about him?
14. Has Eveline romanticized Frank in any way? Is her Father's objection to him perhaps justified?
15. What is Eveline's duty to her father? What promise did she make to her dying mother?
16. What is her duty to herself? Does she really think she has a "right to happiness"? Why or why not?
17. How does Eveline feel about leaving her brother?
18. In what ways is Eveline "like a helpless animal"? What is she afraid of?
19. Why do you think her eyes give Frank "no sign of love or farewell or recognition"?
20. Do you think Eveline made the right decision? Why?

DIRECTED FREE WRITING

Many people find that they can best bring ideas to the surface by writing freely, with no restrictions about correctness. When you engage in free writing in order to "free" ideas from your subconscious mind, you should think of a pertinent question and just start writing.

Consider this: What kind of person is Eveline? As you think, start writing. Set down everything that comes to mind. Think about how Eveline became the person she is. Write in sentences, but do not concern yourself with correctness or word choice or organization. You are writing for your own benefit, attempting to discover everything that you have in mind about Eveline after reading and thinking about the story.

PROBLEM-SOLVING

After you have examined Eveline's character, pose yourself this problem to solve: Explain the ending of the story so that it is understandable and believable. As you seek a solution, ask yourself these questions: Why does she refuse to leave her pinched, narrow life? Is there anything about the way she was brought up that makes this decision believable—perhaps inevitable? Would her life have been different if she had been born male? What happened to her brothers, for instance? Does her religion have any bearing on her decision? Write down all the reasons you can find to help explain why Eveline does not leave home.

Do these reasons shed any light on the theme—the overall meaning of the story? Do you now perhaps see a point you could develop that is related to the theme of the story?

What Point Should I Make?

Besides providing a thorough understanding of the story, these prewriting activities serve to stir up ideas for a thesis—the controlling idea for your paper—and to help you discover evidence to support convincingly the observations you will make in developing that thesis.

RELATE A PART TO THE WHOLE

One bit of advice that will help you write meaningful literary papers is this:

> Devise a thesis that makes its point by relating some aspect of the work to its theme, i.e., to the meaning of the whole.

Our questions so far have led you to approach Joyce's story by analyzing character, particularly the main character, Eveline. But writing a simple character sketch (in which you discuss what sort of person she is, as we asked you to do in the directed free-writing assignment) would not produce a satisfactory literary paper. You need to go beyond that one-dimensional approach and make your essay say something about the story itself. In short, you must relate your analysis of her character to the theme.

FINDING THE THEME

You may have learned that the theme of a work is the moral. In a sense that is true, but a moral suggests a neatly-stated, preachy comment on some vice or virtue, whereas a literary theme will seldom be so pat and should never sound preachy. In order to discover theme you need to decide what you have learned from reading the story. What did the author reveal about the behavior of human beings, about the conduct of society? Rather than looking for a moral, look for some insight into the human condition.

Sometimes you may have a theme in mind but be unable to express it except in a cliché. You could, for instance, see the theme of "Eveline" as an acceptance of the old adage, "Better the devil you know than the devil you don't." Although this idea is acceptable as a theme, a clearer statement would relate the concept more closely to the story, like this: "In 'Eveline' Joyce focuses on the painful choices a young woman faces concerning her desire for a better life, her duty to her family, and her fear of leaving home." Certainly her character—the kind of person she is—relates directly to this theme. If, for instance, Eveline had been a willful, disobedient child who grew up into a rebellious, irresponsible young woman, the outcome of the story would surely have been different.

The problem is thus to find a thesis that will allow you to explain how Eveline's upbringing has conditioned her for the inevitable failure of nerve, the return to servitude and security, the relinquishing of hopes and dreams.

STATING THE THESIS

A good thesis statement should be a *complete sentence* that clearly conveys the point you plan to make in your paper. It should be broad enough to include all the ideas that are necessary as evidence but narrow enough to make a precise statement of your main point and focus your thoughts. If your thesis is too broad—as, for example, "Joyce's characterization of Eveline is extremely well drawn"—you may end up skimming the surface, never providing meaningful interpretation of the work. Notice that this overly broad thesis is unsatisfactory for another reason: it fails to make a real point.

A better thesis for a paper on "Eveline" might be stated in any of the following ways:

> Eveline's Catholic upbringing as a dutiful daughter makes impossible her hopes for a happier life.
>
> If Eveline had been born male instead of female, she might have escaped her unhappy home life.

Eveline, "trapped like a helpless animal" by her deathbed promise to her mother, is morally unable to break her vow and flee her miserable home to seek a new life for herself.

Having been thoroughly beaten down by her brutal, domineering father, Eveline lacks the courage to flee in search of her own life.

Most of the ideas and details you need to support any of these thesis statements will appear in the prewriting that you have already completed. In the next chapter, we will suggest some ways in which you might arrange this material in the paper itself.

2

The Writing Process

Now that you have examined your reactions to "Eveline," collected your ideas, and formulated a thesis sentence, you are ready to organize this material into a workable arrangement for writing.

How Should I Organize My Ideas?

A traditional but effective format includes three parts: the beginning (the introduction), the middle (the body), and the end (the conclusion). This simple plan will serve for almost any piece of writing.

The Basic Structure: Beginning, Middle, and End

The *beginning* of the paper has two main functions: to engage your readers' interest and to let them know what point you expect to make. The *middle* portion of your paper develops and supports the main point with details, examples, reasons, and explanations that make the general thesis more specific and more understandable. The *end* of the paper returns your readers to the main point by summarizing or stressing the general idea you want them to perceive from reading your essay. Later in the chapter, we will offer you more specific suggestions about how to begin and end a paper effectively. For now we want to wrestle with the problem of organizing the body—or the middle part—of your paper about "Eveline."

The Basic Approach

ANALYZING A CHARACTER

The thesis statements that we presented in Chapter 1 approached Joyce's story by relating Eveline's character to the meaning of the work. In the prewriting activities, you generated ample insights and observations about Eveline. Now you must find some arrangement for your ideas in order to present them clearly to your audience. Here is a general plan for writing a paper about a character in literature:

1. *Beginning*. Identify the character you are analyzing and state the main point you intend to make about him or her (this point will serve as your thesis sentence).
2. *Middle*. Present the details of the character's personality that led you to your thesis. Pay attention to the following: what the character says, thinks, and does; what other characters say and think about the person; and what the narrator tells about the character.
3. *End*. Summarize your view and reinforce how this character's role functions to reveal theme.

The middle section of your paper can be organized in several ways. You could organize your writing, for instance, around *central traits*, like "timidity, cowardice, passivity," or around *central events* in the work that make the character's nature clear. Because "Eveline" contains so few events or incidents, you will probably choose to organize this character analysis around central traits. Here is a brief plan for a paper based on one of our sample thesis statements:

1. *Beginning*. Eveline lacks courage to flee from her domineering father and seek her own happiness.
2. *Middle*. Evidence of Eveline's lack of courage can be seen in the following:
   a. Her passivity as a female who lacks the resources and imagination to challenge her traditional role;
   b. Her physical fear of her father, which is generalized to all men;
   c. Her reverence for her mother's memory and the promise she made to keep the family together.
3. *End*. Eveline exemplifies how a woman may be trapped by passivity, fear, and obligation.

This plan states the thesis and then indicates the subpoints that will become topic sentences for several paragraphs of development and support.

The following plan organizes the middle of a paper on the same thesis by stating the topic sentences as specific fears that contribute to Eveline's lack of courage:

Eveline's lack of courage is illustrated in these ways:

a. She is afraid to go against her religious beliefs;
b. She is afraid something will happen to her father if she leaves him;
c. She is afraid her mother's memory will continue to haunt her;
d. She is afraid Frank will treat her as her father treated her mother.

By writing out the subpoints, you provide yourself with a plan to follow in writing the paragraphs that will make up the middle (or body) of your character analysis.

ORDERING THE IDEAS

As you write the middle section of your essay, you will have to decide which point to take up first and which ones to use later in the development of your thesis. Ordinarily, you can arrange your topic sentences in two ways: logical order or chronological order.

Logical order involves arranging ideas in a way that will appeal to your readers' intelligence and good sense. Many writers begin with a less than crucial idea and work up to their most important one. The logic behind this arrangement is based on the assumption that since your final point is the one your readers are most likely to remember, it should also be your strongest point.

In the second plan just presented to you for a paper on "Eveline," the topic sentences about fears are arranged according to the increasing strength of Eveline's feelings: the plan starts with a general point about religion, moves to more specific fears about leaving her father and remembering her mother, and concludes with a shocking insight about Frank. The last idea is particularly appropriate, as it sums up the previous two points by relating Eveline's anxiety about Frank to her feelings about her parents' relationship.

Chronological order, which is based on time, involves writing about events in the order in which they occur. Most narratives, such as short stories and novels, use a chronological approach. Because you will be writing about literature, your organization for a paper could simply follow the chronology of the work under consideration. Logical order is preferable, though, as it provides a more analytical arrangement that will keep your paper from seeming like a mere plot summary.

MAINTAINING A CRITICAL FOCUS

Even though you arrange your ideas logically, the paper could still sound like a plot summary if you imbed your critical* insights in the middle of paragraphs. In order to achieve a critical focus, the topic sentences (usually the first one of each paragraph in the body of the paper) should be critical observations supporting or relating to your thesis. In academic writing, placing the topic sentences at the beginning of paragraphs helps your instructor to follow your thinking. You should in each paragraph use the plot details to support or prove the critical generalization in the topic sentence.

Notice the difference between a critical comment and a plot detail:

Plot detail: Jackson's story opens on a balmy summer day.

Critical comment: By setting her story on a balmy summer day, Jackson creates a false sense of well being.

Plot detail: The oiler, who dies, was the strongest of the four men in the boat.

Critical comment: The oiler's death is ironic because it upsets our expectations of survival of the fittest.

If you want to use both a critical observation and a plot detail in your topic sentence, be sure that the critical comment appears in the independent (main) clause and that the plot detail is placed in a subordinate position:

Plot detail: Granny detests Cordelia's blue lampshades.

Critical comment: One of Cordelia's blue lampshades becomes the image of Granny's diminishing spark of life.

Combined: Although Granny detests Cordelia's blue lampshades, one of them becomes the image of her diminishing spark of life.

Plot detail: The dog in "To Build a Fire" knows better than to go out in weather fifty below zero.

Critical comment: The dog serves as a foil for the foolish man in Jack London's "To Build a Fire."

Combined: In "To Build a Fire" the dog, who knows better than to go out in weather fifty below zero, serves as a foil for the foolish man.

DEVELOPING WITH DETAILS

No matter what organization you choose for the body of your paper, remember to state each critical generalization clearly and to support each one with enough specific references to the story to be convincing. Sort through the observations that you made in your prewriting,

---

* As you probably know, the term *critical*, as applied to literature, means an *evaluative assessment*, not fault-finding.

and select those that relate to the topic sentences in your plan. The following sample paragraph shows how a writer uses specific detail and brief quotations from the story to develop the idea stated in the topic sentence:

> Eveline lacks courage to seek a life of her own because she fears that her father will not be able to cope if she leaves him. Her anxiety is heightened as she recalls that she and her brothers and sisters are grown up and that her mother is dead. If she leaves, her father will be all alone. She realizes that he is "usually fairly bad on a Saturday night" and recognizes that his drinking problem will not get any better after she leaves. Also she has noticed that "Her father was becoming old lately" and assumes that "he would miss her." As a dutiful daughter, Eveline seems to feel that going away with Frank means abandoning her aging father, and that may be why she has written a letter to him—to ease the blow of her departure and to soothe her own conscience.

QUESTIONS FOR CONSIDERATION

In the sample paragraph has the writer given adequate support for the topic sentence? What details from the story has the writer cited to develop the main point? What other details could be used? Where does the writer bring in personal opinion (or interpretation)? Is the interpretation accurate?

How Should I Begin?

Your introduction is crucial to the effectiveness of your essay—and often proves to be the most difficult to write. Try to think of this part as challenging (rather than merely hard to do), and you may find yourself rising to new heights of accomplishment.

POSTPONE IF NOTHING COMES

Remember that you do not have to write your introduction first just because it appears first in the finished essay. As long as you have your thesis clearly in mind (or clearly written out on your planning sheet), you can start at once on the body of the paper. Once you begin generating material, you may suddenly perceive an idea that will serve nicely as a beginning. Or, if you postpone your introduction until the next day, your subconscious mind may provide you with the perfect opening. You may find that some of your best ideas come to you in the shower.

WRITE AN APPEALING OPENING

Work especially hard on your opening sentence. You want to engage the interest of your readers at once. If you begin like this,

> "Eveline" is a very interesting short story by James Joyce.

no one other than your loving mother is likely to read any further unless paid to. You should mention the author and title somewhere in your introduction (even though both may appear in your title). But try also to incorporate something specific in that first sentence. You might want to focus your readers' attention on an incident that you consider significant:

> In his excellent short story "Eveline," James Joyce portrays a young woman paralyzed by the need to make a decision that will change the course of her life.

Or you could start this way:

> In James Joyce's "Eveline," we see a tired young woman accustomed to the "odour of dusty cretonne" trying to muster courage to exchange her dreary existence for the unknown excitements of life with a "sailor chap" in exotic Buenos Ayres.

Or you might try this:

> In the closing lines of James Joyce's "Eveline," the young woman of the title stands "passive, like a helpless animal," watching her dreams of romance and excitement fade into the mist.

STATE THE THESIS

Even more important than an arresting opening sentence is the need to let your readers know somewhere in the introductory paragraph what the paper is going to be about. But try to avoid stating your main point baldly:

> I am going to show that Eveline stays home with her domineering father because she lacks courage to go with Frank.

The "I am going to show" is much too blunt. Try to suggest a bit more indirectly the direction of your thought, the case that you propose to present within the course of your essay. Your thesis should sound more like this:

> Having been thoroughly beaten down by her brutal, domineering father, Eveline lacks the will to flee from him in search of her own happiness.

If you combine your thesis with a general statement about the story, you should produce a worthwhile introduction for a short paper:

> In James Joyce's "Eveline," we see a tired young woman accustomed to the "odour of dusty cretonne," trying to muster courage to exchange her dreary existence for the unknown excitements of life with a "sailor chap" in exotic Buenos Ayres. But, having been thoroughly beaten down by her brutal father, Eveline lacks the will to flee from him in search of her own happiness.

How Should I End?

Your conclusion is just as important as your introduction—perhaps even more so. You want to leave your audience feeling satisfied that you have written something worth reading, that their time has not been wasted. Do not give them a chance to ask, "Well, so what?" at the end.

RELATE THE DISCUSSION TO THEME

Impress your readers with the value of your discussion by reinforcing in the conclusion how your analysis illuminates the theme, or meaning, of the work. Often this process may involve echoing your thesis statement in the introduction. But take care to avoid simply repeating what you said at the beginning. Your conclusion should offer a clear expression of the theme that was suggested as part of your thesis in the introduction.

POSTPONE OR WRITE AHEAD

Conclusions, like introductions, do not necessarily have to be written when you come to them. If you should get some additional insight concerning the theme as you work on composing the main part of the paper, take a minute to jot down the idea so that you can later incorporate this insight into your ending. Or, you could stop right then, write the final paragraph, and put it aside until you come to it. Chances are that you may change this conclusion later, but having something to work with is an enormous help—especially if you are getting tired.

If you write your way through the entire paper and still have no inspiration for the conclusion, then force yourself. Write something and keep revising it until you produce a version that pleases you. The following suggestions may help.

WRITE AN EMPHATIC FINAL SENTENCE

No matter how exhausted you are when you compose your final paragraph, do not risk ruining the effect of your entire essay by letting your conclusion trail off at the end with a limp last sentence. Regardless of the brilliance of your middle paragraphs, your readers are going to feel dejected if you end like this:

> All in all, I think "Eveline" was a fine story, and I think anyone would enjoy reading it and maybe even learn something from it.

We have advice for you in the next chapter on how to compose emphatic sentences. Study those suggestions before you rewrite your conclusion. Work *hard* on that last line. Try to come up with a final paragraph that will crystalize your meaning, something like this one:

> Joyce makes clear throughout the story that Eveline's personality has been heavily influenced by her dutiful upbringing; her passivity has been reinforced by her promise to her dying mother. She is herself now doomed to endure that "life of commonplace sacrifices" that led her mother into despair.

Composing the First Draft

At this point you should be ready to compose the first draft of your essay on "Eveline." You have completed the prewriting activities, worked out a thesis statement, arranged your main supporting points, and selected the details to use for development. You may have even written some of your introduction and conclusion. Now it is time to move beyond these preliminary stages and write a complete draft of your paper. As you launch into the actual composition process, take a minute to get fully prepared for writing.

PAUSING TO RESCAN

You may have been told to get your first draft down on paper as quickly as possible and then, once it is completed, to revise it. This is probably not bad advice if you suffer from writer's block, but you should know that recent studies show that most skilled writers go about it in a different way. Experienced writers tend to pause frequently as they compose—to rescan and perhaps reword what they have just written; to think about what to say next; to make additions, substitutions, or deletions; to be sure a sentence says precisely what they want it to say. These accomplished writers revise still further after the first draft is completed, preferably several hours or even days later so that they can reexamine their writing from a reader's perspective.

If you tend to write headlong without pausing once you begin, perhaps you should try to slow down. Mina Shaughnessy, a noted composition expert, speaks of "the messy process that leads to clarity" in writing. This messy process involves pausing and thinking and reviewing and revising if you expect to do it well.

Sample Student Paper with Revisions

If you would like to see what a student literary paper looks like, here is one written by a freshman at Eastern Illinois University. The first draft of the introduction went like this:

Although the young woman in James Joyce's
"Eveline" has a miserable home life, she refuses
to abandon it. Eveline could not leave her home
in search of a new life because of her sex, the
security her home offers, and a promise made to
her dying mother.

Notice, as you read the essay, how the revised introduction offers
a more general thesis statement in order to avoid repeating these
ideas in the conclusion.

Bound to Home

Although the young woman in James Joyce's   [1]
"Eveline" has a miserable home life, she refuses
to abandon it. On first reading, this refusal
seems difficult to understand, but a closer
analysis of Eveline's character reveals several
reasons why she could not leave her home in
search of a new life.

If Eveline had been born male, her situation   [2]
would have been much different. First of all,
her mother did not ask Eveline's brother Harry
to keep the family together. It seems unlikely
that the mother would have made this request of
another son. Also, in those times it was
considered the female's duty to take care of the
family; thus it was only natural that the mother
would expect Eveline, the daughter, to take over
the household. Finally, if Eveline had been a
boy, she probably would have left the home just
as Harry did. Although the story does not
explicitly state that Harry does not live at
home, he is evidently gone most of the time. The
remarks that "Harry . . . was nearly always down
somewhere in the country" and "Harry always sent
up what he could" suggest that her brother is
seldom around to offer support for Eveline.[1] If

Eveline had been a male, she too would probably have gotten away as soon as possible.

Another factor which keeps Eveline from [3] leaving home is the need for the security that she feels there. This house is where Eveline grew up, and even though home life was not perfect, she seems to have some fond memories of her childhood. She reminisces about the times when "the children of the avenue used to play together" (4). This line, along with the line "Still they seemed to have been rather happy then" (4), suggests that Eveline enjoyed her youth. When she starts to look around the house and sees objects "from which she had never dreamed of being divided" (4), the reader senses that Eveline would really miss her home if she were to go away. Her need for security is strongly suggested when she thinks to herself that "in her home anyway she had shelter and food; she had those whom she had known all her life about her" (4).

Furthermore, although Eveline realizes she has [4] had some hard times, now "she did not find it a wholly undesirable life" (5). She may be afraid of her father, but she also has some happy memories of him—for example, the time the family went on a picnic and her father put on her mother's bonnet "to make the children laugh" (6). There was also the time not long ago when her father cared for her when she was sick. Eveline thinks that her father would miss her, but there are suggestions that she will miss him, too.

Lastly, Eveline's promise to her dying mother [5] unfairly tied her to home forever. On her deathbed, the mother asked Eveline "to keep the family together as long as she could" (6). From

the passage in which Eveline is remembering her
mother's last moments, the reader can understand
how it would be impossible for Eveline to go
back on her word to her mother, especially when
she contemplates "the pitiful vision of her
mother's life" (6). Clearly, Eveline feels sorry
for her mother and the joyless way her life
turned out. Eveline perhaps thinks that it would
bring her mother a small measure of happiness if
she knew the family would be kept together and
cared for.

Eveline's feelings for her mother are strong   [6]
because the daughter unconsciously identifies
with her mother. When Eveline is thinking of how
her life would be with Frank, she tells herself
she will "not be treated as her mother had been"
(5). Actually, Eveline is afraid that her life
will indeed turn out like her mother's because
she knows she is much like her. Both of them
seem to be quite passive and not confident.
Otherwise, they would not have let this man—
Eveline's father—overpower and abuse them. Both
also appear to be devoutly religious, which must
have reinforced Eveline's decision. Having a
picture of a priest and a list of promises
made to Blessed Margaret Mary Alacoque in
the home suggests a religious atmosphere.
Eveline must have felt it would be morally and
spiritually wrong to break her promise to her
mother.

Many who read this story will probably feel   [7]
that Eveline should go off with Frank and leave
behind her gloomy life. Careful readers, though,
will see that Eveline cannot leave her family
because she is female, because she needs the
security of her home, and because she promised

her dying mother to keep the family together.
Eveline is indeed "trapped like a helpless
animal."   [775 words]

                                    —Jane Pfeiffer

Notes

[1] James Joyce, "Eveline." Literature and the
Writing Process. Elizabeth McMahan, Susan Day,
Robert Funk. New York: Macmillan, 1986:5.

Here is the conclusion that Jane first drafted for her paper:

In this story, the reader can find many
reasons Eveline should go off with Frank and
leave behind her gloomy life, yet she refuses to
go away. The major influences on her decision to
stay are the fact she is a female, the
reliability of the home, and her dying mother's
wish which Eveline vowed to uphold.

In what ways does the final conclusion improve on the first version?

Alternative Suggestions

Analyze the title character of James Thurber's "The Secret Life of Walter Mitty." Read the story (pp. 51–54) and complete the prewriting assignment that follows it. Then, using the material generated in the prewriting process, write a draft of a paper focusing on one of the following thesis statements:

1. Mrs. Mitty's character contributes to the meaning of the story by helping us understand Walter Mitty's behavior.
2. The central incidents dramatizing Walter Mitty's secret selves all share certain qualities, revealing what he lacks in his real life.
3. Walter Mitty's seemingly fertile imagination is actually limited to the conventions of cheap novels and Hollywood's glamorized adventure films.
4. Walter Mitty's incompetence in real life is both a cause and an effect of his pervasive fantasy life.

5. Because Walter Mitty is easily bullied, he retreats into fantasies that allow him to rebel in secret.

6. Walter Mitty's statement near the end of the story, "Things close in," provides a concise summary of his situation.

Peer Evaluation Checklist for Revision

The following questions and guidelines will help you evaluate your own or another student's first draft. If you are doing peer evaluation in class, exchange papers; read your partner's thoroughly; then write out, in full sentences, responses to the questions and suggestions below. Your conscientious evaluation will be valuable to your partner in the revision stage. You will also learn about composition by doing close analysis, and, of course, another student will give you helpful remarks and advice on your own essay.

If you are not doing peer evaluation in the classroom, try to talk a friend into reading your paper and thoughtfully answering these questions.

1. Does the paper have a clear purpose? What is the main point? Does the whole paper relate to the main point? Is the main point interesting or too predictable?

2. Are the ideas consistently clear? Make a note of any sentences or paragraphs that you needed to reread. Make a note of any words you found confusing.

3. Does the paper seem well-organized? Is it logical? Do the opening and closing need revision? Make suggestions for improvement. Is there perhaps a better order for the body paragraphs? Are there any paragraphs that do not seem to belong?

4. Is there enough material in the essay? Does it need further details or examples? Make note of places where you would like to see more details or examples. Write questions to help your partner add details. For example, if the essay says, "Eveline did not much like her father," you could ask, "Exactly how did she feel about him?"

5. Are all the quotations from the story accurate? Do they appear within quotation marks?

6. Are the overall tone and level of formality consistent throughout the essay? Note any words or passages that seem inappropriate. Has the writer developed enough sentence variety and emphasis? Note sentences that you consider too long, too short, or in need of rephrasing for a more pleasing effect.

CHAPTER

3

The Rewriting Process

You are probably relieved and pleased that you have completed the first draft of your essay. A large portion of your work is finished. But do not rush off to the typist or the typewriter yet. You need first to do a careful revision of your paper.

What Is Revision?

Revision involves more than just tidying your prose. The process of correcting your spelling, punctuation, and mechanics is called *editing*, but your paper is not ready for that yet. First you need *re-vision*, seeing again to discover ways to make your writing better. Schedule your time so that you are able to lay the rough draft aside at least overnight before attempting to revise. While a draft is still warm from the writing, you cannot look at it objectively. And looking at it objectively is the basis of revision. Your fondness for a well-turned paragraph should not prevent you from cutting it when, in the cold light of morning, you realize that it does not quite relate to your thesis. Your relief at having the words down on paper should not interfere with your crossing them out and rewriting when necessary.

As you examine your cooled-down essay, you may even see that while you were writing, your main point shifted somewhat. Sometimes writers discover what they actually want to say while trying to write something slightly different. You may need to go back and change the thesis, rewrite paragraphs, cut others, and find new support from the literary work before you can consider the paper finished. For example, one student made the point, in a first draft of a paper on Tennessee Williams' play *The Glass Menagerie* (see Chapter

16), that all of the characters practice deception, thus providing read-ers with a negative view of human nature. As she reread her rough draft the following day, she noticed that she had written far more about Laura's deceptions than about those of the other characters. After some reflection, she then decided she should have emphasized the idea that although all of the characters practice deception, Laura seems the least *self*-deceived. Ironically, Laura is the character who has the least contact with the outside world. The student totally revised the paper using her new, more specific and more sophisti-cated insight as the main point.

That student was able to get some distance from her own writing, to look at it as another reader might. In revising, *look at your paper from the readers' point of view*. What questions might a reader want to ask you? These must be answered in the paper, because you will not be around to supply information. Would a reader find your essay consistent? Interesting? Convincing? Are there enough details, illustrations, facts, and evidence from the work you are writing about? Because these considerations may lead you to lengthy rewrit-ing, remember to plan at least as much time for revision as for writing the first draft.

What Should I Add or Take Out?

Revising is hard work, and you may wonder just where and how to start. If you have not been following a plan carefully worked out before you began writing, you should begin the revising process by outlining your first draft.

OUTLINING AFTER THE FIRST DRAFT

To be sure that your discussion is unified and complete—i.e., to discover whether anything needs to be taken out or added—you should briefly outline your rough draft. It may seem odd to make an outline *after* you have written the paper, but listing your main ideas and supporting details will enable you to review your essay quickly and easily. You can examine its skeleton and decide whether everything fits together properly. First write down your thesis state-ment; then add the topic sentences of your paragraphs and the main supporting points for each one. Remember that this step in the revising process is *essential* if you have written the first draft without an outline or a detailed plan.

First, make sure that the idea in every topic sentence is a critical observation relating directly to your thesis.

If not, you should change it until it clearly supports your thesis—or else you should take it out.

Then, examine your supporting details to see if any are irrele-vant or overlapping and need to be cut.

Next, consider whether your support is adequate. It is possible to develop a topic sentence fully with only two subpoints, but you will probably want at least three or four. Is there any important evidence that you have overlooked? If you fail to find adequate support for a topic sentence, perhaps you need to rethink it, omit it, or combine it with another main idea. Continue to be on the lookout for any digressions or unintended repetition of ideas.

CHECKING OUT A PARAGRAPH

For practice in checking the relevance and organization of ideas, examine the sample paragraph from Chapter 2 (p. 18). Outline it in the way we just described. Do you see any irrelevant points? Can you think of any important ideas or details that have been omitted? Are the points arranged in an effective order? Would another arrangement be more effective?

Now look at the following outline of the same paragraph and see whether it matches yours:

Topic sentence—Eveline fears her father will not be able to manage if she leaves him.
1. Eveline thinks about his loneliness—children grown, wife dead.
2. She fears his drinking problem worsening.
3. She worries that he is becoming old lately.
4. She assumes "he would miss her."
5. She writes letter to ease the blow.

Your outline may not come out exactly like this one, but the main idea is to be sure you have included all of the supporting details.

Here are some observations to consider for a revision of the sample paragraph, based on the outline of its major points:

1. Point 1 could be expanded to include details about the neighbors who have died (Tizzie Dunn) and moved away (the Waters).
2. An earlier draft of the paragraph included the point about Eveline's promise to her mother, but it was dropped as being irrelevant to the topic sentence. Do you agree?
3. The paragraph's supporting points appear in the same order as they do in the story. Is this chronological organization effective? Would some logical order be better?

What Should I Rearrange?

A crucial part of revision involves giving some thought to the order of your paragraphs and the order of the supporting details within them. The order in which they came to your mind is not necessarily the best. Luckily, rearranging is fairly easy once you apply yourself to the task.

Remember that neatness does not count at this stage. If you need to add only a sentence or two you can perhaps squeeze the new material in between the lines or draw an arrow to the top or bottom margin and write there. If you discover the need to make major additions or to move whole paragraphs, you may want to use scissors on your rough draft. Cut your paper apart, quite literally, and tape in an added section. Or include an extra sheet of paper (numbered, for example, "p. 3–A"), with a bold notation in the margin at the place you want to include the insert from page 3–A.

The two principles you need use in considering how well your points are arranged are *logic* and *emphasis*. Both principles allow you to arrange ideas in a certain sequence. The following questions will help you devise an appropriate arrangement:

1. Should I arrange the paragraphs and details in my essay in the same order that they occupy in the work I am analyzing?

   If you are writing a paragraph supporting the topic that Eveline is timid, you might collect details from throughout the story. You could then put those details in the same order in which they appear in the story.

2. Should I organize the descriptions in terms of space?

   In a paper examining the significance of the objects in Eveline's home, you might take up these objects as though presented in a tour around the room. Other descriptions may be arranged from near to far, from outside to inside, from small to large.

3. Should I arrange my main points along a scale of value, of power, of weight, or of forcefulness? Could I use an arrangement of
   negative to positive?
   universal to individual?
   most influential to least influential?
   general to specific?
   least impressive to most impressive?

   You can arrange your ideas in either direction along any of these scales–negative to positive or positive to negative, for instance. It is usually effective to place the most emphatic point last in any essay. If you are writing about several of Eveline's reasons for not going with Frank, and you believe that the most influential reason was her promise to her dying mother, you would include that idea in the last paragraph of the body of your paper, opening with a transition like this:
   Though her timidity in general and her fear of her father in particular affected Eveline's final decision, her promise to her mother was the most powerful influence.

The strongest-point rule is just a guideline, of course. Try to arrange your ideas in a way your readers will find effective.

What Sentences Should I Combine?

Once you are satisfied that your ideas proceed smoothly, you need to consider the possibility of combining sentences to avoid needless repetition of words and to eliminate choppiness. You may also decide to use sentence combining to achieve emphasis and variety. Probably you can discover many ways to improve your sentences.

REARRANGING FOR CONCISENESS

If you find that sometimes you are repeating the same word without meaning to, you may eliminate the problem by combining sentences. For instance, you might have written something like this:

> Twain savagely attacks conformity in the scene where the villagers stone the woman. The woman is suspected of being a witch.

As the repetition of "the woman" serves no useful purpose, the two statements can be more effectively phrased in a single sentence:

> In a scene showing the villagers stoning a woman suspected of being a witch, Twain savagely attacks conformity.

When you combine sentences in this way, you take the main idea from one sentence and tuck it, usually as a modifier of some sort, within another sentence. We can illustrate the process in reverse to help you see more clearly what the technique involves. Notice that this sentence contains two simple statements:

> Theodore, who did not wish to throw a stone, was horrified by the cruelty.

The two main ideas in that sentence are these:

> Theodore was horrified by the cruelty.
> Theodore did not wish to throw a stone.

You can recombine those sentences in various ways, depending upon which idea you choose to emphasize:

> Horrified by the cruelty, Theodore did not wish to throw a stone.
> Not wishing to throw a stone, Theodore was horrified by the cruelty.

Sentence combining not only eliminates wordiness but also adds variety and focus. The various combinations provide numerous stylistic choices.

SENTENCE COMBINING EXERCISE

The following sentences, all written by students, include needless repetition and wordiness that can be eliminated by sentence combining. Decide which idea in each pair of sentences should be emphasized, and put that idea in the main (independent) clause. You will, of course, need to change, add, or omit words as you work to improve these sentences, but try not to leave out any significant ideas.

1. The second common stereotype is the dark lady. Usually the dark lady stereotype symbolizes sexual temptation.

2. Kate Chopin wrote a short story called "The Storm." As the title of the story suggests, it is about a rain storm and shows how people respond to the storm.

3. Emily Dickinson's poetry is sometimes elliptical. It is thus sometimes difficult for readers to get even the literal meaning of her poems.

4. There are three major things to consider in understanding Walter Mitty's character. These things include what the author tells us about Mitty, what Mitty himself says and does, and how other people respond to him.

5. Most of the incidents that inspire Mitty's fantasies have humorous connotations associated with them. These can be broken down into basically two groups, with the first one being his desire to be in charge of a situation.

REARRANGING FOR EMPHASIS AND VARIETY

When you rewrite to gain emphasis and variety, you probably will restructure sentences as well as combining them. In fact, you may find yourself dividing a sentence occasionally for easier reading or to produce a short emphatic sentence. The following are some techniques to help you in polishing your sentence structure.

VARYING THE PATTERN

The usual way of forming sentences in English is to begin with the subject, follow with the verb, and add a complement (something that completes the verb), like this:

> Walter Mitty is not a brave person.

Any time you depart from this expected pattern, you gain variety and some degree of emphasis. Notice the difference:

> A brave person Walter Mitty is not.

Here are other variations that you may want to try:

A Dash at the End.

> Twain found constant fault with humanity—with what he called "the damned human race."

An Interrupter Set Off by Dashes or Commas.

> Twain considered humanity in general—"the damned human race"—inferior to the so-called lower animals.

A Modifier at the Beginning.

> Although he loved individual human beings, Twain professed to loathe what he called "the damned human race."

A Short-short Sentence.   Because most of the sentences you will write are moderately long, you gain considerable emphasis when you follow a sentence of normal length with an extremely short one:

> Plagiarizing, which means borrowing the words or ideas of another writer without giving proper credit, is a serious infraction. Do not do it.

Deliberate Repetition.   Just a few pages ago, we cautioned you to combine sentences rather than to repeat words needlessly. That caution still holds. But repeating words for emphasis is a different matter. Purposeful repetition can produce effective and emphatic sentences:

> Twain believed that organized religion was folly, a folly to be ridiculed discreetly.
> One cannot talk well, study well, or write well if one cannot think well.

That last sentence (modeled after one written by Virginia Woolf) repeats the same grammatical structure as well as the same words to achieve a powerful effect.

WRITING EXERCISE

Rewrite the following ordinary sentences to achieve greater emphasis, variety, and conciseness.

1. Edith Wharton was born into a rich, upper-class family, but she was not even allowed to have paper on which to write when she was a child.

2. Her governesses never taught her how to organize ideas in writing, so when she decided to write a book on the decoration of houses, she had to ask her friend Walter Berry to help her write it.

3. She married Teddy Wharton when she was twenty-three years old, and he always carried a one-thousand dollar bill in case she wanted anything.

4. Her good friend, Henry James, gave her advice to help her improve her novels, yet her novels invariably sold far more copies than James's did.

5. She was awarded the Legion of Honor, which is the highest award given by the French government, following World War I for her refugee relief activities.

What Words Should I Change?

You may have a good thesis and convincing, detailed support for it—but your writing style can make the difference between a dull, boring presentation and a rich, engaging one.

CHECK YOUR VERBS

After examining the construction of your sentences, you should look at the specific language you have used. Read through the rough draft and underline the verbs. Look for forms of these useful but weatherbeaten words:

is (are, was, were, etc.)		go	has	
get	do	make	come	move

Consider substituting a different verb—one that presents an image, visual or otherwise—to your readers. For example, this sentence is grammatically correct, but dull:

> Eveline does her work with reluctance.

Searching for a more precise verb than "does," you might write:

> Eveline reluctantly plods through her work.

"Plods" suggests a picture of poor Eveline with slumped shoulders and slow steps, dragging through the day.

Occasionally you can pick up a lively word from somewhere else in a limp sentence and convert it into the main verb:

> Eveline is unable to leave her home because she is trapped by a promise to her dead mother.

"Trapped" is an arresting word in that sentence, and you could shift it to an earlier position to good effect:

> A promise to her dead mother traps Eveline in her miserable home.

This revision also cuts the unnecessary words out of the first version.

EXERCISE

Rewrite the following sentences using livelier verbs and fewer words.

1. The narrator's most unusual characteristic is an overactive sense of humor.
2. Jim's constant practical joking finally makes the readers disgusted.
3. Readers of the story get the message that some people are entertained by the misfortunes of others.

4. The readers come to the conclusion that Jim gets what he deserves.
5. Since the narrator's talk makes up the whole story, we have only his point of view.

USE ACTIVE VOICE MOST OF THE TIME

Although the passive voice sometimes offers the best way to construct a sentence, the habitual use of the passive sprinkles your prose with colorless helping verbs, like "is" and "was." If a sentence is in passive voice, the subject does *not* perform the action implied by the verb:

> The paper was written by Janet, Jo's roommate.
> The assignment was given poorly.
> Her roommate's efforts were hindered by a lack of understanding.

The paper, the assignment, and the roommate's efforts did *not* carry out the writing, the giving, or the hindering. In active voice the subjects of the sentences are the doers or the causes of the action:

> Jo's roommate Janet wrote the paper.
> The teacher gave the assignment poorly.
> Lack of understanding hindered her roommate's efforts.

USE PASSIVE IF APPROPRIATE

Sometimes, of course, you may have a good reason for writing in the passive voice. For example, you may want to give a certain word the important position of subject even though it is not the agent of the action. In the sentence,

> Sensory details are emphasized in this paragraph.

the *details* are the key point. The writer of the paragraph (the agent of the action) is not important enough even to include. In active voice, the key term would be pushed to the middle of the sentence, a much weaker position:

> The writer emphasizes sensory details in this paragraph.

Clearly, you need not shun the passive, but if any of your sentences sound stilted or awkward, check to see if the passive voice may be the culprit.

EXERCISE

Change passive voice to active in the following sentences. Feel free to add, delete, or change words.

1. Antigone is treated brutally by Creon because of her struggle to achieve justice.
2. Creon was not convinced by her tirade against his unbending authority.

3. Conflict between male and female was portrayed in the play by the author.

4. If even a small point is won against a tyrant by society, considerable benefit may be experienced.

5. The tragedy was caused by the iron-bound authority exercised by Creon.

FEEL THE WORDS

Words have emotional meanings (*connotations*) as well as direct dictionary meanings (*denotations*). You may be invited to a get-together, a soiree, a social gathering, a blowout, a blast, a reception, a bash, or a do, and although all are words for parties, the connotations tell you whether to wear jeans or feathers, whether to bring a case of cheap beer or a bottle of expensive wine.

In writing, take into account the emotional content of the words you use. One of our favorite essays, "The Discus Thrower," opens with this sentence:

"I spy on my patients."

The word "spy" immediately captures the imagination with its connotations of intrigue and mystery and its slight flavor of deception. "I watch my patients when they don't know it" is still an interesting sentence because of its denotative content, but essayist Richard Selzer's version commands emotional as well as intellectual engagement.

We are not encouraging you to puff up your prose with strings of adverbs and adjectives; indeed, a single emotionally charged word in a simple sentence can be quite powerful.

ATTEND TO TONE

Tone—the stylistic reflection of a writer's attitude—is usually described in terms of emotion: serious, solemn, satirical, humorous, sly, mournful, expectant, and so on. Although most writing about literature calls for a plain, direct tone, other attitudes can be conveyed. Negative book reviews, for instance, sometimes have a sarcastic tone. A writer unsympathetic to Eveline might describe her as "a spineless drudge who enjoys her oppression," while a sympathetic reader might state that Eveline is "a pitiful victim of a brutal home life." Someone who wants to remain neutral could describe Eveline as "a young woman trapped by duty and her own fears." These variations in tone, conveyed by word choice, reflect the writers' differing attitudes toward what is being discussed.

Once you establish a tone, you should stick with it. A humorous or sarcastic section set unexpectedly in a straightforward, direct essay will distract or disconcert your readers. Be sure to set your tone in the first paragraph; then your readers will unconsciously adjust their expectations about the rest of the paper.

USE FORMAL LANGUAGE

The nature of your audience will also determine the level of usage for your writing. Essays for college classes usually require *formal language,* a style that takes a serious or neutral tone and avoids such informal usage as contractions, slang, and sentence fragments, even intentional ones. (See the "Handbook for Correcting Errors," at the end of this text, for information about fragments.) Formal writing usually involves a third-person approach:

> One can sympathize with Eveline, at the same time regretting her weakness.
> The reader sympathizes with Eveline, ...

Most people today consider the use of first-person plural quite acceptable in formal papers:

> We sympathize with Eveline, ...
> Eveline gains our sympathy, ...

But avoid the informal second person, "you." Do *not* write, "You can see that Eveline is caught in a terrible bind."

Does It Flow?

The best way to examine the flow (the *coherence*) of your prose is to read it aloud. Recording your essays on tape and playing them back enables you to hear with some objectivity how your writing sounds. You might also entice a friend to read your paper aloud to you. Whatever method you use, listen for choppiness or abruptness. Your ideas should be arranged in a clear sequence that is easy to follow. Will your readers experience any confusion when a new idea comes up? If so, you need stronger connections between sentences or between paragraphs—*transitions* that indicate how one idea is related to the next.

For example, when you see the words "for example," you know what to expect. When you see "furthermore" opening a paragraph, your mind gets ready for some addition to the previous point. By contrast, when you see phrases like "on the other hand" or "by contrast," you are prepared for something different from the previous point.

These clearly transitional phrases can be supplemented by more subtle echo transitions (in this paragraph, the words "transitional phrases" above echo the main idea of the preceding paragraph); and by pronoun reference (in this paragraph, the word "these" above refers to the examples in the preceding paragraph). Another technique that increases coherence of writing is the repetition of key terms and structures. In the paragraph you are reading, the key terms are forms of the words "transition," "echo," "refer," and "repeat." In the paragraph preceding this one, notice the repetition of the phrase, "When you see . . ." and, in this paragraph, the repetition of "in this instance, the word(s). . . ." Parallel ideas are presented in parallel ways.

In short, here are the techniques for achieving coherence:

1. A clearly sequenced flow of ideas.
2. Transitional terms (see Chart 3–1 for a handy list).

CHART 3–1. Transitional Terms for All Occasions

TO CONTINUE TO A NEW POINT:

next, second, third, besides, further, finally

TO MAKE AN ADDITION TO A POINT:

too, moreover, in addition, for example, such as, that is, as an illustration, for instance, furthermore

TO SHOW CAUSE AND EFFECT:

therefore, consequently, as a result, accordingly, then, thus, so, hence

TO SHOW CONTRAST:

but, still, on the other hand, nevertheless, however, conversely, notwithstanding, yet

TO SHOW SIMILARITY:

too, similarly, in the same way, likewise, also

TO EMPHASIZE OR RESTATE:

again, namely, in other words, finally, especially, without doubt, indeed, in short, in brief, primarily, chiefly, as a matter of fact, no doubt

TO CONCLUDE A POINT:

finally, in conclusion, to summarize, to sum up, in sum

---

3. Echo transitions.
4. Repetition of key terms.
5. Repetition of sentence structures.

EXERCISE

Look up the words *cohere, coherent,* and *coherence* in a collegiate dictionary. Which definitions most closely fit the way we use these terms in our discussion? What relationship can you see among the definitions given in the dictionary?

Revising Checklist

1. Is the thesis idea intelligent and clearly stated?
2. Is the main idea of every paragraph directly related to the thesis?
3. Is every paragraph fully developed with plenty of specific examples or illustrations?
4. Do all of my ideas flow coherently? Is every transition easy to follow?
5. Is every word, every sentence, completely clear?
6. Is every sentence well-structured and accurately worded?
7. Is my introduction pleasing? Does it make clear what the paper will be about without giving all the content away?
8. Is the concluding sentence emphatic or at least graceful?
9. Have I accomplished my purpose? Does the paper make the point I set out to prove?
10. Have I used formal English throughout?
11. Is my manuscript form acceptable?

   —Have I skipped three lines between the title and the first line of the essay?
   —Have I double-spaced throughout?
   —Did I leave at least one-inch margins on all sides, including top and bottom?
   —Have I prepared a title sheet (if requested to do so)?

How Do I Proofread?

When you get to the editing stage, you can cease being creative. Try to think not about the ideas you have written but about the way you have written them. In order to become a competent editor, you must train yourself to see your own mistakes.

READ IT BACKWARDS

To avoid getting so interested in what you have written that you fail to see your errors, try reading your sentences from the last one on the page to the first, that is, from the bottom to the top. Because your ideas will lack continuity in reverse order, you stand a better chance of keeping your attention focused on each sentence *as* a sentence. Be sure that every word is correctly spelled, that each sentence is complete and correctly punctuated.

LOOK FOR YOUR TYPICAL ERRORS

If you know that you often have problems with certain elements of punctuation or diction, be on guard for these particular errors as you examine each sentence.

1. Make sure that each sentence really is a sentence, not a fragment— especially those beginning with *because, since, which, that, although, as, when,* and *what.*
2. Make sure that independent clauses joined by *indeed, moreover, however, nevertheless, thus,* and *hence* have a semicolon before those words, not just a comma.
3. Make sure that every modifying phrase or clause is close to the word it modifies.
4. If you know you have a problem with spelling, check every word and look up all questionable ones.
5. Be especially alert for words that you know you consistently get wrong. If you are aware that you sometimes confuse words that sound alike (*it's/its, your/you're, there/their/they're, effect/affect*), check the accuracy of your usage.

If you are in doubt about how to correct any of the errors just mentioned, you will find advice in the "Handbook for Correcting Errors" at the end of this text.

SEE EACH WORD SEPARATELY

If you find that you still miss spelling and typographical errors even when reading carefully sentence by sentence from the bottom of the page, you need to go through the paper a second time using an index card with a slit cut in it that allows you to see only a word or two at a time. Fold the card in half and, using a pair of scissors, snip out a viewing slot about a quarter of an inch wide and an inch and a half long. (Cut a somewhat larger opening if your finished drafts are handwritten.) Then, beginning at the bottom of the page, move the card slowly across from *right to left*, checking the spelling of each word as you go. If you are unsure about the spelling of any word, look it up in a dictionary. The easier a word is to spell, the more important it becomes to spell it correctly.

FIND A FRIEND TO HELP

If you are writing an important paper and have a literate friend who will help you proofread, you are in luck. Ask this kind person to point out errors and also to let you know whether your thesis is made plain at the beginning, whether every sentence is clear throughout, and whether the paper as a whole makes good sense. You risk, of course, having to do further revising should any of your friend's responses prove negative, but try to be grateful for the help. You want to turn in a paper that you can be proud of.

Relying entirely on someone else to do your proofreading, though, is probably unwise. You are sure to encounter writing situations in college that preclude your bringing a friend to help—essay examinations, for instance, and in-class essays. You need to learn to find and correct your own errors as best you can, so that you will not risk failure when forced to go it alone.

CHART 3–2. Proofreading Checklist

1. Have I mixed up any of these easily confused words?

its/it's	their/they're/there	lie/lay
effect/affect	suppose/supposed	our/are
your/you're	woman/women	use/used
to/too/two	prejudice/prejudiced	then/than
who's/whose	accept/except	cite/site

2. Have I put an apostrophe appropriately in each of my possessive nouns?
3. Have I carelessly repeated any word?
4. Have I carelessly left any words out?
5. Have I omitted the first or final letter from any words?
6. Have I used the proper punctuation at the end of every sentence?
7. Have I spelled every word correctly?

PART TWO

Writing about Short Fiction

This section, focusing on the short story, covers the literary and rhetorical elements that you need to understand in order to write effectively about short fiction.

CHAPTER

4

How Do I Read Short Fiction?

As noted author Joyce Carol Oates has observed, short fiction can be difficult to understand "because it demands compression; each sentence must contribute to the effect of the whole. Its strategy is not to include an excess of detail but to exclude, to select, to focus as sharply as possible."[1] In order to grasp the full meaning of a story, you need to read it at least twice. Preferably, let some time elapse between readings so that you can mull the story over in your mind. Your initial reading can be purely for pleasure, but the second reading should involve careful and deliberate study of all the elements that combine to produce a unified whole. You should gain both pleasure and knowledge from reading short fiction. The knowledge frequently stems from understanding the *theme* that usually provides some insight into the human condition, although sometimes contemporary short stories simply raise moral or ethical questions and make no pretense of providing answers.

Notice the Structure

During the second reading, you should notice the way the story is structured. The action (i.e., what happens) is called the *plot* and usually is spurred by some conflict involving the main character (the *protagonist*). Except in some modern works, most short stories have a clear beginning, middle, and end in which the conflict produc-

[1] Joyce Carol Oates, *Story.* Preface, Part Two. New York: Heath, 1985:830.

ing the action becomes increasingly intense, building to a climax that sometimes resolves the conflict and sometimes simply concludes it—often in catastrophe. Do not expect many happy endings in serious fiction. A somber conclusion is more likely.

Usually stories proceed in regular chronological order following a time sequence similar to that in real life. But occasionally an author employs flashbacks, stopping the forward action to recount something that happened in the past, in order to supply necessary background material or to maintain suspense. By paying close attention to the numerous flashbacks in Porter's "The Jilting of Granny Weatherall," we come to the realization that Granny has been jilted twice. And if Faulkner had written "A Rose for Emily" chronologically, without the distorted time sequence, we would not feel the stunning impact of his surprise conclusion.

Consider Point of View and Setting

Sometimes the *point of view*—the position from which an author chooses to relate a story—can be crucial to the effectiveness, even the understanding, of short fiction. In Thurber's "The Secret Life of Walter Mitty" we enjoy with Mitty the flashes of fantasy playing through his mind. In Porter's "The Jilting of Granny Weatherall" the point of view perfectly conveys the distorted impressions and nostalgic recollections fleeting in and out of an old woman's fading consciousness. At other times, the point of view provides access to the thoughts and feelings of more than one character. In Crane's "The Bride Comes to Yellow Sky," for example, we know the thoughts of both husband and wife. Hemingway, in "Hills Like White Elephants," chooses to allow his characters to tell the story themselves through dialogue. This objective (*dramatic*) point of view is suggested by a glance at the pages, which consist primarily of conversation. Some authors choose to let one character tell the story in the first person, as the young boy does in Anderson's "I Want to Know Why." Part of our pleasure in reading this story derives from the child's naiveté: his speculations on adult behavior are limited by his ignorance of human sexuality. In Poe's "The Fall of the House of Usher" the first-person narrator is essentially an observer, a peripheral character who is present during all of the action reported but who is not himself the focus of it.

The *setting* of a story, like the point of view, can sometimes be consequential, sometimes not. In most of the stories included in this anthology, setting plays a role of some importance. The dark forest setting and the communal atmosphere of the village perhaps carry symbolic significance in Hawthorne's "Young Goodman Brown." The luminous white pear tree outside the window in Mansfield's "Bliss" can be seen as symbolic of the protagonist's fragile innocence. As you study a short story, give some thought to the setting. Could the events just as well take place somewhere else? How does its place in time affect the story? Or does the setting seem to play an integral part? Does it in some way add to the meaning of the story?

Study the Characters

Pay special attention as you reread dialogue, those passages in quotation marks that characters speak to each other. You can begin to determine characterization from these exchanges, just as you come to know real people partly by what they say. As you form an understanding of a character, you also need to notice what other people in the story say about that person, how they respond to that person, as well as what the author reveals of that person's thoughts and past behavior. Since fiction often allows us access to what the characters are thinking (as well as doing), we can sometimes know fictional persons better than we do our closest friends and family members. Sometimes we can be certain of a character's motivation for behaving in a certain way; at other times this motivation becomes one of the elements we must figure out before we can fully appreciate the story. In Chopin's "The Storm," in order to see the love-making as natural and innocent and cleansing, we should be aware that neither Calixta nor her lover intends to commit adultery. The action and the dialogue make clear that neither character planned this coupling, and Chopin also provides numerous images of whiteness to reinforce our impression of Calixta's purity. Understanding the innocent motives of the two main characters helps us to perceive Chopin's playful theme: that a single, spontaneous, undetected adultery can revitalize two languishing marriages, just as a rainstorm refreshes the thirsty landscape.

Look for Specialized Literary Techniques

As you study a story on second reading, you may notice irony and foreshadowing that you missed the first time through. Since *irony* involves an upsetting of expectations—having the opposite happen from what would be usual—you sometimes need to know the outcome of an action in order to detect the full extent of the irony. *Foreshadowing* works the same way: you may not be aware of these hints of future happenings until the happenings finally occur. But when you go through a story again, both irony and foreshadowing become easily apparent and contribute to its meaning and effectiveness.

Be alert also for *images*—for words and phrases that put a picture in your mind. These images increase the enjoyment of reading fiction and, if deliberately repeated, can become *motifs* that emphasize some important element in the story and thus convey meaning. The constant images of fungus and decay in Poe's "The Fall of the House of Usher" reinforce our impression of the deterioration of Roderick Usher's mind. If a repeated image gathers significant meaning, it then becomes a *symbol*—to be clearly related to something else in the story. The moldering of the Usher mansion probably symbolizes the decay of Usher's psyche, just as the repeated images of dust and decay in Faulkner's "A Rose for Emily" symbolize the deterioration of Miss Emily's mind and of the fortunes of her once revered family.

Continue Questioning to Discover Theme

Your entire study of these various elements of fiction should lead to an understanding of the meaning, the *theme*, of the story. The title may in some way point toward or be related to the meaning. If you ask yourself why Mansfield entitled her poignant story "Bliss," you will probably decide that she was either being ironic or that she wanted us to see how fleeting is the young wife's blindly trusting happiness. Sometimes the title identifies the controlling symbol, as in Steinbeck's "The Chrysanthemums" and Gilman's "The Yellow Wall-Paper." Conrad's title "The Heart of Darkness" directs us straight to his subject: the evil that lurks at the core of human nature.

You need to ponder everything about a short story in order to discover its theme. Keep asking yourself questions until you come up with some meaningful observation about human behavior or the conduct of society. The questions that follow will guide you in exploring any story and perhaps spark that essential insight that leads to understanding.

Critical Questions for Reading the Short Story

Before planning an analysis of any of the selections in the anthology of short stories, write out the answers to the following questions to be sure you understand the piece and to help you generate material for your paper.

1. Who is the main character? Does this person's character change during the course of the story? Do you feel sympathetic toward the main character? What sort of person is she or he?

2. What pattern or structure is there to the development of the plot? Can you describe the way the events are organized?

3. Does surprise play an important role in the plot? Is there foreshadowing? Does the author use flashbacks?

4. Is anything about the story ironic?

5. Is there any symbolism in the story? How does the author make you aware of symbolic actions, people, or objects?

6. What is the setting—the time and location? How important are these elements in the story? Could it be set in another time or place just as well?

7. Describe the atmosphere of the story, if it is important. How does the author create this atmosphere?

8. Who narrates the story? Is the narrator reliable? What effect does the point of view have on your understanding of the story? What would be gained or lost if the story were told from a different point of view (for example, by another character)?

9. How does the title relate to the other elements in the story and to the overall meaning?

10. What is the theme of the story? Can you state it in a single sentence? How is this theme carried out?

11. Does the author's style of writing affect your reading (i.e., interpretation) of the story? If so, how would you describe the style? For example, is it conversational or formal? Familiar or unfamiliar? Simple or ornate? Ironic or satiric?

5

Writing about Structure

When you focus on structure in discussing a literary work, you are examining the way the parts fit together to form a whole. Examining the structure often proves an excellent means of understanding a short story, novel, poem, or play and is also a good way to approach a written literary analysis.

What Is Structure?

Most works of literature have an underlying, reasoned pattern that serves as a framework or *structure*. Consider the key terms in our definition.

Underlying: We mean that the structure is probably not immediately or visually evident. As an analogy, consider the skeleton that gives structure to the body.

Reasoned: We use this term because structure is usually logically appropriate for the plot and theme of the work.

Pattern: We use this term to suggest that the structure serves as a plan or design, like an outline for an essay.

Looking at Structure

With our definition of structure in mind, read James Thurber's "The Secret Life of Walter Mitty" and try to determine what holds the story together.

James Thurber *1894–1961*

THE SECRET LIFE OF WALTER MITTY

"We're going through!" The Commander's voice was like thin ice breaking. He wore his full-dress uniform, with the heavily braided white cap pulled down rakishly over one cold gray eye. "We can't make it, sir. It's spoiling for a hurricane, if you ask me." "I'm not asking you, Lieutenant Berg," said the Commander. "Throw on the power lights! Rev her up to 8,500! We're going through!" The pounding of the cylinders increased: ta-pocketa-pocketa-pocketa-*pocketa-pocketa*. The Commander stared at the ice forming on the pilot window. He walked over and twisted a row of complicated dials. "Switch on No. 8 auxiliary!" he shouted. "Switch on No. 8 auxiliary!" repeated Lieutenant Berg. "Full strength in No. 3 turret!" shouted the Commander. "Full strength in No. 3 turret!" The crew, bending to their various tasks in the huge, hurtling eight-engined Navy hydroplane, looked at each other and grinned. "The Old Man'll get us through," they said to one another. "The Old Man ain't afraid of Hell!" . . .

"No so fast! You're driving too fast!" said Mrs. Mitty. "What are you driving so fast for?"

"Hmm?" said Walter Mitty. He looked at his wife, in the seat beside him, with shocked astonishment. She seemed grossly unfamiliar, like a strange woman who had yelled at him in a crowd. "You were up to fifty-five," she said. "You know I don't like to go more than forty. You were up to fifty-five." Walter Mitty drove on toward Waterbury in silence, the roaring of the SN202 through the worst storm in twenty years of Navy flying fading in the remote, intimate airways of his mind. "You're tensed up again," said Mrs. Mitty. "It's one of your days. I wish you'd let Dr. Renshaw look you over."

Walter Mitty stopped the car in front of the building where his wife went to have her hair done. "Remember to get those overshoes while I'm having my hair done," she said. "I don't need overshoes," said Mitty. She put her mirror back into her bag. "We've been all through that," she said, getting out of the car. "You're not a young man any longer." He raced the engine a little. "Why don't you wear your gloves? Have you lost your gloves?" Walter Mitty reached in a pocket and brought out the gloves. He put them on, but after she had turned and gone into the building and he had driven on to a red light, he took them off again. "Pick it up, brother!" snapped a cop as the light changed, and Mitty hastily pulled on his gloves and lurched ahead. He drove around the streets aimlessly for a time, and then he drove past the hospital on his way to the parking lot.

. . . "It's the millionaire banker, Wellington McMillan," said the pretty nurse. "Yes?" said Walter Mitty, removing his gloves slowly. "Who has the case?" "Dr. Renshaw and Dr. Benbow, but there are two specialists here, Dr. Remington from New York and Mr. Pritchard-Mitford from London. He flew over." A door opened down a long, cool corridor and

51

Dr. Renshaw came out. He looked distraught and haggard. "Hell, Mitty," he said. "We're having the devil's own time with McMillan, the millionaire banker and close personal friend of Roosevelt. Obstreosis of the ductal tract. Tertiary. Wish you'd take a look at him." "Glad to," said Mitty.

In the operating room there were whispered introductions: "Dr. Remington, Dr. Mitty. Mr. Pritchard-Mitford, Dr. Mitty." "I've read your book on streptothricosis," said Pritchard-Mitford, shaking hands. "A brilliant performance, sir." "Thank you," said Walter Mitty. "Didn't know you were in the States, Mitty," grumbled Remington. "Coals to Newcastle, bringing Mitford and me here for a tertiary." "You are very kind," said Mitty. A huge, complicated machine, connected to the operating table, with many tubes and wires, began at this moment to go pocketa-pocketa-pocketa. "The new anesthetizer is giving way!" shouted an interne. "There is no one in the East who knows how to fix it!" "Quiet, man!" said Mitty, in a low, cool voice. He sprang to the machine, which was now going pocketa-pocketa-queep-pocketa-queep. He began fingering delicately a row of glistening dials. "Give me a fountain pen!" he snapped. Someone handed him a fountain pen. He pulled a faulty piston out of the machine and inserted the pen in its place. "That will hold for ten minutes," he said. "Get on with the operation." A nurse hurried over and whispered to Renshaw, and Mitty saw the man turn pale. "Coreopsis has set in," said Renshaw nervously. "If you would take over, Mitty?" Mitty looked at him and at the craven figure of Benbow, who drank, and at the grave, uncertain faces of the two great specialists. "If you wish," he said. They slipped a white gown on him; he adjusted a mask and drew on thin gloves; nurses handed him shining. . . .

"Back it up, Mac! Look out for that Buick!" Walter Mitty jammed on the brakes. "Wrong lane, Mac," said the parking-lot attendant, looking at Mitty closely. "Gee. Yeh," muttered Mitty. He began cautiously to back out of the lane marked "Exit Only." "Leave her sit there," said the attendant. "I'll put her away." Mitty got out of the car. "Hey, better leave the key." "Oh," said Mitty, handing the man the ignition key. The attendant vaulted into the car, backed it up with insolent skill, and put it where it belonged.

They're so damn cocky, thought Walter Mitty, walking along Main Street; they think they know everything. Once he had tried to take his chains off, outside New Milford, and he had got them wound around the axles. A man had had to come out in a wrecking car and unwind them, a young, grinning garageman. Since then Mrs. Mitty always made him drive to a garage to have the chains taken off. The next time, he thought, I'll wear my right arm in a sling; they won't grin at me then. I'll have my right arm in a sling and they'll see I couldn't possibly take the chains off myself. He kicked at the slush on the sidewalk. "Overshoes," he said to himself, and he began looking for a shoe store.

When he came out into the street again, with the overshoes in a box under his arm, Walter Mitty began to wonder what the other thing was his wife had told him to get. She had told him twice, before they set out from their house for Waterbury. In a way he hated these weekly trips to town—he was always getting something wrong. Kleenex, he thought, Squibb's, razor blades? No. Toothpaste, toothbrush, bicarbonate, carborundum, initiative and referendum? He gave it up. But she would remember it. "Where's the what's-its-name?" she would ask. "Don't tell me you forgot the what's-its-name?" A newsboy went by shouting something about the Waterbury trial.

. . . "Perhaps this will refresh your memory." The District Attorney suddenly thrust a heavy automatic at the quiet figure on the witness stand. "Have you ever seen this before?" Walter Mitty took the gun and examined it expertly. "This is my Webley-Vickers 50.80," he said calmly. An excited buzz ran around the courtroom. The judge rapped for order. "You are a crack shot with any sort of firearms, I believe?" said the District Attorney, insinuatingly. "Objection!" shouted Mitty's attorney. "We have shown that the defendant could not have fired the shot. We have shown that he wore his right arm in a sling on the night of the fourteenth of July." Walter Mitty raised his hand briefly and the bickering attorneys were stilled. "With any known make of gun," he said evenly, "I could have killed Gregory Fitzhurst at three hundred feet *with my left hand*." Pandemonium broke loose in the courtroom. A woman's scream rose above the bedlam and suddenly a lovely, dark-haired girl was in Walter Mitty's arms. The District Attorney struck at her savagely. Without rising from his chair, Mitty let the man have it on the point of the chin. "You miserable cur!" . . .

"Puppy biscuit," said Walter Mitty. He stopped walking and the buildings of Waterbury rose up out of the misty courtroom and surrounded him again. A woman who was passing laughed. "He said 'Puppy biscuit,' " she said to her companion. "That man said 'Puppy biscuit' to himself." Walter Mitty hurried on. He went into an A & P, not the first one he came to but a smaller one farther up the street. "I want some biscuit for small, young dogs," he said to the clerk. "Any special brand, sir?" The greatest pistol shot in the world thought a moment, "It says, 'Puppies Bark for It' on the box," said Walter Mitty.

His wife would be through at the hairdresser's in fifteen minutes, Mitty saw in looking at his watch, unless they had trouble drying it; sometimes they had trouble drying it. She didn't like to get to the hotel first; she would want him to be there waiting for her as usual. He found a big leather chair in the lobby, facing a window, and he put the overshoes and the puppy biscuit on the floor beside it. He picked up an old copy of *Liberty* and sank down into the chair. "Can Germany Conquer the World Through the Air?" Walter Mitty looked at the pictures of bombing planes and of ruined streets.

. . . "The cannonading has got the wind up in young Raleigh, sir," said the sergeant. Captain Mitty looked up at him through tousled hair. "Get him to bed," he said wearily. "With the others. I'll fly alone." "But you can't, sir," said the sergeant anxiously. "It takes two men to handle that bomber and the Archies are pounding hell out of the air. Von Richtman's circus is between here and Saulier." "Somebody's got to get that ammunition dump," said Mitty. "I'm going over. Spot of brandy?" He poured a drink for the sergeant and one for himself. War thundered and whined around the dugout and battered at the door. There was a rending of wood and splinters flew through the room. "A bit of a near thing," said Captain Mitty carelessly. "The box barrage is closing in," said the sergeant. "We only live once, Sergeant," said Mitty, with his faint, fleeting smile. "Or do we?" He poured another brandy and tossed it off. "I never see a man could hold his brandy like you, sir," said the sergeant. "Begging your pardon, sir." Captain Mitty stood up and strapped on his huge Webley-Vickers automatic. "It's forty kilometers through hell, sir," said the sergeant. Mitty finished one last brandy. "After all," he said softly, "what isn't?" The pounding of the cannon increased; there was the rat-tat-tatting of machine guns, and from somewhere came the menacing pocketa-pocketa-pocketa of the new flame-throwers. Walter Mitty walked to the door of the dugout humming "Auprès de Ma Blonde." He turned and waved to the sergeant. "Cheerio!" he said. . . .

Something struck his shoulder. "I've been looking all over this hotel for you," said Mrs. Mitty. "Why do you have to hide in this old chair? How do you expect me to find you?" "Things close in," said Walter Mitty vaguely. "What?" Mrs. Mitty said. "Did you get the what's-its-name? The puppy biscuit? What's in the box?" "Overshoes," said Mitty. "Couldn't you have put them on in the store?" "I was thinking," said Walter Mitty. "Does it ever occur to you that I am sometimes thinking?" She looked at him. "I'm going to take your temperature when I get you home," she said.

They went out through the revolving doors that made a faintly derisive whistling sound when you pushed them. It was two blocks to the parking lot. At the drugstore on the corner she said, "Wait here for me. I forgot something. I won't be a minute." She was more than a minute. Walter Mitty lighted a cigarette. It began to rain, rain with sleet in it. He stood up against the wall of the drugstore, smoking. . . . He put his shoulders back and his heels together. "To hell with the handkerchief," said Walter Mitty scornfully. He took one last drag on his cigarette and snapped it away. Then, with that faint, fleeting smile playing about his lips, he faced the firing squad; erect and motionless, proud and disdainful, Walter Mitty the Undefeated, inscrutable to the last.

(1942)

Prewriting

Before you can begin to write about structure, you must first determine the underlying patterns that serve as a framework for the story.

FINDING PATTERNS

Read the following questions; then carefully reread the story. Write down your answers to the questions.

1. What does the title mean?

2. What are the two main parts of Mitty's life?

3. How many fantasies does Mitty have in the course of the story?

4. Finish this list of similarities among Mitty's fantasies:
> heroic task or feat
> impressive machinery
> sound effects

5. Finish this list of similarities among the real-life episodes:
> rude awakening
> wife or other authority figure

Writing

Once you understand the structure of the story, you need to discover a framework within which you can effectively present your observations—that is, a structure for your own paper.

GROUPING DETAILS

Try to write one sentence that describes the general pattern of Mitty's fantasies. Then write another sentence describing the general pattern of the real-life episodes in the story. After you have written sentences that you find satisfactory, discuss which details would belong under each descriptive term in your sentences. For example, you will probably mention

Heroic Tasks or Feats
> piloting Navy craft through storm
> saving millionaire banker's life
> bombing ammunition dump

RELATING DETAILS TO THEME

An accurate description of the general pattern and a convincing list of supporting details will be crucial to any essay about structure. But you also need to work out a thesis—a controlling idea for your paper that relates the structure to the overall impact or meaning of the work. For example, an essay about the structure of "Eveline" might have this thesis:

> The flashbacks to Eveline's family life and to her romance with Frank, which interrupt the basic chronological flow of the story, serve to give us key information explaining her final, fateful decision.

IDEAS FOR WRITING

The following writing ideas relate structure to meaning. Adopt one of them, revise one, or create your own for a paper on "The Secret Life of Walter Mitty."

1. The sharp contrast between the repeated elements in Mitty's fantasies and the repeated elements in his real life explains his inability to integrate his real self and his ideal self.

2. The pattern established in four fully developed fantasies invites readers to fill out the details in the abbreviated closing fantasy, enhancing the humor and pathos of the story.

3. The twist in the expected pattern of fantasy number three (the courtroom scene) adds another dimension to Mitty's "secret life" and gives credibility to his last fantasy.

Rewriting

Our advice in this section will focus on problems peculiar to writing about literature.

INTEGRATING QUOTATIONS GRACEFULLY

In any literary essay you will need quotations from the text of the work you are examining. Be sure that you enclose these borrowings in quotation marks as you gracefully introduce them or integrate them into your own sentences, like this:

> Impressive machinery, emitting "pocketa-pocketa-pocketa" noises, haunts Mitty's fantasies.
>
> In real life Walter Mitty feels threatened by authority—or even by competence—as we see in the episode with the "young, grinning garageman" who untangles the snow chains.
>
> In Mitty's view, a parking attendant "backed it [Mitty's car] up with insolent skill," although the insolence may be imagined.

That last example shows how you may add your own words to explain a possibly confusing word in a quotation: use brackets. Most of the time, though, you can devise a way to avoid this awkwardness by rewriting the sentence:

> After Mitty failed to maneuver his car, a parking attendant "backed it up with insolent skill," but we must wonder whether the insolence was imagined.

CREDITING SOURCES

When writing a paper on a single literary source, you need not use a note number every time you quote. Instead, type a raised 1 directly after your first quotation from the source, like this:

> Mitty's relationship with reality is so weak that at one point he finds his own wife "grossly unfamiliar, like a strange woman who had yelled at him in a crowd."[1]

Then provide an informational note, also numbered with a raised 1, at the end of the paper:

[1] Thurber, James. "The Secret Life of Walter Mitty." *Literature and the Writing Process.* Elizabeth McMahan, Susan Day, and Robert Funk. New York: Macmillan, 1985: 51. Page numbers for subsequent references to this story will be included in parentheses within the text.

Notice that when giving credit within the paper, you close the quotation, put in the parentheses, and end with the period:

We know poor Mitty feels irritated by the competence of others: "They're so damned cocky, thought Walter Mitty, walking along Main Street; they think they know everything" (52).

6

Writing about Symbolism

Symbolism, one of the most important aspects of serious imaginative literature, is often difficult for the unpracticed reader to detect and understand, but this interpretive skill can be developed with practice. Because the meaning or theme of a literary work is often conveyed through symbolism, you can effectively devote an entire paper to an examination of a key symbol or a pattern of symbolism.

What Are Symbols?

A symbol is something concrete that stands for or suggests more than itself: a flag, a piece of colored cloth, stands for a nation; yellowed falling leaves may suggest death; rain can signify rebirth. A symbol makes an abstraction tangible, often visible. The rose in Robert Burns's "Oh, my love is like a red, red rose" makes us appreciate the beauty and vitality of the loved one celebrated in the poem.

HOW DO SYMBOLS FUNCTION?

In fiction, symbols convey significance in an immediate, vivid way. By associating Eveline with dust, for instance, Joyce communicates more about her dreary life than if he had written two paragraphs on passivity and dullness.

Symbols in fiction are often inanimate objects, animals, or people, but other things may function symbolically: colors, names, a line from a song, a repeated phrase—such as the "ta-pocketa-pocketa" in Walter Mitty's fantasies. These recurring items or images, some-times called *motifs*, unify a story and provide important clues to meaning.

Literary symbols frequently have several meanings; sometimes these may even be almost inexpressible. The color and the mysteri-ous, writhing patterns in the wallpaper constitute a strong symbol in Charlotte Perkins Gilman's "The Yellow Wall-Paper," but pre-cisely what the paper "stands for" is difficult to express briefly and satisfactorily. Though some symbols may be hard to interpret, you should not ignore them: they convey significant meaning. Recogniz-ing symbols and responding to them sensitively are requirements for an informed reading of serious fiction.

Looking at Symbols

Read the following story by Shirley Jackson and see if you are aware, on first reading, of her pervasive use of symbolism.

Shirley Jackson *1919–1965*

THE LOTTERY

The morning of June 27th was clear and sunny, with the fresh warmth of a full-summer day; the flowers were blossoming profusely and the grass was richly green. The people of the village began to gather in the square, between the post office and the bank, around ten o'clock; in some towns there were so many people that the lottery took two days and had to be started on June 26th, but in this village, where there were only about three hundred people, the whole lottery took less than two hours, so it could begin at ten o'clock in the morning and still be through in time to allow the villagers to get home for noon dinner.

The children assembled first, of course. School was recently over for the summer, and the feeling of liberty sat uneasily on most of them; they tended to gather together quietly for a while before they broke into boisterous play, and their talk was still of the classroom and the teacher, of books and reprimands. Bobby Martin had already stuffed his pockets full of stones, and the other boys soon followed his example, selecting the smoothest and roundest stones; Bobby and Harry Jones and Dickie Delacroix—the villagers pronounced his name "Dellacroy"—eventually made a great pile of stones in one corner of the square and guarded it against the raids of the other boys. The girls stood aside, talking among themselves, looking over their shoulders at the boys, and the very small children rolled in the dust or clung to the hands of their older brothers or sisters.

Soon the men began to gather, surveying their own children, speaking of planting and rain, tractors and taxes. They stood together, away from the pile of stones in the corner, and their jokes were quiet and they smiled rather than laughed. The women, wearing faded house dresses and sweaters, came shortly after their menfolk. They greeted one another and exchanged bits of gossip as they went to join their husbands. Soon the women, standing by their husbands, began to call to their children, and the children came reluctantly, having to be called four or five times. Bobby Martin ducked under his mother's grasping hand and ran, laughing, back to the pile of stones. His father spoke up sharply, and Bobby came quickly and took his place between his father and his oldest brother.

The lottery was conducted—as were the square dances, the teen-age club, the Halloween program—by Mr. Summers, who had time and energy to devote to civic activities. He was a round-faced, jovial man and he ran the coal business, and people were sorry for him, because he had no children and his wife was a scold. When he arrived in the square, carrying the black wooden box, there was a murmur of conversation among the villagers, and he waved and called, "Little late today, folks." The postmaster, Mr. Graves, followed him, carrying a three-legged stool, and the stool was put in the center of the square and Mr. Summers set the black box down on it. The villagers kept their distance, leaving a space between themselves and the stool, and when Mr. Summers said, "Some of you fellows want to give me a hand?" there was a hesitation before two men, Mr. Martin and his oldest son, Baxter, came forward to hold the box steady on the stool while Mr. Summers stirred up the papers inside it.

The original paraphernalia for the lottery had been lost long ago, and the black box now resting on the stool had been put into use even before Old Man Warner, the oldest man in town, was born. Mr. Summers spoke frequently to the villagers about making a new box, but no one liked to upset even as much tradition as was represented by the black box. There was a story that the present box had been made with some pieces of the box that had preceded it, the one that had been constructed when the first people settled down to make a village here. Every year, after the lottery, Mr. Summers began talking again about a new box, but every year the subject was allowed to fade off without anything's being done. The black box grew shabbier each year; by now it was no longer completely black but splintered badly along one side to show the original wood color, and in some places faded or stained.

Mr. Martin and his oldest son, Baxter, held the black box securely on the stool until Mr. Summers had stirred the papers thoroughly with his hand. Because so much of the ritual had been forgotten or discarded, Mr. Summers had been successful in having slips of paper substituted for the chips of wood that had been used for generations. Chips of wood, Mr. Summers had argued, had been all very well when the village was tiny, but now that the population was more than three hundred and likely to keep on growing, it was necessary to use something that would fit more easily into the black box. The night before the lottery, Mr. Summers and Mr. Graves made up the slips of paper and put them in the box, and it was then taken to the safe of Mr. Summers' coal company and locked up until Mr. Summers was ready to take it to the square next morning. The rest of the year, the box was put away, sometimes one place, sometimes another; it had spent one year in Mr. Graves's barn and another year underfoot in the post office, and sometimes it was set on a shelf in the Martin grocery and left there.

There was a great deal of fussing to be done before Mr. Summers declared the lottery open. There were the lists to make up—of heads of families, heads of households in each family, members of each household in each family. There was the proper swearing-in of Mr. Summers by the postmaster, as the official of the lottery; at one time, some people remembered, there had been a recital of some sort, performed by the official of the lottery, a perfunctory, tuneless chant that had been rattled off duly each year; some people believed that the official of the lottery used to stand just so when he said or sang it, others believed that he was supposed to walk among the people, but years and years ago this part of the ritual had been allowed to lapse. There had been, also, a ritual salute, which the official of the lottery had had to use in addressing each person who came up to draw from the box, but this also had changed with time, until now it was felt necessary only for the official to speak to each person approaching. Mr. Summers was very good at all this; in his clean white shirt and blue jeans, with one hand resting carelessly on the black box, he seemed very proper and important as he talked interminably to Mr. Graves and the Martins.

Just as Mr. Summers finally left off talking and turned to the assembled villagers, Mrs. Hutchinson came hurriedly along the path to the square, her sweater thrown over her shoulders, and slid into place in the back of the crowd. "Clean forgot what day it was," she said to Mrs. Delacroix, who stood next to her, and they both laughed softly. "Thought my old man was out back stacking wood," Mrs. Hutchinson went on, "and then I looked out the window and the kids were gone, and then I remembered it was the twenty-seventh and came a-running." She dried her hands on her apron, and Mrs. Delacroix said, "You're in time, though. They're still talking away up there."

Mrs. Hutchinson craned her neck to see through the crowd and found her husband and children standing near the front. She tapped Mrs. Delacroix on the arm as a farewell and began to make her way through the crowd. The people separated good-humoredly to let her through; two or three people said, in voices just loud enough to be heard across the crowd, "Here comes your Missus, Hutchinson," and "Bill, she made it after all." Mrs. Hutchinson reached her husband, and Mr. Summers, who had been waiting, said cheerfully, "Thought we were going to have to get on without you, Tessie." Mrs. Hutchinson said, grinning, "Wouldn't have me leave m'dishes in the sink, now, would you, Joe?," and soft laughter ran through the crowd as the people stirred back into position after Mrs. Hutchinson's arrival.

"Well, now," Mr. Summers said soberly, "guess we better get started, get this over with, so's we can go back to work. Anybody ain't here?"

"Dunbar," several people said. "Dunbar, Dunbar."

Mr. Summers consulted his list. "Clyde Dunbar," he said. "That's right. He's broke his leg, hasn't he? Who's drawing for him?"

"Me, I guess," a woman said, and Mr. Summers turned to look at her. "Wife draws for her husband," Mr. Summers said. "Don't you have a grown boy to do it for you, Janey?" Although Mr. Summers and everyone else in the village knew the answer perfectly well, it was the business of the official of the lottery to ask such questions formally. Mr. Summers waited with an expression of polite interest while Mrs. Dunbar answered.

"Horace's not but sixteen yet," Mrs. Dunbar said regretfully. "Guess I gotta fill in for the old man this year."

"Right," Mr. Summers said. He made a note on the list he was holding. Then he asked, "Watson boy drawing this year?"

A tall boy in the crowd raised his hand. "Here," he said. "I'm drawing for m'mother and me." He blinked his eyes nervously and ducked his head as several voices in the crowd said things like "Good fellow, Jack," and "Glad to see your mother's got a man to do it."

"Well," Mr. Summers said, "guess that's everyone. Old Man Warner make it?"

"Here," a voice said, and Mr. Summers nodded.

A sudden hush fell on the crowd as Mr. Summers cleared his throat and looked at the list. "All ready?" he called. "Now, I'll read the names—heads of families first—and the men come up and take a paper out of the box. Keep the paper folded in your hand without looking at it until everyone has had a turn. Everything clear?"

The people had done it so many times that they only half listened to the directions; most of them were quiet, wetting their lips, not looking around. Then Mr. Summers raised one hand high and said, "Adams." A man disengaged himself from the crowd and came forward. "Hi, Steve," Mr. Summers said, and Mr. Adams said, "Hi, Joe." They grinned at one another humorlessly and nervously. Then Mr. Adams reached into the black box and took out a folded paper. He held it firmly by one corner as he turned and went hastily back to his place in the crowd, where he stood a little apart from his family, not looking down at his hand.

"Allen." Mr. Summers said. "Anderson. . . . Bentham."

"Seems like there's no time at all between lotteries any more," Mrs. Delacroix said to Mrs. Graves in the back row. "Seems like we got through with the last one only last week."

"Time sure goes fast," Mrs. Graves said.

"Clark. . . . Delacroix."

"There goes my old man," Mrs. Delacroix said. She held her breath while her husband went forward.

"Dunbar," Mr. Summers said, and Mrs. Dunbar went steadily to the box while one of the women said, "Go on, Janey," and another said, "There she goes."

"We're next," Mrs. Graves said. She watched while Mr. Graves came around from the side of the box, greeted Mr. Summers gravely, and selected a slip of paper from the box. By now, all through the crowd there were men holding the small folded papers in their large hands, turning them over and over nervously. Mrs. Dunbar and her two sons stood together, Mrs. Dunbar holding the slip of paper.

"Harburt. . . . Hutchinson."

"Get up there, Bill," Mrs. Hutchinson said, and the people near her laughed.

"Jones."

"They do say," Mr. Adams said to Old Man Warner, who stood next to him, "that over in the north village they're talking of giving up the lottery."

Old Man Warner snorted. "Pack of crazy fools," he said. "Listening to the young folks, nothing's good enough for *them*. Next thing you know, they'll be wanting to go back to living in caves, nobody work any more, live *that* way for a while. Used to be a saying about 'Lottery in June, corn be heavy soon.' First thing you know, we'd all be eating stewed chickweed and acorns. There's *always* been a lottery," he added petulantly. "Bad enough to see young Joe Summers up there joking with everybody."

"Some places have already quit lotteries," Mrs. Adams said.

"Nothing but trouble in *that*," Old Man Warner said stoutly. "Pack of young fools."

"Martin." And Bobby Martin watched his father go forward. "Overdyke . . . . Percy."

"I wish they'd hurry," Mrs. Dunbar said to her oldest son. "I wish they'd hurry."

"They're almost through," her son said.

"You get ready to run tell Dad," Mrs. Dunbar said.

Mr. Summers called his own name and then stepped forward precisely and selected a slip from the box. Then he called, "Warner."

"Seventy-seventh year I been in the lottery," Old Man Warner said as he went through the crowd. "Seventy-seventh time."

"Watson." The tall boy came awkwardly through the crowd. Someone said, "Don't be nervous, Jack," said Mr. Summers said, "Take your time, son."

"Zanini."

After that, there was a long pause, a breathless pause, until Mr. Summers, holding his slip of paper in the air, said, "All right, fellows." For a minute, no one moved, and then all the slips of paper were opened. Suddenly, all the women began to speak at once, saying, "Who is it?," "Who's got it?," "Is it the Dunbars?," "Is it the Watsons?" Then the voices began to say, "It's Hutchinson. It's Bill," "Bill Hutchinson's got it."

"Go tell your father," Mrs. Dunbar said to her older son.

People began to look around to see the Hutchinsons. Bill Hutchinson was standing quiet, staring down at the paper in his hand. Suddenly, Tessie Hutchinson shouted to Mr. Summers, "You didn't give him time enough to take any paper he wanted. I saw you. It wasn't fair!"

"Be a good sport, Tessie," Mrs. Delacroix called, and Mrs. Graves said, "All of us took the same chance."

"Shut up, Tessie," Bill Hutchinson said.

"Well, everyone," Mr. Summers said, "that was done pretty fast, and now we've got to be hurrying a little more to get it done in time." He consulted his next list. "Bill," he said, "you draw for the Hutchinson family. You got any other households in the Hutchinsons?"

"There's Don and Eva," Mrs. Hutchinson yelled. "Make *them* take their chance!"

"Daughters draw with their husbands' families, Tessie," Mr. Summers said gently. "You know that as well as anyone else."

"It wasn't *fair*," Tessie said.

"I guess not, Joe," Bill Hutchinson said regretfully. "My daughter draws with her husband's family, that's only fair. And I've got no other family except the kids."

"Then, as far as drawing for families is concerned, it's you," Mr. Summers said in explanation, "and as far as drawing for households is concerned, that's you, too. Right?"

"Right," Bill Hutchinson said.

"How many kids, Bill?" Mr. Summers asked formally.

"Three," Bill Hutchinson said. "There's Bill, Jr., and Nancy, and little Dave. And Tessie and me."

"All right, then," Mr. Summers said. "Harry, you got their tickets back?"

Mr. Graves nodded and held up the slips of paper. "Put them in the box, then," Mr. Summers directed. "Take Bill's and put it in."

"I think we ought to start over," Mrs. Hutchinson said, as quietly as she could. "I tell you it wasn't *fair*. You didn't give him time enough to choose. *Every*body saw that."

Mr. Graves had selected the five slips and put them in the box, and he dropped all the papers but those onto the ground, where the breeze caught them and lifted them off.

"Listen, everybody," Mrs. Hutchinson was saying to the people around her.

"Ready, Bill?" Mr. Summers asked, and Bill Hutchinson, with one quick glance around at his wife and children, nodded.

"Remember," Mr. Summers said, "take the slips and keep them folded until each person has taken one. Harry, you help little Dave." Mr. Graves took the hand of the little boy, who came willingly with him up to the box. "Take a paper out of the box, Davy," Mr. Summers said. Davy put his hand into the box and laughed. "Take just *one* paper," Mr. Summers said. "Harry, you hold it for him." Mr. Graves took the child's hand and removed the folded paper from the tight fist and held it while little Dave stood next to him and looked up at him wonderingly.

"Nancy, next," Mr. Summers said. Nancy was twelve, and her school friends breathed heavily as she went forward, switching her skirt, and took a slip daintily from the box. "Bill, Jr.," Mr. Summers said, and Billy, his face red and his feet over-large, nearly knocked the box over as he got a paper out. "Tessie," Mr. Summers said. She hesitated for a minute, looking around defiantly, and then set her lips and went up to the box. She snatched a paper out and held it behind her.

"Bill," Mr. Summers said, and Bill Hutchinson reached into the box and felt around, bringing his hand out at last with the slip of paper in it.

The crowd was quiet. A girl whispered, "I hope it's not Nancy," and the sound of the whisper reached the edges of the crowd.

"It's not the way it used to be," Old Man Warner said clearly. "People ain't the way they used to be."

"All right," Mr. Summers said. "Open the papers. Harry, you open little Dave's."

Mr. Graves opened the slip of paper and there was a general sigh through the crowd as he held it up and everyone could see that it was blank. Nancy and Bill, Jr., opened theirs at the same time, and both beamed and laughed, turning around to the crowd and holding their slips of paper above their heads.

"Tessie," Mr. Summers said. There was a pause, and then Mr. Summers looked at Bill Hutchinson, and Bill unfolded his paper and showed it. It was blank.

"It's Tessie," Mr. Summers said, and his voice was hushed. "Show us her paper, Bill."

Bill Hutchinson went over to his wife and forced the slip of paper out of her hand. It had a black spot on it, the black spot Mr. Summers had made the night before with the heavy pencil in the coal-company office. Bill Hutchinson held it up, and there was a stir in the crowd.

"All right, folks," Mr. Summers said. "Let's finish quickly."

Although the villagers had forgotten the ritual and lost the original black box, they still remembered to use stones. The pile of stones the boys had made earlier was ready; there were stones on the ground with the blowing scraps of paper that had come out of the box. Mrs. Delacroix selected a stone so large she had to pick it up with both hands and turned to Mrs. Dunbar. "Come on," she said. "Hurry up."

Mrs. Dunbar had small stones in both hands, and she said, gasping for breath, "I can't run at all. You'll have to go ahead and I'll catch up with you."

The children had stones already, and someone gave little Davy Hutchinson a few pebbles.

Tessie Hutchinson was in the center of a cleared space by now, and she held her hands out desperately as the villagers moved in on her. "It isn't fair," she said. A stone hit her on the side of the head.

Old Man Warner was saying, "Come on, come on, everyone." Steve Adams was in the front of the crowd of villagers, with Mrs. Graves beside him.

"It isn't fair, it isn't right," Mrs. Hutchinson screamed, and then they were upon her.

(1948)

Prewriting

Symbols in fiction are not difficult to recognize. Usually an author will give a symbol particular emphasis—by mentioning it repeatedly (like the dust in "Eveline") or even by naming the work after it (as in "The Yellow Wall-Paper"). A crucial symbol will sometimes be placed in the story's opening or ending.

INTERPRETING SYMBOLS

Shirley Jackson directs our attention to the lottery by making it the title of her story. She also gives us abundant detail about this traditional ritual: we know the exact date and time, how the lottery is conducted, who draws and in what order, what the box and the slips of paper look like, and so forth. Clearly the lottery is the story's central symbol as well as its title. The meaning of the lottery is the meaning of "The Lottery."

Here are some points and questions to consider as you read the story a second time and try to work out your interpretation of its symbolism.

1. We are told a lot about the lottery, but not its exact purpose. Do the townspeople know? Is this omission significant? Intentional?

2. Why is much of the history of the lottery and the black box uncertain and vague? Why does Mr. Summers have to ask a question that he and everybody else already know the answer to?

3. The box used in the lottery is mentioned almost thirty times in the story—more than ten times in the phrase "the black box." Why does the author emphasize this object and its color so strongly?

4. The stones are mentioned five times near the beginning of the
   story and then five or six times more at the end. Why is their
   presence so important? What are the historical/biblical
   associations of a "stoning"? Do they apply in this situation?

5. Which characters seem to stand for particular ideas or views?
   What about Old Man Warner? Look at his speeches and comments
   throughout the story. Tessie Hutchinson also gets a lot of
   attention, of course. What is ironic about her being the chosen
   victim?

Writing

The key to a successful essay is a good *thesis,* or controlling idea.
Before you get too far in your writing, you should try to state your
main point in a single sentence.

PRODUCING A WORKABLE THESIS

A useful thesis should narrow the topic to an idea you can cover
within your word limit. It should indicate the direction of your
thinking—what you intend to *say* about that idea. Be sure to state
your thesis in a complete sentence to indicate the point you plan
to make.

EXERCISE

The following thesis statements are too broad to be workable. Figure
out how each one can be narrowed and given direction; then write
an improved version.

Here is an example of the kind of revisions we hope you will
produce.

> Too broad: Shirley Jackson's "The Lottery" contains a number of
> significant symbols.
>
> Improved: In "The Lottery" Shirley Jackson uses simple objects—
> a box, some stones, some slips of paper—to symbolize
> the narrow-mindedness and brutality that result from
> superstitious thinking.

1. Shirley Jackson's "The Lottery" is a compelling story about
   scapegoats.

2. The ritual of the lottery itself serves as a symbol in Shirley
   Jackson's story.

3. The setting of Shirley Jackson's "The Lottery" is an important
   element in contributing to the effectiveness of the story.

4. The characters function symbolically in Shirley Jackson's "The
   Lottery."

5. Shirley Jackson's "The Lottery" reveals a great deal about society and human nature.

IDEAS FOR WRITING

1. Look up the word "scapegoat" in a good dictionary. Then look it up in the *Micropaedia* of the new *Encyclopaedia Britannica* (1979), which will give you some historical examples of the use of scapegoats. Formulate a thesis that relates the symbolism of "The Lottery" to the notion of a scapegoat. You should also think of modern uses of scapegoats to give relevance to your observations.

2. What is Shirley Jackson saying about traditional rituals? How do the symbols in the story contribute to our understanding of her viewpoint?

3. Write an essay about the symbolism of the characters in "The Lottery," especially Tessie Hutchinson, Old Man Warner, Bill Hutchinson, Mr. Graves, and Mr. Summers.

Rewriting

As you revise your first draft, you will try to improve it in every way possible. Our advice at this point involves ideas for improving your introduction.

SHARPENING THE INTRODUCTION

Look at your introductory paragraph. Does it give your readers a clear idea of the topic and purpose? Will it arouse curiosity and interest, as well as lead into your subject?

One strategy for catching the attention of your readers involves using a pertinent quotation:

> "The less there is to justify a traditional custom," wrote Mark Twain, "the harder it is to get rid of it." This comment accurately describes the situation that Shirley Jackson presents in "The Lottery." Her story illustrates how ignorance and superstition become instilled in human society and lead to unnecessary violence.

Another relevant quotation for this introduction might be Gathorne Cranbrook's observation that "The tradition of preserving traditions became a tradition." Useful quotations like these are available in your library in reference books such as *Bartlett's Familiar Quotations*.

You can also take an arresting or tantalizing quotation from the story itself. Tessie Hutchinson's final scream, "It isn't fair, it isn't right," or Old Man Warner's "There's *always* been a lottery," might serve as an effective opening for an essay on this story.

Another strategy is to pose a startling question, like this:

Why would the people in a quiet, peaceful village publicly murder one of their neighbors every summer? This is the shocking question that Shirley Jackson forces us to consider in her symbolic story "The Lottery."

Or you can combine some suspense with a brief overview of the story:

The weather is sunny and clear. The residents of a peaceful village have gathered for an important annual event. They smile and chat with one another, while the children scurry about in play. Then someone brings out a black box, and the ordinary people of this ordinary town begin the process of choosing which one of their neighbors they are going to stone to death this summer. This shocking turn of events is the premise for Shirley Jackson's story about the fear and violence that lie beneath the placid surface of human societies. The story is called "The Lottery."

Another way to introduce a critical essay is to use interesting details about the author or the story's background that relate to the focus of your essay:

In June of 1948 *The New Yorker* magazine published "The Lottery," a story by Shirley Jackson. Within days the magazine began to receive a flood of telephone calls and letters, more than for any other piece of fiction they had ever published. Almost all of those who wrote were outraged or bewildered—sometimes both. Why did this story prompt such reactions? Why does it still shock readers? The answer may lie in the story's strong symbolic representation of the pointless violence and casual inhumanity that exist in all our lives.

Whatever approach you choose, keep the reader in mind. Think about reading an essay yourself: what do you expect from the introduction? Remember that the reader forms an important first impression from your opening paragraph.

Sample Student Paper

On the left-hand pages following appears the uncorrected second draft of an essay written by Todd Hageman, a student at Eastern Illinois University. On the right-hand pages you will see Todd's finished version. The questions in the margins of the final version ask you to consider the changes Todd made when he revised the paper.

Symbollism in The Lottery

Shirley Jackson's "The Lottery" uses subtle
symbollism along with inconngruities to exemplify
the loss of significance of some rituals &
traditions, and supersitions and flaws of human
nature. The first incongruity used is the day the
story takes place, June 27th. Jackson paints a
picture of a nice, sunny summer day in a small
"Anytown, USA." While Jackson paints this
picture, though, the reader feels an uneasy mood
and senses something is going to happen. Jackson
does this by using the words "hesitant" and
"reluctant" to describe the crowd while they
"smile at jokes instead of laugh."

The next, and one of the biggest symbols
used in the story, is the box--the black box to be
more exact. The box is mentioned repeatedly to
bring significance to it, although the reader
isn't sure why until toward the end of the story.
As the lottery symbolizes traition, the box

SAMPLE STUDENT PAPER--FINISHED VERSION

Why did Todd make the changes that he did in this opening sentence?

Why did Todd eliminate the second part of this thesis statement (about "incongruities" as well as symbolism)?

Symbolism in "The Lottery"

In "The Lottery" Shirley Jackson uses subtle symbolism to exemplify the emptiness of some rituals and traditions, as well as to illustrate several flaws of human nature. She begins with an incongruity in the setting on the day the story takes place, June 27th. Jackson paints a picture of a sunny summer day in a small "Anytown, USA." While Jackson introduces this pleasant setting, though, the reader feels uneasy and senses that something bad is going to happen. Jackson creates this tension by using the words "hesitant" and "reluctant" to describe the crowd and mentions that they "smile at jokes instead of laugh."

Why did he change "Jackson does this..." to "Jackson creates this tension..."?

How did he improve the opening sentence of this paragraph?

The controlling symbol in the story is the box--the black box suggestive of death. The box is mentioned repeatedly to increase its significance, although the reader is not sure why she stresses its importance until toward the end of the story. As the lottery symbolizes empty

symbolizes the lottery. Mr. Summers, the lottery
official, tells about getting a new box every
year, but the talk seems to "fade off." The box
was described as "faded," "splintered," and "grew
shabbyier each year." The condition of the box
symbolize the tradition of the lottery, and the
need for a new box symbolizes the need for a new
tradition.

There was a need for a new tradition because
the lottery itself had lost its significance.
Parts of the original lottery ritual had been
allowed to lapse, and other parts, such as the
salute of the official had "changed with the
times." The lottery had lapsed and changed so
much from the original lottery that the people
really didn't know why they were going through it
any more. Probably the only reason they were
going through it was the intellectual argument
used by Old Man Warner, who said, "There's always
been a lottery." When Mr. Warner is informed that
some places have stopped the lottery, he comes
back with such wit as "Nothing but trouble in
that," and "pack of young fools." The latter idea
expressed brings out the idea that all change is
bad and the young are the ones who make changes.
It is generally aknowledged that the preceeding

tradition, the box symbolizes the lottery itself.
Mr. Summers, the lottery official, speaks about
getting a new box every year but his talk seems to
"fade off." The box is described as "faded,"
"splintered," and growing "shabbier each year."
The worn out condition of the box symbolizes the
tradition of the lottery, while the need for a new
box symbolizes the need for a new tradition, but
the townspeople fail to see the need for change.

Why did Todd change this quotation from "grew shabbier each year"?

Why did Todd add this information?

There is a need for a new tradition because
the lottery itself has lost its significance.
Parts of the original lottery ritual have been
allowed to lapse, and other parts, such as the
salute of the official, have "changed with the
times." The lottery has lapsed and changed so
much from the original that the people really do
not know why they are going through it any more.
Probably the only reason they continue is solemnly
stated by Old Man Warner: "There's always been a
lottery." When Mr. Warner is informed that some
places have stopped the lottery, he comes back
with such meaningless arguments as "Nothing but
trouble in that," and "pack of young fools." He
simply believes that all change is bad and the
young are the ones who make changes. Most people

Why did he eliminate the sarcasm directed at Old Man Warner?

statement is false, leaving Mr. Warner on thin
ice from which to argue. I think the author
shows the uselessness of the lottery through Mr.
Warner's ignorance.

Human nature is shown very clearliy through
Tessie in the story. Tessie shows up late at
the lottery very lackadaisical and in a joking
mood before she was picked. She even gave her
husband an extra nudge as he went to draw. When
Tessie found out one of her family would be
chosen, her mood changed rather quickly,
screaming "unfair!" She even wanted her two
daughters to take their chances; which she knew
was wrong. Her "friends" around her showed their
flaws by saying, "Be a good sport," and "We all
took the same chance," and not showing a bit of
pity. Tessie's kids also showed no pity, as they
opened their blank pieces of paper, they were
described as "beaming and laughing" with the
crowd, even though they knew it was going to be
Mom or Dad picked. The final part of human
nature exemplified was when Tessie drew the black
dot. Every time she said, "It isn't fair," the
following sentence was always her getting hit
with a stone, almost as punishment for saying
it. The stones seem to be saying, "You thought

Can you think of another way to revise the stilted, wordy language of Todd's original statement, "It is generally acknowledged that the preceding statement is false..."?

would disagree, for Mr. Warner has little evidence to support his ideas. I think the author emphasizes the uselessness of the lottery through Mr. Warner's ignorant defense of it.

How does the addition of one word—"selfishness"—in the opening sentence improve this whole paragraph?

The selfishness in human nature is shown clearly in the story through Tessie. She shows up late at the lottery, lackadaisically joking with her neighbors before she is picked. She even gives her husband an encouraging nudge as he goes to draw. When Tessie finds out one of her family will be chosen, her mood changes quickly, and she screams, "Unfair!" She even wants her two daughters to take their chances along with her, which hardly suggests mother-love. Her "friends" around her show their lack of pity by saying, "Be a good sport," and "We all took the same chance!"

Would you have put the period in the same place in revising Todd's comma splice? Or would you have used a semicolon? Why or why not?

Tessie's children also show no sympathy. As they open their blank pieces of paper, they are described as "beaming and laughing" with the crowd, even though they know one of their parents is going to be picked. Human cruelty is also exemplified after Tessie draws the black dot. Every time she cries, "It isn't fair!" she gets hit immediately with a stone, almost as punishment for objecting. The stones seem to be saying, "You

it was fair until you were picked; now take your
medicine."

The story has one key sentence which puts
the whole theme in a nutshell: "Although the
villagers had forgotten the ritual and lost the
original box, they still remembered to use
stones." Through the symbollism being used, the
sentence can be translated into a theme for the
story. The ritual had changed with the times and
lost the original purpose, but people still
remember to look out for themselves. Every time
a villager threw a stone, he was probably
thinking, "Better you than me."

A final thought could be about the slips of
paper and what they symbolized. Jackson
mentioned that the unused papers were "dropped to
the ground where the breeze caught them and
lifted them off." The papers could be meant to
symbolize the people who had been sacrificed
through the lottery. The village people had used
both the papers and the sacrificed people and had
discarded them as trash.

thought it was fair until you were picked; now take your medicine."

Why did Todd move this final paragraph to this position?

The slips of paper also serve a symbolic purpose. Jackson mentions that the unused papers "dropped to the ground where the breeze caught them and lifted them off." The papers could symbolize the people who have been sacrificed through the lottery. The village people make use of both the papers and the sacrificed people, then discard them as trash.

The story has one key sentence which captures the whole theme: "Although the villagers had forgotten the ritual and lost the original box, they still remembered to use stones." Considering the symbolism in the story, the sentence can be translated into a theme. Although the ritual had changed with the times and lost the original purpose, people still remember to look out for themselves. Every time the villagers threw a stone, they were probably thinking, "Better you than me." Jackson dramatizes for us the harm done by ignorance which causes people to cling to outworn rituals. She also shows the selfishness and cruelty which lie just beneath the civilized surface of human behavior.

Why did he replace the phrase "in a nutshell"?

How do these last two sentences that he added improve the paper?

7

Writing about Point of View

Learning about point of view in fiction will help you understand some of the choices that a writer has to make in deciding the best way to present a story. When the point of view is unusual, you may want to focus your written analysis on the narrator or on the significance of the writer's choice of narrator.

What Is Point of View?

In identifying point of view, you decide who tells the story—that is, whose thoughts and feelings the reader has access to. The storyteller, called the *narrator*, is a creation of the author and should not be confused with the author. In the following passage from a story by Colette, for example, the author takes the reader into the private world of her narrator:

> Surely, until tomorrow, I will sink into the depths of a dark sleep, a sleep so stubborn, so shut off from the world, that the wings of dream will come to beat in vain.

And the narrator's position as major character is clear in the opening lines of Sherwood Anderson's story "I'm a Fool":

> It was a hard jolt for me, one of the most bitterest I ever had to face. And it all came about through my own foolishness, too.

But in the following passage, also by Colette, we cannot tell whether we are getting the thoughts of Marcel, Gloria, or another observer:

On the sly, Marcel looks at Gloria with indiscreet persistence, as if he were choosing in advance the proper place to implant a kiss.

In this description, from Stephen Crane's "The Open Boat," we are not conscious of a narrator at all:

On the distant dunes were set many little black cottages, and a tall white windmill reared above them. No man, nor dog, nor bicycle appeared on the beach.

Several systems exist for labelling the point of view in a work of literature. They classify the position and identity of the person who records the action—that is, the person whose eyes and mind become ours as we read the story.

When the writer freely relates many or all of the characters' thoughts, feelings, and actions, the point of view is called *omniscient*—all-knowing. No one character seems to be the central teller of the story. Within the omniscient point of view, an author has a range of approaches from which to choose. On one end of the range, the narration is *objective* (or dramatic), a recording of actions, speech, and gestures, leaving us to 1) infer the thoughts and feelings behind them, and 2) come to our own conclusions about their significance. On the other end of the range, the narration is *editorial*, freely exposing the characters' inner lives and commenting on the story as it progresses. Here are examples of the two extremes:

Objective
    Athena drove through the thick white California fog, frowning as she followed the orange center marks on the winding road. In the back seat, Bob slumped, mumbling to himself.

Editorial
    Athena worried vaguely as she peered through the menacing white California fog, trying to stay on the winding road by following the orange center markers. Bob, in the back seat, drunkenly reviewed the afternoon's confrontation with Marianne. His confusion about the scene was not only the product of cheap wine—the mysterious relationship between the sexes baffles even the soberest thinker.

Notice that in the second, the *editorial* version, the reader 1) has access to Athena's and Bob's minds, 2) gets a personified description of the fog, and 3) is given an outside narrative remark about the situation. Most stories written from an *omniscient* point of view fall somewhere between being completely objective and fully editorial.

The other major classification of point of view is usually called *limited*, because we can identify one character as the storyteller. In detective fiction, for example, often we observe the plot unfold strictly from the main character's (the detective's) point of view. But sometimes our preceptions are limited to those of a minor character, as in the Sherlock Holmes stories, which are narrated by the

great detective's sidekick, Dr. Watson. His admiration and awe of
Holmes' superior skill become ours.

If a writer tells the same story twice, once through one character
and again through a different character, the point of view is still
limited, but *shifting.* John Fowles' novel *The Collector* narrates a kid-
napping first from the kidnapper's point of view and then from
the victim's point of view. The point of view is also called *shifting*
when, within one telling of the story, the writer limits the narrative
position to two (seldom more) characters and switches back and
forth between them. Katherine Ann Porter's story "Rope" exposes
with bitter humor the conflicts of a young married couple by shifting
from the man's point of view to the woman's and back during a
vicious argument—over a thoughtlessly purchased piece of rope.
If the narrator misrepresents or misinterprets the facts, purposely
or naively, the narrator is considered *unreliable:* a child, an insane
person, or a villain, for example, would sometimes be unable or
unwilling to give a fully truthful presentation. Writers often use
unreliable narrators to emphasize the subjectivity of experience, as
you will see in the following story by Ring Lardner.

Here is an outline of the basic terminology for discussing point
of view:

> *Omniscient*
>   Objective<--------------------------->Editorial
>   (range of narrative commentary)
>
> *Limited*
>   Major character
>   Minor character
>   Special types: shifting narrator, unreliable narrator

Looking at Point of View

As you read Ring Lardner's "Haircut," notice how much the narrator reveals about himself and his social circle.

Ring Lardner *1885–1933*

HAIRCUT

I got another barber that comes over from Carterville and helps me out Saturdays, but the rest of the time I can get along all right alone. You can see for yourself that this ain't no New York City and besides that, the most of the boys works all day and don't have no leisure to drop in here and get themselves prettied up.

You're a newcomer, ain't you? I thought I hadn't seen you round before. I hope you like it good enough to stay. As I say, we ain't no New York City or Chicago, but we have pretty good times. Not as good, though, since Jim Kendall got killed. When he was alive, him and Hod Meyers used to keep this town in an uproar. I bet they was more laughin' done here than any town its size in America.

Jim was comical, and Hod was pretty near a match for him. Since Jim's gone, Hod tries to hold his end up just the same as ever, but it's rough goin' when you ain't got nobody to kind of work with.

They used to be plenty fun in here Saturdays. This place is jam-packed Saturdays, from four o'clock on. Jim and Hod would show up right after their supper, round six o'clock. Jim would set himself down in that big chair, nearest the blue spittoon. Whoever had been settin' in that chair, why they'd get up when Jim come in and give it to him.

You'd of thought it was a reserved seat like they have sometimes in a theayter. Hod would generally always stand or walk up and down, or some Saturdays, of course, he'd be settin' in this chair part of the time, gettin' a haircut.

Well, Jim would set there a w'ile without openin' his mouth only to spit, and then finally he'd say to me, "Whitey,"—my right name, that is, my right first name, is Dick, but everybody round here calls me Whitey— Jim would say, "Whitey, your nose looks like a rosebud tonight. You must of been drinkin' some of your aw de cologne."

So I'd say, "No, Jim, but you look like you'd been drinking somethin' of that kind or somethin' worse."

Jim would have to laugh at that, but then he'd speak up and say, "No, I ain't had nothin' to drink, but that ain't sayin' I wouldn't like somethin'. I wouldn't even mind if it was wood alcohol."

Then Hod Meyers would say, "Neither would your wife." That would set everybody to laughin' because Jim and his wife wasn't on very good terms. She'd of divorced him only they wasn't no chance to get alimony and she didn't have no way to take care of herself and the kids. She couldn't never understand Jim. He *was* kind of rough, but a good fella at heart.

Him and Hod had all kinds of sport with Milt Sheppard. I don't suppose you've seen Milt. Well, he's got an Adam's apple that looks more like a mushmelon. So I'd be shavin' Milt and when I'd start to shave down here on his neck, Hod would holler, "Hey, Whitey, wait a minute! Before you cut into it, let's make up a pool and see who can guess closest to the number of seeds."

And Jim would say, "If Milt hadn't of been so hoggish, he'd of ordered a half a canteloupe instead of a whole one and it might not of stuck in his throat."

All the boys would roar at this and Milt himself would force a smile, though the joke was on him. Jim certainly was a card!

There's his shavin' mug, settin' on the shelf, right next to Charley Vail's. "Charles M. Vail." That's the druggist. He comes in regular for his shave, three times a week. And Jim's is the cup next to Charley's. "James H. Kendall." Jim won't need no shavin' mug no more, but I'll leave it there just the same for old time's sake. Jim certainly was a character!

Years ago, Jim used to travel for a canned goods concern over in Carterville. They sold canned goods. Jim had the whole northern half of the State and was on the road five days out of every week. He'd drop in here Saturdays and tell his experiences for that week. It was rich.

I guess he paid more attention to playin' jokes than makin' sales. Finally the concern let him out and he come right home here and told everybody he'd been fired instead of sayin' he'd resigned like most fellas would of.

It was a Saturday and the shop was full and Jim got up out of that chair and says, "Gentlemen, I got an important announcement to make. I been fired from my job."

Well, they asked him if he was in earnest and he said he was and nobody could think of nothin' to say till Jim finally broke the ice himself. He says, "I been sellin' canned goods and now I'm canned goods myself."

You see, the concern he'd been workin' for was a factory that made canned goods. Over in Carterville. And now Jim said he was canned himself. He was certainly a card!

For instance, they'd be a sign, "Henry Smith, Dry Goods." Well, Jim would write down the name and the name of the town and when he got to wherever he was goin' he'd mail back a postal card to Henry Smith at Benton and not sign no name to it, but he'd write on the card, well, somethin' like "Ask your wife about that book agent that spent the afternoon last week," or "Ask your Missus who kept her from gettin' lonesome the last time you was in Carterville." And he'd sign the card, "A Friend."

Of course, he never knew what really come of none of these jokes, but he could picture what *probably* happened and that was enough.

Jim didn't work very steady after he lost his position with the Carterville people. What he did earn, doin' odd jobs round town, why he spent pretty near all of it on gin and his family might of starved if the stores hadn't of carried them along. Jim's wife tried her hand at dressmakin', but they ain't nobody goin' to get rich makin' dresses in this town.

As I say, she'd of divorced Jim, only she seen that she couldn't support herself and the kids and she was always hopin' that some day Jim would cut his habits and give her more than two or three dollars a week.

There was a time when she would go to whoever he was workin' for and ask them to give her his wages, but after she done this once or twice, he beat her to it by borrowin' most of his pay in advance. He told it all round town, how he had outfoxed his Missus. He certainly was a caution!

But he wasn't satisfied with just outwittin' her. He was sore the way she had acted, tryin' to grab off his pay. And he made up his mind he'd get even. Well, he waited till Evan's Circus was advertised to come to town. Then he told his wife and kiddies that he was goin' to take them to the circus. The day of the circus, he told them he would get the tickets and meet them outside the entrance to the tent.

Well, he didn't have no intentions of bein' there or buyin' tickets or nothin'. He got full of gin and laid round Wright's poolroom all day. His wife and the kids waited and waited and of course he didn't show up. His wife didn't have a dime with her, or nowhere else, I guess. So she finally had to tell the kids it was all off and they cried like they wasn't never goin' to stop.

Well, it seems, w'ile they was cryin', Doc Stair came along and he asked what was the matter, but Mrs. Kendall was stubborn and wouldn't tell him, but the kids told him and he insisted on takin' them and their mother in the show. Jim found this out afterwards and it was one reason why he had it in for Doc Stair.

Doc Stair come here about a year and a half ago. He's a mighty handsome young fella and his clothes always look like he has them made to order. He goes to Detroit two or three times a year and w'ile he's there he must have a tailor take his measure and then make him a suit to order. They cost pretty near twice as much, but they fit a whole lot better than if you just bought them in a store.

For a w'ile everybody was wonderin' why a young doctor like Doc Stair should come to a town like this where we already got old Doc Gamble and Doc Foote that's both been here for years and all the practice in town was always divided between the two of them.

Then they was a story got round that Doc Stair's gal had thrown him over, a gal up in the Northern Peninsula somewheres, and the reason he come here was to hide himself away and forget it. He said himself that he thought they wasn't nothin' like general practice in a place like ours to fit a man to be a good all round doctor. And that's why he'd came.

Anyways, it wasn't long before he was makin' enough to live on, though they tell me that he never dunned nobody for what they owed him, and the folks here certainly has got the owin' habit, even in my business. If I had all that was comin' to me for just shaves alone, I could go to Carterville and put up at the Mercer for a week and see a different picture every night. For instance, they's old George Purdy—but I guess I shouldn't ought to be gossipin'.

Well, last year, our coroner died, died of the flu. Ken Beatty, that was his name. He was the coroner. So they had to choose another man to be coroner in his place and they picked Doc Stair. He laughed at first and said he didn't want it, but they made him take it. It ain't no job nobody would fight for and what a man makes out of it in a year would just about buy seeds for their garden. Doc's the kind, though, that can't say no to nothin', if you keep at him long enough.

But I was goin' to tell you about a poor boy we got here in town— Paul Dickson. He fell out of a tree when he was about ten years old. Lit on his head and it done somethin' to him and he ain't never been right. No harm in him, but just silly. Jim Kendall used to call him cuckoo; that's a name Jim had for anybody that was off their head, only he called people's head their bean. That was another of his gags, callin' head bean and callin' crazy people cuckoo. Only poor Paul ain't crazy, but just silly.

You can imagine that Jim used to have all kinds of fun with Paul. He'd send him to the White Front Garage for a left-handed monkey wrench. Of course they ain't no such a thing as a left-handed monkey wrench.

And once we had a kind of fair here and they was a baseball game between the fats and the leans and before the game started Jim called Paul over and sent him down to Schrader's hardware store to get a key for the pitcher's box.

They wasn't nothin' in the way of gags that Jim couldn't think up, when he put his mind to it.

Poor Paul was always kind of suspicious of people, maybe on account of how Jim had kept foolin' him. Paul wouldn't have much to do with anybody only his own mother and Doc Stair and a girl here in town named Julie Gregg. That is, she ain't a girl no more, but pretty near thirty or over.

When Doc first come to town, Paul seemed to feel like here was a real friend and he hung around Doc's office most of the w'ile; the only time he wasn't there was when he'd go home to eat or sleep or when he seen Julie Gregg doin' her shoppin'.

When he looked out Doc's window and seen her, he'd run downstairs and join her and tag along with her to the different stores. The poor boy was crazy about Julie and she always treated him mighty nice and made him feel like he was welcome, though of course it wasn't nothin' but pity on her side.

Doc done all he could to improve Paul's mind and he told me once that he really thought the boy was gettin' better, that they was times when he was as bright and sensible as anybody else.

But I was goin' to tell you about Julie Gregg. Old Man Gregg was in the lumber business, but got to drinkin' and lost most of his money and when he died, he didn't leave nothin' but the house and just enough insurance for the girl to skimp along on.

Her mother was a kind of invalid and didn't hardly ever leave the house. Julie wanted to sell the place and move somewheres else after the old man died, but the mother said she was born here and would die here. It was tough on Julie, as the young people round this town—well, she's too good for them.

She's been away to school and Chicago and New York and different places and they ain't no subject she can't talk on, where you take the rest of the young folks here and you mention anything to them outside of Gloria Swanson or Tommy Meighan and they think you're delirious. Did you see Gloria in *Wages of Virtue*? You missed somethin'!

Well, Doc Stair hadn't been here more than a week when he come in one day to get shaved and I recognized who he was as he had been pointed out to me, so I told him about my old lady. She's been ailin' for a couple years and either Doc Gamble or Doc Foote, neither one, seemed to be helpin' her. So he said he would come out and see her, but if she was able to get out herself, it would be better to bring her to his office where he could make a completer examination.

So I took her to his office and w'ile I was waiting for her in the reception room, in come Julie Gregg. When somebody comes in Doc Stair's office, they's a bell that rings in his inside office so he can tell they's somebody to see him.

So he left my old lady inside and come out to the front office and that's the first time him and Julie met and I guess it was what they call love at first sight. But it wasn't fifty-fifty. This young fella was the slickest lookin' fella she'd ever seen in this town and she went wild over him. To him she was just a young lady that wanted to see the doctor.

She'd came on about the same business I had. Her mother had been doctorin' for years with Doc Gamble and Doc Foote and without no results. So she'd heard they was a new doc in town and decided to give him a try. He promised to call and see her mother that same day.

I said a minute ago that it was love at first sight on her part. I'm not only judgin' by how she acted afterwards but how she looked at him that first day in his office. I ain't no mind reader, but it was wrote all over her face that she was gone.

Now Jim Kendall, besides bein' a jokesmith and a pretty good drinker, well, Jim was quite a lady-killer. I guess he run pretty wild durin' the time he was on the road for them Carterville people, and besides that, he'd had a couple little affairs of the heart right here in town. As I say, his wife could of divorced him, only she couldn't.

But Jim was like the majority of men, and women, too, I guess. He wanted what he couldn't get. He wanted Julie Gregg and worked his head off tryin' to land her. Only he'd of said bean instead of head.

Well, Jim's habits and his jokes didn't appeal to Julie and of course he was a married man, so he didn't have no more chance than, well, than a rabbit. That's an expression of Jim's himself. When somebody didn't have no chance to get elected or somethin', Jim would always say they didn't have no more chance than a rabbit.

He didn't make no bones about how he felt. Right in here, more than once, in front of the whole crowd, he said he was stuck on Julie and anybody that could get her for him was welcome to his house and his wife and kids included. But she wouldn't have nothin' to do with him; wouldn't even speak to him on the street. He finally seen he wasn't gettin' nowheres with his usual line so he decided to try the rough stuff. He went right up to her house one evenin' and when she opened the door he forced his way in and grabbed her. But she broke loose and before he could stop her, she run in the next room and locked the door and phoned to Joe Barnes. Joe's the marshal. Jim could hear who she was phonin' to and he beat it before Joe got there.

Joe was an old friend of Julie's pa. Joe went to Jim the next day and told him what would happen if he ever done it again.

I don't know how the news of this little affair leaked out. Chances is that Joe Barnes told his wife and she told somebody else's wife and they told their husband. Anyways, it did leak out and Hod Meyers had the nerve to kid Jim about it, right here in this shop. Jim didn't deny nothin' and kind of laughed it off and said for us all to wait; that lots of people had tried to make a monkey out of him, but he always got even.

Meanw'ile everybody in town was wise to Julie's bein' wild mad over the Doc. I don't suppose she had any idear how her face changed when him and her was together; of course she couldn't of, or she'd of kept away from him. And she didn't know that we was all noticin' how many times she made excuses to go up to his office or pass it on the other side of the street and look up in his window to see if he was there. I felt sorry for her and so did most other people.

Hod Meyers kept rubbin' it into Jim about how the Doc had cut him out. Jim didn't pay no attention to the kiddin' and you could see he was plannin' one of his jokes.

One trick Jim had was the knack of changin' his voice. He could make you think he was a girl talkin' and he could mimic any man's voice. To show you how good he was along this line, I'll tell you the joke he played on me once.

You know, in most towns of any size, when a man is dead and needs a shave, why the barber that shaves him soaks him five dollars for the job; that is, he don't soak *him*, but whoever ordered the shave. I just charge three dollars because personally I don't mind much shavin' a dead person. They lay a whole lot stiller than live customers. The only thing is that you don't feel like talkin' to them and you get kind of lonesome.

Well, about the coldest day we ever had here, two years ago last winter, the phone rung at the house w'ile I was home to dinner and I answered the phone and it was a woman's voice and she said she was Mrs. John Scott and her husband was dead and would I come out and shave him.

Old John had always been a good customer of mine. But they live seven miles out in the country, on the Streeter road. Still I didn't see how I could say no.

So I said I would be there, but would have to come in a jitney and it might cost three or four dollars besides the price of the shave. So she, or the voice, said that was all right, so I got Frank Abbott to drive me out to the place and when I got there, who should open the door but old John himself! He wasn't no more dead than, well, than a rabbit.

It didn't take no private detective to figure out who had played me this little joke. Nobody could of thought it up but Jim Kendall. He certainly was a card!

I tell you this incident just to show you how he could disguise his voice and make you believe it was somebody else talkin'. I'd of swore it was Mrs. Scott had called me. Anyways, some woman.

Well, Jim waited till he had Doc Stair's voice down pat; then he went after revenge.

He called Julie up on a night when he knew Doc was over in Carterville. She never questioned but what it was Doc's voice. Jim said he must see her that night; he couldn't wait no longer to tell her somethin'. She was all excited and told him to come to the house. But he said he was expectin' an important long distance call and wouldn't she please forget her manners for once and come to his office. He said they couldn't nothin' hurt her and nobody would see her and he just *must* talk to her a little w'ile. Well, poor Julie fell for it.

Doc always keeps a night light in his office, so it looked to Julie like they was somebody there.

Meanw'ile Jim Kendall had went to Wright's poolroom, where they was a whole gang amusin' themselves. The most of them had drunk plenty of gin, and they was a rough bunch even when sober. They was always strong for Jim's jokes and when he told them to come with him and see some fun they give up their card games and pool games and followed along.

Doc's office is on the second floor. Right outside his door they's a flight of stairs leadin' to the floor above. Jim and his gang hid in the dark behind these stairs.

Well, Julie come up to Doc's door and rung the bell and they was nothin' doin'. She rung it again and she rung it seven or eight times. Then she tried the door and found it locked. Then Jim made some kind of a noise and she heard it and waited a minute, and then she says, "Is that you, Ralph?" Ralph is Doc's first name.

They was no answer and it must of came to her all of a sudden that she'd been bunked. She pretty near fell downstairs and the whole gang after her. They chased her all the way home, hollerin', "Is that you, Ralph?" and "Oh, Ralphie, dear, is that you?" Jim says he couldn't holler it himself, as he was laughin' too hard.

Poor Julie! She didn't show up here on Main Street for a long, long time afterward.

And of course Jim and his gang told everybody in town, everybody but Doc Stair. They was scared to tell him, and he might of never knowed only for Paul Dickson. The poor cuckoo, as Jim called him, he was here in the shop one night when Jim was still gloatin' yet over what he'd done to Julie. And Paul took in as much of it as he could understand and he run to Doc with the story.

It's a cinch Doc went up in the air and swore he'd make Jim suffer. But it was a kind of delicate thing, because if it got out that he had beat Jim up, Julie was bound to hear of it and then she'd know that Doc knew and of course knowin' that he knew would make it worse for her than ever. He was goin' to do somethin', but it took a lot of figurin'.

Well, it was a couple of days later when Jim was here in the shop again, and so was the cuckoo. Jim was goin' duck-shootin' the next day and had come in lookin' for Hod Meyers to go with him. I happened to know that Hod went over to Carterville and wouldn't be home till the end of the week. So Jim said he hated to go alone and he guessed he would call if off. Then poor Paul spoke up and said if Jim would take him he would go along. Jim thought a w'ile and then he said, well, he guessed a half-wit was better than nothin'.

I suppose he was plottin' to get Paul out in the boat and play some joke on him, like pushin' him in the water. Anyways, he said Paul could go. He asked him had he ever shot a duck and Paul said no, he'd never even had a gun in his hands. So Jim said he could set in the boat and watch him and if he behaved himself, he might lend him his gun for a couple of shots. They made a date to meet in the mornin' and that's the last I seen of Jim alive.

Next mornin', I hadn't been open more than ten minutes when Doc Stair come in. He looked kind of nervous. He asked me had I seen Paul Dickson. I said no, but I knew where he was, out duck-shootin' with Jim

Kendall. So Doc says that's what he had heard, and he couldn't understand it because Paul had told him he wouldn't never have no more to do with Jim as long as he lived.

He said Paul had told him about the joke Jim played on Julie. He said Paul had asked him what he thought of the joke and the Doc had told him anybody that would do a thing like that ought not to be let live.

I said it had been a kind of raw thing, but Jim just couldn't resist no kind of a joke, no matter how raw. I said I thought he was all right at heart, but just bubblin' over with mischief. Doc turned and walked out.

At noon he got a phone call from old John Scott. The lake where Jim and Paul had went shootin' is on John's place. Paul had come runnin' up to the house a few minutes before and said they'd been an accident. Jim had shot a few ducks and then give the gun to Paul and told him to try his luck. Paul hadn't never handled a gun and he was nervous. He was shakin' so hard that he couldn't control the gun. He let fire and Jim sunk back in the boat, dead.

Doc Stair, bein' the coroner, jumped in Frank Abbott's flivver and rushed out to Scott's farm. Paul and old John was down on the shore of the lake. Paul had rowed the boat to shore, but they'd left the body in it, waitin' for Doc to come.

Doc examined the body and said they might as well fetch it back to town. They was no use leavin' it there or callin' a jury, as it was a plain case of accidental shootin'.

Personally I wouldn't never leave a person shoot a gun in the same boat I was in unless I was sure they knew somethin' about guns. Jim was a sucker to leave a new beginner have his gun, let alone a half-wit. It probably served Jim right, what he got. But still we miss him round here. He certainly was a card!

Comb it wet or dry?

(1925)

Prewriting

To help you examine the point of view and to see how it affects other elements of the story, write out answers to the following questions.

IDENTIFYING POINT OF VIEW

1. Reread the first two paragraphs of the story. Who is speaking? Identify words and phrases in the first two paragraphs that give you an impression of the speaker. How would you summarize that impression?

2. Reread the rest of "Haircut." Who is really the main character of the story?

3. Is the narrator reliable in his perceptions or not? Give examples. What do you think of Whitey's conclusions about Jim's death?

4. Does what Whitey says match Ring Lardner's view? Why or why not?

5. Why is the story not told from Hod's or Julie's point of view?

Writing

Before you decide to focus your paper on point of view, you need to determine its importance in the story. An analysis of point of view may not always merit a full-length paper: a limited, first-person, reliable main character's narration of a personal story is such a natural and appropriate choice that there is little to say about it. But often, as in "Haircut," analysis of the point of view is the key to the story.

RELATING POINT OF VIEW TO THEME

Once we become aware that Whitey has been unconsciously exposing Jim Kendall's viciousness, we need to relate that perception to the main point or impact of the story. Why is this particular point of view effective for this particular story? Here are some writing ideas that combine a discussion of point of view with an analysis of the meaning of the story.

IDEAS FOR WRITING

1. The narrator's attitude toward Jim Kendall and his pranks slowly reveals the backbiting nature of small-town life and of the narrator himself.

2. Ring Lardner uses an unreliable narrator, developing his unreliability throughout the story so that readers are allowed to draw their own conclusions about Jim's death.

3. Whitey's mostly innocent lack of sympathy and self-awareness enhances, by comparison, our discovery of the malice of Jim Kendall, "the card," the main character.

4. Whitey, seemingly a normal resident of the little town, is the perfect choice of narrator for "Haircut," a story fundamentally about small-town life.

5. Using the stories in the anthology, compare the effects of the limited, main-character point of veiw in "Araby" by James Joyce and "A&P" by John Updike.

Rewriting

When you revise, do not neglect your conclusion just because it comes last. It has a psychologically important place in your paper.

Ask yourself, "Does my closing restate the main idea in a too obvious, repetitive way? Will the readers feel let down, dropped off, cut short?" If so, consider some of these ways to make your ending more lively.

SHARPENING THE CONCLUSION

1. *Description.* After a discussion of the viciousness that underlies the placid, small-town life in "Haircut," you might write the following:

   > Finally, the reader may envision Whitey's customer leaving the barbershop, settling his hat on his new haircut as he surveys the sleepy, serene streets of town, getting into his car, and leaving as fast as possible, forever.

2. *Humor or irony,* if appropriate to the tone of your essay. You can probably never match Lardner's gem, "Comb it wet or dry?" which stands in telling ironic contrast to the previous description of murder.

3. *A quotation from the story.* Remember that it must be integrated into your own sentence, perhaps like this:

   > The design of the story surely leads us to question the breadth of the "we" in Whitey's statement about Jim, "But still we miss him around here."

4. *An echo from your introduction.* If you wrote of "Jim Kendall's ten 'jokes' " in your opening, for example, you could conclude with "Jim Kendall played ten big jokes; the eleventh one was on him."

5. *A thought-provoking question, suggestion, or statement.*

   > Does Lardner imply that such human cruelty is inevitable?
   > Is a neighborhood in a big city that different from the world of "Haircut"?

CHAPTER

8

Writing about Setting and Atmosphere

Setting and atmosphere contribute to the effectiveness of short stories in various ways. Sometimes these elements assume enough importance to become the focus of a literary analysis.

What Are Setting and Atmosphere?

Of course you know the meaning of *setting* in reference to a work of literature: the setting includes the location and time of the action in a story, novel, play, or poem. Sometimes the setting conveys an *atmosphere*—the emotional effect of the setting and events—that contributes to the impact or to the meaning of the work. Atmosphere (or mood) is that feeling of chill foreboding that Poe creates by setting his tale of "The Fall of the House of Usher" in a remote, moldering mansion on the edge of a black, stagnant pool and then having eerie things happen. Atmosphere can also be used to increase irony, as Shirley Jackson does in "The Lottery" by conveying the deceptive feeling of carefree summer festivity just before turning her tale abruptly toward ritual murder. Usually, though, setting and atmosphere reflect the dominant tone and theme of a work.

In deciding whether to focus on setting or atmosphere in writing a literary paper, you need to ask yourself not only how much the effect of the work would be changed if these elements were different but also how much you have to say about them—especially concerning their contribution to the effectiveness of the piece. For instance,

the barbershop in which Ring Lardner's "Haircut" takes place seems
the perfect setting for that story. We can scarcely imagine its being
set as effectively anywhere else. How much more can you think
of to say about the setting and atmosphere?

Looking at Setting and Atmosphere

As you read the following story, first published in 1892, consider
how crucial setting and atmosphere are in contributing to its effect.

Charlotte Perkins Gilman *1860–1935*

THE YELLOW WALL-PAPER

It is very seldom that mere ordinary people like John and myself secure ancestral halls for the summer.

A colonial mansion, a hereditary estate, I would say a haunted house, and reach the height of romantic felicity—but that would be asking too much of fate!

Still I will proudly declare that there is something queer about it.

Else, why should it be let so cheaply? And why have stood so long untenanted?

John laughs at me, of course, but one expects that in marriage.

John is practical in the extreme. He has no patience with faith, an intense horror of superstition, and he scoffs openly at any talk of things not to be felt or seen and put down in figures.

John is a physician, and *perhaps*—(I would not say it to a living soul, of course, but this is dead paper and a great relief to my mind)—*perhaps* that is one reason I do not get well faster.

You see he does not believe I am sick! And what can one do?

If a physician of high standing, and one's own husband, assures friends and relatives that there is really nothing the matter with one but temporary nervous depression—a slight hysterical tendency—what is one to do?

My brother is also a physician, and also of high standing, and he says the same thing.

So I take phosphates or phosphites—whichever it is—and tonics, and journeys, and air, and exercise, and am absolutely forbidden to "work" until I am well again.

Personally, I disagree with their ideas.

Personally, I believe that congenial work, with excitement and change, would do me good.

But what is one to do?

I did write for a while in spite of them; but it *does* exhaust me a good deal—having to be so sly about it, or else meet with heavy opposition.

I sometimes fancy that in my condition if I had less opposition and more society and stimulus—but John says the very worst thing I can do is to think about my condition, and I confess it always makes me feel bad.

So I will let it alone and talk about the house.

The most beautiful place! It is quite alone, standing well back from the road, quite three miles from the village. It makes me think of English places that you read about, for there are hedges and walls and gates that lock, and lots of separate little houses for the gardeners and people.

There is a *delicious* garden! I never saw such a garden—large and shady, full of box-bordered paths, and lined with long grape-covered arbors with seats under them.

There were greenhouses, too, but they are all broken now.

There was some legal trouble, I believe, something about the heirs and co-heirs; anyhow, the place has been empty for years.

That spoils my ghostliness, I am afraid, but I don't care—there is something strange about the house—I can feel it.

I even said so to John one moonlight evening, but he said what I felt was a draft, and shut the window.

I get unreasonably angry with John sometimes. I'm sure I never used to be so sensitive. I think it is due to this nervous condition.

But John says if I feel so I shall neglect proper self-control; so I take pains to control myself—before him, at least, and that makes me very tired.

I don't like our room a bit. I wanted one downstairs that opened on the piazza and had roses all over the window, and such pretty old-fashioned chintz hangings! But John would not hear of it.

He said there was only one window and not room for two beds, and no near room for him if he took another.

He is very careful and loving, and hardly lets me stir without special direction.

I have a schedule prescription for each hour in the day; he takes all care from me, and so I feel basely ungrateful not to value it more.

He said we came here solely on my account, that I was to have perfect rest and all the air I could get. "Your exercise depends on your strength, my dear," said he, "and your food somewhat on your appetite; but air you can absorb all the time." So we took the nursery at the top of the house.

It is a big, airy room, the whole floor nearly, with windows that look all ways, and air and sunshine galore. It was nursery first and then playroom and gymnasium, I should judge; for the windows are barred for little children, and there are rings and things in the walls.

The paint and paper look as if a boys' school had used it. It is stripped off—the paper—in great patches all around the head of my bed, about as far as I can reach, and in a great place on the other side of the room low down. I never saw a worse paper in my life.

One of those sprawling flamboyant patterns committing every artistic sin.

It is dull enough to confuse the eye in following, pronounced enough constantly to irritate and provoke study, and when you follow the lame uncertain curves for a little distance they suddenly commit suicide—plunge off at outrageous angles, destroy themselves in unheard of contradictions.

The color is repellent, almost revolting; a smoldering unclean yellow, strangely faded by the slow-turning sunlight.

It is a dull yet lurid orange in some places, a sickly sulphur tint in others.

No wonder the children hated it! I should hate it myself if I had to live in this room long.

There comes John, and I must put this away—he hates to have me write a word.

We have been here two weeks, and I haven't felt like writing before, since that first day.

I am sitting by the window now, up in this atrocious nursery, and there is nothing to hinder my writing as much as I please, save lack of strength.

John is away all day, and even some nights when his cases are serious. I am glad my case is not serious!

But these nervous troubles are dreadfully depressing.

John does not know how much I really suffer. He knows there is no *reason* to suffer, and that satisfies him.

Of course it is only nervousness. It does weigh on me so not to do my duty in any way!

I meant to be such a help to John, such a real rest and comfort, and here I am a comparative burden already!

Nobody would believe what an effort it is to do what little I am able— to dress and entertain, and order things.

It is fortunate Mary is so good with the baby. Such a dear baby!

And yet I *cannot* be with him, it makes me so nervous.

I suppose John never was nervous in his life. He laughs at me so about this wall-paper!

At first he meant to repaper the room, but afterwards he said that I was letting it get the better of me, and that nothing was worse for a nervous patient than to give way to such fancies.

He said that after the wall-paper was changed it would be the heavy bedstead, and then the barred windows, and then that gate at the head of the stairs, and so on.

"You know the place is doing you good," he said, "and really, dear, I don't care to renovate the house just for a three months' rental."

"Then do let us go downstairs," I said, "there are such pretty rooms there."

Then he took me in his arms and called me a blessed little goose, and said he would go down cellar, if I wished, and have it whitewashed into the bargain.

But he is right enough about the beds and windows and things.

It is an airy and comfortable room as any one need wish, and, of course, I would not be so silly as to make him uncomfortable just for a whim.

I'm really getting quite fond of the big room, all but that horrid paper.

Out of one window I can see the garden, those mysterious deep-shaded arbors, the riotous old-fashioned flowers, and bushes and gnarly trees.

Out of another I get a lovely view of the bay and a little private wharf belonging to the estate. There is a beautiful shaded lane that runs down there from the house. I always fancy I see people walking in these numerous paths and arbors, but John has cautioned me not to give way to fancy in the least. He says that with my imaginative power and habit of story-making, a nervous weakness like mine is sure to lead to all manner of excited fancies, and that I ought to use my will and good sense to check the tendency. So I try.

I think sometimes that if I were only well enough to write a little it would relieve the press of ideas and rest me.

But I find I get pretty tired when I try.

It is so discouraging not to have any advice and companionship about my work. When I get really well, John says we will ask Cousin Henry and Julia down for a long visit; but he says he would as soon put fireworks in my pillowcase as to let me have those stimulating people about now.

I wish I could get well faster.

But I must not think about that. This paper looks to me as if it *knew* what a vicious influence it had!

There is a recurrent spot where the pattern lolls like a broken neck and two bulbous eyes stare at you upside down.

I get positively angry with the impertinence of it and the everlastingness. Up and down and sideways they crawl, and those absurd, unblinking eyes are everywhere. There is one place where two breadths didn't match, and the eyes go all up and down the line, one a little higher than the other.

I never saw so much expression in an inanimate thing before, and we all know how much expression they have! I used to lie awake as a child and get more entertainment and terror out of blank walls and plain furniture than most children could find in a toy-store.

I remember what a kindly wink the knobs of our big, old bureau used to have, and there was one chair that always seemed like a strong friend.

I used to feel that if any of the other things looked too fierce I could always hop into that chair and be safe.

The furniture in this room is no worse than inharmonious, however, for we had to bring it all from downstairs. I suppose when this was used as a playroom they had to take the nursery things out, and no wonder! I never saw such ravages as the children have made here.

The wall-paper, as I said before, is torn off in spots, and it sticketh closer than a brother—they must have had perseverance as well as hatred.

Then the floor is scratched and gouged and splintered, the plaster itself is dug out here and there, and this great heavy bed which is all we found in the room, looks as if it had been through the wars.

But I don't mind it a bit—only the paper.

There comes John's sister. Such a dear girl as she is, and so careful of me! I must not let her find me writing.

She is a perfect and enthusiastic housekeeper, and hopes for no better profession. I verily believe she thinks it is the writing which made me sick!

But I can write when she is out, and see her a long way off from these windows.

There is one that commands the road, a lovely shaded winding road, and one that just looks off over the country. A lovely country, too, full of great elms and velvet meadows.

This wall-paper has a kind of sub-pattern in a different shade, a particularly irritating one, for you can only see it in certain lights, and not clearly then.

But in the places where it isn't faded and where the sun is just so—I can see a strange, provoking, formless sort of figure, that seems to skulk about behind that silly and conspicuous front design.

There's sister on the stairs!

Well, the Fourth of July is over! The people are all gone and I am tired out. John thought it might do me good to see a little company, so we just had mother and Nellie and the children down for a week.

Of course I didn't do a thing. Jennie sees to everything now.

But it tired me all the same.

John says if I don't pick up faster he shall send me to Weir Mitchell[1] in the fall.

But I don't want to go there at all. I had a friend who was in his hands once, and she says he is just like John and my brother, only more so!

Besides, it is such an undertaking to go so far.

I don't feel as if it was worth while to turn my hand over for anything, and I'm getting dreadfully fretful and querulous.

I cry at nothing, and cry most of the time.

Of course I don't when John is here, or anybody else, but when I am alone.

And I am alone a good deal just now. John is kept in town very often by serious cases, and Jennie is good and lets me alone when I want her to.

So I walk a little in the garden or down that lovely lane, sit on the porch under the roses, and lie down up here a good deal.

I'm getting really fond of the room in spite of the wall-paper. Perhaps *because* of the wall-paper.

It dwells in my mind so!

I lie here on this great immovable bed—it is nailed down, I believe—and follow that pattern about by the hour. It is as good as gymnastics, I assure you. I start, we'll say, at the bottom, down in the corner over there where it has not been touched, and I determine for the thousandth time that I *will* follow that pointless pattern to some sort of a conclusion.

I know a little of the principle of design, and I know this thing was not arranged on any laws of radiation, or alternation, or repetition, or symmetry, or anything else that I ever heard of.

It is repeated, of course, by the breadths, but not otherwise.

Looked at in one way each breadth stands alone, the bloated curves and flourishes—a kind of "debased Romanesque" with delirium tremens—go waddling up and down in isolated columns of fatuity.

But, on the other hand, they connect diagonally, and the sprawling outlines run off in great slanting waves of optic horror, like a lot of wallowing seaweeds in full chase.

The whole thing goes horizontally, too, at least it seems so, and I exhaust myself trying to distinguish the order of its going in that direction.

They have used a horizontal breadth for a frieze, and that adds wonderfully to the confusion.

There is one end of the room where it is almost intact, and there, when the crosslights fade and the low sun shines directly upon it, I can almost fancy radiation after all,—the interminable grotesques seem to form around a common center and rush off in headlong plunges of equal distraction.

It makes me tired to follow it. I will take a nap I guess.

I don't know why I should write this.

I don't want to.

---

[1] S. Weir Mitchell (1829–1914), a noted physician who specialized in treating neurasthenic women, attended both Charlotte Perkins Gilman and Edith Wharton when they suffered from "nerves."

I don't feel able.

And I know John would think it absurd. But I *must* say what I feel and think in some way—it is such a relief!

But the effort is getting to be greater than the relief.

Half the time now I am awfully lazy, and lie down ever so much.

John says I mustn't lose my strength, and has me take cod liver oil and lots of tonics and things, to say nothing of ale and wine and rare meat.

Dear John! He loves me very dearly, and hates to have me sick. I tried to have a real earnest reasonable talk with him the other day, and tell him how I wish he would let me go and make a visit to Cousin Henry and Julia.

But he said I wasn't able to go, nor able to stand it after I got there; and I did not make out a very good case for myself, for I was crying before I had finished.

It is getting to be a great effort for me to think straight. Just this nervous weakness I suppose.

And dear John gathered me up in his arms, and just carried me upstairs and laid me on the bed, and sat by me and read to me till it tired my head.

He said I was his darling and his comfort and all he had, and that I must take care of myself for his sake, and keep well.

He says no one but myself can help me out of it, that I must use my will and self-control and not let any silly fancies run away with me.

There's one comfort, the baby is well and happy, and does not have to occupy this nursery with the horrid wall-paper.

If we had not used it, that blessed child would have! What a fortunate escape! Why, I wouldn't have a child of mine, an impressionable little thing, live in such a room for worlds.

I never thought of it before, but it is lucky that John kept me here after all, I can stand it so much easier than a baby, you see.

Of course I never mention it to them any more—I am too wise—but I keep watch for it all the same.

There are things in that paper that nobody knows but me, or ever will.

Behind that outside pattern the dim shapes get clearer every day.

It is always the same shape, only very numerous.

And it is like a woman stooping down and creeping about behind that pattern. I don't like it a bit. I wonder—I begin to think—I wish John would take me away from here!

It is so hard to talk with John about my case, because he is so wise, and because he loves me so.

But I tried it last night.

It was moonlight. The moon shines in all around just as the sun does.

I hate to see it sometimes, it creeps so slowly, and always comes in by one window or another.

John was asleep and I hated to waken him, so I kept still and watched the moonlight on that undulating wall-paper till I felt creepy.

The faint figure behind seemed to shake the pattern, just as if she wanted to get out.

I got up softly and went to feel and see if the paper *did* move, and when I came back John was awake.

"What is it, little girl?" he said. "Don't go walking about like that— you'll get cold."

I thought it was a good time to talk so I told him that I really was not gaining here, and that I wished he would take me away.

"Why darling!" said he, "our lease will be up in three weeks, and I can't see how to leave before.

"The repairs are not done at home, and I cannot possibly leave town just now. Of course if you were in any danger, I could and would, but you really are better, dear, whether you can see it or not. I am a doctor, dear, and I know. You are gaining flesh and color, your appetite is better. I feel really much easier about you."

"I don't weigh a bit more," said I, "nor as much; and my appetite may be better in the evening when you are here, but it is worse in the morning when you are away!"

"Bless her little heart!" said he with a big hug, "she shall be as sick as she pleases! But now let's improve the shining hours by going to sleep, and talk about it in the morning!"

"And you won't go away?" I asked gloomily.

"Why, how can I, dear? It is only three weeks more and then we will take a nice little trip of a few days while Jennie is getting the house ready. Really, dear, you are better!"

"Better in body perhaps—" I began, and stopped short, for he sat up straight and looked at me with such a stern, reproachful look that I could not say another word.

"My darling," said he, "I beg of you, for my sake and for our child's sake, as well as for your own, that you will never for one instant let that idea enter your mind! There is nothing so dangerous, so fascinating, to a temperament like yours. It is a false and foolish fancy. Can you not trust me as a physician when I tell you so?"

So of course I said no more on that score, and we went to sleep before long. He thought I was asleep first, but I wasn't, and lay there for hours trying to decide whether that front pattern and the back pattern really did move together or separately.

On a pattern like this, by daylight, there is a lack of sequence, a defiance of law, that is a constant irritant to a normal mind.

The color is hideous enough, and unreliable enough, and infuriating enough, but the pattern is torturing.

You think you have mastered it, but just as you get well underway in following, it turns a back-somersault and there you are. It slaps you in the face, knocks you down, and tramples upon you. It is like a bad dream.

The outside pattern is a florid arabesque, reminding one of a fungus. If you can imagine a toadstool in joints, an interminable string of toadstools, budding and sprouting in endless convolutions—why, that is something like it.

That is, sometimes!

There is one marked peculiarity about this paper, a thing nobody seems to notice but myself, and that is that it changes as the light changes.

When the sun shoots in through the east window—I always watch for that first, long, straight ray—it changes so quickly that I never can quite believe it.

That is why I watch it always.

By moonlight—the moon shines in all night when there is a moon—I wouldn't know it was the same paper.

At night in any kind of light, in twilight, candlelight, lamplight, and worst of all by moonlight, it becomes bars! The outside pattern I mean, and the woman behind it is as plain as can be.

I didn't realize for a long time what the thing was that showed behind, that dim sub-pattern, but now I am quite sure it is a woman.

By daylight she is subdued, quiet. I fancy it is the pattern that keeps her so still. It is so puzzling. It keeps me quiet by the hour.

I lie down ever so much now. John says it is good for me, and to sleep all I can.

Indeed he started the habit by making me lie down for an hour after each meal.

It is a very bad habit I am convinced, for you see I don't sleep.

And that cultivates deceit, for I don't tell them I'm awake—O, no!

The fact is I am getting a little afraid of John.

He seems very queer sometimes, and even Jennie has an inexplicable look.

It strikes me occasionally, just as a scientific hypothesis, that perhaps it is the paper!

I have watched John when he did not know I was looking, and come into the room suddenly on the most innocent excuses, and I've caught him several times *looking at the paper!* And Jennie too. I caught Jennie with her hand on it once.

She didn't know I was in the room, and when I asked her in a quiet, a very quiet voice, with the most restrained manner possible, what she was doing with the paper—she turned around as if she had been caught stealing, and looked quite angry—asked me why I should frighten her so!

Then she said that the paper stained everything it touched, that she had found yellow smooches on all my clothes and John's, and she wished we would be more careful!

Did not that sound innocent? But I know she was studying that pattern, and I am determined that nobody shall find it out but myself!

Life is very much more exciting now than it used to be. You see I have something more to expect, to look forward to, to watch. I really do eat better, and am more quiet than I was.

John is so pleased to see me improve! He laughed a little the other day, and said I seemed to be flourishing in spite of my wall-paper.

I turned it off with a laugh. I had no intention of telling him it was *because* of the wall-paper—he would make fun of me. He might even want to take me away.

I don't want to leave now until I have found it out. There is a week more, and I think that will be enough.

I'm feeling ever so much better! I don't sleep much at night, for it is so interesting to watch developments; but I sleep a good deal in the daytime.

In the daytime it is tiresome and perplexing.

There are always new shoots on the fungus, and new shades of yellow all over it. I cannot keep count of them, though I have tried conscientiously.

It is the strangest yellow, that wall-paper! It makes me think of all the yellow things I ever saw—not beautiful ones like buttercups, but old foul, bad yellow things.

But there is something else about that paper—the smell! I noticed it the moment we came into the room, but with so much air and sun it was not bad. Now we have had a week of fog and rain, and whether the windows are open or not, the smell is here.

It creeps all over the house.

I find it hovering in the dining-room, skulking in the parlor, hiding in the hall, lying in wait for me on the stairs.

It gets into my hair.

Even when I go to ride, if I turn my head suddenly and surprise it— there is that smell!

Such a peculiar odor, too! I have spent hours in trying to analyze it, to find what it smelled like.

It is not bad—at first, and very gentle, but quite the subtlest, most endur- ing odor I ever met.

In this damp weather it is awful, I wake up in the night and find it hanging over me.

It used to disturb me at first. I thought seriously of burning the house— to reach the smell.

But now I am used to it. The only thing I can think of that it is like is the *color* of the paper! A yellow smell.

There is a very funny mark on this wall, low down, near the mopboard. A streak that runs round the room. It goes behind every piece of furniture, except the bed, a long, straight, even *smooch,* as if it had been rubbed over and over.

I wonder how it was done and who did it, and what they did it for. Round and round and round—round and round and round—it makes me dizzy!

I really have discovered something at last.

Through watching so much at night, when it changes so, I have finally found out.

The front pattern *does* move—and no wonder! The woman behind shakes it!

Sometimes I think there are a great many women behind, and some- times only one, and she crawls around fast, and her crawling shakes it all over.

Then in the very bright spots she keeps still, and in the very shady spots she just takes hold of the bars and shakes them hard.

And she is all the time trying to climb through. But nobody could climb through that pattern—it strangles so; I think that is why it has so many heads.

They get through, and then the pattern strangles them off and turns them upside down, and makes their eyes white!

If those heads were covered or taken off it would not be half so bad.

I think that woman gets out in the daytime!

And I'll tell you why—privately—I've seen her!

I can see her out of every one of my windows!

It is the same woman, I know, for she is always creeping, and most women do not creep by daylight.

I see her in that long shaded lane, creeping up and down. I see her in those dark grape arbors, creeping all around the garden.

I see her on that long road under the trees, creeping along, and when a carriage comes she hides under the blackberry vines.

I don't blame her a bit. It must be very humiliating to be caught creeping by daylight!

I always lock the door when I creep by daylight. I can't do it at night, for I know John would suspect something at once.

And John is so queer now, that I don't want to irritate him. I wish he would take another room! Besides, I don't want anybody to get that woman out at night but myself.

I often wonder if I could see her out of all the windows at once.

But, turn as fast as I can, I can only see out of one at one time.

And though I always see her, she *may* be able to creep faster than I can turn!

I have watched her sometimes away off in the open country, creeping as fast as a cloud shadow in a high wind.

If only that top pattern could be gotten off from the under one! I mean to try it, little by little.

I have found out another funny thing, but I shan't tell it this time! It does not do to trust people too much.

There are only two more days to get this paper off, and I believe John is beginning to notice. I don't like the look in his eyes.

And I heard him ask Jennie a lot of professional questions about me. She had a very good report to give.

She said I slept a good deal in the daytime.

John knows I don't sleep very well at night, for all I'm so quiet!

He asked me all sorts of questions, too, and pretended to be very loving and kind.

As if I couldn't see through him!

Still, I don't wonder he acts so, sleeping under this paper for three months.

It only interests me, but I feel sure John and Jennie are secretly affected by it.

Hurrah! This is the last day, but it is enough. John to stay in town over night, and won't be out until this evening.

Jennie wanted to sleep with me—the sly thing! but I told her I should undoubtedly rest better for a night all alone.

That was clever, for really I wasn't alone a bit! As soon as it was moonlight and that poor thing began to crawl and shake the pattern, I got up and ran to help her.

I pulled and she shook, I shook and she pulled, and before morning we had peeled off yards of that paper.

A strip about as high as my head and half around the room.

And then when the sun came and that awful pattern began to laugh at me, I declared I would finish it to-day!

We go away to-morrow, and they are moving all my furniture down again to leave things as they were before.

Jennie looked at the wall in amazement, but I told her merrily that I did it out of pure spite at the vicious thing.

She laughed and said she wouldn't mind doing it herself, but I must not get tired.

How she betrayed herself that time!

But I am here, and no person touches this paper but Me—not *alive!*

She tried to get me out of the room—it was too patent! But I said it was so quiet and empty and clean now that I believed I would lie down again and sleep all I could; and not to wake me even for dinner—I would call when I woke.

So now she is gone, and the servants are gone, and the things are gone, and there is nothing left but the great bedstead nailed down, with the canvas mattress we found on it.

We shall sleep downstairs to-night, and take the boat home to-morrow.

I quite enjoy the room, now it is bare again.

How those children did tear about here!

This bedstead is fairly gnawed!

But I must get to work

I have locked the door and thrown the key down into the front path.

I don't want to go out, and I don't want to have anybody come in, till John comes.

I want to astonish him.

I've got a rope up here that even Jennie did not find. If that woman does get out, and tries to get away, I can tie her!

But I forgot I could not reach far without anything to stand on!

This bed will *not* move!

I tried to lift and push it until I was lame, and then I got so angry I bit off a little piece at one corner—but it hurt my teeth.

Then I peeled off all the paper I could reach standing on the floor. It sticks horribly and the pattern just enjoys it! All those strangled heads and bulbous eyes and waddling fungus growths just shriek with derision!

I am getting angry enough to do something desperate. To jump out of the window would be admirable exercise, but the bars are too strong even to try.

Besides I wouldn't do it. Of course not. I know well enough that a step like that is improper and might be misconstrued.

I don't like to *look* out the windows even—there are so many of those creeping women, and they creep so fast.

I wonder if they all come out of that wallpaper as I did?

But I am securely fastened now by my well-hidden rope—you don't get *me* out in the road there!

I suppose I shall have to get back behind the pattern when it comes night, and that is hard!

It is so pleasant to be out in this great room and creep around as I please!

I don't want to go outside. I won't, even if Jennie asks me to.

For outside you have to creep on the ground, and eveything is green instead of yellow.

But here I can creep smoothly on the floor, and my shoulder just fits in that long smooch around the wall, so I cannot lose my way.

Why there's John at the door!

It is no use, young man, you can't open it!

How he does call and pound!

Now he's crying for an axe.

It would be a shame to break down that beautiful door!

"John dear!" said I in the gentlest voice, "the key is down by the front steps, under a plantain leaf!"

That silenced him for a few moments.

Then he said, very quietly indeed, "Open the door, my darling!"

"I can't," said I. "The key is down by the front door under a plantain leaf!"

And then I said it again, several times, very gently and slowly, and said it so often that he had to go and see, and he got it of course, and came in. He stopped short by the door.

"What is the matter?" he cried. "For God's sake, what are you doing!"

I kept on creeping just the same, but I looked at him over my shoulder.

"I've got out at last," said I, "in spite of you and Jane. And I've pulled off most of the paper, so you can't put me back!"

Now why should that man have fainted? But he did, and right across my path by the wall, so that I had to creep over him every time!

(1892)

Prewriting

As you read the story carefully a second time, pay particular attention to the descriptive passages that appeal to the senses—especially, in this story, to sight and smell. Underline any specific words or phrases that you think contribute to the atmosphere. List, as you go along, the unusual words that Gilman uses in her descriptions, like *skulk, waddling, smooches.*

PREWRITING EXERCISE

A. List at least five words that describe the atmosphere created in this story. Use your thesaurus if you get stuck. Your instructor might want to have you discuss these word choices with the class. Try to decide which are the most appropriate—and why.

B. In a paragraph of about one hundred words, describe the house—and especially the room—in which the narrator is confined. Decide which details are crucial to the story. As you read the story again, be sure you have not overlooked any significant descriptive details.

C. Before planning your paper, write your responses to the following questions.

1. Why is it fitting that the narrator's husband chooses the nursery as her room? (Is it indeed a nursery?)
2. What would the narrator *like* to be doing? Why can't she? Does her illness alone prevent her from doing as she wishes?
3. What do the sunshine and the moonlight contribute to the story?
4. What would be gained or lost if the wallpaper were the kind found in a typical bathroom or kitchen or child's room today (e.g., with little animals)?
5. What are the similarities between the narrator and the woman she sees behind the wallpaper?
6. What significance can you attach to the narrator's discovery that the woman escapes and creeps around outside? Why do you think the narrator asserts that "most women do not creep by daylight"? Is it significant that by the end of the story the narrator sees *many* women creeping about the countryside?
7. Who does the narrator think she is at the end of the story?

Writing

Now that you have become familiar with the story, you need to ask yourself still more questions: How can I make a statement about the function of setting in relation to theme? What, indeed, does the setting contribute to the overall effectiveness of the story? What does the atmosphere contribute? How do both relate to the meaning of the story? Do they simply *heighten* the theme or do they actually help the reader to understand what the story is about? As you think about answers to these questions, review your prewriting material and continue consulting the story for clues.

DISCOVERING AN ORGANIZATION

As you are trying to solve the problems posed by the questions in the preceding paragraph, write down all the likely ideas that strike you. Do you trust your memory, or some of your best inspirations may slip away. Then try to think of some point you can make about the story that will allow you to use this information. Once you have discovered an interesting point to pursue, write out this idea in a single, clear sentence. This idea will be your thesis. Then sort through the details related to setting in the story and ask yourself: What generalizations can I make about these details in support of my thesis? You might, for instance, group your material spatially—arranging details describing the landscape outside the house, details of the inside, details within the narrator's room, and finally of the yellow wallpaper itself. Conclude with a statement summarizing the effectiveness of these details in documenting the narrator's descent into madness.

IDEAS FOR WRITING

1. Discuss the importance of the nursery setting in understanding the dominant/submissive relationship between the husband and wife that ultimately drives the narrator insane.
2. Show how the atmosphere of "strangeness" that Gilman creates throughout the story intensifies her portrayal of the narrator's growing mental imbalance.

Rewriting: Style

During the revising process, you will, as usual, be concerned with the messy business of trying to improve every element of the paper—the ideas, the focus, the organization, the paragraph development, the transitions, the sentence structure, the word choice, the introduction, and the conclusion. But our advice in this section will focus on ways to achieve emphasis through writing balanced sentences.

IMITATING BALANCED STRUCTURE

Balanced (or parallel) sentences are both graceful and emphatic. Of course, all items in any series should be named in the same grammatical form—all nouns, all adjectives, all phrases, all clauses, and so on—whether emphasis is intended or not, like this. Note the following sentences:

> Chopin is admired for the *grace, precision,* and *economy* of her style.
> Good writers acknowledge the necessity of *thinking, planning, writing, revising, resting,* and then *thinking* and *revising* still further.

In the following sentence, though, the third item in the italicized series does not match. Compare it to the corrected version:

> Unbalanced: The main character would not willingly give up the *carefree, extravagant,* and *drinking and staying out late* as he did when a bachelor.
> Balanced: The main character would not willingly give up the *carefree, extravagant, carousing* ways of his bachelorhood.

Probably you can already handle such balancing in ordinary sentences. But pay attention during revising to make sure that all items in series are indeed balanced.

If you need an emphatic sentence for your introduction or conclusion, a good way to learn to write impressive balanced sentences is through *sentence modeling.* Many expert writers—Robert Louis Stevenson, Abraham Lincoln, Winston Churchill, Somerset Maugham—attest that they perfected their writing by studiously copying and imitating the sentences of stylists whom they admired.

SENTENCE MODELING EXERCISE

Examine the model sentence below to discover its structure. How is it formed? Does it use balanced phrases, clauses, or single words? Does it include any deliberate repetition of words as well as structures? Does it build to a climax at the end? If so, how? By adding ideas of increasing importance? By establishing a pattern that gathers momentum?

Once you have discovered the structure of the model sentence, write one as nearly like it as possible *using your own words and subject matter.* Then, repeat this process of imitation four more times, changing your ideas with each new sentence, like this:

Model	"Until the young are informed as much about the courage of pacifists as about the obedience of soldiers, they aren't educated." *—Coleman McCarthy*
Imitation:	Until Americans become as interested in the speeches of candidates as about the performance of athletes, they aren't ideal citizens.
Imitation:	Until men are fascinated as much by the minds of females as by the bodies of females, they will be seen as sexist.

First, copy each of the numbered sentences carefully—including the exact punctuation. Then imitate each one at least five times.

1. "He sees no seams or joints or points of intersection—only irrevocable wholes."

—Mina Shaughnessy

2. "We made meals and changed diapers and took out the garbage and paid bills—while other people died."

—Ellen Goodman

3. "The refrigerator was full of sulfurous scraps, dark crusts, furry oddments."

   —*Alice Munro*

4. "It is sober without being dull; massive without being oppressive."

   —*Sir Kenneth Clark*

5. "Joint by joint, line by line, pill by pill, the use of illegal drugs has become a crisis for American business."

   —*Newsweek* Magazine (1983)

CHAPTER

9

Writing about Theme

A story's theme or meaning grows out of all the elements of imaginative fiction—character, structure, symbolism, point of view, and setting. The theme is usually not an obvious moral or message, and it may be difficult to sum up succinctly. But thinking about the theme of a story and trying to state it in your own words will help to focus your scattered reactions and to make your understanding of the author's purpose more certain.

What is Theme?

Theme has been defined in many ways: the central idea or thesis; the central thought; the underlying meaning, either implied or directly stated; the general idea or insight revealed by the entire story; the central truth; the dominating idea; the abstract concept which is made concrete through representation in person, action, and image.

Because the theme involves ideas and insights, we usually state it in general terms. "Eveline," for instance, concerns the conflicts of a specific character, but the story's central truth—its theme—relates to abstract qualities like *duty* and *fear*. If someone asks what "Eveline" is about, we might respond with details about the title character's encounter with Frank and her failure to go away with him. But if someone asks for the story's theme, we would answer with a general statement of ideas or values: "Eveline" shows how people can be trapped by fear and obligation.

It is easy to confuse *subject* with *theme*. The subject is the topic or material the story examines—love, death, war, human relations, growing up, and so forth. But the theme is the direct or implied

statement that the story makes *about* the subject. For example, the
fantasies of Walter Mitty constitute the subject of Thurber's story,
but the theme is what the story says about those fantasies and why
Mitty has them. The theme, then, is the idea (or ideas) that we
gain from thinking about what we have read.

Looking at Theme

As you read "The Pedestrian" by Ray Bradbury, think about how
this view of the future relates to present-day life.

Ray Bradbury *1920–*

THE PEDESTRIAN

To enter out into that silence that was the city at eight o'clock of a misty evening in November, to put your feet upon that buckling concrete walk, to step over grassy seams and make your way, hands in pockets, through the silences, that was what Mr. Leonard Mead most dearly loved to do. He would stand upon the corner of an intersection and peer down long moonlit avenues of sidewalk in four directions, deciding which way to go, but it really made no difference; he was alone in this world of 2053 A.D., or as good as alone, and with a final decision made, a path selected, he would stride off, sending patterns of frosty air before him like the smoke of a cigar.

Sometimes he would walk for hours and miles and return only at midnight to his house. And on his way he would see the cottages and homes with their dark windows, and it was not unequal to walking through a graveyard where only the faintest glimmers of firefly light appeared in flickers behind the windows. Sudden gray phantoms seemed to manifest upon inner room walls where a curtain was still undrawn against the night, or there were whisperings and murmurs where a window in a tomb-like building was still open.

Mr. Leonard Mead would pause, cock his head, listen, look, and march on, his feet making no noise on the lumpy walk. For long ago he had wisely changed to sneakers when strolling at night, because the dogs in intermittent squads would parallel his journey with barkings if he wore hard heels, and lights might click on and faces appear and an entire street be startled by the passing of a lone figure, himself, in the early November evening.

On this particular evening he began his journey in a westerly direction, toward the hidden sea. There was a good crystal frost in the air; it cut the nose and made the lungs blaze like a Christmas tree inside; you could feel the cold light going on and off, all the branches filled with invisible snow. He listened to the faint push of his soft shoes through autumn leaves with satisfaction, and whistled a cold quiet whistle between his teeth, occasionally picking up a leaf as he passed, examining its skeletal pattern in the infrequent lamplights as he went on, smelling its rusty smell.

"Hello, in there," he whispered to every house on every side as he moved. "What's up tonight on Channel 4, Channel 7, Channel 9? Where are the cowboys rushing, and do I see the United States Cavalry over the next hill to the rescue?"

The street was silent and long and empty, with only his shadow moving like the shadow of a hawk in mid-country. If he closed his eyes and stood very still, frozen, he could imagine himself upon the center of a plain, a wintry, windless Arizona desert with no house in a thousand miles, and only dry river beds, the streets, for company.

"What is it now?" he asked the houses, noticing his wrist watch. "Eight-thirty P.M.? Time for a dozen assorted murders? A quiz? A revue? A comedian falling off the stage?"

Was that a murmur of laughter from within a moon-white house? He hesitated, but went on when nothing more happened. He stumbled over a particularly uneven section of sidewalk. The cement was vanishing under flowers and grass. In ten years of walking by night or day, for thousands of miles, he had never met another person walking, not one in all that time.

He came to a cloverleaf intersection which stood silent where two main highways crossed the town. During the day it was a thunderous surge of cars, the gas stations open, a great insect rustling and a ceaseless jockeying for position as the scarab-beetles, a faint incense puttering from their exhausts, skimmed homeward to the far directions. But now these highways, too, were like streams in a dry season, all stone and bed and moon radiance.

He turned back on a side street, circling around toward his home. He was within a block of his destination when the lone car turned a corner quite suddenly and flashed a fierce white cone of light upon him. He stood entranced, not unlike a night moth, stunned by the illumination, and then drawn toward it.

A metallic voice called to him:

"Stand still. Stay where you are! Don't move!"

He halted.

"Put up your hands!"

"But———" he said.

"Your hands up! Or we'll shoot!"

The police, of course, but what a rare, incredible thing; in a city of three million, there was only *one* police car left, wasn't that correct? Ever since a year ago, 2052, the election year, the force had been cut down from three cars to one. Crime was ebbing; there was no need now for the police, save for this one lone car wandering and wandering the empty streets.

"Your name?" said the police car in a metallic whisper. He couldn't see the men in it for the bright light in his eyes.

"Leonard Mead," he said.

"Speak up!"

"Leonard Mead!"

"Business or profession?"

"I guess you'd call me a writer."

"No profession," said the police car, as if talking to itself. The light held him fixed, like a museum specimen, needle thrust through the chest.

"You might say that," said Mr. Mead. He hadn't written in years. Magazines and books didn't sell any more. Everything went on in the tomblike houses at night now, he thought, continuing his fancy. The tombs, ill-lit by television light, where the people sat like the dead, the gray or multi-colored lights touching their faces, but never really touching them.

"No profession," said the phonograph voice, hissing. "What are you doing out?"

"Walking," said Leonard Mead.

"Walking!"

"Just walking," he said simply, but his face felt cold.

"Walking, just walking, walking?"

"Yes, sir."

"Walking where? For what?"

"Walking for air. Walking to *see.*"

"Your address!"

"Eleven South Saint James Street."

"And there is air *in* your house, you have an air *conditioner,* Mr. Mead?"

"Yes."

"And you have a viewing screen in your house to see with?"

"No."

"No!" There was a crackling quiet that in itself was an accusation.

"Are you married, Mr. Mead?"

"No."

"Not married," said the police voice behind the fiery beam. The moon was high and clear among the stars and the houses were gray and silent.

"Nobody wanted me," said Leonard Mead with a smile.

"Don't speak unless you're spoken to!"

Leonard Mead waited in the cold night.

"Just *walking*, Mr. Mead?"

"Yes."

"But you haven't explained for what purpose."

"I explained; for air, and to see, and just to walk."

"Have you done this often?"

"Every night for years."

The police car sat in the center of the street with its radio throat faintly humming.

"Well, Mr. Mead," it said.

"Is that all?" he asked politely.

"Yes," said the voice. "Here." There was a sigh, a pop. The back door of the police car sprang wide. "Get in."

"Wait a minute, I haven't done anything!"

"Get in."

"I protest."

"Mr. Mead."

He walked like a man suddenly drunk. As he passed the front window of the car he looked in. As he had expected, there was no one in the front seat, no one in the car at all.

"Get in."

He put his hand to the door and peered into the back seat, which was a little cell, a little black jail with bars. It smelled of riveted steel. It smelled of harsh antiseptic; it smelled too clean and hard and metallic. There was nothing soft there.

"Now if you had a wife to give you an alibi," said the iron voice. "But——"

"Where are you taking me?"

The car hesitated, or rather gave a faint whirring click, as if information, somewhere, was dropping card by punch-slotted card under electric eyes. "To the Psychiatric Center for Research on Regressive Tendencies."

He got in. The door shut with a soft thud. The police car rolled through the night avenues, flashing its dim lights ahead.

They passed one house on one street a moment later, one house in an entire city of houses that were dark, but this one particular house had all of its electric lights brightly lit, every window a loud yellow illumination, square and warm in the cool darkness.

"That's *my* house," said Leonard Mead.

No one answered him.

The car moved down the empty river-bed streets and off away, leaving the empty streets with the empty sidewalks, and no sound and no motion all the rest of the chill November night.

(1951)

Prewriting

Because understanding the theme of a literary work involves figuring out what the whole thing means, your main prewriting task entails asking yourself questions that lead to the meaning of the work. You must then express that idea briefly and intelligently.

ANALYZING THEME

Reread "The Pedestrian" and formulate specific leading questions about the following items in the story:

1. The title.
2. The setting, especially the repeated descriptions of the silence, emptiness, and aloneness.
3. Any unusual objects and images, like the metallic voice, the references to tombs and graveyards, Leonard Mead's brightly lit house.

After writing out the answers to the questions you have set for yourself, sum up the theme of this story in a single statement. Then express the theme in another way, using other words. Are both statements valid? Take the one that strikes you as more accurate and write it at the top of a blank sheet of paper. Fill the page with free writing about this idea, expressing as quickly as you can your thoughts and feelings about Bradbury's vision of life in the future.

Writing

We have emphasized that your essays should be plump with supporting details from your source. Without specific references to the literary work, your writing will be vague and unconvincing.

CHOOSING SUPPORTING DETAILS

During a close second reading of a story, pay special attention to the descriptive details. In "The Pedestrian," you will notice that images of light—lights of varying qualities—appear frequently. After picking up on these images, go back through the story one more time and put a check mark next to each one. During this third examination, you may come up with an insight about the meaning of these images—perhaps something like, "A pattern of flickering, dim, and disturbing lights develops through the story, providing a contrast with the appearance of Mead's warmly, steadily lit house." You now have a good topic sentence for a paragraph. A list of specific examples from the story could support the statement but would seem fairly mechanical. So, if possible, *classify* the details. In this case, one kind of disturbing light is cast by the television and another kind is cast by the police prowler car. Quote one or two examples of each kind, and then comment on the significance of these details. In this story, for instance, both types are signs of dehumanization. To further support your point, you could provide a count: eighteen descriptions of light quality in a short, three-page story.

Approach the following writing ideas by rereading the story with the topic in mind. Jot down any details that seem relevant. Review your notes and see what general observations you can make; then sort out these supporting details and comment on their significance.

IDEAS FOR WRITING

1. Write a description of life in 2053 A.D., as suggested by "The Pedestrian." Why does the author present us with this view of the future?

2. Why is Leonard Mead taken to the Psychiatric Center for Research on Regressive Tendencies? What is "regressive" about his behavior? Could Bradbury be making a statement about "progress" and "regression" in this story? Write an essay that explores this idea as the main theme of "The Pedestrian."

3. Write an essay on "The Pedestrian" in which you show how the theme of this story about the future actually makes a comment on present-day life.

Rewriting

When you revise, you should make sure your paper *flows*—that your readers can follow your ideas easily.

ACHIEVING COHERENCE

The best way to make your writing *coherent*—to make it hold together and easy to follow—is to have a clear thesis and to make sure that all your subpoints pertain to that thesis. If you organize the development of your ideas carefully, your paragraphs should unfold in a logical, connected way. Continuity also comes when you think out your ideas completely and develop them adequately. Leaps in thought and shifts in meaning often result from too much generalization and too little development.

Here are some other ways to help you achieve coherence:

Repeated Words and Synonyms.   Repeat key words for coherence as well as for emphasis:

> I do not want *to read another gothic romance.* I especially do not want *to read another* long *gothic romance.*

If repetition is tiresome or you want more variety, use a synonym:

> It was a rare *caper,* planned to the last second. Such elaborate *heists* seem to come right from a detective novel.

Take care when you repeat words. These words should be important or emphatic. Do not repeat a common, limp term because you are too lazy to find a synonym.* The following introduction to a student paper suffers because the writer needlessly repeats "scapegoats" and some form of the same uninteresting verb:

> Shirley Jackson's "The Lottery" is a complex story that deals with a fundamental part of human psychology, the *using* of scapegoats. Scapegoats have been *used* throughout history to justify actions. Many times scapegoats are *used* to conceal human errors or misbeliefs. Scapegoats are, in fact, still *used* today. [italics added]

Notice that the repetition of the key word *scapegoats* is emphatic. The ineffective repetition can be revised this way:

> Shirley Jackson's "The Lottery" is a complex story that deals with a fundamental element of human psychology—*using* scapegoats. Scapegoats have been *created* throughout history to justify actions. Many times they are *employed* to conceal human errors or misbeliefs. In fact, scapegoats still *exist* today.

Parallel Structure.   Repeat a grammatical pattern to tie points and details together:

> In the morning Madame Bovary ate breakfast with her husband; in the afternoon she picnicked with her paramour.

> The play was about to end: the lovers kissed, the curtain fell, and the audience applauded wildly.

Be sure that your grammatical pattern actually *is* parallel. If your phrases or clauses are not precisely balanced (i.e., all grammatically similar), you will lose the good effect:

---

* But you must be aware that synonyms are not always interchangeable. Be sure to check the meaning of any word you are not sure of.

Not Parallel—In "The Lottery" these characteristics include *unwillingness to change, being stuck in tradition, fear of peer pressure,* and *fear itself.*

Parallel—In "The Lottery" these characteristics include *unwillingness to change, enslavement to tradition, fear of peer pressure,* and *fear of the unknown.*

Not Parallel—Many times scapegoats are used to conceal *human errors* or *misbeliefs people have.*

Parallel—Many times scapegoats are used to conceal human *errors* or *misbeliefs.*

EXERCISE

Examine the first three paragraphs of "The Pedestrian" and notice how Bradbury achieves coherence in his writing. Number the sentences (1 to 7) and write down the transitional devices, repeated words, synonyms, pronoun references, parallel structures, and other connectives in each sentence.

Anthology of Short Fiction

Nathaniel Hawthorne *1804–1864*

YOUNG GOODMAN BROWN

Young Goodman Brown came forth at sunset, into the street of Salem village, but put his head back, after crossing the threshold, to exchange a parting kiss with his young wife. And Faith, as the wife was aptly named, thrust her own pretty head into the street, letting the wind play with the pink ribbons of her cap, while she called to Goodman Brown.

"Dearest heart," whispered she, softly and rather sadly, when her lips were close to his ear, "prithee, put off your journey until sunrise, and sleep in your own bed to-night. A lone woman is troubled with such dreams and such thoughts, that she's afeard of herself, sometimes. Pray, tarry with me this night, dear husband, of all nights in the year!"

"My love and my Faith," replied young Goodman Brown, "of all nights in the year, this one night must I tarry away from thee. My journey, as thou callest it, forth and back again, must needs be done 'twixt now and sunrise. What, my sweet, pretty wife, dost thou doubt me already, and we but three months married!"

"Then God bless you!" said Faith with the pink ribbons, "and may you find all well, when you come back."

"Amen!" cried Goodman Brown. "Say thy prayers, dear Faith, and go to bed at dusk, and no harm will come to thee."

So they parted; and the young man pursued his way, until, being about to turn the corner by the meeting-house, he looked back and saw the head of Faith still peeping after him, with a melancholy air, in spite of her pink ribbons.

"Poor little Faith!" thought he, for his heart smote him. "What a wretch am I to leave her on such an errand! She talks of dreams, too. Methought, as she spoke, there was trouble in her face, as if a dream had warned her what work is to be done to-night. But no, no! 't would kill her to think it. Well; she's a blessed angel on earth; and after this one night, I'll cling to her skirts and follow her to Heaven."

With this excellent resolve for the future, Goodman Brown felt himself justified in making more haste on his present evil purpose. He had taken a dreary road, darkened by all the gloomiest trees of the forest, which barely stood aside to let the narrow path creep through, and closed immediately behind. It was as lonely as could be; and there is this peculiarity in such a solitude, that the traveller knows not who may be concealed by the innumerable trunks and the thick boughs overhead; so that, with lonely footsteps, he may yet be passing through an unseen multitude.

"There may be a devilish Indian behind every tree," said Goodman Brown to himself; and he glanced fearfully behind him, as he added, "What if the devil himself should be at my very elbow!"

His head being turned back, he passed a crook of the road, and looking forward again, beheld the figure of a man, in grave and decent attire, seated at the foot of an old tree. He arose at Goodman Brown's approach, and walked onward, side by side with him.

"You are late, Goodman Brown," said he. "The clock of the Old South was striking, as I came through Boston; and that is full fifteen minutes agone."

"Faith kept me back awhile," replied the young man, with a tremor in his voice, caused by the sudden appearance of his companion, though not wholly unexpected.

It was now deep dusk in the forest, and deepest in that part of it where these two were journeying. As nearly as could be discerned, the second traveller was about fifty years old, apparently in the same rank of life as Goodman Brown, and bearing a considerable resemblance to him, though perhaps more in expression than features. Still, they might have been taken for father and son. And yet, though the elder person was as simply clad as the younger, and as simple in manner too, he had an indescribable air of one who knew the world, and would not have felt abashed at the governor's dinner-table, or in King William's court, were it possible that his affairs should call him thither. But the only thing about him that could be fixed upon as remarkable, was his staff, which bore the likeness of a great black snake, so curiously wrought, that it might almost be seen to twist and wriggle itself like a living serpent. This, of course, must have been an ocular deception, assisted by the uncertain light.

"Come, Goodman Brown!" cried his fellow-traveller, "this is a dull pace for the beginning of a journey. Take my staff, if you are so soon weary."

"Friend," said the other, exchanging his slow pace for a full stop, "having kept covenant by meeting thee here, it is my purpose now to return whence I came. I have scruples, touching the matter thou wot'st of."

"Sayest thou so?" replied he of the serpent, smiling apart. "Let us walk on, nevertheless, reasoning as we go, and if I convince thee not, thou shalt turn back. We are but a little way in the forest, yet."

"Too far, too far!" exclaimed the goodman, unconsciously resuming his walk. "My father never went into the woods on such an errand, nor his father before him. We have been a race of honest men and good Christians, since the days of the martyrs. And shall I be the first of the name of Brown that ever took this path and kept—"

"Such company, thou wouldst say," observed the elder person, interrupting his pause. "Well said, Goodman Brown! I have been as well acquainted with your family as with ever a one among the Puritans; and that's no trifle to say. I helped your grandfather, the constable, when he lashed the Quaker woman so smartly through the streets of Salem. And it was I that brought your father a pitch-pine knot, kindled at my own hearth, to set fire to an Indian village, in King Philip's war. They were my good friends, both; and many a pleasant walk have we had along this path, and returned merrily after midnight. I would fain be friends with you, for their sake."

"If it be as thou sayest," replied Goodman Brown, "I marvel they never spoke of these matters. Or, verily, I marvel not, seeing that the least rumor of the sort would have driven them from New England. We are a people of prayer, and good works to boot, and abide no such wickedness."

"Wickedness or not," said the traveller with the twisted staff, "I have a very general acquaintance here in New England. The deacons of many a church have drunk the communion wine with me; the selectmen, of divers towns, make me their chairman; and a majority of the Great and General Court are firm supporters of my interest. The governor and I, too—but these are state secrets."

"Can this be so!" cried Goodman Brown, with a stare of amazement at his undisturbed companion. "Howbeit, I have nothing to do with the governor and council; they have their own ways, and are no rule for a simple husbandman like me. But, were I to go on with thee, how should I meet the eye of that good old man, our minister, at Salem village? Oh, his voice would make me tremble, both Sabbath-day and lecture-day!"

Thus far, the elder traveller had listened with due gravity, but now burst into a fit of irrepressible mirth, shaking himself so violently, that his snakelike staff actually seemed to wriggle in sympathy.

"Ha, ha, ha!" shouted he, again and again; then composing himself. "Well, go on, Goodman Brown, go on; but, prithee, don't kill me with laughing!"

"Well, then, to end the matter at once," said Goodman Brown, considerably nettled, "there is my wife, Faith. It would break her dear little heart; and I'd rather break my own!"

"Nay, if that be the case," answered the other, "e'en go thy ways, Goodman Brown. I would not, for twenty old women like the one hobbling before us, that Faith should come to any harm."

As he spoke, he pointed his staff at a female figure on the path, in whom

Goodman Brown recognized a very pious and exemplary dame, who had taught him his catechism in youth, and was still his moral and spiritual adviser, jointly with the minister and Deacon Gookin.

"A marvel, truly, that Goody Cloyse should be so far in the wilderness, at nightfall!" said he. "But, with your leave, friend, I shall take a cut through the woods, until we have left this Christian woman behind. Being a stranger to you, she might ask whom I was consorting with, and whither I was going."

"Be it so," said his fellow-traveller. "Betake you to the woods, and let me keep the path."

Accordingly, the young man turned aside, but took care to watch his companion, who advanced softly along the road, until he had come within a staff's length of the old dame. She, meanwhile, was making the best of her way, with singular speed for so aged a woman, and mumbling some indistinct words, a prayer, doubtless, as she went. The traveller put forth his staff, and touched her withered neck with what seemed the serpent's tail.

"The devil!" screamed the pious old lady.

"Then Goody Cloyse knows her old friend?" observed the traveller, confronting her, and leaning on his writhing stick.

"Ah, forsooth, and is it your worship, indeed?" cried the good dame. "Yea, truly is it, and in the very image of my old gossip, Goodman Brown, the grandfather of the silly fellow that now is. But, would your worship believe it? my broomstick hath strangely disappeared, stolen, as I suspect, by that unhanged witch, Goody Cory, and that, too, when I was all anointed with the juice of smallage and cinque-foil and wolf's-bane—"

"Mingled with fine wheat and the fat of a new-born babe," said the shape of old Goodman Brown.

"Ah, your worship knows the recipe," cried the old lady, cackling aloud. "So, as I was saying, being all ready for the meeting, and no horse to ride on, I made up my mind to foot it; for they tell me there is a nice young man to be taken into communion to-night. But now your good worship will lend me your arm, and we shall be there in a twinkling."

"That can hardly be," answered her friend. "I may not spare you my arm, Goody Cloyse, but here is my staff, if you will."

So saying, he threw it down at her feet, where, perhaps, it assumed life, being one of the rods which its owner had formerly lent to the Egyptian Magi. Of this fact, however, Goodman Brown could not take cognizance. He had cast up his eyes in astonishment, and looking down again, beheld neither Goody Cloyse nor the serpentine staff, but his fellow-traveller alone, who waited for him as calmly as if nothing had happened.

"That old woman taught me my catechism!" said the young man; and there was a world of meaning in this simple comment.

They continued to walk onward, while the elder traveller exhorted his companion to make good speed and persevere in the path, discoursing so aptly, that his arguments seemed rather to spring up in the bosom of his auditor, than to be suggested by himself. As they went he plucked a branch of maple, to serve for a walking-stick, and began to strip it of the twigs and little boughs, which were wet with evening dew. The moment his fingers touched them, they became strangely withered and dried up, as with a week's sunshine. Thus the pair proceeded, at a good free pace, until suddenly, in a gloomy hollow of the road, Goodman Brown sat himself down on the stump of a tree, and refused to go any farther.

"Friend," said he, stubbornly, "my mind is made up. Not another step will I budge on this errand. What if a wretched old woman do choose to go to the devil, when I thought she was going to Heaven! Is that any reason why I should quit my dear Faith, and go after her?"

"You will think better of this by and by," said his acquaintance, composedly. "Sit here and rest yourself awhile; and when you feel like moving again, there is my staff to help you along."

Without more words, he threw his companion the maple stick, and was as speedily out of sight as if he had vanished into the deepening gloom. The young man sat a few moments by the roadside, applauding himself greatly, and thinking with how clear a conscience he should meet the minister, in his morning walk, nor shrink from the eye of good old Deacon Gookin. And what calm sleep would be his, that very night, which was to have been spent so wickedly, but purely and sweetly now, in the arms of Faith! Amidst these pleasant and praiseworthy meditations, Goodman Brown heard the tramp of horses along the road, and deemed it advisable to conceal himself within the verge of the forest, conscious of the guilty purpose that had brought him thither, though now so happily turned from it.

On came the hoof-tramps and the voices of the riders, two grave old voices, conversing soberly as they drew near. These mingled sounds appeared to pass along the road, within a few yards of the young man's hiding-place; but owing, doubtless, to the depth of the gloom, at that particular spot, neither the travellers nor their steeds were visible. Though their figures brushed the small boughs by the wayside, it could not be seen that they intercepted, even for a moment, the faint gleam from the strip of bright sky, athwart which they must have passed. Goodman Brown alternately crouched and stood on tiptoe, pulling aside the branches, and thrusting forth his head as far as he durst, without discerning so much as a shadow. It vexed him the more, because he could have sworn, were such a thing possible, that he recognized the voices of the minister and Deacon Gookin, jogging along quietly, as they were wont to do, when bound to some ordination or ecclesiastical council. While yet within hearing, one of the riders stopped to pluck a switch.

"Of the two, reverend Sir," said the voice like the deacon's, "I had rather miss an ordination dinner than to-night's meeting. They tell me that some of our community are to be here from Falmouth and beyond, and others from Connecticut and Rhode Island; besides several of the Indian pow-wows, who, after their fashion, know almost as much deviltry as the best of us. Moreover, there is a goodly young woman to be taken into communion."

"Mighty well, Deacon Gookin!" replied the solemn old tones of the minister. "Spur up, or we shall be late. Nothing can be done, you know, until I get on the ground."

The hoofs clattered again, and the voices, talking so strangely in the empty air, passed on through the forest, where no church had ever been gathered, nor solitary Christian prayed. Whither, then, could these holy men be journeying, so deep into the heathen wilderness? Young Goodman Brown caught hold of a tree, for support, being ready to sink down on the ground, faint and over-burthened with the heavy sickness of his heart. He looked up to the sky, doubting whether there really was a Heaven above him. Yet, there was the blue arch, and the stars brightening in it.

"With Heaven above, and Faith below, I will yet stand firm against the devil!" cried Goodman Brown.

While he still gazed upward, into the deep arch of the firmament, and had lifted his hands to pray, a cloud, though no wind was stirring, hurried across the zenith, and hid the brightening stars. The blue sky was still visible, except directly overhead, where this black mass of cloud was sweeping swiftly northward. Aloft in the air, as if from the depths of the cloud, came a confused and doubtful sound of voices. Once, the listener fancied that he could distinguish the accents of townspeople of his own, men and women, both pious and ungodly, many of whom he had met at the communion-table, and had seen others rioting at the tavern. The next moment, so indistinct were the sounds, he doubted whether he had heard aught but the murmur of the old forest, whispering without a wind. Then came a stronger swell of those familiar tones, heard daily in the sunshine, at Salem village, but never, until now, from a cloud at night. There was one voice, of a young woman, uttering lamentations, yet with an uncertain sorrow, and entreating for some favor, which, perhaps, it would grieve her to obtain. And all the unseen multitude, both saints and sinners, seemed to encourage her onward.

"Faith!" shouted Goodman Brown, in a voice of agony and desperation; and the echoes of the forest mocked him, crying—"Faith! Faith!" as if bewildered wretches were seeking her, all through the wilderness.

The cry of grief, rage, and terror was yet piercing the night, when the unhappy husband held his breath for a response. There was a scream, drowned immediately in a louder murmur of voices fading into far-off laughter, as the dark cloud swept away, leaving the clear and silent sky above Goodman Brown. But something fluttered lightly down through the air, and caught on the branch of a tree. The young man seized it and beheld a pink ribbon.

"My Faith is gone!" cried he, after one stupefied moment. "There is no good on earth, and sin is but a name. Come, devil! for to thee is this world given."

And maddened with despair, so that he laughed loud and long, did Goodman Brown grasp his staff and set forth again, at such a rate, that he seemed to fly along the forest path, rather than to walk or run. The road grew wilder and drearier, and more faintly traced, and vanished at length, leaving him in the heart of the dark wilderness, still rushing onward, with the instinct that guides mortal man to evil. The whole forest was peopled with frightful sounds: the creaking of the trees, the howling of wild beasts, and the yell of Indians; while, sometimes, the wind tolled like a distant church bell, and sometimes gave a broad roar around the traveller, as if all Nature was laughing him to scorn. But he was himself the chief horror of the scene, and shrank not from its other horrors.

"Ha! ha! ha!" roared Goodman Brown, when the wind laughed at him. "Let us hear which will laugh loudest! Think not to frighten me with your deviltry! Come witch, come wizard, come Indian powwow, come devil himself! and here comes Goodman Brown. You may as well fear him as he fear you!"

In truth, all through the haunted forest, there could be nothing more frightful than the figure of Goodman Brown. On he flew, among the black pines, brandishing his staff with frenzied gestures, now giving vent to an inspiration of horrid blasphemy, and now shouting forth such laughter, as set all the echoes of the forest laughing like demons around him. The fiend in his own shape is less hideous, than when he rages in the breast of man. Thus sped the demoniac on his course, until, quivering among the trees, he saw a red light before him, as when the felled trunks and branches of a clearing have been set on fire, and throw up their lurid blaze against the sky, at the hour of midnight. He paused, in a lull of the tempest that had driven him onward, and heard the swell of what seemed a hymn, rolling solemnly from a distance, with the weight of many voices. He knew the tune. It was a familiar one in the choir of the village meeting-house. The verse died heavily away, and was lengthened by a chorus, not of human voices, but of all the sounds of the benighted wilderness, pealing in awful harmony together. Goodman Brown cried out; and his cry was lost to his own ear, by its unison with the cry of the desert.

In the interval of silence, he stole forward, until the light glared full upon his eyes. At one extremity of an open space, hemmed in by the dark wall of the forest, arose a rock, bearing some rude, natural resemblance either to an altar or a pulpit, and surrounded by four blazing pines, their tops aflame, their stems untouched, like candles at an evening meeting. The mass of foliage, that had overgrown the summit of the rock, was all on fire, blazing high into the night, and fitfully illuminating the whole field. Each pendent twig and leafy festoon was in a blaze. As the red light arose and fell, a numerous congregation alternately shone forth, then disappeared in shadow, and again grew, as it were, out of the darkness, peopling the heart of the solitary woods at once.

"A grave and dark-clad company!" quoth Goodman Brown.

In truth, they were such. Among them, quivering to-and-fro, between gloom and splendor, appeared faces that would be seen, next day, at the council-board of the province, and others which, Sabbath after Sabbath, looked devoutly heavenward, and benignantly over the crowded pews, from the holiest pulpits in the land. Some affirm, that the lady of the governor was there. At least, there were high dames well known to her, and wives of honored husbands, and widows a great multitude, and ancient maidens, all of excellent repute, and fair young girls, who trembled lest their mothers should espy them. Either the sudden gleams of light, flashing over the obscure field, bedazzled Goodman Brown, or he recognized a score of the church members of Salem village, famous for their especial sanctity. Good old Deacon Gookin had arrived, and waited at the skirts of that venerable saint, his reverend pastor. But, irreverently consorting with these grave, reputable, and pious people, these elders of the church, these chaste dames and dewy virgins, there were men of dissolute lives and women of spotted fame, wretches given over to all mean and filthy vice, and suspected even of horrid crimes. It was strange to see, that the good shrank not from the wicked, nor were the sinners abashed by the saints. Scattered, also, among their pale-faced enemies, were the Indian priests, or powwows, who had often scared their native forest with more hideous incantations than any known to English witchcraft.

"But, where is Faith?" thought Goodman Brown; and, as hope came into his heart, he trembled.

Another verse of the hymn arose, a slow and mournful strain, such as the pious love, but joined to words which expressed all that our nature can conceive of sin, and darkly hinted at far more. Unfathomable to mere mortals is the lore of fiends. Verse after verse was sung, and still the chorus of the desert swelled between, like the deepest tone of a mighty organ. And, with the final peal of that dreadful anthem, there came a sound, as if the roaring wind, the rushing streams, the howling beasts, and every other voice of the unconverted wilderness were mingling and according with the voice of guilty man, in homage to the prince of all. The four blazing pines threw up a loftier flame, and obscurely discovered shapes and visages of horror on the smoke-wreaths, above the impious assembly. At the same moment, the fire on the rock shot redly forth, and formed a glowing arch above its base, where now appeared a figure. With reverence be it spoken, the apparition bore no slight similitude, both in garb and manner, to some grave divine of the New England churches.

"Bring forth the converts!" cried a voice, that echoed through the field and rolled into the forest.

At the word, Goodman Brown stepped forth from the shadow of the trees, and approached the congregation, with whom he felt a loathful brotherhood, by the sympathy of all that was wicked in his heart. He could have well-nigh sworn, that the shape of his own dead father beckoned him to advance, looking downward from a smoke-wreath, while a woman, with dim features of despair, threw out her hand to warn him back. Was it his mother? But he had no power to retreat one step, nor to resist, even in thought, when the minister and good old Deacon Gookin seized his arms, and led him to the blazing rock. Thither came also the slender form of a veiled female, led between Goody Cloyse, that pious teacher of the catechism, and Martha Carrier, who had received the devil's promise to be queen of hell. A rampant hag was she! And there stood the proselytes, beneath the canopy of fire.

"Welcome, my children," said the dark figure, "to the communion of your race! Ye have found, thus young, your nature and your destiny. My children, look behind you!"

They turned; and flashing forth, as it were, in a sheet of flame, the fiend-worshippers were seen; the smile of welcome gleamed darkly on every visage.

"There," resumed the sable form, "are all whom ye have reverenced from youth. Ye deemed them holier than yourselves, and shrank from your own sin, contrasting it with their lives of righteousness and prayerful aspirations heavenward. Yet, here are they all, in my worshipping assembly! This night it shall be granted you to know their secret deeds; how hoary-bearded elders of the church have whispered wanton words to the young maids of their households; how many a woman, eager for widow's weeds, has given her husband a drink at bedtime, and let him sleep his last sleep in her bosom; how beardless youths have made haste to inherit their father's wealth; and how fair damsels—blush not, sweet ones!—have dug little graves in the garden, and bidden me, the sole guest, to an infant's funeral. By the sympathy of your human hearts for sin, ye shall scent out all the places—whether in church, bed-chamber, street, field, or forest—where crime has been committed, and shall exult to behold the whole earth one stain of guilt, one mighty blood-spot. Far more than this! It shall be yours to penetrate, in every bosom, the deep mystery of sin, the fountain of all wicked arts, and which inexhaustibly supplies more evil impulses than human power—than my power, at its utmost—can make manifest in deeds. And now, my children, look upon each other."

They did so; and, by the blaze of the hell-kindled torches, the wretched man beheld his Faith, and the wife her husband, trembling before that unhallowed altar.

"Lo! there ye stand, my children," said the figure, in a deep and solemn tone, almost sad, with its despairing awfulness, as if his once angelic nature could yet mourn for our miserable race. "Depending upon one another's hearts, ye had still hoped that virtue were not all a dream! Now are ye undeceived!—Evil is the nature of mankind. Evil must be your only happiness. Welcome, again, my children, to the communion of your race!"

"Welcome!" repeated the fiend-worshippers, in one cry of despair and triumph.

And there they stood, the only pair, as it seemed, who were yet hesitating on the verge of wickedness, in this dark world. A basin was hollowed, naturally, in the rock. Did it contain water, reddened by the lurid light? or was it blood? or, perchance, a liquid flame? Herein did the Shape of Evil dip his hand, and prepare to lay the mark of baptism upon their foreheads, that they might be partakers of the mystery of sin, more conscious of the secret guilt of others, both in deed and thought, than they could now be of their own. The husband cast one look at his pale wife, and Faith at him. What polluted wretches would the next glance show them to each other, shuddering alike at what they disclosed and what they saw!

"Faith! Faith!" cried the husband. "Look up to Heaven, and resist the Wicked One!"

Whether Faith obeyed, he knew not. Hardly had he spoken, when he found himself amid calm night and solitude, listening to a roar of the wind, which died heavily away through the forest. He staggered against the rock, and felt it chill and damp, while a hanging twig, that had been all on fire, besprinkled his cheek with the coldest dew.

The next morning, young Goodman Brown came slowly into the street of Salem village staring around him like a bewildered man. The good old minister was taking a walk along the grave-yard, to get an appetite for breakfast and meditate his sermon, and bestowed a blessing, as he passed, on Goodman Brown. He shrank from the venerable saint, as if to avoid an anathema. Old Deacon Gookin was at domestic worship, and the holy words of his prayer were heard through the open window. "What God doth the wizard pray to?" quoth Goodman Brown. Goody Cloyse, that excellent old Christian, stood in the early sunshine, at her own lattice, catechising a little girl, who had brought her a pint of morning's milk. Goodman Brown snatched away the child, as from the grasp of the fiend himself. Turning the corner by the meeting-house, he spied the head of Faith, with the pink ribbons, gazing anxiously forth, and bursting into such joy at sight of him that she skipt along the street, and almost kissed her husband before the whole village. But Goodman Brown looked sternly and sadly into her face, and passed on without a greeting.

Had Goodman Brown fallen asleep in the forest, and only dreamed a wild dream of a witch-meeting?

Be it so, if you will. But, alas! it was a dream of evil omen for young Goodman Brown. A stern, a sad, a darkly meditative, a distrustful, if not a desperate man did he become, from the night of that fearful dream. On the Sabbath day, when the congregation were singing a holy psalm, he could not listen, because an anthem of sin rushed loudly upon his ear, and drowned all the blessed strain. When the minister spoke from the pulpit, with power and fervid eloquence, and with his hand on the open Bible, of the sacred truths of our religion, and of saint-like lives and triumphant deaths, and of future bliss or misery unutterable, then did Goodman Brown turn pale, dreading lest the roof should thunder down upon the gray blasphemer and his hearers. Often, awaking suddenly at midnight, he shrank from the bosom of Faith, and at morning or eventide, when the family knelt down at prayer, he scowled, and muttered to himself, and gazed sternly at his wife, and turned away. And when he had lived long, and was borne to his grave, a hoary corpse, followed by Faith, an aged woman, and children and grand-children, a goodly procession, besides neighbors not a few, they carved no hopeful verse upon his tombstone; for his dying hour was gloom.

(1835)

Edgar Allan Poe   *1809–1849*

THE FALL OF THE HOUSE OF USHER

Son coeur est un luth suspendu;
Sitôt qu'on le touche il résonne.[1]
—DE BÉRANGER

During the whole of a dull, dark, and soundless day in the autumn of
the year, when the clouds hung oppressively low in the heavens, I had
been passing alone, on horseback, through a singularly dreary tract of
country, and at length found myself, as the shades of the evening drew
on, within view of the melancholy House of Usher. I know not how it
was—but, with the first glimpse of the building, a sense of insufferable
gloom pervaded my spirit. I say insufferable; for the feeling was unrelieved
by any of that half-pleasurable, because poetic, sentiment with which the
mind usually receives even the sternest natural images of the desolate or
terrible. I looked upon the scene before me—upon the mere house, and
the simple landscape features of the domain—upon the bleak walls—upon
the vacant eye-like windows—upon a few rank sedges—and upon a few
white trunks of decayed trees—with an utter depression of soul which I
can compare to no earthly sensation more properly than to the after-dream
of the reveller upon opium—the bitter lapse into everyday life—the hideous
dropping off of the veil. There was an iciness, a sinking, a sickening of
the heart—an unredeemed dreariness of thought which no goading of the
imagination could torture into aught of the sublime. What was it—I paused
to think—what was it that so unnerved me in the contemplation of the
House of Usher? It was a mystery all insoluble; nor could I grapple with
the shadowy fancies that crowded upon me as I pondered. I was forced
to fall back upon the unsatisfactory conclusion, that while, beyond doubt,
there *are* combinations of very simple natural objects which have the power
of thus affecting us, still the analysis of this power lies among considerations
beyond our depth. It was possible, I reflected, that a mere different arrangement of the particulars of the scene, of the details of the picture, would
be sufficient to modify, or perhaps to annihilate its capacity for sorrowful
impression; and, acting upon this idea, I reined my horse to the precipitous
brink of a black and lurid tarn that lay in unruffled lustre by the dwelling,
and gazed down—but with a shudder even more thrilling than before—
upon the remodelled and inverted images of the gray sedge, and the ghastly
tree-stems, and the vacant and eye-like windows.

Nevertheless, in this mansion of gloom I now proposed to myself a
sojourn of some weeks. Its proprietor, Roderick Usher, had been one of
my boon companions in boyhood; but many years had elapsed since our
last meeting. A letter, however, had lately reached me in a distant part
of the country—a letter from him—which, in its wildly importunate nature,
had admitted of no other than a personal reply. The MS. gave evidence

[1] His heart is a suspended lute; As soon as one touches it, it resounds.

of nervous agitation. The writer spoke of acute bodily illness—of a mental disorder which oppressed him—and of an earnest desire to see me, as his best and indeed his only personal friend, with a view of attempting, by the cheerfulness of my society, some alleviation of his malady. It was the manner in which all this, and much more, was said—it was the apparent *heart* that went with his request—which allowed me no room for hesitation; and I accordingly obeyed forthwith what I still considered a very singular summons.

Although, as boys, we had been intimate associates, yet I really knew little of my friend. His reserve had been always excessive and habitual. I was aware, however, that his very ancient family had been noted, time out of mind, for a peculiar sensibility of temperament, displaying itself, through long ages, in many works of exalted art, and manifested, of late, in repeated deeds of munificent yet unobtrusive charity, as well as in a passionate devotion to the intricacies, perhaps even more than to the orthodox and easily recognizable beauties, of musical science. I had learned, too, the very remarkable fact, that the stem of the Usher race, all time-honored as it was, had put forth, at no period, any enduring branch; in other words, that the entire family lay in the direct line of descent, and had always, with very trifling and very temporary variation, so lain. It was this deficiency, I considered, while running over in thought the perfect keeping of the character of the premises with the accredited character of the people, and while speculating upon the possible influence which the one, in the long lapse of centuries, might have exercised upon the other— it was this deficiency, perhaps, of collateral issue, and the consequent undeviating transmission, from sire to son, of the patrimony with the name, which had, at length, so identified the two as to merge the original title of the estate in the quaint and equivocal appellation of the "House of Usher"—an appellation which seemed to include, in the minds of the peasantry who used it, both the family and the family mansion.

I have said the sole effect of my somewhat childish experiment—that of looking down within the tarn—had been to deepen the first singular impression. There can be no doubt that the consciousness of the rapid increase of my superstition—for why should I not so term it?—served mainly to accelerate the increase itself. Such, I have long known, is the paradoxical law of all sentiments having terror as a basis. And it might have been for this reason only, that, when I again uplifted my eyes to the house itself, from its image in the pool, there grew in my mind a strange fancy—a fancy so ridiculous, indeed, that I but mention it to show the vivid force of the sensations which oppressed me. I had so worked upon my imagination as really to believe that about the whole mansion and domain there hung an atmosphere peculiar to themselves and their immediate vicinity—an atmosphere which had no affinity with the air of heaven, but which had reeked up from the decayed trees, and the gray wall, and the silent tarn—a pestilent and mystic vapor, dull, sluggish, faintly discernible, and leaden-hued.

Shaking off from my spirit what *must* have been a dream, I scanned more narrowly the real aspect of the building. Its principal feature seemed to be that of an excessive antiquity. The discoloration of ages had been great. Minute fungi overspread the whole exterior, hanging in a fine tangled web-work from the eaves. Yet all this was apart from any extraordinary dilapidation. No portion of the masonry had fallen; and there appeared to be a wild inconsistency between its still perfect adaptation of parts, and the crumbling condition of the individual stones. In this there was much that reminded me of the specious totality of old woodwork which has rotted for long years in some neglected vault, with no disturbance from the breath of the external air. Beyond this indication of extensive decay, however, the fabric gave little token of instability. Perhaps the eye of a scrutinizing observer might have discovered a barely perceptible fissure, which, extending from the roof of the building in front, made its way down the wall in a zigzag direction, until it became lost in the sullen waters of the tarn.

Noticing these things, I rode over a short causeway to the house. A servant in waiting took my horse, and I entered the Gothic archway of the hall. A valet, of stealthy step, thence conducted me, in silence, through many dark and intricate passages in my progress to the studio of his master. Much that I encountered on the way contributed, I know not how, to heighten the vague sentiments of which I have already spoken. While the objects around me—while the carvings of the ceilings, the somber tapestries of the walls, the ebon blackness of the floors, and the phantasmagoric armorial trophies which rattled as I strode, were but matters to which, or to such as which, I had been accustomed from my infancy—while I hesitated not to acknowledge how familiar was all this—I still wondered to find how unfamiliar were the fancies which ordinary images were stirring up. On one of the staircases, I met the physician of the family. His countenance, I thought, wore a mingled expression of low cunning and perplexity. He accosted me with trepidation and passed on. The valet now threw open a door and ushered me into the presence of his master.

The room in which I found myself was very large and lofty. The windows were long, narrow, and pointed, and at so vast a distance from the black oaken floor as to be altogether inaccessible from within. Feeble gleams of encrimsoned light made their way through the trellised panes, and served to render sufficiently distinct the more prominent objects around; the eye, however, struggled in vain to reach the remoter angles of the chamber, or the recesses of the vaulted and fretted ceiling. Dark draperies hung upon the walls. The general furniture was profuse, comfortless, antique, and tattered. Many books and musical instruments lay scattered about, but failed to give any vitality to the scene. I felt that I breathed an atmosphere of sorrow. An air of stern, deep, and irredeemable gloom hung over and pervaded all.

Upon my entrance, Usher arose from a sofa on which he had been lying at full length, and greeted me with a vivacious warmth which had much in it, I at first thought, of an overdone cordiality—of the constrained effort of the *ennuyé* man of the world. A glance, however, at his countenance convinced me of his perfect sincerity. We sat down; and for some moments, while he spoke not, I gazed upon him with a feeling of pity, half of awe. Surely, man had never before so terribly altered, in so brief a period, as had Roderick Usher! It was with difficulty that I could bring myself to admit the identity of the wan being before me with the companion of my early boyhood. Yet the character of his face had been at all times remarkable. A cadaverousness of complexion; an eye large, liquid, and luminous beyond comparison; lips somewhat thin and very pallid, but of a surpassingly beautiful curve; a nose of a delicate Hebrew model, but with a breadth of nostril unusual in similar formations; a finely molded chin, speaking, in its want of prominence, of a want of moral energy; hair of a more than web-like softness and tenuity; these features, with an inordinate expansion above the regions of the temple, made up altogether a countenance not easily to be forgotten. And now in the mere exaggeration of the prevailing character of these features, and of the expression they were wont to convey, lay so much of change that I doubted to whom I spoke. The now ghastly pallor of the skin, and the now miraculous luster of the eye, above all things startled and even awed me. The silken hair, too, had been suffered to grow all unheeded, and as, in its wild gossamer texture, it floated rather than fell about the face, I could not, even with effort, connect its Arabesque expression with any idea of simple humanity.

In the manner of my friend I was at once struck with an incoherence— an inconsistency; and I soon found this to arise from a series of feeble and futile struggles to overcome an habitual trepidancy—an excessive nervous agitation. For something of this nature I had indeed been prepared, no less by his letter, than by reminiscences of certain boyish traits, and by conclusions deduced from his peculiar physical conformation and temperament. His action was alternately vivacious and sullen. His voice varied rapidly from a tremulous indecision (when the animal spirits seemed utterly in abeyance) to that species of energetic concision—that abrupt, weighty, unhurried, and hollow-sounding enunciation—that leaden, self-balanced, and perfectly modulated guttural utterance, which may be observed in the lost drunkard, or the irreclaimable eater of opium, during the periods of his most intense excitement.

It was thus that he spoke of the object of my visit, of his earnest desire to see me, and of the solace he expected me to afford him. He entered, at some length, into what he conceived to be the nature of his malady. It was, he said, a constitutional and a family evil, and one for which he despaired to find a remedy—a mere nervous affection, he immediately added, which would undoubtedly soon pass off. It displayed itself in a host of unnatural sensations. Some of these, as he detailed them, interested and bewildered me; although, perhaps, the terms and the general manner of their narration had their weight. He suffered much from a morbid acuteness of the senses; the most insipid food was alone endurable; he could wear only garments of certain texture; the odors of all flowers were oppressive; his eyes were tortured by even a faint light; and there were but peculiar sounds, and these from stringed instruments, which did not inspire him with horror.

To an anomalous species of terror I found him a bounden slave. "I shall perish," said he, "I *must* perish in this deplorable folly. Thus, thus, and not otherwise, shall I be lost. I dread the events of the future, not in themselves, but in their results. I shudder at the thought of any, even the most trivial, incident, which may operate upon this intolerable agitation of soul. I have, indeed, no abhorrence of danger, except in its absolute effect—in terror. In this unnerved—in this pitiable condition—I feel that the period will sooner or later arrive when I must abandon life and reason together, in some struggle with the grim phantasm, Fear."

I learned, moreover, at intervals, and through broken and equivocal hints, another singular feature of his mental condition. He was enchained by certain superstitious impressions in regard to the dwelling which he tenanted, and whence, for many years, he had never ventured forth—in regard to an influence whose suppositious force was conveyed in terms too shadowy here to be re-stated—an influence which some peculiarities in the mere form and substance of his family mansion had, by dint of long sufferance, he said, obtained over his spirit—an effect which the *physique* of the gray walls and turrets, and of the dim tarn into which they all looked down, had, at length, brought about upon the morale of his existence.

He admitted, however, although with hesitation, that much of the peculiar gloom which thus afflicted him could be traced to a more natural and far more palpable origin—to the severe and long-continued illness—indeed to the evidently approaching dissolution—of a tenderly beloved sister, his sole companion for long years, his last and only relative on earth. "Her decease," he said, with a bitterness which I can never forget, "would leave him (him, the hopeless and the frail) the last of the ancient race of the Ushers." While he spoke, the lady Madeline (for so was she called) passed slowly through a remote portion of the apartment, and, without having noticed my presence, disappeared. I regarded her with an utter astonishment not unmingled with dread; and yet I found it impossible to account for such feelings A sensation of stupor oppressed me, as my eyes followed her retreating steps. When a door, at length, closed upon her, my glance sought instinctively and eagerly the countenance of the brother—but he had buried his face in his hands, and I could only perceive that a far more than ordinary wanness had overspread the emaciated fingers through which trickled many passionate tears.

The disease of the lady Madeline had long baffled the skill of her physicians. A settled apathy, a gradual wasting away of the person, and frequent although transient affections of a partially cataleptical character were the unusual diagnosis. Hitherto she had steadily borne up against the pressure of her malady, and had not betaken herself finally to bed; but on the closing in of the evening of my arrival at the house, she succumbed (as her brother told me at night with inexpressible agitation) to the prostrating power of the destroyer; and I learned that the glimpse I had obtained of her person would thus probably be the last I should obtain—that the lady, at least while living, would be seen by me no more.

For several days ensuing, her name was unmentioned by either Usher or myself: and during this period I was busied in earnest endeavors to alleviate the melancholy of my friend. We painted and read together, or I listened, as if in a dream, to the wild improvisations of his speaking guitar. And thus, as a closer and still closer intimacy admitted me more unreservedly into the recesses of his spirit, the more bitterly did I perceive the futility of all attempt at cheering a mind from which darkness, as if an inherent positive quality, poured forth upon all objects of the moral and physical universe in one unceasing radiation of gloom.

I shall ever bear about me a memory of the many solemn hours I thus spent alone with the master of the House of Usher. Yet I should fail in any attempt to convey an idea of the exact character of the studies, or of the occupations, in which he involved me, or led me the way. An excited and highly distempered ideality threw a sulphureous luster over all. His long improvised dirges will ring forever in my ears. Among other things, I hold painfully in mind a certain singular perversion and amplification of the wild air of the last waltz of Von Weber.[2] From the paintings over which his elaborate fancy brooded, and which grew, touch by touch, into vaguenesses at which I shuddered the more thrillingly, because I shuddered knowing not why;—from these paintings (vivid as their images now are before me) I would in vain endeavor to educe more than a small portion which should lie within the compass of merely written words. By the utter simplicity, by the nakedness of his designs, he arrested and overawed attention. If ever mortal painted an idea, that mortal was Roderick Usher. For me at least, in the circumstances then surrounding me, there arose out of the pure abstractions which the hypochondriac contrived to throw upon his canvas, an intensity of intolerable awe, no shadow of which felt I ever yet in the contemplation of the certainly glowing yet too concrete reveries of Fuseli.[3]

One of the phantasmagoric conceptions of my friend, partaking not so rigidly of the spirit of abstraction, may be shadowed forth, although feebly, in words. A small picture presented the interior of an immensely long and rectangular vault or tunnel, with low walls, smooth, white, and without interruption or device. Certain accessory points of the design served well to convey the idea that this excavation lay at an exceeding depth below the surface of the earth. No outlet was observed in any portion of its vast extent, and no torch or other artificial source of light was discernible; yet a flood of intense rays rolled throughout, and bathed the whole in a ghastly and inappropriate splendor.

I have just spoken of that morbid condition of the auditory nerve which rendered all music intolerable to the sufferer, with the exception of certain effects of stringed instruments. It was, perhaps, the narrow limits to which he thus confined himself upon the guitar which gave birth, in great measure, to the fantastic character of his performances. But the fervid facility of his impromptus could not be so accounted for. They must have been, and were, in the notes, as well as in the words of his wild fantasias (for he not unfrequently accompanied himself with rhymed verbal improvisations), the result of that intense mental collectedness and concentration to which I have previously alluded as observable only in particular moments of the highest artificial excitement. The words of one of these rhapsodies I have easily remembered. I was, perhaps, the more forcibly impressed with it as he gave it, because, in the under or mystic current of its meaning, I fancied that I perceived, and for the first time, a full consciousness on the part of Usher of the tottering of his lofty reason upon her throne. The verses, which were entitled "The Haunted Palace," ran very nearly, if not accurately, thus:

[2] Carl Maria von Weber, German composer.
[3] Henry Fuseli, Swiss-born painter of "The Nightmare."

I

In the greenest of our valleys,
By good angels tenanted,
Once a fair and stately palace—
Radiant palace—reared its head.
In the monarch Thought's dominion—
It stood there!
Never seraph spread a pinion
Over fabric half so fair.

II

Banners yellow, glorious, golden,
On its roof did float and flow
(This—all this—was in the olden
Time long ago)
And every gentle air that dallied,
In that sweet day,
Along the ramparts plumed and pallid,
A winged odor went away.

III

Wanderers in that happy valley
Through two luminous windows saw
Spirits moving musically
To a lute's well-tunéd law,
Round about a throne, where sitting
(Porphyrogene!)[4]
In state his glory well befitting,
The ruler of the realm was seen.

IV

And all with pearl and ruby glowing
Was the fair palace door,
Through which came flowing, flowing, flowing
And sparkling evermore,
A troop of Echoes whose sweet duty
Was but to sing,
In voices of surpassing beauty,
The wit and wisdom of their king.

V

But evil things, in robes of sorrow,
Assailed the monarch's high estate;
(Ah, let us mourn, for never morrow
Shall dawn upon him, desolate!)
And, round about his home, the glory

---

[4] Born to royalty.

That blushed and bloomed
Is but a dim-remembered story
Of the old time entombed.

VI

And travelers now within that valley,
Through the red-litten windows see
Vast forms that move fantastically
To a discordant melody;
While, like a rapid ghastly river,
Through the pale door, ⸳
A hideous throng rush out forever,
And laugh—but smile no more.

I well remember that suggestions arising from this ballad led us into a train of thought, wherein there became manifest an opinion of Usher's which I mention not so much on account of its novelty, (for other men have thought thus,) as on account of the pertinacity with which he maintained it. This opinion, in its general form, was that of the sentience of all vegetable things. But, in his disordered fancy, the idea had assumed a more daring character, and trespassed, under certain conditions, upon the kingdom of inorganization. I lack words to express the full extent, or the earnest *abandon* of his persuasion. The belief, however, was connected (as I have previously hinted) with the gray stones of the home of his forefathers. The conditions of the sentience had been here, he imagined, fulfilled in the method of collocation of these stones—in the order of their arrangement, as well as in that of the many fungi which overspread them, and of the decayed trees which stood around—above all, in the long undisturbed endurance of this arrangement, and in its reduplication in the still waters of the tarn. Its evidence—the evidence of the sentience—was to be seen, he said (and I here started as he spoke), in *the gradual yet certain condensation of an atmosphere of their own about the waters and the walls.* The result was discoverable, he added, in that silent yet importunate and terrible influence which for centuries had molded the destinies of his family, and which made *him* what I now saw him—what he was. Such opinions need no comment, and I will make none.

Our books—the books which, for years, had formed no small portion of the mental existence of the invalid—were, as might be supposed, in strict keeping with this character of phantasm. We pored together over such works as the *Ververt et Chartreuse* of Gresset; the *Belphegor* of Machiavelli; the *Heaven and Hell* of Swedenborg; the *Subterranean Voyage* of Nicholas Klimm of Holberg; the *Chiromancy* of Robert Flud, of Jean D'Indaginé, and of De la Chambre; the *Journey into the Blue Distance* of Tieck; and the *City of the Sun* of Campanella. One favorite volume was a small octavo edition of the *Directorium Inquisitorum,* by the Dominican Eymeric de Gironne; and there were passages in Pomponius Mela, about the old African Satyrs and Ægipans, over which Usher would sit dreaming for hours. His chief delight, however, was found in the perusal of an exceedingly rare and curious book in quarto Gothic—the manual of a forgotten church—the *Vigilæ Mortuorum secundum Chorum Ecclesiæ Maguntinæ.*[5]

I could not help thinking of the wild ritual of this work, and of its probable influence upon the hypochondriac, when, one evening, having informed me abruptly that the lady Madeline was no more, he stated his intention of preserving her corpse for a fortnight, (previously to its final interment,) in one of the numerous vaults within the main walls of the building. The worldly reason, however, assigned for this singular proceeding, was one which I did not feel at liberty to dispute. The brother had been led to his resolution (so he told me) by consideration of the unusual character of the malady of the deceased, of certain obtrusive and eager inquiries on the part of her medical men, and of the remote and exposed situation of the burial-ground of the family. I will not deny that when I called to mind the sinister countenance of the person whom I met upon the staircase, on the day of my arrival at the house, I had no desire to oppose what I regarded as at best but a harmless, and by no means an unnatural, precaution.

At the request of Usher, I personally aided him in the arrangements for the temporary entombment. The body having been encoffined, we two alone bore it to its rest. The vault in which we placed it (and which had been so long unopened that our torches, half smothered in its oppressive atmosphere, gave us little opportunity for investigation) was small, damp, and entirely without means of admission for light; lying, at great depth, immediately beneath that portion of the building in which was my own sleeping apartment. It had been used, apparently, in remote feudal times, for the worst purposes of a donjon-keep, and, in later days, as a place of deposit for powder, or some other highly combustible substance, as a portion of its floor, and the whole interior of a long archway through which we reached it, were carefully sheathed with copper. The door, of massive iron, had been, also, similarly protected. Its immense weight caused an unusually sharp grating sound, as it moved upon its hinges.

Having deposited our mournful burden upon trestles within this region of horror, we partially turned aside the yet unscrewed lid of the coffin, and looked upon the face of the tenant. A striking similitude between the brother and sister now first arrested my attention; and Usher, divining, perhaps, my thoughts, murmured out some few words from which I learned that the deceased and himself had been twins, and that sympathies of a scarcely intelligible nature had always existed between them. Our glances, however, rested not long upon the dead—for we could not regard her unawed. The disease which had thus entombed the lady in the maturity of youth, had left, as usual in all maladies of a strictly cataleptical character, the mockery of a faint blush upon the bosom and the face, and that suspiciously lingering smile upon the lip which is so terrible in death. We replaced and screwed down the lid, and, having secured the door of iron, made our way, with toil, into the scarcely less gloomy apartments of the upper portion of the house.

And now, some days of bitter grief having elapsed, an observable change came over the features of the mental disorder of my friend. His ordinary

[5] All metaphysical and occult works from the Middle Ages almost to Poe's time.

manner had vanished. His ordinary occupations were neglected or forgotten. He roamed from chamber to chamber with hurried, unequal, and objectless step. The pallor of his countenance had assumed, if possible, a more ghastly hue—but the luminousness of his eye had utterly gone out. The once occasional huskiness of his tone was heard no more; and a tremulous quaver, as if of extreme terror, habitually characterized his utterance. There were times, indeed, when I thought his unceasingly agitated mind was laboring with some oppressive secret, to divulge which he struggled for the necessary courage. At times, again, I was obliged to resolve all into the mere inexplicable vagaries of madness, for I beheld him gazing upon vacancy for long hours, in an attitude of the profoundest attention, as if listening to some imaginary sound. It was no wonder that his condition terrified—that it infected me. I felt creeping upon me, by slow yet certain degrees, the wild influences of his own fantastic yet impressive superstitions.

It was, especially, upon retiring to bed late in the night of the seventh or eighth day after the placing of the lady Madeline within the donjon, that I experienced the full power of such feelings. Sleep came not near my couch—while the hours waned and waned away. I struggled to reason off the nervousness which had dominion over me. I endeavored to believe that much, if not all of what I felt, was due to the bewildering influence of the gloomy furniture of the room—of the dark and tattered draperies, which, tortured into motion by the breath of a rising tempest, swayed fitfully to and fro upon the walls, and rustled uneasily about the decorations of the bed. But my efforts were fruitless. An irrepressible tremor gradually pervaded my frame; and, at length, there sat upon my very heart an incubus of utterly causeless alarm. Shaking this off with a gasp and a struggle, I uplifted myself upon the pillows, and, peering earnestly within the intense darkness of the chamber, hearkened—I know not why, except that an instinctive spirit prompted me—to certain low and indefinite sounds which came, through the pauses of the storm, at long intervals, I knew not whence. Overpowered by an intense sentiment of horror, unaccountable yet unendurable, I threw on my clothes with haste, (for I felt that I should sleep no more during the night,) and endeavored to arouse myself from the pitiable condition into which I had fallen, by pacing rapidly to and fro through the apartment.

I had taken but few turns in this manner, when a light step on an adjoining staircase arrested my attention. I presently recognized it as that of Usher. In an instant afterward he rapped, with a gentle touch, at my door, and entered, bearing a lamp. His countenance was, as usual, cadaverously wan—but, moreover, there was a species of mad hilarity in his eyes—an evidently restrained hysteria in his whole demeanor. His air appalled me—but anything was preferable to the solitude which I had so long endured, and I even welcomed his presence as a relief.

"And you have not seen it?" he said abruptly, after having stared about him for some moments in silence—"you have not then seen it?—but, stay! you shall." Thus speaking, and having carefully shaded his lamp, he hurried to one of the casements, and threw it freely open to the storm.

The impetuous fury of the entering gust nearly lifted us from our feet. It was, indeed, a tempestuous yet sternly beautiful night, and one wildly singular in its terror and its beauty. A whirlwind had apparently collected its force in our vicinity; for there were frequent and violent alterations in the direction of the wind; and the exceeding density of the clouds (which hung so low as to press upon the turrets of the house) did not prevent our perceiving the life-like velocity with which they flew careering from all points against each other, without passing away into the distance. I say that even their exceeding density did not prevent our perceiving this— yet we had no glimpse of the moon or stars—nor was there any flashing forth of the lightning. But the under surfaces of the huge masses of agitated vapor, as well as all terrestrial objects immediately around us, were glowing in the unnatural light of a faintly luminous and distinctly visible gaseous exhalation which hung about and enshrouded the mansion.

"You must not—you shall not behold this!" said I, shuddering, to Usher, as I led him, with a gentle violence, from the window to a seat. "These appearances, which bewilder you, are merely electrical phenomena not uncommon—or it may be that they have their ghastly origin in the rank miasma of the tarn. Let us close this casement;—the air is chilling and dangerous to your frame. Here is one of your favorite romances. I will read, and you shall listen;—and so we will pass away this terrible night together."

The antique volume which I had taken up was the *Mad Tryst* of Sir Launcelot Canning; but I had called it a favorite of Usher's more in sad jest than in earnest; for, in truth, there is little in its uncouth and unimaginative prolixity which could have had interest for the lofty and spiritual ideality of my friend. It was, however, the only book immediately at hand; and I indulged a vague hope that the excitement which now agitated the hypochondriac, might find relief (for the history of mental disorder is full of similar anomalies) even in the extremeness of the folly which I should read. Could I have judged, indeed, by the wild overstrained air of vivacity with which he hearkened, or apparently hearkened, to the words of the tale, I might well have congratulated myself upon the success of my design.

I had arrived at that well-known portion of the story where Ethelred, the hero of the *Tryst*, having sought in vain for peaceable admission into the dwelling of the hermit, proceeds to make good an entrance by force. Here, it will be remembered, the words of the narrative run thus:

"And Ethelred, who was by nature of a doughty heart, and who was now mighty withal, on account of the powerfulness of the wine which he had drunken, waited no longer to hold parley with the hermit, who, in sooth, was of an obstinate and maliceful turn, but, feeling the rain upon his shoulders, and fearing the rising of the tempest, uplifted his mace outright, and, with blows, made quickly room in the plankings of the door for his gauntleted hand; and now pulling therewith sturdily, he so cracked, and ripped, and tore all asunder, that the noise of the dry and hollow-sounding wood alarumed and reverberated throughout the forest."

At the termination of this sentence I started and, for a moment, paused; for it appeared to me (although I at once concluded that my excited fancy had deceived me)—it appeared to me that, from some very remote portion of the mansion, there came, indistinctly, to my ears, what might have been, in its exact similarity of character, the echo (but a stifled and dull one certainly) of the very cracking and ripping sound which Sir Launcelot had so particularly described. It was, beyond doubt, the coincidence alone which had arrested my attention; for, amid the rattling of the sashes of the casements, and the ordinary commingled noises of the still increasing storm, the sound, in itself, had nothing, surely, which should have interested or disturbed me. I continued the story:

"But the good champion Ethelred, now entering within the door, was sore enraged and amazed to perceive no signal of the maliceful hermit; but, in the stead thereof, a dragon of a scaly and prodigious demeanor, and of a fiery tongue, which sate in guard before a palace of gold, with a floor of silver; and upon the wall there hung a shield of shining brass with this legend enwritten—

> *Who entereth herein, a conqueror hath bin;*
> *Who slayeth the dragon, the shield he shall win.*

And Ethelred uplifted his mace, and struck upon the head of the dragon, which fell before him, and gave up his pesty breath, with a shriek so horrid and harsh, and withal so piercing, that Ethelred had fain to close his ears with his hands against the dreadful noise of it, the like whereof was never before heard."

Here again I paused abruptly, and now with a feeling of wild amazement—for there could be no doubt whatever that, in this instance, I did actually hear (although from what direction it proceeded I found it impossible to say) a low and apparently distant, but harsh, protracted, and most unusual screaming or grating sound—the exact counterpart of what my fancy had already conjured up for the dragon's unnatural shriek as described by the romancer.

Oppressed, as I certainly was, upon the occurrence of this second and most extraordinary coincidence, by a thousand conflicting sensations, in which wonder and extreme terror were predominant, I still retained sufficient presence of mind to avoid exciting, by any observation, the sensitive nervousness of my companion. I was by no means certain that he had noticed the sounds in question; although, assuredly, a strange alteration had, during the last few minutes, taken place in his demeanor. From a position fronting my own, he had gradually brought round his chair, so as to sit with his face to the door of the chamber; and thus I could but partially perceive his features, although I saw that his lips trembled as if he were murmuring inaudibly. His head had dropped upon his breast—yet I knew that he was not asleep, from the wide and rigid opening of the eye as I caught a glance of it in profile. The motion of his body, too, was at variance with this idea—for he rocked from side to side with a gentle yet constant and uniform sway. Having rapidly taken notice of all this, I resumed the narrative of Sir Launcelot, which thus proceeded:

"And now, the champion, having escaped from the terrible fury of the dragon, bethinking himself of the brazen shield, and of the breaking up of the enchantment which was upon it, removed the carcass from out of the way before him, and approached valorously over the silver pavement of the castle to where the shield was upon the wall; which in sooth tarried not for his full coming, but fell down at his feet upon the silver floor, with a mighty great and terrible ringing sound."

No sooner had these syllables passed my lips, than—as if a shield of brass had indeed, at the moment, fallen heavily upon a floor of silver—I became aware of a distinct, hollow, metallic, and clangorous, yet apparently muffled, reverberation. Completely unnerved, I leaped to my feet; but the measured rocking movement of Usher was undisturbed. I rushed to the chair in which he sat. His eyes were bent fixedly before him, and throughout his whole countenance there reigned a stony rigidity. But, as I placed my hand upon his shoulder, there came a strong shudder over his whole person; a sickly smile quivered about his lips; and I saw that he spoke in a low, hurried, and gibbering murmur, as if unconscious of my presence. Bending closely over him, I at length drank in the hideous import of his words.

"Not hear it?—yes, I hear it, and *have* heard it. Long—long—long— many minutes, many hours, many days, have I heard it—yet I dared not— oh, pity me, miserable wretch that I am!—I dared not—I *dared* not speak! *We have put her living in the tomb!* Said I not that my senses were acute? I *now* tell you that I heard her first feeble movements in the hollow coffin. I heard them—many days, many days ago—yet I dared not—I *dared not speak!* And now—tonight—Ethelred—ha! ha!—the breaking of the hermit's door, and the death-cry of the dragon, and the clangor of the shield!— say, rather, the rending of her coffin, and the grating of the iron hinges of her prison, and her struggles within the coppered archway of the vault! Oh whither shall I fly? Will she not be here anon? Is she not hurrying to upbraid me for my haste? Have I not heard her footstep on the stair? Do I not distinguish that heavy and horrible beating of her heart? Mad- man!"—here he sprang furiously to his feet, and shrieked out his syllables, as if in the effort he were giving up his soul—"Madman! I tell you that she now stands without the door!"

As if in the superhuman energy of his utterance there had been found the potency of a spell, the huge antique panels to which the speaker pointed threw slowly back, upon the instant, their ponderous and ebony jaws. It was the work of the rushing gust—but then without those doors there did stand the lofty and enshrouded figure of the lady Madeline of Usher. There was blood upon her white robes, and the evidence of some bitter struggle upon every portion of her emaciated frame. For a moment she remained trembling and reeling to and fro upon the threshold, then, with a low moaning cry, fell heavily inward upon the person of her brother, and in her violent and now final death-agonies, bore him to the floor a corpse, and a victim of the terrors he had anticipated.

From that chamber, and from that mansion, I fled aghast. The storm was still abroad in all its wrath as I found myself crossing the old causeway. Suddenly there shot along the path a wild light, and I turned to see whence a gleam so unusual could have issued; for the vast house and its shadows were alone behind me. The radiance was that of the full, setting, and blood-red moon, which now shone vividly through that once barely discer- nible fissure, of which I have before spoken as extending from the roof of the building, in a zigzag direction, to the base. While I gazed, this fissure rapidly widened—there came a fierce breath of the whirlwind—the entire orb of the satellite burst at once upon my sight—my brain reeled as I saw the mighty walls rushing asunder—there was a long tumultuous shouting sound like the voice of a thousand waters—and the deep and dank tarn at my feet closed sullenly and silently over the fragments of the "House of Usher."

(1839)

Anton Chekhov *1860–1904*

THE LAMENT

It is twilight. A thick wet snow is slowly twirling around the newly lighted street lamps, and lying in soft thin layers on roofs, on horses' backs, on people's shoulders and hats. The cab-driver Iona Potapov is quite white, and looks like a phantom; he is bent double as far as a human body can bend double; he is seated on his box; he never makes a move. If a whole snowdrift fell on him, it seems as if he would not find it necessary to shake it off. His little horse is also quite white, and remains motionless; its immobility, its angularity, and its straight wooden-looking legs, even close by, give it the appearance of a gingerbread horse worth a *kopek*. It is, no doubt, plunged in deep thought. If you were snatched from the plow, from your usual gray surroundings, and were thrown into this slough full of monstrous lights, unceasing noise, and hurrying people, you too would find it difficult not to think.

Iona and his little horse have not moved from their place for a long while. They left their yard before dinner, and up to now, not a fare. The evening mist is descending over the town, the white lights of the lamps replacing brighter rays, and the hubbub of the street getting louder. "Cabby for Viborg way!" suddenly hears Iona. "Cabby!"

Iona jumps, and through his snow-covered eyelashes sees an officer in a greatcoat, with his hood over his head.

"Viborg way!" the officer repeats. "Are you asleep, eh? Viborg way!"

With a nod of assent Iona picks up the reins, in consequence of which layers of snow slip off the horse's back and neck. The officer seats himself in the sleigh, the cabdriver smacks his lips to encourage his horse, stretches out his neck like a swan, sits up, and, more from habit than necessity, brandishes his whip. The little horse also stretches its neck, bends its wooden-looking legs, and makes a move undecidedly.

"What are you doing, werewolf!" is the exclamation Iona hears from the dark mass moving to and fro, as soon as they have started.

"Where the devil are you going? To the r-r-right!"

"You do not know how to drive. Keep to the right!" calls the officer angrily.

A coachman from a private carriage swears at him; a passerby, who has run across the road and rubbed his shoulder against the horse's nose, looks at him furiously as he sweeps the snow from his sleeve. Iona shifts about on his seat as if he were on needles, moves his elbows as if he were trying to keep his equilibrium, and gapes about like someone suffocating, who does not understand why and wherefore he is there.

"What scoundrels they all are!" jokes the officer; "one would think they had all entered into an agreement to jostle you or fall under your horse."

Iona looks round at the officer, and moves his lips. He evidently wants to say something, but the only sound that issues is a snuffle.

"What?" asks the officer.

Iona twists his mouth into a smile, and with an effort says hoarsely:

"My son, *barin*, died this week."

"Hm! What did he die of?"

Iona turns with his whole body toward his fare, and says:

"And who knows! They say high fever. He was three days in the hospital, and then died. . . . God's will be done."

"Turn round! The devil!" sounds from the darkness. "Have you popped off, old doggie, eh? Use your eyes!"

"Go on, go on," says the officer, "otherwise we shall not get there by tomorrow. Hurry up a bit!"

The cabdriver again stretches his neck, sits up, and, with a bad grace, brandishes his whip. Several times again he turns to look at his fare, but the latter has closed his eyes, and apparently is not disposed to listen. Having deposited the officer in the Viborg, he stops by the tavern, doubles himself up on his seat, and again remains motionless, while the snow once more begins to cover him and his horse. An hour, and another. . . . Then, along the footpath, with a squeak of galoshes, and quarreling, come three young men, two of them tall and lanky, the third one short and hump-backed.

"Cabby, to the Police Bridge!" in a cracked voice calls the humpback. "The three of us for two *griveniks!*"

Iona picks up his reins, and smacks his lips. Two *griveniks* is not a fair price, but he does not mind whether it is a *rouble* or five *kopeks*—to him it is all the same now, so long as they are fares. The young men, jostling each other and using bad language, approach the sleigh, and all three at once try to get onto the seat; then begins a discussion as to which two shall sit and who shall be the one to stand. After wrangling, abusing each other, and much petulance, it is at last decided that the humpback shall stand, as he is the smallest.

"Now then, hurry up!" says the humpback in a twanging voice, as he takes his place and breathes in Iona's neck. "Old furry! Here, mate, what a cap you have! There is not a worse one to be found in all Petersburg! . . ."

"He-he!—he-he!" giggles Iona. "Such a . . ."

"Now you, 'such a,' hurry up, are you going the whole way at this pace? Are you? . . . Do you want it in the neck?"

"My head feels like bursting," says one of the lanky ones. "Last night at the Donkmasovs, Vaska and I drank the whole of four bottles of cognac."

"I don't understand what you lie for," says the other lanky one angrily; "you lie like a brute."

"God strike me, it's the truth!"

"It's as much the truth as that a louse coughs!"

"He, he," grins Iona, "what gay young gentlemen!"

"Pshaw, go to the devil!" says the humpback indignantly.

"Are you going to get on or not, you old pest? Is that the way to drive? Use the whip a bit! Go on, devil, go on, give it to him well!"

Iona feels at his back the little man wriggling, and the tremble in his voice. He listens to the insults hurled at him, sees the people, and little by little the feeling of loneliness leaves him. The humpback goes on swearing until he gets mixed up in some elaborate six-foot oath, or chokes with coughing. The lankies begin to talk about a certain Nadejda Petrovna.

Iona looks round at them several times; he waits for a temporary silence, then, turning round again, he murmurs:

"My son . . . died this week."

"We must all die," sighs the humpback, wiping his lips after an attack of coughing. "Now, hurry up, hurry up! Gentlemen, I really cannot go any farther like this! When will he get us there?"

"Well, just you stimulate him a little in the neck!"

"You old pest, do you hear, I'll bone your neck for you! If one treated the like of you with ceremony one would have to go on foot! Do you hear, old serpent Gorinytch![1] Or do you not care a spit?"

Iona hears rather than feels the blows they deal him.

"He, he," he laughs. "They are gay young gentlemen, God bless 'em!"

"Cabby, are you married?" asks a lanky one.

"I? He, he, gay young gentlemen! Now I have only a wife and the moist ground. . . . He, ho, ho . . . that is to say, the grave. My son has died, and I am alive. . . . A wonderful thing, death mistook the door . . . instead of coming to me, it went to my son. . . ."

Iona turns round to tell them how his son died, but at this moment, the humpback, giving a little sigh, announces, "Thank God, we have at last reached our destination," and Iona watches them disappear through the dark entrance. Once more he is alone, and again surrounded by silence. . . . His grief, which has abated for a short while, returns and rends his heart with greater force. With an anxious and hurried look, he searches among the crowds passing on either side of the street to find whether there may be just one person who will listen to him. But the crowds hurry by without noticing him or his trouble. Yet it is such an immense, illimitable grief. Should his heart break and the grief pour out, it would flow over the whole earth, so it seems, and yet no one sees it. It has managed to conceal itself in such an insignificant shell that no one can see it even by day and with a light.

Iona sees a hall porter with some sacking, and decides to talk to him.

"Friend, what sort of time is it?" he asks.

"Past nine. What are you standing here for? Move on."

Iona moves on a few steps, doubles himself up, and abandons himself to his grief. He sees it is useless to turn to people for help. In less than five minutes he straightens himself, holds up his head as if he felt some sharp pain, and gives a tug at the reins; he can bear it no longer. "The stables," he thinks, and the little horse, as if it understood, starts off at a trot.

About an hour and a half later Iona is seated by a large dirty stove. Around the stove, on the floor, on the benches, people are snoring; the air is thick and suffocatingly hot. Iona looks at the sleepers, scratches himself, and regrets having returned so early.

"I have not even earned my fodder," he thinks. "That's what's my trouble. A man who knows his job, who has had enough to eat, and his horse too, can always sleep peacefully."

A young cabdriver in one of the corners half gets up, grunts sleepily, and stretches towards a bucket of water.

[1] A character in Russian folklore.

"Do you want a drink?" Iona asks him.

"Don't I want a drink!"

"That's so? Your good health! But listen, mate—you know, my son is dead. . . . Did you hear? This week, in the hospital. . . . It's a long story."

Iona looks to see what effect his words have, but sees none—the young man has hidden his face and is fast asleep again. The old man sighs, and scratches his head. Just as much as the young one wants to drink, the old man wants to talk. It will soon be a week since his son died, and he has not been able to speak about it properly to anyone. One must tell it slowly and carefully; how his son fell ill, how he suffered, what he said before he died, how he died. One must describe every detail of the funeral, and the journey to the hospital to fetch the dead son's clothes. His daughter Anissia has remained in the village—one must talk about her too. Is it nothing he has to tell? Surely the listener would gasp and sigh, and sympathize with him? It is better, too, to talk to women; although they are stupid, two words are enough to make them sob.

"I'll go and look after my horse," thinks Iona; "there's always time to sleep. No fear of that!"

He puts on his coat, and goes to the stables to his horse; he thinks of the corn, the hay, the weather. When he is alone, he dares not think of his son; he can speak about him to anyone, but to think of him, and picture him to himself, is unbearably painful.

"Are you tucking in?" Iona asks his horse, looking at its bright eyes; "go on, tuck in, though we've not earned our corn, we can eat hay. Yes! I am too old to drive—my son could have, not I. He was a first-rate cab-driver. If only he had lived!"

Iona is silent for a moment, then continues:

"That's how it is, my old horse. There's no more Kuzma Ionitch. He has left us to live, and he went off pop. Now let's say, you had a foal, you were the foal's mother, and suddenly, let's say, that foal went and left you to live after him. It would be sad, wouldn't it?"

The little horse munches, listens, and breathes over its master's hand. . . .

Iona's feelings are too much for him, and he tells the little horse the whole story.

                                                                                     (1885)

Kate Chopin *1850–1904*

THE STORM

I

The leaves were so still that even Bibi thought it was going to rain. Bobinôt, who was accustomed to converse on terms of perfect equality with his little son, called the child's attention to certain sombre clouds that were rolling with sinister intention from the west, accompanied by a sullen, threatening roar. They were at Friedheimer's store and decided to remain there till the storm had passed. They sat within the door on two empty kegs. Bibi was four years old and looked very wise.

"Mama'll be 'fraid, yes," he suggested with blinking eyes.

"She'll shut the house. Maybe she got Sylvie helpin' her this evenin'," Bobinôt responded reassuringly.

"No; she ent got Sylvie. Sylvie was helpin' her yistiday," piped Bibi.

Bobinôt arose and going across to the counter purchased a can of shrimps, of which Calixta was very fond. Then he returned to his perch on the keg and sat stolidly holding the can of shrimps while the storm burst. It shook the wooden store and seemed to be ripping great furrows in the distant field. Bibi laid his little hand on his father's knee and was not afraid.

II

Calixta, at home, felt no uneasiness for their safety. She sat at a side window sewing furiously on a sewing machine. She was greatly occupied and did not notice the approaching storm. But she felt very warm and often stopped to mop her face on which the perspiration gathered in beads. She unfastened her white sacque at the throat. It began to grow dark, and suddenly realizing the situation she got up hurriedly and went about closing windows and doors.

Out on the small front gallery she had hung Bobinôt's Sunday clothes to air and she hastened out to gather them before the rain fell. As she stepped outside, Alcée Laballière rode in at the gate. She had not seen him very often since her marriage, and never alone. She stood there with Bobinôt's coat in her hands, and the big rain drops began to fall. Alcée rode his horse under the shelter of a side projection where the chickens had huddled and there were plows and a harrow piled up in the corner.

"May I come and wait on your gallery till the storm is over, Calixta?" he asked.

"Come 'long in, M'sieur Alcée."

His voice and her own startled her as if from a trance, and she seized Bobinôt's vest. Alcée, mounting to the porch, grabbed the trousers and snatched Bibi's braided jacket that was about to be carried away by a sudden gust of wind. He expressed an intention to remain outside, but it was soon apparent that he might as well have been out in the open: the water beat in upon the boards in driving sheets, and he went inside, closing the door after him. It was even necessary to put something beneath the door to keep the water out.

"My! what a rain! It's good two years sence it rain' like that," exclaimed Calixta as she rolled up a piece of bagging and Alcée helped her to thrust it beneath the crack.

She was a little fuller of figure than five years before when she married; but she had lost nothing of her vivacity. Her blue eyes still retained their melting quality; and her yellow hair, dishevelled by the wind and rain, kinked more stubbornly than ever about her ears and temples.

The rain beat upon the low, shingled roof with a force and clatter that threatened to break an entrance and deluge them there. They were in the dining room—the sitting room—the general utility room. Adjoining was her bed room, with Bibi's couch along side her own. The door stood open, and the room with its white, monumental bed, its closed shutters, looked dim and mysterious.

Alcée flung himself into a rocker and Calixta nervously began to gather up from the floor the lengths of a cotton sheet which she had been sewing.

"If this keeps up, *Dieu sait* if the levees goin' to stan' it!" she exclaimed.

"What have you got to do with the leeves?"

"I got enough to do! An' there's Bobinôt with Bibi out in that storm— if he only didn' left Friedheimer's!"

"Let us hope, Calixta, that Bobinôt's got sense enough to come in out of a cyclone."

She went and stood at the window with a greatly disturbed look on her face. She wiped the frame that was clouded with moisture. It was stiffingly hot. Alcée got up and joined her at the window, looking over her shoulder. The rain was coming down in sheets obscuring the view of far-off cabins and enveloping the distant wood in a gray mist. The playing of the lightning was incessant. A bolt struck a tall chinaberry tree at the edge of the field. It filled all visible space with a blinding glare and the crash seemed to invade the very boards they stood upon.

Calixta put her hands to her eyes, and with a cry, staggered backward. Alcée's arm encircled her, and for an instant he drew her close and spasmodically to him.

"*Bonté*" she cried, releasing herself from his encircling arm and retreating from the window, "the house'll go next! If I only knew w'ere Bibi was!" She would not compose herself; she would not be seated. Alcée clasped her shoulders and looked into her face. The contact of her warm, palpitating body when he had unthinkingly drawn her into his arms, had aroused all the old-time infatuation and desire for her flesh.

"Calixta," he said, "don't be frightened. Nothing can happen. The house is too low to be struck, with so many tall trees standing about. There! aren't you going to be quiet? say, aren't you?" He pushed her hair back from her face that was warm and steaming. Her lips were as red and moist as pomegranate seed. Her white neck and a glimpse of her full, firm bosom disturbed him powerfully. As she glanced up at him the fear in her liquid blue eyes had given place to a drowsy gleam that unconsciously betrayed a senuous desire. He looked down into her eyes and there was nothing for him to do but to gather her lips in a kiss. It reminded him of Assumption.

"Do you remember—in Assumption, Calixta?" he asked in a low voice broken by passion. Oh! she remembered; for in Assumption he had kissed her and kissed her and kissed her; until his senses would well nigh fail, and to save her he would resort to a desperate flight. If she was not an immaculate dove in those days, she was still inviolate; a passionate creature whose very defenselessness had made her defense, against which his honor forbade him to prevail. Now—well, now—her lips seemed in a manner free to be tasted, as well as her round, white throat and her whiter breasts.

They did not heed the crashing torrents, and the roar of the elements made her laugh as she lay in his arms. She was a revelation in that dim, mysterious chamber; as white as the couch she lay upon. Her firm, elastic flesh that was knowing for the first time its birthright, was like a creamy lily that the sun invites to contribute its breath and perfume to the undying life of the world.

The generous abundance of her passion, without guile or trickery, was like a white flame which penetrated and found response in depths of his own senuous nature that had never yet been reached.

When he touched her breasts they gave themselves up in quivering ecstasy, inviting his lips. Her mouth was a fountain of delight. And when he possessed her, they seemed to swoon together at the very borderland of life's mystery.

He stayed cushioned upon her, breathless, dazed, enervated, with his heart beating like a hammer upon her. With one hand she clasped his head, her lips lightly touching his forehead. The other hand stroked with a soothing rhythm his muscular shoulders.

The growl of the thunder was distant and passing away. The rain beat softly upon the shingles, inviting them to drowsiness and sleep. But they dared not yield.

The rain was over; and the sun was turning the glistening green world into a palace of gems. Calixta, on the gallery, watched Alcée ride away. He turned and smiled at her with a beaming face; and she lifted her pretty chin in the air and laughed aloud.

III

Bobinôt and Bibi, trudging home, stopped without at the cistern to make themselves presentable.

"My! Bibi, w'at will yo' mama say! You ought to be ashame'. You oughtn' put on those good pants. Look at 'em! An' that mud on yo' collar! How you got that mud on yo' collar, Bibi? I never saw such a boy!" Bibi was the picture of pathetic resignation. Bobinôt was the embodiment of serious solicitude as he strove to remove from his own person and his son's the signs of their tramp over heavy roads and through wet fields. He scraped the mud off Bibi's bare legs and feet with a stick and carefully removed all traces from his heavy brogans. Then, prepared for the worst—the meeting with an over-scrupulous housewife, they entered cautiously at the back door.

Calixta was preparing supper. She had set the table and was dripping coffee at the hearth. She sprang up as they came in.

"Oh, Bobinôt! You back! My! but I was uneasy. W'ere you been during the rain? An' Bibi? he ain't wet? he ain't hurt?" She had clasped Bibi and was kissing him effusively. Bobinôt's explanations and apologies which he had been composing all along the way, died on his lips as Calixta felt him to see if he were dry, and seemed to express nothing but satisfaction at their safe return.

"I brought you some shrimps, Calixta," offered Bobinôt, hauling the can from his ample side pocket and laying it on the table.

"Shrimps! Oh, Bobinôt! you too good fo' anything!" and she gave him a smacking kiss on the cheek that resounded. *"J'vous réponds,* we'll have a feas' to-night! umph-umph!"

Bobinôt and Bibi began to relax and enjoy themselves, and when the three seated themselves at table they laughed much and so loud that anyone might have heard them as far away as Laballière's.

IV

Alcée Laballière wrote to his wife, Clarisse, that night. It was a loving letter, full of tender solicitude. He told her not to hurry back, but if she and the babies liked it at Biloxi, to stay a month longer. He was getting on nicely; and though he missed them, he was willing to bear the separation a while longer—realizing that their health and pleasure were the first things to be considered.

V

As for Clarisse, she was charmed upon receiving her husband's letter. She and the babies were doing well. The society was agreeable; many of her old friends and acquaintances were at the bay. And the first free breath since her marriage seemed to restore the pleasant liberty of her maiden days. Devoted as she was to her husband, their intimate conjugal life was something which she was more than willing to forego for a while.

So the storm passed and every one was happy.

(Written, 1898; published, 1969)

Stephen Crane *1871–1900*

THE BRIDE COMES TO YELLOW SKY

The great Pullman was whirling onward with such dignity of motion that a glance from the window seemed simply to prove that the plains of Texas were pouring eastward. Vast flats of green grass, dull-hued spaces of mesquite and cactus, little groups of frame houses, woods of light and tender trees, all were sweeping into the east, sweeping over the horizon, a precipice.

A newly married pair had boarded this coach at San Antonio. The man's face was reddened from many days in the wind and sun, and a direct result of new black clothes was that his brick-colored hands were constantly performing in a most conscious fashion. From time to time he looked down respectfully at his attire. He sat with a hand on each knee, like a man waiting in a barber's shop. The glances he devoted to other passengers were furtive and shy.

The bride was not pretty, nor was she very young. She wore a dress of blue cashmere, with small reservations of velvet here and there, and with steel buttons abounding. She continually twisted her head to regard her puff sleeves, very stiff, straight, and high. They embarrassed her. It was quite apparent that she had cooked, and that she expected to cook, dutifully. The blushes caused by the careless scrutiny of some passengers as she had entered the car were strange to see upon this plain, underclass countenance, which was drawn in placid, almost emotionless lines.

They were evidently very happy. "Ever been in a parlor car before?" he asked, smiling with delight.

"No," she answered. "I never was. It's fine, ain't it?"

"Great! And then after a while we'll go forward to the diner, and get a big layout. Finest meal in the world. Charge a dollar."

"Oh, do they?" cried the bride. "Charge a dollar? Why, that's too much—for us—ain't it, Jack?"

"Not this trip, anyhow," he answered bravely. "We're going to go the whole thing."

Later, he explained to her about the trains. "You see, it's a thousand miles from one end of Texas to the other; and this train runs right across it, and never stops but four times." He had the pride of an owner. He pointed out to her the dazzling fittings of the coach; and in truth her eyes opened wider as she contemplated the sea-green figured velvet, the shining brass, silver, and glass, the wood that gleamed as darkly brilliant as the surface of a pool of oil. At one end a bronze figure sturdily held a support for a separated chamber, and at convenient places on the ceiling were frescoes in olive and silver.

To the minds of the pair, their surroundings reflected the glory of their marriage that morning in San Antonio. This was the environment of their new estate, and the man's face in particular beamed with an elation that made him appear ridiculous to the negro porter. This individual at times surveyed them from afar with an amused and superior grin. On other

151

occasions he bullied them with skill in ways that did not make it exactly plain to them that they were being bullied. He subtly used all the manners of the most unconquerable kind of snobbery. He oppressed them; but of this oppression they had small knowledge, and they speedily forgot that infrequently a number of travelers covered them with stares of derisive enjoyment. Historically there was supposed to be something infinitely humorous in their situation.

"We are due in Yellow Sky at 3:42," he said, looking tenderly into her eyes.

"Oh, are we?" she said, as if she had not been aware of it. To evince surprise at her husband's statement was part of her wifely amiability. She took from a pocket a little silver watch; and as she held it before her, and stared at it with a frown of attention, the new husband's face shone.

"I bought it in San Anton' from a friend of mine," he told her gleefully.

"It's seventeen minutes past twelve," she said, looking up at him with a kind of shy and clumsy coquetry. A passenger, noting this play, grew excessively sardonic, and winked at himself in one of the numerous mirrors.

At last they went to the dining car. Two rows of negro waiters, in glowing white suits, surveyed their entrance with the interest, and also the equanimity, of men who had been forewarned. The pair fell to the lot of a waiter who happened to feel pleasure in steering them through their meal. He viewed them with the manner of a fatherly pilot, his countenance radiant with benevolence. The patronage, entwined with the ordinary deference, was not plain to them. And yet, as they returned to their coach, they showed in their faces a sense of escape.

To the left, miles down a long purple slope, was a little ribbon of mist where moved the keening Rio Grande. The train was approaching it at an angle, and the apex was Yellow Sky. Presently it was apparent that, as the distance from Yellow Sky grew shorter, the husband became commensurately restless. His brick-red hands were more insistent in their prominence. Occasionally he was even rather absent-minded and faraway when the bride leaned forward and addressed him.

As a matter of truth, Jack Potter was beginning to find the shadow of a deed weigh upon him like a leaden slab. He, the town marshal of Yellow Sky, a man known, liked, and feared in his corner, a prominent person, had gone to San Antonio to meet a girl he believed he loved, and there, after the usual prayers, had actually induced her to marry him, without consulting Yellow Sky for any part of the transaction. He was now bringing his bride before an innocent and unsuspecting community.

Of course people in Yellow Sky married as it pleased them, in accordance with a general custom; but such was Potter's thought of his duty to his friends, or of their idea of his duty, or of an unspoken form which does not control men in these matters, that he felt he was heinous. He had committed an extraordinary crime. Face to face with this girl in San Antonio, and spurred by his sharp impulse, he had gone headlong over all the social hedges. At San Antonio he was like a man hidden in the dark. A knife to sever any friendly duty, any form, was easy to his hand in that remote city. But the hour of Yellow Sky—the hour of daylight—was approaching.

He knew full well that his marriage was an important thing to his town. It could only be exceeded by the burning of the new hotel. His friends could not forgive him. Frequently he had reflected on the advisability of telling them by telegraph, but a new cowardice had been upon him. He feared to do it. And now the train was hurrying him toward a scene of amazement, glee, and reproach. He glanced out of the window at the line of haze swinging slowly in toward the train.

Yellow Sky had a kind of brass band, which played painfully, to the delight of the populace. He laughed without heart as he thought of it. If the citizens could dream of his prospective arrival with his bride, they would parade the band at the station and escort them, amid cheers and laughing congratulations, to his adobe home.

He resolved that he would use all the devices of speed and plains-craft in making the journey from the station to his house. Once within that safe citadel, he could issue some sort of a vocal bulletin, and then not go among the citizens until they had time to wear off a little of their enthusiasm.

The bride looked anxiously at him. "What's worrying you, Jack?"

He laughed again. "I'm not worrying, girl. I'm only thinking of Yellow Sky."

She flushed in comprehension.

A sense of mutual guilt invaded their minds and developed a finer tenderness. They looked at each other with eyes softly aglow. But Potter often laughed the same nervous laugh. The flush upon the bride's face seemed quite permanent.

The traitor to the feelings of Yellow Sky narrowly watched the speeding landscape. "We're nearly there," he said.

Presently the porter came and announced the proximity of Potter's home. He held a brush in his hand, and, with all his airy superiority gone, he brushed Potter's new clothes as the latter slowly turned this way and that way. Potter fumbled out a coin and gave it to the porter, as he had seen others do. It was a heavy and muscle-bound business, as that of a man shoeing his first horse.

The porter took their bag, and as the train began to slow they moved forward to the hooded platform of the car. Presently the two engines and their long string of coaches rushed into the station of Yellow Sky.

"They have to take water here," said Potter, from a constricted throat and in mournful cadence, as one announcing death. Before the train stopped, his eye had swept the length of the platform, and he was glad and astonished to see there was none upon it but the station-agent, who, with a slightly hurried and anxious air, was walking toward the water tanks. When the train had halted, the porter alighted first, and placed in position a little temporary step.

"Come on, girl," said Potter, hoarsely. As he helped her down they each laughed on a false note. He took the bag from the negro, and bade his wife cling to his arm. As they slunk rapidly away, his hangdog glance perceived that they were unloading the two trunks, and also that the station-agent, far ahead near the baggage car, had turned and was running toward him, making gestures. He laughed, and groaned as he laughed, when he noted the first effect of his marital bliss upon Yellow Sky. He gripped his wife's arm firmly to his side, and they fled. Behind them the porter stood, chuckling fatuously.

II

The California express on the Southern Railway was due at Yellow Sky in twenty-one minutes. There were six men at the bar of the Weary Gentleman saloon. One was a drummer who talked a great deal and rapidly; three were Texans who did not care to talk at that time; and two were Mexican sheepherders, who did not talk as a general practice in the Weary Gentleman saloon. The barkeeper's dog lay on the boardwalk that crossed in front of the door. His head was on his paws, and he glanced drowsily here and there with the constant vigilance of a dog that is kicked on occasion. Across the sandy street were some vivid green grass-plots, so wonderful in appearance, amid the sands that burned near them in a blazing sun, that they caused a doubt in the mind. They exactly resembled the grass mats used to represent lawns on the stage. At the cooler end of the railway station, a man without a coat sat in a tilted chair and smoked his pipe. The fresh-cut bank of the Rio Grande circled near the town, and there could be seen beyond it a great plum-colored plain of mesquite.

Save for the busy drummer and his companions in the saloon, Yellow Sky was dozing. The newcomer leaned gracefully upon the bar, and recited many tales with the confidence of a bard who has come upon a new field.

"—and at the moment that the old man fell downstairs with the bureau in his arms, the old woman was coming up with two scuttles of coal, and of course—"

The drummer's tale was interrupted by a young man who suddenly appeared in the open door. He cried: "Scratchy Wilson's drunk, and has turned loose with both hands." The two Mexicans at once set down their glasses and faded out of the rear entrance of the saloon.

The drummer, innocent and jocular, answered: "All right, old man. S'pose he has? Come in and have a drink, anyhow."

But the information had made such an obvious cleft in every skull in the room that the drummer was obliged to see its importance. All had become instantly solemn. "Say," said he, mystified, "what is this?" His three companions made the introductory gesture of eloquent speech, but the young man at the door forestalled them.

"It means, my friend," he answered, as he came into the saloon, "that for the next two hours this town won't be a health resort."

The barkeeper went to the door and locked and barred it. Reaching out of the window, he pulled in heavy wooden shutters and barred them. Immediately a solemn, chapel-like gloom was upon the place. The drummer was looking from one to another.

"But say," he cried, "what is this, anyhow? You don't mean there is going to be a gunfight?"

"Don't know whether there'll be a fight or not," answered one man, grimly. "But there'll be some shootin'—some good shootin'."

The young man who had warned them waved his hand. "Oh, there'll be a fight fast enough, if any one wants it. Anybody can get a fight out there in the street. There's a fight just waiting."

The drummer seemed to be swayed between the interest of a foreigner and a perception of personal danger.

"What did you say his name was?" he asked.

"Scratchy Wilson," they answered in chorus.

"And will he kill anybody? What are you going to do? Does this happen often? Does he rampage around like this once a week or so? Can he break in that door?"

"No; he can't break down that door," replied the barkeeper. "He's tried it three times. But when he comes you'd better lay down on the floor, stranger. He's dead sure to shoot at it, and a bullet may come through."

Thereafter the drummer kept a strict eye upon the door. The time had not yet been called for him to hug the floor, but, as a minor precaution, he sidled near to the wall. "Will he kill anybody?" he said again.

The men laughed low and scornfully at the question.

"He's out to shoot, and he's out for trouble. Don't see any good in experimentin' with him."

"But what do you do in a case like this? What do you do?"

A man responded: "Why, he and Jack Potter—"

"But," in chorus the other men interrupted, "Jack Potter's in San Anton'."

"Well, who is he? What's he got to do with it?"

"Oh, he's the town marshal. He goes out and fights Scratchy when he gets on one of these tears."

"Wow!" said the drummer, mopping his brow. "Nice job he's got."

The voices had toned away to mere whisperings. The drummer wished to ask further questions, which were born of an increasing anxiety and bewilderment; but when he attempted them, the men merely looked at him in irritation and motioned him to remain silent. A tense waiting hush was upon them. In the deep shadows of the room their eyes shone as they listened for sounds from the street. One man made three gestures at the barkeeper; and the latter, moving like a ghost, handed him a glass and a bottle. The man poured a full glass of whiskey, and set down the bottle noiselessly. He gulped the whiskey in a swallow, and turned again toward the door in immovable silence. The drummer saw that the barkeeper, without a sound, had taken a Winchester from beneath the bar. Later he saw this individual beckoning to him, so he tiptoed across the room.

"You better come with me back of the bar."

"No, thanks," said the drummer, perspiring. "I'd rather be where I can make a break for the back door."

Whereupon the man of bottles made a kindly but peremptory gesture. The drummer obeyed it, and, finding himself seated on a box with his head below the level of the bar, balm was laid upon his soul at sight of various zinc and copper fittings that bore a resemblance to armor plate. The barkeeper took a seat comfortably upon an adjacent box.

"You see," he whispered, "this here Scratchy Wilson is a wonder with a gun—a perfect wonder—and when he goes on the war trail, we hunt our holes—naturally. He's about the last one of the old gang that used to hang out along the river here. He's a terror when he's drunk. When he's sober he's all right—kind of simple—wouldn't hurt a fly—nicest fellow in town. But when he's drunk—whoo!"

There were periods of stillness. "I wish Jack Potter was back from San Anton'," said the barkeeper. "He shot Wilson up once—in the leg—and he would sail in and pull out the kinks in this thing."

Presently they heard from a distance the sound of a shot, followed by three wild yowls. It instantly removed a bond from the men in the darkened saloon. There was a shuffling of feet. They looked at each other. "Here he comes," they said.

III

A man in a maroon-colored flannel shirt, which had been purchased for purposes of decoration, and made principally by some Jewish women on the East Side of New York, rounded a corner and walked into the middle of the main street of Yellow Sky. In either hand the man held a long, heavy, blue-black revolver. Often he yelled, and these cries rang through a semblance of a deserted village, shrilly flying over the roofs in a volume that seemed to have no relation to the ordinary vocal strength of a man. It was as if the surrounding stillness formed the arch of a tomb over him. These cries of ferocious challenge rang against walls of silence. And his boots had red tops with gilded imprints, of the kind beloved in winter by little sledding boys on the hillsides of New England.

The man's face flamed in a rage begot of whiskey. His eyes, rolling, and yet keen for ambush, hunted the still doorways and windows. He walked with the creeping movement of the midnight cat. As it occurred to him, he roared menacing information. The long revolvers in his hands were as easy as straws; they were moved with an electric swiftness. The little fingers of each hand played sometimes in a musician's way. Plain from the low collar of the shirt, the cords of his neck straightened and sank, straightened and sank, as passion moved him. The only sounds were his terrible invitations. The calm adobes preserved their demeanor at the passing of this small thing in the middle of the street.

There was no offer of fight—no offer of fight. The man called to the sky. There were no attractions. He bellowed and fumed and swayed his revolvers here and everywhere.

The dog of the barkeeper of the Weary Gentleman saloon had not appreciated the advance of events. He yet lay dozing in front of his master's door. At sight of the dog, the man paused and raised his revolver humorously. At sight of the man, the dog sprang up and walked diagonally away, with a sullen head, and growling. The man yelled, and the dog broke into a gallop. As it was about to enter an alley, there was a loud noise, a whistling, and something spat the ground directly before it. The dog screamed, and, wheeling in terror, galloped headlong in a new direction. Again there was a noise, a whistling, and sand was kicked viciously before it. Fear-stricken, the dog turned and flurried like an animal in a pen. The man stood laughing, his weapons at his hips.

Ultimately the man was attracted by the closed door of the Weary Gentleman saloon. He went to it and, hammering with a revolver, demanded drink.

The door remaining imperturbable, he picked a bit of paper from the walk, and nailed it to the framework with a knife. He then turned his back contemptuously upon this popular resort and, walking to the opposite side of the street and spinning there on his heel quickly and lithely, fired at the bit of paper. He missed it by a half-inch. He swore at himself, and went away. Later, he comfortably fusilladed the windows of his most intimate friend. The man was playing with this town. It was a toy for him.

But still there was no offer of fight. The name of Jack Potter, his ancient antagonist, entered his mind, and he concluded that it would be a glad thing if he should go to Potter's house, and by bombardment induce him to come out and fight. He moved in the direction of his desire, chanting Apache scalp-music.

When he arrived at it, Potter's house presented the same still front as had the other adobes. Taking up a strategic position, the man howled a challenge. But this house regarded him as might a great stone god. It gave no sign. After a decent wait, the man howled further challenges, mingling with them wonderful epithets.

Presently there came the spectacle of a man churning himself into deepest rage over the immobility of a house. He fumed at it as the winter wind attacks a prairie cabin in the North. To the distance there should have gone the sound of a tumult like the fighting of two hundred Mexicans. As necessity bade him, he paused for breath or to reload his revolvers.

IV

Potter and his bride walked sheepishly and with speed. Sometimes they laughed together shamefacedly and low.

"Next corner, dear," he said finally.

They put forth the efforts of a pair walking bowed against a strong wind. Potter was about to raise a finger to point the first appearance of the new home when, as they circled the corner, they came face to face with a man in a maroon-colored shirt, who was feverishly pushing cartridges into a large revolver. Upon the instant the man dropped his revolver to the ground, and, like lightning, whipped another from its holster. The second weapon was aimed at the bridegroom's chest.

There was a silence. Potter's mouth seemed to be merely a grave for his tongue. He exhibited an instinct to at once loosen his arm from the woman's grip, and he dropped the bag to the sand. As for the bride, her face had gone as yellow as old cloth. She was a slave to hideous rites, gazing at the apparitional snake.

The two men faced each other at a distance of three paces. He of the revolver smiled with a new and quiet ferocity.

"Tried to sneak up on me," he said. "Tried to sneak up on me!" His eyes grew more baleful. As Potter made a slight movement, the man thrust his revolver venomously forward. "No; don't you do it, Jack Potter. Don't you move a finger toward a gun just yet. Don't you move an eyelash. The time has come for me to settle with you, and I'm goin' to do it my own way, and loaf along with no interferin'. So if you don't want a gun bent on you, just mind what I tell you."

Potter looked at his enemy. "I ain't got a gun on me, Scratchy," he said. "Honestly, I ain't." He was stiffening and steadying, but yet somewhere at the back of his mind a vision of the Pullman floated; the sea-green figured velvet, the shining brass, silver, and glass, the wood that gleamed as darkly brilliant as the surface of a pool of oil—all the glory of the marriage, the environment of the new estate. "You know I fight when it comes to fighting, Scratchy Wilson; but I ain't got a gun on me. You'll have to do all the shootin' yourself."

His enemy's face went livid. He stepped forward, and lashed his weapon to and fro before Potter's chest. "Don't you tell me you ain't got no gun on you, you whelp. Don't tell me no lie like that. There ain't a man in Texas ever seen you without no gun. Don't take me for no kid." His eyes blazed with light, and his throat worked like a pump.

"I ain't takin' you for no kid," answered Potter. His heels had not moved an inch backward. "I'm takin' you for a damn fool. I tell you I ain't got a gun, and I ain't. If you're goin' to shoot me up, you better begin now. You'll never get a chance like this again."

So much enforced reasoning had told on Wilson's rage. He was calmer. "If you ain't got a gun, why ain't you got a gun?" he sneered. "Been to Sunday school?"

"I ain't got a gun because I've just come from San Anton' with my wife. I'm married," said Potter. "And if I'd thought there was going to be any galoots like you prowling around when I brought my wife home, I'd had a gun, and don't you forget it."

"Married!" said Scratchy, not at all comprehending.

"Yes, married. I'm married," said Potter, distinctly.

"Married?" said Scratchy. Seemingly for the first time, he saw the drooping, drowning woman at the other man's side. "No!" he said. He was like a creature allowed a glimpse of another world. He moved a pace backward, and his arm, with the revolver, dropped to his side. "Is this the lady?" he asked.

"Yes; this is the lady," answered Potter.

There was another period of silence.

"Well," said Wilson at last, slowly, "I s'pose it's all off now."

"It's all off if you say so, Scratchy. You know I didn't make the trouble." Potter lifted his valise.

"Well, I 'low it's off, Jack." said Wilson. He was looking at the ground. "Married!" He was not a student of chivalry; it was merely that in the presence of this foreign condition he was a simple child of the earlier plains. He picked up his starboard revolver, and, placing both weapons in their holsters, he went away. His feet made funnel-shaped tracks in the heavy sand.

(1898)

Joseph Conrad *1857–1924*

HEART OF DARKNESS

I

The *Nellie*, a cruising yawl, swung to her anchor without a flutter of the sails, and was at rest. The flood had made, the wind was nearly calm, and being bound down the river, the only thing for it was to come to and wait for the turn of the tide.

The sea-reach of the Thames stretched before us like the beginning of an interminable waterway. In the offing the sea and the sky were welded together without a joint, and in the luminous space the tanned sails of the barges drifting up with the tide seemed to stand still in red clusters of canvas sharply peaked, with gleams of varnished sprits. A haze rested on the low shores that ran out to sea in vanishing flatness. The air was dark above Gravesend,[1] and farther back still seemed condensed into a mournful gloom, brooding motionless over the biggest, and the greatest, town on earth.

The Director of Companies was our captain and our host. We four affectionately watched his back as he stood in the bows looking to seaward. On the whole river there was nothing that looked half so nautical. He resembled a pilot, which to a seaman is trustworthiness personified. It was difficult to realize his work was not out there in the luminous estuary, but behind him, within the brooding gloom.

Between us there was, as I have already said somewhere, the bond of the sea. Besides holding our hearts together through long periods of separation, it had the effect of making us tolerant of each other's yarns—and even convictions. The Lawyer—the best of old fellows—had, because of his many years and many virtues, the only cushion on deck, and was lying on the only rug. The Accountant had brought out already a box of dominoes, and was toying architecturally with the bones. Marlow sat cross-legged right aft, leaning against the mizzen-mast. He had sunken cheeks, a yellow complexion, a straight back, an ascetic aspect, and, with his arms dropped, the palms of hands outwards, resembled an idol. The director, satisfied the anchor had good hold, made his way aft and sat down amongst us. We exchanged a few words lazily. Afterwards there was silence on board the yacht. For some reason or other we did not begin that game of dominoes. We felt meditative, and fit for nothing but placid staring. The day was ending in a serenity of still and exquisite brilliance. The water shone pacifically; the sky, without a speck, was a benign immensity of unstained light; the very mist on the Essex marshes was like a gauzy and radiant fabric, hung from the wooded rises inland, and draping the low shores in diaphanous folds. Only the gloom to the west, brooding over the upper reaches, became more sombre every minute, as if angered by the approach of the sun.

---

[1] Seaport on the Thames, 26 miles east of London.

And at last, in its curved and imperceptible fall, the sun sank low, and from glowing white changed to a dull red without rays and without heat, as if about to go out suddenly, stricken to death by the touch of that gloom brooding over a crowd of men.

Forthwith a change came over the waters, and the serenity became less brilliant but more profound. The old river in its broad reach rested unruffled at the decline of day, after ages of good service done to the race that peopled its banks, spread out in the tranquil dignity of a waterway leading to the uttermost ends of the earth. We looked at the venerable stream not in the vivid flush of a short day that comes and departs for ever, but in the august light of abiding memories. And indeed nothing is easier for a man who has, as the phrase goes, "followed the sea" with reverence and affection, than to evoke the great spirit of the past upon the lower reaches of the Thames. The tidal current runs to and fro in its unceasing service, crowded with memories of men and ships it had borne to the rest of home or to the battles of the sea. It had known and served all the men of whom the nation is proud, from Sir Francis Drake to Sir John Franklin, knights all, titled and untitled—the great knights-errant of the sea. It had borne all the ships whose names are like jewels flashing in the night of time, from the *Golden Hind* returning with her round flanks full of treasure, to be visited by the Queen's Highness and thus pass out of the gigantic tale, to the *Erebus* and *Terror*, bound on other conquests— and that never returned. It had known the ships and the men. They had sailed from Deptford, from Greenwich, from Erith—the adventurers and the settlers; kings' ships and the ships of men on 'Change; captains, admirals, the dark "interlopers" of the Eastern trade, and the commissioned "generals" of East India fleets. Hunters for gold or pursuers of fame, they all had gone out on that stream, bearing the sword, and often the torch, messengers of the might within the land, bearers of a spark from the sacred fire. What greatness had not floated on the ebb of that river into the mystery of an unknown earth! . . . The dreams of men, the seed of commonwealths, the germs of empires.

The sun set; the dusk fell on the stream, and lights began to appear along the shore. The Chapman lighthouse, a three-legged thing erect on a mud-flat, shone strongly. Lights of ships moved in the fairway—a great stir of lights going up and going down. And farther west on the upper reaches the place of the monstrous town was still marked ominously on the sky, a brooding gloom in sunshine, a lurid glare under the stars.

"And this also," said Marlow suddenly, "has been one of the dark places on the earth."

He was the only man of us who still "followed the sea." The worst that could be said of him was that he did not represent his class. He was a seaman, but he was a wanderer, too, while most seamen lead, if one may so express it, a sedentary life. Their minds are of the stay-at-home order, and their home is always with them—the ship; and so is their country—the sea. One ship is very much like another, and the sea is always the same. In the immutability of their surroundings the foreign shores, the foreign faces, the changing immensity of life, glide past, veiled not by a sense of mystery but by a slightly disdainful ignorance; for there is nothing mysterious to a seaman unless it be the sea itself, which is the mistress of his existence and as inscrutable as Destiny. For the rest, after his hours of work, a casual stroll or a casual spree on shore suffices to unfold for him the secret of a whole continent, and generally he finds the secret not worth knowing. The yarns of seamen have a direct simplicity, the whole meaning of which lies within the shell of a cracked nut. But Marlow was not typical (if his propensity to spin yarns be excepted), and to him the meaning of an episode was not inside like a kernel but outside, enveloping the tale which brought it out only as a glow brings out a haze, in the likeness of one of these misty halos that sometimes are made visible by the spectral illumination of moonshine.

His remark did not seem at all surprising. It was just like Marlow. It was accepted in silence. No one took the trouble to grunt even; and presently he said, very slow—

"I was thinking of very old times, when the Romans first came here, nineteen hundred years ago—the other day. . . . Light came out of this river since—you say Knights? Yes; but it is like a running blaze on a plain, like a flash of lightning in the clouds. We live in the flicker—may it last as long as the old earth keeps rolling! But darkness was here yesterday. Imagine the feelings of a commander of a fine—what d'ye call 'em?— trireme[2] in the Mediterranean, ordered suddenly to the north; run overland across the Gauls in a hurry; put in charge of one of these craft the legionaries—a wonderful lot of handy men they must have been, too—used to build, apparently by the hundred, in a month or two, if we may believe what we read. Imagine him here—the very end of the world, a sea the colour of lead, a sky the colour of smoke, a kind of ship about as rigid as a concertina—and going up this river with stores, or orders, or what you like. Sand-banks, marshes, forests, savages,—precious little to eat fit for a civilized man, nothing but Thames water to drink. No Falernian wine[3] here, no going ashore. Here and there a military camp lost in a wilderness, like a needle in a bundle of hay—cold, fog, tempests, disease, exile, and death,—death skulking in the air, in the water, in the bush. They must have been dying like flies here. Oh, yes—he did it. Did it very well, too, no doubt, and without thinking much about it either, except afterwards to brag of what he had gone through in his time, perhaps. They were men enough to face the darkness. And perhaps he was cheered by keeping his eye on a chance of promotion to the fleet of Ravenna by and by, if he had good friends in Rome and survived the awful climate. Or think of a decent young citizen in a toga—perhaps too much dice, you know— coming out here in the train of some prefect, or tax-gatherer, or trader even, to mend his fortunes. Land in a swamp, march through the woods, and in some inland post feel the savagery, the utter savagery, had closed round him,—all that mysterious life of the wilderness that stirs in the forest, in the jungles, in the hearts of wild men. There's no initiation either into such mysteries. He has to live in the midst of the incomprehensible, which is also detestable. And it has a fascination, too, that goes to work upon him. The fascination of the abomination—you know, imagine

[2] Roman galley propelled by three tiers of oars.
[3] Wine celebrated among the Romans.

the growing regrets, the longing to escape, the powerless disgust, the surrender, the hate."

He paused.

"Mind," he began again, lifting one arm from the elbow, the palm of the hand outwards, so that, with his legs folded before him, he had the pose of a Buddha preaching in European clothes and without a lotus-flower—"Mind, none of us would feel exactly like this. What saves us is efficiency—the devotion to efficiency. But these chaps were not much account, really. There were no colonists; their administration was merely a squeeze, and nothing more, I suspect. They were conquerors, and for that you want only brute force—nothing to boast of, when you have it, since your strength is just an accident arising from the weakness of others. They grabbed what they could get for the sake of what was to be got. It was just robbery with violence, aggravated murder on a great scale, and men going at it blind—as is very proper for those who tackle a darkness. The conquest of the earth, which mostly means the taking it away from those who have a different complexion or slightly flatter noses than ourselves, is not a pretty thing when you look into it too much. What redeems it is the idea only. An idea at the back of it; not a sentimental pretence but an idea; and an unselfish belief in the idea—something you can set up, and bow down before, and offer a sacrifice to. . . ."

He broke off. Flames glided in the river, small green flames, red flames, white flames, pursuing, overtaking, joining, crossing each other—then separating slowly or hastily. The traffic of the great city went on in the deepening night upon the sleepless river. We looked on, waiting patiently—there was nothing else to do till the end of the flood; but it was only after a long silence, when he said, in a hesitating voice, "I suppose you fellows remember I did once turn fresh-water sailor for a bit," that we knew we were fated, before the ebb began to run, to hear about one of Marlow's inconclusive experiences.

"I don't want to bother you much with what happened to me personally," he began, showing in this remark the weakness of many tellers of tales who seem so often unaware of what their audience would best like to hear; "yet to understand the effect of it on me you ought to know how I got out there, what I saw, how I went up that river to the place where I first met the poor chap. It was the farthest point of navigation and the culminating point of my experience. It seemed somehow to throw a kind of light on everything about me—and into my thoughts. It was sombre enough, too—and pitiful—not extraordinary in any way—not very clear either. No, not very clear. And yet it seemed to throw a kind of light.

"I had then, as you remember, just returned to London after a lot of Indian Ocean, Pacific, China Seas—a regular dose of the East—six years or so, and I was loafing about, hindering you fellows in your work and invading your homes, just as though I had got a heavenly mission to civilize you. It was very fine for a time, but after a bit I did get tired of resting. Then I began to look for a ship—I should think the hardest work on earth. But the ships wouldn't even look at me. And I got tired of that game, too.

"Now when I was a little chap I had a passion for maps. I would look for hours at South America, or Africa, or Australia, and lose myself in all the glories of exploration. At that time there were many blank spaces on the earth, and when I saw one that looked particularly inviting on a map (but they all look that) I would put my finger on it and say, When I grow up I will go there. The North Pole was one of these places, I remember. Well, I haven't been there yet, and shall not try now. The glamour's off. Other places were scattered about the Equator, and in every sort of latitude all over the two hemispheres. I have been in some of them, and . . . well, we won't talk about that. But there was one[4] yet—the biggest, the most blank, so to speak—that I had a hankering after.

"True, by this time it was not a blank space any more. It had got filled since my boyhood with rivers and lakes and names. It had ceased to be a blank space of delightful mystery—a white patch for a boy to dream gloriously over. It had become a place of darkness. But there was in it one river especially, a mighty big river, that you could see on the map, resembling an immense snake uncoiled, with its head in the sea, its body at rest curving afar over a vast country, and its tail lost in the depths of the land. And as I looked at the map of it in a shop window, it fascinated me as a snake would a bird—a silly little bird. Then I remembered there was a big concern, a Company for trade on that river. Dash it all! I thought to myself, they can't trade without using some kind of craft on that lot of fresh water—steamboats! Why shouldn't I try to get charge of one? I went on along Fleet Street, but could not shake off the idea. The snake had charmed me.

"You understand it was a Continental concern, that Trading society; but I have a lot of relations living on the Continent, because it's cheap and not so nasty as it looks, they say.

"I am sorry to own I began to worry them. This was already a fresh departure for me. I was not used to get things that way, you know. I always went my own road and on my own legs where I had a mind to go. I wouldn't have believed it of myself; but, then—you see—I felt somehow I must get there by hook or by crook. So I worried them. The men said 'My dear fellow,' and did nothing. Then—would you believe it?—I tried the women. I, Charlie Marlow, set the women to work—to get a job. Heavens! Well, you see, the notion drove me. I had an aunt, a dear enthusiastic soul. She wrote: 'It will be delightful. I am ready to do anything, anything for you. It is a glorious idea. I know the wife of a very high personage in the Administration, and also a man who has lots of influence with,' etc., etc. She was determined to make no end of fuss to get me appointed skipper of a river steamboat, if such was my fancy.

"I got my appointment—of course; and I got it very quick. It appears the Company had received news that one of their captains had been killed in a scuffle with the natives. This was my chance, and it made me the more anxious to go. It was only months and months afterwards, when I made the attempt to recover what was left of the body, that I heard the original quarrel arose from a misunderstanding about some hens. Yes, two black hens. Fresleven—that was the fellow's name, a Dane—thought himself wronged somehow in the bargain, so he went ashore and started to

[4] The Congo Free State (now Zaire); at the time the personal domain of Leopold II, King of Belgium; it was centered on the Congo River basin.

hammer the chief of the village with a stick. Oh, it didn't surprise me in
the least to hear this, and at the same time to be told that Fresleven was
the gentlest, quietest creature that ever walked on two legs. No doubt
he was; but he had been a couple of years already out there engaged in
the noble cause, you know, and he probably felt the need at last of asserting
his self-respect in some way. Therefore he whacked the old nigger merci-
lessly, while a big crowd of his people watched him, thunderstruck, till
some man—I was told the chief's son—in desperation at hearing the old
chap yell, made a tentative jab with a spear at the white man—and of
course it went quite easy between the shoulderblades. Then the whole
population cleared into the forest, expecting all kinds of calamities to happen, while, on the other hand, the steamer Fresleven commanded left also
in a bad panic, in charge of the engineer, I believe. Afterwards nobody
seemed to trouble much about Fresleven's remains, till I got out and stepped
into his shoes. I couldn't let it rest, though; but when an opportunity
offered at last to meet my predecessor, the grass growing through his ribs
was tall enough to hide his bones. They were all there. The supernatural
being had not been touched after he fell. And the village was deserted,
the huts gaped black, rotting, all askew within the fallen enclosures. A
calamity had come to it, sure enough. The people had vanished. Mad terror
had scattered them, men, women, and children, through the bush, and
they had never returned. What became of the hens I don't know either.
I should think the cause of progress got them, anyhow. However, through
this glorious affair I got my appointment, before I had fairly begun to
hope for it.

"I flew around like mad to get ready, and before forty-eight hours I
was crossing the Channel to show myself to my employers, and sign the
contract. In a very few hours I arrived in a city[5] that always makes me
think of a whited sepulchre. Prejudice no doubt. I had no difficulty in
finding the Company's offices. It was the biggest thing in the town, and
everybody I met was full of it. They were going to run an over-sea empire,
and make no end of coin by trade.

"A narrow and deserted street in deep shadow, high houses, innumerable
windows with venetian blinds, a dead silence, grass sprouting between
the stones, imposing carriage archways right and left, immense double
doors standing ponderously ajar. I slipped through one of these cracks,
went up a swept and ungarnished staircase, as arid as a desert, and opened
the first door I came to. Two women, one fat and the other slim, sat on
straw-bottomed chairs, knitting black wool. The slim one got up and walked
straight at me—still knitting with down-cast eyes—and only just as I began
to think of getting out of her way, as you would for a somnambulist,
stood still, and looked up. Her dress was as plain as an umbrella-cover,
and she turned round without a word and preceded me into a waiting-
room. I gave my name, and looked about. Deal table in the middle, plain
chairs all round the walls, on one end a large shining map, marked with
all the colours of a rainbow.[6] There was a vast amount of red—good to

[5] Brussels.

[6] The colors indicate the countries controlling each colony or area: red for British, blue
for French, green for Italian, orange for Portuguese, purple for German, yellow for Belgian.

see at any time, because one knows that some real work is done in there, a deuce of a lot of blue, a little green, smears of orange, and, on the East Coast, a purple patch, to show where the jolly pioneers of progress drink the jolly lager-beer. However, I wasn't going into any of these. I was going into the yellow. Dead in the centre. And the river was there—fascinating—deadly—like a snake. Ough! A door opened, a white-haired secretarial head, but wearing a compassionate expression, appeared, and a skinny forefinger beckoned me into the sanctuary. Its light was dim, and a heavy writing-desk squatted in the middle. From behind that structure came out an impression of pale plumpness in a frock-coat. The great man himself. He was five feet six, I should judge, and had his grip on the handle-end of ever so many millions. He shook hands, I fancy, murmured vaguely, was satisfied with my French. *Bon voyage.*

"In about forty-five seconds I found myself again in the waiting-room with the compassionate secretary, who, full of desolation and sympathy, made me sign some document. I believe I undertook amongst other things not to disclose any trade secrets. Well, I am not going to.

"I began to feel slightly uneasy. You know I am not used to such ceremonies, and there was something ominous in the atmosphere. It was just as though I had been let into some conspiracy—I don't know—something not quite right; and I was glad to get out. In the outer room the two women knitted black wool feverishly. People were arriving, and the younger one was walking back and forth introducing them. The old one sat on her chair. Her flat cloth slippers were propped up on a foot-warmer, and a cat reposed on her lap. She wore a starched white affair on her head, had a wart on one cheek, and silver-rimmed spectacles hung on the tip of her nose. She glanced at me above the glasses. The swift and indifferent placidity of that look troubled me. Two youths with foolish and cheery countenances were being piloted over, and she threw at them the same quick glance of unconcerned wisdom. She seemed to know all about them and about me, too. An eerie feeling came over me. She seemed uncanny and fateful. Often far away there I thought of these two, guarding the door of Darkness, knitting black wool as for a warm pall, one introducing, introducing continuously to the unknown, the other scrutinizing the cheery and foolish faces with unconcerned old eyes. *Ave!* Old knitter of black wool. *Morituri te salutant.* [7] Not many of those she looked at ever saw her again—not half, by a long way.

"There was yet a visit to the doctor. 'A simple formality,' assured me the secretary, with an air of taking an immense part in all my sorrows. Accordingly a young chap wearing his hat over the left eyebrow, some clerk I suppose,—there must have been clerks in the business, though the house was as still as a house in a city of the dead—came from somewhere up-stairs, and led me forth. He was shabby and careless, with inkstains on the sleeves of his jacket, and his cravat was large and billowy, under a chin shaped like the toe of an old boot. It was a little too early for the doctor, so I proposed a drink, and thereupon he developed a vein of joviality. As we sat over our vermouths he glorified the Company's business, and

---

[7] "Hail! Those who are about to die salute you."—the Roman gladiators supposedly greeted Caesar in this way.

by and by I expressed casually my surprise at him not going out there. He became very cool and collected all at once. 'I am not such a fool as I look, quoth Plato to his disciples,' he said sententiously, emptied his glass with great resolution, and we rose.

"The old doctor felt my pulse, evidently thinking of something else the while. 'Good, good for there,' he mumbled, and then with a certain eagerness asked me whether I would let him measure my head. Rather surprised, I said Yes, when he produced a thing like calipers and got the dimensions back and front and every way, taking notes carefully. He was an unshaven little man in a threadbare coat like a gaberdine, with his feet in slippers, and I thought him a harmless fool. 'I always ask leave, in the interests of science, to measure the crania of those going out there,' he said. 'And when they come back, too?' I asked. 'Oh, I never see them,' he remarked; 'and, moreover, the changes take place inside, you know.' He smiled, as if at some quiet joke. 'So you are going out there. Famous. Interesting, too.' He gave me a searching glance, and made another note. 'Ever any madness in your family?' he asked, in a matter-of-fact tone. I felt very annoyed. 'Is that question in the interest of science, too?' 'It would be,' he said, without taking notice of my irritation, 'interesting for science to watch the mental changes of individuals, on the spot, but . . .' 'Are you an alienist?'[8] I interrupted. 'Every doctor should be—a little,' answered that original, imperturbably. 'I have a little theory which you Messieurs who go out there must help me to prove. This is my share in the advantages my country shall reap from the possession of such a magnificent dependency. The mere wealth I leave to others. Pardon my questions but you are the first Englishman coming under my observation . . .' I hastened to assure him I was not in the least typical. 'If I were,' said I, 'I wouldn't be talking like this with you.' 'What you say is rather profound, and probably erroneous,' he said, with a laugh. 'Avoid irritation more than exposure to the sun. Adieu. How do you English say, eh? Goodbye. Ah! Good-bye. Adieu. In the tropics one must before everything keep calm.' . . . He lifted a warning forefinger. . . . *'Du calme, du calme. Adieu.'*

"One thing more remained to do—say good-bye to my excellent aunt. I found her triumphant. I had a cup of tea—the last decent cup of tea for many days—and in a room that most soothingly looked just as you would expect a lady's drawing room to look, we had a long quiet chat by the fireside. In the course of these confidences it became quite plain to me I had been represented to the wife of the high dignitary, and goodness knows to how many more people besides, as an exceptional and gifted creature—a piece of good fortune for the Company—a man you don't get hold of every day. Good heavens! and I was going to take charge of a two-penny-half-penny river-steamboat with a penny whistle attached! It appeared, however, I was also one of the Workers, with a capital— you know. Something like an emissary of light, something like a lower sort of apostle. There had been a lot of such rot let loose in print and talk just about that time, and the excellent woman, living right in the rush of all that humbug, got carried off her feet. She talked about 'weaning

----

[8] Doctor who treats mental disorders.

those ignorant millions from their horrid ways,' till, upon my word, she made me quite uncomfortable. I ventured to hint that the Company was run for profit.

" 'You forget, dear Charlie, that the labourer is worthy of his hire,' she said, brightly. It's queer how out of touch with truth women are. They live in a world of their own, and there has never been anything like it, and never can be. It is too beautiful altogether, and if they were to set it up it would go to pieces before the first sunset. Some confounded fact we men have been living contentedly with ever since the day of creation would start up and knock the whole thing over.

"After this I got embraced, told to wear flannel, be sure to write often, and so on—and I left. In the street—I don't know why—a queer feeling came to me that I was an imposter. Odd thing that I, who used to clear out for any part of the world at twenty-four hours' notice, with less thought than most men give to the crossing of a street, had a moment—I won't say of hesitation, but of startled pause, before this commonplace affair. The best way I can explain it to you is by saying that, for a second or two, I felt as though, instead of going to the centre of a continent, I were about to set off for the centre of the earth.

"I left in a French steamer, and she called in every blamed port they have out there, for, as far as I could see, the sole purpose of landing soldiers and custom-house officers. I watched the coast. Watching a coast as it slips by the ship is like thinking about an enigma. There it is before you—smiling, frowning, inviting, grand, mean, insipid, or savage, and always mute with an air of whispering, Come and find out. This one was almost featureless, as if still in the making, with an aspect of monotonous grimness. The edge of a colossal jungle, so dark-green as to be almost black, fringed with surf, ran straight, like a ruled line, far, far away along a blue sea whose glitter was blurred by a creeping mist. The sun was fierce, the land seemed to glisten and drip with steam. Here and there grayish-whitish specks showed up clustered inside the white surf, with a flag flying above them perhaps. Settlements some centuries old, and still no bigger than pinheads on the untouched expanse of their background. We pounded along, stopped, landed soldiers; went on, landed custom-house clerks to levy toll in what looked like a God-forsaken wilderness, with a tin shed and a flagpole lost in it; landed more soldiers—to take care of the custom-house clerks, presumably. Some, I heard, got drowned in the surf; but whether they did or not, nobody seemed particularly to care. They were just flung out there, and on they went. Every day the coasts looked the same, as though we had not moved; but we passed various places—trading places—with names like Gran' Bassan, Little Popo; names that seemed to belong to some sordid farce acted in front of a sinister back-cloth. The idleness of a passenger, my isolation amongst all these men with whom I had no point of contact, the oily and languid sea, the uniform sombreness of the coast, seemed to keep me away from the truth of things, within the toil of a mournful and senseless delusion. The voice of the surf heard now and then was a positive pleasure, like the speech of a brother. It was something natural, that had its reason, that had a meaning. Now and then a boat from the shore gave one a momentary contact with reality. It was paddled by black fellows. You could see from afar the white of their eyeballs glistening. They shouted, sang; their bodies streamed with perspiration; they had faces like grotesque masks—these chaps; but they had bone, muscle, a wild vitality, an intense energy of movement, that was as natural and true as the surf along their coast. They wanted no excuse for being there. They were a great comfort to look at. For a time I would feel I belonged still to a world of straightforward facts; but the feeling would not last long. Something would turn up to scare it away. Once, I remember, we came upon a man-of-war anchored off the coast. There wasn't even a shed there, and she was shelling the bush. It appears the French had one of their wars going on thereabouts. Her ensign dropped limp like a rag; the muzzles of the long six-inch guns stuck out all over the low hull; the greasy, slimy swell swung her up lazily and let her down, swaying her thin masts. In the empty immensity of earth, sky, and water, there she was, incomprehensible, firing into a continent. Pop, would go one of the six-inch guns; a small flame would dart and vanish, a little white smoke would disappear, a tiny projectile would give a feeble screech—and nothing happened. Nothing could happen. There was a touch of insanity in the proceeding, a sense of lugubrious drollery in the sight; and it was not dissipated by somebody on board assuring me earnestly there was a camp of natives—he called them enemies!—hidden out of sight somewhere.

"We gave her her letters (I heard the men in that lonely ship were dying of fever at the rate of three a day) and went on. We called at some more places with farcical names, where the merry dance of death and trade goes on in a still and earthy atmosphere as of an overheated catacomb; all along the formless coast bordered by dangerous surf, as if Nature herself had tried to ward off intruders; in and out of rivers, streams of death in life, whose banks were rotting into mud, whose waters, thickened into slime, invaded the contorted mangroves, that seemed to writhe at us in the extremity of an impotent despair. Nowhere did we stop long enough to get a particularized impression, but the general sense of vague and oppressive wonder grew upon me. It was like a weary pilgrimage amongst hints for nightmares.

"It was upward of thirty days before I saw the mouth of the big river. We anchored off the seat of the government.[9] But my work would not begin till some two hundred miles farther on. So as soon as I could I made a start for a place thirty miles higher up.

"I had my passage on a little sea-going steamer. Her captain was a Swede, and knowing me for a seaman, invited me on the bridge. He was a young man, lean, fair, and morose, with lanky hair and a shuffling gait. As we left the miserable little wharf, he tossed his head contemptuously at the shore. 'Been living there?' he asked. I said, 'Yes,' 'Fine lot these government chaps—are they not?' he went on, speaking English with great precision and considerable bitterness. 'It is funny what some people will do for a few francs a month. I wonder what becomes of that kind when it goes up country?' I said to him I expected to see that soon. 'So-o-o!' he exclaimed. He shuffled athwart, keeping one eye ahead vigilantly. 'Don't be too sure,' he continued. 'The other day I took up a man who hanged himself on

[9] Boma, in the mouth of the Congo River.

the road. He was a Swede, too.' 'Hanged himself! Why, in God's name?'
I cried. He kept on looking out watchfully. 'Who knows? The sun too
much for him, or the country perhaps.'

"At last we opened a reach.[10] A rocky cliff appeared, mounds of turned-
up earth by the shore, houses on a hill, others with iron roofs, amongst
a waste of excavations, or hanging to the declivity.[11] A continuous noise
of the rapids above hovered over this scene of inhabited devastation. A
lot of people, mostly black and naked, moved about like ants. A jetty projected into the river. A blinding sunlight drowned all this at times in a
sudden recrudescence of glare. 'There's your Company's station,' said the
Swede, pointing to three wooden barrack-like structures on the rocky slope.
'I will send your things up. Four boxes did you say? So. Farewell.'

"I came upon a boiler wallowing in the grass, then found a path leading
up the hill. It turned aside for the boulders, and also for an undersized
railway-truck lying there on its back with its wheels in the air. One was
off. The thing looked as dead as the carcass of some animal. I came upon
more pieces of decaying machinery, a stack of rusty rails. To the left a
clump of trees made a shady spot, where dark things seemed to stir feebly.
I blinked, the path was steep. A horn tooted to the right, and I saw the
black people run. A heavy and dull detonation shook the ground, a puff
of smoke came out of the cliff and that was all. No change appeared on
the face of the rock. They were building a railway. The cliff was not in
the way or anything; but the objectless blasting was all the work going
on.

"A slight clinking behind me made me turn my head. Six black men
advanced in a file, toiling up the path. They walked erect and slow, balancing small baskets full of earth on their heads, and the clink kept time
with their footsteps. Black rags were wound round their loins, and the
short ends behind waggled to and fro like tails. I could see every rib, the
joints of their limbs were like knots in a rope; each had an iron collar
on his neck, and all were connected together with a chain whose bights[12]
swung between them, rhythmically clinking. Another report from the cliff
made me think suddenly of that ship of war I had seen firing into a continent. It was the same kind of ominous voice; but these men could by no
stretch of imagination be called enemies. They were called criminals, and
the outraged law, like the bursting shells, had come to them, an insoluble
mystery from the sea. All their meagre breasts panted together, the violently
dilated nostrils quivered, the eyes stared stonily up-hill. They passed me
within six inches, without a glance, with that complete, deathlike indifference of unhappy savages. Behind this raw matter one of the reclaimed,
the product of the new forces at work, strolled despondently, carrying a
rifle by its middle. He had a uniform jacket with one button off, and
seeing a white man on the path, hoisted his weapon to his shoulder with
alacrity. This was simple prudence, white men being so much alike at a
distance that he could not tell who I might be. He was speedily reassured,
and with a large, white, rascally grin, and a glance at his charge, seemed

---

[10] Came to a clear stretch in the river.
[11] Town of Matadi.
[12] Loops.

to take me into partnership in his exalted trust. After all, I also was a part of the great cause of these high and just proceedings.

"Instead of going up, I turned and descended to the left. My idea was to let that chain-gang get out of sight before I climbed the hill. You know I am not particularly tender; I've had to strike and to fend off. I've had to resist and to attack sometimes—that's only one way of resisting—without counting the exact cost, according to the demands of such sort of life as I had blundered into. I've seen the devil of violence, and the devil of greed, and the devil of hot desire; but, by all the stars! these were strong, lusty, red-eyed devils, that swayed and drove men—men, I tell you. But as I stood on this hillside, I foresaw that in the blinding sunshine of that land I would become acquainted with a flabby, pretending, weak-eyed devil of a rapacious and pitiless folly. How insidious he could be, too, I was only to find out several months later and a thousand miles farther. For a moment I stood appalled, as though by a warning. Finally I descended the hill, obliquely, towards the trees I had seen.

"I avoided a vast artificial hole somebody had been digging on the slope, the purpose of which I found it impossible to divine. It wasn't a quarry or a sandpit, anyhow. It was just a hole. It might have been connected with the philanthropic desire of giving the criminals something to do. I don't know. Then I nearly fell into a very narrow ravine, almost no more than a scar in the hillside. I discovered that a lot of imported drainage-pipes for the settlement had been tumbled in there. There wasn't one that was not broken. It was a wanton smash-up. At last I got under the trees. My purpose was to stroll into the shade for a moment; but no sooner within than it seemed to me I had stepped into the gloomy circle of some Inferno. The rapids were near, and an uninterrupted, uniform, headlong, rushing noise filled the mournful stillness of the grove, where not a breath stirred, not a leaf moved, with a mysterious sound—as though the tearing pace of the launched earth had suddenly become audible.

"Black shapes crouched, lay, sat between the trees leaning against the trunks, clinging to the earth, half coming out, half effaced within the dim light, in all the attitudes of pain, abandonment, and despair. Another mine on the cliff went off, followed by a slight shudder of the soil under my feet. The work was going on. The work! And this was the place where some of the helpers had withdrawn to die.

"They were dying slowly—it was very clear. They were not enemies, they were not criminals, they were nothing earthly now,—nothing but black shadows of disease and starvation, lying confusedly in the greenish gloom. Brought from all the recesses of the coast in all the legality of time contracts, lost in uncongenial surroundings, fed on unfamiliar food, they sickened, became inefficient, and were then allowed to crawl away and rest. These moribund shapes were free as air—and nearly as thin. I began to distinguish the gleam of the eyes under the trees. Then, glancing down, I saw a face near my hand. The black bones reclined at full length with one shoulder against the tree, and slowly the eyelids rose and the sunken eyes looked up at me, enormous and vacant, a kind of blind, white flicker in the depths of the orbs, which died out slowly. The man seemed young—almost a boy—but you know with them it's hard to tell. I found nothing else to do but to offer him one of my good Swede's ship's biscuits

I had in my pocket. The fingers closed slowly on it and held—there was no other movement and no other glance. He had tied a bit of white worsted round his neck—Why? Where did he get it? Was it a badge—an ornament— a charm—a propitiatory act? Was there any idea at all connected with it? It looked startling round his black neck, this bit of white thread from beyond the seas.

"Near the same tree two more bundles of acute angles sat with their legs drawn up. One, with his chin propped on his knees, stared at nothing, in an intolerable and appalling manner: his brother phantom rested its forehead, as if overcome with a great weariness; and all about others were scattered in every pose of contorted collapse, as in some picture of a massacre or a pestilence. While I stood horror-struck, one of those creatures rose to his hands and knees, and went off on all-fours towards the river to drink. He lapped out of his hand, then sat up in the sunlight, crossing his shins in front of him, and after a time let his woolly head fall on his breastbone.

"I didn't want any more loitering in the shade, and I made haste towards the station. When near the buildings I met a white man, in such an unexpected elegance of get-up that in the first moment I took him for a sort of vision. I saw a high starched collar, white cuffs, a light alpaca jacket, snowy trousers, a clean necktie, and varnished boots. No hat. Hair parted, brushed, oiled, under a green-lined parasol held in a big white hand. He was amazing, and had a pen-holder behind his ear.

"I shook hands with this miracle, and I learned he was the Company's chief accountant, and that all the book-keeping was done at this station. He had come out for a moment, he said, 'to get a breath of fresh air.' The expression sounded wonderfully odd, with its suggestion of sedentary desk-life. I wouldn't have mentioned the fellow to you at all, only it was from his lips that I first heard the name of the man who is so indissolubly connected with the memories of that time. Moreover, I respected the fellow. Yes; I respected his collars, his vast cuffs, his brushed hair. His appearance was certainly that of a hairdresser's dummy; but in the great demoralization of the land he kept up his appearance. That's backbone. His starched collars and got-up shirt-fronts were achievements of character. He had been out nearly three years; and, later, I could not help asking him how he managed to sport such linen. He had just the faintest blush, and said modestly, 'I've been teaching one of the native women about the station. It was difficult. She had a distaste for the work.' Thus this man had verily accomplished something. And he was devoted to his books, which were in apple-pie order.

"Everything else in the station was in a muddle,—heads, things, buildings. Strings of dusty niggers with splay feet arrived and departed; a stream of manufactured goods, rubbishy cottons, beads, and brass-wire sent into the depths of darkness, and in return came a precious trickle of ivory.

"I had to wait in the station for ten days—an eternity. I lived in a hut in the yard, but to be out of the chaos I would sometimes get into the accountant's office. It was built of horizontal planks, and so badly put together that, as he bent over his high desk, he was barred from neck to heels with narrow strips of sunlight. There was no need to open the big shutter to see. It was hot there, too; big flies buzzed fiendishly, and did not sting, but stabbed. I sat generally on the floor, while, of faultless appearance (and even slightly scented), perching on a high stool, he wrote, he wrote. Sometimes he stood up for exercise. When a truckle-bed with a sick man (some invalid agent from up-country) was put in there, he exhibited a gentle annoyance. 'The groans of this sick person,' he said, 'distract my attention. And without that it is extremely difficult to guard against clerical errors in this climate.'

"One day he remarked, without lifting his head, 'In the interior you will no doubt meet Mr. Kurtz.' On my asking who Mr. Kurtz was, he said he was a first-class agent; and seeing my disappointment at this information, he added slowly, laying down his pen, 'He is a very remarkable person.' Further questions elicited from him that Mr. Kurtz was at present in charge of a trading post, a very important one, in the true ivory-country, at 'the very bottom of there. Sends in as much ivory as all the others put together. . . .' He began to write again. The sick man was too ill to groan. The flies buzzed in a great peace.

"Suddenly there was a growing murmur of voices and a great tramping of feet. A caravan had come in. A violent babble of uncouth sounds burst out on the other side of the planks. All the carriers were speaking together, and in the midst of the uproar the lamentable voice of the chief agent was heard 'giving it up' tearfully for the twentieth time that day. . . . He rose slowly. 'What a frightful row,' he said. He crossed the room gently to look at the sick man, and returning, said to me. 'He does not hear.' 'What! Dead?' I asked, startled. 'No, not yet,' he answered, with great composure. Then, alluding with a toss of the head to the tumult in the station-yard, 'When one has got to make correct entries, one comes to hate those savages—hate them to the death.' He remained thoughtful for a moment. 'When you see Mr. Kurtz,' he went on, 'tell him from me that everything here'—he glanced at the desk—'is very satisfactory. I don't like to write to him—with those messengers of ours you never know who may get hold of your letter—at that Central Station.' He stared at me for a moment with his mild, bulging eyes. 'Oh, he will go far, very far,' he began again. 'He will be a somebody in the Administration before long. They, above—the Council in Europe, you know—mean him to be.'

"He turned to his work. The noise outside had ceased, and presently in going out I stopped at the door. In the steady buzz of flies the homeward-bound agent was lying flushed and insensible; the other, bent over his books, was making correct entries of perfectly correct transactions; and fifty feet below the doorstep I could see the still tree-tops of the grove of death.

"Next day I left that station at last, with a caravan of sixty men, for a two-hundred-mile tramp.

"No use telling you much about that. Paths, paths, everywhere; a stamped-in network of paths spreading over the empty land, through long grass, through burnt grass, through thickets, down and up chilly ravines, up and down stony hills ablaze with heat; and a solitude, a solitude, nobody, not a hut. The population had cleared out a long time ago. Well, if a lot of mysterious niggers armed with all kinds of fearful weapons suddenly took to traveling on the road between Deal and Gravesend,[13] catching

---

[13] English coastal towns.

the yokels right and left to carry heavy loads for them, I fancy every farm and cottage thereabouts would get empty very soon. Only here the dwellings were gone, too. Still I passed through several abandoned villages. There's something pathetically childish in the ruins of grass walls. Day after day, with the stamp and shuffle of sixty pair of bare feet behind me, each pair under a 60-lb. load. Camp, cook, sleep, strike camp, march. Now and then a carrier dead in harness, at rest in the long grass near the path, with an empty water-gourd and his long staff lying by his side. A great silence around and above. Perhaps on some quiet night the tremor of far-off drums, sinking, swelling, a tremor vast, faint; a sound weird, appealing, suggestive, and wild—and perhaps with as profound a meaning as the sound of bells in a Christian country. Once a white man in an unbuttoned uniform, camping on the path with an armed escort of lank Zanzibaris,[14] very hospitable and festive—not to say drunk. Was looking after the upkeep of the road, he declared. Can't say I saw any road or any upkeep, unless the body of a middle-aged negro, with a bullet-hole in the forehead, upon which I absolutely stumbled three miles farther on, may be considered as a permanent improvement. I had a white companion, too, not a bad chap, but rather too fleshy and with the exasperating habit of fainting on the hot hillsides, miles away from the least bit of shade and water. Annoying, you know, to hold your own coat like a parasol over a man's head while he is coming-to. I couldn't help asking him once what he meant by coming there at all. 'To make money, of course. What do you think?' he said, scornfully. Then he got fever, and had to be carried in a hammock slung under a pole. As he weighed sixteen stone[15] I had no end of rows with the carriers. They jibbed, ran away, sneaked off with their loads in the night—quite a mutiny. So, one evening, I made a speech in English with gestures, not one of which was lost to the sixty pairs of eyes before me, and the next morning I started the hammock off in front all right. An hour afterwards I came upon the whole concern wrecked in a bush—man, hammock, groans, blankets, horrors. The heavy pole had skinned his poor nose. He was very anxious for me to kill somebody, but there wasn't the shadow of a carrier near. I remembered the old doctor—'It would be interesting for science to watch the mental changes of individuals, on the spot.' I felt I was becoming scientifically interesting. However, all that is to no purpose. On the fifteenth day I came in sight of the big river again, and hobbled into the Central Station. It was on a back water surrounded by scrub and forest, with a pretty border of smelly mud on one side, and on the three others enclosed by a crazy fence of rushes. A neglected gap was all the gate it had, and the first glance at the place was enough to let you see the flabby devil was running that show. White men with long staves in their hands appeared languidly from amongst the buildings, strolling up to take a look at me, and then retired out of sight somewhere. One of them, a stout, excitable chap with black moustaches, informed me with great volubility and many digressions, as soon as I told him who I was, that my steamer was at the bottom of the

[14] Mercenaries from Zanzibar, an island off the east coast of Africa.
[15] 224 pounds (a stone, a British unit of weight, equals 14 pounds).

river. I was thunderstruck. What, how, why? Oh, it was 'all right.' The 'manager himself' was there. All quite correct. 'Everybody had behaved splendidly! splendidly!'—'You must,' he said in agitation, 'go and see the general manager at once. He is waiting!'

"I did not see the real significance of that wreck at once. I fancy I see it now, but I am not sure—not at all. Certainly the affair was too stupid—when I think of it—to be altogether natural. Still . . . But at the moment it presented itself simply as a confounded nuisance. The steamer was sunk. They had started two days before in a sudden hurry up the river with the manager on board, in charge of some volunteer skipper, and before they had been out three hours they tore the bottom out of her on stones, and she sank near the south bank. I asked myself what I was to do there, now my boat was lost. As a matter of fact, I had plenty to do in fishing my command out of the river. I had to set about it the very next day. That, and the repairs when I brought the pieces to the station, took some months.

"My first interview with the manager was curious. He did not ask me to sit down after my twenty-mile walk that morning. He was commonplace in complexion, in feature, in manners, and in voice. He was of middle size and of ordinary build. His eyes, of the usual blue, were perhaps remarkably cold, and he certainly could make his glance fall on one as trenchant and heavy as an axe. But even at these times the rest of his person seemed to disclaim the intention. Otherwise there was only an indefinable, faint expression of his lips, something stealthy—a smile—not a smile—I remember it, but I can't explain. It was unconscious, this smile was, though just after he had said something it got intensified for an instant. It came at the end of his speeches like a seal applied on the words to make the meaning of the commonest phrase appear absolutely inscrutable. He was a common trader, from his youth up employed in these parts—nothing more. He was obeyed, yet he inspired neither love nor fear, nor even respect. He inspired uneasiness. That was it! Uneasiness. Not a definite mistrust—just uneasiness—nothing more. You have no idea how effective such a . . . a . . . faculty can be. He had no genius for organizing, for initiative, or for order even. That was evident in such things as the deplorable state of the station. He had no learning, and no intelligence. His position had come to him—why? Perhaps because he was never ill . . . He had served three terms of three years out there . . . Because triumphant health in the general rout of constitutions is a kind of power in itself. When he went home on leave he rioted on a large scale—pompously. Jack ashore[16] —with a difference—in externals only. This one could gather from his casual talk. He originated nothing, he could keep the routine going—that's all. But he was great. He was great by this little thing that it was impossible to tell what could control such a man. He never gave that secret away. Perhaps there was nothing within him. Such a suspicion made one pause—for out there there were no external checks. Once when various tropical diseases had laid low almost every 'agent' in the station, he was heard to say, 'Men who come out here should have no entrails.' He sealed the utterance with that smile of his, as though it had been a door opening

---

[16] A sailor on shore leave.

into a darkness he had in his keeping. You fancied you had seen things—but the seal was on. When annoyed at mealtimes by the constant quarrels of the white men about precedence, he ordered an immense round table to be made, for which a special house had to be built. This was the station's mess-room. Where he sat was the first place—the rest was nowhere. One felt this to be his unalterable conviction. He was neither civil nor uncivil. He was quiet. He allowed his 'boy'—an overfed young negro from the coast—to treat the white men, under his very eyes, with provoking insolence.

"He began to speak as soon as he saw me. I had been very long on the road. He could not wait. Had to start without me. The up-river stations had to be relieved. There had been so many delays already that he did not know who was dead and who was alive, and how they got on—and so on, and so on. He paid no attention to my explanations, and, playing with a stick of sealing-wax, repeated several times that the situation was 'very grave, very grave.' There were rumours that a very important station was in jeopardy, and its chief, Mr. Kurtz, was ill. Hoped it was not true. Mr. Kurtz was . . . I felt weary and irritable. Hang Kurtz, I thought. I interrupted him by saying I had heard of Mr. Kurtz on the coast. 'Ah! So they talk of him down there,' he murmured to himself. Then he began again, assuring me Mr. Kurtz was the best agent he had, an exceptional man, of the greatest importance to the Company; therefore I could understand his anxiety. He was, he said, 'very, very uneasy.' Certainly he fidgeted on his chair a good deal, exclaimed, 'Ah, Mr. Kurtz!' broke the stick of sealing-wax and seemed dumfounded by the accident. Next thing he wanted to know 'how long it would take to' . . . I interrupted him again. Being hungry, you know, and kept on my feet too, I was getting savage. 'How can I tell?' I said. 'I haven't even seen the wreck yet—some months, no doubt.' All this talk seemed to me so futile. 'Some months,' he said. 'Well, let us say three months before we can make a start. Yes. That ought to do the affair.' I flung out of his hut (he lived all alone in a clay hut with a sort of verandah) muttering to myself my opinion of him. He was a chattering idiot. Afterwards I took it back when it was borne in upon me startlingly with what extreme nicety he had estimated the time requisite for the 'affair.'

"I went to work the next day, turning, so to speak, my back on that station. In that way only it seemed to me I could keep my hold on the redeeming facts of life. Still, one must look about sometimes; and then I saw this station, these men strolling aimlessly about in the sunshine of the yard. I asked myself sometimes what it all meant. They wandered here and there with their absurd long staves in their hands, like a lot of faithless pilgrims bewitched inside a rotten fence. The word 'ivory' rang in the air, was whispered, was sighed. You would think they were praying to it. A taint of imbecile rapacity blew through it all, like a whiff from some corpse. By Jove! I've never seen anything so unreal in my life. And outside, the silent wilderness surrounding this cleared speck on the earth struck me as something great and invincible, like evil or truth, waiting patiently for the passing away of this fantastic invasion.

"Oh, these months! Well, never mind. Various things happened. One evening a grass shed full of calico, cotton prints, beads, and I don't know

what else, burst into a blaze so suddenly that you would have thought
the earth had opened to let an avenging fire consume all that trash. I
was smoking my pipe quietly by my dismantled steamer, and saw them
all cutting capers in the light, with their arms lifted high, when the stout
man with moustaches came tearing down to the river, a tin pail in his
hand, assured me that everybody was 'behaving splendidly, splendidly,'
dipped about a quart of water and tore back again. I noticed there was a
hole in the bottom of his pail.

"I strolled up. There was no hurry. You see the thing had gone off
like a box of matches. It had been hopeless from the very first. The flame
had leaped high, driven everybody back, lighted up everything—and collapsed. The shed was already a heap of embers glowing fiercely. A nigger
was being beaten near by. They said he had caused the fire in some way;
be that as it may, he was screeching most horribly. I saw him, later, for
several days, sitting in a bit of shade looking very sick and trying to recover
himself: afterwards he arose and went out—and the wilderness without
a sound took him into its bosom again. As I approached the glow from
the dark I found myself at the back of two men, talking. I heard the name
of Kurtz pronounced, then the words, 'take advantage of this unfortunate
accident.' One of the men was the manager. I wished him a good evening.
'Did you ever see anything like it—eh? it is incredible,' he said, and walked
off. The other man remained. He was a first-class agent, young, gentle-
manly, a bit reserved, with a forked little beard and a hooked nose. He
was stand-offish with the other agents, and they on their side said he was
the manager's spy upon them. As to me, I had hardly ever spoken to
him before. We got into talk, and by and by we strolled away from the
hissing ruins. Then he asked me to his room, which was in the main
building of the station. He struck a match, and I perceived that this young
aristocrat had not only a silver-mounted dressing-case but also a whole
candle all to himself. Just at that time the manager was the only man
supposed to have any right to candles. Native mats covered the clay walls;
a collection of spears, assegais,[17] shields, knives was hung up in trophies.
The business intrusted to this fellow was the making of bricks—so I had
been informed; but there wasn't a fragment of a brick anywhere in the
station, and he had been there more than a year—waiting. It seems he
could not make bricks without something, I don't know what—straw
maybe. Anyways, it could not be found there, and as it was not likely to
be sent from Europe, it did not appear clear to me what he was waiting
for. An act of special creation perhaps. However, they were all waiting—
all the sixteen or twenty pilgrims of them—for something; and upon my
word it did not seem an uncongenial occupation, from the way they took
it, though the only thing that ever came to them was disease—as far as I
could see. They beguiled the time by backbiting and intriguing against
each other in a foolish kind of way. There was an air of plotting about
that station, but nothing came of it, of course. It was as unreal as everything
else—as the philanthropic pretence of the whole concern, as their talk,
as their government, as their show of work. The only real feeling was a
desire to get appointed to a trading-post where ivory was to be had, so

[17] Slender javelins.

that they could earn percentages. They intrigued and slandered and hated each other only on that account,—but as to effectually lifting a little finger—oh, no. By heavens! there is something after all in the world allowing one man to steal a horse while another must not look at a halter. Steal a horse straight out. Very well. He had done it. Perhaps he can ride. But there is a way of looking at a halter that would provoke the most charitable of saints into a kick.

"I had no idea why he wanted to be sociable, but as we chatted in there it suddenly occurred to me the fellow was trying to get at something—in fact, pumping me. He alluded constantly to Europe, to the people I was supposed to know there—putting leading questions as to my acquaintances in the sepulchral city, and so on. His little eyes glittered like mica discs—with curiosity—though he tried to keep up a bit of superciliousness. At first I was astonished, but very soon I became awfully curious to see what he would find out from me. I couldn't possibly imagine what I had in me to make it worth his while. It was very pretty to see how he baffled himself, for in truth my body was full only of chills, and my head had nothing in it but that wretched steamboat business. It was evident he took me for a perfectly shameless prevaricator. At last he got angry, and, to conceal a movement of furious annoyance, he yawned. I rose. Then I noticed a small sketch in oils, on a panel, representing a woman, draped and blindfolded, carrying a lighted torch. The background was sombre—almost black. The movement of the woman was stately, and the effect of the torch-light on the face was sinister.

"It arrested me, and he stood by civilly, holding an empty half-pint champagne bottle (medical comforts) with the candle stuck in it. To my question he said Mr. Kurtz had painted this—in this very station more than a year ago—while waiting for means to go to his trading-post. 'Tell me, pray,' said I, 'who is this Mr. Kurtz?'

" 'The chief of the Inner Station,' he answered in a short tone, looking away. 'Much obliged,' I said, laughing. 'And you are the brickmaker of the Central Station. Everyone knows that.' He was silent for a while. 'He is a prodigy,' he said at last. 'He is an emissary of pity, and science, and progress, and devil knows what else. We want,' he began to declaim suddenly, 'for the guidance of the cause intrusted to us by Europe, so to speak, higher intelligence, wide sympathies, a singleness of purpose.' 'Who says that?' I asked. 'Lots of them,' he replied. 'Some even write that; and so *he* comes here, a special being, as you ought to know.' 'Why ought I to know?' I interrupted, really surprised. He paid no attention. 'Yes. Today he is chief of the best station, next year he will be assistant-manager, two years more and . . . but I daresay you know what he will be in two years' time. You are of the new gang—the gang of virtue. The same people who sent him specially also recommended you. Oh, don't say no. I've my own eyes to trust.' Light dawned upon me. My dear aunt's influential acquaintances were producing an unexpected effect upon that young man. I nearly burst into a laugh. 'Do you read the Company's confidential correspondence?' I asked. He hadn't a word to say. It was great fun. 'When Mr. Kurtz,' I continued, severely, 'is General Manager, you won't have the opportunity.'

"He blew the candle out suddenly, and we went outside. The moon had risen. Black figures strolled about listlessly, pouring water on the glow, whence proceeded a sound of hissing; steam ascended in the moonlight, the beaten nigger groaned somewhere. 'What a row the brute makes!' said the indefatigable man with the moustaches, appearing near us. 'Serve him right. Transgression—punishment—bang! Pitiless, pitiless. That's the only way. This will prevent all conflagrations for the future. I was just telling the manager . . .' He noticed my companion, and became crestfallen all at once. 'Not in bed yet,' he said, with a kind of servile heartiness; 'it's so natural. Ha! Danger—agitation.' He vanished. I went on to the river-side, and the other followed me. I heard a scathing murmur at my ear. 'Heap of muffs—go to.' The pilgrims could be seen in knots gesticulating, discussing. Several had still their staves in their hands. I verily believe they took these sticks to bed with them. Beyond the fence the forest stood up spectrally in the moonlight, and through the dim stir, through the faint sounds of that lamentable courtyard, the silence of the land went home to one's very heart—its mystery, its greatness, the amazing reality of its concealed life. The hurt nigger moaned feebly somewhere near by, and then fetched a deep sigh that made me mend my pace away from there. I felt a hand introducing itself under my arm. 'My dear sir,' said the fellow, 'I don't want to be misunderstood, and especially by you, who will see Mr. Kurtz long before I can have that pleasure. I wouldn't like him to get a false idea of my disposition. . . .'

"I let him run on, this papier-mâché Mephistopheles, and it seemed to me that if I tried I could poke my forefinger through him, and would find nothing inside but a little loose dirt, maybe. He, don't you see, had been planning to be assistant-manager by and by under the present man, and I could see that the coming of that Kurtz had upset them both not a little. He talked precipitately, and I did not try to stop him. I had my shoulders against the wreck of my steamer, hauled up on the slope like a carcass of some big river animal. The smell of mud, of primeval mud, by Jove! was in my nostrils, the high stillness of primeval forest was before my eyes; there were shiny patches on the black creek. The moon had spread over everything a thin layer of silver—over the rank grass, over the mud, upon the wall of matted vegetation standing higher than the wall of a temple, over the great river I could see through a sombre gap glittering, glittering, as it flowed broadly by without a murmur. All this was great, expectant, mute, while the man jabbered about himself. I wondered whether the stillness on the face of the immensity looking at us two were meant as an appeal or as a menace. What were we who strayed in here? Could we handle that dumb thing, or would it handle us? I felt how big, how confoundedly big, was that thing that couldn't talk, and perhaps was deaf as well. What was in there? I could see a little ivory coming out from there, and I had heard Mr. Kurtz was in there. I had heard enough about it, too—God knows! Yet somehow it didn't bring any image with it—no more than if I had been told an angel or a fiend was in there. I believed it in the same way one of you might believe there are inhabitants in the planet Mars. I knew once a Scotch sailmaker who was certain, dead sure, there were people in Mars. If you asked him for some idea how they looked and behaved, he would get shy and mutter something about 'walking on all fours.' If you as much as smiled, he would—

though a man of sixty—offer to fight you. I would not have gone so far as to fight for Kurtz, but I went for him near enough to a lie. You know I hate, detest, and can't bear a lie, not because I am straighter than the rest of us, but simply because it appalls me. There is a taint of death, a flavour of mortality in lies—which is exactly what I hate and detest in the world—what I want to forget. It makes me miserable and sick, like biting something rotten would do. Temperament, I suppose. Well, I went near enough to it by letting the young fool there believe anything he liked to imagine as to my influence in Europe. I became in an instant as much of a pretence as the rest of the bewitched pilgrims. This simply because I had a notion it somehow would be of help to that Kurtz whom at the time I did not see—you understand. He was just a word for me. I did not see the man in the name any more than you do. Do you see him? Do you see the story? Do you see anything? It seems to me I am trying to tell you a dream—making a vain attempt, because no relation of a dream can convey the dream-sensation, that commingling of absurdity, surprise, and bewilderment in a tremor of struggling revolt, that notion of being captured by the incredible which is of the very essence of dreams . . ."

He was silent for a while.

". . . No, it is impossible; it is impossible to convey the life-sensation of any given epoch of one's existence—that which makes its truth, its meaning—its subtle and penetrating essence. It is impossible. We live, as we dream—alone. . . ."

He paused again as if reflecting, then added—

"Of course in this you fellows see more than I could then. You see me, whom you know. . . ."

It had become so pitch dark that we listeners could hardly see one another. For a long time already he, sitting apart, had been no more to us than a voice. There was not a word from anybody. The others might have been asleep, but I was awake. I listened, I listened on the watch for the sentence, for the word, that would give me the clue to the faint uneasiness inspired by this narrative that seemed to shape itself without human lips in the heavy night-air of the river.

". . . Yes—I let him run on," Marlow began again, "and think what he pleased about the powers that were behind me. I did! And there was nothing behind me! There was nothing but that wretched, old, mangled steamboat I was leaning against, while he talked fluently about 'the necessity for every man to get on.' 'And when one comes out here, you conceive, it is not to gaze at the moon.' Mr. Kurtz was a 'universal genius,' but even a genius would find it easier to work with 'adequate tools—intelligent men.' He did not make bricks—why, there was a physical impossibility in the way—as I was well aware; and if he did secretarial work for the manager, it was because 'no sensible man rejects wantonly the confidence of his superiors.' Did I see it? I saw it. What more did I want? What I really wanted was rivets, by heaven! Rivets. To get on with the work—to stop the hole. Rivets I wanted. There were cases of them down at the coast—cases—piled up—burst—split! You kicked a loose rivet at every second step in that station yard on the hillside. Rivets had rolled into the grove of death. You could fill your pockets with rivets for the trouble of stooping down—and there wasn't one rivet to be found where it was wanted. We had plates that would do, but nothing to fasten them with. And every week the messenger, a lone negro, letter-bag on shoulder and staff in hand, left our station for the coast. And several times a week a coast caravan came in with trade goods—ghastly glazed calico that made you shudder only to look at it, glass beads, valued about a penny a quart, confounded spotted cotton handkerchiefs. And no rivets. Three carriers could have brought all that was wanted to set that steamboat afloat.

"He was becoming confidential now, but I fancy my unresponsive attitude must have exasperated him at last, for he judged it necessary to inform me he feared neither God nor devil, let alone any mere man. I said I could see that very well, but what I wanted was a certain quantity of rivets—and rivets were what really Mr. Kurtz wanted, if he had only known it. Now letters went to the coast every week. . . . 'My dear sir,' he cried, 'I write from dictation.' I demanded rivets. There was a way— for an intelligent man. He changed his manner; became very cold, and suddenly began to talk about a hippopotamus; wondered whether sleeping on board the steamer (I stuck to my salvage night and day) I wasn't disturbed. There was an old hippo that had the bad habit of getting out on the bank and roaming at night over the station grounds. The pilgrims used to turn out in a body and empty every rifle they could lay hands on at him. Some even had sat up o' nights for him. All this energy was wasted, though. 'That animal has a charmed life,' he said; 'but you can say this only of brutes in this country. No man—you apprehend me?— no man here bears a charmed life.' He stood there for a moment in the moonlight with his delicate hooked nose set a little askew, and his mica eyes glittering without a wink, then, with a curt Good-night, he strode off. I could see he was disturbed and considerably puzzled, which made me feel more hopeful than I had been for days. It was a great comfort to turn from that chap to my influential friend, the battered, twisted, ruined, tin-pot steamboat. I clambered on board. She rang under my feet like an empty Huntley & Palmer biscuit-tin kicked along a gutter; she was nothing so solid in make, and rather less pretty in shape, but I had expended enough hard work on her to make me love her. No influential friend would have served me better. She had given me a chance to come out a bit—to find out what I could do. No, I don't like work. I had rather laze about and think of all the fine things that can be done. I don't like work—no man does—but I like what is in the work,—the chance to find yourself. Your own reality—for yourself, not for others—what no other man can ever know. They can only see the mere show, and never can tell what it really means.

"I was not surprised to see somebody sitting aft, on the deck, with his legs dangling over the mud. You see I rather chummed with the few mechanics there were in that station, whom the other pilgrims naturally despised—on account of their imperfect manners, I suppose. This was the foreman—a boiler-maker by trade—a good worker. He was a lank, bony, yellow-faced man, with big intense eyes. His aspect was worried, and his head was as bald as the palm of my hand; but his hair in falling seemed to have stuck to his chin, and had prospered in the new locality, for his beard hung down to his waist. He was a widower with six young children (he had left them in charge of a sister of his to come out there), and the passion of his life was pigeon-flying. He was an enthusiast and a connoisseur. He would rave about pigeons. After work hours he used sometimes to come over from his hut for a talk about his children and his pigeons; at work, when he had to crawl in the mud under the bottom of the steamboat, he would tie up that beard of his in a kind of white serviette[18] he brought for the purpose. It had loops to go over his ears. In the evening he could be seen squatted on the bank rinsing that wrapper in the creek with great care, then spreading it solemnly on a bush to dry.

"I slapped him on the back and shouted, 'We shall have rivets!' He scrambled to his feet exclaiming, 'No! Rivets!' as though he couldn't believe his ears. Then in a low voice, 'You . . . eh?' I don't know why we behaved like lunatics. I put my finger to the side of my nose and nodded mysteriously. 'Good for you!' he cried, snapped his fingers above his head, lifting one foot. I tried a jig. We capered on the iron deck. A frightful clatter came out of that hulk, and the virgin forest on the other bank of the creek sent it back in a thundering roll upon the sleeping station. It must have made some of the pilgrims sit up in their hovels. A dark figure obscured the lighted doorway of the manager's hut, vanished, then, a second or so after, the doorway itself vanished, too. We stopped, and the silence driven away by the stamping of our feet flowed back again from the recesses of the land. The great wall of vegetation, an exuberant and entangled mass of trunks, branches, leaves, boughs, festoons, motionless in the moonlight, was like a rioting invasion of soundless life, a rolling wave of plants, piled up, crested, ready to topple over the creek, to sweep every little man of us out of his little existence. And it moved not. A deadened burst of mighty splashes and snorts reached us from afar, as though an ichthyosaurus[19] had been taking a bath of glitter in the great river. 'After all,' said the boiler-maker in a reasonable tone, 'why shouldn't we get the rivets?' Why not, indeed! I did not know of any reason why we shouldn't 'They'll come in three weeks,' I said, confidently.

"But they didn't. Instead of rivets there came an invasion, an infliction, a visitation. It came in sections during the next three weeks, each section headed by a donkey carrying a white man in new clothes and tan shoes, bowing from that elevation right and left to the impressed pilgrims. A quarrelsome band of footsore sulky niggers trod on the heels of the donkey; a lot of tents, camp-stools, tin boxes, white cases, brown bales would be shot down in the courtyard, and the air of mystery would deepen a little over the muddle of the station. Five such installments came, with their absurd air of disorderly flight with the loot of innumerable outfit shops and provision stores, that, one would think, they were lugging, after a raid, into the wilderness for equitable division. It was an inextricable mess of things decent in themselves but that human folly made look like the spoils of thieving.

"This devoted band called itself the Eldorado Exploring Expedition, and I believe they were sworn to secrecy. Their talk, however, was the talk of sordid buccaneers: it was reckless without hardihood, greedy without audacity, and cruel without courage; there was not an atom of foresight

---

[18] Napkin.
[19] Extinct marine reptile.

or of serious intention in the whole batch of them, and they did not seem aware these things are wanted for the work of the world. To tear treasure out of the bowels of the land was their desire, with no more moral purpose at the back of it than there is in burglars breaking into a safe. Who paid the expenses of the noble enterprise I don't know; but the uncle of our manager was leader of that lot.

"In exterior he resembled a butcher in a poor neighbourhood, and his eyes had a look of sleepy cunning. He carried his fat paunch with ostentation on his short legs, and during the time his gang infested the station spoke to no one but his nephew. You could see these two roaming about all day long with their heads close together in an everlasting confab.

"I had given up worrying myself about the rivets. One's capacity for that kind of folly is more limited than you would suppose. I said Hang!— and let things slide. I had plenty of time for meditation, and now and then I would give some thought to Kurtz. I wasn't very interested in him. No. Still, I was curious to see whether this man, who had come out equipped with moral ideas of some sort, would climb to the top after all and how he would set about his work when there."

II

"One evening as I was lying flat on the deck of my steamboat, I heard voices approaching—and there were the nephew and the uncle strolling along the bank. I laid my head on my arm again, and had nearly lost myself in a doze, when somebody said in my ear, as it were: 'I am as harmless as a little child, but I don't like to be dictated to. Am I the manager—or am I not? I was ordered to send him there. It's incredible.' . . . I became aware that the two were standing on the shore alongside the forepart of the steamboat, just below my head. I did not move; it did not occur to me to move: I was sleepy. 'It *is* unpleasant,' grunted the uncle. 'He has asked the Administration to be sent there,' said the other, 'with the idea of showing what he could do; and I was instructed accordingly. Look at the influence that man must have. Is it not frightful?' They both agreed it was frightful, then made several bizarre remarks: 'Make rain and fine weather—one man—the Council—by the nose'—bits of absurd sentences that got the better of my drowsiness, so that I had pretty near the whole of my wits about me when the uncle said, 'The climate may do away with this difficulty for you. Is he alone there?' 'Yes,' answered the manager; 'he sent his assistant down the river with a note to me in these terms: "Clear this poor devil out of the country, and don't bother sending more of that sort. I had rather be alone than have the kind of men you can dispose of with me." It was more than a year ago. Can you imagine such impudence!' 'Anything since then?' asked the other, hoarsely. 'Ivory,' jerked the nephew; 'lots of it—prime sort—lots—most annoying, from him.' 'And with that?' questioned the heavy rumble. 'Invoice,' was the reply fired out, so to speak. Then silence. They had been talking about Kurtz.

"I was broad awake by this time, but, lying perfectly at ease, remained still, having no inducement to change my position. 'How did that ivory come all of this way?' growled the elder man, who seemed very vexed. The other explained that it had come with a fleet of canoes in charge of an English half-caste clerk Kurtz had with him; that Kurtz had apparently intended to return himself, the station being by that time bare of goods and stores, but after coming three hundred miles, had suddenly decided to go back, which he started to do alone in a small dugout with four paddlers, leaving the half-caste to continue down the river with the ivory. The two fellows there seemed astounded at anybody attempting such a thing. They were at a loss for an adequate motive. As to me, I seemed to see Kurtz for the first time. It was a distinct glimpse: the dugout, four paddling savages, and the lone white man turning his back suddenly on the headquarters, on relief, on thoughts of home—perhaps; setting his face towards the depths of the wilderness, towards his empty and desolate station. I did not know the motive. Perhaps he was just simply a fine fellow who stuck to his work for its own sake. His name, you understand, had not been pronounced once. He was 'that man.' The half-caste, who, as far as I could see, had conducted a difficult trip with great prudence and pluck, was invariably alluded to as 'that scoundrel.' The 'scoundrel' had reported that the 'man' had been very ill—had recovered imperfectly. . . . The two below me moved away then a few paces, and strolled back and forth at some little distance. I heard: 'Military post—doctor—two hundred miles—quite alone now—unavoidable delays—nine months—no news—strange rumors.' They approached again, just as the manager was saying, 'No one, as far as I know, unless a species of wandering trader—a pestilential fellow, snapping ivory from the natives.' Who was it they were talking about now? I gathered in snatches that this was some man supposed to be in Kurtz's district, and of whom the manager did not approve. 'We will not be free from unfair competition till one of these fellows is hanged for an example,' he said. 'Certainly,' grunted the other; 'get him hanged! Why not? Anything—anything can be done in this country. That's what I say; nobody here, you understand, *here*, can endanger your position. And why? You stand the climate—you outlast them all. The danger is in Europe; but there before I left I took care to————' They moved off and whispered, then their voices rose again. 'The extraordinary series of delays is not my fault. I did my best.' The fat man sighed. 'Very sad.' 'And the pestiferous absurdity of his talk,' continued the other; 'he bothered me enough when he was here. "Each station should be like a beacon on the road towards better things, a centre for trade of course, but also for humanizing, improving, instructing." Conceive you—that ass! And he wants to be manager! No, it's————' Here he got choked by excessive indignation, and I lifted my head the least bit. I was surprised to see how near they were—right under me. I could have spat upon their hats. They were looking on the ground, absorbed in thought. The manager was switching his leg with a slender twig: his sagacious relative lifted his head. 'You have been well since you came out this time?' he asked. The other gave a start. 'Who? I? Oh! Like a charm—like a charm. But the rest—oh, my goodness! All sick. They die so quick, too, that I haven't the time to send them out of the country—it's incredible!' 'H'm. Just so,' grunted the uncle. 'Ah! my boy, trust to this—I say, trust to this.' I saw him extend his short flipper of an arm for a gesture that took in the forest, the creek, the mud, the river,—seemed to beckon with a dishonouring flourish before the sunlit face of the land, a treacherous appeal to the lurking death, to the hidden evil, to the profound darkness of its heart. It was so startling that I leaped to my feet and looked back at the edge of the forest, as though I had expected an answer of some sort to that black display of confidence. You know the foolish notions that come to one sometimes. The high stillness confronted these two figures with its ominous patience, waiting for the passing away of a fantastic invasion.

"They swore aloud together—out of sheer fright, I believe—then pretending not to know anything of my existence, turned back to the station. The sun was low; and leaning forward side by side, they seemed to be tugging painfully uphill their two ridiculous shadows of unequal length, that trailed behind them slowly over the tall grass without bending a single blade.

"In a few days the Eldorado Expedition went into the patient wilderness, that closed upon it as the sea closes over a diver. Long afterwards the news came that all the donkeys were dead. I know nothing as to the fate of the less valuable animals. They, no doubt, like the rest of us, found what they deserved. I did not inquire. I was then rather excited at the prospect of meeting Kurtz very soon. When I say very soon I mean it comparatively. It was just two months from the day we left the creek when we came to the bank below Kurtz's station.

"Going up that river was like travelling back to the earliest beginnings of the world, when vegetation rioted on the earth and the big trees were kings. An empty stream, a great silence, an impenetrable forest. The air was warm, thick, heavy, sluggish. There was no joy in the brilliance of sunshine. The long stretches of the waterway ran on, deserted, into the gloom of overshadowed distances. On silvery sandbanks hippos and alligators sunned themselves side by side. The broadening waters flowed through a mob of wooded islands; you lost your way on that river as you would in a desert, and butted all day long against shoals, trying to find the channel, till you thought yourself bewitched and cut off for ever from everything you had known once—somewhere—far away—in another existence perhaps. There were moments when one's past came back to one, as it will sometimes when you have not a moment to spare to yourself; but it came in the shape of an unrestful and noisy dream, remembered with wonder amongst the overwhelming realities of this strange world of plants, and water, and silence. And this stillness of life did not in the least resemble a peace. It was the stillness of an implacable force brooding over an inscrutable intention. It looked at you with a vengeful aspect. I got used to it afterwards; I did not see it any more; I had no time. I had to keep guessing at the channel; I had to discern, mostly by inspiration, the signs of hidden banks; I watched for sunken stones; I was learning to clap my teeth smartly before my heart flew out, when I shaved by a fluke some infernal sly old snag that would have ripped the life out of the tin-pot steamboat and drowned all the pilgrims; I had to keep a look-out for the signs of dead wood we would cut up in the night for next day's steaming. When you have to attend to things of that sort, to the mere incidents of the surface, the reality—the reality, I tell you—fades. The inner truth is hidden—luckily, luckily. But I felt it all the same; I felt often its mysterious stillness watching me at my monkey tricks, just as it watches you fellows performing on your respective tight-ropes for—what is it? Half-a-crown a tumble———"

"Try to be civil, Marlow," growled a voice, and I knew there was at least one listener awake besides myself.

"I beg your pardon. I forgot the heartache which makes up the rest of the price. And indeed what does the price matter, if the trick be well done? You do your tricks very well. And I didn't do badly either, since I managed not to sink that steamboat on my first trip. It's a wonder to me yet. Imagine a blindfolded man set to drive a van over a bad road. I sweated and shivered over that business considerably, I can tell you. After all, for a seaman, to scrape the bottom of the thing that's supposed to float all the time under his care is the unpardonable sin. No one may know of it, but you never forget the thump—eh? A blow on the very heart. You remember it, you dream of it, you wake up at night and think of it—years after—and go hot and cold all over. I don't pretend to say that steamboat floated all the time. More than once she had to wade for a bit, with twenty cannibals splashing around and pushing. We had enlisted some of these chaps on the way for a crew. Fine fellows—cannibals—in their place. They were men one could work with, and I am grateful to them. And, after all, they did not eat each other before my face: they had brought along a provision of hippo-meat which went rotten, and made the mystery of the wilderness stink in my nostrils. Phoo! I can sniff it now. I had the manager on board and three or four pilgrims with their staves—all complete. Sometimes we came upon a station close by the bank, clinging to the skirts of the unknown, and the white men rushing out of a tumble-down hovel, with great gestures of joy and surprise and welcome, seemed very strange—had the appearance of being held there captive by a spell. The word ivory would ring in the air for a while—and on we went again into the silence, along empty reaches, round the still bends, between the high walls of our winding way, reverberating in hollow claps the ponderous beat of the stern-wheel. Trees, trees, millions of trees, massive, immense, running up high; and at their foot, hugging the bank against the steam, crept the little begrimed steamboat, like a sluggish beetle crawling on the floor of a lofty portico. It made you feel very small, very lost, and yet it was not altogether depressing, that feeling. After all, if you were small, the grimy beetle crawled on—which was just what you wanted it to do. Where the pilgrims imagined it crawled to I don't know. To some place where they expected to get something, I bet! For me it crawled towards Kurtz—exclusively; but when the steam-pipes started leaking we crawled very slow. The reaches opened before us and closed behind, as if the forest had stepped leisurely across the water to bar the way for our return. We penetrated deeper and deeper into the heart of darkness. It was very quiet there. At night sometimes the roll of drums behind the curtain of trees would run up the river and remain sustained faintly, as if hovering in the air high over our heads, till the first break of day. Whether it meant war, peace, or prayer we could not tell. The dawns were heralded by the descent of a chill stillness; the wood-cutters slept, their fires burned low; the snapping of a twig would make you start. We were wanderers on a prehistoric earth, on an earth that wore the aspect of an unknown planet. We could have fancied ourselves the first of men taking possession of an accursed inheritance, to be subdued at the cost of profound anguish and of excessive toil. But suddenly, as we struggled round a bend, there would be a glimpse of rush walls, of peaked grass-roofs, a burst of yells, a whirl of black limbs, a mass of hands clapping, of feet stamping, of bodies swaying, of eyes rolling, under the droop of heavy and motionless foliage. The steamer toiled along slowly on the edge of a black and incomprehensible frenzy. The prehistoric man was cursing us, praying to us, welcoming us—who could tell? We were cut off from the comprehension of our surroundings; we glided past like phantoms, wondering and secretly appalled, as sane men would be before an enthusiastic outbreak in a madhouse. We could not understand because we were too far and could not remember, because we were travelling in the night of first ages, of those ages that are gone, leaving hardly a sign—and no memories.

"The earth seemed unearthly. We are accustomed to look upon the shackled form of a conquered monster, but there—there you could look at a thing monstrous and free. It was unearthly, and the men were————No, they were not inhuman. Well, you know, that was the worst of it—this suspicion of their not being inhuman. It would come slowly to one. They howled and leaped, and spun, and made horrid faces; but what thrilled you was just the thought of their humanity—like yours—the thought of your remote kinship with this wild and passionate uproar. Ugly. Yes, it was ugly enough; but if you were man enough you would admit to yourself that there was in you just the faintest trace of a response to the terrible frankness of that noise, a dim suspicion of there being a meaning in it which you—you so remote from the night of first ages—could comprehend. And why not? The mind of man is capable of anything—because everything is in it, all the past as well the future. What was there after all? Joy, fear, sorrow, devotion, valour, rage—who can tell?—but truth—truth stripped of its cloak of time. Let the fool gape and shudder—the man knows, and can look on without a wink. But he must at least be as much of a man as these on the shore. He must meet that truth with his own true stuff—with his own inborn strength. Principles won't do. Acquisitions, clothes, pretty rags—rags that would fly off at the first good shake. No; you want a deliberate belief. An appeal to me in this fiendish row—is there? Very well; I hear; I admit, but I have a voice, too, and for good or evil mine is the speech that cannot be silenced. Of course, a fool, what with sheer fright and fine sentiments, is always safe. Who's that grunting? You wonder I didn't go ashore for a howl and a dance? Well, no—I didn't. Fine sentiments, you say? Fine sentiments, be hanged! I had no time. I had to mess about with white-lead and strips of woollen blanket helping to put bandages on those leaky steampipes—I tell you. I had to watch the steering, and circumvent those snags, and get the tin-pot along by hook or by crook. There was surface-truth enough in these things to save a wiser man. And between whiles I had to look after the savage who was fireman. He was an improved specimen; he could fire up a vertical boiler. He was there below me, and, upon my word, to look at him was as edifying as seeing a dog in a parody of breeches and a feather hat, walking on his hind-legs. A few months of training had done for that really fine chap. He squinted at the steam-gauge and at the water-gauge with an evident effort of intrepidity—and he had filed teeth, too, the poor devil, and the wool of his pate shaved into queer patterns, and three ornamental scars on each of his cheeks. He ought to have been clapping his hands and stamping his feet on the bank, instead of which he was hard at work, a thrall to strange witchcraft, full of improving knowledge. He was useful because he had been instructed; and what he knew was this— that should the water in that transparent thing disappear, the evil spirit inside the boiler would get angry through the greatness of his thirst, and take a terrible vengeance. So he sweated and fired up and watched the glass fearfully (with an impromptu charm, made of rags, tied to his arm, and a piece of polished bone, as big as a watch, stuck flatways through his lower lip), while the wooded banks slipped past us slowly, the short noise was left behind, the interminable miles of silence—and we crept on, towards Kurtz. But the snags were thick, the water was treacherous and shallow, the boiler seemed indeed to have a sulky devil in it, and thus neither that fireman nor I had any time to peer into our creepy thoughts.

"Some fifty miles below the Inner Station we came upon a hut of reeds, an inclined and melancholy pole, with the unrecognizable tatters of what had been a flag of some sort flying from it, and a neatly stacked wood-pile. This was unexpected. We came to the bank, and on the stack of firewood found a flat piece of board with some faded pencil-writing on it. When deciphered it said: 'Wood for you. Hurry up. Approach cautiously.' There was a signature, but it was illegible—not Kurtz—a much longer word. 'Hurry up.' Where? Up the river? 'Approach cautiously.' We had not done so. But the warning could not have been meant for the place where it could be only found after approach. Something was wrong above. But what—and how much? That was the question. We commented adversely upon the imbecility of that telegraphic style. The bush around said nothing, and would not let us look very far, either. A torn curtain of red twill hung in the doorway of the hut, and flapped sadly in our faces. The dwelling was dismantled; but we could see a white man had lived there not very long ago. There remained a rude table—a plank on two posts; a heap of rubbish reposed in a dark corner, and by the door I picked up a book. It had lost its covers, and the pages had been thumbed into a state of extremely dirty softness; but the back had been lovingly stitched afresh with white cotton thread, which looked clean yet. It was an extraordinary find. Its title was, *An Inquiry into Some Points of Seamanship*, by a man Towser, Towson—some such name—Master in his Majesty's Navy. The matter looked dreary reading enough, with illustrative diagrams and repulsive tables of figures, and the copy was sixty years old. I handled this amazing antiquity with the greatest possible tenderness, lest it should dissolve in my hands. Within, Towson or Towser was inquiring earnestly into the breaking strain of ships' chains and tackle, and other such matters. Not a very enthralling book; but at the first glance you could see there a singleness of intention, an honest concern for the right way of going to work, which made these humble pages, thought out so many years ago, luminous with another than a professional light. The simple old sailor, with his talk of chains and purchases,[20] made me forget the jungle and the pilgrims in a delicious sensation of having come upon something unmistakably real. Such a book being there was wonderful enough; but still more astounding were the notes penciled in the margin, and plainly referring to the text. I couldn't believe my eyes! They were in cipher! Yes, it looked like cipher. Fancy a man lugging with him a book of that description into this nowhere and studying it—and making notes—in cipher at that! It was an extravagant mystery.

"I had been dimly aware for some time of a worrying noise, and when I lifted my eyes I saw the wood-pile was gone, and the manager, aided by all the pilgrims, was shouting at me from the river-side. I slipped the book into my pocket. I assure you to leave off reading was like tearing myself away from the shelter of an old and solid friendship.

"I started the lame engine ahead. 'It must be this miserable trader—this intruder,' exclaimed the manager, looking back malevolently at the place we had left. 'He must be English,' I said. 'It will not save him from getting into trouble if he is not careful,' muttered the manager darkly. I observed with assumed innocence that no man was safe from trouble in this world.

"The current was more rapid now, the steamer seemed at her last gasp, the stern-wheel flopped languidly, and I caught myself listening on tiptoe for the next beat of the float,[21] for in sober truth I expected the wretched thing to give up every moment. It was like watching the last flickers of a life. But still we crawled. Sometimes I would pick out a tree a little way ahead to measure our progress towards Kurtz by, but I lost it invariably before we got abreast. To keep the eyes so long on one thing was too much for human patience. The manager displayed a beautiful resignation. I fretted and fumed and took to arguing with myself whether or no I would talk openly with Kurtz; but before I could come to any conclusion it occurred to me that my speech or my silence, indeed any action of mine, would be a mere futility. What did it matter what any one knew or ignored? What did it matter who was manager? One gets sometimes such a flash of insight. The essentials of this affair lay deep under the surface, beyond my reach, and beyond my power of meddling.

"Towards the evening of the second day we judged ourselves about eight miles from Kurtz's station. I wanted to push on; but the manager looked grave, and told me the navigation up there was so dangerous that it would be advisable, the sun being very low already, to wait where we were till next morning. Moreover, he pointed out that if the warning to approach cautiously were to be followed, we must approach in daylight—not at dusk, or in the dark. This was sensible enough. Eight miles meant nearly three hours' steaming for us, and I could also see suspicious ripples at the upper end of the reach. Nevertheless, I was annoyed beyond expression at the delay, and most unreasonably, too, since one night more could not matter much after so many months. As we had plenty of wood, and caution was the word, I brought up in the middle of the stream. The

[20] Rigging used to apply leverage.
[21] Blade of the paddle wheel.

reach was narrow, straight, with high sides like a railway cutting. The dusk came gliding into it long before the sun had set. The current ran smooth and swift, but a dumb immobility sat on the banks. The living trees, lashed together by the creepers and every living bush of the undergrowth, might have been changed into stone, even to the slenderest twig, to the lightest leaf. It was not sleep—it seemed unnatural, like a state of trance. Not the faintest sound of any kind could be heard. You looked on amazed, and began to suspect yourself of being deaf—then the night came suddenly, and struck you blind as well. About three in the morning some large fish leaped, and the loud splash made me jump as though a gun had been fired. When the sun rose there was a white fog, very warm and clammy, and more blinding than the night. It did not shift or drive; it was just there, standing all round you like something solid. At eight or nine, perhaps, it lifted as a shutter lifts. We had a glimpse of the towering multitude of trees, of the immense matted jungle, with the blazing little ball of the sun hanging over it—all perfectly still—and then the white shutter came down again, smoothly, as if sliding in greased grooves. I ordered the chain, which we had begun to heave in, to be paid out again. Before it stopped running with a muffled rattle, a cry, a very loud cry as of infinite desolation, soared slowly in the opaque air. It ceased. A complaining clamour, modulated in savage discords, filled our ears. The sheer unexpectedness of it made my hair stir under my cap. I don't know how it struck the others: to me it seemed as though the mist itself had screamed, so suddenly, and apparently from all sides at once, did this tumultuous and mournful uproar arise. It culminated in a hurried outbreak of almost intolerably excessive shrieking, which stopped short, leaving us stiffened in a variety of silly attitudes, and obstinately listening to the nearly as appalling and excessive silence. 'Good God! What is the meaning———' stammered at my elbow one of the pilgrims, a little fat man, with sandy hair and red whiskers, who wore side-spring boots, and pink pyjamas tucked into his socks. Two others remained open-mouthed a whole minute, then dashed into the little cabin, to rush out incontinently and stand darting scared glances, with Winchesters[22] at 'ready' in their hands. What we could see was just the steamer we were on, her outlines blurred as though she had been on the point of dissolving, and a misty strip of water, perhaps two feet broad, around her—and that was all. The rest of the world was nowhere, as far as our eyes and ears were concerned. Just nowhere. Gone, disappeared; swept off without leaving a whisper or a shadow behind.

"I went forward, and ordered the chain to be hauled in short, so as to be ready to trip the anchor and move the steamboat at once if necessary. 'Will they attack?' whispered an awed voice. 'We will be all butchered in this fog,' murmured another. The faces twitched with the strain, the hands trembled slightly, the eyes forgot to wink. It was very curious to see the contrast of expressions of the white men and of the black fellows of our crew, who were as much strangers to that part of the river as we, though their homes were only eight hundred miles away. The whites, of course greatly discomposed, had besides a curious look of being painfully shocked by such an outrageous row. The others had an alert, naturally interested

---

[22] American repeating rifles.

expression; but their faces were essentially quiet, even those of the one or two who grinned as they hauled at the chain. Several exchanged short, grunting phrases, which seemed to settle the matter to their satisfaction. Their headman, a young, broad-chested black, severely draped in dark-blue fringed cloths, with fierce nostrils and his hair all done up artfully in oily ringlets, stood near me. 'Aha!' I said, just for good fellowship's sake. 'Catch 'im,' he snapped, with bloodshot widening of his eyes and a flash of sharp teeth—'catch 'im. Give 'im to us.' 'To you, eh?' I asked; 'what would you do with them?' 'Eat 'im!' he said, curtly, and, leaning his elbow on the rail, looked out into the fog in a dignified and profoundly pensive attitude. I would no doubt have been properly horrified, had it not occurred to me that he and his chaps must be very hungry; that they must have been growing increasingly hungry for at least this month past. They had been engaged for six months (I don't think a single one of them had any clear idea of time, as we at the end of countless ages have. They still belonged to the beginnings of time—had no inherited experience to teach them as it were), and of course, as long as there was a piece of paper written over in accordance with some farcical law or other made down the river, it didn't enter anybody's head to trouble how they would live. Certainly they had brought with them some rotten hippo-meat, which couldn't have lasted very long, anyway, even if the pilgrims hadn't, in the midst of a shocking hullabaloo, thrown a considerable quantity of it overboard. It looked like a high-handed proceeding; but it was really a case of legitimate self-defense. You can't breathe dead hippo waking, sleeping, and eating, and at the same time keep your precarious grip on existence. Besides that, they had given them every week three pieces of brass wire, each about nine inches long; and the theory was they were to buy their provisions with that currency in river-side villages. You can see how *that* worked. They were either no villages, or the people were hostile, or the director, who like the rest of us fed out of tins, with an occasional old he-goat thrown in, didn't want to stop the steamer for some more or less recondite reason. So, unless they swallowed the wire itself, or made loops of it to snare the fishes with, I don't see what good their extravagant salary could be to them. I must say it was paid with a regularity worthy of a large and honourable trading company. For the rest, the only thing to eat—though it didn't look eatable in the least—I saw in their possession was a few lumps of some stuff like half-cooked dough, of a dirty lavender colour, they kept wrapped in leaves, and now and then swallowed a piece of, but so small that it seemed done more for the looks of the thing than for any serious purpose of sustenance. Why in the name of all the gnawing devils of hunger they didn't go for us—they were thirty to five—and have a good tuck-in[23] for once, amazes me now when I think of it. They were big powerful men, with not much capacity to weigh the consequences, with courage, with strength, even yet, though their skins were no longer glossy and their muscles no longer hard. And I saw that something restraining, one of those human secrets that baffle probability, had come into play there. I looked at them with a swift quickening of interest—not because it occurred to me I might be eaten by them before very long, though I

---

[23] British slang, a good meal.

own to you that just then I perceived—in a new light, as it were—how unwholesome the pilgrims looked, and I hoped, yes I positively hoped, that my aspect was not so—what shall I say?—so—unappetizing: a touch of fantastic vanity which fitted well with the dream-sensation that pervaded all my days at that time. Perhaps I had a little fever, too. One can't live with one's finger everlastingly on one's pulse. I had often 'a little fever,' or a little touch of other things—the playful paw-strokes of the wilderness, the preliminary trifling before the more serious onslaught which came in due course. Yes; I looked at them as you would on any human being, with a curiosity of their impulses, motives, capacities, weaknesses, when brought to the test of an inexorable physical necessity. Restraint! What possible restraint? Was it superstition, disgust, patience, fear—or some kind of primitive honour? No fear can stand up to hunger, no patience can wear it out, disgust simply does not exist where hunger is; and as to superstition, beliefs, and what you may call principles, they are less than chaff in a breeze. Don't you know the devilry of lingering starvation, its exasperating torment, its black thoughts, its sombre and brooding ferocity? Well, I do. It takes a man all his inborn strength to fight hunger properly. It's really easier to face bereavement, dishonour, and the perdition of one's soul—than this kind of prolonged hunger. Sad, but true. And these chaps, too, had no earthly reason for any kind of scruple. Restraint! I would just as soon have expected restraint from a hyena prowling amongst the corpses of a battlefield. But there was the fact facing me—the fact dazzling, to be seen, like the foam on the depths of the sea, like a ripple on an unfathomable enigma, a mystery greater—when I thought of it—than the curious, inexplicable note of desperate grief in this savage clamour that had swept by us on the river-bank, behind the blind whiteness of the fog.

"Two pilgrims were quarrelling in hurried whispers as to which bank. 'Left.' 'No, no; how can you? Right, right, of course.' 'It is very serious,' said the manager's voice behind me; 'I would be desolated if anything should happen to Mr. Kurtz before we came up.' I looked at him, and had not the slightest doubt he was sincere. He was just the kind of man who would wish to preserve appearances. That was his restraint. But when he muttered something about going on at once, I did not even take the trouble to answer him. I knew, and he knew, that it was impossible. Were we to let go our hold of the bottom, we would be absolutely in the air—in space. We wouldn't be able to tell where we were going to—whether up or down stream, or across—till we fetched against one bank or the other,—and then we wouldn't know at first which it was. Of course I made no move. I had no mind for a smash-up. You couldn't imagine a more deadly place for a shipwreck. Whether drowned at once or not, we were sure to perish speedily in one way or another. 'I authorize you to take all the risks,' he said, after a short silence. 'I refuse to take any,' I said, shortly; which was just the answer he expected, though its tone might have surprised him. 'Well, I must defer to your judgment. You are captain,' he said, with marked civility. I turned my shoulder to him in sign of my appreciation, and looked into the fog. How long would it last? It was the most hopeless look-out. The approach to this Kurtz grubbing for ivory in the wretched bush was beset by as many dangers as though he had been an enchanted princess sleeping in a fabulous castle. 'Will they attack, do you think?' asked the manager, in a confidential tone.

"I did not think they would attack, for several obvious reasons. The thick fog was one. If they left the bank in their canoes they would get lost in it, as we would be if we attempted to move. Still, I had also judged the jungle of both banks quite impenetrable—and yet eyes were in it, eyes that had seen us. The river-side bushes were certainly very thick; but the undergrowth behind was evidently penetrable. However, during the short lift I had seen no canoes anywhere in the reach—certainly not abreast of the steamer. But what made the idea of attack inconceivable to me was the nature of the noise—of the cries we had heard. They had not the fierce character boding immediate hostile intention. Unexpected, wild, and violent as they had been, they had given me an irresistible impression of sorrow. The glimpse of the steamboat had for some reason filled those savages with unrestrained grief. The danger, if any, I expounded, was from our proximity to a great human passion let loose. Even extreme grief may ultimately vent itself in violence—but more generally takes the form of apathy. . . .

"You should have seen the pilgrims stare! They had no heart to grin, or even to revile me: but I believe they thought me gone mad—with fright, maybe. I delivered a regular lecture. My dear boys, it was no good bothering. Keep a lookout? Well, you may guess I watched the fog for the signs of lifting as a cat watches a mouse; but for anything else our eyes were of no more use to us than if we had been buried miles deep in a heap of cotton-wool. It felt like it, too—choking, warm, stifling. Besides, all I said, though it sounded extravagant, was absolutely true to fact. What we afterwards alluded to as an attack was really an attempt at repulse. The action was very far from being aggressive—it was not even defensive, in the usual sense: it was undertaken under the stress of desperation, and in its essence was purely protective.

"It developed itself, I should say, two hours after the fog lifted, and its commencement was at a spot, roughly speaking, about a mile and a half below Kurtz's station. We had just floundered and flopped round a bend, when I saw an islet, a mere grassy hummock of bright green, in the middle of the stream. It was the only thing of the kind; but as we opened the reach more, I perceived it was the head of a long sandbank, or rather of a chain of shallow patches stretching down the middle of the river. They were discoloured, just awash, and the whole lot was seen just under the water, exactly as a man's backbone is seen running down the middle of his back under the skin. Now, as far as I did see, I could go to the right or to the left of this. I didn't know either channel, of course. The banks looked pretty well alike, the depth appeared the same; but as I had been informed the station was on the west side, I naturally headed for the western passage.

"No sooner had we fairly entered it than I became aware it was much narrower than I had supposed. To the left of us there was the long uninterrupted shoal, and to the right a high, steep bank heavily overgrown with bushes. Above the bush the trees stood in serried ranks. The twigs overhung the current thickly, and from distance to distance a large limb of some tree projected rigidly over the stream. It was then well on in the afternoon, the face of the forest was gloomy, and a broad strip of shadow had already fallen on the water. In this shadow we steamed up—very slowly, as you may imagine. I sheered her well inshore—the water being deepest near the bank, as the sounding-pole informed me.

"One of my hungry and forbearing friends was sounding[24] in the bows just below me. This steamboat was exactly like a decked scow. On the deck, there were two little teak-wood houses, with doors and windows. The boiler was in the fore-end, and the machinery right astern. Over the whole there was a light roof, supported on stanchions. The funnel projected through that roof, and in front of the funnel a small cabin built of light planks served for a pilot-house. It contained a couch, two camp-stools, a loaded Martini-Henry[25] leaning in one corner, a tiny table, and the steering-wheel. It had a wide door in front and a broad shutter at each side. All these were always thrown open, of course. I spent my days perched up there on the extreme fore-end of that roof, before the door. At night I slept, or tried to, on the couch. An athletic black belonging to some coast tribe, and educated by my poor predecessor, was the helmsman. He sported a pair of brass earrings, wore a blue cloth wrapper from the waist to the ankles, and thought all the world of himself. He was the most unstable kind of fool I had ever seen. He steered with no end of a swagger while you were by; but if he lost sight of you, he became instantly the prey of an abject funk, and would let that cripple of a steamboat get the upper hand of him in a minute.

"I was looking down at the sounding-pole, and feeling much annoyed to see at each try a little more of it stick out of that river, when I saw my poleman give up the business suddenly, and stretch himself flat on the deck, without even taking the trouble to haul his pole in. He kept hold on it though, and it trailed in the water. At the same time the fireman, whom I could also see below me, sat down abruptly before his furnace and ducked his head. I was amazed. Then I had to look at the river mighty quick, because there was a snag in the fairway. Sticks, little sticks, were flying about—thick: they were whizzing before my nose, dropping below me, striking behind me against my pilot-house. All this time the river, the shore, the woods, were very quiet—perfectly quiet. I could only hear the heavy splashing thump of the stern-wheel and the patter of these things. We cleared the snag clumsily. Arrows, by Jove! We were being shot at! I stepped in quickly to close the shutter on the land-side. That fool-helmsman, his hands on the spokes, was lifting his knees high, stamping his feet, champing his mouth, like a reined-in horse. Confound him! And we were staggering within ten feet of the bank. I had to lean right out to swing the heavy shutter, and I saw a face amongst the leaves on the level with my own, looking at me very fierce and steady; and then suddenly, as though a veil had been removed from my eyes, I made out, deep in the tangled gloom, naked breasts, arms, legs, glaring eyes,—the bush was swarming with human limbs in movement, glistening, of bronze colour. The twigs shook, swayed, and rustled, the arrows flew out of them, and then the shutter came to. 'Steer her straight,' I said to the helmsman. He held his

---

[24] Measuring the water's depth by means of a weighted line.
[25] A heavy military rifle.

head rigid, face forward; but his eyes rolled, he kept on lifting and setting down his feet gently, his mouth foamed a little. 'Keep quiet!' I said in a fury. I might just as well have ordered a tree not to sway in the wind. I darted out. Below me there was a great scuffle of feet on the iron deck; confused exclamations; a voice screamed, 'Can you turn back?' I caught sight of a V-shaped ripple on the water ahead. What? Another snag! A fusillade burst out under my feet. The pilgrims had opened with their Winchesters, and were simply squirting lead into that bush. A deuce of a lot of smoke came up and drove slowly forward. I swore at it. Now I couldn't see the ripple of the snag either. I stood in the doorway, peering, and the arrows came in swarms. They might have been poisoned, but they looked as though they wouldn't kill a cat. The bush began to howl. Our wood-cutters raised a warlike whoop; the report of a rifle just at my back deafened me. I glanced over my shoulder, and the pilot-house was yet full of noise and smoke when I made a dash at the wheel. The fool-nigger had dropped everything, to throw the shutter open and let off that Martini-Henry. He stood before the wide opening, glaring, and I yelled at him to come back, while I straightened the sudden twist out of that steamboat. There was no room to turn even if I had wanted to, the snag was somewhere very near ahead in that confounded smoke, there was no time to lose, so I just crowded her into the bank—right into the bank, where I knew the water was deep.

"We tore slowly along the overhanging bushes in a whirl of broken twigs and flying leaves. The fusillade below stopped short, as I had foreseen it would when the squirts got empty. I threw my head back to a glinting whizz that traversed the pilot-house, in at one shutter hole and out at the other. Looking past that mad helmsman, who was shaking the empty rifle and yelling at the shore, I saw vague forms of men running bent double, leaping, gliding, distinct, incomplete, evanescent. Something big appeared in the air before the shutter, the rifle went overboard, and the man stepped back swiftly, looked at me over his shoulder in an extraordinary, profound, familiar manner, and fell upon my feet. The side of his head hit the wheel twice, and the end of what appeared a long cane clattered round and knocked over a little camp-stool. It looked as though after wrenching that thing from somebody ashore he had lost his balance in the effort. The thin smoke had blown away, we were clear of the snag, and looking ahead I could see that in another hundred yards or so I would be free to sheer off, away from the bank; but my feet felt so very warm and wet that I had to look down. The man had rolled on his back and stared straight up at me; both his hands clutched that cane. It was the shaft of a spear that, either thrown or lunged through the opening, had caught him in the side just below the ribs; the blade had gone in out of sight, after making a frightful gash; my shoes were full; a pool of blood lay very still, gleaming dark-red under the wheel; his eyes shown with an amazing lustre. The fusillade burst out again. He looked at me anxiously, gripping the spear like something precious, with an air of being afraid I would try to take it away from him. I had to make an effort to free my eyes from his gaze and attend to the steering. With one hand I felt above my head for the line of the steam whistle, and jerked out screech after screech hurriedly. The tumult of angry and warlike yells was checked instantly, and then from the depths of the woods went out such a tremulous and prolonged wail of mournful fear and utter despair as may be imagined to follow the flight of the last hope from the earth. There was a great commotion in the bush; the shower of arrows stopped, a few dropping shots rang out sharply—then silence, in which the languid beat of the stern-wheel came plainly to my ears. I put the helm hard a-starboard at the moment when the pilgrim in pink pyjamas, very hot and agitated, appeared in the doorway. 'The manager sends me———' he began in an official tone, and stopped short. 'Good God!' he said, glaring at the wounded man.

"We two whites stood over him, and his lustrous and inquiring glance enveloped us both. I declare it looked as though he would presently put to us some question in an understandable language; but he died without uttering a sound, without moving a limb, without twitching a muscle. Only in the very last moment, as though in response to some sign we could not see, to some whisper we could not hear, he frowned heavily, and that frown gave to his black death-mask an inconceivably sombre, brooding, and menacing expression. The lustre of inquiring glance faded swiftly into vacant glassiness. 'Can you steer?' I asked the agent eagerly. He looked very dubious; but I made a grab at his arm, and he understood at once I meant him to steer whether or no. To tell you the truth, I was morbidly anxious to change my shoes and socks. 'He is dead,' murmured the fellow, immensely impressed. 'No doubt about it,' said I, tugging like mad at the shoe-laces. 'And by the way, I suppose Mr. Kurtz is dead as well by this time.'

"For the moment that was the dominant thought. There was a sense of extreme disappointment, as though I had found out I had been striving after something altogether without a substance. I couldn't have been more disgusted if I had travelled all this way for the sole purpose of talking with Mr. Kurtz. Talking with . . . I flung one shoe overboard, and became aware that that was exactly what I had been looking forward to—a talk with Kurtz. I made the strange discovery that I had never imagined him as doing, you know, but as discoursing. I didn't say to myself, 'Now I will never see him,' or 'Now I will never shake him by the hand,' but, 'now I will never hear him.' The man presented himself as a voice. Not of course that I did not connect him with some sort of action. Hadn't I been told in all the tones of jealousy and admiration that he had collected, bartered, swindled, or stolen more ivory than all the other agents together? That was not the point. The point was in his being a gifted creature, and that of all his gifts the one that stood out preëminently, that carried with it a sense of real presence, was his ability to talk, his words—the gift of expression, the bewildering, the illuminating, the most exalted and the most contemptible, the pulsating stream of light, or the deceitful flow from the heart of an impenetrable darkness.

"The other shoe went flying unto the devil-god of that river. I thought, By Jove! it's all over. We are too late; he has vanished—the gift has vanished, by means of some spear, arrow, or club. I will never hear that chap speak after all,—and my sorrow had a startling extravagance of emotion, even such as I had noticed in the howling sorrow of these savages in the bush. I couldn't have felt more of lonely desolation somehow, had I been robbed of a belief or had missed my destiny in life. . . . Why do you sigh in this beastly way, somebody? Absurd? Well, absurd. Good Lord! mustn't a man ever——— Here, give me some tobacco." . . .

There was a pause of profound stillness, then a match flared, and Marlow's lean face appeared, worn, hollow, with downward folds and dropped eyelids, with an aspect of concentrated attention; and as he took vigorous draws at his pipe, it seemed to retreat and advance out of the night in the regular flicker of the tiny flame. The match went out.

"Absurd!" he cried. "This is the worst of trying to tell. . . . Here you all are, each moored with two good addresses, like a hulk with two anchors, a butcher round one corner, a policeman round another, excellent appetites, and temperature normal—you hear—normal from year's end to year's end. And you say, Absurd! Absurd be—exploded! Absurd! My dear boys, what can you expect from a man who out of sheer nervousness had just flung overboard a pair of new shoes! Now I think of it, it is amazing I did not shed tears. I am, upon the whole, proud of my fortitude. I was cut to the quick at the idea of having lost the inestimable privilege of listening to the gifted Kurtz. Of course I was wrong. The privilege was waiting for me. Oh, yes, I heard more than enough. And I was right, too. A voice. He was very little more than a voice. And I heard—him—it—this voice— other voices—all of them were so little more than voices—and the memory of that time itself lingers around me, impalpable, like a dying vibration of one immense jabber, silly, atrocious, sordid, savage, or simply mean, without any kind of sense. Voices, voices—even the girl herself—now—"

He was silent for a long time.

"I laid the ghost of his gifts at last with a lie," he began, suddenly. "Girl! What? Did I mention a girl? Oh, she is out of it—completely. They— the women I mean—are out of it—should be out of it. We must help them to stay in that beautiful world of their own, lest ours gets worse. Oh, she had to be out of it. You should have heard the disinterred body of Mr. Kurtz saying, 'My Intended.' You would have perceived directly then how completely she was out of it. And the lofty frontal bone of Mr. Kurtz! They say the hair goes on growing sometimes, but this—ah— specimen, was impressively bald. The wilderness had patted him on the head, and, behold, it was like a ball—an ivory ball; it had caressed him, and—lo!—he had withered; it had taken him, loved him, embraced him, got into his veins, consumed his flesh, and sealed his soul to its own by the inconceivable ceremonies of some devilish initiation. He was its spoiled and pampered favourite. Ivory? I should think so. Heaps of it, stacks of it. The old mud shanty was bursting with it. You would think there was not a single tusk left either above or below the ground in the whole country. 'Mostly fossil,' the manager had remarked disparagingly. It was no more fossil than I am; but they call it fossil when it is dug up. It appears these niggers do bury the tusks sometimes—but evidently they couldn't bury this parcel deep enough to save the gifted Mr. Kurtz from his fate. We filled the steamboat with it, and had to pile a lot on the deck. Thus he could see and enjoy as long as he could see, because the appreciation of this favour had remained with him to the last. You should have heard him say, 'My ivory.' Oh yes, I heard him. 'My Intended, my ivory, my station, my river, my——' everything belonged to him. It made me hold my breath in expectation of hearing the wilderness burst into a prodigious peal of laughter that would shake the fixed stars in their places. Everything belonged to him—but that was a trifle. The thing was to know what he belonged to, how many powers of darkness claimed him for their own. That was the reflection that made you creepy all over. It was impossible— it was not good for one either—trying to imagine. He had taken a high seat amongst the devils of the land—I mean literally. You can't understand. How could you?—with solid pavement under your feet, surrounded by kind neighbours ready to cheer you or to fall on you, stepping delicately between the butcher and the policeman, in the holy terror of scandal and gallows and lunatic asylums—how can you imagine what particular region of the first ages a man's untrammelled feet may take him into by the way of solitude—utter solitude without a policeman—by the way of si- lence—utter silence, where no warning voice of a kind neighbour can be heard whispering of public opinion? These little things make all the great difference. When they are gone you must fall back upon your own innate strength, upon your own capacity for faithfulness. Of course you may be too much of a fool to go wrong—too dull even to know you are being assaulted by the powers of darkness. I take it, no fool ever made a bargain for his soul with the devil: the fool is too much of a fool, or the devil too much of a devil—I don't know which. Or you may be such a thunder- ingly exalted creature as to be altogether deaf and blind to anything but heavenly sights and sounds. Then the earth for you is only a standing place—and whether to be like this is your loss or your gain I won't pretend to say. But most of us are neither one nor the other. The earth for us is a place to live in, where we must put up with sights, with sounds, with smells, too, by Jove!—breathe dead hippo, so to speak, and not be contami- nated. And there, don't you see? your strength comes in, the faith in your ability for the digging of unostentatious holes to bury the stuff in—your power of devotion, not to yourself, but to an obscure, back-breaking busi- ness. And that's difficult enough. Mind, I am not trying to excuse or even explain—I am trying to account to myself for—for—Mr. Kurtz—for the shade of Mr. Kurtz. This initiated wraith from the back of Nowhere hon- oured me with its amazing confidence before it vanished altogether. This was because it could speak English to me. The original Kurtz had been educated partly in England, and—as he was good enough to say himself— his sympathies were in the right place. His mother was half-English, his father was half-French. All Europe contributed to the making of Kurtz; and by and by I learned that, most appropriately, the International Society for the Suppression of Savage Customs had intrusted him with the making of a report, for its future guidance. And he had written it, too. I've seen it. I've read it. It was eloquent, vibrating with eloquence, but too high- strung, I think. Seventeen pages of close writing he had found time for! But this must have been before his—let us say—nerves, went wrong, and caused him to preside at certain midnight dances ending with unspeakable rites, which—as far as I reluctantly gathered from what I heard at various times—were offered up to him—do you understand?—to Mr. Kurtz himself. But it was a beautiful piece of writing. The opening paragraph, however, in the light of later information, strikes me now as ominous. He began with the argument that we whites, from the point of development we

had arrived at, 'must necessarily appear to them [savages] in the nature
of supernatural beings—we approach them with the might as of a deity,'
and so on, and so on. 'By the simple exercise of our will we can exert a
power for good practically unbounded,' etc., etc. From that point he soared
and took me with him. The peroration was magnificent, though difficult
to remember, you know. It gave me the notion of an exotic Immensity
ruled by an august Benevolence. It made me tingle with enthusiasm. This
was the unbounded power of eloquence—of words—of burning noble
words. There were no practical hints to interrupt the magic current of
phrases, unless a kind of note at the foot of the last page, scrawled evidently
much later, in an unsteady hand, may be regarded as the exposition of a
method. It was very simple, and at the end of that moving appeal to every
altruistic sentiment it blazed at you, luminous and terrifying, like a flash
of lightning in a serene sky: 'Exterminate all the brutes!' The curious
part was that he had apparently forgotten all about that valuable postscriptum, because, later on, when he in a sense came to himself, he repeatedly
entreated me to take good care of 'my pamphlet' (he called it), as it was
sure to have in the future a good influence upon his career. I had full
information about all these things, and, besides, as it turned out, I was
to have the care of his memory. I'd done enough for it to give me the
indisputable right to lay it, if I choose, for an everlasting rest in the dust-
bin of progress amongst all the sweepings and, figuratively speaking, all
the dead cats of civilization. But then, you see, I can't choose. He won't
be forgotten. Whatever he was, he was not common. He had the power
to charm or frighten rudimentary souls into an aggravated witch-dance
in his honour; he could also fill the small souls of the pilgrims with bitter
misgivings: he had one devoted friend at least, and he had conquered one
soul in the world that was neither rudimentary nor tainted with self-seek-
ing. No; I can't forget him, though I am not prepared to affirm the fellow
was exactly worth the life we lost in getting to him. I missed my late
helmsman awfully,—I missed him even while his body was still lying in
the pilot-house. Perhaps you will think it passing strange this regret for
a savage who was no more account than a grain of sand in a black Sahara.
Well, don't you see, he had done something, he had steered; for months
I had him at my back—a help—an instrument. It was a kind of partnership.
He steered for me—I had to look after him, I worried about his deficiencies,
and thus a subtle bond had been created, of which I only became aware
when it was suddenly broken. And the intimate profundity of that look
he gave me when he received his hurt remains to this day in my memory—
like a claim of distant kinship affirmed in a supreme moment.

"Poor fool! If he had only left that shutter alone. He had no restraint,
no restraint—just like Kurtz—a tree swayed by the wind. As soon as I
had put on a dry pair of slippers, I dragged him out after first jerking
the spear out of his side, which operation I confess I performed with my
eyes shut tight. His heels leaped together over the little door-step; his
shoulders were pressed to my breast; I hugged him from behind desperately.
Oh! he was heavy, heavy; heavier than any man on earth, I should imagine.
Then without more ado I tipped him overboard. The current snatched
him as though he had been a wisp of grass, and I saw the body roll over

twice before I lost sight of it for ever. All the pilgrims and the manager were then congregated on the awning-deck about the pilot-house, chattering at each other like a flock of excited magpies, and there was a scandalized murmur at my heartless promptitude. What they wanted to keep that body hanging about for I can't guess. Embalm it, maybe. But I had also heard another, and a very ominous, murmur on the deck below. My friends the wood-cutters were likewise scandalized and with a better show of rea-son—though I admit that the reason itself was quite inadmissible. Oh, quite! I had made up my mind that if my late helmsman was to be eaten, the fishes alone should have him. He had been a very second-rate helmsman while alive, but now he was dead he might have become a first-class tempta-tion, and possibly cause some startling trouble. Besides, I was anxious to take the wheel, the man in pink pyjamas showing himself a hopeless duffer at the business.

"This I did directly the simple funeral was over. We were going half-speed, keeping right in the middle of the stream, and I listened to the talk about me. They had given up Kurtz, they had given up the station; Kurtz was dead, and the station had been burnt—and so on—and so on. The red-haired pilgrim was beside himself with the thought that at least this poor Kurtz had been properly avenged. 'Say! We must have made a glorious slaughter of them in the bush. Eh? What do you think? Say?' He positively danced, the bloodthirsty little gingery beggar. And he had nearly fainted when he saw the wounded man! I could not help saying, 'You made a glorious lot of smoke, anyhow.' I had seen, from the way the tops of the bushes rustled and flew, that almost all the shots had gone too high. You can't hit anything unless you take aim and fire from the shoulder; but these chaps fired from the hip with their eyes shut. The retreat, I maintained—and I was right—was caused by the screeching of the steam-whistle. Upon this they forgot Kurtz, and began to howl at me with indignant protests.

"The manager stood by the wheel murmuring confidentially about the necessity of getting well away down the river before dark at all events, when I saw in the distance a clearing on the river-side and the outlines of some sort of building. 'What's this?' I asked. He clapped his hands in wonder. 'The station!' he cried. I edged in at once, still going half-speed.

"Through my glasses I saw the slope of a hill interspersed with rare trees and perfectly free from undergrowth. A long decaying building on the summit was half buried in the high grass; the large holes in the peaked roof gaped black from afar; the jungle and the woods made a background. There was no enclosure or fence of any kind; but there had been one apparently, for near the house half-a-dozen slim posts remained in a row, roughly trimmed, and with their upper ends ornamented with round carved balls. The rails, or whatever there had been between, had disappeared. Of course the forest surrounded all that. The river-bank was clear, and on the water-side I saw a white man under a hat like a cartwheel beckoning persistently with his whole arm. Examining the edge of the forest above and below, I was almost certain I could see movements—human forms gliding here and there. I steamed past prudently, then stopped the engines and let her drift down. The man on the shore began to shout, urging us to land. 'We have been attacked,' screamed the manager. 'I know—I know. It's all right,' yelled back the other, as cheerful as you please. 'Come along. It's all right. I am glad.'

"His aspect reminded me of something I had seen—something funny I had seen somewhere. As I manoeuvred to get alongside, I was asking myself, 'What does this fellow look like?' Suddenly I got it. He looked like a harlequin. His clothes had been made of some stuff that was brown holland probably, but it was covered with patches all over, with bright patches, blue, red, and yellow,—patches on the back, patches on the front, patches on elbows, on knees; coloured binding around his jacket, scarlet edging at the bottom of his trousers; and the sunshine made him look extremely gay and wonderfully neat withal, because you could see how beautifully all this patching had been done. A beardless, boyish face, very fair, no features to speak of, nose peeling, little blue eyes, smiles and frowns chasing each other over that open countenance like sunshine and shadow on a wind-swept plain. 'Look out, captain!' he cried; 'there's a snag lodged in here last night.' What! Another snag? I confess I swore shamefully. I had nearly holed my cripple, to finish off that charming trip. The harlequin on the bank turned his little pug-nose up to me. 'You English?' he asked, all smiles. 'Are you?' I shouted from the wheel. The smiles vanished, and he shook his head as if sorry for my disappointment. Then he brightened up. 'Never mind!' he cried, encouragingly. 'Are we in time?' I asked. 'He is up there,' he replied, with a toss of the head up the hill, and becoming gloomy all of a sudden. His face was like the autumn sky, overcast one moment and bright the next.

"When the manager, escorted by the pilgrims, all of them armed to the teeth, had gone to the house this chap came on board. 'I say, I don't like this. These natives are in the bush,' I said. He assured me earnestly it was all right. 'They are simple people,' he added; 'well, I am glad you came. It took me all my time to keep them off.' 'But you said it was all right,' I cried. 'Oh, they meant no harm,' he said; and as I stared he corrected himself, 'Not exactly.' Then vivaciously, 'My faith, your pilot-house wants a clean-up!' In the next breath he advised me to keep enough steam on the boiler to blow the whistle in case of any trouble. 'One good screech will do more for you than all your rifles. They are simple people,' he repeated. He rattled away at such a rate he quite overwhelmed me. He seemed to be trying to make up for lots of silence, and actually hinted, laughing, that such was the case. 'Don't you talk with Mr. Kurtz?' I said. 'You don't talk with that man—you listen to him,' he exclaimed with severe exaltation. 'But now———' He waved his arm, and in the twinkling of an eye was in the uttermost depths of despondency. In a moment he came up again with a jump, possessed himself of both my hands, shook them continuously, while he gabbled: 'Brother, sailor . . . honour . . . pleasure . . . delight . . . introduce myself . . . Russian . . . son of an arch-priest . . . Government of Tambov . . . What? Tobacco. English tobacco; the excellent English tobacco! Now, that's brotherly. Smoke? Where's a sailor that does not smoke?'

"The pipe soothed him, and gradually I made out he had run away from school, had gone to sea in a Russian ship; ran away again; served some time in English ships; was now reconciled with the arch-priest. He made a point of that. 'But when one is young one must see things, gather experience, ideas; enlarge the mind.' 'Here!' I interrupted. 'You can never tell! Here I met Mr. Kurtz,' he said, youthfully solemn and reproachful. I held my tongue after that. It appears he had persuaded a Dutch trading-house on the coast to fit him out with stores and goods, and had started for the interior with a light heart, and no more idea of what would happen to him than a baby. He had been wandering about that river for nearly two years alone, cut off from everybody and everything. 'I am not so young as I look. I am twenty-five,' he said. 'At first old Van Shuyten would tell me to go to the devil,' he narrated with keen enjoyment; 'but I stuck to him, and talked and talked, till at last he got afraid I would talk the hind-leg off his favourite dog, so he gave me some cheap things and a few guns, and told me he hoped he would never see my face again. Good old Dutchman, Van Shuyten. I've sent him one small lot of ivory a year ago, so that he can't call me a little thief when I get back. I hope he got it. And for the rest I don't care. I had some wood stacked for you. That was my old house. Did you see?'

"I gave him Towson's book. He made as though he would kiss me, but restrained himself. 'The only book I had left, and I thought I had lost it,' he said, looking at it ecstatically. 'So many accidents happen to a man going about alone, you know. Canoes get upset sometimes—and some-times you've got to clear out so quick when the people get angry.' He thumbed the pages. 'You made notes in Russian?' I asked. He nodded. 'I thought they were written in cipher,' I said. He laughed, then became serious. 'I had lots of trouble to keep these people off,' he said. 'Did they want to kill you?' I asked. 'Oh, no!' he cried, and checked himself. 'Why did they attack us?' I pursued. He hesitated, then said shamefacedly, 'They don't want him to go.' 'Don't they?' I said, curiously. He nodded a nod full of mystery and wisdom. 'I tell you,' he cried, 'this man has enlarged my mind.' He opened his arms wide, staring at me with his little blue eyes that were perfectly round."

III

"I looked at him, lost in astonishment. There he was before me, in motley, as though he had absconded from a troupe of mimes, enthusiastic, fabulous. His very existence was improbable, inexplicable, and altogether bewilder-ing. He was an insoluble problem. It was inconceivable how he had existed, how he had succeeded in getting so far, how he had managed to remain—why he did not instantly disappear. 'I went a little farther,' he said, 'then still a little farther—till I had gone so far that I don't know how I'll ever get back. Never mind. Plenty time. I can manage. You take Kurtz away quick—quick—I tell you.' The glamour of youth enveloped his particol-oured rags, his destitution, his loneliness, the essential desolation of his futile wanderings. For months—for years—his life hadn't been worth a day's purchase; and there he was gallantly, thoughtlessly alive, to all appear-ance indestructible solely by the virtue of his few years and of his unreflect-ing audacity. I was seduced into something like admiration—like envy. Glamour urged him on, glamour kept him unscathed. He surely wanted nothing from the wilderness but space to breathe in and to push on through. His need was to exist, and to move onwards at the greatest possible risk, and with a maximum of privation. If the absolutely pure, uncalculating, unpractical spirit of adventure had ever ruled a human being, it ruled this be-patched youth. I almost envied him the possession of this modest and clear flame. It seemed to have consumed all thought of self so completely, that even while he was talking to you, you forgot that it was he—the man before your eyes—who had gone through these things. I did not envy him his devotion to Kurtz, though. He had not meditated over it. It came to him, and he accepted it with a sort of eager fatalism. I must say that to me it appeared about the most dangerous thing in every way he had come upon so far.

"They had come together unavoidably, like two ships becalmed near each other, and lay rubbing sides at last. I suppose Kurtz wanted an audience, because on a certain occasion, when encamped in the forest, they had talked all night, or more probably Kurtz had talked. 'We talked of everything,' he said, quite transported at the recollection. 'I forgot there was such a thing as sleep. The night did not seem to last an hour. Everything! Everything! . . . Of love, too.' 'Ah, he talked to you of love!' I said, much amused. 'It isn't what you think,' he cried, almost passionately. 'It was in general. He made me see things—things.'

"He threw his arms up. We were on deck at the time, and the headman of my wood-cutters, lounging near by, turned upon him his heavy and glittering eyes. I looked around, and I don't know why, but I assure you that never, never before, did this land, this river, this jungle, the very arch of this blazing sky, appear to me so hopeless and so dark, so impenetrable to human thought, so pitiless to human weakness. 'And, ever since, you have been with him, of course?' I said.

"On the contrary. It appears their intercourse had been very much broken by various causes. He had, as he informed me proudly, managed to nurse Kurtz through two illnesses (he alluded to it as you would to some risky feat), but as a rule Kurtz wandered alone, far in the depths of the forest. 'Very often coming to this station, I had to wait days and days before he would turn up,' he said. 'Ah, it was worth waiting for!—sometimes.' 'What was he doing? exploring or what?' I asked. 'Oh, yes, of course'; he had discovered lots of villages, a lake, too—he did not know exactly in what direction; it was dangerous to inquire too much—but mostly his expeditions had been for ivory. 'But he had no goods to trade with by that time,' I objected. 'There's a good lot of cartridges left even yet,' he answered, looking away. 'To speak plainly, he raided the country,' I said. He nodded. 'Not alone, surely!' He muttered something about the villages round that lake. 'Kurtz got the tribe to follow him, did he?' I suggested. He fidgeted a little. 'They adored him,' he said. The tone of these words was so extraordinary that I looked at him searchingly. It was curious to see his mingled eagerness and reluctance to speak of Kurtz. The man filled his life, occupied his thoughts, swayed his emotions. 'What can you expect?' he burst out; 'he came to them with thunder and lightning, you know—and they had never seen anything like it—and very terrible. He could be very terrible. You can't judge Mr. Kurtz as you would an ordinary man. No, no, no! Now—just to give you an idea—I don't mind telling you, he wanted to shoot me, too, one day—but I don't judge him.' 'Shoot you!' I cried. 'What for?' 'Well, I had a small lot of ivory the chief of that village near my house gave me. You see I used to shoot game for them. Well, he wanted it, and wouldn't hear reason. He declared he would shoot me unless I gave him the ivory and then cleared out of the country, because he could do so, and had a fancy for it, and there was nothing on earth to prevent him killing whom he jolly well pleased. And it was true, too. I gave him the ivory. What did I care! But I didn't clear out. No, no. I couldn't leave him. I had to be careful, of course, till we got friendly again for a time. He had his second illness then. Afterwards I had to keep out of the way; but I didn't mind. He was living for the most part in those villages on the lake. When he came down to the river, sometimes he would talk to me, and sometimes it was better for me to be careful. This man suffered too much. He hated all this, and somehow he couldn't get away. When I had a chance I begged him to try and leave while there was time; I offered to go back with him. And he would say yes, and then he would remain; go off on another ivory hunt; disappear for weeks; forget himself amongst these people—forget himself—you know.' 'Why! he's mad,' I said. He protested indignantly. Mr. Kurtz couldn't be mad. If I had heard him talk, only two days ago, I wouldn't dare hint at such a thing. . . . I had taken up my binoculars while we talked, and was looking at the shore, sweeping the limit of the forest at each side and at the back of the house. The consciousness of there being people in that bush, so silent, so quiet—as silent and quiet as the ruined house on the hill—made me uneasy. There was no sign on the face of nature of this amazing tale that was not so much told as suggested to me in desolate exclamations, completed by shrugs, in interrupted phrases, in hints ending in deep signs. The woods were unmoved, like a mask—heavy, like the closed door of a prison—they looked with their air of hidden knowledge, of patient expectation, of unapproachable silence. The Russian was explaining to me that it was only lately that Mr. Kurtz had come down to the river, bringing along with him all the fighting men of that lake tribe. He had been absent for several months—getting himself adored, I suppose—and had come down unexpectedly, with the intention to all appearance of making a raid either across the river or down stream. Evidently the appetite for more ivory had got the better of the—what shall I say?—less material aspirations. However he had got much worse suddenly. 'I heard he was lying helpless, and so I came up—took my chance,' said the Russian. 'Oh, he is bad, very bad.' I directed my glass to the house. There were no signs of life, but there was the ruined roof, the long mud wall peeping above the grass, with three little square window-holes, no two of the same size; all this brought within reach of my hand, as it were. And then I made a brusque movement, and one of the remaining posts of that vanished fence leaped up in the field of my glass. You remember I told you I had been struck at the distance by certain attempts at ornamentation, rather remarkable in the ruinous aspect of the place. Now I had suddenly a nearer view, and its first result was to make me throw my head back as if before a blow. Then I went carefully from post to post with my glass, and I saw my mistake. These round knobs were not ornamental but symbolic; they were expressive and puzzling, striking and disturbing—food for thought and also for vultures if there had been any looking down from the sky; but at all events for such ants as were industrious enough to ascend the pole. They would have been even more impressive, those heads on the stakes, if their faces had not been turned to the house. Only one, the first I had made out, was facing my way. I was not so shocked as you may think. The start back I had given was really nothing but a movement of surprise. I had expected to see a knob of wood there, you know. I returned deliberately to the first I had seen—and there it was, black, dried, sunken, with closed eyelids,—a head that seemed to sleep at the top of that pole, and with the shrunken dry lips showing a narrow white line of the teeth, was smiling, too, smiling continuously at some endless and jocose dream of that eternal slumber.

"I am not disclosing any trade secrets. In fact, the manager said afterwards that Mr. Kurtz's methods had ruined the district. I have no opinion on that point, but I want you clearly to understand that there was nothing exactly profitable in these heads being there. They only showed that Mr. Kurtz lacked restraint in the gratification of his various lusts, that there was something wanting in him—some small matter which, when the pressing need arose, could not be found under his magnificent eloquence. Whether he knew of this deficiency himself I can't say. I think the knowledge came to him at last—only at the very last. But the wilderness had found him out early, and had taken on him a terrible vengeance for the fantastic invasion. I think it had whispered to him things about himself which he did not know, things of which he had no conception till he took counsel with this great solitude—and the whisper had proved irresistibly fascinating. It echoed loudly within him because he was hollow at the core. . . . I put down the glass, and the head that had appeared near enough to be spoken to seemed at once to have leaped away from me into inaccessible distance.

"The admirer of Mr. Kurtz was a bit crestfallen. In a hurried, indistinct voice he began to assure me he had not dared to take these—say, symbols—down. He was not afraid of the natives; they would not stir till Mr. Kurtz gave the word. His ascendancy was extraordinary. The camps of these people surrounded the place, and the chiefs came every day to see him. They would crawl. . . . 'I don't want to know anything of the ceremonies used when approaching Mr. Kurtz,' I shouted. Curious, this feeling that came over me that such details would be more intolerable than those heads drying on the stakes under Mr. Kurtz's windows. After all, that was only a savage sight, while I seemed at one bound to have been transported into some lightless region of subtle horrors, where pure, uncomplicated savagery was a positive relief, being something that had a right to exist—obviously—in the sunshine. The young man looked at me with surprise. I suppose it did not occur to him that Mr. Kurtz was no idol of mine. He forgot I hadn't heard any of these splendid monologues on, what was it? on love, justice, conduct of life—or what not. If it had come to crawling before Mr. Kurtz, he crawled as much as the veriest savage of them all. I had no idea of the conditions, he said: these heads were the heads of rebels. I shocked him excessively by laughing. Rebels! What would be the next definition I was to hear? There had been enemies, criminals, workers—and these were rebels. Those rebellious heads looked very subdued to me on their sticks. 'You don't know how such a life tries a man like

Kurtz,' cried Kurtz's last disciple. 'Well, and you?' I said. 'I! I! I am a simple man. I have no great thoughts. I want nothing from anybody. How can you compare me to . . . ?' His feelings were too much for speech, and suddenly he broke down. 'I don't understand,' he groaned. 'I've been doing my best to keep him alive, and that's enough. I had no hand in all this. I have no abilities. There hasn't been a drop of medicine or a mouthful of invalid food for months here. He was shamefully abandoned. A man like this, with such ideas. Shamefully! Shamefully! I—I—haven't slept for the last ten nights . . .'

"His voice lost itself in the calm of the evening. The long shadows of the forest had slipped down hill while we talked, had gone far beyond the ruined hovel, beyond the symbolic row of stakes. All this was in the gloom, while we down there were yet in the sunshine, and the stretch of the river abreast of the clearing glittered in a still and dazzling splendour, with a murky and overshadowed bend above and below. Not a living soul was seen on the shore. The bushes did not rustle.

"Suddenly round the corner of the house a group of men appeared, as though they had come up from the ground. They waded waist-deep in the grass, in a compact body, bearing an improvised stetcher in their midst. Instantly, in the emptiness of the landscape, a cry arose whose shrillness pierced the still air like a sharp arrow flying straight to the very heart of the land; and, as if by enchantment, streams of human beings—of naked human beings—with spears in their hands, with bows, with shields, with wild glances and savage movements, were poured into the clearing by the dark-faced and pensive forest. The bushes shook, the grass swayed for a time, and then everything stood still in attentive immobility.

" 'Now, if he does not say the right thing to them we are all done for,' said the Russian at my elbow. The knot of men with the stretcher had stopped, too, half-way to the steamer, as if petrified. I saw the man on the stretcher sit up, lank and with an uplifted arm, above the shoulders of the bearers. 'Let us hope that the man who can talk so well of love in general will find some particular reason to spare us this time,' I said. I resented bitterly the absurd danger of our situation, as if to be at the mercy of that atrocious phantom had been a dishonouring necessity. I could not hear a sound, but through my glasses I saw the thin arm extended commandingly, the lower jaw moving, the eyes of that apparition shining darkly far in its bony head that nodded with grotesque jerks. Kurtz—Kurtz—that means short in German—don't it? Well, the name was as true as everything else in his life—and death. He looked at least seven feet long. His covering had fallen off, and his body emerged from it pitiful and appalling as from a winding-sheet. I could see the cage of his ribs all astir, the bones of his arm waving. It was as though an animated image of death carved out of old ivory had been shaking its hand with menaces at a motionless crowd of men made of dark and glittering bronze. I saw him open his mouth wide—it gave him a weirdly voracious aspect, as though he had wanted to swallow all the air, all the earth, all the men before him. A deep voice reached me faintly. He must have been shouting. He fell back suddenly. The stretcher shook as the bearers staggered forward again, and almost at the same time I noticed that the crowd of savages was vanishing without any perceptible movement of retreat, as if the forest that had ejected these beings so suddenly had drawn them in again as the breath is drawn in a long aspiration.

"Some of the pilgrims behind the stretcher carried his arms—two shot-guns, a heavy rifle, and a light revolver-carbine—the thunderbolts of that pitiful Jupiter. The manager bent over him murmuring as he walked beside his head. They laid him down in one of the little cabins—just a room for a bedplace and a camp-stool or two, you know. We had brought his belated correspondence, and a lot of torn envelopes and open letters littered his bed. His hand roamed feebly amongst these pages. I was struck by the fire of his eyes and the composed languor of his expression. It was not so much the exhaustion of disease. He did not seem in pain. This shadow looked satiated and calm, as though for the moment it had had its fill of all the emotions.

"He rustled one of the letters, and looking straight in my face said, 'I am glad.' Somebody had been writing to him about me. These special recommendations were turning up again. The volume of tone he emitted without effort, almost without the trouble of moving his lips, amazed me. A voice! a voice! It was grave, profound, vibrating, while the man did not seem capable of a whisper. However, he had enough strength in him—factitious no doubt—to very nearly make an end of us, as you shall hear directly.

"The manager appeared silently in the doorway; I stepped out at once and he drew the curtain after me. The Russian, eyed curiously by the pilgrims, was staring at the shore. I followed the direction of his glance.

"Dark human shapes could be made out in the distance, flitting indistinctly against the gloomy border of the forest, and near the river two bronze figures, leaning on tall spears, stood in the sunlight under fantastic head-dresses of spotted skins, warlike and still in statuesque repose. And from right to left along the light shore moved a wild and gorgeous apparition of a woman.

"She walked with measured steps, draped in striped and fringed cloths, treading the earth proudly, with a slight jingle and flash of barbarous ornaments. She carried her head high; her hair was done in the shape of a helmet; she had brass leggings to the knee, brass wire gauntlets to the elbow, a crimson spot on her tawny cheek, innumerable necklaces of glass beads on her neck; bizarre things, charms, gifts of witch-men, that hung about her, glittered and trembled at every step. She must have had the value of several elephant tusks upon her. She was savage and superb, wild-eyed and magnificent; there was something ominous and stately in her deliberate progress. And in the hush that had fallen suddenly upon the whole sorrowful land, the immense wilderness, the colossal body of the fecund and mysterious life seemed to look at her, pensive, as though it had been looking at the image of its own tenebrous and passionate soul.

"She came abreast of the steamer, stood still, and faced us. Her long shadow fell to the water's edge. Her face had a tragic and fierce aspect of wild sorrow and of dumb pain mingled with the fear of some struggling half-shaped resolve. She stood looking at us without a stir, and like the wilderness itself, with an air of brooding over an inscrutable purpose. A whole minute passed, and then she made a step forward. There was a low jingle, a glint of yellow metal, a sway of fringed draperies, and she stopped as if her heart had failed her. The young fellow by my side growled. The pilgrims murmured at my back. She looked at us all as if her life had depended upon the unswerving steadiness of her glance. Suddenly she opened her bared arms and threw them up rigid above her head, as though in an uncontrollable desire to touch the sky, and at the same time the swift shadows darted out on the earth, swept around on the river, gathering the steamer into a shadowy embrace. A formidable silence hung over the scene.

"She turned away slowly, walked on, following the bank, and passed into the bushes to the left. Once only her eyes gleamed back at us in the dusk of the thickets before she disappeared.

" 'If she had offered to come aboard I really think I would have tried to shoot her,' said the man of patches, nervously. 'I have been risking my life every day for the last fortnight to keep her out of the house. She got in one day and kicked up a row about those miserable rags I picked up in a storeroom to mend my clothes with. I wasn't decent. At least it must have been that, for she talked like a fury to Kurtz for an hour, pointing at me now and then. I don't understand the dialect of this tribe. Luckily for me, I fancy Kurtz felt too ill that day to care, or there would have been mischief. I don't understand. . . . No—it's too much for me. Ah, well, it's all over now.'

"At this moment I heard Kurtz's deep voice behind the curtain: 'Save me!—save the ivory, you mean. Don't tell me. Save *me!* Why, I've had to save you. You are interrupting my plans now. Sick! Sick! Not so sick as you would like to believe. Never mind. I'll carry my ideas out yet—I will return. I'll show you what can be done. You with your little peddling notions—you are interfering with me. I will return. I. . . .'

"The manager came out. He did me the honour to take me under the arm and lead me aside. 'He is very low, very low,' he said. He considered it necessary to sigh, but neglected to be consistently sorrowful. 'We have done all we could for him—haven't we? But there is no disguising the fact, Mr. Kurtz has done more harm than good to the Company. He did not see the time was not ripe for vigorous action. Cautiously, cautiously—that's my principle. We must be cautious yet. The district is closed to us for a time. Deplorable! Upon the whole, the trade will suffer. I don't deny there is a remarkable quantity of ivory—mostly fossil. We must save it, at all events—but look how precarious the position is—and why? Because the method is unsound.' 'Do you,' said I, looking at the shore, 'call it "unsound method?" ' 'Without doubt,' he exclaimed, hotly. 'Don't you?' . . . 'No method at all,' I murmured after a while. 'Exactly,' he exulted. 'I anticipated this. Shows a complete want of judgment. It is my duty to point it out in the proper quarter.' 'Oh,' said I, 'that fellow—what's his name?—the brickmaker, will make a readable report for you.' He appeared confounded for a moment. It seemed to me I had never breathed an atmosphere so vile, and I turned mentally to Kurtz for relief—positively for relief. 'Nevertheless I think Mr. Kurtz is a remarkable man,' I said with emphasis. He started, dropped on me a cold heavy glance, said very quietly, 'he *was*,' and turned his back on me. My hour of favour was over; I found myself lumped along with Kurtz as a partisan of methods for which the time was not ripe: I was unsound! Ah! but it was something to have at least a choice of nightmares.

"I had turned to the wilderness really, not to Mr. Kurtz, who, I was ready to admit, was as good as buried. And for a moment it seemed to me as if I also were buried in a vast grave full of unspeakable secrets. I felt an intolerable weight oppressing my breast, the smell of the damp earth, the unseen presence of victorious corruption, the darkness of an impenetrable night. . . . The Russian tapped me on the shoulder. I heard him mumbling and stammering something about 'brother seaman— couldn't conceal—knowledge of matters that would affect Mr. Kurtz's repu- tation.' I waited. For him evidently Mr. Kurtz was not in his grave; I suspect that for him Mr. Kurtz was one of the immortals. 'Well!' said I at last, 'speak out. As it happens, I am Mr. Kurtz's friend—in a way.'

"He stated with a good deal of formality that had we not been 'of the same profession,' he would have kept the matter to himself without regard to consequences. 'He suspected there was an active ill will towards him on the part of these white men that———' 'You are right,' I said, remember- ing a certain conversation I had overheard. 'The manager thinks you ought to be hanged.' He showed a concern at this intelligence which amused me at first. 'I had better get out of the way quietly,' he said, earnestly. 'I can do no more for Kurtz now, and they would soon find some excuse. What's to stop them? There's a military post three hundred miles from here.' 'Well, upon my word,' said I, 'perhaps you had better go if you have any friends amongst the savages near by.' 'Plenty,' he said. 'They are simple people—and I want nothing, you know.' He stood biting his lip, then: 'I don't want any harm to happen to these whites here, but of course I was thinking of Mr. Kurtz's reputation—but you are a brother seaman and———' 'All right,' said I, after a time. 'Mr. Kurtz's reputation is safe with me.' I did not know how truly I spoke.

"He informed me, lowering his voice, that it was Kurtz who had ordered the attack to be made on the steamer. 'He hated sometimes the idea of being taken away—and then again. . . . But I don't understand these mat- ters. I am a simple man. He thought it would scare you away—that you would give it up, thinking him dead. I could not stop him. Oh, I had an awful time of it this last month.' 'Very well,' I said. 'He is all right now.' 'Ye-e-es,' he muttered, not very convinced apparently. 'Thanks,' said I; 'I shall keep my eyes open.' 'But quiet—eh?' he urged, anxiously. 'It would be awful for his reputation if anybody here———' I promised a complete discretion with great gravity. 'I have a canoe and three black fellows waiting not very far. I am off. Could you give me a few Martini-Henry cartridges?' I could, and did, with proper secrecy. He helped himself, with a wink at me, to a handful of my tobacco. 'Between sailors—you know—good English tobacco.' At the door of the pilot-house he turned round—'I say, haven't you a pair of shoes you could spare?' He raised one leg. 'Look.' The soles were tied with knotted strings sandal-wise under his bare feet. I rooted out an old pair, at which he looked with admiration before tucking it under his left arm. One of his pockets (bright red) was bulging with car- tridges, from the other (dark blue) peeped 'Towson's Inquiry,' etc., etc. He seemed to think himself excellently well equipped for a renewed en- counter with the wilderness. 'Ah! I'll never, never meet such a man again.

You ought to have heard him recite poetry—his own, too, it was, he told me. Poetry!' He rolled his eyes at the recollection of these delights. 'Oh, he enlarged my mind!' 'Good-bye,' said I. He shook hands and vanished in the night. Sometimes I ask myself whether I had ever really seen him—whether it was possible to meet such a phenomenon! . . .

"When I woke up shortly after midnight his warning came to my mind with its hint of danger that seemed, in the starred darkness, real enough to make me get up for the purpose of having a look round. On the hill a big fire burned, illuminating fitfully a crooked corner of the station-house. One of the agents with a picket of a few of our blacks, armed for the purpose, was keeping guard over the ivory; but deep within the forest, red gleams that wavered, that seemed to sink and rise from the ground amongst confused columnar shapes of intense blackness, showed the exact position of the camp where Mr. Kurtz's adorers were keeping their uneasy vigil. The monotonous beating of a big drum filled the air with muffled shocks and a lingering vibration. A steady droning sound of many men chanting each to himself some weird incantation came out from the black, flat wall of the woods as the humming of bees comes out of a hive, and had a strange narcotic effect upon my half-awake senses. I believe I dozed off leaning over the rail, till an abrupt burst of yells, an overwhelming outbreak of a pent-up and mysterious frenzy, woke me up in a bewildered wonder. It was cut short all at once, and the low droning went on with an effect of audible and soothing silence. I glanced casually into the little cabin. A light was burning within, but Mr. Kurtz was not there.

"I think I would have raised an outcry if I had believed my eyes. But I didn't believe them at first—the thing seemed so impossible. The fact is I was completely unnerved by a sheer blank fright, pure abstract terror, unconnected with any distinct shape of physical danger. What made this emotion so overpowering was—how shall I define it?—the moral shock I received, as if something altogether monstrous, intolerable to thought and odious to the soul, had been thrust upon me unexpectedly. This lasted of course the merest fraction of a second, and then the usual sense of commonplace, deadly danger, the possibility of a sudden onslaught and massacre, or something of the kind, which I saw impending, was positively welcome and composing. It pacified me, in fact, so much, that I did not raise an alarm.

"There was an agent buttoned up inside an ulster and sleeping on a chair on deck within three feet of me. The yells had not awakened him; he snored very slightly; I left him to his slumbers and leaped ashore. I did not betray Mr. Kurtz—it was ordered I should never betray him—it was written I should be loyal to the nightmare of my choice. I was anxious to deal with this shadow by myself alone,—and to this day I don't know why I was so jealous of sharing with any one the peculiar blackness of that experience.

"As soon as I got on the bank I saw a trail—a broad trail through the grass. I remember the exultation with which I said to myself, 'He can't walk—he is crawling on all-fours—I've got him.' The grass was wet with dew. I strode rapidly with clenched fists. I fancy I had some vague notion of falling upon him and giving him a drubbing. I don't know. I had some imbecile thoughts. The knitting old woman with the cat obtruded herself upon my memory as a most improper person to be sitting at the other end of such an affair. I saw a row of pilgrims squirting lead in the air out of Winchesters held to the hip. I thought I would never get back to the steamer, and imagined myself living alone and unarmed in the woods to an advanced age. Such silly things—you know. And I remember I confounded the beat of the drum with the beating of my heart, and was pleased at its calm regularity.

"I kept to the track though—then stopped to listen. The night was very clear; a dark blue space, sparkling with dew and starlight, in which black things stood very still. I thought I could see a kind of motion ahead of me. I was strangely cocksure of everything that night. I actually left the track and ran in a wide semicircle (I verily believe chuckling to myself) so as to get in front of that stir, of that motion I had seen—if indeed I had seen anything. I was circumventing Kurtz as though it had been a boyish game.

"I came upon him, and, if he had not heard me coming, I would have fallen over him, too, but he got up in time. He rose, unsteady, long, pale, indistinct, like a vapour exhaled by the earth, and swayed slightly, misty and silent before me; while at my back the fires loomed between the trees, and the murmur of many voices issued from the forest. I had cut him off cleverly; but when actually confronting him I seemed to come to my senses, I saw the danger in its right proportion. It was by no means over yet. Suppose he began to shout? Though he could hardly stand, there was still plenty of vigour in his voice. 'Go away—hide yourself,' he said, in that profound tone. It was very awful. I glanced back. We were within thirty yards from the nearest fire. A black figure stood up, strode on long black legs, waving long black arms, across the glow. It had horns—antelope horns, I think—on its head. Some sorceror, some witch-man, no doubt: it looked fiend-like enough. 'Do you know what you are doing?' I whispered. 'Perfectly,' he answered, raising his voice for that single word: it sounded to me far off and yet loud, like a hail through a speaking-trumpet. If he makes a row we are lost, I thought to myself. This clearly was not a case for fisticuffs, even apart from the very natural aversion I had to beat that Shadow—this wandering and tormented thing. 'You will be lost,' I said—'utterly lost.' One gets sometimes such a flash of inspiration, you know. I did say the right thing, though indeed he could not have been more irretrievably lost than he was at this very moment, when the foundations of our intimacy were being laid—to endure—to endure—even to the end—even beyond.

"'I had immense plans,' he muttered irresolutely. 'Yes,' said I; 'but if you try to shout I'll smash your head with———' There was not a stick or a stone near. 'I will throttle you for good,' I corrected myself. 'I was on the threshold of great things,' he pleaded, in a voice of longing, with a wistfulness of tone that made my blood run cold. 'And now for this stupid scoundrel———' 'Your success in Europe is assured in any case,' I affirmed, steadily. I did not want to have the throttling of him, you understand—and indeed it would have been very little use for any practical purpose. I tried to break the spell—the heavy, mute spell of the wilderness— that seemed to draw him to its pitiless breast by the awakening of forgotten and brutal instincts, by the memory of gratified and monstrous passions.

This alone, I was convinced, had driven him out to the edge of the forest, to the bush, towards the gleam of fires, the throb of drums, the drone of weird incantations; this alone had beguiled his unlawful soul beyond the bounds of permitted aspirations. And, don't you see, the terror of the position was not in being knocked on the head—though I had a very lively sense of that danger, too—but in this, that I had to deal with a being to whom I could not appeal in the name of anything high or low. I had, even like the niggers, to invoke him—himself—his own exalted and incredible degradation. There was nothing either above or below him, and I knew it. He had kicked himself loose of the earth. Confound the man! he had kicked the very earth to pieces. He was alone, and I before him did not know whether I stood on the ground or floated in the air. I've been telling you what we said—repeating the phrases we pronounced—but what's the good? They were common everyday words—the familiar, vague sounds exchanged on every waking day of life. But what of that? They had behind them, to my mind, the terrific suggestiveness of words heard in dreams, of phrases spoken in nightmares. Soul! If anybody had ever struggled with a soul, I am the man. And I wasn't arguing with a lunatic either. Believe me or not, his intelligence was perfectly clear—concentrated, it is true, upon himself with horrible intensity, yet clear; and therein was my only chance—barring, of course, the killing him there and then, which wasn't so good, on account of unavoidable noise. But his soul was mad. Being alone in the wilderness, it had looked within itself, and, by heavens! I tell you, it had gone mad. I had—for my sins, I suppose—to go through the ordeal of looking into it myself. No eloquence could have been so withering to one's belief in mankind as his final burst of sincerity. He struggled with himself, too. I saw it,—I heard it. I saw the inconceivable mystery of a soul that knew no restraint, no faith, and no fear, yet struggling blindly with itself. I kept my head pretty well; but when I had him at last stretched on the couch, I wiped my forehead, while my legs shook under me as though I had carried half a ton on my back down that hill. And yet I had only supported him, his bony arm clasped round my neck— and he was not much heavier than a child.

"When next day we left at noon, the crowd, of whose presence behind the curtain of trees I had been acutely conscious all the time, flowed out of the woods again, filled the clearing, covered the slope with a mass of naked, breathing, quivering, bronze bodies. I steamed up a bit, then swung downstream, and two thousand eyes followed the evolutions of the splashing, thumping, fierce river-demon beating the water with its terrible tail and breathing black smoke into the air. In front of the first rank, along the river, three men, plastered with bright red earth from head to foot, strutted to and fro restlessly. When we came abreast again, they faced the river, stamped their feet, nodded their horned heads, swayed their scarlet bodies; they shook towards the fierce river-demon a bunch of black feathers, a mangy skin with a pendent tail—something that looked like a dried gourd; they shouted periodically together strings of amazing words that resembled no sounds of human language; and the deep murmurs of the crowd, interrupted suddenly, were like the response of some satanic litany.

"We had carried Kurtz into the pilot-house: there was more air there.

Lying on the couch, he stared through the open shutter. There was an eddy in the mass of human bodies, and the woman with helmeted head and tawny cheeks rushed out to the very brink of the stream. She put out her hands, shouted something, and all that wild mob took up the shout in a roaring chorus of articulated, rapid, breathless utterance.

" 'Do you understand this?' I asked.

"He kept on looking out past me with fiery, longing eyes, with a mingled expression of wistfulness and hate. He made no answer, but I saw a smile, a smile of indefinable meaning, appear on his colourless lips that a moment after twitched convulsively. 'Do I not?' he said slowly, gasping, as if the words had been torn out of him by a supernatural power.

"I pulled the string of the whistle, and I did this because I saw the pilgrims on deck getting out their rifles with an air of anticipating a jolly lark. At the sudden screech there was a movement of abject terror through that wedged mass of bodies. 'Don't! don't you frighten them away,' cried someone on deck disconsolately. I pulled the string time after time. They broke and ran, they leaped, they crouched, they swerved, they dodged the flying terror of the sound. The three red chaps had fallen flat, face down on the shore, as though they had been shot dead. Only the barbarous and superb woman did not so much as flinch, and stretched tragically her bare arms after us over the sombre and glittering river.

"And then that imbecile crowd down on the deck started their little fun, and I could see nothing more for smoke.

"The brown current ran swiftly out of the heart of darkness, bearing us down towards the sea with twice the speed of our upward progress; and Kurtz's life was running swiftly, too, ebbing, ebbing out of his heart into the sea of inexorable time. The manager was very placid, he had no vital anxieties now, he took us both in with a comprehensive and satisfied glance: the 'affair' had come off as well as could be wished. I saw the time approaching when I would be left alone of the party of 'unsound method.' The pilgrims looked upon me with disfavour. I was, so to speak, numbered with the dead. It is strange how I accepted this unforeseen partnership, this choice of nightmares forced upon me in the tenebrous land invaded by these mean and greedy phantoms.

"Kurtz discoursed. A voice! a voice! It rang deep to the very last. It survived his strength to hide in the magnificent folds of eloquence the barren darkness of his heart. Oh, he struggled! he struggled! The wastes of his weary brain were haunted by shadowy images now—images of wealth and fame revolving obsequiously round his unextinguishable gift of noble and lofty expression. My Intended, my station, my career, my ideas—these were the subjects for the occasional utterances of elevated sentiments. The shade of the original Kurtz frequented the bedside of the hollow sham, whose fate it was to be buried presently in the mould of primeval earth. But both the diabolic love and the unearthly hate of mysteries it had penetrated fought for the possession of that soul satiated with primitive emotions, avid of lying fame, of sham distinction, of all the appearances of success and power.

"Sometimes he was contemptibly childish. He desired to have kings meet him at railway-stations on his return from some ghastly Nowhere, where he intended to accomplish great things. 'You show them you have in you something that is really profitable, and then there will be no limits to the recognition of your ability,' he would say. 'Of course you must take care of the motives—right motives—always.' The long reaches that were like one and the same reach, monotonous bends that were exactly alike, slipped past the steamer with their multitude of secular[26] trees looking patiently after this grimy fragment of another world, the forerunner of change, of conquest, of trade, of massacres, of blessings. I looked ahead—piloting. 'Close the shutter,' said Kurtz suddenly one day; 'I can't bear to look at this.' I did so. There was a silence. 'Oh, but I will wring your heart yet!' he cried at the invisible wilderness.

"We broke down—as I had expected—and had to lie up for repairs at the head of an island. This delay was the first thing that shook Kurtz's confidence. One morning he gave me a packet of papers and a photograph—the lot tied together with a shoe-string. 'Keep this for me,' he said. 'This noxious fool' (meaning the manager) 'is capable of prying into my boxes when I am not looking.' In the afternoon I saw him. He was lying on his back with closed eyes, and I withdrew quietly, but I heard him mutter, 'Live rightly, die, die . . .' I listened. There was nothing more. Was he rehearsing some speech in his sleep, or was it a fragment of a phrase from some newspaper article? He had been writing for the papers and meant to do so again, 'for the furthering of my ideas. It's a duty.'

"His was an impenetrable darkness. I looked at him as you peer down at a man who is lying at the bottom of a precipice where the sun never shines. But I had not much time to give him, because I was helping the engine-driver to take to pieces the leaky cylinders, to straighten a bent connecting-rod, and in other such matters. I lived in an infernal mess of rust, filings, nuts, bolts, spanners, hammers, ratchet-drills—things I abominate, because I don't get on with them. I tended the little forge we fortunately had aboard; I toiled wearily in a wretched scrap-heap—unless I had the shakes too bad to stand.

"One evening coming in with a candle I was startled to hear him say a little tremulously, 'I am lying here in the dark waiting for death.' The light was within a foot of his eyes. I forced myself to murmur, 'Oh, nonsense!' and stood over him as if transfixed.

"Anything approaching the change that came over his features I have never seen before, and hope never to see again. Oh, I wasn't touched. I was fascinated. It was as though a veil had been rent. I saw on that ivory face the expression of sombre pride, of ruthless power, of craven terror—of an intense and hopeless despair. Did he live his life again in every detail of desire, temptation, and surrender during that supreme moment of complete knowledge? He cried in a whisper at some image, at some vision—he cried out twice, a cry that was no more than a breath—

" 'The horror! The horror!'

"I blew the candle out and left the cabin. The pilgrims were dining in the mess-room, and I took my place opposite the manager, who lifted his eyes to give me a questioning glance, which I successfully ignored. He leaned back, serene, with that peculiar smile of his sealing the unexpressed depths of his meanness. A continuous shower of small flies streamed upon

[26] Centuries old.

the lamp, upon the cloth, upon our hands and faces. Suddenly the manager's boy put his insolent black head in the doorway, and said in a tone of scathing contempt—

" 'Mistah Kurtz—he dead.'

"All the pilgrims rushed out to see. I remained, and went on with my dinner. I believe I was considered brutally callous. However, I did not eat much. There was a lamp in there—light, don't you know—and outside it was so beastly, beastly dark. I went no more near the remarkable man who had pronounced a judgment upon the adventures of his soul on this earth. The voice was gone. What else had been there? But I am of course aware that next day the pilgrims buried something in a muddy hole.

"And then they very nearly buried me.

"However, as you see, I did not go to join Kurtz there and then. I did not. I remained to dream the nightmare out to the end, and to show my loyalty to Kurtz once more. Destiny. My destiny! Droll thing life is— that mysterious arrangement of merciless logic for a futile purpose. The most you can hope from it is some knowledge of yourself—that comes too late—a crop of unextinguishable regrets. I have wrestled with death. It is the most unexciting contest you can imagine. It takes place in an impalpable grayness, with nothing under foot, with nothing around, without spectators, without clamour, without glory, without the great desire of victory, without the great fear of defeat, in a sickly atmosphere of tepid scepticism, without much belief in your own right, and still less in that of your adversary. If such is the form of ultimate wisdom, then life is a greater riddle than some of us think it to be. I was within a hair's breadth of the last opportunity for pronouncement, and I found with humiliation that probably I would have nothing to say. This is the reason why I affirm that Kurtz was a remarkable man. He had something to say. He said it. Since I had peeped over the edge myself, I understand better the meaning of his stare, that could not see the flame of the candle, but was wide enough to embrace the whole universe, piercing enough to penetrate all the hearts that beat in the darkness. He had summed up—he had judged. 'The horror!' He was a remarkable man. After all, this was the expression of some sort of belief; it had candour, it had conviction, it had a vibrating note of revolt in its whisper, it had the appalling face of a glimpsed truth—the strange commingling of desire and hate. And it is not my own extremity I remember best—a vision of grayness without form filled with physical pain, and a careless contempt for the evanescence of all things—even of this pain itself. No! It is his extremity that I seem to have lived through. True, he had made that last stride, he had stepped over the edge, while I had been permitted to draw back my hesitating foot. And perhaps in this is the whole difference; perhaps all the wisdom, and all truth, and all sincerity, are just compressed into that inappreciable moment of time in which we step over the threshold of the invisible. Perhaps! I like to think my sum- ming-up would not have been a word of careless contempt. Better his cry—much better. It was an affirmation, a moral victory paid for by innu- merable defeats, by abominable terrors, by abominable satisfactions. But it was a victory! That is why I have remained loyal to Kurtz to the last, and even beyond, when a long time after I heard once more, not his own voice, but the echo of his magnificent eloquence thrown to me from a soul as translucently pure as a cliff of crystal.

"No, they did not bury me, though there is a period of time which I remember mistily, with a shuddering wonder, like a passage through some inconceivable world that had no hope in it and no desire. I found myself back in the sepulchral city resenting the sight of people hurrying through the streets to filch a little money from each other, to devour their infamous cookery, to gulp their unwholesome beer, to dream their insignificant and silly dreams. They trespassed upon my thoughts. They were intruders whose knowledge of life was to me an irritating pretence, because I felt so sure they could not possibly know the things I knew. Their bearing, which was simply the bearing of commonplace individuals going about their business in the assurance of perfect safety, was offensive to me like the outrageous flauntings of folly in the face of a danger it is unable to comprehend. I had no particular desire to enlighten them, but I had some difficulty in restraining myself from laughing in their faces, so full of stupid importance. I daresay I was not very well at that time. I tottered about the streets—there were various affairs to settle—grinning bitterly at perfectly respectable persons. I admit my behaviour was inexcusable, but then my temperature was seldom normal in these days. My dear aunt's endeavours to 'nurse up my strength' seemed altogether beside the mark. It was not my strength that wanted nursing, it was my imagination that wanted soothing. I kept the bundle of papers given me by Kurtz, not knowing exactly what to do with it. His mother had died lately, watched over, as I was told, by his Intended. A clean-shaved man, with an official manner and wearing gold-rimmed spectacles, called on me one day and made inquiries, at first circuitous, afterwards suavely pressing, about what he was pleased to denominate certain 'documents.' I was not surprised, because I had had two rows with the manager on the subject out there. I had refused to give up the smallest scrap out of that package, and I took the same attitude with the spectacled man. He became darkly menacing at last, and with much heat argued that the Company had the right to every bit of information about its 'territories.' And said he, 'Mr. Kurtz's knowledge of unexplored regions must have been necessarily extensive and peculiar—owing to his great abilities and to the deplorable circumstances in which he had been placed: therefore———' I assured him Mr. Kurtz's knowledge, however extensive, did not bear upon the problems of commerce or administration. He invoked then the name of science. 'It would be an incalculable loss if,' etc., etc. I offered him the report on the 'Suppression of Savage Customs,' with the postscriptum torn off. He took it eagerly, but ended by sniffing at it with an air of contempt. 'This is not what we had a right to expect,' he remarked. 'Expect nothing else,' I said. 'There are only private letters.' He withdrew upon some threat of legal proceedings, and I saw him no more; but another fellow, calling himself Kurtz's cousin, appeared two days later, and was anxious to hear all the details about his dear relative's last moments. Incidentally he gave me to understand that Kurtz had been essentially a great musician. 'There was the making of an immense success,' said the man, who was an organist, I believe, with lank gray hair flowing over a greasy coat-collar. I had no reason to doubt his statement; and to this day I am unable to say what was Kurtz's profession, whether he ever had any—which was the greatest of his talents. I had taken him for a painter who wrote for the papers, or else for a journalist who could paint—but even the cousin (who took snuff during the interview) could not tell me what he had been—exactly. He was a universal genius—on that point I agreed with the old chap, who thereupon blew his nose noisily into a large cotton handkerchief and withdrew in a senile agitation, bearing off some family letters and memoranda without importance. Ultimately, a journalist anxious to know something of the fate of his 'dear colleague' turned up. This visitor informed me Kurtz's proper sphere ought to have been politics 'on the popular side.' He had furry straight eyebrows, bristly hair cropped short, an eyeglass on a broad ribbon, and becoming expansive, confessed his opinion that Kurtz really couldn't write a bit—'but heavens! how that man could talk. He electrified large meetings. He had faith—don't you see?—he had the faith. He could get himself to believe anything—anything. He would have been a splendid leader of an extreme party.' 'What party?' I asked. 'Any party,' answered the other. 'He was an—an—extremist.' Did I not think so? I assented. Did I know, he asked, with a sudden flash of curiosity, 'what it was that had induced him to go out there?' 'Yes,' said I, and forthwith handed him the famous Report for publication, if he thought fit. He glanced through it hurriedly, mumbling all the time, judged 'it would do,' and took himself off with this plunder.

"Thus I was left at last with a slim packet of letters and the girl's portrait. She struck me as beautiful—I mean she had a beautiful expression. I know that the sunlight can be made to lie, too, yet one felt that no manipulation of light and pose could have conveyed the delicate shade of truthfulness upon those features. She seemed ready to listen without mental reservation, without suspicion, without a thought for herself. I concluded I would go and give her back her portrait and those letters myself. Curiosity? Yes; and also some other feeling perhaps. All that had been Kurtz's had passed out of my hands: his soul, his body, his station, his plans, his ivory, his career. There remained only his memory and his Intended—and I wanted to give that up, too, to the past, in a way—to surrender personally all that remained of him with me to that oblivion which is the last word of our common fate. I don't defend myself. I had no clear perception of what it was I really wanted. Perhaps it was an impulse of unconscious loyalty, or the fulfillment of one of those ironic necessities that lurk in the facts of human existence. I don't know. I can't tell. But I went.

"I thought his memory was like the other memories of the dead that accumulate in every man's life—a vague impress on the brain of shadows that had fallen on it in their swift and final passage; but before the high and ponderous door, between the tall houses of a street as still and decorous as a well-kept alley in a cemetery, I had a vision of him on the stretcher, opening his mouth voraciously, as if to devour all the earth with all its mankind. He lived then before me; he lived as much as he had ever lived— a shadow insatiable of splendid appearances, of frightful realities; a shadow darker than the shadow of the night, and draped nobly in the folds of a gorgeous eloquence. The vision seemed to enter the house with me—the stretcher, the phantom-bearers, the wild crowd of obedient worshippers, the gloom of the forests, the glitter of the reach between the murky bends, the beat of the drum, regular and muffled like the beating of a heart— the heart of a conquering darkness. It was a moment of triumph for the wilderness, an invading and vengeful rush which, it seemed to me, I would have to keep back alone for the salvation of another soul. And the memory of what I had heard him say afar there, with the horned shapes stirring at my back, in the glow of fires, within the patient woods, those broken phrases came back to me, were heard again in their ominous and terrifying simplicity. I remembered his abject pleading, his abject threats, the colossal scale of his vile desires, the meanness, the torment, the tempestuous anguish of his soul. And later on I seemed to see his collected languid manner, when he said one day, 'This lot of ivory now is really mine. The Company did not pay for it. I collected it myself at a very great personal risk. I am afraid they will try to claim it as theirs though. H'm. It is a difficult case. What do you think I ought to do—resist? Eh? I want no more than justice.' . . . He wanted no more than justice—no more than justice. I rang the bell before a mahogany door on the first floor, and while I waited he seemed to stare at me out of the glassy panel—stare with that wide and immense stare embracing, condemning, loathing all the universe. I seemed to hear the whispered cry, 'The horror! The horror!'

"The dusk was falling. I had to wait in a lofty drawing-room with three long windows from floor to ceiling that were like three luminous and bedraped columns. The bent gilt legs and backs of the furniture shone in indistinct curves. The tall marble fireplace had a cold and monumental whiteness. A grand piano stood massively in a corner; with dark gleams on the flat surfaces like a sombre and polished sarcophagus. A high door opened—closed. I rose.

"She came forward, all in black, with a pale head, floating towards me in the dusk. She was in mourning. It was more than a year since his death, more than a year since the news came; she seemed as though she would remember and mourn forever. She took both my hands in hers and murmured, 'I had heard you were coming.' I noticed she was not very young—I mean not girlish. She had a mature capacity for fidelity, for belief, for suffering. The room seemed to have grown darker, as if all the sad light of the cloudy evening had taken refuge on her forehead. This fair hair, this pale visage, this pure brow, seemed surrounded by an ashy halo from which the dark eyes looked out at me. Their glance was guileless, profound, confident, and trustful. She carried her sorrowful head as though she were proud of that sorrow, as though she would say, I—I alone know how to mourn for him as he deserves. But while we were still shaking hands, such a look of awful desolation came upon her face that I perceived she was one of those creatures that are not the play-things of Time. For her he had died only yesterday. And, by Jove! the impression was so powerful that for me, too, he seemed to have died only yesterday—nay, this very minute. I saw her and him in the same instant of time—his death and her sorrow—I saw her sorrow in the very moment of his death. Do you understand? I saw them together—I heard them to-gether. She had said, with a deep catch of the breath, 'I have survived' while my strained ears seemed to hear distinctly, mingled with her tone of despairing regret, the summing up whisper of his eternal condemnation. I asked myself what I was doing there, with a sensation of panic in my heart as though I had blundered into a place of cruel and absurd mysteries not fit for a human being to behold. She motioned me to a chair. We sat down. I laid the packet gently on the little table, and she put her hand over it. . . . 'You knew him well,' she murmured, after a moment of mourning silence.

" 'Intimacy grows quickly out there,' I said. 'I knew him as well as it is possible for one man to know another.'

" 'And you admired him,' she said. 'It was impossible to know him and not to admire him. Was it?'

" 'He was a remarkable man,' I said, unsteadily. Then before the appealing fixity of her gaze, that seemed to watch for more words on my lips, I went on, 'It was impossible not to———'

" 'Love him,' she finished eagerly, silencing me into an appalled dumbness. 'How true! how true! But when you think that no one knew him so well as I! I had all his noble confidence. I knew him best.'

" 'You knew him best,' I repeated. And perhaps she did. But with every word spoken the room was growing darker, and only her forehead, smooth and white, remained illumined by the unextinguishable light of belief and love.

" 'You were his friend,' she went on. 'His friend,' she repeated, a little louder. 'You must have been, if he had given you this, and sent you to me. I feel I can speak to you—and oh! I must speak. I want you—you who have heard his last words—to know I have been worthy of him. . . . It is not pride. . . . Yes! I am proud to know I understood him better than any one on earth—he told me so himself. And since his mother died I have had no one—no one—to—to———'

"I listened. The darkness deepened. I was not even sure whether he had given me the right bundle. I rather suspect he wanted me to take care of another batch of his papers which, after his death, I saw the manager examining under the lamp. And the girl talked, easing her pain in the certitude of my sympathy; she talked as thirsty men drink. I had heard that her engagement with Kurtz had been disapproved by her people. He wasn't rich enough or something. And indeed I don't know whether he had not been a pauper all his life. He had given me some reason to infer that it was his impatience of comparative poverty that drove him out there.

" '. . . Who was not his friend who had heard him speak once?' she was saying. 'He drew men towards him by what was best in them.' She looked at me with intensity. 'It is the gift of the great,' she went on, and the sound of her low voice seemed to have the accompaniment of all the other sounds, full of mystery, desolation, and sorrow, I had ever heard—the ripple of the river, the soughing of the trees swayed by the wind, the murmurs of the crowds, the faint ring of incomprehensible words cried from afar, the whisper of a voice speaking from beyond the threshold of an eternal darkness. 'But you have heard him! You know!' she cried.

" 'Yes, I know,' I said with something like despair in my heart, but bowing my head before the faith that was in her, before that great and saving illusion that shone with an unearthly glow in the darkness, in the triumphant darkness from which I could not have defended her—from which I could not even defend myself.

" 'What a loss to me—to us!'—she corrected herself with beautiful generosity; then added in a murmur, 'To the world.' By the last gleams of twilight I could see the glitter of her eyes, full of tears—of tears that would not fall.

" 'I have been very happy—very fortunate—very proud,' she went on. 'Too fortunate. Too happy for a little while. And now I am unhappy for—for life.'

"She stood up; her fair hair seemed to catch all the remaining light in a glimmer of gold. I rose, too.

" 'And of all this,' she went on, mournfully, 'of all his promise, and of all his greatness, of his generous mind, of his noble heart, nothing remains—nothing but a memory. You and I———'

" 'We shall always remember him,' I said, hastily.

" 'No!' she cried. 'It is impossible that all this should be lost—that such a life should be sacrificed to leave nothing—but sorrow. You know what vast plans he had. I knew of them, too—I could not perhaps understand—but others knew of them. Something must remain. His words, at least, have not died.'

" 'His words will remain,' I said.

" 'And his example,' she whispered to herself. 'Men looked up to him—his goodness shone in every act. His example———'

" 'True,' I said; 'his example, too. Yes, his example. I forgot that.'

" 'But I do not. I cannot—I cannot believe—not yet. I cannot believe that I shall never see him again, that nobody will see him again, never, never, never.'

"She put out her arms as if after a retreating figure, stretching them back and with clasped pale hands across the fading and narrow sheen of the window. Never see him! I saw him clearly enough then. I shall see this eloquent phantom as long as I live, and I shall see her, too, a tragic and familiar Shade, resembling in this gesture another one, tragic also, and bedecked with powerless charms, stretching bare brown arms over the glitter of the infernal stream, the stream of darkness. She said suddenly very low. 'He died as he lived.'

" 'His end,' said I, with dull anger stirring in me, 'was in every way worthy of his life.'

" 'And I was not with him,' she murmured. My anger subsided before a feeling of infinite pity.

" 'Everything that could be done———' I mumbled.

" 'Ah, but I believed in him more than any one on earth—more than his own mother, more than—himself. He needed me! Me! I would have treasured every sigh, every word, every sign, every glance.'

"I felt like a chill grip on my chest. 'Don't,' I said, in a muffled voice.

" 'Forgive me. I—I—have mourned so long in silence—in silence. . . . You were with him—to the last? I think of his loneliness. Nobody near to understand him as I would have understood. Perhaps no one to hear. . . .'

" 'To the very end,' I said, shakily. 'I heard his very last words. . . .' I stopped in a fright.

" 'Repeat them,' she murmured in a heart-broken tone. 'I want—I want—something—something—to—live with.'

"I was on the point of crying at her, 'Don't you hear them?' The dusk was repeating them in a persistent whisper all around us, in a whisper that seemed to swell menacingly like the first whisper of a rising wind. 'The horror! the horror!'

" 'His last word—to live with,' she insisted. 'Don't you understand I loved him—I loved him—I loved him!'

"I pulled myself together and spoke slowly.

" 'The last word he pronounced was—your name.'

"I heard a light sigh and then my heart stood still, stopped dead short by an exulting and terrible cry, by the cry of inconceivable triumph and of unspeakable pain. 'I knew it—I was sure!' . . . She knew. She was sure. I heard her weeping; she had hidden her face in her hands. It seemed to me that the house would collapse before I could escape, that the heavens would fall upon my head. But nothing happened. The heavens do not fall for such a trifle. Would they have fallen, I wonder, if I had rendered Kurtz that justice which was his due? Hadn't he said he wanted only justice? But I couldn't. I could not tell her. It would have been too dark—too dark altogether. . . ."

Marlow ceased, and sat apart, indistinct and silent, in the pose of a meditating Buddha. Nobody moved for a time. "We have lost the first of the ebb," said the Director, suddenly. I raised my head. The offing was barred by a black bank of clouds, and the tranquil waterway leading to the uttermost ends of the earth flowed sombre under an overcast sky—seemed to lead into the heart of an immense darkness.

(1902)

James Joyce *1882–1941*

ARABY

North Richmond Street, being blind, was a quiet street except at the hour when the Christian Brothers' School set the boys free. An uninhabited house of two storeys stood at the blind end, detached from its neighbours in a square ground. The other houses of the street, conscious of decent lives within them, gazed at one another with brown imperturbable faces.

The former tenant of our house, a priest, had died in the back drawing-room. Air, musty from having been long enclosed, hung in all the rooms, and the waste room behind the kitchen was littered with old useless papers. Among these I found a few paper-covered books, the pages of which were curled and damp: *The Abbot,* by Walter Scott, *The Devout Communicant* and *The Memoirs of Vidocq.* I liked the last best because its leaves were yellow. The wild garden behind the house contained a central apple-tree and a few straggling bushes under one of which I found the late tenant's rusty bicycle-pump. He had been a very charitable priest; in his will he had left all his money to institutions and the furniture of his house to his sister.

When the short days of winter came dusk fell before we had well eaten our dinners. When we met in the street the houses had grown sombre. The space of sky above us was the colour of ever-changing violet and towards it the lamps of the street lifted their feeble lanterns. The cold air stung us and we played till our bodies glowed. Our shouts echoed in the silent street. The career of our play brought us through the dark muddy lanes behind the houses where we ran the gauntlet of the rough tribes from the cottages, to the back doors of the dark dripping gardens where odours arose from the ashpits, to the dark odorous stables where a coachman smoothed and combed the horse or shook music from the buckled harness. When we returned to the street light from the kitchen windows had filled the areas. If my uncle was seen turning the corner we hid in the shadow until we had seen him safely housed. Or if Mangan's sister came out on the doorstep to call her brother in to his tea we watched her from our shadow peer up and down the street. We waited to see whether she would remain or go in and, if she remained, we left our shadow and walked up to Mangan's steps resignedly. She was waiting for us, her figure defined by the light from the half-opened door. Her brother always teased her before he obeyed and I stood by the railings looking at her. Her dress swung as she moved her body and the soft rope of her hair tossed from side to side.

Every morning I lay on the floor in the front parlour watching her door. The blind was pulled down to within an inch of the sash so that I could not be seen. When she came out on the doorstep my heart leaped. I ran to the hall, seized my books and followed her. I kept her brown figure always in my eye and, when we came near the point at which our ways diverged, I quickened my pace and passed her. This happened morning after morning. I had never spoken to her, except for a few casual

221

words, and yet her name was like a summons to all my foolish blood.

Her image accompanied me even in places the most hostile to romance. On Saturday evenings when my aunt went marketing I had to go to carry some of the parcels. We walked through the flaring streets, jostled by drunken men and bargaining women, amid the curse of labourers, the shrill litanies of shop-boys who stood on guard by the barrels of pigs' cheeks, the nasal chanting of street-singers, who sang a *come-all-you* about O'Donovan Rossa, or a ballad about the troubles in our native land. These noises converged in a single sensation of life for me: I imagined that I bore my chalice safely through a throng of foes. Her name sprang to my lips at moments in strange prayers and praises which I myself did not understand. My eyes were often full of tears (I could not tell why) and at times a flood from my heart seemed to pour itself out into my bosom. I thought little of the future. I did not know whether I would ever speak to her or not or, if I spoke to her, how I could tell her of my confused adoration. But my body was like a harp and her words and gestures were like fingers running upon the wires.

One evening I went into the back drawing-room in which the priest had died. It was a dark rainy evening and there was no sound in the house. Through one of the broken panes I heard the rain impinge upon the earth, the fine incessant needles of water playing in the sodden beds. Some distant lamp or lighted window gleamed below me. I was thankful that I could see so little. All my senses seemed to desire to veil themselves and, feeling that I was about to slip from them, I pressed the palms of my hands together until they trembled, murmuring: "*O love! O love!*" many times.

At last she spoke to me. When she addressed the first words to me I was so confused that I did not know what to answer. She asked me was I going to *Araby*. I forgot whether I answered yes or no. It would be a splendid bazaar, she said; she would love to go.

"And why can't you?" I asked.

While she spoke she turned a silver bracelet round and round her wrist. She could not go, she said, because there would be a retreat that week in her convent. Her brother and two other boys were fighting for their caps and I was alone at the railings. She held one of the spikes, bowing her head towards me. The light from the lamp opposite our door caught the white curve of her neck, lit up her hair that rested there and, falling, lit up the hand upon the railing. It fell over one side of her dress and caught the white border of a petticoat just visible as she stood at ease.

"It's well for you," she said.

"If I go," I said, "I will bring you something."

What innumerable follies laid waste my waking and sleeping thoughts after that evening! I wished to annihilate the tedious intervening days. I chafed against the work of school. At night in my bedroom and by day in the classroom her image came between me and the page I strove to read. The syllables of the word *Araby* were called to me through the silence in which my soul luxuriated and cast an Eastern enchantment over me. I asked for leave to go to the bazaar on Saturday night. My aunt was surprised and hoped it was not some Freemason affair. I answered few questions in class. I watched my master's face pass from amiability to sternness; he hoped I was not beginning to idle. I could not call my wandering thoughts together. I had hardly any patience with the serious work of life which, now that it stood between me and my desire, seemed to me child's play, ugly monotonous child's play.

On Saturday morning I reminded my uncle that I wished to go to the bazaar in the evening. He was fussing at the hall-stand, looking for the hat-brush, and answered me curtly:

"Yes, boy, I know."

As he was in the hall I could not go into the front parlour and lie at the window. I left the house in bad humour and walked slowly towards the school. The air was pitilessly raw and already my heart misgave me.

When I came home to dinner my uncle had not yet been home. Still it was early. I sat staring at the clock for some time and, when its ticking began to irritate me, I left the room. I mounted the staircase and gained the upper part of the house. The high cold empty gloomy rooms liberated me and I went from room to room singing. From the front window I saw my companions playing below in the street. Their cries reached me weakened and indistinct and, leaning my forehead against the cool glass, I looked over at the dark house where she lived. I may have stood there for an hour, seeing nothing but the brown-clad figure cast by my imagination, touched discreetly by the lamplight at the curved neck, at the hand upon the railings and at the border below the dress.

When I came downstairs again I found Mrs. Mercer sitting at the fire. She was an old garrulous woman, a pawnbroker's widow, who collected used stamps for some pious purpose. I had to endure the gossip of the tea-table. The meal was prolonged beyond an hour and still my uncle did not come. Mrs. Mercer stood up to go: she was very sorry she couldn't wait any longer, but it was after eight o'clock and she did not like to be out late, as the night air was bad for her. When she had gone I began to walk up and down the room, clenching my fists. My aunt said:

"I'm afraid you may put off your bazaar for this night of Our Lord."

At nine o'clock I heard my uncle's latchkey in the halldoor. I heard him talking to himself and heard the hallstand rocking when it had received the weight of his overcoat. I could interpret these signs. When he was midway through his dinner I asked him to give me the money to go to the bazaar. He had forgotten.

"The people are in bed and after their first sleep now," he said.

I did not smile. My aunt said to him energetically:

"Can't you give him the money and let him go? You've kept him late enough as it is."

My uncle said he was very sorry he had forgotten. He said he believed in the old saying: "All work and no play makes Jack a dull boy." He asked me where I was going and, when I had told him a second time he asked me did I know *The Arab's Farewell to his Steed.* When I left the kitchen he was about to recite the opening lines of the piece to my aunt.

I held a florin tightly in my hand as I strode down Buckingham Street towards the station. The sight of the streets thronged with buyers and glaring with gas recalled to me the purpose of my journey. I took my seat in a third-class carriage of a deserted train. After an intolerable delay the train moved out of the station slowly. It crept onward among ruinous houses and over the twinkling river. At Westland Row Station a crowd of people pressed to the carriage doors; but the porters moved them back, saying that it was a special train for the bazaar. I remained alone in the bare carriage. In a few minutes the train drew up beside an improvised wooden platform. I passed out on to the road and saw by the lighted dial of a clock that it was ten minutes to ten. In front of me was a large building which displayed the magical name.

I could not find any sixpenny entrance and, fearing that the bazaar would be closed, I passed quickly through a turnstile, handing a shilling to a weary-looking man. I found myself in a big hall girdled at half its height by a gallery. Nearly all the stalls were closed and the greater part of the hall was in darkness. I recognized a silence like that which pervades a church after a service. I walked into the centre of the bazaar timidly. A few people were gathered about the stalls which were still open. Before a curtain, over which the words *Café Chantant* were written in coloured lamps, two men were counting money on a salver. I listened to the fall of the coins.

Remembering with difficulty why I had come I went over to one of the stalls and examined porcelain vases and flowered tea-sets. At the door of the stall a young lady was talking and laughing with two young gentlemen. I remarked their English accents and listened vaguely to their conversation.

"O, I never said such a thing!"

"O, but you did!"

"O, but I didn't!"

"Didn't she say that?"

"Yes. I heard her."

"O, there's a . . . fib!"

Observing me the young lady came over and asked me did I wish to buy anything. The tone of her voice was not encouraging; she seemed to have spoken to me out of a sense of duty. I looked humbly at the great jars that stood like eastern guards at either side of the dark entrance to the stall and murmured:

"No, thank you."

The young lady changed the position of one of the vases and went back to the two young men. They began to talk of the same subject. Once or twice the young lady glanced at me over her shoulder.

I lingered before her stall, though I knew my stay was useless, to make my interest in her wares seem the more real. Then I turned away slowly and walked down the middle of the bazaar. I allowed the two pennies to fall against the sixpence in my pocket. I heard a voice call from one end of the gallery that the light was out. The upper part of the hall was now completely dark.

Gazing up into the darkness I saw myself as a creature driven and derided by vanity; and my eyes burned with anguish and anger.

(1914)

Katherine Mansfield *1888–1923*

BLISS

Although Bertha Young was thirty she still had moments like this when she wanted to run instead of walk, to take dancing steps on and off the pavement, to bowl a hoop, to throw something up in the air and catch it again, or to stand still and laugh at—nothing—at nothing, simply.

What can you do if you are thirty and, turning the corner of your own street, you are overcome, suddenly, by a feeling of bliss—absolute bliss!—as though you'd suddenly swallowed a bright piece of that late afternoon sun and it burned in your bosom, sending out a little shower of sparks into every particle, into every finger and toe? . . .

Oh, is there no way you can express it without being "drunk and disorderly"? How idiotic civilization is! Why be given a body if you have to keep it shut up in a case like a rare, rare fiddle?

"No, that about the fiddle is not quite what I mean," she thought, running up the steps and feeling in her bag for the key—she'd forgotten it, as usual—and rattling the letter-box. "It's not what I mean, because—Thank you, Mary"—she went into the hall. "Is nurse back?"

"Yes, M'm."

"And has the fruit come?"

"Yes, M'm. Everything's come."

"Bring the fruit up to the dining-room, will you? I'll arrange it before I go upstairs."

It was dusky in the dining-room and quite chilly. But all the same Bertha threw off her coat; she could not bear the tight clasp of it another moment, and the cold air fell on her arms.

But in her bosom there was still that bright glowing place—that shower of little sparks coming from it. It was almost unbearable. She hardly dared to breathe for fear of fanning it higher, and yet she breathed deeply, deeply. She hardly dared to look into the cold mirror—but she did look, and it gave her back a woman, radiant, with smiling, trembling lips, with big, dark eyes and an air of listening, waiting for something . . . divine to happen . . . that she knew must happen . . . infallibly.

Mary brought in the fruit on a tray and with it a glass bowl, and a blue dish, very lovely, with a strange sheen on it as though it had been dipped in milk.

"Shall I turn on the light, M'm?"

"No, thank you. I can see quite well."

There were tangerines and apples stained with strawberry pink. Some yellow pears, smooth as silk, some white grapes covered with a silver bloom and a big cluster of purple ones. These last she had bought to tone in with the new dining-room carpet. Yes, that did sound rather far-fetched and absurd, but it was really why she had bought them. She had thought in the shop: "I must have some purple ones to bring the carpet up to the table." And it had seemed quite sense at the time.

When she had finished with them and had made two pyramids of these

bright round shapes, she stood away from the table to get the effect—
and it really was most curious. For the dark table seemed to melt into
the dusky light and the glass dish and the blue bowl to float in the air.
This, of course in her present mood, was so incredibly beautiful. . . .
She began to laugh.

"No, no. I'm getting hysterical." And she seized her bag and coat and
ran upstairs to the nursery.

Nurse sat at a low table giving Little B her supper after her bath. The
baby had on a white flannel gown and a blue woollen jacket, and her
dark, fine hair was brushed up into a funny little peak. She looked up
when she saw her mother and began to jump.

"Now, my lovey, eat it up like a good girl," said Nurse, setting her
lips in a way that Bertha knew, and that meant she had come into the
nursery at another wrong moment.

"Has she been good, Nanny?"

"She's been a little sweet all the afternoon," whispered Nanny. "We
went to the park and I sat down on a chair and took her out of the pram
and a big dog came along and put its head on my knee and she clutched
its ear, tugged it. Oh, you should have seen her."

Bertha wanted to ask if it wasn't rather dangerous to let her clutch at
a strange dog's ear. But she did not dare to. She stood watching them,
her hands by her side, like the poor little girl in front of the rich little
girl with the doll.

The baby looked up at her again, stared, and then smiled so charmingly
that Bertha couldn't help crying:

"Oh, Nanny, do let me finish giving her her supper while you put the
bath things away."

"Well, M'm, she oughtn't to be changed hands while she's eating,"
said Nanny, still whispering. "It unsettles her; it's very likely to upset
her."

How absurd it was. Why have a baby if it had to be kept—not in a
case like a rare, rare fiddle—but in another woman's arms?

"Oh, I must!" said she.

Very offended, Nanny handed her over.

"Now, don't excite her after her supper. You know you do, M'm. And
I have such a time with her after!"

Thank heaven! Nanny went out of the room with the bath towels.

"Now I've got you to myself, my little precious," said Bertha, as the
baby leaned against her.

She ate delightfully, holding up her lips for the spoon and then waving
her hands. Sometimes she wouldn't let the spoon go; and sometimes, just
as Bertha had filled it, she waved it away to the four winds.

When the soup was finished Bertha turned round to the fire.

"You're nice—you're very nice!" said she, kissing her warm baby. "I'm
fond of you. I like you."

And, indeed, she loved Little B so much—her neck as she bent forward,
her exquisite toes as they shone transparent in the firelight—that all her
feeling of bliss came back again, and again she didn't know how to express
it—what to do with it.

"You're wanted on the telephone," said Nanny, coming back in triumph and seizing *her* Little B.

Down she flew. It was Harry.

"Oh, is that you, Ber? Look here. I'll be late. I'll take a taxi and come along as quickly as I can, but get dinner put back ten minutes—will you? All right?"

"Yes, perfectly. Oh, Harry!"

"Yes?"

What had she to say? She'd nothing to say. She only wanted to get in touch with him for a moment. She couldn't absurdly cry: "Hasn't it been a divine day!"

"What is it?" rapped out the little voice.

"Nothing. *Entendu,*" said Bertha, and hung up the receiver, thinking how more than idiotic civilization was.

They had people coming to dinner. The Norman Knights—a very sound couple—he was about to start a theatre, and she was awfully keen on interior decoration, a young man, Eddie Warren, who had just published a little book of poems and whom everybody was asking to dine, and a "find" of Bertha's called Pearl Fulton. What Miss Fulton did, Bertha didn't know. They had met at the club and Bertha had fallen in love with her, as she always did fall in love with beautiful women who had something strange about them.

The provoking thing was that, though they had been about together and met a number of times and really talked, Bertha couldn't yet make her out. Up to a certain point Miss Fulton was rarely, wonderfully frank, but the certain point was there, and beyond that she would not go.

Was there anything beyond it? Harry said "No." Voted her dullish, and "cold like all blond women, with a touch, perhaps, of anæmia of the brain." But Bertha wouldn't agree with him; not yet, at any rate.

"No, the way she has of sitting with her head a little on one side, and smiling, has something behind it, Harry, and I must find out what that something is."

"Most likely it's a good stomach," answered Harry.

He made a point of catching Bertha's heels with replies of that kind . . . "liver frozen, my dear girl," or "pure flatulence," or "kidney disease," . . . and so on. For some strange reason Bertha liked this, and almost admired it in him very much.

She went into the drawing-room and lighted the fire; then, picking up the cushions, one by one, that Mary had disposed so carefully, she threw them back on to the chairs and the couches. That made all the difference; the room came alive at once. As she was about to throw the last one she surprised herself by suddenly hugging it to her, passionately, passionately. But it did not put out the fire in her bosom. Oh, on the contrary!

The windows of the drawing-room opened on to a balcony overlooking the garden. At the far end, against the wall, there was a tall, slender pear tree in fullest, richest bloom; it stood perfect, as though becalmed against the jade-green sky. Bertha couldn't help feeling, even from this distance, that it had not a single bud or a faded petal. Down below, in the garden beds, the red and yellow tulips, heavy with flowers, seemed to lean upon the dusk. A grey cat, dragging its belly, crept across the lawn, and a black one, its shadow, trailed after. The sight of them, so intent and so quick, gave Bertha a curious shiver.

"What creepy things cats are!" she stammered, and she turned away from the window and began walking up and down. . . .

How strong the jonquils smelled in the warm room. Too strong? Oh, no. And yet, as though overcome, she flung down on a couch and pressed her hands to her eyes.

"I'm too happy—too happy!" she murmured.

And she seemed to see on her eyelids the lovely pear tree with its wide open blossoms as a symbol of her own life.

Really—really—she had everything. She was young. Harry and she were as much in love as ever, and they got on together splendidly and were really good pals. She had an adorable baby. They didn't have to worry about money. They had this absolutely satisfactory house and garden. And friends—modern, thrilling friends, writers and painters and poets or people keen on social questions—just the kind of friends they wanted. And then there were books, and there was music, and she had found a wonderful little dressmaker, and they were going abroad in the summer, and their new cook made the most superb omelettes. . . .

"I'm absurd. Absurd!" She sat up; but she felt quite dizzy, quite drunk. It must have been the spring.

Yes, it was the spring. Now she was so tired she could not drag herself upstairs to dress.

A white dress, a string of jade beads, green shoes and stockings. It wasn't intentional. She had thought of this scheme hours before she stood at the drawing-room window.

Her petals rustled softly into the hall, and she kissed Mrs. Norman Knight, who was taking off the most amusing orange coat with a procession of black monkeys round the hem and up the fronts.

". . . Why! Why! Why is the middle-class so stodgy—so utterly without a sense of humour! My dear, it's only by a fluke that I am here at all— Norman being the protective fluke. For my darling monkeys so upset the train that it rose to a man and simply ate me with its eyes. Didn't laugh— wasn't amused—that I should have loved. No, just stared—and bored me through and through."

"But the cream of it was," said Norman, pressing a large tortoiseshell-rimmed monocle into his eye, "you don't mind me telling this, Face, do you?" (In their home and among their friends they called each other Face and Mug.) "The cream of it was when she, being full fed, turned to the woman beside her and said: 'Haven't you ever seen a monkey before?' "

"Oh, yes!" Mrs. Norman Knight joined in the laughter. "Wasn't that too absolutely creamy?"

And a funnier thing still was that now her coat was off she did look like a very intelligent monkey—who had even made that yellow silk dress out of scraped banana skins. And her amber ear-rings; they were like little dangling nuts.

"This is a sad, sad fall!" said Mug, pausing in front of Little B's perambulator. "When the perambulator comes into the hall—" and he waved the rest of the quotation away.

The bell rang. It was lean, pale Eddie Warren (as usual) in a state of acute distress.

"It *is* the right house, *isn't* it?" he pleaded.

"Oh, I think so—I hope so," said Bertha brightly.

"I have had such a *dreadful* experience with a taxi-man; he was *most* sinister. I couldn't get him to *stop*. The *more* I knocked and called the *faster* he went. And *in* the moonlight this *bizarre* figure with the *flattened* head *crouching* over the *lit-tle* wheel. . . ."

He shuddered, taking off an immense white silk scarf. Bertha noticed that his socks were white, too—most charming.

"But how dreadful!" she cried.

"Yes, it really was," said Eddie, following her into the drawing-room. "I saw myself *driving* through Eternity in a *timeless* taxi."

He knew the Norman Knights. In fact, he was going to write a play for N. K. when the theatre scheme came off.

"Well, Warren, how's the play?" said Norman Knight, dropping his monocle and giving his eye a moment in which to rise to the surface before it was screwed down again.

And Mrs. Norman Knight: "Oh, Mr. Warren, what happy socks!"

"I *am* so glad you like them," said he, staring at his feet. "They seem to have got so *much* whiter since the moon rose." And he turned his lean sorrowful young face to Bertha. "There *is* a moon, you know."

She wanted to cry: "I am sure there is—often—often!"

He really was a most attractive person. But so was Face, crouched before the fire in her banana skins, and so was Mug, smoking a cigarette and saying as he flicked the ash: "Why doth the bridegroom tarry?"

"There he is, now."

Bang went the front door open and shut. Harry shouted: "Hullo, you people. Down in five minutes." And they heard him swarm up the stairs. Bertha couldn't help smiling; she knew how he loved doing things at high pressure. What, after all, did an extra five minutes matter? But he would pretend to himself that they mattered beyond measure. And then he would make a great point of coming into the drawing-room, extravagantly cool and collected.

Harry had such a zest for life. Oh, how she appreciated it in him. And his passion for fighting—for seeking in everything that came up against him another test of his power and of his courage—that, too, she understood. Even when it made him just occasionally, to other people, who didn't know him well, a little ridiculous perhaps. . . . For there were moments when he rushed into battle where no battle was. . . . She talked and laughed and positively forgot until he had come in (just as she had imagined) that Pearl Fulton had not turned up.

"I wonder if Miss Fulton has forgotten?"

"I expect so," said Harry. "Is she on the 'phone?"

"Ah! There's a taxi, now." And Bertha smiled with that little air of proprietorship that she always assumed while her women finds were new and mysterious. "She lives in taxis."

"She'll run to fat if she does," said Harry coolly, ringing the bell for dinner. "Frightful danger for blond women."

"Harry—don't," warned Bertha, laughing up at him.

Came another tiny moment, while they waited, laughing and talking, just a trifle too much at their ease, a trifle too unaware. And then Miss Fulton, all in silver, with a silver fillet binding her pale blond hair, came in smiling, her head a little on one side.

"Am I late?"

"No, not at all," said Bertha. "Come along." And she took her arm and they moved into the dining-room.

What was there in the touch of that cool arm that could fan—fan—start blazing—blazing—the fire of bliss that Bertha did not know what to do with?

Miss Fulton did not look at her; but then she seldom did look at people directly. Her heavy eyelids lay upon her eyes and the strange half smile came and went upon her lips as though she lived by listening rather than seeing. But Bertha knew, suddenly, as if the longest, most intimate look had passed between them—as if they had said to each other: "You, too?"—that Pearl Fulton, stirring the beautiful red soup in the grey plate, was feeling just what she was feeling.

And the others? Face and Mug, Eddie and Harry, their spoons rising and falling—dabbing their lips with their napkins, crumbling bread, fiddling with the forks and glasses and talking.

"I met her at the Alpha show—the weirdest little person. She'd not only cut off her hair, but she seemed to have taken a dreadfully good snip off her legs and arms and her neck and her poor little nose as well."

"Isn't she very *liée* with Michael Oat?"

"The man who wrote *Love in False Teeth?*"

"He wants to write a play for me. One act. One man. Decides to commit suicide. Gives all the reasons why he should and why he shouldn't. And just as he has made up his mind either to do it or not to do it—curtain. Not half a bad idea."

"What's he going to call it—'Stomach Trouble'?"

"I *think* I've come across the *same* idea in a lit-tle French review, *quite* unknown in England."

No, they didn't share it. They were dears—dears—and she loved having them there, at her table, and giving them delicious food and wine. In fact, she longed to tell them how delightful they were, and what a decorative group they made, how they seemed to set one another off and how they reminded her of a play by Tchekof!

Harry was enjoying his dinner. It was part of his—well, not his nature, exactly, and certainly not his pose—his—something or other—to talk about food and to glory in his "shameless passion for the white flesh of the lobster" and "the green of pistachio ices—green and cold like the eyelids of Egyptian dancers."

When he looked up at her and said: "Bertha, this is a very admirable *soufflée!*" she almost could have wept with child-like pleasure.

Oh, why did she feel so tender towards the whole world tonight? Everything was good—was right. All that happened seemed to fill again her brimming cup of bliss.

And still, in the back of her mind, there was the pear tree. It would be silver now, in the light of poor dear Eddie's moon, silver as Miss Fulton, who sat there turning a tangerine in her slender fingers that were so pale a light seemed to come from them.

What she simply couldn't make out—what was miraculous—was how she should have guessed Miss Fulton's mood so exactly and so instantly. For she never doubted for a moment that she was right, and yet what had she to go on? Less than nothing.

"I believe this does happen very, very rarely between women. Never between men," thought Bertha. "But while I am making the coffee in the drawing-room perhaps she will 'give a sign.'"

What she meant by that she did not know, and what would happen after that she could not imagine.

While she thought like this she saw herself talking and laughing. She had to talk because of her desire to laugh.

"I must laugh or die."

But when she noticed Face's funny little habit of tucking something down the front of her bodice—as if she kept a tiny, secret hoard of nuts there, too—Bertha had to dig her nails into her hands—so as not to laugh too much.

It was over at last. And: "Come and see my new coffee machine," said Bertha.

"We only have a new coffee machine once a fortnight," said Harry. Face took her arm this time; Miss Fulton bent her head and followed after.

The fire had died down in the drawing-room to a red, flickering "nest of baby phœnixes," said Face.

"Don't turn up the light for a moment. It is so lovely." And down she crouched by the fire again. She was always cold . . . "without her little red flannel jacket, of course," thought Bertha.

At that moment Miss Fulton "gave the sign."

"Have you a garden?" said the cool, sleepy voice.

This was so exquisite on her part that all Bertha could do was to obey. She crossed the room, pulled the curtains apart, and opened those long windows.

"There!" she breathed.

And the two women stood side by side looking at the slender, flowering tree. Although it was so still it seemed, like the flame of a candle, to stretch up, to point, to quiver in the bright air, to grow taller and taller as they gazed—almost to touch the rim of the round, silver moon.

How long did they stand there? Both, as it were, caught in that circle of unearthly light, understanding each other perfectly, creatures of another world, and wondering what they were to do in this one with all this blissful treasure that burned in their bosoms and dropped, in silver flowers, from their hair and hands?

For ever—for a moment? And did Miss Fulton murmur: "Yes. Just *that*." Or did Bertha dream it?

Then the light was snapped on and Face made the coffee and Harry said: "My dear Mrs. Knight, don't ask me about my baby. I never see

her. I shan't feel the slightest interest in her until she has a lover," and
Mug took his eye out of the conservatory for a moment and then put it
under glass again and Eddie Warren drank his coffee and set down the
cup with a face of anguish as though he had drunk and seen the spider.

"What I want to do is to give the young men a show. I believe London
is simply teeming with first-chop, unwritten plays. What I want to say
to 'em is: 'Here's the theatre. Fire ahead.' "

"You know, my dear, I am going to decorate a room for the Jacob Na-
thans. Oh, I am so tempted to do a fried-fish scheme, with the backs of
the chairs shaped like frying pans and lovely chip potatoes embroidered
all over the curtains."

"The trouble with our young writing men is that they are still too romantic. You can't put out to sea without being seasick and wanting a basin.
Well, why won't they have the courage of those basins?"

"A *dreadful* poem about a *girl* who was *violated* by a beggar *without* a
nose in a lit-tle wood. . . ."

Miss Fulton sank into the lowest, deepest chair and Harry handed round
the cigarettes.

From the way he stood in front of her shaking the silver box and saying
abruptly: "Egyptian? Turkish? Virginia? They're all mixed up," Bertha
realized that she not only bored him; he really disliked her. And she decided
from the way Miss Fulton said: "No, thank you, I won't smoke," that
she felt it, too, and was hurt.

"Oh, Harry, don't dislike her. You are quite wrong about her. She's
wonderful, wonderful. And, besides, how can you feel so differently about
someone who means so much to me? I shall try to tell you when we are
in bed to-night what has been happening. What she and I have shared."

At those last words something strange and almost terrifying darted into
Bertha's mind. And this something blind and smiling whispered to her:
"Soon these people will go. The house will be quiet—quiet. The lights
will be out. And you and he will be alone together in the dark room—
the warm bed. . . ."

She jumped up from her chair and ran over to the piano.

"What a pity someone does not play!" she cried. "What a pity somebody
does not play."

For the first time in her life Bertha Young desired her husband.

Oh, she'd loved him—she'd been in love with him, of course, in every
other way, but just not in that way. And, equally, of course, she'd understood that he was different. They'd discussed it so often. It had worried
her dreadfully at first to find that she was so cold, but after a time it
had not seemed to matter. They were so frank with each other—such
good pals. That was the best of being modern.

But now—ardently! ardently! The word ached in her ardent body! Was
this what that feeling of bliss had been leading up to? But then, then—

"My dear," said Mrs. Norman Knight, "you know our shame. We are
the victims of time and train. We live in Hampstead. It's been so nice."

"I'll come with you into the hall," said Bertha. "I loved having you.
But you must not miss the last train. That's so awful, isn't it?"

"Have a whisky, Knight, before you go?" called Harry.

"No, thanks, old chap."

Bertha squeezed his hand for that as she shook it.

"Good night, good-bye," she cried from the top step, feeling that this self of hers was taking leave of them for ever.

When she got back into the drawing-room the others were on the move.

". . . Then you can come part of the way in my taxi."

"I shall be *so* thankful *not* to have to face *another* drive *alone* after my *dreadful* experience."

"You can get a taxi at the rank just at the end of the street. You won't have to walk more than a few yards."

"That's a comfort. I'll go and put on my coat."

Miss Fulton moved towards the hall and Bertha was following when Harry almost pushed past.

"Let me help you."

Bertha knew that he was repenting his rudeness—she let him go. What a boy he was in some ways—so impulsive—so—simple.

And Eddie and she were left by the fire.

"I *wonder* if you have seen Bilks' *new* poem called *Table d'Hôte*," said Eddie softly. "It's *so* wonderful. In the last Anthology. Have you got a copy? I'd *so* like to *show* it to you. It begins with an *incredibly* beautiful line: 'Why Must it Always be Tomato Soup?' "

"Yes," said Bertha. And she moved noiselessly to a table opposite the drawing-room door and Eddie glided noiselessly after her. She picked up the little book and gave it to him; they had not made a sound.

While he looked it up she turned her head towards the hall. And she saw . . . Harry with Miss Fulton's coat in his arms and Miss Fulton with her back turned to him and her head bent. He tossed the coat away, put his hands on her shoulders and turned her violently to him. His lips said: "I adore you," and Miss Fulton laid her moonbeam fingers on his cheeks and smiled her sleepy smile. Harry's nostrils quivered; his lips curled back in a hideous grin while he whispered: "To-morrow," and with her eyelids Miss Fulton said: "Yes."

"Here it is," said Eddie. " 'Why Must it Always be Tomato Soup?' It's so *deeply* true, don't you feel? Tomato soup is so *dreadfully* eternal."

"If you prefer," said Harry's voice, very loud, from the hall, "I can phone you a cab to come to the door."

"Oh, no. It's not necessary," said Miss Fulton, and she came up to Bertha and gave her the slender fingers to hold.

"Good-bye. Thank you so much."

"Good-bye," said Bertha.

Miss Fulton held her hand a moment longer.

"Your lovely pear tree!" she murmured.

And then she was gone, with Eddie following, like the black cat following the grey cat.

"I'll shut up shop," said Harry, extravagantly cool and collected.

"Your lovely pear tree—pear tree—pear tree!"

Bertha simply ran over to the long windows.

"Oh, what is going to happen now?" she cried.

But the pear tree was as lovely as ever and as full of flower and as still.

(1920)

Sherwood Anderson *1876–1941*

NOBODY KNOWS

Looking cautiously about, George Willard arose from his desk in the office of the *Winesburg Eagle* and went hurriedly out at the back door. The night was warm and cloudy and although it was not yet eight o'clock, the alleyway back of the *Eagle* office was pitch dark. A team of horses tied to a post somewhere in the darkness stamped on the hard-baked ground. A cat sprang from under George Willard's feet and ran away into the night. The young man was nervous. All day he had gone about his work like one dazed by a blow. In the alleyway he trembled as though with fright.

In the darkness George Willard walked along the alleyway, going carefully and cautiously. The back doors of the Winesburg stores were open and he could see men sitting about under the store lamps. In Myerbaum's Notion Store Mrs. Willy the saloon keeper's wife stood by the counter with a basket on her arm. Sid Green the clerk was waiting on her. He leaned over the counter and talked earnestly.

George Willard crouched and then jumped through the path of light that came out at the door. He began to run forward in the darkness. Behind Ed Griffith's saloon old Jerry Bird the town drunkard lay asleep on the ground. The runner stumbled over the sprawling legs. He laughed brokenly.

George Willard had set forth upon an adventure. All day he had been trying to make up his mind to go through with the adventure and now he was acting. In the office of the *Winesburg Eagle* he had been sitting since six o'clock trying to think.

There had been no decision. He had just jumped to his feet, hurried past Will Henderson who was reading proof in the printshop and started to run along the alleyway.

Through street after street went George Willard, avoiding the people who passed. He crossed and recrossed the road. When he passed a street lamp he pulled his hat down over his face. He did not dare think. In his mind there was a fear but it was a new kind of fear. He was afraid the adventure on which he had set out would be spoiled, that he would lose courage and turn back.

George Willard found Louise Trunnion in the kitchen of her father's house. She was washing dishes by the light of a kerosene lamp. There she stood behind the screen door in the little shedlike kitchen at the back of the house. George Willard stopped by a picket fence and tried to control the shaking of his body. Only a narrow potato patch separated him from the adventure. Five minutes passed before he felt sure enough of himself to call to her. "Louise! Oh, Louise!" he called. The cry stuck in his throat. His voice became a hoarse whisper.

Louise Trunnion came out across the potato patch holding the dish cloth in her hand. "How do you know I want to go out with you," she said sulkily. "What makes you so sure?"

George Willard did not answer. In silence the two stood in the darkness with the fence between them. "You go on along," she said. "Pa's in there. I'll come along. You wait by Williams' barn."

The young newspaper reporter had received a letter from Louise Trunnion. It had come that morning to the office of the *Winesburg Eagle*. The letter was brief. "I'm yours if you want me," it said. He thought it annoying that in the darkness by the fence she had pretended there was nothing between them. "She has a nerve! Well, gracious sakes, she has a nerve," he muttered as he went along the street and passed a row of vacant lots where corn grew. The corn was shoulder high and had been planted right down to the sidewalk.

When Louise Trunnion came out of the front door of her house she still wore the gingham dress in which she had been washing dishes. There was no hat on her head. The boy could see her standing with the doorknob in her hand talking to someone within, no doubt to old Jake Trunnion, her father. Old Jake was half deaf and she shouted. The door closed and everything was dark and silent in the little side street. George Willard trembled more violently than ever.

In the shadows by Williams' barn George and Louise stood, not daring to talk. She was not particularly comely and there was a black smudge on the side of her nose. George thought she must have rubbed her nose with her finger after she had been handling some of the kitchen pots.

The young man began to laugh nervously. "It's warm," he said. He wanted to touch her with his hand. "I'm not very bold," he thought. Just to touch the folds of the soiled gingham dress would, he decided, be an exquisite pleasure. She began to quibble. "You think you're better than I am. Don't tell me, I guess I know," she said drawing closer to him.

A flood of words burst from George Willard. He remembered the look that had lurked in the girl's eyes when they had met on the streets and thought of the note she had written. Doubt left him. The whispered tales concerning her that had gone about town gave him confidence. He became wholly the male, bold and aggressive. In his heart there was no sympathy for her. "Ah, come on, it'll be all right. There won't be anyone know anything. How can they know?" he urged.

They began to walk along a narrow brick sidewalk between the cracks of which tall weeds grew. Some of the bricks were missing and the sidewalk was rough and irregular. He took hold of her hand that was also rough and thought it delightfully small. "I can't go far," she said and her voice was quiet, unperturbed.

They crossed a bridge that ran over a tiny stream and passed another vacant lot in which corn grew. The street ended. In the path at the side of the road they were compelled to walk one behind the other. Will Overton's berry field lay beside the road and there was a pile of boards. "Will is going to build a shed to store berry crates here," said George and they sat down upon the boards.

When George Willard got back into Main Street it was past ten o'clock and had begun to rain. Three times he walked up and down the length of Main Street. Sylvester West's Drug Store was still open and he went in and bought a cigar. When Shorty Crandall the clerk came out at the door with him he was pleased. For five minutes the two stood in the shelter

of the store awning and talked. George Willard felt satisfied. He had wanted
more than anything else to talk to some man. Around the corner toward
the New Willard House he went whistling softly.

On the sidewalk at the side of Winney's Dry Goods Store where there
was a high board fence covered with circus pictures, he stopped whistling
and stood perfectly still in the darkness, attentive, listening as though for
a voice calling his name. Then again he laughed nervously. "She hasn't
got anything on me. Nobody knows," he muttered doggedly and went
on his way.

(1919)

Franz Kafka *1883–1924*

A HUNGER ARTIST

During these last decades the interest in professional fasting has markedly
diminished. It used to pay very well to stage such great performances
under one's own management, but today that is quite impossible. We live
in a different world now. At one time the whole town took a lively interest
in the hunger artist; from day to day of his fast the excitement mounted;
everybody wanted to see him at least once a day; there were people who
bought season tickets for the last few days and sat from morning till night
in front of his small barred cage; even in the nighttime there were visiting
hours, when the whole effect was heightened by torch flares; on fine days
the cage was set out in the open air, and then it was the children's special
treat to see the hunger artist; for their elders he was often just a joke
that happened to be in fashion, but the children stood open-mouthed, holding each other's hands for greater security, marvelling at him as he sat
there pallid in black tights, with his ribs sticking out so prominently,
not even on a seat but down among straw on the ground, sometimes giving
a courteous nod, answering questions with a constrained smile, or perhaps
stretching an arm through the bars so that one might feel how thin it
was, and then again withdrawing deep into himself, paying no attention
to anyone or anything, not even to the all-important striking of the clock
that was the only piece of furniture in his cage, but merely staring into
vacancy with half-shut eyes, now and then taking a sip from a tiny glass
of water to moisten his lips.

Besides casual onlookers there were also relays of permanent watchers
selected by the public, usually butchers, strangely enough, and it was their
task to watch the hunger artist day and night, three of them at a time,
in case he should have some secret recourse to nourishment. This was
nothing but a formality, instituted to reassure the masses, for the initiates
knew well enough that during his fast the artist would never in any circumstances, not even under forcible compulsion, swallow the smallest morsel
of food; the honor of his profession forbade it. Not every watcher, of

course, was capable of understanding this, there were often groups of night watchers who were very lax in carrying out their duties and deliberately huddled together in a retired corner to play cards with great absorption, obviously intending to give the hunger artist the chance of a little refreshment, which they supposed he could draw from some private hoard. Nothing annoyed the artist more than such watchers; they made him miserable; they made his fast seem unendurable; sometimes he mastered his feebleness sufficiently to sing during their watch for as long as he could keep going, to show them how unjust their suspicions were. But that was of little use; they only wondered at his cleverness in being able to fill his mouth even while singing. Much more to his taste were the watchers who sat close up to the bars, who were not content with the dim night lighting of the hall but focused him in the full glare of the electric pocket torch given them by the impresario. The harsh light did not trouble him at all. In any case he could never sleep properly, and he could always drowse a little, whatever the light, at any hour, even when the hall was thronged with noisy onlookers. He was quite happy at the prospect of spending a sleepless night with such watchers; he was ready to exchange jokes with them, to tell them stories out of his nomadic life, anything at all to keep them awake and demonstrate to them again that he had no eatables in his cage and that he was fasting as not one of them could fast. But his happiest moment was when the morning came and an enormous breakfast was brought them, at his expense, on which they flung themselves with the keen appetite of healthy men after a weary night of wakefulness. Of course there were people who argued that this breakfast was an unfair attempt to bribe the watchers, but that was going rather too far, and when they were invited to take on a night's vigil without a breakfast, merely for the sake of the cause, they made themselves scarce, although they stuck stubbornly to their suspicions.

Such suspicions, anyhow, were a necessary accompaniment to the profession of fasting. No one could possibly watch the hunger artist continuously, day and night, and so no one could produce first-hand evidence that the fast had really been rigorous and continuous; only the artist himself could know that; he was therefore bound to be the sole completely satisfied spectator of his own fast. Yet for other reasons he was never satisfied; it was not perhaps mere fasting that had brought him to such skeleton thinness that many people had regretfully to keep away from his exhibitions, because the sight of him was too much for them, perhaps it was dissatisfaction with himself that had worn him down. For he alone knew, what no other initiate knew, how easy it was to fast. It was the easiest thing in the world. He made no secret of this, yet people did not believe him; at the best they set him down as modest, most of them, however, thought he was out for publicity or else was some kind of cheat who found it easy to fast because he had discovered a way of making it easy, and then had the impudence to admit the fact, more or less. He had to put up with all that, and in the course of time had got used to it, but his inner dissatisfaction always rankled, and never yet, after any term of fasting—this must be granted to his credit—had he left the cage of his own free will. The longest period of fasting was fixed by his impresario at forty days, beyond that term he was not allowed to go, not even in great cities, and there was good reason for it, too. Experience had proved that for about forty days the interest of the public could be stimulated by a steadily increasing pressure of advertisement, but after that the town began to lose interest, sympathetic support began notably to fall off; there were of course local variations as between one town and another or one country and another, but as a general rule forty days marked the limit. So on the fortieth day the flower-bedecked cage was opened, enthusiastic spectators filled the hall, a military band played, two doctors entered the cage to measure the results of the fast, which were announced through a megaphone, and finally two young ladies appeared, blissful at having been selected for the honor, to help the hunger artist down the few steps leading to a small table on which was spread a carefully chosen invalid repast. And at this very moment the artist always turned stubborn. True, he would entrust his bony arms to the outstretched helping hands of the ladies bending over him, but stand up he would not. Why stop fasting at this particular moment, after forty days of it? He had held out for a long time, an illimitably long time; why stop now, when he was in his best fasting form, or rather, not yet quite in his best fasting form? Why should he be cheated of the fame he would get for fasting longer, for being not only the record hunger artist of all time, which presumably he was already, but for beating his own record by a performance beyond human imagination, since he felt that there were no limits to his capacity for fasting? His public pretended to admire him so much, why should it have so little patience with him; if he could endure fasting longer, why shouldn't the public endure it? Besides, he was tired, he was comfortable sitting in the straw, and now he was supposed to lift himself to his full height and go down to a meal the very thought of which gave him a nausea that only the presence of the ladies kept him from betraying, and even that with an effort. And he looked up into the eyes of the ladies who were apparently so friendly and in reality so cruel, and shook his head, which felt too heavy on its strengthless neck. But then there happened yet again what always happened. The impresario came forward, without a word—for the band made speech impossible—lifted his arms in the air above the artist, as if inviting Heaven to look down upon its creature here in the straw, this suffering martyr, which indeed he was, although in quite another sense; grasped him round the emaciated waist, with exaggerated caution, so that the frail condition he was in might be appreciated; and committed him to the care of the blenching ladies, not without secretly giving him a shaking so that his legs and body tottered and swayed. The artist now submitted completely; his head lolled on his breast as if it had landed there by chance; his body was hollowed out; his legs in a spasm of self-preservation clung close to each other at the knees, yet scraped on the ground as if it were not really solid ground, as if they were only trying to find solid ground; and the whole weight of his body, a featherweight after all, relapsed onto one of the ladies, who, looking round for help and panting a little—this post of honor was not at all what she had expected it to be—first stretched her neck as far as she could to keep her face at least free from contact with the artist, then finding this impossible, and her more fortunate companion not coming to her aid but merely holding extended on her own trembling hand the little bunch of knucklebones that was the artist's, to the great delight of the spectators burst into tears and had to be replaced by an attendant who had long been stationed in readiness. Then came the food, a little of which the impresario managed to get between the artist's lips, while he sat in a kind of half-fainting trance, to the accompaniment of cheerful patter designed to distract the public's attention from the artist's condition; after that, a toast was drunk to the public, supposedly prompted by a whisper from the artist in the impresario's ear; the band confirmed it with a mighty flourish, the spectators melted away, and no one had any cause to be dissatisfied with the proceedings, no one except the hunger artist himself, he only, as always.

So he lived for many years, with small regular intervals of recuperation, in visible glory, honored by the world, yet in spite of that troubled in spirit, and all the more troubled because no one would take his trouble seriously. What comfort could he possibly need? What more could he possibly wish for? And if some good-natured person, feeling sorry for him, tried to console him by pointing out that his melancholy was probably caused by fasting, it could happen, especially when he had been fasting for some time, then he reacted with an outburst of fury and to the general alarm began to shake the bars of his cage like a wild animal. Yet the impresario had a way of punishing these outbreaks which he rather enjoyed putting into operation. He would apologize publicly for the artist's behavior, which was only to be excused, he admitted, because of the irritability caused by fasting; a condition hardly to be understood by well-fed people; then by natural transition he went on to mention the artist's equally incomprehensible boast that he could fast for much longer than he was doing; he praised the high ambition, the good will, the great self-denial undoubtedly implicit in such a statement; and then quite simply countered it by bringing out photographs, which were also on sale to the public, showing the artist on the fortieth day of a fast lying in bed almost dead from exhaustion. This perversion of the truth, familiar to the artist though it was, always unnerved him afresh and proved too much for him. What was a consequence of the premature ending of his fast was here presented as the cause of it! To fight against this lack of understanding, against a whole world of non-understanding, was impossible. Time and again in good faith he stood by the bars listening to the impresario, but as soon as the photographs appeared he always let go and sank with a groan back onto his straw, and the reassured public could once more come close and gaze at him.

A few years later when the witnesses of such scenes called them to mind, they often failed to understand themselves at all. For meanwhile the aforementioned change in public interest had set in; it seemed to happen almost overnight; there may have been profound causes for it, but who was going to bother about that; at any rate the pampered hunger artist suddenly found himself deserted one fine day by the amusement seekers, who went streaming past him to other more favored attractions. For the last time the impresario hurried him over half Europe to discover whether the old interest might still survive here and there; all in vain; everywhere, as if by secret agreement, a positive revulsion from professional fasting was in evidence. Of course it could not really have sprung up so suddenly as all that, and many premonitory symptoms which had not been sufficiently remarked or suppressed during the rush and glitter of success now came retrospectively to mind, but it was now too late to take any counter-measures. Fasting would surely come into fashion again at some future date, yet that was no comfort for those living in the present. What, then, was the hunger artist to do? He had been applauded by thousands in his time and could hardly come down to showing himself in a street booth at village fairs, and as for adopting another profession, he was not only too old for that but too fanatically devoted to fasting. So he took leave of the impresario, his partner in an unparalleled career, and hired himself to a large circus; in order to spare his own feelings he avoided reading the conditions of his contract.

A large circus with its enormous traffic in replacing and recruiting men, animals and apparatus can always find a use for people at any time, even for a hunger artist, provided of course that he does not ask too much, and in this particular case anyhow it was not only the artist who was taken on but his famous and long-known name as well; indeed considering the peculiar nature of his performance, which was not impaired by advancing age, it could not be objected that here was an artist past his prime, no longer at the height of his professional skill, seeking a refuge in some quiet corner of a circus; on the contrary, the hunger artist averred that he could fast as well as ever, which was entirely credible; he even alleged that if he were allowed to fast as he liked, and this was at once promised him without more ado, he could astound the world by establishing a record never yet achieved, a statement which certainly provoked a smile among the other professionals, since it left out of account the change in public opinion, which the hunger artist in his zeal conveniently forgot.

He had not, however, actually lost his sense of the real situation and took it as a matter of course that he and his cage should be stationed, not in the middle of the ring as a main attraction, but outside, near the animal cages, on a site that was after all easily accessible. Large and gaily painted placards made a frame for the cage and announced what was to be seen inside it. When the public came thronging out in the intervals to see the animals, they could hardly avoid passing the hunger artist's cage and stopping there for a moment, perhaps they might even have stayed longer had not those pressing behind them in the narrow gangway, who did not understand why they should be held up on their way towards the excitements of the menagerie, made it impossible for anyone to stand gazing quietly for any length of time. And that was the reason why the hunger artist, who had of course been looking forward to these visiting hours as the main achievement of his life, began instead to shrink from them. At first he could hardly wait for the intervals; it was exhilarating to watch the crowds come streaming his way, until only too soon—not even the most obstinate self-deception, clung to almost consciously, could hold out against the fact—the conviction was borne in upon him that these people, most of them, to judge from their actions, again and again, without exception, were all on their way to the menagerie. And the first sight of them from the distance remained the best. For when they reached his cage he was at once deafened by the storm of shouting and abuse that arose from the two contending factions, which renewed themselves continuously, of those who wanted to stop and stare at him—he soon began to dislike them more than the others—not out of real interest but only out of obstinate self-assertiveness, and those who wanted to go straight on to the animals. When the first great rush was past, the stragglers came along, and these, whom nothing could have prevented from stopping to look at him as long as they had breath, raced past with long strides, hardly even glancing at him, in their haste to get to the menagerie in time. And all too rarely did it happen that he had a stroke of luck, when some father of a family fetched up before him with his children, pointed a finger at the hunger artist and explained at length what the phenomenon meant, telling stories of earlier years when he himself had watched similar but much more thrilling performances, and the children, still rather uncomprehending, since neither inside nor outside school had they been sufficiently prepared for this lesson—what did they care about fasting?—yet showed by the brightness of their intent eyes that new and better times might be coming. Perhaps, said the hunger artist to himself many a time, things would be a little better if his cage were set not quite so near the menagerie. That made it too easy for people to make their choice, to say nothing of what he suffered from the stench of the menagerie, the animals' restlessness by night, the carrying past of raw lumps of flesh for the beasts of prey, the roaring at feeding times, which depressed him continually. But he did not dare to lodge a complaint with the management; after all, he had the animals to thank for the troops of people who passed his cage, among whom there might always be one here and there to take an interest in him, and who could tell where they might seclude him if he called attention to his existence and thereby to the fact that, strictly speaking, he was only an impediment on the way to the menagerie.

A small impediment, to be sure, one that grew steadily less. People grew familiar with the strange idea that they could be expected, in times like these, to take an interest in a hunger artist, and with this familiarity the verdict went out against him. He might fast as much as he could, and he did so; but nothing could save him now, people passed him by. Just try to explain to anyone the art of fasting! Anyone who has no feeling for it cannot be made to understand it. The fine placards grew dirty and illegible, they were torn down; the little notice board telling the number of fast days achieved, which at first was changed carefully every day, had long stayed at the same figure, for after the first few weeks even this small task seemed pointless to the staff; and so the artist simply fasted on and on, as he had once dreamed of doing, and it was no trouble to him, just as he had always foretold, but no one counted the days, no one, not even the artist himself, knew what records he was already breaking, and his heart grew heavy. And when once in a time some leisurely passer-by stopped, made merry over the old figure on the board and spoke of swindling, that was in its way the stupidest lie ever invented by indifference and inborn malice, since it was not the hunger artist who was cheating; he was working honestly, but the world was cheating him of his reward.

Many more days went by, however, and that too came to an end. An overseer's eye fell on the cage one day and he asked the attendants why this perfectly good stage should be left standing there unused with dirty straw inside it; nobody knew, until one man, helped out by the notice board, remembered about the hunger artist. They poked into the straw with sticks and found him in it. "Are you still fasting?" asked the overseer. "When on earth do you mean to stop?" "Forgive me, everybody," whispered the hunger artist; only the overseer, who had his ear to the bars, understood him. "Of course," said the overseer, and tapped his forehead with a finger to let the attendants know what state the man was in, "we forgive you." "I always wanted you to admire my fasting," said the hunger artist. "We do admire it," said the overseer, affably. "But you shouldn't admire it," said the hunger artist. "Well, then we don't admire it," said the overseer, "but why shouldn't we admire it?" "Because I have to fast, I can't help it," said the hunger artist. "What a fellow you are," said the overseer, "and why can't you help it?" "Because," said the hunger artist, lifting his head a little and speaking, with his lips pursed, as if for a kiss, right into the overseer's ear, so that no syllable might be lost, "because I couldn't find the food I liked. If I had found it, believe me, I should have made no fuss and stuffed myself like you or anyone else. These were his last words, but in his dimming eyes remained the firm though no longer proud persuasion that he was still continuing to fast.

"Well, clear this out now!" said the overseer, and they buried the hunger artist, straw and all. Into the cage they put a young panther. Even the most insensitive felt it refreshing to see this wild creature leaping around the cage that had so long been dreary. The panther was all right. The food he liked was brought him without hesitation by the attendants; he seemed not even to miss his freedom; his noble body, furnished almost to the bursting point with all that it needed, seemed to carry freedom around with it too; somewhere in his jaws it seemed to lurk; and the joy of life streamed with such ardent passion from his throat that for the onlookers it was not easy to stand the shock of it. But they braced themselves, crowded round the cage, and did not want ever to move away.

(1922)

Translated by Willa and Edwin Muir

Ernest Hemingway   *1899–1961*

HILLS LIKE WHITE ELEPHANTS

The hills across the valley of the Ebro were long and white. On this side there was no shade and no trees and the station was between two lines of rails in the sun. Close against the side of the station there was the warm shadow of the building and a curtain, made of strings of bamboo beads, hung across the open door into the bar, to keep out flies. The American and the girl with him sat at a table in the shade, outside the building. It was very hot and the express from Barcelona would come in forty minutes. It stopped at this junction for two minutes and went on to Madrid.

"What should we drink?" the girl asked. She had taken off her hat and put it on the table.

"It's pretty hot," the man said.

"Let's drink beer."

"Dos cervezas," the man said into the curtain.

"Big ones?" a woman asked from the doorway.

"Yes. Two big ones."

The woman brought two glasses of beer and two felt pads. She put the felt pads and the beer glasses on the table and looked at the man and the girl. The girl was looking off at the line of hills. They were white in the sun and the country was brown and dry.

"They look like white elephants," she said.

"I've never seen one," the man drank his beer.

"No, you wouldn't have."

"I might have," the man said. "Just because you say I wouldn't have doesn't prove anything."

The girl looked at the bead curtain. "They've painted something on it," she said. "What does it say?"

"Anis del Toro. It's a drink."

"Could we try it?"

The man called "Listen" through the curtain. The woman came out from the bar.

"Four reales."

"We want two Anis del Toro."

"With water?"

"Do you want it with water?"

"I don't know," the girl said. "Is it good with water?"

"It's all right."

"You want them with water?" asked the woman.

"Yes, with water."

"It tastes like licorice," the girl said and put the glass down.

"That's the way with everything."

"Yes," said the girl. "Everything tastes of licorice. Especially all the things you've waited so long for, like absinthe."

"Oh, cut it out."

"You started it," the girl said. "I was being amused. I was having a fine time."

"Well, let's try and have a fine time."

"All right. I was trying. I said the mountains looked like white elephants. Wasn't that bright?"

"That was bright."

"I wanted to try this new drink. That's all we do, isn't it—look at things and try new drinks?"

"I guess so."

The girl looked across at the hills.

"They're lovely hills," she said. "They don't really look like white elephants. I just meant the coloring of their skin through the trees."

"Should we have another drink?"

"All right."

The warm wind blew the bead curtain against the table.

"The beer's nice and cool," the man said.

"It's lovely," the girl said.

"It's really an awfully simple operation, Jig," the man said. "It's not really an operation at all."

The girl looked at the ground the table legs rested on.

"I know you wouldn't mind it, Jig. It's really not anything. It's just to let the air in."

The girl did not say anything.

"I'll go with you and I'll stay with you all the time. They just let the air in and then it's all perfectly natural."

"Then what will we do afterward?"

"We'll be fine afterward. Just like we were before."

"What makes you think so?"

"That's the only thing that bothers us. It's the only thing that's made us unhappy."

The girl looked at the bead curtain, put her hand out and took hold of two of the strings of beads.

"And you think then we'll be all right and be happy."

"I know we will. You don't have to be afraid. I've known lots of people that have done it."

"So have I," said the girl. "And afterward they were all so happy."

"Well," the man said, "if you don't want to you don't have to. I wouldn't have you do it if you didn't want to. But I know it's perfectly simple."

"And you really want to?"

"I think it's the best thing to do. But I don't want you to do it if you don't really want to."

"And if I do it you'll be happy and things will be like they were and you'll love me?"

"I love you now. You know I love you."

"I know. But if I do it, then it will be nice again if I say things are like white elephants, and you'll like it?"

"I'll love it. I love it now but I just can't think about it. You know how I get when I worry."

"If I do it you won't ever worry?"

"I won't worry about that because it's perfectly simple."

"Then I'll do it. Because I don't care about me."

"What do you mean?"

"I don't care about me."

"Well, I care about you."

"Oh, yes. But I don't care about me. And I'll do it and then everything will be fine."

"I don't want you to do it if you feel that way."

The girl stood up and walked to the end of the station. Across, on the other side, were fields of grain and trees along the banks of the Ebro. Far away, beyond the river, were mountains. The shadow of a cloud moved across the field of grain and she saw the river through the trees.

"And we could have all this," she said. "And we could have everything and every day we make it more impossible."

"What did you say?"

"I said we could have everything."

"We can have everything."

"No, we can't."

"We can have the whole world."

"No, we can't."

"We can go everywhere."

"No, we can't. It isn't ours any more."

"It's ours."

"No, it isn't. And once they take it away, you never get it back."

"But they haven't taken it away."

"We'll wait and see."

"Come on back in the shade," he said. "You mustn't feel that way."

"I don't feel any way," the girl said. "I just know things."

"I don't want you to do anything that you don't want to do—"

"Nor that isn't good for me," she said. "I know. Could we have another beer?"

"All right. But you've got to realize—"

"I realize," the girl said. "Can't we maybe stop talking?"

They sat down at the table and the girl looked across at the hills on the dry side of the valley and the man looked at her and at the table.

"You've got to realize," he said, "that I don't want you to do it if you don't want to. I'm perfectly willing to go through with it if it means anything to you."

"Doesn't it mean anything to you? We could get along."

"Of course it does. But I don't want anybody but you. I don't want anyone else. And I know it's perfectly simple."

"Yes, you know it's perfectly simple."

"It's all right for you to say that, but I do know it."

"Would you do something for me now?"

"I'd do anything for you."

"Would you please please please please please please please stop talking?"

He did not say anything but looked at the bags against the wall of the station. There were labels on them from all the hotels where they had spent nights.

"But I don't want you to," he said. "I don't care anything about it."

"I'll scream," the girl said.

The woman came out through the curtains with two glasses of beer and put them down on the damp felt pads. "The train comes in five minutes," she said.

"What did she say?" asked the girl.

"That the train is coming in five minutes."

The girl smiled brightly at the woman, to thank her.

"I'd better take the bags over to the other side of the station," the man said. She smiled at him.

"All right. Then come back and we'll finish the beer."

He picked up the two heavy bags and carried them around the station to the other tracks. He looked up the tracks but could not see the train. Coming back, he walked through the barroom, where people waiting for the train were drinking. He drank an Anis at the bar and looked at the people. They were all waiting reasonably for the train. He went out through the bead curtain. She was sitting at the table and smiled at him.

"Do you feel better?" he asked.

"I feel fine," she said. "There's nothing wrong with me. I feel fine."

(1927)

Katherine Anne Porter *1890—1980*

THE JILTING OF GRANNY WEATHERALL

She flicked her wrist neatly out of Doctor Harry's pudgy careful fingers and pulled the sheet up to her chin. The brat ought to be in knee breeches. Doctoring around the country with spectacles on his nose! "Get along now, take your schoolbooks and go. There's nothing wrong with me."

Doctor Harry spread a warm paw like a cushion on her forehead where the forked green vein danced and made her eyelids twitch. "Now, now, be a good girl, and we'll have you up in no time."

"That's no way to speak to a woman nearly eighty years old just because she's down. I'd have you respect your elders, young man."

"Well, Missy, excuse me." Doctor Harry patted her cheek. "But I've got to warn you, haven't I? You're a marvel, but you must be careful or you're going to be good and sorry."

"Don't tell me what I'm going to be. I'm on my feet now, morally speaking. It's Cornelia. I had to go to bed to get rid of her."

Her bones felt loose, and floated around in her skin, and Doctor Harry floated like a balloon around the foot of the bed. He floated and pulled down his waistcoat and swung his glasses on a cord. "Well, stay where you are, it certainly can't hurt you."

"Get along and doctor your sick," said Granny Weatherall. "Leave a well woman alone. I'll call for you when I want you. . . . Where were you forty years ago when I pulled through milk-leg and double pneumonia? You weren't even born. Don't let Cornelia lead you on," she shouted, because Doctor Harry appeared to float up to the ceiling and out. "I pay my own bills, and I don't throw my money away on nonsense!"

She meant to wave good-by, but it was too much trouble. Her eyes closed of themselves, it was like a dark curtain drawn around the bed. The pillow rose and floated under her, pleasant as a hammock in a light wind. She listened to the leaves rustling outside the window. No, somebody was swishing newspapers: no, Cornelia and Doctor Harry were whispering together. She leaped broad awake, thinking they whispered in her ear.

"She was never like this, *never* like this!" "Well, what can we expect?" "Yes, eighty years old. . . ."

Well, and what if she was? She still had ears. It was like Cornelia to whisper around doors. She always kept things secret in such a public way.

She was always being tactful and kind. Cornelia was dutiful; that was the trouble with her. Dutiful and good: "So good and dutiful," said Granny, "that I'd like to spank her." She saw herself spanking Cornelia and making a fine job of it.

"What'd you say, Mother?"

Granny felt her face tying up in hard knots.

"Can't a body think, I'd like to know?"

"I thought you might want something."

"I do. I want a lot of things. First off, go away and don't whisper."

She lay and drowsed, hoping in her sleep that the children would keep out and let her rest a minute. It had been a long day. Not that she was tired. It was always pleasant to snatch a minute now and then. There was always so much to be done, let me see: tomorrow.

Tomorrow was far away and there was nothing to trouble about. Things were finished somehow when the time came; thank God there was always a little margin over for peace: then a person could spread out the plan of life and tuck in the edges orderly. It was good to have everything clean and folded away, with the hair brushes and tonic bottles sitting straight on the white embroidered linen: the day started without fuss and the pantry shelves laid out with rows of jelly glasses and brown jugs and white stone-china jars with blue whirligigs and words painted on them: coffee, tea, sugar, ginger, cinnamon, allspice: and the bronze clock with the lion on top nicely dusted off. The dust that lion could collect in twenty-four hours! The box in the attic with all those letters tied up, well she'd have to go through that tomorrow. All those letters—George's letters and John's letters and her letters to them both—lying around for the children to find afterwards made her uneasy. Yes, that would be tomorrow's business. No use to let them know how silly she had been once.

While she was rummaging around she found death in her mind and it felt clammy and unfamiliar. She had spent so much time preparing for death there was no need for bringing it up again. Let it take care of itself now. When she was sixty she had felt very old, finished, and went around making farewell trips to see her children and grandchildren, with a secret in her mind: This is the very last of your mother, children! Then she made her will and came down with a long fever. That was all just a notion like a lot of other things, but it was lucky too, for she had once for all got over the idea of dying for a long time. Now she couldn't be worried. She hoped she had better sense now. Her father had lived to be one hundred and two years old and had drunk a noggin of strong hot toddy on his last birthday. He told the reporters it was his daily habit, and he owed his long life to that. He had made quite a scandal and was very pleased about it. She believed she'd just plague Cornelia a little.

"Cornelia! Cornelia!" No footsteps, but a sudden hand on her cheek. "Bless you, where have you been?"

"Here, mother."

"Well, Cornelia, I want a noggin of hot toddy."

"Are you cold, darling?"

"I'm chilly, Cornelia. Lying in bed stops the circulation. I must have told you that a thousand times."

Well, she could just hear Cornelia telling her husband that Mother was getting childish and they'd have to humor her. The thing that most annoyed her was that Cornelia thought she was deaf, dumb, and blind. Little hasty glances and tiny gestures tossed around her and over her head saying, "Don't cross her, let her have her way, she's eighty years old," and she sitting there as if she lived in a thin glass cage. Sometimes Granny almost made up her mind to pack up and move back to her own house where nobody could remind her every minute that she was old. Wait, wait, Cornelia, till your own children whisper behind your back!

In her day she had kept a better house and had got more work done. She wasn't too old yet for Lydia to be driving eighty miles for advice when one of the children jumped the track, and Jimmy still dropped in and talked things over: "Now, Mammy, you've a good business head, I want to know what you think of this? . . ." Old Cornelia couldn't change the furniture around without asking. Little things, little things! They had been so sweet when they were little. Granny wished the old days were back again with the children young and everything to be done over. It had been a hard pull, but not too much for her. When she thought of all the food she had cooked, and all the clothes she had cut and sewed, and all the gardens she had made—well, the children showed it. There they were, made out of her, and they couldn't get away from that. Sometimes she wanted to see John again and point to them and say, Well, I didn't do so badly, did I? But that would have to wait. That was for tomorrow. She used to think of him as a man, but now all the children were older than their father, and he would be a child beside her if she saw him now. It seemed strange and there was something wrong in the idea. Why, he couldn't possibly recognize her. She had fenced in a hundred acres once, digging the post holes herself and clamping the wires with just a negro boy to help. That changed a woman. John would be looking for a young woman with the peaked Spanish comb in her hair and the painted fan. Digging post holes changed a woman. Riding country roads in the winter when women had their babies was another thing: sitting up nights with sick horses and sick negroes and sick children and hardly ever losing one. John, I hardly ever lost one of them! John would see that in a minute, that would be something he could understand, she wouldn't have to explain anything!

It made her feel like rolling up her sleeves and putting the whole place to rights again. No matter if Cornelia was determined to be everywhere at once, there were a great many things left undone on this place. She would start tomorrow and do them. It was good to be strong enough for everything, even if all you made melted and changed and slipped under your hands, so that by the time you finished you almost forgot what you were working for. What was it I set out to do? she asked herself intently, but she could not remember. A fog rose over the valley, she saw it marching across the creek swallowing the trees and moving up the hill like an army of ghosts. Soon it would be at the near edge of the orchard, and then it was time to go in and light the lamps. Come in, children, don't stay out in the night air.

Lighting the lamps had been beautiful. The children huddled up to her and breathed like little calves waiting at the bars in the twilight. Their eyes followed the match and watched the flame rise and settle in a blue curve, then they moved away from her. The lamp was lit, they didn't have to be scared and hang on to mother any more. Never, never, never more. God, for all my life I thank Thee. Without Thee, my God, I could never have done it. Hail, Mary, full of grace.

I want you to pick all the fruit this year and see that nothing is wasted. There's always someone who can use it. Don't let good things rot for want of using. You waste life when you waste good food. Don't let things get lost. It's bitter to lose things. Now, don't let me get to thinking, not when I am tired and taking a little nap before supper. . . .

The pillow rose about her shoulders and pressed against her heart and the memory was being squeezed out of it: oh, push down the pillow, somebody: it would smother her if she tried to hold it. Such a fresh breeze blowing and such a green day with no threats in it. But he had not come, just the same. What does a woman do when she has put on the white veil and set out the white cake for a man and he doesn't come? She tried to remember. No, I swear he never harmed me but in that. He never harmed me but in that . . . and what if he did? There was the day, the day, but a whirl of dark smoke rose and covered it, crept up and over into the bright field where everything was planted so carefully in orderly rows. That was hell, she knew hell when she saw it. For sixty years she had prayed against remembering him and against losing her soul in the deep pit of hell, and now the two things were mingled in one and the thought of him was a smoky cloud from hell that moved and crept in her head when she had just got rid of Doctor Harry and was trying to rest a minute. Wounded vanity, Ellen, said a sharp voice in the top of her mind. Don't let your wounded vanity get the upper hand of you. Plenty of girls get jilted. You were jilted, weren't you? Then stand up to it. Her eyelids wavered and let in streamers of blue-gray light like tissue paper over her eyes. She must get up and pull the shades down or she'd never sleep. She was in bed again and the shades were not down. How could that happen? Better turn over, hide from the light, sleeping in the light gave you nightmares. "Mother, how do you feel now?" and a stinging wetness on her forehead. But I don't like having my face washed in cold water!

Hapsy? George? Lydia? Jimmy? No, Cornelia, and her features were swollen and full of little puddles. "They're coming, darling, they'll all be here soon." Go wash your face, child, you look funny.

Instead of obeying, Cornelia knelt down and put her head on the pillow. She seemed to be talking but there was no sound. "Well, are you tongue-tied? Whose birthday is it? Are you going to give a party?"

Cornelia's mouth moved urgently in strange shapes. "Don't do that, you bother me, daughter."

"Oh, no, Mother, Oh, no. . . ."

Nonsense. It was strange about children. They disputed your every word. "No what, Cornelia?"

"Here's Doctor Harry."

"I won't see that boy again. He just left five minutes ago."

"That was this morning, Mother. It's night now. Here's the nurse."

"This is Doctor Harry, Mrs. Weatherall. I never saw you look so young and happy!"

"Ah, I'll never be young again—but I'd be happy if they'd let me lie in peace and get rested."

She thought she spoke up loudly, but no one answered. A warm weight on her forehead, a warm bracelet on her wrist, and a breeze went on whispering, trying to tell her something. A shuffle of leaves in the everlasting hand of God. He blew on them and they danced and rattled. "Mother, don't mind, we're going to give you a little hypodermic." "Look here, daughter, how do ants get in this bed? I saw sugar ants yesterday." Did you send for Hapsy too?

It was Hapsy she really wanted. She had to go a long way back through a great many rooms to find Hapsy standing with a baby on her arm. She seemed to herself to be Hapsy also, and the baby on Hapsy's arm was Hapsy and himself and herself, all at once, and there was no surprise in the meeting. Then Hapsy melted from within and turned flimsy as gray gauze and the baby was a gauzy shadow, and Hapsy came up close and said, "I thought you'd never come," and looked at her very searchingly and said, "You haven't changed a bit!" They leaned forward to kiss, when Cornelia began whispering from a long way off, "Oh, is there anything you want to tell me? Is there anything I can do for you?"

Yes, she had changed her mind after sixty years and she would like to see George. I want you to find George. Find him and be sure to tell him I forgot him. I want him to know I had my husband just the same and my children and my house like any other woman. A good house too and a good husband that I loved and fine children out of him. Better than I hoped for even. Tell him I was given back everything he took away and more. Oh, no, oh, God, no, there was something else besides the house and the man and the children. Oh, surely they were not all? What was it? Something not given back. . . . Her breath crowded down under her ribs and grew into a monstrous frightening shape with cutting edges; it bored up into her head, and the agony was unbelievable: Yes, John, get the doctor now, no more talk, my time has come.

When this one was born it should be the last. The last. It should have been born first, for it was the one she had truly wanted. Everything came in good time. Nothing left out, left over. She was strong, in three days she would be as well as ever. Better. A woman needed milk in her to have her full health.

"Mother, do you hear me?"

"I've been telling you—"

"Mother, Father Connolly's here."

"I went to Holy Communion only last week. Tell him I'm not so sinful as all that."

"Father just wants to speak to you."

He could speak as much as he pleased. It was like him to drop in and inquire about her soul as if it were a teething baby, and then stay on for a cup of tea and a round of cards and gossip. He always had a funny story of some sort, usually about an Irishman who made his little mistakes and confessed them, and the point lay in some absurd thing he would blurt out in the confessional showing his struggles between native piety and original sin. Granny felt easy about her soul. Cornelia, where are your manners? Give Father Connolly a chair. She had her secret, comfortable understanding with a few favorite saints who cleared a straight road to God for her. All as surely signed and sealed as the papers for the new Forty Acres. Forever . . . heirs and assigns forever. Since the day the wedding cake was not cut, but thrown out and wasted. The whole bottom dropped out of the world, and there she was blind and sweating with nothing under her feet and the walls falling away. His hand had caught her under the breast, she had not fallen, there was the freshly polished floor with the green rug on it, just as before. He had cursed like a sailor's parrot and said, "I'll kill him for you." Don't lay a hand on him, for my sake leave something to God. "Now, Ellen, you must believe what I tell you. . . ."

So there was nothing, nothing to worry about any more, except sometimes in the night one of the children screamed in a nightmare, and they both hustled out shaking and hunting for the matches and calling, "There, wait a minute, here we are!" John, get the doctor now. Hapsy's time has come. But there was Hapsy standing by the bed in a white cap. "Cornelia, tell Hapsy to take off her cap. I can't see her plain."

Her eyes opened very wide and the room stood out like a picture she had seen somewhere. Dark colors with the shadows rising towards the ceiling in long angles. The tall black dresser gleamed with nothing on it but John's picture, enlarged from a little one, with John's eyes very black when they should have been blue. You never saw him, so how do you know how he looked? But the man insisted the copy was perfect, it was very rich and handsome. For a picture, yes, but it's not my husband. The table by the bed had a linen cover and a candle and a crucifix. The light was blue from Cornelia's silk lampshades. No sort of light at all, just frippery. You had to live forty years with kerosene lamps to appreciate honest electricity. She felt very strong and she saw Doctor Harry with a rosy nimbus around him.

"You look like a saint, Doctor Harry, and I vow that's as near as you'll ever come to it."

"She's saying something."

"I heard you, Cornelia. What's all this carrying-on?"

"Father Connolly's saying—"

Cornelia's voice staggered and bumped like a cart in a bad road. It rounded corners and turned back again and arrived nowhere. Granny stepped up in the cart very lightly and reached for the reins, but a man sat beside her and she knew him by his hands, driving the cart. She did not look in his face, for she knew without seeing, but looked instead down the road where the trees leaned over and bowed to each other and a thousand birds were singing a Mass. She felt like singing too, but she put her hand in the bosom of her dress and pulled out a rosary, and Father Connolly murmured Latin in a very solemn voice and tickled her feet. My God, will you stop that nonsense? I'm a married woman. What if he did run away and leave me to face the priest by myself? I found another a whole world better. I wouldn't have exchanged my husband for anybody except St. Michael himself, and you may tell him that for me with a thank you in the bargain.

Light flashed on her closed eyelids, and a deep roaring shook her. Cornelia, is that lightning? I hear thunder. There's going to be a storm. Close all the windows. Call the children in. . . . "Mother, here we are, all of us." "Is that you, Hapsy?" "Oh, no, I'm Lydia. We drove as fast as we could." Their faces drifted above her, drifted away. The rosary fell out of her hands and Lydia put it back. Jimmy tried to help, their hands fumbled together, and Granny closed two fingers around Jimmy's thumb. Beads wouldn't do, it must be something alive. She was so amazed her thoughts ran round and round. So, my dear Lord, this is my death and I wasn't even thinking about it. My children have come to see me die. But I can't, it's not time. Oh, I always hated surprises. I wanted to give Cornelia the amethyst set—Cornelia, you're to have the amethyst set, but Hapsy's to wear it when she wants, and, Doctor Harry, do shut up. Nobody sent for you. Oh, my dear Lord, do wait a minute. I meant to do something about the Forty Acres, Jimmy doesn't need it and Lydia will later on, with that worthless husband of hers. I meant to finish the altar cloth and send six bottles of wine to Sister Borgia for her dyspepsia. I want to send six bottles of wine to Sister Borgia, Father Connolly, now don't let me forget.

Cornelia's voice made short turns and tilted over and crashed. "Oh, Mother, oh, Mother, oh, Mother. . . ."

"I'm not going Cornelia. I'm taken by surprise. I can't go."

You'll see Hapsy again. What about her? "I thought you'd never come." Granny made a long journey outward, looking for Hapsy. What if I don't find her? What then? Her heart sank down and down, there was no bottom to death, she couldn't come to the end of it. The blue light from Cornelia's lampshade drew into a tiny point in the center of her brain, it flickered and winked like an eye, quietly it fluttered and dwindled. Granny lay curled down within herself, amazed and watchful, staring at the point of light that was herself; her body was now only a deeper mass of shadow in an endless darkness and this darkness would curl around the light and swallow it up. God, give a sign!

For the second time there was no sign. Again no bridegroom and the priest in the house. She could not remember any other sorrow because this grief wiped them all away. Oh, no, there's nothing more cruel than this—I'll never forgive it. She stretched herself with a deep breath and blew out the light.

(1930)

William Faulkner *1897–1962*

A ROSE FOR EMILY

I

When Miss Emily Grierson died, our whole town went to her funeral: the men through a sort of respectful affection for a fallen monument, the women mostly out of curiosity to see the inside of her house, which no one save an old manservant—a combined gardener and cook—had seen in at least ten years.

It was a big, squarish frame house that had once been white, decorated with cupolas and spires and scrolled balconies in the heavily lightsome style of the seventies, set on what had once been our most select street. But garages and cotton gins had encroached and obliterated even the august names of that neighborhood, only Miss Emily's house was left, lifting its stubborn and coquettish decay above the cotton wagons and the gasoline pumps—an eyesore among eyesores. And now Miss Emily had gone to join the representatives of those august names where they lay in the cedar-bemused cemetery among the ranked and anonymous graves of Union and Confederate soldiers who fell at the battle of Jefferson.

Alive, Miss Emily had been a tradition, a duty, and a care; a sort of hereditary obligation upon the town, dating from that day in 1894 when Colonel Sartoris, the mayor—he who fathered the edict that no Negro woman should appear on the streets without an apron—remitted her taxes, the dispensation dating from the death of her father on into perpetuity. Not that Miss Emily would have accepted charity. Colonel Sartoris invented an involved tale to the effect that Miss Emily's father had loaned money to the town, which the town, as a matter of business, preferred this way of repaying. Only a man of Colonel Sartoris' generation and thought could have invented it, and only a woman could have believed it.

When the next generation, with its more modern ideas, became mayors and aldermen, this arrangement created some little dissatisfaction. On the first of the year they mailed her a tax notice. February came, and there was no reply. They wrote her a formal letter, asking her to call at the sheriff's office at her convenience. A week later the mayor wrote her himself, offering to call or to send his car for her, and received in reply a note on paper of an archaic shape, in a thin, flowing calligraphy in faded ink, to the effect that she no longer went out at all. The tax notice was also enclosed, without comment.

They called a special meeting of the Board of Aldermen. A deputation waited upon her, knocked at the door through which no visitor had passed since she ceased giving china-painting lessons eight or ten years earlier. They were admitted by the old Negro into a dim hall from which a stairway mounted into still more shadow. It smelled of dust and disuse—a close, dank smell. The Negro led them into the parlor. It was furnished in heavy, leather-covered furniture. When the Negro opened the blinds of one window, they could see that the leather was cracked; and when they sat down, a faint dust rose sluggishly about their thighs, spinning with slow motes in the single sun-ray. On a tarnished gilt easel before the fireplace stood a crayon portrait of Miss Emily's father.

They rose when she entered—a small, fat woman in black, with a thin gold chain descending to her waist and vanishing into her belt, leaning on an ebony cane with a tarnished gold head. Her skeleton was small and spare; perhaps that was why what would have been merely plumpness in another was obesity in her. She looked bloated, like a body long submerged in motionless water, and of that pallid hue. Her eyes, lost in the fatty ridges of her face, looked like two small pieces of coal pressed into a lump of dough as they moved from one face to another while the visitors stated their errand.

She did not ask them to sit. She just stood in the door and listened quietly until the spokesman came to a stumbling halt. Then they could hear the invisible watch ticking at the end of the gold chain.

Her voice was dry and cold. "I have no taxes in Jefferson. Colonel Sartoris explained it to me. Perhaps one of you can gain access to the city records and satisfy yourselves."

"But we have. We are the city authorities, Miss Emily. Didn't you get a notice from the sheriff, signed by him?"

"I received a paper, yes," Miss Emily said. "Perhaps he considers himself the sheriff. . . . I have no taxes in Jefferson."

"But there is nothing on the books to show that, you see. We must go by the—"

"See Colonel Sartoris. I have no taxes in Jefferson."

"But, Miss Emily—"

"See Colonel Sartoris." (Colonel Sartoris had been dead almost ten years.) "I have no taxes in Jefferson. Tobe!" The Negro appeared. "Show these gentlemen out."

II

So she vanquished them, horse and foot, just as she had vanquished their fathers thirty years before about the smell. That was two years after her father's death and a short time after her sweetheart—the one we believed would marry her—had deserted her. After her father's death she went out very little; after her sweetheart went away, people hardly saw her at all. A few ladies had the temerity to call, but were not received, and the only sign of life about the place was the Negro man—a young man then—going in and out with a market basket.

"Just as if a man—any man—could keep a kitchen properly," the ladies said; so they were not surprised when the smell developed. It was another link between the gross, teeming world and the high and mighty Griersons.

A neighbor, a woman, complained to the mayor, Judge Stevens, eighty years old.

"But what will you have me do about it, madam?" he said.

"Why, send her word to stop it," the woman said.

"Isn't there a law?"

"I'm sure that won't be necessary," Judge Stevens said. "It's probably just a snake or a rat that nigger of hers killed in the yard. I'll speak to him about it."

The next day he received two more complaints, one from a man who came in diffident deprecation. "We really must do something about it, Judge. I'd be the last one in the world to bother Miss Emily, but we've got to do something." That night the Board of Aldermen met—three graybeards and one younger man, a member of the rising generation.

"It's simple enough," he said. "Send her word to have her place cleaned up. Give her a certain time to do it in, and if she don't . . ."

"Dammit, sir," Judge Stevens said, "will you accuse a lady to her face of smelling bad?"

So the next night, after midnight, four men crossed Miss Emily's lawn and slunk about the house like burglars, sniffing along the base of the brickwork and at the cellar openings while one of them performed a regular sowing motion with his hand out of a sack slung from his shoulder. They broke open the cellar door and sprinkled lime there, and in all the outbuildings. As they recrossed the lawn, a window that had been dark was lighted and Miss Emily sat in it, the light behind her, and her upright torso motionless as that of an idol. They crept quietly across the lawn and into the shadow of the locusts that lined the street. After a week or two the smell went away.

That was when people had begun to feel really sorry for her. People in our town, remembering how old lady Wyatt, her great-aunt, had gone completely crazy at last, believed that the Griersons held themselves a little too high for what they really were. None of the young men were quite good enough for Miss Emily and such. We had long thought of them as a tableau: Miss Emily a slender figure in white in the background, her father a spraddled silhouette in the foreground, his back to her and clutching a horsewhip, the two of them framed by the back-flung front door. So when she got to be thirty and was still single, we were not pleased exactly, but vindicated; even with insanity in the family she wouldn't have turned down all of her chances if they had really materialized.

When her father died, it got about that the house was all that was left to her; and in a way, people were glad. At last they could pity Miss Emily. Being left alone, and a pauper, she had become humanized. Now she too would know the old thrill and the old despair of a penny more or less.

The day after his death all the ladies prepared to call at the house and offer condolence and aid, as is our custom. Miss Emily met them at the door, dressed as usual and with no trace of grief on her face. She told them that her father was not dead. She did that for three days, with the ministers calling on her, and the doctors, trying to persuade her to let them dispose of the body. Just as they were about to resort to law and force, she broke down, and they buried her father quickly.

We did not say she was crazy then. We believed she had to do that. We remembered all the young men her father had driven away, and we knew that with nothing left, she would have to cling to that which had robbed her, as people will.

III

She was sick for a long time. When we saw her again, her hair was cut short, making her look like a girl, with a vague resemblance to those angels in colored church windows—sort of tragic and serene.

The town had just let the contracts for paving the sidewalks, and in the summer after her father's death they began the work. The construction company came with niggers and mules and machinery, and a foreman named Homer Barron, a Yankee—a big, dark, ready man, with a big voice and eyes lighter than his face. The little boys would follow in groups to hear him cuss the niggers, and the niggers singing in time to the rise and fall of picks. Pretty soon he knew everybody in town. Whenever you heard a lot of laughing anywhere about the square, Homer Barron would be in the center of the group. Presently we began to see him and Miss Emily on Sunday afternoons driving in the yellow-wheeled buggy and the matched team of bays from the livery stable.

At first we were glad that Miss Emily would have an interest, because the ladies all said, "Of course a Grierson would not think seriously of a Northerner, a day laborer." But there were still others, older people, who said that even grief could not cause a real lady to forget *noblesse oblige*— without calling it *noblesse oblige*. They just said, "Poor Emily. Her kinsfolk should come to her." She had some kin in Alabama; but years ago her father had fallen out with them over the estate of old lady Wyatt, the crazy woman, and there was no communication between the two families. They had not even been represented at the funeral.

And as soon as the old people said, "Poor Emily," the whispering began. "Do you suppose it's really so?" they said to one another. "Of course it is. What else could . . ." This behind their hands; rustling of craned silk and satin behind jalousies closed upon the sun of Sunday afternoon as the thin, swift clop-clop-clop of the matched team passed: "Poor Emily."

She carried her head high enough—even when we believed that she was fallen. It was as if she demanded more than ever the recognition of her dignity as the last Grierson; as if it had wanted that touch of earthiness to reaffirm her imperviousness. Like when she bought the rat poison, the arsenic. That was over a year after they had begun to say "Poor Emily," and while the two female cousins were visiting her.

"I want some poison," she said to the druggist. She was over thirty then, still a slight woman, though thinner than usual, with cold, haughty black eyes in a face the flesh of which was strained across the temples and about the eyesockets as you imagine a lighthouse-keeper's face ought to look. "I want some poison," she said.

"Yes, Miss Emily. What kind? For rats and such? I'd recom—"

"I want the best you have. I don't care what kind."

The druggist named several. "They'll kill anything up to an elephant. But what you want is—"

"Arsenic," Miss Emily said. "Is that a good one?"

"Is . . . arsenic? Yes, ma'am. But what you want—"

"I want arsenic."

The druggist looked down at her. She looked back at him, erect, her face like a strained flag. "Why, of course," the druggist said. "If that's what you want. But the law requires you to tell what you are going to use it for."

Miss Emily just stared at him, her head tilted back in order to look him eye for eye, until he looked away and went and got the arsenic and wrapped it up. The Negro delivery boy brought her the package; the druggist didn't come back. When she opened the package at home there was written on the box, under the skull and bones: "For rats."

IV

So the next day we all said, "She will kill herself"; and we said it would be the best thing. When she had first begun to be seen with Homer Barron, we had said, "She will marry him." Then we said, "She will persuade him yet," because Homer himself had remarked—he liked men, and it was known that he drank with the younger men in the Elk's Club—that he was not a marrying man. Later we said, "Poor Emily," behind the jalousies as they passed on Sunday afternoon in the glittering buggy, Miss Emily with her head high and Homer Barron with his hat cocked and a cigar in his teeth, reins and whip in a yellow glove.

Then some of the ladies began to say that it was a disgrace to the town and a bad example to the young people. The men did not want to interfere, but at last the ladies forced the Baptist minister—Miss Emily's people were Episcopal—to call upon her. He would never divulge what happened during that interview, but he refused to go back again. The next Sunday they again drove about the streets, and the following day the minister's wife wrote to Miss Emily's relations in Alabama.

So she had blood-kin under her roof again and we sat back to watch developments. At first nothing happened. Then we were sure that they were to be married. We learned that Miss Emily had been to the jeweler's and ordered a man's toilet set in silver, with the letters H.B. on each piece. Two days later we learned that she had bought a complete outfit of men's clothing, including a nightshirt, and we said "They are married." We were really glad. We were glad because the two female cousins were even more Grierson than Miss Emily had ever been.

So we were not surprised when Homer Barron—the streets had been finished some time since—was gone. We were a little disappointed that there was not a public blowing-off, but we believed that he had gone on to prepare for Miss Emily's coming, or to give her a chance to get rid of the cousins. (By that time it was a cabal, and we were all Miss Emily's allies to help circumvent the cousins.) Sure enough, after another week they departed. And, as we had expected all along, within three days Homer Barron was back in town. A neighbor saw the Negro man admit him at the kitchen door at dusk one evening.

And that was the last we saw of Homer Barron. And of Miss Emily for some time. The Negro man went in and out with the market basket, but the front door remained closed. Now and then we would see her at a window for a moment, as the men did that night when they sprinkled the lime, but for almost six months she did not appear on the streets. Then we knew that this was to be expected too; as if that quality of her father which had thwarted her woman's life so many times had been too virulent and too furious to die.

When we next saw Miss Emily, she had grown fat and her hair was turning gray. During the next few years it grew grayer and grayer until it attained an even pepper-and-salt iron-gray, when it ceased turning. Up to the day of her death at seventy-four it was still that vigorous iron-gray, like the hair of an active man.

From that time on her front door remained closed, save for a period of six or seven years, when she was about forty, during which she gave lessons in china-painting. She fitted up a studio in one of the downstairs rooms, where the daughters and granddaughters of Colonel Sartoris' contemporaries were sent to her with the same regularity and in the same spirit that they were sent on Sundays with a twenty-five cent piece for the collection plate. Meanwhile her taxes had been remitted.

Then the newer generation became the backbone and the spirit of the town, and the painting pupils grew up and fell away and did not send their children to her with boxes of color and tedious brushes and pictures cut from the ladies' magazines. The front door closed upon the last one and remained closed for good. When the town got free postal delivery Miss Emily alone refused to let them fasten the metal numbers above her door and attach a mailbox to it. She would not listen to them.

Daily, monthly, yearly we watched the Negro grow grayer and more stooped, going in and out with the market basket. Each December we sent her a tax notice, which would be returned by the post office a week later, unclaimed. Now and then we would see her in one of the downstairs windows—she had evidently shut up the top floor of the house—like the carven torso of an idol in a niche, looking or not looking at us, we could never tell which. Thus she passed from generation to generation—dear, inescapable, impervious, tranquil, and perverse.

And so she died. Fell ill in the house filled with dust and shadows, with only a doddering Negro man to wait on her. We did not even know she was sick; we had long since given up trying to get any information from the Negro. He talked to no one, probably not even to her, for his voice had grown harsh and rusty, as if from disuse.

She died in one of the downstairs rooms, in a heavy walnut bed with a curtain, her gray head propped on a pillow yellow and moldy with age and lack of sunlight.

V

The Negro met the first of the ladies at the front door and let them in, with their hushed, sibilant voices and their quick, curious glances, and then he disappeared. He walked right through the house and out the back and was not seen again.

The two female cousins came at once. They held the funeral on the second day, with the town coming to look at Miss Emily beneath a mass of bought flowers, with the crayon face of her father musing profoundly above the bier and the ladies sibilant and macabre; and the very old men— some in their brushed Confederate uniforms—on the porch and the lawn, talking of Miss Emily as if she had been a contemporary of theirs, believing that they had danced with her and courted her perhaps, confusing time with its mathematical progression, as the old do, to whom all the past is not a diminishing road, but, instead, a huge meadow which no winter ever quite touches, divided from them now by the narrow bottleneck of the most recent decade of years.

Already we knew that there was one room in that region above stairs which no one had seen in forty years, and which would have to be forced. They waited until Miss Emily was decently in the ground before they opened it.

The violence of breaking down the door seemed to fill this room with pervading dust. A thin, acrid pall as of the tomb seemed to lie everywhere upon this room decked and furnished as for a bridal: upon the valance curtains of faded rose color, upon the rose-shaded lights, upon the dressing table, upon the delicate array of crystal and the man's toilet things backed with tarnished silver, silver so tarnished that the monogram was obscured. Among them lay a collar and tie, as if they had just been removed, which, lifted, left upon the surface a pale crescent in the dust. Upon a chair hung the suit, carefully folded; beneath it the two mute shoes and the discarded socks.

The man himself lay in the bed.

For a long while we just stood there, looking down at the profound and fleshless grin. The body had apparently once lain in the attitude of an embrace, but now the long sleep that outlasts love, that conquers even the grimace of love, had cuckolded him. What was left of him, rotted beneath what was left of the nightshirt, had become inextricable from the bed in which he lay; and upon him and upon the pillow beside him lay that even coating of the patient and biding dust.

Then we noticed that in the second pillow was the indentation of a head. One of us lifted something from it, and leaning forward, that faint and invisible dust dry and acrid in the nostrils, we saw a long strand of iron-gray hair.

(1931)

D. H. Lawrence *1885–1930*

THE ROCKING-HORSE WINNER

There was a woman who was beautiful, who started with all the advantages, yet she had no luck. She married for love, and the love turned to dust. She had bonny children, yet she felt they had been thrust upon her, and she could not love them. They looked at her coldly, as if they were finding fault with her. And hurriedly she felt she must cover up some fault in herself. Yet what it was that she must cover up she never knew. Nevertheless, when her children were present, she always felt the centre of her heart go hard. This troubled her, and in her manner she was all the more gentle and anxious for her children, as if she loved them very much. Only she herself knew that at the centre of her heart was a hard little place that could not feel love, no, not for anybody. Everybody else said of her: "She is such a good mother. She adores her children." Only she herself, and her children themselves, knew it was not so. They read it in each other's eyes.

There were a boy and two little girls. They lived in a pleasant house, with a garden, and they had discreet servants, and felt themselves superior to anyone in the neighbourhood.

Although they lived in style, they felt always an anxiety in the house. There was never enough money. The mother had a small income, and the father had a small income, but not nearly enough for the social position which they had to keep up. The father went into town to some office. But though he had good prospects, these prospects never materialised. There was always the grinding sense of the shortage of money, though the style was always kept up.

At last the mother said: "I will see if *I* can't make something." But she did not know where to begin. She racked her brains, and tried this thing and the other, but could not find anything successful. The failure made deep lines come into her face. Her children were growing up, they would have to go to school. There must be more money, there must be more money. The father, who was always very handsome and expensive in his tastes, seemed as if he never *would* be able to do anything worth doing. And the mother, who had a great belief in herself, did not succeed any better, and her tastes were just as expensive.

And so the house came to be haunted by the unspoken phrase: *There must be more money! There must be more money!* The children could hear it all the time, though nobody said it aloud. They heard it at Christmas, when the expensive and splendid toys filled the nursery. Behind the shining modern rocking-horse, behind the smart doll's house, a voice would start whispering: "There *must* be more money! There *must* be more money!" And the children would stop playing, to listen for a moment. They would look into each other's eyes, to see if they had all heard. And each one saw in the eyes of the other two that they too had heard. "There *must* be more money! There *must* be more money!"

It came whispering from the springs of the still-swaying rocking-horse, and even the horse, bending his wooden, champing head, heard it. The big doll, sitting so pink and smirking in her new pram, could hear it quite plainly, and seemed to be smirking all the more self-consciously because of it. The foolish puppy, too, that took the place of the teddybear, he was looking so extraordinarily foolish for no other reason but that he heard the secret whisper all over the house: "There *must* be more money!"

Yet nobody ever said it aloud. The whisper was everywhere, and therefore no one spoke it. Just as no one ever says: "We are breathing!" in spite of the fact that breath is coming and going all the time.

"Mother," said the boy Paul one day, "why don't we keep a car of our own? Why do we always use uncle's, or else a taxi?"

"Because we're the poor members of the family," said the mother.

"But why *are* we, mother?"

"Well—I suppose," she said slowly and bitterly, "it's because your father has no luck."

The boy was silent for some time.

"Is luck money, mother?" he asked, rather timidly.

"No, Paul. Not quite. It's what causes you to have money."

"Oh!" said Paul vaguely. "I thought when Uncle Oscar said *filthy lucker*, it meant money."

"*Filthy lucre* does mean money," said the mother. "But it's lucre, not luck."

"Oh!" said the boy. "Then what *is* luck, mother?"

"It's what causes you to have money. If you're lucky you have money. That's why it's better to be born lucky than rich. If you're rich, you may lose your money. But if you're lucky, you will always get more money."

"Oh! Will you? And is father not lucky?"

"Very unlucky, I should say," she said bitterly.

The boy watched her with unsure eyes.

"Why?" he asked.

"I don't know. Nobody ever knows why one person is lucky and another unlucky."

"Don't they? Nobody at all? Does *nobody* know?"

"Perhaps God. But He never tells."

"He ought to, then. And aren't you lucky either, mother?"

"I can't be, if I married an unlucky husband."

"But by yourself, aren't you?"

"I used to think I was, before I married. Now I think I am very unlucky indeed."

"Why?"

"Well—never mind! Perhaps I'm not really," she said.

The child looked at her to see if she meant it. But he saw, by the lines of her mouth, that she was only trying to hide something from him.

"Well, anyhow," he said stoutly, "I'm a lucky person."

"Why?" said his mother, with a sudden laugh.

He stared at her. He didn't even know why he had said it.

"God told me," he asserted, brazening it out.

"I hope He did, dear!" she said, again with a laugh, but rather bitter.

"He did, mother!"

"Excellent!" said the mother, using one of her husband's exclamations.

The boy saw she did not believe him; or rather, that she paid no attention to his assertion. This angered him somewhere, and made him want to compel her attention.

He went off by himself, vaguely, in a childish way, seeking for the clue to 'luck.' Absorbed, taking no heed of other people, he went about with a sort of stealth, seeking inwardly for luck. He wanted luck, he wanted it, he wanted it. When the two girls were playing dolls in the nursery, he would sit on his big rocking-horse, charging madly into space, with a frenzy that made the little girls peer at him uneasily. Wildly the horse careered, the waving dark hair of the boy tossed, his eyes had a strange glare in them. The little girls dared not speak to him.

When he had ridden to the end of his mad little journey, he climbed down and stood in front of his rocking-horse, staring fixedly into its lowered face. Its red mouth was slightly open, its big eye was wide and glassy-bright.

"Now!" he would silently command the snorting steed. "Now, take me to where there is luck! Now take me!"

And he would slash the horse on the neck with the little whip he had asked Uncle Oscar for. He *knew* the horse could take him to where there was luck, if only he forced it. So he would mount again and start on his furious ride, hoping at last to get there. He knew he could get there.

"You'll break your horse, Paul!" said the nurse.

"He's always riding like that! I wish he'd leave off!" said his elder sister Joan.

But he only glared down on them in silence. Nurse gave him up. She could make nothing of him. Anyhow, he was growing beyond her.

One day his mother and his Uncle Oscar came in when he was on one of his furious rides. He did not speak to them.

"Hallo, you young jockey! Riding a winner?" said his uncle.

"Aren't you growing too big for a rocking-horse? You're not a very little boy any longer, you know," said his mother.

But Paul only gave a blue glare from his big, rather close-set eyes. He would speak to nobody when he was in full tilt. His mother watched him with an anxious expression on her face.

At last he suddenly stopped forcing his horse into the mechanical gallop and slid down.

"Well, I got there!" he announced fiercely, his blue eyes still flaring, and his sturdy long legs straddling apart.

"Where did you get to?" asked his mother.

"Where I wanted to go," he flared back at her.

"That's right, son!" said Uncle Oscar. "Don't you stop till you get there. What's the horse's name?"

"He doesn't have a name," said the boy.

"Gets on without all right?" asked the uncle.

"Well, he has different names. He was called Sansovino last week."

"Sansovino, eh? Won the Ascot.[1] How did you know this name?"

"He always talks about horse-races with Bassett," said Joan.

---

[1] A famous horse race.

The uncle was delighted to find that his small nephew was posted with all the racing news. Bassett, the young gardener, who had been wounded in the left foot in the war and had got his present job through Oscar Cresswell, whose batman he had been, was a perfect blade of the 'turf.' He lived in the racing events, and the small boy lived with him.

Oscar Cresswell got it all from Bassett.

"Master Paul comes and asks me, so I can't do more than tell him, sir," said Bassett, his face terribly serious, as if he were speaking of religious matters.

"And does he ever put anything on a horse he fancies?"

"Well—I don't want to give him away—he's a young sport, a fine sport, sir. Would you mind asking him himself? He sort of takes a pleasure in it, and perhaps he'd feel I was giving him away, sir, if you don't mind."

Bassett was serious as a church.

The uncle went back to his nephew and took him off for a ride in the car.

"Say, Paul, old man, do you ever put anything on a horse?" the uncle asked.

The boy watched the handsome man closely.

"Why, do you think I oughtn't to?" he parried.

"Not a bit of it! I thought perhaps you might give me a tip for the Lincoln."[2]

The car sped on into the country, going down to Uncle Oscar's place in Hampshire.

"Honour bright?" said the nephew.

"Honour bright, son!" said the uncle.

"Well, then, Daffodil."

"Daffodil! I doubt it, sonny. What about Mirza?"

"I only know the winner," said the boy. "That's Daffodil."

"Daffodil, eh?"

There was a pause. Daffodil was an obscure horse comparatively.

"Uncle!"

"Yes, son?"

"You won't let it go any further, will you? I promised Bassett."

"Bassett be damned, old man! What's he got to do with it?"

"We're partners. We've been partners from the first. Uncle, he lent me my first five shillings, which I lost. I promised him, honour bright, it was only between me and him; only you gave me that ten-shilling note I started winning with, so I thought you were lucky. You won't let it go any further, will you?"

The boy gazed at his uncle from those big, hot, blue eyes, set rather close together. The uncle stirred and laughed uneasily.

"Right you are, son! I'll keep your tip private. Daffodil, eh? How much are you putting on him?"

"All except twenty pounds," said the boy. "I keep that in reserve."

The uncle thought it a good joke.

---

[2] Another horse race.

"You keep twenty pounds in reserve, do you, you young romancer? What are you betting, then?"

"I'm betting three hundred," said the boy gravely. "But it's between you and me, Uncle Oscar! Honour bright?"

The uncle burst into a roar of laughter.

"It's between you and me all right, you young Nat Gould,"[3] he said, laughing. "But where's your three hundred?"

"Bassett keeps it for me. We're partners."

"You are, are you! And what is Bassett putting on Daffodil?"

"He won't go quite as high as I do, I expect. Perhaps he'll go a hundred and fifty."

"What, pennies?" laughed the uncle.

"Pounds," said the child, with a surprised look at his uncle. "Bassett keeps a bigger reserve than I do."

Between wonder and amusement Uncle Oscar was silent. He pursued the matter no further, but he determined to take his nephew with him to the Lincoln races.

"Now, son," he said, "I'm putting twenty on Mirza, and I'll put five on for you on any horse you fancy. What's your pick?"

"Daffodil, uncle."

"No, not the fiver on Daffodil!"

"I should if it was my own fiver," said the child.

"Good! Good! Right you are! A fiver for me and a fiver for you on Daffodil."

The child had never been to a race-meeting before, and his eyes were blue fire. He pursed his mouth tight and watched. A Frenchman just in front had put his money on Lancelot. Wild with excitement, he flayed his arms up and down, yelling *Lancelot! Lancelot!* in his French accent.

Daffodil came in first, Lancelot second, Mirza third. The child, flushed and with eyes blazing, was curiously serene. His uncle brought him four five-pound notes, four to one.

"What am I to do with these?" he cried, waving them before the boy's eyes.

"I suppose we'll talk to Bassett," said the boy. "I expect I have fifteen hundred now; and twenty in reserve; and this twenty."

His uncle studied him for some moments.

"Look here, son!" he said. "You're not serious about Bassett and that fifteen hundred, are you?"

"Yes, I am. But it's between you and me, uncle. Honour bright?"

"Honour bright all right, son! But I must talk to Bassett."

"If you'd like to be a partner, uncle, with Bassett and me, we could all be partners. Only, you'd have to promise, honour bright, uncle, not to let it go beyond us three. Bassett and I are lucky, and you must be lucky, because it was your ten shillings I started winning with. . . ."

Uncle Oscar took both Bassett and Paul into Richmond Park for an afternoon, and there they talked.

"It's like this, you see, sir," Bassett said. "Master Paul would get me talking about racing events, spinning yarns, you know, sir. And he was

---

[3] Nathaniel Gould (1857–1919), who wrote about horse racing.

always keen on knowing if I'd made or if I'd lost. It's about a year since, now, that I put five shillings on Blush of Dawn for him: and we lost. Then the luck turned, with that ten shillings he had from you: that we put on Singhalese. And since that time, it's been pretty steady, all things considering. What do you say, Master Paul?"

"We're all right when we're sure," said Paul. "It's when we're not quite sure that we go down."

"Oh, but we're careful then," said Bassett.

"But when are you *sure*?" smiled Uncle Oscar.

"It's Master Paul, sir," said Bassett in a secret, religious voice. "It's as if he had it from heaven. Like Daffodil, now, for the Lincoln. That was as sure as eggs."

"Did you put anything on Daffodil?" asked Oscar Cresswell.

"Yes, sir. I made my bit."

"And my nephew?"

Bassett was obstinately silent, looking at Paul.

"I made twelve hundred, didn't I, Bassett? I told uncle I was putting three hundred on Daffodil."

"That's right," said Bassett, nodding.

"But where's the money?" asked the uncle.

"I keep it safe locked up, sir. Master Paul he can have it any minute he likes to ask for it."

"What, fifteen hundred pounds?"

"And twenty! And *forty*, that is, with the twenty he made on the course."

"It's amazing!" said the uncle.

"If Master Paul offers you to be partners, sir, I would, if I were you: if you'll excuse me," said Bassett.

Oscar Cresswell thought about it.

"I'll see the money," he said.

They drove home again, and, sure enough, Bassett came round to the garden-house with fifteen hundred pounds in notes. The twenty pounds reserve was left with Joe Glee, in the Turf Commission deposit.

"You see, it's all right, uncle, when I'm *sure!* Then we go strong, for all we're worth. Don't we, Bassett?"

"We do that, Master Paul."

"And when are you sure?" said the uncle, laughing.

"Oh, well, sometimes I'm *absolutely* sure, like about Daffodil," said the boy; "and sometimes I have an idea; and sometimes I haven't even an idea, have I, Bassett? Then we're careful, because we mostly go down."

"You do, do you! And when you're sure, like about Daffodil, what makes you sure, sonny?"

"Oh, well, I don't know," said the boy uneasily. "I'm sure, you know, uncle; that's all."

"It's as if he had it from heaven, sir," Bassett reiterated.

"I should say so!" said the uncle.

But he became a partner. And when the Leger[4] was coming on Paul was 'sure' about Lively Spark, which was a quite inconsiderable horse. The boy insisted on putting a thousand on the horse, Bassett went for

---

[4] A horse race.

five hundred, and Oscar Cresswell two hundred. Lively Spark came in first, and the betting had been ten to one against him. Paul had made ten thousand.

"You see," he said, "I was absolutely sure of him."

Even Oscar Cresswell had cleared two thousand.

"Look here, son," he said, "this sort of thing makes me nervous."

"It needn't, uncle! Perhaps I shan't be sure again for a long time."

"But what are you going to do with your money?" asked the uncle.

"Of course," said the boy, "I started it for mother. She said she had no luck, because father is unlucky, so I thought if *I* was lucky, it might stop whispering."

"What might stop whispering?"

"Our house. I *hate* our house for whispering."

"What does it whisper?"

"Why—why"—the boy fidgeted—"why, I don't know. But it's always short of money, you know, uncle."

"I know it, son, I know it."

"You know people send mother writs, don't you, uncle?"

"I'm afraid I do," said the uncle.

"And then the house whispers, like people laughing at you behind your back. It's awful, that is! I thought if I was lucky——"

"You might stop it," added the uncle.

The boy watched him with big blue eyes, that had an uncanny cold fire in them, and he said never a word.

"Well, then!" said the uncle. "What are we doing?"

"I shouldn't like mother to know I was lucky," said the boy.

"Why not, son?"

"She'd stop me."

"I don't think she would."

"Oh!"—and the boy writhed in an odd way—"I *don't* want her to know, uncle."

"All right, son! We'll manage it without her knowing."

They managed it very easily. Paul, at the other's suggestion, handed over five thousand pounds to his uncle, who deposited it with the family lawyer, who was then to inform Paul's mother that a relative had put five thousand pounds into his hands, which sum was to be paid out a thousand pounds at a time, on the mother's birthday, for the next five years.

"So she'll have a birthday present of a thousand pounds for five successive years," said Uncle Oscar. "I hope it won't make it all the harder for her later."

Paul's mother had her birthday in November. The house had been 'whispering' worse than ever lately, and, even in spite of his luck, Paul could not bear up against it. He was very anxious to see the effect of the birthday letter, telling his mother about the thousand pounds.

When there were no visitors, Paul now took his meals with his parents, as he was beyond the nursery control. His mother went into town nearly every day. She had discovered that she had an odd knack of sketching furs and dress materials, so she worked secretly in the studio of a friend who was the chief 'artist' for the leading drapers. She drew the figures of ladies in furs and ladies in silk and sequins for the newspaper advertisements. This young woman artist earned several thousand pounds a year, but Paul's mother only made several hundreds, and she was again dissatisfied. She so wanted to be first in something, and she did not succeed, even in making sketches for drapery advertisements.

She was down to breakfast on the morning of her birthday. Paul watched her face as she read her letters. He knew the lawyer's letter. As his mother read it, her face hardened and became more expressionless. Then a cold, determined look came on her mouth. She hid the letter under the pile of others, and said not a word about it.

"Didn't you have anything nice in the post for your birthday, mother?" said Paul.

"Quite moderately nice," she said, her voice cold and absent.

She went away to town without saying more.

But in the afternoon Uncle Oscar appeared. He said Paul's mother had had a long interview with the lawyer, asking if the whole five thousand could not be advanced at once, as she was in debt.

"What do you think, uncle?" asked the boy.

"I leave it to you, son."

"Oh, let her have it, then! We can get some more with the other," said the boy.

"A bird in the hand is worth two in the bush, laddie!" said Uncle Oscar.

"But I'm sure to *know* for the Grand National; or the Lincolnshire; or else the Derby.[5] I'm sure to know for *one* of them," said Paul.

So Uncle Oscar signed the agreement, and Paul's mother touched the whole five thousand. Then something very curious happened. The voices in the house suddenly went mad, like a chorus of frogs on a spring evening. There were certain new furnishings, and Paul had a tutor. He was *really* going to Eton, his father's school, in the following autumn. There were flowers in the winter, and a blossoming of the luxury Paul's mother had been used to. And yet the voices in the house, behind the sprays of mimosa and almond-blossom, and from under the piles of iridescent cushions, simply trilled and screamed in a sort of ecstasy: "There *must* be more money! Oh-h-h; there *must* be more money. Oh, now, now-w! Now-w-w—there *must* be more money!—more than ever! More than ever!"

It frightened Paul terribly. He studied away at his Latin and Greek with his tutor. But his intense hours were spent with Bassett. The Grand National had gone by: he had not 'known,' and had lost a hundred pounds. Summer was at hand. He was in agony for the Lincoln. But even for the Lincoln he didn't 'know,' and he lost fifty pounds. He became wild-eyed and strange, as if something were going to explode in him.

"Let it alone, son! Don't you bother about it!" urged Uncle Oscar. But it was as if the boy couldn't really hear what his uncle was saying.

"I've got to know for the Derby! I've got to know for the Derby!" the child reiterated, his big blue eyes blazing with a sort of madness.

His mother noticed how overwrought he was.

[5] Other famous horse races.

"You'd better go to the seaside. Wouldn't you like to go now to the seaside, instead of waiting? I think you'd better," she said, looking down at him anxiously, her heart curiously heavy because of him.

But the child lifted his uncanny blue eyes.

"I couldn't possibly go before the Derby, mother!" he said. "I couldn't possibly!"

"Why not?" she said, her voice becoming heavy when she was opposed. "Why not? You can still go from the seaside to see the Derby with your Uncle Oscar, if that's what you wish. No need for you to wait here. Besides, I think you care too much about these races. It's a bad sign. My family has been a gambling family, and you won't know till you grow up how much damage it has done. But it has done damage. I shall have to send Bassett away, and ask Uncle Oscar not to talk racing to you, unless you promise to be reasonable about it: go away to the seaside and forget it. You're all nerves!"

"I'll do what you like, mother, so long as you don't send me away till after the Derby," the boy said.

"Send you away from where? Just from this house?"

"Yes," he said, gazing at her.

"Why, you curious child, what makes you care about this house so much, suddenly? I never knew you loved it."

He gazed at her without speaking. He had a secret within a secret, something he had not divulged, even to Bassett or to his Uncle Oscar.

But his mother, after standing undecided and a little bit sullen for some moments, said:

"Very well, then! Don't go to the seaside till after the Derby, if you don't wish it. But promise me you won't let your nerves go to pieces. Promise you won't think so much about horse-racing and *events*, as you call them!"

"Oh no," said the boy casually. "I won't think much about them, mother. You needn't worry. I wouldn't worry, mother, if I were you."

"If you were me and I were you," said his mother, "I wonder what we *should* do!"

"But you know you needn't worry, mother, don't you?" the boy repeated.

"I should be awfully glad to know it," she said wearily.

"Oh, well, you *can*, you know. I mean, you *ought* to know you needn't worry," he insisted.

"Ought I? Then I'll see about it," she said.

Paul's secret of secrets was his wooden horse, that which had no name. Since he was emancipated from a nurse and a nursery-governess, he had had his rocking-horse removed to his own bedroom at the top of the house.

"Surely you're too big for a rocking-horse!" his mother had remonstrated.

"Well, you see, mother, till I can have a *real* horse, I like to have *some* sort of animal about," had been his quaint answer.

"Do you feel he keeps you company?" she laughed.

"Oh yes! He's very good, he always keeps me company, when I'm there," said Paul.

So the horse, rather shabby, stood in an arrested prance in the boy's bedroom.

The Derby was drawing near, and the boy grew more and more tense.

He hardly heard what was spoken to him, he was very frail, and his eyes were really uncanny. His mother had sudden strange seizures of uneasiness about him. Sometimes, for half an hour, she would feel a sudden anxiety about him that was almost anguish. She wanted to rush to him at once, and know he was safe.

Two nights before the Derby, she was at a big party in town, when one of her rushes of anxiety about her boy, her firstborn, gripped her heart till she could hardly speak. She fought with the feeling, might and main, for she believed in common sense. But it was too strong. She had to leave the dance and go downstairs to telephone to the country. The children's nursery-governess was terribly surprised and startled at being rung up in the night.

"Are the children all right, Miss Wilmot?"

"Oh yes, they are quite all right."

"Master Paul? Is he all right?"

"He went to bed as right as a trivet. Shall I run up and look at him?"

"No," said Paul's mother reluctantly. "No! Don't trouble. It's all right. Don't sit up. We shall be home fairly soon." She did not want her son's privacy intruded upon.

"Very good," said the governess.

It was about one o'clock when Paul's mother and father drove up to their house. All was still. Paul's mother went to her room and slipped off her white fur cloak. She had told her maid not to wait up for her. She heard her husband downstairs, mixing a whisky and soda.

And then, because of the strange anxiety at her heart, she stole upstairs to her son's room. Noiselessly she went along the upper corridor. Was there a faint noise? What was it?

She stood, with arrested muscles, outside his door, listening. There was a strange, heavy, and yet not loud noise. Her heart stood still. It was a soundless noise, yet rushing and powerful. Something huge, in violent, hushed motion. What was it? What in God's name was it? She ought to know. She felt that she knew the noise. She knew what it was.

Yet she could not place it. She couldn't say what it was. And on and on it went, like a madness.

Softly, frozen with anxiety and fear, she turned the door-handle.

The room was dark. Yet in the space near the window, she heard and saw something plunging to and fro. She gazed in fear and amazement.

Then suddenly she switched on the light, and saw her son, in his green pyjamas, madly surging on the rocking-horse. The blaze of light suddenly lit him up, as he urged the wooden horse, and lit her up, as she stood, blonde, in her dress of pale green and crystal, in the doorway.

"Paul!" she cried. "Whatever are you doing?"

"It's Malabar!" he screamed in a powerful, strange voice. "It's Malabar!"

His eyes blazed at her for one strange and senseless second, as he ceased urging his wooden horse. Then he fell with a crash to the ground, and she, all her tormented motherhood flooding upon her, rushed to gather him up.

But he was unconscious, and unconscious he remained, with some brain-fever. He talked and tossed, and his mother sat stonily by his side.

"Malabar! It's Malabar! Bassett, Bassett, I *know!* It's Malabar!"

So the child cried, trying to get up and urge the rocking-horse that gave him his inspiration.

"What does he mean by Malabar?" asked the heart-frozen mother.

"I don't know," said the father stonily.

"What does he mean by Malabar?" she asked her brother Oscar.

"It's one of the horses running for the Derby," was the answer.

And, in spite of himself, Oscar Cresswell spoke to Bassett, and himself put a thousand on Malabar: at fourteen to one.

The third day of the illness was critical: they were waiting for a change. The boy, with his rather long, curly hair, was tossing ceaselessly on the pillow. He neither slept nor regained consciousness, and his eyes were like blue stones. His mother sat, feeling her heart had gone, turned actually into a stone.

In the evening, Oscar Cresswell did not come, but Bassett sent a message, saying could he come up for one moment, just one moment? Paul's mother was very angry at the intrusion, but on second thoughts she agreed. The boy was the same. Perhaps Bassett might bring him to consciousness.

The gardener, a shortish fellow with a little brown moustache and sharp little brown eyes, tiptoed into the room, touched his imaginary cap to Paul's mother, and stole to the bedside, staring with glittering, smallish eyes at the tossing, dying child.

"Master Paul!" he whispered. "Master Paul! Malabar came in first all right, a clean win. I did as you told me. You've made over seventy thousand pounds, you have; you've got over eighty thousand. Malabar came in all right, Master Paul."

"Malabar! Malabar! Did I say Malabar, mother? Did I say Malabar? Do you think I'm lucky, mother? I knew Malabar, didn't I? Over eighty thousand pounds! I call that lucky, don't you, mother? Over eighty thousand pounds! I knew, didn't I know I knew? Malabar came in all right. If I ride my horse till I'm sure, then I tell you, Bassett, you can go as high as you like. Did you go for all you were worth, Bassett?"

"I went a thousand on it, Master Paul."

"I never told you, mother, that if I can ride my horse, and *get there*, then I'm absolutely sure—oh, absolutely! Mother, did I ever tell you? I *am* lucky!"

"No, you never did," said his mother.

But the boy died in the night.

And even as he lay dead, his mother heard her brother's voice saying to her: "My God, Hester, you're eighty-odd thousand to the good, and a poor devil of a son to the bad. But, poor devil, poor devil, he's best gone out of a life where he rides his rocking-horse to find a winner."

(1932)

Arna Bontemps   *1902–1973*

A SUMMER TRAGEDY

Old Jeff Patton, the black share farmer, fumbled with his bow tie. His fingers trembled and the high, stiff collar pinched his throat. A fellow loses his hand for such vanities after thirty or forty years of simple life. Once a year, or maybe twice if there's a wedding among his kinfolks, he may spruce up, but generally fancy clothes do nothing but adorn the wall of the big room and feed the moths. That had been Jeff Patton's experience. He had not worn his stiff-bosomed shirt more than a dozen times in all his married life. His swallow-tailed coat lay on the bed beside him, freshly brushed and pressed, but it was as full of holes as the overalls in which he worked on weekdays. The moths had used it badly. Jeff twisted his mouth into a hideous toothless grimace as he contended with the obstinate bow. He stamped his good foot and decided to give up the struggle.

"Jennie," he called.

"What's that, Jeff?" His wife's shrunken voice came out of the adjoining room like an echo. It was hardly bigger than a whisper.

"I reckon you'll have to he'p me wid this heah bow tie, baby," he said meekly. "Dog if I can hitch it up."

Her answer was not strong enough to reach him, but presently the old woman came to the door, feeling her way with a stick. She had a wasted, dead-leaf appearance. Her body, as scrawny and gnarled as a string bean, seemed less than nothing in the ocean of frayed and faded petticoats that surrounded her. These hung an inch or two above the tops of her heavy unlaced shoes and showed little grotesque piles where the stockings had fallen down from her negligible legs.

"You oughta could do a heap mo' wid a thing like that'n me—beingst as you got yo' good sight."

"Looks like I oughta could," he admitted. "But my fingers is gone democrat on me. I get all mixed up in the looking glass an' can't tell wicha way to twist the devilish thing."

Jennie sat on the side of the bed, and old Jeff Patton got down on one knee while she tied the bow knot. It was a slow and painful ordeal for each of them in this position. Jeff's bones cracked, his knee ached, and it was only after a half dozen attempts that Jennie worked a semblance of a bow into the tie.

"I got to dress maself now," the old woman whispered. "These is ma old shoes an' stockings, and I ain't so much as unwrapped ma dress."

"Well, don't worry 'bout me no mo', baby," Jeff said. "That 'bout finishes me. All I gotta do now is slip on that old coat 'n ves' an' I'll be fixed to leave."

Jennie disappeared again through the dim passage into the shed room. Being blind was no handicap to her in that black hole. Jeff heard the cane placed against the wall beside the door and knew that his wife was on easy ground. He put on his coat, took a battered top hat from the bed post, and hobbled to the front door. He was ready to travel. As soon

271

as Jennie could get on her Sunday shoes and her old black silk dress, they would start.

Outside the tiny log house, the day was warm and mellow with sunshine. A host of wasps were humming with busy excitement in the trunk of a dead sycamore. Gray squirrels were searching through the grass for hickory nuts, and blue jays were in the trees, hopping from branch to branch. Pine woods stretched away to the left like a black sea. Among them were scattered scores of log houses like Jeff's, houses of black share farmers. Cows and pigs wandered freely among the trees. There was no danger of loss. Each farmer knew his own stock and knew his neighbor's as well as he knew his neighbor's children.

Down the slope to the right were the cultivated acres on which the colored folks worked. They extended to the river, more than two miles away, and they were today green with the unmade cotton crop. A tiny thread of a road, which passed directly in front of Jeff's place, ran through these green fields like a pencil mark.

Jeff, standing outside the door, with his absurd hat in his left hand, surveyed the wide scene tenderly. He had been forty-five years on these acres. He loved them with the unexplained affection that others have for the countries to which they belong.

The sun was hot on his head, his collar still pinched his throat, and the Sunday clothes were intolerably hot. Jeff transferred the hat to his right hand and began fanning with it. Suddenly the whisper that was Jennie's voice came out of the shed room.

"You can bring the car round front whilst you's waitin'," it said feebly. There was a tired pause; then it added, "I'll soon be fixed to go."

"A'right, baby," Jeff answered. "I'll get it in a minute."

But he didn't move. A thought struck him that made his mouth fall open. The mention of the car brought to his mind with new intensity, the trip he and Jennie were about to take. Fear came into his eyes; excitement took his breath. Lord, Jesus!

"Jeff. . . . O Jeff," the old woman's whisper called.

He awakened with a jolt. "Hunh, baby?"

"What you doin'?"

"Nuthin. Jes studyin'. I jes been turnin' things round 'n round in ma mind."

"You could be gettin' the car," she said.

"Oh yes, right away, baby."

He started round to the shed, limping heavily on his bad leg. There were three frizzly chickens in the yard. All his other chickens had been killed or stolen recently. But the frizzly chickens had been saved somehow. That was fortunate indeed, for these curious creatures had a way of devouring "poison" from the yard and in that way protecting against conjure and black luck and spells. But even the frizzly chickens seemed now to be in a stupor. Jeff thought they had some ailment; he expected all three of them to die shortly.

The shed in which the old T-model Ford stood was only a grass roof held up by four corner poles. It had been built by tremulous hands at a time when the little rattletrap car had been regarded as a peculiar treasure. And, miraculously, despite wind and downpour, it still stood.

Jeff adjusted the crank and put his weight upon it. The engine came to life with a sputter and bang that rattled the old car from radiator to tail light. Jeff hopped into the seat and put his foot on the accelerator. The sputtering and banging increased. The rattling became more violent. That was good. It was good banging, good sputtering and rattling, and it meant that the aged car was still in running condition. She could be depended on for this trip.

Again Jeff's thought halted as if paralyzed. The suggestion of the trip fell into the machinery of his mind like a wrench. He felt dazed and weak. He swung the car out into the yard, made a half turn, and drove around to the front door. When he took his hands off the wheel, he noticed that he was trembling violently. He cut off the motor and climbed to the ground to wait for Jennie.

A few minutes later she was at the window, her voice rattling against the pane like a broken shutter.

"I'm ready, Jeff."

He did not answer, but limped into the house and took her by the arm. He led her slowly through the big room, down the step, and across the yard.

"You reckon I'd oughta lock the do'?" he asked softly.

They stopped and Jennie weighed the question. Finally she shook her head.

"Ne' mind the door'," she said. "I don't see no cause to lock up things."

"You right," Jeff agreed. "No cause to lock up."

Jeff opened the door and helped his wife into the car. A quick shudder passed over him. Jesus! Again he trembled.

"How come you shaking so?" Jennie whispered.

"I don't know," he said.

"You mus' be scairt, Jeff."

"No, baby, I ain't scairt."

He slammed the door after her and went around to crank up again. The motor started easily. Jeff wished that it had not been so responsive. He would have liked a few more minutes in which to turn things around in his head. As it was, with Jennie chiding him about being afraid, he had to keep going. He swung the car into the little pencil-mark road and started off toward the river, driving very slowly, very cautiously.

Chugging across the green countryside, the small battered Ford seemed tiny indeed. Jeff felt a familiar excitement, a thrill, as they came down the first slope to the immense levels on which the cotton was growing. He could not help reflecting that the crops were good. He knew what that meant, too; he had made forty-five of them with his own hands. It was true that he had worn out nearly a dozen mules, but that was the fault of old man Stevenson, the owner of the land. Major Stevenson had the old notion that one mule was all a share farmer needed to work a thirty-acre plot. It was an expensive notion, the way it killed mules from overwork but the old man held to it. Jeff thought it killed a good many share farmers as well as mules, but he had no sympathy for them. He had always been strong, and he had been taught to have no patience with weakness in men. Women or children might be tolerated if they were puny, but a weak man was a curse. Of course, his own children—

Jeff's thought halted there. He and Jennie never mentioned their dead children any more. And naturally, he did not wish to dwell upon them in his mind. Before he knew it, some remark would slip out of his mouth and that would make Jennie feel blue. Perhaps she would cry. A woman like Jennie could not easily throw off the grief that comes from losing five grown children within two years. Even Jeff was still staggered by the blow. His memory had not been much good recently. He frequently talked to himself. And, although he had kept it a secret, he knew that his courage had left him. He was terrified by the least unfamiliar sound at night. He was reluctant to venture far from home in the daytime. And that habit of trembling when he felt fearful was now far beyond his control. Sometimes he became afraid and trembled without knowing what had frightened him. The feeling would just come over him like a chill.

The car rattled slowly over the dusty road. Jennie sat erect and silent with a little absurd hat pinned to her hair. Her useless eyes seemed very large, very white in their deep sockets. Suddenly Jeff heard her voice, and he inclined his head to catch the words.

"Is we passed Delia Moore's house yet?" she asked.

"Not yet," he said.

"You must be drivin' mighty slow, Jeff."

"We just as well take our time, baby."

There was a pause. A little puff of steam was coming out of the radiator of the car. Heat wavered above the hood. Delia Moore's house was nearly half a mile away. After a moment Jennie spoke again.

"You ain't really scairt, is you, Jeff?"

"Nah, baby, I ain't scairt."

"You know how we agreed—we gotta keep on goin'."

Jewels of perspiration appeared on Jeff's forehead. His eyes rounded, blinked, became fixed on the road.

"I don't know," he said with a shiver, "I reckon it's the only thing to do."

"Hm."

A flock of guinea fowls, pecking in the road, were scattered by the passing car. Some of them took to their wings; others hid under bushes. A blue jay, swaying on a leafy twig, was annoying a roadside squirrel. Jeff held an even speed till he came near Delia's place. Then he slowed down noticeably.

Delia's house was really no house at all, but an abandoned store building converted into a dwelling. It sat near a crossroads, beneath a single black cedar tree. There Delia, a cattish old creature of Jennie's age, lived alone. She had been there more years than anybody could remember, and long ago had won the disfavor of such women as Jennie. For in her young days Delia had been gayer, yellower, and saucier than seemed proper in those parts. Her ways with menfolks had been dark and suspicious. And the fact that she had had as many husbands as children did not help her reputation.

"Yonder's old Delia," Jeff said as they passed.

"What she doin'?"

"Jes sittin' in the do'," he said.

"She see us?"

"Hm," Jeff said. "Musta did."

That relieved Jennie. It strengthened her to know that her old enemy had seen her pass in her best clothes. That would give the old she-devil something to chew her gums and fret about, Jennie thought. Wouldn't she have a fit if she didn't find out? Old evil Delia! This would be just the thing for her. It would pay her back for being so evil. It would also pay her, Jennie thought, for the way she used to grin at Jeff—long ago, when her teeth were good.

The road became smooth and red, and Jeff could tell by the smell of the air that they were nearing the river. He could see the rise where the road turned and ran along parallel to the stream. The car chugged on monotonously. After a long silent spell, Jennie leaned against Jeff and spoke.

"How many bale o' cotton you think we got standin'?" she said.

Jeff wrinkled his forehead as he calculated.

" 'Bout twenty-five, I reckon."

"How many you make las' year?"

"Twenty-eight," he said. "How come you ask that?"

"I's jes thinkin'," Jennie said quietly.

"It don't make a speck o' difference though," Jeff reflected. "If we get much or if we get little, we still gonna be in debt to old man Stevenson when he gets through counting up agin us. It's took us a long time to learn that."

Jennie was not listening to these words. She had fallen into a trancelike meditation. Her lips twitched. She chewed her gums and rubbed her gnarled hands nervously. Suddenly, she leaned forward, buried her face in the nervous hands, and burst into tears. She cried aloud in a dry, cracked voice that suggested the rattle of fodder on dead stalks. She cried aloud like a child, for she had never learned to suppress a genuine sob. Her slight old frame shook heavily and seemed hardly able to sustain such violent grief.

"What's the matter, baby?" Jeff asked awkwardly. "Why you cryin' like all that?"

"I's jes thinkin'," she said.

"So you the one what's scairt now, hunh?"

"I ain't scairt, Jeff. I's jes thinkin' 'bout leavin' eve'thing like this—eve'-thing we been used to. It's right sad-like."

Jeff did not answer, and presently Jennie buried her face again and cried.

The sun was almost overhead. It beat down furiously on the dusty wagon-path road, on the parched roadside grass and the tiny battered car. Jeff's hands, gripping the wheel, became wet with perspiration; his forehead sparkled. Jeff's lips parted. His mouth shaped a hideous grimace. His face suggested the face of a man being burned. But the torture passed and his expression softened again.

"You mustn't cry, baby," he said to his wife. "We gotta be strong. We can't break down."

Jennie waited a few seconds, then said, "You reckon we oughta do it, Jeff? You reckon we oughta go 'head an' do it, really?"

Jeff's voice choked; his eyes blurred. He was terrified to hear Jennie say the thing that had been in his mind all morning. She had egged him on when he had wanted more than anything in the world to wait, to reconsider, to think things over a little longer. Now she was getting cold feet. Actually, there was no need of thinking the question through again. It would only end in making the same painful decision once more. Jeff knew that. There was no need of fooling around longer.

"We jes as well to do like we planned," he said. "They ain't nothin' else for us now—it's the bes' thing."

Jeff thought of the handicaps, the near impossibility, of making another crop with his leg bothering him more and more each week. Then there was always the chance that he would have another stroke, like the one that had made him lame. Another one might kill him. The least it could do would be to leave him helpless. Jeff gasped—Lord Jesus! He could not bear to think of being helpless, like a baby, on Jennie's hands. Frail, blind Jennie.

The little pounding motor of the car worked harder and harder. The puff of steam from the cracked radiator became larger. Jeff realized that they were climbing a little rise. A moment later the road turned abruptly, and he looked down upon the face of the river.

"Jeff."

"Hunh?"

"Is that the water I hear?"

"Hm. Tha's it."

"Well, which way you goin' now?"

"Down this-a way," he said. "The road runs 'long 'side o' the water a lil piece."

She waited a while calmly. Then she said, "Drive faster."

"A'right, baby," Jeff said.

The water roared in the bed of the river. It was fifty or sixty feet below the level of the road. Between the road and the water there was a long smooth slope, sharply inclined. The slope was dry, the clay hardened by prolonged summer heat. The water below, roaring in a narrow channel, was noisy and wild.

"Jeff."

"Hunh?"

"How far you goin'?"

"Jes a lil piece down the road."

"You ain't scairt, is you, Jeff?"

"Nah, baby," he said trembling. "I ain't scairt."

"Remember how we planned it, Jeff. We gotta do it like we said. Brave-like."

"Hm."

Jeff's brain darkened. Things suddenly seemed unreal, like figures in a dream. Thoughts swam in his mind foolishly, hysterically, like little blind fish in a pool within a dense cave. They rushed again. Jeff soon became dizzy. He shuddered violently and turned to his wife.

"Jennie, I can't do it. I can't." His voice broke pitifully.

She did not appear to be listening. All the grief had gone from her face. She sat erect, her unseeing eyes wide open, strained and frightful. Her glossy black skin had become dull. She seemed as thin, as sharp and bony, as a starved bird. Now, having suffered and endured the sadness of tearing herself away from beloved things, she showed no anguish. She was absorbed with her own thoughts, and she didn't even hear Jeff's voice shouting in her ear.

Jeff said nothing more. For an instant there was light in his cavernous brain. The great chamber was, for less than a second, peopled by characters he knew and loved. They were simple, healthy creatures, and they behaved in a manner that he could understand. They had quality. But since he had already taken leave of them long ago, the remembrance did not break his heart again. Young Jeff Patton was among them, the Jeff Patton of fifty years ago who went down to New Orleans with a crowd of country boys to the Mardi Gras doings. The gay young crowd, boys with candy-striped shirts and rouged brown girls in noisy silks, was like a picture in his head. Yet it did not make him sad. On that very trip Slim Burns had killed Joe Beasley—the crowd had been broken up. Since then Jeff Patton's world had been the Greenbriar Plantation. If there had been other Mardi Gras carnivals, he had not heard of them. Since then there had been no time; the years had fallen on him like waves. Now he was old, worn out. Another paralytic stroke (like the one he had already suffered) would put him on his back for keeps. In that condition, with a frail blind woman to look after him, he would be worse off than if he were dead.

Suddenly Jeff's hands became steady. He actually felt brave. He slowed down the motor of the car and carefully pulled off the road. Below, the water of the stream boomed, a soft thunder in the deep channel. Jeff ran the car onto the clay shope, pointed it directly toward the stream, and put his foot heavily on the accelerator. The little car leaped furiously down the steep incline toward the water. The movement was nearly as swift and direct as a fall. The two old black folks, sitting quietly side by side, showed no excitement. In another instant the car hit the water and dropped immediately out of sight.

A little later it lodged in the mud of a shallow place. One wheel of the crushed and upturned little Ford became visible above the rushing water.

(1933)

John Steinbeck *1902–1968*

THE CHRYSANTHEMUMS

The high gray-flannel fog of winter closed off the Salinas Valley from the sky and from all the rest of the world. On every side it sat like a lid on the mountains and made of the great valley a closed pot. On the broad, level land floor the gang plows bit deep and left the black earth shining like metal where the shares had cut. On the foothill ranches across the Salinas River, the yellow stubble fields seemed to be bathed in pale cold sunshine, but there was no sunshine in the valley now in December. The thick willow scrub along the river flamed with sharp and positive yellow leaves.

It was a time of quiet and of waiting. The air was cold and tender. A light wind blew up from the southwest so that the farmers were mildly hopeful of a good rain before long; but fog and rain do not go together.

Across the river, on Henry Allen's foothill ranch there was little work to be done, for the hay was cut and stored and the orchards were plowed up to receive the rain deeply when it should come. The cattle on the higher slopes were becoming shaggy and rough-coated.

Elisa Allen, working in her flower garden, looked down across the yard and saw Henry, her husband, talking to two men in business suits. The three of them stood by the tractor shed, each man with one foot on the side of the little Fordson. They smoked cigarettes and studied the machine as they talked.

Elisa watched them for a moment and then went back to her work. She was thirty-five. Her face was lean and strong and her eyes were as clear as water. Her figure looked blocked and heavy in her gardening costume, a man's black hat pulled down over her eyes, clodhopper shoes, a figured print dress almost completely covered by a big corduroy apron with four big pockets to hold the snips, the trowel and scratcher, the seeds and the knife she worked with. She wore heavy leather gloves to protect her hands while she worked.

She was cutting down the old year's chrysanthemum stalks with a pair of short and powerful scissors. She looked down toward the men by the tractor shed now and then. Her face was eager and mature and handsome; even her work with the scissors was over-eager, over-powerful. The chrysanthemum stems seemed too small and easy for her energy.

She brushed a cloud of hair out of her eyes with the back of her glove, and left a smudge of earth on her cheek in doing it. Behind her stood the neat white farm house with red geraniums close-banked around it as high as the windows. It was a hard-swept looking little house, with hard-polished windows, and a clean mud-mat on the front steps.

Elisa cast another glance toward the tractor shed. The strangers were getting into their Ford coupe. She took off a glove and put her strong fingers down into the forest of new green chrysanthemum sprouts that were growing around the old roots. She spread the leaves and looked down among the close-growing stems. No aphids were there, no sowbugs or snails or cutworms. Her terrier fingers destroyed such pests before they could get started.

Elisa started at the sound of her husband's voice. He had come near quietly, and he leaned over the wire fence that protected her flower garden from cattle and dogs and chickens.

"At it again," he said. "You've got a strong new crop coming."

Elisa straightened her back and pulled on the gardening glove again. "Yes. They'll be strong this coming year." In her tone and on her face there was a little smugness.

"You've got a gift with things," Henry observed. "Some of those yellow chrysanthemums you had this year were ten inches across. I wish you'd work out in the orchard and raise some apples that big."

Her eyes sharpened. "Maybe I could do it, too. I've a gift with things, all right. My mother had it. She could stick anything in the ground and make it grow. She said it was having planters' hands that knew how to do it."

"Well, it sure works with flowers," he said.

"Henry, who were those men you were talking to?"

"Why, sure, that's what I came to tell you. They were from the Western Meat Company. I sold them those thirty head of three-year-old steers. Got nearly my own price, too."

"Good," she said. "Good for you."

"And I thought," he continued, "I thought how it's Saturday afternoon, and we might go into Salinas for dinner at a restaurant, and then to a picture show—to celebrate, you see."

"Good," she repeated. "Oh, yes. That will be good."

Henry put on his joking tone. "There's fights tonight. How'd you like to go to the fights?"

"Oh, no," she said breathlessly. "No, I wouldn't like fights."

"Just fooling, Elisa. We'll go to a movie. Let's see. It's two now. I'm going to take Scotty and bring down those steers from the hill. It'll take us maybe two hours. We'll go in town about five and have dinner at the Cominos Hotel. Like that?"

"Of course I'll like it. It's good to eat away from home."

"All right, then. I'll go get up a couple of horses."

She said, "I'll have plenty of time to transplant some of these sets, I guess."

She heard her husband calling Scotty down by the barn. And a little later she saw the two men ride up the pale yellow hillside in search of the steers.

There was a little square sandy bed kept for rooting the chrysanthemums. With her trowel she turned the soil over and over, and smoothed it and patted it firm. Then she dug ten parallel trenches to receive the sets. Back at the chrysanthemum bed she pulled out the little crisp shoots, trimmed off the leaves of each one with her scissors and laid it on a small orderly pile.

A squeak of wheels and plod of hoofs came from the road. Elisa looked up. The country road ran along the dense bank of willows and cottonwoods that bordered the river, and up this road came a curious vehicle, curiously drawn. It was an old spring-wagon, with a round canvas top on it like the cover of a prairie schooner. It was drawn by an old bay horse and a little gray-and-white burro. A big stubble-bearded man sat between the cover flaps and drove the crawling team. Underneath the wagon, between the hind wheels, a lean and rangy mongrel dog walked sedately. Words were painted on the canvas, in clumsy, crooked letters. "Pots, pans, knives, sisors, lawn mores, Fixed." Two rows of articles, and the triumphantly definitive "Fixed" below. The black paint had run down in little sharp points beneath each letter.

Elisa, squatting on the ground, watched to see the crazy, loose-jointed wagon pass by. But it didn't pass. It turned into the farm road in front of her house, crooked old wheels skirling and squeaking. The rangy dog darted from between the wheels and ran ahead. Instantly the two ranch shepherds flew out at him. Then all three stopped and with stiff and quivering tails, with taut straight legs, with ambassadorial dignity, they slowly circled, sniffing daintily. The caravan pulled up to Elisa's wire fence and stopped. Now the newcomer dog, feeling out-numbered, lowered his tail and retired under the wagon with raised hackles and bared teeth.

The man on the wagon seat called out, "That's a bad dog in a fight when he gets started."

Elisa laughed. "I see he is. How soon does he generally get started?"

The man caught up her laughter and echoed it heartily. "Sometimes not for weeks and weeks," he said. He climbed stiffly down, over the wheel. The horse and the donkey drooped like unwatered flowers.

Elisa saw that he was a very big man. Although his hair and beard were graying, he did not look old. His worn black suit was wrinkled and spotted with grease. The laughter had disappeared from his face and eyes the moment his laughing voice ceased. His eyes were dark, and they were full of the brooding that gets in the eyes of teamsters and of sailors. The calloused hands he rested on the wire fence were cracked, and every crack was a black line. He took off his battered hat.

"I'm off my general road, ma'am," he said. "Does this dirt road cut over across the river to the Los Angeles highway?"

Elisa stood up and shoved the thick scissors in her apron pocket. "Well, yes, it does, but it winds around and then fords the river. I don't think your team could pull through the sand."

He replied with some asperity, "It might surprise you what them beasts can pull through."

"When they get started?" she asked.

He smiled for a second. "Yes. When they get started."

"Well," said Elisa, "I think you'll save time if you go back to the Salinas road and pick up the highway there."

He drew a big finger down the chicken wire and made it sing. "I ain't in any hurry, ma'am. I go from Seattle to San Diego and back every year. Takes all my time. About six months each way. I aim to follow nice weather."

Elisa took off her gloves and stuffed them in the apron pocket with the scissors. She touched the under edge of her man's hat, searching for fugitive hairs. "That sounds like a nice kind of way to live," she said.

He leaned confidentially over the fence. "Maybe you noticed the writing on my wagon. I mend pots and sharpen knives and scissors. You got any of them things to do?"

"Oh, no," she said quickly. "Nothing like that." Her eyes hardened with resistance.

"Scissors is the worst thing," he explained. "Most people just ruin scissors trying to sharpen 'em, but I know how. I got a special tool. It's a little bobbit kind of thing, and patented. But it sure does the trick."

"No. My scissors are all sharp."

"All right, then. Take a pot," he continued earnestly, "a bent pot, or a pot with a hole. I can make it like new so you don't have to buy no new ones. That's a saving for you."

"No," she said shortly. "I tell you I have nothing like that for you to do."

His face fell to an exaggerated sadness. His voice took on a whining undertone. "I ain't had a thing to do today. Maybe I won't have no supper tonight. You see I'm off my regular road. I know folks on the highway clear from Seattle to San Diego. They save their things for me to sharpen up because they know I do it so good and save them money."

"I'm sorry," Elisa said irritably. "I haven't anything for you to do."

His eyes left her face and fell to searching the ground. They roamed about until they came to the chrysanthemum bed where she had been working. "What's them plants, ma'am?"

The irritation and resistance melted from Elisa's face. "Oh, those are chrysanthemums, giant whites and yellows. I raise them every year, bigger than anybody around here."

"Kind of a long-stemmed flower? Looks like a quick puff of colored smoke?" he asked.

"That's it. What a nice way to describe them."

"They smell kind of nasty till you get used to them," he said.

"It's a good bitter smell," she retorted, "not nasty at all."

He changed his tone quickly. "I like the smell myself."

"I had ten-inch blooms this year," she said.

The man leaned farther over the fence. "Look. I know a lady down the road a piece, has got the nicest garden you ever seen. Got nearly every kind of flower but no chrysanthemums. Last time I was mending a copper-bottom washtub for her (that's a hard job but I do it good), she said to me, 'If you ever run acrost some nice chrysanthemums I wish you'd try to get me a few seeds.' That's what she told me."

Elisa's eyes grew alert and eager. "She couldn't have known much about chrysanthemums. You *can* raise them from seed, but it's much easier to root the little sprouts you see there."

"Oh," he said. "I s'pose I can't take none to her, then."

"Why yes you can," Elisa cried. "I can put some in damp sand, and you can carry them right along with you. They'll take root in the pot if you keep them damp. And then she can transplant them."

"She'd sure like to have some, ma'am. You say they're nice ones?"

"Beautiful," she said. "Oh, beautiful." Her eyes shone. She tore off the battered hat and shook out her dark pretty hair. "I'll put them in a flower pot, and you can take them right with you. Come into the yard."

While the man came through the picket gate Elisa ran excitedly along the geranium-bordered path to the back of the house. And she returned carrying a big red flower pot. The gloves were forgotten now. She kneeled on the ground by the starting bed and dug up the sandy soil with her fingers and scooped it into the bright new flower pot. Then she picked up the little pile of shoots she had prepared. With her strong fingers she pressed them into the sand and tamped around them with her knuckles. The man stood over her. "I'll tell you what to do," she said. "You remember so you can tell the lady."

"Yes, I'll try to remember."

"Well, look. These will take root in about a month. Then she must set them out, about a foot apart in good rich earth like this, see?" She lifted a handful of dark soil for him to look at. "They'll grow fast and tall. Now remember this: In July tell her to cut them down, about eight inches from the ground."

"Before they bloom?" he asked.

"Yes, before they bloom." Her face was tight with eagerness. "They'll grow right up again. About the last of September the buds will start."

She stopped and seemed perplexed. "It's the budding that takes the most care," she said hesitantly. "I don't know how to tell you." She looked deep into his eyes, searchingly. Her mouth opened a little, and she seemed to be listening. "I'll try to tell you," she said. "Did you ever hear of planting hands?"

"Can't say I have, ma'am."

"Well, I can only tell you what it feels like. It's when you're picking off the buds you don't want. Everything goes right down into your finger-tips. You watch your fingers work. They do it themselves. You can feel how it is. They pick and pick the buds. They never make a mistake. They're with the plant. Do you see? Your fingers and the plant. You can feel that, right up your arm. They know. They never make a mistake. You can feel it. When you're like that you can't do anything wrong. Do you see that? Can you understand that?"

She was kneeling on the ground looking up at him. Her breast swelled passionately.

The man's eyes narrowed. He looked away self-consciously. "Maybe I know," he said. "Sometimes in the night in the wagon there——"

Elisa's voice grew husky. She broke in on him, "I've never lived as you do, but I know what you mean. When the night is dark—why, the stars are sharp-pointed, and there's quiet. Why, you rise up and up! Every pointed star gets driven into your body. It's like that. Hot and sharp and—lovely."

Kneeling there, her hand went out toward his legs in the greasy black trousers. Her hesitant fingers almost touched the cloth. Then her hand dropped to the ground. She crouched low like a fawning dog.

He said, "It's nice, just like you say. Only when you don't have no dinner, it ain't."

She stood up then, very straight, and her face was ashamed. She held the flower pot out to him and placed it gently in his arms. "Here. Put it in your wagon, on the seat, where you can watch it. Maybe I can find something for you to do."

At the back of the house she dug in the can pile and found two old and battered aluminum saucepans. She carried them back and gave them to him. "Here, maybe you can fix these."

His manner changed. He became professional. "Good as new I can fix them." At the back of his wagon he set a little anvil, and out of an oily tool box dug a small machine hammer. Elisa came through the gate to watch him while he pounded out the dents in the kettles. His mouth grew sure and knowing. At a difficult part of the work he sucked his underlip.

"You sleep right in the wagon?" Elisa asked.

"Right in the wagon, ma'am. Rain or shine I'm dry as a cow in there."

"It must be nice," she said. "It must be very nice. I wish women could do such things."

"It ain't the right kind of life for a woman."

Her upper lip raised a little, showing her teeth. "How do you know? How can you tell?" she said.

"I don't know, ma'am," he protested. "Of course I don't know. Now here's your kettles, done. You don't have to buy no new ones."

"How much?"

"Oh, fifty cents'll do. I keep my prices down and my work good. That's why I have all them satisfied customers up and down the highway."

Elisa brought him a fifty-cent piece from the house and dropped it in his hand. "You might be surprised to have a rival some time. I can sharpen scissors, too. And I can beat the dents out of little pots. I could show you what a woman might do."

He put his hammer back in the oily box and shoved the little anvil out of sight. "It would be a lonely life for a woman, ma'am, and a scarey life, too, with animals creeping under the wagon all night." He climbed over the singletree, steadying himself with a hand on the burro's white rump. He settled himself in the seat, picked up the lines. "Thank you kindly, ma'am," he said. "I'll do like you told me; I'll go back and catch the Salinas road."

"Mind," she called, "if you're long in getting there, keep the sand damp."

"Sand, ma'am? . . . Sand? Oh, sure. You mean around the chrysanthemums. Sure I will." He clucked his tongue. The beasts leaned luxuriously into their collars. The mongrel dog took his place between the back wheels. The wagon turned and crawled out the entrance road and back the way it had come, along the river.

Elisa stood in front of her wire fence watching the slow progress of the caravan. Her shoulders were straight, her head thrown back, her eyes half-closed, so that the scene came vaguely into them. Her lips moved silently, forming the words "Good-bye—good-bye." Then she whispered, "That's a bright direction. There's a glowing there." The sound of her whisper startled her. She shook herself free and looked about to see whether anyone had been listening. Only the dogs had heard. They lifted their heads toward her from their sleeping in the dust, and then stretched out their chins and settled asleep again. Elisa turned and ran hurriedly into the house.

In the kitchen she reached behind the stove and felt the water tank. It was full of hot water from the noonday cooking. In the bathroom she tore off her soiled clothes and flung them into the corner. And then she scrubbed herself with a little block of pumice, legs and thighs, loins and chest and arms, until her skin was scratched and red. When she had dried herself she stood in front of a mirror in her bedroom and looked at her body. She tightened her stomach and threw out her chest. She turned and looked over her shoulder at her back.

After a while she began to dress slowly. She put on her newest under-clothing and her nicest stockings and the dress which was the symbol of her prettiness. She worked carefully on her hair, penciled her eyebrows and rouged her lips.

Before she was finished she heard the little thunder of hoofs and the shouts of Henry and his helper as they drove the red steers into the corral. She heard the gate bang shut and set herself for Henry's arrival.

His steps sounded on the porch. He entered the house calling, "Elisa, where are you?"

"In my room dressing. I'm not ready. There's hot water for your bath. Hurry up. It's getting late."

When she heard him splashing in the tub, Elisa laid his dark suit on the bed, and shirt and socks and tie beside it. She stood his polished shoes on the floor beside the bed. Then she went to the porch and sat primly and stiffly down. She looked toward the river road where the willow-line was still yellow with frosted leaves so that under the high gray fog they seemed a thin band of sunshine. This was the only color in the gray after-noon. She sat unmoved for a long time. Her eyes blinked rarely.

Henry came banging out of the door, shoving his tie inside his vest as he came. Elisa stiffened and her face grew tight. Henry stopped short and looked at her. "Why—why, Elisa. You look so nice!"

"Nice? You think I look nice? What do you mean by 'nice'?"

Henry blundered on. "I don't know. I mean you look different, strong and happy."

"I am strong? Yes, strong. What do you mean 'strong'?"

He looked bewildered. "You're playing some kind of a game," he said helplessly. "It's a kind of a play. You look strong enough to break a calf over your knee, happy enough to eat it like a watermelon."

For a second she lost her rigidity. "Henry! Don't talk like that. You didn't know what you said." She grew complete again. "I'm strong," she boasted. "I never knew before how strong."

Henry looked down toward the tractor shed, and when he brought his eyes back to her, they were his own again. "I'll get out the car. You can put on your coat while I'm starting."

Elisa went into the house. She heard him drive to the gate and idle down his motor, and then she took a long time to put on her hat. She pulled it here and pressed it there. When Henry turned the motor off she slipped into her coat and went out.

The little roadster bounced along on the dirt road by the river, raising the birds and driving the rabbits into the brush. Two cranes flapped heavily over the willow-line and dropped into the riverbed.

Far ahead on the road Elisa saw a dark speck. She knew.

She tried not to look as they passed it, but her eyes would not obey. She whispered to herself sadly, "He might have thrown them off the road. That wouldn't have been much trouble, not very much. But he kept the pot," she explained. "He had to keep the pot. That's why he couldn't get them off the road."

The roadster turned a bend and she saw the caravan ahead. She swung full around toward her husband so she could not see the little covered wagon and the mismatched team as the car passed them.

In a moment it was over. The thing was done. She did not look back.

She said loudly, to be heard above the motor, "It will be good, tonight, a good dinner."

"Now you're changed again," Henry complained. He took one hand from the wheel and patted her knee. "I ought to take you in to dinner oftener. It would be good for both of us. We get so heavy out on the ranch."

"Henry," she asked, "could we have wine at dinner?"

"Sure we could. Say! That will be fine."

She was silent for a while; then she said, "Henry, at those prize fights, do the men hurt each other very much?"

"Sometimes a little, not often. Why?"

"Well, I've read how they break noses, and blood runs down their chests. I've read how the fighting gloves get heavy and soggy with blood."

He looked around at her. "What's the matter, Elisa? I didn't know you read things like that." He brought the car to a stop, then turned to the right over the Salinas River bridge.

"Do any women ever go to the fights?" she asked.

"Oh, sure, some. What's the matter, Elisa? Do you want to go? I don't think you'd like it, but I'll take you if you really want to go."

She relaxed limply in the seat. "Oh, no. No. I don't want to go. I'm sure I don't." Her face was turned away from him. "It will be enough if we can have wine. It will be plenty." She turned up her coat collar so he could not see that she was crying weakly—like an old woman.

(1937)

Eudora Welty *1909–*

A WORN PATH

It was December—a bright frozen day in the early morning. Far out in the country there was an old Negro woman with her head tied in a red rag, coming along a path through the pinewoods. Her name was Phoenix Jackson. She was very old and small and she walked slowly in the dark pine shadows, moving a little from side to side in her steps, with the balanced heaviness and lightness of a pendulum in a grandfather clock. She carried a thin, small cane made from an umbrella, and with this she kept tapping the frozen earth in front of her. This made a grave and persistent noise in the still air, that seemed meditative like the chirping of a solitary little bird.

She wore a dark striped dress reaching down to her shoe tops, and an equally long apron of bleached sugar sacks, with a full pocket: all neat and tidy, but every time she took a step she might have fallen over her shoelaces, which dragged from her unlaced shoes. She looked straight ahead. Her eyes were blue with age. Her skin had a pattern all its own of numberless branching wrinkles and as though a whole little tree stood in the middle of her forehead, but a golden color ran underneath, and the two knobs of her cheeks were illumined by a yellow burning under the dark. Under the red rag her hair came down on her neck in the frailest of ringlets, still black, and with an odor like copper.

Now and then there was a quivering in the thicket. Old Phoenix said, "Out of my way, all you foxes, owls, beetles, jack rabbits, coons and wild animals! . . . Keep out from under these feet, little bob-whites. . . . Keep the big wild hogs out of my path. Don't let none of those come running my direction. I got a long way." Under her small black-freckled hand her cane, limber as a buggy whip, would switch at the brush as if to rouse up any hiding things.

On she went. The woods were deep and still. The sun made the pine needles almost too bright to look at, up where the wind rocked. The cones dropped as light as feathers. Down in the hollow was the mourning dove—it was not too late for him.

The path ran up a hill. "Seem like there is chains about my feet, time I get this far," she said, in the voice of argument old people keep to use with themselves. "Something always take a hold of me on this hill—pleads I should stay."

After she got to the top she turned and gave a full, severe look behind her where she had come. "Up through pines," she said at length. "Now down through oaks."

Her eyes opened their widest, and she started down gently. But before she got to the bottom of the hill a bush caught her dress.

Her fingers were busy and intent, but her skirts were full and long, so that before she could pull them free in one place they were caught in another. It was not possible to allow the dress to tear. "I in the thorny bush," she said. "Thorns, you doing your appointed work. Never want to let folks pass, no sir. Old eyes thought you was a pretty little *green* bush."

Finally, trembling all over, she stood free, and after a moment dared to stoop for her cane.

"Sun so high!" she cried, leaning back and looking, while the thick tears went over her eyes. "The time getting all gone here."

At the foot of this hill was a place where a log was laid across the creek.

"Now comes the trial," said Phoenix.

Putting her right foot out, she mounted the log and shut her eyes. Lifting her skirt, leveling her cane fiercely before her, like a festival figure in some parade, she began to march across. Then she opened her eyes and she was safe on the other side.

"I wasn't as old as I thought," she said.

But she sat down to rest. She spread her skirts on the bank around her and folded her hands over her knees. Up above her was a tree in a pearly cloud of mistletoe. She did not dare to close her eyes, and when a little boy brought her a plate with a slice of marble-cake on it she spoke to him. "That would be acceptable," she said. But when she went to take it there was just her own hand in the air.

So she left that tree, and had to go through a barbed-wire fence. There she had to creep and crawl, spreading her knees and stretching her fingers like a baby trying to climb the steps. But she talked loudly to herself: she could not let her dress be torn now, so late in the day, and she could not pay for having her arm or her leg sawed off if she got caught fast where she was.

At last she was safe through the fence and risen up out in the clearing. Big dead trees, like black men with one arm, were standing in the purple stalks of the withered cotton field. There sat a buzzard.

"Who you watching?"

In the furrow she made her way along.

"Glad this not the season for bulls," she said, looking sideways, "and the good Lord made his snakes to curl up and sleep in the winter. A pleasure I don't see no two-headed snake coming around that tree, where it come once. It took a while to get by him, back in the summer."

She passed through the old cotton and went into a field of dead corn. It whispered and shook and was taller than her head. "Through the maze now," she said, for there was no path.

Then there was something tall, black, and skinny there, moving before her.

At first she took it for a man. It could have been a man dancing in the field. But she stood still and listened, and it did not make a sound. It was as silent as a ghost.

"Ghost," she said sharply, "who be you the ghost of? For I have heard of nary death close by."

But there was no answer—only the ragged dancing in the wind.

She shut her eyes, reached out her hand, and touched a sleeve. She found a coat and inside that an emptiness, cold as ice.

"You scarecrow," she said. Her face lighted. "I ought to be shut up for good," she said with laughter. "My senses is gone. I too old. I the oldest people I ever know. Dance, old scarecrow," she said, "while I dancing with you."

She kicked her foot over the furrow and, with mouth drawn down, shook her head once or twice in a little strutting way. Some husks blew down and whirled in streamers about her skirts.

Then she went on, parting her way from side to side with the cane, through the whispering field. At last she came to the end, to a wagon track where the silver grass blew between the red ruts. The quail were walking around like pullets, seeming all dainty and unseen.

"Walk pretty," she said. "This the easy place. This the easy going."

She followed the track, swaying through the quiet bare fields, through the little strings of trees silver in their dead leaves, past cabins silver from weather, with the doors and windows boarded shut, all like old women under a spell sitting there. "I walking in their sleep," she said, nodding her head vigorously.

In a ravine she went where a spring was silently flowing through a hollow log. Old Phoenix bent and drank. "Sweet-gum makes the water sweet," she said, and drank more. "Nobody know who made this well, for it was here when I was born."

The track crossed a swampy part where the moss hung as white as lace from every limb. "Sleep on, alligators, and blow your bubbles." Then the track went into the road.

Deep, deep the road went down between the high green-colored banks. Overhead the live-oaks met, and it was as dark as a cave.

A black dog with a lolling tongue came up out of the weeds by the ditch. She was meditating, and not ready, and when he came at her she only hit him a little with her cane. Over she went in the ditch, like a little puff of milkweed.

Down there, her senses drifted away. A dream visited her, and she reached her hand up, but nothing reached down and gave her a pull. So she lay there and presently went to talking. "Old woman," she said to herself, "That black dog come up out of the weeds to stall you off, and now there he sitting on his fine tail, smiling at you."

A white man finally came along and found her—a hunter, a young man, with his dog on a chain.

"Well, Granny!" he laughed. "What are you doing there?"

"Lying on my back like a June-bug waiting to be turned over, mister," she said, reaching up her hand.

He lifted her up, gave her a swing in the air, and set her down. "Anything broken, Granny?"

"No sir, them old dead weeds is springy enough," said Phoenix, when she had got her breath. "I thank you for your trouble."

"Where do you live, Granny?" he asked, while the two dogs were growling at each other.

"Away back yonder, sir, behind the ridge. You can't even see it from here."

"On your way home?"

"No sir, I going to town."

"Why, that's too far! That's as far as I walk when I come out myself, and I get something for my trouble." He patted the stuffed bag he carried, and there hung down a little closed claw. It was one of the bob-whites, with its beak hooked bitterly to show it was dead. "Now you go on home, Granny!"

"I bound to go to town, mister," said Phoenix. "The time come around."

He gave another laugh, filling the whole landscape. "I know you old colored people! Wouldn't miss going to town to see Santa Claus!"

But something held old Phoenix very still. The deep lines in her face went into a fierce and different radiation. Without warning, she had seen with her own eyes a flashing nickel fall out of the man's pocket onto the ground.

"How old are you, Granny?" he was saying.

"There is no telling, mister," she said, "no telling."

Then she gave a little cry and clapped her hands and said, "Git on away from here, dog! Look! Look at that dog!" She laughed as if in admiration. "He ain't scared of nobody. He a big black dog." She whispered, "Sic him!"

"Watch me get rid of that cur," said the man. "Sic him, Pete! Sic him!"

Phoenix heard the dogs fighting, and heard the man running and throwing sticks. She even heard a gunshot. But she was slowly bending forward by that time, further and further forward, the lids stretched down over her eyes, as if she were doing this in her sleep. Her chin was lowered almost to her knees. The yellow palm of her hand came out from the fold of her apron. Her fingers slid down and along the ground under the piece of money with the grace and care they would have in lifting an egg from under a setting hen. Then she slowly straightened up, she stood erect, and the nickel was in her apron pocket. A bird flew by. Her lips moved. "God watching me the whole time. I come to stealing."

The man came back, and his own dog panted about them. "Well, I scared him off that time," he said, and then he laughed and lifted his gun and pointed it at Phoenix.

She stood straight and faced him.

"Doesn't the gun scare you?" he said, still pointing it.

"No, sir, I seen plenty go off closer by, in my day, and for less than what I done," she said, holding utterly still.

He smiled, and shouldered the gun. "Well, Granny," he said, "you must be a hundred years old, and scared of nothing. I'd give you a dime if I had any money with me. But you take my advice and stay home, and nothing will happen to you."

"I bound to go on my way, mister," said Phoenix. She inclined her head in the red rag. Then they went in different directions, but she could hear the gun shooting again and again over the hill.

She walked on. The shadows hung from the oak trees to the road like curtains. Then she smelled wood-smoke, and smelled the river, and she saw a steeple and the cabins on their steep steps. Dozens of little black children whirled around her. There ahead was Natchez shining. Bells were ringing. She walked on.

In the paved city it was Christmas time. There were red and green electric lights strung and criss-crossed everywhere, and all turned on in the daytime. Old Phoenix would have been lost if she had not distrusted her eyesight and depended on her feet to know where to take her.

She paused quietly on the sidewalk where people were passing by. A lady came along in the crowd, carrying an armful of red-, green- and silver-wrapped presents: she gave off perfume like the red roses in hot summer, and Phoenix stopped her.

"Please, missy, will you lace up my shoe?" She held up her foot.

"What do you want, Grandma?"

"See my shoe," said Phoenix. "Do all right for out in the country, but wouldn't look right to go in a big building."

"Stand still then, Grandma," said the lady. She put her packages down on the sidewalk beside her and laced and tied both shoes tightly.

"Can't lace 'em with a cane," said Phoenix. "Thank you, missy, I doesn't mind asking a nice lady to tie up my shoe, when I gets out on the street."

Moving slowly and from side to side, she went into the big building, and into a tower of steps, where she walked up and around and around until her feet knew to stop.

She entered a door, and there she saw nailed up on the wall the document that had been stamped with the gold seal and framed in the gold frame, which matched the dream that was hung up in her head.

"Here I be," she said. There was a fixed and ceremonial stiffness over her body.

"A charity case, I suppose," said an attendant who sat at the desk before her.

But Phoenix only looked above her head. There was sweat on her face, the wrinkles in her skin shone like a bright net.

"Speak up, Grandma," the woman said. "What's your name? We must have your history, you know. Have you been here before? What seems to be the trouble with you?"

Old Phoenix only gave a twitch to her face as if a fly were bothering her.

"Are you deaf?" cried the attendant.

But then the nurse came in.

"Oh, that's just old Aunt Phoenix," she said. "She doesn't come for herself—she has a little grandson. She makes these trips just as regular as clockwork. She lives away back off the Old Natchez Trace." She bent down. "Well, Aunt Phoenix, why don't you just take a seat? We won't keep you standing after your long trip." She pointed.

The old woman sat down, bolt upright in the chair.

"Now, how is the boy?" asked the nurse.

Old Phoenix did not speak.

"I said, how is the boy?"

But Phoenix only waited and stared straight ahead, her face very solemn and withdrawn into rigidity.

"Is his throat any better?" asked the nurse. "Aunt Phoenix, don't you hear me? Is your grandson's throat any better since the last time you came for the medicine?"

With her hands on her knees, the old woman waited, silent, erect and motionless, just as if she were in armor.

"You musn't take up our time this way, Aunt Phoenix," the nurse said. "Tell us quickly about your grandson, and get it over. He isn't dead, is he?"

At last there came a flicker and then a flame of comprehension across her face, and she spoke.

"My grandson. It was my memory had left me. There I sat and forgot why I made my long trip."

"Forgot?" The nurse frowned. "After you came so far?"

Then Phoenix was like an old woman begging a dignified forgiveness for waking up frightened in the night. "I never did go to school, I was too old at the Surrender," she said in a soft voice. "I'm an old woman without an education. It was my memory fail me. My little grandson, he is just the same, and I forgot it in the coming."

"Throat never heals, does it?" said the nurse, speaking in a loud, sure voice to old Phoenix. By now she had a card with something written on it, a little list. "Yes. Swallowed lye. When was it?—January—two-three years ago—"

Phoenix spoke unasked now. "No, missy, he not dead, he just the same. Every little while his throat begin to close up again, and he not able to swallow. He not get his breath. He not able to help himself. So the time came around, and I go on another trip for the soothing medicine."

"All right. The doctor said as long as you came to get it, you could have it," said the nurse. "But it's an obstinate case."

"My little grandson, he sit up there in the house all wrapped up, waiting by himself," Phoenix went on. "We is the only two left in the world. He suffer and it don't seem to put him back at all. He got a sweet look. He going to last. He wear a little patch quilt and peep out holding his mouth open like a little bird. I remembers so plain now. I not going to forget him again, no, the whole enduring time. I could tell him from all the others in creation."

"All right." The nurse was trying to hush her now. She brought her a bottle of medicine. "Charity," she said, making a checkmark in a book.

Old Phoenix held the bottle close to her eyes, and then carefully put it into her pocket.

"I thank you," she said.

"It's Christmas time, Grandma," said the attendant. "Could I give you a few pennies out of my purse?"

"Five pennies is a nickel," said Phoenix stiffly.

"Here's a nickel," said the attendant.

Phoenix rose carefully and held out her hand. She received the nickel and then fished the other nickel out of her pocket and laid it beside the new one. She stared at her palm closely, with her head on one side.

Then she gave a tap with her cane on the floor.

"This is what come to me to do," she said. "I going to the store and buy my child a little windmill they sells, made out of paper. He going to find it hard to believe there such a thing in the world. I'll march myself back where he waiting, holding it straight up in this hand."

She lifted her free hand, gave a little nod, turned around, and walked out of the doctor's office. Then her slow step began on the stairs, going down.

(1941)

Alberto Moravia *1907–*

THE CHASE

I have never been a sportsman—or, rather, I have been a sportsman only once, and that was the first and last time. I was a child, and one day, for some reason or other, I found myself together with my father, who was holding a gun in his hand, behind a bush, watching a bird that had perched on a branch not very far away. It was a large, gray bird—or perhaps it was brown—with a long—or perhaps a short—beak; I don't remember. I only remember what I felt at that moment as I looked at it. It was like watching an animal whose vitality was rendered more intense by the very fact of my watching it and of the animal's not knowing that I was watching it.

At that moment, I say, the notion of wildness entered my mind, never again to leave it: everything is wild which is autonomous and unpredictable and does not depend upon us. Then all of a sudden there was an explosion; I could no longer see the bird and I thought it had flown away. But my father was leading the way, walking in front of me through the undergrowth. Finally he stooped down, picked up something and put it in my hand. I was aware of something warm and soft and I lowered my eyes: there was the bird in the palm of my hand, its dangling, shattered head crowned with a plume of already-thickening blood. I burst into tears and dropped the corpse on the ground, and that was the end of my shooting experience.

I thought again of this remote episode in my life this very day after watching my wife, for the first and also the last time, as she was walking through the streets of the city. But let us take things in order.

What had my wife been like; what was she like now? She once had been, to put it briefly, "wild"—that is, entirely autonomous and unpredictable; latterly she had become "tame"—that is, predictable and dependent. For a long time she had been like the bird that, on that far-off morning in my childhood, I had seen perching on the bough; latterly, I am sorry to say, she had become like a hen about which one knows everything in advance—how it moves, how it eats, how it lays eggs, how it sleeps, and so on.

Nevertheless I would not wish anyone to think that my wife's wildness consisted of an uncouth, rough, rebellious character. Apart from being extremely beautiful, she is the gentlest, politest, most discreet person in the world. Rather her wildness consisted of the air of charming unpredictability, of independence in her way of living, with which during the first years of our marriage she acted in my presence, both at home and abroad. Wildness signified intimacy, privacy, secrecy. Yes, my wife as she sat in front of her dressing table, her eyes fixed on the looking glass, passing the hairbrush with a repeated motion over her long, loose hair, was just as wild as the solitary quail hopping forward along a sun-filled furrow or the furtive fox coming out into a clearing and stopping to look around before running on. She was wild because I, as I looked at her, could never

manage to foresee when she would give a last stroke with the hairbrush
and rise and come toward me; wild to such a degree that sometimes when
I went into our bedroom the smell of her, floating in the air, would have
something of the acrid quality of a wild beast's lair.

Gradually she became less wild, tamer. I had had a fox, a quail, in the
house, as I have said; then one day I realized that I had a hen. What
effect does a hen have on someone who watches it? It has the effect of
being, so to speak, an automaton in the form of a bird; automatic are the
brief, rapid steps with which it moves about; automatic its hard, terse
pecking; automatic the glance of the round eyes in its head that nods and
turns; automatic its ready crouching down under the cock; automatic the
dropping of the egg wherever it may be and the cry with which it announces
that the egg has been laid. Good-by to the fox; good-by to the quail. And
her smell—this no longer brought to my mind, in any way, the innocent
odor of a wild animal; rather I detected in it the chemical suavity of some
ordinary French perfume.

Our flat is on the first floor of a big building in a modern quarter of
the town; our windows look out on a square in which there is a small
public garden, the haunt of nurses and children and dogs. One day I was
standing at the window, looking in a melancholy way at the garden. My
wife, shortly before, had dressed to go out; and once again, watching her,
I had noticed the irrevocable and, so to speak, invisible character of her
gestures and personality: something which gave one the feeling of a thing
already seen and already done and which therefore evaded even the most
determined observation. And now, as I stood looking at the garden and
at the same time wondering why the adorable wildness of former times
had so completely disappeared, suddenly my wife came into my range of
vision as she walked quickly across the garden in the direction of the
bus stop. I watched her and then I almost jumped for joy; in a movement
she was making to pull down a fold of her narrow skirt and smooth it
over her thigh with the tips of her long, sharp nails, in this movement I
recognized the wildness that in the past had made me love her. It was
only an instant, but in that instant I said to myself: She's become wild
again because she's convinced that I am not there and am not watching
her. Then I left the window and rushed out.

But I did not join her at the bus stop; I felt that I must not allow
myself to be seen. Instead I hurried to my car, which was standing nearby,
got in and waited. A bus came and she got in together with some other
people; the bus started off again and I began following it. Then there
came back to me the memory of that one shooting expedition in which I
had taken part as a child, and I saw that the bus was the undergrowth
with its bushes and trees, my wife the bird perching on the bough while
I, unseen, watched it living before my eyes. And the whole town, during
this pursuit, became, as though by magic, a fact of nature like the countryside: the houses were hills, the streets valleys, the vehicles hedges and
woods, and even the passers-by on the pavements had something unpredictable and autonomous—that is, wild—about them. And in my mouth, behind
my clenched teeth, there was the acrid, metallic taste of gunfire; and my
eyes, usually listless and wandering, had become sharp, watchful, attentive.

These eyes were fixed intently upon the exit door when the bus came
to the end of its run. A number of people got out, and then I saw my
wife getting out. Once again I recognized, in the manner in which she
broke free of the crowd and started off toward a neighboring street, the
wildness that pleased me so much. I jumped out of the car and started
following her.

She was walking in front of me, ignorant of my presence, a tall woman
with an elegant figure, long-legged, narrow-hipped, broad-backed, her
brown hair falling on her shoulders.

Men turned around as she went past; perhaps they were aware of what
I myself was now sensing with an intensity that quickened the beating
of my heart and took my breath away: the unrestricted, steadily increasing,
irresistible character of her mysterious wildness.

She walked hurriedly, having evidently some purpose in view, and even
the fact that she had a purpose of which I was ignorant added to her
wildness; I did not know where she was going, just as on that far-off morning I had not known what the bird perching on the bough was about to
do. Moreover I thought the gradual, steady increase in this quality of wildness came partly from the fact that as she drew nearer to the object of
this mysterious walk there was an increase in her—how shall I express
it?—of biological tension, of existential excitement, of vital effervescence.
Then, unexpectedly, with the suddenness of a film, her purpose was revealed.

A fair-haired young man in a leather jacket and a pair of corduroy trousers was leaning against the wall of a house in that ancient, narrow street.
He was idly smoking as he looked in front of him. But as my wife passed
close to him, he threw away his cigarette with a decisive gesture, took a
step forward and seized her arm. I was expecting her to rebuff him, to
move away from him, but nothing happened: evidently obeying the rules
of some kind of erotic ritual, she went on walking beside the young man.
Then after a few steps, with a movement that confirmed her own complic-
ity, she put her arm around her companion's waist and he put his around
her.

I understood then that this unknown man who took such liberties with
my wife was also attracted by wildness. And so, instead of making a conventional appointment with her, instead of meeting in a café with a handshake,
a falsely friendly and respectful welcome, he had preferred, by agreement
with her, to take her by surprise—or, rather, to pretend to do so—while
she was apparently taking a walk on her own account. All this I perceived
by intuition, noticing that at the very moment when he stepped forward
and took her arm her wildness had, so to speak, given an upward bound.
It was years since I had seen my wife so alive, but alas, the source of
this life could not be traced to me.

They walked on thus entwined and then, without any preliminaries,
just like two wild animals, they did an unexpected thing: they went into
one of the dark doorways in order to kiss. I stopped and watched them
from a distance, peering into the darkness of the entrance. My wife was
turned away from me and was bending back with the pressure of his
body, her hair hanging free. I looked at that long, thick mane of brown

hair, which as she leaned back fell free of her shoulders, and I felt at that moment her vitality reached its diapason, just as happens with wild animals when they couple and their customary wildness is redoubled by the violence of love. I watched for a long time and then, since this kiss went on and on and in fact seemed to be prolonged beyond the limits of my power of endurance, I saw that I would have to intervene.

I would have to go forward, seize my wife by the arm—or actually by that hair, which hung down and conveyed so well the feeling of feminine passivity—then hurl myself with clenched fists upon the blond young man. After this encounter I would carry off my wife, weeping, mortified, ashamed, while I was raging and broken-hearted, upbraiding her and pouring scorn upon her.

But what else would this intervention amount to but the shot my father fired at that free, unknowing bird as it perched on the bough? The disorder and confusion, the mortification, the shame, that would follow would irreparably destroy the rare and precious moment of wildness that I was witnessing inside the dark doorway. It was true that this wildness was directed against me; but I had to remember that wildness, always and everywhere, is directed against everything and everybody. After the scene of my intervention it might be possible for me to regain control of my wife, but I should find her shattered and lifeless in my arms like the bird that my father placed in my hand so that I might throw it into the shooting bag.

The kiss went on and on: well, it was a kiss of passion—that could not be denied. I waited until they finished, until they came out of the doorway, until they walked on again still linked together. Then I turned back.

(1969)
Translated by Angus Davidson

Flannery O'Connor *1925–1964*

GOOD COUNTRY PEOPLE

Besides the neutral expression that she wore when she was alone, Mrs. Freeman had two others, forward and reverse, that she used for all her human dealings. Her forward expression was steady and driving like the advance of a heavy truck. Her eyes never swerved to left or right but turned as the story turned as if they followed a yellow line down the center of it. She seldom used the other expression because it was not often necessary for her to retract a statement, but when she did, her face came to a complete stop, there was an almost imperceptible movement of her black eyes, during which they seemed to be receding, and then the observer would see that Mrs. Freeman, though she might stand there as real as several grain sacks thrown on top of each other, was no longer there in spirit. As for getting anything across to her when this was the case, Mrs. Hopewell had given it up. She might talk her head off. Mrs. Freeman could never be brought to admit herself wrong on any point. She would stand there and if she could be brought to say anything, it was something like, "Well, I wouldn't of said it was and I wouldn't of said it wasn't" or letting her gaze range over the top kitchen shelf where there was an assortment of dusty bottles, she might remark, "I see you ain't ate many of them figs you put up last summer."

They carried on their most important business in the kitchen at breakfast. Every morning Mrs. Hopewell got up at seven o'clock and lit her gas heater and Joy's. Joy was her daughter, a large blonde girl who had an artificial leg. Mrs. Hopewell thought of her as a child though she was thirty-two years old and highly educated. Joy would get up while her mother was eating and lumber into the bathroom and slam the door, and before long, Mrs. Freeman would arrive at the back door. Joy would hear her mother call, "Come on in," and then they would talk for a while in low voices that were indistinguishable in the bathroom. By the time Joy came in, they had usually finished the weather report and were on one or the other of Mrs. Freeman's daughters, Glynese or Carramae. Joy called them Glycerin and Caramel. Glynese, a redhead, was eighteen and had many admirers; Carramae, a blonde, was only fifteen but already married and pregnant. She could not keep anything on her stomach. Every morning Mrs. Freeman told Mrs. Hopewell how many times she had vomited since the last report.

Mrs. Hopewell liked to tell people that Glynese and Carramae were two of the finest girls she knew and that Mrs. Freeman was a *lady* and that she was never ashamed to take her anywhere or introduce her to anybody they might meet. Then she would tell how she had happened to hire the Freemans in the first place and how they were a godsend to her and how she had had them four years. The reason for her keeping them so long was that they were not trash. They were good country people. She had telephoned the man whose name they had given as reference and he had told her that Mr. Freeman was a good farmer but that his wife was the nosiest woman ever to walk the earth. "She's got to be into everything," the man said. "If she don't get there before the dust settles, you can bet she's dead, that's all. She'll want to know all your business. I can stand him real good," he had said, "but me nor my wife neither could have stood that woman one more minute on this place." That had put Mrs. Hopewell off for a few days.

She had hired them in the end because there were no other applicants but she had made up her mind beforehand exactly how she would handle the woman. Since she was the type who had to be into everything, then, Mrs. Hopewell had decided, she would not only let her be into everything, she would *see to it* that she was into everything—she would give her the responsibility of everything, she would put her in charge. Mrs. Hopewell had no bad qualities of her own but she was able to use other people's in such a constructive way that she had kept them four years.

Nothing is perfect. This was one of Mrs. Hopewell's favorite sayings. Another was: that is life! And still another, the most important, was: well, other people have their opinions too. She would make these statements, usually at the table, in a tone of gentle insistence as if no one held them but her, and the large hulking Joy, whose constant outrage had obliterated every expression from her face, would stare just a little to the side of her, her eyes icy blue, with the look of someone who has achieved blindness by an act of will and means to keep it.

When Mrs. Hopewell said to Mrs. Freeman that life was like that, Mrs. Freeman would say, "I always said so myself." Nothing had been arrived at by anyone that had not first been arrived at by her. She was quicker than Mr. Freeman. When Mrs. Hopewell said to her after they had been on the place a while, "You know, you're the wheel behind the wheel," and winked, Mrs. Freeman had said, "I know it. I've always been quick. It's some that are quicker than others."

"Everybody is different," Mrs. Hopewell said.

"Yes, most people is," Mrs. Freeman said.

"It takes all kinds to make the world."

"I always said it did myself."

The girl was used to this kind of dialogue for breakfast and more of it for dinner; sometimes they had it for supper too. When they had no guest they ate in the kitchen because that was easier. Mrs. Freeman always managed to arrive at some point during the meal and to watch them finish it. She would stand in the doorway if it were summer but in the winter she would stand with one elbow on top of the refrigerator and look down on them, or she would stand by the gas heater, lifting the back of her skirt slightly. Occasionally she would stand against the wall and roll her head from side to side. At no time was she in any hurry to leave. All this was very trying on Mrs. Hopewell but she was a woman of great patience. She realized that nothing is perfect and that in the Freemans she had good country people and that if, in this day and age, you get good country people, you had better hang onto them.

She had had plenty of experience with trash. Before the Freemans she had averaged one tenant family a year. The wives of these farmers were not the kind you would want to be around you for very long. Mrs. Hopewell, who had divorced her husband long ago, needed someone to walk over the fields with her; and when Joy had to be impressed for these services, her remarks were usually so ugly and her face so glum that Mrs. Hopewell would say, "If you can't come pleasantly, I don't want you at all," to which the girl, standing square and rigid-shouldered with her neck thrust slightly forward, would reply, "If you want me, here I am—LIKE I AM."

Mrs. Hopewell excused this attitude because of the leg (which had been shot off in a hunting accident when Joy was ten). It was hard for Mrs. Hopewell to realize that her child was thirty-two now and that for more than twenty years she had had only one leg. She thought of her still as a child because it tore her heart to think instead of the poor stout girl in her thirties who had never danced a step or had any *normal* good times. Her name was really Joy but as soon as she was twenty-one and away from home, she had had it legally changed. Mrs. Hopewell was certain that she had thought and thought until she had hit upon the ugliest name in any language. Then she had gone and had the beautiful name, Joy, changed without telling her mother until after she had done it. Her legal name was Hulga.

When Mrs. Hopewell thought the name, Hulga, she thought of the broad blank hull of a battleship. She would not use it. She continued to call her Joy to which the girl responded but in a purely mechanical way.

Hulga had learned to tolerate Mrs. Freeman who saved her from taking walks with her mother. Even Glynese and Carramae were useful when they occupied attention that might otherwise have been directed at her. At first she had thought she could not stand Mrs. Freeman for she had found that it was not possible to be rude to her. Mrs. Freeman would take on strange resentments and for days together she would be sullen but the source of her displeasure was always obscure; a direct attack, a positive leer, blatant ugliness to her face—these never touched her. And without warning one day, she began calling her Hulga.

She did not call her that in front of Mrs. Hopewell who would have been incensed but when she and the girl happened to be out of the house together, she would say something and add the name Hulga to the end of it, and the big spectacled Joy-Hulga would scowl and redden as if her privacy had been intruded upon. She considered the name her personal affair. She had arrived at it first purely on the basis of its ugly sound and then the full genius of its fitness had struck her. She had a vision of the name working like the ugly sweating Vulcan who stayed in the furnace and to whom, presumably, the goddess had to come when called. She saw it as the name of her highest creative act. One of her major triumphs was that her mother had not been able to turn her dust into Joy, but the greater one was that she had been able to turn it herself into Hulga. However, Mrs. Freeman's relish for using the name only irritated her. It was as if Mrs. Freeman's beady steel-pointed eyes had penetrated far enough behind her face to reach some secret fact. Something about her seemed to fascinate Mrs. Freeman and then one day Hulga realized that it was the artificial leg. Mrs. Freeman had a special fondness for the details of secret infections, hidden deformities, assaults upon children. Of diseases, she preferred the lingering or incurable. Hulga had heard Mrs. Hopewell give her the details of the hunting accident, how the leg had been literally blasted off, how she had never lost consciousness. Mrs. Freeman could listen to it any time as if it had happened an hour ago.

When Hulga stumped into the kitchen in the morning (she could walk without making the awful noise but she made it—Mrs. Hopewell was certain—because it was ugly-sounding), she glanced at them and did not speak. Mrs. Hopewell would be in her red kimono with her hair tied around her head in rags. She would be sitting at the table, finishing her breakfast and Mrs. Freeman would be hanging by her elbow outward from the refrigerator, looking down at the table. Hulga always put her eggs on the stove to boil and then stood over them with her arms folded, and Mrs. Hopewell would look at her—a kind of indirect gaze divided between her and Mrs. Freeman—and would think that if she would only keep herself up a little, she wouldn't be so bad looking. There was nothing wrong with her face that a pleasant expression wouldn't help. Mrs. Hopewell said that people who looked on the bright side of things would be beautiful even if they were not.

Whenever she looked at Joy this way, she could not help but feel that it would have been better if the child had not taken the Ph.D. It had certainly not brought her out any and now that she had it, there was no more excuse for her to go to school again. Mrs. Hopewell thought it was nice for girls to go to school to have a good time but Joy had "gone through." Anyhow, she would not have been strong enough to go again. The doctors had told Mrs. Hopewell that with the best of care, Joy might see forty-five. She had a weak heart. Joy had made it plain that if it had not been for this condition, she would be far from these red hills and good country people. She would be in a university lecturing to people who knew what she was talking about. And Mrs. Hopewell could very well picture her there, looking like a scarecrow and lecturing to more of the same. Here she went about all day in a six-year-old skirt and a yellow sweat shirt with a faded cowboy on a horse embossed on it. She thought this was funny; Mrs. Hopewell thought it was idiotic and showed simply that she was still a child. She was brilliant but she didn't have a grain of sense. It seemed to Mrs. Hopewell that every year she grew less like other people and more like herself—bloated, rude, and squint-eyed. And she said such strange things! To her own mother she had said—without warning, without excuse, standing up in the middle of a meal with her face purple and her mouth half full—"Woman! do you ever look inside? Do you ever look inside and see what you are *not*? God!" she had cried sinking down again and staring at her plate, "Malebranche[1] was right: we are not our own light. We are not our own light!" Mrs. Hopewell had no idea to this day what brought that on. She had only made the remark, hoping Joy would take it in, that a smile never hurt anyone.

The girl had taken the Ph.D. in philosophy and this left Mrs. Hopewell at a complete loss. You could say, "My daughter is a nurse," or "My daughter is a school teacher," or even, "My daughter is a chemical engineer." You could not say, "My daughter is a philosopher." That was something that had ended with the Greeks and Romans. All day Joy sat on her neck

---

[1] Nicolas Malebranche, 1638–1715, French philosopher.

in a deep chair, reading. Sometimes she went for walks but she didn't like dogs or cats or birds or flowers or nature or nice young men. She looked at nice young men as if she could smell their stupidity.

One day Mrs. Hopewell had picked up one of the books the girl had just put down and opening it at random, she read, "Science, on the other hand, has to assert its soberness and seriousness afresh and declare that it is concerned solely with what-is. Nothing—how can it be for science anything but a horror and a phantasm? If science is right, then one thing stands firm: science wishes to know nothing of nothing. Such is after all the strictly scientific approach to Nothing. We know it by wishing to know nothing of Nothing." These words had been underlined with a blue pencil and they worked on Mrs. Hopewell like some evil incantation in gibberish. She shut the book quickly and went out of the room as if she were having a chill.

This morning when the girl came in, Mrs. Freeman was on Carramae. "She thrown up four times after supper," she said, "and was up twict in the night after three o'clock. Yesterday she didn't do nothing but ramble in the bureau drawer. All she did. Stand up there and see what she could run up on."

"She's got to eat," Mrs. Hopewell muttered, sipping her coffee, while she watched Joy's back at the stove. She was wondering what the child had said to the Bible salesman. She could not imagine what kind of a conversation she could possibly have had with him.

He was a tall gaunt hatless youth who had called yesterday to sell them a Bible. He had appeared at the door, carrying a large black suitcase that weighted him so heavily on one side that he had to brace himself against the door facing. He seemed on the point of collapse but he said in a cheerful voice, "Good morning, Mrs. Cedars!" and set the suitcase down on the mat. He was not a bad-looking young man though he had on a bright blue suit and yellow socks that were not pulled up far enough. He had prominent face bones and a streak of sticky-looking brown hair falling across his forehead.

"I'm Mrs. Hopewell," she said.

"Oh!" he said, pretending to look puzzled but with his eyes sparkling, "I saw it said 'The Cedars,' on the mailbox so I thought you was Mrs. Cedars!" and he burst out in a pleasant laugh. He picked up the satchel and under cover of a pant, he fell forward into her hall. It was rather as if the suitcase had moved first, jerking him after it. "Mrs. Hopewell!" he said and grabbed her hand. "I hope you are well!" and he laughed again and then all at once his face sobered completely. He paused and gave her a straight earnest look and said, "Lady, I've come to speak of serious things."

"Well, come in," she muttered, none too pleased because her dinner was almost ready. He came into the parlor and sat down on the edge of a straight chair and put the suitcase between his feet and glanced around the room as if he were sizing her up by it. Her silver gleamed on the two sideboards; she decided he had never been in a room as elegant as this.

"Mrs. Hopewell," he began, using her name in a way that sounded almost intimate, "I know you believe in Chrustian service."

"Well yes," she murmured.

"I know," he said and paused, looking very wise with his head cocked on one side, "that you're a good woman. Friends have told me."

Mrs. Hopewell never liked to be taken for a fool. "What are you selling?" she asked.

"Bibles," the young man said and his eye raced around the room before he added, "I see you have no family Bible in your parlor, I see that is the one lack you got!"

Mrs. Hopewell could not say, "My daughter is an atheist and won't let me keep the Bible in the parlor." She said, stiffening slightly, "I keep my Bible by my bedside." This was not the truth. It was in the attic somewhere.

"Lady," he said, "the word of God ought to be in the parlor."

"Well, I think that's a matter of taste," she began. "I think . . ."

"Lady," he said, "for a Chrustian, the word of God ought to be in every room in the house besides in his heart. I know you're a Chrustian because I can see it in every line of your face."

She stood up and said, "Well, young man, I don't want to buy a Bible and I smell my dinner burning."

He didn't get up. He began to twist his hands and looking down at them, he said softly, "Well lady, I'll tell you the truth—not many people want to buy one nowadays and besides, I know I'm real simple. I don't know how to say a thing but to say it. I'm just a country boy." He glanced up into her unfriendly face. "People like you don't like to fool with country people like me!"

"Why!" she cried, "good country people are the salt of the earth! Besides, we all have different ways of doing, it takes all kinds to make the world go 'round. That's life!"

"You said a mouthful," he said.

"Why, I think there aren't enough good country people in the world!" she said, stirred. "I think that's what's wrong with it!"

His face had brightened. "I didn't inraduce myself," he said. "I'm Manley Pointer from out in the country around Willohobie, not even from a place, just from near a place."

"You wait a minute," she said. "I have to see about my dinner." She went out to the kitchen and found Joy standing near the door where she had been listening.

"Get rid of the salt of the earth," she said, "and let's eat."

Mrs. Hopewell gave her a pained look and turned the heat down under the vegetables. "I can't be rude to anybody," she murmured and went back into the parlor.

He had opened the suitcase and was sitting with a Bible on each knee.

"You might as well put those up," she told him. "I don't want one."

"I appreciate your honesty," he said. "You don't see any more real honest people unless you go way out in the country."

"I know," she said, "real genuine folks!" Through the crack in the door she heard a groan.

"I guess a lot of boys come telling you they're working their way through college," he said, "but I'm not going to tell you that. Somehow," he said, "I don't want to go to college. I want to devote my life to Chrustian service. See," he said, lowering his voice, "I got this heart condition. I may not live long. When you know it's something wrong with you and you may not live long, well then, lady . . ." He paused, with his mouth open, and stared at her.

He and Joy had the same condition! She knew that her eyes were filling with tears but she collected herself quickly and murmured, "Won't you stay for dinner? We'd love to have you!" and was sorry the instant she heard herself say it.

"Yes mam," he said in an abashed voice, "I would sher love to do that!"

Joy had given him one look on being introduced to him and then throughout the meal had not glanced at him again. He had addressed several remarks to her, which she had pretended not to hear. Mrs. Hopewell could not understand deliberate rudeness, although she lived with it, and she felt she had always to overflow with hospitality to make up for Joy's lack of courtesy. She urged him to talk about himself and he did. He said he was the seventh child of twelve and that his father had been crushed under a tree when he himself was eight year old. He had been crushed very badly, in fact, almost cut in two and was practically not recognizable. His mother had got along the best she could by hard working and she had always seen that her children went to Sunday School and that they read the Bible every evening. He was now nineteen years old and he had been selling Bibles for four months. In that time he had sold seventy-seven Bibles and had the promise of two more sales. He wanted to become a missionary because he thought that was the way you could do most for people. "He who losest his life shall find it," he said simply and he was so sincere, so genuine and earnest that Mrs. Hopewell would not for the world have smiled. He prevented his peas from sliding onto the table by blocking them with a piece of bread which he later cleaned his plate with. She could see Joy observing sidewise how he handled his knife and fork and she saw too that every few minutes, the boy would dart a keen appraising glance at the girl as if he were trying to attract her attention.

After dinner Joy cleared the dishes off the table and disappeared and Mrs. Hopewell was left to talk with him. He told her again about his childhood and his father's accident and about various things that had happened to him. Every five minutes or so she would stifle a yawn. He sat for two hours until finally she told him she must go because she had an appointment in town. He packed his Bibles and thanked her and prepared to leave, but in the doorway he stopped and wrung her hand and said that not on any of his trips had he met a lady as nice as her and he asked if he could come again. She had said she would always be happy to see him.

Joy had been standing in the road, apparently looking at something in the distance, when he came down the steps toward her, bent to the side with his heavy valise. He stopped where she was standing and confronted her directly. Mrs. Hopewell could not hear what he said but she trembled to think what Joy would say to him. She could see that after a minute Joy said something and that then the boy began to speak again, making an excited gesture with his free hand. After a minute Joy said something else at which the boy began to speak once more. Then to her amazement,

Mrs. Hopewell saw the two of them walk off together, toward the gate. Joy had walked all the way to the gate with him and Mrs. Hopewell could not imagine what they had said to each other, and she had not yet dared to ask.

Mrs. Freeman was insisting upon her attention. She had moved from the refrigerator to the heater so that Mrs. Hopewell had to turn and face her in order to seem to be listening. "Glynese gone out with Harvey Hill again last night," she said. "She had this sty."

"Hill," Mrs. Hopewell said absently, "is that the one who works in the garage?"

"Nome, he's the one that goes to chiropracter school," Mrs. Freeman said. "She had this sty. Been had it two days. So she says when he brought her in the other night he says, 'Lemme get rid of that sty for you,' and she says, 'How?' and he says, 'You just lay yourself down acrost the seat of that car and I'll show you.' So she done it and he popped her neck. Kept on a-popping it several times until she made him quit. This morning," Mrs. Freeman said, "she ain't got no sty. She ain't got no traces of a sty."

"I never heard of that before," Mrs. Hopewell said.

"He ast her to marry him before the Ordinary."[2] Mrs. Freeman went on, "and she told him she wasn't going to be married in no *office.*"

"Well, Glynese is a fine girl," Mrs. Hopewell said. "Glynese and Carramae are both fine girls."

"Carramae said when her and Lyman was married Lyman said it sure felt sacred to him. She said he said he wouldn't take five hundred dollars for being married by a preacher."

"How much would he take?" the girl asked from the stove.

"He said he wouldn't take five hundred dollars," Mrs. Freeman repeated.

"Well we all have work to do," Mrs. Hopewell said.

"Lyman said it just felt more sacred to him," Mrs. Freeman said. "The doctor wants Carramae to eat prunes. Says instead of medicine. Says them cramps is coming from pressure. You know where I think it is?"

"She'll be better in a few weeks," Mrs. Hopewell said.

"In the tube," Mrs. Freeman said. "Else she wouldn't be as sick as she is."

Hulga had cracked her two eggs into a saucer and was bringing them to the table along with a cup of coffee that she had filled too full. She sat down carefully and began to eat, meaning to keep Mrs. Freeman there by questions if for any reason she showed an inclination to leave. She could perceive her mother's eye on her. The first round-about question would be about the Bible salesman and she did not wish to bring it on. "How did he pop her neck?" she asked.

Mrs. Freeman went into a description of how he had popped her neck. She said he owned a '55 Mercury but that Glynese said she would rather marry a man with only a '36 Plymouth who would be married by a preacher. The girl asked what if he had a '32 Plymouth and Mrs. Freeman said what Glynese had said was a '36 Plymouth.

Mrs. Hopewell said there were not many girls with Glynese's common sense. She said what she admired in those girls was their common sense.

[2] Judge of probate.

She said that reminded her that they had had a nice visitor yesterday, a young man selling Bibles. "Lord," she said, "he bored me to death but he was so sincere and genuine I couldn't be rude to him. He was just good country people, you know," she said, "—just the salt of the earth."

"I seen him walk up," Mrs. Freeman said, "and then later—I seen him walk off," and Hulga could feel the slight shift in her voice, the slight insinuation, that he had not walked off alone, had he? Her face remained expressionless but the color rose into her neck and she seemed to swallow it down with the next spoonful of egg. Mrs. Freeman was looking at her as if they had a secret together.

"Well, it takes all kinds of people to make the world go 'round," Mrs. Hopewell said, "It's very good we aren't all alike."

"Some people are more alike than others," Mrs. Freeman said.

Hulga got up and stumped, with about twice the noise that was necessary, into her room and locked the door. She was to meet the Bible salesman at ten o'clock at the gate. She had thought about it half the night. She had started thinking of it as a great joke and then she had begun to see profound implications in it. She had lain in bed imagining dialogues for them that were insane on the surface but that reached below to depths that no Bible salesman would be aware of. Their conversation yesterday had been of this kind.

He had stopped in front of her and had simply stood there. His face was bony and sweaty and bright, with a little pointed nose in the center of it, and his look was different from what it had been at the dinner table. He was gazing at her with open curiosity, with fascination, like a child watching a new fantastic animal at the zoo, and he was breathing as if he had run a great distance to reach her. His gaze seemed somehow familiar but she could not think where she had been regarded with it before. For almost a minute he didn't say anything. Then on what seemed an insuck of breath, he whispered, "You ever ate a chicken that was two days old?"

The girl looked at him stonily. He might have just put this question up for consideration at the meeting of a philosophical association. "Yes," she presently replied as if she had considered it from all angles.

"It must have been mighty small!" he said triumphantly and shook all over with little nervous giggles, getting very red in the face, and subsiding finally into his gaze of complete admiration, while the girl's expression remained exactly the same.

"How old are you?" he asked softly.

She waited some time before she answered. Then in a flat voice she said, "Seventeen."

His smiles came in succession like waves breaking on the surface of a little lake. "I see you got a wooden leg," he said. "I think you're real brave. I think you're real sweet."

The girl stood blank and solid and silent.

"Walk to the gate with me," he said. "You're a brave sweet little thing and I liked you the minute I seen you walk in the door."

Hulga began to move forward.

"What's your name?" he asked, smiling down on the top of her head.

"Hulga," she said.

"Hulga," he murmured, "Hulga. Hulga. I never heard of anybody name Hulga before. You're shy, aren't you, Hulga?" he asked.

She nodded, watching his large red hand on the handle of the giant valise.

"I like girls that wear glasses," he said. "I think a lot. I'm not like these people that a serious thought don't ever enter their heads. It's because I may die."

"I may die too," she said suddenly and looked up at him. His eyes were very small and brown, glittering feverishly.

"Listen," he said, "don't you think some people was meant to meet on account of what all they got in common and all? Like they both think serious thoughts and all?" He shifted the valise to his other hand so that the hand nearest her was free. He caught hold of her elbow and shook it a little. "I don't work on Saturday," he said. "I like to walk in the woods and see what Mother Nature is wearing. O'er the hills and far away. Picnics and things. Couldn't we go on a picnic tomorrow? Say yes, Hulga," he said and gave her a dying look as if he felt his insides about to drop out of him. He had even seemed to sway slightly toward her.

During the night she had imagined that she seduced him. She imagined that the two of them walked on the place until they came to the storage barn beyond the two back fields and there, she imagined, that things came to such a pass that she very easily seduced him and that then, of course, she had to reckon with his remorse. True genius can get an idea across even to an inferior mind. She imagined that she took his remorse in hand and changed it into a deeper understanding of life. She took all his shame away and turned it into something useful.

She set off for the gate at exactly ten o'clock, escaping without drawing Mrs. Hopewell's attention. She didn't take anything to eat, forgetting that food is usually taken on a picnic. She wore a pair of slacks and a dirty white shirt, and as an afterthought, she had put some Vapex on the collar of it since she did not own any perfume. When she reached the gate no one was there.

She looked up and down the empty highway and had the furious feeling that she had been tricked, that he had only meant to make her walk to the gate after the idea of him. Then suddenly he stood up very tall, from behind a bush on the opposite embankment. Smiling, he lifted his hat which was new and wide-brimmed. He had not worn it yesterday and she wondered if he had bought it for the occasion. It was toast-colored with a red and white band around it and was slightly too large for him. He stepped from behind the bush still carrying the black valise. He had on the same suit and the same yellow socks sucked down in his shoes from walking. He crossed the highway and said, "I knew you'd come!"

The girl wondered acidly how he had known this. She pointed to the valise and asked, "Why did you bring your Bibles?"

He took her elbow, smiling down on her as if he could not stop. "You can never tell when you'll need the word of God, Hulga," he said. She had a moment in which she doubted that this was actually happening and then they began to climb the embankment. They went down into the pasture toward the woods. The boy walked lightly by her side, bouncing on his toes. The valise did not seem to be heavy today; he even swung it. They crossed half the pasture without saying anything and then, putting his hand easily on the small of her back, he asked softly, "Where does your wooden leg join on?"

She turned an ugly red and glared at him and for an instant the boy looked abashed. "I didn't mean you no harm," he said. "I only meant you're so brave and all. I guess God takes care of you."

"No," she said, looking forward and walking fast, "I don't even believe in God."

At this he stopped and whistled. "No!" he exclaimed as if he were too astonished to say anything else.

She walked on and in a second he was bouncing at her side, fanning with his hat. "That's very unusual for a girl," he remarked, watching her out of the corner of his eye. When they reached the edge of the wood, he put his hand on her back again and drew her against him without a word and kissed her heavily.

The kiss, which had more pressure than feeling behind it, produced that extra surge of adrenalin in the girl that enables one to carry a packed trunk out of a burning house, but in her, the power went at once to the brain. Even before he released her, her mind, clear and detached and ironic anyway, was regarding him from a great distance, with amusement but with pity. She had never been kissed before and she was pleased to discover that it was an unexceptional experience and all a matter of the mind's control. Some people might enjoy drain water if they were told it was vodka. When the boy, looking expectant but uncertain, pushed her gently away, she turned and walked on, saying nothing as if such business, for her, were common enough.

He came along panting at her side, trying to help her when he saw a root that she might trip over. He caught and held back the long swaying blades of thorn vine until she had passed beyond them. She led the way and he came breathing heavily behind her. Then they came out on a sunlit hillside, sloping softly into another one a little smaller. Beyond, they could see the rusted top of the old barn where the extra hay was stored.

The hill was sprinkled with small pink weeds. "Then you ain't saved?" he asked suddenly, stopping.

The girl smiled. It was the first time she had smiled at him at all. "In my economy," she said, "I'm saved and you are damned but I told you I didn't believe in God."

Nothing seemed to destroy the boy's look of admiration. He gazed at her now as if the fantastic animal at the zoo had put its paw through the bars and given him a loving poke. She thought he looked as if he wanted to kiss her again and she walked on before he had the chance.

"Ain't there somewheres we can sit down sometime?" he murmured, his voice softening toward the end of the sentence.

"In that barn," she said.

They made for it rapidly as if it might slide away like a train. It was a large two-story barn, cool and dark inside. The boy pointed up the ladder that led into the loft and said, "It's too bad we can't go up there."

"Why can't we?" she asked.

"Yer leg," he said reverently.

The girl gave him a contemptuous look and putting both hands on the ladder, she climbed it while he stood below, apparently awestruck. She pulled herself expertly through the opening and then looked down at him and said. "Well, come on if you're coming," and he began to climb the ladder, awkwardly bringing the suitcase with him.

"We won't need the Bible," she observed.

"You never can tell," he said, panting. After he had got into the loft, he was a few seconds catching his breath. She had sat down in a pile of straw. A wide sheath of sunlight, filled with dust particles, slanted over her. She lay back against a bale, her face turned away, looking out the front opening of the barn where hay was thrown from a wagon into the loft. The two pink-speckled hillsides lay back against a dark ridge of woods. The sky was cloudless and cold blue. The boy dropped down by her side and put one arm under her and the other over her and began methodically kissing her face, making little noises like a fish. He did not remove his hat but it was pushed far enough back not to interfere. When her glasses got in his way, he took them off of her and slipped them into his pocket.

The girl at first did not return any of the kisses but presently she began to and after she had put several on his cheek, she reached his lips and remained there, kissing him again and again as if she were trying to draw all the breath out of him. His breath was clear and sweet like a child's and the kisses were sticky like a child's. He mumbled about loving her and about knowing when he first seen her that he loved her, but the mumbling was like the sleepy fretting of a child being put to sleep by his mother. Her mind, throughout this, never stopped or lost itself for a second to her feelings. "You ain't said you loved me none," he whispered finally, pulling back from her. "You got to say that."

She looked away from him off into the hollow sky and then down at a black ridge and then down farther into what appeared to be two green swelling lakes. She didn't realize he had taken her glasses but this landscape could not seem exceptional to her for she seldom paid any close attention to her surroundings.

"You got to say it," he repeated. "You got to say you love me."

She was always careful how she committed herself. "In a sense," she began, "if you use the word loosely, you might say that. But it's not a word I use. I don't have illusions. I'm one of those people who see *through* to nothing."

The boy was frowning. "You got to say it. I said it and you got to say it," he said.

The girl looked at him almost tenderly. "You poor baby," she murmured. "It's just as well you don't understand," and she pulled him by the neck, face-down, against her. "We are all damned," she said, "but some of us have taken off our blindfolds and see that there's nothing to see. It's a kind of salvation."

The boy's astonished eyes looked blankly through the ends of her hair. "Okay," he almost whined, "but do you love me or don'tcher?"

"Yes," she said and added, "in a sense. But I must tell you something. There mustn't be anything dishonest between us." She lifted his head and looked him in the eye. "I am thirty years old," she said. "I have a number of degrees."

The boy's look was irritated but dogged. "I don't care," he said. "I don't care a thing about what all you done. I just want to know if you love me or don'tcher?" and he caught her to him and wildly planted her face with kisses until she said, "Yes, yes."

"Okay then," he said, letting her go. "Prove it."

She smiled, looking dreamily out on the shifty landscape. She had seduced him without even making up her mind to try. "How?" she asked, feeling that he should be delayed a little.

He leaned over and put his lips to her ear. "Show me where your wooden leg joins on," he whispered.

The girl uttered a sharp little cry and her face instantly drained of color. The obscenity of the suggestion was not what shocked her. As a child she had sometimes been subject to feelings of shame but education had removed the last traces of that as a good surgeon scrapes for cancer; she would no more have felt it over what he was asking than she would have believed in his Bible. But she was as sensitive about the artificial leg as a peacock about his tail. No one ever touched it but her. She took care of it as someone else would his soul, in private and almost with her own eyes turned away. "No," she said.

"I known it," he muttered, sitting up. "You're just playing me for a sucker."

"Oh no no!" she cried. "It joins on at the knee. Only at the knee. Why do you want to see it?"

The boy gave her a long penetrating look. "Because," he said, "it's what makes you different. You ain't like anybody else."

She sat staring at him. There was nothing about her face or her round freezing-blue eyes to indicate that this had moved her; but she felt as if her heart had stopped and left her mind to pump her blood. She decided that for the first time in her life she was face to face with real innocence. This boy, with an instinct that came from beyond wisdom, had touched the truth about her. When after a minute, she said in a hoarse high voice, "All right," it was like surrendering to him completely. It was like losing her own life and finding it again, miraculously, in his.

Very gently he began to roll the slack leg up. The artificial limb, in a white sock and brown flat shoe, was bound in a heavy material like canvas and ended in an ugly jointure where it was attached to the stump. The boy's face and his voice were entirely reverent as he uncovered it and said, "Now show me how to take it off and on."

She took it off for him and put it back on again and then he took it off himself, handling it as tenderly as if it were a real one. "See!" he said with a delighted child's face. "Now I can do it myself!"

"Put it back on," she said. She was thinking that she would run away with him and that every night he would take the leg off and every morning put it back on again. "Put it back on," she said.

"Not yet," he murmured, setting it on its foot out of her reach. "Leave it off for awhile. You got me instead."

She gave a little cry of alarm but he pushed her down and began to kiss her again. Without the leg she felt entirely dependent on him. Her brain seemed to have stopped thinking altogether and to be about some other function that it was not very good at. Different expressions raced back and forth over her face. Every now and then the boy, his eyes like two steel spikes, would glance behind him, where the leg stood. Finally she pushed him off and said, "Put it back on me now."

"Wait," he said. He leaned the other way and pulled the valise toward him and opened it. It had a pale blue spotted lining and there were only two Bibles in it. He took one of these out and opened the cover of it. It was hollow and contained a pocket flask of whiskey, a pack of cards, and a small blue box with printing on it. He laid these out in front of her one at a time in an evenly-spaced row, like one presenting offerings at the shrine of a goddess. He put the blue box in her hand. THIS PRODUCT TO BE USED ONLY FOR THE PREVENTION OF DISEASE, she read, and dropped it. The boy was unscrewing the top of the flask. He stopped and pointed, with a smile, to the deck of cards. It was not an ordinary deck but one with an obscene picture on the back of each card. "Take a swig," he said, offering her the bottle first. He held it in front of her, but like one mesmerized, she did not move.

Her voice when she spoke had an almost pleading sound. "Aren't you," she murmured, "aren't you just good country people?"

The boy cocked his head. He looked as if he were just beginning to understand that she might be trying to insult him. "Yeah," he said, curling his lip slightly, "but it ain't held me back none. I'm as good as you any day in the week."

"Give me my leg," she said.

He pushed it farther away with his foot. "Come on now, let's begin to have us a good time," he said coaxingly. "We ain't got to know one another good yet."

"Give me my leg!" she screamed and tried to lunge for it but he pushed her down easily.

"What's the matter with you all of a sudden?" he asked, frowning as he screwed the top on the flask and put it quickly back inside the Bible. "You just a while ago said you didn't believe in nothing. I thought you was some girl!"

Her face was almost purple. "You're a Christian!" she hissed. "You're a fine Christian! You're just like them all—say one thing and do another. You're a perfect Christian, you're . . ."

The boy's mouth was set angrily. "I hope you don't think," he said in a lofty indignant tone, "that I believe in that crap! I may sell Bibles but I know which end is up and I wasn't born yesterday and I know where I'm going!"

"Give me my leg!" she screeched. He jumped up so quickly that she barely saw him sweep the cards and the blue box back into the Bible and throw the Bible into the valise. She saw him grab the leg and then she saw it for an instant slanted forlornly across the inside of the suitcase with a Bible at either side of its opposite ends. He slammed the lid shut and snatched up the valise and swung it down the hole and then stepped through himself.

When all of him had passed but his head, he turned and regarded her with a look that no longer had any admiration in it. "I've gotten a lot of interesting things," he said. "One time I got a woman's glass eye this way. And you needn't to think you'll catch me because Pointer ain't really my name. I use a different name at every house I call at and don't stay nowhere long. And I'll tell you another thing, Hulga," he said, using the name as if he didn't think much of it, "you ain't so smart. I been believing in nothing ever since I was born!" and then the toast-colored hat disappeared down the hole and the girl was left, sitting on the straw in the dusty sunlight. When she turned her churning face toward the opening, she saw his blue figure struggling successfully over the green speckled lake.

Mrs. Hopewell and Mrs. Freeman, who were in the back pasture, digging up onions, saw him emerge a little later from the woods and head across the meadow toward the highway. "Why, that looks like that nice dull young man that tried to sell me a Bible yesterday," Mrs. Hopewell said, squinting. "He must have been selling them to the Negroes back in there. He was so simple," she said, "but I guess the world would be better off if we were all that simple."

Mrs. Freeman's gaze drove forward and just touched him before he disappeared under the hill. Then she returned her attention to the evil-smelling onion shoot she was lifting from the ground. "Some can't be that simple," she said. "I know I never could."

(1955)

James Baldwin *1924–*

SONNY'S BLUES

I read about it in the paper, in the subway, on my way to work. I read it, and I couldn't believe it, and I read it again. Then perhaps I just stared at it, at the newsprint spelling out his name, spelling out the story. I stared at it in the swinging lights of the subway car, and in the faces and bodies of the people, and in my own face, trapped in the darkness which roared outside.

It was not to be believed and I kept telling myself that, as I walked from the subway station to the high school. And at the same time I couldn't doubt it. I was scared, scared for Sonny. He became real to me again. A great block of ice got settled in my belly and kept melting there slowly all day long, while I taught my classes algebra. It was a special kind of ice. It kept melting, sending trickles of ice water all up and down my veins, but it never got less. Sometimes it hardened and seemed to expand until I felt my guts were going to come spilling out or that I was going to choke or scream. This would always be at a moment when I was remembering some specific thing Sonny had once said or done.

When he was about as old as the boys in my classes his face had been bright and open, there was a lot of copper in it; and he'd had wonderfully direct brown eyes, and great gentleness and privacy. I wondered what he looked like now. He had been picked up, the evening before, in a raid on an apartment downtown, for peddling and using heroin.

I couldn't believe it: but what I mean by that is that I couldn't find any room for it anywhere inside me. I had kept it outside me for a long time. I hadn't wanted to know. I had had suspicions, but I didn't name them, I kept putting them away. I told myself that Sonny was wild, but he wasn't crazy. And he'd always been a good boy, he hadn't ever turned hard or evil or disrespectful, the way kids can, so quick, so quick, especially in Harlem. I didn't want to believe that I'd ever see my brother going down, coming to nothing, all that light in his face gone out, in the condition I'd already seen so many others. Yet it had happened and here I was, talking about algebra to a lot of boys who might, every one of them for all I knew, be popping off needles every time they went to the head. Maybe it did more for them than algebra could.

I was sure that the first time Sonny had ever had horse, he couldn't have been much older than these boys were now. These boys, now, were living as we'd been living then, they were growing up with a rush and their heads bumped abruptly against the low ceiling of their actual possibilities. They were filled with rage. All they really knew were two darknesses, the darkness of their lives, which was now closing in on them, and the darkness of the movies, which had blinded them to that other darkness, and in which they now, vindictively, dreamed, at once more together than they were at any other time, and more alone.

When the last bell rang, the last class ended, I let out my breath. It seemed I'd been holding it for all that time. My clothes were wet—I may have looked as though I'd been sitting in a steam bath, all dressed up, all afternoon. I sat alone in the classroom a long time. I listened to the boys outside, downstairs, shouting and cursing and laughing. Their laughter struck me for perhaps the first time. It was not the joyous laughter which— God knows why—one associates with children. It was mocking and insular, its intent was to denigrate. It was disenchanted, and in this, also, lay the authority of their curses. Perhaps I was listening to them because I was thinking about my brother and in them I heard my brother. And myself.

One boy was whistling a tune, at once very complicated and very simple, it seemed to be pouring out of him as though he were a bird, and it sounded very cool and moving through all that harsh, bright air, only just holding its own through all those other sounds.

I stood up and walked over to the window and looked down into the courtyard. It was the beginning of the spring and the sap was rising in the boys. A teacher passed through them every now and again, quickly, as though he or she couldn't wait to get out of that courtyard, to get those boys out of their sight and off their minds. I started collecting my stuff. I thought I'd better get home and talk to Isabel.

The courtyard was almost deserted by the time I got downstairs. I saw this boy standing in the shadow of a doorway, looking just like Sonny. I almost called his name. Then I saw that it wasn't Sonny, but somebody we used to know, a boy from around our block. He'd been Sonny's friend. He'd never been mine, having been too young for me, and, anyway, I'd never liked him. And now, even though he was a grown-up man, he still hung around that block, still spent hours on the street corners, was always high and raggy. I used to run into him from time to time and he'd often work around to asking me for a quarter or fifty cents. He always had some real good excuse, too, and I always gave it to him. I don't know why.

But now, abruptly, I hated him. I couldn't stand the way he looked at me, partly like a dog, partly like a cunning child. I wanted to ask him what the hell he was doing in the school courtyard.

He sort of shuffled over to me, and he said, "I see you got the papers. So you already know about it."

"You mean about Sonny? Yes, I already know about it. How come they didn't get you?"

He grinned. It made him repulsive and it also brought to mind what he'd looked like as a kid. "I wasn't there. I stay away from them people."

"Good for you." I offered him a cigarette and I watched him through the smoke. "You come all the way down here just to tell me about Sonny?"

"That's right." He was sort of shaking his head and his eyes looked strange, as though they were about to cross. The bright sun deadened his damp dark brown skin and it made his eyes look yellow and showed up the dirt in his kinked hair. He smelled funky. I moved a little away from him and I said, "Well, thanks. But I already know about it and I got to get home."

"I'll walk you a little ways," he said. We started walking. There were a couple of kids still loitering in the courtyard and one of them said good-night to me and looked strangely at the boy beside me.

"What're you going to do?" he asked me. "I mean, about Sonny?"

"Look. I haven't seen Sonny for over a year, I'm not sure I'm going to do anything. Anyway, what the hell *can* I do?"

"That's right," he said quickly, "ain't nothing you can do. Can't much help old Sonny no more, I guess."

It was what I was thinking and so it seemed to me he had no right to say it.

"I'm surprised at Sonny, though," he went on—he had a funny way of talking, he looked straight ahead as though he were talking to himself—"I thought Sonny was a smart boy, I thought he was too smart to get hung."

"I guess he thought so too," I said sharply, "and that's how he got hung. And how about you? You're pretty goddamn smart, I bet."

Then he looked directly at me, just for a minute. "I ain't smart," he said. "If I was smart, I'd have reached for a pistol a long time ago."

"Look. Don't tell *me* your sad story, if it was up to me, I'd give you one." Then I felt guilty—guilty, probably, for never having supposed that the poor bastard *had* a story of his own, much less a sad one, and I asked, quickly, "What's going to happen to him now?"

He didn't answer this. He was off by himself some place.

"Funny thing," he said, and from his tone we might have been discussing the quickest way to get to Brooklyn, "when I saw the papers this morning, the first thing I asked myself was if I had anything to do with it. I felt sort of responsible."

I began to listen more carefully. The subway station was on the corner, just before us, and I stopped. He stopped, too. We were in front of a bar and he ducked slightly, peering in, but whoever he was looking for didn't seem to be there. The juke box was blasting away with something black and bouncy and I half watched the barmaid as she danced her way from the juke box to her place behind the bar. And I watched her face as she laughingly responded to something someone said to her, still keeping time to the music. When she smiled one saw the little girl, one sensed the doomed, still struggling woman beneath the battered face of the semi-whore.

"I never *give* Sonny nothing," the boy said finally, "but a long time ago I come to school high and Sonny asked me how it felt." He paused, I couldn't bear to watch him, I watched the barmaid, and I listened to the music which seemed to be causing the pavement to shake. "I told him it felt great." The music stopped, the barmaid paused and watched the juke box until the music began again. "It did."

All this was carrying me some place I didn't want to go. I certainly didn't want to know how it felt. It filled everything, the people, the houses, the music, the dark, quicksilver barmaid, with menace; and this menace was their reality.

"What's going to happen to him now?" I asked again.

"They'll send him away some place and they'll try to cure him." He shook his head. "Maybe he'll even think he's kicked the habit. Then they'll let him loose"—he gestured, throwing his cigarette into the gutter. "That's all."

"What do you mean, that's *all*?"

But I knew what he meant.

"I *mean*, that's *all*." He turned his head and looked at me, pulling down the corners of his mouth. "Don't you know what I mean?" he asked, softly.

"How the hell *would* I know what you mean?" I almost whispered it, I don't know why.

"That's right," he said to the air, "how would *he* know what I mean?" He turned toward me again, patient and calm, and yet I somehow felt him shaking, shaking as though he were going to fall apart. I felt that ice in my guts again, the dread I'd felt all afternoon; and again I watched the barmaid, moving about the bar, washing glasses, and singing. "Listen. They'll let him out and then it'll just start all over again. That's what I mean."

"You mean—they'll let him out. And then he'll just start working his way back in again. You mean he'll never kick the habit. Is that what you mean?"

"That's right," he said, cheerfully. "*You* see what I mean."

"Tell me," I said at last, "why does he want to die? He must want to die, he's killing himself, why does he want to die?"

He looked at me in surprise. He licked his lips. "He don't want to die. He wants to live. Don't nobody want to die, ever."

Then I wanted to ask him—too many things. He could not have answered, or if he had, I could not have borne the answers. I started walking. "Well, I guess it's none of my business."

"It's going to be rough on old Sonny," he said. We reached the subway station. "This is your station?" he asked. I nodded. I took one step down. "Damn!" he said, suddenly. I looked up at him. He grinned again. "Damn it if I didn't leave all my money home. You ain't got a dollar on you, have you? Just for a couple of days, is all."

All at once something inside gave and threatened to come pouring out of me. I didn't hate him any more. I felt that in another moment I'd start crying like a child.

"Sure," I said. "Don't sweat." I looked in my wallet and didn't have a dollar, I only had a five. "Here," I said. "That hold you?"

He didn't look at it—he didn't want to look at it. A terrible, closed look came over his face, as though he were keeping the number on the bill a secret from him and me. "Thanks," he said, and now he was dying to see me go. "Don't worry about Sonny. Maybe I'll write him or something."

"Sure," I said. "You do that. So long."

"Be seeing you," he said. I went on down the steps.

And I didn't write Sonny or send him anything for a long time. When I finally did, it was just after my little girl died, and he wrote me back a letter which made me feel like a bastard.

Here's what he said:

Dear brother,

You don't know how much I needed to hear from you. I wanted to write you many a time but I dug how much I must have hurt you and so I didn't write. But now I feel like a man who's been trying to climb up out of some deep, real deep and funky hole and just saw the sun up there, outside. I got to get outside.

I can't tell you much about how I got here. I mean I don't know how to tell you. I guess I was afraid of something or I was trying to escape from something and you know I have never been very strong in the head (smile). I'm glad Mama and Daddy are dead and can't see what's happened to their son and I swear if I'd known what I was doing I would never have hurt you so, you and a lot of other fine people who were nice to me and who believed in me.

I don't want you to think it had anything to do with me being a musician. It's more than that. Or maybe less than that. I can't get anything straight in my head down here and I try not to think about what's going to happen to me when I get outside again. Sometime I think I'm going to flip and *never* get outside and sometime I think I'll come straight back. I tell you one thing, though, I'd rather blow my brains out than go through this again. But that's what they all say, so they tell me. If I tell you when I'm coming to New York and if you could meet me, I sure would appreciate it. Give my love to Isabel and the kids and I was sure sorry to hear about little Gracie. I wish I could be like Mama and say the Lord's will be done, but I don't know it seems to me that trouble is the one thing that never does get stopped and I don't know what good it does to blame it on the Lord. But maybe it does some good if you believe it.

Your brother,
Sonny

Then I kept in constant touch with him and I sent him whatever I could and I went to meet him when he came back to New York. When I saw him many things I thought I had forgotten came flooding back to me. This was because I had begun, finally, to wonder about Sonny, about the life that Sonny lived inside. This life, whatever it was, had made him older and thinner and it had deepened the distant stillness in which he had always moved. He looked very unlike my baby brother. Yet, when he smiled, when we shook hands, the baby brother I'd never known looked out from the depths of his private life, like an animal waiting to be coaxed into the light.

"How you been keeping?" he asked me.

"All right. And you?"

"Just fine." He was smiling all over his face. "It's good to see you again."

"It's good to see you."

The seven years' difference in our ages lay between us like a chasm: I wondered if these years would ever operate between us as a bridge. I was remembering, and it made it hard to catch my breath, that I had been there when he was born; and I had heard the first words he had ever spoken. When he started to walk, he walked from our mother straight to me. I caught him just before he fell when he took the first steps he ever took in this world.

"How's Isabel?"

"Just fine. She's dying to see you."

"And the boys?"

"They're fine, too. They're anxious to see their uncle."

"Oh, come on. You know they don't remember me."

"Are you kidding? Of course they remember you."

He grinned again. We got into a taxi. We had a lot to say to each other, far too much to know how to begin.

As the taxi began to move, I asked, "You still want to go to India?"

He laughed. "You still remember that. Hell, no. This place is Indian enough for me."

"It used to belong to them," I said.

And he laughed again. "They damn sure knew what they were doing when they got rid of it."

Years ago, when he was around fourteen, he'd been all hipped on the idea of going to India. He read books about people sitting on rocks, naked, in all kinds of weather, but mostly bad, naturally, and walking barefoot through hot coals and arriving at wisdom. I used to say that it sounded to me as though they were getting away from wisdom as fast as they could. I think he sort of looked down on me for that.

"Do you mind," he asked, "if we have the driver drive alongside the park? On the west side—I haven't seen the city in so long."

"Of course not," I said. I was afraid that I might sound as though I were humoring him, but I hoped he wouldn't take it that way.

So we drove along, between the green of the park and the stony, lifeless elegance of hotels and apartment buildings, toward the vivid, killing streets of our childhood. These streets hadn't changed, though housing projects jutted up out of them now like rocks in the middle of a boiling sea. Most of the houses in which we had grown up had vanished, as had the stores from which we had stolen, the basements in which we had first tried sex, the rooftops from which we had hurled tin cans and bricks. But houses exactly like the houses of our past yet dominated the landscape, boys exactly like the boys we once had been found themselves smothering in these houses, came down into the streets for light and air and found themselves encircled by disaster. Some escaped the trap, most didn't. Those who got out always left something of themselves behind, as some animals amputate a leg and leave it in the trap. It might be said, perhaps, that I had escaped, after all, I was a school teacher; or that Sonny had, he hadn't lived in Harlem for years. Yet, as the cab moved uptown through streets which seemed, with a rush, to darken with dark people, and as I covertly studied Sonny's face, it came to me that what we both were seeking through our separate cab windows was that part of ourselves which had been left behind. It's always at the hour of trouble and confrontation that the missing member aches.

We hit 110th Street and started rolling up Lenox Avenue. And I'd known this avenue all my life, but it seemed to me again, as it had seemed on the day I'd first heard about Sonny's trouble, filled with a hidden menace which was its very breath of life.

"We almost there," said Sonny.

"Almost." We were both too nervous to say anything more.

We live in a housing project. It hasn't been up long. A few days after it was up it seemed uninhabitably new, now, of course, it's already run-

down. It looks like a parody of the good, clean, faceless life—God knows
the people who live in it do their best to make it a parody. The beat-
looking grass lying around isn't enough to make their lives green, the
hedges will never hold out the streets, and they know it. The big windows
fool no one, they aren't big enough to make space out of no space. They
don't bother with the windows, they watch the TV screen instead. The
playground is most popular with the children who don't play at jacks,
or skip rope, or roller skate, or swing, and they can be found in it after
dark. We moved in partly because it's not too far from where I teach,
and partly for the kids; but it's really just like the houses in which Sonny
and I grew up. The same things happen, they'll have the same things to
remember. The moment Sonny and I started into the house I had the
feeling that I was simply bringing him back into the danger he had almost
died trying to escape.

Sonny has never been talkative. So I don't know why I was sure he'd
be dying to talk to me when supper was over the first night. Everything
went fine, the oldest boy remembered him, and the youngest boy liked
him, and Sonny had remembered to bring something for each of them;
and Isabel, who is really much nicer than I am, more open and giving,
had gone to a lot of trouble about dinner and was genuinely glad to see
him. And she's always been able to tease Sonny in a way that I haven't.
It was nice to see her face so vivid again and to hear her laugh and watch
her make Sonny laugh. She wasn't, or, anyway, she didn't seem to be, at
all uneasy or embarrassed. She chatted as though there were no subject
which had to be avoided and she got Sonny past his first, faint stiffness.
And thank God she was there, for I was filled with that icy dread again.
Everything I did seemed awkward to me, and everything I said sounded
freighted with hidden meaning. I was trying to remember everything I'd
heard about dope addiction and I couldn't help watching Sonny for signs.
I wasn't doing it out of malice. I was trying to find out something about
my brother. I was dying to hear him tell me he was safe.

"Safe!" my father grunted, whenever Mama suggested trying to move
to a neighborhood which might be safer for children. "Safe, hell! Ain't
no place safe for kids, nor nobody."

He always went on like this, but he wasn't, ever, really as bad as he
sounded, not even on weekends, when he got drunk. As a matter of fact,
he was always on the lookout for "something a little better," but he died
before he found it. He died suddenly, during a drunken weekend in the
middle of the war, when Sonny was fifteen. He and Sonny hadn't ever
got on too well. And this was partly because Sonny was the apple of his
father's eye. It was because he loved Sonny so much and was frightened
for him, that he was always fighting with him. It doesn't do any good to
fight with Sonny. Sonny just moves back, inside himself, where he can't
be reached. But the principal reason that they never hit it off is that they
were so much alike. Daddy was big and rough and loud-talking, just the
opposite of Sonny, but they both had—that same privacy.

Mama tried to tell me something about this, just after Daddy died. I
was home on leave from the army.

This was the last time I ever saw my mother alive. Just the same, this picture gets all mixed up in my mind with pictures I had of her when she was younger. The way I always see her is the way she used to be on a Sunday afternoon, say, when the old folks were talking after the big Sunday dinner. I always see her wearing pale blue. She'd be sitting on the sofa. And my father would be sitting in the easy chair, not far from her. And the living room would be full of church folks and relatives. There they sit, in chairs all around the living room, and the night is creeping up outside, but nobody knows it yet. You can see the darkness growing against the windowpanes and you hear the street noises every now and again, or maybe the jangling beat of a tambourine from one of the churches close by, but it's real quiet in the room. For a moment nobody's talking, but every face looks darkening, like the sky outside. And my mother rocks a little from the waist, and my father's eyes are closed. Everyone is looking at something a child can't see. For a minute they've forgotten the children. Maybe a kid is lying on the rug, half asleep. Maybe somebody's got a kid in his lap and is absentmindedly stroking the kid's head. Maybe there's a kid, quiet and big-eyed, curled up in a big chair in the corner. The silence, the darkness coming, and the darkness in the faces frighten the child obscurely. He hopes that the hand which strokes his forehead will never stop—will never die. He hopes that there will never come a time when the old folks won't be sitting around the living room, talking about where they've come from, and what they've seen, and what's happened to them and their kinfolk.

But something deep and watchful in the child knows that this is bound to end, is already ending. In a moment someone will get up and turn on the light. Then the old folks will remember the children and they won't talk any more that day. And when light fills the room, the child is filled with darkness. He knows that every time this happens he's moved just a little closer to that darkness outside. The darkness outside is what the old folks have been talking about. It's what they've come from. It's what they endure. The child knows that they won't talk any more because if he knows too much about what's happened to *them*, he'll know too much too soon, about what's going to happen to *him*.

The last time I talked to my mother, I remember I was restless. I wanted to get out and see Isabel. We weren't married then and we had a lot to straighten out between us.

There Mama sat, in black, by the window. She was humming an old church song, *Lord, you brought me from a long ways off*. Sonny was out somewhere. Mama kept watching the streets.

"I don't know," she said, "if I'll ever see you again, after you go off from here. But I hope you'll remember the things I tried to teach you."

"Don't talk like that," I said, and smiled. "You'll be here a long time yet."

She smiled, too, but she said nothing. She was quiet for a long time. And I said, "Mama, don't you worry about nothing. I'll be writing all the time, and you be getting the checks. . . ."

"I want to talk to you about your brother," she said, suddenly. "If anything happens to me he ain't going to have nobody to look out for him."

"Mama," I said, "ain't nothing going to happen to you *or* Sonny. Sonny's all right. He's a good boy and he's got good sense."

"It ain't a question of his being a good boy," Mama said, "nor of his having good sense. It ain't only the bad ones, nor yet the dumb ones that gets sucked under." She stopped, looking at me. "Your Daddy once had a brother," she said, and she smiled in a way that made me feel she was in pain. "You didn't never know that, did you?"

"No," I said, "I never knew that," and I watched her face.

"Oh, yes," she said, "your Daddy had a brother." She looked out of the window again. "I know you never saw your Daddy cry. But *I* did— many a time, through all these years."

I asked her, "What happened to his brother? How come nobody's ever talked about him?"

This was the first time I ever saw my mother look old.

"His brother got killed," she said, "when he was just a little younger than you are now. I knew him. He was a fine boy. He was maybe a little full of the devil, but he didn't mean nobody no harm."

Then she stopped and the room was silent, exactly as it had sometimes been on those Sunday afternoons. Mama kept looking out into the streets.

"He used to have a job in the mill," she said, "and, like all young folks, he just liked to perform on Saturday nights. Saturday nights, him and your father would drift around to different places, go to dances and things like that, or just sit around with people they knew, and your father's brother would sing, he had a fine voice, and play along with himself on his guitar. Well, this particular Saturday night, him and your father was coming home from some place, and they were both a little drunk and there was a moon that night, it was bright like day. Your father's brother was feeling kind of good, and he was whistling to himself, and he had his guitar slung over his shoulder. They was coming down a hill and beneath them was a road that turned off from the highway. Well, your father's brother, being always kind of frisky, decided to run down this hill, and he did, with that guitar banging and clanging behind him, and he ran across the road, and he was making water behind a tree. And your father was sort of amused at him and he was still coming down the hill, kind of slow. Then he heard a car motor and that same minute his brother stepped from behind the tree, into the road, in the moonlight. And he started to cross the road. And your father started to run down the hill, he says he don't know why. This car was full of white men. They was all drunk, and when they seen your father's brother they let out a great whoop and holler and they aimed the car straight at him. They was having fun, they ;ust wanted to scare him, the way they do sometimes, you know. But they was drunk. And I guess the boy, being drunk, too, and scared, kind of lost his head. By the time he jumped it was too late. Your father says he heard his brother scream when the car rolled over him, and he heard the wood of that guitar when it give, and he heard them strings go flying, and he heard them white men shouting, and the car kept on a-going and it ain't stopped till this day. And, time your father got down the hill, his brother weren't nothing but blood and pulp."

Tears were gleaming on my mother's face. There wasn't anything I could say.

"He never mentioned it," she said, "because I never let him mention it before you children. Your Daddy was like a crazy man that night and for many a night thereafter. He says he never in his life seen anything as dark as that road after the lights of that car had gone away. Weren't nothing, weren't nobody on that road, just your Daddy and his brother and that busted guitar. Oh, yes. Your Daddy never did really get right again. Till the day he died he weren't sure but that every white man he saw was the man that killed his brother."

She stopped and took out her handkerchief and dried her eyes and looked at me.

"I ain't telling you all this," she said, "to make you scared or bitter or to make you hate nobody. I'm telling you this because you got a brother. And the world ain't changed."

I guess I didn't want to believe this. I guess she saw this in my face. She turned away from me, toward the window again, searching those streets.

"But I praise my Redeemer," she said at last, "that He called your Daddy home before me. I ain't saying it to throw no flowers at myself, but, I declare, it keeps me from feeling too cast down to know I helped your father get safely through this world. Your father always acted like he was the roughest, strongest man on earth. And everybody took him to be like that. But if he hadn't had me there—to see his tears!"

She was crying again. Still, I couldn't move. I said, "Lord, Lord, Mama, I didn't know it was like that."

"Oh, honey," she said, "there's a lot that you don't know. But you are going to find out." She stood up from the window and came over to me. "You got to hold on to your brother," she said, "and don't let him fall, no matter what it looks like is happening to him and no matter how evil you gets with him. You going to be evil with him many a time. But don't you forget what I told you, you hear?"

"I won't forget," I said. "Don't you worry, I won't forget. I won't let nothing happen to Sonny."

My mother smiled as though she were amused at something she saw in my face. Then, "You may not be able to stop nothing from happening. But you got to let him know you's *there*."

Two days later I was married, and then I was gone. And I had a lot of things on my mind and I pretty well forgot my promise to Mama until I got shipped home on a special furlough for her funeral.

And, after the funeral, with just Sonny and me alone in the empty kitchen, I tried to find out something about him.

"What do you want to do?" I asked him.

"I'm going to be a musician," he said.

For he had graduated, in the time I had been away, from dancing to the juke box to finding out who was playing what, and what they were doing with it, and he had bought himself a set of drums.

"You mean, you want to be a drummer?" I somehow had the feeling that being a drummer might be all right for other people but not for my brother Sonny.

"I don't think," he said, looking at me very gravely, "that I'll ever be a good drummer. But I think I can play a piano."

I frowned. I'd never played the role of the older brother quite so seriously before, had scarcely ever, in fact, *asked* Sonny a damn thing. I sensed myself in the presence of something I didn't really know how to handle, didn't understand. So I made my frown a little deeper as I asked: "What kind of musician do you want to be?"

He grinned. "How many kinds do you think there are?"

"Be *serious*," I said.

He laughed, throwing his head back, and then looked at me. "I *am* serious."

"Well, then, for Christ's sake, stop kidding around and answer a serious question. I mean, do you want to be a concert pianist, you want to play classical music and all that, or—or what?" Long before I finished he was laughing again. "For Christ's *sake*, Sonny!"

He sobered, but with difficulty. "I'm sorry. But you sound so—*scared!*" and he was off again.

"Well, you may think it's funny now, baby, but it's not going to be so funny when you have to make your living at it, let me tell you *that*." I was furious because I knew he was laughing at me and I didn't know why.

"No," he said, very sober now, and afraid, perhaps, that he'd hurt me, "I don't want to be a classical pianist. That isn't what interests me. I mean"—he paused, looking hard at me, as though his eyes would help me to understand, and then gestured helplessly, as though perhaps his hand would help—"I mean, I'll have a lot of studying to do, and I'll have to study *everything*, but, I mean, I want to play *with*—jazz musicians." He stopped. "I want to play jazz," he said.

Well, the word had never before sounded as heavy, as real, as it sounded that afternoon in Sonny's mouth. I just looked at him and I was probably frowning a real frown by this time. I simply couldn't see why on earth he'd want to spend his time hanging around nightclubs, clowning around on bandstands, while people pushed each other around a dance floor. It seemed—beneath him, somehow. I had never thought about it before, had never been forced to, but I suppose I had always put jazz musicians in a class with what Daddy called "good-time people."

"Are you *serious?*"

"Hell, *yes*, I'm serious."

He looked more helpless than ever, and annoyed, and deeply hurt.

I suggested, helpfully: "You mean—like Louis Armstrong?"[1]

His face closed as though I'd struck him. "No. I'm not talking about none of that old-time, down home crap."

"Well, look, Sonny, I'm sorry, don't get mad. I just don't altogether get it, that's all. Name somebody—you know, a jazz musician you admire."

"Bird."[2]

"Who?"

"Bird! Charlie Parker! Don't they teach you nothing in the goddamn army?"

I lit a cigarette. I was surprised and then a little amused to discover

[1] Louis "Satchmo" Armstrong (1900–1971), jazz trumpeter, singer, and band leader.
[2] Charlie "Bird" Parker (1920–1955), modern jazz saxophonist and band leader.

that I was trembling. "I've been out of touch," I said. "You'll have to be patient with me. Now. Who's this Parker character?"

"He's just one of the greatest jazz musicians alive," said Sonny, sullenly, his hands in his pockets, his back to me. "Maybe *the* greatest," he added, bitterly, "that's probably why *you* never heard of him."

"All right," I said, "I'm ignorant. I'm sorry. I'll go out and buy all the cat's records right away, all right?"

"It don't," said Sonny, with dignity, "make any difference to me. I don't care what you listen to. Don't do me no favors."

I was beginning to realize that I'd never seen him so upset before. With another part of my mind I was thinking that this would probably turn out to be one of those things kids go through and that I shouldn't make it seem important by pushing it too hard. Still, I didn't think it would do any harm to ask: "Doesn't all this take a lot of time? Can you make a living at it?"

He turned back to me and half leaned, half sat, on the kitchen table. "Everything takes time," he said, "and—well, yes, sure, I can make a living at it. But what I don't seem to be able to make you understand is that it's the only thing I want to do."

"Well, Sonny," I said, gently, "you know people can't always do exactly what they *want* to do—"

"*No,* I don't know that," said Sonny, surprising me. "I think people *ought* to do what they want to do, what else are they alive for?"

"You getting to be a big boy," I said desperately, "it's time you started thinking about your future."

"I'm thinking about my future," said Sonny, grimly. "I think about it all the time."

I gave up. I decided, if he didn't change his mind, that we could always talk about it later. "In the meantime," I said, "you got to finish school." We had already decided that he'd have to move in with Isabel and her folks. I knew this wasn't the ideal arrangement because Isabel's folks are inclined to be dicty[3] and they hadn't especially wanted Isabel to marry me. But I didn't know what else to do. "And we have to get you fixed up at Isabel's."

There was a long silence. He moved from the kitchen table to the window. "That's a terrible idea. You know it yourself."

"Do you have a *better* idea?"

He just walked up and down the kitchen for a minute. He was as tall as I was. He had started to shave. I suddenly had the feeling that I didn't know him at all.

He stopped at the kitchen table and picked up my cigarettes. Looking at me with a kind of mocking, amused defiance, he put one between his lips. "You mind?"

"You smoking already?"

He lit the cigarette and nodded, watching me through the smoke. "I just wanted to see if I'd have the courage to smoke in front of you." He grinned and blew a great cloud of smoke to the ceiling. "It was easy."

[3] Bossy (dictatorial).

He looked at my face. "Come on, now. I bet you was smoking at my age, tell the truth."

I didn't say anything but the truth was on my face, and he laughed. But now there was something very strained in his laugh. "Sure. And I bet that ain't all you was doing."

He was frightening me a little. "Cut the crap," I said. "We already decided that you was going to go and live at Isabel's. Now what's got into you all of a sudden?"

"*You* decided it," he pointed out. "*I* didn't decide nothing." He stopped in front of me, leaning against the stove, arms loosely folded. "Look, brother. I don't want to stay in Harlem no more, I really don't." He was very earnest. He looked at me, then over toward the kitchen window. There was something in his eyes I'd never seen before, some thoughtfulness, some worry all his own. He rubbed the muscle of one arm. "It's time I was getting out of here."

"Where do you want to *go*, Sonny?"

"I want to join the army. Or the navy, I don't care. If I say I'm old enough, they'll believe me."

Then I got mad. It was because I was so scared. "You must be crazy. You goddamn fool, what the hell do you want to go and join the *army* for?"

"I just told you. To get out of Harlem."

"Sonny, you haven't even finished *school*. And if you really want to be a musician, how do you expect to study if you're in the *army*?"

He looked at me, trapped, and in anguish. "There's ways. I might be able to work out some kind of deal. Anyway, I'll have the G.I. Bill when I come out."

"*If* you come out." We stared at each other. "Sonny, please. Be reasonable. I know the setup is far from perfect. But we got to do the best we can."

"I ain't learning nothing in school," he said. "Even when I go." He turned away from me and opened the window and threw his cigarette out into the narrow alley. I watched his back. "At least, I ain't learning nothing you'd want me to learn." He slammed the window so hard I thought the glass would fly out, and turned back to me. "And I'm sick of the stink of these garbage cans!"

"Sonny," I said, "I know how you feel. But if you don't finish school now, you're going to be sorry later that you didn't." I grabbed him by the shoulders. "And you only got another year. It ain't so bad. And I'll come back and I swear I'll help you do *whatever* you want to do. Just try to put up with it till I come back. Will you please do that? For me?"

He didn't answer and he wouldn't look at me.

"Sonny. You hear me?"

He pulled away. "I hear you. But you never hear anything *I* say."

I didn't know what to say to that. He looked out of the window and then back at me. "OK," he said, and sighed. "I'll try."

Then I said, trying to cheer him up a little, "They got a piano at Isabel's. You can practice on it."

And as a matter of fact, it did cheer him up for a minute. "That's right," he said to himself. "I forgot that." His face relaxed a little. But the worry, the thoughtfulness, played on it still, the way shadows play on a face which is staring into the fire.

But I thought I'd never hear the end of that piano. At first, Isabel would write me, saying how nice it was that Sonny was so serious about his music and how, as soon as he came in from school, or wherever he had been when he was supposed to be at school, he went straight to that piano and stayed there until suppertime. And, after supper, he went back to that piano and stayed there until everybody went to bed. He was at the piano all day Saturday and all day Sunday. Then he bought a record player and started playing records. He'd play one record over and over again, all day long sometimes, and he'd improvise along with it on the piano. Or he'd play one section of the record, one chord, one change, one progression, then he'd do it on the piano. Then back to the record. Then back to the piano.

Well, I really don't know how they stood it. Isabel finally confessed that it wasn't like living with a person at all, it was like living with sound. And the sound didn't make any sense to her, didn't make any sense to any of them—naturally. They began, in a way, to be afflicted by this presence that was living in their home. It was as though Sonny were some sort of god, or monster. He moved in an atmosphere which wasn't like theirs at all. They fed him and he ate, he washed himself, he walked in and out of their door; he certainly wasn't nasty or unpleasant or rude, Sonny isn't any of those things; but it was as though he were all wrapped up in some cloud, some fire, some vision all his own; and there wasn't any way to reach him.

At the same time, he wasn't really a man yet, he was still a child, and they had to watch out for him in all kinds of ways. They certainly couldn't throw him out. Neither did they dare to make a great scene about that piano because even they dimly sensed, as I sensed, from so many thousands of miles away, that Sonny was at that piano playing for his life.

But he hadn't been going to school. One day a letter came from the school board and Isabel's mother got it—there had, apparently, been other letters but Sonny had torn them up. This day, when Sonny came in, Isabel's mother showed him the letter and asked where he'd been spending his time. And she finally got it out of him that he'd been down in Greenwich Village, with musicians and other characters, in a white girl's apartment. And this scared her and she started to scream at him and what came up, once she began—though she denies it to this day—was what sacrifices they were making to give Sonny a decent home and how little he appreciated it.

Sonny didn't play the piano that day. By evening, Isabel's mother had calmed down but then there was the old man to deal with, and Isabel herself. Isabel says she did her best to be calm but she broke down and started crying. She says she just watched Sonny's face. She could tell, by watching him, what was happening with him. And what was happening was that they penetrated his cloud, they had reached him. Even if their fingers had been a thousand times more gentle than human fingers ever are, he could hardly help feeling that they had stripped him naked and were spitting on that nakedness. For he also had to see that his presence, that music, which was life or death to him, had been torture for them and that they had endured it, not at all for his sake, but only for mine. And Sonny couldn't take that. He can take it a little better today than he could then but he's still not very good at it and, frankly, I don't know anybody who is.

The silence of the next few days must have been louder than the sound of all the music ever played since time began. One morning, before she went to work, Isabel was in his room for something and she suddenly realized that all of his records were gone. And she knew for certain that he was gone. And he was. He went as far as the navy would carry him. He finally sent me a postcard from some place in Greece and that was the first I knew that Sonny was still alive. I didn't see him any more until we were both back in New York and the war had long been over.

He was a man by then, of course, but I wasn't willing to see it. He came by the house from time to time, but we fought almost every time we met. I didn't like the way he carried himself, loose and dreamlike all the time, and I didn't like his friends, and his music seemed to be merely an excuse for the life he led. It sounded just that weird and disordered.

Then we had a fight, a pretty awful fight, and I didn't see him for months. By and by I looked him up, where he was living, in a furnished room in the Village, and I tried to make it up. But there were lots of other people in the room and Sonny just lay on his bed, and he wouldn't come downstairs with me, and he treated these other people as though they were his family and I weren't. So I got mad and then he got mad, and then I told him that he might just as well be dead as live the way he was living. Then he stood up and he told me not to worry about him any more in life, that he *was* dead as far as I was concerned. Then he pushed me to the door and the other people looked on as though nothing were happening, and he slammed the door behind me. I stood in the hallway, staring at the door. I heard somebody laugh in the room and then the tears came to my eyes. I started down the steps, whistling to keep from crying, I kept whistling to myself, *You going to need me, baby, one of these cold, rainy days.*

I read about Sonny's trouble in the spring. Little Grace died in the fall. She was a beautiful little girl. But she only lived a little over two years. She died of polio and she suffered. She had a slight fever for a couple of days, but it didn't seem like anything and we just kept her in bed. And we would certainly have called the doctor, but the fever dropped, she seemed to be all right. So we thought it had just been a cold. Then, one day, she was up, playing, Isabel was in the kitchen fixing lunch for the two boys when they'd come in from school, and she heard Grace fall down in the living room. When you have a lot of children you don't always start running when one of them falls, unless they start screaming or something. And, this time, Gracie was quiet. Yet, Isabel says that when she heard that *thump* and then that silence, something happened to her to make her afraid. And she ran to the living room and there was little Grace on the floor, all twisted up, and the reason she hadn't screamed was that she couldn't get her breath. And when she did scream, it was the worst sound, Isabel says, that she'd ever heard in all her life, and she still hears it sometimes in her dreams. Isabel will sometimes wake me up with a

low, moaning, strangling sound and I have to be quick to awaken her
and hold her to me and where Isabel is weeping against me seems a mortal
wound.

I think I may have written Sonny the very day that little Grace was
buried. I was sitting in the living room in the dark, by myself, and I
suddenly thought of Sonny. My trouble made his real.

One Saturday afternoon, when Sonny had been living with us, or anyway, been in our house, for nearly two weeks, I found myself wandering
aimlessly about the living room, drinking from a can of beer, and trying
to work up courage to search Sonny's room. He was out, he was usually
out whenever I was home, and Isabel had taken the children to see their
grandparents. Suddenly I was standing still in front of the living room
window, watching Seventh Avenue. The idea of searching Sonny's room
made me still. I scarcely dared to admit to myself what I'd be searching
for. I didn't know what I'd do if I found it. Or if I didn't.

On the sidewalk across from me, near the entrance to a barbecue joint,
some people were holding an old-fashioned revival meeting. The barbecue
cook, wearing a dirty white apron, his conked[4] hair reddish and metallic
in the pale sun, and a cigarette between his lips, stood in the doorway,
watching them. Kids and older people paused in their errands and stood
there, along with some older men and a couple of very tough-looking
women who watched everything that happened on the avenue, as though
they owned it, or were maybe owned by it. Well, they were watching
this, too. The revival was being carried on by three sisters in black, and
a brother. All they had were their voices and their Bibles and a tambourine.
The brother was testifying and while he testified two of the sisters stood
together, seeming to say, amen, and the third sister walked around with
the tambourine outstretched and a couple of people dropped coins into
it. Then the brother's testimony ended and the sister who had been taking
up the collection dumped the coins into her palm and transferred them
to the pocket of her long black robe. Then she raised both hands, striking
the tambourine against the air, and then against one hand, and she started
to sing. And the two other sisters and the brother joined in.

It was strange, suddenly, to watch, though I had been seeing these meetings all my life. So, of course, had everybody else down there. Yet, they
paused and watched and listened and I stood still at the window. *"'Tis
the old ship of Zion,"* they sang, and the sister with the tambourine kept a
steady, jangling beat, *"it has rescued many a thousand!"* Not a soul under
the sound of their voices was hearing this song for the first time, not
one of them had been rescued. Nor had they seen much in the way of
rescue work being done around them. Neither did they especially believe
in the holiness of the three sisters and the brother, they knew too much
about them, knew where they lived, and how. The woman with the tambourine, whose voice dominated the air, whose face was bright with joy, was
divided by very little from the woman who stood watching her, a cigarette
between her heavy, chapped lips, her hair a cuckoo's nest, her face scarred
and swollen from many beatings, and her black eyes glittering like coal.
Perhaps they both knew this, which was why, when, as rarely, they ad-

---

[4] Artificially straightened.

dressed each other, they addressed each other as Sister. As the singing filled the air the watching, listening faces underwent a change, the eyes focusing on something within; the music seemed to soothe a poison out of them; and time seemed, nearly, to fall away from the sullen, belligerent, battered faces, as though they were fleeing back to their first condition, while dreaming of their last. The barbecue cook half shook his head and smiled, and dropped his cigarette and disappeared into his joint. A man fumbled in his pockets for change and stood holding it in his hand impatiently, as though he had just remembered a pressing appointment further up the avenue. He looked furious. Then I saw Sonny, standing on the edge of the crowd. He was carrying a wide, flat notebook with a green cover, and it made him look, from where I was standing, almost like a schoolboy. The coppery sun brought out the copper in his skin, he was very faintly smiling, standing very still. Then the singing stopped, the tambourine turned into a collection plate again. The furious man dropped in his coins and vanished, so did a couple of the women, and Sonny dropped some change in the plate, looking directly at the woman with a little smile. He started across the avenue, toward the house. He has a slow, loping walk, something like the way Harlem hipsters walk, only he's imposed on this his own half-beat. I had never really noticed it before.

I stayed at the window, both relieved and apprehensive. As Sonny disappeared from my sight, they began singing again. And they were still singing when his key turned in the lock.

"Hey," he said.

"Hey, yourself. You want some beer?"

"No. Well, maybe." But he came up to the window and stood beside me, looking out. "What a warm voice," he said.

They were singing *If I could only hear my mother pray again!*

"Yes," I said, "and she can sure beat that tambourine."

"But what a terrible song," he said, and laughed. He dropped his notebook on the sofa and disappeared into the kitchen. "Where's Isabel and the kids?"

"I think they went to see their grandparents. You hungry?"

"No." He came back into the living room with his can of beer. "You want to come some place with me tonight?"

I sensed, I don't know how, that I couldn't possibly say no. "Sure. Where?"

He sat down on the sofa and picked up his notebook and started leafing through it. "I'm going to sit in with some fellows in a joint in the Village."

"You mean, you're going to play, tonight?"

"That's right." He took a swallow of his beer and moved back to the window. He gave me a sidelong look. "If you can stand it."

"I'll try," I said.

He smiled to himself and we both watched as the meeting across the way broke up. The three sisters and the brother, heads bowed, were singing *God be with you till we meet again.* The faces around them were very quiet. Then the song ended. The small crowd dispersed. We watched the three women and the lone man walk slowly up the avenue.

"When she was singing before," said Sonny, abruptly, "her voice reminded me for a minute of what heroin feels like sometimes—when it's in your veins. It makes you feel sort of warm and cool at the same time. And distant. And—and sure." He sipped his beer, very deliberately not looking at me. I watched his face. "It makes you feel—in control. Sometimes you've got to have that feeling."

"Do you?" I sat down slowly in the easy chair.

"Sometimes." He went to the sofa and picked up his notebook again. "Some people do."

"In order," I asked, "to play?" And my voice was very ugly, full of contempt and anger.

"Well"—he looked at me with great, troubled eyes, as though, in fact, he hoped his eyes would tell me things he could never otherwise say— "they *think* so. And *if* they think so—!"

"And what do *you* think?" I asked.

He sat on the sofa and put his can of beer on the floor. "I don't know," he said, and I couldn't be sure if he were answering my question or pursuing his thoughts. His face didn't tell me. "It's not so much to *play*. It's to *stand* it, to be able to make it at all. On any level." He frowned and smiled: "In order to keep from shaking to pieces."

"But these friends of yours," I said, "they seem to shake themselves to pieces pretty goddamn fast."

"Maybe." He played with the notebook. And something told me that I should curb my tongue, that Sonny was doing his best to talk, that I should listen. "But of course you only know the ones that've gone to pieces. Some don't—or at least they haven't *yet* and that's just about all *any* of us can say." He paused. "And then there are some who just live, really, in hell, and they know it and they see what's happening and they go right on. I don't know." He sighed, dropped the notebook, folded his arms. "Some guys, you can tell from the way they play, they on something *all* the time. And you can see that, well, it makes something real for them. But of course," he picked up his beer from the floor and sipped it and put the can down again, "they *want* to, too, you've got to see that. Even some of them that say they don't—*some*, not all."

"And what about you?" I asked—I couldn't help it. "What about you? Do *you* want to?"

He stood up and walked to the window and I remained silent for a long time. Then he sighed. "Me," he said. Then: "While I was downstairs before, on my way here, listening to that woman sing, it struck me all of a sudden how much suffering she must have had to go through—to sing like that. It's *repulsive* to think you have to suffer that much."

I said: "But there's no way not to suffer—is there, Sonny?"

"I believe not," he said and smiled, "but that's never stopped anyone from trying." He looked at me. "Has it?" I realized, with this mocking look, that there stood between us, forever, beyond the power of time or forgiveness, the fact that I had held silence—so long!—when he had needed human speech to help him. He turned back to the window. "No, there's no way not to suffer. But you try all kinds of ways to keep from drowning in it, to keep on top of it, and to make it seem—well, like *you*. Like you did something, all right, and now you're suffering for it. You know?" I said nothing. "Well you know," he said, impatiently, "why *do* people suffer? Maybe it's better to do something to give it a reason, *any* reason."

"But we just agreed," I said, "that there's no way not to suffer. Isn't it better, then, just to—take it?"

"But nobody just takes it," Sonny cried, "that's what I'm telling you! *Everybody* tries not to. You're just hung up on the *way* some people try—it's not *your* way!"

The hair on my face began to itch, my face felt wet. "That's not true," I said, "that's not true. I don't give a damn what other people do, I don't even care how they suffer. I just care how *you* suffer." And he looked at me. "Please believe me," I said, "I don't want to see you—die—trying not to suffer."

"I won't," he said flatly, "die trying not to suffer. At least, not any faster than anybody else."

"But there's no need," I said, trying to laugh, "is there? in killing yourself."

I wanted to say more, but I couldn't. I wanted to talk about will power and how life could be—well, beautiful. I wanted to say that it was all within; but was it? or, rather, wasn't that exactly the trouble? And I wanted to promise that I would never fail him again. But it would all have sounded—empty words and lies.

So I made the promise to myself and prayed that I would keep it.

"It's terrible sometimes, inside," he said, "that's what's the trouble. You walk these streets, black and funky and cold, and there's not really a living ass to talk to, and there's nothing shaking, and there's no way of getting it out—that storm inside. You can't talk it and you can't make love with it, and when you finally try to get with it and play it, you realize *nobody's* listening. So *you've* got to listen. You got to find a way to listen."

And then he walked away from the window and sat on the sofa again, as though all the wind had suddenly been knocked out of him. "Sometimes you'll do *anything* to play, even cut your mother's throat." He laughed and looked at me. "Or your brother's." Then he sobered. "Or your own." Then: "Don't worry. I'm all right now and I think I'll *be* all right. But I can't forget—where I've been. I don't mean just the physical place I've been, I mean where I've *been*. And *what* I've been."

"What have you been, Sonny?" I asked.

He smiled—but sat sideways on the sofa, his elbow resting on the back, his fingers playing with his mouth and chin, not looking at me. "I've been something I didn't recognize, didn't know I could be. Didn't know anybody could be." He stopped, looking inward, looking helplessly young, looking old. "I'm not talking about it now because I feel *guilty* or anything like that—maybe it would be better if I did, I don't know. Anyway, I can't really talk about it. Not to you, not to anybody," and now he turned and faced me. "Sometimes, you know, and it was actually when I was most *out* of the world, I felt that I was in it, that I was *with* it, really, and I could play or I didn't really have to *play*, it just came out of me, it was there. And I don't know how I played, thinking about it now, but I know I did awful things, those times, sometimes, to people. Or it wasn't that I *did* anything to them—it was that they weren't real." He picked up the beer can; it was empty; he rolled it between his palms: "And other times—well, I needed a fix, I needed to find a place to lean, I needed to clear a space to *listen*—and I couldn't find it, and I—went crazy, I did terrible things to *me*, I was terrible *for* me." He began pressing the beer can between his hands, I watched the metal begin to give. It glittered, as he played with it like a knife, and I was afraid he would cut himself, but I said nothing. "Oh well, I can never tell you. I was all by myself at the bottom of something, stinking and sweating and crying and shaking, and I smelled it, you know? *my* stink, and I thought I'd die if I couldn't get away from it and yet, all the same, I knew that everything I was doing was just locking me in with it. And I didn't know," he paused, still flattening the beer can, "I didn't know, I still *don't* know, something kept telling me that maybe it was good to smell your own stink, but I didn't think that *that* was what I'd been trying to do—and—who can stand it?" and he abruptly dropped the ruined beer can, looking at me with a small, still smile, and then rose, walking to the window as though it were the lodestone rock. I watched his face, he watched the avenue. "I couldn't tell you when Mama died—but the reason I wanted to leave Harlem so bad was to get away from drugs. And then, when I ran away, that's what I was running from—really. When I came back, nothing had changed, *I* hadn't changed, I was just—older." And he stopped, drumming with his fingers on the windowpane. The sun had vanished, soon darkness would fall. I watched his face. "It can come again," he said, almost as though speaking to himself. Then he turned to me. "It can come again," he repeated. "I just want you to know that."

"All right," I said, at last. "So it can come again. All right."

He smiled, but the smile was sorrowful. "I had to try to tell you," he said.

"Yes," I said. "I understand that."

"You're my brother," he said, looking straight at me, and not smiling at all.

"Yes," I repeated, "yes. I understand that."

He turned back to the window, looking out. "All that hatred down there," he said, "all that hatred and misery and love. It's a wonder it doesn't blow the avenue apart."

We went to the only nightclub on a short, dark street, downtown. We squeezed through the narrow, chattering, jampacked bar to the entrance of the big room, where the bandstand was. And we stood there for a moment, for the lights were very dim in this room and we couldn't see. Then, "Hello, boy," said the voice and an enormous black man, much older than Sonny or myself, erupted out of all that atmospheric lighting and put an arm around Sonny's shoulder. "I been sitting right here," he said, "waiting for you."

He had a big voice, too, and heads in the darkness turned toward us.

Sonny grinned and pulled a little away, and said, "Creole, this is my brother. I told you about him."

Creole shook my hand. "I'm glad to meet you, son," he said, and it was clear that he was glad to meet me *there*, for Sonny's sake. And he smiled, "You got a real musician in *your* family," and he took his arm from Sonny's shoulder and slapped him, lightly, affectionately, with the back of his hand.

"Well. Now I've heard it all," said a voice behind us. This was another musician, and a friend of Sonny's, a coal-black, cheerful-looking man, built close to the ground. He immediately began confiding to me, at the top of his lungs, the most terrible things about Sonny, his teeth gleaming like a lighthouse and his laugh coming up out of him like the beginning of an earthquake. And it turned out that everyone at the bar knew Sonny, or almost everyone; some were musicians, working there, or nearby, or not working, some were simply hangers-on, and some were there to hear Sonny play. I was introduced to all of them and they were all very polite to me. Yet, it was clear that, for them, I was only Sonny's brother. Here, I was in Sonny's world. Or, rather: his kingdom. Here, it was not even a question that his veins bore royal blood.

They were going to play soon and Creole installed me, by myself, at a table in a dark corner. Then I watched them, Creole, and the little black man, and Sonny, and the others, while they horsed around, standing just below the bandstand. The light from the bandstand spilled just a little short of them and, watching them laughing and gesturing and moving about, I had the feeling that they, nevertheless, were being most careful not to step into that circle of light too suddenly: that if they moved into the light too suddenly, without thinking, they would perish in flame. Then, while I watched, one of them, the small black man, moved into the light and crossed the bandstand and started fooling around with his drums. Then—being funny and being, also, extremely ceremonious—Creole took Sonny by the arm and led him to the piano. A woman's voice called Sonny's name and a few hands started clapping. And Sonny, also being funny and being ceremonious, and so touched, I think, that he could have cried, but neither hiding it nor showing it, riding it like a man, grinned, and put both hands to his heart and bowed from the waist.

Creole then went to the bass fiddle and a lean, very bright-skinned brown man jumped up on the bandstand and picked up his horn. So there they were, and the atmosphere on the bandstand and in the room began to change and tighten. Someone stepped up to the microphone and announced them. Then there were all kinds of murmurs. Some people at the bar shushed others. The waitress ran around, frantically getting in the last orders, guys and chicks got closer to each other, and the lights on the bandstand, on the quartet, turned to a kind of indigo. Then they all looked different there. Creole looked about him for the last time, as though he were making certain that all his chickens were in the coop, and then he—jumped and struck the fiddle. And there they were.

All I know about music is that not many people ever really hear it. And even then, on the rare occasions when something opens within, and the music enters, what we mainly hear, or hear corroborated, are personal, private, vanishing evocations. But the man who creates the music is hearing something else, is dealing with the roar rising from the void and imposing order on it as it hits the air. What is evoked in him, then, is of another order, more terrible because it has no words, and triumphant, too, for that same reason. And his triumph, when he triumphs, is ours. I just watched Sonny's face. His face was troubled, he was working hard, but he wasn't with it. And I had the feeling that, in a way, everyone on the bandstand was waiting for him, both waiting for him and pushing him along. But as I began to watch Creole, I realized that it was Creole who held them all back. He had them on a short rein. Up there, keeping the beat with his whole body, wailing on the fiddle, with his eyes half closed, he was listening to everything, but he was listening to Sonny. He was having a dialogue with Sonny. He wanted Sonny to leave the shoreline and strike out for the deep water. He was Sonny's witness that deep water and drowning were not the same thing—he had been there, and he knew. And he wanted Sonny to know. He was waiting for Sonny to do the things on the keys which would let Creole know that Sonny was in the water.

And, while Creole listened, Sonny moved, deep within, exactly like some-one in torment. I had never before thought of how awful the relationship must be between the musician and his instrument. He has to fill it, this instrument, with the breath of life, his own. He has to make it do what he wants it to do. And a piano is just a piano. It's made out of so much wood and wires and little hammers and big ones, and ivory. While there's only so much you can do with it, the only way to find this out is to try; to try and make it do everything.

And Sonny hadn't been near a piano for over a year. And he wasn't on much better terms with his life, not the life that stretched before him now. He and the piano stammered, started one way, got scared, stopped; started another way, panicked, marked time, started again; then seemed to have found a direction, panicked again, got stuck. And the face I saw on Sonny I'd never seen before. Everything had been burned out of it, and, at the same time, things usually hidden were being burned in, by the fire and fury of the battle which was occurring in him up there.

Yet, watching Creole's face as they neared the end of the first set, I had the feeling that something had happened, something I hadn't heard. Then they finished, there was scattered applause, and then, without an instant's warning, Creole started into something else, it was almost sar-donic, it was *Am I Blue*. And, as though he commanded, Sonny began to play. Something began to happen. And Creole let out the reins. The dry, low, black man said something awful on the drums, Creole answered, and the drums talked back. Then the horn insisted, sweet and high, slightly detached perhaps, and Creole listened, commenting now and then, dry, and driving, beautiful and calm and old. Then they all came together again, and Sonny was part of the family again. I could tell this from his face. He seemed to have found, right there beneath his fingers, a damn brand-new piano. It seemed that he couldn't get over it. Then, for a while, just being happy with Sonny, they seemed to be agreeing with him that brand-new pianos certainly were a gas.

Then Creole stepped forward to remind them that what they were play-ing was the blues. He hit something in all of them, he hit something in me, myself, and the music tightened and deepened, apprehension began to beat the air. Creole began to tell us what the blues were all about. They were not about anything very new. He and his boys up there were keeping it new, at the risk of ruin, destruction, madness, and death, in order to find new ways to make us listen. For, while the tale of how we suffer, and how we are delighted, and how we may triumph is never new, it always must be heard. There isn't any other tale to tell, it's the only light we've got in all this darkness.

And this tale, according to that face, that body, those strong hands on those strings, has another aspect in every country, and a new depth in every generation. Listen, Creole seemed to be saying, listen. Now these are Sonny's blues. He made the little black man on the drums know it, and the bright, brown man on the horn. Creole wasn't trying any longer to get Sonny in the water. He was wishing him Godspeed. Then he stepped back, very slowly, filling the air with the immense suggestion that Sonny speak for himself.

Then they all gathered around Sonny and Sonny played. Every now and again one of them seemed to say, amen. Sonny's fingers filled the air with life, his life. But that life contained so many others. And Sonny went all the way back, he really began with the spare, flat statement of the opening phrase of the song. Then he began to make it his. It was very beautiful because it wasn't hurried and it was no longer a lament. I seemed to hear with what burning he had made it his, with what burning we had yet to make it ours, how we could cease lamenting. Freedom lurked around us and I understood, at last, that he could help us to be free if we would listen, that he would never be free until we did. Yet, there was no battle in his face now, I heard what he had gone through, and would continue to go through until he came to rest in earth. He had made it his: that long line, of which we knew only Mama and Daddy. And he was giving it back, as everything must be given back, so that, passing through death, it can live forever. I saw my mother's face again, and felt, for the first time, how the stones of the road she had walked on must have bruised her feet. I saw the moonlit road where my father's brother died. And it brought something else back to me, and carried me past it, I saw my little girl again and felt Isabel's tears again, and I felt my own tears begin to rise. And I was yet aware that this was only a moment, that the world waited outside, as hungry as a tiger, and that trouble stretched above us, longer than the sky.

Then it was over. Creole and Sonny let out their breath, both soaking wet, and grinning. There was a lot of applause and some of it was real. In the dark, the girl came by and I asked her to take drinks to the bandstand. There was a long pause, while they talked up there in the indigo light and after a while I saw the girl put a Scotch and milk on top of the piano for Sonny. He didn't seem to notice it, but just before they started playing again, he sipped from it and looked toward me, and nodded. Then he put it back on top of the piano. For me, then, as they began to play again, it glowed and shook above my brother's head like the very cup of trembling.[5]

(1957)

[5] From Isaiah 51:22, "Thus saith thy Lord the Lord . . . , Behold, I have taken out of thine hand the cup of trembling, even the dregs of the cup of my fury; thou shalt no more drink it again."

Doris Lessing   *1919–*

A WOMAN ON A ROOF

It was during the week of hot sun, that June.

Three men were at work on the roof, where the leads got so hot they had the idea of throwing water on to cool them. But the water steamed, then sizzled; and they made jokes about getting an egg from some woman in the flats under them, to poach it for their dinner. By two it was not possible to touch the guttering they were replacing, and they speculated about what workmen did in regularly hot countries. Perhaps they should borrow kitchen gloves with the egg? They were all a bit dizzy, not used to the heat; and they shed their coats and stood side by side squeezing themselves into a foot-wide patch of shade against a chimney, careful to keep their feet in the thick socks and boots out of the sun. There was a fine view across several acres of roofs. Not far off a man sat in a deck chair reading the newspapers. Then they saw her, between chimneys, about fifty yards away. She lay face down on a brown blanket. They could see the top part of her: black hair, a flushed solid back, arms spread out.

"She's stark naked," said Stanley, sounding annoyed.

Harry, the oldest, a man of about forty-five, said: "Looks like it."

Young Tom, seventeen, said nothing, but he was excited and grinning.

Stanley said: "Someone'll report her if she doesn't watch out."

"She thinks no one can see," said Tom, craning his head all ways to see more.

At this point the woman, still lying prone, brought her two hands up behind her shoulders with the ends of a scarf in them, tied it behind her back, and sat up. She wore a red scarf tied around her breasts and brief red bikini pants. This being the first day of the sun she was white, flushing red. She sat smoking, and did not look up when Stanley let out a wolf whistle. Harry said: "Small things amuse small minds," leading the way back to their part of the roof, but it was scorching. Harry said: "Wait, I'm going to rig up some shade," and disappeared down the skylight into the building. Now that he'd gone, Stanley and Tom went to the farthest point they could to peer at the woman. She had moved, and all they could see were two pink legs stretched on the blanket. They whistled and shouted but the legs did not move. Harry came back with a blanket and shouted: "Come on, then." He sounded irritated with them. They clambered back to him and he said to Stanley: "What about your missus?" Stanley was newly married, about three months. Stanley said, jeering: "What about my missus?"—preserving his independence. Tom said nothing, but his mind was full of the nearly naked woman. Harry slung the blanket, which he had borrowed from a friendly woman downstairs, from the stem of a television aerial to a row of chimney pots. This shade fell across the piece of gutter they had to replace. But the shade kept moving, they had to adjust the blanket, and not much progress was made. At last some of the heat left the roof, and they worked fast, making up for lost time. First Stanley, then Tom, made a trip to the end of the roof to see the woman.

"She's on her back," Stanley said, adding a jest which made Tom snicker, and the older man smile tolerantly. Tom's report was that she hadn't moved, but it was a lie. He wanted to keep what he had seen to himself: he had caught her in the act of rolling down the little red pants over her hips, till they were no more than a small triangle. She was on her back, fully visible, glistening with oil.

Next morning, as soon as they came up, they went to look. She was already there, face down, arms spread out, naked except for the little red pants. She had turned brown in the night. Yesterday she was a scarlet and white woman, today she was a brown woman. Stanley let out a whistle. She lifted her head, startled, as if she'd been asleep, and looked straight over at them. The sun was in her eyes, she blinked and stared, then she dropped her head again. At this gesture of indifference, they all three, Stanley, Tom, and old Harry, let out whistles and yells. Harry was doing it in parody of the younger men, making fun of them, but he was also angry. They were all angry because of her utter indifference to the three men watching her.

"Bitch," said Stanley.

"She should ask us over," said Tom, snickering.

Harry recovered himself and reminded Stanley: "If she's married, her old man wouldn't like that."

"Christ," said Stanley virtuously, "if my wife lay about like that, for everyone to see, I'd soon stop her."

Harry said, smiling: "How do you know, perhaps she's sunning herself at this very moment?"

"Not a chance, not on our roof." The safety of his wife put Stanley into a good humour, and they went to work. But today it was hotter than yesterday; and several times one or the other suggested they should tell Matthew, the foreman, and ask to leave the roof until the heat wave was over. But they didn't. There was work to be done in the basement of the big block of flats, but up here they felt free, on a different level from ordinary humanity shut in the streets or the buildings. A lot more people came out onto the roofs that day, for an hour at midday. Some married couples sat side by side in deck chairs, the women's legs stockingless and scarlet, the men in vests with reddening shoulders.

The woman stayed on her blanket, turning herself over and over. She ignored them, no matter what they did. When Harry went off to fetch more screws, Stanley said: "Come on." Her roof belonged to a different system of roofs, separated from theirs at one point by about twenty feet. It meant a scrambling climb from one level to another, edging along parapets, clinging to chimneys, while their big boots slipped and slithered, but at last they stood on a small square projecting roof looking straight down at her, close. She sat smoking, reading a book. Tom thought she looked like a poster, or a magazine cover, with the blue sky behind her and her legs stretched out. Behind her a great crane at work on a new building in Oxford Street swung its black arm across the roofs in a great arc. Tom imagined himself at work on the crane, adjusting the arm to swing over and pick her up and swing her back across the sky to drop her near him.

They whistled. She looked up at them, cool and remote, then went on reading. Again, they were furious. Or rather, Stanley was. His sun-heated face was screwed into rage as he whistled again and again, trying to make her look up. Young Tom stopped whistling. He stood beside Stanley, excited, grinning; but he felt as if he were saying to the woman: "Don't associate me with *him*," for his grin was apologetic. Last night he had thought of the unknown woman before he slept, and she had been tender with him. This tenderness he was remembering as he shifted his feet by the jeering, whistling Stanley, and watched the indifferent, healthy brown woman a few feet off, with the gap that plunged to the street between them. Tom thought it was romantic, it was like being high on two hilltops. But there was a shout from Harry, and they clambered back. Stanley's face was hard, really angry. The boy kept looking at him and wondered why he hated the woman so much, for by now he loved her.

They played their little games with the blanket, trying to trap shade to work under; but again it was not until nearly four that they could work seriously, and they were exhausted, all three of them. They were grumbling about the weather, by now. Stanley was in a thoroughly bad humour. When they made their routine trip to see the woman before they packed up for the day, she was apparently asleep, face down, her back all naked save for the scarlet triangle on her buttocks. "I've got a good mind to report her to the police," said Stanley, and Harry said: "What's eating you? What harm's she doing?"

"I tell you, if she was my wife!"

"But she isn't, is she?" Tom knew that Harry, like himself, was uneasy at Stanley's reaction. He was normally a sharp young man, quick at his work, making a lot of jokes, good company.

"Perhaps it will be cooler tomorrow," said Harry.

But it wasn't, it was hotter, if anything, and the weather forecast said the good weather would last. As soon as they were on the roof, Harry went over to see if the woman were there, and Tom knew it was to prevent Stanley going, to put off his bad humour. Harry had grown-up children, a boy the same age as Tom, and the youth trusted and looked up to him.

Harry came back and said: "She's not there."

"I bet her old man has put his foot down," said Stanley, and Harry and Tom caught each other's eyes and smiled behind the young married man's back.

Harry suggested they should get permission to work in the basement, and they did, that day. But before packing up Stanley said: "Let's have a breath of fresh air." Again Harry and Tom smiled at each other as they followed Stanley up to the roof, Tom in the devout conviction that he was there to protect the woman from Stanley. It was about five-thirty, and a calm, full sunlight lay over the roofs. The great crane still swung its black arm from Oxford Street to above their heads. She was not there. Then there was a flutter of white from behind a parapet, and she stood up, in a belted, white dressing gown. She had been there all day, probably, but on a different patch of roof, to hide from them. Stanley did not whistle, he said nothing, but watched the woman bend to collect papers, books, cigarettes, then fold the blanket over her arm. Tom was thinking: If they weren't here, I'd go over and say . . . what? But he knew from his nightly dreams of her that she was kind and friendly. Perhaps she would ask him down to her flat? Perhaps. . . . He stood watching her disappear down the skylight. As she went, Stanley let out a shrill derisive yell; she started, and it seemed as if she nearly fell. She clutched to save herself, they could hear things falling. She looked straight at them, angry. Harry said, facetiously: "Better be careful on those slippery ladders, love." Tom knew he said it to save her from Stanley, but she could not know it. She vanished, frowning. Tom was full of a secret delight, because he knew her anger was for the others, not for him.

"Roll on some rain," said Stanley, bitterly looking at the blue evening sky.

Next day was cloudless, and they decided to finish the work in the basement. They felt excluded, shut in the grey cement basement fitting pipes, from the holiday atmosphere of London in a heat wave. At lunchtime they came up for some air, but while the married couples, and the men in shirt-sleeves or vests, were there, she was not there, either on her usual patch of roof or where she had been yesterday. They all, even Harry, clambered about, between chimney pots, over parapets, the hot leads stinging their fingers. There was not a sign of her. They took off their shirts and vests and exposed their chests, feeling their feet sweaty and hot. They did not mention the woman. But Tom felt alone again. Last night she had asked him into her flat: it was big and had fitted white carpets and a bed with a padded white leather headtop. She wore a black filmy negligée and her kindness to Tom thickened his throat as he remembered it. He felt she had betrayed him by not being there.

And again after work they climbed up, but still there was nothing to be seen of her. Stanley kept repeating that if it was as hot as this tomorrow he wasn't going to work and that's all there was to it. But they were all there next day. By ten the temperature was in the middle seventies, and it was eighty long before noon. Harry went to the foreman to say it was impossible to work on the leads in that heat; but the foreman said there was nothing else he could put them on, and they'd have to. At midday they stood, silent, watching the skylight on her roof open, and then she slowly emerged in her white gown, holding a bundle of blanket. She looked at them, gravely, then went to the part of the roof where she was hidden from them. Tom was pleased. He felt she was more his when the other men couldn't see her. They had taken off their shirts and vests, but now they put them back again, for they felt the sun bruising their flesh. "She must have the hide of a rhino," said Stanley, tugging at guttering and swearing. They stopped work, and sat in the shade, moving around behind chimney stacks. A woman came to water a yellow window box just opposite them. She was middle-aged, wearing a flowered summer dress. Stanley said to her: "We need a drink more than them." She smiled and said: "Better drop down to the pub quick, it'll be closing in a minute." They exchanged pleasantries, and she left them with a smile and a wave.

"Not like Lady Godiva," said Stanley. "She can give us a bit of a chat and a smile."

"You didn't whistle at *her*," said Tom, reproving.

"Listen to him," said Stanley, "you didn't whistle, then?"

But the boy felt as if he hadn't whistled, as if only Harry and Stanley had. He was making plans, when it was time to knock off work, to get left behind and somehow make his way over to the woman. The weather report said the hot spell was due to break, so he had to move quickly. But there was no chance of being left. The other two decided to knock off work at four, because they were exhausted. As they went down, Tom quickly climbed a parapet and hoisted himself higher by pulling his weight up a chimney. He caught a glimpse of her lying on her back, her knees up, eyes closed, a brown woman lolling in the sun. He slipped and clattered down, as Stanley looked for information: "She's gone down," he said. He felt as if he had protected her from Stanley, and that she must be grateful to him. He could feel the bond between the woman and himself.

Next day, they stood around on the landing below the roof, reluctant to climb up into the heat. The woman who had lent Harry the blanket came out and offered them a cup of tea. They accepted gratefully, and sat around Mrs. Pritchett's kitchen an hour or so, chatting. She was married to an airline pilot. A smart blonde, of about thirty, she had an eye for the handsome sharp-faced Stanley; and the two teased each other while Harry sat in a corner, watching, indulgent, though his expression reminded Stanley that he was married. And young Tom felt envious of Stanley's ease in badinage; felt, too, that Stanley's getting off with Mrs. Pritchett left his romance with the woman on the roof safe and intact.

"I thought they said the heat wave'd break," said Stanley, sullen, as the time approached when they really would have to climb up into the sunlight.

"You don't like it, then?" asked Mrs. Pritchett.

"All right for some," said Stanley. "Nothing to do but lie about as if it was a beach up there. Do you ever go up?"

"Went up once," said Mrs. Pritchett. "But it's a dirty place up there, and it's too hot."

"Quite right too," said Stanley.

Then they went up, leaving the cool neat little flat and the friendly Mrs. Pritchett.

As soon as they were up they saw her. The three men looked at her, resentful at her ease in this punishing sun. Then Harry said, because of the expression on Stanley's face: "Come on, we've got to pretend to work, at least."

They had to wrench another length of guttering that ran beside a parapet out of its bed, so that they could replace it. Stanley took it in his two hands, tugged, swore, stood up. "Fuck it," he said, and sat down under a chimney. He lit a cigarette. "Fuck them," he said. "What do they think we are, lizards? I've got blisters all over my hands." Then he jumped up and climbed over the roofs and stood with his back to them. He put his fingers either side of his mouth and let out a shrill whistle. Tom and Harry squatted, not looking at each other, watching him. They could just see the woman's head, the beginnings of her brown shoulders. Stanley whistled again. Then he began stamping with his feet, and whistled and yelled and screamed at the woman, his face getting scarlet. He seemed quite mad, as he stamped and whistled, while the woman did not move, she did not move a muscle.

"Barmy," said Tom.

"Yes," said Harry, disapproving.

Suddenly the older man came to a decision. It was, Tom knew, to save some sort of scandal or real trouble over the woman. Harry stood up and began packing tools into a length of oily cloth. "Stanley," he said, commanding. At first Stanley took no notice, but Harry said: "Stanley, we're packing it in, I'll tell Matthew."

Stanley came back, cheeks mottled, eyes glaring.

"Can't go on like this," said Harry. "It'll break in a day or so. I'm going to tell Matthew we've got sunstroke, and if he doesn't like it, it's too bad." Even Harry sounded aggrieved, Tom noted. The small, competent man, the family man with his grey hair, who was never at a loss, sounded really off balance. "Come on," he said, angry. He fitted himself into the open square in the roof, and went down, watching his feet on the ladder. Then Stanley went, with not a glance at the woman. Then Tom who, his throat beating with excitement, silently promised her in a backward glance: Wait for me, wait, I'm coming.

On the pavement Stanley said: "I'm going home." He looked white now, so perhaps he really did have sunstroke. Harry went off to find the foreman who was at work on the plumbing of some flats down the street. Tom slipped back, not into the building they had been working on, but the building on whose roof the woman lay. He went straight up, no one stopping him. The skylight stood open, with an iron ladder leading up. He emerged onto the roof a couple of yards from her. She sat up, pushing back her black hair with both hands. The scarf across her breasts bound them tight, and brown flesh bulged around it. Her legs were brown and smooth. She stared at him in silence. The boy stood grinning, foolish, claiming the tenderness he expected from her.

"What do you want?" she asked.

"I . . . I came to . . . make your acquaintance," he stammered, grinning, pleading with her.

They looked at each other, the slight, scarlet-faced excited boy, and the serious, nearly naked woman. Then, without a word, she lay down on her brown blanket, ignoring him.

"You like the sun, do you?" he enquired of her glistening back.

Not a word. He felt panic, thinking of how she had held him in her arms, stroked his hair, brought him where he sat, lordly, in her bed, a glass of some exhilarating liquor he had never tasted in life. He felt that if he knelt down, stroked her shoulders, her hair, she would turn and clasp him in her arms.

He said: "The sun's all right for you, isn't it?"

She raised her head, set her chin on two small fists. "Go away," she said. He did not move. "Listen," she said, in a slow reasonable voice, where anger was kept in check, though with difficulty; looking at him, her face weary with anger: "If you get a kick out of seeing women in bikinis, why don't you take a six-penny bus ride to the Lido? You'd see dozens of them, without all this mountaineering."

She hadn't understood him. He felt her unfairness pale him. He stammered: "But I like you, I've been watching you and . . ."

"Thanks," she said, and dropped her face again, turned away from him.

She lay there. He stood there. She said nothing. She had simply shut him out. He stood, saying nothing at all, for some minutes. He thought:

She'll have to say something if I stay. But the minutes went past, with no sign of them in her, except in the tension of her back, her thighs, her arms—the tension of waiting for him to go.

He looked up at the sky, where the sun seemed to spin in heat; and over the roofs where he and his mates had been earlier. He could see the heat quivering where they had worked. "And they expect us to work in these conditions!" he thought, filled with righteous indignation. The woman hadn't moved. A bit of hot wind blew her black hair softly, it shone, and was iridescent. He remembered how he had stroked it last night.

Resentment of her at last moved him off and away down the ladder, through the building, into the street. He got drunk then, in hatred of her.

Next day when he woke the sky was grey. He looked at the wet grey and thought, vicious: "Well, that's fixed you, hasn't it now? That's fixed you good and proper."

The three men were at work early on the cool leads, surrounded by damp drizzling roofs where no one came to sun themselves, black roofs, slimy with rain. Because it was cool now, they would finish the job that day, if they hurried.

(1958)

John Updike *1932–*

A & P

In walks these three girls in nothing but bathing suits. I'm in the third checkout slot, with my back to the door, so I don't see them until they're over by the bread. The one that caught my eye first was the one in the plaid green two-piece. She was a chunky kid, with a good tan and a sweet broad soft-looking can with those two crescents of white just under it, where the sun never seems to hit, at the top of the backs of her legs. I stood there with my hand on a box of HiHo crackers trying to remember if I rang it up or not. I ring it up again and the customer starts giving me hell. She's one of these cash-register-watchers, a witch about fifty with rouge on her cheekbones and no eyebrows, and I know it made her day to trip me up. She'd been watching cash registers for fifty years and probably never seen a mistake before.

By the time I got her feathers smoothed and her goodies into a bag— she gives me a little snort in passing, if she'd been born at the right time they would have burned her over in Salem—by the time I get her on her way the girls had circled around the bread and were coming back, without a pushcart, back my way along the counters, in the aisle between the checkouts and the Special bins. They didn't even have shoes on. There was this chunky one, with the two-piece—it was bright green and the seams on the bra were still sharp and her belly was still pretty pale so I guessed she just got it (the suit)—there was this one, with one of those chubby berry-faces, the lips all bunched together under her nose, this one, and a tall one, with black hair that hadn't quite frizzed right, and one of these sunburns right across under the eyes, and a chin that was too long— you know, the kind of girl other girls think is very "striking" and "attractive" but never quite makes it, as they very well know, which is why they like her so much—and then the third one, that wasn't quite so tall. She was the queen. She kind of led them, the other two peeking around and making their shoulders round. She didn't look around, not this queen, she just walked straight on slowly, on these long white primadonna legs. She came down a little hard on her heels, as if she didn't walk in bare feet that much, putting down her heels and then letting the weight move along to her toes as if she was testing the floor with every step, putting a little deliberate extra action into it. You never know for sure how girls' minds work (do you really think it's a mind in there or just a little buzz like a bee in a glass jar?) but you got the idea she had talked the other two into coming in here with her, and now she was showing them how to do it, walk slow and hold yourself straight.

She had on a kind of dirty-pink—beige maybe, I don't know—bathing suit with a little nubble all over it and, what got me, the straps were down. They were off her shoulders looped loose around the cool tops of her arms, and I guess as a result the suit had slipped a little on her, so all around the top of the cloth there was this shining rim. If it hadn't been there you wouldn't have known there could have been anything whiter than those shoulders. With the straps pushed off, there was nothing between the top of the suit and the top of her head except just *her*, this clean bare plane of the top of her chest down from the shoulder bones like a dented sheet of metal tilted in the light. I mean, it was more than pretty.

She had a sort of oaky hair that the sun and salt had bleached, done up in a bun that was unravelling, and a kind of prim face. Walking into the A & P with your straps down, I suppose it's the only kind of face you *can* have. She held her head so high her neck, coming up out of those white shoulders, looked kind of stretched, but I didn't mind. The longer her neck was, the more of her there was.

She must have felt in the corner of her eye me and over my shoulder Stokesie in the second slot watching, but she didn't tip. Not this queen. She kept her eyes moving across the racks, and stopped, and turned so slow it made my stomach rub the inside of my apron, and buzzed to the other two, who kind of huddled against her for relief, and then they all three of them went up the cat-and-dog-food - breakfast-cereal - maca-roni - rice - raisins - seasonings - spreads - spaghetti - soft-drinks - crackers -and-cookies aisle. From the third slot I look straight up this aisle to the meat counter, and I watched them all the way. The fat one with the tan sort of fumbled with the cookies, but on second thought she put the package back. The sheep pushing their carts down the aisle—the girls were walking against the usual traffic (not that we have one-way signs or anything)— were pretty hilarious. You could see them, when Queenie's white shoulders dawned on them, kind of jerk, or hop, or hiccup, but their eyes snapped back to their own baskets and on they pushed. I bet you could set off dynamite in an A & P and the people would by and large keep reaching and checking oatmeal off their lists and muttering "Let me see, there was a third thing, began with A, asparagus, no, ah, yes, applesauce!" or whatever it is they do mutter. But there was no doubt, this jiggled them. A few houseslaves in pin curlers even looked around after pushing their carts past to make sure what they had seen was correct.

You know, it's one thing to have a girl in a bathing suit down on the beach, where what with the glare nobody can look at each other much anyway, and another thing in the cool of the A & P, under the fluorescent lights, against all those stacked packages, with her feet paddling along naked over our checker-board green-and-cream rubber-tile floor.

"Oh Daddy," Stokesie said beside me. "I feel so faint."

"Darling," I said. "Hold me tight." Stokesie's married, with two babies chalked up on his fuselage already, but as far as I can tell that's the only difference. He's twenty-two, and I was nineteen this April.

"Is it done?" he asks, the responsible married man finding his voice. I forgot to say he thinks he's going to be manager some sunny day, maybe in 1990 when it's called the Great Alexandrov and Petrooshki Tea Company or something.

What he meant was, our town is five miles from a beach with a big summer colony out on the Point, but we're right in the middle of town, and the women generally put on a shirt or shorts or something before they get out of the car into the street. And anyway these are usually women with six children and varicose veins mapping their legs and nobody, includ-ing them, could care less. As I say, we're right in the middle of town, and if you stand at our front doors you can see two banks and the Congregational church and the newspaper store and three real-estate offices and about twenty-seven old freeloaders tearing up Central Street because the sewer broke again. It's not as if we're on the Cape; we're north of Boston and there's people in this town haven't seen the ocean for twenty years.

The girls had reached the meat counter and were asking McMahon something. He pointed, they pointed, and they shuffled out of sight behind a pyramid of Diet Delight peaches. All that was left for us to see was old McMahon patting his mouth and looking after them sizing up their joints. Poor kids, I began to feel sorry for them, they couldn't help it.

Now here comes the sad part of the story, at least my family says it's sad, but I don't think it's so sad myself. The store's pretty empty, it being Thursday afternoon, so there was nothing much to do except lean on the register and wait for the girls to show up again. The whole store was like a pinball machine and I didn't know which tunnel they'd come out of. After a while they come around out of the far aisle, around the light bulbs, records at discount of the Caribbean Six or Tony Martin Sings or some such gunk you wonder they waste the wax on, six-packs of candy bars, and plastic toys done up in cellophane that fall apart when a kid looks at them anyway. Around they come, Queenie still leading the way, and holding a little gray jar in her hand. Slots Three through Seven are unmanned and I could see her wondering between Stokes and me, but Stokesie with his usual luck draws an old party in baggy gray pants who stumbles up with four giant cans of pineapple juice (what do these bums *do* with all that pineapple juice? I've often asked myself) so the girls come to me. Queenie puts down the jar and I take it into my fingers icy cold. Kingfish Fancy Herring Snacks in Pure Sour Cream: 49¢. Now her hands are empty, not a ring or a bracelet, bare as God made them, and I wonder where the money's coming from. Still with that prim look she lifts a folded dollar bill out of the hollow at the center of her nubbled pink top. The jar went heavy in my hand. Really, I thought that was so cute.

Then everybody's luck begins to run out. Lengel comes in from haggling with a truck full of cabbages on the lot and is about to scuttle into that door marked MANAGER behind which he hides all day when the girls touch his eye. Lengel's pretty dreary, teaches Sunday school and the rest, but he doesn't miss that much. He comes over and says, "Girls, this isn't the beach."

Queenie blushes, though maybe it's just a brush of sunburn I was noticing for the first time, now that she was so close. "My mother asked me to pick up a jar of herring snacks." Her voice kind of startled me, the way voices do when you see the people first, coming out so flat and dumb yet kind of tony, too, the way it ticked over "pick up" and "snacks." All of a sudden I slid right down her voice into her living room. Her father and the other men were standing around in ice-cream coats and bow ties and the women were in sandals picking up herring snacks on toothpicks off a big glass plate and they were all holding drinks the color of water with olives and sprigs of mint in them. When my parents have somebody over they get lemonade and if it's a real racy affair Schlitz in tall glasses with "They'll Do It Every Time" cartoons stencilled on.

"That's all right," Lengel said. "But this isn't the beach." His repeating this struck me as funny, as if it had just occurred to him, and he had been thinking all these years the A & P was a great big dune and he was the head lifeguard. He didn't like my smiling—as I say he doesn't miss much—but he concentrates on giving the girls that sad Sunday-school-superintendent stare.

Queenie's blush is no sunburn now, and the plump one in plaid, that I liked better from the back—a really sweet can—pipes up, "We weren't doing any shopping. We just came in for the one thing."

"That makes no difference," Lengel tells her, and I could see from the way his eyes went that he hadn't noticed she was wearing a two-piece before. "We want you decently dressed when you come in here."

"We *are* decent," Queenie says suddenly, her lower lip pushing, getting sore now that she remembers her place, a place from which the crowd that runs the A & P must look pretty crummy. Fancy Herring Snacks flashed in her very blue eyes.

"Girls, I don't want to argue with you. After this come in here with your shoulders covered. It's our policy." He turns his back. That's policy for you. Policy is what the kingpins want. What the others want is juvenile delinquency.

All this while, the customers had been showing up with their carts, but, you know, sheep, seeing a scene, they had all bunched up on Stokesie, who shook open a paper bag as gently as peeling a peach, not wanting to miss a word. I could feel in the silence everybody getting nervous, most of all Lengel, who asks me, "Sammy, have you rung up their purchase?"

I thought and said, "No" but it wasn't about that I was thinking. I go through the punches, 4, 9, GROC, TOT—it's more complicated than you think, and after you do it often enough, it begins to make a little song, that you hear words to, in my case "Hello (*bing*) there, you (*gung*) hap-py pee-pul (*splat*)!"—the *splat* being the drawer flying out. I uncrease the bill, tenderly as you may imagine, it just having come from between the two smoothest scoops of vanilla I had ever known there were, and pass a half and a penny into her narrow pink palm, and nestle the herrings in a bag and twist its neck and hand it over, all the time thinking.

The girls, and who'd blame them, are in a hurry to get out, so I say "I quit" to Lengel quick enough for them to hear, hoping they'll stop and watch me, their unsuspected hero. They keep right on going, into the electric eye; the door flies open and they flicker across the lot to their car, Queenie and Plaid and Big Tall Goony-Goony (not that as raw material she was so bad), leaving me with Lengel and a kink in his eyebrow.

"Did you say something, Sammy?"

"I said I quit."

"I thought you did."

"You didn't have to embarrass them."

"It was they who were embarrassing us."

I started to say something that came out "Fiddle-de-do." It's a saying of my grandmother's, and I know she would have been pleased.

"I don't think you know what you're saying," Lengel said.

"I know you don't," I said. "But I do." I pull the bow at the back of my apron and start shrugging it off my shoulders. A couple of customers that had been heading for my slot begin to knock against each other, like scared pigs in a chute.

Lengel sighs and begins to look very patient and old and gray. He's been a friend of my parents for years. "Sammy, you don't want to do this to your Mom and Dad," he tells me. It's true, I don't. But it seems to me that once you begin a gesture it's fatal not to go through with it. I fold the apron, "Sammy" stitched in red on the pocket, and put it on the counter, and drop the bow tie on top of it. The bow tie is theirs, if you've ever wondered. "You'll feel this for the rest of your life," Lengel says, and I know that's true, too, but remembering how he made that pretty girl blush makes me so scrunchy inside I punch the No Sale tab and the machine whirs "pee-pul" and the drawer splats out. One advantage to this scene taking place in summer, I can follow this up with a clean exit, there's no fumbling around getting your coat and galoshes, I just saunter into the electric eye in my white shirt that my mother ironed the night before, and the door heaves itself open, and outside the sunshine is skating around on the asphalt.

I look around for my girls, but they're gone, of course. There wasn't anybody but some young married screaming with her children about some candy they didn't get by the door of a powder-blue Falcon station wagon. Looking back in the big windows, over the bags of peat moss and aluminum lawn furniture stacked on the pavement, I could see Lengel in my place in the slot, checking the sheep through. His face was dark gray and his back stiff, as if he's just had an injection of iron, and my stomach kind of fell as I felt how hard the world was going to be to me hereafter.

(1962)

Joyce Carol Oates *1938–*

WHERE ARE YOU GOING, WHERE HAVE YOU BEEN?

For Bob Dylan

Her name was Connie. She was fifteen and she had a quick, nervous giggling habit of craning her neck to glance into mirrors or checking other people's faces to make sure her own was all right. Her mother, who noticed everything and knew everything and who hadn't much reason any longer to look at her own face, always scolded Connie about it. "Stop gawking at yourself. Who are you? You think you're so pretty?" she would say. Connie would raise her eyebrows at these familiar old complaints and look right through her mother, into a shadowy vision of herself as she was right at that moment: she knew she was pretty and that was everything. Her mother had been pretty once too, if you could believe those old snapshots in the album, but now her looks were gone and that was why she was always after Connie.

"Why don't you keep your room clean like your sister? How've you got your hair fixed—what the hell stinks? Hair spray? You don't see your sister using that junk."

Her sister June was twenty-four and still lived at home. She was a secretary in the high school Connie attended, and if that wasn't bad enough—with her in the same building—she was so plain and chunky and steady that Connie had to hear her praised all the time by her mother and her mother's sisters. June did this, June did that, she saved money and helped clean the house and cooked and Connie couldn't do a thing, her mind was all filled with trashy daydreams. Their father was away at work most of the time and when he came home he wanted supper and he read the newspaper at supper and after supper he went to bed. He didn't bother talking much to them, but around his bent head Connie's mother kept picking at her until Connie wished her mother was dead and she herself was dead and it was all over. "She makes me want to throw up sometimes," she complained to her friends. She had a high, breathless, amused voice that made everything she said sound a little forced, whether it was sincere or not.

There was one good thing: June went places with girl friends of hers, girls who were just as plain and steady as she, and so when Connie wanted to do that her mother had no objections. The father of Connie's best girl friend drove the girls the three miles to town and left them at a shopping plaza so they could walk through the stores or go to a movie, and when he came to pick them up again at eleven he never bothered to ask what they had done.

They must have been familiar sights, walking around the shopping plaza in their shorts and flat ballerina slippers that always scuffed the sidewalk, with charm bracelets jingling on their thin wrists; they would lean together to whisper and laugh secretly if someone passed who amused or interested them. Connie had long dark blond hair that drew anyone's eye to it, and she wore part of it pulled up on her head and puffed out and the rest of it she let fall down her back. She wore a pull-over jersey blouse that looked one way when she was at home and another way when she was away from home. Everything about her had two sides to it, one for home and one for anywhere that was not home: her walk, which could be childlike and bobbing, or languid enough to make anyone think she was hearing music in her head; her mouth, which was pale and smirking most of the time, but bright and pink on these evenings out; her laugh, which was cynical and drawling at home—"Ha, ha, very funny,"—but high-pitched and nervous anywhere else, like the jingling of the charms on her bracelet.

Sometimes they did go shopping or to a movie, but sometimes they went across the highway, ducking fast across the busy road, to a drive-in restaurant where older kids hung out. The restaurant was shaped like a big bottle, though squatter than a real bottle, and on its cap was a revolving figure of a grinning boy holding a hamburger aloft. One night in midsummer they ran across, breathless with daring, and right away someone leaned out a car window and invited them over, but it was just a boy from high school they didn't like. It made them feel good to be able to ignore him. They went up through the maze of parked and cruising cars to the bright-lit, fly-infested restaurant, their faces pleased and expectant as if they were entering a sacred building that loomed up out of the night to give them what haven and blessing they yearned for. They sat at the counter and crossed their legs at the ankles, their thin shoulders rigid with excitement, and listened to the music that made everything so good: the music was always in the background, like music at a church service; it was something to depend upon.

A boy named Eddie came in to talk with them. He sat backwards on his stool turning himself jerkily around in semicircles and then stopping and turning back again, and after a while he asked Connie if she would like something to eat. She said she would and so she tapped her friend's arm on her way out—her friend pulled her face up into a brave, droll look—and Connie said she would meet her at eleven, across the way. "I just hate to leave her like that," Connie said earnestly, but the boy said that she wouldn't be alone for long. So they went out to his car, and on the way Connie couldn't help but let her eyes wander over the windshields and faces all around her, her face gleaming with a joy that had nothing to do with Eddie or even this place; it might have been the music. She drew her shoulders up and sucked in her breath with the pure pleasure of being alive, and just at that moment she happened to glance at a face just a few feet from hers. It was a boy with shaggy black hair, in a convertible jalopy painted gold. He stared at her and then his lips widened into a grin. Connie slit her eyes at him and turned away, but she couldn't help glancing back and there he was, still watching her. He wagged a finger and laughed and said, "Gonna get you, baby," and Connie turned away again without Eddie noticing anything.

She spent three hours with him, at the restaurant where they ate hamburgers and drank Cokes in wax cups that were always sweating, and then down an alley a mile or so away, and when he left her off at five to eleven only the movie house was still open at the plaza. Her girl friend was there, talking with a boy. When Connie came up, the two girls smiled at each other and Connie said, "How was the movie?" and the girl said, "*You* should know." They rode off with the girl's father, sleepy and pleased, and Connie couldn't help but look back at the darkened shopping plaza with its big empty parking lot and its signs that were faded and ghostly now, and over at the drive-in restaurant where cars were still circling tirelessly. She couldn't hear the music at this distance.

Next morning June asked her how the movie was and Connie said, "So-so."

She and that girl and occasionally another girl went several times a week, and the rest of the time Connie spent around the house—it was summer vacation—getting in her mother's way and thinking, dreaming about the boys she met. But all the boys fell back and dissolved into a single face that was not even a face but an idea, a feeling, mixed up with the urgent insistent pounding of the music and the humid night air of July. Connie's mother kept dragging her back to the daylight by finding things for her to do or saying suddenly, "What's this about the Pettinger girl?"

And Connie would say nervously, "Oh, her. That dope." She always drew thick clear lines between herself and such girls, and her mother was simple and kind enough to believe it. Her mother was so simple, Connie thought, that it was maybe cruel to fool her so much. Her mother went scuffling around the house in old bedroom slippers and complained over the telephone to one sister about the other, then the other called up and the two of them complained about the third one. If June's name was mentioned her mother's tone was approving, and if Connie's name was mentioned it was disapproving. This did not really mean she disliked Connie, and actually Connie thought that her mother preferred her to June just because she was prettier, but the two of them kept up a pretense of exasperation, a sense that they were tugging and struggling over something of little value to either of them. Sometimes, over coffee, they were almost friends, but something would come up—some vexation that was like a fly buzzing suddenly around their heads—and their faces went hard with contempt.

One Sunday Connie got up at eleven—none of them bothered with church—and washed her hair so that it could dry all day long in the sun. Her parents and sister were going to a barbecue at an aunt's house and Connie said no, she wasn't interested, rolling her eyes to let her mother know just what she thought of it. "Stay home alone then," her mother said sharply. Connie sat out back in a lawn chair and watched them drive away, her father quiet and bald, hunched around so that he could back the car out, her mother with a look that was still angry and not at all softened through the windshield, and in the back seat poor old June, all dressed up as if she didn't know what a barbecue was, with all the running yelling kids and the flies. Connie sat with her eyes closed in the sun, dreaming and dazed with the warmth about her as if this were a kind of love, the caresses of love, and her mind slipped over onto thoughts of the boy she had been with the night before and how nice he had been, how sweet it always was, not the way someone like June would suppose but sweet, gentle, the way it was in movies and promised in songs; and when she opened her eyes she hardly knew where she was, the back yard ran off into weeds and a fence-like line of trees and behind it the sky was perfectly blue and still. The asbestos "ranch house" that was now three years old startled her—it looked small. She shook her head as if to get awake.

It was too hot. She went inside the house and turned on the radio to drown out the quiet. She sat on the edge of her bed, barefoot, and listened for an hour and a half to a program called XYZ Sunday Jamboree, record after record of hard, fast, shrieking songs she sang along with, interspersed by exclamations from "Bobby King": "An' look here, you girls at Napoleon's—Son and Charley want you to pay real close attention to this song coming up!"

And Connie paid close attention herself, bathed in a glow of slow-pulsed joy that seemed to rise mysteriously out of the music itself and lay languidly about the airless little room, breathed in and breathed out with each gentle rise and fall of her chest.

After a while she heard a car coming up the drive. She sat up at once, startled, because it couldn't be her father so soon. The gravel kept crunching all the way in from the road—the driveway was long—and Connie ran to the window. It was a car she didn't know. It was an open jalopy, painted a bright gold that caught the sunlight opaquely. Her heart began to pound and her fingers snatched at her hair, checking it, and she whispered, "Christ. Christ," wondering how bad she looked. The car came to a stop at the side door and the horn sounded four short taps, as if this were a signal Connie knew.

She went into the kitchen and approached the door slowly, then hung out the screen door, her bare toes curling down off the step. There were two boys in the car and now she recognized the driver: he had shaggy, shabby black hair that looked crazy as a wig and he was grinning at her.

"I ain't late, am I?" he said.

"Who the hell do you think you are?" Connie said.

"Toldja I'd be out, didn't I?"

"I don't even know who you are."

She spoke sullenly, careful to show no interest or pleasure, and he spoke in a fast, bright monotone. Connie looked past him to the other boy, taking her time. He had fair brown hair, with a lock that fell onto his forehead. His sideburns gave him a fierce, embarrassed look, but so far he hadn't even bothered to glance at her. Both boys wore sunglasses. The driver's glasses were metallic and mirrored everything in miniature.

"You wanta come for a ride?" he said.

Connie smirked and let her hair fall loose over one shoulder.

"Don'tcha like my car? New paint job," he said. "Hey."

"What?"

"You're cute."

She pretended to fidget, chasing flies away from the door.

"Don'tcha believe me, or what?" he said.

"Look, I don't even know who you are," Connie said in disgust.

"Hey, Ellie's got a radio, see. Mine broke down." He lifted his friend's arm and showed her the little transistor radio the boy was holding, and now Connie began to hear the music. It was the same program that was playing inside the house.

"Bobby King?" she said.

"I listen to him all the time. I think he's great."

"He's kind of great," Connie said reluctantly.

"Listen, that guy's *great*. He knows where the action is."

Connie blushed a little, because the glasses made it impossible for her to see just what this boy was looking at. She couldn't decide if she liked him or if he was just a jerk, and so she dawdled in the doorway and wouldn't come down or go back inside. She said, "What's all that stuff painted on your car?"

"Can'tcha read it?" He opened the door very carefully, as if he were afraid it might fall off. He slid out just as carefully, planting his feet firmly on the ground, the tiny metallic world in his glasses slowing down like gelatine hardening, and in the midst of it Connie's bright green blouse. "This here is my name, to begin with," he said. ARNOLD FRIEND was written in tarlike black letters on the side, with a drawing of a round, grinning face that reminded Connie of a pumpkin, except it wore sunglasses. "I wanta introduce myself, I'm Arnold Friend and that's my real name and I'm gonna be your friend, honey, and inside the car's Ellie Oscar, he's kinda shy." Ellie brought his transistor radio up to his shoulder and balanced it there. "Now, these numbers are a secret code, honey," Arnold Friend explained. He read off the numbers 33, 19, 17 and raised his eyebrows at her to see what she thought of that, but she didn't think much of it. The left rear fender had been smashed and around it was written, on the gleaming gold background: DONE BY CRAZY WOMAN DRIVER. Connie had to laugh at that. Arnold Friend was pleased at her laughter and looked up at her. "Around the other side's a lot more—you wanta come and see them?"

"No."

"Why not?"

"Why should I?"

"Don'tcha wanta see what's on the car? Don'tcha wanta go for a ride?"

"I don't know."

"Why not?"

"I got things to do."

"Like what?"

"Things."

He laughed as if she had said something funny. He slapped his thighs. He was standing in a strange way, leaning back against the car as if he were balancing himself. He wasn't tall, only an inch or so taller than she would be if she came down to him. Connie liked the way he was dressed, which was the way all of them dressed: tight faded jeans stuffed into black, scuffed boots, a belt that pulled his waist in and showed how lean he was, and a white pull-over shirt that was a little soiled and showed the hard small muscles of his arms and shoulders. He looked as if he probably did hard work, lifting and carrying things. Even his neck looked muscular. And his face was a familiar face, somehow: the jaw and chin and cheeks slightly darkened because he hadn't shaved for a day or two, and the nose long and hawklike, sniffing as if she were a treat he was going to gobble up and it was all a joke.

"Connie, you ain't telling the truth. This is your day set aside for a ride with me and you know it," he said, still laughing. The way he straightened and recovered from his fit of laughing showed that it had been all fake.

"How do you know what my name is?" she said suspiciously.

"It's Connie."

"Maybe and maybe not."

"I know my Connie," he said, wagging his finger. Now she remembered him even better, back at the restaurant, and her cheeks warmed at the thought of how she had sucked in her breath just at the moment she passed him—how she must have looked to him. And he had remembered her. "Ellie and I come out here especially for you," he said. "Ellie can sit in back. How about it?"

"Where?"

"Where what?"

"Where're we going?"

He looked at her. He took off the sunglasses and she saw how pale the skin around his eyes was, like holes that were not in shadow but instead in light. His eyes were like chips of broken glass that catch the light in an amiable way. He smiled. It was as if the idea of going for a ride somewhere, to someplace, was a new idea to him.

"Just for a ride, Connie sweetheart."

"I never said my name was Connie," she said.

"But I know what it is. I know your name and all about you, lots of things," Arnold Friend said. He had not moved yet but stood still leaning back against the side of his jalopy. "I took a special interest in you, such a pretty girl, and found out all about you—like I know your parents and sister are gone somewheres and I know where and how long they're going to be gone, and I know who you were with last night, and your best girl friend's name is Betty. Right?"

He spoke in a simple lilting voice, exactly as if he were reciting the words to a song. His smile assured her that everything was fine. In the car Ellie turned up the volume on his radio and did not bother to look around at them.

"Ellie can sit in the back seat," Arnold Friend said. He indicated his friend with a casual jerk of his chin, as if Ellie did not count and she should not bother with him.

"How'd you find out all that stuff?" Connie said.

"Listen: Betty Schultz and Tony Fitch and Jimmy Pettinger and Nancy Pettinger," he said in a chant. "Raymond Stanley and Bob Hutter—"

"Do you know all those kids?"

"I know everybody."

"Look, you're kidding. You're not from around here."

"Sure."

"But—how come we never saw you before?"

"Sure you saw me before," he said. He looked down at his boots, as if he were a little offended. "You just don't remember."

"I guess I'd remember you," Connie said.

"Yeah?" He looked up at this, beaming. He was pleased. He began to mark time with the music from Ellie's radio, tapping his fists lightly together. Connie looked away from his smile to the car, which was painted so bright it almost hurt her eyes to look at it. She looked at that name, ARNOLD FRIEND. And up at the front fender was an expression that was familiar—MAN THE FLYING SAUCERS. It was an expression kids had used the year before but didn't use this year. She looked at it for a while as if the words meant something to her that she did not yet know.

"What're you thinking about? Huh?" Arnold Friend demanded. "Not worried about your hair blowing around in the car, are you?"

"No."

"Think I maybe can't drive good?"

"How do I know?"

"You're a hard girl to handle. How come?" he said. "Don't you know I'm your friend? Didn't you see me put my sign in the air when you walked by?"

"What sign?"

"My sign." And he drew an X in the air, leaning out toward her. They were maybe ten feet apart. After his hand fell back to his side the X was still in the air, almost visible. Connie let the screen door close and stood perfectly still inside it, listening to the music from her radio and the boy's blend together. She stared at Arnold Friend. He stood there so stiffly relaxed, pretending to be relaxed, with one hand idly on the door handle as if he were keeping himself up that way and had no intention of ever moving again. She recognized most things about him, the tight jeans that showed his thighs and buttocks and the greasy leather boots and the tight shirt, and even that slippery friendly smile of his, that sleepy dreamy smile that all the boys used to get across ideas they didn't want to put into words. She recognized all this and also, the sing-song way he talked, slightly mocking, kidding, but serious and a little melancholy, and she recognized the way he tapped one fist against the other in homage to the perpetual music behind him. But all these things did not come together.

She said suddenly, "Hey, how old are you?"

His smile faded. She could see then that he wasn't a kid, he was much older—thirty, maybe more. At this knowledge her heart began to pound faster.

"That's a crazy thing to ask. Can'tcha see I'm your own age?"

"Like hell you are."

"Or maybe a coupla years older. I'm eighteen."

"Eighteen?" she said doubtfully.

He grinned to reassure her and lines appeared at the corners of his mouth. His teeth were big and white. He grinned so broadly his eyes became slits and she saw how thick the lashes were, thick and black as if painted with a black tarlike material. Then, abruptly, he seemed to become embarrassed and looked over his shoulder at Ellie. "*Him*, he's crazy," he said. "Ain't he a riot? He's a nut, a real character." Ellie was still listening to the music. His sunglasses told nothing about what he was thinking. He wore a bright orange shirt unbuttoned halfway to show his chest,

which was a pale, bluish chest and not muscular like Arnold Friend's.
His shirt collar was turned up all around and the very tips of the collar
pointed out past his chin as if they were protecting him. He was pressing
the transistor radio up against his ear and sat there in a kind of daze,
right in the sun.

"He's kinda strange," Connie said.

"Hey, she says you're kinda strange! Kinda strange!" Arnold Friend
cried. He pounded on the car to get Ellie's attention. Ellie turned for
the first time and Connie saw with shock that he wasn't a kid either—he
had a fair, hairless face, cheeks reddened slightly as if the veins grew too
close to the surface of his skin, the face of a forty-year-old baby. Connie
felt a wave of dizziness rise in her at this sight and she stared at him as
if waiting for something to change the shock of the moment, make it all
right again. Ellie's lips kept shaping words, mumbling along with the words
blasting in his ear.

"Maybe you two better go away," Connie said faintly.

"What? How come?" Arnold Friend cried, "We come out here to take
you for a ride. It's Sunday." He had the voice of the man on the radio
now. It was the same voice, Connie thought. "Don'tcha know it's Sunday
all day? And honey, no matter who you were with last night, today you're
with Arnold Friend and don't you forget it! Maybe you better step out
here," he said, and this last was in a different voice. It was a little flatter,
as if the heat was finally getting to him.

"No. I got things to do."

"Hey."

"You two better leave."

"We ain't leaving until you come with us."

"Like hell I am—"

"Connie, don't fool around with me. I mean—I mean, don't fool *around*,"
he said, shaking his head. He laughed incredulously. He placed his sunglasses on top of his head, carefully, as if he were indeed wearing a wig,
and brought the stems down behind his ears. Connie stared at him, another
wave of dizziness and fear rising in her so that for a moment he wasn't
even in focus but was just a blur standing there against his gold car, and
she had the idea that he had driven up the driveway all right but had
come from nowhere before that and belonged nowhere and that everything
about him and even about the music that was so familiar to her was only
half real.

"If my father comes and sees you—"

"He ain't coming. He's at a barbecue."

"How do you know that?"

"Aunt Tillie's. Right now they're—uh—they're drinking. Sitting
around," he said vaguely, squinting as if he were staring all the way to
town and over to Aunt Tillie's back yard. Then the vision seemed to get
clear and he nodded energetically. "Yeah. Sitting around. There's your
sister in a blue dress, huh? And high heels, the poor sad bitch—nothing
like you, sweetheart! And your mother's helping some fat woman with
the corn, they're cleaning the corn—husking the corn—"

"What fat woman?" Connie cried.

"How do I know what fat woman, I don't know every goddamn fat woman in the world!" Arnold Friend laughed.

"Oh, that's Mrs. Hornsby. . . . Who invited her?" Connie said. She felt a little lightheaded. Her breath was coming quickly.

"She's too fat. I don't like them fat. I like them the way you are, honey," he said, smiling sleepily at her. They stared at each other for a while through the screen door. He said softly, "Now, what you're going to do is this: you're going to come out that door. You're going to sit up front with me and Ellie's going to sit in the back, the hell with Ellie, right? This isn't Ellie's date. You're my date. I'm your lover, honey."

"What? You're crazy—"

"Yes, I'm your lover. You don't know what that is but you will," he said. "I know that too. I know all about you. But look: it's real nice and you couldn't ask for nobody better than me, or more polite. I always keep my word. I'll tell you how it is, I'm always nice at first, the first time. I'll hold you so tight you won't think you have to try to get away or pretend anything because you'll know you can't. And I'll come inside you where it's all secret and you'll give in to me and you'll love me—"

"Shut up! You're crazy!" Connie said. She backed away from the door. She put her hands up against her ears as if she'd heard something terrible, something not meant for her. "People don't talk like that, you're crazy," she muttered. Her heart was almost too big now for her chest and its pumping made sweat break out all over her. She looked out to see Arnold Friend pause and then take a step toward the porch, lurching. He almost fell. But, like a clever drunken man, he managed to catch his balance. He wobbled in his high boots and grabbed hold of one of the porch posts.

"Honey?" he said. "You still listening?"

"Get the hell out of here!"

"Be nice, honey. Listen."

"I'm going to call the police—"

He wobbled again and out of the side of his mouth came a fast spat curse, an aside not meant for her to hear. But even this "Christ!" sounded forced. Then he began to smile again. She watched this smile come, awkward as if he were smiling from inside a mask. His whole face was a mask, she thought wildly, tanned down to his throat but then running out as if he had plastered make-up on his face but had forgotten about his throat.

"Honey—? Listen, here's how it is. I always tell the truth and I promise you this: I ain't coming in that house after you."

"You better not! I'm going to call the police if you—if you don't—"

"Honey," he said, talking right through her voice, "honey, I'm not coming in there but you are coming out here. You know why?"

She was panting. The kitchen looked like a place she had never seen before, some room she had run inside but that wasn't good enough, wasn't going to help her. The kitchen window had never had a curtain, after three years, and there were dishes in the sink for her to do—probably— and if you ran your hand across the table you'd probably feel something sticky there.

"You listening, honey? Hey?"

"—going to call the police—"

"Soon as you touch the phone I don't need to keep my promise and can come inside. You won't want that."

She rushed forward and tried to lock the door. Her fingers were shaking. "But why lock it," Arnold Friend said gently, talking right into her face. "It's just a screen door. It's just nothing." One of his boots was at a strange angle, as if his foot wasn't in it. It pointed out to the left, bent at the ankle. "I mean, anybody can break through a screen door and glass and wood and iron or anything else if he needs to, anybody at all, and specially Arnold Friend. If the place got lit up with a fire, honey, you'd come runnin' out into my arms, right into my arms an' safe at home—like you knew I was your lover and'd stopped fooling around. I don't mind a nice shy girl but I don't like no fooling around." Part of those words were spoken with a slight rhythmic lilt, and Connie somehow recognized them—the echo of a song from last year, about a girl rushing into her boy friend's arms and coming home again—

Connie stood barefoot on the linoleum floor, staring at him. "What do you want?" she whispered.

"I want you," he said.

"What?"

"Seen you that night and thought, that's the one, yes sir. I never needed to look anymore."

"But my father's coming back. He's coming to get me. I had to wash my hair first—" She spoke in a dry, rapid voice, hardly raising it for him to hear.

"No, your daddy is not coming and yes, you had to wash your hair and you washed it for me. It's nice and shining and all for me. I thank you sweetheart," he said with a mock bow, but again he almost lost his balance. He had to bend and adjust his boots. Evidently his feet did not go all the way down; the boots must have been stuffed with something so that he would seem taller. Connie stared out at him and behind him at Ellie in the car, who seemed to be looking off toward Connie's right, into nothing. This Ellie said, pulling the words out of the air one after another as if he were just discovering them, "You want me to pull out the phone?"

"Shut your mouth and keep it shut," Arnold Friend said, his face red from bending over or maybe from embarrassment because Connie had seen his boots. "This ain't none of your business."

"What—what are you doing? What do you want?" Connie said. "If I call the police they'll get you, they'll arrest you—"

"Promise was not to come in unless you touch that phone, and I'll keep that promise," he said. He resumed his erect position and tried to force his shoulders back. He sounded like a hero in a movie, declaring something important. But he spoke too loudly and it was as if he were speaking to someone behind Connie. "I ain't made plans for coming in that house where I don't belong but just for you to come out to me, the way you should. Don't you know who I am?"

"You're crazy," she whispered. She backed away from the door but did not want to go into another part of the house, as if this would give him permission to come through the door. "What do you . . . you're crazy, you. . . ."

"Huh? What're you saying, honey?"

Her eyes darted everywhere in the kitchen. She could not remember what it was, this room.

"This is how it is, honey: you come out and we'll drive away, have a nice ride. But if you don't come out we're gonna wait till your people come home and then they're all going to get it."

"You want that telephone pulled out?" Ellie said. He held the radio away from his ear and grimaced, as if without the radio the air was too much for him.

"I toldja shut up, Ellie," Arnold Friend said, "you're deaf, get a hearing aid, right? Fix yourself up. This little girl's no trouble and's gonna be nice to me, so Ellie keep to yourself, this ain't your date—right? Don't hem in on me, don't hog, don't crush, don't bird dog, don't trail me," he said in a rapid, meaningless voice, as if he were running through all the expressions he'd learned but was no longer sure which of them was in style, then rushing on to new ones, making them up with his eyes closed. "Don't crawl under my fence, don't squeeze in my chipmunk hole, don't sniff my glue, suck my popsicle, keep your own greasy fingers on yourself!" He shaded his eyes and peered in at Connie, who was backed against the kitchen table. "Don't mind him, honey, he's just a creep. He's a dope. Right? I'm the boy for you and like I said, you come out here nice like a lady and give me your hand, and nobody else gets hurt, I mean, your nice old bald-headed daddy and your mummy and your sister in her high heels. Because listen: why bring them in this?"

"Leave me alone," Connie whispered.

"Hey, you know that old woman down the road, the one with the chickens and stuff—you know her?"

"She's dead!"

"Dead? What? You know her?" Arnold Friend said.

"She's dead—"

"Don't you like her?"

"She's dead—she's—she isn't here any more—"

"But don't you like her, I mean, you got something against her? Some grudge or something?" Then his voice dipped as if he were conscious of a rudeness. He touched the sunglasses perched up on top of his head as if to make sure they were still there. "Now, you be a good girl."

"What are you going to do?"

"Just two things, or maybe three," Arnold Friend said. "But I promise it won't last long and you'll like me the way you get to like people you're close to. You will. It's all over for you here, so come on out. You don't want your people in any trouble, do you?"

She turned and bumped against a chair or something, hurting her leg, but she ran into the back room and picked up the telephone. Something roared in her ear, a tiny roaring, and she was so sick with fear that she could do nothing but listen to it—the telephone was clammy and very heavy and her fingers groped down to the dial but were too weak to touch it. She began to scream into the phone, into the roaring. She cried out, she cried for her mother, she felt her breath start jerking back and forth in her lungs as if it were something Arnold Friend was stabbing her with again and again with no tenderness. A noisy sorrowful wailing rose all about her and she was locked inside it the way she was locked inside this house.

After a while she could hear again. She was sitting on the floor with her wet back against the wall.

Arnold Friend was saying from the door, "That's a good girl. Put the phone back."

She kicked the phone away from her.

"No, honey. Pick it up. Put it back right."

She picked it up and put it back. The dial tone stopped.

"That's a good girl. Now, you come outside."

She was hollow with what had been fear but what was now just an emptiness. All that screaming had blasted it out of her. She sat, one leg cramped under her, and deep inside her brain was something like a pinpoint of light that kept going and would not let her relax. She thought, I'm not going to see my mother again. She thought, I'm not going to sleep in my bed again. Her bright green blouse was all wet.

Arnold Friend said, in a gentle-loud voice that was like a stage voice, "The place where you came from ain't there any more, and where you had in mind to go is cancelled out. This place you are now—inside your daddy's house—is nothing but a cardboard box I can knock down any time. You know that and always did know it. You hear me?"

She thought, I have got to think. I have got to know what to do.

"We'll go out to a nice field, out in the country here where it smells so nice and it's sunny," Arnold Friend said. "I'll have my arms tight around you so you won't need to try to get away and I'll show you what love is like, what it does. The hell with this house! It looks solid all right," he said. He ran a fingernail down the screen and the noise did not make Connie shiver, as it would have the day before. "Now, put your hand on your heart, honey. Feel that? That feels solid too but we know better. Be nice to me, be sweet like you can because what else is there for a girl like you but to be sweet and pretty and give in?—and get away before her people come back?"

She felt her pounding heart. Her hand seemed to enclose it. She thought for the first time in her life that it was nothing that was hers, that belonged to her, but just a pounding, living thing inside this body that wasn't really hers, either.

"You don't want them to get hurt," Arnold Friend went on. "Now, get up, honey. Get up all by yourself."

She stood.

"Now, turn this way. That's right. Come over here to me.—Ellie, put that away, didn't I tell you? You dope. You miserable creepy dope," Arnold Friend said. His words were not angry but only part of an incantation. The incantation was kindly. "Now, come out through the kitchen to me, honey, and let's see a smile, try it, you're a brave, sweet little girl and now they're eating corn and hot dogs cooked to bursting over an outdoor fire, and they don't know one thing about you and never did and honey, you're better than them because not a one of them would have done this for you."

Connie felt the linoleum under her feet; it was cool. She brushed her hair back and out of her eyes. Arnold Friend let go of the post tentatively and opened his arms for her, his elbows pointing in toward each other and his wrists limp, to show that this was an embarrassed embrace and a little mocking, he didn't want to make her self-conscious.

She put out her hand against the screen. She watched herself push the door slowly open as if she were back safe somewhere in the other doorway, watching this body and this head of long hair moving out into the sunlight where Arnold Friend waited.

"My sweet little blue-eyed girl," he said in a half-sung sigh that had nothing to do with her brown eyes but was taken up just the same by the vast sunlit reaches of the land behind him and on all sides of him—so much land that Connie had never seen before and did not recognize except to know that she was going to it.

(1966)

Yukio Mishima *1925–1970*

PATRIOTISM

I

On the twenty-eighth of February, 1936 (on the third day, that is, of the
February 26 Incident), Lieutenant Shinji Takeyama of the Konoe Transport
Battalion—profoundly disturbed by the knowledge that his closest colleagues had been with the mutineers from the beginning, and indignant
at the imminent prospect of Imperial troops attacking Imperial troops—
took his officer's sword and ceremonially disemboweled himself in the
eight-mat room of his private residence in the sixth block of Aoba-chō,
in Yotsuya Ward. His wife, Reiko, followed him, stabbing herself to death.
The lieutenant's farewell note consisted of one sentence: "Long live the
Imperial Forces." His wife's, after apologies for her unfilial conduct in
thus preceding her parents to the grave, concluded: "The day which, for
a soldier's wife, had to come, has come. . . ." The last moments of this
heroic and dedicated couple were such as to make the gods themselves
weep. The lieutenant's age, it should be noted, was thirty-one, his wife's
twenty-three; and it was not half a year since the celebration of their
marriage.

II

Those who saw the bride and bridegroom in the commemorative photograph—perhaps no less than those actually present at the lieutenant's wedding—had exclaimed in wonder at the bearing of this handsome couple.
The lieutenant, majestic in military uniform, stood protectively beside his
bride, his right hand resting upon his sword, his officer's cap held at his
left side. His expression was severe, and his dark brows and wide-gazing
eyes well conveyed the clear integrity of youth. For the beauty of the
bride in her white over-robe no comparisons were adequate. In the eyes,
round beneath soft brows, in the slender, finely shaped nose, and in the
full lips, there was both sensuousness and refinement. One hand, emerging
shyly from a sleeve of the over-robe, held a fan, and the tips of the fingers,
clustering delicately, were like the bud of a moonflower.

After the suicide, people would take out this photograph and examine
it, and sadly reflect that too often there was a curse on these seemingly
flawless unions. Perhaps it was no more than imagination, but looking
at the picture after the tragedy it almost seemed as if the two young people
before the gold-lacquered screen were gazing, each with equal clarity, at
the deaths which lay before them.

Thanks to the good offices of their go-between, Lieutenant General Ozeki,
they had been able to set themselves up in a new home at Aoba-chō in
Yotsuya. "New home" is perhaps misleading. It was an old three-room
rented house backing onto a small garden. As neither the six- nor the
four-and-a-half-mat room downstairs was favored by the sun, they used
the upstairs eight-mat room as both bedroom and guest room. There was

no maid, so Reiko was left alone to guard the house in her husband's absence.

The honeymoon trip was dispensed with on the grounds that these were times of national emergency. The two of them had spent the first night of their marriage at this house. Before going to bed, Shinji, sitting erect on the floor with his sword laid before him, had bestowed upon his wife a soldierly lecture. A woman who had become the wife of a soldier should know and resolutely accept that her husband's death might come at any moment. It could be tomorrow. It could be the day after. But, no matter when it came—he asked—was she steadfast in her resolve to accept it? Reiko rose to her feet, pulled open a drawer of the cabinet, and took out what was the most prized of her new possessions, the dagger her mother had given her. Returning to her place, she laid the dagger without a word on the mat before her, just as her husband had laid his sword. A silent understanding was achieved at once, and the lieutenant never again sought to test his wife's resolve.

In the first few months of her marriage Reiko's beauty grew daily more radiant, shining serene like the moon after rain.

As both were possessed of young, vigorous bodies, their relationship was passionate. Nor was this merely a matter of the night. On more than one occasion, returning home straight from maneuvers, and begrudging even the time it took to remove his mud-splashed uniform, the lieutenant had pushed his wife to the floor almost as soon as he had entered the house. Reiko was equally ardent in her response. For a little more or a little less than a month, from the first night of their marriage Reiko knew happiness, and the lieutenant, seeing this, was happy too.

Reiko's body was white and pure, and her swelling breasts conveyed a firm and chaste refusal; but, upon consent, those breasts were lavish with their intimate, welcoming warmth. Even in bed these two were frighteningly and awesomely serious. In the very midst of wild, intoxicating passions, their hearts were sober and serious.

By day the lieutenant would think of his wife in the brief rest periods between training; and all day long, at home, Reiko would recall the image of her husband. Even when apart, however, they had only to look at the wedding photograph for their happiness to be once more confirmed. Reiko felt not the slightest surprise that a man who had been a complete stranger until a few months ago should now have become the sun about which her whole world revolved.

All these things had a moral basis, and were in accordance with the Education Rescript's injunction that "husband and wife should be harmonious." Not once did Reiko contradict her husband, nor did the lieutenant ever find reason to scold his wife. On the god shelf below the stairway, alongside the tablet from the Great Ise Shrine, were set photographs of their Imperial Majesties, and regularly every morning, before leaving for duty, the lieutenant would stand with his wife at this hallowed place and together they would bow their heads low. The offering water was renewed each morning, and the sacred sprig of *sasaki* was always green and fresh. Their lives were lived beneath the solemn protection of the gods and were filled with an intense happiness which set every fiber in their bodies trembling.

III

Although Lord Privy Seal Saitō's house was in their neighborhood, neither of them heard any noise of gunfire on the morning of February 26. It was a bugle, sounding muster in the dim, snowy dawn, when the ten-minute tragedy had already ended, which first disrupted the lieutenant's slumbers. Leaping at once from his bed, and without speaking a word, the lieutenant donned his uniform, buckled on the sword held ready for him by his wife, and hurried swiftly out into the snow-covered streets of the still darkened morning. He did not return until the evening of the twenty-eighth.

Later, from the radio news, Reiko learned the full extent of this sudden eruption of violence. Her life throughout the subsequent two days was lived alone, in complete tranquility, and behind locked doors.

In the lieutenant's face, as he hurried silently out into the snowy morning, Reiko had read the determination to die. If her husband did not return, her own decision was made: she too would die. Quietly she attended to the disposition of her personal possessions. She chose her sets of visiting kimonos as keepsakes for friends of her schooldays, and she wrote a name and address on the stiff paper wrapping in which each was folded. Constantly admonished by her husband never to think of the morrow, Reiko had not even kept a diary and was now denied the pleasure of assiduously rereading her record of the happiness of the past few months and consigning each page to the fire as she did so. Ranged across the top of the radio were a small china dog, a rabbit, a squirrel, a bear, and a fox. There were also a small vase and a water pitcher. These comprised Reiko's one and only collection. But it would hardly do, she imagined, to give such things as keepsakes. Nor again would it be quite proper to ask specifically for them to be included in the coffin. It seemed to Reiko, as these thoughts passed through her mind, that the expressions on the small animals' faces grew even more lost and forlorn.

Reiko took the squirrel in her hand and looked at it. And then, her thoughts turning to a realm far beyond these child-like affections, she gazed up into the distance at the great sunlike principle which her husband embodied. She was ready, and happy, to be hurtled along to her destruction in that gleaming sun chariot—but now, for these few moments of solitude, she allowed herself to luxuriate in this innocent attachment to trifles. The time when she had genuinely loved these things, however, was long past. Now she merely loved the memory of having once loved them, and their place in her heart had been filled by more intense passions, by a more frenzied happiness. . . . For Reiko had never, even to herself, thought of those soaring joys of the flesh as a mere pleasure. The February cold, and the icy touch of the china squirrel, had numbed Reiko's slender fingers; yet, even so, in her lower limbs, beneath the ordered repetition of the pattern which crossed the skirt of her trim *meisen* kimono, she could feel now, as she thought of the lieutenant's powerful arms reaching out toward her, a hot moistness of the flesh which defied the snows.

She was not in the least afraid of the death hovering in her mind. Waiting alone at home, Reiko firmly believed that everything her husband was feeling or thinking now, his anguish and distress, was leading her—just as surely as the power in his flesh—to a welcome death. She felt as if her body could melt away with ease and be transformed to the merest fraction of her husband's thought.

Listening to the frequent announcements on the radio, she heard the names of several of her husband's colleagues mentioned among those of the insurgents. This was news of death. She followed the developments closely, wondering anxiously, as the situation became daily more irrevocable, why no Imperial ordinance was sent down, and watching what had at first been taken as a movement to restore the nation's honor come gradually to be branded with the infamous name of mutiny. There was no communication from the regiment. At any moment, it seemed, fighting might commence in the city streets, where the remains of the snow still lay.

Toward sundown on the twenty-eighth Reiko was startled by a furious pounding on the front door. She hurried downstairs. As she pulled with fumbling fingers at the bolt, the shape dimly outlined beyond the frosted-glass panel made no sound, but she knew it was her husband. Reiko had never known the bolt on the sliding door to be so stiff. Still it resisted. The door just would not open.

In a moment, almost before she knew she had succeeded, the lieutenant was standing before her on the cement floor inside the porch, muffled in a khaki greatcoat, his top boots heavy with slush from the street. Closing the door behind him, he returned the bolt once more to its socket. With what significance, Reiko did not understand.

"Welcome home."

Reiko bowed deeply, but her husband made no response. As he had already unfastened his sword and was about to remove his greatcoat, Reiko moved around behind to assist. The coat, which was cold and damp and had lost the odor of horse dung it normally exuded when exposed to the sun, weighed heavily upon her arm. Draping it across a hanger, and cradling the sword and leather belt in her sleeves, she waited while her husband removed his top boots and then followed behind him into the "living room." This was the six-mat room downstairs.

Seen in the clear light from the lamp, her husband's face, covered with a heavy growth of bristle, was almost unrecognizably wasted and thin. The cheeks were hollow, their luster and resilience gone. In his normal good spirits he would have changed into old clothes as soon as he was home and have pressed her to get supper at once, but now he sat before the table still in his uniform, his head drooping dejectedly. Reiko refrained from asking whether she should prepare the supper.

After an interval the lieutenant spoke.

"I knew nothing. They hadn't asked me to join. Perhaps out of consideration, because I was newly married. Kanō, and Homma too, and Yamaguchi."

Reiko recalled momentarily the faces of high-spirited young officers, friends of her husband, who had come to the house occasionally as guests.

"There may be an Imperial ordinance sent down tomorrow. They'll be posted as rebels, I imagine. I shall be in command of a unit with orders to attack them. . . . I can't do it. It's impossible to do a thing like that."

He spoke again.

"They've taken me off guard duty, and I have permission to return home for one night. Tomorrow morning, without question, I must leave to join the attack. I can't do it, Reiko."

Reiko sat erect with lowered eyes. She understood clearly that her husband had spoken of his death. The lieutenant was resolved. Each word, being rooted in death, emerged sharply and with powerful significance against this dark, unmovable background. Although the lieutenant was speaking of his dilemma, already there was no room in his mind for vacillation.

However, there was a clarity, like the clarity of a stream fed from melting snows, in the silence which rested between them. Sitting in his own home after the long two-day ordeal, and looking across at the face of his beautiful wife, the lieutenant was for the first time experiencing true peace of mind. For he had at once known, though she said nothing, that his wife divined the resolve which lay beneath his words.

"Well, then . . ." The lieutenant's eyes opened wide. Despite his exhaustion they were strong and clear, and now for the first time they looked straight into the eyes of his wife. "To-night I shall cut my stomach."

Reiko did not flinch.

Her round eyes showed tension, as taut as the clang of a bell.

"I am ready," she said. "I ask permission to accompany you."

The lieutenant felt almost mesmerized by the strength in those eyes. His words flowed swiftly and easily, like the utterances of a man in delirium, and it was beyond his understanding how permission in a matter of such weight could be expressed so casually.

"Good. We'll go together. But I want you as a witness, first, for my own suicide. Agreed?"

When this was said a sudden release of abundant happiness welled up in both their hearts. Reiko was deeply affected by the greatness of her husband's trust in her. It was vital for the lieutenant, whatever else might happen, that there should be no irregularity in his death. For that reason there had to be a witness. The fact that he had chosen his wife for this was the first mark of his trust. The second, and even greater mark, was that though he had pledged that they should die together he did not intend to kill his wife first—he had deferred her death to a time when he would no longer be there to verify it. If the lieutenant had been a suspicious husband, he would doubtless, as in the usual suicide pact, have chosen to kill his wife first.

When Reiko said, "I ask permission to accompany you," the lieutenant felt these words to be the final fruit of the education which he had himself given his wife, starting on the first night of their marriage, and which had schooled her, when the moment came, to say what had to be said without a shadow of hesitation. This flattered the lieutenant's opinion of himself as a self-reliant man. He was not so romantic or conceited as to imagine that the words were spoken spontaneously, out of love for her husband.

With happiness welling almost too abundantly in their hearts, they could not help smiling at each other. Reiko felt as if she had returned to her wedding night.

Before her eyes was neither pain nor death. She seemed to see only a free and limitless expanse opening out into vast distances.

"The water is hot. Will you take your bath now?"

"Ah yes, of course."

"And supper . . . ?"

The words were delivered in such level, domestic tones that the lieutenant came near to thinking, for the fraction of a second, that everything had been a hallucination.

"I don't think we'll need supper. But perhaps you could warm some sake?"

"As you wish."

As Reiko rose and took a *tanzen* gown from the cabinet for after the bath, she purposely directed her husband's attention to the opened drawer. The lieutenant rose, crossed to the cabinet, and looked inside. From the ordered array of paper wrappings he read, one by one, the addresses of the keepsakes. There was no grief in the lieutenant's response to this demonstration of heroic resolve. His heart was filled with tenderness. Like a husband who is proudly shown the childish purchases of a young wife, the lieutenant, overwhelmed by affection, lovingly embraced his wife from behind and implanted a kiss upon her neck.

Reiko felt the roughness of the lieutenant's unshaven skin against her neck. This sensation, more than being just a thing of this world, was for Reiko almost the world itself, but now—with the feeling that it was soon to be lost forever—it had freshness beyond all her experience. Each moment had its own vital strength, and the senses in every corner of her body were reawakened. Accepting her husband's caresses from behind, Reiko raised herself on the tips of her toes, letting the vitality seep through her entire body.

"First the bath, and then, after some sake . . . lay out the bedding upstairs, will you?"

The lieutenant whispered the words into his wife's ear. Reiko silently nodded.

Flinging off his uniform, the lieutenant went to the bath. To faint background noises of slopping water Reiko tended the charcoal brazier in the living room and began the preparations for warming the sake.

Taking the *tanzen*, a sash, and some underclothes, she went to the bathroom to ask how the water was. In the midst of a coiling cloud of steam the lieutenant was sitting cross-legged on the floor, shaving, and she could dimly discern the rippling movements of the muscles on his damp, powerful back as they responded to the movement of his arms.

There was nothing to suggest a time of any special significance. Reiko, going busily about her tasks, was preparing side dishes from odds and ends in stock. Her hands did not tremble. If anything, she managed even more efficiently and smoothly than usual. From time to time, it is true, there was a strange throbbing deep within her breast. Like distant lightning, it had a moment of sharp intensity and then vanished without trace. Apart from that, nothing was in any way out of the ordinary.

The lieutenant, shaving in the bathroom, felt his warmed body miraculously healed at last of the desperate tiredness of the days of indecision and filled—in spite of the death which lay ahead—with pleasurable anticipation. The sound of his wife going about her work came to him faintly. A healthy physical craving, submerged for two days, reasserted itself.

The lieutenant was confident there had been no impurity in that joy they had experienced when resolving upon death. They had both sensed at that moment—though not, of course, in any clear and conscious way— that those permissible pleasures which they shared in private were once more beneath the protection of Righteousness and Divine Power, and of a complete and unassailable morality. On looking into each other's eyes and discovering there an honorable death, they had felt themselves safe once more behind steel walls which none could destroy, encased in an impenetrable armor of Beauty and Truth. Thus, so far from seeing any inconsistency or conflict between the urges of his flesh and the sincerity of his patriotism, the lieutenant was even able to regard the two as parts of the same thing.

Thrusting his face close to the dark, cracked, misted wall mirror, the lieutenant shaved himself with great care. This would be his death face. There must be no unsightly blemishes. The clean-shaven face gleamed once more with a youthful luster, seeming to brighten the darkness of the mirror. There was a certain elegance, he even felt, in the association of death with this radiantly healthy face.

Just as it looked now, this would become his death face! Already, in fact, it had half departed from the lieutenant's personal possession and had become the bust above a dead solider's memorial. As an experiment he closed his eyes tight. Everything was wrapped in blackness, and he was no longer a living, seeing creature.

Returning from the bath, the traces of the shave glowing faintly blue beneath his smooth cheeks, he seated himself beside the now well-kindled charcoal brazier. Busy though Reiko was, he noticed, she had found time lightly to touch up her face. Her cheeks were gay and her lips moist. There was no shadow of sadness to be seen. Truly, the lieutenant felt, as he saw this mark of his young wife's passionate nature, he had chosen the wife he ought to have chosen.

As soon as the lieutenant had drained his sake cup he offered it to Reiko. Reiko had never before tasted sake, but she accepted without hesitation and sipped timidly.

"Come here," the lieutenant said.

Reiko moved to her husband's side and was embraced as she leaned backward across his lap. Her breast was in violent commotion, as if sadness, joy, and the potent sake were mingling and reacting within her. The lieutenant looked down into his wife's face. It was the last face he would see in this world, the last face he would see of his wife. The lieutenant scrutinized the face minutely, with the eyes of a traveler bidding farewell to splendid vistas which he will never revisit. It was a face he could not tire of looking at—the features regular yet not cold, the lips lightly closed with a soft strength. The lieutenant kissed those lips, unthinkingly. And suddenly, though there was not the slightest distortion of the face into the unsightliness of sobbing, he noticed that tears were welling slowly from beneath the long lashes of the closed eyes and brimming over into a glistening stream.

When, a little later, the lieutenant urged that they should move to the upstairs bedroom, his wife replied that she would follow after taking a bath. Climbing the stairs alone to the bedroom, where the air was already warmed by the gas heater, the lieutenant lay down on the bedding with arms outstretched and legs apart. Even the time at which he lay waiting for his wife to join him was no later and no earlier than usual.

He folded his hands beneath his head and gazed at the dark boards of the ceiling in the dimness beyond the range of the standard lamp. Was it death he was now waiting for? Or a wild ecstasy of the senses? The two seemed to overlap, almost as if the object of this bodily desire was death itself. But, however that might be, it was certain that never before had the lieutenant tasted such total freedom.

There was the sound of a car outside the window. He could hear the screech of its tires skidding in the snow piled at the side of the street. The sound of its horn re-echoed from near-by walls. . . . Listening to these noises he had the feeling that this house rose like a solitary island in the ocean of a society going as restlessly about its business as ever. All around, vastly and untidily, stretched the country for which he grieved. He was to give his life for it. But would that great country, with which he was prepared to remonstrate to the extent of destroying himself, take the slightest heed of his death? He did not know; and it did not matter. His was a battlefield without glory, a battlefield where none could display deeds of valor: it was the front line of the spirit.

Reiko's footsteps sounded on the stairway. The steep stairs in this old house creaked badly. There were fond memories in that creaking, and many a time, while waiting in bed, the lieutenant had listened to its welcome sound. At the thought that he would hear it no more he listened with intense concentration, striving for every corner of every moment of this precious time to be filled with the sound of those soft footfalls on the creaking stairway. The moments seemed transformed to jewels, sparkling with inner light.

Reiko wore a Nagoya sash about the waist of her *yukata*, but as the lieutenant reached toward it, its redness sobered by the dimness of the light, Reiko's hand moved to his assistance and the sash fell away, slithering swiftly to the floor. As she stood before him, still in her *yukata*, the lieutenant inserted his hands through the side slits beneath each sleeve, intending to embrace her as she was; but at the touch of his finger tips upon the warm naked flesh, and as the armpits closed gently about his hands, his whole body was suddenly aflame.

In a few moments the two lay naked before the glowing gas heater.

Neither spoke the thought, but their hearts, their bodies, and their pounding breasts blazed with the knowledge that this was the very last time. It was as if the words "The Last Time" were spelled out, in invisible brushstrokes, across every inch of their bodies.

The lieutenant drew his wife close and kissed her vehemently. As their tongues explored each other's mouths, reaching out into the smooth, moist interior, they felt as if the still-unknown agonies of death had tempered their senses to the keenness of red-hot steel. The agonies they could not yet feel, the distant pains of death, had refined their awareness of pleasure.

"This is the last time I shall see your body," said the lieutenant. "Let me look at it closely." And, tilting the shade on the lampstand to one side, he directed the rays along the full length of Reiko's outstretched form.

Reiko lay still with her eyes closed. The light from the low lamp clearly revealed the majestic sweep of her white flesh. The lieutenant, not without a touch of egocentricity, rejoiced that he would never see this beauty crumble in death.

At his leisure, the lieutenant allowed the unforgettable spectacle to engrave itself upon his mind. With one hand he fondled the hair, with the other he softly stroked the magnificent face, implanting kisses here and there where his eyes lingered. The quiet coldness of the high, tapering forehead, the closed eyes with their long lashes beneath faintly etched brows, the set of the finely shaped nose, the gleam of teeth glimpsed between full, regular lips, the soft cheeks and the small, wise chin . . . these things conjured up in the lieutenant's mind the vision of a truly radiant death face, and again and again he pressed his lips tight against the white throat—where Reiko's own hand was soon to strike—and the throat reddened faintly beneath his kisses. Returning to the mouth he laid his lips against it with the gentlest of pressures, and moved them rhythmically over Reiko's with the light rolling motion of a small boat. If he closed his eyes, the world became a rocking cradle.

Wherever the lieutenant's eyes moved his lips faithfully followed. The high, swelling breasts, surmounted by nipples like the buds of a wild cherry, hardened as the lieutenant's lips closed about them. The arms flowed smoothly downward from each side of the breast, tapering toward the wrists, yet losing nothing of their roundness of symmetry, and at their tips were those delicate fingers which had held the fan at the wedding ceremony. One by one, as the lieutenant kissed them, the fingers withdrew behind their neighbor as if in shame. . . . The natural hollow curving between the bosom and the stomach carried in its lines a suggestion not only of softness but of resilient strength, and while it gave forewarning of the rich curves spreading outward from here to the hips, it had, in itself, an appearance only of restraint and proper discipline. The whiteness and richness of the stomach and hips was like milk brimming in a great bowl, and the sharply shadowed dip of the navel could have been the fresh impress of a raindrop, fallen there that very moment. Where the shadows gathered more thickly, hair clustered, gentle and sensitive, and as the agitation mounted in the now no longer passive body there hung over this region a scent like the smoldering of fragrant blossoms, growing steadily more pervasive.

At length, in a tremulous voice, Reiko spoke.

"Show me. . . . Let me look too, for the last time."

Never before had he heard from his wife's lips so strong and unequivocal a request. It was as if something which her modesty had wished to keep hidden to the end had suddenly burst its bonds of constraint. The lieutenant obediently lay back and surrendered himself to his wife. Lithely she raised her white, trembling body, and—burning with an innocent desire to return to her husband what he had done for her—placed two white fingers on the lieutenant's eyes, which gazed fixedly up at her, and gently stroked them shut.

Suddenly overwhelmed by tenderness, her cheeks flushed by a dizzying uprush of emotion, Reiko threw her arms about the lieutenant's close-cropped head. The bristly hairs rubbed painfully against her breast, the prominent nose was cold as it dug into her flesh, and his breath was hot. Relaxing her embrace, she gazed down at her husband's masculine face. The severe brows, the closed eyes, the splendid bridge of the nose, the shapely lips drawn firmly together . . . the blue, clean-shaven cheeks reflecting the light and gleaming smoothly. Reiko kissed each of these. She kissed the broad nape of the neck, the strong, erect shoulders, the powerful chest with its twin circles like shields and its russet nipples. In the armpits, deeply shadowed by the ample flesh of the shoulders and chest, a sweet and melancholy odor emanated from the growth of hair, and in the sweetness of this odor was contained, somehow, the essence of young death. The lieutenant's naked skin glowed like a field of barley, and everywhere the muscles showed in sharp relief, converging on the lower abdomen about the small, unassuming navel. Gazing at the youthful, firm stomach, modestly covered by a vigorous growth of hair, Reiko thought of it as it was soon to be, cruelly cut by the sword, and she laid her head upon it, sobbing in pity, and bathed it with kisses.

At the touch of his wife's tears upon his stomach the lieutenant felt ready to endure with courage the cruelest agonies of his suicide.

What ecstasies they experienced after these tender exchanges may well be imagined. The lieutenant raised himself and enfolded his wife in a powerful embrace, her body now limp with exhaustion after her grief and tears. Passionately they held their faces close, rubbing cheek against cheek. Reiko's body was trembling. Their breasts, moist with sweat, were tightly joined, and every inch of the young and beautiful bodies had become so much one with the other that it seemed impossible there should ever again be a separation. Reiko cried out. From the heights they plunged into the abyss, and from the abyss they took wing and soared once more to dizzying heights. The lieutenant panted like the regimental standard-bearer on a route march. . . . As one cycle ended, almost immediately a new wave of passion would be generated, and together—with no trace of fatigue—they would climb again in a single breathless movement to the very summit.

IV

When the lieutenant at last turned away, it was not from weariness. For one thing, he was anxious not to undermine the considerable strength he would need in carrying out his suicide. For another, he would have been sorry to mar the sweetness of these last memories by over-indulgence.

Since the lieutenant had clearly desisted, Reiko too, with her usual compliance, followed his example. The two lay naked on their backs, with fingers interlaced, staring fixedly at the dark ceiling. The room was warm from the heater, and even when the sweat had ceased to pour from their bodies they felt no cold. Outside, in the hushed night, the sounds of passing traffic had ceased. Even the noises of the trains and streetcars around Yotsuya station did not penetrate this far. After echoing through the region bounded by the moat, they were lost in the heavily wooded park fronting the broad driveway before Akasaka Palace. It was hard to believe in the tension gripping this whole quarter, where the two factions of the bitterly divided Imperial Army now confronted each other, poised for battle.

Savoring the warmth glowing within themselves, they lay still and recalled the ecstasies they had just known. Each moment of the experience was relived. They remembered the taste of kisses which had never wearied, the touch of naked flesh, episode after episode of dizzying bliss. But already, from the dark boards of the ceiling, the face of death was peering down. These joys had been final, and their bodies would never know them again. Not that joy of this intensity—and the same thought had occurred to them both—was ever likely to be reexperienced, even if they should live on to old age.

The feel of their fingers intertwined—this too would soon be lost. Even the wood-grain patterns they now gazed at on the dark ceiling boards would be taken from them. They could feel death edging in, nearer and nearer. There could be no hesitation now. They must have the courage to reach out to death themselves, and to seize it.

"Well, let's make our preparations," said the lieutenant. The note of determination in the words was unmistakable, but at the same time Reiko had never heard her husband's voice so warm and tender.

After they had risen, a variety of tasks awaited them.

The lieutenant, who had never once before helped with the bedding, now cheerfully slid back the door of the closet, lifted the mattress across the room by himself, and stowed it away inside.

Reiko turned off the gas heater and put away the lamp standard. During the lieutenant's absence she had arranged this room carefully, sweeping and dusting it to a fresh cleanness, and now—if one overlooked the rose-wood table drawn into one corner—the eight-mat room gave all the appearance of a reception room ready to welcome an important guest.

"We've seen some drinking here, haven't we? With Kanō and Homma and Noguchi . . ."

"Yes, they were great drinkers, all of them."

"We'll be meeting them before long, in the other world. They'll tease us, I imagine, when they find I've brought you with me."

Descending the stairs, the lieutenant turned to look back into this calm, clean room, now brightly illuminated by the ceiling lamp. There floated across his mind the faces of the young officers who had drunk there, and laughed, and innocently bragged. He had never dreamed then that he would one day cut open his stomach in this room.

In the two rooms downstairs husband and wife busied themselves smoothly and serenely with their respective preparations. The lieutenant went to the toilet, and then to the bathroom to wash. Meanwhile Reiko folded away her husband's padded robe, placed his uniform tunic, his trousers, and a newly cut bleached loincloth in the bathroom, and set out sheets of paper on the living-room table for the farewell notes. Then she removed the lid from the writing box and began rubbing ink from the ink tablet. She had already decided upon the wording of her own note.

Reiko's fingers pressed hard upon the cold gilt letters of the ink table, and the water in the shallow well at once darkened, as if a black cloud had spread across it. She stopped thinking that this repeated action, this pressure from her fingers, this rise and fall of faint sound, was all and solely for death. It was a routine domestic task, a simple paring away of time until death should finally stand before her. But somehow, in the increasingly smooth motion of the tablet rubbing on the stone, and in the scent from the thickening ink, there was unspeakable darkness.

Neat in his uniform, which he now wore next to his skin, the lieutenant emerged from the bathroom. Without a word he seated himself at the table, bolt upright, took a brush in his hand, and stared undecidedly at the paper before him.

Reiko took a white silk kimono with her and entered the bathroom. When she reappeared in the living room, clad in the white kimono and with her face lightly made up, the farewell note lay completed on the table beneath the lamp. The thick black brushstrokes said simply:

"Long Live the Imperial Forces—Army Lieutenant Takeyama Shinji."

While Reiko sat opposite him writing her own note, the lieutenant gazed in silence, intensely serious, at the controlled movement of his wife's pale fingers as they manipulated the brush.

With their respective notes in their hands— the lieutenant's sword strapped to his side, Reiko's small dagger thrust into the sash of her white kimono—the two of them stood before the god shelf and silently prayed. Then they put out all the downstairs lights. As he mounted the stairs the lieutenant turned his head and gazed back at the striking, white-clad figure of his wife, climbing behind him, with lowered eyes, from the darkness beneath.

The farewell notes were laid side by side in the alcove of the upstairs room. They wondered whether they ought not to remove the hanging scroll, but since it had been written by their go-between, Lieutenant General Ozeki, and consisted moreover, of two Chinese characters signifying "Sincerity," they left it where it was. Even if it were to become stained with splashes of blood, they felt that the lieutenant general would understand.

The lieutenant, sitting erect with his back to the alcove, laid his sword on the floor before him.

Reiko sat facing him, a mat's width away. With the rest of her so severely white the touch of rouge on her lips seemed remarkably seductive.

Across the dividing mat they gazed intently into each other's eyes. The lieutenant's sword lay before his knees. Seeing it, Reiko recalled their first night and was overwhelmed with sadness. The lieutenant spoke, in a hoarse voice:

"As I have no second to help me I shall cut deep. It may look unpleasant, but please do not panic. Death of any sort is a fearful thing to watch. You must not be discouraged by what you see. Is that all right?"

"Yes."

Reiko nodded deeply.

Looking at the slender white figure of his wife the lieutenant experienced a bizarre excitement. What he was about to perform was an act in his public capacity as a soldier, something he had never previously shown his wife. It called for a resolution equal to the courage to enter battle; it was a death of no less degree and quality than death in the front line. It was his conduct on the battlefield that he was now to display.

Momentarily the thought led the lieutenant to a strange fantasy. A lonely death on the battlefield, a death beneath the eyes of his beautiful wife . . . in the sensation that he was now to die in these two dimensions, realizing an impossible union of them both, there was sweetness beyond words. This must be the very pinnacle of good fortune, he thought. To have every moment of his death observed by those beautiful eyes—it was like being borne to death on a gentle, fragrant breeze. There was some special favor here. He did not understand precisely what it was, but it was a domain unknown to others: a dispensation granted to no one else had been permitted to himself. In the radiant, bridelike figure of his white-robed wife the lieutenant seemed to see a vision of all those things he had loved and for which he was to lay down his life—the Imperial House-hold, the Nation, the Army Flag. All these, no less than the wife who sat before him, were presences observing him closely with clear and never-faltering eyes.

Reiko too was gazing intently at her husband, so soon to die, and she thought that never in this world had she seen anything so beautiful. The lieutenant always looked well in uniform, but now, as he contemplated death with severe brows and firmly closed lips, he revealed what was per-haps masculine beauty at its most superb.

"It's time to go," the lieutenant said at last.

Reiko bent her body low to the mat in a deep bow. She could not raise her face. She did not wish to spoil her make-up with tears, but the tears could not be held back.

When at length she looked up she saw hazily through the tears that her husband had wound a white bandage around the blade of his now unsheathed sword, leaving five or six inches of naked steel showing at the point.

Resting the sword in its cloth wrapping on the mat before him, the lieutenant rose from his knees, resettled himself cross-legged, and unfas-tened the hooks of his uniform collar. His eyes no longer saw his wife. Slowly, one by one, he undid the flat brass buttons. The dusky brown chest was revealed, and then the stomach. He unclasped his belt and undid the buttons of his trousers. The pure whiteness of the thickly coiled loin-cloth showed itself. The lieutenant pushed the cloth down with both hands, further to ease his stomach, and then reached for the white-bandaged blade of his sword. With his left hand he massaged his abdomen, glancing down-ward as he did so.

To reassure himself on the sharpness of his sword's cutting edge the lieutenant folded back the left trouser flap, exposing a little of his thigh, and lightly drew the blade across the skin. Blood welled up in the wound at once, and several streaks of red trickled downward, glistening in the strong light.

It was the first time Reiko had ever seen her husband's blood, and she felt a violent throbbing in her chest. She looked at her husband's face. The lieutenant was looking at the blood with calm appraisal. For a mo-ment—though thinking at the same time that it was hollow comfort—Reiko experienced a sense of relief.

The lieutenant's eyes fixed his wife with an intense, hawk-like stare. Moving the sword around to his front, he raised himself slightly on his hips and let the upper half of his body lean over the sword point. That he was mustering his whole strength was apparent from the angry tension of the uniform at his shoulders. The lieutenant aimed to strike deep into the left of his stomach. His sharp cry pierced the silence of the room.

Despite the effort he had himself put into the blow, the lieutenant had the impression that someone else had struck the side of his stomach agonizingly with a thick rod of iron. For a second or so his head reeled and he had no idea what had happened. The five or six inches of naked point had vanished completely into his flesh, and the white bandage, gripped in his clenched fist, pressed directly against his stomach.

He returned to consciousness. The blade had certainly pierced the wall of the stomach, he thought. His breathing was difficult, his chest thumped violently, and in some far deep region, which he could hardly believe was a part of himself, a fearful and excruciating pain came welling up as if the ground had split open to disgorge a boiling stream of molten rock. The pain came suddenly nearer, with terrifying speed. The lieutenant bit his lower lip and stifled an instinctive moan.

Was this *seppuku?*—he was thinking. It was a sensation of utter chaos, as if the sky had fallen on his head and the world was reeling drunkenly. His will power and courage, which had seemed so robust before he made the incision, had now dwindled to something like a single hair-like thread of steel, and he was assailed by the uneasy feeling that he must advance along this thread, clinging to it with desperation. His clenched fist had grown moist. Looking down, he saw that both his hand and the cloth about the blade were drenched in blood. His loincloth too was dyed a deep red. It struck him as incredible that, amidst this terrible agony, things which could be seen could still be seen, and existing things existed still.

The moment the lieutenant thrust the sword into his left side and she saw the deathly pallor fall across his face, like an abruptly lowered curtain, Reiko had to struggle to prevent herself from rushing to his side. Whatever happened, she must watch. She must be a witness. That was the duty her husband had laid upon her. Opposite her, a mat's space away, she could clearly see her husband biting his lip to stifle the pain. The pain was there, with absolute certainty, before her eyes. And Reiko had no means of rescuing him from it.

The sweat glistened on her husband's forehead. The lieutenant closed his eyes, and then opened them again, as if experimenting. The eyes had lost their luster, and seemed innocent and empty like the eyes of a small animal.

The agony before Reiko's eyes burned as strong as the summer sun, utterly remote from the grief which seemed to be tearing herself apart within. The pain grew steadily in stature, stretching upward. Reiko felt that her husband had already become a man in a separate world, a man whose whole being had been resolved into pain, a prisoner in a cage of pain where no hand could reach out to him. But Reiko felt no pain at all. Her grief was not pain. As she thought about this, Reiko began to feel as if someone had raised a cruel wall of glass high between herself and her husband.

Ever since her marriage her husband's existence had been her own existence, and every breath of his had been a breath drawn by herself. But now, while her husband's existence in pain was a vivid reality, Reiko could find in this grief of hers no certain proof at all of her own existence.

With only his right hand on the sword the lieutenant began to cut sideways across his stomach. But as the blade became entangled with the entrails it was pushed constantly outward by their soft resilience; and the lieutenant realized that it would be necessary, as he cut, to use both hands to keep the point pressed deep into his stomach. He pulled the blade across. It did not cut as easily as he had expected. He directed the strength of his whole body into his right hand and pulled again. There was a cut of three or four inches.

The pain spread slowly outward from the inner depths until the whole stomach reverberated. It was like the wild clanging of a bell. Or like a thousand bells which jangled simultaneously at every breath he breathed and every throb of his pulse, rocking his whole being. The lieutenant could no longer stop himself from moaning. But by now the blade had cut its way through to below the navel, and when he noticed this he felt a sense of satisfaction, and a renewal of courage.

The volume of blood had steadily increased, and now it spurted from the wound as if propelled by the beat of the pulse. The mat before the lieutenant was drenched red with splattered blood, and more blood overflowed onto it from pools which gathered in the folds of the lieutenant's khaki trousers. A spot, like a bird, came flying across to Reiko and settled on the lap of her white silk kimono.

By the time the lieutenant had at last drawn the sword across to the right side of his stomach, the blade was already cutting shallow and had revealed its naked tip, slippery with blood and grease. But, suddenly stricken by a fit of vomiting, the lieutenant cried out hoarsely. The vomiting made the fierce pain fiercer still, and the stomach, which had thus far remained firm and compact, now abruptly heaved, opening wide its wound, and the entrails burst through, as if the wound too were vomiting. Seemingly ignorant of their master's suffering, the entrails gave an impression of robust health and almost disagreeable vitality as they slipped smoothly out and spilled over into the crotch. The lieutenant's head drooped, his shoulders heaved, his eyes opened to narrow slits, and a thin trickle of saliva dribbled from his mouth. The gold markings on his epaulettes caught the light and glinted.

Blood was scattered everywhere. The lieutenant was soaked in it to his knees, and he sat now in a crumpled and listless posture, one hand on the floor. A raw smell filled the room. The lieutenant, his head drooping, retched repeatedly, and the movement showed vividly in his shoulders. The blade of the sword, now pushed back by the entrails and exposed to its tip, was still in the lieutenant's right hand.

It would be difficult to imagine a more heroic sight than that of the lieutenant at this moment, as he mustered his strength and flung back his head. The movement was performed with sudden violence, and the back of his head struck with a sharp crack against the alcove pillar. Reiko had been sitting until now with her face lowered, gazing in fascination at the tide of blood advancing toward her knees, but the sound took her by surprise and she looked up.

The lieutenant's face was not the face of a living man. The eyes were hollow, the skin parched, the once so lustrous cheeks and lips the color of dried mud. The right hand alone was moving. Laboriously gripping the sword, it hovered shakily in the air like the hand of a marionette and strove to direct the point at the base of the lieutenant's throat. Reiko watched her husband make this last, most heart-rending, futile exertion. Glistening with blood and grease, the point was thrust at the throat again and again. And each time it missed its aim. The strength to guide it was no longer there. The straying point struck the collar and the collar badges. Although its hooks had been unfastened, the stiff military collar had closed together again and was protecting the throat.

Reiko could bear the sight no longer. She tried to go to her husband's help, but she could not stand. She moved through the blood on her knees, and her white skirts grew deep red. Moving to the rear of her husband, she helped no more than by loosening the collar. The quivering blade at last contacted the naked flesh of the throat. At that moment Reiko's impression was that she herself had propelled her husband forward; but that was not the case. It was movement planned by the lieutenant himself, his last exertion of strength. Abruptly he threw his body at the blade, and the blade pierced his neck, emerging at the nape. There was a tremendous spurt of blood and the lieutenant lay still, cold blue-tinged steel protruding from his neck at the back.

V

Slowly, her socks slippery with blood, Reiko descended the stairway. The upstairs room was now completely still.

Switching on the ground-floor lights, she checked the gas jet and the main gas plug and poured water over the smoldering, half-buried charcoal in the brazier. She stood before the upright mirror in the four-and-a-half mat room and held up her skirts. The bloodstains made it seem as if a bold, vivid pattern was printed across the lower half of her white kimono. When she sat down before the mirror, she was conscious of the dampness and coldness of her husband's blood in the region of her thighs, and she shivered. Then, for a long while, she lingered over her toilet preparations. She applied the rouge generously to her cheeks, and her lips too she painted heavily. This was no longer make-up to please her husband. It was make-up for the world which she would leave behind, and there was a touch of the magnificent and the spectacular in her brushwork. When she rose, the mat before the mirror was wet with blood. Reiko was not concerned about this.

Returning from the toilet, Reiko stood finally on the cement floor of the porchway. When her husband had bolted the door here last night it had been in preparation for death. For a while she stood immersed in the consideration of a simple problem. Should she now leave the bolt drawn? If she were to lock the door, it could be that the neighbors might not notice their suicide for several days. Reiko did not relish the thought of their two corpses putrefying before discovery. After all, it seemed, it would be best to leave it open. . . . She released the bolt, and also drew open the frosted-glass door a fraction. . . . At once a chill wind blew in. There was no sign of anyone in the midnight streets, and stars glittered ice-cold through the trees in the large house opposite.

Leaving the door as it was, Reiko mounted the stairs. She had walked here and there for some time and her socks were no longer slippery. About halfway up, her nostrils were already assailed by a peculiar smell.

The lieutenant was lying on his face in a sea of blood. The point protruding from his neck seemed to have grown even more prominent than before. Reiko walked heedlessly across the blood. Sitting beside the lieutenant's corpse, she stared intently at the face, which lay on one cheek on the mat. The eyes were opened wide, as if the lieutenant's attention had been attracted by something. She raised the head, folding it in her sleeve, wiped the blood from the lips, and bestowed a last kiss.

Then she rose and took from the closet a new white blanket and a waist cord. To prevent any derangement of her skirts, she wrapped the blanket about her waist and bound it there firmly with the cord.

Reiko sat herself on a spot about one foot distant from the lieutenant's body. Drawing the dagger from her sash, she examined its dully gleaming blade intently, and held it to her tongue. The taste of the polished steel was slightly sweet.

Reiko did not linger. When she thought how the pain which had previously opened such a gulf between herself and her dying husband was now to become a part of her own experience, she saw before her only the joy of herself entering a realm her husband had already made his own. In her husband's agonized face there had been something inexplicable which she was seeing for the first time. Now she would solve that riddle. Reiko sensed that at last she too would be able to taste the true bitterness and sweetness of that great moral principle in which her husband believed. What had until now been tasted only faintly through her husband's example she was about to savor directly with her own tongue.

Reiko rested the point of the blade against the base of her throat. She thrust hard. The wound was only shallow. Her head blazed, and her hands shook uncontrollably. She gave the blade a strong pull sideways. A warm substance flooded into her mouth, and everything before her eyes reddened, in a vision of spouting blood. She gathered her strength and plunged the point of the blade deep into her throat.

(1966)

Translated by Geoffrey W. Sargent

Ursula K. Le Guin *1929–*

THE ONES WHO WALK AWAY FROM OMELAS

With a clamor of bells that set the swallows soaring, the Festival of Summer came to the city Omelas, bright-towered by the sea. The rigging of the boats in harbor sparkled with flags. In the streets between houses with red roofs and painted walls, between old moss-grown gardens and under avenues of trees, past great parks and public buildings, processions moved. Some were decorous: old people in long stiff robes of mauve and gray, grave master workmen, quiet, merry women carrying their babies and chatting as they walked. In other streets the music beat faster, a shimmering of gong and tambourine, and the people went dancing, the procession was a dance. Children dodged in and out, their high calls rising like the swallows' crossing flights over the music and the singing. All the processions wound towards the north side of the city, where on the great water-meadow called the Green Fields boys and girls, naked in the bright air, with mud-stained feet and ankles and long, lithe arms, exercised their restive horses before the race. The horses wore no gear at all but a halter without bit. Their manes were braided with streamers of silver, gold, and green. They flared their nostrils and pranced and boasted to one another; they were vastly excited, the horse being the only animal who has adopted our ceremonies as his own. Far off to the north and west the mountains stood up half encircling Omelas on her bay. The air of morning was so clear that the snow still crowning the Eighteen Peaks burned with white-gold fire across the miles of sunlit air, under the dark blue of the sky. There was just enough wind to make the banners that marked the race-course snap and flutter now and then. In the silence of the broad green meadows one could hear the music winding through the city streets, farther and nearer and ever approaching, a cheerful faint sweetness of the air that from time to time trembled and gathered together and broke out into the great joyous clanging of the bells.

Joyous! How is one to tell about joy? How describe the citizens of Omelas?

They were not simple folk, you see, though they were happy. But we do not say the words of cheer much any more. All smiles have become archaic. Given a description such as this one tends to make certain assumptions. Given a description such as this one tends to look next for the King, mounted on a splendid stallion and surrounded by his noble knights, or perhaps in a golden litter borne by great-muscled slaves. But there was no king. They did not use swords, or keep slaves. They were not barbarians. I do not know the rules and laws of their society, but I suspect that they were singularly few. As they did without monarchy and slavery, so they also got on without the stock exchange, the advertisement, the secret police, and the bomb. Yet I repeat that these were not simple folk, not dulcet shepherds, noble savages, bland utopians. They were not less complex than us. The trouble is that we have a bad habit, encouraged by pedants and sophisticates, of considering happiness as something rather stupid. Only pain is intellectual, only evil interesting. This is the treason of the artist: a refusal to admit the banality of evil and the terrible boredom of pain. If you can't lick 'em, join 'em. If it hurts, repeat it. But to praise despair is to condemn delight, to embrace violence is to lose hold of everything else. We have almost lost hold; we can no longer describe a happy man, nor make any celebration of joy. How can I tell you about the people of Omelas? They were not naïve and happy children—though their children were, in fact, happy. They were mature, intelligent, passionate adults whose lives were not wretched. O miracle! but I wish I could describe it better. I wish I could convince you. Omelas sounds in my words like a city in a fairy tale, long ago and far away, once upon a time. Perhaps it would be best if you imagined it as your own fancy bids, assuming it will rise to the occasion, for certainly I cannot suit you all. For instance, how about technology? I think that there would be no cars or helicopters in and above the streets; this follows from the fact that the people of Omelas are happy people. Happiness is based on a just discrimination of what is necessary, what is neither necessary nor destructive, and what is destructive. In the middle category, however—that of the unnecessary but undestructive, that of comfort, luxury, exuberance, etc.—they could perfectly well have central heating, subway trains, washing machines, and all kinds of marvelous devices not yet invented here, floating light-sources, fuelless power, a cure for the common cold. Or they could have none of that: it doesn't matter. As you like it. I incline to think that people from towns up and down the coast have been coming in to Omelas during the last days before the Festival on very fast little trains and double-decked trams, and that the train station of Omelas is actually the handsomest building in town, though plainer than the magnificent Farmers' Market. But even granted trains, I fear that Omelas so far strikes some of you as goody-goody. Smiles, bells, parades, horses, bleh. If so, please add an orgy. If an orgy would help, don't hesitate. Let us not, however, have temples from which issue beautiful nude priests and priestesses already half in ecstasy and ready to copulate with any man or woman, lover or stranger, who desires union with the deep godhead of the blood, although that was my first idea. But really it would be better not to have any temples in Omelas—at least, not manned temples. Religion yes, clergy no. Surely the beautiful nudes can just wander about, offering themselves like divine soufflés to the hunger of the needy and the rapture of the flesh. Let them join the processions. Let tambourines be struck above the copulations, and the glory of desire be proclaimed upon the gongs, and (a not unimportant point) let the offspring of these delightful rituals be beloved and looked after by all. One thing I know there is none of in Omelas is guilt. But what else should there be? I thought at first there were no drugs, but that is puritanical. For those who like it, the faint insistent sweetness of *drooz* may perfume the ways of the city, *drooz* which first brings a great lightness and brilliance to the mind and limbs, and then after some hours a dreamy languor, and wonderful visions at last of the very arcana and inmost secrets of the Universe, as well as exciting the pleasure of sex beyond all belief; and it is not habit-forming. For more modest tastes I think there ought to be beer. What else, what else belongs in the joyous city? The sense of victory, surely, the celebration of courage. But as we did without clergy, let us do without soldiers. The joy built upon successful slaughter is not the right kind of joy; it will not do; it is fearful and it is trivial. A boundless and generous contentment, a magnanimous triumph felt not against some outer enemy but in communion with the finest and fairest in the souls of all men everywhere and the splendor of the world's summer: this is what swells the hearts of the people of Omelas, and the victory they celebrate is that of life. I really don't think many of them need to take *drooz*.

Most of the processions have reached the Green Fields by now. A marvelous smell of cooking goes forth from the red and blue tents of the provisioners. The faces of small children are amiably sticky; in the benign gray beard of a man a couple of crumbs of rich pastry are entangled. The youths and girls have mounted their horses and are beginning to group around the starting line of the course. An old woman, small, fat, and laughing, is passing out flowers from a basket, and tall young men wear her flowers in their shining hair. A child of nine or ten sits at the edge of the crowd, alone, playing on a wooden flute. People pause to listen, and they smile, but they do not speak to him; for he never ceases playing and never sees them, his dark eyes wholly rapt in the sweet, thin magic of the tune.

He finishes and slowly lowers his hands holding the wooden flute.

As if that little private silence were the signal, all at once a trumpet sounds from the pavilion near the starting line: imperious, melancholy, piercing. The horses rear on their slender legs, and some of them neigh in answer. Sober-faced, the young riders stroke the horses' necks and soothe them, whispering, "Quiet, quiet, there my beauty, my hope. . . ." They begin to form in rank along the starting line. The crowds along the racecourse are like a field of grass and flowers in the wind. The Festival of Summer has begun.

Do you believe? Do you accept the festival, the city, the joy? No? Then let me describe one more thing.

In a basement under one of the beautiful public buildings of Omelas, or perhaps in the cellar of one of its spacious private homes, there is a room. It has one locked door, and no window. A little light seeps in dustily between cracks in the boards, second-hand from a cobwebbed window somewhere across the cellar. In one corner of the little room a couple of mops, with stiff, clotted, foul-smelling heads, stand near a rusty bucket. The floor is dirt, a little damp to the touch, as cellar dirt usually is. The room is about three paces long and two wide: a mere broom closet or disused tool room. In the room a child is sitting. It could be a boy or a girl. It looks about six, but actually is nearly ten. It is feeble-minded. Perhaps it was born defective, or perhaps it has become imbecile through fear, malnutrition, and neglect. It picks its nose and occasionally fumbles vaguely with its toes or genitals, as it sits hunched in the corner farthest from the bucket and the two mops. It is afraid of the mops. It finds them horrible. It shuts its eyes, but it knows the mops are still standing there; and the door is locked; and nobody will come. The door is always locked; and nobody ever comes, except that sometimes—the child has no understanding of time or interval—sometimes the door rattles terribly and opens, and a person, or several people, are there. One of them may come in and kick the child to make it stand up. The others never come close, but peer in at it with frightened, disgusted eyes. The food bowl and the water jug are hastily filled, the door is locked, the eyes disappear. The people at the door never say anything, but the child, who has not always lived in the tool room, and can remember sunlight and its mother's voice, sometimes speaks. "I will be good," it says. "Please let me out. I will be good!" They never answer. The child used to scream for help at night, and cry a good deal, but now it only makes a kind of whining, "eh-haa, eh-haa," and it speaks less and less often. It is so thin there are no calves to its legs; its belly protrudes; it lives on a half-bowl of corn meal and grease a day. It is naked. Its buttocks and thighs are a mass of festered sores, as it sits in its own excrement continually.

They all know it is there, all the people of Omelas. Some of them have come to see it, others are content merely to know it is there. They all know that it has to be there. Some of them understand why, and some do not, but they all understand that their happiness, the beauty of their city, the tenderness of their friendships, the health of their children, the wisdom of their scholars, the skill of their makers, even the abundance of their harvest and the kindly weathers of their skies, depend wholly on this child's abominable misery.

This is usually explained to children when they are between eight and twelve, whenever they seem capable of understanding; and most of those who come to see the child are young people, though often enough an adult comes, or comes back, to see the child. No matter how well the matter has been explained to them, these young spectators are always shocked and sickened at the sight. They feel disgust, which they had thought themselves superior to. They feel anger, outrage, impotence, despite all the explanations. They would like to do something for the child. But there is nothing they can do. If the child were brought up into the sunlight out of that vile place, if it were cleaned and fed and comforted, that would be a good thing, indeed; but if it were done, in that day and hour all the prosperity and beauty and delight of Omelas would wither and be destroyed. Those are the terms. To exchange all the goodness and grace of every life in Omelas for that single, small improvement: to throw away the happiness of thousands for the chance of the happiness of one: that would be to let guilt within the walls indeed.

The terms are strict and absolute; there may not even be a kind word spoken to the child.

Often the young people go home in tears, or in a tearless rage, when they have seen the child and faced this terrible paradox. They may brood over it for weeks or years. But as time goes on they begin to realize that even if the child could be released, it would not get much good of its freedom: a little vague pleasure of warmth and food, no doubt, but little more. It is too degraded and imbecile to know any real joy. It has been afraid too long ever to be free of fear. Its habits are too uncouth for it to respond to humane treatment. Indeed, after so long it would probably be wretched without walls about it to protect it, and darkness for its eyes, and its own excrement to sit in. Their tears at the bitter injustice dry when they begin to perceive the terrible justice of reality, and to accept it. Yet it is their tears and anger, the trying of their generosity and the acceptance of their helplessness, which are perhaps the true source of the splendor of their lives. Theirs is no vapid, irresponsible happiness. They know that they, like the child, are not free. They know compassion. It is the existence of the child, and their knowledge of its existence, that makes possible the nobility of their architecture, the poignancy of their music, the profundity of their science. It is because of the child that they are so gentle with children. They know that if the wretched one were not there sniveling in the dark, the other one, the flute-player, could make no joyful music as the young riders line up in their beauty for the race in the sunlight of the first morning of summer.

Now do you believe in them? Are they not more credible? But there is one more thing to tell, and this is quite incredible.

At times one of the adolescent girls or boys who go to see the child does not go home to weep or rage, does not, in fact, go home at all. Sometimes also a man or woman much older falls silent for a day or two, and then leaves home. These people go out into the street, and walk down the street alone. They keep walking, and walk straight out of the city of Omelas, through the beautiful gates. They keep walking across the farmlands of Omelas. Each one goes alone, youth or girl, man or woman. Night falls; the traveler must pass down village streets, between the houses with yellow-lit windows, and on out into the darkness of the fields. Each alone, they go west or north, towards the mountains. They go on. They leave Omelas, they walk ahead into the darkness, and they do not come back. The place they go towards is a place even less imaginable to most of us than the city of happiness. I cannot describe it at all. It is possible that it does not exist. But they seem to know where they are going, the ones who walk away from Omelas.

                                                                    (1975)

PART THREE

Writing about Poetry

The language of poetry is even more compressed than the language of the short story. You need to give yourself willingly to the understanding of poetry. The pleasure of reading it derives from the beauty of the language—the delight of the sounds and the images—as well as the power of the emotion and the depth of the insights conveyed. Poetry may seem difficult, but it can also be intensely rewarding.

10

How Do I Read Poetry?

In order to enjoy discovering the meaning of poetry, you must approach it with a positive attitude—a willingness to understand. Poetry invites your creative participation. More than any other form of literature, poetry allows you as reader to inform its meaning as you bring your own knowledge and experience to bear in interpreting images, motifs, and symbols.

Begin by reading the poem aloud—or at least by sounding the words aloud in your mind. Rhyme and rhythm work in subtle ways to emphasize key words and clarify meaning. As you reread, go slowly, paying careful attention to every word and examining again and again any difficult parts.

Get the Literal Meaning First

Before you begin interpreting a poem, you must be sure that you understand the literal meaning. Because one of the delights of poetry stems from the unusual ways in which poets put words together, you may sometimes need to straighten out the syntax. For instance, Thomas Hardy writes,

> And why unblooms the best hope ever sown?

The usual way of expressing that question would be something like this:

> And why does the best hope ever sown not bloom?

Occasionally you may need to fill in words that the poet deliberately omitted through ellipsis. When Walt Whitman writes,

> But I with mournful tread,
> Walk the deck my captain lies,
> Fallen cold and dead,

we can tell that he means "the deck [on which] my Captain lies,/ Fallen cold and dead."

Pay close attention to punctuation; it can provide clues to meaning. But do not be distressed if you discover that poets (like Emily Dickinson and Stevie Smith) sometimes use punctuation in strange ways or (like e e cummings) not at all. Along with the deliberate fracturing of syntax, this unusual use of punctuation comes under the heading of poetic license.

Always you must look up any words that you do not know—as well as any familiar words that fail to make complete sense in the context. When you read this line from Whitman,

> Passing the apple-tree blows of white and pink in the orchards,

the word "blows" seems a strange choice. If you consult your dictionary, you will discover an unusual definition of blows: "masses of blossoms," a meaning which fits exactly.

Make Associations for Meaning

Once you understand the literal meaning of a poem, you can begin to expand that meaning into an interpretation. As you do so, keep asking yourself questions: Who is the speaker? Who is being addressed? What is the message? What do the images add? What do the symbols suggest? How does it all fit together?

When, for instance, Emily Dickinson in the following lines envisions "Rowing in Eden," how do you respond to this image?

> Rowing in Eden—
> Ah, the Sea!
> Might I but moor—Tonight—
> In Thee!

Can she mean *literally* rowing in Eden? Not unless you picture a lake in the Garden, which is, of course, a possibility. What do you associate with Eden? Complete bliss? Surely. Innocence, perhaps— the innocence of Adam and Eve before the Fall? Or their lustful sensuality after the Fall? Given the opening lines of the poem,

> Wild Nights—Wild Nights!
> Were I with thee
> Wild Nights should be
> Our luxury!

one fitting response might be that "Rowing in Eden" suggests paddling through sexual innocence in a far from chaste anticipation of reaching the port of ecstasy: to "Moor—Tonight—/ In Thee!"

Sometimes poems, like stories and plays, contain *allusions* (indirect references to famous persons, events, places, or to other works of literature) that add to the meaning. Some allusions are fairly easy to perceive. When Eliot's Prufrock, in his famous love song, observes,

> No! I am not Prince Hamlet, nor was meant to be,

we know that he declines to compare himself with Shakespeare's Hamlet, a character who also had difficulty taking decisive action. Some allusions, though, are more subtle. You need to know these lines from Ernest Dowson,

> Last night, ah, yesternight, betwixt her lips and mine,
> There fell thy shadow, Cynara!

in order to catch the allusion to them in Eliot's "The Hollow Men":

> Between the motion
> And the act
> Falls the shadow.

Many allusions you can simply look up. If you are puzzled by Swinburne's line

> Thou has conquered, O pale Galilean,

your dictionary will identify the Galilean as Jesus Christ. For less well-known figures or events, you may need to consult a dictionary of Biblical characters, a dictionary of classical mythology, or a good encyclopedia.

Other valuable reference tools are Sir James Frazer's *The Golden Bough*, which discusses pre-classical myth, magic, and religion; and Cirlot's *A Dictionary of Symbols*, which traces through mythology and world literature the significance of various archetypal (i.e., universal) symbols—the sea, the seasons, colors, numbers, islands, serpents, and a host of others.

Thus, learning to understand poetry—like learning to understand any imaginative literature—involves asking yourself questions, then speculating and researching until you come up with satisfying answers.

Critical Questions for Reading Poetry

Before planning an analysis of any of the selections in the anthology of poetry, write out your answers to the following questions to confirm your understanding of the poem and to generate material for the paper.

1. Can you paraphrase the poem?
2. Who is the speaker in the poem? How would you describe this persona?

3. What is the speaker's tone? Which words reveal this tone? Is the poem perhaps ironic?

4. What heavily connotative words are used? What words have unusual or special meanings? Are any words or phrases repeated? If so, why? Which words do you need to look up?

5. What images does the poet use? How do the images relate to one another? Do these images form a unified pattern (a motif) throughout the poem?

6. What figures of speech are used? How do they contribute to the tone and meaning of the poem?

7. Are there any symbols? What do they mean? Are they universal symbols, or do they arise from the particular context of this poem?

8. Is the occasion for or the setting of the poem important in understanding its meaning? If so, why?

9. What is the theme (the central idea) of this poem? Can you state it in a single sentence?

10. How important is the role of sound effects, such as rhyme and rhythm? How do they affect tone and meaning?

11. How important is the contribution of form, such as rhyme scheme and line arrangement? How does the form influence the overall effect of the poem?

11

Writing about Persona and Tone

Tone, which, you remember, can be important in analyzing a short story, is crucial to the interpretation of poetry. Persona is closely related to tone. In order to identify persona and determine tone, you need (as usual) to ask yourself questions about the poem.

Who Is Speaking?

A good question to begin with is this: Who is the speaker in the poem? Often the most obvious answer seems to be "the poet," especially if the poem is written in the first person. When Emily Dickinson begins,

> This is my letter to the world
> That never wrote to me—

we can be fairly sure that she is writing in her own voice—that the poem itself is her "letter to the world." But poets often adopt a *persona;* that is, they speak through the voice of a character they have created. Stevie Smith, herself a middle-aged woman, adopts a persona of a different age and of the opposite sex in these lines:

> An old man of seventy-three
> I lay with my young bride in my arms. . . .

Thomas Hardy in "The Ruined Maid" (on p. 389) composes a dramatic monologue with a dual persona (or two personae), two young women who converse throughout the poem. The speaker in Auden's

387

"The Unknown Citizen" (on p. 390) is apparently a spokesperson for the bureaucracy—but most certainly is not Auden himself. Thus, in order to be strictly accurate, you should avoid "The poet says . . ." and use instead, "The speaker in the poem says . . ." or "The persona in the poem says. . . ."

What Is Tone?

After deciding who the speaker is, your next question might be, "What is the tone of this poetic voice?" Tone in poetry is essentially the same as in fiction: the attitude of the writer toward the subject matter of the poem. And tone in a piece of writing is always similar to tone of voice in speaking. If a friend finds you on the verge of tears and comments, "You certainly look cheerful today," the tone of voice—as well as the absurdity of the statement—lets you know that your friend is being ironic—that she means the opposite of what she says. When Stephen Crane begins a poem,

> Do not weep, maiden, for war is kind,

any alert person perceives his ironic tone at once from the word "kind," which war definitely is not. But irony can be much more subtle. Sometimes you need to put together a number of verbal clues in order to be sure of the irony.

One of your chief problems in identifying tone involves finding exactly the right word or words to describe it. Even after you have detected that a work is ironic, you sometimes need to decide whether the irony is gentle or bitter, whether it is light or scathing in tone. You need a number of adjectives at your command. As you analyze tone in the poems that follow, keep these terms in mind to see whether any may prove useful: humorous, joyous, playful, light, hopeful, brisk, lyrical, admiring, celebratory, laudatory, expectant, wistful, sad, mournful, dreary, tragic, elegiac, solemn, somber, poignant, earnest, blasé, disillusioned, straightforward, curt, hostile, sarcastic, cynical, ambivalent.

Looking at Persona and Tone

Read the following five poems for pleasure. Then, as you read through them again slowly and carefully, pay attention to the persona and try to identify the tone of this speaker's voice. Is the speaker angry, frightened, astonished, admiring? Or perhaps sincere, sarcastic, humorous, or deceptive?

Theodore Roethke *1908–1963*

MY PAPA'S WALTZ

The whiskey on your breath
Could make a small boy dizzy;
But I hung on like death:
Such waltzing was not easy.

We romped until the pans
Slid from the kitchen shelf;
My mother's countenance
Could not unfrown itself.

The hand that held my wrist
Was battered on one knuckle;   10
At every step you missed
My right ear scraped a buckle.

You beat time on my head
With a palm caked hard by dirt,
Then waltzed me off to bed
Still clinging to your shirt.

(1948)

Thomas Hardy *1840–1928*

THE RUINED MAID

"O 'Melia, my dear, this does everything crown!
Who could have supposed I should meet you in Town?
And whence such fair garments, such prosperi-ty?"—
"O didn't you know I'd been ruined?" said she.

—"You left us in tatters, without shoes or socks,
Tired of digging potatoes, and spudding up docks;
And now you've gay bracelets and bright feathers three!"—
"Yes: that's how we dress when we're ruined," said she.

—"At home in the barton[1] you said 'thee' and 'thou,'
And 'thik oon,' and 'theas oon,' and 't'other'; but now   10
Your talking quite fits 'ee for high compa-ny!"—
"Some polish is gained with one's ruin," said she.

[1] Farmyard.

—"Your hands were like paws then, your face blue and bleak,
But now I'm bewitched by your delicate cheek,
And your little gloves fit as on any la-dy!"—
"We never do work when we're ruined," said she.

—"You used to call home-life a hag-ridden dream,
And you'd sigh, and you'd sock;[2] but at present you seem
To know not of megrims[3] or melancho-ly!"—
"True. One's pretty lively when ruined," said she.   20

—"I wish I had feathers, a fine sweeping gown,
And a delicate face, and could strut about Town!"—
"My dear—a raw country girl, such as you be,
Cannot quite expect that. You ain't ruined," said she.

                                                                    (1866)

W. H. Auden   *1907–1973*

THE UNKNOWN CITIZEN

(To JS/07/M/378
This Marble Monument
Is Erected by the State)

He was found by the Bureau of Statistics to be
One against whom there was no official complaint,
And all the reports on his conduct agree
That, in the modern sense of an old-fashioned word, he was a saint,
For in everything he did he served the Greater Community.
Except for the War till the day he retired
He worked in a factory and never got fired,
But satisfied his employers, Fudge Motors Inc.
Yet he wasn't a scab or odd in his views,
For his Union reports that he paid his dues,   10
(Our report on his Union shows it was sound)
And our Social Psychology workers found
That he was popular with his mates and liked a drink.
The Press are convinced that he bought a paper every day
And that his reactions to advertisements were normal in every way.
Policies taken out in his name prove that he was fully insured.
And his Health-card shows he was once in hospital but left it cured.
Both Producers Research and High-Grade Living declare
He was fully sensible to the advantages of the Installment Plan
And had everything necessary to the Modern Man,   20

[2] Moan.
[3] Sadness.

A phonograph, a radio, a car and a frigidaire.
Our researchers into Public Opinion are content
That he held the proper opinions for the time of year;
When there was peace, he was for peace; when there was war, he
    went.
He was married and added five children to the population,
Which our Eugenist says was the right number for a parent of his
    generation,
And our teachers report that he never interfered with their education.
Was he free? Was he happy? The question is absurd: 30
Had anything been wrong, we should certainly have heard.

(1940)

Edmund Waller *1607–1687*

GO, LOVELY ROSE

Go, lovely Rose,
Tell her That wastes her time and me,
    that now she knows,
When I resemble her to thee,
How sweet and fair she seems to be.

Tell her That's young,
And shuns to have her graces spied,
    that had'st thou sprung
In deserts where no men abide,
Thou must have uncommended died.   10

Small is the worth
Of beauty from the light retir'd:
    Bid her come forth,
Suffer herself to be desir'd,
And not blush so to be admir'd.

Then die, that she
The common fate of all things rare
    May read in thee,
How small a part of time they share,
That are so wondrous sweet and fair.   20

(1645)

Dorothy Parker *1893–1967*

ONE PERFECT ROSE

A single flow'r he sent me, since we met.
    All tenderly his messenger he chose;
Deep-hearted, pure, with scented dew still wet—
    One perfect rose.

I knew the language of the floweret;
    "My fragile leaves," it said, "his heart enclose."
Love long has taken for his amulet
    One perfect rose.

Why is it no one ever sent me yet
    One perfect limousine, do you suppose?   10
Ah no, it's always just my luck to get
    One perfect rose.

                                    (1926)

Prewriting

As you search for a fuller understanding of a poem and for a possible writing approach, remember to keep rereading the poem (or at least pertinent parts of it). The questions you pose for yourself will then be easier to answer and your responses more accurate.

ASKING QUESTIONS ABOUT THE SPEAKER

If a poem lends itself to an approach through persona or tone, you will, of course, find something unusual or perhaps puzzling about the speaker or the poetic voice. Consider Theodore Roethke's "My Papa's Waltz," which you just read. Ask yourself first, Who is the speaker? You know from line 2: "a small boy." But the past tense verbs suggest that the boy may be grown now, remembering a childhood experience. Sometimes this adult perspective can be important.

Next, ask yourself, What is the speaker's attitude toward his father? This is the crucial issue in determining the tone of the poem. You need to look carefully at details and word choice to discover your answer. Consider, for instance, these questions:

1. Is it pleasant or unpleasant to be made dizzy from the smell of whiskey on someone's breath?
2. Does it sound like fun to hang on "like death"?
3. How does it change the usually pleasant experience of waltzing to call it "not easy"?

4. What sort of "romping" would be necessary to cause pans to slide from a shelf?

5. Is it unusual to hold your dancing partner by the wrist? How is this different from being held by the hand?

6. Would it be enjoyable or painful to have your ear scraped repeatedly by a buckle?

7. Would you like or resent having someone "beat time" on your head with a hard, dirty hand?

8. If the father is gripping the boy's wrist with one hand and thumping his head with the other, does this explain why the boy must hang on for dear life?

9. What other line in the poem does the last line echo?

If your answers to these questions lead you to conclude that this waltzing was not fun for the boy, then you could describe the tone as ironic (because of the discrepancy between the pleasant idea of the waltz and the boy's unpleasant experience). You could, possibly, describe the tone as detached, because the boy gives no clear indication of his feelings. We have to deduce them from details in the poem. You could even describe the tone as reminiscent, but this term is too general to indicate the meaning carried by the tone.

We all bring our own experience to bear in interpreting a poem. What you must guard against is allowing your personal experience to carry too much weight in your response. If, for instance, you had an abusive father, you might so strongly identify with the boy's discomfort that you would call the tone resentful. On the other hand, if you enjoyed a loving relationship with your father, you might well find (as does X. J. Kennedy) "the speaker's attitude toward his father warmly affectionate, and take this recollection of childhood to be a happy one" (*An Introduction to Poetry*, 4th ed. Boston: Little, Brown, 1971: 10). Kennedy cites as evidence "the rollicking rhythms of the poem; the playfulness of a rhyme like *dizzy* and *easy*; the joyful suggestions of the words *waltz, waltzing,* and *romped.*" He suggests that a reader who sees the tone as resentful fails "to visualize this scene in all its comedy, with kitchen pans falling and the father happily using his son's head for a drum." Kennedy also feels in the last line the suggestion of "the boy *still clinging* with persistent love."

DESCRIBING THE TONE

You can see by now that speaker and tone are all but impossible to separate. In order to get at the tone of the other poems that you just read, write out the responses to the following questions and be prepared to discuss the tone of each poem in class.

"THE RUINED MAID"

1. Who are the two speakers in this poem?

2. What does the term "maid" mean in the title? Look it up in your dictionary if you are not sure.

3. What different meanings does your dictionary give for "ruined"? Which one applies in the poem?

4. How does the ruined maid probably make her living? What details suggest this?

5. Describe how the tone of the country maid's speeches changes during the course of the poem.

6. What tone does the ruined maid use in addressing her former friend?

7. How does the final line undercut the ruined maiden's boast that she gained "polish" with her ruin?

8. What is Hardy's tone—that is, the tone of the poem itself?

"THE UNKNOWN CITIZEN"

1. How is the "he" being referred to in the poem identified in the italicized epigraph?

2. Who is the speaker in the poem? Why does the speaker use "our" and "we" instead of "my" and "I"?

3. Is *Fudge Motors Inc.* a serious name for a corporation? What is the effect of rhyming "Inc." (line 8) with "drink" (line 13)?

4. Why does Auden capitalize so many words and phrases that normally would not be capitalized (like Greater Community, Installment Plan, Modern Man, Public Opinion, etc.)?

5. What is the attitude of the poetic voice toward the Unknown Citizen? What is Auden's attitude toward the Unknown Citizen? What is Auden's attitude toward the speaker in the poem?

6. What, then, is the tone of the poem?

"GO, LOVELY ROSE"

1. What has happened between the speaker and the woman before the poem was written?

2. Why does he choose a rose to carry his message?

3. What does "uncommended" mean in line 10?

4. Can you detect a tone slightly different in lines 2 and 7 from the speaker's admiring tone in the poem as a whole?

5. How do you respond to his telling the rose to die so that the woman may be reminded of how quickly her beauty will also die?

6. Does the title "Song," as the poem is sometimes called, convey any hint about the tone?

7. How would you describe the tone of this poem?

"ONE PERFECT ROSE"

1. What are the similarities between Parker's poem and Waller's?

2. What are the major differences?

3. Why does Parker put an apostrophe in "flow'r"?

4. What is an "amulet"?

5. How does the tone of the poem change in the last stanza? Can you explain why this happens?

6. What is the tone of the entire poem?

Writing

Because you may find poetry more difficult to write about than short stories, be sure that you understand the poem thoroughly before you commit your thoughts to paper. After you are sure that you have grasped the literal level, you then need to begin to examine the images, make associations, and flesh out the meanings that will eventually lead you to a complete interpretation of the poem. By this time you should have generated sufficient material to write about the work. The writing process at this stage is essentially the same as it is for discussing a short story.

EXPLICATING AND ANALYZING

Some people consider explicating and analyzing poetry to be about the same thing. Others make a distinction. For some people an explication involves an almost line-by-line explanation of the poem, leading ultimately to the theme; an analysis involves focusing on some element of the poem and examining how that element contributes to an understanding of theme. You can see that analysis is more challenging to write because you must exercise more options in selecting and organizing your material. An explication can proceed from beginning to end in a more or less chronological fashion. Your instructor will let you know if it matters which type of paper you compose. Before you begin writing, you should turn to pages 407–410 and examine the sample student paper on poetry and its revision.

IDEAS FOR WRITING

1. Both "My Papa's Waltz" (page 389) and "Piano" by D. H. Lawrence (page 501) concern the childhood experience of a young boy. Study both poems; then compare or contrast their tones.

2. Discuss the ambivalent tone of "My Papa's Waltz," making clear (either as you compare the two readings or in the conclusion) which interpretation you consider most convincing.

3. Compare Waller's "Go, Lovely Rose" with Parker's parody "One Perfect Rose" by focusing on the differences in tone.

4. Stevie Smith's "Not Waving But Drowning" (see p. 519) seems difficult until you realize that two voices are speaking—the "I" of the first and third stanzas and the "they" of the second. Once you understand the implications of this dual perspective, write an explication of the poem.

5. Discuss the satirical effectiveness of Auden's deadpan narrator in "The Unknown Citizen."

Rewriting: Style

Toward the end of your revising process, you should always devote some attention to style. Your writing *must* be clear and coherent, but your readers will be even more favorably impressed if also your sentences are shapely, your words well chosen and your statements precise.

TRY SENTENCE COMBINING

As you revise your first draft, examine your sentence structure to determine whether any of your statements might be more effective if combined. Consider these two observations:

> These recurring images are sometimes called motifs. They unify a work and provide important clues to meaning.

By writing two sentences you give equal importance to the definition of motifs and to the explanation of their function. If you choose to stress the definition, you can do so by combining the sentences this way:

> These recurring images, which unify a work and provide important clues to meaning, are sometimes called motifs.

Probably, though, you would want to emphasize the way motifs function by subordinating the definition this way:

> These recurring images, sometimes called motifs, unify a work and provide important clues to meaning.

Sentence combining, as you can see, enables you to express ideas with greater precision and to show their relationship.

EXERCISE

We have decombined a series of sentences from a well-written passage in a paper by one of our students, Sherry Young. Read through the entire passage; then, using sentence combining, create a paragraph in which the main ideas appear in the main clauses and the less important details are effectively subordinated to them. Some sentences may be fine as they are. There is, of course, no single right way to revise these choppy sentences. Try to produce a version you consider stylistically effective.

The story opens with the two characters at odds.

Dr. Ed is giving medical advice to Rosicky.

Rosicky has a heart problem.

Dr. Ed sounds much like the typical doctor.

He is all-knowing.

He is gruff but loveable.

But Rosicky jokes with the doctor.

He seems amused by Dr. Ed's pronouncements.

"Well, I guess you ain't got no pills for a bad heart, Dr. Ed. I guess the only thing is fur me to git me a new one."

Dr. Ed takes slight offense at this attitude.

He does not like having a patient take his judgment lightly.

He proceeds to give old Rosicky a list of things he must not do.

He hopes this careful routine will prolong Rosicky's life.

The key line in the scene comes from Rosicky.

"I can't make my heart go no longer'n it wants to, can I, Dr. Ed?"

Of course not.

Dr. Ed has skill.

He has a great deal of medical training.

Yet he cannot fix the old man's heart.

He can only give advice.

He wants him to give up working his farm.

Perhaps this is why the doctor is displeased.

He "frowned at [his stethoscope] as if he were seriously annoyed with the instrument."

12

Writing about Poetic Language

In no other form of literature are words so important as in poetry. As you study the language of poetry—its freshness, precision, and beauty—you can learn ways in which to use words effectively in your own prose writing.

What Do the Words Suggest?

Your sensitivity to poetic language will be enhanced if you learn a few terms used in literary criticism.

CONNOTATION AND DENOTATION

"I crawled back to him."

What do those five words mean to you? You may picture a scene of a battle or adventure in which one person must move to another on hands and knees. Or you may envision an emotional scene in which a spurned lover accepts a humiliating reconciliation.

Which scene you picture depends on whether you are thinking of the *denotative* or *connotative* meaning of the word *crawl*. The first choice uses the denotative meaning—the definition of *crawl* that you would find in a dictionary. The second choice involves the connotative meaning of the word—the one that carries emotional weight. For another example of the importance of connotation, consider the variations in emotional message in the following three statements:

I lost.
I was defeated.
I was mastered.

Connotation is the reason a cashier at Disney World is called a Merchandise Host. You might, if you wanted to be facetious, consider your teacher in this course as a Written Communications Group Consultant. These are *euphemisms*, which substitute words with high-class connotations for plain-sounding words.

FIGURES OF SPEECH, IMAGERY, SYMBOL, AND PARADOX

"Merchandise Host" is a figure of speech, a variation of the usual denotative way words would be used. Figures of speech show up all the time in our everyday talk, but even more frequently in poetic language. Three kinds that you should know so that you can write about poetry are *metaphor, simile,* and *personification.*

Metaphors and *similes* are comparisons that make use of the connotative values of words. When Shakespeare writes to a young lover that "Thy eternal summer shall not fade," he is comparing her youth to the joys of summertime. In "Dulce Et Decorum Est," a compelling anti-war poem, Wilfred Owen uses the metaphors "drunk with fatigue," "blood-shod," "like old beggars under sacks," "coughing like hags," "flound'ring like a man in fire or lime," and "his hanging face, like a devil's sick of sin." The last four of these singularly grim comparisons would usually be called *similes* because they include the connective *like,* but you can also find similes that use *as* and other explicitly comparative words.

"Daylight is nobody's friend," writes Anne Sexton in a metaphor that compares daylight to a friend, but more exactly it is a *personification,* because it makes a nonhuman thing sound like a human being. T. S. Eliot uses personification when he writes ". . . the afternoon, the evening, sleeps so peacefully," as does Andrew Marvell in "fate with jealous eyes does see."

Perhaps personification is so widely used in poetry because it gives us a clear image of something otherwise vague or abstract, like daylight or fate. *Imagery* is the term we use to speak of these sensory impressions literature gives us. Robert Frost, in a famous poem, describes a sleigh driver ". . . stopping here/ To watch his woods fill up with snow," providing a visual image that most readers find easy to picture. In the same poem, Frost gives us an apt auditory image: "The only other sound's the sweep/ Of easy wind and downy flake." And anyone who has spent time in a big airport must agree with Yvor Winters' image of one: ". . . the light gives perfect vision, false and hard;/ The metal glitters, deep and bright."

A *symbol* is an image that becomes so suggestive that it takes on much more meaning than its descriptive value. The connotations of the words, repetition, placement, or other indications of emphasis help identify an image as a symbol. Blue skies and fresh spring breezes can certainly be just that, but they can also symbolize freedom. Look at the first stanza of a W. H. Auden poem:

> As I walked out one evening
> > Walking down Bristol Street
> The people on the pavement
> > Were fields of harvest wheat.

The image in lines three and four is descriptive: you can envision a crowd of moving people seeming to ripple like wheat. The observation is also symbolic, because harvest wheat is just about to be cut down; the rest of the poem endorses a rather dim view of human hopes and dreams. The same poem says, "You shall love your crooked neighbor/ With your crooked heart." An inexperienced reader might say, "Now, that doesn't make any sense! 'Crooked heart' and 'love' seem contradictory." Others, though, would be sensitive to the paradox in those lines. A *paradox* is a phrase or statement that on the surface seems contradictory but makes some kind of emotional sense. Looking back at the Yvor Winters description of the San Francisco airport at night, you will find the phrase "perfect vision, false and hard." How can perfect vision be false instead of true? Only as a paradox. So are "the sounds of silence," "grim humor," "lonely in a crowd," "icy hot saxophone work." And popular singer Carly Simon tells her lover paradoxically that "Nobody does it better/ Makes me feel bad so good."

Looking at Poetic Language

The six poems you are about to study exemplify elements of poetic language. As you read them over several times, identify figures of speech, imagery, symbol, and paradox.

Walt Whitman *1819–1892*

A NOISELESS PATIENT SPIDER

A noiseless patient spider,
I mark'd where on a little promontory it stood isolated,
Mark'd how to explore the vacant vast surrounding,

It launched forth filament, filament, filament, out of itself,
Ever unreeling them, ever tirelessly speeding them.

And you O my soul where you stand,
Surrounded, detached, in measureless oceans of space,
Ceaselessly musing, venturing, throwing, seeking the spheres to
    connect them,
Till the bridge you will need be form'd, till the ductile anchor hold,
Till the gossamer thread you fling catch somewhere, O my soul.   10

(1881)

William Shakespeare *1564–1616*

SONNET 18

Shall I compare thee to a summer's day?
Thou art more lovely and more temperate:
Rough winds do shake the darling buds of May,
And summer's lease hath all too short a date:
Sometimes too hot the eye of heaven shines,
And often is his gold complexion dimmed;
And every fair from fair sometimes declines,
By chance or nature's changing course untrimmed;
But thy eternal summer shall not fade,
Nor lose possession of that fair thou ow'st;   10
Nor shall death brag thou wander'st in his shade,
When in eternal lines to time thou grow'st:
So long as men can breathe, or eyes can see,
So long lives this, and this gives life to thee.

(1609)

H. D. *1886–1961*

HEAT

Oh wind, rend open the heat,
cut apart the heat,
rend it to tatters.

Fruit cannot drop
through this thick air—
fruit cannot fall into heat
that presses up and blunts

the points of pears
and rounds the grapes.

Cut the heat—   10
plough through it,
turning it on either side
of your path.

(1916)

Robert Frost *1874–1963*

THE SILKEN TENT

She is as in a field a silken tent
At midday when a sunny summer breeze
Has dried the dew and all its ropes relent,
So that in guys it gently sways at ease,
And its supporting central cedar pole,
That is its pinnacle to heavenward
And signifies the sureness of the soul,
Seems to owe naught to any single cord,
But strictly held by none, is loosely bound
By countless silken ties of love and thought   10
To everything on earth the compass round,
And only by one's going slightly taut
In the capriciousness of summer air
Is of the slightest bondage made aware.

(1942)

Donald Hall *1928–*

MY SON, MY EXECUTIONER

My son, my executioner,
    I take you in my arms,
Quiet and small and just astir,
    And whom my body warms.

Sweet death, small son, our instrument
    Of immortality,
Your cries and hungers document
    Our bodily decay.

We twenty-five and twenty-two,
Who seemed to live forever,   10
Observe enduring life in you
And start to die together.

(1955)

Adrienne Rich *1929–*

AUNT JENNIFER'S TIGERS

Aunt Jennifer's tigers prance across a screen,
Bright topaz denizens of a world of green.
They do not fear the men beneath the tree;
They pace in sleek chivalric certainty.

Aunt Jennifer's fingers fluttering through her wool
Find even the ivory needle hard to pull.
The massive weight of Uncle's wedding band
Sits heavily upon Aunt Jennifer's hand.

When Aunt is dead, her terrified hands will lie
Still ringed with ordeals she was mastered by.   10
The tigers in the panel that she made
Will go on prancing, proud and unafraid.

(1951)

Prewriting

The following exercises will help you analyze the use of language in the poems that you just read in preparation for writing a paper focusing on that approach.

EXAMINING POETIC LANGUAGE

1. Why could one say that Sonnet 18 presents contrast rather than comparison?

2. In a group of classmates, attempt to write a companion poem to Sonnet 18, only with the extended metaphor being, "Shall I compare thee to a winter's day?" Try to use connotative language.

3. What is the main comparison made in "A Noiseless Patient Spider"? What is personified? Using a thesaurus, rewrite the poem, substituting near synonyms for some of the original words. Comment on the differences in meaning and tone you create. (Imagine, for example, if the spider "launched forth string, string, string, out of itself.")

4. "Heat" identifies the abstract conditions of heat and wind with concrete things, but does not do so explicitly. What concrete things represent the heat and the wind in the poem's basic image?

5. Make a sketch of the silken tent in Frost's poem. What do the different parts of the tent symbolize? What is Frost's attitude toward "She," and what words let you know it?

6. Explain the paradox that is central to "My Son, My Executioner."

7. The basic comparison in "Aunt Jennifer's Tigers" is the one between the woman herself and the tigers she embroiders. Make a paired list of words that describe Aunt Jennifer and words that describe the tigers. What does "Uncle's wedding band" symbolize?

Writing

Poetic language is one of the richest veins of material for writing. You could, for example, analyze the role of nature imagery in "Heat," in "Shall I compare thee to a summer's day?" and in "A Noiseless, Patient Spider." Or you could examine the cumulative effect of the extended simile in "The Silken Tent." One way to approach a paper on poetic language is through comparison.

COMPARING AND CONTRASTING

Noticing similarities and differences between poems will sharpen your sensitivity to each of them. If you listed all the words in the short poem "My Son, My Executioner" and scrambled them, then listed all the words in "Heat" and scrambled them, putting the two lists side by side, you might see for the first time that "Heat" has no words over two syllables, that it has few abstract terms, and that in contrast with "My Son, My Executioner" it has few words that convey emotion. Taking the comparison further, you might say that "Heat" focuses on creating a strong, simple image, while "My Son, My Executioner" focuses on expression of ideas and feelings.

Also, as you have seen from your pre-writing exercise on "Aunt Jennifer's Tigers," comparisons of images and language within a poem may give you access to its meaning. The following writing assignments suggest some meaningful comparisons to explore.

IDEAS FOR WRITING

1. Analyze the poetic language of "The Silken Tent" and "Aunt Jennifer's Tigers" to make a statement about the poem's attitudes toward traditional women's roles.

2. Compare the two kinds of love described in "A Valediction: Forbidding Mourning" (page 442 in the anthology), using the images associated with each kind.

3. Discuss the symbol of the spider in "Design" (page 497 in the anthology) and "A Noiseless Patient Spider" (pages 400–401).

4. Show how the language of "To the Mercy Killers" (page 528) and Dickinson's "She dealt her pretty words like Blades" (page 478) is similarly effective.

5. Compare and contrast the nature imagery in Shakespeare's Sonnet 18 ("Shall I compare thee to a summer's day?") (page 401) and Sonnet 73 ("That time of year thou mayst in me behold" on page 439 in the anthology).

Rewriting: Style

After looking so closely at poetic language, you should have a grasp of how important every word is to the total effect of a piece of writing.

CHOOSING VIVID, DESCRIPTIVE TERMS

Dudley Randall's "To the Mercy Killers" draws its strength almost exclusively from the vividness of its language: he describes himself as "a clot, an aching clench,/ A stub, a stump, a butt, a scab, a knob,/ A roaring pain, a putrefying stench." While your expository prose should not be quite so packed with arresting terminology, it can probably be improved by some attention to descriptive wording. Look at some of your back papers from this class. See whether you can identify your pet vacant words: Do you always express positive evaluations with *nice* or *beautiful?* Do you usually intensify an adjective with the word *very?* Do you refer to everything from ideas to irises as *things?* And do you describe anything that causes a faint stir in your being as *interesting,* causing you to come up with vapid sentences like, "This beautiful poem is full of very interesting things"? If so, you need to find livelier, more exact terms.

FINDING LIVELY WORDS

Two quite different sources of help can work together in your quest for more descriptive style. The first is your imagination: when you see that word "interesting" crop up as you write your rough draft, put a check in the margin; later, as you rewrite, ask yourself what you really meant. Sometimes you mean *significant* or *meaningful;* sometimes you mean *unusual* or *odd;* sometimes you even mean *perplexing* or *disturbing.*

If you are not completely pleased with your efforts, try using a thesaurus to jog your memory. Under *interesting* in our Roget's *Thesaurus*, we find "racy, spicy, breezy, salty; succulent, piquant, appealing, zestful, glamorous, colorful, picturesque; absorbing, enthralling, engrossing, fascinating, entertaining, ageless, dateless," as well as cross-references to more lists at *amusement, attention, attraction, and right.* Somewhere in this large selection you should be able to find a word that conveys a clearer image than *interesting* does. Never choose an unfamiliar word, though, without first looking it up in a collegiate dictionary to be sure it conveys the exact meaning you want.

EXERCISE

Find five to ten sentences in your back papers (from this class or others) that can be improved by the use of livelier, more descriptive words. Write down the original, using every other line on your page. Then revise the sentence, crossing out vacant words and writing in the new ones on the blank lines.

Sample Student Paper

Following you will find a second draft followed by a final version of a student paper analyzing imagery.

EXERCISE

Reread the two drafts, making point-by-point comparisons. Notice that the writer went beyond the instructor's specific suggestions in her final revision. Write a paragraph on one of these three topics:

1. Identify five cases in which the writer made changes in word choice (diction). Using a dictionary, explain the rationale for the changes.
2. Identify two sentences that have been significantly changed. Explain the reasons for the changes.
3. Closely analyze all the alterations in one paragraph of the essay.

SAMPLE STUDENT PAPER--SECOND DRAFT

Images of a Love

The speaker in John Donne's poem "A Valediction:
Forbidding Mourning" is an unromantic man who is sternly
forbidding his wife to be sorrowful at his parting.
This description is not true of course, but it is the
way the speaker might be perceived if all comparisons,
contrasts, and images were taken out of the poem. In
order to appreciate the beauty of this poem and
interpret it correctly, it is necessary to take a close
look at each image or comparison.

The first comparison we come to likens the speaker's
parting to the quiet and easy death of virtuous men.
The speaker paints a picture of a virtuous or upright
man who, because he does not fear it, is passing
peacefully into death. His deathbed is surrounded by
his friends who are having trouble deciding if he has
actually passed away or if he is still quietly
breathing. The speaker says that his departure from his
wife should be just as calm. He says, "let us melt,"
which implies slowly and easily parting without any
noise or tears. He explains that showing great emotion
would expose their love to the common people and he does
not want this because he believes their love is
special, and that exposure would lower their love.

[margin note: *vague reference*]
[margin note: *Best word choice?*]

The speaker next contrasts their love to the love
of common people. He states that common people notice
earthquakes, but not trepidations or tremblings that
take place among the stars. He is illustrating that
common people's love is earthly, but that their love is
heavenly. He goes on to say that "sublunary" or earthly
lovers cannot be apart from each other because when they
are, they lose their love because it is only physical.
He claims that he and his wife are not like this. He
feels that their love (his and his wife's) is spiritual
and refined and that it is so great that it is above
their understanding ("ourselves know not what it is").
They do not have to worry about their spouse being

[margin note: *misleading reference?*]
[margin note: *needs rephrasing*]
[margin note: *weak reference*]
[margin note: *rephrase*]

unfaithful, as earthly lovers do, because their love is
not just physical.

Next the speaker compares the malleability of gold
to the distance that their souls can stretch. The
speaker says that temporary separation should not be
viewed as a break. He believes that even though they
may be many miles apart, they are still one. He claims
their souls can expand over distances equal to the
malleability of gold or 250 square feet. This is a
truly beautiful image.

Maybe expand with other associations of gold

clarify

The last image is another very beautiful one. It
compares their two souls to twin compasses. The speaker
believes that if their souls are two (instead of one),
they are still linked to each other, as are the parts of
a compass. He likens his wife to the foot in the
center. She makes no attempt on her own to move. She
does so only if he does. She is also like the center
foot in that if he leaves, she leans after him and then
becomes upright when he returns home as does the center
foot of a compass when the outer foot is at a distance
drawing a circle. He says that there will be times when
he must leave but that he will always return to her even
as a compass returns to its starting point upon
completion of a circle.

Without its images, this poem would be nothing more
than a husband prohibiting his wife from being sad at
his departure. However, Donne's images transform this
rough message into a beautiful and romantic love poem.
Images *are* important!

weak closing line

--Sonya Weaver

*This is a good second draft, showing
sensitivity to the images. I have marked
a few places where your style needs
more clarity and grace, as well as one
paragraph whose content could be
expanded.*

FINAL DRAFT

Images of a Love

The speaker in John Donne's poem "A Valediction:
Forbidding Mourning" is an unromantic man who is sternly
forbidding his wife to be sorrowful at his parting.
This description is not true, of course, but it is the
way the speaker might be perceived if all comparisons,
contrasts, and images were taken out of the poem. In
order to appreciate the beauty of this poem and
interpret it accurately, each image or comparison must
be closely analyzed.

The first comparison we come to likens the
speaker's parting to the quiet and easy death of
virtuous men. The speaker paints a picture of a
virtuous or upright man who, because he does not fear
it, is passing peacefully into death. His deathbed is
surrounded by his friends who are having trouble
deciding if he has actually passed away or if he is
still quietly breathing. The speaker suggests that his
departure from his wife should be just as calm. He
says, "let us melt," which implies slow and easy
movement, without any clamor or sobbing. He explains
that showing great emotion would display their love to
the common people, and he does not want this display
because he believes it would make their special love
seem common.

The speaker next contrasts their special love to
common love. He states that common people notice
earthquakes, but not trepidations or tremblings that
take place among the stars. He is illustrating that
common people's love is earthly, but that the love
between him and his wife is heavenly. He goes on to say
that "sublunary" or earthly lovers mourn physical
separation because their love is limited to the physical
realm. He claims that he and his wife are not thus
limited. Their love is so spiritual and refined that it
is even beyond their own understanding ("ourselves know
not what it is"). They do not have to worry about

unfaithfulness, as earthly lovers do, because their love is not merely defined by the physical.

Next the speaker compares their love to the rare, precious, and beautiful metal gold. Not only does the comparison suggest that their love shares these three qualities, but it also shares gold's malleability. An ounce of gold can be spread thin enough to cover 250 square feet. The speaker compares this span to the distance that their souls can stretch. The speaker says that temporary separation should not be viewed as a break. He believes that even though they may be many miles apart, they are still one, like a continuous sheet of spread gold--an unusual and expressive image.

The last image is another very eloquent one. It compares their two souls to twin compasses. The speaker believes that if their souls are two (instead of one), they are still linked to each other, as are the parts of a compass. He likens his wife to the foot in the center. She makes no attempt on her own to move but does so only if he does. She is also like the center foot in that if he leaves, she leans after him and then becomes upright when he returns home, behaving like the center foot of a compass when the outer foot draws a circle and then folds into the center. He says that there will be times when he must leave but that he will always return to her even as a compass returns to its starting point upon completion of a circle.

Without its images, this poem would be nothing more than a husband's prohibiting his wife from being sad at his departure. However, Donne's often extraordinary images transform this austere message into a beautiful and romantic love poem. --Sonya Weaver

13

Writing about Poetic Form

When we say that poetry has *form,* we mean it has design or structure. All poems have some kind of form. Many elements go into
making the forms of poetry, but they all involve arranging the words
in patterns. Sometimes sound controls the pattern; sometimes the
number of words or the length of the lines determines the form.

What Are the Forms of Poetry?

Poetic form can be divided into those that use sound effects (rhythm,
rhyme), those that involve the length and organization of lines
(stanza), and those that artistically manipulate word order (syntax).

RHYTHM AND RHYME

Sound effects are produced by organized repetition. Systematically
stressing or accenting words and syllables produces *rhythm;* repeating similar sounds in an effective scheme produces *rhyme.* Both effects intensify the meaning of a poem, arouse interest, and give
pleasure. Once we notice a pattern of sound, we expect it to continue,
and this expectation makes us more attentive to subtleties in the
entire poem.

   Rhythm can affect us powerfully. We respond almost automatically
to the beat of a drum, the thumping of our heart, the pulsing of
an engine. Poetic rhythm, usually more subtle, is made by repeating

stresses and pauses. Rhythm conveys no verbal meaning itself, but when used skillfully it enforces the meaning and tone of a poem. Consider how Theodore Roethke captures the raucous spirit of "My Papa's Waltz" in the recurring three-stress rhythm of these lines:

> We romped until the pans
> Slid from the kitchen shelf; . . .
>
> Then waltzed me off to bed
> Still clinging to your shirt.

Rhyme, a recurring pattern of similar sounds, also enhances tone and meaning. Because rhymed language is special language, it helps to set poetry apart from ordinary expression and calls attention to the sense, feeling, and tone of the words. Rhyme also gives a certain pleasure to the reader by fulfilling the expectation of the sound patterns. Rhyme, which usually depends on sound, not spelling, occurs when accented syllables contain the same or similar vowel sound with identical consonants following the vowel: *right* and *bite,* *knuckle* and *buckle.* Rhymes are commonly used at regular intervals within a poem, often at the ends of lines:

> Yet he wasn't a scab or odd in his views,
> For his Union reports that he paid his dues.

Closely allied to rhyme are other verbal devices that depend on the correspondence of sounds. *Alliteration* is the repetition of consonant sounds either at the beginning of words or in stressed syllables: "The Soul selects her own Society—" or "Peter Piper picked a peck of pickled peppers." *Assonance* is the repetition of similar vowel sounds that are not followed by identical consonant sounds: *grave* and *gain, shine* and *bright. Consonance* is a kind of half-rhyme in which the consonants are parallel but the vowels change: *blade* and *blood, flash* and *flesh.* Alliteration, assonance, and consonance are likely to be used occasionally and not in regular, recurring patterns; but these devices of sound do focus our attention and affect the tone, melody, and tempo of poetic expression.

EXERCISE

Listen to a favorite popular song and copy down the lyrics (you may have to listen several times). Now arrange the lines on the page as you think they would be printed. What patterns of rhythm and sound do you see? Did you notice them before you wrote the words down and arranged the lines? Does the lineation (the arrangement into lines of poetry) help make the meaning any clearer? If possible, compare your written version with a printed one (on the album cover or album liner or in a magazine that publishes song lyrics).

STANZAIC FORM: CLOSED AND OPEN FORMS

In the past, almost all poems were written in *closed form:* poetry with lines of equal length arranged in fixed patterns of stress and rhyme. Although these elements of form are still much in evidence today, modern poets prefer the greater freedom of *open form poetry,* which uses lines of varying length and avoids rigid patterns of rhyme or rhythm.

Closed forms give definition and shape to poetic expression. *Rhyme schemes* and *stanza* patterns demand the careful arrangement of words and lines into units of meaning that guide both writer and reader in understanding poetry.

Stanzas can be created on the basis of the number of lines, the length of the lines, the pattern of stressed syllables (the meter), and the rhyme scheme (the order in which rhymed words recur). The simplest stanza form is the *couplet:* two rhymed lines, usually of equal length and similar meter. W. H. Auden's "The Unknown Citizen" (p. 390) is written in rhyming couplets, although the lines vary in length and sometimes in rhythm. The most common stanza in English poetry is the *quatrain,* a group of four lines with any number of rhyme schemes. "Aunt Jennifer's Tigers" (p. 403) is composed of three quatrains in which the lines rhyme as couplets (critics indicate this pattern of rhyme with letters: *a a b b*). The same rhyme scheme and stanza form are used in "The Ruined Maid" (p. 389), while the quatrains of "My Papa's Waltz" (p. 389) employ an alternating rhyme pattern (*a b a b*).

Longer stanza patterns are used, of course, but the quatrain and the couplet remain the basic components of closed form poetry. The fixed form that has been used most frequently by the greatest variety of notable poets in England and America is the *sonnet.* Originated in Italy in the fourteenth century, the sonnet became a staple of English poetry in the sixteenth century and has continued to attract practitioners ever since.

The form of the sonnet is firmly fixed: fourteen lines, with ten syllables per line, arranged in a set rhyme scheme. The *Shakespearean sonnet* uses the rhyme scheme most common for sonnets in English: *a b a b, c d c d, e f e f, g g.* You will notice the rhyme scheme falls into three quatrains and an ending couplet, with a total of seven rhymes. The *Italian sonnet,* not found much in English poetry, uses fewer rhymes (five) and has only two groupings of lines, the first eight (called the *octave*) and the last six (the *sestet*). "Shall I Compare Thee to a Summer's Day?" (p. 401) and "That Time of Year Thou Mayst in Me Behold" (p. 439) are splendid examples of Shakespeare's mastery of the sonnet (he wrote 154 of them) and illustrate why this traditional verse form continues to entice and stir both poets and readers. Robert Frost's "The Silken Tent" (p. 402) is an intriguing example of a modern sonnet.

A poem written in *open form* generally has no rhyme scheme and no basic meter for the entire selection. Rhyme and rhythm do occur, of course, but not in the fixed patterns that are required of stanzas and sonnets. Many readers think that open form poetry is easy to write, but that is not the case. Only careless poetry is easy to write, and even closed forms can be sloppily written. Open forms demand their own special arrangements; without the fixed patterns of traditional forms to guide them, modern poets must discover these structures on their own. Walt Whitman's "A Noiseless Patient Spider" (p. 400) demonstrates how open form still uses sound and rhythm to create tone, enhance meaning, and guide the responses of the reader.

SYNTAX

Rhyme, rhythm, and stanza are not the only resources of form available to poets. Writers can also manipulate the way the words are arranged into sentences. For instance, the short, staccato sentences of "We Real Cool" (p. 415) impress us in a way entirely different from the effect of the intricate expression of "The Silken Tent" (p. 402), which is a single compound-complex sentence stretching over fourteen lines. Words in English sentences must be arranged in fairly standard patterns. If we reverse the order of "John struck the ball" to "The ball struck John," the words take on a new meaning altogether. As with stanza form and rhyme scheme, poets can either stick with the rigidity of English sentence structure (syntax) or try to achieve unusual effects through inversion. e e cummings, for example, forces his readers to pay close attention to the line "anyone lived in a pretty how town" by rearranging the words in an unexpected way. (In the standard pattern of an exclamation, the line would read "How pretty a town anyone lived in!")

Looking at the Forms of Poetry

The following poems illustrate many of the variations of sound and organization that we have just discussed. As you read these poems, be alert for the special effects that the poets create with rhythm, rhyme, stanza form, and syntax. You may have to read some selections several times to appreciate how thoroughly form and meaning work together.

Gwendolyn Brooks *1917–*

WE REAL COOL

The Pool Players.
Seven at the Golden Shovel.

> We real cool. We
> Left school. We
>
> Lurk late. We
> Strike straight. We
>
> Sing sin. We
> Thin gin. We
>
> Jazz June. We
> Die soon.

(1960)

A. E. Housman *1859–1936*

EIGHT O'CLOCK

He stood, and heard the steeple
   Sprinkle the quarters on the morning town.
One, two, three, four, to market-place and people
   It tossed them down.

Strapped, noosed, nighing his hour,
   He stood and counted them and cursed his luck;
And then the clock collected in the tower
   Its strength, and struck.

(1922)

T. S. Eliot *1888–1965*

THE HOLLOW MEN

Mistah Kurtz—he dead. [1]

                                              A penny for the Old Guy [2]

                                I

We are the hollow men
We are the stuffed men
Leaning together
Headpiece filled with straw. Alas!
Our dried voices, when
We whisper together
Are quiet and meaningless
As wind in dry grass
Or rats' feet over broken glass
In our dry cellar   10

    Shape without form, shade without colour,
Paralysed force, gesture without motion;

    Those who have crossed
With direct eyes, to death's other Kingdom
Remember us—if at all—not as lost
Violent souls, but only
As the hollow men
The stuffed men.

                                II

Eyes I dare not meet in dreams
In death's dream kingdom   20
These do not appear:
There, the eyes are
Sunlight on a broken column
There, is a tree swinging
And voices are
In the wind's singing
More distant and more solemn
Than a fading star.

    Let me be no nearer
In death's dream kingdom   30
Let me also wear
Such deliberate disguises
Rat's coat, crowskin, crossed staves

---

[1] This is a reference to the character Kurtz in Joseph Conrad's *Heart of Darkness*. Kurtz is associated with the confrontation with evil.

[2] The Gunpowder Plot of 1605 was a failed plan to blow up the English Houses of Parliament. Guy Fawkes, one of the plotters, is still burned in effigy on the anniversary of that attempt, Nov. 5, and children traditionally beg "a penny for the Old Guy."

In a field
Behaving as the wind behaves
No nearer—

    Not that final meeting
In the twilight kingdom

III

This is the dead land
This is cactus land   40
Here the stone images
Are raised, here they receive
The supplication of a dead man's hand
Under the twinkle of a fading star.

    Is it like this
In death's other kingdom
Waking alone
At the hour when we are
Trembling with tenderness
Lips that would kiss   50
Form prayers to broken stone.

IV

The eyes are not here
There are no eyes here
In this valley of dying stars
In this hollow valley
This broken jaw of our lost kingdoms

    In this last of meeting places
We grope together
And avoid speech
Gathered on this beach of the tumid river   60

    Sightless, unless
The eyes reappear
As the perpetual star
Multifoliate rose
Of death's twilight kingdom
The hope only
Of empty men.

V

Here we go round the prickly pear
Prickly pear prickly pear
Here we go round the prickly pear   70
At five o'clock in the morning.

    Between the idea
And the reality
Between the motion
And the act
Falls the Shadow

For Thine is the Kingdom

 Between the conception
And the creation
Between the emotion   80
And the response
Falls the Shadow
     Life is very long

 Between the desire
And the spasm
Between the potency
And the existence
Between the essence
And the descent
Falls the Shadow   90
    For Thine is the Kingdom

 For Thine is
Life is
For Thine is the

 This is the way the world ends
This is the way the world ends
This is the way the world ends
Not with a bang but a whimper.

           (1925)

e e cummings *1894–1962*

ANYONE LIVED IN A PRETTY HOW TOWN

  anyone lived in a pretty how town
  (with up so floating many bells down)
  spring summer autumn winter
  he sang his didn't he danced his did.

  Women and men (both little and small)
  cared for anyone not at all
  they sowed their isn't they reaped their same
  sun moon stars rain

  children guessed (but only a few
  and down they forgot as up they grew   10
  autumn winter spring summer)
  that noone loved him more by more

  when by now and tree by leaf
  she laughed his joy she cried his grief

bird by snow and stir by still
anyone's any was all to her

someones married their everyones
laughed their cryings and did their dance
(sleep wake hope and then) they
said their nevers they slept their dream   20

stars rain sun moon
(and only the snow can begin to explain
how children are apt to forget to remember
with up so floating many bells down)

one day anyone died i guess
(and noone stooped to kiss his face)
busy folk buried them side by side
little by little and was by was

all by all and deep by deep
and more by more they dream their sleep   30
noone and anyone earth by april
wish by spirit and if by yes.

Women and men (both dong and ding)
summer autumn winter spring
reaped their sowing and went their came
sun moon stars rain

                                                                    (1940)

Prewriting

Writing about poetic form is challenging. Because it is impossible to separate form from meaning, you must be sure that you understand what a poem says before you try to analyze how its formal characteristics contribute to your understanding and appreciation. In completing the following exercises, you should read the poems aloud, if possible, and reread the difficult passages a number of times before you decide upon your answers.

EXPERIMENTING WITH POETIC FORM

1. Write out the following poem, filling in the blanks with one of the choices given in parentheses to the right of each line. Use sound, rhyme, and context to determine your choices.

THE DEATH OF THE BALL TURRET GUNNER

From my mother's _____ I fell   (womb, sleep)
   into the State,

And I _____ in its belly   (hunched, crouched)
   till my wet _____ froze.   (skin, fur)
Six miles from earth, _____ from   (freed, loosed)
   its dream of life,
I woke to black flak and the
   _____ fighters.   (loud, nightmare)
When I died they _____ me   (washed, flushed)
   out of the turret with a _____ .   (mop, hose)

Now turn to page 528 and compare your choices with the poet's.
Can you explain why each word was chosen?

2. Examine "We Real Cool" by Gwendolyn Brooks (p. 415). How
   would you describe the rhythm of this poem? How does the
   rhythm affect your perception of the speakers (the "We" of the
   poem)? Why are all the sentences in the last four stanzas only
   three words long? What is the effect of placing the subject of
   those sentences ("We") at the ends of the lines?

3. Look at the alliteration in "Eight O'Clock" by A. E. Housman
   (p. 415). What events or feelings are emphasized by alliteration?
   How do other elements of form—rhyme, stress, stanza pattern—
   influence the tone and point of the brief drama described in the
   poem? Write an objective account of the events in "Eight
   O'Clock." What did you have to leave out of your account?

4. Study the rhyme schemes and line variations of the following
   poems, all of which are written in quatrains:

   "Eight O'Clock" (p. 415)   "My Son, My Executioner" (p. 402)
   "London" (p. 453)   "One Perfect Rose" (p. 392)
   "anyone lived in a pretty   "Piano" (p. 501)
      how town" (p. 418)
   "A Valediction: Forbidding Mourning" (p. 442)

   In which of the poems do the stanza divisions indicate a change
   of time or the beginning of a new point? Do any of the poets
   disregard the stanza patterns? Try to decide why all of these
   poets used quatrains.

5. Complete as many of the following quatrains as you can by
   supplying a last line. Try to write a line which puts a picture
   in the reader's mind.

              She even thinks that up in heaven
                 Her class lies late and snores,
              While poor black cherubs rise at seven

                   _____ .

> The golf links lie so near the mill
>   That almost every day
> The laboring children can look out
>
> _____ .
>
> As I walked out one evening,
>   Walking down Bristol Street,
> The crowds upon the pavement
>
> _____ .
>
> Whose woods these are I think I know.
> His house is in the village though;
> He will not see me stopping here
>
> _____ .

Compare your creations with the originals, which your teacher can supply.

6. Is "The Hollow Men" written in closed form or open form? Make a list of the parts of the poem that appear "closed" and another list of the sections that use "open" form. Why does the poet use parts of old nursery rhymes?

7. Rewrite the following lines—from "The Unknown Citizen" and "anyone lived in a pretty how town"—putting them in the word order you would ordinarily expect them to follow:

> For in everything he did he served the Greater Community.
>
> Except for the War till the day he retired
> He worked in a factory. . . .
>
> Anyone lived in a pretty how town
> (with up so floating many bells down)
>
> Women and men (both little and small)
> cared for anyone not at all

8. Ogden Nash was the whimsical master of outrageous rhymes and comical couplets. Often playful and nonsensical, Nash's verse could also be pointed and critical. Read the following rhymed couplets by Ogden Nash and then try to imitate them. In writing your own couplets you will probably want to follow Nash's practice of using a title to set up the theme of your two-line commentaries.

COMMON SENSE

> Why did the Lord give us agility
> If not to evade responsibility?

THE COW
The cow is of the bovine ilk;
One end is moo, the other, milk.

REFLECTION ON INGENUITY
Here's a good rule of thumb:
Too clever is dumb.

THE PARENT
Children aren't happy with nothing to ignore,
And that's what parents were created for.

GRANDPA IS ASHAMED
A child need not be very clever
To learn that "Later, dear" means "Never."

Writing

Since rhythm, rhyme, syntax, and stanza convey no meaning in themselves, you probably will not write an entire essay on form alone. Instead you can use what you have learned about poetic form to help you analyze and interpret a poem (or poems) with greater understanding and confidence.

RELATING FORM TO THEME

You can use observations about form to confirm and develop your ideas about the meaning or theme of a poem. Looking at a poem's formal characteristics will help you to answer such important questions as these: What is the tone? Is the speaker being ironic? What are the key words and images? And how does the main idea advance through the poem?

Specifically, elements of form offer clues like these:

1. Close, obvious rhyme often indicates a comic or ironic tone. Subtle rhymes support more serious tones.
2. Heavy stress can be humorous, but it can also suggest anger, defiance, strength, or fear.
3. Rhythm and repetition emphasize key words.
4. Stanzas and rhyme schemes mark out patterns of thought and show how the theme develops.
5. Important images are often underscored with rhyme and stress.
6. Syntax calls attention to complex ideas.
7. A combination of elements can indicate a change in speaker or a shift in tone or thought.

8. Typographical effects can call attention to significant feelings or ideas.

This list does not exhaust the possibilities, but it should alert you to the various ways that form relates to thought and meaning in poetry.

IDEAS FOR WRITING

1. Compare and contrast one of Shakespeare's sonnets (p. 401 or p. 439) with Frost's "The Silken Tent" or "Design" (p. 497) or with Dudley Randall's "To the Mercy Killers" (p. 528), which are also sonnets. Why do the modern poems *not* seem like sonnets? Pay particular attention to the syntax and the way the rhyme scheme subdivides each poem. How do Shakespeare, Frost, and Randall keep their sonnets fresh and original?

2. Explicate "anyone lived in a pretty how town," giving special attention to the functions of rhyme, rhythm, alliteration, syntax and stanza form.

3. Show how rhythm, repetition, and rhyme operate in "We Real Cool" and "Eight O'Clock." Are the effects the same in both poems?

4. Write an original haiku, limerick, or sonnet.
   A *haiku* is a rhymeless Japanese poem. Its form is based on syllables: seventeen syllables usually arranged in three lines, often following a pattern of five, seven, and five. Haiku written in English, however, do not always follow the original Japanese syllable pattern and may even be rhymed. Because of their brevity, haiku compress their expression by focusing on images and letting the closely observed details suggest the feelings and meanings. The following haiku, some translated from Japanese originals and some written in English, provide a variety of models for you to follow:

> The piercing chill I feel:
>   my dead wife's comb, in our bedroom,
>   under my heel . . .
>   —*Taniguchi Buson (trans. Harold G. Henderson)*

> Sprayed with strong poison
>   my roses are crisp this year
> in the crystal vase.
>   —*Paul Goodman*

the old woman holds
lilac buds
to her good ear
                        —*Raymond Roseliep*

Heat-lightning streak—
        through darkness pierces
the heron's shriek.
                        —*Matsuo Basho*

Notice that the images in these haiku convey strong sensory experiences implying a great deal more than a mere description would suggest.

The *limerick* is a form of humorous verse popularized in the nineteenth century by Englishman Edward Lear. Its form is fairly simple—a five-line stanza built on two rhymes (*a a b b a*) with the third and fourth lines one beat shorter than the other three. The meter (or rhythm pattern) usually involves two unstressed syllables followed by an accented syllable, giving the lines a kind of playful skipping or jogging sound when they are recited or read aloud.

Lear's limericks depended on a curious or fantastic "plot" for their effects:

There was a Young Lady whose chin
Resembled the point of a pin;
    So she had it made sharp
    And purchased a harp,
And played several tunes with her chin.

More contemporary limericks take delight in giving the last line an extra twist with a surprise rhyme or an absurd idea. Some modern limericks make their point by using outrageous spellings or tricks of typography:

There was a young fellow named Tate
Who dined with his girl at 8.8,
    But I'd hate to relate
    What that person named Tate
And his tête-à-tête ate at 8.8.
                        —*Carolyn Wells*

There was a young lady of Warwick,
Who lived in a castle histarwick,
    On the damp castle mould
    She contracted a could,
And the doctor prescribed paregarwick.
                        —*Anonymous*

These often ingenious and slightly mad little verses continue to entertain readers and writers alike.

WEAR AND TEAR

There was an old man of the Cape,
Who made himself garments of crêpe.
    When asked, "Do they tear?"
    He replied, "Here and there,
But they're perfectly splendid for shape!"
                —Robert Louis Stevenson

There was a young virgin named Wilde,
Who kept herself quite undefiled,
    By thinking of Jesus,
    Contagious diseases,
And the bother of having a child.
                —Anonymous

Rewriting: Style

As a writer, you must choose your words carefully. Many English words are to some extent synonymous, even interchangeable, but often the distinctions between synonyms are as important as their similarities. "The difference between the right word and the almost right word," said Mark Twain, "is the difference between lightning and the lightning bug." When you revise your essay, focus on the accuracy and precision of the words you use.

FINDING THE EXACT WORD

You must take care that both the denotations and connotations of the words you use are the ones you intend. You do not want to write *heroics* when you really mean *heroism*. You do not want to "*expose* three main topics" when you really intend to *explore* them. Here are some problem areas to consider as you look at the words you have used in your essay:

1. **Distinguish among synonyms.**
   Exact writing demands that you choose among different shades of meaning. Although *feeling* and *sensation* are synonyms, they are certainly not interchangeable. Neither are *funny* and *laughable* or *famous* and *notorious*. Consult your dictionary for help in choosing the word that says exactly what you mean.

EXERCISE

Explain the differences in meaning among the following groups of words and phrases:

a. a *renowned* politician, a *famous* politician, a *notorious* politician
b. an *indifferent* parent, a *detached* parent, an *unconcerned* parent
c. to *condone* an action, to *excuse* an action, to *forgive* an action
d. *pilfer, steal, rob, burglarize, loot, ransack*

   e. an *apparent* error, a *visible* error, an *egregious* error
   f. a *proud* person, a *pompous* person, an *arrogant* person

2. **Watch out for words with similar sound or spelling.**
   Homonyms (words that have the same pronunciation but different meanings and different spellings) are sometimes a source of confusion. The student who wrote that a song conveyed the composer's "piece of mind" let the sound of the word override her knowledge of spelling and meaning. Words that are similar in sound and spelling can also be confusing. If you are not careful, you can easily confuse *eminent* with *imminent* or write *quiet* when you mean *quite*.

EXERCISE

Explain the difference in meaning in the following pairs of words:

  a. apprise, appraise
  b. anecdote, antidote
  c. chord, cord
  d. elicit, illicit
  e. martial, marital
  f. statue, statute
  g. human, humane
  h. lose, loose
  i. idol, idle
  j. accept, except
  k. beside, besides
  l. isle, aisle
m. weather, whether
  n. incidence, incident

3. **Choose the precise adjective form.**
   Many words have two or more adjective forms: a *questioning* remark is not the same as a *questionable* remark. As with homonyms and other words that sound alike, do not let the similarity in spelling and pronunciation mislead you.

EXERCISE

Point out the connotative differences in meaning in the following pairs of adjectives:

  a. an intelligible essay, an intelligent essay
  b. a hateful sibling, a hated sibling
  c. a likely roommate, a likable roommate
  d. an informed speaker, an informative speaker
  e. a workable thesis, a working thesis
  f. a liberal man, a liberated man

4. **Watch out for malapropisms.**

Misused words are often unintentionally funny. These humorous confusions and near-misses are called malapropisms. You may get a laugh from your readers if you write "My car insurance collapsed last week," but you will not be impressing them with your command of the language.

EXERCISE

In the following sentences, what do you think the writer probably meant to say?
a. He has only a *supercilious* knowledge of the subject.
b. She was the *pineapple* of perfection.
c. They burned the *refuge.*
d. He passed his civil service *eliminations.*
e. They are in for a *shrewd* awakening.

5. **Be sure the words fit the context.**

Sentences can be unclear if all the words do not have the same emotional associations. For instance, "The thief brandished his gun and angrily requested the money" is confusing because *brandished* and *angrily* suggest a different emotion from *requested.*

EXERCISE

Explain why the italicized words are inappropriate in the following sentences. What words would you use as replacements?
a. Her *stubbornness* in the face of danger saved our lives.
b. The use of violence to obtain a goal is too *poignantly* barbaric for most people to *sympathize* with.
c. The mob shouted in *displeasure.*

Anthology of Poetry

Anonymous   *(English lyric)*

WESTERN WIND

Western wind, when wilt thou blow,
The small rain down can rain?
Christ, if my love were in my arms
And I in my bed again!

(about 1500)

Anonymous   *(traditional Scottish ballad)*

SIR PATRICK SPENS

The king sits in Dumferling toune,
   Drinking the blude-reid wine:
"O whar will I get guid sailor,
   To sail this schip of mine?"

Up and spak an eldern knicht,
   Sat at the kings richt kne:
"Sir Patrick Spens is the best sailor,
   That sails upon the se."

The king has written a braid letter,
   And signd it wi his hand,   10
And sent it to Sir Patrick Spens,
   Was walking on the sand.

The first line that Sir Patrick red,
   A loud lauch lauchéd[1] he;
The next line that Sir Patrick red,
   The teir blinded his ee.

"O wha is this has don this deid,
   This ill deid don to me,
To send me out this time o' the yeir,
   To sail upon the se!   20

"Mak hast, make hast, my mirry men all
   Our guid schip sails the morne":
"O say na sae, my master deir,
   For I feir a deadlie storme.

"Late, late yestreen I saw the new moone,
   Wi the auld moone in hir arme,
And I feir, I feir, my deir master,
   That we will cum to harme."

O our Scots nobles wer richt laith[2]
   To weet their cork-heild schoone,[3]   30
Bot lang owre[4] a' the play wer playd,
   Their hats they swam aboone.

O lang, lang may their ladies sit,
   Wi thair fans into their hand,
Or eir they se Sir Patrick Spens
   Cum sailing to the land.

O lang, lang may the ladies stand,
   Wi thair gold kems in their hair
Waiting for thar ain deir lords,
   For they'll se thame na mair.   40

Half owre,[5] half owre to Aberdour,
   It's fiftie fadom deip,
And thair lies guid Sir Patrick Spens,
   Wi the Scots lords at his feit.

                  (probably 13th century)

---

[1] Laughed.   [2] Loath (reluctant).
[3] Shoes.   [4] Before.   [5] Halfway over.

Anonymous (*traditional Scottish ballad*)

BONNY BARBARA ALLAN

It was in and about the Martinmas[1] time,
　　When the green leaves were afalling,
That Sir John Graeme, in the West Country,
　　Fell in love with Barbara Allan.

He sent his men down through the town,
　　To the place where she was dwelling:
"O haste and come to my master dear,
　　Gin ye be Barbara Allan."

O hooly,[2] hooly rose she up,
　　To the place where he was lying,　　　　　　　　10
And when she drew the curtain by:
　　"Young man, I think you're dying."

"O it's I'm sick, and very, very sick,
　　And 'tis a' for Barbara Allan."—
"O the better for me ye's never be
　　Tho your heart's blood were aspilling."

"O dinna ye mind,[3] young man," said she,
　　"When ye was in the tavern adrinking,
That ye made the health gae round and round,
　　And slighted Barbara Allan?"　　　　　　　　　20

He turned his face unto the wall,
　　And death was with him dealing:
"Adieu, adieu, my dear friends all,
　　And be kind to Barbara Allan."

And slowly, slowly raise she up,
　　And slowly, slowly left him,
And sighing said she could not stay,
　　Since death of life had reft him.

She had not gane a mile but twa,
　　When she heard the dead-bell ringing,　　　　　30
And every jow[4] that the dead-bell geid,
　　It cried, "Woe to Barbara Allan!"

"O mother, mother, make my bed!
　　O make it saft and narrow!
Since my love died for me today,
　　I'll die for him tomorrow."

(probably 14th century)

---

[1] Saint Martin's day, November 11.　　[2] Slowly.
[3] Don't you remember.　　[4] Stroke.

Anonymous

THERE IS A LADY SWEET AND KIND

There is a lady sweet and kind,
Was never face so pleased my mind;
I did but see her passing by,
And yet I love her till I die.

Her gesture, motion and her smiles,
Her wit, her voice, my heart beguiles,
Beguiles my heart, I know not why,
And yet I love her till I die.

Her free behavior, winning looks,
Will make a lawyer burn his books.   10
I touched her not, alas, not I,
And yet I love her till I die.

Had I her fast betwixt mine arms,
Judge you that think such sports were harms,
Were't any harm? No, no, fie, fie!
For I will love her till I die.

Should I remain confinéd there,
So long as Phoebus in his sphere,
I to request, she to deny,
Yet would I love her till I die.   20

Cupid is wingéd and doth range;
Her country so my love doth change,
But change she earth, or change she sky,
Yet will I love her till I die.

                                                        (1607)

Geoffrey Chaucer   *1340?–1400*

LACK OF STEADFASTNESS

Somtyme this world was so stedfast and stable
That mannes word was obligacioun;
And now it is so fals and deceivable
That word and werk, as in conclusioun,
Ben nothing lyk, for turned up-so-doun
Is al this world for mede[1] and wilfulnesse,
That al is lost for lak of stedfastnesse.

[1] Gain.

What maketh this world to be so variable
But lust[2] that folk have in dissensioun?
For among us now a man is holde unable,   10
But if he can, by som collusioun,
Don his neighbour wrong or oppressioun.
What causeth this but wilful wrecchednesse,
That al is lost for lak of stedfastnesse?

Trouthe is put doun, resoun is holden fable;
Vertu hath now no dominacioun;
Pitee exyled, no man is merciable;
Through covetyse is blent[3] discrecioun.
The world hath mad a permutacioun.
Fro right to wrong, fro trouthe to fikelnesse,   20
That al is lost for lak of stedfastnesse.

LENVOY TO KING RICHARD

O prince, desyre for to be honourable,
Cherish thy folk and hate extorcioun!
Suffre nothing that may be reprevable[4]
To thyn estat don in thy regioun.
Shew forth thy swerd of castigacioun,
Dred God, do law, love trouthe and worthinesse,   30
And wed thy folk ageyn to stedfastnesse.

(c. 1397)

THE COMPLAINT OF CHAUCER TO HIS PURSE

To you, my purse, and to non other wight
Compleyne I, for ye be my lady dere!
I am so sorry, now that ye be light;
For certes, but ye make hevy chere,
Me were as leef by leyd up-on my bere;
For whiche un-to your mercy thus I crye:
Beth hevy ageyn, or elles mot I dye!

Now voucheth sauf this day, or[1] hit be night,
That I of you the blisful soun may here,
Or see your colour lyk the sonne bright,   10
That of yelownesse hadde never pere.
Ye be my lyf, ye be myn hertes stere,[2]
Quene of comfort and of good companye:
Beth hevy ageyn, or elles mot I dye!

---

[2] Pleasure or desire.   [3] Blinded.   [4] Shameful, deserving blame.
[1] Ere (before).   [2] Star or rudder.

Now purs, that be to me my lyves light,
And saveour, as doun in this worlde here,
Out of this toune help me through your might,
Sin that ye wole nat been my tresorere;
For I am shave as ny as any frere.
But yit I pray un-to your curtesye: 20
Beth hevy ageyn, or elles mot I dye!

LENVOY DE CHAUCER

O conquerour of Brutes Albioun!
Which that by lyne[3] and free eleccioun
Ben verray king, this song to you I sende;
And ye, that mowen al our harm amende,
Have minde up-on my supplicacioun!

(1399?)

Sir Thomas Wyatt   *1503–1542*

WHOSO LIST TO HUNT

Whoso list to hunt, I know where is an hind,[1]
But as for me—alas, I may no more.
The vain travail hath wearied me so sore,
I am of them that farthest come behind.
Yet may I, by no means, my wearied mind
Draw from the deer; but as she fleeth afore,
Fainting I follow. I leave off therefore,
Since in a net I seek to hold the wind.
Who list her hunt, I put him out of doubt,
As well as I, may spend his time in vain.   10
And graven with diamonds in letters plain
There is written her fair neck round about:
Noli me tangere,[2] for Caesar's I am,
And wild for to hold, though I seem tame.

(ca. 1526)

[3] Line; i.e., by hereditary right.
[1] Female deer: this sonnet is traditionally associated with Anne Boleyn, then Henry VIII's mistress.
[2] *Noli me tangere:* don't touch me.

THEY FLEE FROM ME

They flee from me, that sometime did me seek,
With naked foot, stalking in my chamber:
I have seen them gentle, tame, and meek,
That now are wild, and do not remember
That sometime they put themselves in danger
To take bread at my hand; and now they range,
Busily seeking with a continual change.

Thankéd be fortune, it hath been otherwise
Twenty times better; but once, in special,
In thin array, after a pleasant guise,   10
When her loose gown from her shoulders did fall,
And she me caught in her arms long and small,
Therewithal sweetly did me kiss,
And softly said, "Dear heart, how like you this?"

It was no dream; I lay broad waking.
But all is turned, thorough my gentleness,
Into a strange fashion of forsaking;
And I have leave to go of her goodness,
And she also to use new-fangleness.
But since that I so kindely am served,   20
I would fain know what she hath deserved.

                                        (ca. 1535)

Sir Philip Sidney *1554–1586*

WITH HOW SAD STEPS, O MOON

With how sad steps, O Moon, thou climb'st the skies!
How silently, and with how wan a face!
What! may it be that even in heavenly place
That busy archer his sharp arrows tries?
Sure, if that long-with-love-acquainted eyes
Can judge of love, thou feel'st a lover's case;
I read it in thy looks; thy languished grace
To me, that feel the like, thy state descries.
Then, even of fellowship, O Moon, tell me,
Is constant love deemed there but want of wit?   10
Are beauties there as proud as here they be?
Do they above, love to be loved, and yet
Those lovers scorn whom that love doth possess?
Do they call virtue there ungratefulness?

                                        (ca. 1581)

Edmund Spenser *1552–1599*

ONE DAY I WROTE HER NAME UPON THE STRAND

One day I wrote her name upon the strand,[1]
  But came the waves and washed it away:
Again I wrote it with a second hand,
  But came the tide and made my pains his prey.
"Vain man," said she, "that doest in vain assay,
  A mortal thing so to immortalize,
  For I myself shall like to this decay,
  And eek[2] my name be wiped out likewise."
"Not so," quod I, "let baser things devise
  To die in dust, but you shall live by fame: 10
  My verse your virtues rare shall eternize,
  And in the heavens write your glorious name.
Where whenas death shall all the world subdue,
  Our love shall live, and later life renew."

(1595)

Christopher Marlowe *1564–1593*

THE PASSIONATE SHEPHERD TO HIS LOVE

Come live with me and be my love,
And we will all the pleasures prove,
That valleys, groves, hills and fields,
Woods, or steepy mountain yields.

And we will sit upon the rocks,
And see the shepherds feed their flocks,
By shallow rivers to whose falls
Melodious birds sing madrigals.

And I will make thee beds of roses
With a thousand fragrant posies,   10
A cap of flowers, and a kirtle
Embroidered all with leaves of myrtle;

A gown made of the finest wool
Which from our pretty lambs we pull;
Fair lined slippers for the cold,
With buckles of the purest gold;

---

[1] Beach.   [2] Also.

A belt of straw and ivy buds,
With coral clasps and amber studs:
And if these pleasures may thee move,
Come live with me and be my love.   20

The shepherds' swains shall dance and sing
For thy delight each May morning:
If these delights thy mind may move,
Then live with me and be my love.

(1600)

Sir Walter Raleigh   *1552?–1618*

THE NYMPH'S REPLY TO THE SHEPHERD

If all the world and love were young,
And truth in every shepherd's tongue,
These pretty pleasures might me move,
To live with thee, and be thy love.

Time drives the flocks from field to fold,
When rivers rage, and rocks grow cold,
And Philomel becometh dumb,
The rest complains of cares to come.

The flowers do fade, and wanton fields,
To wayward winter reckoning yields,   10
A honey tongue, a heart of gall,
Is fancy's spring, but sorrow's fall.

Thy gowns, thy shoes, thy beds of roses,
Thy cap, thy kirtle, and thy posies,
Soon break, soon wither, soon forgotten:
In folly ripe, in reason rotten.

Thy belt of straw and ivy buds,
Thy coral clasps and amber studs,
All these in me no means can move,
To come to thee, and be thy love.   20

But could youth last, and love still breed,
Had joys no date, nor age no need,
Then these delights my mind might move,
To live with thee and be thy love.

(1600)

William Shakespeare *1564–1616*

WHEN IN DISGRACE WITH FORTUNE AND MEN'S EYES

When in disgrace with fortune and men's eyes
I all alone beweep my outcast state,
And trouble deaf heaven with my bootless cries,
And look upon myself, and curse my fate,
Wishing me like to one more rich in hope,
Featured like him, like him with friends possessed,
Desiring this man's art, and that man's scope,
With what I most enjoy contented least;
Yet in these thoughts myself almost despising,
Haply I think on thee, and then my state,   10
Like to the lark at break of day arising
From sullen earth, sings hymns at heaven's gate;
For thy sweet love remembered such wealth brings
That then I scorn to change my state with kings.

(1609)

LET ME NOT TO THE MARRIAGE OF TRUE MINDS

Let me not to the marriage of true minds
Admit impediments. Love is not love
Which alters when it alteration finds,
Or bends with the remover to remove:
O, no! it is an ever-fixéd mark
That looks on tempests and is never shaken;
It is the star to every wandering bark,
Whose worth's unknown, although his height be taken.
Love's not Time's fool, though rosy lips and cheeks
Within his bending sickle's compass come;   10
Love alters not with his brief hours and weeks,
But bears it out even to the edge of doom.
If this be error and upon me proved,
I never writ, nor no man ever loved.

(1609)

THAT TIME OF YEAR THOU MAYST IN ME BEHOLD

That time of year thou mayst in me behold
When yellow leaves, or none, or few, do hang
Upon those boughs which shake against the cold,
Bare ruined choirs, where late the sweet birds sang.
In me thou see'st the twilight of such day
As after sunset fadeth in the west,
Which by and by black night doth take away,
Death's second self that seals up all in rest.
In me thou see'st the glowing of such fire,
That on the ashes of his youth doth lie,   10
As the death-bed, whereon it must expire
Consumed with that which it was nourished by.
This thou perceiv'st, which makes thy love more strong
To love that well, which thou must leave ere long.

(1609)

MY MISTRESS' EYES ARE NOTHING LIKE THE SUN

My mistress' eyes are nothing like the sun;
Coral is far more red than her lips' red;
If snow be white, why then her breasts are dun;
If hairs be wires, black wires grow on her head.
I have seen roses damask'd, red and white,
But no such roses see I in her cheeks,
And in some perfumes there is more delight
Than in the breath that from my mistress reeks.
I love to hear her speak, yet well I know
That music hath a far more pleasing sound.   10
I grant I never saw a goddess go;
My mistress, when she walks, treads on the ground:
And yet, by heaven, I think my love as rare
As any she belied with false compare.

(1609)

WHEN MY LOVE SWEARS THAT SHE IS MADE OF TRUTH

When my love swears that she is made of truth,
I do believe her, though I know she lies,
That she might think me some untutored youth,
Unlearnéd in the world's false subtleties.
Thus vainly thinking that she thinks me young,
Although she knows my days are past the best,
Simply I credit her false-speaking tongue:
On both sides thus is simple truth suppressed.
But wherefore says she not she is unjust?
And wherefore say not I that I am old?   10
O, love's best habit is in seeming trust,
And age in love loves not to have years told:
Therefore I lie with her and she with me,
And in our faults by lies we flattered be.

(1609)

John Donne *1572–1631*

SONG

Go and catch a falling star,
    Get with child a mandrake root,
Tell me where all past years are,
    Or who cleft the devil's foot,
Teach me to hear mermaids singing,
Or to keep off envy's stinging,
        And find
        What wind
Serves to advance an honest mind.

If thou be'st born to strange sights,   10
    Things invisible to see,
Ride ten thousand days and nights,
    Till age snow white hairs on thee.
Thou, when thou return'st, wilt tell me,
All strange wonders that befell thee,
        And swear,
        No where
Lives a woman true and fair.

If thou find'st one, let me know;
    Such a pilgrimage were sweet.   20
Yet do not, I would not go,
    Though at next door we might meet:
Though she were true when you met her,
And last till you write your letter,
       Yet she
       Will be
False, ere I come, to two or three.

                                (1633)

THE BAIT

Come live with me, and be my love,
And we will some new pleasures prove,[1]
Of golden sands, and crystal brooks,
With silken lines, and silver hooks.

There will the river whispering run,
Warmed by thy eyes more than the sun.
And there th' enamoured fish will stay,
Begging themselves they may betray.

When thou wilt swim in that live bath,
Each fish, which every channel hath,   10
Will amorously to thee swim,
Gladder to catch thee, than thou him.

If thou, to be so seen, beest loath,
By sun or moon, thou dark'nest both;
And if myself have leave to see,
I need not their light, having thee.

Let others freeze with angling reeds,
And cut their legs with shells and weeds,
Or treacherously poor fish beset
With strangling snare, or windowy net.   20

Let coarse bold hands from slimy nest
The bedded fish in banks out-wrest,
Or curious traitors, sleave-silk flies,
Bewitch poor fishes' wandering eyes.

For thee, thou need'st no such deceit,
For thou thyself art thine own bait;
That fish that is not catched thereby,
Alas, is wiser far than I.

                                (1633)

[1] Test.

A VALEDICTION: FORBIDDING MOURNING

As virtuous men pass mildly away,
    And whisper to their souls, to go,
Whilst some of their sad friends do say,
    The breath goes now, and some say, no:

So let us melt, and make no noise,
    No tear-floods, nor sigh-tempests move,
T'were profanation of our joys
    To tell the laity our love.

Moving of th' earth brings harms and fears,
    Men reckon what it did and meant,   10
But trepidation of the spheres,
    Though greater far, is innocent.

Dull sublunary lovers' love
    (Whose soul is sense) cannot admit
Absence, because it doth remove
    Those things which elemented it.

But we by a love, so much refined
    That our selves know not what it is,
Inter-assuréd of the mind,
    Care less, eyes, lips, and hands to miss.   20

Our two souls therefore, which are one,
    Though I must go, endure not yet
A breach, but an expansion,
    Like gold to airy thinness beat.

If they be two, they are two so
    As stiff twin compasses are two,
Thy soul, the fixt foot, makes no show
    To move, but doth, if th' other do.

And though it in the center sit,
    Yet when the other far doth roam,   30
It leans, and hearkens after it,
    And grows erect, as that comes home.

Such wilt thou be to me, who must
    Like th' other foot, obliquely run;
Thy firmness makes my circle just,
    And makes me end, where I begun.

                                                    (1633)

DEATH BE NOT PROUD

Death, be not proud, though some have calléd thee
Mighty and dreadful, for thou art not so,
For those whom thou think'st thou dost overthrow
Die not, poor Death, nor yet canst thou kill me.
From rest and sleep, which but thy pictures be,
Much pleasure, then from thee much more must flow;
And soonest our best men with thee do go—
Rest of their bones and souls' delivery!
Thou'rt slave to fate, chance, kings, and desperate men,
And dost with poison, war, and sickness dwell, 10
And poppy or charms can make us sleep as well,
And better than thy stroke; why swell'st thou then?
One short sleep past, we wake eternally,
And death shall be no more: Death, thou shalt die!

(1633)

Robert Herrick *1591–1674*

TO THE VIRGINS, TO MAKE MUCH OF TIME

Gather ye rosebuds while ye may,
    Old Time is still a-flying:
And this same flower that smiles today
    Tomorrow will be dying.

The glorious lamp of heaven, the sun,
    The higher he's a-getting,
The sooner will his race be run,
    And nearer he's to setting.

That age is best which is the first,
    When youth and blood are warmer; 10
But being spent, the worse, and worst
    Times still succeed the former.

Then be not coy, but use your time,
    And while ye may, go marry:
For having lost but once your prime,
    You may for ever tarry.

(1648)

DELIGHT IN DISORDER

A sweet disorder in the dress
Kindles in clothes a wantonness:
A lawn[1] about the shoulders thrown
Into a fine distraction:
An erring lace, which here and there
Enthrals the crimson stomacher:[2]
A cuff neglectful, and thereby
Ribbands[3] to flow confusedly:
A winning wave, deserving note,
In the tempestuous petticoat: 10
A careless shoe-string, in whose tie
I see a wild civility:
Do more bewitch me than when art
Is too precise in every part.

                                                    (1648)

John Milton *1608–1674*

WHEN I CONSIDER HOW MY LIGHT IS SPENT

When I consider how my light is spent
Ere half my days in this dark world and wide,
And that one talent which is death to hide
Lodged with me useless, though my soul more bent
To serve therewith my Maker, and present
My true account, lest He returning chide,
"Doth God exact day-labor, light denied?"
I fondly ask. But Patience, to prevent
That murmur, soon replies, "God doth not need
Either man's work or his own gifts. Who best   10
Bear His mild yoke, they serve Him best. His state
Is kingly: thousands at His bidding speed,
And post o'er land and ocean without rest;
They also serve who only stand and wait."

                                                    (1652?)

---

[1] Linen shawl.   [2] Decorative garment worn over the chest and stomach.
[3] Ribbons.

Richard Lovelace *1618–1657*

TO LUCASTA, ON GOING TO THE WARS

Tell me not, sweet, I am unkind,
    That from the nunnery
Of thy chaste breast and quiet mind
    To war and arms I fly.

True, a new mistress now I chase,
    The first foe in the field;
And with a stronger faith embrace
    A sword, a horse, a shield.

Yet this inconstancy is such
    As thou too shalt adore;
I could not love thee, dear, so much,   10
    Loved I not honor more.

                                 (1649)

TO AMARANTHA, THAT SHE WOULD DISHEVEL HER HAIR

Amarantha sweet and fair,
Ah, braid no more that shining hair!
As my curious hand or eye
Hovering round thee, let it fly!

Let it fly as unconfined
As its calm ravisher the wind,
Who hath left his darling, th' East,
To wanton o'er that spicy nest.

Every tress must be confest,
But neatly tangled at the best;   10
Like a clew[1] of golden thread
Most excellently ravellèd.

Do not then wind up that light
In ribbands, and o'ercloud in night,
Like the Sun in 's early ray;
But shake your head, and scatter day!

See, 'tis broke! Within this grove,
The bower and the walks of love,

---

[1] Ball.

Weary lie we down and rest
And fan each other's panting breast.   20

Here we'll strip and cool our fire
In cream below, in milk-baths higher;
And when all wells are drawn dry,
I'll drink a tear out of thine eye,

Which our very joys shall leave,
That sorrows thus we can deceive;
Or our very sorrows weep,
That joys so ripe so little keep.

(1649)

Andrew Marvell *1621–1678*

TO HIS COY MISTRESS

Had we but world enough, and time,
This coyness,[1] lady, were no crime.
We would sit down, and think which way
To walk, and pass our long love's day.
Thou by the Indian Ganges' side
Shouldst rubies find: I by the tide
Of Humber[2] would complain. I would
Love you ten years before the Flood:
And you should if you please refuse
Till the conversion of the Jews.   10
My vegetable love should grow
Vaster than empires, and more slow.
An hundred years should go to praise
Thine eyes, and on thy forehead gaze.
Two hundred to adore each breast:
But thirty thousand to the rest.
An age at least to every part,
And the last age should show your heart.
For, lady, you deserve this state;
Nor would I love at lower rate.   20
     But at my back I always hear
Time's wingéd chariot hurrying near:
And yonder all before us lie
Deserts of vast eternity.
Thy beauty shall no more be found,
Nor, in thy marble vault, shall sound
My echoing song; then worms shall try
That long preserved virginity:

---

[1] Modesty, reluctance.   [2] A river in northern England.

And your quaint honour turn to dust;
And into ashes all my lust.   30
The grave's a fine and private place,
But none, I think, do there embrace.
　　　Now therefore, while the youthful hue
Sits on thy skin like morning dew,
And while thy willing soul transpires
At every pore with instant fires,
Now let us sport us while we may;
And now, like am'rous birds of prey,
Rather at once our time devour,
Than languish in his slow-chapped[3] pow'r.   40
Let us roll all our strength, and all
Our sweetness, up into one ball:
And tear our pleasures with rough strife,
Through the iron gates of life.
Thus, though we cannot make our sun
Stand still, yet we will make him run.

                                                              (1681)

Jonathan Swift *1667–1745*

A DESCRIPTION OF THE MORNING

Now hardly here and there a hackney-coach[1]
Appearing, showed the ruddy morn's approach.
Now Betty from her master's bed had flown,
And softly stole to discompose her own;
The slip-shod 'prentice from his master's door
Had pared the dirt and sprinkled round the floor.
Now Moll had whirled her mop with dext'rous airs,
Prepared to scrub the entry and the stairs.
The youth with broomy stumps began to trace[2]
The kennel-edge,[3] where wheels had worn the place.   10
The small-coal man was heard with cadence deep,
Till drowned in shriller notes of chimney-sweep:
Duns[4] at his lordship's gate began to meet;
And brickdust Moll[5] had screamed through half the street.
The turnkey now his flock returning sees,
Duly let out a-nights to steal for fees.
The watchful bailiffs take their silent stands,
And schoolboys lag with satchels in their hands.

                                                              (1709)

---

[3] Slow-jawed.
[1] Horse-drawn carriage.　　[2] Search for old nails.
[3] Gutter edge.　　[4] Bill collectors.
[5] Woman selling brickdust to be used for scouring.

A DESCRIPTION OF A CITY SHOWER

Careful observers may foretell the hour
(By sure prognostics) when to dread a shower:
While rain depends,[1] the pensive cat gives o'er
Her frolics, and pursues her tail no more.
Returning home at night, you'll find the sink
Strike your offended sense with double stink.
If you be wise, then go not far to dine;
You'll spend in coach hire more than save in wine.
A coming shower your shooting corns presage,
Old achés throb, your hollow tooth will rage.   10
Sauntering in coffeehouse is Dulman seen;
He damns the climate and complains of spleen.
    Meanwhile the South, rising with dabbled wings,
A sable cloud athwart the welkin flings,
That swilled more liquor than it could contain,
And, like a drunkard, gives it up again.
Brisk Susan whips her linen from the rope,
While the first drizzling shower is borne aslope:
Such is that sprinkling which some careless quean[2]
Flirts on you from her mop, but not so clean: 20
You fly, invoke the gods; then turning, stop
To rail; she singing, still whirls on her mop.
Not yet the dust had shunned the unequal strife,
But, aided by the wind, fought still for life,
And wafted with its foe by violent gust,
'Twas doubtful which was rain and which was dust.
Ah! where must needy poet seek for aid,
When dust and rain at once his coat invade?
Sole coat, where dust cemented by the rain
Erects the nap, and leaves a mingled stain.   30
    Now in contiguous drops the flood comes down,
Threatening with deluge this devoted town.
To shops in crowds the daggled females fly,
Pretend to cheapen[3] goods, but nothing buy.
The templar[4] spruce, while every spout's abroach,
Stays till 'tis fair, yet seems to call a coach.
The tucked-up sempstress walks with hasty strides,
While streams run down her oiled umbrella's sides.
Here various kinds, by various fortunes led,
Commence acquaintance underneath a shed.   40
Triumphant Tories and desponding Whigs
Forget their feuds, and join to save their wigs.
Boxed in a chair the beau impatient sits,

---

[1] Is pending.   [2] Disreputable woman, prostitute.
[3] Bargain or haggle for.   [4] Law student who lives in one of the inns of court, either the Inner Temple or the Middle Temple.

While spouts run clattering o'er the roof by fits,
And ever and anon with frightful din
The leather[5] sounds; he trembles from within.
So when Troy chairmen bore the wooden steed,
Pregnant with Greeks impatient to be freed
(Those bully Greeks, who, as the moderns do,
Instead of paying chairmen, run them through),   50
Laocoön struck the outside with his spear,
And each imprisoned hero quaked for fear.
    Now from all parts the swelling kennels[6] flow,
And bear their trophies with them as they go:
Filth of all hues and odors seem to tell
What street they sailed from, by their sight and smell.
They, as each torrent drives with rapid force,
From Smithfield or St. Pulchre's shape their course,
And in huge confluence joined at Snow Hill ridge,
Fall from the conduit prone to Holborn Bridge,   60
Sweepings from butchers' stalls, dung, guts, and blood, ⎫
Drowned puppies, stinking sprats, all drenched in mud, ⎬
Dead cats, and turnip tops, come tumbling down the flood. ⎭

                    (1710)

Alexander Pope   *1688–1744*

FROM AN ESSAY ON CRITICISM

FROM PART II

    Of all the causes which conspire to blind
Man's erring judgment, and misguide the mind,
What the weak head with strongest bias rules,
Is *Pride*, the never-failing vice of fools.
Whatever Nature has in worth denied,
She gives in large recruits of needful pride;
For as in bodies, thus in souls, we find
What wants in blood and spirits, swelled with wind:
Pride, where wit fails, steps in to our defence,
And fills up all the mighty void of sense.   10
If once right reason drives that cloud away,
Truth breaks upon us with resistless day.
Trust not yourself: but your defects to know,
Make use of ev'ry friend—and ev'ry foe.

---

[5] Sedan chair roof.   [6] Gutters.

A little learning is a dang'rous thing;
Drink deep, or taste not the Pierian spring:[1]
There shallow draughts intoxicate the brain,
And drinking largely sobers us again.
Fired at first sight with what the Muse imparts,
In fearless youth we tempt the heights or arts,   20
While from the bounded level of our mind,
Short views we take, nor see the lengths behind;
But more advanced, behold with strange surprise
New distant scenes of endless science rise!
So pleased at first the tow'ring Alps we try,
Mount o'er the vales, and seem to tread the sky,
Th' eternal snows appear already past,
And the first clouds and mountains seem the last:
But, those attained, we tremble to survey
The growing labours of the lengthened way,   30
Th' increasing prospect tires our wand'ring eyes,
Hills peep o'er hills, and Alps on Alps arise!

                                                                        (1711)

From AN ESSAY ON MAN

From *EPISTLE II*

I. Know then thyself, presume not God to scan;[1]
The proper study of mankind is Man.
Placed on this isthmus of a middle state,
A being darkly wise, and rudely[2] great;
With too much knowledge for the Sceptic side,
With too much weakness for the Stoic's pride,
He hangs between; in doubt to act, or rest,
In doubt to deem himself a god, or beast;
In doubt his mind or body to prefer,
Born but to die, and reasoning but to err;
Alike in ignorance, his reason such,
Whether he thinks too little, or too much:
Chaos of thought and passion, all confused;
Still by himself abused, or disabused;
Created half to rise, and half to fall;
Great lord of all things, yet a prey to all;
Sole judge of truth, in endless error hurled:
The glory, jest, and riddle of the world!

                                                                        (1733)

[1] A spring sacred to the muses; source of poetic inspiration.
[1] Scrutinize.   [2] Crudely.

William Blake *1757–1827*

THE CHIMNEY SWEEPER

FROM *Songs of Innocence*

When my mother died I was very young,
And my father sold me while yet my tongue
Could scarcely cry " 'weep! 'weep! 'weep! 'weep!"
So your chimneys I sweep and in soot I sleep.

There's little Tom Dacre, who cried when his head
That curled like a lamb's back, was shaved, so I said,
"Hush, Tom! never mind it, for when your head's bare,
You know that the soot cannot spoil your white hair."

And so he was quiet, and that very night,
As Tom was a-sleeping he had such a sight!   10
That thousands of sweepers, Dick, Joe, Ned, and Jack,
Were all of them locked up in coffins of black;

And by came an angel who had a bright key,
And he opened the coffins and set them all free;
Then down a green plain, leaping, laughing they run,
And wash in a river and shine in the sun;

Then naked and white, all their bags left behind,
They rise upon clouds and sport in the wind.
And the angel told Tom, if he'd be a good boy,
He'd have God for his father and never want joy.   20

And so Tom awoke; and we rose in the dark
And got with our bags and our brushes to work.
Tho' the morning was cold, Tom was happy and warm;
So if all do their duty, they need not fear harm.

(1789)

THE CHIMNEY SWEEPER

FROM *Songs of Experience*

A little black thing among the snow:
Crying weep, weep, in notes of woe!
Where are thy father and mother? Say?
They are both gone up to the church to pray.

Because I was happy upon the heath,
And smiled among the winter's snow:
They clothed me in the clothes of death,
And taught me to sing the notes of woe.

And because I am happy, and dance and sing,
They think they have done me no injury: 10
And are gone to praise God and his priest and king
Who make up a heaven of our misery.

(1794)

THE SICK ROSE

O rose, thou art sick!
The invisible worm
That flies in the night,
In the howling storm,

Has found out thy bed
Of crimson joy,
And his dark secret love
Does thy life destroy.

(1794)

THE LAMB

FROM *Songs of Innocence*
Little Lamb, who made thee?
Dost thou know who made thee?
Gave thee life, and bid thee feed
By the stream and o'er the mead;
Gave thee clothing of delight,
Softest clothing, wooly, bright;
Gave thee such a tender voice,
Making all the vales rejoice?
 Little Lamb, who made thee?
 Dost thou know who made thee? 10
 Little Lamb, I'll tell thee,
 Little Lamb, I'll tell thee:
He is calléd by thy name,
For he calls himself a Lamb.
He is meek, and he is mild;
He became a little child.
I a child, and thou a lamb,
We are calléd by his name.
 Little Lamb, God bless thee!
 Little Lamb, God bless thee! 20

(1789)

THE TYGER

From *Songs of Experience*

Tyger, Tyger, burning bright
In the forests of the night,
What immortal hand or eye
Could frame thy fearful symmetry?

In what distant deeps or skies
Burnt the fire of thine eyes?
On what wings dare he aspire?
What the hand dare seize the fire?

And what shoulder and what art
Could twist the sinews of thy heart?   10
And, when thy heart began to beat,
What dread hand? and what dread feet?

What the hammer? What the chain?
In what furnace was thy brain?
What the anvil? What dread grasp
Dare its deadly terrors clasp?

When the stars threw down their spears,
And watered heaven with their tears,
Did He smile his work to see?
Did He who made the lamb make thee?   20

Tyger, Tyger, burning bright
In the forests of the night,
What immortal hand or eye
Dare frame thy fearful symmetry?

(1794)

LONDON

I wander through each chartered street,
Near where the chartered Thames does flow,
And mark in every face I meet
Marks of weakness, marks of woe.

In every cry of every man,
In every infant's cry of fear,
In every voice, in every ban,
The mind-forged manacles I hear.

How the Chimney-sweeper's cry
Every black'ning church appalls;   10
And the hapless soldier's sigh
Runs in blood down palace walls.

But most through midnight streets I hear
How the youthful harlot's curse
Blasts the new-born infant's tear,
And blights with plagues the marriage hearse.

(1794)

THE GARDEN OF LOVE

I went to the Garden of Love,
And saw what I never had seen:
A Chapel was built in the midst,
Where I used to play on the green.

And the gates of this Chapel were shut,
And "Thou shalt not" writ over the door;
So I turned to the Garden of Love
That so many sweet flowers bore;

And I saw it was filled with graves,
And tombstones where flowers should be;   10
And priests in black gowns were walking their rounds,
And binding with briars my joys and desires.

(1794)

Robert Burns   *1759–1796*

A RED, RED ROSE

O, my luve is like a red red rose
    That's newly sprung in June:
O, my luve is like the melodie
    That's sweetly played in tune.

As fair art thou, my bonie lass,
    So deep in luve am I;
And I will luve thee still, my dear,
    Till a' the seas gang dry.

Till a' the seas gang dry, my dear,
    And the rocks melt wi' the sun;   10
And I will luve thee still, my dear,
    While the sands o' life shall run.

And fare thee weel, my only luve!
And fare thee weel a while!
And I will come again, my luve,
Tho' it were ten thousand mile.

(ca. 1788)

William Wordsworth *1770–1850*

COMPOSED UPON WESTMINSTER BRIDGE

SEPT. 3, 1802

Earth has not anything to show more fair:
Dull would he be of soul who could pass by
A sight so touching in its majesty:
This city now doth, like a garment, wear
The beauty of the morning; silent, bare,
Ships, towers, domes, theatres, and temples lie
Open unto the fields, and to the sky;
All bright and glittering in the smokeless air.
Never did sun more beautifully steep
In his first splendour, valley, rock, or hill;   10
Ne'er saw I, never felt, a calm so deep!
The river glideth at his own sweet will:
Dear God! the very houses seem asleep;
And all that mighty heart is lying still!

(1802)

THE WORLD IS TOO MUCH WITH US

The world is too much with us; late and soon,
Getting and spending, we lay waste our powers:
Little we see in Nature that is ours;
We have given our hearts away, a sordid boon!
The sea that bares her bosom to the moon;
The winds that will be howling at all hours,
And are up-gathered now like sleeping flowers;
For this, for everything, we are out of tune;
It moves us not.—Great God! I'd rather be
A pagan suckled in a creed outworn;   10
So might I, standing on this pleasant lea,
Have glimpses that would make me less forlorn;
Have sight of Proteus rising from the sea;
Or hear old Triton blow his wreathèd horn.

(1806)

Samuel Taylor Coleridge *1772–1834*

FROST AT MIDNIGHT

The frost performs its secret ministry,
Unhelped by any wind. The owlet's cry
Came loud—and hark, again! loud as before.
The inmates of my cottage, all at rest,
Have left me to that solitude, which suits
Abstruser musings: save that at my side
My cradled infant slumbers peacefully.
'Tis calm indeed! so calm, that it disturbs
And vexes meditation with its strange
And extreme silentness. Sea, hill, and wood,   10
This populous village! Sea, and hill, and wood,
With all the numberless goings-on of life,
Inaudible as dreams! the thin blue flame
Lies on my low-burnt fire, and quivers not;
Only that film,[1] which fluttered on the grate,
Still flutters there, the sole unquiet thing.
Methinks, its motion in this hush of nature
Gives it dim sympathies with me who live,
Making it a companionable form,
Whose puny flaps and freaks the idling Spirit   20
By its own moods interprets, everywhere
Echo or mirror seeking of itself,
And makes a toy of Thought.

                                   But O! how oft,
How oft, at school, with most believing mind,
Presageful, have I gazed upon the bars,
To watch that fluttering *stranger!* and as oft
With unclosed lids, already had I dreamt
Of my sweet birth-place, and the old church-tower,
Whose bells, the poor man's only music, rang
From morn to evening, all the hot Fair-day,   30
So sweetly, that they stirred and haunted me
With a wild pleasure, falling on mine ear
Most like articulate sounds of things to come!
So gazed I, till the soothing things, I dreamt,
Lulled me to sleep, and sleep prolonged my dreams!
And so I brooded all the following morn,
Awed by the stern preceptor's face, mine eye
Fixed with mock study on my swimming book:
Save if the door half opened, and I snatched
A hasty glance, and still my heart leaped up,

[1] A piece of soot on the bar of the grate, supposed to foretell the arrival of a stranger or a friend.

40

For still I hoped to see the *stranger's* face,
Townsman, or aunt, or sister more beloved,
My playmate when we both were clothed alike!

Dear Babe, that sleepest cradled by my side,
Whose gentle breathing, heard in this deep calm,
Fill up the interspersèd vacancies
And momentary pauses of the thought!
My babe so beautiful! it thrills my heart
With tender gladness, thus to look at thee,
And think that thou shalt learn far other lore,   50
And in far other scenes! For I was reared
In the great city, pent 'mid cloisters dim,
And saw nought lovely but the sky and stars.
But *thou*, my babe! shalt wander like a breeze
By lakes and sandy shores, beneath the crags
Of ancient mountain, and beneath the clouds,
Which image in their bulk both lakes and shores
And mountain crags: so shalt thou see and hear
The lovely shapes and sounds intelligible
Of that eternal language, which thy God   60
Utters, who from eternity doth teach
Himself in all, and all things in himself.
Great universal Teacher! he shall mold
Thy spirit, and by giving make it ask.

Therefore all seasons shall be sweet to thee,
Whether the summer clothe the general earth
With greenness, or the redbreast sit and sing
Betwixt the tufts of snow on the bare branch
Of mossy apple-tree, while the nigh thatch
Smokes in the sun-thaw; whether the eavesdrops fall   70
Heard only in the trances of the blast,
Or if the secret ministry of frost
Shall hang them up in silent icicles,
Quietly shining to the quiet Moon.

(1798)

KUBLA KHAN

In Xanadu did Kubla Khan
   A stately pleasure-dome decree:
Where Alph, the sacred river, ran
Through caverns measureless to man
   Down to a sunless sea.
So twice five miles of fertile ground
   With walls and towers were girdled round:
And there were gardens bright with sinuous rills
Where blossomed many an incense-bearing tree;

And here were forests ancient as the hills,   10
Enfolding sunny spots of greenery.

But O, that deep romantic chasm which slanted
Down the green hill athwart a cedarn cover![1]
A savage place! as holy and enchanted
As e'er beneath a waning moon was haunted
By woman wailing for her demon-lover!
And from this chasm, with ceaseless turmoil seething
As if this earth in fast thick pants were breathing,
A mighty fountain momently[2] was forced;
Amid whose swift half-intermitted burst   20
Huge fragments vaulted like rebounding hail,
Or chaffy grain beneath the thresher's flail:
And 'mid these dancing rocks at once and ever
It flung up momently the sacred river.
Five miles meandering with a mazy motion
Through wood and dale the sacred river ran,
Then reached the caverns measureless to man,
And sank in tumult to a lifeless ocean:
And 'mid this tumult Kubla heard from far
Ancestral voices prophesying war!   30
          The shadow of the dome of pleasure
              Floated midway on the waves;
          Where was heard the mingled measure
              From the fountain and the caves.
          It was a miracle of rare device,
          A sunny pleasure-dome with caves of ice!

          A damsel with a dulcimer
              In a vision once I saw:
          It was an Abyssinian maid,
              And on her dulcimer she played,   40
          Singing of Mount Abora.
          Could I revive within me,
              Her symphony and song,
          To such a deep delight 'twould win me,
          That with music loud and long,
          I would build that dome in air,
          That sunny dome! those caves of ice!
          And all who heard should see them there,
          And all should cry, Beware! Beware!
          His flashing eyes, his floating hair!   50
          Weave a circle round him thrice,
              And close your eyes with holy dread,
              For he on honey-dew hath fed,
          And drunk the milk of Paradise.

                                                              (1816)

---

[1] Across a cedar woods.   [2] Every moment.

George Gordon, Lord Byron   *1788–1824*

SHE WALKS IN BEAUTY

She walks in beauty, like the night
    Of cloudless climes and starry skies;
And all that's best of dark and bright
    Meet in her aspect and her eyes:
Thus mellowed to that tender light
    Which Heaven to gaudy day denies.

One shade the more, one ray the less,
    Had half impaired the nameless grace
Which waves in every raven tress,
    Or softly lightens o'er her face;   10
Where thoughts serenely sweet express,
    How pure, how dear their dwelling-place.

And on that cheek, and o'er that brow,
    So soft, so calm, yet eloquent,
The smiles that win, the tints that glow,
    But tell of days in goodness spent,
A mind at peace with all below,
    A heart whose love is innocent!

                  (1814)

Percy Bysshe Shelley   *1792–1822*

OZYMANDIAS

I met a traveller from an antique land
Who said: Two vast and trunkless legs of stone
Stand in the desert . . . Near them, on the sand,
Half sunk, a shattered visage lies, whose frown,
And wrinkled lip, and sneer of cold command,
Tell that its sculptor well those passions read
Which yet survive, stamped on these lifeless things,
The hand that mocked them, and the heart that fed:
And on the pedestal these words appear:
"My name is Ozymandias, king of kings: 10
Look on my works, ye Mighty, and despair!"
Nothing beside remains. Round the decay
Of that colossal wreck, boundless and bare
The lone and level sands stretch far away.

                  (1817)

ODE TO THE WEST WIND

I

O wild West Wind, thou breath of Autumn's being,
Thou, from whose unseen presence the leaves dead
Are driven, like ghosts from an enchanter fleeing,

Yellow, and black, and pale, and hectic red,
Pestilence-stricken multitudes: O thou,
Who chariotest to their dark wintry bed

The wingéd seeds, where they lie cold and low,
Each like a corpse within its grave, until
Thine azure sister of the Spring shall blow

Her clarion o'er the dreaming earth, and fill   10
(Driving sweet buds like flocks to feed in air)
With living hues and odours plain and hill:

Wild Spirit, which art moving everywhere;
Destroyer and preserver; hear, oh hear!

II

Thou on whose stream, mid the steep sky's commotion,
Loose clouds like earth's decaying leaves are shed,
Shook from the tangled boughs of Heaven and Ocean,

Angels of rain and lightning: there are spread
On the blue surface of thine aëry surge,
Like the bright hair uplifted from the head   20

Of some fierce Maenad,[1] even from the dim verge
Of the horizon to the zenith's height,
The locks of the approaching storm. Thou dirge

Of the dying year, to which this closing night
Will be the dome of a vast sepulchre,
Vaulted with all thy congregated might

Of vapours, from whose solid atmosphere
Black rain, and fire, and hail will burst: oh, hear!

III

Thou who didst waken from his summer dreams
The blue Mediterranean, where he lay,   30
Lulled by the coil of his crystálline streams,

Beside a pumice isle in Baiae's bay,[2]
And saw in sleep old palaces and towers
Quivering within the wave's intenser day,

All overgrown with azure moss and flowers
So sweet, the sense faints picturing them! Thou
For whose path the Atlantic's level powers

[1] Frenzied female worshipper of Dionysus, the Greek god of vegetation and fertility.
[2] West coast of Italy, where Roman emperors built villas.

Cleave themselves into chasms, while far below
The sea-blooms and the oozy woods which wear
The sapless foliage of the ocean, know 40

Thy voice, and suddenly grow gray with fear,
And tremble and despoil themselves: oh, hear!

IV

If I were a dead leaf thou mightest bear;
If I were a swift cloud to fly with thee;
A wave to pant beneath thy power, and share

The impulse of thy strength, only less free
Than thou, O uncontrollable! If even
I were as in my boyhood, and could be

The comrade of thy wanderings over Heaven,
As then, when to outstrip thy skiey speed 50
Scarce seemed a vision; I would ne'er have striven

As thus with thee in prayer in my sore need.
O, lift me as a wave, a leaf, a cloud!
I fall upon the thorns of life! I bleed!

A heavy weight of hours has chained and bowed
One too like thee: tameless, and swift, and proud.

V

Make me thy lyre, even as the forest is:
What if my leaves are falling like its own!
The tumult of thy mighty harmonies

Will take from both a deep, autumnal tone, 60
Sweet though in sadness. Be thou, Spirit fierce,
My spirit! Be thou me, impetuous one!

Drive my dead thoughts over the universe
Like withered leaves to quicken a new birth!
And, by the incantation of this verse,

Scatter, as from an unextinguished hearth
Ashes and sparks, my words among mankind!
Be through my lips to unawakened earth

The trumpet of a prophecy! O, Wind,
If Winter comes, can Spring be far behind? 70

(1819)

John Keats *1795–1821*

ON FIRST LOOKING INTO CHAPMAN'S HOMER[1]

Much have I travelled in the realms of gold,
And many goodly states and kingdoms seen:
Round many western islands have I been
Which bards in fealty to Apollo[2] hold.
Oft of one wide expanse had I been told
That deep-browed Homer ruled as his demesne;[3]
Yet did I never breathe its pure serene
Till I heard Chapman speak out loud and bold:
Then felt I like some watcher of the skies
When a new planet swims into his ken;   10
Or like stout Cortez[4] when with eagle eyes
He stared at the Pacific—and all his men
Looked at each other with a wild surmise—
Silent, upon a peak in Darien.

(1816)

ODE ON A GRECIAN URN

Thou still unravished bride of quietness,
　　Thou foster-child of silence and slow time,
Sylvan historian, who canst thus express
　　A flowery tale more sweetly than our rhyme:
What leaf-fringed legend haunts about thy shape
Of deities or mortals, or of both,
　　In Tempe[1] or the dales of Arcady?[2]
What men or gods are these? What maidens loth?
　　What mad pursuit? What struggle to escape?
　　　　What pipes and timbrels? What wild ecstasy?   10

Heard melodies are sweet, but those unheard
　　Are sweeter; therefore, ye soft pipes, play on;
Not to the sensual ear, but, more endeared,
　　Pipe to the spirit ditties of no tone:

---

[1] George Chapman published translations of both *The Iliad* (1611) and *The Odyssey* (1616).
[2] God of poetic inspiration.   [3] Domain.
[4] Actually Vasco de Balboa first sighted the Pacific.
[1] Valley in Thessaly, noted for its natural beauty.
[2] Region in Greece, a traditional setting for pastoral poetry.

Fair youth, beneath the trees, thou canst not leave
    Thy song, nor ever can those trees be bare;
        Bold Lover, never, never canst thou kiss,
Though winning near the goal—yet, do not grieve;
    She cannot fade, though thou hast not thy bliss,
        For ever wilt thou love, and she be fair!   20

Ah, happy, happy boughs! that cannot shed
    Your leaves, nor ever bid the spring adieu;
And, happy melodist, unweariéd,
    For ever piping songs for ever new;
More happy love! more happy, happy love!
    For ever warm and still to be enjoyed,
        For ever panting, and for ever young;
All breathing human passion far above,
    That leaves a heart high-sorrowful and cloyed,
        A burning forehead, and a parching tongue.   30

Who are these coming to the sacrifice?
    To what green altar, O mysterious priest,
Lead'st thou that heifer lowing at the skies,
    And all her silken flanks with garlands dressed?
What little town by river or sea shore,
    Or mountain-built with peaceful citadel,
        Is emptied of this folk, this pious morn?
And, little town, thy streets for evermore
    Will silent be; and not a soul to tell
        Why thou art desolate, can e'er return.   40

O Attic[3] shape! Fair attitude! with brede[4]
    Of marble men and maidens overwrought,
With forest branches and the trodden weed;
    Thou, silent form, dost tease us out of thought
As doth eternity: Cold Pastoral!
    When old age shall this generation waste,
        Thou shalt remain, in midst of other woe
Than ours, a friend to man, to whom thou say'st,
    "Beauty is truth, truth beauty,"—that is all
        Ye know on earth, and all ye need to know.   50
                             (1819)

TO AUTUMN

Season of mists and mellow fruitfulness,
    Close bosom-friend of the maturing sun;

---

[3] Of Attica, thus, classic in grace and simplicity.
[4] Design, embroidery.

Conspiring with him how to load and bless
　　With fruit the vines that round the thatch-eves run;
To bend with apples the mossed cottage-trees,
　　And fill all fruit with ripeness to the core;
　　　　To swell the gourd, and plump the hazel shells
　　With a sweet kernel; to set budding more,
And still more, later flowers for the bees,
Until they think warm days will never cease,　　　　　　　　10
　　　　For Summer has o'er-brimmed their clammy cells.

Who hath not seen thee oft amid thy store?
　　Sometimes whoever seeks abroad may find
Thee sitting careless on a granary floor,
　　Thy hair soft-lifted by the winnowing wind;
Or on a half-reaped furrow sound asleep,
　　Drowsed with the fume of poppies, while thy hook
　　　　Spares the next swath and all its twinéd flowers:
And sometimes like a gleaner thou dost keep
　　Steady thy laden head across a brook;　　　　　　　　20
　　Or by a cider-press, with patient look,
　　　　Thou watchest the last oozings hours by hours.

Where are the songs of Spring? Ay, where are they?
　　Think not of them, thou hast thy music too,—
While barred clouds bloom the soft-dying day,
　　And touch the stubble-plains with rosy hue;
Then in a wailful choir the small gnats mourn
　　Among the river sallows[1] borne aloft
　　　　Or sinking as the light wind lives or dies;
And full-grown lambs loud bleat from hilly bourn;[2]　　　30
　　Hedge-crickets sing; and now with treble soft
　　The red-breast whistles from a garden-croft;[3]
　　　　And gathering swallows twitter in the skies.

　　　　　　　　　　　　　　　　　　　　　　　　(1819)

Oliver Wendell Holmes *1809–1894*

THE CHAMBERED NAUTILUS[1]

This is the ship of pearl, which, poets feign,
　　Sails the unshadowed main,—
　　The venturous bark that flings

---

[1] Willows.　　[2] Field.　　[3] Garden plot.
[1] A mollusk having a spiral shell with a series of air-filled chambers.

On the sweet summer wind its purpled wings
In gulfs enchanted, where the Siren[2] sings.
   And coral reefs lie bare,
Where the cold sea-maids rise to sun their streaming hair.

Its webs of living gauze no more unfurl;
   Wrecked is the ship of pearl!
   And every chambered cell,   10
Where its dim dreaming life was wont to dwell,
As the frail tenant shaped his growing shell,
   Before thee lies revealed,—
Its irised ceiling rent, its sunless crypt unsealed!

Year after year beheld the silent toil
   That spread his lustrous coil;
   Still, as the spiral grew,
He left the past year's dwelling for the new,
Stole with soft step its shining archway through,
   Built up its idle door,   20
Stretched in his last-found home, and knew the old no more.

Thanks for the heavenly message brought by thee,
   Child of the wandering sea,
   Cast from her lap, forlorn!
From thy dead lips a clearer note is born
Than ever Triton[3] blew from wreathéd horn!
   While on mine ear it rings,
Through the deep caves of thought I hear a voice that sings:—

Build thee more stately mansions, O my soul,
   As the swift seasons roll!   30
   Leave thy low-vaulted past!
Let each new temple, nobler than the last,
Shut thee from heaven with a dome more vast,
   Till thou at length art free,
Leaving thine outgrown shell by life's unresting sea!

                             (1858)

Edgar Allan Poe *1809–1849*

TO HELEN

Helen,[1] thy beauty is to me
   Like those Nicéan[2] barks of yore,

---

[2] Sea nymph whose song lured sailors to destruction on the rocks.
[3] God of the sea, son of Poseidon, who blew his horn to calm the waves.
[1] Helen of Troy, probably.   [2] Nicea, a city in Asia Minor.

That gently, o'er a perfumed sea,
    The weary, way-worn wanderer bore
    To his own native shore.

On desperate seas long wont to roam,
    Thy hyacinth[3] hair, thy classic face,
Thy Naiad airs[4] have brought me home
    To the glory that was Greece
And the grandeur that was Rome.   10

Lo! in yon brilliant window-niche
    How statue-like I see thee stand,
    The agate lamp within thy hand!
Ah, Psyche,[5] from the regions which
    Are Holy Land!

               (1831)

SONNET: TO SCIENCE

Science! true daughter of Old Time thou art!
Who alterest all things with thy peering eyes.
Why preyest thou thus upon the poet's heart,
Vulture, whose wings are dull realities?
How should he love thee? or how deem thee wise,
Who wouldst not leave him in his wandering
To seek for treasure in the jewelled skies,
Albeit he soared with an undaunted wing?
Hast thou not dragged Diana[1] from her car?
And driven the Hamadryad[2] from the wood   10
To seek a shelter in some happier star?
Hast thou not torn the Naiad[3] from her flood,
The Elfin[4] from the green grass, and from me
The summer dream beneath the tamarind tree?

               (1829)

---

[3] Classical reference to hair, its color and curl.
[4] Gracefulness of a water nymph.   [5] The soul.
[1] Goddess of the moon.   [2] Wood nymph.   [3] Water nymph.   [4] Elf.

Alfred, Lord Tennyson   *1809–1892*

ULYSSES[1]

It little profits that an idle king,
By this still hearth, among these barren crags,
Matched with an agéd wife,[2] I mete and dole
Unequal laws unto a savage race,
That hoard, and sleep, and feed, and know not me.
I cannot rest from travel; I will drink
Life to the lees. All times I have enjoyed
Greatly, have suffered greatly, both with those
That loved me, and alone; on shore, and when
Through scudding drifts the rainy Hyades[3]   10
Vext the dim sea. I am become a name;
For always roaming with a hungry heart
Much have I seen and known,—cities of men
And manners, climates, councils, governments,
Myself not least, but honored of them all,—
And drunk delight of battle with my peers,
Far on the ringing plains of windy Troy.
I am a part of all that I have met;
Yet all experience is an arch wherethrough
Gleams that untravelled world whose margin fades   20
For ever and for ever when I move.
How dull it is to pause, to make an end,
To rust unburnished, not to shine in use!
As though to breathe were life! Life piled on life
Were all too little, and of one to me
Little remains; but every hour is saved
From that eternal silence, something more,
A bringer of new things; and vile it were
For some three suns to store and hoard myself,
And this gray spirit yearning in desire   30
To follow knowledge like a sinking star,
Beyond the utmost bound of human thought.
        This is my son, mine own Telemachus,
To whom I leave the sceptre and the isle,[4]
Well-loved of me, discerning to fulfill
This labor, by slow prudence to make mild
A rugged people, and through soft degrees
Subdue them to the useful and the good.

[1] Tennyson's depiction of the hero of *The Odyssey* owes much to *The Inferno* of Dante, who presented a restless man eager to continue searching for knowledge and truth.
[2] Penelope.   [3] Constellation which, when rising with the sun, was thought to be a sign of rain.
[4] Ithaca.

Most blameless is he, centred in the sphere
Of common duties, decent not to fail   40
In offices of tenderness, and pay
Meet adoration to my household gods,
When I am gone. He works his work, I mine.
    There lies the port; the vessel puffs her sail;
There gloom the dark, broad seas. My mariners,
Souls that have toiled, and wrought, and thought with me,—
That ever with a frolic welcome took
The thunder and the sunshine, and opposed
Free hearts, free foreheads,—you and I are old;
Old age hath yet his honor and his toil.   50
Death closes all; but something ere the end,
Some work of noble note, may yet be done,
Not unbecoming men that strove with Gods.
The lights begin to twinkle from the rocks;
The long day wanes; the slow moon climbs; the deep
Moans round with many voices. Come, my friends.
'T is not too late to seek a newer world.
Push off, and sitting well in order smite
The sounding furrows; for my purpose holds
To sail beyond the sunset, and the baths   60
Of all the western stars, until I die.
It may be that the gulfs will wash us down;
It may be we shall touch the Happy Isles,[5]
And see the great Achilles,[6] whom we knew.
Though much is taken, much abides; and though
We are not now that strength which in old days
Moved earth and heaven, that which we are, we are,—
One equal temper of heroic hearts,
Made weak by time and fate, but strong in will
To strive, to seek, to find, and not to yield.   70
                                                                    (1842)

BREAK, BREAK, BREAK

Break, break, break,
    On thy cold gray stones, O Sea!
And I would that my tongue could utter
    The thoughts that arise in me.

O well for the fisherman's boy,
    That he shouts with his sister at play!
O well for the sailor lad,
    That he sings in his boat on the bay!

[5] Elysium, a paradise thought to lie in the western extremity of the ocean.
[6] Major hero of the Trojan War, in which he was killed.

And the stately ships go on
　　To their haven under the hill; 　　　　　　　　10
But O for the touch of a vanished hand,
　　And the sound of a voice that is still!

Break, break, break,
　　At the foot of thy crags, O Sea!
But the tender grace of a day that is dead
　　Will never come back to me.

(1842)

Robert Browning *1812–1889*

PORPHYRIA'S LOVER

The rain set early in tonight,
　　The sullen wind was soon awake,
It tore the elm-tops down for spite,
　　And did its worst to vex the lake:
　　I listened with heart fit to break.
When glided in Porphyria; straight
　　She shut the cold out and the storm,
And kneeled and made the cheerless grate
　　Blaze up, and all the cottage warm;
　　Which done, she rose, and from her form 　　　　　10
Withdrew the dripping cloak and shawl,
　　And laid her soiled gloves by, untied
Her hat and let the damp hair fall,
　　And, last, she sat down by my side
　　And called me. When no voice replied,
She put my arm about her waist,
　　And made her smooth white shoulder bare,
And all her yellow hair displaced,
　　And, stooping, made my cheek lie there,
　　And spread, o'er all, her yellow hair, 　　　　　　20
Murmuring how she loved me—she
　　Too weak, for all her heart's endeavour,
To set its struggling passion free
　　From pride, and vainer ties dissever,
　　And give herself to me for ever.
But passion sometimes would prevail,
　　Nor could tonight's gay feast restrain
A sudden thought of one so pale
　　For love of her, and all in vain:
　　So, she was come through wind and rain. 　　　　30

Be sure I looked up at her eyes
    Happy and proud; at last I knew
Porphyria worshipped me; surprise
    Made my heart swell, and still it grew
    While I debated what to do.
That moment she was mine, mine, fair,
    Perfectly pure and good: I found
A thing to do, and all her hair
    In one long yellow string I wound
    Three times her little throat around,   40
And strangled her. No pain felt she;
    I am quite sure she felt no pain.
As a shut bud that holds a bee,
    I warily oped her lids: again
    Laughed the blue eyes without a stain.
And I untightened next the tress
    About her neck; her cheek once more
Blushed bright beneath my burning kiss:
    I propped her head up as before,
    Only, this time my shoulder bore   50
Her head, which droops upon it still:
    The smiling rosy little head,
So glad it has its utmost will,
    That all it scorned at once is fled,
    And I, its love, am gained instead!
Porphyria's love: she guessed not how
    Her darling one wish would be heard.
And thus we sit together now,
    And all night long we have not stirred,
    And yet God has not said a word!   60
                          (1836)

MY LAST DUCHESS

FERRARA

That's my last Duchess painted on the wall,
Looking as if she were alive; I call
That piece a wonder, now: Frà Pandolf's[1] hands
Worked busily a day, and there she stands.
Will't please you sit and look at her? I said
"Frà Pandolf" by design, for never read
Strangers like you that pictured countenance,
The depth and passion of its earnest glance,
But to myself they turned (since none puts by
The curtain I have drawn for you, but I)   10
And seemed as they would ask me, if they durst,

---

[1] A fictitious artist.

How such a glance came there; so, not the first
Are you to turn and ask thus. Sir, 'twas not
Her husband's presence only, called that spot
Of joy into the Duchess' cheek: perhaps
Frà Pandolf chanced to say "Her mantle laps
Over my Lady's wrist too much," or "Paint
Must never hope to reproduce the faint
Half-flush that dies along her throat": such stuff
Was courtesy, she thought, and cause enough   20
For calling up that spot of joy. She had
A heart—how shall I say?—too soon made glad,
Too easily impressed; she liked whate'er
She looked on, and her looks went everywhere.
Sir, 'twas all one! My favor at her breast,
The dropping of the daylight in the West,
The bough of cherries some officious fool
Broke in the orchard for her, the white mule
She rode with round the terrace—all and each
Would draw from her alike the approving speech,   30
Or blush, at least. She thanked men,—good; but thanked
Somehow—I know not how—as if she ranked
My gift of a nine-hundred-years-old name
With anybody's gift. Who'd stoop to blame
This sort of trifling? Even had you skill
In speech—(which I have not)—to make your will
Quite clear to such an one, and say, "Just this
Or that in you disgusts me; here you miss,
Or there exceed the mark"—and if she let
Herself be lessoned so, nor plainly set   40
Her wits to yours, forsooth, and made excuse,
—E'en then would be some stooping, and I choose
Never to stoop. Oh, Sir, she smiled, no doubt,
Whene'er I passed her; but who passed without
Much the same smile? This grew; I gave commands;
Then all smiles stopped together. There she stands
As if alive. Will't please you rise? We'll meet
The company below, then. I repeat,
The Count your Master's known munificence
Is ample warrant that no just pretence   50
Of mine for dowry will be disallowed;
Though his fair daughter's self, as I avowed
At starting, is my object. Nay, we'll go
Together down, Sir! Notice Neptune, though,
Taming a sea-horse, thought a rarity,
Which Claus of Innsbruck[2] cast in bronze for me.

                                                          (1842)

---

[2] Another fictitious artist.

SOLILOQUY OF THE SPANISH CLOISTER

Gr-r-r—there go, my heart's abhorrence!
    Water your damned flower-pots, do!
If hate killed men, Brother Lawrence,
    God's blood, would not mine kill you!
What? your myrtle-bush wants trimming?
    Oh, that rose has prior claims—
Needs its leaden vase filled brimming?
    Hell dry you up with its flames!

At the meal we sit together;
    Salve tibi![1] I must hear   10
Wise talk of the kind of weather,
    Sort of season, time of year:
Not a plenteous cork-crop: scarcely
    Dare we hope oak-galls, I doubt;
What's the Latin name for "parsley"?
    What's the Greek name for Swine's Snout?

Whew! We'll have our platter burnished,
    Laid with care on our own shelf!
With a fire-new spoon we're furnished,
    And a goblet for ourself,   20
Rinsed like something sacrificial
    Ere 'tis fit to touch our chaps—
Marked with L for our initial!
    (He-he! There his lily snaps!)

Saint, forsooth! While brown Dolores
    Squats outside the Convent bank
With Sanchicha, telling stories,
    Steeping tresses in the tank,
Blue-black, lustrous, thick like horsehairs,
    —Can't I see his dead eye glow,   30
Bright as 'twere a Barbary corsair's?
    (That is, if he'd let it show!)

When he finishes refection,
    Knife and fork he never lays
Cross-wise, to my recollection,
    As do I, in Jesu's praise.
I the Trinity illustrate,
    Drinking watered orange-pulp—
In three sips the Arian[2] frustrate;
    While he drains his at one gulp!   40

Oh, those melons? If he's able
    We're to have a feast! so nice!

[1] Hail to thee!
[2] A follower of Arius, heretic who denied the doctrine of the Trinity.

One goes to the Abbot's table,
 All of us get each a slice.
How go on your flowers? None double?
 Not one fruit-sort can you spy?
Strange!—And I, too, at such trouble,
 Keep them close-nipped on the sly!

There's a great text in Galatians,
 Once you trip on it, entails   50
Twenty-nine distinct damnations,
 One sure, if another fails:
If I trip him just a-dying,
 Sure of heaven as sure can be,
Spin him round and send him flying
 Off to hell, a Manichee?[3]

Or, my scrofulous French novel
 On grey paper with blunt type!
Simply glance at it, you grovel
 Hand and foot in Belial's[4] gripe: 60
If I double down its pages
 At the woeful sixteenth print,
When he gathers his greengages,
 Ope a sieve and slip it in't?

Or, there's Satan!—one might venture
 Pledge one's soul to him, yet leave
Such a flaw in the indenture
 As he'd miss till, past retrieve,
Blasted lay that rose-acacia
 We're so proud of! *Hy, Zy, Hine.* . . . 70
'St there's Vespers! *Plena gratiâ*
 Ave, Virgo![5] Gr-r-r—you swine!

            (1842)

Walt Whitman *1819–1892*

WHEN I HEARD THE LEARNED ASTRONOMER

When I heard the learned astronomer,
When the proofs, the figures, were ranged in columns before me,
When I was shown the charts and diagrams, to add, divide, and
 measure them,

[3] One who accepts the heresy of Manes, who denied the primacy of God and saw good and evil constantly in struggle.
[4] Satan, also a name of wickedness.
[5] Hail, Virgin, full of grace!

When I sitting heard the astronomer where he lectured with much
    applause in the lecture-room,
How soon unaccountable I became tired and sick,
Till rising and gliding out I wandered off by myself,
In the mystical moist night-air, and from time to time,
Looked up in perfect silence at the stars.   10

(1865)

FROM SONG OF MYSELF

SECTION 11

Twenty-eight young men bathe by the shore,
Twenty-eight young men and all so friendly;
Twenty-eight years of womanly life and all so lonesome.

She owns the fine house by the rise of the bank,
She hides handsome and richly drest aft the blinds of the window.

Which of the young men does she like the best?
Ah the homeliest of them is beautiful to her.

Where are you off to, lady? for I see you,
You splash in the water there, yet stay stock still in your room.

Dancing and laughing along the beach came the twenty-ninth bather,
The rest did not see her, but she saw them and loved them.

The beards of the young men glistn'd with wet, it ran from their
    long hair,
Little streams pass'd all over their bodies.

An unseen hand also pass'd over their bodies,
It descended tremblingly from their temples and ribs.

The young men float on their backs, their white bellies bulge to the
    sun, they do not ask who seizes fast to them,
They do not know who puffs and declines with pendant and bending
    arch,
They do not think whom they souse with spray.

(1881)

Lewis Carroll *1832–1898*

JABBERWOCKY

'Twas brillig,[1] and the slithy toves
    Did gyre and gimble in the wabe;
All mimsy were the borogoves,
    And the mome raths outgrabe.

"Beware the Jabberwock, my son!
    The jaws that bite, the claws that catch!
Beware the Jubjub bird, and shun
    The frumious Bandersnatch!"

He took his vorpal sword in hand;
    Long time the manxome foe he sought—   10
So rested he by the Tumtum tree,
    And stood awhile in thought.

And, as in uffish thought he stood,
    The Jabberwock, with eyes of flame,
Came whiffling through the tulgey wood,
    And burbled as it came!

One, two! One, two! And through and through
    The vorpal blade went snicker-snack!
He left it dead, and with its head
    He went galumphing back.   20

"And hast thou slain the Jabberwock?
    Come to my arms, my beamish boy!
O frabjous day! Callooh! Callay!"
    He chortled in his joy.

---

[1] "Jabberwocky" appeared in *Through the Looking-Glass*, where Humpty Dumpty offered these explanations of some of the words in the poem:

brillig—four o'clock in the afternoon, when you begin boiling things for dinner

slithy—lithe and slimy; a "portmanteau word" which packs up two meanings into one word

toves—something like badgers, something like lizards, something like corkscrews

gyre—to go round and round like a gyroscope

gimble—to make holes like a gimlet

wabe—the grass plot around a sundial: it goes a long way before it, a long way behind it, and a long way beyond it on each side

mimsy—flimsy and miserable

borogove—a thin shabby-looking bird with its feathers sticking out all around, something like a live mop

mome—perhaps short for "from home," meaning that they had lost their way

rath—a sort of green pig

outgrabe—past tense of "outgribe," something between to bellow and to whistle, with a kind of sneeze in the middle.

'Twas brillig, and the slithy toves
    Did gyre and gimble in the wabe;
All mimsy were the borogoves,
    And the mome raths outgrabe.

                   (1855)

Matthew Arnold *1822–1888*

DOVER BEACH

The sea is calm to-night,
The tide is full, the moon lies fair
Upon the Straits;—on the French coast, the light
Gleams, and is gone; the cliffs of England stand,
Glimmering and vast, out in the tranquil bay.
Come to the window, sweet is the night air!
Only, from the long line of spray
Where the ebb meets the moon-blanched sand,
Listen! you hear the grating roar
Of pebbles which the waves suck back, and fling,   10
At their return, up the high strand,
Begin, and cease, and then again begin,
With tremulous cadence slow, and bring
The eternal note of sadness in.

    Sophocles[1] long ago
Heard it on the Aegean, and it brought
Into his mind the turbid ebb and flow
Of human misery; we
Find also in the sound a thought,
Hearing it by this distant northern sea.   20

The sea of faith
Was once, too, at the full, and round earth's shore
Lay like the folds of a bright girdle furled;
But now I only hear
Its melancholy, long, withdrawing roar,
Retreating to the breath
Of the night-wind down the vast edges drear
And naked shingles[2] of the world.

Ah, love, let us be true
To one another! for the world, which seems   30
To lie before us like a land of dreams,

---

[1] In *Antigone* the Greek dramatist Sophocles likens the curse of heaven to the ebb and flow of the sea.
[2] Gravel beaches.

So various, so beautiful, so new,
Hath really neither joy, nor love, nor light,
Nor certitude, nor peace, nor help for pain;
And we are here as on a darkling[3] plain
Swept with confused alarms of struggle and flight,
Where ignorant armies clash by night.

(1867)

Emily Dickinson *1830–1886*

HE PUT THE BELT AROUND MY LIFE

He put the Belt around my life—
I heard the Buckle snap—
And turned away, imperial,
My Lifetime folding up—
Deliberate, as a Duke would do
A Kingdom's Title Deed—
Henceforth, a Dedicated sort—
A Member of the Cloud.

Yet not too far to come at call—
And do the little Toils   10
That make the Circuit of the Rest—
And deal occasional smiles
To lives that stoop to notice mine—
And kindly ask it in—
Whose invitation, know you not
For Whom I must decline?

(c. 1861)

MUCH MADNESS IS DIVINEST SENSE

Much Madness is divinest Sense—
To a discerning Eye—
Much Sense—the starkest Madness—
'Tis the Majority
In this, as All, prevail—
Assent—and you are sane—
Demur—you're straightway dangerous—
And handled with a Chain—

(c. 1862)

---

[3] Darkened or darkening.

THE SOUL SELECTS HER OWN SOCIETY

The Soul selects her own Society—
Then—shuts the Door—
To her divine Majority—
Present no more—

Unmoved—she notes the Chariots—pausing—
At her low Gate—
Unmoved—an Emperor be kneeling
Upon her Mat—

I've known her—from an ample nation—
Choose One—   10
Then—close the Valves of her attention—
Like Stone—

                                                    (c. 1862)

I HEARD A FLY BUZZ WHEN I DIED

I heard a Fly buzz—when I died—
The Stillness in the Room
Was like the Stillness in the Air—
Between the Heaves of Storm—

The Eyes around—had wrung them dry—
And Breaths were gathering firm
For that last Onset—when the King
Be witnessed—in the Room—

I willed my Keepsakes—Signed away
What portion of me be   10
Assignable—and then it was
There interposed a Fly—

With Blue—uncertain stumbling Buzz—
Between the light—and me—
And then the Windows failed—and then
I could not see to see—

                                                    (c. 1862)

SHE DEALT HER PRETTY WORDS LIKE BLADES

She dealt her pretty words like Blades—
How glittering they shone—

And every One unbared a Nerve
Or wantoned with a Bone—

She never deemed—she hurt—
That—is not Steel's Affair—
A vulgar grimace in the Flesh—
How ill the Creatures bear—

To Ache is human—not polite—
The Film upon the eye   10
Mortality's old Custom—
Just locking up—to Die.

(c. 1862)

IT WAS NOT DEATH, FOR I STOOD UP

It was not Death, for I stood up,
And all the Dead, lie down—
It was not Night, for all the Bells
Put out their Tongues, for Noon.

It was not Frost, for on my Flesh
I felt Siroccos—crawl—
Nor Fire—for just my Marble feet
Could keep a Chancel, cool—

And yet, it tasted, like them all,
The Figures I have seen   10
Set orderly, for Burial,
Reminded me, of mine—

As if my life were shaven,
And fitted to a frame,
And could not breathe without a key,
And 'twas like Midnight, some—

When everything that ticked—has stopped—
And Space stares all around—
Or Grisly frosts—first Autumn morns,
Repeal the Beating Ground—   20

But, most, like Chaos—Stopless—cool—
Without a Chance, or Spar—
Or even a Report of Land—
To justify—Despair.

(c. 1862)

BECAUSE I COULD NOT STOP FOR DEATH

Because I could not stop for Death—
He kindly stopped for me—
The Carriage held but just Ourselves—
And Immortality—

We slowly drove—He knew no haste
And I had put away
My labor and my leisure too,
For His Civility—

We passed the School, where Children strove
At Recess—in the Ring—   10
We passed the Fields of Gazing Grain—
We passed the Setting Sun—

Or rather—He passed Us—
The Dews drew quivering and chill—
For only Gossamer,[1] my Gown—
My Tippet[2] —only Tulle[3]—

We paused before a House that seemed
A Swelling of the Ground—
The Roof was scarcely visible—
The Cornice—in the Ground—   20

Since then—'tis Centuries—and yet
Feels shorter than the Day
I first surmised the Horses' Heads
Were toward Eternity—

(c. 1863)

SHE ROSE TO HIS REQUIREMENT

She rose to His Requirement—dropt
The Playthings of Her Life
To take the honorable Work
Of Woman, and of Wife—

If ought She missed in Her new Day,
Of Amplitude, or Awe—
Or first Prospective—Or the Gold
In using, wear away,

It lay unmentioned—as the Sea
Develop Pearl, and Weed,   10
But only to Himself—be known
The Fathoms they abide—

(c.1863)

[1] Soft, sheer, gauzy fabric.   [2] A scarf.   [3] Thin, netted fabric.

Christina Rossetti *1830–1894*

IN AN ARTIST'S STUDIO

One face looks out from all his canvases,
    One selfsame figure sits or walks or leans:
    We found her hidden just behind those screens,
That mirror gave back all her loveliness.
A queen in opal or in ruby dress,
    A nameless girl in freshest summer-greens,
    A saint, an angel—every canvas means
The same one meaning, neither more nor less.
He feeds upon her face by day and night,
    And she with true kind eyes looks back on him,   10
Fair as the moon and joyful as the light:
    Not wan with waiting, not with sorrow dim;
Not as she is, but was when hope shone bright;
    Not as she is, but as she fills his dream.

        (1861)

Thomas Hardy *1840–1928*

THE DARKLING THRUSH

DECEMBER 31, 1900

I leant upon a coppice[1] gate
    When Frost was spectre-gray,
And Winter's dregs made desolate
    The weakening eye of day.
The tangled bine-stems[2] scored the sky
    Like strings of broken lyres,
And all mankind that haunted nigh
    Had sought their household fires.

The land's sharp features seemed to be
    The Century's corpse outleant,   10
His crypt the cloudy canopy,
    The wind his death-lament.
The ancient pulse of germ and birth
    Was shrunken hard and dry,
And every spirit upon earth
    Seemed fervorless as I.

---

[1] A small thicket.   [2] Twining shoots of a climbing plant.

At once a voice arose among
    The bleak twigs overhead
In a full-hearted evensong
    Of joy illimited;   20
An agéd thrush, frail, gaunt, and small,
    In blast-beruffled plume,
Had chosen thus to fling his soul
    Upon the growing gloom.

So little cause for carolings
    Of such ecstatic sound
Was written on terrestrial things
    Afar or nigh around,
That I could think there trembled through
    His happy good-night air   30
Some blessed Hope, whereof he knew
    And I was unaware.

                                   (1902)

CHANNEL FIRING

That night your great guns, unawares,
Shook all our coffins as we lay,
And broke the chancel window squares,
We thought it was the Judgment-day

And sat upright. While drearisome
Arose the howl of wakened hounds:
The mouse let fall the altar-crumb,
The worms drew back into the mounds,

The glebe cow drooled. Till God called, "No;
It's gunnery practice out at sea   10
Just as before you went below;
The world is as it used to be:

"All nations striving strong to make
Red war yet redder. Mad as hatters
They do no more for Christés sake
Than you who are helpless in such matters.

"That this is not the judgment-hour
For some of them's a blesséd thing,
For if it were they'd have to scour
Hell's floor for so much threatening . . .   20

"Ha, ha. It will be warmer when
I blow the trumpet (if indeed
I ever do; for you are men,
And rest eternal sorely need)."

So down we lay again. "I wonder,
Will the world ever saner be,"
Said one, "than when He sent us under
In our indifferent century!"

And many a skeleton shook his head.
"Instead of preaching forty years,"   30
My neighbor Parson Thirdly said,
"I wish I had stuck to pipes and beer."

Again the guns disturbed the hour,
Roaring their readiness to avenge,
As far inland as Stourton tower,[1]
And Camelot,[2] and starlit Stonehenge.[3]

                                                                    (1914)

Gerard Manley Hopkins *1844–1889*

PIED BEAUTY

Glory be to God for dappled things—
    For skies of couple-color as a brinded[1] cow;
        For rose-moles all in stipple[2] upon trout that swim;
Fresh-firecoal chestnut-falls;[3] finches' wings;
    Landscape plotted and pieced—fold, fallow, and plow;
        And áll trádes, their gear and tackle and trim.

All things counter, original, spare, strange;
    Whatever is fickle, freckled (who knows how?)
        With swift, slow; sweet, sour; adazzle, dim;
He fathers-forth whose beauty is past change: 10
        Praise him.

                                                                    (1877)

BINSEY POPLARS

FELLED 1879

My aspens dear, whose airy cages quelled,
Quelled or quenched in leaves the leaping sun,

---

[1] Monument to King Alfred, who defeated the Danes in 879 A.D.
[2] Legendary city of King Arthur's court.
[3] Circle of massive upright stones on Salisbury Plain.
[1] Streaked.   [2] Shaded with small dots.   [3] Fallen chestnuts as bright as coals of fire.

All felled, felled, are all felled;
 Of a fresh and following folded rank
   Not spared, not one
   That dandled a sandalled
  Shadow that swam or sank
On meadow and river and wind-wandering weed-winding bank.

 O if we but knew what we do
   When we delve or hew—   10
  Hack and rack the growing green!
   Since country is so tender
  To touch, her being só slender,
  That, like this sleek and seeing ball
  But a prick will make no eye at all,
  Where we, even where we mean
    To mend her we end her,
   When we hew or delve:
After-comers cannot guess the beauty been.
  Ten or twelve, only ten or twelve   20
  Strokes of havoc únselve
   The sweet especial scene,
  Rural scene, a rural scene,
  Sweet especial rural scene.

               (1879)

SPRING AND FALL:

TO A YOUNG CHILD

Márgarét áre you gríeving
Over Goldengrove unleaving?
Leáves, líke the things of man, you
With your fresh thoughts care for, can you?
Áh! ás the heart grows older
It will come to such sights colder
By and by, nor spare a sigh
Though worlds of wanwood[1] leafmeal[2] lie;
And yet you *will* weep and know why.
Now no matter, child, the name: 10
Sórrow's spríngs áre the same.
Nor mouth had, no nor mind, expressed
What heart heard of, ghost[3] guessed:
It ís the blight man was born for,
It is Margaret you mourn for.

               (1880)

[1] Pale woods, as though bloodless.
[2] Fallen leaf by leaf.
[3] Spirit, soul.

A. E. Housman *1859–1936*

TO AN ATHLETE DYING YOUNG

The time you won your town the race
We chaired you through the market-place;
Man and boy stood cheering by,
And home we brought you shoulder-high.

To-day, the road all runners come,
Shoulder-high we bring you home,
And set you at your threshold down,
Townsman of a stiller town.

Smart lad, to slip betimes away
From fields where glory does not stay,   10
And early though the laurel grows
It withers quicker than the rose.

Eyes the shady night has shut
Cannot see the record cut,
And silence sounds no worse than cheers
After earth has stopped the ears.

Now you will not swell the rout
Of lads that wore their honors out,
Runners whom renown outran
And the name died before the man.   20

So set, before its echoes fade,
The fleet foot on the sill of shade,
And hold to the low lintel up
The still-defended challenge-cup.

And round that early-laurelled head
Will flock to gaze the strengthless dead,
And find unwithered on its curls
The garland briefer than a girl's.

(1896)

LOVELIEST OF TREES

Loveliest of trees, the cherry now
Is hung with bloom along the bough,
And stands about the woodland ride,
Wearing white for Eastertide.

Now, of my threescore years and ten,
Twenty will not come again,
And take from seventy springs a score,
It only leaves me fifty more.

And since to look at things in bloom
Fifty springs are little room,   10
About the woodlands I will go
To see the cherry hung with snow.

(1896)

WHEN I WAS ONE-AND-TWENTY

When I was one-and-twenty
    I heard a wise man say,
"Give crowns and pounds and guineas
    But not your heart away;
Give pearls away and rubies
    But keep your fancy free."
But I was one-and-twenty,
    No use to talk to me.

When I was one-and-twenty
    I heard him say again,   10
"The heart out of the bosom
    Was never given in vain;
'Tis paid with sighs a plenty
    And sold for endless rue."
And I am two-and-twenty,
    And oh, 'tis true, 'tis true.

(1896)

William Butler Yeats *1865–1939*

THE WILD SWANS AT COOLE[1]

The trees are in their autumn beauty,
The woodland paths are dry,
Under the October twilight the water
Mirrors a still sky;
Upon the brimming water among the stones
Are nine-and-fifty swans.

---

[1] Coole Park, the country estate of the poet's friend Lady Augusta Gregory; Yeats was
often a guest there.

The nineteenth autumn has come upon me
Since I first made my count;
I saw, before I had well finished,
All suddenly mount   10
And scatter wheeling in great broken rings
Upon their clamorous wings.

I have looked upon those brilliant creatures,
And now my heart is sore.
All's changed since I, hearing at twilight,
The first time on this shore,
The bell-beat of their wings above my head,
Trod with a lighter tread.

Unwearied still, lover by lover,
They paddle in the cold   20
Companionable streams or climb the air;
Their hearts have not grown old;
Passion or conquest, wander where they will,
Attend upon them still.

But now they drift on the still water,
Mysterious, beautiful;
Among what rushes will they build,
By what lake's edge or pool
Delight men's eyes when I awake some day
To find they have flown away?   30
                                                        (1916)

THE SECOND COMING

Turning and turning in the widening gyre[1]
The falcon cannot hear the falconer;
Things fall apart; the centre cannot hold;
Mere anarchy is loosed upon the world,
The blood-dimmed tide is loosed, and everywhere
The ceremony of innocence is drowned;
The best lack all conviction, while the worst
Are full of passionate intensity.

Surely some revelation is at hand;
Surely the Second Coming is at hand.   10
The Second Coming! Hardly are those words out
When a vast image out of *Spiritus Mundi*[2]

---

[1] A spiral motion, used by Yeats to suggest the cycles of history.
[2] The Soul of the World, a collective unconscious from which humans draw memories, symbols, dreams.

Troubles my sight: somewhere in sands of the desert
A shape with lion body and the head of a man,
A gaze blank and pitiless as the sun,
Is moving its slow thighs, while all about it
Reel shadows of the indignant desert birds.
The darkness drops again; but now I know
That twenty centuries of stony sleep
Were vexed to nightmare by a rocking cradle,   20
And what rough beast, its hour come round at last,
Slouches towards Bethlehem to be born?

                                                        (1921)

SAILING TO BYZANTIUM[1]

That is no country for old men. The young
In one another's arms, birds in the trees
—Those dying generations—at their song,
The salmon-falls, the mackerel-crowded seas,
Fish, flesh, or fowl, commend all summer long
Whatever is begotten, born, and dies.
Caught in that sensual music all neglect
Monuments of unageing intellect.

An agéd man is but a paltry thing,
A tattered coat upon a stick, unless   10
Soul clap its hands and sing, and louder sing
For every tatter in its mortal dress,
Nor is there singing school but studying
Monuments of its own magnificence;
And therefore I have sailed the seas and come
To the holy city of Byzantium.

O sages standing in God's holy fire
As in the gold mosaic of a wall,
Come from the holy fire, perne in a gyre,[2]
And be the singing-masters of my soul.   20
Consume my heart away; sick with desire
And fastened to a dying animal
It knows not what it is; and gather me
Into the artifice of eternity.

Once out of nature I shall never take
My bodily form from any natural thing,

---

[1] The capital of the Byzantine Empire, the city now called Istanbul; for Yeats, a symbol of life perfected by art.

[2] The spiraling motion that Yeats associates with the whirling of fate; see "The Second Coming."

But such a form as Grecian goldsmiths make
Of hammered gold and gold enamelling
To keep a drowsy Emperor awake;
Or set upon a golden bough to sing   30
To lords and ladies of Byzantium
Of what is past, or passing, or to come.

(1928)

Ernest Dowson *1867–1900*

CYNARA[1]

Last night, ah, yesternight, betwixt her lips and mine
There fell thy shadow, Cynara! thy breath was shed
Upon my soul between the kisses and the wine;
And I was desolate and sick of an old passion,
    Yea, I was desolate and bowed my head:
I have been faithful to thee, Cynara! in my fashion.

All night upon mine heart I felt her warm heart beat,
Night-long within mine arms in love and sleep she lay;
Surely the kisses of her bought red mouth were sweet;
But I was desolate and sick of an old passion,   10
    When I awoke and found the dawn was gray:
I have been faithful to thee, Cynara! in my fashion.

I have forgot much, Cynara! gone with the wind,
Flung roses, roses riotously with the throng,
Dancing, to put thy pale, lost lilies out of mind;
But I was desolate and sick of an old passion,
    Yea, all the time, because the dance was long:
I have been faithful to thee, Cynara! in my fashion.

I cried for madder music and for stronger wine,
But when the feast is finished and the lamps expire,   20
Then falls thy shadow, Cynara! the night is thine;
And I am desolate and sick of an old passion,
    Yea hungry for the lips of my desire:
I have been faithful to thee, Cynara! in my fashion.

(1896)

[1] The complete title, "*Non sum qualis eram bonae sub regno Cynarae,*" is a line from the Latin poet Horace (65–8 B.C.). and means "I am not as I was under the reign of kind Cynara."

Edwin Arlington Robinson   *1869–1935*

REUBEN BRIGHT

Because he was a butcher and thereby
Did earn an honest living (and did right),
I would not have you think that Reuben Bright
Was any more a brute than you or I:
For when they told him that his wife must die,
He stared at them, and shook with grief and fright,
And cried like a great baby half that night,
And made the women cry to see him cry.

And after she was dead, and he had paid
The singers and the sexton and the rest,   10
He packed a lot of things that she had made
Most mournfully away in an old chest
Of hers, and put some chopped-up cedar boughs
In with them, and tore down the slaughter house.

                                                    (1896)

EROS TURANNOS[1]

She fears him, and will always ask
    What fated her to choose him;
She meets in his engaging mask
    All reasons to refuse him;
But what she meets and what she fears
Are less than are the downward years,
Drawn slowly to the foamless weirs
    Of age, were she to lose him.

Between a blurred sagacity
    That once had power to sound him,   10
And Love, that will not let him be
    The Judas that she found him,
Her pride assuages her almost,
As if it were alone the cost.
He sees that he will not be lost,
    And waits and looks around him.

A sense of ocean and old trees
    Envelops and allures him;

---

[1] Tyrannic love.

Tradition, touching all he sees,
   Beguiles and reassures him;   20
And all her doubts of what he says
Are dimmed with what she knows of days—
Till even prejudice delays
   And fades, and she secures him.

The falling leaf inaugurates
   The reign of her confusion;
The pounding wave reverberates
   The dirge of her illusion;
And home, where passion lived and died,
Becomes a place where she can hide,   30
While all the town and harbor-side
   Vibrate with her seclusion.

We tell you, tapping on our brows,
   The story as it should be,
As if the story of a house
   Were told, or ever could be;
We'll have no kindly veil between
Her visions and those we have seen,—
As if we guessed what hers have been,
   Or what they are or would be.   40

Meanwhile we do no harm; for they
   That with a god have striven,
Not hearing much of what we say,
   Take what the god has given;
Though like waves breaking it may be,
Or like a changed familiar tree,
Or like a stairway to the sea
   Where down the blind are driven.

(1916)

Stephen Crane *1871–1900*

THE IMPACT OF A DOLLAR UPON THE HEART

The impact of a dollar upon the heart
Smiles warm red light
Sweeping from the hearth rosily upon the white table,
With the hanging cool velvet shadows
Moving softly upon the door.

The impact of a million dollars
Is a crash of flunkeys
And yawning emblems of Persia
Cheeked against oak, France and a sabre,
The outcry of old beauty   10
Whored by pimping merchants
To submission before wine and chatter.
Silly rich peasants stamp the carpets of men,
Dead men who dreamed fragrance and light
Into their woof, their lives;
The rug of an honest bear
Under the foot of a cryptic slave
Who speaks always of baubles,
Forgetting place, multitude, work and state,
Champing and mouthing of hats   20
Making ratful squeak of hats,
Hats.

                                                                    (1899)

A MAN SAID TO THE UNIVERSE

A man said to the universe:
"Sir, I exist!"
"However," replied the universe,
"The fact has not created in me
A sense of obligation."

                                                                    (1899)

WAR IS KIND

Do not weep, maiden, for war is kind.
Because your lover threw wild hands toward the sky
And the affrighted steed ran on alone,
Do not weep.
War is kind.

            Hoarse, booming drums of the regiment,
            Little souls who thirst for fight,
            These men were born to drill and die.
            The unexplained glory flies above them,
            Great is the Battle-God, great, and his Kingdom—   10
            A field where a thousand corpses lie.

Do not weep, babe, for war is kind.
Because your father tumbled in the yellow trenches,
Raged at his breast, gulped and died,
Do not weep.
War is kind.

> Swift blazing flag of the regiment,
> Eagle with crest of red and gold,
> These men were born to drill and die.
> Point for them the virtue of slaughter,   20
> Make plain to them the excellence of killing
> And a field where a thousand corpses lie.

Mother whose heart hung humble as a button
On the bright splendid shroud of your son,
Do not weep.
War is kind.

                                                             (1899)

Paul Laurence Dunbar *1872–1906*

WE WEAR THE MASK

> We wear the mask that grins and lies,
> It hides our cheeks and shades our eyes,—
> This debt we pay to human guile;
> With torn and bleeding hearts we smile,
> And mouth with myriad subtleties.
>
> Why should the world be overwise,
> In counting all our tears and sighs?
> Nay, let them only see us, while
>   We wear the mask.
>
> We smile, but, O great Christ, our cries   10
> To thee from tortured souls arise.
> We sing, but oh the clay is vile
> Beneath our feet, and long the mile;
> But let the world dream otherwise,
>   We wear the mask!

                                                             (1895)

Robert Frost   *1874–1963*

MENDING WALL

Something there is that doesn't love a wall,
That sends the frozen-ground-swell under it
And spills the upper boulders in the sun,
And makes gaps even two can pass abreast.
The work of hunters is another thing:
I have come after them and made repair
Where they have left not one stone on a stone,
But they would have the rabbit out of hiding,
To please the yelping dogs. The gaps I mean,
No one has seen them made or heard them made,   10
But at spring mending-time we find them there.
I let my neighbor know beyond the hill;
And on a day we meet to walk the line
And set the wall between us once again.
We keep the wall between us as we go.
To each the boulders that have fallen to each.
And some are loaves and some so nearly balls
We have to use a spell to make them balance:
"Stay where you are until our backs are turned!"
We wear our fingers rough with handling them.   20
Oh, just another kind of outdoor game,
One on a side. It comes to little more:
There where it is we do not need the wall:
He is all pine and I am apple orchard.
My apple trees will never get across
And eat the cones under his pines, I tell him.
He only says, "Good fences make good neighbors."
Spring is the mischief in me, and I wonder
If I could put a notion in his head:
"*Why* do they make good neighbors? Isn't it   30
Where there are cows? But here there are no cows.
Before I built a wall I'd ask to know
What I was walling in or walling out,
And to whom I was like to give offense.
Something there is that doesn't love a wall,
That wants it down." I could say "Elves" to him,
But it's not elves exactly, and I'd rather
He said it for himself. I see him there,
Bringing a stone grasped firmly by the top
In each hand, like an old-stone savage armed.   40
He moves in darkness as it seems to me,
Not of woods only and the shade of trees.
He will not go behind his father's saying,

And he likes having thought of it so well
He says again, "Good fences make good neighbors."

(1914)

BIRCHES

When I see birches bend to left and right
Across the lines of straighter darker trees,
I like to think some boy's been swinging them.
But swinging doesn't bend them down to stay
As ice storms do. Often you must have seen them
Loaded with ice a sunny winter morning
After a rain. They click upon themselves
As the breeze rises, and turn many-colored
As the stir cracks and crazes their enamel.
Soon the sun's warmth makes them shed crystal shells   10
Shattering and avalanching on the snow crust—
Such heaps of broken glass to sweep away
You'd think the inner dome of heaven had fallen.
They are dragged to the withered bracken by the load,
And they seem not to break; though once they are bowed
So low for long, they never right themselves:
You may see their trunks arching in the woods
Years afterwards, trailing their leaves on the ground
Like girls on hands and knees that throw their hair
Before them over their heads to dry in the sun.   20
But I was going to say when Truth broke in
With all her matter of fact about the ice storm,
I should prefer to have some boy bend them
As he went out and in to fetch the cows—
Some boy too far from town to learn baseball,
Whose only play was what he found himself,
Summer or winter, and could play alone.

One by one he subdued his father's trees
By riding them down over and over again
Until he took the stiffness out of them,   30
And not one but hung limp, not one was left
For him to conquer. He learned all there was
To learn about not launching out too soon
And so not carrying the tree away
Clear to the ground. He always kept his poise
To the top branches, climbing carefully
With the same pains you use to fill a cup
Up to the brim, and even above the brim,
Then he flung outward, feet first, with a swish,
Kicking his way down through the air to the ground.   40

So was I once myself a swinger of birches.
And so I dream of going back to be.
It's when I'm weary of considerations,
And life is too much like a pathless wood
Where your face burns and tickles with the cobwebs
Broken across it, and one eye is weeping
From a twig's having lashed across it open.
I'd like to get away from earth awhile
And then come back to it and begin over.
May no fate willfully misunderstand me   50
And half grant what I wish and snatch me away
Not to return. Earth's the right place for love:
I don't know where it's likely to go better.
I'd like to go by climbing a birch tree,
And climb black branches up a snow-white trunk
Toward heaven, till the tree could bear no more,
But dipped its top and set me down again.
That would be good both going and coming back.
One could do worse than be a swinger of birches.

(1915)

FIRE AND ICE

Some say the world will end in fire,
Some say in ice.
From what I've tasted of desire
I hold with those who favor fire.
But if it had to perish twice,
I think I know enough of hate
To say that for destruction ice
Is also great
And would suffice.

(1923)

DESERT PLACES

Snow falling and night falling fast, oh, fast
In a field I looked into going past,
And the ground almost covered smooth in snow,
But a few weeds and stubble showing last.

The woods around it have it—it is theirs.
All animals are smothered in their lairs.
I am too absent-spirited to count;
The loneliness includes me unawares.

And lonely as it is, that loneliness
Will be more lonely ere it will be less— 10
A blanker whiteness of benighted snow
With no expression, nothing to express.

They cannot scare me with their empty spaces
Between stars—on stars where no human race is.
I have it in me so much nearer home
To scare myself with my own desert places.

(1934)

NEITHER OUT FAR NOR IN DEEP

The people along the sand
All turn and look one way.
They turn their back on the land.
They look at the sea all day.

As long as it takes to pass
A ship keeps raising its hull;
The wetter ground like glass
Reflects a standing gull.

The land may vary more;
But wherever the truth may be— 10
The water comes ashore,
And the people look at the sea.

They cannot look out far.
They cannot look in deep.
But when was that ever a bar
To any watch they keep?

(1934)

DESIGN

I found a dimpled spider, fat and white,
On a white heal-all, holding up a moth
Like a white piece of rigid satin cloth—
Assorted characters of death and blight
Mixed ready to begin the morning right,
Like the ingredients of a witches' broth—
A snow-drop spider, a flower like a froth,
And dead wings carried like a paper kite.

What had that flower to do with being white,
The wayside blue and innocent heal-all? 10

What brought the kindred spider to that height,
Then steered the white moth thither in the night?
What but design of darkness to appall?—
If design govern in a thing so small.

(1936)

Carl Sandburg *1878–1967*

FOG

The fog comes
on little cat feet.

It sits looking
over harbor and city
on silent haunches
and then moves on.

(1916)

GRASS

Pile the bodies high at Austerlitz and Waterloo.[1]
Shovel them under and let me work—
            I am the grass; I cover all.

And pile them high at Gettysburg[2]
And pile them high at Ypres and Verdun.[3]
Shovel them under and let me work.
Two years, ten years, and passengers ask the conductor:
            What place is this?
            Where are we now?

            I am the grass.   10
            Let me work.

(1918)

---

[1] Battlefields of the Napoleonic Wars.
[2] Civil War battlefield.   [3] Battlefields in World War I.

Wallace Stevens 1879–1954

THE SNOW MAN

One must have a mind of winter
To regard the frost and the boughs
Of the pine-trees crusted with snow;

And have been cold a long time
To behold the junipers shagged with ice,
The spruces rough in the distant glitter

Of the January sun; and not to think
Of any misery in the sound of the wind,
In the sound of a few leaves,

Which is the sound of the land   10
Full of the same wind
That is blowing in the same bare place

For the listener, who listens in the snow,
And, nothing himself, beholds
Nothing that is not there and the nothing that is.

(1921)

ANECDOTE OF THE JAR

I placed a jar in Tennessee,
And round it was, upon a hill.
It made the slovenly wilderness
Surround that hill.

The wilderness rose up to it,
And sprawled around, no longer wild.
The jar was round upon the ground
And tall and of a port in air.

It took dominion everywhere.
The jar was gray and bare.   10
It did not give of bird or bush,
Like nothing else in Tennessee.

(1923)

THE EMPEROR OF ICE-CREAM

Call the roller of big cigars,
The muscular one, and bid him whip
In kitchen cups concupiscent curds.
Let the wenches dawdle in such dress
As they are used to wear, and let the boys
Bring flowers in last month's newspapers.
Let be be finale of seem.
The only emperor is the emperor of ice-cream.

Take from the dresser of deal,
Lacking the three glass knobs, that sheet   10
On which she embroidered fantails once
And spread it so as to cover her face.
If her horny feet protrude, they come
To show how cold she is, and dumb.
Let the lamp affix its beam.
The only emperor is the emperor of ice-cream.

(1923)

William Carlos Williams *1883–1963*

DANSE RUSSE

If when my wife is sleeping
and the baby and Kathleen
are sleeping
and the sun is a flame-white disc
in silken mists
above shining trees,—
if I in my north room
dance naked, grotesquely
before my mirror
waving my shirt round my head   10
and singing softly to myself:
"I am lonely, lonely.
I was born to be lonely,
I am best so!"
If I admire my arms, my face,
my shoulders, flanks, buttocks
against the yellow drawn shades,—

Who shall say I am not
the happy genius of my household?

(1916)

THE RED WHEELBARROW

so much depends
upon

a red wheel
barrow

glazed with rain
water

beside the white
chickens.

(1923)

D. H. Lawrence   *1885–1930*

PIANO

Softly, in the dusk, a woman is singing to me;
Taking me back down the vista of years, till I see
A child sitting under the piano, in the boom of the tingling strings
And pressing the small, poised feet of a mother who smiles as she
      sings.

In spite of myself, the insidious mastery of song
Betrays me back, till the heart of me weeps to belong
To the old Sunday evenings at home, with winter outside
And hymns in the cozy parlour, the tinkling piano our guide.

So now it is vain for the singer to burst into clamour
With the great black piano appassionato. The glamour   10
Of childish days is upon me, my manhood is cast
Down in the flood of remembrance, I weep like a child for the past.

(1918)

SNAKE

A snake came to my water-trough
On a hot, hot day, and I in pyjamas for the heat,
To drink there.

In the deep, strange-scented shade of the great dark carob tree
I came down the steps with my pitcher

And must wait, must stand and wait, for there he was at the trough
    before me.

He reached down from a fissure in the earth-wall in the gloom
And trailed his yellow-brown slackness soft-bellied down, over the
    edge of the stone trough
And rested his throat upon the stone bottom,   10
And where the water had dripped from the tap, in a small clearness,
He sipped with his straight mouth,
Softly drank through his straight gums, into his slack long body,
Silently.

Someone was before me at my water-trough,
And I, like a second comer, waiting.

He lifted his head from his drinking, as cattle do,
And looked at me vaguely, as drinking cattle do,
And flickered his two-forked tongue from his lips, and mused a
    moment,
And stooped and drank a little more,   20
Being earth-brown, earth-golden from the burning bowels of the earth
On the day of Sicilian July, with Etna smoking.

The voice of my education said to me
He must be killed,
For in Sicily the black, black snakes are innocent, the gold are
    venomous.
And voices in me said, If you were a man
You would take a stick and break him now, and finish him off.

But must I confess how I liked him,
How glad I was he had come like a guest in quiet, to drink at my
    water-trough
And depart peaceful, pacified, and thankless.   30
Into the burning bowels of this earth?

Was it cowardice, that I dared not kill him?
Was it perversity, that I longed to talk to him?
Was it humility, to feel so honoured?
I felt so honoured.

And yet those voices:
If you were not afraid, you would kill him!

And truly I was afraid, I was most afraid,
But even so, honoured still more
That he should seek my hospitality   40
From out the dark door of the secret earth.

He drank enough
And lifted his head, dreamily, as one who has drunken,
And flickered his tongue like a forked night on the air, so black,
Seeming to lick his lips,
And looked around like a god, unseeing, into the air,

And slowly turned his head,
And slowly, very slowly, as if thrice adream,
Proceeded to draw his slow length curving round
And climb again the broken bank of my wall-face.

And as he put his head into that dreadful hole,
And as he slowly drew up, snake-easing his shoulders, and entered
    farther,
A sort of horror, a sort of protest again his withdrawing into that
    horrid black hole,   50
Deliberately going into the blackness, and slowly drawing himself
    after,
Overcame me now his back was turned.

I looked around, I put down my pitcher,
I picked up a clumsy log
And threw it at the water-trough with a clatter.

I think I did not hit him,
But suddenly that part of him that was left behind convulsed in
    undignified haste,
Writhed like lightning, and was gone   60
Into the black hole, the earth-lipped fissure in the wall-front,
At which, in the intense still noon, I stared with fascination.

And immediately I regretted it.
I thought how paltry, how vulgar, what a mean act!
I despised myself and the voices of my accursed human education.

And I thought of the albatross,
And I wished he would come back, my snake.

For he seemed to me again like a king,
Like a king in exile, uncrowned in the underworld.
Now due to be crowned again.   70

And so, I missed my chance with one of the lords
Of life.
And I have something to expiate;
A pettiness.

          (1923)

Ezra Pound *1885–1972*

IN A STATION OF THE METRO[1]

The apparition of these faces in the crowd;
Petals on a wet, black bough.

          (1913)

[1] Subway in Paris.

THE RIVER-MERCHANT'S WIFE: A LETTER

While my hair was still cut straight across my forehead
I played about the front gate, pulling flowers.
You came by on bamboo stilts, playing horse,
You walked about my seat, playing with blue plums.
And we went on living in the village of Chokan:
Two small people, without dislike or suspicion.

At fourteen I married My Lord you.
I never laughed, being bashful.
Lowering my head, I looked at the wall.
Called to, a thousand times, I never looked back.   10

At fifteen I stopped scowling,
I desired my dust to be mingled with yours
Forever and forever and forever.
Why should I climb the look out?

At sixteen you departed,
You went into far Ku-to-yen, by the river of swirling eddies,
And you have been gone five months.
The monkeys make sorrowful noise overhead.

You dragged your feet when you went out.
By the gate now, the moss is grown, the different mosses,   20
Too deep to clear them away!
The leaves fall early this autumn, in wind.
The paired butterflies are already yellow with August
Over the grass in the West garden;
They hurt me. I grow older.
If you are coming down through the narrows of the river Kiang,
Please let me know beforehand,
And I will come out to meet you
              As far as Cho-fu-Sa.

By Rihaku[1]
(1915)

Robinson Jeffers *1887–1962*

HURT HAWKS

I

The broken pillar of the wing jags from the clotted shoulder,
The wing trails like a banner in defeat,

[1] Japanese name for the Chinese poet Li Po (8th century).

No more to use the sky forever but live with famine
And pain a few days: cat nor coyote
Will shorten the week of waiting for death, there is game without
    talons.
He stands under the oak-bush and waits
The lame feet of salvation; at night he remembers freedom
And flies in a dream, the dawns ruin it.
He is strong and pain is worse to the strong, incapacity is worse.
The curs of the day come and torment him   10
At distance, no one but death the redeemer will humble that head,
The intrepid readiness, the terrible eyes.
The wild God of the world is sometimes merciful to those
That ask mercy, not often to the arrogant.
You do not know him, you communal people, or you have forgotten
    him;
Intemperate and savage, the hawk remembers him;
Beautiful and wild, the hawks, and men that are dying, remember
    him.

II

I'd sooner, except the penalties, kill a man than a hawk, but the
    great redtail
Had nothing left but unable misery
From the bone too shattered for mending, the wing that trailed under
    his talons when he moved.   20
We had fed him six weeks, I gave him freedom,
He wandered over the foreland hill and returned in the evening,
    asking for death,
Not like a beggar, still eyed with the old
Implacable arrogance. I gave him the lead gift in the twilight. What
    fell was relaxed,
Owl-downy, soft feminine feathers; but what
Soared: the fierce rush: the night-herons by the flooded river cried
    fear at its rising
Before it was quite unsheathed from reality.

(1928)

NOVEMBER SURF

Some lucky day each November great waves awake and are drawn
Like smoking mountains bright from the west
And come and cover the cliff with white violent cleanness: then
    suddenly
The old granite forgets half a year's filth:
The orange-peel, eggshells, papers, pieces of clothing, the clots
Of dung in corners of the rock, and used
Sheaths that make light love safe in the evenings: all the droppings
    of the summer

Idlers washed off in a winter ecstasy:
I think this cumbered continent envies its cliff then. . . . But all
    seasons
The earth, in her childlike prophetic sleep,   10
Keeps dreaming of the bath of a storm that prepares up the long
    coast
Of the future to scour more than her sea-lines:
The cities gone down, the people fewer and the hawks more
    numerous,
The rivers mouth to source pure; when the two-footed
Mammal, being someways one of the nobler animals, regains
The dignity of room, the value of rareness.

                                      (1932)

Marianne Moore *1887–1972*

POETRY

I, too, dislike it: there are things that are important beyond all this
    fiddle.
    Reading it, however, with a perfect contempt for it, one discovers
        in
        it after all, a place for the genuine.
            Hands that can grasp, eyes
            that can dilate, hair that can rise
                if it must, these things are important not because a

high-sounding interpretation can be put upon them but because they
    are
    useful. When they become so derivative as to become
        unintelligible,
    the same thing may be said for all of us, that we
        do not admire what   10
        we cannot understand: the bat
            holding on upside down or in quest of something to

eat, elephants pushing, a wild horse taking a roll, a tireless wolf under
    a tree, the immovable critic twitching his skin like a horse that
        feels a flea, the base-
    ball fan, the statistician—
        nor is it valid
        to discriminate against "business documents and

school-books";[1] all these phenomena are important. One must make
    a distinction

---

[1] Quotation from Russian author Leo Tolstoy, who wrote: ". . . poetry is everything with
the exception of business documents and school books."

however: when dragged into prominence by half poets, the result
    is not poetry,   20
  nor till the poets among us can be
    "literalists of
    the imagination"[2] —above
      insolence and triviality and can present

for inspection, "imaginary gardens with real toads in them," shall
    we have
  it. In the meantime, if you demand on the one hand,
    the raw material of poetry in
      all its rawness and
      that which is on the other hand
        genuine, you are interested in poetry.

                                      (1921)

T. S. Eliot *1888–1965*

THE LOVE SONG OF J. ALFRED PRUFROCK

> *S'io credesse che mia risposta fosse*
> *A persona che mai tornasse al mondo,*
> *Questa fiamma staria senza piu scosse.*
> *Ma perciocche giammai di questo fondo*
> *Non torno vivo alcun, s'i'odo il vero,*
> *Senze tema d'infamia ti rispondo.*[1]

Let us go then, you and I,
When the evening is spread out against the sky
Like a patient etherised upon a table;
Let us go, through certain half-deserted streets,
The muttering retreats
Of restless nights in one-night cheap hotels
And sawdust restaurants with oyster-shells:
Streets that follow like a tedious argument
Of insidious intent

---

[2] Quotation from poet W. B. Yeats, who characterized William Blake as "a too literal realist of imagination."

[1] The epigraph is from Dante's *Inferno*—the speech of one dead and damned, Count Guido da Montefeltro, who thinks his hearer is also going to remain in Hell; he offers to tell Dante his story: "If I thought my reply were to someone who could ever return to the world, this flame would waver no more. But since, I'm told, nobody ever escapes from this pit, I'll tell you without fear of ill fame."

To lead you to an overwhelming question . . .   10
Oh, do not ask, "What is it?"
Let us go and make our visit.
In the room the women come and go
Talking of Michelangelo.

The yellow fog that rubs its back upon the window-panes,
The yellow smoke that rubs its muzzle on the window-panes
Licked its tongue into the corners of the evening,
Lingered upon the pools that stand in drains,
Let fall upon its back the soot that falls from chimneys,
Slipped by the terrace, made a sudden leap,   20
And seeing that it was a soft October night,
Curled once about the house, and fell asleep.

And indeed there will be time
For the yellow smoke that slides along the street
Rubbing its back upon the window-panes;
There will be time, there will be time
To prepare a face to meet the faces that you meet;
There will be time to murder and create,
And time for all the works and days of hands
That lift and drop a question on your plate;   30
Time for you and time for me,
And time yet for a hundred indecisions,
And for a hundred visions and revisions,
Before the taking of a toast and tea.

In the room the women come and go
Talking of Michelangelo.

And indeed there will be time
To wonder, "Do I dare?" and, "Do I dare?"
Time to turn back and descend the stair,
With a bald spot in the middle of my hair—   40
(They will say: "How his hair is growing thin!")
My morning coat, my collar mounting firmly to the chin,
My necktie rich and modest, but asserted by a simple pin—
(They will say: "But how his arms and legs are thin!")
Do I dare
Disturb the universe?
In a minute there is time
For decisions and revisions which a minute will reverse.

For I have known them all already, known them all—
Have known the evenings, mornings, afternoons,   50
I have measured out my life with coffee spoons;
I know the voices dying with a dying fall
Beneath the music from a farther room.
      So how should I presume?

And I have known the eyes already, known them all—
The eyes that fix you in a formulated phrase,
And when I am formulated, sprawling on a pin,
When I am pinned and wriggling on the wall,
Then how should I begin
To spit out all the butt-ends of my days and ways?   60
    And how should I presume?

And I have known the arms already, known them all—
Arms that are braceleted and white and bare
(But in the lamplight, downed with light brown hair!)
Is it perfume from a dress
That makes me so digress?
Arms that lie along a table, or wrap about a shawl.
    And should I then presume?
    And how should I begin?

    . . .

Shall I say, I have gone at dusk through narrow streets   70
And watched the smoke that rises from the pipes
Of lonely men in shirt-sleeves, leaning out of windows? . . .

I should have been a pair of ragged claws
Scuttling across the floors of silent seas.

    . . .

After the afternoon, the evening, sleep so peacefully!
Smoothed by long fingers,
Asleep . . . tired . . . or it malingers,
Stretched on the floor, here beside you and me.
Should I, after tea and cakes and ices,
Have the strength to force the moment to its crisis?   80
But though I have wept and fasted, wept and prayed,
Though I have seen my head (grown slightly bald) brought in
   upon a platter,[2]
I am no prophet—and here's no great matter;
I have seen the moment of my greatness flicker,
And I have seen the eternal Footman hold my coat, and snicker,
And in short, I was afraid.

And would it have been worth it, after all,
After the cups, the marmalade, the tea,
Among the porcelain, among some talk of you and me,
Would it have been worth while,   90
To have bitten off the matter with a smile,
To have squeezed the universe into a ball
To roll it toward some overwhelming question,
To say: "I am Lazarus,[3] come from the dead,

    [2] The head of John the Baptist was presented to Salome on a platter. See Matthew 14:1–
11.
    [3] Jesus raised Lazarus from the dead. See John 11:1–44.

Come back to tell you all, I shall tell you all"—
If one, settling a pillow by her head,
    Should say: "That is not what I meant at all;
    That is not it, at all."

And would it have been worth it, after all,
Would it have been worth while,   100
After the sunsets and the dooryards and the sprinkled streets,
After the novels, after the teacups, after the skirts that trail along the
    floor—
And this, and so much more?—
It is impossible to say just what I mean!
But as if a magic lantern threw the nerves in patterns on a screen:
Would it have been worth while
If one, settling a pillow or throwing off a shawl,
And turning toward the window, should say:
    "That is not it at all,   110
    That is not what I meant, at all."
              . . .

No! I am not Prince Hamlet, nor was meant to be;
Am an attendant lord, one that will do
To swell a progress, start a scene or two,
Advise the prince; no doubt, an easy tool,
Deferential, glad to be of use,
Politic, cautious, and meticulous;
Full of high sentence, but a bit obtuse;
At times, indeed, almost ridiculous—
Almost, at times, the Fool.

I grow old . . . I grow old . . .   120
I shall wear the bottoms of my trousers rolled.

Shall I part my hair behind? Do I dare to eat a peach?
I shall wear white flannel trousers, and walk upon the beach.
I have heard the mermaids singing, each to each.

I do not think that they will sing to me.

I have seen them riding seaward on the waves
Combing the white hair of the waves blown back
When the wind blows the water white and black.

We have lingered in the chambers of the sea
By sea-girls wreathed with seaweed red and brown   130
Till human voices wake us, and we drown.

                                  (1917)

John Crowe Ransom *1888–1974*

BELLS FOR JOHN WHITESIDE'S DAUGHTER

There was such speed in her little body,
And such lightness in her footfall,
It is no wonder her brown study
Astonishes us all.

Her wars were bruited in our high window.
We looked among orchard trees and beyond,
Where she took arms against her shadow,
Or harried unto the pond
The lazy geese, like a snow cloud
Dripping their snow on the green grass,   10
Tricking and stopping, sleepy and proud,
Who cried in goose, Alas,

For the tireless heart within the little
Lady with rod that made them rise
From their noon apple-dreams and scuttle
Goose-fashion under the skies!

But now go the bells, and we are ready,
In one house we are sternly stopped
To say we are vexed at her brown study,
Lying so primly propped.   20
                                            (1924)

Claude McKay *1890–1948*

AMERICA

Although she feeds me bread of bitterness,
And sinks into my throat her tiger's tooth,
Stealing my breath of life, I will confess
I love this cultured hell that tests my youth!
Her vigor flows like tides into my blood,
Giving me strength erect against her hate.
Her bigness sweeps my being like a flood,
Yet as a rebel fronts a king in state,
I stand within her walls with not a shred
Of terror, malice, not a word of jeer.   10
Darkly I gaze into the days ahead,
And see her might and granite wonders there,

Beneath the touch of Time's unerring hand,
Like priceless treasures sinking in the sand.

(1920)

Edna St. Vincent Millay *1892–1950*

LOVE IS NOT ALL

Love is not all; it is not meat nor drink
Nor slumber nor a roof against the rain,
Nor yet a floating spar to men that sink
And rise and sink and rise and sink again;
Love can not fill the thickened lung with breath,
Nor clean the blood, nor set the fractured bone;
Yet many a man is making friends with death
Even as I speak, for lack of love alone.
It well may be that in a difficult hour,
Pinned down by pain and moaning for release,   10
Or nagged by want past resolution's power,
I might be driven to sell your love for peace,
Or trade the memory of this night for food.
It well may be. I do not think I would.

(1931)

FIRST FIG

My candle burns at both ends;
    It will not last the night;
But ah, my foes, and oh, my friends—
    It gives a lovely light.

(1920)

Archibald MacLeish *1892–1982*

ARS POETICA

A poem should be palpable and mute
As a globed fruit,

Dumb
As old medallions to the thumb,

Silent as the sleeve-worn stone
Of casement ledges where the moss has grown—

A poem should be wordless
As the flight of birds.

      . . .

A poem should be motionless in time
As the moon climbs,   10

Leaving, as the moon releases
Twig by twig the night-entangled trees,

Leaving, as the moon behind the winter leaves,
Memory by memory the mind—

A poem should be motionless in time
As the moon climbs

      . . .

A poem should be equal to:
Not true

For all the history of grief
An empty doorway and a maple leaf   20

For love
The leaning grasses and two lights above the sea—

A poem should not mean
But be

                                     (1926)

Wilfred Owen   *1893–1918*

DULCE ET DECORUM EST

Bent double, like old beggars under sacks,
Knock-kneed, coughing like hags, we cursed through sludge,
Till on the haunting flares we turned our backs
And towards our distant rest began to trudge.
Men marched asleep. Many had lost their boots
But limped on, blood-shod. All went lame; all blind;
Drunk with fatigue; deaf even to the hoots
Of tired, outstripped Five-Nines that dropped behind.

Gas! Gas! Quick, boys!—An ecstasy of fumbling,
Fitting the clumsy helmets just in time;   10
But someone still was yelling out and stumbling
And flound'ring like a man in fire or lime . . .
Dim, through the misty panes and thick green light,
As under a green sea, I saw him drowning.

In all my dreams before my helpless sight,
He plunges at me, guttering, choking, drowning.

If in some smothering dreams you too could pace
Behind the wagon that we flung him in,
And watch the white eyes writhing in his face,
His hanging face, like a devil's sick of sin;   20
If you could hear, at every jolt, the blood
Come gargling from the froth-corrupted lungs,
Obscene as cancer, bitter as the cud
Of vile, incurable sores on innocent tongues,—
My friend, you would not tell with such high zest
To children ardent for some desperate glory,
The old Lie: Dulce et decorum est
Pro patria mori.[1]

                                                          (1920)

e. e. cummings   *1894–1962*

O SWEET SPONTANEOUS

O sweet spontaneous
earth how often have
the
doting

　　　fingers of
prurient philosophers pinched
and
poked

thee
, has the naughty thumb   10
of science prodded
thy

　　　beauty   . how
often have religions taken
thee upon their scraggy knees

squeezing and

buffeting thee that thou mightest conceive
gods
　　　(but
true   20

---

[1] The quotation is from the Latin poet Horace, meaning "It is sweet and fitting to die for one's country."

to the incomparable
couch of death thy
rhythmic
lover

        thou answerest

them only with
           spring)

                            (1920)

NEXT TO OF COURSE GOD AMERICA I

"next to of course god america i
love you land of the pilgrims' and so forth oh
say can you see by the dawn's early my
country 'tis of centuries come and go
and are no more what of it we should worry
in every language even deafanddumb
thy sons acclaim your glorious name by gorry
by jingo by gee by gosh by gum
why talk of beauty what could be more beautiful than these heroic happy dead   10
who rushed like lions to the roaring slaughter
they did not stop to think they died instead
then shall the voice of liberty be mute?"

He spoke.   And drank rapidly a glass of water

                            (1926)

SINCE FEELING IS FIRST

since feeling is first
who pays any attention
to the syntax of things
will never wholly kiss you;

wholly to be a fool
while Spring is in the world

my blood approves,
and kisses are a better fate
than wisdom
lady i swear by all flowers. Don't cry   10
—the best gesture of my brain is less than
your eyelids' flutter which says

we are for each other: then
laugh, leaning back in my arms
for life's not a paragraph

And death i think is no parenthesis

(1926)

PITY THIS BUSY MONSTER,MANUNKIND

pity this busy monster,manunkind,

not. Progress is a comfortable disease:
your victim(death and life safely beyond)

plays with the bigness of his littleness
—electrons deify one razorblade
into a mountainrange;lenses extend

unwish through curving wherewhen till unwish
return on its unself

                    A world of made
is not a world of born—pity poor flesh   10

and trees,poor stars and stones,but never this
fine specimen of hypermagical

ultraomnipotence. We doctors know

a hopeless case if—listen:there's a hell
of a good universe next door;let's go

(1944)

Jean Toomer *1894–1967*

REAPERS

Black reapers with the sound of steel on stones
Are sharpening scythes. I see them place the hones
In their hip-pockets as a thing that's done,
And start their silent swinging, one by one.

Black horses drive a mower through the weeds,
And there, a field rat, startled, squealing bleeds,
His belly close to ground. I see the blade,
Blood-stained, continue cutting weeds and shade.

(1923)

Robert Graves *1895–*

THE COOL WEB

Children are dumb to say how hot the day is,
How hot the scent is of the summer rose,
How dreadful the black wastes of evening sky,
How dreadful the tall soldiers drumming by.

But we have speech, to chill the angry day,
And speech, to dull the rose's cruel scent.
We spell away the overhanging night,
We spell away the soldiers and the fright.

There's a cool web of language winds us in,
Retreat from too much joy or too much fear: 10
We grow sea-green at last and coldly die
In brininess and volubility.

But if we let our tongues lose self-possession,
Throwing off language and its watery clasp
Before our death, instead of when death comes,
Facing the wide glare of the children's day,
Facing the rose, the dark sky and the drums,
We shall go mad no doubt and die that way.

(1926)

Langston Hughes *1902–1967*

HARLEM

What happens to a dream deferred?

    Does it dry up
    like a raisin in the sun?
    Or fester like a sore—
    And then run?
    Does it stink like rotten meat?
    Or crust and sugar over—
    like a syrupy sweet?

    Maybe it just sags
    like a heavy load.   10

    Or does it explode?

(1951)

SAME IN BLUES

I said to my baby,
Baby, take it slow.
I can't, she said, I can't!
I got to go!

> *There's a certain*
> *amount of traveling*
> *in a dream deferred.*

Lulu said to Leonard,
I want a diamond ring.
Leonard said to Lulu,   10
You won't get a goddamn thing!

> *A certain*
> *amount of nothing*
> *in a dream deferred.*

Daddy, daddy, daddy,
All I want is you.
You can have me, baby—
but my lovin' days is through.

> *A certain*
> *amount of impotence*   20
> *in a dream deferred.*

Three parties
On my party line—
But that third party,
Lord, ain't mine!

> *There's liable*
> *to be confusion*
> *in a dream deferred.*

From river to river,
Uptown and down,   30
There's liable to be confusion
when a dream gets kicked around.

                                                        (1951)

Stevie Smith *1902–1971*

NOT WAVING BUT DROWNING

Nobody heard him, the dead man,
But still he lay moaning:
I was much further out than you thought
And not waving but drowning.

Poor chap, he always loved larking
And now he's dead
It must have been too cold for him his heart gave way,
They said.

Oh, no no no, it was too cold always
(Still the dead one lay moaning)   10
I was much too far out all my life
And not waving but drowning.

(1957)

Countee Cullen *1903–1946*

INCIDENT

(For Eric Walrond)

Once riding in old Baltimore,
    Heart-filled, head-filled with glee,
I saw a Baltimorean
    Keep looking straight at me.

Now I was eight and very small,
    And he was no whit bigger,
And so I smiled, but he poked out
    His tongue, and called me, "Nigger."

I saw the whole of Baltimore
    From May until December;   10
Of all the things that happened there
    That's all that I remember.

(1925)

Richard Eberhart   *1904–*

THE FURY OF AERIAL BOMBARDMENT

You would think the fury of aerial bombardment
Would rouse God to relent; the infinite spaces
Are still silent. He looks on shock-pried faces.
History, even, does not know what is meant.

You would feel that after so many centuries
God would give man to repent; yet he can kill
As Cain could, but with multitudinous will,
No farther advanced than in his ancient furies.

Was man made stupid to see his own stupidity?
Is God by definition indifferent, beyond us all?   10
Is the eternal truth man's fighting soul
Wherein the Beast ravens in its own avidity?

Of Van Wettering I speak, and Averill,
Names on a list, whose faces I do not recall
But they are gone to early death, who late in school
Distinguished the belt feed lever from the belt holding pawl.

                                                                    (1944)

John Betjeman   *1906–1984*

IN WESTMINSTER ABBEY

Let me take this other glove off
    As the *vox humana*[1] swells,
And the beauteous fields of Eden
    Bask beneath the Abbey bells.
Here, where England's statesmen lie,
Listen to a lady's cry.

Gracious Lord, oh bomb the Germans.
    Spare their women for Thy Sake,
And if that is not too easy
    We will pardon Thy Mistake.   10
But, gracious Lord, whate'er shall be,
Don't let anyone bomb me.

[1] Organ stop (setting) intended to suggest the human voice.

Keep our Empire undismembered
    Guide our Forces by Thy Hand,
Gallant blacks from far Jamaica,
    Honduras and Togoland;
Protect them Lord in all their fights,
And, even more, protect the whites.

Think of what our Nation stands for,
    Books from Boots'[2] and country lanes,   20
Free speech, free passes, class distinction,
    Democracy and proper drains.
Lord, put beneath Thy special care
One-eighty-nine Cadogan Square.

Although dear Lord I am a sinner,
    I have done no major crime;
Now I'll come to Evening Service
    Whensoever I have time.
So, Lord, reserve for me a crown,
And do not let my shares go down.   30

I will labour for Thy Kingdom,
    Help our lads to win the war,
Send white feathers to the cowards,
    Join the Women's Army Corps,
Then wash the Steps around Thy Throne
In the Eternal Safety Zone.

Now I feel a little better,
    What a treat to hear Thy Word,
Where the bones of leading statesmen
    Have so often been interred.   40
And now, dear Lord, I cannot wait
Because I have a luncheon date.

(1940)

W. H. Auden *1907–1973*

MUSÉE DES BEAUX ARTS[1]

About suffering they were never wrong,
The Old Masters: how well they understood
Its human position; how it takes place

---

[2] Chain of British drug stores that include lending libraries.
[1] Museum of Fine Arts.

While someone else is eating or opening a window or just walking
    dully along;
How, when the aged are reverently, passionately waiting
For the miraculous birth, there always must be
Children who did not specially want it to happen, skating
On a pond at the edge of the wood:
They never forgot   10
That even the dreadful martyrdom must run its course
Anyhow in a corner, some untidy spot
Where the dogs go on with their doggy life and the torturer's horse
Scratches its innocent behind on a tree.

In Brueghel's *Icarus*,[2] for instance: how everything turns away
Quite leisurely from the disaster; the ploughman may
Have heard the splash, the forsaken cry,
But for him it was not an important failure; the sun shone
As it had to on the white legs disappearing into the green
Water; and the expensive delicate ship that must have seen   20
Something amazing, a boy falling out of the sky,
Had somewhere to get to and sailed calmly on.

                                             (1940)

LULLABY

Lay your sleeping head, my love,
Human on my faithless arm;
Time and fevers burn away
Individual beauty from
Thoughtful children, and the grave
Proves the child ephemeral:
But in my arms till break of day
Let the living creature lie,
Mortal, guilty, but to me
The entirely beautiful.   10

Soul and body have no bounds:
To lovers as they lie upon
Her tolerant enchanted slope
In their ordinary swoon,
Grave the vision Venus sends
Of supernatural sympathy,
Universal love and hope;
While an abstract insight wakes
Among the glaciers and the rocks
The hermit's sensual ecstasy.   20

---

[2] Painting by Pieter Brueghel (1520–1569) which depicts the fall of Icarus, who in Greek
mythology had flown too close to the sun on wings made of feathers and wax.

Certainty, fidelity
On the stroke of midnight pass
Like vibrations of a bell,
And fashionable madmen raise
Their pedantic boring cry:
Every farthing of the cost,
All the dreaded cards foretell,
Shall be paid, but from this night
Not a whisper, not a thought,
Not a kiss nor look be lost.   30

Beauty, midnight, vision dies:
Lets the winds of dawn that blow
Softly round your dreaming head
Such a day of sweetness show
Eye and knocking heart may bless,
Find the mortal world enough;
Noons of dryness see you fed
By the involuntary powers,
Nights of insult let you pass
Watched by every human love.   40
                                        (1940)

Theodore Roethke *1908–1963*

ELEGY FOR JANE

(MY STUDENT, THROWN BY A HORSE)

I remember the neckcurls, limp and damp as tendrils,
And her quick look, a sidelong pickerel smile;
And how, once startled into talk, the light syllables leaped for her,
And she balanced in the delight of her thought,
A wren, happy, tail into the wind,
Her song trembling the twigs and small branches.
The shade sang with her;
The leaves, their whispers turned to kissing;
And the mould sang in the bleached valleys under the rose.

Oh, when she was sad, she cast herself down into such a pure depth, 10
Even a father could not find her;
Scraping her cheek against straw;
Stirring the clearest water.

My sparrow, you are not here,
Waiting like a fern, making a spiny shadow.
The sides of wet stones cannot console me,
Nor the moss, wound with the last light.

If only I could nudge you from this sleep,
My maimed darling, my skittery pigeon.
Over this damp grave I speak the words of my love: 20
I, with no rights in this matter,
Neither father nor lover.

(1953)

I KNEW A WOMAN

I knew a woman, lovely in her bones,
When small birds sighed, she would sigh back at them;
Ah, when she moved, she moved more ways than one:
The shapes a bright container can contain!
Of her choice virtues only gods should speak,
Or English poets who grew up on Greek
(I'd have them sing in chorus, cheek to cheek).

How well her wishes went! She stroked my chin,
She taught me Turn, and Counter-turn, and Stand;
She taught me Touch, that undulant white skin;   10
I nibbled meekly from her proffered hand;
She was the sickle; I, poor I, the rake,
Coming behind her for her pretty sake
(But what prodigious mowing we did make).

Love likes a gander, and adores a goose:
Her full lips pursed, the errant note to seize;
She played it quick, she played it light and loose;
My eyes, they dazzled at her flowing knees;
Her several parts could keep a pure repose,
Or one hip quiver with a mobile nose
(She moved in circles, and those circles moved).

Let seed be grass, and grass turn into hay:
I'm martyr to a motion not my own;
What's freedom for? To know eternity.
I swear she cast a shadow white as stone.
But who would count eternity in days?
These old bones live to learn her wanton ways:
(I measure time by how a body sways).

(1958)

Stephen Spender *1909–*

AN ELEMENTARY SCHOOL CLASSROOM
IN A SLUM

Far far from gusty waves, these children's faces.
Like rootless weeds the torn hair round their paleness.
The tall girl with her weighed-down head. The paper-
seeming boy with rat's eyes. The stunted unlucky heir
Of twisted bones, reciting a father's gnarled disease,
His lesson from his desk. At back of the dim class,
One unnoted, sweet and young: his eyes live in a dream
Of squirrels' game, in tree room, other than this.

On sour cream walls, donations. Shakespeare's head
Cloudless at dawn, civilized dome riding all cities.   10
Belled, flowery, Tyrolese valley. Open-handed map
Awarding the world its world. And yet, for these
Children, these windows, not this world, are world,
Where all their future's painted with a fog,
A narrow street sealed in with a lead sky,
Far far from rivers, capes, and stars of words.

Surely Shakespeare is wicked, the map a bad example
With ships and sun and love tempting them to steal—
For lives that slyly turn in their cramped holes
From fog to endless night? On their slag heap, these children   20
Wear skins peeped through by bones and spectacles of steel
With mended glass, like bottle bits on stones.
All of their time and space are foggy slum
So blot their maps with slums as big as doom.

Unless, governor, teacher, inspector, visitor,
This map becomes their window and these windows
That open on their lives like crouching tombs
Break, O break open, till they break the town
And show the children to the fields and all their world
Azure on their sands, to let their tongues   30
Run naked into books, the white and green leaves open
The history theirs whose language is the sun.

                                          (1939)

Karl Shapiro *1913–*

AUTO WRECK

Its quick soft silver bell beating, beating,
And down the dark one ruby flare
Pulsing out red light like an artery,
The ambulance at top speed floating down
Past beacons and illuminated clocks
Wings in a heavy curve, dips down,
And brakes speed, entering the crowd.
The doors leap open, emptying light;
Stretchers are laid out, the mangled lifted
And stowed into the little hospital.   10
Then the bell, breaking the hush, tolls once,
And the ambulance with its terrible cargo
Rocking, slightly rocking, moves away,
As the doors, an afterthought, are closed.
We are deranged, walking among the cops
Who sweep glass and are large and composed.
One is still making notes under the light.
One with a bucket douches ponds of blood
Into the street and gutter.
One hangs lanterns on the wrecks that cling,   20
Empty husks of locusts, to iron poles.
Our throats were tight as tourniquets,
Our feet were bound with splints, but now,
Like convalescents intimate and gauche,
We speak through sickly smiles and warn
With the stubborn saw of common sense,
The grim joke and the banal resolution.
The traffic moves around with care,
But we remain, touching a wound
That opens to our richest horror.   30
Already old, the question Who shall die?
Becomes unspoken Who is innocent?
For death in war is done by hands;
Suicide has cause and stillbirth, logic;
And cancer, simple as a flower, blooms.
But this invites the occult mind,
Cancels our physics with a sneer,
And spatters all we knew of denouement
Across the expedient and wicked stones.

(1942)

Dudley Randall *1914–*

BALLAD OF BIRMINGHAM

"Mother dear, may I go downtown
instead of out to play,
and march the streets of Birmingham
in a freedom march today?"

"No, baby, no, you may not go,
for the dogs are fierce and wild,
and clubs and hoses, guns and jails
aren't good for a little child."

"But, mother, I won't be alone.
Other children will go with me,   10
and march the streets of Birmingham
to make our country free."

"No, baby, no, you may not go,
for I fear those guns will fire.
But you may go to church instead,
and sing in the children's choir."

She has combed and brushed her nightdark hair,
and bathed rose petal sweet,
and drawn white gloves on her small brown hands,
and white shoes on her feet.   20

The mother smiled to know her child
was in the sacred place,
but that smile was the last smile
to come upon her face.

For when she heard the explosion,
her eyes grew wet and wild.
She raced through the streets of Birmingham
calling for her child.

She clawed through bits of glass and brick,
then lifted out a shoe.   30
"O, here's the shoe my baby wore,
but, baby, where are you?"

(1968)

TO THE MERCY KILLERS

If ever mercy move you murder me,
I pray you, kindly killers, let me live.
Never conspire with death to set me free,
but let me know such life as pain can give.
Even though I be a clot, an aching clench,
a stub, a stump, a butt, a scab, a knob,
a screaming pain, a putrefying stench,
still let me live, so long as life shall throb.
Even though I turn such traitor to myself
as beg to die, do not accomplice me.   10
Even though I seem not human, a mute shelf
of glucose, bottled blood, machinery
to swell the lung and pump the heart—even so,
do not put out my life. Let me still glow.

                                                   (1973)

Randall Jarrell *1914–1965*

THE DEATH OF THE BALL TURRET GUNNER

From my mother's sleep I fell into the State,
And I hunched in its belly till my wet fur froze.
Six miles from earth, loosed from its dream of life,
I woke to black flak and the nightmare fighters.
When I died they washed me out of the turret with a hose.

                                                   (1945)

John Berryman *1914–1972*

LIFE, FRIENDS, IS BORING. WE MUST NOT SAY SO

Life, friends, is boring. We must not say so.
After all, the sky flashes, the great sea yearns,
we ourselves flash and yearn,
and moreover my mother told me as a boy
(repeatingly) 'Ever to confess you're bored
means you have no

Inner Resources.' I conclude now I have no
inner resources, because I am heavy bored.
Peoples bore me.
literature bores me, especially great literature,   10
Henry bores me, with his plights & gripes
as bad as achilles,

who loves people and valiant art, which bores me.
And the tranquil hills, & gin, look like a drag
and somehow a dog
has taken itself & its tail considerably away
into mountains or sea or sky, leaving
behind: me, wag.

           (1964)

Henry Reed   *1914–*

NAMING OF PARTS

Today we have naming of parts. Yesterday,
We had daily cleaning. And tomorrow morning,
We shall have what to do after firing. But today,
Today we have naming of parts. Japonica
Glistens like coral in all of the neighbouring gardens,
     And today we have naming of parts.

This is the lower sling swivel. And this
Is the upper sling swivel, whose use you will see,
When you are given your slings. And this is the piling swivel,
Which in your case you have not got. The branches   10
Hold in the gardens their silent, eloquent gestures,
     Which in our case we have not got.

This is the safety-catch, which is always released
With an easy flick of the thumb. And please do not let me
See anyone using his finger. You can do it quite easy
If you have any strength in your thumb. The blossoms
Are fragile and motionless, never letting anyone see
     Any of them using their finger.

And this you can see is the bolt. The purpose of this
Is to open the breech, as you see. We can slide it   20
Rapidly backwards and forwards: we call this
Easing the spring. And rapidly backwards and forwards
The early bees are assaulting and fumbling the flowers:
     They call it easing the Spring.

They call it easing the Spring: it is perfectly easy
If you have any strength in your thumb: like the bolt,
And the breech, and the cocking-piece, and the point of balance,
Which in our case we have not got; and the almond-blossom
Silent in all of the gardens and the bees going backwards and forwards,
    For today we have naming of parts.   30
                                      (1947)

Dylan Thomas *1914–1953*

THE FORCE THAT THROUGH THE GREEN FUSE DRIVES THE FLOWER

The force that through the green fuse drives the flower
Drives my green age; that blasts the roots of trees
Is my destroyer.
And I am dumb to tell the crooked rose
My youth is bent by the same wintry fever.

The force that drives the water through the rocks
Drives my red blood; that dries the mouthing streams
Turns mine to wax.
And I am dumb to mouth unto my veins
How at the mountain spring the same mouth sucks.   10

The hand that whirls the water in the pool
Stirs the quicksand; that ropes the blowing wind
Hauls my shroud sail.
And I am dumb to tell the hanging man
How of my clay is made the hangman's lime.

The lips of time leech to the fountain head;
Love drips and gathers, but the fallen blood
Shall calm her sores.
And I am dumb to tell a weather's wind
How time has ticked a heaven round the stars.   20

And I am dumb to tell the lover's tomb
How at my sheet goes the same crooked worm.

                                      (1934)

THE HAND THAT SIGNED THE PAPER

The hand that signed the paper felled a city;
Five sovereign fingers taxed the breath,
Doubled the globe of dead and halved a country;
These five kings did a king to death.

The mighty hand leads to a sloping shoulder,
The finger joints are cramped with chalk;
A goose's quill has put an end to murder
That put an end to talk.

The hand that signed the treaty bred a fever,
And famine grew, and locusts came;   10
Great is the hand that holds dominion over
Man by a scribbled name.

The five kings count the dead but do not soften
The crusted wound nor stroke the brow;
A hand rules pity as a hand rules heaven;
Hands have no tears to flow.

(1936)

DO NOT GO GENTLE INTO THAT GOOD NIGHT

Do not go gentle into that good night,
Old age should burn and rave at close of day;
Rage, rage against the dying of the light.

Though wise men at their end know dark is right,
Because their words had forked no lightning they
Do not go gentle into that good night.

Good men, the last wave by, crying how bright
Their frail deeds might have danced in a green bay,
Rage, rage against the dying of the light.

Wild men who caught and sang the sun in flight,   10
And learn, too late, they grieved it on its way,
Do not go gentle into that good night.

Grave men, near death, who see with blinding sight
Blind eyes could blaze like meteors and be gay,
Rage, rage against the dying of the light.

And you, my father, there on the sad height,
Curse, bless, me now with your fierce tears, I pray.
Do not go gentle into that good night.
Rage, rage against the dying of the light.

(1952)

Gwendolyn Brooks *1917–*

A SONG IN THE FRONT YARD

I've stayed in the front yard all my life.
I want a peek at the back
Where it's rough and untended and hungry weed grows.
A girl gets sick of a rose.

I want to go in the back yard now
And maybe down the alley,
To where the charity children play.
I want a good time today.

They do some wonderful things.
They have some wonderful fun: 10
My mother sneers, but I say it's fine
How they don't have to go in at quarter to nine.
My mother, she tells me that Johnnie Mae
Will grow up to be a bad woman.
That George'll be taken to Jail soon or late
(On account of last winter he sold our back gate).

But I say it's fine. Honest, I do.
And I'd like to be a bad woman, too,
And wear the brave stockings of night-black lace
And strut down the streets with paint on my face.   20
                                                                    (1945)

KITCHENETTE BUILDING

We are things of dry hours and the involuntary plan,
Grayed in, and gray. "Dream" makes a giddy sound, not strong
Like "rent," "feeding a wife," "satisfying a man."

But could a dream send up through onion fumes
Its white and violet, fight with fried potatoes
And yesterday's garbage ripening in the hall,
Flutter, or sing an aria down these rooms

Even if we were willing to let it in,
Had time to warm it, keep it very clean,
Anticipate a message, let it begin?   10

We wonder. But not well! not for a minute!
Since Number Five is out of the bathroom now,
We think of lukewarm water, hope to get in it.

                                                                    (1945)

Robert Lowell *1917–1977*

SKUNK HOUR

(*FOR ELIZABETH BISHOP*)

Nautilus Island's hermit
heiress still lives through winter in her Spartan cottage;
her sheep still graze above the sea.
Her son's a bishop. Her farmer
is first selectman in our village;
she's in her dotage.

Thirsting for
the hierarchic privacy
of Queen Victoria's century,
she buys up all   10
the eyesores facing her shore,
and lets them fall.

The season's ill—
we've lost our summer millionaire,
who seemed to leap from an L. L. Bean[1]
catalogue. His nine-knot yawl
was auctioned off to lobstermen.
A red fox stain covers Blue Hill.

And now our fairy
decorator brightens his shop for fall;   20
his fishnet's filled with orange cork,
orange, his cobbler's bench and awl;
there is no money in his work,
he'd rather marry.

One dark night,
my Tudor Ford climbed the hill's skull;
I watched for love-cars. Lights turned down,
they lay together, hull to hull,
where the graveyard shelves on the town. . . .
My mind's not right.   30

A car radio bleats,
"Love, O careless Love. . . ." I hear
my ill-spirit sob in each blood cell,
as if my hand were at its throat. . . .
I myself am hell;
nobody's here—

only skunks, that search
in the moonlight for a bite to eat.

[1] A store that sells outdoor equipment and clothing.

They march on their soles up Main Street:
white stripes, moonstruck eyes' red fire   40
under the chalk-dry and spar spire
of the Trinitarian Church.

I stand on top
of our back steps and breathe the rich air—
a mother skunk with her column of kittens swills the garbage pail.
She jabs her wedge-head in a cup
of sour cream, drops her ostrich tail,
and will not scare.

                                                                    (1959)

Reed Whittemore *1919–*

CLAMMING

I go digging for clams once every two or three years
Just to keep my hand in (I usually cut it),
And I'm sure that whenever I do so I tell the same story
Of how, at the age of four, I was trapped by the tide
As I clammed a sandbar. It's no story at all,
But I tell it and tell it. It serves my small lust
To be thought of as someone who's lived.
I've a war too to fall back on, and some years of flying,
As well as a high quota of drunken parties,
A wife and children; but somehow the clamming thing   10
Gives me an image of me that soothes my psyche
Like none of the louder events: me helpless,
Alone with my sandpail,
As fate in the form of soupy Long Island Sound
Comes stalking me.

I've a son now at that age.
He's spoiled. He's been sickly.
He's handsome and bright, affectionate and demanding.
I think of the tides when I look at him.
I'd have him alone and sea-girt, poor little boy.   20

The self, what a brute it is. It wants, wants.
It will not let go of its even most fictional grandeur,
But must grope, grope down in the muck of its past
For some little squirting life and bring it up tenderly
To the lo and behold of death, that it may weep
And pass on the weeping, keep the thing going.

Son, when you clam,
Watch out for the tides and take care of yourself,
Yet no great care,
Lest you care too much and talk of the caring   30
And bore your best friends and inhibit your children and sicken
At last into opera on somebody's sandbar. Son, when you clam,
Clam.

(1965)

THE FALL OF THE HOUSE OF USHER

It was a big boxy wreck of a house
Owned by a classmate of mine named Rod Usher,
Who lived in the thing with his twin sister.
He was a louse and she was a souse.

While I was visiting them one wet summer, she died.
We buried her,
Or rather we stuck her in a back room for a bit,
    meaning to bury her
When the graveyard dried.

But the weather got wetter.   10
One night we were both waked by a twister,
Plus a screeching and howling outside that
    turned out to be sister
Up and dying again, making it hard for Rod to
    forget her.

He didn't. He and she died in a heap, and I left
    quick,
Which was lucky since the house fell in right after,

                    Like a ton of brick.

(1970)

Howard Nemerov   *1920–*

THE TOWN DUMP

"The art of our necessities is strange
That can make vile things precious."

A mile out in the marshes, under a sky
Which seems to be always going away
In a hurry, on that Venetian land threaded
With hidden canals, you will find the city
Which seconds ours (so cemeteries, too,
Reflect a town from hillsides out of town),
Where Being most Becomingly ends up
Becoming some more. From cardboard tenements,
Windowed with cellophane, or simply tenting
In paper bags, the angry mackerel eyes   10
Glare at you out of stove-in, sunken heads
Far from the sea; the lobster, also, lifts
An empty claw in his most minatory
Of gestures; oyster, crab, and mussel shells
Lie here in heaps, savage as money hurled
Away at the gate of hell. If you want results,
These are results.
                          Objects of value or virtue,
However, are also to be picked up here,
Though rarely, lying with bones and rotten meat,
Eggshells and mouldy bread, banana peels   20
No one will skid on, apple cores that caused
Neither the fall of man nor a theory
Of gravitation. People do throw out
The family pearls by accident, sometimes,
Not often; I've known dealers in antiques
To prowl this place by night, with flashlights, on
The off-chance of somebody's having left
Derelict chairs which will turn out to be
By Hepplewhite, a perfect set of six
Going to show, I guess, that in any sty   30
Someone's heaven may open and shower down
Riches responsive to the right dream; though
It is a small chance, certainly, that sends
The ghostly dealer, heavy with fly-netting
Over his head, across these hills in darkness,
Stumbling in cut-glass goblets, lacquered cups,
And other products of his dreamy midden
Pencilled with light and guarded by the flies.

For there are flies, of course. A dynamo
Composed, by thousands, of our ancient black					40
Retainers, hums here day and night, steady
As someone telling beads, the hum becoming
A high whine at any disturbance; then,
Settled again, they shine under the sun
Like oil-drops, or are invisible as night,
By night.
                All this continually smoulders,
Crackles, and smokes with mostly invisible fires
Which, working deep, rarely flash out and flare,
And never finish. Nothing finishes;
The flies, feeling the heat, keep on the move.					50

Among the flies, the purifying fires,
The hunters by night, acquainted with the art
Of our necessities, and the new deposits
That each day wastes with treasure, you may say
There should be ratios. You may sum up
The results, if you want results. But I will add
That wild birds, drawn to the carrion and flies,
Assemble in some numbers here, their wings
Shining with light, their flight enviably free,
Their music marvelous, though sad, and strange.					60
                                    (1958)

Richard Wilbur *1921–*

FIRST SNOW IN ALSACE

The snow came down last night like moths
Burned on the moon; it fell till dawn,
Covered the town with simple cloths.

Absolute snow lies rumpled on
What shellbursts scattered and deranged,
Entangled railings, crevassed lawn.

As if it did not know they'd changed,
Snow smoothly clasps the roofs of homes
Fear-gutted, trustless and estranged.

The ration stacks are milky domes;					10
Across the ammunition pile
The snow has climbed in sparkling combs.

You think: beyond the town a mile
Or two, this snowfall fills the eyes
Of soldiers dead a little while.

Persons and persons in disguise,
Walking the new air white and fine,
Trade glances quick with shared surprise.

At children's windows, heaped, benign,
As always, winter shines the most,   20
And frost makes marvelous designs.

The night guard coming from his post,
Ten first-snows back in thought, walks slow
And warms him with a boyish boast:

He was the first to see the snow.

                                                            (1947)

Philip Larkin *1922–*

POETRY OF DEPARTURES

Sometimes you hear, fifth-hand,
As epitaph:
He chucked up everthing
And just cleared off,
And always the voice will sound
Certain you approve
This audacious, purifying,
Elemental move.
And they are right, I think.
We all hate home   10
And having to be there:
I detest my room,
Its specially-chosen junk,
The good books, the good bed,
And my life, in perfect order:
So to hear it said
He walked out on the whole crowd
Leaves me flushed and stirred,
Like *Then she undid her dress*
Or *Take that you bastard;*   20
Surely I can, if he did?
And that helps me stay
Sober and industrious.
But I'd go today,
Yes, swagger the nut-strewn roads,

Crouch in the fo'c'sle
Stubbly with goodness, if
It weren't so artificial,
Such a deliberate step backwards
To create an object: 30
Books; china; a life
Reprehensibly perfect.

(1955)

Denise Levertov *1923–*

THE ACHE OF MARRIAGE

The ache of marriage:

thigh and tongue, beloved,
are heavy with it,
it throbs in the teeth

We look for communion
and are turned away, beloved,
each and each

It is leviathan and we
in its belly
looking for joy, some joy 10
not to be known outside it

two by two in the ark of
the ache of it.

(1964)

Maxine Kumin *1925–*

WOODCHUCKS

Gassing the woodchucks didn't turn out right.
The knockout bomb from the Feed and Grain Exchange
was featured as merciful, quick at the bone
and the case we had against them was airtight,
both exits shoehorned shut with puddingstone,
but they had a sub-sub-basement out of range.

Next morning they turned up again, no worse
for the cyanide than we for our cigarettes
and state-store Scotch, all of us up to scratch.
They brought down the marigolds as a matter of course   10
and then took over the vegetable patch
nipping the broccoli shoots, beheading the carrots.

The food from our mouths, I said, righteously thrilling
to the feel of the .22, the bullets' neat noses.
I, a lapsed pacifist fallen from grace
puffed with Darwinian pieties for killing,
now drew a bead on the littlest woodchuck's face.
He died down in the everbearing roses.

Ten minutes later I dropped the mother. She
flipflopped in the air and fell, her needle teeth   20
still hooked in a leaf of early Swiss chard.
Another baby next. O one-two-three
the murderer inside me rose up hard,
the hawkeye killer came on stage forthwith.

There's one chuck left. Old wily fellow, he keeps
me cocked and ready day after day after day.
All night I hunt his humped-up form. I dream
I sight along the barrel in my sleep.
If only they'd all consented to die unseen
gassed underground the quiet Nazi way.   30
                                                              (1972)

W. D. Snodgrass *1926–*

APRIL INVENTORY

The green catalpa tree has turned
All white; the cherry blooms once more.
In one whole year I haven't learned
A blessed thing they pay you for.
The blossoms snow down in my hair;
The trees and I will soon be bare.

The trees have more than I to spare.
The sleek, expensive girls I teach,
Younger and pinker every year,
Bloom gradually out of reach.   10
The pear tree lets its petals drop
Like dandruff on a tabletop.

The girls have grown so girlish now
I have to nudge myself to stare.
This year they smile and mind me how
My teeth are falling with my hair.
In thirty years I may not get
Younger, shrewder, or out of debt.

The tenth time, just a year ago,
I made myself a little list   20
Of all the things I'd ought to know,
Then told my parents, analyst,
And everyone who's trusted me
I'd be substantial, presently.

I haven't read one book about
A book or memorized one plot.
Or found a mind I did not doubt.
I learned one date. And then forgot.
And one by one the solid scholars
Get the degrees, the jobs, the dollars.   30

And smile above their starchy collars.
I taught my classes Whitehead's[1] notions;
One lovely girl, a song of Mahler's.[2]
Lacking a source book and promotions,
I taught one child the colors of
A luna moth and how to love.

I taught myself to name my name,
To bark back, loosen love and crying;
To ease my woman so she came,
To ease an old man who was dying.   40
I have not learned how often I
Can win, can love, but choose to die.

I have not learned there is a lie
Love shall be blonder, slimmer, younger;
That my equivocating eye
Loves only by my body's hunger;
That I have forces, true to feel,
Or that the lovely world is real.

While scholars speak authority
And wear their ulcers on their sleeves,   50
My eyes in spectacles shall see
These trees procure and spend their leaves.
There is a value underneath
The gold and silver in my teeth.

---

[1] Alfred North Whitehead (1861–1947), British mathematician and philosopher.
[2] Gustav Mahler (1860–1911), Austrian composer.

Though trees turn bare and girls turn wives,
We shall afford our costly seasons;
There is a gentleness survives
That will outspeak and has its reasons.
There is a loveliness exists,
Preserves us; not for specialists.   60

                                                  (1957)

Robert Creeley *1926–*

A MARRIAGE

The first retainer
he gave to her
was a golden
wedding ring.

The second—late at night
he woke up,
leaned over on an elbow,
and kissed her.

The third and the last—
he died with   10
and gave up loving
and lived with her.

                                                  (1958)

Allen Ginsberg *1926–*

A SUPERMARKET IN CALIFORNIA

What thoughts I have of you tonight, Walt Whitman, for I walked down the sidestreets under the trees with a headache self-conscious looking at the full moon.

In my hungry fatigue, and shopping for images, I went into the neon fruit supermarket, dreaming of your enumerations!

What peaches and what penumbras! Whole families shopping at night! Aisles full of husbands! Wives in the avocados, babies in the tomatoes!—and you, Garcia Lorca, what were you doing down by the watermelons?

I saw you, Walt Whitman, childless, lonely old grubber, poking among the meats in the refrigerator and eyeing the grocery boys.

I heard you asking questions of each: Who killed the pork chops? What price bananas? Are you my Angel?

I wandered in and out of the brilliant stacks of cans following you, and followed in my imagination by the store detective.

We strode down the open corridors together in our solitary fancy tasting artichokes, possessing every frozen delicacy, and never passing the cashier.

Where are we going, Walt Whitman? The doors close in an hour. Which way does your beard point tonight?

(I touch your book and dream of our odyssey in the supermarket and feel absurd.)

Will we walk all night through solitary streets? The trees add shade to shade, lights out in the houses, we'll both be lonely.   10

Will we stroll dreaming of the lost America of love past blue automobiles in driveways, home to our silent cottage?

Ah, dear father, graybeard, lonely old courage-teacher, what America did you have when Charon quit poling his ferry and you got out on a smoking bank and stood watching the boat disappear on the black waters of Lethe?

(1956)

Robert Bly *1926–*

DRIVING TO TOWN LATE TO MAIL A LETTER

It is a cold and snowy night. The main street is deserted.
The only things moving are swirls of snow.
As I lift the mailbox door, I feel its cold iron.
There is a privacy I love in this snowy night.
Driving around, I will waste more time.

(1962)

W. S. Merwin *1927–*

FOR THE ANNIVERSARY OF MY DEATH

Every year without knowing it I have passed the day
When the last fires will wave to me
And the silence will set out
Tireless traveller
Like the beam of a lightless star

Then I will no longer
Find myself in life as in a strange garment
Surprised at the earth
And the love of one woman
And the shamelessness of men   10
As today writing after three days of rain
Hearing the wren sing and the falling cease
And bowing not knowing to what

(1967)

James Wright *1927–1980*

A BLESSING

Just off the highway to Rochester, Minnesota,
Twilight bounds softly forth on the grass.
And the eyes of those two Indian ponies
Darken with kindness.
They have come gladly out of the willows
To welcome my friend and me.
We step over the barbed wire into the pasture
Where they have been grazing all day, alone.
They ripple tensely, they can hardly contain their happiness
That we have come.   10
They bow shyly as wet swans. They love each other.
There is no loneliness like theirs.
At home once more,
They begin munching the young tufts of spring in the darkness.
I would like to hold the slenderer one in my arms,
For she has walked over to me
And nuzzled my left hand.
She is black and white,
Her mane falls wild on her forehead,
And the light breeze moves me to caress her long ear   20

That is delicate as the skin over a girl's wrist.
Suddenly I realize
That if I stepped out of my body I would break
Into blossom.

(1961)

Anne Sexton *1928–1974*

YOU ALL KNOW THE STORY OF THE OTHER WOMAN

It's a little Walden.
She is private in her breathbed
as his body takes off and flies,
flies straight as an arrow.
But it's a bad translation.
Daylight is nobody's friend.
God comes in like a landlord
and flashes on his brassy lamp.
Now she is just so-so.
He puts his bones back on,   10
turning the clock back an hour.
She knows flesh, that skin balloon,
the unbound limbs, the boards,
the roof, the removable roof.
She is his selection, part time.
You know the story too! Look,
when it is over he places her,
like a phone, back on the hook.

(1967)

Adrienne Rich *1929–*

LIVING IN SIN

She had thought the studio would keep itself;
No dust upon the furniture of love.
Half heresy, to wish the taps less vocal,
The panes relieved of grime. A plate of pears,
A piano with a Persian shawl, a cat
Stalking the picturesque amusing mouse

Had been her vision when he pleaded "Come."
Not that at five each separate stair would writhe
Under the milkman's tramp; that morning light
So coldly would delineate the scraps   10
Of last night's cheese and blank sepulchral bottles;
That on the kitchen shelf among the saucers
A pair of beetle-eyes would fix her own—
Envoy from some black village in the mouldings . . .
Meanwhile her night's companion, with a yawn
Sounded a dozen notes upon the keyboard,
Declared it out of tune, inspected whistling
A twelve hours' beard, went out for cigarettes;
While she, contending with a woman's demons,
Pulled back the sheets and made the bed and found   20
A fallen towel to dust the table-top,
And wondered how it was a man could wake
From night to day and take the day for granted.
By evening she was back in love again,
Though not so wholly but throughout the night
She woke sometimes to feel the daylight coming
Like a relentless milkman up the stairs.

                                                                              (1955)

THE MIDDLE-AGED

Their faces, safe as an interior
Of Holland tiles and Oriental carpet,
Where the fruit-bowl, always filled, stood in a light
Of placid afternoon—their voices' measure,
Their figures moving in the Sunday garden
To lay the tea outdoors or trim the borders,
Afflicted, haunted us. For to be young
Was always to live in other peoples' houses
Whose peace, if we sought it, had been made by others,
Was ours at second-hand and not for long.   10
The custom of the house, not ours, the sun
Fading the silver-blue Fortuny[1] curtains,
The reminiscence of a Christmas party
Of fourteen years ago—all memory,
Signs of possession and of being possessed,
We tasted, tense with envy. They were so kind,
Would have given us anything; the bowl of fruit
Was filled for us, there was a room upstairs
We must call ours: but twenty years of living
They could not give. Nor did they ever speak   20
Of the coarse stain on that polished balustrade,

[1] Elegant fabric based on Moorish tile designs.

The crack in the study window, or the letters
Locked in a drawer and the key destroyed.
All to be understood by us, returning
Late, in our own time—how that peace was made,
Upon what terms, with how much left unsaid.

(1955)

Gary Snyder *1930–*

RUNNING WATER MUSIC

under the trees
under the clouds
by the river
on the beach,

"sea roads."
whales   great sea-path beasts—
        salt; cold
        water; smoky fire.
steam, cereal,
        stone, wood boards.   10
bone awl, pelts,
        bamboo pins and spoons.
unglazed bowl.
a band around the hair.

      beyond wounds.

sat on a rock in the sun,
watched the old pine
wave
over blinding fine white
      river sand.   20

(1970)

Sylvia Plath *1932–1963*

THE RIVAL

If the moon smiled, she would resemble you.
You leave the same impression
Of something beautiful, but annihilating.
Both of you are great light borrowers.

Her O-mouth grieves at the world; yours is unaffected,

And your first gift is making stone out of everything.
I wake to a mausoleum; you are here,
Ticking your fingers on the marble table, looking for cigarettes,
Spiteful as a woman, but not so nervous,
And dying to say something unanswerable.   10

The moon, too, abases her subjects,
But in the daytime she is ridiculous.
Your dissatisfactions, on the other hand,
Arrive through the mailslot with loving regularity,
White and blank, expansive as carbon monoxide.

No day is safe from news of you,
Walking about in Africa maybe, but thinking of me.

                                                              (1962)

DADDY

You do not do, you do not do
Any more, black shoe
In which I have lived like a foot
For thirty years, poor and white,
Barely daring to breathe or Achoo.

Daddy, I have had to kill you.
You died before I had time——
Marble-heavy, a bag full of God,
Ghastly statue with one grey toe
Big as a Frisco seal   10

And a head in the freakish Atlantic
Where it pours bean green over blue
In the waters off beautiful Nauset.[1]
I used to pray to recover you.
Ach, du.[2]

In the German tongue, in the Polish town
Scraped flat by the roller
Of wars, wars, wars.
But the name of the town is common.
My Polack friend   20

Says there are a dozen or two.
So I never could tell where you
Put your foot, your root,
I never could talk to you.
The tongue stuck in my jaw.

[1] Beach and harbor on Cape Cod.   [2] German for "Ah, you."

It stuck in a barb wire snare.
Ich, ich, ich, ich,[3]
I could hardly speak.
I thought every German was you.
And the language obscene   30

An engine, an engine
Chuffing me off like a Jew.
A Jew to Dachau, Auschwitz, Belsen.[4]
I began to talk like a Jew.
I think I may well be a Jew.

The snows of the Tyrol, the clear beer of Vienna
Are not very pure or true.
With my gypsy ancestress and my weird luck
And my Taroc pack[5] and my Taroc pack
I may be a bit of a Jew.   40

I have always been scared of *you*,
With your Luftwaffe,[6] your gobbledygoo.
And your neat moustache
And your Aryan eye, bright blue.
Panzer[7]-man, panzer-man, O You——

Not God but a swastika
So black no sky could squeak through.
Every woman adores a Fascist,
The boot in the face, the brute
Brute heart of a brute like you.   50

You stand at the blackboard, daddy,
In the picture I have of you,
A cleft in your chin instead of your foot
But no less a devil for that, no not
Any less the black man who

Bit my pretty red heart in two.
I was ten when they buried you.
At twenty I tried to die
And get back, back, back to you.
I thought even the bones would do.   60

But they pulled me out of the sack,
And they stuck me together with glue.
And then I knew what to do.
I made a model of you,
A man in black with a Meinkampf[8] look

---

[3] German for "I, I, I, I."   [4] Nazi concentration camps.
[5] Tarot cards, used in fortune telling.
[6] The German air force in World War II.
[7] Referring to a German tank unit in World War II.
[8] *My Struggle*, the title of Adolf Hitler's political autobiography.

And a love of the rack and the screw.
And I said I do, I do.
So daddy, I'm finally through.
The black telephone's off at the root,
The voices just can't worm through.   70

If I've killed one man, I've killed two——
The vampire who said he was you
And drank my blood for a year,
Seven years, if you want to know.
Daddy, you can lie back now.

There's a stake in your fat black heart
And the villagers never liked you.
They are dancing and stamping on you.
They always *knew* it was you.
Daddy, daddy, you bastard, I'm through.   80
                                                            (1963)

Imamu Amiri Baraka *1934–*

IN MEMORY OF RADIO

Who has ever stopped to think of the divinity of Lamont Cranston?[1]
(Only Jack Kerouac, that I know of: & me.
The rest of you probably had on WCBS and Kate Smith,
Or something equally unattractive.)

What can I say?
It is better to have loved and lost
Than to put linoleum in your living rooms?

Am I a sage or something?
Mandrake's hypnotic gesture of the week?[2]
(Remember, I do not have the healing powers of Oral Roberts . . .   10
I cannot, like F. J. Sheen,[3] tell you how to get saved & *rich!*
I cannot even order you to gaschamber satori[4] like Hitler or
        Goody Knight[5]

---

[1] Hero of "The Shadow," radio series (1931–54) in which Cranston had the powers to become invisible and "to cloud men's minds."

[2] Comic strip hero Mandrake the Magician used hypnotic powers to fight evil.

[3] Bishop Fulton J. Sheen, known for his radio sermons in the 1930s and '40s.

[4] Zen Buddhist state of spiritual enlightenment.

[5] Governor of California (1953–59) at a time when the use of the gas chamber for capital punishment was hotly debated.

& Love is an evil word.
Turn it backwards/see, see what I mean?
An evol word. & besides
who understands it?
I certainly wouldn't like to go out on that kind of limb.

Saturday mornings we listened to *Red Lantern* & his undersea folk.
At 11, *Let's Pretend* /& we did/& I, the poet, still do, Thank God!

What was it he used to say (after the transformation, when he was   20
safe & invisible & the unbelievers couldn't throw stones?) "Heh, heh,
heh,
Who knows what evil lurks in the hearts of men? The Shadow knows."

O, yes he does
O, yes he does.
An evil word it is,
This Love.

(1961)

Ishmael Reed   *(1938–*

beware: do not read this poem

tonite , *thriller* was
abt an ol woman , so vain she
surrounded her self w/
     many mirrors

it got so bad that finally she
locked herself indoors & her
whole life became the
     mirrors

one day the villagers broke
into her house , but she was too   10
swift for them . she disappeared
     into a mirror
each tenant who bought the house
after that, lost a loved one to
     the ol woman in the mirror :
     first a little girl
     then a young woman
     then the young woman/s husband

the hunger of this poem is legendary   20
it has taken in many victims

back off from this poem
it has drawn in yr feet
back off from this poem
it has drawn in yr legs
back off from this poem
it is a greedy mirror
you are into this poem . from
 the waist down
nobody can hear you can they ?
this poem has had you up to here   30
  belch
this poem aint got no manners
you cant call out frm this poem
relax now & go w/this poem
move & roll on to this poem

do not resist this poem
this poem has yr eyes
this poem has his head
this poem has his arms
this poem has his fingers   40
this poem has his fingertips

this poem is the reader & the
reader this poem

statistic: the us bureau of missing persons reports
  that in 1968 over 100,000 people disappeared
  leaving no solid clues
   nor trace   only
a space in the lives of their friends 50
           (1972)

Nikki Giovanni *1943–*

DREAMS

in my younger years
before i learned
black people aren't
suppose to dream
i wanted to be
a raelet
and say "dr o wn d in my youn tears"
or "tal kin bout tal kin bout"

or marjorie hendricks and grind
all up against the mic   10
and scream
"baaaaaby nightanddday
baaaaaby nightanddday"
then as i grew and matured
i became more sensible
and decided i would
settle down
and just become
a sweet inspiration

(1968)

WOMAN POEM

you see, my whole life
is tied up
to unhappiness
its father cooking breakfast
and me getting fat as a hog
or having no food
at all and father proving
his incompetence
again
i wish i knew how it would feel   10
to be free

its having a job
they won't let you work
or no work at all
castrating me
(yes it happens to women too)

its a sex object if you're pretty
and no love
or love and no sex if you're fat
get back fat black woman be a mother   20
grandmother strong thing but not woman
gameswoman romantic woman love needer
man seeker dick eater sweat getter
fuck needing love seeking woman

its a hole in your shoe
and buying lil sis a dress
and her saying you shouldn't
when you know
all too well—that you shouldn't

but smiles are only something we give   30
to properly dressed social workers
not each other
only smiles of i know
your game sister
which isn't really
a smile

joy is finding a pregnant roach
and squashing it
not finding someone to hold
let go get off get back don't turn   40
me on you black dog
how dare you care
about me
you ain't got no good sense
cause i ain't shit you must be lower
than that to care

its a filthy house
with yesterday's watermelon
and monday's tears
cause true ladies don't   50
know how to clean

its intellectual devastation
of everybody
to avoid emotional commitment
"yeah honey i would've married
him but he didn't have no degree"

its knock-kneed mini skirted
wig wearing died blond mamma's scar
born dead my scorn your whore
rough heeled broken nailed powdered   60
face me
whose whole life is tied
up to unhappiness
cause its the only
for real thing
i
know

                                        (1969)

PART FOUR

Writing about Drama

*This section, focusing on drama and including brief
discussions of its beginnings and more recent developments
in contemporary theater, completes our literary and
rhetorical instruction.*

14

How Do I Read a Play?

A play is written to be performed. Although most drama begins with a written script, the author of a play counts on the collaboration of others—actors, directors, set designers, costumers, make-up artists, lighting and sound engineers—to translate the written words into a performance on stage or film or videotape. Unlike novelists and poets, playwrights do not necessarily expect their words to be read by the audience.

The performance goal of drama does not mean, however, that you cannot read and study a play as you would a story or a poem. Plays share many literary qualities with other types of creative writing: character, plot, structure, atmosphere, theme, symbolism, and point of view. But it is important to recognize the differences between reading a play and seeing one performed.

Listen to the Lines

The major difference between reading and watching a play is that, as reader, you do not have the actors' voices and gestures to interpret the lines and establish the characters for you. Because playwrights rely almost entirely on speeches or conversations (called *dialogue*) to define character, develop plot, and convey theme, it will be your task as a reader to listen to the lines in your mind. Read the dialogue as you would expect to hear it spoken. For example, when you read Antigone's response to Creon,

> Your edict, King, was strong,
> But all your strength is weakness itself against
> The immortal unrecorded laws of God,

557

do you hear the assurance and defiance in her voice? Or when you read Tom's farewell speech to his sister in *The Glass Menagerie,* can you detect the mixture of tenderness and regret in his words, "Oh, Laura, Laura, I tried to leave you behind me, but I am more faithful than I intended to be! . . . Blow out your candles, Laura—and so goodbye. . . ."? Of course the tone of these lines is not as clear when they are taken out of context, but even these brief quotations illustrate the charged nature of language you should expect when you read a play.

You can actually read the lines out loud to yourself or enlist some fellow students to act out some scenes with you. These oral readings will force you to decide how to interpret the words. But most of the time you will have to use your imagination to re-create the sound of the spoken medium. If you do get to see a performance of a play you are reading or to hear a recording of it, you will appreciate the extraordinary liveliness of dramatic literature when it is lifted from the page and provided with sound and action.

Reading a play does have some advantage over viewing a live performance. Unlike a theatergoer, a reader can stop and return to lines or speeches that seem especially complicated or meaningful. Close reading gives you the opportunity to examine and consider the playwright's exact words, which often fly by quickly, sometimes in altered form, in an actual performance.

Visualize the Scene

In addition to imagining the sound of the dialogue, you will also want to picture what is supposed to be happening on stage. The poet and playwright Ezra Pound pointed out that the "medium of drama is not words, but persons moving about on a stage using words." This observation underlines the importance of movement, gesture, and setting in the performance of a play. These nonverbal elements of the language of drama are sometimes described in the author's *stage directions.* Oftentimes, though, you will find the cues for gestures, movements, and facial expressions in the words themselves, just as the director and the actors do when they are preparing a script for production. For example, these lines of Othello, spoken when he has been roused from his bed by a fight among his men, suggest the physical performance that would accompany the words:

> Why, how now, ho! from whence ariseth this?
> Are we turn'd Turks, and to ourselves do that
> Which heaven hath forbid the Ottomites?
> For Christian shame, put by this barbarous brawl:
> He that stirs next to carve for his own rage
> Holds his soul light; he dies upon his motion.
> Silence that dreadful bell.

Reading this speech with an actor's or director's imagination, you can see in your mind the character stride angrily into the fight scene, gesture threateningly at the men who are poised to continue the fight, and then point suddenly off-stage in the direction of the clamoring alarm bell. Such a detailed reading will take time, but you will be rewarded by the fun and satisfaction of catching the full dramatic quality of the play.

In more recent years, playwrights like Arthur Miller and Tennessee Williams have tried to keep artistic control over the interpretations of their works by including detailed stage directions in their scripts. The extensive production notes for Williams' *The Glass Menagerie* sometimes read like descriptions from a novel or poem:

> Friday evening. It is about five o'clock of a late spring evening which comes "scattering poems in the sky." A delicate lemony light is in the Wingfield apartment. . . . A fragile, unearthly prettiness has come out in Laura: she is like a piece of translucent glass touched by light, given a momentary radiance, not actual, not lasting.

With or without notes like this, your imagination will be working full time when you read a play. You will not be at the mercy of some designer's taste or the personal interpretation of a director or actor. You will be free to produce the play in the theater of your mind.

Critical Questions for Reading Plays

Before planning an analysis of any of the plays in this text, write out your answers to the following questions to be sure you understand the play and to help you generate material for your paper.

1. What is the central conflict in the play? How is it resolved?
2. Does the play contain any secondary conflicts (subplots)? How do they relate to the main conflict?
3. Does the play follow a traditional dramatic structure (see Chapter 15)? What is the climax? Is there a denouement?
4. Who is the main character or protagonist (see Chapter 15)? What sort of person is he or she? Does this protagonist have a fatal flaw? Is the protagonist a hero (see Chapter 16)?
5. Is the antagonist—the one who opposes the protagonist—a person, an environment, or a social force (see Chapter 15)? If a person, does the antagonist cause conflict intentionally?
6. Do the other characters provide exposition (background information)? Are they used as *foils* to oppose, contrast, criticize, and thus help develop the main characters?

7. What are the time and setting of the play? How important are these elements? Could the play be set just as effectively in another time or place?

8. Does the title provide any clues to an understanding of the play? If you had to give the play another title, what would it be?

9. What is the theme of the play? Can you state it in a single sentence?

10. Is the play a tragedy, a comedy, or a mixture (see Chapter 16)? Is this classification important?

11. Is the presentation a realistic one? Does the playwright use any special theatrical devices? If so, what effect do they have on your impression of the play?

15

Writing about
Dramatic Structure

Drama is not as flexible as other forms of literature. A writer of fiction can take as much time as needed to inform the reader about character, setting, motivation, or theme. The dramatist must do everything quickly and clearly. Audiences will not sit through a tedious first act; neither can they stop the play, pick it up tomorrow, or go back to Act One to refresh their memories. Even with the technology of video recording, most plays, including film and television drama, are seen in a single, relatively brief sitting.

What Is Dramatic Structure?

More than 2000 years ago the Greek philosopher Aristotle pointed out that the most important element of drama is the *fable*, what we call the *story* or *plot*. The fable, said Aristotle, has to have a beginning, a middle, and an end. As obvious as this observation seems, it emphasizes the dramatist's special need to engage an audience early and keep it engaged until the conclusion of the play.

Recognizing the drama's strict time limits, Aristotle set down a number of conditions for developing the fable, or plot, in a clear and interesting way. According to Aristotle, the heart of the dramatic story is the *agon*, or *argument*, and the conflict surrounding this argument creates tension and incites interest. The two sides of the conflict, the pros and cons of the argument, are represented on stage by the *protagonist* and the *antagonist*. The protagonist may be one person or many, and the antagonist may be a person, a group, a thing, or a force (supernatural or natural). We often call the protagonist of a play its *hero* or *heroine,* and sometimes the antagonist is also the *villain.*

The fundamental struggle between the protagonist and the antagonist is developed according to a set pattern that theater audiences have come to recognize and expect. This conventional structure can be varied, of course, but most dramatic literature contains the following components:

1. *Point of attack*—the starting point from which the dramatist leads the audience into the plot. A playwright can begin at the story's beginning and allow the audience to discover what is going on at the same time the characters do; or the writer can begin in the middle of things (*in medias res*), or even near the end, and gradually reveal the events that have already taken place.

2. *Exposition*—the revelation of facts, circumstances, and past events. Establishing the essential facts about the characters and the conflict can be accomplished in a number of ways: from having minor characters reveal information through conversation to plunging the audience right into the action.

3. *Rising action*—the building of interest through complication of the conflict. In this stage the protagonist and antagonist move steadily toward a confrontation.

4. *Climax*—the play's high point, the decisive showdown between protagonist and antagonist. The climax—the play's turning point—can be a single moment or a series of events, but once reached, it becomes a point of no return.

5. *Falling action*—the unraveling of the plot, where events fall into place and the conflict moves toward final resolution.

6. *Denouement*—the play's conclusion; the explanation or outcome of the action. The term denouement (literally an "untying") may be applied to both comedy and tragedy, but the Greeks used the word *catastrophe* for a tragic denouement, probably because it involved the death of the hero or heroine.

Whatever it is called, the denouement marks the end of the play: the lovers kiss, the bodies are carried off the stage, and the audience goes home. Most dramatists employ this traditional pattern. Even when they mix in other devices, rearrange elements, and invent new ways to exhibit their materials, dramatists still establish a conflict, develop both sides of the argument, and reach a credible conclusion. After centuries of theater history, the basic structure of drama has changed very little.

Looking at Dramatic Structure

ANTIGONE BY SOPHOCLES

As you read *Antigone*, written in 442 B.C., notice that the play's central conflict is introduced, developed, and resolved according to the pattern we have just described.

Although written first, *Antigone* is the third and last play in the chronology of events that concern Sophocles' Oedipus cycle, which also includes *Oedipus Rex* and *Oedipus at Colonus*. According to Greek legend, King Laius of Thebes and his descendants were doomed by the god Apollo. Warned by the Oracle of Delphi that his own son would kill him, Laius leaves the son, Oedipus, to die in the mountains. But Oedipus survives and unknowingly kills his father, whom he encounters on the road to Thebes. Oedipus solves the riddle of the Sphinx for the Thebans and becomes their king, marrying his mother, the widow Jocasta. Several years later, when he learns what he has done, Oedipus blinds himself and leaves Thebes. His two sons, Eteocles and Polyneices, quarrel over the succession, and Polyneices is driven out of the city. He returns with an army, but he and Eteocles kill each other in battle, while Creon, brother of Jocasta, succeeds to the throne. Antigone and Ismene, daughters of Oedipus, are discussing Creon's first official decree as the play opens.

Sophocles *c.496–c.405* B.C.

An English Version by Dudley Fitts and Robert Fitzgerald

ANTIGONE

THE CHARACTERS

ANTIGONE, *daughter of Oedipus, former banished king.*
ISMENE, *her elder sister.*
CREON, *their maternal uncle, now King of Thebes.*
HAIMON, *Creon's son, beloved of Antigone.*
EURYDICE, *the Queen, his mother, whose other son has* just been killed defending Thebes from attack.
TEIRESIAS, *the old and blind seer or prophet.*
A SENTRY *and* A MESSENGER
THE CHORUS *of fifteen Thebans, elder citizens, among whom the* CHORAGOS *is the leader.*

TIME: *The legendary past of Ancient Greece.*
PLACE: *The walled city of Thebes with its seven gates.*

PROLOGUE

SCENE:

Before the palace of CREON, *King of Thebes. A central double door, and two lateral doors. A platform extends the length of the façade, and from this platform three steps lead down into the "orchestra," or chorus-ground. Time: Dawn of the day after the repulse of the Argive army from the assault on Thebes.*

[ANTIGONE *and* ISMENE *enter from the central door of the Palace.*]
ANTIGONE. Ismenê, dear sister,
  You would think that we had already suffered enough
  For the curse on Oedipus:
  I cannot imagine any grief
  That you and I have not gone through. And now—
  Have they told you of the new decree of our King Creon?
ISMENE. I have heard nothing: I know
  That two sisters lost two brothers, a double death
  In a single hour; and I know that the Argive army
  Fled in the night; but beyond this, nothing.   10
ANTIGONE. I thought so. And that is why I wanted you
  To come out here with me. There is something we must do.
ISMENE. Why do you speak so strangely?
ANTIGONE. Listen, Ismenê:
  Creon buried our brother Eteoclês

564

With military honors, gave him a soldier's funeral,
And it was right that he should; but Polyneicês,
Who fought as bravely and died as miserably,—
They say that Creon has sworn
No one shall bury him, no one mourn for him,   20
But his body must lie in the fields, a sweet treasure
For carrion birds to find as they search for food.
That is what they say, and our good Creon is coming here
To announce it publicly; and the penalty—
Stoning to death in the public square! There it is,
And now you can prove what you are:
A true sister, or a traitor to your family.
ISMENE. Antigonê, you are mad! What could I possibly do?
ANTIGONE. You must decide whether you will help me or not.
ISMENE. I do not understand you. Help you in what?   30
ANTIGONE. Ismenê, I am going to bury him. Will you come?
ISMENE. Bury him! You have just said the new law forbids it.
ANTIGONE. He is my brother. And he is your brother, too.
ISMENE. But think of the danger! Think what Creon will do!
ANTIGONE. Creon is not strong enough to stand in my way.
ISMENE. Ah sister!
Oedipus died, everyone hating him
For what his own search brought to light, his eyes
Ripped out by his own hand; and Iocastê died,
His mother and wife at once: she twisted the cords   40
That strangled her life; and our two brothers died,
Each killed by the other's sword. And we are left:
But oh, Antigonê,
Think how much more terrible than these
Our own death would be if we should go against Creon
And do what he has forbidden! We are only women,
We cannot fight with men, Antigonê!
The law is strong, we must give in to the law
In this thing, and in worse. I beg the Dead
To forgive me, but I am helpless: I must yield   50
To those in authority. And I think it is dangerous business
To be always meddling.
ANTIGONE.   If that is what you think,
I should not want you, even if you asked to come.
You have made your choice, you can be what you want to be.
But I will bury him; and if I must die,
I say that this crime is holy: I shall lie down
With him in death, and I shall be as dear
To him as he to me.
                    It is the dead,
Not the living, who make the longest demands:
We die for ever . . .
                    You may do as you like,   60
Since apparently the laws of the gods mean nothing to you.

ISMENE. They mean a great deal to me; but I have no strength
   To break laws that were made for the public good.
ANTIGONE. That must be your excuse, I suppose. But as for me,
   I will bury the brother I love.
ISMENE.   Antigonê,
   I am so afraid for you!
ANTIGONE.   You need not be:
   You have yourself to consider, after all.
ISMENE. But no one must hear of this, you must tell no one!
   I will keep it a secret, I promise!
ANTIGONE. Oh, tell it! Tell everyone!   70
   Think how they'll hate you when it all comes out
   If they learn that you knew about it all the time!
ISMENE. So fiery! You should be cold with fear.
ANTIGONE. Perhaps. But I am doing only what I must.
ISMENE. But can you do it? I say that you cannot.
ANTIGONE. Very well: when my strength gives out, I shall do no more.
ISMENE. Impossible things should not be tried at all.
ANTIGONE. Go away, Ismenê:
   I shall be hating you soon, and the dead will too,
   For your words are hateful. Leave me my foolish plan: 80
   I am not afraid of the danger; if it means death,
   It will not be the worst of deaths—death without honor.
ISMENE. Go then, if you feel that you must.
   You are unwise,
   But a loyal friend indeed to those who love you.
                          [*Exit into the Palace.* ANTIGONE *goes off, L.*]
                      [*Enter the* CHORUS.]

                          PÁRODOS

                                                          [*strophe 1*]
CHORUS. Now the long blade of the sun, lying
   Level east to west, touches with glory
   Thebes of the Seven Gates. Open, unlidded
   Eye of golden day! O marching light
   Across the eddy and rush of Dircê's stream,
   Striking the white shields of the enemy
   Thrown headlong backward from the blaze of morning!

CHORAGOS. Polyneicês their commander
   Roused them with windy phrases,
   He the wild eagle screaming   10
   Insults above our land,
   His wings their shields of snow,
   His crest their marshaled helms.

                                                      [*antistrophe 1*]
CHORUS. Against our seven gates in a yawning ring
   The famished spears came onward in the night;
   But before his jaws were sated with our blood,
   Or pinefire took the garland of our towers,

He was thrown back; and as he turned, great Thebes—
No tender victim for his noisy power—
Rose like a dragon behind him, shouting war.   20

CHORAGOS. For God hates utterly
    The bray of bragging tongues;
    And when he beheld their smiling,
    Their swagger of golden helms,
    The frown of his thunder blasted
    Their first man from our walls.

                                  [strophe 2]

CHORUS. We heard his shout of triumph high in the air
    Turn to a scream; far out in a flaming arc
    He fell with his windy torch, and the earth struck him.
    And others storming in fury no less than his   30
    Found shock of death in the dusty job of battle.

CHORAGOS. Seven captains at seven gates
    Yielded their clanging arms to the god
    That bends the battle-line and breaks it.
    These two only, brothers in blood,
    Face to face in matchless rage,
    Mirroring each of the other's death,
    Clashed in long combat.

                                [antistrophe 2]

CHORUS. But now in the beautiful morning of victory
    Let Thebes of the many chariots sing for joy!   40
    With hearts dancing we'll take leave of war:
    Our temples shall be sweet with hymns of praise,
    And the long night shall echo with our chorus.

     SCENE I

CHORAGOS. But now at last our new King is coming:
    Creon of Thebes, Menoiceus' son.
    In this auspicious dawn of his reign
    What are the new complexities
    That shifting Fate has woven for him?
    What is his counsel? Why has he summoned
    The old men to hear him?

[*Enter* CREON *from the Palace, C. He addresses the* CHORUS *from the top step.*]

CREON. Gentlemen: I have the honor to inform you that our Ship of State,
    which recent storms have threatened to destroy, has come safely to har-
    bor at last, guided by the merciful wisdom of Heaven. I have sum-   10
    moned you here this morning because I know that I can depend upon
    you: your devotion to King Laïos was absolute; you never hesitated in
    your duty to our late ruler Oedipus; and when Oedipus died, your
    loyalty was transferred to his children. Unfortunately, as you know,
    his two sons, the princes Eteoclês and Polyneicês, have killed each other

in battle; and I, as the next in blood, have succeeded to the full power
of the throne.

I am aware, of course, that no Ruler can expect complete loyalty
from his subjects until he has been tested in office. Nevertheless, I say
to you at the very outset that I have nothing but contempt for   20
the kind of Governor who is afraid, for whatever reason, to follow the
course that he knows is best for the State; and as for the man who
sets private friendship above the public welfare,—I have no use for
him, either. I call God to witness that if I saw my country headed for
ruin, I should not be afraid to speak out plainly; and I need hardly
remind you that I would never have any dealings with an enemy of
the people. No one values friendship more highly than I; but we must
remember that friends made at the risk of wrecking our Ship are not
real friends at all.

These are my principles, at any rate, and that is why I have   30
made the following decision concerning the sons of Oedipus: Eteoclês,
who died as a man should die, fighting for his country, is to be buried
with full military honors, with all the ceremony that is usual when
the greatest heroes die; but his brother Polyneicês, who broke his exile
to come back with fire and sword against his native city and the shrines
of his fathers' gods, whose one idea was to spill the blood of his blood
and sell his own people into slavery—Polyneicês, I say, is to have no
burial: no man is to touch him or say the least prayer for him; he shall
lie on the plain, unburied; and the birds and the scavenging dogs can
do with him whatever they like.   40

This is my command, and you can see the wisdom behind it. As
long as I am King, no traitor is going to be honored with the loyal
man. But whoever shows by word and deed that he is on the side of
the State,—he shall have my respect while he is living, and my reverence
when he is dead.

CHORAGOS. If that is your will, Creon son of Menoiceus,
    You have the right to enforce it: we are yours.
CREON. That is my will. Take care that you do your part.
CHORAGOS. We are old men: let the younger ones carry it out.
CREON. I do not mean that: the sentries have been appointed.   50
CHORAGOS. Then what is it that you would have us do?
CREON. You will give no support to whoever breaks this law.
CHORAGOS. Only a crazy man is in love with death!
CREON. And death it is; yet money talks, and the wisest
    Have sometimes been known to count a few coins too many.

[*Enter* SENTRY *from L.*]

SENTRY. I'll not say that I'm out of breath from running, King, because
    every time I stopped to think about what I have to tell you, I felt like
    going back. And all the time a voice kept saying, "You fool, don't you
    know you're walking straight into trouble?"; and then another voice:
    "Yes, but if you let somebody else get the news to Creon first,   60
    it will be even worse than that for you!" But good sense won out, at
    least I hope it was good sense, and here I am with a story that makes

no sense at all; but I'll tell it anyhow, because, as they say, what's going
to happen's going to happen, and—

CREON. Come to the point. What have you to say?
SENTRY. I did not do it. I did not see who did it. You must not punish
   me for what someone else has done.
CREON. A comprehensive defense! More effective, perhaps,
   If I knew its purpose. Come: what is it?
SENTRY. A dreadful thing . . . I don't know how to put it—   70
CREON. Out with it!
SENTRY.   Well, then;
   The dead man—
            Polyneicês—
Pause. The SENTRY *is overcome, fumbles for words.* CREON *waits impassively.*
           out there—
                someone,—
   New dust on the slimy flesh!
Pause. No sign from CREON.
   Someone has given it burial that way, and
   Gone . . .
   [*Long pause.* CREON *finally speaks with deadly control.*]
CREON. And the man who dared do this?
SENTRY.   I swear I
   Do not know! You must believe me!
                    Listen:
   The ground was dry, not a sign of digging, no,
   Not a wheeltrack in the dust, no trace of anyone.
   It was when they relieved us this morning: and one of them,
   The corporal, pointed to it.
                There it was,   80
   The strangest—
        Look:
   The body, just mounded over with light dust: you see?
   Not buried really, but as if they'd covered it
   Just enough for the ghost's peace. And no sign
   Of dogs or any wild animal that had been there.
   And then what a scene there was! Every man of us
   Accusing the other: we all proved the other man did it,
   We all had proof that we could not have done it.
   We were ready to take hot iron in our hands,
   Walk through fire, swear by all the gods,   90
   It was not I!
   I do not know who it was, but it was not I!
   [CREON's *rage has been mounting steadily, but the* SENTRY *is too intent upon
   his story to notice it.*]
   And then, when this came to nothing, someone said
   A thing that silenced us and made us stare
   Down at the ground: you had to be told the news,
   And one of us had to do it! We threw the dice,
   And the bad luck fell to me. So here I am,

No happier to be here than you are to have me:
Nobody likes the man who brings bad news.
CHORAGOS. I have been wondering, King: can it be that the gods have
    done this?   100
CREON [*furiously*]. Stop.
    Must you doddering wrecks
    Go out of your heads entirely? "The gods!"
    Intolerable!
    The gods favor this corpse? Why? How had he served them?
    Tried to loot their temples, burn their images,
    Yes, and the whole State, and its laws with it!
    Is it your senile opinion that the gods love to honor bad men?
    A pious thought!—
                  No, from the very beginning
    There have been those who have whispered together,   110
    Stiff-necked anarchists, putting their heads together,
    Scheming against me in alleys. These are the men,
    And they have bribed my own guard to do this thing.
    [*Sententiously*]   Money!
    There's nothing in the world so demoralising as money.
    Down go your cities,
    Homes gone, men gone, honest hearts corrupted,
    Crookedness of all kinds, and all for money!
    [*To* SENTRY]   But you—!
    I swear by God and by the throne of God,
    The man who has done this thing shall pay for it!
    Find that man, bring him here to me, or your death   120
    Will be the least of your problems: I'll string you up
    Alive, and there will be certain ways to make you
    Discover your employer before you die;
    And the process may teach you a lesson you seem to have missed:
    The dearest profit is sometimes all too dear:
    That depends on the source. Do you understand me?
    A fortune won is often misfortune.
SENTRY. King, may I speak?
CREON.   Your very voice distresses me.
SENTRY. Are you sure that it is my voice, and not your conscience?
CREON. By God, he wants to analyse me now!   130
SENTRY. It is not what I say, but what has been done, that hurts you.
CREON. You talk too much.
SENTRY. Maybe; but I've done nothing.
CREON. Sold your soul for some silver: that's all you've done.
SENTRY. How dreadful it is when the right judge judges wrong!
CREON. Your figures of speech
    May entertain you now; but unless you bring me the man,
    You will get little profit from them in the end.

                                [*Exit* CREON *into the Palace.*]

SENTRY. "Bring me the man"—!
    I'd like nothing better than bringing him the man!   140

But bring him or not, you have seen the last of me here.
At any rate, I am safe!

[Exit S<small>ENTRY</small>.]

ODE I

[strophe 1]

C<small>HORUS</small>. Numberless are the world's wonders, but none
    More wonderful than man; the stormgray sea
    Yields to his prows, the huge crests bear him high;
    Earth, holy and inexhaustible, is graven
    With shining furrows where his plows have gone
    Year after year, the timeless labor of stallions.

[antistrophe 1]

    The lightboned birds and beasts that cling to cover,
    The lithe fish lighting their reaches of dim water,
    All are taken, tamed in the net of his mind;
    The lion on the hill, the wild horse windy-maned,
    Resign to him; and his blunt yoke has broken
    The sultry shoulders of the mountain bull.

[strophe 2]

    Words also, and thought as rapid as air,
    He fashions to his good use; statecraft is his,
    And his the skill that deflects the arrows of snow,
    The spears of winter rain: from every wind
    He has made himself secure—from all but one:
    In the late wind of death he cannot stand.

[antistrophe 2]

    O clear intelligence, force beyond all measure!
    O fate of man, working both good and evil!
    When the laws are kept, how proudly his city stands!
    When the laws are broken, what of his city then?
    Never may the anarchic man find rest at my hearth,
    Never be it said that my thoughts are his thoughts.

S<small>CENE</small> II

[Re-enter S<small>ENTRY</small> leading A<small>NTIGONE</small>.]

C<small>HORAGOS</small>. What does this mean? Surely this captive woman
    Is the Princess, Antigonê. Why should she be taken?
S<small>ENTRY</small>. Here is the one who did it! We caught her
    In the very act of burying him.—Where is Creon?
C<small>HORAGOS</small>. Just coming from the house.

[Enter C<small>REON</small>, C.]

C<small>REON</small>.   What has happened?
    Why have you come back so soon?
S<small>ENTRY</small> [expansively].   O King,
    A man should never be too sure of anything:
    I would have sworn
    That you'd not see me here again: your anger

Frightened me so, and the things you threatened me with;   10
But how could I tell then
That I'd be able to solve the case so soon?
No dice-throwing this time: I was only too glad to come!
Here is this woman. She is the guilty one:
We found her trying to bury him.
Take her, then; question her; judge her as you will.
I am through with the whole thing now, and gláderof it.
CREON. But this is Antigonê! Why have you brought her here?
SENTRY. She was burying him, I tell you!
CREON [*severely*].   Is this the truth?
SENTRY. I saw her with my own eyes. Can I say more?   20
CREON. The details: come, tell me quickly!
SENTRY.   It was like this:
  After those terrible threats of yours, King,
  We went back and brushed the dust away from the body.
  The flesh was soft by now, and stinking,
  So we sat on a hill to windward and kept guard.
  No napping this time! We kept each other awake.
  But nothing happened until the white round sun
  Whirled in the center of the round sky over us:
  Then, suddenly,
  A storm of dust roared up from the earth, and the sky   30
  Went out, the plain vanished with all its trees
  In the stinging dark. We closed our eyes and endured it.
  The whirlwind lasted a long time, but it passed;
  And then we looked, and there was Antigonê!
  I have seen
  A mother bird come back to a stripped nest, heard
  Her crying bitterly a broken note or two
  For the young ones stolen. Just so, when this girl
  Found the bare corpse, and all her love's work wasted,
  She wept, and cried on heaven to damn the hands   40
  That had done this thing.
                            And then she brought more dust
  And sprinkled wine three times for her brother's ghost.
  We ran and took her at once. She was not afraid,
  Not even when we charged her with what she had done.
  She denied nothing.
                    And this was a comfort to me,
  And some uneasiness: for it is a good thing
  To escape from death, but it is no great pleasure
  To bring death to a friend.
                            Yet I always say
  There is nothing so comfortable as your own safe skin!
CREON. [*slowly, dangerously*]. And you, Antigonê?   50
  You with your head hanging,—do you confess this thing?
ANTIGONE. I do. I deny nothing.
CREON [*to* SENTRY].   You may go.

                                                        [*Exit* SENTRY.]

[*To* ANTIGONE.] Tell me, tell me briefly:
Had you heard my proclamation touching this matter?
ANTIGONE. It was public. Could I help hearing it?
CREON. And yet you dared defy the law.
ANTIGONE.   I dared.
   It was not God's proclamation. That final Justice
   That rules the world below makes no such laws.
   Your edict, King, was strong,
   But all your strength is weakness itself against   60
   The immortal unrecorded laws of God.
   They are not merely now: they were, and shall be,
   Operative for ever, beyond man utterly.
   I knew I must die, even without your decree:
   I am only mortal. And if I must die
   Now, before it is my time to die,
   Surely this is no hardship: can anyone
   Living, as I live, with evil all about me,
   Think Death less than a friend? This death of mine
   Is of no importance; but if I had left my brother   70
   Lying in death unburied, I should have suffered.
   Now I do not.
                 You smile at me. Ah Creon,
   Think me a fool, if you like; but it may well be
   That a fool convicts me of folly.
CHORAGOS. Like father, like daughter: both headstrong, deaf to reason!
   She has never learned to yield.
CREON.   She has much to learn.
   The inflexible heart breaks first, the toughest iron
   Cracks first, and the wildest horses bend their necks
   At the pull of the smallest curb.
                                    Pride? In a slave?
   This girl is guilty of a double insolence,   80
   Breaking the given laws and boasting of it.
   Who is the man here,
   She or I, if this crime goes unpunished?
   Sister's child, or more than sister's child,
   Or closer yet in blood—she and her sister
   Win bitter death for this!
   [*To* SERVANTS.]   Go, some of you,
   Arrest Ismenê. I accuse her equally.
   Bring her: you will find her sniffling in the house there.
   Her mind's a traitor: crimes kept in the dark
   Cry for light, and the guardian brain shudders;   90
   But how much worse than this
   Is brazen boasting of barefaced anarchy!
ANTIGONE. Creon, what more do you want than my death?
CREON.   Nothing.
   That gives me everything.
ANTIGONE. Then I beg you: kill me.
   This talking is a great weariness: your words

Are distasteful to me, and I am sure that mine
Seem so to you. And yet they should not seem so:
I should have praise and honor for what I have done.
All these men here would praise me   100
Were their lips not frozen shut with fear of you.
[*Bitterly.*] Ah the good fortune of kings,
Licensed to say and do whatever they please!
CREON. You are alone here in that opinion.
ANTIGONE. No, they are with me.
  But they keep their tongues in leash.
CREON. Maybe. But you are guilty, and they are not.
ANTIGONE. There is no guilt in reverence for the dead.
CREON. But Eteoclês—was he not your brother too?
ANTIGONE. My brother too.
CREON.   And you insult his memory?   110
ANTIGONE [*softly*]. The dead man would not say that I insult it.
CREON. He would: for you honor a traitor as much as him.
ANTIGONE. His own brother, traitor or not, and equal in blood.
CREON. He made war on his country.
  Eteoclês defended it.
ANTIGONE. Nevertheless, there are honors due all the dead.
CREON. But not the same for the wicked as for the just.
ANTIGONE. Ah Creon, Creon.
  Which of us can say what the gods hold wicked?
CREON. An enemy is an enemy, even dead.   120
ANTIGONE. It is my nature to join in love, not hate.
CREON [*finally losing patience*]. Go join them, then; if you must have your
  love,
Find it in hell!
CHORAGOS.   But see, Ismenê comes:

               [*Enter* ISMENE, *guarded.*]
  Those tears are sisterly, the cloud
  That shadows her eyes rains down gentle sorrow.
CREON. You too, Ismenê,
  Snake in my ordered house, sucking my blood
  Stealthily—and all the time I never knew
  That these two sisters were aiming at my throne!
                                              Ismenê,
Do you confess your share in this crime, or deny it?   130
Answer me.
ISMENE. Yes, if she will let me say so. I am guilty.
ANTIGONE [*coldly*]. No, Ismenê. You have no right to say so.
  You would not help me, and I will not have you help me.
ISMENE. But now I know what you meant; and I am here
  To join you, to take my share of punishment.
ANTIGONE. The dead man and the gods who rule the dead
  Know whose act this was. Words are not friends.
ISMENE. Do you refuse me, Antigonê? I want to die with you:
  I too have a duty that I must discharge to the dead.   140

ANTIGONE. You shall not lessen my death by sharing it.
ISMENE. What do I care for life when you are dead?
ANTIGONE. Ask Creon. You're always hanging on his opinions.
ISMENE. You are laughing at me. Why, Antigone?
ANTIGONE. It's a joyless laughter, Ismenê.
ISMENE.   But can I do nothing?
ANTIGONE. Yes. Save yourself. I shall not envy you.
   There are those who will praise you; I shall have honor, too.
ISMENE. But we are equally guilty!
ANTIGONE.   No more, Ismenê.
   You are alive, but I belong to Death.
CREON [*to the* CHORUS]. Gentlemen, I beg you to observe these girls: 150
   One has just now lost her mind; the other,
   It seems, has never had a mind at all.
ISMENE. Grief teaches the steadiest minds to waver, King.
CREON. Yours certainly did, when you assumed guilt with the guilty!
ISMENE. But how could I go on living without her?
CREON.   You are.
   She is already dead.
ISMENE.   But, your own son's bride!
CREON. There are places enough for him to push his plow.
   I want no wicked women for my sons!
ANTIGONE. O dearest Haimon, how your father wrongs you!
CREON. I've had enough of your childish talk of marriage!   160
CHORAGOS. Do you really intend to steal this girl from your son?
CREON. No; Death will do that for me.
CHORAGOS.   Then she must die?
CREON [*ironically*]. You dazzle me.
                          —But enough of this talk!
   [*To* GUARDS.] You, there, take them away and guard them well:
   For they are but women, and even brave men run
   When they see Death coming.
                          [*Exeunt* ISMENE, ANTIGONE *and* GUARDS.]

                          ODE II

                                                      [*strophe 1*]
CHORUS. Fortunate is the man who has never tasted God's vengeance!
   Where once the anger of heaven has struck, that house is shaken
   For ever: damnation rises behind each child
   Like a wave cresting out of the black northeast,
   When the long darkness under sea roars up
   And bursts drumming death upon the windwhipped sand.

                                                      [*antistrophe 1*]
   I have seen this gathering sorrow from time long past
   Loom upon Oedipus' children: generation from generation
   Takes the compulsive rage of the enemy god.
   So lately this last flower of Oedipus' line   10
   Drank the sunlight! but now a passionate word
   And a handful of dust have closed up all its beauty.

[*strophe 2*]

What mortal arrogance
Transcends the wrath of Zeus?
Sleep cannot lull him, nor the effortless long months
Of the timeless gods: but he is young for ever,
And his house is the shining day of high Olympos.
     All that is and shall be,
     And all the past, is his.
No pride on earth is free of the curse of heaven.   20

[*antistrophe 2*]

The straying dreams of men
     May bring them ghosts of joy:
But as they drowse, the waking embers burn them;
Or they walk with fixed éyes, as blind men walk.
But the ancient wisdom speaks for our own time:
     Fate works most for woe
     With Folly's fairest show.
Man's little pleasure is the spring of sorrow.

SCENE III

CHORAGOS. But here is Haimon, King, the last of all your sons.
   Is it grief for Antigonê that brings him here,
   And bitterness at being robbed of his bride?

               [*Enter* HAIMON.]
CREON. We shall soon see, and no need of diviners.

                        —Son,
   You have heard my final judgment on that girl:
   Have you come here hating me, or have you come
   With deference and with love, whatever I do?
HAIMON. I am your son, father. You are my guide.
   You make things clear for me, and I obey you.
   No marriage means more to me than your continuing wisdom.   10
CREON. Good. That is the way to behave: subordinate
   Everything else, my son, to your father's will.
   This is what a man prays for, that he may get
   Sons attentive and dutiful in his house,
   Each one hating his father's enemies,
   Honoring his father's friends. But if his sons
   Fail him, if they turn out unprofitably,
   What has he fathered but trouble for himself
   And amusement for the malicious?
                    So you are right   20
   Not to lose your head over this woman.
   Your pleasure with her would soon grow cold, Haimon,
   And then you'd have a hellcat in bed and elsewhere.
   Let her find her husband in Hell!
   Of all the people in this city, only she
   Has had contempt for my law and broken it.
   Do you want me to show myself weak before the people?

Or to break my sworn word? No, and I will not.
The woman dies.
I suppose she'll plead "family ties." Well, let her.
If I permit my own family to rebel,   30
How shall I earn the world's obedience?
Show me the man who keeps his house in hand,
He's fit for public authority.
                             I'll have no dealings
With law-breakers, critics of the government:
Whoever is chosen to govern shall be obeyed—
Must be obeyed, in all things, great and small,
Just and unjust! O Haimon,
The man who knows how to obey, and that man only,
Knows how to give commands when the time comes.
You can depend on him, no matter how fast   40
The spears come: he's a good soldier, he'll stick it out.
Anarchy, anarchy! Show me a greater evil!
This is why cities tumble and the great houses rain down,
This is what scatters armies!
No, no: good lives are made so by discipline.
We keep the laws then, and the lawmakers,
And no woman shall seduce us. If we must lose,
Let's lose to a man, at least! Is a woman stronger than we?
CHORAGOS. Unless time has rusted my wits,
What you say, King, is said with point and dignity.
HAIMON [*boyishly earnest*].   Father.   50
Reason is God's crowning gift to man, and you are right
To warn me against losing mine. I cannot say—
I hope that I shall never want to say—that you
Have reasoned badly. Yet there are other men
Who can reason, too; and their opinions might be helpful.
You are not in a position to know everything
That people say or do, or what they feel:
Your temper terrifies them—everyone
Will tell you only what you like to hear.
But I, at any rate, can listen; and I have heard them   60
Muttering and whispering in the dark about this girl.
They say no woman has ever, so unreasonably,
Died so shameful a death for a generous act:
"She covered her brother's body. Is this indecent?
"She kept him from dogs and vultures. Is this a crime?
"Death?—She should have all the honor that we can give her!"
This is the way they talk out there in the city.
You must believe me:
Nothing is closer to me than your happiness.
What could be closer? Must not any son   70
Value his father's fortune as his father does his?
I beg you, do not be unchangeable:
Do not believe that you alone can be right.
The man who thinks that,

The man who maintains that only he has the power
To reason correctly, the gift to speak, the soul—
A man like that, when you know him, turns out empty.
It is not reason never to yield to reason!
In flood time you can see how some trees bend,
And because they bend, even their twigs are safe,   80
While stubborn trees are torn up, roots and all.
And the same thing happens in sailing:
Make your sheet fast, never slacken,—and over you go,
Head over heels and under: and there's your voyage.
Forget you are angry! Let yourself be moved!
I know I am young; but please let me say this:
The ideal condition
Would be, I admit, that men should be right by instinct;
But since we are all too likely to go astray,
The reasonable thing is to learn from those who can teach.   90
CHORAGOS. You will do well to listen to him, King,
    If what he says is sensible. And you, Haimon,
    Must listen to your father.—Both speak well.
CREON. You consider it right for a man of my years and experience
    To go to school to a boy?
HAIMON.   It is not right
    If I am wrong. But if I am young, and right,
    What does my age matter?
CREON. You think it right to stand up for an anarchist?
HAIMON. Not at all. I pay no respect to criminals.
CREON. Then she is not a criminal?   100
HAIMON. The City would deny it, to a man.
CREON. And the City proposes to teach me how to rule?
HAIMON. Ah. Who is it that's talking like a boy now?
CREON. My voice is the one voice giving orders in this City!
HAIMON. It is no City if it takes orders from one voice.
CREON. The State is the King!
HAIMON. Yes, if the State is a desert.

                                                         [*Pause.*]

CREON. This boy, it seems, has sold out to a woman.
HAIMON. If you are a woman: my concern is only for you.
CREON. So? Your "concern"! In a public brawl with your father!   110
HAIMON. How about you, in a public brawl with justice?
CREON. With justice, when all that I do is within my rights?
HAIMON. You have no right to trample on God's right.
CREON [*completely out of control*]. Fool, adolescent fool! Taken in by a woman!
HAIMON. You'll never see me taken in by anything vile.
CREON. Every word you say is for her!
HAIMON [*quietly, darkly*]. And for you.
    And for me. And for the gods under the earth.
CREON. You'll never marry her while she lives.
HAIMON. Then she must die.—But her death will cause another.   120
CREON. Another?
    Have you lost your senses? Is this an open threat?

HAIMON. There is no threat in speaking to emptiness.
CREON. I swear you'll regret this superior tone of yours!
    You are the empty one!
HAIMON. If you were not my father, I'd say you were perverse.
CREON. You girlstruck fool, don't play at words with me!
HAIMON. I am sorry. You prefer silence.
CREON.   Now, by God—!
    I swear, by all the gods in heaven above us,
    You'll watch it, I swear you shall!
    [*To the* SERVANTS]   Bring her out!   130
    Bring the woman out! Let her die before his eyes!
    Here, this instant, with her bridegroom beside her!
HAIMON. Not here, no; she will not die here, King.
    And you will never see my face again.
    Go on raving as long as you've a friend to endure you.

                                      [*Exit* HAIMON.]
CHORAGOS.   Gone, gone.
    Creon, a young man in a rage is dangerous!
CREON. Let him do, or dream to do, more than a man can.
    He shall not save these girls from death.
CHORAGOS.   These girls?
    You have sentenced them both?
CREON.   No, you are right.
    I will not kill the one whose hands are clean.   140
CHORAGOS. But Antigonê?
CREON [*somberly*].   I will carry her far away
    Out there in the wilderness, and lock her
    Living in a vault of stone. She shall have food,
    As the custom is, to absolve the State of her death.
    And there let her pray to the gods of hell:
    They are her only gods:
    Perhaps they will show her an escape from death,
    Or she may learn, though late,
    That piety shown the dead is pity in vain.

                                      [*Exit* CREON.]

ODE III

                                    [*strophe*]

CHORUS. Love, unconquerable
    Waster of rich men, keeper
    Of warm lights and all-night vigil
    In the soft face of a girl:
    Sea-wanderer, forest-visitor!
    Even the pure Immortals cannot escape you,
    And mortal man, in his one day's dusk,
    Trembles before your glory.

                                   [*antistrophe*]

    Surely you swerve upon ruin
    The just man's consenting heart,   10
    As here you have made bright anger

Strike between father and son—
And none has conquered but Love!
A girl's glánce wórking the will of heaven:
Pleasure to her alone who mocks us,
Merciless Aphroditê.[1]

SCENE IV

[ANTIGONE *enters guarded.*]

CHORAGOS. But I can no longer stand in awe of this,
    Nor, seeing what I see, keep back my tears.
    Here is Antigonê, passing to that chamber
    Where all find sleep at last.

                                                   [strophe 1]

ANTIGONE. Look upon me, friends, and pity me
    Turning back at the night's edge to say
    Goodbye to the sun that shines for me no longer;
    Now sleepy Death
    Summons me down to Acheron,[1] that cold shore:
    There is no bridesong there, nor any music.   10

CHORUS. Yet not unpraised, not without a kind of honor.
    You walk at last into the underworld;
    Untouched by sickness, broken by no sword.
    What woman has ever found your way to death?

                                        [antistrophe 1]

ANTIGONE. How often I have heard the story of Niobê,
    Tantalos' wretched daughter, how the stone
    Clung fast about her, ivy-close: and they say
    The rain falls endlessly
    And sifting soft snow; her tears are never done.[2]
    I feel the loneliness of her death in mine.   20

CHORUS. But she was born of heaven, and you
    Are woman, woman-born. If her death is yours,
    A mortal woman's, is this not for you
    Glory in our world and in the world beyond?

                                              [strophe 2]

ANTIGONE. You laugh at me. Ah, friends, friends,
    Can you not wait until I am dead? O Thebes,
    O men many-charioted, in love with Fortune,
    Dear springs of Dircê, sacred Theban grove,
    Be witness for me, denied all pity,
    Unjustly judged! and think a word of love   30
    For her whose path turns
    Under dark earth, where there are no more tears.

---

[1] Goddess of love.
[1] The river over which the souls cross into Hades.
[2] Niobe wept ceaselessly over the loss of her children and was eventually turned into stone.

CHORUS. You have passed beyond human daring and come at last
    Into a place of stone where Justice sits.
    I cannot tell
    What shape of your father's guilt appears in this.

[antistrophe 2]

ANTIGONE. You have touched it at last: that bridal bed
    Unspeakable, horror of son and mother mingling:
    Their crime, infection of all our family!
    O Oedipus, father and brother!   40
    Your marriage strikes from the grave to murder mine.
    I have been a stranger here in my own land:
    All my life
    The blasphemy of my birth has followed me.

CHORUS. Reverence is a virtue, but strength
    Lives in established law: that must prevail.
    You have made your choice,
    Your death is the doing of your conscious hand.

[epode]

ANTIGONE. Then let me go, since all your words are bitter,
    And the very light of the sun is cold to me.   50
    Lead me to my vigil, where I must have
    Neither love nor lamentation; no song, but silence.
    [CREON *interrupts impatiently.*]
CREON. If dirges and planned lamentations could put off death,
    Men would be singing for ever.
    [*To the* SERVANTS]   Take her, go!
    You know your orders: take her to the vault
    And leave her alone there. And if she lives or dies,
    That's her affair, not ours: our hands are clean.
ANTIGONE. O tomb, vaulted bridebed in eternal rock,
    Soon I shall be with my own again
    Where Persephonê[3] welcomes the thin ghosts underground: 60
    And I shall see my father again, and you, mother,
    And dearest Polyneicês—
                dearest indeed
    To me, since it was my hand
    That washed him clean and poured the ritual wine:
    And my reward is death before my time!
    And yet, as men's hearts know, I have done no wrong,
    I have not sinned before God. Or if I have,
    I shall know the truth in death. But if the guilt
    Lies upon Creon who judged me, then, I pray,
    May his punishment equal my own.
CHORAGOS.   O passionate heart,   70
    Unyielding, tormented still by the same winds!
CREON. Her guards shall have good cause to regret their delaying.

---

[3] Queen of the underworld.

ANTIGONE. Ah! That voice is like the voice of death!
CREON. I can give you no reason to think you are mistaken.
ANTIGONE. Thebes, and you my fathers' gods,
    And rulers of Thebes, you see me now, the last
    Unhappy daughter of a line of kings,
    Your kings led away to death. You will remember
    What things I suffer, and at what men's hands,
    Because I would not transgress the laws of heaven.   80
    [*To the* GUARDS, *simply*] Come: let us wait no longer.

                         [*Exit* ANTIGONE, *L., guarded*]

ODE IV

[*strophe 1*]

CHORUS. All Danaê's beauty was locked away
    In a brazen cell where the sunlight could not come:
    A small room, still as any grave, enclosed her.
    Yet she was a princess too,
    And Zeus in a rain of gold poured love upon her.[4]
    O child, child,
    No power in wealth or war
    Or tough sea-blackened ships
    Can prevail against untiring Destiny!

[*antistrophe 1*]
                               10

    And Dryas' son also, that furious king,
    Bore the god's prisoning anger for his bride:
    Sealed up by Dionysos in deaf stone,
    His madness died among echoes.
    So at the last he learned what dreadful power
    His tongue had mocked:
    For he had profaned the revels,
    And fired the wrath of the nine
    Implacable Sisters that love the sound of the flute.[5]

[*strophe 2*]

    And old men tell a half-remembered tale
    Of horror done where a dark ledge splits the sea   20
    And a double surf beats on the gráy shóres:
    How a king's new woman, sick
    With hatred for the queen he had imprisoned,
    Ripped out his two sons' eyes with her bloody hands
    While grinning Arês[6] watched the shuttle plunge
    Four times: four blind wounds crying for revenge,

[*antistrophe 2*]

    Crying, tears and blood mingled.—Piteously born,
    Those sons whose mother was of heavenly birth!

---

    [4] Danae was the mother of Perseus by Zeus, who visited her in the form of a shower of gold during her imprisonment.
    [5] Dryas' son, Lycurgus, opposed Dionysus and was punished by madness and imprisonment.
    [6] The god of war.

Her father was the god of the North Wind
And she was cradled by gales,   30
She raced with young colts on the glittering hills
And walked untrammeled in the open light:
But in her marriage deathless Fate found means
To build a tomb like yours for all her joy.[7]

SCENE V

[*Enter blind* TEIRESIAS,[1] *led by a boy. The opening speeches of*
TEIRESIAS *should be in singsong contrast to the realistic lines of*
CREON.]

TEIRESIAS. This is the way the blind man comes, Princess, Princess,
    Lock-step, two heads lit by the eyes of one.
CREON. What new thing have you to tell us, old Teiresias?
TEIRESIAS. I have much to tell you: listen to the prophet, Creon.
CREON. I am not aware that I have ever failed to listen.
TEIRESIAS. Then you have done wisely, King, and ruled well.
CREON. I admit my debt to you. But what have you to say?
TEIRESIAS. This, Creon: you stand once more on the edge of fate.
CREON. What do you mean? Your words are a kind of dread.
TEIRESIAS. Listen, Creon: 10
    I was sitting in my chair of augury, at the place
    Where the birds gather about me. They were all a-chatter,
    As is their habit, when suddenly I heard
    A strange note in their jangling, a scream, a
    Whirring fury; I knew that they were fighting,
    Tearing each other, dying
    In a whirlwind of wings clashing. And I was afraid.
    I began the rites of burnt-offering at the altar,
    But Hephaistos[2] failed me: instead of bright flame,
    There was only the sputtering slime of the fat thigh-flesh   20
    Melting: the entrails dissolved in gray smoke,
    The bare bone burst from the welter. And no blaze!
    This was a sign from heaven. My boy described it,
    Seeing for me as I see for others.
    I tell you, Creon, you yourself have brought
    This new calamity upon us. Our hearths and altars
    Are stained with the corruption of dogs and carrion birds
    That glut themselves on the corpse of Oedipus' son.
    The gods are deaf when we pray to them, their fire
    Recoils from our offering, their birds of omen   30
    Have no cry of comfort, for they are gorged
    With the thick blood of the dead.
                            O my son,
    These are no trifles! Think: all men make mistakes,

---

[7] The second wife of King Phineus blinded her stepsons; their mother, Cleopatra, the
daughter of the North Wind, was imprisoned in a cave.

[1] The old blind prophet of Thebes who frequently appears in Greek literature.

[2] God of fire and metal-working.

But a good man yields when he knows his course is wrong,
And repairs the evil. The only crime is pride.
Give in to the dead man, then: do not fight with a corpse—
What glory is it to kill a man who is dead?
Think, I beg you:
It is for your own good that I speak as I do.
You should be able to yield for your own good.   40
CREON. It seems that prophets have made me their especial province.
All my life long
I have been a kind of butt for the dull arrows
Of doddering fortune-tellers!
                         No, Teiresias:
If your birds—if the great eagles of God himself
Should carry him stinking bit by bit to heaven,
I would not yield. I am not afraid of pollution:
No man can defile the gods.
                         Do what you will,
Go into business, make money, speculate
In India gold or that synthetic gold from Sardis,   50
Get rich otherwise than by my consent to bury him.
Teiresias, it is a sorry thing when a wise man
Sells his wisdom, lets out his words for hire!
TEIRESIAS. Ah Creon! Is there no man left in the world—
CREON. To do what—Come, let's have the aphorism!
TEIRESIAS. No man who knows that wisdom outweighs any wealth?
CREON. As surely as bribes are baser than any baseness.
TEIRESIAS. You are sick, Creon! You are deathly sick!
CREON. As you say: it is not my place to challenge a prophet.
TEIRESIAS. Yet you have said my prophecy is for sale.   60
CREON. The generation of prophets has always loved gold.
TEIRESIAS. The generation of kings has always loved brass.
CREON. You forget yourself! You are speaking to your King.
TEIRESIAS. I know it. You are a king because of me.
CREON. You have a certain skill; but you have sold out.
TEIRESIAS. King, you will drive me to words that—
CREON.   Say them, say them!
Only remember: I will not pay you for them.
TEIRESIAS. No, you will find them too costly.
CREON.   No doubt. Speak:
Whatever you say, you will not change my will.
TEIRESIAS. Then take this, and take it to heart!   70
The time is not far off when you shall pay back
Corpse for corpse, flesh of your own flesh.
You have thrust the child of this world into living night,
You have kept from the gods below the child that is theirs:
The one in a grave before her death, the other,
Dead, denied the grave. This is your crime:
And the Furies[3] and the dark gods of Hell

---

[3] The three spirits who pursue and punish doers of unavenged crimes.

Are swift with terrible punishment for you.
Do you want to buy me now, Creon?
                                        Not many days,
And your house will be full of men and women weeping,   80
And curses will be hurled at you from far
Cities grieving for sons unburied, left to rot
Before the walls of Thebes.
These are my arrows, Creon: they are all for you.
[*To* Boy] But come, child: lead me home
Let him waste his fine anger upon younger men.
Maybe he will learn at last
To control a wiser tongue in a better head.

                                                    [*Exit* TEIRESIAS.]

CHORAGOS. The old man has gone, King, but his words
  Remain to plague us. I am old, too,   90
  But I cannot remember that he was ever false.
CREON. That is true. . . . It troubles me.
  Oh it is hard to give in! but it is worse
  To risk everything for stubborn pride.
CHORAGOS. Creon: take my advice.
CREON.   What shall I do?
CHORAGOS. Go quickly: free Antigonê from her vault
  And build a tomb for the body of Polyneicês.
CREON. You would have me do this?
CHORAGOS.   Creon, yes!
  And it must be done at once: God moves
  Swiftly to cancel the folly of stubborn men.   100
CREON. It is hard to deny the heart! But I
  Will do it: I will not fight with destiny.
CHORAGOS. You must go yourself, you cannot leave it to others.
CREON. I will go.
            —Bring axes, servants:
  Come with me to the tomb. I buried her, I
  Will set her free.
            Oh, quickly!
  My mind misgives—
  The laws of the gods are mighty, and a man must serve them   110
  To the last day of his life!

                                                    [*Exit* CREON.]

                        PAEAN
                                                    [*strophe 1*]

CHORAGOS. God of many names
CHORUS.   O Iacchos
                              son
    of Cadmeian Sémelê
                    O born of the Thunder!
  Guardian of the West
                    Regent
    of Eleusis' plain

O Prince of mænad Thebes
and the Dragon Field by rippling Ismenos:

[antistrophe 1]

CHORAGOS. God of many names[4]
CHORUS.   the flame of torches
    flares on our hills
                the nymphs of Iacchos
    dance at the spring of Castalia:
    from the vine-close mountain
                                come ah come in ivy:
    Evohé evohé! sings through the streets of Thebes   10

[strophe 2]

CHORAGOS. God of many names
CHORUS.   Iacchos of Thebes
    heavenly Child
                of Sémelê bride of the Thunderer!
    The shadow of plague is upon us:
                                    come
    with clement feet
                oh come from Parnasos
    down the long slopes
                    across the lamenting water

[antistrophe 2]

CHORAGOS. Iô Fire! Chorister of the throbbing stars!
    O purest among the voices of the night!
    Thou son of God, blaze for us!
CHORUS. Come with choric rapture of circling Mænads[5]
    Who cry *Iô Iacche!*
            God of many names!   20

ÉXODOS

[Enter MESSENGER, L.]

MESSENGER. Men of the line of Cadmos, you who live
    Near Amphion's citadel:
                    I cannot say
Of any condition of human life, "This is fixed,
This is clearly good, or bad." Fate raises up,
And Fate casts down the happy and unhappy alike:
No man can foretell his Fate.
                    Take the case of Creon:
Creon was happy once, as I count happiness:
Victorious in battle, sole governor of the land,
Fortunate father of children nobly born.
And now it has all gone from him! Who can say   10
That a man is still alive when his life's joy fails?

---

[4] Dionysus, the god of wine and of an orgiastic religion celebrating the power and fertility of nature, was also called Bacchus as well as the many names and epithets given in these lines.

[5] Female members of the cult of Dionysus.

He is a walking dead man. Grant him rich,
Let him live like a king in his great house:
If his pleasure is gone, I would not give
So much as the shadow of smoke for all he owns.
CHORAGOS. Your words hint at sorrow: what is your news for us?
MESSENGER. They are dead. The living are guilty of their death.
CHORAGOS. Who is guilty? Who is dead? Speak!
MESSENGER. Haimon.
Haimon is dead; and the hand that killed him
Is his own hand.
CHORAGOS. His father's? or his own? 20
MESSENGER. His own, driven mad by the murder his father had done.
CHORAGOS. Teiresias, how clearly you saw it all!
MESSENGER. This is my news: you must draw what conclusions you can
from it.
CHORAGOS. But look: Eurydicê, our Queen:
Has she overheard us?

[*Enter* EURYDICE *from the Palace, C.*]
EURYDICE. I have heard something, friends:
As I was unlocking the gate of Pallas' shrine,
For I needed her help today, I heard a voice
Telling of some new sorrow. And I fainted
There at the temple with all my maidens about me. 30
But speak again: whatever it is, I can bear it:
Grief and I are no strangers.
MESSENGER. Dearest Lady,
I will tell you plainly all that I have seen.
I shall not try to comfort you: what is the use,
Since comfort could lie only in what is not true?
The truth is always best.
I went with Creon
To the outer plain where Polyneicês was lying,
No friend to pity him, his body shredded by dogs.
We made our prayers in that place to Hecatê
And Pluto, that they would be merciful. And we bathed 40
The corpse with holy water, and we brought
Fresh-broken branches to burn what was left of it,
And upon the urn we heaped up a towering barrow
Of the earth of his own land.
When we were done, we ran
To the vault where Antigonê lay on her couch of stone.
One of the servants had gone ahead,
And while he was yet far off he heard a voice
Grieving within the chamber, and he came back
And told Creon. And as the King went closer,
The air was full of wailing, the words lost, 50
And he begged us to make all haste. "Am I a prophet?"
He said, weeping, "And must I walk this road,
"The saddest of all that I have gone before?

"My son's voice calls me on. Oh quickly, quickly!
"Look through the crevice there, and tell me
"If it is Haimon, or some deception of the gods!"
We obeyed; and in the cavern's farthest corner
We saw her lying:
She had made a noose of her fine linen veil
And hanged herself. Haimon lay beside her,   60
His arms about her waist, lamenting her,
His love lost under ground, crying out
That his father had stolen her away from him.
When Creon saw him the tears rushed to his eyes
And he called to him: "What have you done, child? Speak to me.
"What are you thinking that makes your eyes so strange?
"O my son, my son, I come to you on my knees!"
But Haimon spat in his face. He said not a word,
Staring—
         And suddenly drew his sword
And lunged. Creon shrank back, the blade missed; and the boy,   70
Desperate against himself, drove it half its length
Into his own side, and fell. And as he died
He gathered Antigonê close in his arms again,
Choking, his blood bright red on her white cheek.
And now he lies dead with the dead, and she is his
At last, his bride in the houses of the dead.

                              [*Exit* EURYDICE *into the Palace.*]
CHORAGOS. She has left us without a word. What can this mean?
MESSENGER. It troubles me, too; yet she knows what is best,
   Her grief is too great for public lamentation,
   And doubtless she has gone to her chamber to weep   80
   For her dead son, leading her maidens in his dirge.
CHORAGOS. It may be so: but I fear this deep silence.   [*Pause.*]
MESSENGER. I will see what she is doing. I will go in.

                              [*Exit* MESSENGER *into the Palace.*]
         [*Enter* CREON *with attendants, bearing* HAIMON'S *body.*]
CHORAGOS. But here is the King himself: oh look at him,
   Bearing his own damnation in his arms.
CREON. Nothing you say can touch me any more.
   My own blind heart has brought me
   From darkness to final darkness. Here you see
   The father murdering, the murdered son—
   And all my civic wisdom!   90
   Haimon my son, so young, so young to die,
   I was the fool, not you; and you died for me.
CHORAGOS. That is the truth; but you were late in learning it.
CREON. This truth is hard to bear. Surely a god
   Has crushed me beneath the hugest weight of heaven,
   And driven me headlong a barbaric way
   To trample out the thing I held most dear.
   The pains that men will take to come to pain!

[*Enter* MESSENGER *from the Palace.*]

MESSENGER. The burden you carry in your hands is heavy,
But it is not all: you will find more in your house.   100
CREON. What burden worse than this shall I find there?
MESSENGER. The Queen is dead.
CREON.   O port of death, deaf world,
Is there no pity for me? And you, Angel of evil,
I was dead, and your words are death again.
Is it true, boy? Can it be true?
Is my wife dead? Has death bred death?
MESSENGER. You can see for yourself.

[*The doors are opened, and the body of* EURYDICE *is disclosed within.*]

CREON.   Oh pity!
All true, all true, and more than I can bear!
O my wife, my son!
MESSENGER. She stood before the altar, and her heart   110
Welcomed the knife her own hand guided,
And a great cry burst from her lips for Megareus dead,
And for Haimon dead, her sons; and her last breath
Was a curse for their father, the murderer of her sons.
And she fell, and the dark flowed in through her closing eyes.
CREON. O God, I am sick with fear.
Are there no swords here? Has no one a blow for me?
MESSENGER. Her curse is upon you for the deaths of both.
CREON. It is right that it should be. I alone am guilty.
I know it, and I say it. Lead me in,
Quickly, friends.
I have neither life nor substance. Lead me in.   120
CHORAGOS. You are right, if there can be right in so much wrong.
The briefest way is best in a world of sorrow.
CREON.   Let it come,
Let death come quickly, and be kind to me.
I would not ever see the sun again.
CHORAGOS. All that will come when it will; but we, meanwhile,
Have much to do. Leave the future to itself.
CREON. All my heart was in that prayer!
CHORAGOS. Then do not pray any more: the sky is deaf.   130
CREON. Lead me away. I have been rash and foolish.
I have killed my son and my wife.
I look for comfort; my comfort lies here dead.
Whatever my hands have touched has come to nothing.
Fate has brought all my pride to a thought of dust.

[*As* CREON *is being led into the house, the* CHORAGOS *advances and speaks directly to the audience.*]

CHORAGOS. There is no happiness where there is no wisdom;
No wisdom but in submission to the gods.
Big words are always punished,
And proud men in old age learn to be wise.

(c. 442 B.C.)

Prewriting

Now that you have read *Antigone* and have some sense of its basic structure, read the play again carefully and write out the answers to the questions below. Your responses will not only help you to sharpen your understanding of dramatic structure; they will also lead you to clarify your reactions to *Antigone*'s characters and themes.

ANALYZING DRAMATIC STRUCTURE

1. What background are we given in the Prologue? List the main points of information that this scene between Antigone and Ismene reveals.

2. What exposition do the Chorus and the Choragos (the leader of the chorus) give in the section called the Parados (page 566)?

3. How does Sophocles use the Sentry in Scene One? Does this character provide more than factual exposition?

4. What do you think the main conflict is? State it as specifically as you can in a single sentence.

5. Identify the protagonist and the antagonist. Is it fair to apply the labels *heroine* or *villain* to them?

6. Where does the climax occur? Identify the scene and describe what happens. Why do you think this is the play's turning point?

7. Does the climax seem to come early in the play? How does Sophocles maintain interest after the turning point? Did you expect such dramatic developments after the climax? Do you think Creon expected them?

8. When does the catastrophe occur? Was this outcome inevitable? Did you feel different about the outcome the second time you read the play?

9. State what you consider the play's theme to be.

10. A *foil* is a contrasting character who sets off or helps to define another character. How is Ismene a foil to Antigone? Are there any foils to Creon?

11. Why is Eurydice included in the plot? How do you feel about her fate?

Having answered these questions about the structure of *Antigone*, devise a graph or chart that illustrates the pattern of events in the play. Make sure your graph shows the six structural components discussed on page 562.

Writing

Your understanding of the structure of *Antigone* will enable you to write more easily about the play's arguments. As you watched the conflict develop between Antigone and Creon, you undoubtedly became aware of the opposing values that these two characters represent. As one critic has observed about *Antigone*, "the characters *are* the issues, and the issues the characters" (Charles Paul Segal, "Sophocles' Praise of Man and the Conflicts of *Antigone*," *Sophocles: A Collection of Critical Essays*, ed. T. Woodward, Englewood Cliffs: Prentice Hall, 1966:63). It is now your turn to examine these issues and decide where you stand.

ARGUING AN ISSUE

Argument means dispute; it implies that there are opposing sides. Any matter worth arguing will involve at least one "issue"—that is, an essential point in question or disagreement. You need not always take sides, but once you have decided what issues are involved in an argument, you can write an effective paper by taking a stand and explaining why you have chosen one side over the other.

Your approach to *Antigone* will have to take into account the controversial nature of the play's conflict. Review your responses to the prewriting questions about the disagreement and about the antagonist and protagonist. Can you identify an issue that you think is central to the play's meaning? Are there other issues involved in the conflict? Try to get the main issues stated as clearly and specifically as you can before you begin to write. The ideas for writing that follow should help you to work out the important issues of the play.

You can argue an issue in two ways. You can take an affirmative position on one side of the question and present reasons and evidence to support your stand. Or you can anticipate the arguments of the opposing side and show how the evidence does not support this side, indicating where the fallacies or errors lie in the opposition's reasoning. You will probably want to combine both techniques in writing about *Antigone*.

Whatever your approach, you need to study the evidence and examine the ideas on both sides for flaws in logical thinking. One way to make this examination involves listing the main arguments, pro and con, in two columns on a sheet of paper:

Creon	*Antigone*
Public interest outweighs private loyalties.	Eternal unwritten laws take precedence.
Polyneices made war on his own country.	All the dead deserve honor.

You can make a similar listing of speeches or lines from the play that serve as evidence for the two sides of the argument. For instance, you may want to note such revealing statements by Creon as these:

> "Whoever is chosen to govern should be obeyed."
> "If we must lose, / Let's lose to a man, at least! Is a woman stronger than we?"
> "The State is the King!"

Compare these lists and see which side has the stronger arguments and the greater amount of evidence. You can then decide which side you are going to support; you also have a convenient listing of specific ideas and quotations to use in developing your essay.

IDEAS FOR WRITING

1. Is Creon a politician concerned with imposing and maintaining order? Is Antigone an anarchist whose action will destroy that order? Or is she a private citizen determined to follow the dictates of her personal beliefs? Write about the issues in *Antigone* as a struggle between public policy and individual conscience, supporting the side that you think is "right."

2. Can you analyze the conflict between Antigone and Creon as a psychological clash between a woman and a man? Write an essay that focuses on the male-female opposition in the play. You may want to work Ismene, Haimon, and Eurydice into your scheme of opposing values.

QUOTING FROM A PLAY

When writing a paper on a single play, you need to cite your source in a note only the first time you quote from the play. For subsequent quotations give act and scene numbers in parentheses at the end of the quoted material; for verse plays give act, scene, and line numbers. Because *Antigone* is not divided into acts, give the scene and line numbers for the quotations you use. Long quotations (more than two lines) should be indented with *no* quotation marks. Also, indicate the speaker when quoting a passage in which more than one character speaks. Here are some samples:

> It is up to Ismene to point out the obvious: "We are only women/ We cannot fight with the men, Antigone!" (Pro.46–47).
>
> [Only two lines quoted—separated with a slash and enclosed in quotation marks]
>
> Creon's speeches show his contempt for women:
>
>> Gentlemen, I beg you to observe these girls:
>> One has just now lost her mind; the other,

> It seems, has never had a mind at all. (2.148–49)
> [Long quotation—indented, no quotation marks]

Iago is a master of understatement and insinuation:

> *Othello.* Is he not honest?
> *Iago.* Honest, my lord!
> *Othello.* Honest! ay, honest.
> *Iago.* My lord, for aught I know.
> *Othello.* What dost thou think?
> *Iago.* Think, my lord! (3.3.103–105)
> [Change of speakers indicated]

Remember to introduce each quotation carefully. You may want to review the material in Chapter Five on integrating quotations gracefully (pp. 56–57).

Rewriting

You will want to be certain that your arguments about *Antigone* are perfectly clear. Take some time to insure that what you have written cannot be misunderstood. If you can, coax a friend or classmate into reading your first draft; ask your reader to point out sentences that do not make sense or are unclear.

AVOIDING UNCLEAR LANGUAGE

Multisyllabic words and long, involved sentences may dazzle your readers, but they can also hinder clear communication. Your first goal in writing should be to convey ideas and information. Trying to impress your readers with big words and fancy phrases may lead to one or more forms of unclear expression:

1. **Engfish.** Writing specialist Ken Macrorie uses this term to call attention to artificial language that does not represent a writer's own experience and education. Engfish is phony, pretentious, stuffy, and often impossible to decode. Writers use Engfish, it seems, when they are unsure of which attitude to take toward their subject and their audience. The student who wrote

   > Antigone's unacceptable posture toward the designated governmental powers inevitably entailed the termination of her existence,

   no doubt thought that this inflated diction was appropriate for a serious paper on a classical play. But most readers probably would prefer to see that sentence revised to read more clearly, like this:

   > Antigone's defiance led to her death.

   In the long run, clarity will impress your readers more than Engfish ever can.

2. **Jargon.** This term applies to the specialized language used by a particular group of people. Computer operators, sociologists, teenagers, architects, hockey players, mobsters—all sorts of interest groups and professions—employ words and terms that relate only to their particular activities. The problem with jargon is that outsiders do not understand it. Writing about a "love game" or the "ad court" will be all right for an audience of tennis buffs, but you will have to change your language for more general readers. Jargon may not come up in your essay about *Antigone*, but it can creep in from other sources. For instance, the student who wrote

> Antigone's behavior is marked by regressive reaction formation toward authoritarian figures.

was apparently influenced by the jargon of her psychology class. Unless you are writing for an audience of fellow psychoanalysts, you would do better to say the following:

> Antigone sometimes acted like a disobedient daughter.

3. **Abstract words.** Abstract terms and general expressions do not automatically make your writing intellectual and impressive. Although it is true that writing an argumentative essay requires using abstract ideas, your paper will still be more persuasive if it is factual, concrete, and clear. Abstractions tend to be hazy and difficult to define. Words like *duty, anarchy, patriotism,* and *truth* have different meanings for different people. When writing about an abstract concept, make certain that you have a definite meaning in your own mind. If, for instance, you write that

> Antigone is a woman of honor,

it is a good idea to check the dictionary to see if your understanding of the word "honor" coincides with a standard definition. *The American Heritage Dictionary* gives thirteen entries for "honor." Which one does the above sentence convey? Would "a woman's chastity" be accurate in this context? It might be more meaningful to say

> Antigone is a woman of principle and integrity,

although those words are also abstract. Try, if possible, to specify the meaning you want when using an abstract term:

> Above all, Creon is a master politician—a man of ambition intent on holding his power.

Sample Student Paper on Drama

The following paper analyzing the power struggle between male and female in *Antigone* was written by Laurie Dahlberg, a student at Illinois State University. Notice how she uses and documents quoted material from the play. Your "Notes" section at the end belongs on a separate page.

"A Woman Stronger Than We?"

Antigone is a drama built around two basic conflicts. Beneath the more obvious conflict of the individual versus the state lies a struggle of male against female. The protagonist, Antigone, becomes a criminal by choice, but a feminist by chance. The antagonist, Creon, is fighting to retain control over Antigone, not only as king over subject but also as man over woman.

Antigone knows that she has violated the king's order not to bury her brother Etiocles, but she seems not to notice that she has also violated the social code by stepping outside the boundaries of acceptable feminine behavior. Her act of defiance is courageous, self-reliant, and completely contrary to the obedience expected of women in her society. She fearlessly assures her sister, Ismene, that "Creon is not strong enough to stand in my way."[1] It is up to Ismene, then, to point out the obvious: "We are only women, / We cannot fight with the men, Antigone!" (Pro.46-47). A perfect foil for Antigone, Ismene epitomizes the good Theban woman--she is deferential, passive, and timid. Though she loves Antigone dearly, Ismene is still bound to her male masters and cannot follow her sister: "I must yield to authority," she says. "And I think it is a dangerous business to be always meddling" (Pro.50-51). Eventually, Ismene is rewarded for her passivity when Creon spares her life.

When Antigone is arrested, King Creon expresses shock that a woman in his court has committed the crime. But his disbelief soon turns to perverse pleasure at the opportunity to punish

this woman for her audacity. Creon's speeches show his contempt
for women:

>   Gentlemen, I beg you to observe these girls:
>
>   One has just now lost her mind; the other,
>
>   It seems, has never had a mind at all. (2.148-49)

Antigone, however, rises above the pettiness of sexual rivalry
by responding only to the conflict between king and subject.
Unlike Creon, Antigone acts out of a heartfelt moral obligation,
not pride: "There is no guilt in reverence for the dead," she
cries (2.106). As Antigone calmly and eloquently argues the
righteousness of her action, instead of quivering with fear
under Creon's threats, the king's feeling of triumph slowly
turns to rage. At the close of her defense, Antigone states:

>   You smile at me. Ah Creon,
>
>   Think me a fool, if you like; but it may well be
>
>   That a fool convicts me of folly. (2.72-74)

To which Creon angrily replies:

>   Pride? In a slave?
>
>   This girl is guilty of a double insolence,
>
>   Breaking the given laws and boasting of it.
>
>   Who is the man here,
>
>   She or I, if this crime goes unpunished? (2.79-83)

Though Antigone's illegal act is punishable by death, it
is the fact that a mere woman has defied him that enrages Creon.
Her death alone will not satisfy him. He needs to master her
willfulness and make her regret her arrogance. Instead of killing her, he entombs her, where she will die slowly. This
method of execution, Creon says, will teach the woman a lesson:

>   And there let her pray to the gods of hell:
>
>   They are her only gods:
>
>   Perhaps they will show her an escape from death,
>
>   Or she may learn, though late,
>
>   That piety shown the dead is pity in vain. (3.145-49)

The key to Creon's personality is found in his comment to
Haimon when he is explaining why he (the king) has sentenced
his son's bride to death:

> We keep the laws then, and the lawmakers,
>
> And no woman shall seduce us. If we must lose,
>
> Let's lose to a man, at least! Is a woman stronger
>
> than we? (3.46-48)

Creon refuses to listen to Haimon's reasoning, and the young
man, disgusted by his father's cruelty, rejects him. This rejection makes the king even more bitter. Creon's pride has made
him blind to his mistake.

Throughout the course of the play, Creon changes from a
strict but competent leader to a wildly insecure man, plagued
by imaginary enemies. He has come to suspect that anyone who
disagrees with him is involved in a plot against him:

> You, too, Ismene,
>
> Snake in my ordered house, sucking my blood,
>
> Stealthily--and all the time I never knew
>
> That these two sisters were aiming at my throne!
>
> (2.124-27)

Creon has mistaken Antigone's act of piety for a wild attempt
by a power-hungry woman to undermine his rule. Out of his own
fear of being beaten by a woman, Creon begins a chain of events
which finally destroy him, fulfilling Antigone's prediction:

> . . . if the guilt
>
> Lies upon Creon who judged me, then, I pray,
>
> May his punishment equal my own. (4.66-70)

Notes

[1] Sophocles, <u>Antigone</u>.   Trans. Dudley Fitts and Robert Fitzgerald. <u>Literature</u> <u>and</u> <u>the</u> <u>Writing</u> <u>Process</u>.   Elizabeth McMahan, Susan Day, Robert Funk, eds. New York: Macmillan, 1986: Prologue, line 35. Subsequent references to this source will be cited in parentheses within the essay.

Questions for Discussion

1. Do you think this essay overemphasizes the gender issue in analyzing the conflict between Creon and Antigone? Has the author slighted or ignored more important issues?
2. Can you find any additional evidence which the author of the essay overlooked or chose not to use? Would the case be strengthened by including Eurydice in the analysis?
3. The author says that Antigone rises above sexual rivalry in her defiant behavior. Is this view entirely true? Can you find any evidence to suggest that Antigone is also caught up in the power struggle between male and female?
4. In carrying out her approach, the author of the essay analyzes Creon more than Antigone. Why is that? Is this strategy productive? Do you agree with the conclusion about Creon's character development?

16

Writing about Character

Pondering people's characters comes quite naturally and easily. You will remember that we began our approach to literature with the study of character in the short story. Drama also provides us with carefully drawn examples of human speech and behavior. Whether the presentation is realistic or not, the characters are at the heart of the play.

What Is the Modern Hero?

In everyday life, we use the word *heroic* to describe people who save others' lives while risking their own, acts of great self-sacrifice or self-control, feats that we hold in awe. Before you read on, think of the last time you remember calling something heroic or referring to someone as a hero. Note down the situation, and think about what you meant by the word. We often use it lightly—the person who supplies a much needed extension cord or an emergency ten dollar loan may temporarily be a hero. But drama practically forces us into deeper consideration of what a hero is.

THE TRAGIC HERO

In the fourth century B.C. Aristotle described the classic concept of the tragic hero. He wrote that the hero must be someone "who is highly renowned and prosperous." Classical tragedy involves the inevitable destruction of a noble person by means of a character flaw, usually a disproportionate measure of a specific human attribute such as pride or jealousy or indecision. The Aristotelian definition implies a basic premise that there is a natural, right ordering and proportion of characteristics within the human being which, if violated, produces calamity. Many critics cite Antigone's "difficult willfulness" as the explanation of her fate. One claims that "she can assert what she is only by staking her entire being, her life. It is by this extreme defense of her beliefs that she rises to heroic and deeply tragic stature" (Charles Segal, "Sophocles' Praise of Man and the Conflicts of the *Antigone*," *Sophocles: A Collection of Critical Essays*, ed. Thomas Woodard. Englewood Cliffs: Prentice-Hall, 1966: 65).

THE MODERN HERO

In 1949, the famous playwright Arthur Miller described what he considers a new kind of hero. In an article called "Tragedy and the Common Man" (*New York Times*, 27 Feb. 1949, 3.1.3.), he challenges Aristotle's idea that the hero must be a "highly renowned and prosperous" figure who has a tragic flaw. In contrast to disorder exclusively within the human character of the hero, Miller's idea of the modern hero emphasizes a clash between the character and the environment, especially social environment. He says that each person has a chosen image of self and position and that tragedy results when the character's environment denies the fulfillment of this self-concept. The hero no longer must be born into the nobility but gains stature in the action of pitting self against cosmos. The tragedy is "the disaster inherent in being torn away from our chosen image of what and who we are in this world." Feelings of displacement and indignity, then, are the driving forces for Miller's modern tragic hero. In his own play *Death of a Salesman*, the character Willy Loman imagines himself as a well-liked, successful, worldly businessman. Tragically, he is really an object of ridicule and contempt, always on the edge of poverty. Such conflicts between ideal self-image and reality occur over and over in the modern play you are about to read.

Looking at the Modern Hero

THE GLASS MENAGERIE BY TENNESSEE WILLIAMS

As you read the play for pleasure, take note of the characters especially. Who is the hero? the heroine?—or are there none? Which characters do you respond positively to? Are there any to whom you respond negatively?

Tennessee Williams *1911–1983*

THE GLASS MENAGERIE

Nobody, not even the rain, has such small hands.
E. E. CUMMINGS

SCENE An Alley in St. Louis
Part I. Preparation for a Gentleman Caller
Part II. The Gentleman calls.
Time: Now and the Past.

THE CHARACTERS

AMANDA WINGFIELD (*the mother*): A little woman of great but confused vitality clinging frantically to another time and place. Her characterization must be carefully created, not copied from type. She is not paranoiac, but her life is paranoia. There is much to admire in Amanda, and as much to love and pity as there is to laugh at. Certainly she has endurance and a kind of heroism, and though her foolishness makes her unwittingly cruel at times, there is tenderness in her slight person.

LAURA WINGFIELD (*her daughter*): Amanda, having failed to establish contact with reality, continues to live vitally in her illusions, but Laura's situation is even graver. A childhood illness has left her crippled, one leg slightly shorter than the other, and held in a brace. This defect need not be more than suggested on the stage. Stemming from this, Laura's separation increases till she is like a piece of her own glass collection, too exquisitely fragile to move from the shelf.

TOM WINGFIELD (*her son*): And the narrator of the play. A poet with a job in a warehouse. His nature is not remorseless, but to escape from a trap he has to act without pity.

JIM O'CONNOR (*the gentleman caller*): A nice, ordinary, young man.

SCENE I

The Wingfield apartment is in the rear of the building, one of those vast hive-like conglomerations of cellular living-units that flower as warty growths in overcrowded urban centers of lower middle-class population and are symptomatic of the impulse of this largest and fundamentally enslaved section of American society to avoid fluidity and differentiation and to exist and function as one interfused mass of automatism.

The apartment faces an alley and is entered by a fire escape, a structure whose name is a touch of accidental poetic truth, for all of these huge buildings are always burning with the slow and implacable fires of human desperation. The fire escape is part of what we see—that is, the landing of it and steps descending from it.

The scene is memory and is therefore nonrealistic. Memory takes a lot of poetic license. It omits some details; others are exaggerated, according to the emotional value of the articles it touches, for memory is seated predominantly in the heart. The interior is therefore rather dim and poetic.

At the rise of the curtain, the audience is faced with the dark, grim rear wall of the Wingfield tenement. This building is flanked on both sides by dark, narrow alleys which run into murky canyons of tangled clotheslines, garbage cans, and the sinister latticework of neighboring fire escapes. It is up and down these side alleys that exterior entrances and exits are made during the play. At the end of TOM's opening commentary, the dark tenement wall slowly becomes transparent and reveals the interior of the ground-floor Wingfield apartment.

Nearest the audience is the living room, which also serves as a sleeping room for LAURA, the sofa unfolding to make her bed. Just beyond, separated from the living room by a wide arch or second proscenium with transparent faded portieres (or second curtain), is the dining room. In an old-fashioned whatnot in the living room are seen scores of transparent glass animals. A blown-up photograph of the father hangs on the wall of the living room, to the left of the archway. It is the face of a very handsome young man in a doughboy's First World War cap. He is gallantly smiling, ineluctably smiling, as if to say "I will be smiling forever."

Also hanging on the wall, near the photograph, are a typewriter keyboard chart and a Gregg shorthand diagram. An upright typewriter on a small table stands beneath the charts.

The audience hears and sees the opening scene in the dining room through both the transparent fourth wall of the building and the transparent gauze portieres of the dining-room arch. It is during this revealing scene that the fourth wall slowly ascends, out of sight. This transparent exterior wall is not brought down again until the very end of the play, during TOM's final speech.

The narrator is an undisguised convention of the play. He takes whatever license with dramatic convention is convenient to his purposes.

Tom enters, dressed as a merchant sailor, and strolls across to the fire escape. There he stops and lights a cigarette. He addresses the audience.

TOM. Yes, I have tricks in my pocket, I have things up my sleeve. But I am the opposite of a stage magician. He gives you illusion that has the appearance of truth. I give you truth in the pleasant disguise of illusion.

To begin with, I turn back time. I reverse it to that quaint period, the thirties, when the huge middle class of America was matriculating in a school for the blind. Their eyes had failed them, or they had failed their eyes, and so they were having their fingers pressed forcibly down on the fiery Braille alphabet of a dissolving economy.

In Spain there was revolution. Here there was only shouting and confusion. In Spain there was Guernica.[1] Here there were disturbances of labor, sometimes pretty violent, in otherwise peaceful cities such as Chicago, Cleveland, Saint Louis . . .

This is the social background of the play. [*Music begins to play.*]

The play is memory. Being a memory play, it is dimly lighted, it is sentimental, it is not realistic. In memory everything seems to happen to music. That explains the fiddle in the wings.

I am the narrator of the play, and also a character in it. The other characters are my mother, Amanda, my sister, Laura, and a gentleman caller who appears in the final scenes. He is the most realistic character in the play, being an emissary from a world of reality that we were somehow set apart from. But since I have a poet's weakness for symbols, I am using this character also as a symbol; he is the long-delayed but always expected something that we live for.

There is a fifth character in the play who doesn't appear except in this larger-than-life-size photograph over the mantel. This is our father who left us a long time ago. He was a telephone man who fell in love with long distances; he gave up his job with the telephone company and skipped the light fantastic out of town . . .

The last we heard of him was a picture postcard from Mazatlan, on the Pacific coast of Mexico, containing a message of two words: "Hello—Goodbye!" and no address.

I think the rest of the play will explain itself. . . . [Amanda's *voice becomes audible through the portieres.*] [*Legend on screen:* "Ou sont les neiges d'antan?"[2]] [Tom *divides the portieres and enters the dining room.* Amanda *and* Laura *are seated at a drop-leaf table. Eating is indicated by gestures without food or utensils.* Amanda *faces the audience.* Tom *and* Laura *are seated in profile. The interior is lit up softly and through the scrim we see* Amanda *and* Laura *seated at the table.*]

Amanda [*calling*]. Tom?

Tom. Yes, Mother.

Amanda. We can't say grace until you come to the table!

Tom. Coming, Mother. [*He bows slightly and withdraws, reappearing a few moments later in his place at the table.*]

Amanda [*to her son*]. Honey, don't *push* with your *fingers*. If you have to push with something, the thing to push with is a crust of bread. And chew—chew! Animals have secretions in their stomachs which enable them to digest food without mastication, but human beings are supposed

---

[1] Spanish town bombed by fascists in the Spanish Civil War, 1937.

[2] "Where are the snows of yester-year?" A quotation from a poem by Francois Villon, fifteenth century.

to chew their food before they swallow it down. Eat food leisurely, son, and really enjoy it. A well-cooked meal has lots of delicate flavors that have to be held in the mouth for appreciation. So chew your food and give your salivary glands a chance to function! [TOM *deliberately lays his imaginary fork down and pushes his chair back from the table.*]

TOM. I haven't enjoyed one bite of this dinner because of your constant directions on how to eat it. It's you that make me rush through meals with your hawklike attention to every bite I take. Sickening—spoils my appetite—all this discussion of—animals' secretion—salivary glands—mastication!

AMANDA [*lightly*]. Temperament like a Metropolitan star! [TOM *rises and walks toward the living room.*] You're not excused from the table.

TOM. I'm getting a cigarette.

AMANDA. You smoke too much. [LAURA *rises.*]

LAURA. I'll bring in the blanc mange. [TOM *remains standing with his cigarette by the portieres.*]

AMANDA [*rising*]. No, sister, no, sister—you be the lady this time and I'll be the darky.

LAURA. I'm already up.

AMANDA. Resume your seat, little sister—I want you to stay fresh and pretty—for gentlemen callers!

LAURA [*sitting down*]. I'm not expecting any gentlemen callers.

AMANDA [*crossing out to the kitchenette, airily*]. Sometimes they come when they are least expected! Why, I remember one Sunday afternoon in Blue Mountain— [*She enters the kitchenette.*]

TOM. I know what's coming!

LAURA. Yes. But let her tell it.

TOM. Again?

LAURA. She loves to tell it. [AMANDA *returns with a bowl of dessert.*]

AMANDA. One Sunday afternoon in Blue Mountain—your mother received—*seventeen!*—gentlemen callers! Why, sometimes there weren't chairs enough to accommodate them all. We had to send the nigger over to bring in folding chairs from the parish house.

TOM [*remaining at the portieres*]. How did you entertain those gentlemen callers?

AMANDA. I understood the art of conversation!

TOM. I bet you could talk.

AMANDA. Girls in those days *knew* how to talk, I can tell you.

TOM. Yes? [*Image on screen: Amanda as a girl on a porch, greeting callers.*]

AMANDA. They knew how to entertain their gentlemen callers. It wasn't enough for a girl to be possessed of a pretty face and a graceful figure— although I wasn't slighted in either respect. She also needed to have a nimble wit and a tongue to meet all occasions.

TOM. What did you talk about?

AMANDA. Things of importance going on in the world! Never anything coarse or common or vulgar. [*She addresses* TOM *as though he were seated in the vacant chair at the table though he remains by the portieres. He plays this scene as though reading from a script.*] My callers were gentlemen— all! Among my callers were some of the most prominent young planters of the Mississippi Delta—planters and sons of planters! [TOM *motions* for music and a spot of light on AMANDA. *Her eyes lift, her face glows, her voice becomes rich and elegiac.*] [*Screen legend:* "Ou sont les neiges d'antan?"] There was young Champ Laughlin who later became vice-president of the Delta Planters Bank. Hadley Stevenson who was drowned in Moon Lake and left his widow one hundred and fifty thousand in Government bonds. There were the Cutrere brothers, Wesley and Bates. Bates was one of my bright particular beaux! He got in a quarrel with that wild Wainwright boy. They shot it out on the floor of Moon Lake Casino. Bates was shot through the stomach. Died in the ambulance on his way to Memphis. His widow was also well provided-for, came into eight or ten thousand acres, that's all. She married him on the rebound—never loved her—carried my picture on him the night he died! And there was that boy that every girl in the Delta had set her cap for! That beautiful, brilliant young Fitzhugh boy from Greene County!

TOM. What did he leave his widow?

AMANDA. He never married! Gracious, you talk as though all of my old admirers had turned up their toes to the daisies!

TOM. Isn't this the first you've mentioned that still survives?

AMANDA. That Fitzhugh boy went North and made a fortune—came to be known as the Wolf of Wall Street! He had the Midas touch, whatever he touched turned to gold! And I could have been Mrs. Duncan J. Fitzhugh, mind you! But—I picked your *father!*

LAURA [*rising*]. Mother, let me clear the table.

AMANDA. No, dear, you go in front and study your typewriter chart. Or practice your shorthand a little. Stay fresh and pretty!—It's almost time for our gentlemen callers to start arriving. [*She flounces girlishly toward the kitchenette.*] How many do you suppose we're going to entertain this afternoon? [TOM *throws down the paper and jumps up with a groan.*]

LAURA [*alone in the dining room*]. I don't believe we're going to receive any, Mother.

AMANDA [*reappearing, airily*]. What? No one—not one? You must be joking! [LAURA *nervously echoes her laugh. She slips in a fugitive manner through the half-open portieres and draws them gently behind her. A shaft of very clear light is thrown on her face against the faded tapestry of the curtains. Faintly the music of "The Glass Menagerie" is heard as she continues, lightly.*] Not one gentleman caller? It can't be true! There must be a flood, there must have been a tornado!

LAURA. It isn't a flood, it's not a tornado, Mother. I'm just not popular like you were in Blue Mountain. . . . [TOM *utters another groan.* LAURA *glances at him with a faint, apologetic smile. Her voice catches a little.*] Mother's afraid I'm going to be an old maid. [*The scene dims out with the "Glass Menagerie" music.*]

SCENE II

On the dark stage the screen is lighted with the image of blue roses. Gradually LAURA's *figure becomes apparent and the screen goes out. The music subsides.*

LAURA *is seated in the delicate ivory chair at the small claw-foot table. She wears a dress of soft violet material for a kimono—*

her hair is tied back from her forehead with a ribbon. She is washing and polishing her collection of glass. AMANDA appears on the fire escape steps. At the sound of her ascent, LAURA catches her breath, thrusts the bowl of ornaments away, and sets herself stiffly before the diagram of the typewriter keyboard as though it held her spellbound. Something has happened to AMANDA. It is written in her face as she climbs to the landing: a look that is grim and hopeless and a little absurd. She has on one of those cheap or imitation velvety-looking cloth coats with imitation fur collar. Her hat is five or six years old, one of those dreadful cloche hats that were worn in the late Twenties, and she is clutching an enormous black patent-leather pocketbook with nickel clasps and initials. This is her full-dress outfit, the one she usually wears to the D.A.R.[1] Before entering she looks through the door. She purses her lips, opens her eyes very wide, rolls them upward and shakes her head. Then she slowly lets herself in the door. Seeing her mother's expression LAURA touches her lips with a nervous gesture.

LAURA. Hello, Mother, I was—[*She makes a nervous gesture toward the chart on the wall. AMANDA leans against the shut door and stares at LAURA with a martyred look.*]
AMANDA. Deception? Deception? [*She slowly removes her hat and gloves, continuing the sweet suffering stare. She lets the hat and gloves fall on the floor—a bit of acting.*]
LAURA [*shakily*]. How was the D.A.R. meeting? [*AMANDA slowly opens her purse and removes a dainty white handkerchief which she shakes out delicately and delicately touches to her lips and nostrils.*] Didn't you go to the D.A.R. meeting, Mother?
AMANDA [*faintly, almost inaudibly*]. —No.—No. [*then more forcibly*] I did not have the strength—to go to the D.A.R. In fact, I did not have the courage! I wanted to find a hole in the ground and hide myself in it forever! [*She crosses slowly to the wall and removes the diagram of the typewriter keyboard. She holds it in front of her for a second, staring at it sweetly and sorrowfully—then bites her lips and tears it in two pieces.*]
LAURA [*faintly*]. Why did you do that, Mother? [*AMANDA repeats the same procedure with the chart of the Gregg Alphabet.*] Why are you—
AMANDA. Why? Why? How old are you, Laura?
LAURA. Mother, you know my age.
AMANDA. I thought that you were an adult; it seems that I was mistaken. [*She crosses slowly to the sofa and sinks down and stares at LAURA.*]
LAURA. Please don't stare at me, Mother. [*AMANDA closes her eyes and lowers her head. There is a ten-second pause.*]
AMANDA. What are we going to do, what is going to become of us, what is the future? [*There is another pause.*]
LAURA. Has something happened, Mother? [*AMANDA draws a long breath, takes out the handkerchief again, goes through the dabbing process.*] Mother, has—something happened?

[1] The Daughters of the American Revolution.

AMANDA. I'll be all right in a minute, I'm just bewildered—[*She hesitates.*]—by life. . . .

LAURA. Mother, I wish that you would tell me what's happened!

AMANDA. As you know, I was supposed to be inducted into my office at the D.A.R. this afternoon. [*Screen image:* A swarm of typewriters.] But I stopped off at Rubicam's Business College to speak to your teachers about your having a cold and ask them what progress they thought you were making down there.

LAURA. Oh. . . .

AMANDA. I went to the typing instructor and introduced myself as your mother. She didn't know who you were. "Wingfield," she said, "We don't have any such student enrolled at the school!" I assured her she did, that you had been going to classes since early in January. "I wonder," she said, "If you could be talking about that terribly shy little girl who dropped out of school after only a few days' attendance?" "No," I said, "Laura, my daughter, has been going to school every day for the past six weeks!" "Excuse me," she said. She took the attendance book out and there was your name, unmistakably printed, and all the dates you were absent until they decided that you had dropped out of school. I still said, "No, there must have been some mistake! There must have been some mix-up in the records!" And she said, "No—I remember her perfectly now. Her hands shook so that she couldn't hit the right keys! The first time we gave a speed test, she broke down completely—was sick at the stomach and almost had to be carried into the wash room! After that morning she never showed up any more. We phoned the house but never got any answer"—While I was working at Famous-Barr, I suppose, demonstrating those— [*She indicates a brassiere with her hands.*] Oh, I felt so weak I could barely keep on my feet! I had to sit down while they got me a glass of water! Fifty dollars' tuition, all of our plans—my hopes and ambitions for you—just gone up the spout, just gone up the spout like that. [LAURA *draws a long breath and gets awkwardly to her feet. She crosses to the Victrola and winds it up.*] What are you doing?

LAURA. Oh! [*She releases the handle and returns to her seat.*]

AMANDA. Laura, where have you been going when you've gone out pretending that you were going to business college?

LAURA. I've just been going out walking.

AMANDA. That's not true.

LAURA. It is. I just went walking.

AMANDA. Walking? Walking? In winter? Deliberately courting pneumonia in that light coat? Where did you walk to, Laura?

LAURA. All sorts of places—mostly in the park.

AMANDA. Even after you'd started catching that cold?

LAURA. It was the lesser of two evils, Mother. [*Screen image:* Winter scene in a park.] I couldn't go back there. I—threw up—on the floor!

AMANDA. From half past seven till after five every day you mean to tell me you walked around in the park, because you wanted to make me think that you were still going to Rubicam's Business College?

LAURA. It wasn't as bad as it sounds. I went inside places to get warmed up.

AMANDA. Inside where?

LAURA. I went in the art museum and the bird houses at the Zoo. I visited the penguins every day! Sometimes I did without lunch and went to the movies. Lately I've been spending most of my afternoons in the Jewel Box, that big glass house where they raise the tropical flowers.

AMANDA. You did all this to deceive me, just for deception? [LAURA *looks down.*] Why?

LAURA. Mother, when you're disappointed, you get that awful suffering look on your face, like the picture of Jesus' mother in the museum!

AMANDA. Hush!

LAURA. I couldn't face it. [*There is a pause. A whisper of strings is heard. Legend on screen:* "The Crust of Humility."]

AMANDA [*hopelessly fingering the huge pocketbook*]. So what are we going to do the rest of our lives? Stay home and watch the parades go by? Amuse ourselves with the glass menagerie, darling? Eternally play those worn-out phonograph records your father left as a painful reminder of him? We won't have a business career—we've given that up because it gave us nervous indigestion! [*She laughs wearily.*] What is there left but dependency all our lives? I know so well what becomes of unmarried women who aren't prepared to occupy a position. I've seen such pitiful cases in the South—barely tolerated spinsters living upon the grudging patronage of sister's or brother's wife!—stuck away in some little mousetrap of a room—encouraged by one in-law to visit another—little birdlike women without any nest—eating the crust of humility all their life! Is that the future that we've mapped out for ourselves? I swear it's the only alternative I can think of! [*She pauses.*] It isn't a very pleasant alternative, is it? [*She pauses again.*] Of course—some girls *do marry.* [LAURA *twists her hands nervously.*] Haven't you ever liked some boy?

LAURA. Yes. I liked one once. [*She rises.*] I came across his picture a while ago.

AMANDA [*with some interest*]. He gave you his picture?

LAURA. No, it's in the yearbook.

AMANDA [*disappointed*]. Oh—a high school boy. [*Screen image:* Jim as the high school hero bearing a silver cup.]

LAURA. Yes. His name was Jim. [*She lifts the heavy annual from the claw-foot table.*] Here he is in *The Pirates of Penzance.*

AMANDA [*absently*]. The what?

LAURA. The operetta the senior class put on. He had a wonderful voice and we sat across the aisle from each other Mondays, Wednesdays and Fridays in the Aud. Here he is with the silver cup for debating! See his grin?

AMANDA [*absently*]. He must have had a jolly disposition.

LAURA. He used to call me—Blue Roses. [*Screen image:* Blue roses.]

AMANDA. Why did he call you such a name as that?

LAURA. When I had that attack of pleurosis—he asked me what was the matter when I came back. I said pleurosis—he thought that I said Blue Roses! So that's what he always called me after that. Whenever he saw me, he'd holler, "Hello, Blue Roses!" I didn't care for the girl that he went out with. Emily Meisenbach. Emily was the best-dressed girl at Soldan. She never struck me, though, as being sincere . . . It says in the Personal Section—they're engaged. That's —six years ago! They must be married by now.

AMANDA. Girls that aren't cut out for business careers usually wind up married to some nice man. [*She gets up with a spark of revival.*] Sister, that's what you'll do! [LAURA *utters a startled, doubtful laugh. She reaches quickly for a piece of glass.*]

LAURA. But, Mother—

AMANDA. Yes? [*She goes over to the photograph.*]

LAURA [*in a tone of frightened apology*]. I'm—crippled!

AMANDA. Nonsense! Laura, I've told you never, never to use that word. Why, you're not crippled, you just have a little defect—hardly noticeable, even! When people have some slight disadvantage like that, they cultivate other things to make up for it—develop charm—and vivacity—and— *charm!* That's all you have to do! [*She turns again to the photograph.*] One thing your father had *plenty of*—was *charm!* [*Tom motions to the fiddle in the wings. The scene fades out with music.*]

SCENE III

Legend on screen: "After the fiasco—"
TOM *speaks from the fire escape landing.*

TOM. After the fiasco at Rubicam's Business College, the idea of getting a gentleman caller for Laura began to play a more and more important part in Mother's calculations. It became an obsession. Like some arche-type of the universal unconscious, the image of the gentleman caller haunted our small apartment. . . . [*Screen image:* A young man at the door of a house with flowers.] An evening at home rarely passed without some allusion to this image, this specter, this hope. . . . Even when he wasn't mentioned, his presence hung in Mother's preoccupied look and in my sister's frightened, apologetic manner—hung like a sentence passed upon the Wingfields! Mother was a woman of action as well as words. She began to take logical steps in the planned direction. Late that winter and in the early spring—realizing that extra money would be needed to properly feather the nest and plume the bird—she con-ducted a vigorous campaign on the telephone, roping in subscribers to one of those magazines for matrons called *The Homemaker's Companion,* the type of journal that features the serialized sublimations of ladies of letters who think in terms of delicate cuplike breasts, slim, tapering waists, rich, creamy thighs, eyes like wood smoke in autumn, fingers that soothe and caress like strains of music, bodies as powerful as Etrus-can sculpture. [*Screen image:* The cover of a glamor magazine.] [AMANDA *enters with the telephone on a long extension cord. She is spotlighted in the dim stage.*]

AMANDA. Ida Scott? This is Amanda Wingfield! We *missed* you at the D.A.R. last Monday! I said to myself: She's probably suffering with that sinus condition! How is that sinus condition? Horrors! Heaven have mercy— You're a Christian martyr, yes, that's what you are, a Christian martyr! Well, I just now happened to notice that your subscription to the *Compan-ion's* about to expire! Yes, it expires with the next issue, honey!—just when that wonderful new serial by Bessie Mae Hopper is getting off to such an exciting start. Oh, honey, it's something that you can't miss!

You remember how *Gone with the Wind* took everybody by storm? You simply couldn't go out if you hadn't read it. All everybody *talked* was Scarlett O'Hara. Well, this is a book that critics already compare to *Gone with the Wind*. It's the *Gone with the Wind* of the post-World-War generation!—What?—Burning?—Oh, honey, don't let them burn, go take a look in the oven and I'll hold the wire! Heavens—I think she's hung up! [*The scene dims out.*] [*Legend on screen:* "You think I'm in love with Continental Shoemakers?"] [*Before the lights come up again, the violent voices of* TOM *and* AMANDA *are heard. They are quarreling behind the portieres. In front of them stands* LAURA *with clenched hands and panicky expression. A clear pool of light is on her figure throughout this scene.*]

TOM. What in Christ's name am I—

AMANDA [*shrilly*]. Don't you use that—

TOM. —supposed to do!

AMANDA. —expression! Not in my—

TOM. Ohhh!

AMANDA. —presence! Have you gone out of your senses?

TOM. I have, that's true, *driven* out!

AMANDA. What is the matter with you, you—big—big—IDIOT!

TOM. Look!—I've got *no thing,* no single thing—

AMANDA. Lower your voice!

TOM. —in my life here that I can call my OWN! Everything is—

AMANDA. Stop that shouting!

TOM. Yesterday you confiscated my books! You had the nerve to—

AMANDA. I took that horrible novel back to the library—yes! That hideous book by that insane Mr. Lawrence. [TOM *laughs wildly.*] I cannot control the output of diseased minds or people who cater to them— [TOM *laughs still more wildly.*] BUT I WON'T ALLOW SUCH FILTH BROUGHT INTO MY HOUSE! No, no, no, no, no!

TOM. House, house! Who pays rent on it, who makes a slave of himself to—

AMANDA [*fairly screeching*]. Don't you DARE to—

TOM. No, no, *I* mustn't say things! *I've* got to just—

AMANDA. Let me tell you—

TOM. I don't want to hear any more! [*He tears the portieres open. The dining-room area is lit with a turgid smoky red glow. Now we see* AMANDA; *her hair is in metal curlers and she is wearing a very old bathrobe, much too large for her slight figure, a relic of the faithless Mr. Wingfield. The upright typewriter now stands on the drop-leaf table, along with a wild disarray of manuscripts. The quarrel was probably precipitated by* AMANDA's *interruption of* TOM's *creative labor. A chair lies overthrown on the floor. Their gesticulating shadows are cast on the ceiling by the fiery glow.*]

AMANDA. You *will* hear more, you—

TOM. No, I won't hear more, I'm going out!

AMANDA. You come right back in—

TOM. Out, out, out! Because I'm—

AMANDA. Come back here, Tom Wingfield! I'm not through talking to you!

TOM. Oh, go—

LAURA [*desperately*].—Tom!

AMANDA. You're going to listen, and no more insolence from you! I'm at the end of my patience! [*He comes back toward her.*]

TOM. What do you think I'm at? Aren't I supposed to have any patience to reach the end of, Mother? I know, I know. It seems unimportant to you, what I'm *doing*—what I *want* to do—having a little *difference* between them! You don't think that—

AMANDA. I think you've been doing things that you're ashamed of. That's why you act like this. I don't believe that you go every night to the movies. Nobody goes to the movies night after night. Nobody in their right minds goes to the movies as often as you pretend to. People don't go to the movies at nearly midnight, and movies don't let out at two A.M. Come in stumbling. Muttering to yourself like a maniac! You get three hours' sleep and then go to work. Oh, I can picture the way you're doing down there. Moping, doping, because you're in no condition.

TOM [*wildly*]. No, I'm in no condition!

AMANDA. What right have you got to jeopardize your job? Jeopardize the security of us all? How do you think we'd manage if you were—

TOM. Listen! You think I'm crazy about the *warehouse*? [*He bends fiercely toward her slight figure.*] You think I'm in love with the Continental Shoemakers? You think I want to spend fifty-five *years* down there in that— *celotex interior!* with—*fluorescent—tubes!* Look! I'd rather somebody picked up a crowbar and battered out my brains—than go back mornings! I *go!* Every time you come in yelling that Goddamn *"Rise and Shine!" "Rise and Shine!"* I say to myself, "How *lucky dead* people are!" But I get up. I *go!* For sixty-five dollars a month I give up all that I dream of doing and being *ever!* And you say self—*self's* all I ever think of. Why, listen, if self is what I thought of, Mother, I'd be where he is— GONE! [*He points to his father's picture.*] As far as the system of transportation reaches! [*He starts past her. She grabs his arm.*] Don't grab at me, Mother!

AMANDA. Where are you going?

TOM. I'm going to the *movies!*

ANANDA. I don't believe that lie!

[TOM *crouches toward her, overtowering her tiny figure. She backs away, gasping.*]

TOM. I'm going to opium dens! Yes, opium dens, dens of vice and criminals' hangouts, Mother. I've joined the Hogan Gang, I'm a hired assassin, I carry a tommy gun in a violin case! I run a string of cat houses in the Valley! They call me Killer, Killer Wingfield, I'm leading a double-life, a simple, honest warehouse worker by day, by night a dynamic *czar* of the *underworld, Mother.* I go to gambling casinos, I spin away fortunes on the roulette table! I wear a patch over one eye and a false mustache, sometimes I put on green whiskers. On those occasions they call me—*El Diablo!* Oh, I could tell you many things to make you sleepless! My enemies plan to dynamite this place. They're going to blow us all sky-high some night! I'll be glad, very happy, and so will you! You'll go up, up on a broomstick, over Blue Mountain with seventeen gentlemen callers! You ugly—babbling old—*witch. . . .* [*He goes through a series of violent, clumsy movements, seizing his overcoat, lunging to the door, pulling it fiercely open. The women watch him, aghast. His arm catches in the sleeve of the coat as he struggles to pull it on. For a moment he is pinioned by the bulky garment. With an outraged groan he tears the coat off again, splitting the shoulder of it, and hurls it across the room. It strikes against the shelf of* LAURA's *glass collection, and there is a tinkle of shattering glass.* LAURA *cries out as if wounded.*] [*Music.*] [*Screen legend:* "The Glass Menagerie."]

LAURA [*shrilly*]. My glass!—menagerie. . . .[*She covers her face and turns away.*] [*But* AMANDA *is still stunned and stupefied by the "ugly witch" so that she barely notices this occurrence. Now she recovers her speech.*]

AMANDA [*in an awful voice*]. I won't speak to you—until you apologize! [*She crosses through the portieres and draws them together behind her.* TOM *is left with* LAURA. LAURA *clings weakly to the mantel with her face averted.* TOM *stares at her stupidly for a moment. Then he crosses to the shelf. He drops awkwardly on his knees to collect the fallen glass, glancing at* LAURA *as if he would speak but couldn't.*]

[*"The Glass Menagerie" music steals in as the scene dims out.*]

SCENE IV

The interior of the apartment is dark. There is a faint light in the alley. A deep-voiced bell in a church is tolling the hour of five.

TOM *appears at the top of the alley. After each solemn boom of the bell in the tower, he shakes a little noisemaker or rattle as if to express the tiny spasm of man in contrast to the sustained power and dignity of the Almighty. This and the unsteadiness of his advance make it evident that he has been drinking. As he climbs the few steps to the fire escape landing light steals up inside.* LAURA *appears in the front room in a nightdress. She notices that* TOM's *bed is empty.* TOM *fishes in his pockets for his door key, removing a motley assortment of articles in this search, including a shower of movie ticket stubs and an empty bottle. At last he finds the key, but just as he is about to insert it, it slips from his fingers. He strikes a match and crouches below the door.*

TOM [*bitterly*]. One crack—and it falls through! [LAURA *opens the door.*]

LAURA. Tom! Tom, what are you doing?

TOM. Looking for a door key.

LAURA. Where have you been all this time?

TOM. I have been to the movies.

LAURA. All this time at the movies?

TOM. There was a very long program. There was a Garbo picture and a Mickey Mouse and a travelogue and a newsreel and a preview of coming attractions. And there was an organ solo and a collection for the Milk Fund—simultaneously—which ended up in a terrible fight between a fat lady and an usher!

LAURA [*innocently*]. Did you have to stay through everything?

TOM. Of course! And, oh, I forgot! There was a big stage show! The head-liner on this stage show was Malvolio the Magician. He performed won-derful tricks, many of them such as pouring water back and forth be-tween pitchers. First it turned to wine and then it turned to beer and then it turned to whiskey. I know it was whiskey it finally turned to because he needed somebody to come up out of the audience to help him, and I came up—both shows! It was Kentucky Straight Bourbon. A very generous fellow, he gave souvenirs. [*He pulls from his pocket a shimmering rainbow-colored scarf.*] He gave me this. This is his magic scarf. You can have it, Laura. You wave it over a canary cage and you get a bowl of goldfish. You wave it over the goldfish bowl and they fly away canaries. . . . But the wonderfullest trick of all was the coffin trick. We nailed him into a coffin and he got out of the coffin without removing one nail. [*He has come inside.*] There is a trick that would come in handy for me—get me out of this two-by-four situation! [*He flops onto the bed and starts removing his shoes.*]

LAURA. Tom—shhh!

TOM. What're you shushing me for?

LAURA. You'll wake up Mother.

TOM. Goody, goody! Pay'er back for all those "Rise an' Shines." [*He lies down, groaning.*] You know it don't take much intelligence to get yourself into a nailed-up coffin, Laura. But who in hell ever got himself out of one without removing one nail?

[*As if in answer, the father's grinning photograph lights up. The scene dims out.*]

[*Immediately following, the church bell is heard striking six. At the sixth stroke the alarm clock goes off in* AMANDA's *room, and after a few moments we hear her calling: "Rise and Shine! Rise and Shine!* LAURA *go tell your brother to rise and shine!"*]

TOM [*sitting up slowly*]. I'll rise—but I won't shine. [*The light increases.*]

AMANDA. Laura, tell your brother his coffee is ready. [*Laura slips into the front room.*]

LAURA. Tom—It's nearly seven. Don't make Mother nervous. [*He stares at her stupidly.*]

[*beseechingly:*] Tom, speak to Mother this morning. Make up with her, apologize, speak to her!

TOM. She won't to me. It's her that started not speaking.

LAURA. If you just say you're sorry she'll start speaking.

TOM. Her not speaking—is that such a tragedy?

LAURA. Please—please!

AMANDA (*calling from the kitchenette*). Laura, are you going to do what I asked you to do, or do I have to get dressed and go out myself?

LAURA. Going, going—soon as I get on my coat! [*She pulls on a shapeless felt hat with a nervous, jerky movement, pleadingly glancing at* TOM. *She rushes awkwardly for her coat. The coat is one of* AMANDA's *inaccurately made-over, the sleeves too short for* LAURA.] Butter and what else?

AMANDA [*entering from the kitchenette*]. Just butter. Tell them to charge it.

LAURA. Mother, they make such faces when I do that.

AMANDA. Sticks and stones can break our bones, but the expression on Mr. Garfinkel's face won't harm us! Tell your brother his coffee is getting cold.

LAURA [*at the door*]. Do what I asked you, will you, will you, Tom? [*He looks sullenly away.*]

AMANDA. Laura, go now or just don't go at all!

LAURA [*rushing out*]. Going—going! [*A second later she cries out.* TOM *springs up and crosses to the door.* TOM *opens the door.*]

TOM. Laura?

LAURA. I'm all right. I slipped, but I'm all right.

AMANDA [*peering anxiously after her*]. If anyone breaks a leg on those fire-escape steps, the landlord ought to be sued for every cent he possesses! [*She shuts the door. Now she remembers she isn't speaking to* TOM *and returns to the other room.*] [*As* TOM *comes listlessly for his coffee, she turns her back to him and stands rigidly facing the window on the gloomy gray vault of the areaway. Its light on her face with its aged but childish features is cruelly sharp, satirical as a Daumier print.*] [*The music of "Ave Maria" is heard softly.*] [TOM *glances sheepishly but sullenly at her averted figure and slumps at the table. The coffee is scalding hot; he sips it and gasps and spits it back in the cup. At his gasp,* AMANDA *catches her breath and half turns. Then she catches herself and turns back to the window.* TOM *blows on his coffee, glancing sidewise at his mother. She clears her throat.* TOM *clears his. He starts to rise, sinks back down again, scratches his head, clears his throat again.* AMANDA *coughs.* TOM *raises his cup in both hands to blow on it, his eyes staring over the rim of it at his mother for several moments. Then he slowly sets the cup down and awkwardly and hesitantly rises from the chair.*]

TOM [*hoarsely*]. Mother. I—I apologize, Mother. [AMANDA *draws a quick, shuddering breath. Her face works grotesquely. She breaks into childlike tears.*] I'm sorry for what I said, for everything that I said, I didn't mean it.

AMANDA [*sobbingly*]. My devotion has made me a witch and so I make myself hateful to my children!

TOM. No, you *don't.*

AMANDA. I worry so much, don't sleep, it makes me nervous!

TOM [*gently*]. I understand that.

AMANDA. I've had to put up a solitary battle all these years. But you're my right-hand bower! Don't fall down, don't fail!

TOM [*gently*]. I try, Mother.

AMANDA [*with great enthusiasm*]. Try and you will *succeed!* [*The notion makes her breathless.*] Why, you—you're just *full* of natural endowments! Both of my children—they're *unusual* children! Don't you think I know it? I'm so—*proud!* Happy and—feel I've—so much to be thankful for but—promise me one thing, son!

TOM. What, Mother?

AMANDA. Promise, son, you'll—never be a drunkard!

TOM [*turns to her grinning*]. I will never be a drunkard, Mother.

AMANDA. That's what frightened me so, that you'd be drinking! Eat a bowl of Purina!

TOM. Just coffee, Mother.

AMANDA. Shredded wheat biscuit?

TOM. No. No, Mother, just coffee.

AMANDA. You can't put in a day's work on an empty stomach. You've got ten minutes—don't gulp! Drinking too-hot liquids makes cancer of the stomach. . . . Put cream in.

TOM. No, thank you.

AMANDA. To cool it.

TOM. No! No, thank you, I want it black.

AMANDA. I know, but it's not good for you. We have to do all that we can to build ourselves up. In these trying times we live in, all that we have to cling to is—each other. . . . That's why it's important to—Tom, I—I sent out your sister so I could discuss something with you. If you hadn't spoken I would have spoken to you. [*She sits down.*]

TOM [*gently*]. What is it, Mother, that you want to discuss?

AMANDA. *Laura!* [TOM *puts his cup down slowly*] [*Legend on screen:* "Laura." *Music:* "*The Glass Menagerie.*"]

TOM. —Oh.—Laura . . .

AMANDA [*touching his sleeve*]. You know how Laura is. So quiet but—still water runs deep! She notices things and I think she—broods about them. [TOM *looks up.*] A few days ago I came in and she was crying.

TOM. What about?

AMANDA. You.

TOM. Me?

AMANDA. She has an idea that you're not happy here.

TOM. What gave her that idea?

AMANDA. What gives her any idea? However, you do act strangely. I— I'm not criticizing, understand *that!* I know your ambitions do not lie in the warehouse, that like everybody in the whole wide world—you've had to—make sacrifices, but—Tom—Tom—life's not easy, it calls for— Spartan endurance! There's so many things in my heart that I cannot describe to you! I've never told you but I—*loved* your father. . . .

TOM [*gently*]. I know that, Mother.

AMANDA. And you—when I see you taking after his ways! Staying out late—and—well, you *had* been drinking the night you were in that— terrifying condition! Laura says that you hate the apartment and that you go out nights to get away from it! Is that true, Tom?

TOM. No. You say there's so much in your heart that you can't describe to me. That's true of me, too. There's so much in my heart that I can't describe to *you!* So let's respect each other's—

AMANDA. But, why—*why,* Tom—are you always so *restless?* Where do you *go* to, nights?

TOM. I—go to the movies.

AMANDA. Why do you go to the movies so much, Tom?

TOM. I go to the movies because—I like adventure. Adventure is something I don't have much of at work, so I go to the movies.

AMANDA. But, Tom, you go to the movies *entirely* too *much!*

TOM. I like a lot of adventure. [AMANDA *looks baffled, then hurt. As the familiar inquisition resumes,* TOM *becomes hard and impatient again.* AMANDA *slips back into her querulous attitude toward him.*] [*Image on screen: A sailing vessel with Jolly Roger.*]

AMANDA. Most young men find adventure in their careers.

TOM. Then most young men are not employed in a warehouse.

AMANDA. The world is full of young men employed in warehouses and offices and factories.

TOM. Do all of them find adventure in their careers?

AMANDA. They do or they do without it! Not everybody has a craze for adventure.

TOM. Man is by instinct a lover, a hunter, a fighter, and none of those
instincts are given much play at the warehouse!

AMANDA. Man is by instinct! Don't quote instinct to me! Instinct is something that people have got away from! It belongs to animals! Christian
adults don't want it!

TOM. What do Christian adults want, then, Mother?

AMANDA. Superior things! Things of the mind and the spirit! Only animals
have to satisfy instincts! Surely your aims are somewhat higher than
theirs! Than monkeys—pigs—

TOM. I reckon they're not.

AMANDA. You're joking. However, that isn't what I wanted to discuss.

TOM [*rising*]. I haven't much time.

AMANDA [*pushing his shoulders*]. Sit down.

TOM. You want me to punch in red at the warehouse, Mother?

AMANDA. You have five minutes. I want to talk about Laura. [*Screen legend:*
"Plans and Provisions."]

TOM. All right! What about Laura?

AMANDA. We have to be making some plans and provisions for her. She's
older than you, two years, and nothing has happened. She just drifts
along doing nothing. It frightens me terribly how she just drifts along.

TOM. I guess she's the type that people call home girls.

AMANDA. There's no such type, and if there is, it's a pity! That is unless
the home is hers, with a husband!

TOM. What?

AMANDA. Oh, I can see the handwriting on the wall as plain as I see the
nose in front of my face! It's terrifying! More and more you remind
me of your father! He was out all hours without explanation!—Then
left! Goodbye! And me with the bag to hold. I saw that letter you got
from the Merchant Marine. I know what you're dreaming of. I'm not
standing here blindfolded. [*She pauses.*] Very well, then. Then *do* it! But
not till there's somebody to take your place.

TOM. What do you mean?

AMANDA. I mean that as soon as Laura has got somebody to take care of
her, married, a home of her own, independent—why, then you'll be
free to go wherever you please, on land, on sea, whichever way the
wind blows you! But until that time you've got to look out for your
sister. I don't say me because I'm old and don't matter! I say for your
sister because she's young and dependent.

I put her in business college—a dismal failure! Frightened her so it
made her sick at the stomach. I took her over to the Young People's
League at the church. Another fiasco. She spoke to nobody, nobody
spoke to her. Now all she does is fool with those pieces of glass and
play those worn-out records. What kind of a life is that for a girl to
lead?

TOM. What can I do about it?

AMANDA. Overcome selfishness! Self, self, self is all that you ever think
of! [TOM *springs up and crosses to get his coat. It is ugly and bulky. He pulls
on a cap with earmuffs.*] Where is your muffler? Put your wool muffler
on! [*He snatches it angrily from the closet, tosses it around his neck and pulls
both ends tight.*] Tom! I haven't said what I had in mind to ask you.

Tom. I'm too late to—

Amanda [*catching his arm—very importunately; then shyly*]. Down at the ware-house, aren't there some—nice young men?

Tom. No!

Amanda. There *must* be—*some* . . .

Tom. Mother—[*He gestures.*]

Amanda. Find out one that's clean-living—doesn't drink and ask him out for sister!

Tom. What?

Amanda. For *sister!* To *meet!* Get *acquainted!*

Tom [*stamping to the door*]. Oh, my go-osh!

Amanda. Will you? [*He opens the door. She says, imploringly:*] Will you? [*He starts down the fire escape.*] Will you? *Will* you, dear?

Tom [*calling back*]. Yes! [Amanda *closes the door hesitantly and with a troubled but faintly hopeful expression.*] [*Screen image:* The cover of a glamor maga-zine.] [*The spotlight picks up* Amanda *at the phone.*]

Amanda. Ella Cartwright? This is Amanda Wingfield! How are you, honey? How is that kidney condition? [*There is a five-second pause.*] Horrors! [*There is another pause.*] You're a Christian martyr, yes, honey, that's what you are, a Christian martyr! Well, I just now happened to notice in my little red book that your subscription to the *Companion* has just run out! I knew that you wouldn't want to miss out on the wonderful serial starting in this new issue. It's by Bessie Mae Hopper, the first thing she's written since *Honeymoon for Three*. Wasn't that a strange and inter-esting story? Well, this one is even lovelier, I believe. It has a sophisti-cated, society background. It's all about the horsey set on Long Island! [*The light fades out.*]

SCENE V

Legend on the screen: "Annunciation."

　Music is heard as the light slowly comes on.

　It is early dusk of a spring evening. Supper has just been finished in the Wingfield apartment. Amanda *and* Laura, *in light-colored dresses, are removing dishes from the table in the dining room, which is shadowy, their movements formalized almost as a dance or ritual, their moving forms as pale and silent as moths.* Tom, *in white shirt and trousers, rises from the table and crosses toward the fire escape.*

Amanda [*as he passes her*]. Son, will you do me a favor?

Tom. What?

Amanda. Comb your hair! You look so pretty when your hair is combed! [Tom *slouches on the sofa with the evening paper. Its enormous headline reads:* "Franco Triumphs."[1]] There is only one respect in which I would like you to emulate your father.

Tom. What respect is that?

Amanda. The care he always took of his appearance. He never allowed

[1] Franco headed the fascist forces in the Spanish Civil War.

himself to look untidy. [*He throws down the paper and crosses to the fire escape.*] Where are you going?

TOM. I'm going out to smoke.

AMANDA. You smoke too much. A pack a day at fifteen cents a pack. How much would that amount to in a month? Thirty times fifteen is how much, Tom? Figure it out and you will be astounded at what you could save. Enough to give you a night-school course in accounting at Washington U.! Just think what a wonderful thing that would be for you, son! [TOM *is unmoved by the thought.*]

TOM. I'd rather smoke. [*He steps out on the landing, letting the screen door slam.*]

AMANDA [*sharply*]. I know! That's the tragedy of it. . . . [*Alone, she turns to look at her husband's picture.*] [*Dance music: "The World Is Waiting for the Sunrise!"*]

TOM [*to the audience*]. Across the alley from us was the Paradise Dance Hall. On evenings in spring the windows and doors were open and the music came outdoors. Sometimes the lights were turned out except for a large glass sphere that hung from the ceiling. It would turn slowly about and filter the dusk with delicate rainbow colors. Then the orchestra played a waltz or a tango, something that had a slow and sensuous rhythm. Couples would come outside, to the relative privacy of the alley. You could see them kissing behind ash pits and telephone poles. This was the compensation for lives that passed like mine, without any change or adventure. Adventure and change were imminent in this year. They were waiting around the corner for all these kids. Suspended in the mist over Berchtesgaden, caught in the folds of Chamberlain's[2] umbrella. In Spain there was Guernica! But here there was only hot swing music and liquor, dance halls, bars, and movies, and sex that hung in the gloom like a chandelier and flooded the world with brief, deceptive rainbows. . . . All the world was waiting for bombardments! [AMANDA *turns from the picture and comes outside.*]

AMANDA [*sighing*]. A fire escape landing's a poor excuse for a porch. [*She spreads a newspaper on a step and sits down, gracefully and demurely as if she were settling into a swing on a Mississippi veranda.*] What are you looking at?

TOM. The moon.

AMANDA. Is there a moon this evening?

TOM. It's rising over Garfinkel's Delicatessen.

AMANDA. So it is! A little silver slipper of a moon. Have you made a wish on it yet?

TOM. Um-hum.

AMANDA. What did you wish for?

TOM. That's a secret.

AMANDA. A secret, huh? Well, I won't tell mine either. I will be just as mysterious as you.

TOM. I bet I can guess what yours is.

AMANDA. Is my head so transparent?

---

[2] Chamberlain was the Prime Minister of Great Britain from 1937 to 1940. He met with Hitler at Berchtesgaden, Germany, trying to avoid World War II.

TOM. You're not a sphinx.

AMANDA. No, I don't have secrets. I'll tell you what I wished for on the moon. Success and happiness for my precious children! I wish for that whenever there's a moon, and when there isn't a moon, I wish for it, too.

TOM. I thought perhaps you wished for a gentleman caller.

AMANDA. Why do you say that?

TOM. Don't you remember asking me to fetch one?

AMANDA. I remember suggesting that it would be nice for your sister if you brought home some nice young man from the warehouse. I think that I've made that suggestion more than once.

TOM. Yes, you have made it repeatedly.

AMANDA. Well?

TOM. We are going to have one.

AMANDA. *What?*

TOM. A gentleman caller! [*The annunciation is celebrated with music.*] [AMANDA *rises.*] [*Image on screen:* A caller with a bouquet.]

AMANDA. You mean you have asked some nice young man to come over?

TOM. Yep. I've asked him to dinner.

AMANDA. You really did?

TOM. I did!

AMANDA. You did, and did he—*accept?*

TOM. He did!

AMANDA. Well, well—well, well! That's—lovely!

TOM. I thought that you would be pleased.

AMANDA. It's definite then?

TOM. Very definite.

AMANDA. Soon?

TOM. Very soon.

AMANDA. For heaven's sake, stop putting on and tell me some things, will you?

TOM. What things do you want me to tell you?

AMANDA. *Naturally* I would like to know when he's *coming!*

TOM. He's coming tomorrow.

AMANDA. *Tomorrow?*

TOM. Yep. Tomorrow.

AMANDA. But, Tom!

TOM. Yes, Mother?

AMANDA. Tomorrow gives me no time!

TOM. Time for what?

AMANDA. Preparations! Why didn't you phone me at once, as soon as you asked him, the minute that he accepted? Then, don't you see, I could have been getting ready!

TOM. You don't have to make any fuss.

AMANDA. Oh, Tom, Tom, Tom, of course I have to make a fuss! I want things nice, not sloppy! Not thrown together, I'll certainly have to do some fast thinking, won't I?

TOM. I don't see why you have to think at all.

AMANDA. You just don't know. We can't have a gentleman caller in a pigsty! All my wedding silver has to be polished, the monogrammed table linen

ought to be laundered! The windows have to be washed and fresh curtains put up. And how about clothes? We have to *wear* something, don't
we?

TOM. Mother, this boy is no one to make a fuss over!

AMANDA. Do you realize he's the first young man we've introduced to
your sister? It's terrible, dreadful, disgraceful that poor little sister has
never received a single gentleman caller! Tom, come inside! [*She opens
the screen door.*]

TOM. What for?

AMANDA. I want to ask you some things.

TOM. If you're going to make such a fuss, I'll call it off, I'll tell him not
to come!

AMANDA. You certainly won't do anything of the kind. Nothing offends
people worse than broken engagements. It simply means I'll have to
work like a Turk! We won't be brilliant, but we will pass inspection.
Come on inside. [TOM *follows her inside, groaning.*] Sit down.

TOM. Any particular place you would like me to sit?

AMANDA. Thank heavens I've got that new sofa! I'm also making payments
on a floor lamp I'll have sent out! And put the chintz covers on, they'll
brighten things up! Of course I'd hoped to have these walls re-papered.
. . . What is the young man's name?

TOM. His name is O'Connor.

AMANDA. That, of course, means fish—tomorrow is Friday! I'll have that
salmon loaf—with Durkee's dressing! What does he do? He works at
the warehouse?

TOM. Of course! How else would I—

AMANDA. Tom, he—doesn't drink?

TOM. Why do you ask me that?

AMANDA. Your father *did!*

TOM. Don't get started on that!

AMANDA. He *does* drink, then?

TOM. Not that I know of!

AMANDA. Make sure, be certain! The last thing I want for my daughter's
a boy who drinks!

TOM. Aren't you being a little bit premature? Mr. O'Connor has not yet
appeared on the scene!

AMANDA. But will tomorrow. To meet your sister, and what do I know
about his character? Nothing! Old maids are better off than wives of
drunkards!

TOM. Oh, my God!

AMANDA. Be still!

TOM [*leaning forward to whisper*]. Lots of fellows meet girls whom they
don't marry!

AMANDA. Oh, talk sensibly, Tom—and don't be sarcastic! [*She has gotten a
hairbrush.*]

TOM. What are you doing?

AMANDA. I'm brushing that cowlick down! [*She attacks his hair with the brush.*]
What is this young man's position at the warehouse?

TOM [*submitting grimly to the brush and the interrogation*]. This young man's
position is that of a shipping clerk, Mother.

AMANDA. Sounds to me like a fairly responsible job, the sort of a job *you* would be in if you just had more *get-up.* What is his salary? Have you any idea?

TOM. I would judge it to be approximately eighty-five dollars a month.

AMANDA. Well—not princely, but—

TOM. Twenty more than I make.

AMANDA. Yes, how well I know! But for a family man, eighty-five dollars a month is not much more than you can just get by on. . . .

TOM. Yes, but Mr. O'Connor is not a family man.

AMANDA. He might be, mightn't he? Some time in the future?

TOM. I see. Plans and provisions.

AMANDA. You are the only young man that I know of who ignores the fact that the future becomes the present, the present the past, and the past turns into everlasting regret if you don't plan for it!

TOM. I will think that over and see what I can make of it.

AMANDA. Don't be supercilious with your mother! Tell me some more about this—what do you call him?

TOM. James D. O'Connor. The D. is for Delaney.

AMANDA. Irish on *both* sides! *Gracious!* And doesn't drink?

TOM. Shall I call him up and ask him right this minute?

AMANDA. The only way to find out about those things is to make discreet inquiries at the proper moment. When I was a girl in Blue Mountain and it was suspected that a young man drank, the girl whose attentions he had been receiving, if any girl *was,* would sometimes speak to the minister of his church, or rather her father would if her father was living, and sort of feel him out on the young man's character. That is the way such things are discreetly handled to keep a young woman from making a tragic mistake!

TOM. Then how did you happen to make a tragic mistake?

AMANDA. That innocent look of your father's had everyone fooled! He *smiled*—the world was *enchanted!* No girl can do worse than put herself at the mercy of a handsome appearance! I hope that Mr. O'Connor is not too good-looking.

TOM. No, he's not too good-looking. He's covered with freckles and hasn't too much of a nose.

AMANDA. He's not right-down homely, though?

TOM. Not right-down homely. Just medium homely, I'd say.

AMANDA. Character's what to look for in a man.

TOM. That's what I've always said, Mother.

AMANDA. You've never said anything of the kind and I suspect you would never give it a thought.

TOM. Don't be so suspicious of me.

AMANDA. At least I hope he's the type that's up and coming.

TOM. I think he really goes in for self-improvement.

AMANDA. What reason have you to think so?

TOM. He goes to night school.

AMANDA [*beaming*]. Splendid! What does he do, I mean study?

TOM. Radio engineering and public speaking!

AMANDA. Then he has visions of being advanced in the world! Any young man who studies public speaking is aiming to have an executive job

some day! And radio engineering? A thing for the future! Both of these
facts are very illuminating. Those are the sort of things that a mother
should know concerning any young man who comes to call on her
daughter. Seriously or—not.

TOM. One little warning. He doesn't know about Laura. I didn't let on
that we had dark ulterior motives. I just said, why don't you come
and have dinner with us? He said okay and that was the whole conversation.

AMANDA. I bet it was! You're eloquent as an oyster. However, he'll
know about Laura when he gets here. When he sees how lovely and
sweet and pretty she is, he'll thank his lucky stars he was asked to
dinner.

TOM. Mother, you mustn't expect too much of Laura.

AMANDA. What do you mean?

TOM. Laura seems all those things to you and me because she's ours and
we love her. We don't even notice she's crippled any more.

AMANDA. Don't say crippled! You know that I never allow that word to
be used!

TOM. But face facts, Mother. She is and—that's not all—

AMANDA. What do you mean "not all"?

TOM. Laura is very different from other girls.

AMANDA. I think the difference is all to her advantage.

TOM. Not quite all—in the eyes of others—strangers—she's terribly shy
and lives in a world of her own and those things make her seem a
little peculiar to people outside the house.

AMANDA. Don't say peculiar.

TOM. Face the facts. She is. [*The dance hall music changes to a tango that has
a minor and somewhat ominous tone.*]

AMANDA. In what way is she peculiar—may I ask?

TOM [*gently*]. She lives in a world of her own—a world of little glass ornaments, Mother. . . . [*He gets up.* AMANDA *remains holding the brush, looking
at him, troubled.*] She plays old phonograph records and—that's about
all— [*He glances at himself in the mirror and crosses to the door.*]

AMANDA [*sharply*]. Where are you going?

TOM. I'm going to the movies. [*He goes out the screen door.*]

AMANDA. Not to the movies, every night to the movies! [*She follows quickly
to the screen door.*] I don't believe you always go to the movies! [*He is
gone.* AMANDA *looks worriedly after him for a moment. Then vitality and
optimism return and she turns from the door, crossing to the portieres.*] Laura!
Laura! [LAURA *answers from the kitchenette.*]

LAURA. Yes, Mother.

AMANDA. Let those dishes go and come in front! [LAURA *appears with a
dish towel.* AMANDA *speaks to her gaily.*] Laura, come here and make a
wish on the moon! [*Screen image: The Moon.*]

LAURA [*entering*]. Moon—moon?

AMANDA. A little silver slipper of a moon. Look over your left shoulder,
Laura, and make a wish! [LAURA *looks faintly puzzled as if called out of
sleep.* AMANDA *seizes her shoulders and turns her at an angle by the door.*]
Now! Now, darling, *wish!*

LAURA. What shall I wish for, Mother?

AMANDA [*her voice trembling and her eyes suddenly filling with tears*]. Happiness! Good fortune! [*The sound of the violin rises and the stage dims out.*]

SCENE VI

The light comes up on the fire escape landing. TOM *is leaning against the grill, smoking.* [*Screen image:* The high school hero.]

TOM. And so the following evening I brought Jim home to dinner. I had known Jim slightly in high school. In high school Jim was a hero. He had tremendous Irish good nature and vitality with the scrubbed and polished look of white chinaware. He seemed to move in a continual spotlight. He was a star in basketball, captain of the debating club, president of the senior class and the glee club and he sang the male lead in the annual light operas. He was always running or bounding, never just walking. He seemed always at the point of defeating the law of gravity. He was shooting with such velocity through his adolescence that you would logically expect him to arrive at nothing short of the White House by the time he was thirty. But Jim apparently ran into more interference after his graduation from Soldan. His speed had definitely slowed. Six years after he left high school he was holding a job that wasn't much better than mine. [*Screen image:* The Clerk.] He was the only one at the warehouse with whom I was on friendly terms. I was valuable to him as someone who could remember his former glory, who had seen him win basketball games and the silver cup in debating. He knew of my secret practice of retiring to a cabinet of the washroom to work on poems when business was slack in the warehouse. He called me Shakespeare. And while the other boys in the warehouse regarded me with suspicious hostility, Jim took a humorous attitude toward me. Gradually his attitude affected the others, their hostility wore off and they also began to smile at me as people smile at an oddly fashioned dog who trots across their path at some distance. I knew that Jim and Laura had known each other at Soldan, and I had heard Laura speak admiringly of his voice. I didn't know if Jim remembered her or not. In high school Laura had been as unobtrusive as Jim had been astonishing. If he did remember Laura, it was not as my sister, for when I asked him to dinner, he grinned and said, "You know, Shakespeare, I never thought of you as having folks!" He was about to discover that I did. . . . [*Legend on screen:* "The accent of a coming foot."] [*The light dims out on* TOM *and comes up in the Wingfield living room—a delicate lemony light. It is about five on a Friday evening of late spring which comes "scattering poems in the sky."*] [AMANDA *has worked like a turk in preparation for the gentleman caller. The results are astonishing. The new floor lamp with its rose silk shade is in place, a colored paper lantern conceals the broken light fixture in the ceiling, new billowing white curtains are at the windows, chintz covers are on the chairs and sofa, a pair of new sofa pillows make their initial appearance. Open boxes and tissue paper are scattered on the floor.*] [LAURA *stands in the middle of the room with lifted arms while* AMANDA *crouches before her adjusting the hem of a new dress, devout and ritualistic. The dress is colored and designed by memory. The arrangement of* LAURA's *hair is changed; it is softer and more becoming. A fragile, unearthly prettiness has come out in* LAURA: *she is like a piece of translucent glass touched by light, given a momentary radiance, not actual, not lasting.*]

AMANDA [*impatiently*]. Why are you trembling?

LAURA. Mother, you've made me so nervous!

AMANDA. How have I made you nervous?

LAURA. By all the fuss! You make it seem so important!

AMANDA. I don't understand you, Laura. You couldn't be satisfied with just sitting home, and yet whenever I try to arrange something for you, you seem to resist it. [*She gets up.*] Now take a look at yourself. No, wait! Wait just a moment—I have an idea!

LAURA. What is it now? [AMANDA *produces two powder puffs which she wraps in handkerchiefs and stuffs in* LAURA's *bosom.*]

LAURA. Mother, what are you doing?

AMANDA. They call them "Gay Deceivers"!

LAURA. I won't wear them!

AMANDA. You will!

LAURA. Why should I?

AMANDA. Because, to be painfully honest, your chest is flat.

LAURA. You make it seem like we were setting a trap.

AMANDA. All pretty girls are a trap, a pretty trap, and men expect them to be. [*Legend on screen: "A pretty trap."*] Now look at yourself, young lady. This is the prettiest you will ever be! [*She stands back to admire* LAURA.] I've got to fix myself now! You're going to be surprised by your mother's appearance! [AMANDA *crosses through the portieres, humming gaily.* LAURA *moves slowly to the long mirror and stares solemnly at herself. A wind blows the white curtains inward in a slow, graceful motion and with a faint, sorrowful sighing.*]

AMANDA [*from somewhere behind the portieres*]: It isn't dark enough yet. [LAURA *turns slowly before the mirror with a troubled look.*] [*Legend on screen:* "This is my sister: Celebrate her with strings!" *Music plays.*]

AMANDA [*laughing, still not visible*]. I'm going to show you something. I'm going to make a spectacular appearance!

LAURA. What is it, Mother?

AMANDA. Possess your soul in patience—you will see! Something I've resurrected from that old trunk! Styles haven't changed so terribly much after all. . . . [*She parts the portieres.*] Now just look at your mother! [*She wears a girlish frock of yellowed voile with a blue silk sash. She carries a bunch of jonquils—the legend of her youth is nearly revived. Now she speaks feverishly:*] This is the dress in which I led the cotillion. Won the cakewalk twice at Sunset Hill, wore one Spring to the Governor's Ball in Jackson! See how I sashayed around the ballroom, Laura? [*She raises her skirt and does a mincing step around the room.*] I wore it on Sundays for my gentlemen callers! I had it on the day I met your father. . . . I had malaria fever all that Spring. The change of climate from East Tennessee to the Delta— weakened resistance. I had a little temperature all the time—not enough to be serious—just enough to make me restless and giddy! Invitations poured in—parties all over the Delta! "Stay in bed," said Mother, "you have a fever!"—but I just wouldn't. I took quinine but kept on going, going! Evenings, dances! Afternoons, long, long rides! Picnics—lovely! So lovely, that country in May—all lacy with dogwood, literally flooded with jonquils! That was the spring I had the craze for jonquils. Jonquils became an absolute obsession. Mother said, "Honey, there's no more room for jonquils." And still I kept on bringing in more jonquils. Whenever, wherever I saw them, I'd say, "Stop! Stop! I see jonquils!" I made the young men help me gather the jonquils! It was a joke, Amanda and her jonquils. Finally there were no more vases to hold them, every available space was filled with jonquils. No vases to hold them? All right, I'll hold them myself! And then I—[*She stops in front of the picture. Music plays.*] met your father! Malaria fever and jonquils and then—this—boy. . . . [*She switches on the rose-colored lamp.*] I hope they get here before it starts to rain. [*She crosses the room and places the jonquils in a bowl on the table.*] I gave your brother a little extra change so he and Mr. O'Connor could take the service car home.

LAURA [*with an altered look*]. What did you say his name was?

AMANDA. O'Connor.

LAURA. What is his first name?

AMANDA. I don't remember. Oh, yes, I do. It was—Jim! [LAURA *sways slightly and catches hold of a chair.*] [*Legend on screen:* "Not Jim!"]

LAURA [*faintly*]. Not—Jim!

AMANDA. Yes, that was it, it was Jim! I've never known a Jim that wasn't nice! [*The music becomes ominous.*]

LAURA. Are you sure his name is Jim O'Connor?

AMANDA. Yes. Why?

LAURA. Is he the one that Tom used to know in high school?

AMANDA. He didn't say so. I think he just got to know him at the warehouse.

LAURA. There was a Jim O'Connor we both knew in high school—[*then, with effort*] If that is the one that Tom is bringing to dinner—you'll have to excuse me, I won't come to the table.

AMANDA. What sort of nonsense is this?

LAURA. You asked me once if I'd ever liked a boy. Don't you remember I showed you this boy's picture?

AMANDA. You mean the boy you showed me in the yearbook?

LAURA. Yes, that boy.

AMANDA. Laura, Laura, were you in love with that boy?

LAURA. I don't know, Mother. All I know is I couldn't sit at the table if it was him!

AMANDA. It won't be him! It isn't the least bit likely. But whether it is or not, you will come to the table. You will not be excused.

LAURA. I'll have to be, Mother.

AMANDA. I don't intend to humor your silliness, Laura. I've had too much from you and your brother, both! So just sit down and compose yourself till they come. Tom has forgotten his key so you'll have to let them in, when they arrive.

LAURA [*panicky*]. Oh, Mother—*you* answer the door!

AMANDA [*lightly*]. I'll be in the kitchen—busy!

LAURA. Oh, Mother, please answer the door, don't make me do it.!

AMANDA [*crossing into the kitchenette*]. I've got to fix the dressing for the salmon. Fuss, fuss—silliness!—over a gentleman caller! [*The door swings shut.* LAURA *is left alone.*] [*Legend on screen:* "Terror!"] [*She utters a low moan and turns off the lamp—sits stiffly on the edge of the sofa, knotting her fingers together.*] [*Legend on screen:* "The Opening of a Door!"] [TOM *and* JIM *appear on the fire escape steps and climb to the landing. Hearing their approach,* LAURA *rises with a panicky gesture. She retreats to the portieres. The doorbell.* LAURA *catches her breath and touches her throat. Low drums sound.*]

AMANDA [*calling*]. Laura, sweetheart! The door! [LAURA *stares at it without moving.*]

JIM. I think we just beat the rain.

TOM. Uh-huh. [*He rings again, nervously.* JIM *whistles and fishes for a cigarette.*]

AMANDA [*very, very gaily*]. Laura, that is your brother and Mr. O'Connor! Will you let them in, darling? [LAURA *crosses toward the kitchenette door.*]

LAURA [*breathlessly*]. Mother—you go to the door! [AMANDA *steps out of the kitchenette and stares furiously at* LAURA. *She points imperiously at the door.*]

LAURA. Please, please!

AMANDA [*in a fierce whisper*]. What is the matter with you, you silly thing?

LAURA [*desperately*]. Please, you answer it, *please!*

AMANDA. I told you I wasn't going to humor you, Laura. Why have you chosen this moment to lose your mind?

LAURA. Please, please, you go!

AMANDA. You'll have to go to the door because I can't!

LAURA [*despairingly*]. I can't either!

AMANDA. *Why?*

LAURA. I'm *sick!*

AMANDA. I'm sick, too—of your nonsense! Why can't you and your brother be normal people? Fantastic whims and behavior! [TOM *gives a long ring.*] Preposterous goings on! Can you give me one reason—[*She calls out lyrically.*] *Coming! Just one second!*—why you should be afraid to open a door? Now you answer it, Laura!

LAURA. Oh, oh, oh . . . [*She returns through the portieres, darts to the Victrola, winds it frantically and turns it on.*]

AMANDA. Laura Wingfield, you march right to that door!

LAURA. *Yes*—yes, Mother! [*A faraway, scratchy rendition of "Dardanella" softens the air and gives her strength to move through it. She slips to the door and draws it cautiously open.* TOM *enters with the caller,* JIM O'CONNOR.]

TOM. Laura, this is Jim. Jim, this is my sister, Laura.

JIM [*stepping inside*]. I didn't know that Shakespeare had a sister!

LAURA [*retreating, stiff and trembling, from the door*]. How—how do you do?

JIM [*heartily, extending his hand*]. Okay! [LAURA *touches it hesitantly with hers.*] Your hand's *cold*, Laura!

LAURA. Yes, well—I've been playing the Victrola. . . .

JIM. Must have been playing classical music on it! You ought to play a little hot swing music to warm you up!

LAURA. Excuse me—I haven't finis⌐ ⌐d playing the Victrola. . . . [*She turns awkwardly and hurries into the fro   room. She pauses a second by the Victrola. Then she catches her breath and ⌐. ts through the portieres like a frightened deer.*]

JIM [*grinning*]. What was the matter?

TOM. Oh—with Laura? Laura is—terribly shy.

JIM. Shy, huh? It's unusual to meet a shy girl nowadays. I don't believe you ever mentioned you had a sister.

Tom. Well, now you know. I have one. Here is the *Post Dispatch*. You want a piece of it?

Jim. Uh-huh.

Tom. What piece? The comics?

Jim. Sports! [*He glances at it.*] Ole Dizzy Dean is on his bad behavior.

Tom [*uninterested*]. Yeah? [*He lights a cigarette and goes over to the fire-escape door.*]

Jim. Where are *you* going?

Tom. I'm going out on the terrace.

Jim [*going after him*]. You know, Shakespeare—I'm going to sell you a bill of goods!

Tom. What goods?

Jim. A course I'm taking.

Tom. Huh?

Jim. In public speaking! You and me, we're not the warehouse type.

Tom. Thanks—that's good news. But what has public speaking got to do with it?

Jim. It fits you for—executive positions!

Tom. Awww.

Jim. I tell you it's done a helluva lot for me. [*Image on screen:* Executive at his desk.]

Tom. In what respect?

Jim. In every! Ask yourself what is the difference between you an' me and men in the office down front? Brains?—No!—Ability?—No! Then what? Just one little thing—

Tom. What is that one little thing?

Jim. Primarily it amounts to—social poise! Being able to square up to people and hold your own on any social level!

Amanda [*from the kitchenette*]. Tom?

Tom. Yes, Mother?

Amanda. Is that you and Mr, O'Connor?

Tom. Yes, Mother.

Amanda. Well, you just make yourselves comfortable in there.

Tom. Yes, Mother.

Amanda. Ask Mr. O'Connor if he would like to wash his hands.

Jim. Aw, no—no—thank you—I took care of that at the warehouse. Tom—

Tom. Yes?

Jim. Mr. Mendoza was speaking to me about you.

Tom. Favorably?

Jim. What do you think?

Tom. Well—

Jim. You're going to be out of a job if you don't wake up.

Tom. I am waking up—

Jim. You show no signs.

Tom. The signs are interior. [*Image on screen:* The sailing vessel with the Jolly Roger again.]

Tom. I'm planning to change. [*He leans over the fire-escape rail, speaking with quiet exhilaration. The incandescent marquees and signs of the first-run movie houses light his face from across the alley. He looks like a voyager.*] I'm right at the point of commiting myself to a future that doesn't include the warehouse and Mr. Mendoza or even a night-school course in public speaking.

JIM. What are you gassing about?

TOM. I'm tired of the movies.

JIM. Movies!

TOM. Yes, movies! Look at them—[*a wave toward the marvels of Grand Avenue*] All of those glamorous people—having adventures—hogging it all, gobbling the whole thing up! You know what happens? People go to the *movies* instead of *moving!* Hollywood characters are supposed to have all the adventures for everybody in America, while everybody in America sits in a dark room and watches them have them! Yes, until there's a war. That's when adventure becomes available to the masses! *Everyone's* dish, not only Gable's! Then the people in the dark room come out of the dark room to have some adventures themselves—goody, goody! It's our turn now, to go to the South Sea Island—to make a safari—to be exotic, far-off! But I'm not patient. I don't want to wait till then. I'm tired of the *movies* and I am *about* to *move!*

JIM [*incredulously*]. Move?

TOM. Yes.

JIM. When?

TOM. Soon!

JIM. Where? Where? [*The music seems to answer the question, while* TOM *thinks it over. He searches in his pockets.*]

TOM. I'm starting to boil inside. I know I seem dreamy, but inside—well, I'm boiling! Whenever I pick up a shoe, I shudder a little thinking how short life is and what I am doing! Whatever that means, I know it doesn't mean shoes—except as something to wear on a traveler's feet! [*He finds what he has been searching for in his pockets and holds out a paper to Jim.*] Look—

JIM. What?

TOM. I'm a member.

JIM [*reading*]. The Union of Merchant Seamen.

TOM. I paid my dues this month, instead of the light bill.

JIM. You will regret it when they turn the lights off.

TOM. I won't be here.

JIM. How about your mother?

TOM. I'm like my father. The bastard son of a bastard! Did you notice how he's grinning in his picture in there? And he's been absent going on sixteen years!

JIM. You're just talking, you drip. How does your mother feel about it?

TOM. Shhh! Here comes Mother! Mother is not acquainted with my plans!

AMANDA [*coming through the portieres*]. Where are you all?

TOM. On the terrace, Mother. [*They start inside. She advances to them.* TOM *is distinctly shocked at her appearance. Even* JIM *blinks a little. He is making his first contact with girlish Southern vivacity and in spite of the night-school course in public speaking is somewhat thrown off the beam by the unexpected outlay of social charm. Certain responses are attempted by* JIM *but are swept aside by* AMANDA's *gay laughter and chatter.* TOM *is embarrassed but after the first shock* JIM *reacts very warmly. He grins and chuckles, is altogether won over.*] [*Image on screen:* Amanda as a girl.]

AMANDA [*coyly smiling, shaking her girlish ringlets*]. Well, well, well, so this
is Mr. O'Connor. Introductions entirely unnecessary. I've heard so much
about you from my boy. I finally said to him, Tom—good gracious!—
why don't you bring this paragon to supper? I'd like to meet this nice
young man at the warehouse!—instead of just hearing him sing your
praises so much! I don't know why my son is so stand-offish—that's
not Southern behavior! Let's sit down and—I think we could stand a
little more air in here! Tom, leave the door open. I felt a nice fresh
breeze a moment ago. Where has it gone to? Mmm, so warm already!
And not quite summer, even. We're going to burn up when summer
really gets started. However, we're having—we're having a very light
supper. I think light things are better fo' this time of year. The same
as light clothes are. Light clothes an' light food are what warm weather
calls fo'. You know our blood gets so thick during th' winter—it takes
a while fo' us to *adjust* ou'selves—when the season changes . . . . It's
come so quick this year. I wasn't prepared. All of a sudden—heavens!
Already summer! I ran to the trunk an' pulled out this light dress—
terribly old! Historical almost! But feels so good—so good an' co-ol, y'
know. . . .

TOM. Mother—

AMANDA. Yes, honey?

TOM. How about—supper?

AMANDA. Honey, you go ask Sister if supper is ready! You know that Sister
is in full charge of supper! Tell her you hungry boys are waiting for
it. [*to* JIM] Have you met Laura?

JIM. She—

AMANDA. Let you in? Oh, good, you've met already! It's rare for a girl as
sweet an' pretty as Laura to be domestic! But Laura is, thank heavens,
not only pretty but also very domestic. I'm not at all. I never was a
bit. I never could make a thing but angel-food cake. Well, in the South
we had so many servants. Gone, gone, gone. All vestiges of gracious
living! Gone completely! I wasn't prepared for what the future brought
me. All of my gentlemen callers were sons of planters and so of course
I assumed that I would be married to one and raise my family on a
large piece of land with plenty of servants. But man proposes—and
woman accepts the proposal! To vary that old, old saying a little bit—
I married no planter! I married a man who worked for the telephone
company! That gallantly smiling gentleman over there! [*She points to
the picture.*] A telephone man who—fell in love with long-distance! Now
he travels and I don't even know where! But what am I going on for
about my—tribulations? Tell me yours—I hope you don't have any!
Tom?

TOM [*returning*]. Yes, Mother?

AMANDA. Is supper nearly ready?

TOM. It looks to me like supper is on the table.

AMANDA. Let me look—[*She rises prettily and looks through the portieres.*] Oh,
lovely! But where is Sister?

TOM. Laura is not feeling well and she says that she thinks she'd better
not come to the table.

AMANDA. What? Nonsense! Laura? Oh, Laura!

LAURA [*from the kitchenette, faintly*]. Yes, Mother.

AMANDA. You really must come to the table. We won't be seated until you come to the table! Come in, Mr. O'Connor. You sit over there, and I'll. . . . Laura? Laura Wingfield! You're keeping us waiting, honey! We can't say grace until you come to the table! [*The kitchenette door is pushed weakly open and* LAURA *comes in. She is obviously quite faint, her lips trembling, her eyes wide and staring. She moves unsteadily toward the table.*] [*Screen legend:* "Terror!"] [*Outside a summer storm is coming on abruptly. The white curtains billow inward at the windows and there is a sorrowful murmur from the deep blue dusk.*] [LAURA *suddenly stumbles; she catches at a chair with a faint moan.*]

TOM. Laura!

AMANDA. Laura! [*There is a clap of thunder.*] [*Screen legend:* "Ah!"] [*despairingly*] Why, Laura, you *are* ill, darling! Tom, help your sister into the living room, dear! Sit in the living room, Laura—rest on the sofa. Well! [*to* JIM *as* TOM *helps his sister to the sofa in the living room*] Standing over the hot stove made her ill! I told her it was just too warm this evening, but—[TOM *comes back to the table.*] Is Laura all right now?

TOM. Yes.

AMANDA. What *is* that? Rain? A cool rain has come up! [*She gives* JIM *a frightened look.*] I think we may—have grace—now . . . [TOM *looks at her stupidly.*] Tom, honey—you say grace!

TOM. Oh . . . "For these and all thy mercies—" [*They bow their heads,* AMANDA *stealing a nervous glance at* JIM. *In the living room* LAURA, *stretched on the sofa, clenches her hand to her lips, to hold back a shuddering sob.*] "God's Holy Name be praised—" (*The scene dims out.*]

SCENE VII

It is half an hour later. Dinner is just being finished in the dining room, LAURA *is still huddled upon the sofa, her feet drawn under her, her head resting on a pale blue pillow, her eyes wide and mysteriously watchful. The new floor lamp with its shade of rose-colored silk gives a soft, becoming light to her face, bringing out the fragile, unearthly prettiness which usually escapes attention. From outside there is a steady murmur of rain, but it is slackening and soon stops; the air outside becomes pale and luminous as the moon breaks through the clouds. A moment after the curtain rises, the lights in both rooms flicker and go out.*

JIM. Hey, there, Mr. Light Bulb! [AMANDA *laughs nervously.*] [*Legend on screen:* "Suspension of public service."]

AMANDA. Where was Moses when the lights went out? Ha-ha. Do you know the answer to that one, Mr. O'Connor?

JIM. No, Ma'am, what's the answer?

AMANDA. In the dark! [JIM *laughs appreciatively.*] Everybody sit still. I'll light the candles. Isn't it lucky we have them on the table? Where's a match? Which of you gentlemen can provide a match?

JIM. Here.

AMANDA. Thank you, Sir.

JIM. Not at all, Ma'am!

AMANDA [*as she lights the candles*]. I guess the fuse has burnt out. Mr. O'Connor, can you tell a burnt-out fuse? I know I can't and Tom is a total loss when it comes to mechanics. [*They rise from the table and go into the kitchenette, from where their voices are heard.*] Oh, be careful you don't bump into something. We don't want our gentleman caller to break his neck. Now wouldn't that be a fine howdy-do?

JIM. Ha-ha! Where is the fuse-box?

AMANDA. Right here next to the stove. Can you see anything?

JIM. Just a minute.

AMANDA. Isn't electricity a mysterious thing? Wasn't it Benjamin Franklin who tied a key to a kite? We live in such a mysterious universe, don't we? Some people say that science clears up all the mysteries for us. In my opinion it only creates more! Have you found it yet?

JIM. No, Ma'am. All these fuses look okay to me.

AMANDA. Tom!

TOM. Yes, Mother?

AMANDA. That light bill I gave you several days ago. The one I told you we got the notices about? [*Legend on screen:* "Ha!"]

TOM. Oh—yeah.

AMANDA. You didn't neglect to pay it by any chance?

TOM. Why I—

AMANDA. Didn't! I might have known it!

JIM. Shakespeare probably wrote a poem on that light bill, Mrs. Wingfield.

AMANDA. I might have known better than to trust him with it! There's such a high price for negligence in this world!

JIM. Maybe the poem will win a ten-dollar prize.

AMANDA. We'll just have to spend the remainder of the evening in the nineteenth century, before Mr. Edison made the Mazda lamp!

JIM. Candlelight is my favorite kind of light.

AMANDA. That shows you're romantic! But that's no excuse for Tom. Well, we got through dinner. Very considerate of them to let us get through dinner before they plunged us into everlasting darkness, wasn't it, Mr. O'Connor?

JIM. Ha-ha!

AMANDA. Tom, as a penalty for your carelessness you can help me with the dishes.

JIM. Let me give you a hand.

AMANDA. Indeed you will not!

JIM. I ought to be good for something.

AMANDA. Good for something? [*Her tone is rhapsodic.*] You? Why, Mr. O'Connor, nobody, *nobody's* given me this much entertainment in years—as you have!

JIM. Aw, now, Mrs. Wingfield!

AMANDA. I'm not exaggerating, not one bit! But Sister is all by her lonesome. You go keep her company in the parlor! I'll give you this lovely old candelabrum that used to be on the altar at the church of the Heavenly Rest. It was melted a little out of shape when the church burnt down. Lightning struck it one spring. Gypsy Jones was holding a revival at the time and he intimated that the church was destroyed because the Episcopalians gave card parties.

JIM. Ha-ha.

AMANDA. And how about you coaxing Sister to drink a little wine? I think
it would be good for her! Can you carry both at once?

JIM. Sure. I'm Superman!

AMANDA. Now, Thomas, get into this apron! [JIM *comes into the dining room,
carrying the candelabrum, its candles lighted, in one hand and a glass of wine
in the other. The door of the kitchenette swings closed on* AMANDA's *gay laughter;
the flickering light approaches the portieres.* LAURA *sits up nervously as* JIM
*enters. She can hardly speak from the almost intolerable strain of being alone
with a stranger.*] [*Screen legend:* "I don't suppose you remember me at
all!"] [*At first, before* JIM's *warmth overcomes her paralyzing shyness,* LAURA's
*voice is thin and breathless, as though she had just run up a steep flight of
stairs.* JIM's *attitude is gently humorous. While the incident is apparently unimportant, it is to* LAURA *the climax of her secret life.*]

JIM. Hello there, Laura.

LAURA [*faintly*]. Hello. [*She clears her throat.*]

JIM. How are you feeling now? Better?

LAURA. Yes. Yes, thank you.

JIM. This is for you. A little dandelion wine. [*He extends the glass toward
her with extravagant gallantry.*]

LAURA. Thank you.

JIM. Drink it—but don't get drunk! [*He laughs heartily.* LAURA *takes the glass
uncertainly; she laughs shyly.*] Where shall I set the candles?

LAURA. Oh—oh, anywhere . . .

JIM. How about here on the floor? Any objections?

LAURA. No.

JIM. I'll spread a newspaper under to catch the drippings. I like to sit on
the floor. Mind if I do?

LAURA. Oh, no.

JIM. Give me a pillow?

LAURA. What?

JIM. A pillow!

LAURA. Oh . . . [*She hands him one quickly.*]

JIM. How about you? Don't you like to sit on the floor?

LAURA. Oh—yes.

JIM. Why don't you, then?

LAURA. I—will.

JIM. Take a pillow! [LAURA *does. She sits on the floor on the other side of the
candelabrum.* JIM *crosses his legs and smiles engagingly at her.*] I can't hardly
see you sitting way over there.

LAURA. I can—see you.

JIM. I know, but that's not fair, I'm in the limelight. [LAURA *moves her
pillow closer.*] Good! Now I can see you! Comfortable?

LAURA. Yes.

JIM. So am I. Comfortable as a cow! Will you have some gum?

LAURA. No, thank you.

JIM. I think that I will indulge, with your permission. [*He musingly unwraps
a stick of gum and holds it up.*] Think of the fortune made by the guy
that invented the first piece of chewing gum. Amazing, huh? The Wrig-
ley Building is one of the sights of Chicago—I saw it when I went up

to the Century of Progress. Did you take in the Century of Progress?

LAURA. No, I didn't.

JIM. Well, it was quite a wonderful exposition. What impressed me most was the Hall of Science. Gives you an idea of what the future will be in America, even more wonderful than the present time is! [*There is a pause.* JIM *smiles at her.*] Your brother tells me you're shy. Is that right, Laura?

LAURA. I—don't know.

JIM. I judge you to be an old-fashioned type of girl. Well, I think that's a pretty good type to be. Hope you don't think I'm being too personal— do you?

LAURA [*hastily, out of embarrassment*]. I believe I *will* take a piece of gum, if you—don't mind. [*clearing her throat*] Mr. O'Connor, have you—kept up with your singing?

JIM. Singing? Me?

LAURA. Yes. I remember what a beautiful voice you had.

JIM. When did you hear me sing? [LAURA *does not answer, and in the long pause which follows a man's voice is heard singing offstage.*]

> VOICE:
> O blow, ye winds, heigh-ho,
> A-roving I will go!
> I'm off to my love
> With a boxing glove—
> Ten thousand miles away!

JIM. You say you've heard me sing?

LAURA. Oh, yes! Yes, very often . . . I—don't suppose—you remember me—at all?

JIM [*smiling doubtfully*]. You know I have an idea I've seen you before. I had that idea as soon as you opened the door. It seemed almost like I was about to remember your name. But the name that I started to call you—wasn't a name! And so I stopped myself before I said it.

LAURA. Wasn't it—Blue Roses?

JIM [*springing up, grinning*]. Blue Roses! My gosh, yes—Blue Roses! That's what I had on my tongue when you opened the door! Isn't it funny what tricks your memory plays? I didn't connect you with high school somehow or other. But that's where it was; it was high school. I didn't even know you were Shakespeare's sister! Gosh, I'm sorry.

LAURA. I didn't expect you to. You—barely knew me!

JIM. But we did have a speaking acquaintance, huh?

LAURA. Yes, we—spoke to each other.

JIM. When did you recognize me?

LAURA. Oh, right away!

JIM. Soon as I came in the door?

LAURA. When I heard your name I thought it was probably you. I knew that Tom used to know you a little in high school. So when you came in the door—well, then I was—sure.

JIM. Why didn't you *say* something, then?

LAURA [*breathlessly*]. I didn't know what to say, I was—too surprised!

JIM. For goodness sakes! You know, this sure is funny!

LAURA. Yes! Yes, isn't it, though . . .

JIM. Didn't we have a class in something together?

LAURA. Yes, we did.

JIM. What class was that?

LAURA. It was—singing—chorus!

JIM. Aw!

LAURA. I sat across the aisle from you in the Aud.

JIM. Aw.

LAURA. Mondays, Wednesdays, and Fridays.

JIM. Now I remember—you always came in late.

LAURA. Yes, it was so hard for me, getting upstairs. I had that brace on my leg—it clumped so loud!

JIM. I never heard any clumping.

LAURA [*wincing at the recollection*]. To me it sounded like—thunder!

JIM. Well, well, well, I never even noticed.

LAURA. And everybody was seated before I came in. I had to walk in front of all those people. My seat was in the back row. I had to go clumping all the way up the aisle with everyone watching!

JIM. You shouldn't have been self-conscious.

LAURA. I know, but I was. It was always such a relief when the singing started.

JIM. Aw, yes, I've placed you now! I used to call you Blue Roses. How was it that I got started calling you that?

LAURA. I was out of school a little while with pleurosis. When I came back you asked me what was the matter. I said I had pleurosis—you thought I said *Blue Roses*. That's what you always called me after that.

JIM. I hope you didn't mind.

LAURA. Oh, no—I liked it. You see, I wasn't acquainted with many—people. . . .

JIM. As I remember you sort of stuck by yourself.

LAURA. I—I—never have had much luck at—making friends.

JIM. I don't see why you wouldn't.

LAURA. Well, I—started out badly.

JIM. You mean being—

LAURA. Yes, it sort of—stood between me—

JIM. You shouldn't have let it!

LAURA. I know, but it did, and—

JIM. You were shy with people!

LAURA. I tried not to be but never could—

JIM. Overcome it?

LAURA. No, I—I never could!

JIM. I guess being shy is something you have to work out of kind of gradually.

LAURA [*sorrowfully*]. Yes—I guess it—

JIM. Takes time!

LAURA. Yes—

JIM. People are not so dreadful when you know them. That's what you have to remember! And everybody has problems, not just you, but practically everybody has got some problems. You think of yourself as having the only problems, as being the only one who is disappointed. But just look around you and you will see lots of people as disappointed as you are. For instance, I hoped when I was going to high school that I would be further along at this time, six years later, than I am now. You remember that wonderful write-up I had in *The Torch?*

LAURA. Yes! [*She rises and crosses to the table.*]

JIM. It said I was bound to succeed in anything I went into! [*Laura returns with the high school yearbook.*] Holy Jeez, *The Torch!* [*He accepts it reverently. They smile across the book with mutual wonder. LAURA crouches beside him and they begin to turn the pages. LAURA's shyness is dissolving in his warmth.*]

LAURA. Here you are in *The Pirates of Penzance!*

JIM [*wistfully*]. I sang the baritone lead in that operetta.

LAURA [*raptly*]. So—*beautifully!*

JIM [*protesting*]. Aw—

LAURA. Yes, yes—beautifully—beautifully!

JIM. You heard me?

LAURA. All three times!

JIM. No!

LAURA. Yes!

JIM. All three performances?

LAURA [*looking down*]. Yes.

JIM. Why?

LAURA. I—wanted to ask you to—autograph my program. [*She takes the program from the back of the yearbook and shows it to him.*]

JIM. Why didn't you ask me to?

LAURA. You were always surrounded by your own friends so much that I never had a chance to.

JIM. You should have just—

LAURA. Well, I—thought you might think I was—

JIM. Thought I might think you was—what?

LAURA. Oh—

JIM [*with reflective relish*]. I was beleaguered by females in those days.

LAURA. You were terribly popular!

JIM. Yeah—

LAURA. You had such a friendly way—

JIM. I was spoiled in high school.

LAURA. Everybody—liked you!

JIM. Including you?

LAURA. I—yes, I—did, too—[*She gently closes the book in her lap.*]

JIM. Well, well, well! Give me that program, Laura. [*She hands it to him. He signs it with a flourish.*] There you are—better late than never!

LAURA. Oh, I—what a—surprise!

JIM. My signature isn't worth very much right now. But some day— maybe—it will increase in value! Being disappointed is one thing and being discouraged is something else. I am disappointed but I am not discouraged. I'm twenty-three years old. How old are you?

LAURA. I'll be twenty-four in June.

JIM. That's not old age!

LAURA. No, but—

JIM. You finished high school?

LAURA [*with difficulty*]. I didn't go back.

JIM. You mean you dropped out?

LAURA. I made bad grades in my final examinations. [*She rises and replaces the book and the program on the table. Her voice is strained.*] How is—Emily Meisenbach getting along?

JIM. Oh, that kraut-head!

LAURA. Why do you call her that?

JIM. That's what she was.

LAURA. You're not still—going with her?

JIM. I never see her.

LAURA. It said in the "Personal" section that you were—engaged!

JIM. I know, but I wasn't impressed by that—propaganda!

LAURA. It wasn't—the truth?

JIM. Only in Emily's optimistic opinion!

LAURA. Oh— [*Legend:* "What have you done since high school?"] [JIM *lights a cigarette and leans indolently back on his elbows smiling at* LAURA *with a warmth and charm which lights her inwardly with altar candles. She remains by the table, picks up a piece from the glass menagerie collection, and turns it in her hands to cover her tumult.*]

JIM [*after several reflective puffs on his cigarette*]. What have you done since high school? [*She seems not to hear him.*] Huh? [LAURA *looks up.*] I said what have you done since high school, Laura?

LAURA. Nothing much.

JIM. You must have been doing something these six long years.

LAURA. Yes.

JIM. Well, then, such as what?

LAURA. I took a business course at business college—

JIM. How did that work out?

LAURA. Well, not very—well—I had to drop out, it gave me—indigestion— [JIM *laughs gently.*]

JIM. What are you doing now?

LAURA. I don't do anything—much. Oh, please don't think I sit around doing nothing! My glass collection takes up a good deal of time. Glass is something you have to take good care of.

JIM. What did you say—about glass?

LAURA. Collection I said—I have one—[*She clears her throat and turns away again, acutely shy.*]

JIM [*abruptly*]. You know what I judge to be the trouble with you? Inferiority complex! Know what that is? That's what they call it when someone low-rates himself! I understand it because I had it, too. Although my case was not so aggravated as yours seems to be. I had it until I took up public speaking, developed my voice, and learned that I had an aptitude for science. Before that time I never thought of myself as being outstanding in any way whatsoever! Now I've never made a regular study of it, but I have a friend who says I can analyze people better than doctors that make a profession of it. I don't claim that to be necessarily true, but I can sure guess a person's psychology, Laura! [*He takes out his gum.*] Excuse me, Laura. I always take it out when the flavor is gone. I'll use this scrap of paper to wrap it in. I know how it is to get it stuck on a shoe. [*He wraps the gum in paper and puts it in his pocket.*] Yep—that's what I judge to be your principal trouble. A lack of confidence in yourself as a person. You don't have the proper amount of faith in yourself. I'm basing that fact on a number of your remarks and also on certain observations I've made. For instance that clumping you thought was so awful in high school. You say that you even dreaded to walk into class. You see what you did? You dropped out of school, you gave up an education because of a clump, which as far as I know was practically nonexistent! A little physical defect is what you have. Hardly noticeable even! Magnified thousands of times by imagination! You know what my strong advice to you is? Think of yourself as *superior* in some way!

LAURA. In what way would I think?

JIM. Why, man alive, Laura! Just look about you a little. What do you see? A world full of common people! All of 'em born and all of 'em going to die! Which of them has one-tenth of your good points! Or mine! Or anyone else's, as far as that goes—gosh! Everybody excels in some one thing. Some in many! [*He unconsciously glances at himself in the mirror.*] All you've got to do is discover in *what!* Take me, for instance. [*He adjusts his tie at the mirror.*] My interest happens to lie in electrodynamics. I'm taking a course in radio engineering at night school, Laura, on top of a fairly responsible job at the warehouse. I'm taking that course and studying public speaking.

LAURA. Ohhhh.

JIM. Because I believe in the future of television! [*turning his back to her*] I wish to be ready to go up right along with it. Therefore I'm planning to get in on the ground floor. In fact I've already made the right connections and all that remains is for the industry itself to get under way! Full steam—[*His eyes are starry.*] *Knowledge*—Zzzzzp! *Money*—Zzzzzzp!— *Power!* That's the cycle democracy is built on! [*His attitude is convincingly dynamic.* LAURA *stares at him, even her shyness eclipsed in her absolute wonder. He suddenly grins.*] I guess you think I think a lot of myself!

LAURA. No—o-o-o, I—

JIM. Now how about you? Isn't there something you take more interest in than anything else?

LAURA. Well, I do—as I said—have my—glass collection— [*A peal of girlish laughter rings from the kitchenette.*]

JIM. I'm not right sure I know what you're talking about. What kind of glass is it?

LAURA. Little articles of it, they're ornaments mostly! Most of them are little animals made out of glass, the tiniest little animals in the world. Mother calls them a glass menagerie! Here's an example of one, if you'd like to see it! This one is one of the oldest. It's nearly thirteen. [*Music: "The Glass Menagerie."*] [*He stretches out his hand.*] Oh, be careful—if you breathe, it breaks!

JIM. I'd better not take it. I'm pretty clumsy with things.

LAURA. Go on, I trust you with him! [*She places the piece in his palm.*] There now—you're holding him gently! Hold him over the light, he loves the light! You see how the light shines through him!

JIM. It sure does shine!

LAURA. I shouldn't be partial, but he is my favorite one.

JIM. What kind of a thing is this one supposed to be?

LAURA. Haven't you noticed the single horn on his forehead?
JIM. A unicorn, huh?
LAURA. Mmmm-hmmm!
JIM. Unicorns—aren't they extinct in the modern world?
LAURA. I know!
JIM. Poor little fellow, he must feel sort of lonesome.
LAURA [*smiling*]. Well, if he does, he doesn't complain about it. He stays on a shelf with some horses that don't have horns and all of them seem to get along nicely together.
JIM. How do you know?
LAURA [*lightly*]. I haven't heard any arguments among them!
JIM [*grinning*]. No arguments, huh? Well, that's a pretty good sign! Where shall I set him?
LAURA. Put him on the table. They all like a change of scenery once in a while!
JIM. Well, well, well, well—[*He places the glass piece on the table, then raises his arms and stretches.*] Look how big my shadow is when I stretch!
LAURA. Oh, oh, yes—it stretches across the ceiling!
JIM [*crossing to the door*]. I think it's stopped raining. [*He opens the fire-escape door and the background music changes to a dance tune.*] Where does the music come from?
LAURA. From the Paradise Dance Hall across the alley.
JIM. How about cutting the rug a little, Miss Wingfield?
LAURA. Oh, I—
JIM. Or is your program filled up? Let me have a look at it. [*He grasps an imaginary card.*] Why, every dance is taken! I'll just have to scratch some out. [*Waltz music: "La Golondrina."*] Ahhh, a waltz! [*He executes some sweeping turns by himself, then holds his arms toward* LAURA.]
LAURA [*breathlessly*]. I—can't dance!
JIM. There you go, that inferiority stuff!
LAURA. I've never danced in my life!
JIM. Come on, try!
LAURA. Oh, but I'd step on you!
JIM. I'm not made out of glass.
LAURA. How—how—how do we start?
JIM. Just leave it to me. You hold your arms out a little.
LAURA. Like this?
JIM [*taking her in her arms*]. A little bit higher. Right. Now don't tighten up, that's the main thing about it—relax.
LAURA [*laughing breathlessly*]. It's hard not to.
JIM. Okay.
LAURA. I'm afraid you can't budge me.
JIM. What do you bet I can't? [*He swings her into motion.*]
LAURA. Goodness, yes, you can!
JIM. Let yourself go, now, Laura, just let yourself go.
LAURA. I'm—
JIM. Come on!
LAURA. —trying!
JIM. Not so stiff—easy does it!
LAURA. I know but I'm—

JIM. Loosen th' backbone! There now, that's a lot better.

LAURA. Am I?

JIM. Lots, lots better! [*He moves her about the room in a clumsy waltz.*]

LAURA. Oh, my!

JIM. Ha-ha!

LAURA. Oh, my goodness!

JIM. Ha-ha-ha! [*They suddenly bump into the table, and the glass piece on it falls to the floor. JIM stops the dance.*] What did we hit on?

LAURA. Table.

JIM. Did something fall off it? I think—

LAURA. Yes.

JIM. I hope that it wasn't the little glass horse with the horn!

LAURA. Yes. [*She stoops to pick it up.*]

JIM. Aw, aw, aw. Is it broken?

LAURA. Now it is just like all the other horses.

JIM. It's lost its—

LAURA. Horn! It doesn't matter. Maybe it's a blessing in disguise.

JIM. You'll never forgive me. I bet that that was your favorite piece of glass.

LAURA. I don't have favorites much. It's no tragedy, Freckles. Glass breaks so easily. No matter how careful you are. The traffic jars the shelves and things fall off them.

JIM. Still I'm awfully sorry that I was the cause.

LAURA [*smiling*]. I'll just imagine he had an operation. The horn was removed to make him feel less—freakish! [*They both laugh.*] Now he will feel more at home with the other horses, the ones that don't have horns. . . .

JIM. Ha-ha, that's very funny! [*Suddenly he is serious.*] I'm glad to see that you have a sense of humor. You know—you're—well—very different! Surprisingly different from anyone else I know! [*His voice becomes soft and hesitant with a genuine feeling.*] Do you mind me telling you that? [LAURA *is abashed beyond speech.*] I mean it in a nice way— [LAURA *nods shyly, looking away.*] You make me feel sort of—I don't know how to put it! I'm usually pretty good at expressing things, but—this is something that I don't know how to say! [LAURA *touches her throat and clears it—turns the broken unicorn in her hands. His voice becomes softer.*] Has anyone ever told you that you were pretty? [*There is a pause, and the music rises slightly.* LAURA *looks up slowly, with wonder, and shakes her head.*] Well, you are! In a very different way from anyone else. And all the nicer because of the difference, too. [*His voice becomes low and husky.* LAURA *turns away, nearly faint with the novelty of her emotions.*] I wish that you were my sister. I'd teach you to have some confidence in yourself. The different people are not like other people, but being different is nothing to be ashamed of. Because other people are not such wonderful people. They're one hundred times one thousand. You're one times one! They walk all over the earth. You just stay here. They're common as—weeds, but—you—well, you're—*Blue Roses!* [*Image on screen:* Blue Roses.] [*The music changes.*]

LAURA. But blue is wrong for—roses. . . .

JIM. It's right for you! You're—pretty!

LAURA. In what respect am I pretty?

JIM. In all respects—believe me! Your eyes—your hair—are pretty! Your hands are pretty! [*He catches hold of her hand.*] You think I'm making this up because I'm invited to dinner and have to be nice. Oh, I could do that! I could put on an act for you, Laura, and say lots of things without being very sincere. But this time I am. I'm talking to you sincerely. I happened to notice you had this inferiority complex that keeps you from feeling comfortable with people. Somebody needs to build your confidence up and make you proud instead of shy and turning away and—blushing. Somebody—ought to—*kiss* you, Laura! [*His hand slips slowly up her arm to her shoulder as the music swells tumultuously. He suddenly turns her about and kisses her on the lips. When he releases her,* LAURA *sinks on the sofa with a bright, dazed look.* JIM *backs away and fishes in his pocket for a cigarette.*] [*Legend on screen:* "A souvenir."] Stumblejohn! [*He lights the cigarette, avoiding her look. There is a peal of girlish laughter from* AMANDA *in the kitchenette.* LAURA *slowly raises and opens her hand. It still contains the little broken glass animal. She looks at it with a tender, bewildered expression.*] Stumblejohn! I shouldn't have done that—that was way off the beam. You don't smoke, do you? [*She looks up, smiling, not hearing the question. He sits beside her rather gingerly. She looks at him speechlessly— waiting. He coughs decorously and moves a little farther aside as he considers the situation and senses her feelings, dimly, with perturbation. He speaks gently.*] Would you—care for a—mint? [*She doesn't seem to hear him but her look grows brighter even.*] Peppermint? Life Saver? My pocket's a regular drugstore—wherever I go. . . . [*He pops a mint in his mouth. Then he gulps and decides to make a clean breast of it. He speaks slowly and gingerly.*] Laura, you know, if I had a sister like you, I'd do the same thing as Tom. I'd bring out fellows and—introduce her to them. The right type of boys— of a type to—appreciate her. Only—well—he made a mistake about me. Maybe I've got no call to be saying this. That may not have been the idea in having me over. But what if it was? There's nothing wrong about that. The only trouble is that in my case—I'm not in a situation to—do the right thing. I can't take down your number and say I'll phone. I can't call up next week and—ask for a date. I thought I had better explain the situation in case you—misunderstood it and—I hurt your feelings. . . . [*There is a pause. Slowly, very slowly,* LAURA's *look changes, her eyes returning slowly from his to the glass figure in her palm.* AMANDA *utters another gay laugh in the kitchenette.*]

LAURA [*faintly*]. You—won't—call again?

JIM. No, Laura, I can't. [*He rises from the sofa.*] As I was just explaining, I've—got strings on me. Laura, I've—been going steady! I go out all the time with a girl named Betty. She's a home-girl like you, and Catholic, and Irish, and in a great many ways we—get along fine. I met her last summer on a moonlight boat trip up the river to Alton, on the *Majestic.* Well—right away from the start it was—love! [*Legend: Love!*] [LAURA *sways slightly forward and grips the arm of the sofa. He fails to notice, now enrapt in his own comfortable being.*] Being in love has made a new man of me! [*Leaning stiffly forward, clutching the arm of the sofa,* LAURA *struggles visibly with her storm. But* JIM *is oblivious; she is a long way off.*] The power of love is really pretty tremendous! Love is something that—

changes the whole world, Laura! [*The storm abates a little and* LAURA *leans back. He notices her again.*] It happened that Betty's aunt took sick, she got a wire and had to go to Centralia. So Tom—when he asked me to dinner—I naturally just accepted the invitation, not knowing that you—that he—that I—[*He stops awkwardly.*] Huh—I'm a stumble-john! [*He flops back on the sofa. The holy candles on the altar of* LAURA'S *face have been snuffed out. There is a look of almost infinite desolation.* JIM *glances at her uneasily.*] I wish that you would—say something. [*She bites her lip which was trembling and then bravely smiles. She opens her hand again on the broken glass figure. Then she gently takes his hand and raises it level with her own. She carefully places the unicorn in the palm of his hand, then pushes his fingers closed upon it.*] What are you—doing that for? You want me to have him? Laura? [*She nods.*]

LAURA. A—souvenir. . . . [*She rises unsteadily and crouches beside the Victrola to wind it up.*] [*Legend on screen:* "Things have a way of turning out so badly!" *Or image:* "Gentleman caller waving goodbye—gaily."] [*At this moment* AMANDA *rushes brightly back into the living room. She bears a pitcher of fruit punch in an old-fashioned cut-glass pitbcer, and a plate of macaroons. The plate has a gold border and poppies painted on it.*]

AMANDA. Well, well, well! Isn't the air delightful after the shower? I've made you children a little liquid refreshment. [*She turns gaily to* JIM.] Jim, do you know that song about lemonade?

"Lemonade, lemonade
Made in the shade and stirred with a spade—
Good enough for any old maid!"

JIM [*uneasily*]. Ha-ha! No—I never heard it.
AMANDA. Why, Laura! You look so serious!
JIM. We were having a serious conversation.
AMANDA. Good! Now you're better acquainted!
JIM [*uncertainly*]. Ha-ha! Yes.
AMANDA. You modern young people are much more serious-minded than my generation. I was so gay as a girl!
JIM. You haven't changed, Mrs. Wingfield.
AMANDA. Tonight I'm rejuvenated! The gaiety of the occasion, Mr. O'Connor! [*She tosses her head with a peal of laughter, spilling some lemonade.*] Oooo! I'm baptizing myself!
JIM. Here—let me—
AMANDA [*setting the pitcher down*]. There now. I discovered we had some maraschino cherries. I dumped them in, juice and all!
JIM. You shouldn't have gone to that trouble, Mrs. Wingfield.
AMANDA. Trouble, trouble? Why, it was loads of fun! Didn't you hear me cutting up in the kitchen? I bet your ears were burning! I told Tom how outdone with him I was for keeping you to himself so long a time! He should have brought you over much, much sooner! Well, now that you've found your way, I want you to be a very frequent caller! Not just occasional but all the time. Oh, we're going to have a lot of gay times together! I see them coming! Mmm, just breathe that air! So fresh, and the moon's so pretty! I'll skip back out—I know where my place is when young folks are having a—serious conversation!

JIM. Oh, don't go out, Mrs. Wingfield. The fact of the matter is I've got to be going.

AMANDA. Going, now? You're joking! Why, it's only the shank of the evening, Mr. O'Connor!

JIM. Well, you know how it is.

AMANDA. You mean you're a young workingman and have to keep working-men's hours. We'll let you off early tonight. But only on the condition that next time you stay later. What's the best night for you? Isn't Saturday night the best night for you workingmen?

JIM. I have a couple of time-clocks to punch, Mrs. Wingfield. One at morning, another one at night!

AMANDA. My, but you *are* ambitious! You work at night, too?

JIM. No, Ma'am, not work but—Betty! [*He crosses deliberately to pick up his hat. The band at the Paradise Dance Hall goes into a tender waltz.*]

AMANDA. Betty? Betty? Who's—Betty! [*There is an ominous cracking sound in the sky.*]

JIM. Oh, just a girl. The girl I go steady with! [*He smiles charmingly. The sky falls.*] [*Legend:* "The Sky Falls."]

AMANDA [*a long-drawn exhalation*]. Ohhhh . . . Is it a serious romance, Mr. O'Connor?

JIM. We're going to be married the second Sunday in June.

AMANDA. Ohhhh—how nice! Tom didn't mention that you were engaged to be married.

JIM. The cat is not out of the bag at the warehouse yet. You know how they are. They call you Romeo and stuff like that. [*He stops at the oval mirror to put on his hat. He carefully shapes the brim and the crown to give a discreetly dashing effect.*] It's been a wonderful evening, Mrs. Wingfield. I guess this is what they mean by Southern hospitality.

AMANDA. It really wasn't anything at all.

JIM. I hope it don't seem like I'm rushing off. But I promised Betty I'd pick her up at the Wabash depot, an' by the time I get my jalopy down there her train'll be in. Some women are pretty upset if you keep 'em waiting.

AMANDA. Yes, I know—the tyranny of women! [*She extends her hand.*] Goodbye, Mr. O'Connor. I wish you luck—and happiness—and success! All three of them, and so does Laura! Don't you, Laura?

LAURA. Yes!

JIM [*taking* LAURA's *hand*]. Goodbye, Laura. I'm certainly going to treasure that souvenir. And don't you forget the good advice I gave you. [*He raises his voice to a cheery shout.*] So long, Shakespeare! Thanks again, ladies. Good night! [*He grins and ducks jauntily out. Still bravely grimacing,* AMANDA *closes the door on the gentleman caller. Then she turns back to the room with a puzzled expression. She and* LAURA *don't dare to face each other.* LAURA *crouches beside the Victrola to wind it.*]

AMANDA [*faintly*]. Things have a way of turning out so badly. I don't believe that I would play the Victrola. Well, well—well! Our gentleman caller was engaged to be married! [*She raises her voice.*] Tom!

TOM [*from the kitchenette*]. Yes, Mother?

AMANDA. Come in here a minute. I want to tell you something awfully funny.

Tom [*entering with a macaroon and a glass of the lemonade*]. Has the gentleman caller gotten away already?

AMANDA. The gentleman caller has made an early departure. What a wonderful joke you played on us!

Tom. How do you mean?

AMANDA. You didn't mention that he was engaged to be married.

Tom. Jim? Engaged?

AMANDA. That's what he just informed us.

Tom. I'll be jiggered! I didn't know about that.

AMANDA. That seems very peculiar.

Tom. What's peculiar about it?

AMANDA. Didn't you call him your best friend down at the warehouse?

Tom. He is, but how did I know?

AMANDA. It seems extremely peculiar that you wouldn't know your best friend was going to be married!

Tom. The warehouse is where I work, not where I know things about people!

AMANDA. You don't know things anywhere! You live in a dream; you manufacture illusions! [*He crosses to the door.*] Where are you going?

Tom. I'm going to the movies.

AMANDA. That's right, now that you've had us make such fools of ourselves. The effort, the preparations, all the expense! The new floor lamp, the rug, the clothes for Laura! All for what? To entertain some other girl's fiancé! Go to the movies, go! Don't think about us, a mother deserted, an unmarried sister who's crippled and has no job! Don't let anything interfere with your selfish pleasure! Just go, go, go—to the movies!

Tom. All right, I will! The more you shout about my selfishness to me the quicker I'll go, and I won't go to the movies!

AMANDA. Go, then! Go to the moon—you selfish dreamer! [Tom *smashes his glass on the floor. He plunges out on the fire escape, slamming the door.* LAURA *screams in fright. The dance-hall music becomes louder.* Tom *stands on the fire escape, gripping the rail. The moon breaks through the storm clouds, illuminating his face.*] [Legend on screen: "And so goodbye . . ."] [Tom's *closing speech is timed with what is happening inside the house. We see, as though through soundproof glass, that* AMANDA *appears to be making a comforting speech to* LAURA *who is huddled upon the sofa. Now that we cannot hear the mother's speech, her silliness is gone and she has dignity and tragic beauty.* LAURA's *hair hides her face until, at the end of the speech, she lifts her head to smile at her mother.* AMANDA's *gestures are slow and graceful, almost dancelike, as she comforts her daughter. At the end of her speech she glances a moment at the father's picture—then withdraws through the portieres. At the close of* Tom's *speech,* LAURA *blows out the candles, ending the play.*]

Tom. I didn't go to the moon, I went much further—for time is the longest distance between two places. Not long after that I was fired for writing a poem on the lid of a shoe-box. I left Saint Louis. I descended the steps of this fire escape for a last time and followed, from then on, in my father's footsteps, attempting to find in motion what was lost in space. I traveled around a great deal. The cities swept about me like dead leaves, leaves that were brightly colored but torn away from the branches. I would have stopped, but I was pursued by something. It always came upon me unawares, taking me altogether by surprise. Perhaps it was a familiar bit of music. Perhaps it was only a piece of transparent glass. Perhaps I am walking along a street at night, in some strange city, before I have found companions. I pass the lighted window of a shop where perfume is sold. The window is filled with pieces of colored glass, tiny transparent bottles in delicate colors, like bits of a shattered rainbow. Then all at once my sister touches my shoulder. I turn around and look into her eyes. Oh, Laura, Laura, I tried to leave you behind me, but I am more faithful than I intended to be! I reach for a cigarette, I cross the street, I run into the movies or a bar, I buy a drink, I speak to the nearest stranger—anything that can blow your candles out! [Laura *bends over the candles.*] For nowadays the world is lit by lightning! Blow out your candles, Laura—and so goodbye. . . . [*She blows the candles out.*]

(1944)

Prewriting

Begin your study of *The Glass Menagerie* by writing about and discussing the following six ideas.

ANALYZING THE CHARACTERS

1. One way to look at this play is as a tangle of deceptions. List five deceptions that occur in the play. Compare your list with those of others in your class. Discuss how you would rank the seriousness or harmlessness of the deceptions you have identified. Be sure to consider possible self-deceptions for each character.

2. Reread the opening scene involving Amanda, Tom, and Laura. With two other people, prepare an oral reading of the scene, choosing one quality to emphasize in each of the characters. Present the scene to your class, asking them to identify the qualities you chose. Listen to the other students' interpretations of the scene.

3. In Scene IV, Tom says, "Man is by instinct a lover, a hunter, a fighter, and none of those instincts are given much play at the warehouse!" How does this statement fit in with Miller's concept of tragic heroism? Find statements by each of the characters that imply displacement or indignity. How is the heroism of *Antigone* different?

4. How is tradition important to the characters in both *Antigone* and in *The Glass Menagerie?*

5. Reread Tom's closing speech. Why is he unable to leave Laura behind him?

6. Choose a character from *The Glass Menagerie* and argue that he or she is the hero. Can you argue for more than one character as a hero?

Writing

In your prewriting, you gathered a list of deceptions that you found in *The Glass Menagerie*. Looking at that list, you may come up with a thesis for an essay on the play. "Deception is an important element in *The Glass Menagerie*" is not enough, even though that may be your first reaction to such a long list. You must say *why* deception is important. Here are some possible thesis ideas:

> Though Amanda's deceptions and self-deceptions are the most obvious, every character in the play practices deception. This tempers our attitude toward her.

> One of the moral questions addressed in *The Glass Menagerie* is this: "Which is more damaging to the spirit, deception of others or self-deception?"

> In *The Glass Menagerie*, Williams presents deception on all levels of seriousness, seeming to encourage a view of humanity as suffused with lies and illusions.

CHOOSING A STRUCTURE

Your choice of thesis should determine how you organize your raw material—in this case, your list of examples from the prewriting activity. Perhaps your list looks something like this:

Deception
—Rubicam's Business College—Laura
—Amanda—that Laura isn't crippled or "peculiar," that she is able to have gentleman callers, that her "unusual" children make her proud and happy, that the Gentleman Caller will surely fall in love with Laura, that Tom has constantly praised Jim at home.
—Tom's secret plans to join the Merchant Marine.
—Whatever he *does* if he doesn't go to the movies.
—Pays union dues instead of light bill.
—The father was deceptively charming.
—Powder puffs (gay deceivers).
—Emily tells yearbook that she and Jim are engaged.
—Jim—will a night school course really do all he believes it will? Does he believe it? His stubborn cheerfulness and optimism. Disappointment that he hasn't gone farther often concealed.
—Amanda—that Laura isn't "satisfied with just sitting home." White lie to Jim, "You know Sister is in full charge of supper!"

This unorganized jumble can be structured in several ways. For the first thesis we mentioned, you would probably sort the deceptions character by character, perhaps presenting Amanda's first and then those of the others. For the second thesis, you would separate deceptions of others from self-deceptions and devote a section of your essay to each type, closing with an evaluation of the spiritual damage done by each. For the last thesis, you would have the challenging work of arranging the list from the most trivial to the most serious so that your reader appreciates the full spectrum.

IDEAS FOR WRITING

The following writing suggestions lend themselves to the process of prewriting, devising a thesis, and deciding on a structure appropriate to the thesis. Choose an idea that interests you and reread the play with that topic in mind.

1. Examine the role of imagination and fantasy in each character's life.
2. Show similarities and differences among the characters' use of memory.
3. Expand the comparison made by Williams in the CHARACTERS section: Laura "is like a piece of her own glass collection, too exquisitely fragile to move from the shelf."
4. Consider the character of the gentleman caller: Is he really as Tom describes him in his opening speech, "an emissary from a world of reality that we were somehow set apart from . . . , the long-delayed but always expected something that we live for"?
5. Investigate the ideas of oddness and normality in the play.
6. Explain how the father is an important character even though he never appears onstage.
7. A key element in drama and fiction is character development and change. Does the gentleman caller change Laura? How? Do any of the other characters undergo change?
8. Read, summarize and apply Miller's concept of tragedy and the common man to *The Glass Menagerie.*
9. What character, if any, does the e. e. cummings epigraph, "Nobody, not even the rain, has such small hands," refer to? What is the significance of this statement?
10. Analyze the nondialogue elements of the play: the music, stage business, stage directions, screen images, sets, titles, lighting, and so forth.

Rewriting

The more specifically you support your statements about the work, the more credible you will be to your reader. Another crucial advantage to forcing yourself to be specific is that you will prevent yourself from straying from the printed page into the fields of your own mind, which may be rich and green but not relevant.

DEVELOPING PARAGRAPHS SPECIFICALLY

The following paragraph makes several good observations but lacks specifics:

> In many ways Tom fulfills Arthur Miller's characterization of the modern tragic hero. His ideal image of himself is constantly frustrated both at home and at work. He feels misunderstood, a victim of indignity. He is clearly at odds with his environment.

Although these statements are true, the writer has given the reader no particular cause to believe them. The paragraph should have additional details from the play. Compare the following:

> In many ways Tom fulfills Arthur Miller's characterization of the modern tragic hero. In the list of characters, Williams describes him as "a poet with a job in a warehouse." His ideal image of himself is constantly frustrated both at home and at work. He complains, "Man is by instinct a lover, a hunter, a fighter, and none of those instincts are given much play at the warehouse!" Tom feels misunderstood, a victim of indignity. He accuses Amanda, "It seems unimportant to you, what I'm *doing*—what I *want* to do—having a little *difference* between them!" This is a man clearly at odds with his environment.

The references to the text of the play specifically support the writer's contention. The exercise that follows will give you practice in finding such support.

EXERCISE

For each general statement, provide appropriate quotations from the play. Some of these generalizations may give you further ideas for papers.

1. Amanda is not deeply and completely self-deceived.
2. Human sexuality disturbs Amanda.
3. Characters in the play take both realistic and unrealistic action toward their goals.
4. Both times glass is broken in the play, the forces of masculinity and sexuality are involved.
5. Tom Wingfield may live as much in his imagination as Amanda and Laura do in theirs.

17

Drama for Writing: The Research Paper

Until now, we have been discussing and illustrating how to write papers supported with material from only a *primary source* (i.e., from the literary work under consideration). In this chapter we will focus on the process of writing a paper supported with primary material but also drawing on *secondary sources* (i.e., critical material from the library). As we explain how to incorporate other people's ideas into your own writing, we will also introduce you to a mid-twentieth century development in drama: theater of the absurd. You will thus have two avenues to explore at the library. You may decide to seek further information about theater of the absurd, or you may prefer to examine critical opinions about an absurdist play. You may, perhaps, even become inspired to investigate both.

Keep in mind as you study this chapter that the process we describe here for writing about drama is essentially the same procedure you would employ when writing a documented paper on a work in any literary genre—a short story, a poem, a novel, or a play.

What is Theater of the Absurd?

Primarily a British and European phenomenon, theater of the absurd departs markedly from the realistic representation of events presented on stage in plays such as *The Glass Menagerie* and *Death of a Salesman.* The absurdist playwrights attempt to show that the human condition is itself absurd, pointless—especially when the social order is based on empty rituals that serve as insulation against life's unpleasant realities. Eugene Ionesco in *The Bald Soprano* emphasizes the banality of comfortable middle-class people by presenting characters who do nothing throughout the play except talk earnestly about the obvious—declaring as an observation of great insight, for instance, that life in the city is less peaceful than in the country. Samuel Beckett often departs from a realistic setting to exaggerate the absurdity of life that must end in death. In *Endgame* his two main characters inhabit garbage cans on an otherwise empty stage. Harold Pinter employs more realistic settings, but his plots involve the characters in menacing situations beyond their comprehension, and their incongruous behavior often lacks any conventional motivation. The mindset shared by absurdist playwrights is that the human predicament is anguished, meaningless, and futile.

Looking at Absurdist Drama

PICNIC ON THE BATTLEFIELD

by Fernando Arrabal

Although theater of the absurd sounds depressing and hopeless, the plays are often quite funny, brightened by morbid humor. In the following play, Arrabal, a Spanish playwright living in France, presents a ridiculous situation in which comical characters enact a brief, bizarre drama, illustrating a grimly serious theme.

Fernando Arrabal *1933–*

PICNIC ON THE BATTLEFIELD

CHARACTERS

ZAPO, *A soldier*
MONSIEUR TÉPAN, *The sol-dier's father*
MADAME TÉPAN, *The soldier's mother*

ZÉPO, *An enemy soldier*
FIRST STRETCHER BEARER
SECOND STRETCHER BEARER

A battlefield. The stage is covered with barbed wire and sandbags. The battle is at its height. Rifle shots, exploding bombs and machine guns can be heard.
ZAPO is alone on the stage, flat on his stomach, hidden among the sandbags. He is very frightened. The sound of the fighting stops. Silence.
ZAPO takes a ball of wool and some needles out of a canvas workbag and starts knitting a pullover, which is already quite far advanced. The field telephone, which is by his side, suddenly starts ringing.

ZAPO. Hallo, hallo . . . yes, Captain . . . yes, I'm the sentry of sector 47 . . . Nothing new, Captain . . . Excuse me, Captain, but when's the fighting going to start again? And what am I supposed to do with the hand-grenades? Do I chuck them in front of me or behind me? . . . Don't get me wrong. I didn't mean to annoy you . . . Captain, I really feel terribly lonely, couldn't you send me someone to keep me company? . . . even if it's only a nanny-goat? [*The* CAPTAIN *is obviously severely reprimanding him.*] Whatever you say, Captain, whatever you say. [ZAPO *hangs up. He mutters to himself. Silence. Enter* MONSIEUR *and* MADAME TÉPAN, *carrying baskets as if they were going on a picnic. They address their son, who has his back turned and doesn't see them come in.*]
MONS. T. [*ceremoniously.*] Stand up, my son, and kiss your mother on the brow. [ZAPO, *surprised, gets up and kisses his mother very respectfully on the forehead. He is about to speak, but his father doesn't give him a chance.*] And now, kiss *me.*
ZAPO. But, dear Father and dear Mother, how did you dare to come all this way, to such a dangerous place? You must leave at once.
MONS. T. So you think you've got something to teach your father about war and danger, do you? All this is just a game to me. How many times—to take the first example that comes to mind—have I got off an underground train while it was still moving.
MME. T. We thought you must be bored, so we came to pay you a little visit. This war must be a bit tedious, after all.
ZAPO. It all depends.
MONS. T. I know exactly what happens. To start with you're attracted by the novelty of it all. It's fun to kill people, and throw hand-grenades

650

about, and wear uniforms—you feel smart, but in the end you get bored stiff. You'd have found it much more interesting in my day. Wars were much more lively, much more highly colored. And then, the best thing was that there were horses, plenty of horses. It was a real pleasure; if the Captain ordered us to attack, there we all were immediately, on horseback, in our red uniforms. It was a sight to be seen. And then there were the charges at the gallop, sword in hand, and suddenly you found yourself face to face with the enemy, and he was equal to the occasion too—with his horses—there were always horses, lots of horses, with their well-rounded rumps—in his highly-polished boots, and his green uniform.

Mme. T. No, no, the enemy uniform wasn't green. It was blue. I remember distinctly that it was blue.

Mons. T. I tell you it was green.

Mme. T. When I was little, how many times did I go out on to the balcony to watch the battle and say to the neighbour's little boy: 'I bet you a gum-drop the blues win.' And the blues were our enemies.

Mons. T. Oh, well, you must be right, then.

Mme. T. I've always liked battles. As a child I always said that when I grew up I wanted to be a Colonel of dragoons. But my mother wouldn't hear of it, you know how she will stick to her principles at all costs.

Mons. T. Your mother's just a half-wit.

Zapo. I'm sorry, but you really must go. You can't come into a war unless you're a soldier.

Mons. T. I don't give a damn, we came here to have a picnic with you in the country and to enjoy our Sunday.

Mme. T. And I've prepared an excellent meal, too. Sausage, hard-boiled eggs—you know how you like them!—ham sandwiches, red wine, salad, and cakes.

Zapo. All right, let's have it your way. But if the Captain comes he'll be absolutely furious. Because he isn't at all keen on us having visits when we're at the front. He never stops telling us: 'Discipline and hand-grenades are what's wanted in war, not visits.'

Mons. T. Don't worry, I'll have a few words to say to your Captain.

Zapo. And what if we have to start fighting again?

Mons. T. You needn't think that'll frighten me, it won't be the first fighting I've seen. Now if only it was battles on horseback! Times have changed, you can't understand. [*Pause.*] We came by motor bike. No one said a word to us.

Zapo. They must have thought you were the referees.

Mons. T. We had enough trouble getting through, though. What with all the tanks and jeeps.

Mme. T. And do you remember the bottle-neck that cannon caused, just when we got here?

Mons. T. You mustn't be surprised at anything in wartime, everyone knows that.

Mme. T. Good, let's start our meal.

Mons. T. You're quite right, I feel as hungry as a hunter. It's the smell of gunpowder.

Mme. T. We'll sit on the rug while we're eating.

ZAPO. Can I bring my rifle with me?

MME. T. You leave your rifle alone. It's not good manners to bring your rifle to table with you. [*Pause.*] But you're absolutely filthy, my boy. How on earth did you get into such a state? Let's have a look at your hands.

ZAPO. [*ashamed, holding out his hands*] I had to crawl about on the ground during the manoeuvres.

MME. T. And what about your ears?

ZAPO. I washed them this morning.

MME. T. Well that's all right, then. And your teeth? [*He shows them.*] Very good. Who's going to give her little boy a great big kiss for cleaning his teeth so nicely? [*To her husband*] Well, go on, kiss your son for cleaning his teeth so nicely. [M. TEPAN *kisses his son.*] Because, you know, there's one thing I *will* not have, and that's making fighting a war an excuse for not washing.

ZAPO. Yes, Mother. [*They eat.*]

MONS. T. Well, my boy, did you make a good score?

ZAPO. When?

MONS. T. In the last few days, of course.

ZAPO. Where?

MONS. T. At the moment, since you're fighting a war.

ZAPO. No, nothing much. I didn't make a good score. Hardly ever scored a bull.

MONS. T. Which are you best at shooting, enemy horses or soldiers?

ZAPO. No, not horses, there aren't any horses any more.

MONS. T. Well, soldiers then?

ZAPO. Could be.

MONS. T. Could be? Aren't you sure?

ZAPO. Well you see . . . I shoot without taking aim, [*pause*] and at the same time I say a Pater Noster for the chap I've shot.

MONS. T. You must be braver than that. Like your father.

MME. T. I'm going to put a record on. [*She puts a record on the gramophone— a pasodoble. All three are sitting on the ground, listening.*]

MONS. T. That really *is* music. Yes indeed, ole! [*The music continues. Enter an enemy soldier:* ZÉPO. *He is dressed like* ZAPO. *The only difference is the colour of their uniforms.* ZÉPO *is in green and* ZAPO *is in grey.* ZÉPO *listens to the music openmouthed. He is behind the family so they can't see him. The record ends. As he gets up* ZAPO *discovers* ZÉPO. *Both put their hands up. M. and* MME. TÉPAN *look at them in surprise.*] What's going on? [ZAPO *reacts— he hesitates. Finally, looking as if he's made up his mind, he points his rifle at* ZÉPO.]

ZAPO. Hands up! [ZÉPO *puts his hands up even higher, looking even more terrified.* ZAPO *doesn't know what to do. Suddenly he goes over quickly to* ZÉPO *and touches him gently on the shoulder, like a child playing a game of 'tag'.*] Got you! [*To his father, very pleased.*] There we are! A prisoner!

MONS. T. Fine. And now what're you going to do with him?

ZAPO. I don't know, but, well, could be—they might make me a corporal.

MONS. T. In the meantime you'd better tie him up.

ZAPO. Tie him up? Why?

Mons. T. Prisoners always get tied up!

Zapo. How?

Mons. T. Tie up his hands.

Mme. T. Yes, there's no doubt about it, you must tie up his hands, I've always seen them do that.

Zapo. Right. [*To his prisoner.*] Put your hands together, if you please.

Zépo. Don't hurt me too much.

Zapo. I won't.

Zépo. Ow! You're hurting me.

Mons. T. Now now, don't maltreat your prisoner.

Mme. T. Is that the way I brought you up? How many times have I told you that we must be considerate of our fellow-men?

Zapo. I didn't do it on purpose. [*To* Zépo.] And like that, does it hurt?

Zépo. No, it's all right like that.

Mons. T. Tell him straight out, say what you mean, don't mind us.

Zépo. It's all right like that.

Mons. T. Now his feet.

Zapo. His feet as well, whatever next?

Mons. T. Didn't they teach you the rules?

Zapo. Yes.

Mons. T. Well then!

Zapo. [*very politely, to* Zépo]. Would you be good enough to sit on the ground, please?

Zépo. Yes, but don't hurt me.

Mme. T. You'll see, he'll take a dislike to you.

Zapo. No he won't, no he won't. I'm not hurting you, am I?

Zépo. No, that's perfect.

Zapo. Papa, why don't you take a photo of the prisoner on the ground and me with my foot on his stomach?

Mons. T. Oh, yes that'd look good.

Zépo. Oh no, not that!

Mme. T. Say yes, don't be obstinate.

Zépo. No, I said no, and no it is.

Mme. T. But just a little teeny weeny photo, what harm could that do you? And we could put it in the dining room, next to the life-saving certificate my husband won thirteen years ago.

Zépo. No—you won't shift me.

Zapo. But why won't you let us?

Zépo. I'm engaged. And if she sees the photo one day, she'll say I don't know how to fight a war properly.

Zapo. No she won't, all you'll need to say is that it isn't you, it's a panther.

Mme. T. Come on, do say yes.

Zépo. All right then. But only to please you.

Zapo. Lie down flat. [Zépo *lies down.* Zapo *puts a foot on his stomach and grabs his rifle with a martial air.*]

Mme. T. Stick your chest out a bit further.

Zapo. Like this?

Mme. T. Yes like that, and don't breathe.

Mons. T. Try to look like a hero.

ZAPO. What d'you mean, like a hero?

MONS. T. It's quite simple; try and look like the butcher does when he's boasting about his successes with the girls.

ZAPO. Like this?

MONS. T. Yes, like that.

MME. T. The most important thing is to puff your chest out and not breathe.

ZÉPO. Have you nearly finished?

MONS. T. Just be patient a moment. One . . . two . . . three.

ZAPO. I hope I'll come out well.

MME. T. Yes, you looked very martial.

MONS. T. You were fine.

MME. T. It makes me want to have my photo taken with you.

MONS. T. Now there's a good idea.

ZAPO. Right. I'll take it if you like.

MME. T. Give me your helmet to make me look like a soldier.

ZÉPO. I don't want any more photos. Even one's far too many.

ZAPO. Don't take it like that. After all, what harm can it do you?

ZÉPO. It's my last word.

MONS. T. [*to his wife*] Don't press the point, prisoners are always very sensitive. If we go on he'll get cross and spoil our fun.

ZAPO. Right, what're we going to do with him, then?

MME. T. We could invite him to lunch. What do you say?

MONS. T. I don't see why not.

ZAPO. [*To* ZÉPO]. Well, will you have lunch with us, then?

ZÉPO. Er . . .

MONS. T. We brought a good bottle with us.

ZÉPO. Oh well, all right then.

MME. T. Make yourself at home, don't be afraid to ask for anything you want.

ZÉPO. All right.

MONS. T. And what about you, did you make a good score?

ZÉPO. When?

MONS. T. In the last few days, of course.

ZÉPO. Where?

MONS. T. At the moment, since you're fighting a war.

ZÉPO. No, nothing much. I didn't make a good score, hardly ever scored a bull.

MONS. T. Which are you best at shooting? Enemy horses or soldiers?

ZÉPO. No, not horses, they aren't any horses any more.

MONS. T. Well, soldiers, then?

ZÉPO. Could be.

MONS. T. Could be? Aren't you sure?

ZÉPO. Well you see . . . I shoot without taking aim [*pause*], and at the same time I say an Ave Maria for the chap I've shot.

ZAPO. An Ave Maria? I'd have thought you'd have said a Pater Noster.

ZÉPO. No, always an Ave Maria. [*Pause*] It's shorter.

MONS. T. Come come, my dear fellow, you must be brave.

MME. T. [*to* ZÉPO]. We can untie you if you like.

ZÉPO. No, don't bother, it doesn't matter.

MONS. T. Don't start getting stand-offish with us now. If you'd like us to untie you, say so.

MME. T. Make yourself comfortable.

ZÉPO. Well, if that's how you feel, you can untie my feet, but it's only to please you.

MONS. T. Zapo, untie him. [ZAPO *unties him.*]

MME. T. Well, do you feel better?

ZÉPO. Yes, of course. I really am putting you to a lot of inconvenience.

MONS. T. Not at all, just make yourself at home. And if you'd like us to untie your hands you only have to say so.

ZÉPO. No, not my hands, I don't want to impose upon you.

MONS. T. No no, my dear chap, no no. I tell you, it's no trouble at all.

ZÉPO. Right . . . Well then, untie my hands too. But only for lunch, eh? I don't want you to think that you give me an inch and I take an ell.[1]

MONS. T. Untie his hands, son.

MME. T. Well, since our distinguished prisoner is so charming, we're going to have a marvellous day in the country.

ZÉPO. Don't call me your distinguished prisoner, just call me your prisoner.

MME. T. Won't that embarrass you?

ZÉPO. No, no, not at all.

MONS. T. Well, I must say you're modest. [*Noise of aeroplanes.*]

ZAPO. Aeroplanes. They're sure to be coming to bomb us. [ZAPO *and* ZÉPO *throw themselves on the sandbags and hide.*] [*To his parents*]. Take cover. The bombs will fall on you. [*The noise of the aeroplanes overpowers all the other noises. Bombs immediately start to fall. Shells explode very near the stage but not on it. A deafening noise.* ZAPO *and* ZÉPO *are cowering down between the sandbags.* M. TÉPAN *goes on talking calmly to his wife, and she answers in the same unruffled way. We can't hear what they are saying because of the bombing.* MME. TÉPAN *goes over to one of the baskets and takes an umbrella out of it. She opens it.* M. *and* MME. TÉPAN *shelter under it as if it were raining. They are standing up. They shift rhythmically from one foot to the other and talk about their personal affairs. The bombing continues. Finally the aeroplanes go away. Silence.* M. TÉPAN *stretches an arm outside the umbrella to make sure that nothing more is falling from the heavens.*]

MONS. T. [*to his wife*]. You can shut your umbrella. [MME. TÉPAN *does so. They both go over to their son and tap him lightly on the behind with the umbrella.*] Come on, out you come. The bombing's over. [ZAPO *and* ZÉPO *come out of their hiding place.*]

ZAPO. Didn't you get hit?

MONS. T. What d'you think could happen to your father? [*Proudly.*] Little bombs like that! Don't make me laugh! [*Enter, left, two* RED CROSS SOLDIERS. *They are carrying a stretcher.*]

1ST STRETCHER BEARER. Any dead here?

ZAPO. No, no one around these parts.

1ST STRETCHER BEARER. Are you sure you've looked properly?

ZAPO. Sure.

---

[1] A unit of measure equal to 45 inches.

1st STRETCHER BEARER. And there isn't a single person dead?

ZAPO. I've already told you there isn't.

1st STRETCHER BEARER. No one wounded, even?

ZAPO. Not even that.

2nd STRETCHER BEARER [*to the* 1st S. B.]. Well, now we're in a mess! [*To* ZAPO *persuasively.*] Just look again, search everywhere, and see if you can't find us a stiff.

1st STRETCHER BEARER. Don't keep on about it, they've told you quite clearly there aren't any.

2nd STRETCHER BEARER. What a lousy trick!

ZAPO. I'm terribly sorry. I promise you I didn't do it on purpose.

2nd STRETCHER BEARER. That's what they all say. That no one's dead and that they didn't do it on purpose.

1st STRETCHER BEARER. Oh, let the chap alone!

MONS. T. [*obligingly*]. We should be only too pleased to help you. At your service.

2nd STRETCHER BEARER. Well, really, if things go on like this I don't know what the Captain will say to us.

MONS. T. But what's it all about?

2nd STRETCHER BEARER. Quite simply that the others' wrists are aching with carting so many corpses and wounded men about, and that we haven't found any yet. And it's not because we haven't looked!

MONS. T. Well yes, that really is annoying. [*To* ZAPO.] Are you quite sure no one's dead?

ZAPO. Obviously, Papa.

MONS. T. Have you looked under all the sandbags?

ZAPO. Yes, Papa.

MONS. T. [*angrily*]. Well then, you might as well say straight out that you don't want to lift a finger to help these gentlemen, when they're so nice, too!

1st STRETCHER BEARER. Don't be angry with him. Let him be. We must just hope we'll have more luck in another trench and that all the lot'll be dead.

MONS. T. I should be delighted.

MME. T. Me too. There's nothing I like more than people who put their hearts into their work.

MONS. T. [*indignantly, addressing his remarks to the wings*]. Then is no one going to do anything for these gentlemen?

ZAPO. If it only rested with me, it'd already be done.

ZÉPO. I can say the same.

MONS. T. But look here, is neither of you even wounded?

ZAPO. [*ashamed*]. No, not me.

MONS. T. [*To* ZÉPO]. What about you?

ZÉPO. [*ashamed*]. Me neither. I never have any luck.

MME. T. [*pleased*]. Now I remember! This morning, when I was peeling the onions, I cut my finger. Will that do you?

MONS. T. Of course it will! [*Enthusiastically.*] They'll take you off at once!

1st STRETCHER BEARER. No, that won't work. With ladies it doesn't work.

Mons. T. We're no further advanced, then.

1st Stretcher Bearer. Never mind.

2nd Stretcher Bearer. We may be able to make up for it in the other trenches. [*They start to go off.*]

Mons. T. Don't worry! If we find a dead man we'll keep him for you! No fear of us giving him to anyone else!

2nd Stretcher Bearer. Thank you very much, sir.

Mons. T. Quite all right, old chap, think nothing of it. [*The two stretcher bearers say goodbye. All four answer them. The stretcher bearers go out.*]

Mme. T. That's what's so pleasant about spending a Sunday in the country. You always meet such nice people.

Mons. T. [*Pause.*]. But why are you enemies?

Mme. T. Your father is the only one who's capable of thinking of such ideas; don't forget he's a former student of the Ecole Normale, *and* a philatelist.[2]

Zépo. I don't know, I'm not very well educated.

Mme. T. Was it by birth, or did you become enemies afterwards?

Zépo. I don't know, I don't know anything about it.

Mons. T. Well then, how did you come to be in the war?

Zépo. One day, at home, I was just mending my mother's iron, a man came and asked me: 'Are you Zépo?' 'Yes.' 'Right, you must come to the war.' And so I asked him: 'But what war?' and he said: 'Don't you read the papers then? You're just a peasant!' I told him I did read the papers but not the war bits. . . .

Zapo. Just how it was with me—exactly how it was with me.

Mons. T. Yes, they came to fetch you too.

Mme. T. No, it wasn't quite the same; that day you weren't mending an iron, you were mending the car.

Mons. T. I was talking about the rest of it. [*To* Zépo.] Go on, what happened then?

Zépo. Then I told him I had a fiancée and that if I didn't take her to the pictures on Sundays she wouldn't like it. He said that that wasn't the least bit important.

Zapo. Just how it was with me—exactly how it was with me.

Zépo. And then my father came down, and he said I couldn't go to the war because I didn't have a horse.

Zapo. Just what my father said.

Zépo. The man said you didn't need a horse any more, and I asked him if I could take my fiancée with me. He said no. Then I asked whether I could take my aunt with me so that she could make me one of her custards on Thursdays; I'm very fond of them.

Mme. T. [*realising that she'd forgotten it*]. Oh! The custard!

Zépo. He said no again.

Zapo. Same as with me.

Zépo. And ever since then I've been alone in the trench nearly all the time.

Mme. T. I think you and your distinguished prisoner might play together this afternoon, as you're as close to each other and so bored.

---

[2] Student of the Teacher's College and a stamp collector.

ZAPO. On no, Mother, I'm too afraid, he's an enemy.

MONS. T. Now now, you mustn't be afraid.

ZAPO. If you only knew what the General was saying about the enemy!

MME. T. What did he say?

ZAPO. He said the enemy are very nasty people. When they take prisoners they put little stones in their shoes so that it hurts them to walk.

MME. T. How awful! What barbarians!

MONS. T. [*indignantly, to* ZÉPO]. And aren't you ashamed to belong to an army of criminals?

ZÉPO. I haven't done anything. I don't do anybody any harm.

MME. T. He was trying to take us in, pretending to be such a little saint!

MONS. T. We oughtn't to have untied him. You never know, we only need to turn our backs and he'll be putting a stone in our shoes.

ZÉPO. Don't be so nasty to me.

MONS. T. What'd you think we *should* be, then? I'm indignant. I know what I'll do. I'll go and find the Captain and ask him to let me fight in the war.

ZAPO. He won't let you, you're too old.

MONS. T. Then I'll buy myself a horse and a sword and come and fight on my own account.

MME. T. Bravo! If I were a man I'd do the same.

ZÉPO. Don't be like that with me, Madame. Anyway I'll tell you something—our General told us the same thing about you.

MME. T. How could he dare tell such a lie!

ZAPO. No—but the same thing really?

ZÉPO. Yes, the same thing.

MONS. T. Perhaps it was the same man who talked to you both?

MME. T. Well if it was the same man he might at least have said something different. That's a fine thing—saying the same thing to everyone!

MONS. T. [*To* ZÉPO, *in a different tone of voice*]. Another little drink?

MME. T. I hope you liked our lunch?

MONS. T. In any case, it was better than last Sunday.

ZÉPO. What happened?

MONS. T. Well, we went to the country and we put the food on the rug. While we'd got our backs turned a cow ate up all our lunch, and the napkins as well.

ZÉPO. What a greedy cow!

MONS. T. Yes, but afterwards, to get our own back, we ate the cow. [*They laugh.*]

ZAPO. [*to* ZÉPO]. They couldn't have been very hungry after that!

MONS. T. Cheers! [*They all drink.*]

MME. T. [*to* ZÉPO]. And what do you do to amuse yourself in the trench?

ZÉPO. I spend my time making flowers out of rags, to amuse myself. I get terribly bored.

MME. T. And what do you do with the flowers?

ZÉPO. At the beginning I used to send them to my fiancée, but one day she told me that the greenhouse and the cellar were already full of them and that she didn't know what to do with them any more, and she asked me, if I didn't mind, to send her something else.

MME. T. And what did you do?

ZÉPO. I go on making rag flowers to pass the time.

MME. T. Do you throw them away afterwards, then?

ZÉPO. No, I've found a way to use them now. I give one flower for each pal who dies. That way I know that even if I make an awful lot there'll never be enough.

MONS. T. That's a good solution you've hit on.

ZÉPO. [*shyly*]. Yes.

ZAPO. Well, what I do is knit, so as not to get bored.

MME. T. But tell me, are all the soldiers as bored as you?

ZÉPO. It all depends on what they do to amuse themselves.

ZAPO. It's the same on our side.

MONS. T. Then let's stop the war.

ZÉPO. How?

MONS. T. It's very simple. [*To* ZAPO.] You just tell your pals that the enemy soldiers don't want to fight a war, and you [*to* ZÉPO] say the same to your comrades. And then everyone goes home.

ZAPO. Marvellous!

MME. T. And then you'll be able to finish mending the iron.

ZAPO. How is it that no one thought of such a good idea before?

MME T. Your father is the only one who's capable of thinking of such ideas; don't forget he's a former student of the Ecole Normale, *and* a philatelist.

ZÉPO. But what will the sergeant-majors and corporals do?

MONS. T. We'll give them some guitars and castanets to keep them quite!

ZÉPO. Very good idea.

MONS. T. You see how easy it is. Everything's fixed.

ZÉPO. We shall have a tremendous success.

ZAPO. My pals will be terribly pleased.

MME. T. What d'you say to putting on the pasodoble we were playing just now, to celebrate?

ZÉPO. Perfect.

ZAPO. Yes, put the record on, Mother. [MME. TÉPAN *puts a record on. She turns the handle. She waits. Nothing can be heard.*]

MONS. T. I can't hear a thing.

MME. T. Oh, how silly of me! Instead of putting a record on I put on a beret. [*She puts the record on. A gay pasodoble is heard.* ZAPO *dances with* ZÉPO, *and* MME. TÉPAN *with her husband. They are all very gay. The field telephone rings. None of the four hears it. They go on dancing busily. The telephone rings again. The dance continues.*
The battle starts up again with a terrific din of bombs, shots and bursts of machine-gun fire. None of the four has seen anything and they go on dancing merrily. A burst of machine-gun fire mows them all down. They fall to the ground, stone dead. A shot must have grazed the gramophone; the record keeps repeating the same thing, like a scratched record. The music of the scratched record can be heard till the end of the play. The two STRETCHER BEARERS *enter left. They are carrying the empty stretcher.*]

SUDDEN CURTAIN

(1959)

Using Library Sources in Your Writing

The ability to locate sources of information on a given subject and then incorporate the new ideas you find into your own writing is a valuable skill that every well-educated person needs to learn. In order to begin a documented paper about a literary work, you first should read carefully at least twice the primary source (the piece of literature about which you intend to do research). Our advice will use examples related to Arrabal's *Picnic on the Battlefield,* but remember that the process is the same for writing a library paper on any piece of literature you may choose.

Prewriting

The prewriting stage for a documented paper will necessarily be more complex than just gathering ideas for writing using only your own thoughts. You still need to understand completely the literary work before you begin, and your task will be complicated by the need to find, read, and assimilate the work of others, being careful all the while to credit these ideas when you incorporate them into your own writing.

FINDING A THESIS

In order to write a good paper involving research, you should begin with a *thesis question* which you can eventually turn into a thesis statement once you have discovered the information needed to provide the answer. You might want to approach the matter as a problem to be solved.

Thinking as Problem-solving.   You will write with greater engagement if you can discover some problem concerning your chosen literary work that genuinely interests you and then set out to solve that problem. Do you wonder, for instance, why several of Arrabal's characters seem so callous toward extreme cruelty? By reading about his work, you can probably find the answer to that question and arrive at a more thorough understanding of his plays. The problem, then, that you would work on solving as you write your paper would be this:

> How can I explain convincingly the reasons for Arrabal's casual presentation of cruelty in *Picnic on the Battlefield?*

Your thesis statement involves your solution of that problem and might read something like this:

> Arrabal's casual presentation of cruelty in *Picnic on the Battlefield* underscores the evil of accepting brutal behavior as commonplace in society—an acceptance that ultimately allows us to tolerate, sometimes even to celebrate, war.

Perhaps you find yourself more interested in the techniques used by Arrabal and the absurdist dramatists than by their philosophical stance. If so, you might conceive your problem this way:

> How does Arrabal go about conveying to the audience his conviction that war is absurd?

After completing your background reading, your problem would become finding the most effective way to explain how Arrabal achieves his dramatic purpose by using a pointless plot, stereotypical characters, meaningless actions, and absurd dialogue.

LOCATING SOURCES

At some stage in the writing of a documented paper, you need to visit the library and find out what other people have said about the literary work you have chosen as your subject.

USING THE CARD CATALOGUE OR THE COMPUTER FILE

If your research is going to focus on some aspect of Fernando Arrabal's work, you could profitably make your first stop at the library's card catalogue—or at the handy computer terminal that functions the same way. Each provides a listing of all books with call numbers indicating their locations. Because you will not at this point know the names of these books or their authors, you should look up *Arrabal, Fernando,* in the *subject index* to find books written about him and his work. You should also check *Arrabal* in the author index to discover possible collections of essays in which he may discuss his own plays or offer perceptive comments on theater of the absurd.

TAKING NOTES

Jot down author, title, and call numbers of any books that look useful. When you locate the actual texts, examine the indexes to discover whether they contain material on your literary work. Read any passages that appear relevant and take notes to record the most interesting ideas. Remember to put quotation marks around any material that you copy directly. And be sure to include on your notecards the title, publisher, place of publication, and date of any book from which you take information. On each card, write down the specific page the information came from, even if not a direct quotation.

USING BIBLIOGRAPHIES AND INDEXES

Even though you might find ample material in books to supply a wealth of documentation, your paper will not be well-researched unless you also discover what articles and reviews are available by consulting bibliographies and indexes.

The *MLA International Bibliography* lists (year by year) articles from leading periodicals. You would look under *Arrabal* in the twentieth-century French section because his plays are first published in French. (If you are doing research on an author whose nationality or dates you are unsure of, you must find out this information first from the *Dictionary of American Biography,* the *Dictionary of National Biography* [British], or *World Authors, 1950–1970*).

The *Reader's Guide to Periodical Literature,* which is much easier to use than the *MLA Bibliography,* will enable you to locate theater or book reviews in popular magazines, such as *Harper's,* the *Atlantic, The New Yorker, Time, Newsweek, The Nation,* and *The New Republic.* Entries are listed both by author and by subject.

Should you become interested in the staging of Arrabal's plays or the reviews of the productions or simply in the theater of the absurd, you will need also to consult the *New York Theater Critics' Reviews,* the *New York Times Theater Reviews,* and perhaps *Dramatic Criticism Index* and *Theater and Allied Arts: A Guide to Books.* (If, by the way, you should want to do research on a twentieth-century novel, you would check the *Book Review Digest* for contemporary reviews [since 1905]; for a nineteenth-century novel, *Poole's Index to Periodical Literature.*)

Once you have found titles of articles and reviews that sound pertinent, you need to locate the journal and see whether the actual article or review lives up to the promise of its title. If the material proves useful, take notes. Be sure to record on each notecard the name of the journal, the volume number, date, and pages. You will need this information later in order to credit your sources.

Writing

Before you begin actually writing your first draft, you need to turn the thesis question you were investigating into a thesis statement— a sentence that conveys the point you want to make after studying your primary source and reading your secondary sources. If, for instance, you begin by investigating this question,

> Why do Arrabal's characters in *Picnic on the Battlefield* make such ridiculous statements and engage in such bizarre actions?

you might, after doing your research, end up with a thesis statement something like this:

The ridiculous conversation and bizarre actions of the characters in *Picnic on the Battlefield* effectively convey Arrabal's conviction that war is absurd.

Your thesis may change, of course, as you work with your material, but you need a fairly clear idea of what you want to say and how you will go about saying it before you start.

DEVELOPING A PLAN

Many people strongly recommend taking notes on 3″ by 5″ or 5″ by 7″ notecards during the researching stage of writing a documented paper. These small cards make the material easy to organize. If you have, instead, pages of notes, you may find yourself wasting time as you shuffle through dozens of sheets trying to locate the note you need.

Using Notecards.   After completing your note-taking, you should read each card and try to select a word or two that summarizes the meaning of the passage on each card. Write that heading in the upper right-hand corner of the card. You can do this as you take notes, if you prefer. After all the cards have headings, read through these headings and group the cards with similar ideas together in stacks.

That's the easy part. Next, you must put your mind to work and decide on some reasonable order in which to present these ideas. Then, arrange the stacks according to your plan. As you write, following this plan, the necessary information will be in front of you ready to be incorporated into the first draft of your paper.

WRITING BEFORE RESEARCH

If you are fired with enthusiasm for the play, if you have a number of significant observations that you want to express, you should go right ahead and devise a thesis, marshall your evidence, order your ideas, and write a first draft. Then you can go to the library, locate and read a number of pertinent *secondary sources* written about your chosen literary work (articles, reviews, sections of books, perhaps even whole books if your research needs to be thorough), and incorporate ideas from this reading into your paper at the appropriate places. You may find—especially if you are writing about a popular work by a well-known author—that most of your cogent insights have already appeared in print. Try not to be disheartened. Grit your teeth and give credit to the person who published first.

Say, for example, you had made this comment in your first draft:

Everyone in the play considers war a game.

After reading criticism on Arrabal's play, you would discover that one of the critics, Peter Podol, makes this same observation. Thus you would need to alter your statement to read something like this:

As Podol observes, everyone in the play considers war a game (31).

Or, if a critic has made the point more effectively than you did, you might decide to scrap your sentence and quote the secondary source directly, like this:

> As Podol observes, "The *jeu*, or game, . . . plays a significant role in this first drama" (31).

After giving credit where credit is due throughout your paper, you may want to emphasize—if you can do so gracefully—the remaining ideas that are entirely yours:

> Zapo's knitting and Zépo's making rag flowers suggest, I think, a feminine gentleness quite in keeping with their refusal to shoot the enemy deliberately.

Some people find this method of "plugging in" ideas from their research the easiest way to handle a documented paper. If you are knowledgeable and enthusiastic about your topic, it may be the best way to proceed.

But, on the other hand, if after reading the primary source, you find yourself devoid of ideas, perhaps confused about the work, a better method is the one we described first: go to the library, locate the pertinent secondary sources, and study them carefully. Then, after having gained a thorough understanding of the primary source, you devise a thesis, choose your supporting material (both from the play and from the critics), arrange your ideas in an orderly way, and write your first draft.

Avoiding Plagiarism

Whenever you write a paper after consulting secondary sources, you must take scrupulous care to give credit to those sources for any ideas or phrasings that you may borrow.

Plagiarism involves carelessly—or, far worse, deliberately—presenting the words or ideas of another writer as your own.

You must be careful in taking notes to put quotation marks around any passages—or even phrases—that you copy word for word. Changing an occasional word here and there will not do, either: such close paraphrasing is still considered plagiarism. The examples below may help you to see the difference between plagiarism and paraphrasing (stating another's ideas in your own words), in case you are in doubt.

Original Passage:
> "I hope that it transcends the personal and the private, and has something to do with the anguish of us all" (54).
>   —*Edward Albee on* The American Dream

Plagiarism:
  Albee writes that he hopes his play transcends the personal and the private and has a lot to do with everyone's anguish (54).

Combined Paraphrase and Direct Quotation:
  Albee writes that he wants the play to rise above "the personal and the private" to reveal "the anguish of us all" (54).

Paraphrase:
  Albee says that he hopes the play goes beyond individual problems and deals with universal grief and pain (54).

Direct Quotation:
  "I hope," writes Albee, "that [*The American Dream*] transcends the personal and the private, and has something to do with the anguish of us all" (54).

Introducing Quotations

Whether you are quoting directly or simply paraphrasing someone else's ideas, you should always give credit in the text of your paper to the person from whom you are borrowing. The MLA documentary style now requires you to do so. No longer will you be able to toss in a quotation, put a note number at the end, and trust your reader to fumble for the note page to discover your source. Because you now have to cite all sources within the paper, you need to exercise great skill in varying the way you introduce quotations and borrowed ideas.

As you read your secondary sources, pay attention to the various ways that these writers credit their sources. If you read widely enough, this graceful introducing of other people's ideas will become second nature to you. But in case you still have to work at introducing your quotations, here are a few models for you to go by:

> As critic Lawrence Stone explains, daughters in Shakespeare's England were "often unwanted and might be regarded as no more than a tiresome drain on the economic resources of the family" (112).

> Henry James argues that "The dramatic current stagnates . . ." (654).

> Kettle declares *Middlemarch* to be "the most impressive novel in our language" (1:160).

> According to biographer Joan Givner, the failure of Porter's personal relationship with Josephson caused a temporary inability to write (221).

> Novelist Alice Walker asserts that the mothers and grandmothers of black women were "driven to a numb and bleeding madness by the springs of creativity in them for which there was no release" (31).

As Rachel Brownstein points out, "A beautiful virgin walled off from an imperfect real world is the central figure in romance" (35).

"A beginning as simple as this," observes Mark Schorer, "must overcome corrupted reading habits of long standing . . ." (706–07).

IDEAS FOR RESEARCHED WRITING

1. Examine closely the conversations in *Picnic on the Battlefield*. How does this language help convey Arrabal's theme?
2. How does the language of Pinter's *The Dumb Waiter* illustrate the existential philosophy of the theater of the absurd?
3. What is a dumb waiter? How many meanings does this phrase convey? Why did Pinter call his play *The Dumb Waiter*?
4. How does the staging of *Picnic on the Battlefield* reflect the absurdist philosophy of the playwright?
5. Research the staging of *Hedda Gabler, Death of a Salesman,* and *Picnic on the Battlefield*. Discuss how the staging changes from the traditional to the nonrepresentational to the absurdist.
6. Contrast the characters of Antigone, Desdemona, and Hedda Gabler.

Rewriting

Many people who do researched writing make no attempt to provide complete, accurate documentation of sources in the first draft because pausing to do so interrupts the flow of ideas. You need, of course, to include at least the last name of the person whose words are quoted or paraphrased (or the title of an anonymous source), but you can fill in from your notes the remaining information as part of the revising process.

CITING SOURCES

Various academic disciplines use different documentation styles. Because you are writing about literature, the appropriate one for you to follow is the newly streamlined Modern Language Association style. Sample entries to illustrate the MLA format appear in the following section. You may also use as a model the documentation included in the sample student research paper at the end of this chapter.

Be sure that you follow the models accurately. You should have all the necessary information recorded on your notecards. If you neglected to write down a page number or a date or a publisher, you must now trudge back to the library and track down the book or periodical again. You can see that taking care during the information-gathering stage will save you frustration later during the documenting stage.

INCLUDING INFORMATIONAL NOTES

With the new MLA style you will no longer use footnotes or end-notes to credit your sources. Any numbered notes—whether typed at the bottom of the page or inserted just before the final "Works Cited" entries—will be informational notes. Any brief comment that is important enough to include but that is not precisely to the point of your discussion should be placed in a note. When you type these informational notes, you should entitle them simply "Notes" and place them on a separate page at the end of the paper, just before the "Works Cited" page.

Editing

You must be particularly careful in proofreading and correcting a documented paper. Careless errors in typing will ruin your credibility—as well as your grade. Careless errors in crediting your sources could result in plagiarism, thus threatening your credibility, your grade, and your college career.

CHECKING THE DOCUMENTATION

Besides following your usual procedures for proofreading and editing, you should take time to read through the paper one extra time, checking only the way you have incorporated your sources. Ask yourself these questions:

1. Did I put quotation marks around all sentences and phrases borrowed from my reading?
2. Did I give credit in the text for all ideas borrowed from my reading, whether quoted directly or not?
3. Did I always put periods and commas before the quotation marks except when documentation in parentheses follows the quotation? Here's an example:

    "Arrabal's world," Esslin believes, "derives its absurdity . . . from the fact that his characters see the human situation with uncomprehending eyes of childlike simplicity" (217).

4. Did I include all the required information in the citations?
5. Did I use accurate paraphrases that are not too close to the original wording?

Then, take a few extra minutes to check carefully your "Works Cited" page. Ask yourself these questions:

1. Did I alphabetize correctly? (*A, an* and *the* do not count when alphabetizing the title of an anonymous article.)

2. Did I use hanging indention (Did I indent all lines of an entry five spaces except for the first line)?
3. Did I use colons where colons are needed, periods where periods are needed, parentheses where parentheses are needed?
4. Did I underline the titles of all books and the names of all magazines and scholarly journals?
5. Did I use quotation marks around the titles of articles and chapters from books?
6. Did I convert all Roman numerals to Arabic?
7. Did I include all the necessary data?

Sample Student Documented Paper

The following paper was written by Laurie Dahlberg, a student at Illinois State University. Because she has used the new MLA documentation style, you will be able to see exactly how the system works. Be sure to put your "Notes" and your "Works Cited" list each on separate pages. A complete guide to using this system follows Laurie's paper.

An Analysis of Arrabal's Picnic on the Battlefield

Fernando Arrabal's play Picnic on the Battlefield may at first appear to be simply a war protest, but its simplicity can be misleading. Like other artists, Arrabal himself can be found at the center of the play, projecting his own dismal yet amusing view of human nature at war with itself. Though the playwright's purpose is to expose the utter stupidity of war[1] which, as critic Janet Diaz observes, is "forced on peace-loving men by their governments" (151-2), he nonetheless portrays his characters in a way which causes the audience to wonder whether these people deserve the dignity of peace. Arrabal portrays humanity as innocent yet cruel. Examining the characterization in the play gives us insight into its absurdist philosophical underpinnings.

Arrabal creates a world which is altogether bewildering to its inhabitants and audience alike. "Paradoxes abound," writes Podol: "the lyrical is united with the cruel, humor is

combined with terror, innocence with depravity . . . "(29).
Though Picnic on the Battlefield includes layers of often
confusing paradoxes, Arrabal achieves unity through
repetition--of words, symbols, even characters. Zapo and Zepo
behave exactly alike in order to stress the absurdity of
fighting a war against someone who is no different from
oneself.

Drama specialist Martin Esslin notes that the play's
absurdity derives largely from the characters who see their
situation "through uncomprehending eyes of childlike
simplicity" (217). Thus Zapo knits in the trenches, a
prisoner lunches politely with his captors, and the Tepans
protect themselves from bombs with an ordinary umbrella. Diaz
comments that the action seems illogical only until we
recognize that the "logic is not directly expressed, but
symbolically embodied in the action" (153). Thus, the play
presents a highly subjective form of reality which, in the
words of critic Ruby Cohn, "syncopate[s] incidents in a
dream-like way . . ." (29-30). The bouyant, giddy behavior of
the characters suggests a dream world, but elements of reality
are strongly present. As Arrabal himself has observed, he is
a "realist including the nightmare" (qtd. in Killinger 220).

The characters in the play behave like adult children.
Thomas Donahue notes that they "combine the imaginative,
playful, sadistically cruel behavior of the child with the
chronologically mature body of an adult" (8). They seem
almost blameless in their innocence. Esslin adds that "Like
children, they are often cruel because they have failed to
understand, or even to notice, the existence of a moral law;
and like children, they suffer the cruelty of the world as a
meaningless affliction" (217). These adult children vacillate
between being playful and pouting, generous and
inconsiderate. As the play opens, the lonely Zapo, who cannot
understand the meaning of war, is plaintively asking his
captain to send him someone to keep him company, "even if it's
only a nanny goat." Genevieve Serreau observes that the

simplicity of the language contributes greatly to the
effectiveness of the play. The characters speak, she says,
with "the poetic truth of the language of childhood, a speech
as direct as a shower of stones . . ." (68).

Of course, Zapo, and his double, Zepo, are little more
than children, perhaps eighteen years old. But they at least
have enough understanding of the dangers of war to dive under
the sandbags when bombs begin to fall. Mons. and Mme. Tepan,
on the other hand, do not recognize the slightest danger as
they stroll casually into the middle of a war zone to have a
picnic with their son. Arrabal, in fact, seems to intensify
the immaturity of the older couple, perhaps suggesting that
the longer one is on earth, the more confusing it all
becomes. His characters can only cope with the complexity of
life by retreating into a shell of ignorance, like pulling the
covers up over their heads.

Reacting to war with the incomprehension of children, the
characters relegate war to the status of a childish game.
According to critic Peter Podol, the game, or "jeu," provides
a motif in which war is equated with "a broad range of playful
competitions" (31). The equation of war and game is
reiterated throughout the play, as when Zapo tags the enemy
Zepo on the shoulder, instead of taking him prisoner at
gunpoint. Both characters understand this gesture.

But Arrabal goes beyond the contrast between the
innocence of the adult children and the cruelty of the real
world. He quite honestly includes the darker side of human
nature in order to make his characters not just naive, but
morally naive. This conflict between depravity and innocence
is an emerging force in the play. As T. J. Donahue explains,

> [The characters'] moral systems, if one can
> call them such, tend to be mechanistic. They shoot
> their so-called enemy and then quickly recite the
> Hail Mary or the Our Father. In their eyes, asking
> for pardon is a sufficient safeguard against guilt.

>   . . . Yet their lack of guilt demonstrates that
>   reality never penetrates the fiber of their lives.
>   (8)

We get our first clue about the unfeeling nature of the
characters when Mme. Tepan remarks, "We thought you must be
bored, so we came to pay you a little visit. This war must be
a bit tedious, after all." Tedious is hardly an appropriate
word to use to describe a war. Later, she casually declares,
"I've always liked battles. As a child I always said that
when I grew up I wanted to be a Colonel of the dragoons."[2]
The same callous nature is revealed by degrees in each of the
characters. Gentle Zapo is eager to pose with the captured
Zepo like a hunter with his trophy. Death and destruction
seem only to heighten Mons. Tepan's appetite: "I feel hungry
as a hunter. It's the smell of gunpowder."

Arrabal brilliantly counterpoints this cruelly
indifferent attitude with the excessively polite etiquette
observed by the Tepans--with highly comic results. In theory,
social politeness (supposedly a proud product of
"civilization") grew out of the understanding of accepted
moral laws, like the Golden Rule. And although the Tepans
strictly adhere to the complicated structure of social
decorum, it becomes apparent that the morality which should
underlie this civility is absent, leaving a ridiculous shell
of social niceties devoid of any connection with the
principles which produced them. In a highly ironic scene,
Mme. Tepan is more interested in the cleanliness of her son
than in his safety or his well-being: ". . . you know,
there's one thing I <u>will</u> not have, and that's making fighting
a war an excuse for not washing."

Thus, despite the dull horror and grotesqueries, <u>Picnic</u>
<u>on the Battlefield</u> is often hilariously funny. Donahue
describes the appeal of the black humor this way:

>   From the point of view of the spectator, . . .
>   the distance that is established between what these

hapless children want to be and what they really
are, between what they strive to do and what they
do, gives a comic luster . . . reminiscent of the
type of comedy produced by the pratfalls of
Chaplin's tramp. (24)

By making us laugh, Arrabal clearly hopes to make us see the
flaws of society. As Podol illustrates, Arrabal depends
heavily upon humor--on the "construction of incongruities"--in
order to "render the idea of war totally ludicrous" (30). But
he does not hold human beings to blame for the evils of the
social system. He declares, "My characters are not familiar
with the laws. They try to understand laws that serve no
useful purpose whatsoever. Even in extreme cases, they are
not guilty. It is not my characters who should be changed,
but rather society" (qtd. in Espinasse 72).

NOTES

[1]Fernando Arrabal, born in Spanish Morocco in 1932,
lived in Spain during the Spanish Civil War under a military
dictatorship, which may account for his strong anti-war
sentiments (Serreau 61).

[2]According to Podol, "Zapo's mother, Mme. Tepan,
mirrors Arrabal's own mother both in name (Teran) and in her
blind admiration for the military uniform and its aura" (30).

WORKS CITED

Cohn, Ruby. Currents in Contemporary Drama. Bloomington:
    Indiana UP, 1960.

Diaz, Janet W. "Theatre and Theories of Fernando Arrabal."
    Kentucky Romance Quarterly 2 (1969): 143-54.

Donahue, Thomas John. The Theatre of Fernando Arrabal. New
    York: New York UP, 1980.

Espinasse, Francoise. "An Interview with Fernando Arrabal."
    <u>Evergreen Review</u> 71 (Oct. 1969): 43-47, 72-73.

Esslin, Martin. <u>The Theatre of the Absurd.</u> Garden City:
    Doubleday, 1969.

Killinger, John. "Arrabal and Surrealism." <u>Modern Drama</u> 14
    (Sept. 1971): 210-23.

Podol, Peter L. <u>Fernando Arrabal</u>. Boston: G. K. Hall, 1978.

Serreau, Genevieve. "A New Comic Style: Arrabal." <u>Evergreen
    Review</u> 4 (Nov.-Dec. 1960): 61-69.

Remember that in your paper the "Notes" and "Works Cited" list will each appear on separate pages.

Sample New MLA Documentation Style

1. Instead of concluding with a list of documentary notes or a bibliography, your paper will end with an alphabetized list of "Works Cited" that includes all sources mentioned in your essay.
2. In citing primary sources (i.e., short stories, poems, novels, or plays), include author's name and page number (or line number, if a poem) in the text for the first entry. Thereafter, page number alone will suffice, unless your list of "Works Cited" includes more than one work by that author.[1]

A. Quotation from a novel:

Rhoda Nunn emphasizes the importance of role models as she declares to Monica, "Your mistake was in looking only at the weak women" (Gissing 316).

Gissing's awareness of the importance of role models is evident when Rhoda Nunn tells Monica, "Your mistake was in looking only at weak women" (316).

The "Works Cited" entry is

Gissing, George. The Odd Women. 1893. Rpt. New York: Norton, 1977.

---

[1] You should include a shortened title if you have several works by the same author, like this: (Gissing, *Grub Street* 37).

B. Quotation from a poem:

In "Kubla Khan" Coleridge leaves unresolved the paradox of "caverns measureless to man" from which was "heard the mingled measure" (lines 4, 33).

Coleridge's assertion that poetic life is a "miracle of rare device / A sunny pleasure dome with caves of ice" (35–36) proves paradoxical.

> Do not abbreviate the words "line" or "lines." Once lineation is established (as in the example above), then use only line numbers.

> The "Works Cited" entry is

Coleridge, S. T. "Kubla Khan." Coleridge: Poetical Works. Ed. Ernest H. Coleridge. London: Oxford UP, 1973. 297–98.

C. Quotation from a play:

In Othello, Iago's striking comment, "What you know, you know./ From this time forth I will never speak a word" (5.2.299–300), serves as a philosophic closure.

The ontological level of discourse can be seen in the words of Emilia, who exclaims, "O, the more angel she,/ And you the blacker devil!" (Othello 5.1.129–30).

> [The numbers separated by periods mean: act 5, scene 1, lines 129 through 130.]

> The "Works Cited" entry is

Shakespeare, William. Othello. Literature: An Introduction to Fiction, Poetry, and Drama. Ed. X. J. Kennedy. 3rd ed. Boston: Little, 1983. 875–958.

D. Quotations from nondramatic prose are cited the same way as a novel.

3. Individual citations of secondary sources (books or articles considering the work under discussion) are inserted in the paper by author and page number (or by author, shortened title, and page number if your list of "Works Cited" includes more than one work by that person).

A. Quotation from a work in more than one volume:

Kettle declares Middlemarch to be "the most impressive novel in our language" (1:160).

> The "Works Cited" entry is

Kettle, Arnold. An Introduction to the English Novel. 2 vols. New York: Harper, 1951.

B. Quotation from book with single author:

As Lawrence Stone explains, daughters in Shakespeare's England were "often unwanted and might be regarded as no more than a tiresome drain on the economic resources of the family" (112).

The "Works Cited" entry is

Stone, Lawrence. The Family, Sex and Marriage in England: 1500–1800. New York: Harper, 1977.

C. Quotation from an article:

As Michael Holzman reports, many of his students felt that "Expression and communication were reserved for speech" (235).

The "Works Cited" entry is

Holzman, Michael. "Teaching Is Remembering." College English 46 (1984): 229–38.

According to Tanselle, "The basic technical problem of bibliographical description arises from the difficulty of expressing the visual in verbal terms" (71).

The "Works Cited" entry is

Tanselle, G. Thomas. "The Bibliographical Description of Patterns." Studies in Bibliography 23 (1970): 70–102.

4. Any notes in your paper will be informational; that is, they will contain material of interest that is not essential to your discussion (like the note at the bottom of page 673). These content notes are included as "Notes" just before your list of "Works Cited."

5. Always use Arabic numbers, except when citing pages from a preface, introduction, or table of contents (vi) or when mentioning monarchs (James I, Elizabeth II).

6. If the place of publication of a book is a foreign city, cite the original name and add the English version in brackets: München [Munich].

7. Always omit the abbreviations p. and pp. (for page and pages).

8. In general, lower case for vol., no., chap., trans. in citations.

9. If you cite two or more entries by the same author, do not repeat the author's name. Instead use three hyphens, followed by a period. Then give the remaining information as usual.

Sample Entries For a List of "Works Cited"

Remember: You must alphabetize your list and use hanging indention; i.e., after the first line, indent subsequent lines five spaces.

A. Book with one author:

   Rabkin, Norman. Shakespeare and the Problem of Meaning. Chicago:
       U of Chicago P, 1981.

B. Reprint of an earlier edition:

   Partridge, Eric. Shakespeare's Bawdy. 1948. Rpt. New York: Dutton,
       1969.

C. Revised edition:

   Howe, Irving. William Faulkner: A Critical Study. 3rd ed. Chicago:
       U of Chicago P, 1973.

D. Book with two authors:

   Gilbert, Sandra, and Susan Gubar. The Madwoman in the Attic:
       The Woman Writer and the Nineteenth-Century Literary
       Imagination. New Haven: Yale UP, 1979.

E. Book with more than two authors or editors:

   Spiller, Robert E., et al. LHUS. 3rd ed. London: Macmillan, 1969.

   [*LHUS* means *Literary History of the United States* and is
   abbreviated in citations, as are *PMLA* (*Publication of the Modern
   Language Association*) and *TLS* (London *Times Literary
   Supplement*).]

F. Work in several volumes:

   Kettle, Arnold. An Introduction to the English Novel. 2 vols. New
       York: Harper, 1951.

G. Essay in a collection, casebook, or critical edition:

   Tyndall, William York. "The Form of Billy Budd." *Melville's* Billy
       Budd *and the Critics*. Ed. William T. Stafford. Belmont:
       Wadsworth, 1961. 125–31.

   [If an underlined title contains another title usually underlined,
   leave the second title without underlining.]

H. Work in an anthology:

   Arnold, Matthew. "Dover Beach." The Norton Anthology of English
       Literature. Ed. M. H. Abrams et al. 2 vols. New York: Norton,
       1968. 2: 1039.

I. Work in translation:

Cirlot, J. E. A Dictionary of Symbols. Trans. Jack Sage. 2nd ed. New York: Philosophical Lib., 1976.

J. Anonymous book:

The Statutes of the Realm. London: Record Commissions, 1820–28; facsim. ed. 1968.

[facsim.—abbreviation for facsimile]

K. Anonymous article (magazine with no volume number);

"The Talk of the Town." The New Yorker 30 Jan. 1984: 25–29.

L. Signed article (newspaper):

Harding, D. W. "Father and Daughter in Shakespeare's Last Plays." TLS 30 Nov. 1979: 59–61.

[*TLS* means the London *Times Literary Supplement.*]

Unsigned article (newspaper):

"College Grads Better Consumers." Chicago Tribune 3 May 1976: 2.3.

[means section 2, page 3]

M. Signed article (periodical with no volume number);

Heilbrun, Carolyn. "The Masculine Wilderness of the American Novel." Saturday Review 29 Jan. 1962: 41–44.

N. Signed article (periodical with continuous pagination):

Mason, John B. "Whitman's Catalogues: Rhetorical Means for Two Journeys in 'Song of Myself.'" American Literature 45 (1973): 34–49.

Signed article (periodical with each issue separately paged):

Frey, John R. "America and Her Literature Reviewed by Postwar Germany." American-German Review 10.5 (1954): 4–7.

[means vol. 10, issue 5]

O. Unsigned encyclopedia article:

"Abolitionists." Encyclopedia Americana. 1974 ed.

P. Signed encyclopedia article:

P[ar]k, T[homas]. "Ecology." Encyclopaedia Britannica. 1968 ed.

Q. Article from *Dictionary of American Biography:*

N[evins], A[llan]. "Warren Gamaliel Harding." *DAB* (1932).

R. Anonymous pamphlet:

> Preparing Your Dissertation for Microfilming. Ann Arbor: UMI, n.d.

[UMI means University Microfilms International. n.d. means no date given.]

S. Reference to the Bible:

> The Bible. Trans. J. M. P. Smith, Edgar J. Goodspeed, et al. Chicago:
> U of Chicago P, 1939.

> The Geneva Bible. 1560. Facsim. Rpt. Madison: U of Wisconsin P,
> 1961.

[Do not underline the King James version of the Bible, and do not list the Bible unless you have used a version other than the King James. Cite chapter and verse in parentheses in the text of your paper this way: (Dan. 9.25–27)].

T. Reference to a letter (in a published collection):

> Clemens, Samuel. Mark Twain's Letters. Ed. A. B. Paine. 2 vols. New
> York: Harper, 1917.

U. Reference to a letter (unpublished or personal):

> Wharton, Edith. Letter to William Brownell. 6 Nov. 1907. Wharton
> Archives. Amherst College, Amherst, MA.
> Vidal, Gore. Letter to author. 2 June 1984.

V. Personal or telephone interview:

> Kesey, Ken. Personal interview. 28 May 1983.
> Didion, Joan. Telephone interview. 10 April 1982.

W. Review (signed or unsigned):

> Updike, John. "Who Wants to Know?" Rev. of the Dragons of Eden,
> by Carl Sagan. The New Yorker 22 Aug. 1977: 87–90.

> Rev. of Ring, by Jonathan Yardley. The New Yorker 12 Sept. 1977:
> 159–60.

X. Lecture:

> Axelrod, Rise. "Who Did What with Whom?" MLA Convention.
> Chicago, 30 Dec. 1977.

Y. Film:

> Modern Times. Dir. Charles Chaplin. With Chaplin and Paulette
> Goddard. United Artists, 1936.

[If you are discussing the contribution of an individual, begin with that person's name.]

Z. Document from ERIC (Education Resources Information Center):

> Cooper, Grace C. "The Teaching of Composition and Different
> Cognitive Styles." Mar. 1980. Ed 186 915.

Anthology of Drama

William Shakespeare *1564–1616*

OTHELLO

THE NAMES OF THE ACTORS

OTHELLO, *the Moor.*

BRABANTIO, *a senator, father to Desdemona.*

CASSIO, *an honourable lieutenant to Othello.*

IAGO, *Othello's ancient, a villain.*

RODERIGO, *a gulled gentleman.*

DUKE OF VENICE.

SENATORS *of Venice.*

MONTANO, *governor of Cyprus.*

LODOVICO and GRATIANO, *kinsmen to Brabantio, two noble Venetians.*

SAILORS.

CLOWN.

DESDEMONA, *daughter to Brabantio and wife to Othello.*

EMILIA, *wife to Iago.*

BIANCA, *a courtezan and mistress to Cassio.*

MESSENGER, HERALD, OFFICERS, GENTLEMEN, MUSICIANS, AND ATTENDANTS.

[SCENE: *Venice: A Sea-port in Cyprus.*]

ACT I.

SCENE I. [*Venice. A street.*]

[*Enter* RODERIGO *and* IAGO.]

ROD. Tush! never tell me; I take it much unkindly
  That thou, Iago, who hast had my purse
  As if the strings were thine, shouldst know of this.
IAGO. 'Sblood,° but you'll not hear me:
  If ever I did dream of such a matter,
  Abhor me.
ROD. Thou told'st me thou didst hold him in thy hate.
IAGO. Despise me, if I do not. Three great ones of the city,°
  In personal suit to make me his lieutenant,
  Off-capp'd to him°: and, by the faith of man,   10
  I know my price, I am worth no worse a place:
  But he, as loving his own pride and purposes,
  Evades them, with a bombast circumstance
  Horribly stuff'd with epithets of war;
  And, in conclusion,
  Nonsuits° my mediators; for, 'Certes,' says he,
  'I have already chose my officer.'
  And what was he?
  Forsooth, a great arithmetician,°
  One Michael Cassio, a Florentine,   20
  A fellow almost damn'd in a fair wife;°
  That never set a squadron in the field,
  Nor the division° of a battle knows
  More than a spinster; unless the bookish theoric,°
  Wherein the toged° consuls can propose°
  As masterly as he: mere prattle, without practice,
  Is all his soldiership. But he, sir, had th' election:
  And I, of whom his eyes had seen the proof
  At Rhodes, mat Cyprus° and on other grounds
  Christian and heathen, must be be-lee'd and calm'd   30
  By debitor and creditor: this counter-caster,°
  He, in good time,° must his lieutenant be,
  And I—God bless the mark°!—his Moorship's ancient.°

'Sblood an oath, "by God's blood"   **great ones of the city** Iago means to indicate his importance in the community; this is suggested also by his use of the word *worth* in line 11   **him** Othello   **Nonsuits** rejects   **arithmetician** a man whose military knowledge was merely theoretical, based on books of tactics   **A . . . wife** Cassio does not seem to be married, but his counterpart in Shakespeare's source did have a wife   **division** disposition of a battle line   **theoric** theory   **toged** wearing the toga   **propose** discuss   **Rhodes, Cyprus** islands in the Mediterranean south of Asia Minor, long subject to contention between the Venetians and the Turks   **counter-caster** a sort of bookkeeper; contemptuous term   **in good time** forsooth   **God bless the mark** anciently, a pious interjection to avert evil omens   **ancient** standardbearer, ensign

ROD. By heaven, I rather would have been his hangman.
IAGO. Why, there 's no remedy; 'tis the curse of service,
 Preferment goes by letter and affection,
 And not by old gradation,° where each second
 Stood heir to th' first. Now, sir, be judge yourself,
 Whether I in any just term am affin'd°
 To love the Moor.
ROD.   I would not follow then.   40
IAGO. O, sir, content you;
 I follow him to serve my turn upon him:
 We cannot all be masters, nor all masters
 Cannot be truly follow'd. You shall mark
 Many a duteous and knee-crooking knave,
 That, doting on his own obsequious bondage,
 Wears out his time, much like his master's ass,
 For nought but provender, and when he's old, cashier'd:
 Whip me such honest knaves. Others there are
 Who, trimm'd in forms and visages of duty,   50
 Keep yet their hearts attending on themselves,
 And, throwing but shows of service on their lords,
 Do well thrive by them and when they have lin'd their coats
 Do themselves homage: these fellows have some soul;
 And such a one do I profess myself. For, sir,
 It is as sure as you are Roderigo,
 Were I the Moor, I would not be Iago°:
 In following him, I follow but myself;
 Heaven is my judge, not I for love and duty,
 But seeming so, for my peculiar end: 60
 For when my outward action doth demonstrate
 The native act and figure of my heart
 In compliment extern,° 'tis not long after
 But I will wear my heart upon my sleeve
 For daws to peck at: I am not what I am.
ROD. What a full fortune does the thick-lips° owe,
 If he can carry 't thus!
IAGO.   Call up her father,
 Rouse him: make after him, poison his delight,
 Proclaim him in the streets; incense her kinsmen,
 And, though he in a fertile climate dwell,   70
 Plague him with flies: though that his joy be joy,
 Yet throw such changes of vexation on 't,
 As it may lose some colour.
ROD. Here is her father's house; I'll call aloud.
IAGO. Do, with like timorous° accent and dire yell
 As when, by night and negligence, the fire

---

old gradation seniority. Iago here expresses a characteristic prejudice of professional soldiers. **affin'd** bound   **Were . . . Iago** Were I in the position of the Moor, I should not feel as Iago feels   **compliment extern** outward civilty   **thick-lips** Elizabethans often applied the term *Moor* to Negroes   **timorous** frightening

Is spied in populous cities.

Rod. What, ho, Brabantio! Signior Brabantio, ho!

Iago. Awake! what, ho, Brabantio! thieves! thieves! thieves!
  Look to your house, your daughter and your bags!   80
  Thieves! thieves!

  [Brabantio *appears above at a window.*]

Bra. What is the reason of this terrible summons?
  What is the matter there?

Rod. Signior, is all your family within?

Iago. Are your doors lock'd?

Bra.   Why, wherefore ask you this?

Iago. 'Zounds, sir, y' are robb'd; for shame, put on your gown;
  Your heart is burst, you have lost half your soul;
  Even now, now, very now, an old black ram   90
  Is tupping your white ewe. Arise, arise;
  Awake the snorting° citizens with the bell,
  Or else the devil will make a grandsire of you:
  Arise, I say.

Bra.   What, have you lost your wits?

Rod. Most reverend signior, do you know my voice?

Bra. Not I: what are you?

Rod. My name is Roderigo.

Bra.   The worser welcome:
  I have charg'd thee not to haunt about my doors:
  In honest plainness thou hast heard me say
  My daughter is not for thee; and now, in madness,   100
  Being full of supper and distemp'ring draughts,
  Upon malicious bravery,° doest thou come
  To start° my quiet.

Rod. Sir, sir, sir,—

Bra.   But thou must needs be sure
  My spirit and my place have in them power
  To make this bitter to thee.

Rod.   Patience, good sir.

Bra. What tell'st thou me of robbing? this is Venice;
  My house is not a grange.°

Rod.   Most grave Brabantio,
  In simple and pure soul I come to you.

Iago. 'Zounds, sir, you are one of those that will not serve God, if the
  devil bid you. Because we come to do you service and you think we
  are ruffians, you'll have your daughter covered with a Barbary horse;
  you'll have your nephews° neigh to you; you'll have coursers for cousins
  and gennets° for germans.°

Bra. What profane wretch are thou?

---

snorting snoring   **bravery** defiance, bravado   **start** disrupt   **grange** isolated farm-
house   **nephews** grandsons   **gennets** small Spanish horses   **germans** near relatives

IAGO. I am one, sir, that comes to tell you your daughter and
 the Moor are now making the beast with two backs.
BRA. Thou art a villain.
IAGO.   You are—a senator.
BRA. This thou shalt answer; I know thee, Roderigo.
ROD. Sir, I will answer any thing. But, I beseech you,
 If 't be your pleasure and most wise consent,
 As partly I find it is, that your fair daughter,   120
 At this odd-even° and dull watch o' th' night,
 Transported, with no worse nor better guard
 But with a knave of common hire, a gondolier,
 To the gross clasps of a lascivious Moor,—
 If this be known to you and your allowance,°
 We then have done you bold and saucy wrongs;
 But if you know not this, my manners tell me
 We have your wrong rebuke. Do not believe
 That, from° the sense of all civility,
 I thus would play and trifle with your reverence: 130
 Your daughter, if you have not given her leave,
 I say again, hath made a gross revolt;
 Tying her duty, beauty, wit and fortunes
 In an extravagant° and wheeling° stranger
 Of here and every where. Straight satisfy yourself:
 If she be in her chamber or your house,
 Let loose on me the justice of the state
 For thus deluding you.
BRA.   Strike on the tinder,° ho!
 Give me a taper! call up all my people!
 This accident° is not unlike my dream: 140
 Belief of it oppresses me already.
 Light, I say! light!   [*Exit above.*]
IAGO.   Farewell; for I must leave you:
 It seems not meet, nor wholesome to my place,
 To be produc'd—as, if I stay, I shall—
 Against the Moor: for, I do know, the state,
 However this may gall him with some check,°
 Cannot with safety cast° him, for he's embark'd
 With such loud reason to the Cyprus wars,
 Which even now stand in act,° that, for their souls,
 Another of his fathom° they have none,   150
 To lead their business: in which regard,
 Though I do hate him as I do hell-pains,
 Yet, for necessity of present life,

---

odd-even between night and morning   **allowance** permission   **from** contrary to
extravagant wandering   **wheeling** vagabond   **tinder** charred linen kept in a metal
box, and ignited by a spark from flint and steel   **accident** occurrence, event   **check**
rebuke   **cast** dismiss   **stand in act** are going on   **fathom** ability

I must show out a flag and sign of love,
Which is indeed but sign. That you shall surely find him,
Lead to the Sagittary° the raised search:
And there will I be with him. So, farewell.   [*Exit.*]

      [*Enter below* BRABANTIO, *with* SERVANTS *and torches.*]

BRA. It is too true an evil: gone she is;
  And what's to come of my despised time
  Is nought but bitterness. Now, Roderigo,   160
  Where didst thou see her? O unhappy girl!
  With the Moor, say'st thou? Who would be a father!
  How didst thou know 'twas she? O, she deceives me
  Past thought! What said she to you? Get moe° tapers:
  Raise all my kindred. Are they married, think you?
ROD. Truly, I think they are.
BRA. O heaven! How got she out? O treason of the blood!
  Fathers, from hence trust not your daughters' minds
  By what you see them act. Is° there not charms
  By which the property° of youth and maidhood   170
  May be abus'd? Have you not read, Roderigo,
  Of some such thing?
ROD.   Yes, sir, I have indeed.
BRA. Call up my brother. O, would you° had had her!
  Some one way, some another. Do you know
  Where we may apprehend her and the Moor?
ROD. I think I can discover him, if you please
  To get good guard and go along with me.
BRA. Pray you, lead on. At every house I'll call;
  I may command at most. Get weapons, ho!
  And raise some special officers of night.°   180
  On, good Roderigo: I will deserve your pains.   [*Exeunt.*]

      SCENE II. [*Another street.*]

    [*Enter* OTHELLO, IAGO, ATTENDANTS *with torches.*]

IAGO. Though in the trade of war I have slain men,
  Yet do I hold it very stuff o' th' conscience
  To do no contriv'd murder: I lack iniquity
  Sometime to do me service: nine or ten times
  I had thought t' have yerk'd° him here under the ribs.
OTH. 'Tis better as it is.
IAGO.   Nay, but he prated,
  And spoke such scurvy and provoking terms
  Against your honour
  That, with the little godliness I have,
  I did full hard forbear him. But, I pray you, sir,   10

Sagittary probably an inn   **moe** more   **Is** are   **property** special quality   **you**
Roderigo   **officers of night** police   **yerk'd** stabbed

Are you fast married? Be assur'd of this,
That the magnifico° is much belov'd,
And hath in his effect° a voice potential°
As double° as the duke's: he will divorce you;
Or put upon you what restraint and grievance
The law, with all his might to enforce it on,
Will give him cable.
OTH.   Let him do his spite;
My services which I have done the signiory°
Shall out-tongue his complaints. 'Tis yet to know—
Which, when I know that boasting is an honour,   20
I shall promulgate—I fetch my life and being
From men of royal siege,° and my demerits°
May speak unbonneted° to as proud a fortune
As this that I have reach'd: for know, Iago,
But that I love the gentle Desdemona,
I would not my unhoused free condition
Put into circumscription and confine
For the sea's worth. But, look! what lights come yond?
IAGO. Those are the raised father and his friends:
You were best go in.
OTH.   Not I; I must be found: 30
My parts, my title and my perfect soul°
Shall manifest me rightly. Is it they?
IAGO. By Janus, I think no.

[*Enter* CASSIO *and certain* OFFICERS WITH TORCHES.]

OTH. The servants of the duke, and my lieutenant.
The goodness of the night upon you, friends!
What is the news?
CAS.   The duke does greet you, general,
And he requires your haste-post-haste appearance,
Even on the instant.
OTH.   What is the matter, think you?
CAS. Something from Cyprus, as I may divine:
It is a business of some heat: the galleys   40
Have sent a dozen sequent° messengers
This very night at one another's heels,
And many of the consuls,° rais'd and met,
Are at the duke's already: you have been hotly call'd for;
When, being not at your lodging to be found,
The senate hath sent about three several° quests
To search you out.
OTH.   'Tis well I am found by you.

---

magnifico Venetian grandee (i.e., Brabantio)   **effect** influence   **potential** powerful
double twice as influential as most men's   **signiory** Venetian government   **siege** rank
demerits deserts   **unbonneted** on equal terms   **perfect soul** unflawed conscience
sequent successive   **consuls** senators   **several** separate

I will but spend a word here in the house.
And go with you.   *[Exit.]*
Cas.   Ancient, what makes he here?
Iago. 'Faith, he to-night hath boarded a land carack:°   50
    If it prove lawful prize, he's made for ever.
Cas. I do not understand.
Iago.   He's married.
Cas.   To who?

[*Enter* Othello.]

Iago. Marry, to—Come, captain, will you?
Oth.   Have with you.
Cas. Here comes another troop to seek for you.

[*Enter* Brabantio, Roderigo, *with* Officers *and torches.*]

Iago. It is Brabantio. General, be advis'd;
    He comes to bad intent.
Oth.   Holla! stand there!
Rod. Signior, it is the Moor.
Bra.   Down with him, thief!
                        [*They draw on both sides.*]
Iago. You, Roderigo! come, sir, I am for you.
Oth. Keep up your bright swords, for the dew will rust them.
    Good Signior, you shall more command with years   60
    Than with your weapons.
Bra. O thou foul thief, where hast thou stow'd my daughter?
    Damn'd as thou art, thou hast enchanted her;
    For I'll refer me to all things of sense,°
    If she in chains of magic were not bound,
    Whether a maid so tender, fair and happy,
    So opposite to marriage that she shunn'd
    The wealthy curled darlings of our nation,
    Would ever have, t' incur a general mock
    Run from her guardage° to the sooty bosom   70
    Of such a thing as thou, to fear, not to delight.
    Judge me the world, if 'tis not gross in sense°
    That thou has practis'd on her with foul charms,
    Abus'd her delicate youth with drugs or minerals°
    That weaken motion:° I'll have't disputed on;°
    'Tis probable and palpable to thinking.
    I therefore apprehend and do attach thee
    For an abuser of the world,° a practiser

---

carack large merchant ship   **things of sense** commonsense understandings of the natural order   **guardage** guardianship   **gross in sense** easily discernible in apprehension or perception   **minerals** medicine, poison   **motion** thought, reason   **disputed on** argued in court by professional counsel   **abuser of the world** corrupter of society

Of arts inhibited° and out of warrant.
Lay hold upon him: if he do resist,   80
Subdue him at his peril.
OTH.   Hold your hands,
Both you of my inclining,° and the rest:
Were it my cue to fight, I should have known it
Without a prompter. Wither will you that I go
To answer this charge?
BRA.   To prison, till fit time
Of law and course of direct session°
Call thee to answer.
OTH.   What if I do obey?
How may the duke be therewith satisfied,
Whose messengers are here about my side,
Upon some present business of the state   90
To bring me to him?
FIRST OFF.   'Tis true, most worthy signior;
The duke's in council, and your noble self,
I am sure, is sent for.
BRA.   How! the duke in council!
In this time of night! Bring him away:
Mine's not an idle cause: the duke himself,
Or any of my brothers of the state,
Cannot but feel this wrong as 'twere their own;
For if such actions may have passage free,
Bond-slaves and pagans° shall our statesmen be.

                                                              [*Exeunt.*]

        SCENE III. [*A council-chamber.*]

[Enter DUKE, SENATORS *and* OFFICERS *set at a table, with lights and* ATTEN-
DANTS.]

DUKE. There is no composition in these news
    That gives them credit.
FIRST SEN.   Indeed, they are disproportion'd;°
    My letters say a hundred and seven galleys.
DUKE. And mine, a hundred forty.
SEC. SEN.   And mine, two hundred:
    But though they jump° not on a just account,—
    As in these cases, where the aim° reports,
    'Tis oft with difference—yet do they all confirm
    A Turkish fleet, and bearing up to Cyprus.
DUKE. Nay, it is possible enough to judgment:
    I do not so secure me° in the error,   10

---

inhibited prohibited   **inclining** following, party   **course of direct session** regular
legal proceedings   **Bond-slaves and pagans** contemptuous reference to Othello's past history   **disproportion'd** inconsistent   **jump** agree   **aim** conjecture   **secure me** feel
myself secure

But the main article° I do approve
In fearful sense.
SAILOR.   [*Within*] What, ho! what, ho! what, ho!
FIRST OFF. A messenger from the galleys.

[*Enter* SAILOR.]

DUKE   Now, what's the business?
Sail. The Turkish preparation makes for Rhodes;
   So was I bid report here to the state
   By Signior Angelo.
DUKE How say you by this change?
FIRST SEN.   This cannot be,
   By no assay° of reason: 'tis a pageant,
   To keep us in false gaze. When we consider
   Th' importancy of Cyprus to the Turk,   20
   And let ourselves again but understand,
   That as it more concerns the Turk than Rhodes,
   So may he with more facile question° bear it,
   For that it stands not in such warlike brace,°
   But altogether lacks th' abilities
   That Rhodes is dress'd in: if we make thought of this,
   We must not think the Turk is so unskilful
   To leave that latest which concerns him first,
   Neglecting an attempt of ease and gain,
   To wake and wage a danger profitless.   30
DUKE. Nay, in all confidence, he's not for Rhodes.
FIRST OFF. Here is more news.

[*Enter a* MESSENGER.]

MESS. The Ottomites, reverend and gracious,
   Steering with due course toward the isle of Rhodes,
   Have there injointed them with an after fleet.
FIRST SEN. Ay, so I thought. How many, as you guess?
MESS. Of thirty sail: and now they do re-stem°
   Their backward course, bearing with frank appearance
   Their purposes toward Cyprus. Signior Montano,
   Your trusty and most valiant servitor,   40
   With his free duty recommends you thus,
   And prays you to believe him.
DUKE. 'Tis certain, then, for Cyprus.
   Marcus Luccicos, is not he in town?
FIRST SEN. He's now in Florence.
DUKE. Write from us to him; post-post-haste dispatch.
FIRST SEN. Here comes Brabantio and the valiant Moor.

---

main article i.e, that the Turkish fleet is threatening   **assay** test   **more facile question**
greater facility of effort   **brace** state of defense   **re-stem** steer again

[Enter BRABANTIO, OTHELLO, CASSIO, IAGO, RODERIGO, *and* OFFICERS.]

Duke. Valiant Othello, we must straight employ you
   Against the general enemy Ottoman.
   [*To* BRABANTIO] I did not see you; welcome, gentle signior;   50
   We lack'd your counsel and your help to-night.
BRA. So did I yours. Good your grace, pardon me;
   Neither my place nor aught I heard of business
   Hath rais'd me from my bed, nor doth the general care
   Take hold on me, for my particular grief
   Is of so flood-gate and o'erbearing nature
   That it engluts° and swallows other sorrows
   And it is still itself.
DUKE.   Why, what's the matter?
BRA. My daughter! O, my daughter!
DUKE AND SEN.   Dead?
BRA.   Ay, to me;
   She is abus'd, stol'n from me, and corrupted   60
   By spells and medicines bought of mountebanks;
   For nature so preposterously to err,
   Being not deficient, blind, or lame of sense,
   Sans witchcraft could not.
DUKE. Whoe'er he be that in this foul proceeding
   Hath thus beguil'd your daughter of herself
   And you of her, the bloody book of law
   You shall yourself read in the bitter letter
   After your own sense, yea, though our proper son
   Stood in your action.°
BRA.   Humbly I thank your grace.   70
   Here is the man, this Moor, whom now, it seems,
   Your special mandate for the state-affairs
   Hath hither brought.
DUKE AND SEN.   We are very sorry for 't.
DUKE [*To* OTHELLO]. What, in your own part, can you say to this?
BRA. Nothing, but this is so.
OTH. Most potent, grave, and reverend signiors,
   My very noble and approv'd good masters,
   That I have ta'en away this old man's daughter,
   It is most true; true, I have married her:
   The very head and front of my offending   80
   Hath this extent, no more. Rude am I in my speech,
   And little bless'd with the soft phrase of peace;
   For since these arms of mine had seven years' pith,°
   Till now some nine moons wasted, they have us'd
   Their dearest action in the tented field,
   And little of this great world can I speak,
   More than pertains to feats of broil and battle,
   And therefore little shall I grace my cause

engluts engulfs   **Stood . . . action** was under your accusation   **pith** strength, vigor

In speaking for myself. Yet, by your gracious patience,°
I will a round unvarnish'd tale deliver   90
Of my whole course of love; what drugs, what charms,
What conjuration and what mighty magic,
For such proceeding I am charg'd withal,
I won his daughter.
BRA.   A maiden never bold;
Of spirit so still and quiet, that her motion
Blush'd at herself;° and she, in spite of nature,
Of years, of country, credit, every thing,
To fall in love with what she fear'd to look on!
It is a judgement maim'd and most imperfect
That will confess perfection so could err   100
Against all rules of nature, and must be driven
To find our practices of cunning hell,
Why this should be. I therefore vouch° again
That with some mixtures pow'rful o'er the blood,
Or with some dram conjur'd to this effect,
He wrought upon her.
DUKE.   To vouch this, is no proof,
Without more wider and more overt test
Than these thin habits and poor likelihoods
Of modern seeming do prefer against him.
FIRST SEN. But, Othello, speak: 110
Did you by indirect and forced courses
Subdue and poison this young maid's affections?
Or came it by request and such fair question
As soul to soul affordeth?
OTH.   I do beseech you,
Send for the lady to the Sagittary,
And let her speak of me before her father:
If you do find me foul in her report,
The trust, the office I do hold of you,
Not only take away, but let your sentence
Even fall upon my life.
DUKE.   Fetch Desdemona hither.   120
OTH. Ancient, conduct them; you best know the place.
                                             [*Exeunt* IAGO *and* ATTENDANTS.]
And, till she come, as truly as to heaven
I do confess the vices of my blood,
So justly to your grave ear I'll present
How I did thrive in this fair lady's love.
And she in mine.
DUKE. Say it, Othello.
OTH. Her father lov'd me; oft invited me;
Still question'd me the story of my life,
From year to year, the battles, sieges, fortunes,   130

---

patience sufferance, permission   **motion . . . herself** inward impulses blushed at themselves   **vouch** assert

That I have pass'd.
I ran it through, even from my boyish days,
To th' very moment that he bade me tell it;
Wherein I spake of most disastrous chances,
Of moving accidents by flood and field,
Of hair-breadth scapes i' th' imminent° deadly breach,
Of being taken by the insolent foe
And sold to slavery, of my redemption thence
And portance° in my travels' history:
Wherein of antres° vast and deserts idle,°   140
Rough quarries, rocks and hills whose heads touch heaven,
It was my hint° to speak,—such was the process;
And of the Cannibals that each other eat,°
The Anthropophagi° and men whose heads
Do grow beneath their shoulders. This to hear
Would Desdemona seriously incline:
But still the house-affairs would draw her thence:
Which ever as she could with haste dispatch,
She 'ld come again, and with a greedy ear
Devour up my discourse: which I observing,   150
Took once a pliant hour, and found good means
To draw from her a prayer of earnest heart
That I would all my pilgrimage dilate,°
Whereof by parcels she had something heard,
But not intentively°: I did consent,
And often did beguile her of her tears,
When I did speak of some distressful stroke
That my youth suffer'd. My story being done,
She gave me for my pains a world of sighs:
She swore, in faith, 'twas strange, 'twas passing strange,   160
'Twas pitiful, 'twas wondrous pitiful:
She wish'd she had not heard it, yet she wish'd
That heaven had made her such a man: she thank'd me,
And bade me, if I had a friend that lov'd her,
I should but teach him how to tell my story,
And that would woo her. Upon this hint I spake:
She lov'd me for the dangers I had pass'd,
And I lov'd her that she did pity them.
This only is the witchcraft I have us'd:
Here comes the lady; let her witness it.   170

[*Enter* DESDEMONA, IAGO, *and* ATTENDANTS.]

DUKE. I think this tale would win my daughter too.
   Good Brabantio,

---

imminent i.e., impending parts when a gap has been made in a fortification   **portance**
conduct.   **antres** caverns   **idle** barren, unprofitable   **hint** occasion   **eat** ate   **An-**
thropophagi man-eaters   **dilate** relate in detail   **intentively** with full attention

Take up this mangled matter at the best:
Men do their broken weapons rather use
Than their bare hands.
BRA.   I pray you, hear her speak:
If she confess that she was half the wooer,
Destruction on my head, if my bad blame
Light on the man! Come hither, gentle mistress:
Do you perceive in all this noble company
Where most you owe obedience?
DES.   My noble father,   180
I do perceive here a divided duty°:
To you I am bound for life and education;
My life and education both do learn me
How to respect you; you are the lord of duty;
I am hitherto your daughter: but here's my husband,
And so much duty as my mother show'd
To you, preferring you before her father,
So much I challenge that I may profess
Due to the Moor my lord.
BRA.   God be with you! I have done.
Please it your grace, on to° the state-affairs: 190
I had rather to adopt a child than get° it.
Come hither, Moor:
I here do give thee that with all my heart
Which, but thou hast already, with all my heart
I would keep from thee. For your sake,° jewel,
I am glad at soul I have no other child;
For thy escape would teach me tyranny,
To hang clogs on them. I have done, my lord.
DUKE. Let me speak like yourself,° and lay a sentence,
Which, as a grise° or step, may help these lovers   200
Into your favour.
When remedies are past, the griefs are ended
By seeing the worst, which late on hopes depended.
To mourn a mischief that is past and gone
Is the next° way to draw new mischief on.
What cannot be preserv'd when fortune takes,
Patience her injury a mock'ry makes.
The robb'd that smiles steals something from the thief;
He robs himself that spends a bootless grief.
BRA. So let the Turk of Cyprus us beguile;   210
We lost it not, so long as we can smile.
He bears the sentence well that nothing bears
But the free comfort° which from thence he hears,
But he bears both the sentence and the sorrow

---

divided duty Desdemona recognizes that she still owes a duty to her father even after
marriage   **on to** i.e., proceed with   **get** beget   **For your sake** on your account   **like
yourself** i.e., as you would, in your proper temper   **sentence** maxim   **grise** step   **next**
nearest   **comfort** i.e., the consolation that it may be borne with patience

That, to pay grief, must of poor patience borrow.
These sentences, to sugar, or to gall,
Being strong on both sides, are equivocal:
But words are words; I never yet did hear
That the bruis'd heart was pierced through the ear.
I humbly beseech you, proceed to th' affairs of state. 220

DUKE. The Turk with a most mighty preparation makes for Cyprus.
Othello, the fortitude° of the place is best known to you; and though
we have there a substitute of most allowed° sufficiency, yet opinion, a
sovereign mistress of effects, throws a more safer voice on you°: you
must therefore be content to slubber° the gloss of your new fortunes
with this more subborn and boisterous expedition.

OTH. The tyrant custom, most grave senators,
Hath made the flinty and steel couch of war
My thrice-driven° bed of down: I do agnize°
A natural and prompt alacrity 230
I find in hardness,° and do undertake
These present wars against the Ottomites.
Most humbly therefore bending to your state,
I crave fit disposition for my wife,
Due reference of place and exhibition,°
With such accommodation and besort°
As levels with her breeding.

DUKE.   If you please,
Be 't at her father's.

BRA.   I'll not have it so.

OTH. Nor I.

DES.   Nor I; I would not there reside,
To put my father in impatient thoughts 240
By being in his eye. Most gracious duke,
To my unfolding lend your prosperous° ear;
And let me find a charter° in your voice,
T' assist my simpleness.°

DUKE. What would you, Desdemona?

DES. That I did love the Moor to live with him,
My downright violence and storm of fortunes
May trumpet to the world: my heart's subdu'd
Even to the very quality of my lord:
I saw Othello's visage in his mind, 250
And to his honours and his valiant parts
Did I my soul and fortunes consecrate.
So that, dear lords, if I be left behind,
A moth of peace, and he go to the war,
The rites for why I love him are bereft me,

---

fortitude strength   **allowed** acknowledged   **opinion . . . on you** public opinion, an
important determiner of affairs, chooses you as the best man   **slubber** soil, sully   **thrice-
driven** thrice sifted   **agnize** know in myself   **hardness** hardship   **exhibition** allowance   **besort** suitable company   **prosperous** propitious   **charter** privilege   **simpleness** simplicity

And I a heavy interim shall support
    By his dear absence. Let me go with him.
OTH. Let her have your voices.
    Vouch with me, heaven, I therefore beg it not,
    To please the palate of my appetite,   260
    Nor to comply with heat—the young affects°
    In me defunct—and proper satisfaction,
    But to be free and bounteous to her mind:
    And heaven defend your good souls, that you think
    I will your serious and great business scant
    When she is with me: no, when light-wing'd toys
    Of feather'd Cupid seel° with wanton dullness
    My speculative and offic'd instruments,°
    That° my disports° corrupt and taint° my business,
    Let housewives make a skillet of my helm,   270
    And all indign° and base adversities
    Make head against my estimation°!
DUKE. Be it as you shall privately determine,
    Either for her stay or going: th' affair cries haste,
    And speed must answer it.
FIRST SEN. You must away to-night.
OTH.   With all my heart.
DUKE. At nine i' th' morning here we'll meet again.
    Othello, leave some officer behind,
    And he shall our commission bring to you;
    With such things else of quality and respect   280
    As doth import° you.
OTH.   So please your grace, my ancient;
    A man he is of honesty and trust:
    To his conveyance I assign my wife,
    With what else needful your good grace shall think
    To be sent after me.
DUKE.   Let it be so.
    Good night to every one. [*To* BRA.] And, noble signior,
    If virtue no delighted° beauty lack,
    Your son-in-law is far more fair than black.
FIRST SEN. Adieu, brave Moor; use Desdemona well.
BRA. Look to her, Moor, if thou hast eyes to see;   290
    She has deceiv'd her father, and may thee.
                        [*Exeunt* DUKE, SENATORS, OFFICERS, *& c.*]
OTH. My life upon her faith! Honest Iago,°
    My Desdemona must I leave to thee:
    I prithee, let thy wife attend on her;
    And bring them after in the best advantage.

---

   affects inclinations, desires   **seel** in falconry, to make blind by sewing up the eyes of
the hawk in training   **speculative . . . instruments** ability to see and reason clearly
That so that   **disports** pastimes   **taint** impair   **indign** unworthy, shameful   **esti-
mation** reputation   **import** concern   **delighted** delightful   **Honest Iago** an evidence
of Iago's carefully built reputation

Come, Desdemona; I have but an hour
Of love, of worldly matters and direction,
To spend with thee: we must obey the time.

[Exit with DESDEMONA.*]*

ROD. Iago—
IAGO. What say'st thou, noble heart?   300
ROD. What will I do, thinkest thou?
IAGO. Why, go to bed, and sleep.
ROD. I will incontinently° drown myself.
IAGO. If thou dost, I shall never love thee after. Why, thou silly gentleman!
ROD. It is silliness to live when to live is torment; and then have we a
    prescription to die when death is our physician.
IAGO. O villanous! I have looked upon the world for four times seven years;
    and since I could distinguish betwixt a benefit and an injury, I never
    found man that knew how to love himself. Ere I would say, I would
    drown myself for the love of a guinea-hen, I would change my humanity
    with a baboon.   312
ROD. What should I do? I confess it is my shame to be so fond; but it is
    not in my virtue° to amend it.
IAGO. Virtue! a fig! 'tis in ourselves that we are thus or thus. Our bodies
    are our gardens, to the which our wills are gardeners; so that if we
    will plant nettles, or sow lettuce, set hyssop° and weed up thyme, supply
    it with one gender° of herbs, or distract it with many, either to have
    it sterile with idleness,° or manured with industry, why, the power
    and corrigible authority° of this lies in our wills. If the balance of our
    lives had not one scale of reason to poise another of sensuality, the
    blood and baseness of our natures would conduct us to most preposterous
    conclusions: but we have reason to cool our raging motions,° our carnal
    stings, our unbitted° lusts, whereof I take this that you call love to be
    a sect° or scion.   325
ROD. It cannot be.
IAGO. It is merely a lust of the blood and a permission of the will. Come,
    be a man. Drown thyself! drown cats and blind puppies. I have professed
    me thy friend and I confess me knit to thy deserving with cables of
    perdurable° toughness; I could never better stead thee than now. Put
    money in thy purse; follow thou the wars; defeat thy favour° with an
    usurped beard; I say, put money in thy purse. It cannot be that Desde-
    mona should long continue her love to the Moor,—put money in thy
    purse,—nor he his to her: it was a violent commencement in her, and
    thou shalt see an answerable sequestration°:—put but money in thy
    purse. These Moors are changeable in their wills:—fill thy purse with

---

incontinently immediately   **virtue** strength   **hyssop** an herb of the mint family
gender kind   **idleness** want of cultivation   **corrigible authority** the power to correct
reason . . . motions Iago understands the warfare between reason and sensuality, but his
ethics are totally inverted; reason works in him not good, as it should according to natural law,
but evil, which he has chosen for his good   **motions** appetites   **unbitted** uncontrolled
sect cutting   **perdurable** very durable   **defeat thy favour** disguise and disfigure thy
face   **answerable sequestration** a separation corresponding

money:—the food that to him now is as luscious as locusts,° shall be
to him shortly as bitter as coloquintida.° She must change for youth:
when she is sated with his body, she will find the error of her choice:
she must have change, she must: therefore put money in thy purse. If
thou wilt needs damn thyself, do it a more delicate way than drowning.
Make all the money thou canst: if sanctimony and a frail vow betwixt
an erring° barbarian and a super-subtle Venetian be not too hard for
my wits and all the tribe of hell, thou shalt enjoy her; therefore make
money. A pox of drowning thyself! it is clean out of the way: seek
thou rather to be hanged in compassing thy joy than to be drowned
and go without her.   347

Rod. Wilt thou be fast to my hopes, if I depend on the issue?

Iago. Thou art sure of me:—go, make money:—I have told thee often,
and I re-tell thee again and again, I hate the Moor: my cause is hearted;°
thine hath no less reason. Let us be conjunctive° in our revenge against
him; if thou canst cuckold him, thou dost thyself a pleasure, me a sport.
There are many events in the womb of time which will be delivered.
Traverse!° go, provide thy money. We will have more of this to-morrow.
Adieu.

Rod. Where shall we meet i' the morning?

Iago. At my lodging.

Rod. I'll be with thee betimes.

Iago. Go to; farewell. Do you hear, Roderigo?

Rod. What say you?   360

Iago. No more of drowning, do you hear?

Rod. I am changed: I'll go sell all my land.   [*Exit*]

Iago. Thus do I ever make my fool my purse;
For I mine own gain'd knowledge should profane,
If I would time expend with such a snipe,°
But for my sport and profit. I hate the Moor;
And it is thought abroad, that 'twixt my sheets
H' as done my office: I know not if 't be true;
But I, for mere suspicion in that kind,
Will do as if for surety. He holds me well;   370
The better shall my purpose work on him.
Cassio's a proper man: let me see now:
To get his place and to plume up° my will
In double knavery—How, how?—Let's see:—
After some time, to abuse Othello's ears
That he° is too familiar with his wife.
He hath a person and a smooth dispose°
To be suspected, fram'd to make women false.
The Moor is of a free° and open nature,
That thinks men honest that but seem to be so,   380

---

locusts of doubtful meaning; defined as fruit of the carob tree, as honeysuckle, and as
lollipops or sugar sticks   **coloquintida** colocynth, or bitter apple, a purgative   **erring**
wandering   **hearted** fixed in the heart   **conjunctive** united   **Traverse** go (military
term)   **snipe** gull, fool   **plume up** glorify, gratify   **he** i.e., Cassio   **dispose** external
manner   **free** frank

And will as tenderly be led by th' nose
As asses are.
I have 't. It is engend'red. Hell and night
Must bring this monstrous birth to the world's light.

[*Exit.*]

ACT II.

SCENE I. [*A Sea-port in Cyprus. An open place near the quay.*]

[*Enter* MONTANO *and two* GENTLEMEN.]

MON. What from the cape can you discern at sea?
FIRST GENT. Nothing at all: it is a high-wrought flood;
  I cannot, 'twixt the heaven and the main,
  Descry a sail.
MON. Methinks the wind hath spoke aloud at land;
  A fuller blast ne'er shook our battlements:
  If it hath ruffian'd° so upon the sea,
  What ribs of oak, when mountains melt on them,
  Can hold the mortise°? What shall we hear of this?
SEC. GENT. A segregation° of the Turkish fleet: 10
  For do but stand upon the foaming shore,
  The chidden billow seems to pelt the clouds:
  The wind-shak'd surge, with high and monstrous mane,
  Seems to cast water on the burning bear,°
  And quench the guards° of th' ever-fixed pole:
  I never did like molestation view
  On the enchafed° flood.
MON.   If that the Turkish fleet
  Be not enshelter'd and embay'd, they are drown'd;
  It is impossible they bear it out.

[*Enter a third* GENTLEMAN.]

THIRD GENT. News, lads! our wars are done   20
  The desperate tempest hath so bang'd the Turks,
  That their designment° halts: a noble ship of Venice
  Hath seen a grievous wrack and sufferance°
  On most part of their fleet.
MON. How! is this true?
THIRD GENT.   The ship is here put in,
  A Veronesa; Michael Cassio,
  Lieutenant to the warlike Moor Othello,

---

ruffian'd raged   **mortise** the socket hollowed out in fitting timbers   **segregation** dispersion   **bear** a constellation   **quench the guards** overwhelm the stars near the polestar   **enchafed** angry   **designment** enterprise   **sufferance** disaster

Is come on shore: the Moor himself at sea,
  And is in full commission here for Cyprus.
Mon. I am glad on 't; 'tis a worthy governor.   30
Third Gent. But this same Cassio, though he speak of comfort
  Touching the Turkish loss, yet he looks sadly,
  And prays the Moor be safe; for they were parted
  With foul and violent tempest.
Mon.   Pray heavens he be;
  For I have serv'd him, and the man commands
  Like a full° soldier. Let's to the seaside, ho!
  As well to see the vessel that's come in
  As to throw out our eyes for brave Othello,
  Even till we make the main and th' aerial blue
  An indistinct regard.°
Third Gent.   Come, let's do so;   40
  For every minute is expectancy
  Of more arrivance.°

    [*Enter* Cassio.]

Cas. Thanks, you the valiant of this warlike isle,
  That so approve the Moor! O, let the heavens
  Give him defence against the elements,
  For I have lost him on a dangerous sea.
Mon. Is he well shipp'd?
Cas. His bark is stoutly timber'd, and his pilot
  Of very expert and approv'd allowance;°
  Therefore my hopes, not surfeited to death,   50
  Stand in bold cure. [*A cry within*] 'A sail, a sail, a sail!'

    [*Enter a fourth* Gentleman.]

Cas. What noise?
Fourth Gent. The town is empty; on the brow o' th' sea
  Stand ranks of people, and they cry 'A sail!'
Cas. My hopes do shape him for the governor.
                                [*Guns heard.*]
Sec. Gent. They do discharge their shot of courtesy:
  Our friends at least.
Cas.   I pray you, sir, go forth,
  And give us truth who 'tis that is arriv'd.
Sec. Gent. I shall.   [*Exit.*]
Mon. But, good lieutenant, is your general wiv'd?   60
Cas. Most fortunately: he hath achiev'd a maid
  That paragons° description and wild fame;

---

full perfect   **make. . . regard** cause the blue of the sea and the air to grow indistinguishable in our view   **arrivance** arrival   **allowance** reputation   **paragons** surpasses

One that excels the quirks° of blazoning° pens,
And in th' essential vesture of creation°
Does tire the ingener.°

[*Enter second* Gentleman.]

                           How now! who has put in?
Sec. Gent. 'Tis one Iago, ancient to the general.
Cas. Has had most favourable and happy speed:
  Tempests themselves, high seas and howling winds,
  The gutter'd° rocks and congregated sands,—
  Traitors ensteep'd° to clog the guiltless keel,—   70
  As having sense of beauty, do omit
  Their mortal° natures, letting go safely by
  The divine Desdemona.
Mon.   What is she?
Cas. She that I spake of, our great captain's captain,
  Left in the conduct of the bold Iago,
  Whose footing here anticipates our thoughts
  A se'nnight's° speed. Great Jove, Othello guard,
  And swell his sail with thine own pow'rful breath,
  That he may bless this bay with his tall ship,
  Make love's quick pants in Desdemona's arms,   80
  Give renew'd fire to our extinced spirits,
  And bring all Cyprus comfort!

[*Enter* Desdemona, Iago, Roderigo, *and* Emilia *with* Attendants.]

                     O, behold,
The riches of the ship is come on shore!
You men of Cyprus, let her have your knees.
Hail to thee, lady! and the grace of heaven,
Before, behind thee and on every hand,
Enwheel thee round!
Des.   I thank you, valiant Cassio.
  What tidings can you tell me of my lord?
Cas. He is not yet arriv'd: nor know I aught
  But that he's well and will be shortly here.   90
Des. O, but I fear—How lost you company?
Cas. The great contention of the sea and skies
  Parted our fellowship—But, hark! a sail.
          [*Within*] 'A sail, a sail!' [*Guns heard.*]
Sec. Gent. They give their greeting to the citadel:
  This likewise is a friend.
Cas.   See for the news.   [*Exit* Gentleman.]

---

quirks witty conceits   **blazoning** setting forth honorably in words   **vesture of creation** the real qualities with which creation has invested her   **ingener** inventor, praiser
gutter'd jagged, trenched   **ensteep'd** lying under water   **mortal** deadly   **se'nnight's**
week's

Good ancient, you are welcome. [*To* Emilia] Welcome, mistress:
　Let it not gall your patience, good Iago,
　That I extend my manners; 'tis my breeding
　That gives me this bold show of courtesy.　　　　　　　[*Kissing her.*]
Iago. Sir, would she give you so much of her lips　　　　　　　101
　As of her tongue she oft bestows on me,
　You would have enough.
Des.　　　　　　　　　　Alas, she has no speech.
Iago. In faith, too much;
　I find it still, when I have list to sleep:
　Marry, before your ladyship, I grant,
　She puts her tongue a little in her heart,
　And chides with thinking.
Emil. You have little cause to say so.
Iago. Come on, come on; you are pictures out of doors,　　110
　Bells in your parlours, wild-cats in your kitchens,
　Saints in your injuries, devils being offended,
　Players in your housewifery, and housewives° in your beds.
Des. O, fie upon thee, slanderer!
Iago. Nay, it is true, or else I am a Turk:
　You rise to play and go to bed to work.
Emil. You shall not write my praise.
Iago.　　　　　　　　　　No, let me not.
Des. What wouldst thou write of me, if thou shouldst praise me?
Iago. O gentle lady, do not put me to 't;
　For I am nothing, if not critical.°　　　　　　　　　　120
Des. Come on, assay. There's one gone to the harbour?
Iago. Ay, madam.
Des. I am not merry; but I do beguile
　The thing I am, by seeming otherwise.
　Come, how wouldst thou praise me?
Iago. I am about it; but indeed my invention
　Comes from my pate as birdlime° does from frieze;°
　It plucks out brains and all: but my Muse labours,
　And thus she is deliver'd.
　If she be fair and wise, fairness and wit,　　　　　　　　130
　The one's for use, the other useth it.
Des. Well praised! How if she be black and witty?
Iago. If she be black, and thereto have a wit,
　She'll find a white° that shall her blackness fit.
Des. Worse and worse.
Emil. How if fair and foolish?
Iago. She never yet was foolish that was fair;
　For even her folly help'd her to an heir.
Des. These are old fond° paradoxes to make fools laugh i' the alehouse.
　What miserable praise hast thou for her that's foul and foolish?　140

---

housewives hussies　　**critical** censorious　　**birdlime** sticky substance smeared on twigs
to catch small birds.　　**frieze** coarse woolen cloth　　**white** a fair person, with a wordplay
on 'wight'　　**fond** foolish

IAGO. There's none so foul and foolish thereunto,
  But does foul pranks which fair and wise ones do.
DES. O heavy ignorance! thou praisest the worst best. But what praise
  couldst thou bestow on a deserving woman indeed, one that, in the
  authority of her merit, did justly put on the vouch° of her malice itself?
IAGO. She that was ever fair and never proud,
  Had tongue at will and yet was never loud,
  Never lack'd gold and yet went never gay,
  Fled from her wish and yet said 'Now I may,'
  She that being ang'red, her revenge being nigh,   150
  Bade her wrong stay and her displeasure fly,
  She that in wisdom never was so frail
  To change the cod's head for the salmon's tail,°
  She that could think and ne'er disclose her mind,
  See suitors following and not look behind,
  She was a wight, if ever such wight were,—
DES. To do what?
IAGO. To suckle fools and chronicle small beer.°
DES. O most lame and impotent conclusion! Do not learn of him, Emilia,
  though he be thy husband. How say you, Cassio? is he not a most profane
  and liberal° counsellor?   161
CAS. He speaks home,° madam: you may relish him more in the soldier
  than in the scholar.
IAGO [*Aside*]. He takes her by the palm: ay, well said, whisper: with as
  little a web as this will I ensnare as great a fly as Cassio. Ay, smile
  upon her, do; I will gyve° thee in thine own courtship.° You say true;
  'tis so, indeed: if such tricks as these strip you out of your lieutenantry,
  it had been better you had not kissed your three fingers° so oft, which
  now again you are most apt to play the sir° in. Very good; well kissed!
  an excellent courtesy! 'tis so, indeed. Yet again your fingers to your
  lips? would they were clyster-pipes° for your sake. [*Trumpet within.*]
  The Moor! I know his trumpet.   172
CAS. 'Tis truly so.
DES. Let 's meet him and receive him.
CAS. Lo, where he comes!

        [*Enter* OTHELLO *and* ATTENDANTS.]
OTH. O my fair warrior!
DES.   My dear Othello!
OTH. It gives me wonder great as my content
  To see you here before me. O my soul's joy!
  If after every tempest come such calms,
  May the winds blow till they have waken'd death!   180
  And let the labouring bark climb hills of seas
  Olympus-high and duck again as low

---

put on the vouch compel the approval   **To change . . . tail** to exchange a delicacy
for mere refuse   **chronical small beer** keep petty household accounts   **liberal** licentious
speaks home i.e., without reserve   **gyve** fetter, shackle   **courtship** courtesy
kissed your three fingers He kisses his own hand as a token of reverence   **the sir** i.e.,
the fine gentleman   **clyster-pipes** tubes used for enemas

As hell 's from heaven! If it were now to die,
'Twere now to be most happy; for, I fear,
My soul hath her content so absolute
That not another comfort like to this
Succeeds in unknown fate.

DES.   The heavens forbid
But that our loves and comforts should increase,
Even as our days do grow!

OTH.   Amen to that, sweet powers!
I cannot speak enough of this content;   190
It stops me here; it is too much of joy:
And this, and this, the greatest discords be [*Kissing her.*]
That e'er our hearts shall make!

IAGO.   [*Aside*] O, you are well tun'd now!
But I'll set down the pegs° that make this music,
As honest as I am.

OTH.   Come, let us to the castle.
News, friends; our wars are done, the Turks are drowned.
How does my old acquaintance of this isle?
Honey, you shall be well desir'd in Cyprus;
I have found great love amongst them. O my sweet,
I prattle out of fashion, and I dote   200
In mine own comforts. I prithee, good Iago,
Go to the bay and disembark my coffers:
Bring thou the master to the citadel;
He is a good one, and his worthiness
Does challenge much respect. Come, Desdemona,
Once more, well met at Cyprus.

          [*Exeunt* OTHELLO *and* DESDEMONA *and all but* IAGO *and* RODERIGO.]

IAGO. [*To an* ATTENDANT]. Do thou meet me presently at the harbour.
[*To* ROD.] Come hither. If thou be'st valiant,—as, they say, base men
being in love have then a nobility in their natures more than is native to them,—list me. The lieutenant tonight watches on the court of
guard°. —First, I must tell thee this—Desdemona is directly in love
with him.   212

ROD. With him! why, 'tis not possible.

IAGO. Lay thy finger thus, and let thy soul be instructed. Mark me with
what violence she first loved the Moor, but for bragging and telling
her fantastical lies: and will she love him still for prating? let not thy
discreet heart think it. Her eye must be fed; and what delight shall
she have to look on the devil? When the blood is made dull with the
act of sport, there should be, again to inflame it and to give satiety a
fresh appetite, loveliness in favour, sympathy in years, manners and
beauties; all which the Moor is defective in: now, for want of these
required conveniences, her delicate tenderness will find itself abused,
begin to heave the gorge, disrelish and abhor the Moor; very nature
will instruct her in it and compel her to some second choice. Now,

---

set down the pegs lower the pitch of the strings, i.e., disturb the harmony   **court of
guard** guardhouse

sir, this granted,—as it is a most pregnant and unforced position—who stands so eminent in the degree of this fortune as Cassio does? a knave very voluble; no further conscionable° than in putting on the mere form of civil and humane seeming, for the better compassing of his salt° and most hidden loose affection? why, none; why, none: a slipper° and subtle knave, a finder of occasions, that has an eye can stamp and counterfeit advantages, though true advantage never present itself; a devilish knave. Besides, the knave is handsome, young, and hath all those requisites in him that folly and green minds look after: a pestilent complete knave; and the woman hath found him already.   234

Rod. I cannot believe that in her; she 's full of most blessed condition.

Iago. Blessed fig's-end! the wine she drinks is made of grapes: if she had been blessed, she would never have loved the Moor. Blessed pudding! Didst thou not see her paddle with the palm of his hand? didst not mark that?

Rod. Yes, that I did; but that was but courtesy.

Iago. Lechery, by this hand; an index and obscure prologue to the history of lust and foul thoughts. They met so near with their lips that their breaths embraced together. Villainous thoughts, Roderigo! when these mutualities so marshall the way, hard at hand comes the master and main exercise, the incorporate conclusion. Pish! But, sir, be you ruled by me: I have brought you from Venice. Watch you to-night; for the command, I'll lay't upon you. Cassio knows you not. I'll not be far from you: do you find some occasion to anger Cassio, either by speaking too loud, or tainting° his discipline; or from what other course you please, which the time shall more favourably minister.   250

Rod. Well.

Iago. Sir, he is rash and very sudden in choler, and haply may strike at you: provoke him, that he may; for even out of that will I cause these of Cyprus to mutiny; whose qualification° shall come into no true taste again but by the displanting of Cassio. So shall you have a shorter journey to your desires by the means I shall then have to prefer them; and the impediment most profitably removed, without the which there were no expectation of our prosperity.   258

Rod. I will do this, if I can bring it to any opportunity.

Iago. I warrant thee. Meet me by and by° at the citadel: I must fetch his necessaries ashore. Farewell.

Rod. Adieu.   [*Exit*]

Iago. That Cassio loves her, I do well believe 't;
     That she loves him, 'tis apt° and of great credit°:
     The Moor, howbeit that I endure him not,
     Is of a constant, loving, noble nature,
     And I dare think he'll prove to Desdemona
     A most dear husband. Now, I do love her too;
     Not out of absolute lust, though peradventure
     I stand accountant for as great a sin,   270

---

conscionable conscientious   **salt** licentious   **slipper** slippery   **tainting** disparaging   **qualification** appeasement   **by and by** immediately   **apt** probable   **credit** credibility

But partly led to diet my revenge,
For that I do suspect the lusty Moor
Hath leap'd into my seat; the thought whereof
Doth, like a poisonous mineral, gnaw my inwards;
And nothing can or shall content my soul
Till I am even'd with him, wife for wife,
Or failing so, yet that I put the Moor
At least into a jealousy so strong
That judgement cannot cure. Which thing to do,
If this poor trash° of Venice, whom I trash°   280
For his quick hunting, stand the putting on,°
I'll have our Michael Cassio on the hip,°
Abuse him to the Moor in the rank garb—
For I fear Cassio with my night-cap too—
Make the Moor thank me, love me and reward me,
For making him egregiously an ass
And practising upon his peace and quiet
Even to madness. 'Tis here, but yet confus'd:
Knavery's plain face is never seen till us'd.   [*Exit.*]

SCENE II. [*A street.*]

[*Enter Othello's* HERALD *with a proclamation.*]

HER. It is Othello's pleasure, our noble and valiant general, that, upon
certain tidings now arrived, importing the mere perdition° of the Turkish fleet, every man put himself into triumph; some to dance, some to
make bonfires, each man to what sport and revels his addiction leads
him: for, besides these beneficial news, it is the celebration of his nuptial.
So much was his pleasure should be proclaimed. All offices° are open,
and there is full liberty of feasting from this present hour of five till
the bell have told eleven. Heaven bless the isle of Cyprus and our general
Othello!   [*Exit.*]

SCENE III. [*A hall in the castle.*]

[*Enter* OTHELLO, DESDEMONA, CASSIO, *and* ATTENDANTS.]

OTH. Good Michael, look you to the guard to-night:
Let's teach ourselves that honourable stop,°
Not to outsport discretion.
CAS. Iago hath direction what to do;
But, notwithstanding, with my personal eye
Will I look to 't.

---

trash worthless thing (Roderigo)   **trash** hold in check   **putting on** incitement to quarrel   **on the hip** at my mercy (wrestling term)   **mere perdition** complete destruction
offices rooms where food and drink were kept   **stop** restraint

OTH.   Iago is most honest.
 Michael, goodnight: to-morrow with your earliest
 Let me have speech with you. [*To* DESDEMONA] Come, my dear love,
 The purchase made, the fruits are to ensue;
 That profit's yet to come 'tween me and you.   10
 Good night.   [*Exit* OTHELLO, *with* DESDEMONA *and* ATTENDANTS.]

 [*Enter* IAGO.]

CAS. Welcome, Iago; we must to the watch.
IAGO. Not this hour, lieutenant; 'tis not yet ten o' the clock. Our general cast° us thus early for the love of his Desdemona; who let us not therefore blame: he hath not yet made wanton the night with her; and she is sport for Jove.
CAS. She's a most exquisite lady.
IAGO. And, I'll warrant her, full of game.
CAS. Indeed, she's a most fresh and delicate creature.
IAGO. What an eye she has! methinks it sounds a parley of provocation.
CAS. An inviting eye; and yet methinks right modest.   20
IAGO. And when she speaks, is it not an alarum to love?
CAS. She is indeed perfection.
IAGO. Well, happiness to their sheets! Come, lieutenant, I have a stoup° of wine; and here without are a brace of Cyprus gallants that would fain have a measure to the health of black Othello.
CAS. Not to-night, good Iago: I have very poor and unhappy brains for drinking: I could well wish courtesy would invent some other custom of entertainment.
IAGO. O, they are our friends; but one cup: I'll drink for you. 30
CAS. I have drunk but one cup to-night, and that was craftily qualified° too, and, behold, what innovation° it makes here°: I am unfortunate in the infirmity, and dare not task my weakness with any more.
IAGO. What, man! 'tis a night of revels: the gallants desire it.
CAS. Where are they?
IAGO. Here at the door; I pray you, call them in.
CAS. I'll do 't; but it dislikes me.   [*Exit.*]
IAGO. If I can fasten but one cup upon him,
 With that which he hath drunk to-night already,
 He'll be as full of quarrel and offence   40
 As my young mistress' dog. Now, my sick fool Roderigo,
 Whom love hath turn'd almost the wrong side out,
 To Desdemona hath to-night carous'd
 Potations pottle-deep;° and he's to watch:
 Three lads of Cyprus, noble swelling spirits,
 That hold their honours in a wary distance,°

---

cast dismissed **stoup** measure of liquor, two quarts **qualified** diluted **innovation** disturbance **here** i.e., in Cassio's head **pottle-deep** to the bottom of the tankard **hold . . . distance** i.e, are extremely sensitive of their honor

The very elements° of this warlike isle,
Have I to-night fluster'd with flowing cups,
And they watch° too. Now, 'mongst this flock of drunkards,
Am I to put our Cassio in some action   50
That may offend the isle.—But here they come:

[*Enter* CASSIO, MONTANO, *and* GENTLEMEN; SERVANTS *following with wine.*]

If consequence do but approve° my dream,
My boat sails freely, both with wind and stream.
CAS. 'Fore God, they have given me a rouse° already.
MON. Good faith, a little one; not past a pint, as I am a soldier.
IAGO. Some wine, ho!
[*Sings*] And let me the canakin° clink, clink;
    And let me the canakin clink:
       A soldier's a man;
       A life 's but a span;   60
    Why, then, let a soldier drink.
  Some wine, boys!
CAS. 'Fore God, an excellent song.
IAGO. I learned it in England, where, indeed, they are most potent in pot-
ting: your Dane, your German, and your swag-bellied Hollander—
Drink, ho!—are nothing to your English.
CAS. Is your Englishman so expert in his drinking?
IAGO. Why, he drinks you, with facility, your Dane dead drunk; he sweats
not to overthrow your Almain°; he gives your Hollander a vomit, ere
the next pottle can be filled.   70
CAS. To the health of our general!
MON. I am for it, lieutenant; and I'll do you justice.°
IAGO. O sweet England! [*Sings.*]
  King Stephen was a worthy peer,
    His breeches cost him but a crown;
  He held them sixpence all too dear,
    With that he call'd the tailor lown.°

  He was a wight of high renown,
    And thou art but of low degree:
  'Tis pride that pulls the country down;   80
    Then take thine auld cloak about thee.
  Some wine, ho!
CAS. Why, this is a more exquisite song than the other.
IAGO. Will you hear 't again?
CAS. No; for I hold him to be unworthy of his place that does those things.
Well, God's above all; and there be souls must be saved, and there be
souls must not be saved.
IAGO. It's true, good lieutenant.

---

very elements true representatives   **watch** are members of the guard   **approve** confirm   **rouse** full draft of liquor   **canakin** small drinking vessel   **Almain** German
I'll . . . justice i.e., drink as much as you   **lown** lout, loon

CAS. For mine own part,—no offence to the general, nor any man of quality,—I hope to be saved.   90
IAGO. And so do I too, lieutenant.
CAS. Ay, but, by your leave, not before me; the lieutenant is to be saved
before the ancient. Let 's have no more of this; let 's to our affairs.—
God forgive us our sins!—Gentlemen, let 's look to our business. Do
not think, gentlemen, I am drunk: this is my ancient; this is my right
hand, and this is my left: I am not drunk now; I can stand well enough,
and speak well enough.
ALL. Excellent well.
CAS. Why, very well then; you must not think then that I am drunk.

                                                            [*Exit*]
MON. To th' platform, masters; come, let 's set the watch.   100
IAGO. You see this fellow that is gone before;
    He 's soldier fit to stand by Cæsar
    And give direction: and do but see his vice;
    'Tis to his virtue a just equinox,°
    The one as long as th' other: 'tis pity of him.
    I fear the trust Othello puts him in,
    On some odd time of his infirmity,
    Will shake this island.
MON.   But is he often thus?
IAGO. 'Tis evermore the prologue to his sleep:
    He'll watch the horologe° a double set,°   110
    If drink rock not his cradle.
MON.   It were well
    The general were put in mind of it.
    Perhaps he sees it not; or his good nature
    Prizes the virtue that appears in Cassio,
    And looks not on his evils: is not this true?

    [*Enter* RODERIGO.]

IAGO [*Aside to him*]. How now, Roderigo!
    I pray you, after the lieutenant; go.   [*Exit* RODERIGO.]
                    MON. And 'tis great pity that the noble Moor
    Should hazard such a place as his own second
    With one of an ingraft° infirmity: 120
    It were an honest action to say
    So to the Moor.
IAGO.   Not I, for this fair island:
    I do love Cassio well; and would do much
    To cure him of this evil—But, hark! what noise?
                            [*Cry within: 'Help! help!*]

---

equinox equal length of days and nights; used figuratively to mean "counterpart"   **horo-
loge** clock   **double set** twice around   **ingraft** ingrafted, inveterate

[*Enter* Cassio, *pursuing* Roderigo.]

Cas. 'Zounds, you rogue! you rascal!
Mon.   What's the matter, lieutenant?
Cas. A knave teach me my duty!
  I'll beat the knave into a twiggen° bottle.
Rod. Beat me!
Cas.   Dost thou prate, rogue?   [*Striking* Roderigo.]
Mon.   Nay, good lieutenant;
                         [*Staying him.*]
  I pray you, sir, hold your hand.
Cas.   Let me go, sir,
  Or I'll knock you o'er the mazzard.°
Mon.   Come, come, you're drunk.   130
Cas. Drunk!   [*They fight.*]
Iago [*Aside to* Roderigo]. Away, I say; go out, and cry a mutiny.
                         [*Exit* Roderigo.]
  Nay, good lieutenant,—God's will, gentlemen;—
  Help, ho!—Lieutenant,—sir,—Montano,—sir;—
  Help, masters!—Here's a goodly watch indeed!
                         [*Bell rings.*]
  Who's that which rings the bell?—Diablo,° ho!
  The town will rise°: God's will, lieutenant, hold!
  You'll be asham'd for ever.

[*Enter* Othello *and* Attendants.]

Oth.   What is the matter here?
Mon. 'Zounds, I bleed still; I am hurt to th' death.   140
  He dies!   [*Thrusts at* Cassio.]
Oth. Hold, for your lives!
Iago. Hold, ho! Lieutenant,—sir,—Montano,—gentlemen,—
  Have you forgot all sense of place and duty?
  Hold! the general speaks to you; hold, for shame!
Oth. Why, how now, ho! from whence ariseth this?
  Are we turn'd Turks° and to ourselves do that
  Which heaven hath forbid the Ottomites?
  For Christian shame, put by this barbarous brawl:
  He that stirs next to carve for° his own rage
  Holds his soul light; he dies upon his motion.   150
  Silence that dreadful bell: it frights the isle
  From her propriety.° What is the matter, masters?
  Honest Iago, that looks dead with grieving,
  Speak, who began this? on thy love, I charge thee.

---

    twiggen covered with woven twigs   **mazzard** head   **Diablo** the devil   **rise** grow
riotous   **turn'd Turks** changed completely for the worse; proverbial   **carve for** indulge   **propriety** proper state or condition

Iago. I do not know: friends all but now, even now,
　In quarter,° and in terms like bride and groom
　Devesting them for bed; and then, but now—
　As if some planet had unwitted men—
　Swords out, and tilting one at other's breast,
　In opposition bloody. I cannot speak   160
　Any beginning to this peevish odds;°
　And would in action glorious I had lost
　Those legs that brought me to a part of it!
Oth. How comes it, Michael, you are thus forgot?
Cas. I pray you, pardon me; I cannot speak.
Oth. Worthy Montano, you were wont be civil;
　The gravity and stillness of your youth
　The world hath noted, and your name is great
　In mouths of wisest censure°: what's the matter,
　That you unlace° your reputation thus   170
　And spend your rich opinion for the name
　Of a night-brawler? give me answer to it.
Mon. Worthy Othello, I am hurt to danger:
　Your officer, Iago, can inform you,—
　While I spare speech, which something now offends me,—
　Of all that I do know: nor know I aught
　By me that's said or done amiss this night;
　Unless self-charity be sometimes a vice,
　And to defend ourselves it be a sin
　When violence assails us.
Oth. 　　　　　　　　　Now, by heaven,   180
　My blood begins my safer guides to rule;
　And passion, having my best judgement collied,°
　Assays to lead the way: if I once stir,
　Or do but lift this arm, the best of you
　Shall sink in my rebuke. Give me to know
　How this foul rout began, who set it on;
　And he that is approv'd in° this offence,
　Though he had twinn'd with me, both at a birth,
　Shall lose me. What! in a town of war,
　Yet wild, the people's hearts brimful of fear,   190
　To manage private and domestic quarrel,
　In night, and on the court and guard° of safety!
　'Tis monstrous, Iago, who began 't?
Mon. If partially affin'd,° or leagu'd in office,
　Thou dost deliver more or less than truth,
　Thou art no soldier.
Iago. 　　　　　　　　　Touch me not so near:
　I had rather have this tongue cut from my mouth

In quarter on terms　　**peevish odds** childish quarrel　　**censure** judgment　　**unlace**
degrade　　**collied** darkened　　**approv'd in** found guilty of　　**court and guard** spot and
guarding place, i.e., the main guardhouse　　**affin'd** bound by a tie

Than it should do offence to Michael Cassio;
Yet, I persuade myself, to speak the truth
Shall nothing wrong him. Thus it is, general.   200
Montano and myself being in speech,
There comes a fellow crying out for help;
And Cassio following him with determin'd sword,
To execute° upon him. Sir, this gentleman
Steps in to Cassio, and entreats his pause:
Myself the crying fellow did pursue,
Lest by his clamour—as it so fell out—
The town might fall in fright: he, swift of foot,
Outran my purpose; and I return'd the rather
For that I heard the clink and fall of swords,   210
And Cassio high in oath; which till to-night
I ne'er might say before. When I came back—
For this was brief—I found them close together,
At blow and thrust; even as again they were
When you yourself did part them.
More of this matter cannot I report:
But men are men; the best sometimes forget:
Though Cassio did some little wrong to him,
As men in rage strike those that wish them best,
Yet surely, Cassio, I believe, receiv'd   220
From him that fled some strange indignity,
Which patience could not pass.
OTH.   I know, Iago,
Thy honesty and love doth mince this matter,
Making it light to Cassio. Cassio, I love thee;
But never more be officer of mine.

                    [*Enter* DESDEMONA, *attended.*]

Look, if my gentle love be not rais'd up!
I'll make thee an example.
DES.   What's the matter?
OTH. All 's well now, sweeting; come away to bed.
Sir, for your hurts, myself will be your surgeon: 230
Lead him off.   [*To* MONTANO, *who is led off.*]
Iago, look with care about the town,
And silence those whom this vile brawl distracted.
Come, Desdemona: 'tis the soldiers' life
To have their balmy slumbers wak'd with strife.
                    [*Exit with all but* IAGO *and* CASSIO.]
IAGO. What, are you hurt, lieutenant?
CAS. Ay, past all surgery.
Iago. Marry, God forbid!
CAS. Reputation, reputation, reputation! O, I have lost my reputation! I

---

execute give effect to (his anger)

have lost the immortal part of myself, and what remains is bestial. My
reputation, Iago, my reputation!   240
Iago. As I am an honest man, I thought you had received some bodily
  wound; there is more sense in that than in reputation. Reputation is
  an idle and most false imposition; oft got without merit, and lost without
  deserving: you have lost no reputation at all, unless you repute yourself
  such a loser. What, man! there are ways to recover the general again:
  you are but now cast in his mood, a punishment more in policy than
  in malice; even so as one would beat his offenceless dog to affright an
  imperious lion: sue to him again, and he 's yours.
Cas. I will rather sue to be despised than to deceive so good a commander
  with so slight, so drunken, and so indiscreet an officer. Drunk? and
  speak parrot°? and squabble? swagger? swear? and discourse fustian°
  with one's own shadow? O thou invisible spirit of wine, if thou hast
  no name to be known by, let us call thee devil!   253
Iago. What was he that you followed with your sword? What had he done
  to you?
Cas. I know not.
Iago. Is 't possible?
Cas. I remember a mass of things, but nothing distinctly; a quarrel, but
  nothing wherefore. O God, that men should put an enemy in their
  mouths to steal away their brains! that we should, with joy, pleasance,
  revel and applause, transform ourselves into beasts!   261
Iago. Why, but you are now well enough: how came you thus recovered?
Cas. It hath pleased the devil drunkenness to give place to the devil wrath:
  one unperfectness° shows me another, to make me frankly despise myself.
Iago. Come, you are too severe a moraler: as the time, the place, and the
  condition of this country stands, I could heartily wish this had not
  befallen; but, since it is as it is, mend it for your own good.
Cas. I will ask him for my place again; he shall tell me I am a drunkard!
  had I as many mouths as Hydra,° such an answer would stop them
  all. To be now a sensible man, by and by a fool, and presently a beast!
  O strange! Every inordinate cup is unblessed and the ingredient is a
  devil.   273
Iago. Come, come, good wine is a good familiar creature, if it be well
  used: exclaim no more against it. And, good lieutenant, I think you
  think I love you.
Cas. I have well approved° it, sir. I drunk!
Iago. You or any man living may be a drunk at a time, man. I'll tell
  you what you shall do. Our general's wife is now the general: I may
  say so in this respect, for that he hath devoted and given up himself
  to the contemplation, mark, and denotement° of her parts and graces:
  confess yourself freely to her; importune her help to put you in your
  place again: she is of so free, so kind, so apt, so blessed a disposition,
  she holds it a vice in her goodness not to do more than she is requested:

speak parrot talk nonsense   **discourse fustian** talked nonsense   **unperfectness** imper-
fection   **Hydra** a monster with many heads, slain by Hercules as the second of his twelve
labors   **approved** proved   **denotement** observation

this broken joint between you and her husband entreat her to splinter;°
and, my fortunes against any lay° worth naming, this crack of your
love shall grow stronger than it was before.   287
CAS. You advise me well.
IAGO. I protest, in the sincerity of love and honest kindness.
CAS. I think it freely; and betimes in the morning I will beseech the virtuous
Desdemona to undertake for me: I am desperate of my fortunes if they
check° me here.
IAGO. You are in the right. Good night, lieutenant; I must to the watch.
CAS. Good night, honest Iago.   [*Exit* CASSIO.]
IAGO. And what 's he then that says I play the villain?
    When this advice is free I give and honest,
    Probal° to thinking and indeed the course
    To win the Moor again? For 'tis most easy
    Th' inclining° Desdemona to subdue°
    In any honest suit: she 's fram'd as fruitful   300
    As the free elements. And then for her
    To win the Moor—were 't to renounce his baptism,
    All seals and symbols of redeemed sin,
    His soul is so enfetter'd to her love,
    That she may make, unmake, do what she list,
    Even as her appetite shall play the god
    With his weak function. How am I then a villain
    To counsel Cassio to this parallel° course,
    Directly to his good? Divinity of hell!
    When devils will the blackest sins put on,°   310
    They do suggest° at first with heavenly shows,
    As I do now: for whiles this honest fool
    Plies Desdemona to repair his fortunes
    And she for him pleads strongly to the Moor,
    I'll pour this pestilence into his ear,
    That she repeals him° for her body's lust;
    And by how much she strives to do him good,
    She shall undo her credit with the Moor.
    So will I turn her virtue into pitch,
    And out of her own goodness make the net   320
    That shall enmesh them all.

[*Enter* RODERIGO.]

    How now, Roderigo!
ROD. I do not follow here in the chase, not like a hound that hunts, but
one that fills up the cry.° My money is almost spent; I have been to-

---

    splinter bind with splints   **lay** stake, wager   **check** repulse   **Probal** proba-
ble   **inclining** favorably disposed   **subdue** persuade   **parallel** probably, corresponding to his best interest   **put on** further   **suggest** tempt   **repeals him** i.e., attempts
to get him restored   **cry** pack

night exceedingly well cudgellēd; and I think the issue will be, I shall
have so much experience for my pains, and so, with no money at all
and a little more wit, return again to Venice.

Iago. How poor are they that have not patience!
What wound did ever heal but by degrees?
Thou know'st we work by wit, and not by witchcraft;
And wit depends on dilatory time.   330
Does 't not go well? Cassio hath beaten thee,
And thou, by that small hurt, hast cashier'd° Cassio:
Though other things grow fair against the sun,
Yet fruits that blossom first will first be ripe:
Content thyself awhile. By th' mass, 'tis morning;
Pleasure and action make the hours seem short.
Retire thee; go where thou art billeted:
Away, I say; thou shalt know more hereafter:
Nay, get thee gone.   [*Exit* Roderigo.]
              Two things are to be done: 340
My wife must move for Cassio to her mistress;
I'll set her on;
Myself the while to draw the Moor apart,
And bring him jump° when he may Cassio find
Soliciting his wife: ay, that's the way:
Dull not device by coldness and delay.   [*Exit.*]

ACT III.

scene i. [*Before the castle.*]

[*Enter* Cassio *and* Musicians.]

Cas. Masters, play here; I will content° your pains;
Something that 's brief; and bid 'Good morrow, general.'

                                       [*They play.*]

[*Enter* Clown.]

Clo. Why, masters, have your instruments been in Naples,
    that they speak i' the nose° thus?
First Mus. How, sir, how!
Clo. Are these, I pray you, wind-instruments?
First Mus. Ay, marry, are they, sir.
Clo. O, thereby hangs a tail.
First Mus. Whereby hangs a tale,° sir?
Clo. Marry, sir, by many a wind-instrument that I know. But, masters,

---

    cashier'd dismissed from service   **jump** precisely   **content** reward   **speak i' the nose** i.e., like Neapolitans, who spoke a nasal dialect (with a joke on syphilis, which attacks the nose)   **tale** pun on *tail*, a wind instrument of sorts.

here 's money for you: and the general so likes your music, that he
desires you, for love's sake, to make no more noise with it.   12
FIRST MUS. Well, sir, we will not.
CLO. If you have any music that may not be heard, to 't again: but, as
they say, to hear music the general does not greatly care.
FIRST MUS. We have none such, sir.
CLO. Then put up your pipes in your bag, for I'll away: go; vanish into
air; away!   [*Exeunt* MUSICIANS.]
CAS. Dost thou hear, my honest friend?
CLO. No, I hear not your honest friend; I hear you.   20
CAS. Prithee, keep up thy quillets. There 's a poor piece of gold for thee:
if the gentlewoman that attends the general's wife be stirring, tell her
there 's one Cassio entreats her a little favour of speech: wilt thou do
this?
CLO. She is stirring, sir: if she will stir hither, I shall seem to notify unto
her.
CAS. Do, good my friend.   [*Exit* CLOWN.]

[*Enter* IAGO.]

                              In happy time, Iago.
IAGO. You have not been a-bed, then?
CAS. Why, no; the day had broke
    Before we parted. I have made bold, Iago,   30
    To send in to your wife: my suit to her
    Is, that she will to virtuous Desdemona
    Procure me some access.
IAGO.   I'll send her to you presently;
    And I'll devise a mean to draw the Moor
    Out of the way, that your converse and business
    May be more free.
CAS. I humbly thank you for 't.   [*Exit* IAGO.]
                              I never knew
    A Florentine more kind and honest.

[*Enter* EMILIA.]

EMIL. Good morrow, good lieutenant: I am sorry
    For your displeasure; but all will sure be well.   40
    The general and his wife are talking of it;
    And she speaks for you stoutly: the Moor replies,
    That he you hurt is of great fame in Cyprus
    And great affinity° and that in wholesome wisdom
    He might not but refuse you, but he protests he loves you
    And needs no other suitor but his likings
    To take the safest occasion by the front°
    To bring you in again.
CAS.   Yet, I beseech you,
    If you think fit, or that it may be done,

affinity kindred, family connection   **by the front** i.e., by the forelock

Give me advantage of some brief discourse 50
With Desdemona alone.
EMIL.   Pray you, come in:
I will bestow you where you shall have time
To speak your bosom freely.
CAS. I am much bound to you.   [*Exeunt.*]

       SCENE II. [*A room in the castle.*]

[*Enter* OTHELLO, IAGO, *and* GENTLEMEN.]

OTH. These letters give, Iago, to the pilot;
And by him do my duties to the senate:
That done, I will be walking on the works:°
Repair there to me.
IAGO.   Well, my good lord, I'll do 't.
OTH. This fortification, gentlemen, shall we see't?
GENT. We'll wait upon your lordship.   [*Exeunt.*]

       SCENE III. [*The garden of the castle.*]

[*Enter* DESDEMONA, CASSIO *and* EMILIA.]

DES. Be thou assur'd, good Cassio, I will do
All my abilities in thy behalf.
EMIL. Good madam, do: I warrant it grieves my husband,
As if the case were his.
DES. O, that 's an honest fellow. Do not doubt, Cassio,
But I will have my lord and you again
As friendly as you were.
CAS.   Bounteous madam,
Whatever shall become of Michael Cassio,
He's never any thing but your true servant.
DES. I know 't; I thank you. You do love my lord: 10
You have known him long; and be you well assur'd
He shall in strangeness° stand no farther off
Than in a politic distance.
CAS.   Ay, but lady,
That policy may either last so long
Or feed upon such nice and waterish diet,
Or breed itself so out of circumstance,°
That, I being absent and my place supplied,
My general will forget my love and service.
DES. Do not doubt° that; before Emilia here
I give thee warrant of thy place: assure thee,   20
If I do vow a friendship, I'll perform it
To the last article: my lord shall never rest;

---

works earthworks, fortifications   **strangeness** distant behavior   **breed . . . circum-**
stance increase itself so on account of accidents   **doubt** fear

I'll watch him tame° and talk him out of patience;
His bed shall seem a school, his board a shrift;°
I'll intermingle every thing he does
With Cassio's suit: therefore be merry, Cassio;
For thy solicitor shall rather die
Than give thy cause away.°

[*Enter* OTHELLO *and* IAGO *at a distance*.]

EMIL. Madam, here comes my lord.
CAS. Madam, I'll take my leave.
DES. Why, stay, and hear me speak.   30
CAS. Madam, not now: I am very ill at ease,
  Unfit for mine own purposes.
DES. Well, do your discretion.   [*Exit* CASSIO.]
IAGO. Ha! I like not that.
OTH.   What dost thou say?
IAGO. Nothing, my lord: or if—I know not what.
OTH. Was not that Cassio parted from my wife?
IAGO. Cassio, my lord! No, sure, I cannot think it,
  That he would steal away so guilty-like,
  Seeing you coming.
OTH.   I do believe 'twas he.   40
DES. How now, my lord!
  I have been talking with a suitor here,
  A man that languishes in your displeasure.
OTH. Who is 't you mean?
DES. Why, your lieutenant, Cassio. Good my lord,
  If I have any grace or power to move you,
  His present reconciliation take;
  For if he be not one that truly loves you,
  That errs in ignorance and not in cunning,
  I have no judgement in an honest face: 50
  I prithee, call him back.
OTH.   Went he hence now?
DES. Ay, sooth; so humbled
  That he hath left part of his grief with me,
  To suffer with him. Good love, call him back.
OTH. Not now, sweet Desdemon; some other time.
DES. But shall 't be shortly?
OTH.   The sooner, sweet, for you.
DES. Shall 't be to-night at supper?
OTH.   No, not to-night.
DES. To-morrow dinner, then?
OTH.   I shall not dine at home;
  I meet the captains at the citadel.

---

watch him tame tame him by keeping him from sleeping (a term from falconry)   **shrift**
confessional   **away** up

DES. Why, then, to-morrow night; or Tuesday morn;   60
    On Tuesday noon, or night; on Wednesday morn:
    I prithee, name the time, but let it not
    Exceed three days: in faith, he's penitent;
    And yet his trepass, in our common reason°—
    Save that, they say, the wars must make examples
    Out of their best—is not almost a fault
    T' incur a private check. When shall he come?
    Tell me, Othello: I wonder in my soul,
    What you would ask me, that I should deny,
    Or stand so mamm'ring on.° What! Michael Cassio,   70
    That came a-wooing with you, and so many a time,
    When I have spoke of you dispraisingly,
    Hath ta'en your part; to have so much to do
    To bring him in! Trust me, I could do much,—
OTH. Prithee, no more: let him come when he will;
    I will deny thee nothing.
DES.   Why, this is not a boon;
    'Tis as I should entreat you wear your gloves,
    Or feed on nourishing dishes, or keep you warm,
    Or sue to you to do a peculiar profit
    To your own person: nay, when I have a suit   80
    Wherein I mean to touch your love indeed,
    It shall be full of poise° and difficult weight
    And fearful to be granted.
OTH.   I will deny thee nothing:
    Whereon, I do beseech thee, grant me this,
    To leave me but a little to myself.
DES. Shall I deny you? no: farewell, my lord.
OTH. Farewell, my Desdemona: I'll come to thee straight.
DES. Emilia, come. Be as your fancies teach you;
    Whate'er you be, I am obedient.
                              [*Exit with* EMILIA.]
                                                        90
OTH. Excellent wretch!° Perdition catch my soul,
    But I do love thee! and when I love thee not,
    Chaos is come again.
IAGO. My noble lord,—
OTH.   What dost thou say, Iago?
IAGO. Did Michael Cassio, when you woo'd my lady,
    Know of your love?
OTH. He did, from first to last: why dost thou ask?
IAGO. But for a satisfaction of my thought;
    No further harm.
OTH.   Why of thy thought, Iago?
IAGO. I did not think he had been acquainted with her.
OTH. O, yes; and went between us very oft.   100
IAGO. Indeed!

---

common reason everyday judgments   **mamm'ring on** wavering   **poise** weight, heaviness   **wretch** term of affectionate endearment with a connotation of pity

OTH. Indeed! ay, indeed: discern'st thou aught in that?
  Is he not honest?
IAGO.   Honest, my lord!
OTH.   Honest! ay, honest.
IAGO. My lord, for aught I know.
OTH. What dost thou think?
IAGO.   Think, my lord!
OTH.   Think, my lord!
  By heaven, he echoes me,
  As if there were some monster in his thought
  Too hideous to be shown. Thou dost mean something:
  I heard thee say even now, thou lik'st not that,
  When Cassio left my wife: what didst not like?   110
  And when I told thee he was of my counsel
  In my whole course of wooing, thou criedst 'Indeed!'
  And didst contract and purse thy brow together,
  As if thou then hadst shut up in thy brain
  Some horrible conceit: if thou dost love me,
  Show me thy thought.
IAGO. My lord, you know I love you.
OTH.   I think thou dost;
  And, for I know thou 'rt full of love and honesty,
  And weigh'st thy words before thou giv'st them breath,
  Therefore these stops of thine fright me the more: 120
  For such things in a false disloyal knave
  Are tricks of custom, but in a man that's just
  They 're close delations,° working from the heart
  That passion cannot rule.
IAGO.   For Michael Cassio,
  I dare be sworn I think that he is honest.
OTH. I think so too.
IAGO.   Men should be what they seem;
  Or those that be not, would they might seem none!
OTH. Certain, men should be what they seem.
IAGO. Why, then, I think Cassio 's an honest man.
OTH. Nay, yet there 's more in this: 130
  I prithee, speak to me as to thy thinkings,
  As thou dost ruminate, and give thy worst of thoughts
  The worst of words.
IAGO.   Good my lord, pardon me:
  Though I am bound to every act of duty,
  I am not bound to that all slaves are free to.
  Utter my thoughts? Why, say they are vile and false;
  As where 's that palace whereinto foul things
  Sometimes intrude not? who has a breast so pure,
  But some uncleanly apprehensions
  Keep leets° and law-days° and in sessions sit   140

---

close delations secret or involuntary accusations   **Keep leets** hold courts   **law-days**
court days

With meditations lawful?
OTH. Thou dost conspire against thy friend, Iago,
   If thou but think'st him wrong'd and mak'st his ear
   A stranger to thy thoughts.
IAGO.   I do beseech you—
   Though I perchance am vicious° in my guess,
   As, I confess, it is my nature's plague
   To spy into abuses, and oft my jealousy°
   Shapes faults that are not—that your wisdom yet,
   From one that so imperfectly conceits,°
   Would take no notice, nor build yourself a trouble   150
   Out of his scattering and unsure observance.
   It were not for your quiet nor your good,
   Nor for my manhood, honesty, or wisdom,
   To let you know my thoughts.
OTH.   What dost thou mean?
IAGO. Good name in man and woman, dear my lord,
   Is the immediate jewel of their souls:
   Who steals my purse steals trash; 'tis something, nothing;
   'Twas mine, 'tis his, and has been slave to thousands;
   But he that filches from me my good name
   Robs me of that which not enriches him   160
   And makes me poor indeed.
OTH. By heaven, I'll know thy thoughts.
IAGO. You cannot, if my heart were in your hand;
   Nor shall not, whilst 'tis in my custody.
OTH. Ha!
IAGO.   Oh, beware, my lord, of jealousy;
   It is the green-ey'd monster which doth mock
   The meat it feeds on: that cuckold lives in bliss
   Who, certain of his fate, loves not his wronger;
   But, O, what damned minutes tells he o'er
   Who dotes, yet doubts, suspects, yet strongly loves!   170
OTH. O misery!
IAGO. Poor and content is rich and rich enough,
   But riches fineless° is as poor as winter
   To him that ever fears he shall be poor.
   Good God, the souls of all my tribe defend
   From jealousy!
OTH.   Why, why is this?
   Think'st thou I'ld make a life of jealousy,
   To follow still the changes of the moon
   With fresh suspicions? No; to be once in doubt
   Is once to be resolv'd: exchange me for a goat,   180
   When I shall turn the business of my soul
   To such exsufflicate and blown° surmises,

---

vicious wrong   **jealousy** suspicion of evil   **conceits** judges   **fineless** boundless
exsufflicate and blown unsubstantial and inflated, flyblown

Matching thy inference. 'Tis not to make me jealous
To say my wife is fair, feeds well, loves company,
Is free of speech, sings, plays and dances well;
Where virtue is, these are more virtuous;
Nor from mine own weak merits will I draw
The smallest fear or doubt of her revolt:
For she had eyes, and chose me. No, Iago;
I'll see before I doubt; when I doubt, prove;   190
And on the proof, there is no more but this,—
Away at once with love or jealousy!
IAGO. I am glad of this; for now I shall have reason
    To show the love and duty that I bear you
    With franker spirit: therefore, as I am bound,
    Receive it from me. I speak not yet of proof.
    Look to your wife; observe her well with Cassio;
    Wear your eye thus, not jealous nor secure°:
    I would not have your free and noble nature,
    Out of self-bounty,° be abus'd; look to 't: 200
    I know our country disposition well;
    In Venice they do let heaven see the pranks
    They dare not show their husbands; their best conscience
    Is not to leave 't undone, but keep 't unknown.
OTH. Dost thou say so?
IAGO. She did deceive her father, marrying you;
    And when she seem'd to shake and fear your looks,
    She lov'd them most.
OTH.   And so she did.
IAGO.   Why, go to then;
    She that, so young, could give out such a seeming,°
    To seel° her father's eyes up close as oak—   210
    He thought 'twas witchcraft—but I am much to blame;
    I humbly do beseech you of your pardon
    For too much loving you.
OTH.   I am bound to thee for ever.
IAGO. I see this hath a little dash'd your spirits.
OTH. Not a jot, not a jot.
IAGO.   I' faith, I fear it has.
    I hope you will consider what is spoke
    Comes from my love. But I do see y' are mov'd:
    I am to pray you not to strain my speech
    To grosser issues nor to larger reach°
    Than to suspicion.   220
OTH. I will not.
IAGO.   Should you do so, my lord,
    My speech should fall into such vile success
    As my thoughts aim not at. Cassio 's my worthy friend—

---

secure free from uneasiness   **self-bounty** inherent or natural goodness   **seeming** false
appearance   **seel** blind (a term from falconry)   **reach** meaning

My lord, I see y' are mov'd.
OTH.   No, not much mov'd:
 I do not think but Desdemona's honest.
IAGO. Long live she so! and long live you to think so!
OTH. And yet, how nature erring from itself,—
IAGO. Ay, there 's the point: as—to be bold with you—
 Not to affect many proposed matches
 Of her own clime, complexion, and degree,   230
 Whereto we see in all things nature tends—
 Foh! one may smell in such a will° most rank,
 Foul disproportion,° thoughts unnatural.
 But pardon me; I do not in position°
 Distinctly speak of her; though I may fear
 Her will, recoiling to° her better judgment,
 May fall to match you with her country forms°
 And happily repent.°
OTH.   Farewell, farewell:
 If more thou dost perceive, let me know more;
 Set on thy wife to observe: leave me, Iago.   240
IAGO [*Going*]. My lord, I take my leave.
OTH. Why did I marry? This honest creature doubtless
 Sees and knows more, much more, than he unfolds.
IAGO [*Returning*]. My Lord, I would I might entreat your honour
 To scan this thing no farther; leave it to time:
 Although 'tis fit that Cassio have his place,
 For, sure, he fills it up with great ability,
 Yet, if you please to hold him off awhile,
 You shall by that perceive him and his means:
 Note, if your lady strain his entertainment°   250
 With any strong or vehement importunity;
 Much will be seen in that. In the mean time,
 Let me be thought too busy in my fears—
 As worthy cause I have to fear I am—
 And hold her free,° I do beseech your honour.
OTH. Fear not my government.°
IAGO. I once more take my leave.   [*Exit.*]
OTH. This fellow 's of exceeding honesty,
 And knows all qualities, with a learned spirit,
 Of human dealings. If I do prove her haggard,°   260
 Though that her jesses° were my dear heartstrings,
 I 'ld whistle her off and let her down the wind,
 To prey at fortune.° Haply, for I am black
 And have not those soft parts of conversation

---

will sensuality **disproportion** abnormality **position** general argument **recoiling
to** falling back upon, or recoiling against **fall . . . forms** happen to compare you with
Venetian norms of handsomeness **repent** i.e., of her marriage **strain his entertainment**
urge his reinstatement **hold her free** regard her as innocent **government** self-control
haggard a wild female duck **jesses** straps fastened around the legs of a trained hawk
at fortune at random

That chamberers° have, or for I am declin'd
Into the vale of years,—yet that 's not much—
She 's gone. I am abus'd: and my relief
Must be to loathe her. O curse of marriage,
That we can call these delicate creatures ours,
And not their appetites! I had rather be a toad,   270
And live upon the vapour of a dungeon,
Than keep a corner in the thing I love
For others' uses. Yet, 'tis the plague of great ones;
Prerogativ'd° are they less than the base;
'Tis destiny unshunnable, like death:
Even then this forked° plague is fated to us
When we do quicken.° Look where she comes:

[*Enter* Desdemona *and* Emilia.]

If she be false, O, then heaven mocks itself!
I'll not believe 't.
Des.   How now, my dear Othello!
Your dinner, and the generous islanders   280
By you invited, do attend your presence.
Oth. I am to blame.
Des.   Why do you speak so faintly?
Are you not well?
Oth. I have a pain upon my forehead here.
Des. 'Faith, that 's with watching;° 'twill away again:
Let me but bind it hard, within this hour
It will be well.
Oth.   Your napkin is too little:
                        [*He puts the handkerchief from him; and it drops.*]
Let it alone. Come, I'll go in with you.
Des. I am very sorry that you are not well.

                                            [*Exit with* Othello.]

Emil. I am glad I have found this napkin: 290
This was her first remembrance from the Moor:
My wayward husband hath a hundred times
Woo'd me to steal it; but she so loves the token,
For he conjur'd her she should ever keep it,
That she reserves it evermore about her
To kiss and talk to. I'll have the work ta'en out,°
And give 't Iago: what he will do with it
Heaven knows, not I;
I nothing but to please his fantasy.

[*Enter* Iago.]

Iago. How now! what do you here alone?   300
Emil. Do not you chide; I have a thing for you.

    chamberers gallant   **Prerogativ'd** privileged   **forked** an allusion to the horns of the
cuckold   **quicken** receive life   **generous** noble   **watching** working late   **work ta'en
out** design copied

IAGO. A thing for me? it is a common thing°—
EMIL. Ha!
IAGO. To have a foolish wife.
EMIL. O, is that all? What will you give me now
   For that same handkerchief?
Iago.   What handkerchief?
EMIL. What handkerchief!
   Why, that the Moor first gave to Desdemona;
   That which so often you did bid me steal.
IAGO. Hast stol'n it from her?   310
EMIL. No, 'faith; she let it drop by negligence,
   And, to th' advantage, I, being here, took 't up.
   Look, here it is.
IAGO.   A good wench; give it me.
EMIL. What will you do with 't, that you have been so earnest
   To have me filch it?
IAGO.   *[Snatching it]* Why, what is that to you?
EMIL. If it be not for some purpose of import,
   Give 't me again: poor lady, she'll run mad
   When she shall lack it.
IAGO. Be not acknown on 't;° I have use for it.
   Go, leave me.   *[Exit* EMILIA.*]*
   I will in Cassio's lodging lose this napkin,   320
   And let him find it. Trifles light as air
   Are too the jealous confirmations strong
   As proofs of holy writ: this may do something.
   The Moor already changes with my poison:
   Dangerous conceits are, in their natures, poisons,
   Which at the first are scarce found to distaste,
   But with a little act° upon the blood,
   Burn like the mines of sulphur. I did say so:

[Enter OTHELLO.*]*

   Look, where he comes! Not poppy, nor mandragora,   330
   Nor all the drowsy syrups of the world,
   Shall ever medicine thee to that sweet sleep
   Which thou owedst yesterday.
OTH.   Ha! ha! false to me?
IAGO. Why, how now, general! no more of that.
OTH. Avaunt! be gone! thou has set me on the rack;
   I swear 'tis better to be much abus'd
   Than but to know 't a little.
IAGO.   How now, my lord!
OTH. What sense had I of her stol'n hours of lust?
   I saw 't not, thought it not, it harm'd not me:
   I slept the next night well, fed well, was free and merry;   340

---

common thing (with bawdy suggestion)   **Be . . . on't** do not confess knowledge of
it   **act** action, working

I found not Cassio's kisses on her lips:
He that is robb'd, not wanting what is stol'n,
Let him not know 't, and he 's not robb'd at all.
IAGO. I am sorry to hear this.
OTH. I had been happy, if the general camp,
Pioners° and all, had tasted her sweet body,
So I had nothing known. O, now, for ever
Farewell the tranquil mind! farewell content!
Farewell the plumed troop, and the big wars,
That make ambition virtue! O, farewell!   350
Farewell the neighing steed, and the shrill trump,
The spirit-stirring drum, th' ear-piercing fife,
The royal banner, and all quality,
Pride, pomp and circumstance° of glorious war!
And, O you mortal engines,° whose rude throats
Th' immortal Jove's dread clamours counterfeit,
Farewell! Othello's occupation 's gone!
IAGO. Is 't possible, my lord?
OTH. Villain, be sure thou prove my love a whore,
Be sure of it; give me the ocular proof;   360
Or, by the worth of mine eternal soul,
Thou hadst been better have been born a dog
Than answer my wak'd wrath!
IAGO.   Is 't come to this?
OTH. Make me to see 't; or, at the least, so prove it,
That the probation bear no hinge nor loop
To hang a doubt on; or woe upon thy life!
IAGO. My noble lord,—
OTH. If thou dost slander her and torture me,o
Never pray more; abandon all remorse;
On horror's head horrors° accumulate;   370
Do deeds to make heaven weep, all earth amaz'd;
For nothing canst thou to damnation add
Greater than that.
IAGO.   O grace! O heaven forgive me!
Are you a man? have you a soul or sense?
God be wi' you; take mine office. O wretched fool,
That liv'st to make thine honesty a vice!
O monstrous world! Take note, take note, O world,
To be direct and honest is not safe.
I thank you for this profit; and from hence
I'll love no friend, sith love breeds such offence.   380
OTH. Nay, stay: thou shouldst be honest.
IAGO. I should be wise, for honesty 's a fool
And loses that it works for.
OTH.   By the world,

Pioners sappers, a low grade of soldiers   **circumstance** attendant fact; here, formal display   **mortal engines** i.e., cannon   **horrors** object of *accumulate*

I think my wife be honest and think she is not;
I think that thou are just and think thou art not.
I'll have some proof. Her name, that was as fresh
As Dian's visage, is now begrim'd and black
As mine own face. If there be cords, or knives,
Poison, or fire, or suffocating streams,
I'll not endure it. Would I were satisfied!   390
IAGO. I see, sir, you are eaten up with passion:
   I do repent me that I put it to you.
   You would be satisfied!
OTH.   Would! nay, I will.
IAGO. And may: but, how? how satisfied, my lord?
   Would you, the supervisor, grossly gape on—
   Behold her topp'd?
OTH.   Death and damnation! O!
IAGO. It were a tedious difficulty, I think,
   To bring them to that prospect: damn them then,
   If ever mortal eyes do see them bolster°
   More than their own! What then? how then?   400
   What shall I say? Where 's satisfaction?
   It is impossible you should see this,
   Were they as prime as goats, as hot as monkeys,
   As salt° as wolves in pride, and fools as gross
   As ignorance made drunk. But yet, I say,
   If imputation° and strong circumstances,
   Which lead directly to the door of truth,
   Will give you satisfaction, you may have 't.
OTH. Give me a living reason she 's disloyal.
IAGO. I do not like the office: 410
   But, sith I am ent'red in this cause so far,
   Prick'd to 't by foolish honesty and love,
   I will go on. I lay with Cassio lately;
   And, being troubled with a raging tooth,
   I could not sleep.
   There are a kind of men so loose of soul,
   That in their sleeps will mutter their affairs:
   One of this kind is Cassio:
   In sleep I heard him say 'Sweet Desdemona,
   Let us be wary, let us hide our loves;'   420
   And then, sir, would he gripe and wring my hand,
   Cry 'O sweet creature!' and then kiss me hard,
   As if he pluck'd up kisses by the roots
   That grew upon my lips: then laid his leg
   Over my thigh, and sigh'd, and kiss'd; and then
   Cried 'Cursed fate that gave thee to the Moor!'
OTH. O monstrous! monstrous!
IAGO.   Nay, this was but his dream.

---

bolster lie together   **salt** wanton, sensual   **imputation** i.e., opinion founded on strong
circumstantial evidence

Oth. But this denoted a foregone conclusion°:
  'Tis a shrewd doubt, though it be but a dream.
Iago. And this may help to thicken other proofs   430
  That do demonstrate thinly.
Oth: I'll tear her all to pieces.
Iago. Nay, but be wise: yet we see nothing done;
  She may be honest yet. Tell me but this,
  Have you not sometimes seen a handkerchief
  Spotted with strawberries in your wife's hand?
Oth. I gave her such a one; 'twas my first gift.
Iago. I know not that: but such a handkerchief—
  I am sure it was your wife's—did I to-day
  See Cassio wipe his beard with.
Oth.   If it be that,—
Iago. If it be that, or any that was hers,   440
  It speaks against her with the other proofs.
Oth. O, that the slave had forty thousand lives!
  One is too poor, too weak for my revenge.
  Now do I see 'tis true. Look here, Iago;
  All my fond love thus do I blow to heaven.
  'Tis gone.
  Arise, black vengeance, from the hollow hell!
  Yield up, O love, thy crown and hearted° throne
  To tyrannous hate! Swell, bosom, with thy fraught,°
  For 'tis of aspics'° tongues!
Iago.   Yet be content.   450
Oth. O, blood, blood, blood!
Iago. Patience, I say; your mind perhaps may change.
Oth. Never, Iago. Like to the Pontic sea,
  Whose icy current and compulsive course
  Ne'er feels retiring ebb, but keeps due on
  To the Propontic and the Hellespont,
  Even so my bloody thoughts, with violent pace,
  Shall ne'er look back, ne'er ebb to humble love,
  Till that a capable and wide revenge
  Swallow them up. Now, by yond marble° heaven,   460
  [*Kneels*] In the due reverence of a sacred vow
  I here engage my words.
Iago.   Do not rise yet.
  [*Kneels*] Witness, you ever-burning lights above,
  You elements that clip us round about,
  Witness that here Iago doth give up
  The execution° of his wit, hands, heart,
  To wrong'd Othello's service! Let him command,
  And to obey shall be in me remorse,°

---

foregone conclusion previous trial or experience (not used in our sense)   **hearted** fixed
in the heart   **fraught** freight, burden   **aspics'** venemous serpents'   **marble** i.e., gleaming like marble   **execution** exercise   **remorse** pity for Othello's wrongs

What bloody business ever. [*They rise.*]
OTH.   I greet thy love,
  Not with vain thanks, but with acceptance bounteous,   470
  And will upon the instant put thee to 't:
  Within these three days let me hear thee say
  That Cassio 's not alive.
IAGO. My friend is dead; 'tis done at your request:
  But let her live.
OTH. Damn her, lewd minx! O, damn her! damn her!
  Come, go with me apart; I will withdraw,
  To furnish me with some swift means of death
  For the fair devil. Now art thou my lieutenant.
IAGO. I am your own for ever. [*Exeunt.*]

    SCENE IV. [*Before the castle.*]

  [*Enter* DESDEMONA, EMILIA, *and* CLOWN.]

DES. Do you know, sirrah, where Lieutenant Cassio lies?
CLO. I dare not say he lies any where.
DES. Why, man?
CLO. He 's a soldier, and for one to say a soldier lies, is stabbing.
DES. Go to: where lodges he?
CLO. To tell you where he lodges, is to tell you where I lie.
DES. Can any thing be made of this?
CLO. I know not where he lodges, and for me to devise a lodging and
  say he lies here or he lies there, were to lie in mine own throat.
DES. Can you inquire him out, and be edified by report?   10
CLO. I will catechize the world for him; that is, make questions, and by
  them answer.
DES. Seek him, bid him come hither: tell him I have moved my lord on
  his behalf, and hope all will be well.
CLO. To do this is within the compass of man's wit; and therefore I will
  attempt the doing it.   [*Exit* CLO.]
DES. Where should I lose that handkerchief, Emilia?
EMIL. I know not, madam.
DES. Believe me, I had rather have lost my purse
  Full of crusadoes°: and, but my noble Moor   20
  Is true of mind and made of no such baseness
  As jealous creatures are, it were enough
  To put him to ill thinking.
EMIL.   Is he not jealous?
DES. Who, he? I think the sun where he was born
  Drew all such humours from him.
EMIL.   Look, where he comes.

  [*Enter* OTHELLO.]

crusadoes Portuguese gold coins

DES. I will not leave him now till Cassio
   Be call'd to him.—How is 't with you, my lord?
OTH. Well, my good lady. [*Aside*] O, hardness to dissemble!—
   How do you, Desdemona?
DES.   Well, my good lord.
OTH. Give me your hand: this hand is moist, my lady.   30
DES. It yet hath felt no age nor known no sorrow.
OTH. This argues fruitfulness and liberal heart:
   Hot, hot, and moist: this hand of yours requires
   A sequester° from liberty, fasting and prayer,
   Much castigation, exercise devout;
   For here 's a young and sweating devil here,
   That commonly rebels. 'Tis a good hand,
   A frank one.
DES.   You may, indeed, say so:
   For 'twas that hand that gave away my heart.
OTH. A liberal hand: the hearts of old gave hands;   40
   But our new heraldry is hands, not hearts.°
DES. I cannot speak of this. Come now, your promise.
OTH. What promise, chuck?
DES. I have sent to bid Cassio come speak with you.
OTH. I have a salt and sorry rheum° offends me;
   Lend my thy handkerchief.
DES.   Here, my lord.
OTH. That which I gave you.
DES.   I have it not about me.
OTH. Not?
DES.   No, indeed, my lord.
OTH.   That 's a fault.
   That handkerchief
   Did an Egyptian° to my mother give;   50
   She was a charmer, and could almost read
   The thoughts of people: she told her, while she kept it,
   'Twould make her amiable and subdue my father
   Entirely to her love, but if she lost it
   Or made a gift of it, my father's eye
   Should hold her loathed and his spirits should hunt
   After new fancies: she, dying, gave it me;
   And bid me, when my fate would have me wive,
   To give it her. I did so: and take heed on 't;
   Make it a darling like your precious eye;   60
   To lose 't or give 't away were such perdition
   As nothing else could match.
DES.   Is 't possible?
OTH. 'Tis true: there 's magic in the web of it:

---

sequester separation, sequestration   **new . . . hearts** a current expression referring to marriages in which there is a joining of hands without the giving of hearts   **sorry rheum** distressful head cold   **Egyptian** gypsy

A sibyl, that had numb'red in the world
The sun to course two hundred compasses,
In her prophetic fury sew'd the work;
The worms were hallow'd that did breed the silk;
And it was dy'd in mummy° which the skilful
Conserv'd of° maidens' hearts.
DES.   Indeed! is 't true?
OTH. Most veritable; therefore look to 't well.   70
DES. Then would to God that I had never seen 't!
OTH. Ha! wherefore?
DES. Why do you speak so startingly and rash?
OTH. Is 't lost? is 't gone? speak, is it out o' th' way?
DES. Heaven bless us!
OTH. Say you?
DES. It is not lost; but what an if it were?
OTH. How!
DES. I say, it is not lost.
OTH.   Fetch 't, let me see 't.
DES. Why, so I can, sir, but I will not now.   80
    This is a trick to put me from my suit:
    Pray you, let Cassio be receiv'd again.
OTH. Fetch me the handkerchief: my mind misgives.
DES. Come, come;
    You'll never meet a more sufficient man.
OTH. The handkerchief!
DES.   I pray, talk me of Cassio.
OTH. The handkerchief!
DES.   A man that all his time
    Hath founded his good fortunes on your love,
    Shar'd dangers with you,—
OTH. The handkerchief!   90
DES. In sooth, you are to blame.
OTH. Away!   [*Exit* OTHELLO.]
EMIL. Is not this man jealous?
DES. I ne'er saw this before.
    Sure, there 's some wonder in this handkerchief:
    I am most unhappy in the loss of it.
EMIL. 'Tis not a year or two shows us a man:
    They are all but stomachs, and we all but food;
    They eat us hungerly, and when they are full,
    They belch us.

[*Enter* IAGO *and* CASSIO.]

                    Look you, Cassio and my husband!   100
IAGO. There is no other way; 'tis she must do 't:

---

mummy medicinal or magical preparation drained from the flesh of mummified bodies
Conserv'd of preserved out of

    And, lo, the happiness! go, and importune her.
DES. How now, good Cassio! what 's the news with you?
CAS. Madam, my former suit: I do beseech you
    That by your virtuous means I may again
    Exist, and be a member of his love
    Whom I with all the office of my heart
    Entirely honour: I would not be delay'd.
    If my offence be of such mortal kind
    That nor my service past, nor present sorrows,   110
    Nor purpos'd merit in futurity,
    Can ransom me into his love again,
    But to know so must be my benefit;°
    So shall I clothe me in a forc'd content,
    And shut myself up in some other course,
    To fortune's alms.
DES.   Alas, thrice-gentle Cassio!
    My advocation° is not now in tune;
    My lord is not my lord; nor should I know him,
    Were he in favour as in humour alter'd.
    So help me every spirit sanctified,   120
    As I have spoken for you all my best
    And stood within the blank° of his displeasure
    For my free speech! You must awhile be patient:
    What I can do I will; and more I will
    Than for myself I dare: let that suffice you.
IAGO. Is my lord angry?
EMIL.   He went hence but now,
    And certainly in strange unquietness.
IAGO. Can he be angry? I have seen the cannon,
    When it hath blown his ranks into the air,
    And, like the devil, from his very arm   130
    Puff'd his own brother:—and can he be angry?
    Something of moment then: I will go meet him:
    There 's matter in 't indeed, if he be angry.
DES. I prithee, do so.   [*Exit* IAGO.]
                  Something, sure, of state,
    Either from Venice, or some unhatch'd practice
    Made demonstrable here in Cyprus to him,
    Hath puddled° his clear spirit; and in such cases
    Men's natures wrangle with inferior things,
    Though great ones are their object. 'Tis even so;
    For let our finger ache, and it indues°   140
    Our other healthful members even to a sense
    Of pain: nay, we must think men are not gods,
    Nor of them look for such observancy
    As fits the bridal. Beshrew me much, Emilia,

---

to know . . . benefit to know that my case is hopeless will end my vain endeavor   **advoca-
tion** advocacy   **blank** white spot in the center of a target; here, range   **puddled** sullied
the purity of   **indues** brings to the same conditon

I was, unhandsome° warrior as I am,
Arraigning his unkindness with my soul;
But now I find I had suborn'd the witness,
And he 's indicted falsely.
EMIL. Pray heaven it be state-matters, as you think,
And no conception° nor no jealous toy   150
Concerning you.
DES. Alas the day! I never gave him cause.
EMIL. But jealous souls will not be answer'd so;
They are not ever jealous for the cause,
But jealous for they are jealous: 'tis a monster
Begot upon itself, born on itself.
DES. Heaven keep that monster from Othello's mind!
EMIL. Lady, amen.
DES. I will go seek him. Cassio, walk here about:
If I do find him fit, I'll move your suit   160
And seek to effect it to my uttermost.
CAS. I humbly thank your ladyship.

                          [*Exit* DESDEMONA *with* EMILIA.]

[*Enter* BIANCA.]

BIAN. Save you, friend Cassio!
CAS.   What make you from home?
How is 't with you, my most fair Bianca?
I' faith, sweet love, I was coming to your house.
BIAN. And I was going to your lodging, Cassio.
What, keep a week away? seven days and nights?
Eight score eight hours? and lovers' absent hours,
More tedious than the dial eight score times?
O weary reck'ning!
CAS.   Pardon me, Bianca.   170
I have this while with leaden thoughts been press'd;
But I shall, in a more continuate° time,
Strike off this score of absence. Sweet Bianca,
                    [*Giving her* DESDEMONA'S *handkerchief.*]
Take me this work out.°
BIAN.   O Cassio, whence came this?
This is some token from a newer friend:
To the felt absence now I feel a cause:
Is 't come to this? Well, well.
CAS.   Go to, woman!
Throw your vile guesses in the devil's teeth,
From whence you have them. You are jealous now
That this is from some mistress, some remembrance: 180

---

unhandsome unfair   **conception** mere fancy   **continuate** uninterrupted   **Take
. . out** i.e., copy this embroidery for me

No, in good troth, Bianca.
BIAN.   Why, whose is it?
CAS. I know not, sweet: I found it in my chamber.
   I like the work well: ere it be demanded—
   As like enough it will—I would have it copied:
   Take it, and do 't; and leave me for this time.
BIAN. Leave you! wherefore?
CAS. I do attend here on the general;
   And think it no addition, nor my wish,
   To have him see me woman'd.
BIAN.   Why, I pray you?
CAS. Not that I love you not.   190
BIAN.   But that you do not love me.
   I pray you, bring me on the way a little,
   And say if I shall see you soon at night.
CAS. 'Tis but a little way that I can bring you;
   For I attend here: but I'll see you soon.
BIAN. 'Tis very good; I must be circumstanc'd.°   [*Exeunt omnes.*]

ACT IV.

SCENE I. [*Cyprus. Before the castle.*]

[*Enter* OTHELLO *and* IAGO.]

IAGO. Will you think so?
OTH.   Think so, Iago!
IAGO.   What,
   To kiss in private?
OTH.   An unauthoriz'd kiss.
IAGO. Or to be naked with her friend in bed
   An hour or more, not meaning any harm?
OTH. Naked in bed, Iago, and not mean harm!
   It is hypocrisy against the devil:
   They that mean virtuously, and yet do so,
   The devil their virtue tempts, and they tempt heaven.
IAGO. So° they do nothing, 'tis a venial slip:
   But if I give my wife a handkerchief,—   10
OTH. What then?
IAGO. Why, then, 'tis hers, my lord: and, being hers,
   She may, I think, bestow 't on any man.
OTH. She is protectress of her honour too:
   May she give that?
IAGO. Her honour is an essence that 's not seen;
   They have it very oft that have it not:

___

circumstanc'd governed by circumstances   **So** so long as

But, for the handkerchief,—
OTH. By heaven, I would most gladly have forgot it.
 Thou said'st—O, it comes o'er my memory,   20
 As doth the raven o'er the infected house,°
 Boding to all—he had my handkerchief.
IAGO. Ay, what of that?
OTH.   That 's not so good now.
IAGO.   What,
 If I had said I had seen him do you wrong?
 Or heard him say,—as knaves be such abroad,
 Who having, by their own importunate suit,
 Or voluntary dotage of some mistress,
 Convinced or supplied° them, cannot choose
 But they must blab—
OTH.   Hath he said any thing?
IAGO. He hath, my lord; but be you well assur'd,   30
 No more than he'll unswear.
OTH.   What hath he said?
IAGO. 'Faith, that he did—I know not what he did.
OTH. What? what?
IAGO. Lie—
OTH.   With her?
IAGO.   With her, on her; what you will.
OTH. Lie with her! lie on her! We say lie on her, when they belie her.
 Lie with her! that 's fulsome.—Handkerchief—confessions—handker-
 chief!—To confess, and be hanged for his labour;—first, to be hanged,
 and then to confess.—I tremble at it. Nature would not invest herself
 in such shadowing passion without some instruction.° It is not words
 that shakes me thus. Pish! Noses, ears, and lips.—Is 't possible?—Con-
 fess—handkerchief—O devil!   [*Falls in a trance.*]
IAGO. Work on,   42
 My medicine, work! Thus credulous fools are caught;
 And many worthy and chaste dames even thus,
 All guiltless, meet reproach. What, ho! my lord!
 My lord, I say! Othello!

[*Enter* CASSIO.]

                         How now, Cassio!
CAS. What 's the matter?
IAGO. My lord is fall'n into an epilepsy:
 This is his second fit; he had one yesterday.
CAS. Rub him about the temples.   50

---

 raven . . . house allusion to the belief that the raven hovered over a house of sickness
or infection   **Convinced or supplied** i.e., mistresses gained by importunity and those who
doted voluntarily   **Nature . . . instruction** i.e., my jealousy cannot be merely the result
of natural imagination, but must have some foundation in fact

IAGO.   No, forbear;
  The lethargy° must have his quiet course:
  If not, he foams at mouth and by and by
  Breaks out to savage madness. Look, he stirs:
  Do you withdraw yourself a little while,
  He will recover straight: when he is gone,
  I would on great occasion speak with you.   [*Exit* CASSIO.]
  How is it, general? have you not hurt your head?
OTH. Dost thou mock me?
IAGO.   I mock you! no, by heaven.
  Would you would bear your fortune like a man!
OTH. A horned man 's a monster and a beast.   60
IAGO. There 's many a beast then in a populous city,
  And many a civil° monster.
OTH. Did he confess it?
IAGO.   Good sir, be a man;
  Think every bearded fellow that 's but yok'd
  May draw with you°: there 's millions now alive
  That nightly lie in those unproper° beds
  Which they dare swear peculiar°: your case is better.
  O, 'tis the spite of hell, the fiend's arch-mock,
  To lip a wanton in a secure couch,
  And to suppose her chaste! No, let me know;   70
  And knowing what I am, I know what she shall be.
OTH. O, thou are wise; 'tis certain.
IAGO.   Stand you awhile apart;
  Confine yourself but in a patient list.°
  Whilst you were here o'erwhelmed with your grief—
  A passion most unsuiting such a man—
  Cassio came hither: I shifted him away,
  And laid good 'scuse upon your ecstasy,
  Bade him anon return and here speak with me;
  The which he promis'd. Do but encave° yourself,
  And mark the fleers,° the gibes, and notable scorns,   80
  That dwell in every region of his face;
  For I will make him tell the tale anew,
  Where, how, how oft, how long ago, and when
  He hath, and is again to cope your wife:
  I say, but mark his gesture. Marry, patience;
  Or I shall say y' are all in all in spleen,
  And nothing of a man.
OTH.   Dost thou hear, Iago?
  I will be found most cunning in my patience;
  But—dost thou hear?—most bloody.
IAGO.   That 's not amiss;

---

lethargy unconscious condition   **civil** i.e., in civilized society   **draw with you** i.e.,
share your fate as cuckold   **unproper** not belonging exclusively to an individual   **peculiar** private, one's own   **patient list** within the bounds of patience   **encave** conceal
fleers sneers

But yet keep time° in all. Will you withdraw?   90

[OTHELLO *retires.*]

Now will I question Cassio of Bianca,
A housewife that by selling her desires
Buys herself bread and clothes: it is a creature
That dotes on Cassio; as 'tis the strumpet's plague
To beguile many and be beguil'd by one:
He, when he hears of her, cannot refrain
From the excess of laughter. Here he comes:

[*Enter* CASSIO.]

As he shall smile, Othello shall go mad;
And his unbookish° jealousy must conster°
Poor Cassio's smiles, gestures and light behaviour,   100
Quite in the wrong. How do you now, lieutenant?
CAS. The worser that you give me the addition°
Whose want even kills me.
IAGO. Ply Desdemona well, and you are sure on 't.
[*Speaking lower*] Now, if this suit lay in Bianca's power,
How quickly should you speed!
CAS.   Alas, poor caitiff!
OTH. Look, how he laughs already!
IAGO. I never knew woman love man so.
CAS. Alas, poor rogue! I think, i' faith, she loves me.
OTH. Now he denies it faintly, and laughs it out.   110
IAGO. Do you hear, Cassio?
OTH.   Now he importunes him
To tell o'er: go to; well said, well said.
IAGO. She gives it out that you shall marry her:
Do you intend it?
CAS. Ha, ha, ha!
OTH. Do you triumph, Roman°? do you triumph?
CAS. I marry her! what? a customer!° Prithee, bear some charity to my
wit; do not think it so unwholesome. Ha, ha, ha!
OTH. So, so, so, so: they laugh that win.
IAGO. 'Faith, the cry goes that you shall marry her.   120
CAS. Prithee, say true.
IAGO. I am a very villain else.
OTH. Have you scored me°? Well.
CAS. This is the monkey's own giving out: she is persuaded I will marry
her, out of her own love and flattery, not out of my promise.
OTH. Iago beckons me; now he begins the story.
CAS. She was here even now; she haunts me in every place. I was the
other day talking on the seabank with certain Venetians; and thither
comes the bauble,° and, by this hand, she falls me thus about my neck—

keep time use judgment and order   unbookish uninstructed   conster construe
addition title   Roman epithet arising from the association of the Romans with the
idea of triumph   customer prostitute   scored me made up my reckoning, or branded
me   bauble plaything

OTH. Crying, 'O dear Cassio!' as it were: his gesture imports it.   130
CAS. So hangs, and lolls, and weeps upon me; so shakes, and pulls me:
  ha, ha, ha!
OTH. Now he tells how she plucked him to my chamber. O, I see that
  nose of yours, but not that dog I shall throw it to.
CAS. Well, I must leave her company.
IAGO. Before me!° look, where she comes.

  [*Enter* BIANCA.]

CAS. 'Tis such another fitchew!° marry, a perfumed one.—What do you
  mean by this haunting of me?
BIAN. Let the devil and his dam haunt you! What did you mean by that
  same handkerchief you gave me even now? I was a fine fool to take it.
  I must take out the work?—A likely piece of work, that you should
  find it in your chamber, and not know who left it there! This is some
  minx's token, and I must take out the work? There; give it your hobby-
  horse°: wheresoever you had it, I'll take out no work on 't.   144
CAS. How how, my sweet Bianca! how now! how now!
OTH. By heaven, that should be my handkerchief!
BIAN. An you'll come to supper to-night, you may; an you will not, come
  when you are next prepared for.   [*Exit.*]
IAGO. After her, after her.
CAS. 'Faith, I must; she'll rail in the street else.   150
IAGO. Will you sup there?
CAS. Yes, I intend so.
IAGO. Well, I may chance to see you; for I would very fain speak with
  you.
CAS. Prithee, come; will you?
IAGO. Go to; say no more.   [*Exit* CASSIO.]
OTH [*Advancing*]. How shall I murder him, Iago?
IAGO. Did you perceive how he laughed at his vice?
OTH. O Iago!
IAGO. And did you see the handkerchief?   160
OTH. Was that mine?
IAGO. Yours, by this hand: and to see how he prizes the foolish woman
  your wife! she gave it him, and he hath given it his whore.
OTH. I would have him nine years a-killing. A fine woman! a fair woman!
  a sweet woman!
IAGO. Nay, you must forget that.
OTH. Ay, let her rot, and perish, and be damned to-night; for she shall
  not live: no, my heart is turned to stone; I strike it, and it hurts my
  hand. O, the world hath not a sweeter creature: she might lie by an
  emperor's side and command him tasks.   170
IAGO. Nay, that 's not your way.°

  Before me! On my soul!   **fitchew** polecat (because of her strong perfume; also, slang
word for a prostitute)   **hobby-horse** harlot   **your way** i.e., the way you should think
of her

OTH. Hang her! I do but say what she is: so delicate with her needle: an admirable musician: O! she will sing the savageness out of a bear: of so high and plenteous wit and invention:—

IAGO. She 's the worse for all this.

OTH. O, a thousand thousand times: and then, of so gentle a condition!

IAGO. Ay, too gentle.

OTH. Nay, that 's certain: but yet the pity of it, Iago! O Iago, the pity of it, Iago!

IAGO. If you are so fond over her iniquity, give her patent° to offend; for, if it touch not you, it comes near nobody.   181

OTH. I will chop her into messes°; cuckold me!

IAGO. O, 'tis foul in her.

OTH. With mine officer!

IAGO. That 's fouler.

OTH. Get me some poison, Iago; this night: I'll not expostulate with her, lest her body and beauty unprovide° my mind again: this night, Iago.

IAGO. Do it not with poison, strangle her in her bed, even the bed she hath contaminated.

OTH. Good, good: the justice of it pleases: very good.   190

IAGO. And for Cassio, let me be his undertaker°: you shall hear more by midnight.

OTH. Excellent good. [*A trumpet within.*] What trumpet is that same?

IAGO. I warrant something from Venice.

[*Enter* LODOVICO, DESDEMONA, *and* ATTENDANTS.]

                                        'Tis Lodovico.
This comes from the duke: and, see, your wife's with him.

LOD. God save you, worthy general!

OTH.   With all my heart, sir.

LOD. The duke and the senators of Venice greet you.

                                   [*Gives him a letter.*]

OTH. I kiss the instrument of their pleasures.

                              [*Opens the letter, and reads.*]

DES. And what 's the news, good cousin Lodovico?

IAGO. I am very glad to see you, signior;   200
    Welcome to Cyprus.

LOD. I thank you. How does Lieutenant Cassio?

IAGO. Lives, sir.

DES. Cousin, there 's fall'n between him and my lord
    An unkind breach: but you shall make all well.

OTH. Are you sure of that?

DES. My lord?

OTH. [*Reads*]. 'This fail you not to do, as you will—'

LOD. He did not call; he 's busy in the paper.
    Is there division 'twixt my lord and Cassio?   210

DES. A most unhappy one: I would do much

---

patent license   **messes** dishes of food   **unprovide** weaken, unfit   **let . . . under-taker** i.e., let me settle with him

T' atone them, for the love I bear to Cassio.
OTH. Fire and brimstone!
DES.   My lord?
OTH.   Are you wise?
DES. What, is he angry?
LOD.   May be the letter mov'd him:
   For, as I think, they do command him home,
   Deputing Cassio in his government.°
DES. Trust me, I am glad on 't.
OTH.   Indeed!
DES.   My lord?
OTH. I am glad to see you mad.
DES.   Why, sweet Othello,—
OTH. [*Striking her*]. Devil!
DES. I have not deserv'd this.   220
LOD. My lord, this would not be believ'd in Venice,
   Though I should swear I saw 't; 'tis very much:
   Make her amends; she weeps.
OTH.   O devil, devil!
  If that the earth could teem with woman's tears,
   Each drop she falls would prove a crocodile.°
   Out of my sight!
DES.   I will not stay to offend you.   [*Going.*]
LOD. Truly, an obedient lady:
   I do beseech your lordship, call her back.
OTH. Mistress!
DES.   My lord?
OTH.   What would you with her, sir?
LOD. Who, I, my lord?   230
OTH. Ay; you did wish that I would make her turn:
   Sir, she can turn, and turn, and yet go on,
   And turn again; and she can weep, sir, weep;
   And she 's obedient, as you say, obedient,
   Very obedient. Proceed you in your tears.
   Concerning this, sir,—O well-painted passion°!—
   I am commanded home. Get you away;
   I'll send for you anon. Sir, I obey the mandate,
   And will return to Venice. Hence, avaunt!
                       [*Exit* DESDEMONA.]
   Cassio shall have my place. And, sir, to-night,   240
   I do entreat that we may sup together:
   You are welcome, sir, to Cyprus.—Goats and monkeys!   [*Exit.*]
LOD. Is this the noble Moor whom our full senate
   Call all in all sufficient? Is this the nature
   Whom passion could not shake? whose solid virtue
   The shot of accident, nor dart of chance,

---

government office   **prove a crocodile** i.e., by weeping crocodile tears; it was believed the crocodile shed tears over the body of the person it was eating   **well-painted passion** well-simulated emotion

Could neither graze nor pierce?

IAGO.   He is much chang'd.

LOD. Are his wits safe? is he not light of brain?

IAGO. He 's that he is: I may not breathe my censure
    What he might be: if what he might he is not,   250
    I would to heaven he were!

LOD.   What, strike his wife!

IAGO. 'Faith, that was not so well; yet would I knew
    That stroke would prove the worst!

LOD.   Is it his use?
    Or did the letters work upon his blood,
    And new-create this fault?

IAGO.   Alas, alas!
    It is not honesty in me to speak
    What I have seen and known. You shall observe him,
    And his own courses will denote him so
    That I may save my speech: do but go after,
    And mark how he continues.   260

LOD. I am sorry that I am deceiv'd in him.   [*Exeunt.*]

      SCENE II. [*A room in the castle.*]

[*Enter* OTHELLO *and* EMILIA.]

OTH. You have seen nothing then?

EMIL. Nor ever heard, nor ever did suspect.

OTH. Yes, you have seen Cassio and she together.

EMIL. But then I saw no harm, and then I heard
    Each syllable that breath made up between them.

OTH. What, did they never whisper?

EMIL.   Never, my lord.

OTH. Nor send you out o' th' way?

EMIL. Never.

OTH. To fetch her fan, her gloves, her mask, nor nothing?

EMIL. Never, my lord.   10

OTH. That 's strange.

EMIL. I durst, my lord, to wager she is honest,
    Lay down my soul at stake: if you think other,
    Remove your thought; it doth abuse your bosom.
    If any wretch have put this in your head,
    Let heaven requite it with the serpent's curse!
    For, if she be not honest, chaste, and true,
    There 's no man happy; the purest of their wives
    Is foul as slander.

OTH.   Bid her come hither: go.

                              [*Exit* EMILIA.]

    She says enough; yet she 's a simple bawd   20
    That cannot say as much. This is a subtle whore,
    A closet lock and key° of villanous secrets:
    And yet she'll kneel and pray; I have seen her do 't.

closet lock and key complete storeroom

[*Enter* DESDEMONA *and* EMILIA.]

DES. My lord, what is your will?
OTH.   Pray, chuck, come hither.
DES. What is your pleasure?
OTH.   Let me see your eyes;
   Look in my face.
DES.   What horrible fancy 's this?
OTH. [*To* Emilia]. Some of your function,° mistress;
   Leave procreants° alone and shut the door;
   Cough, or cry 'hem', if any body come:
   Your mystery, your mystery°: nay, dispatch.   30
                                                       [*Exit* EMILIA.]

DES. Upon my knees, what doth your speech import?
   I understand a fury in your words,
   But not the words.
OTH. Why, what art thou?
DES.   Your wife, my lord; your true
   And loyal wife.
OTH.   Come, swear it, damn thyself;
   Lest, being like one of heaven, the devils themselves
   Should fear to seize thee: therefore be double damn'd:
   Swear thou are honest.
DES.   Heaven doth truly know it.
OTH. Heaven truly knows that thou are false as hell.
DES. To whom, my lord? with whom? how am I false?   40
OTH. O Desdemon! away! away! away!
DES. Alas the heavy day! Why do you weep?
   Am I the motive of these tears, my lord?
   If haply you my father do suspect
   An instrument of this your calling back,
   Lay not your blame on me: if you have lost him,
   Why, I have lost him too.
OTH.   Had it pleas'd heaven
   To try me with affliction; had they° rain'd
   All kinds of sores and shames on my bare head,
   Steep'd me in poverty to the very lips,   50
   Given to captivity me and my utmost hopes,
   I should have found in some place of my soul
   A drop of patience: but, alas, to make me
   A fixed figure for the time of scorn
   To point his slow unmoving finger at°!
   Yet could I bear that too; well, very well:
   But there, where I have garner'd up my heart,

Some . . . function i.e., set to work in your chosen profession, that of bawd   **procreants** mating couples   **mystery** trade, occupation   **they** heavenly powers   **A . . . at** Othello possibly thinks of himself as a man set in a pillory at whom the scornful world points in mockery. There seems to be a comparison with the sundial, whose gnomon, or indicator, becomes the finger of scornful time.

Where either I must live, or bear no life;
The fountain from the which my current runs,
Or else dries up; to be discarded thence!   60
Or keep it as a cistern for foul toads
To knot and gender° in! Turn thy complexion° there,
Patience, thou young and rose-lipp'd cherubin,—
Ay, there, look grim as hell!

DES. I hope my noble lord esteems me honest.

OTH. O, ay; as summer flies are in the shambles,°
That quicken° even with blowing. O thou weed,
Who are so lovely fair and smell'st so sweet
That the sense aches at thee, would thou hads't ne'er been born!

DES. Alas, what ignorant sin have I committed?   70

OTH. Was this fair paper, this most goodly book,
Made to write 'whore' upon? What committed!
Committed! O thou public commoner°!
I should make very forges of my cheeks,
That would to cinders burn up modesty,
Did I but speak thy deeds. What committed!
Heaven stops the nose at it and the moon winks,
The bawdy wind that kisses all it meets
Is hush'd within the hollow mine of earth,
And will not hear it. What committed!   80
Impudent strumpet!

DES.   By heaven, you do me wrong.

OTH. Are not you a strumpet?

DES.   No, as I am a Christian:
If to preserve this vessel° for my lord
From any other foul unlawful touch
Be not to be a strumpet, I am none.

OTH. What, not a whore?

DES.   No, as I shall be sav'd.

OTH. Is 't possible?

DES. O, heaven forgive us!

OTH.   I cry you mercy, then:
I took you for the cunning whore of Venice
That married with Othello. [*Raising his voice*] You, mistress,   90
That have the office opposite to Saint Peter,
And keep the gate of hell!

[*Enter* EMILIA.]

                    You, you, ay, you!
We have done our course; there 's money for your pains:
I pray you, turn the key and keep our counsel.   [*Exit.*]

EMIL. Alas, what does this gentleman conceive?

---

gender engender   **Turn thy complexion** grow pale   **shambles** slaughterhouse
quicken come to life   **commoner** prostitute   **vessel** body

How do you, madam? how do you, my good lady?
Des. 'Faith, half asleep.
Emil. Good madam, what 's the matter with my lord?
Des. With who?
Emil. Why, with my lord, madam.   100
Des. Who is thy lord?
Emil.   He that is yours, sweet lady.
Des. I have none: do not talk to me, Emilia;
   I cannot weep; nor answers have I none,
   But what should go by water.° Prithee, tonight
   Lay on my bed my wedding sheets: remember;
   And call thy husband hither.
Emil.   Here 's a change indeed!   [*Exit.*]
Des. 'Tis meet I should be us'd so, very meet.
   How have I been behav'd, that me might stick
   The small'st opinion on my least misuse°?

[*Enter* Iago *and* Emilia.]

Iago. What is your pleasure, madam? How is 't with you?   110
Des. I cannot tell. Those that do teach young babes
   Do it with gentle means and easy tasks:
   He might have chid me so; for, in good faith,
   I am a child to chiding.
Iago.   What is the matter, lady?
Emil. Alas, Iago, my lord hath so bewhor'd her,
   Thrown such despite° and heavy terms upon her,
   As true hearts cannot bear.
Des. Am I that name, Iago?
Iago.   What name, fair lady?
Des. Such as she said my lord did say I was.
Emil. He call'd her whore: a beggar in his drink   120
   Could not have laid such terms upon his callet.°
Iago. Why did he so?
Des. I do not know; I am sure I am none such.
Iago. Do not weep, do not weep. Alas the day!
Emil. Hath she forsook so many noble matches,
   Her father and her country and her friends,
   To be call'd whore? would it not make one weep?
Des. It is my wretched fortune.
Iago.   Beshrew him for 't!
   How comes this trick upon him?
Des.   Nay, heaven doth know.
Emil. I will be hang'd, if some eternal villain,   130
   Some busy and insinuating rogue,
   Some cogging,° cozening slave, to get some office,
   Have not devis'd this slander; I will be hang'd else.

---

go by water be expressed by tears   **misuse** evil conduct   **despite** contempt, scorn
callet lewd woman   **cogging** cheating

IAGO. Fie, there is no such man; it is impossible.

Des. If any such there be, heaven pardon him!

EMIL. A halter pardon him! and hell gnaw his bones!
  Why should he call her whore? who keeps her company?
  What place? what time? what form? what likelihood?
  The Moor's abus'd by some most villainous knave,
  Some base notorious knave, some scurvy fellow.   140
  O heaven, that such companions thou 'ldst unfold,
  And put in every honest hand a whip
  To lash the rascals naked through the world
  Even from the east to th' west!

IAGO.   Speak within door.°

EMIL. O, fie upon them! Some such squire he was
  That turn'd your wit the seamy side without,
  And made you to suspect me with the Moor.

IAGO. You are a fool; go to.

DES.   Alas, Iago.
  What shall I do to win my lord again?
  Good friend, go to him; for, by this light of heaven,   150
  I know not how I lost him. Here I kneel:
  If e'er my will did trespass 'gainst his love,
  Either in discourse of thought or actual deed,
  Or that mine eyes, mine ears, or any sense,
  Delighted them in any other form;
  Or that I do not yet, and ever did,
  And ever will—though he do shake me off
  To beggarly divorcement—love him dearly,
  Comfort forswear me! Unkindness may do much;
  And his unkindness may defeat my life,   160
  But never taint my love. I cannot say 'whore:'
  It doth abhor me now I speak the word;
  To do the act that might the addition° earn
  Not the world's mass of vanity could make me.

IAGO. I pray you, be content; 'tis but his humour:
  The business of the state does him offence,
  And he does chide with you.

DES. If 'twere no other,—

IAGO.   'Tis but so, I warrant.

                           [Trumpets within.]

  Hark, how these instruments summon to supper!
  The messengers of Venice stay the meat°;   170
  Go in, and weep not; all things shall be well.

              [Exeunt DESDEMONA *and* EMILIA.]

[Enter RODERIGO.]

  How now, Roderigo!

ROD. I do not find that thou dealest justly with me.

Speak . . . door i.e., not so loud   **addition** title   **stay the meat** are waiting for supper

Iago. What in the contrary?

Rod. Everyday thou daffest me° with some device, Iago; and rather, as it
seems to me now, keepest from me all conveniency° than suppliest me
with the least advantage of hope. I will indeed no longer endure it,
nor am I yet persuaded to put up° in peace what already I have foolishly
suffered.   180

Iago. Will you hear me, Roderigo?

Rod. 'Faith, I have heard too much, for your words and performances
are no kin together.

Iago. You charge me most unjustly.

Rod. With nought but truth. I have wasted myself out of my means. The
jewels you have had from me to deliver to Desdemona would half have
corrupted a votarist°: you have told me she hath received them and
returned me expectations and comforts of sudden respect and acquaintance, but I find none.

Iago. Well; go to; very well.   190

Rod. Very well! go to! I cannot go to, man; nor 'tis not very well: nay, I
think it is scurvy, and begin to find myself fopped° in it.

Iago. Very well.

Rod. I tell you 'tis not very well. I will make myself known to Desdemona:
if she will return me my jewels, I will give over my suit and repent
my unlawful solicitation; if not, assure yourself I will seek satisfaction
of you.

Iago. You have said now.°

Rod. Ay, and said nothing but what I protest intendment of doing.

Iago. Why, now I see there 's mettle in thee, and even from this instant
do build on thee a better opinion than ever before. Give my thy hand,
Roderigo: thou hast taken against me a most just exception; but yet, I
protest, I have dealt most directly in thy affair.   203

Rod. It hath not appeared.

Iago. I grant indeed it hath not appeared, and your suspicion is not without
wit and judgement. But, Roderigo, if thou hast that in thee indeed,
which I have greater reason to believe now than ever, I mean purpose,
courage and valour, this night show it: if thou the next night following
enjoy not Desdemona, take me from this world with treachery and devise
engines for° my life.   210

Rod. Well, what is it? is it within reason and compass?

Iago. Sir, there is especial commission come from Venice to depute Cassio
in Othello's place.

Rod. Is that true? why, then Othello and Desdemona return again to Venice.

Iago. O, no; he goes into Mauritania° and takes away with him the fair
Desdemona, unless his abode be lingered here by some accident: wherein
none can be so determinate° as the removing of Cassio.

Rod. How do you mean, removing of him?

---

daffest me puts me off with an excuse   **conveniency** advantage, opportunity   **put
up** submit to   **votarist** nun   **fopped** fooled   **You . . . now** well said, quite right
intendment purpose, intention   **engines for** plots against   **Mauritania** Roman name
of northwest Africa, supposed land of the Moors   **determinate** decisive

IAGO. Why, by making him uncapable of Othello's place; knocking out
his brains. 221

ROD. And that you would have me to do?

IAGO. Ay, if you dare do yourself a profit and a right. He sups to-night
with a harlotry,° and thither will I go to him: he knows not yet of
his honourable fortune. If you will watch his going thence, which I
will fashion to fall out between twelve and one, you may take him at
your pleasure: I will be near to second your attempt, and he shall fall
between us. Come, stand not amazed at it, but go along with me; I
will show you such a necessity in his death that you shall think yourself
bound to put it on him. It is now high° supper-time, and the night
grows to waste: about it. 231

ROD. I will hear further reason for this.

IAGO. And you shall be satisfied. [*Exeunt.*]

    SCENE III. [*Another room in the castle.*]

[*Enter* OTHELLO, LODOVICO, DESDEMONA, EMILIA, *and* ATTENDANTS.]

LOD. I do beseech you, sir, trouble yourself no further.

OTH. O, pardon me; 'twill do me good to walk.

LOD. Madam, good night; I humbly thank your ladyship.

DES. Your honour is most welcome.

OTH.   Will you walk, sir?

O,—Desdemona,—

DES. My lord?

OTH. Get you to bed on th' instant; I will be returned forthwith: dismiss
your attendant there: look 't be done.

DES. I will, my lord.

            [*Exit* OTHELLO, *with* LODOVICO *and* ATTENDANTS.]

EMIL. How goes it now? he looks gentler than he did. 10

DES. He says he will return incontinent°:
   He hath commanded me to go to bed,
   And bade me to dismiss you.

EMIL.   Dismiss me!

DES. It was his bidding; therefore, good Emilia,
   Give me my nightly wearing, and adieu:
   We must not now displease him.

EMIL. I would you had never seen him!

DES. So would not I: my love doth so approve him,
   That even his stubbornness,° his checks,° his frowns,—
   Prithee, unpin me,—have grace and favour in them. 20

EMIL. I have laid those sheets you bade me on the bed.

DES. All 's one. Good faith, how foolish are our minds!
   If I do die before thee, prithee, shroud me
   In one of those same sheets.

EMIL.   Come, come, you talk.

DES. My mother had a maid call'd Barbary:

---

harlotry courtesan   **high** quite   **incontinent** immediately   **stubbornness** harsh-
ness   **checks** rebukes

She was in love, and he she lov'd prov'd mad
And did forsake her: she had a song of 'willow;'
An old thing 'twas, but it express'd her fortune,
And she died singing it: that song to-night
Will not go from my mind; I have much to do,   30
But to° go hang my head all at one side,
And sing it like poor Barbary. Prithee, dispatch.

EMIL. Shall I go fetch your night-gown°?

DES.   No, unpin me here.
This Lodovico is a proper man.

EMIN. A very handsome man.

DES. He speaks well.

EMIL. I know a lady in Venice would have walked barefoot to Palestine
for a touch of his nether lip.

DES. [*Singing*]. The poor soul sat sighing by a sycamore tree,
        Sing all a green willow;   40
    Her hand on her bosom, her head on her knee,
        Sing willow, willow, willow:
    The fresh streams ran by her, and murmur'd her moans;
        Sing willow, willow, willow;
    Her salt tears fell from her, and soft'ned the stones;—
Lay by these:—
[*Singing*] Sing willow, willow, willow;
Prithee, hie thee; he'll come anon:—
[*Singing*] Sing all a green willow must be my garland.
        Let nobody blame him; his scorn I approve,—   50
Nay, that 's not next.—Hark! who is 't that knocks?

EMIL. It 's the wind.

DES. [*Singing*]. I call'd my love false love; but what said he then?
        Sing willow, willow, willow:
    If I court moe women, you'll couch with moe men.—
So, get thee gone; good night. Mine eyes do itch;
Doth that bode weeping?

EMIL.   'Tis neither here nor there.

DES. I have heard it said so. O, these men, these men!
Dost thou in conscience think,—tell me, Emilia,—
That there be women do abuse their husbands   60
In such gross kind?

EMIL.   There be some such, no question.

DES. Wouldst thou do such a deed for all the world?

EMIL. Why, would not you?

DES.   No, by this heavenly light!

EMIL. Nor I neither by this heavenly light; I might do 't as well i' the
dark.

DES. Wouldst thou do such a deed for all the world?

EMIL. The world 's a huge thing: it is a great price
For a small vice.

DES. In troth, I think thou wouldst not.

But to not to   **night-gown** dressing gown

EMIL. In troth, I think I should; and undo 't when I had done. Marry, I
would not do such a thing for a joint-ring,° nor for measures of lawn,
nor for gowns, petticoats, nor caps, nor any petty exhibition;° but, for
all the whole world,—why, who would not make her husband a cuckold
to make him a monarch? I should venture purgatory for 't.   74

DES. Beshrew me, if I would do such a wrong
For the whole world.

EMIL. Why, the wrong is but a wrong i' the world; and having the world
for your labour, 'tis a wrong in your own world, and you might quickly
make it right.

DES. I do not think there is any such woman.   80

EMIL. Yes, a dozen; and as many to the vantage° as would store the world
they played for.
But I do think it is their husband's faults
If wives do fall: say that they slack their duties,
And pour our treasures into foreign laps,°
Or else break out in peevish jealousies,
Throwing restraint upon us; or say they strike us,
Or scant our former having in despite;°
Why, we have galls,° and though we have some grace,°
Yet have we some revenge. Let husbands know   90
Their wives have sense like them: they see and smell
And have their palates both for sweet and sour,
As husbands have. What is it that they do
When they change us for others? Is it sport?
I think it is: and doth affection breed it?
I think it doth: is 't frailty that thus errs?
It is so too: and have not we affections,
Desires for sport, and frailty, as men have?
Then let them use us well: else let them know,
The ills we do, their ills instruct us so.   100

DES. Good night, good night: heaven me such uses send,
Not to pick bad from bad, but by bad mend!   [*Exeunt.*]

ACT V.

SCENE I. [*Cyprus. A street.*]

[*Enter* IAGO *and* RODERIGO.]

IAGO. Here stand behind this bulk;° straight will he come:
Wear thy good rapier bare, and put it home:
Quick, quick; fear nothing; I'll be at thy elbow:
It makes us, or it mars us; think on that,
And fix most firm thy resolution.

---

joint-ring a ring made in separable halves as a lover's token   **exhibition** gift, present
to the vantage in addition   **pour . . . laps** i.e., are unfaithful   **scant . . . despite** reduce
our allowance to spite us   **have galls** are capable of resenting injury and insult
grace i.e., to forgive   **bulk** framework projecting from the front of a shop

Rod. Be near at hand; I may miscarry in 't.
Iago. Here, at thy hand: be bold, and take thy stand.

[*Retires.*]

Rod. I have no great devotion to the deed;
  And yet he hath given me satisfying reasons:
  'Tis but a man gone. Forth, my sword: he dies.   10
Iago. I have rubb'd this young quat° almost to the sense,°
  And he grows angry. Now, whether he kill Cassio,
  Or Cassio him, or each do kill the other,
  Every way makes my gain: live Roderigo,
  He calls me to a restitution large
  Of gold and jewels that I bobb'd° from him,
  As gifts to Desdemona;
  It must not be: if Cassio do remain,
  He hath a daily beauty in his life
  That makes me ugly; and, besides, the Moor   20
  May unfold me to him; there stand I in much peril:
  No, he must die. But so: I hear him coming.

[*Enter* Cassio.]

Rod. I know his gait, 'tis he.—Villain, thou diest!

[*Makes a pass at* Cassio.]

Cas. That thrust had been mine enemy indeed,
  But that my coat° is better than thou know'st:
  I will make proof of thine.   [*Draws, and wounds* Roderigo.]
Rod.   O, I am slain!

[Iago *from behind wounds* Cassio *in the leg, and exit.*]

Cas. I am maim'd for ever. Help, ho! murder! murder!

[*Falls.*]

[*Enter* Othello.]

Oth. The voice of Cassio: Iago keeps his word.
Rod. O, villain that I am!
Oth.   It is even so.
Cas. O, help, ho! light! a surgeon!   30
Oth. 'Tis he:—O brave Iago, honest and just,
  That hast such noble sense of thy friend's wrong!
  Thou teachest me. Minion, your dear lies dead,
  And your unblest fate hies: strumpet, I come.
  Forth of my heart those charms, thine eyes, are blotted;
  Thy bed, lust-stain'd, shall with lust's blood be spotted.

[*Exit* Othello.]

[*Enter* Lodovico *and* Gratiano.]

---

quat pimple, pustule; used contemptuously   **to the sense** to the quick   **bobb'd** filched
cunningly   **coat** coat of mail

CAS. What, ho! no watch? no passage°? murder! murder!
GRA. 'Tis some mischance; the cry is very direful.
CAS. O, help!
LOD. Hark!   40
ROD. O wretched villain!
LOD. Two or three groan: it is a heavy° night;
    These may be counterfeits: let 's think 't unsafe
    To come in to the cry without more help.
ROD. Nobody come? then shall I bleed to death.
LOD. Hark!

    [*Enter* IAGO *with a light.*]

GRA. Here 's one comes in his shirt, with light and weapons.
IAGO. Who 's there? whose noise is this that cries on° murder?
LOD. We do not know.
IAGO.   Did not you hear a cry?
CAS. Here, here! for heaven's sake, help me!
IAGO.   What 's the matter?   50
GRA. This is Othello's ancient, as I take it.
LOD. The same indeed; a very valiant fellow.
IAGO. What are you here that cry so grievously?
CAS. Iago? O, I am spoil'd, undone by villains!
    Give me some help.
IAGO. O me, lieutenant! what villains have done this?
CAS. I think that one of them is hereabout,
    And cannot make away.
IAGO.   O treacherous villains!
    What are you there? come in, and give some help.
                            [*To* LODOVICO *and* GRATIANO.]
ROD. O, help me here!   60
CAS. That 's one of them.
IAGO.   O murd'rous slave! O villain!
                              [*Stabs* RODERIGO.]
ROD. O damn'd Iago! O inhuman dog!
IAGO. Kill men i' th' dark!—Where be these bloody thieves?—
    How silent in this town!—Ho! murder! murder!—
    What° may you be? are you of good or evil?
LOD. As you shall prove us, praise us.
IAGO. Signior Lodovico?
LOD. He, sir.
IAGO. I cry you mercy. Here 's Cassio hurt by villains.
GRA. Cassio!   70
IAGO. How is 't, brother!
CAS. My leg is cut in two.
IAGO.   Marry, heaven forbid!
    Light, gentlemen: I'll bind it with my shirt.

---

passage people passing   **heavy** thick, cloudy   **cries on** cries out   **What** who

[Enter BIANCA.]

BIAN. What is the matter, ho? who is 't that cried?
IAGO. Who is 't that cried?
BIAN. O my dear Cassio! my sweet Cassio!
  O Cassio, Cassio, Cassio!
IAGO. O notable strumpet! Cassio, may you suspect
  Who they should be that have thus mangled you?
CAS. No.   80
GRA. I am sorry to find you thus: I have been to seek you.
IAGO. Lend me a garter. So. O, for a chair,°
  To bear him easily hence!
BIAN. Alas, he faints! O Cassio, Cassio, Cassio!
IAGO. Gentlemen all, I do suspect this trash°
  To be a party in this injury.
  Patience awhile, good Cassio. Come, come;
  Lend me a light. Know we this face or no?
  Alas, my friend and my dear countryman
  Roderigo! no:—yes, sure:—O heaven! Roderigo.   90
GRA. What, of Venice?
IAGO. Even he, sir: did you know him?
GRA.   Know him! ay.
IAGO. Signior Gratiano? I cry your gentle pardon;
  These bloody accidents must excuse my manners,
  That so neglected you.
GRA.   I am so glad to see you.
IAGO. How do you, Cassio? O, a chair, a chair!
GRA. Roderigo!
IAGO. He, he, 'tis he. *[A chair brought in.]* O, that 's well said; the chair.
  Some good man bear him carefully from hence;
  I'll fetch the general's surgeon. *[To* BIANCA] For you, mistress,   100
  Save you your labour. He that lies slain here, Cassio,
  Was my dear friend: what malice was between you?
CAS. None in the world; nor do I know the man.
IAGO. *[To* BIAN.] What, look you pale? O, bear him out o' th' air.
                           *[*CASSIO *and* RODERIGO *are borne off.]*
  Stay you, good gentlemen. Look you pale, mistress?
  Do you perceive the gastness° of her eye?
  Nay, if you stare, we shall hear more anon.
  Behold her well; I pray you, look upon her:
  Do you see, gentlemen? nay, guiltiness will speak,
  Though tongues were out of use.   110

[Enter EMILIA.]

EMIL. 'Las, what 's the matter? what 's the matter, husband?
IAGO. Cassio hath here been set on in the dark

---

chair sedan chair   **trash** worthless thing, i.e., Bianca   **gastness** terror, ghastliness

By Roderigo and fellows that are scap'd:
He 's almost slain, and Roderigo dead.
EMIL. Alas, good gentleman! alas, good Cassio!
IAGO. This is the fruit of whoring. Prithee, Emilia,
Go know of Cassio where he supp'd to-night.
[*To* BIANCA] What, do you shake at that?
BIAN. He supp'd at my house; but I therefore shake not.
IAGO. O, did he so? I charge you, go with me. 120
EMIL. Fie, fie upon thee, strumpet!
BIAN. I am no strumpet; but of life as honest
As you that thus abuse me.
EMIL.   As I! foh! fie upon thee!
IAGO. Kind gentlemen, let 's go see poor Cassio dress'd.
Come, mistress, you must tell 's another tale.
Emilia, run you to the citadel,
And tell my lord and lady what hath happ'd.
Will you go on afore? [*Aside*] This is the night
That either makes me or fordoes° me quite.   [*Exeunt.*]

SCENE II. [*A bedchamber in the castle.*]

[*Enter* OTHELLO *with a light*; DESDEMONA *in her bed.*]

OTH. It is the cause, it is the cause,° my soul,—
Let me not name it to you, you chaste stars!—
It is the cause. Yet I'll not shed her blood;
Nor scar that whiter skin of hers than snow,
And smooth as monumental alabaster.
Yet she must die, else she'll betray more men.
Put out the light, and then put out the light:
If I quench thee, thou flaming minister,
I can again thy former light restore,
Should I repent me: but once put out thy light,   10
Thou cunning'st pattern of excelling nature,
I know not where is that Promethean heat°
That can thy light relume.° When I have pluck'd the rose,
I cannot give it vital growth again,
It needs must wither: I'll smell thee on the tree.
                                                   [*Kissing her.*]
O balmy breath, that dost almost persuade
Justice to break her sword! One more, one more.
Be thus when thou art dead, and I will kill thee,
And love thee after. One more, and that 's the last:
So sweet was ne'er so fatal. I must weep,   20
But they are cruel tears: this sorrow 's heavenly°;

---

fordoes undoes, ruins   **It is the cause** i.e., the cause of justice on which Othello must
act, Desdemona's deed, which is too unmentionable to be named to the chaste stars   **Prome-**
thean heat divine fire; allusion to the theft of fire from heaven by Prometheus   **relume**
rekindle   **this . . . heavenly** this tenderness, with which I lament the punishment which
justice compels me to inflict, is a holy passion

It strikes where it doth love. She wakes.

DES. Who 's there? Othello?

OTH.   Ay, Desdemona.

DES. Will you come to bed, my lord?

OTH. Have you pray'd to-night, Desdemon?

DES.   Ay, my lord.

OTH. If you bethink yourself of any crime
    Unreconcil'd as yet to heaven and grace,
    Solicit for it straight.

DES. Alack, my lord, what may you mean by that?

OTH. Well, do it, and be brief; I will walk by: 30
    I would not kill thy unprepared spirit;
    No; heaven forfend! I would not kill thy soul.

DES. Talk you of killing?

OTH.   Ay, I do.

DES.   Then heaven
    Have mercy on me!

OTH.   Amen, with all my heart!

DES. If you say so, I hope you will not kill me.

OTH. Hum!

DES. And yet I fear you; for you 're fatal then
    When your eyes roll so: why I should fear I know not,
    Since guiltiness I know not; but yet I feel I fear.

OTH. Think on thy sins.

DES.   They are loves I bear to you.   40

OTH. Ay, and for that thou diest.

DES. That death 's unnatural that kills for loving.
    Alas, why gnaw you so your nether lip?
    Some bloody passion shakes your very frame:
    These are portents; but yet I hope, I hope,
    They do not point on me.

OTH.   Peace, and be still!

DES. I will so. What 's the matter?

OTH. That handkerchief which I so lov'd and gave thee
    Thou gav'st to Cassio.

DES.   No, by my life and soul!
    Send for the man, and ask him.

OTH.   Sweet soul, take heed,   50
    Take heed of perjury; thou are on thy deathbed.

DES. Ay, but not yet to die.

OTH.   Yes, presently:
    Therefore confess thee freely of thy sin;
    For to deny each article with oath
    Cannot remove nor choke the strong conception°
    That I do groan withal. Thou art to die.

DES. Then Lord have mercy on me!

OTH.   I say, amen.

DES. And have you mercy too! I never did

conception plan, intention

Offend you in my life; never lov'd Cassio
But with such general warranty of heaven   60
As I might love; I never gave him token.
OTH. By heaven, I saw my handkerchief in 's hand.
O perjur'd woman! thou dost stone° my heart,
And makest me call what I intend to do
A murder, which I thought a sacrifice:
I saw the handkerchief.
DES.   He found it then;
I never gave it him: send for him hither;
Let him confess a truth.
OTH.   He hath confess'd.
DES. What, my lord?
OTH. That he hath us'd thee.
DES.   How? unlawfully?
OTH.   Ay.   70
DES. He will not say so.
OTH.   No, his mouth is stopp'd;
Honest Iago hath ta'en order° for 't.
DES. O! my fear interprets: what, is he dead?
OTH. Had all his hairs been lives, my great revenge
Had stomach for them all.
DES. Alas! he is betray'd and I undone.
OTH. Out, strumpet! weep'st thou for him to my face?
DES. O, banish me, my lord, but kill me not!
OTH. Down, strumpet!
DES. Kill me to-morrow: let me live to-night!   80
OTH. Nay, if you strive,—
DES. But half an hour!
OTH.   Being done, there is no pause.°
DES. But while I say one prayer!
OTH.   It is too late.   [*Smothers her.*]
EMIL. [*At the door*]. My lord, my lord! what, ho! my lord, my lord!
OTH. What noise is this? Not dead? not yet quite dead?
I that am cruel am yet merciful;
I would not have thee linger in thy pain:
So, so.
EMIL. [*Within*]. What, ho! my lord, my lord!
OTH.   Who 's there?
EMIL. [*Within*]. O, good my lord, I would speak a word with you!   90
OTH. Yes: 'tis Emilia. By and by. She 's dead.
'Tis like she comes to speak of Cassio's death.—
The noise was here. Ha! no more moving?
Still as the grave. Shall she come in? were 't good?—
I think she stirs again:—no. What 's best to do?

___

stone turn to stone, harden; Othello means that he will be tempted to kill her in sheer
anger because of her perjury   **ta'en order** taken measures   **Being . . . pause** i.e., when
the execution of the deed has once begun, there is no stopping

If she come in, she'll sure speak to my wife:
My wife! my wife! what wife? I have no wife.
O, insupportable! O heavy hour!
Methinks it should be now a huge eclipse
Of sun and moon, and that th' affrighted globe   100
Should yawn° at alteration.°
EMIL.   [*Within*] I do beseech you
    That I may speak with you, O, good my lord!
OTH. I had forgot thee: O, come in, Emilia:
    Soft; by and by. Let me the curtains draw.
    Where art thou?

                              [*Closes bed-curtains and opens door.*]

[*Enter* EMILIA.]

                            What 's the matter with thee now?
EMIL. O, my good lord, yonder 's foul murders done!
OTH. What, now?
EMIL. But now, my lord.
OTH. It is the very error° of the moon;
    She comes more nearer earth than she was wont,   110
    And makes men mad.
EMIL. Cassio, my lord, hath kill'd a young Venetian
    Call'd Roderigo.
OTH.   Roderigo kill'd!
    And Cassio kill'd!
EMIL.   No, Cassio is not kill'd.
OTH. Not Cassio kill'd! then murder 's out of tune,
    And sweet revenge grows harsh.
DES. O, falsely, falsely murder'd!
EMIL.   Alas, what cry is that?
OTH. That! what!
EMIL. Out, and alas! that was my lady's voice.
    Help, help, ho! help. O lady, speak again!   120
    Sweet Desdemona! O sweet mistress, speak!
DES. A guiltless death I die.
EMIL. O, who hath done this deed?
DES. Nobody; I myself. Farewell:
    Commend me to my kind lord: O, farewell!   [*Dies.*]
OTH. Why, how should she be murd'red?
EMIL.   Alas, who knows?
OTH. You heard her say herself, it was not I.
EMIL. She said so: I must needs report the truth.
OTH. She 's, like a liar, gone to burning hell:
    'Twas I that kill'd her.
EMIL.   O, the more angel she,   130
    And you the blacker devil!

yawn gape in amazement   **at alteration** at the change   **error** irregularity

OTH. She turn'd to folly,° and she was a whore.
EMIL. Thou dost belie her, and thou art a devil.
OTH. She was false as water.
EMIL.   Thou art rash as fire, to say
   That she was false: O, she was heavenly true!
OTH. Cassio did top her; ask thy husband else.
   O, I were damned beneath all depth in hell,
   But that I did proceed upon just grounds
   To this extremity. Thy husband knew it all.
EMIL. My husband!   140
OTH. Thy husband.
EMIL. That she was false to wedlock?
OTH. Ay, with Cassio. Nay, had she been true,
   If heaven would make me such another world
   Of one entire and perfect chrysolite,°
   I 'ld not have sold her for it.
EMIL. My husband!
OTH.   Ay, 'twas he that told me first:
   An honest man he is, and hates the slime
   That sticks on filthy deeds.
EMIL.   My husband!
OTH. What needs this iterance,° woman? I say thy husband.   150
EMIL. O mistress, villainy hath made mocks with° love!
   My husband say that she was false!
OTH.   He, woman;
   I say thy husband: dost understand the word?
   My friend, thy husband, honest, honest Iago.
EMIL. If he say so, may his pernicious soul
   Rot half a grain a day! he lies to th' heart:
   She was too fond of her most filthy bargain.
OTH. Ha!
EMIL. Do thy worst:
   This deed of thine is no more worthy heaven   160
   Than thou wast worthy her.
OTH.   Peace, you were best.
EMIL. Thou hast not half that power to do me harm
   As I have to be hurt.° O gull! O dolt!
   As ignorant as dirt! thou hast done a deed—
   I care not for thy sword; I'll make thee known,
   Though I lost twenty lives.—Help! help, ho! help!
   The Moor hath kill'd my mistress! Murder! murder!

[*Enter* MONTANO, GRATIANO, *and* IAGO *with others*.]

MON. What is the matter! How now, general!
EMIL. O, are you come, Iago? you have done well,

---

   folly unchastity   **chrysolite** the golden stone; a name given to various precious stones
of green color   **iterance** iteration, repetition   **made mocks with** derided, made sport
of   **to be hurt** i.e., to endure hurting

That men must lay their murders on your neck.   170
Gra. What is the matter?
Emil. Disprove this villain, if thou be'st a man:
    He says thou told'st him that his wife was false:
    I know thou didst not, thou 'rt not such a villain:
    Speak, for my heart is full.
Iago. I told him what I thought, and told no more
    Than what he found himself was apt° and true.
Emil. But did you ever tell him she was false?
Iago. I did.
Emil. You told a lie; an odious, damned lie;   180
    Upon my soul, a lie, a wicked lie.
    She false with Cassio!—did you say with Cassio?
Iago. With Cassio, mistress. Go to, charm° your tongue.
Emil. I will not charm my tongue; I am bound to speak:
    My mistress here lies murdered in her bed,—
All. O heavens forfend!
Emil. And your reports have set the murder on.
Oth. Nay, stare not, masters: it is true, indeed.
Gra. 'Tis a strange truth.
Mon. O monstrous act!
Emil.   Villainy, villainy, villainy!   190
    I think upon 't, I think: I smell 't: O villiany—
    I thought so then°: I'll kill myself for grief:—
    O villainy, villainy!
Iago. What, are you mad? I charge you, get you home.
Emil. Good gentlemen, let me have leave to speak:
    'Tis proper I obey him, but not now.
    Perchance, Iago, I will ne'er go home.
Oth. O! O! O!   [*He falls on the bed.*]
Emil.   Nay, lay thee down and roar;
    For thou hast kill'd the sweetest innocent
    That e'er did lift up eye.
Oth.   [*Rising*] O, she was foul!   200
    I scarce did know you, uncle: there lies your niece,
    Whose breath, indeed, these hands have newly stopp'd:
    I know this act shows horrible and grim.
Gra. Poor Desdemon! I am glad thy father 's dead:
    Thy match was mortal to him, and pure grief
    Shore° his old thread in twain: did he live now,
    This sight would make him do a desperate turn,
    Yea, curse his better angel from his side,
    And fall to reprobation.°
Oth. 'Tis pitiful; but yet Iago knows   210

---

    apt natural, likely   **charm** keep silent   **then** i.e., at some earlier time, probably IV,
ii, when she suspected the machinations of *some eternal villain:* she did not, however, know
that villain to be Iago until this moment   **Shore** cut   **reprobation** damnation, rejection
by God

That she with Cassio hath the act of shame   210
A thousand times committed; Cassio confess'd it:
And she did gratify his amorous works
With that recognizance° and pledge of love
Which I first gave her; I saw it in his hand:
It was a handkerchief, an antique token
My father gave my mother.
EMIL. O heaven! O heavenly pow'rs!
IAGO. Come, hold your peace.
EMIL.   'Twill out, 'twill out: I peace!
No, I will speak as liberal as the north°:   220
Let heaven and men and devils, let them all,
All, all, cry shame against me, yet I'll speak.
IAGO. Be wise, and get you home.
EMIL.   I will not. [IAGO *offers to stab* EMILIA.]
GRA.   Fie!
Your sword upon a woman?
EMIL. O thou dull Moor! that handkerchief thou speak'st of
I found by fortune° and did give my husband;
For often, with a solemn earnestness,
More than indeed belong'd to such a trifle,
He begg'd of me to steal it.
IAGO.   Villainous whore!
EMIL. She give it Cassio! no, alas! I found it,   230
And I did give 't my husband.
IAGO.   Filth, thou liest!
EMIL. By heaven, I do not, I do not, gentlemen.
O murd'rous coxcomb°! what should such a fool
Do with so good a wife!
OTH.   Are there no stones in heaven°
But what serves for the thunder?—Precious villain!
          [*He runs at* IAGO: IAGO, *from behind, stabs* EMILIA, *and exits.*]
GRA. The woman falls; sure, he hath kill'd his wife.
EMIL. Ay, ay: O, lay me by my mistress' side.
GRA. He 's gone, but his wife 's kill'd.
MON. 'Tis a notorious villain. Take you this weapon,
Which I have here recover'd from the Moor: 240
Come, guard the door without; let him not pass,
But kill him rather. I'll after that same villain,
For 'tis a damned slave.
              [*Exit with all but* OTHELLO *and* EMILIA.]
OTH.   I am not valiant neither,
But every puny whipster° gets my sword:
But why should honour outlive honesty°?

---

recognizance token   **liberal as the north** freely as the north wind   **fortune** chance
coxcomb fool; addressed to Othello   **stones in heaven** thunderbolts. It was supposed that
real stones fell with the thunder and caused the damage.   **whipster** contemptible
fellow   **honour outlive honesty** Othello realizes that he has done a shameful deed;
he asks why his reputation for valor should endure.

Let it go all.
EMIL.   What did thy song bode, lady?
  Hark, canst thou hear me? I will play the swan,
  And die in music. [*Singing*] Willow, willow, willow.—
  Moor, she was chaste; she lov'd thee, cruel Moor;
  So come my soul to bliss, as I speak true;   250
  So speaking as I think, I die, I die.   [*Dies.*]
OTH. I have another weapon in this chamber;
  It is a sword of Spain, the ice-brook's temper°:—
  O, here it is. Uncle, I must come forth.
GRA. [*Within*]. If thou attempt it, it will cost thee dear:
  Thou hast no weapon, and perforce must suffer.
OTH. Look in upon me then and speak with me,
  Or, naked° as I am, I will assault thee.

                    [*Enter* GRATIANO.]

GRA. What is the matter?
OTH.   Behold, I have a weapon;
  A better never did itself sustain   260
  Upon a soldier's thigh: I have seen the day,
  That, with this little arm and this good sword,
  I have made my way through more impediments
  Than twenty times your stop°: but, O vain boast!
  Who can control his fate? 'tis not so now.
  Be not afraid, though you do see me weapon'd;
  Here is my journey's end, here is my butt,°
  And very sea-mark° of my utmost sail.
  Do you go back dismay'd? 'tis a lost fear;
  Man° but a rush° against Othello's breast,   270
  And he retires. Where should Othello go?
  Now, how dost thou look now? O ill-starr'd wench!
  Pale as thy smock! when we shall meet at compt,°
  This look of thine will hurl my soul from heaven,
  And fiends will snatch at it. Cold, cold, my girl!
  Even like thy chastity. O cursed, cursed slave!
  Whip me, ye devils,
  From the possession of this heavenly sight!
  Blow me about in winds! roast me in sulphur!
  Wash me in steep-down gulfs of liquid fire!   280
  O Desdemon! Dead Desdemon! dead!
  Oh! Oh!

[*Enter* LODOVICO, CASSIO *carried in a chair*, MONTANO, *and* IAGO,
    prisoner, with OFFICERS.]

---

ice-brook's temper usually defined as "tempered in ice-cold water"   **naked** unarmed   **stop** power   **butt** mark for archery, goal, limit   **sea-mark** beacon (marking
his destination or limit)   **Man** provide, as in manning a gun   **rush** reed   **compt** account, judgment day

LOD. Where is this rash and most unfortunate man?
OTH. That 's he that was Othello: here I am.
LOD. Where is that viper? bring the villain forth.
OTH. I look down towards his feet;° but that 's a fable.
   If that thou be'st a devil, I cannot kill thee.

                              [*Wounds* IAGO.]

LOD. Wrench his sword from him.
IAGO.   I bleed, sir; but not kill'd.
OTH. I am not sorry neither: I 'ld have thee live;
   For, in my sense, 'tis happiness to die.   290
LOD. O thou Othello, that wert once so good,
   Fall'n in the practice of a damned slave,
   What shall be said to thee?
OTH.   Why, any thing:
   An honourable murderer, if you will;
   For nought I did in hate, but all in honour.
LOD. This wretch hath part confess'd his villainy:
   Did you and he consent in Cassio's death?
OTH. Ay.
CAS. Dear general, I never gave you cause.
OTH. I do believe it, and I ask you pardon.   300
   Will you, I pray, demand that demi-devil
   Why he hath thus ensnar'd my soul and body?
IAGO. Demand me nothing: what you know, you know:
   From this time forth I never will speak word.
LOD. What, not to pray?
GRA.   Torments will ope your lips.
OTH. Well, thou dost best.
LOD. Sir, you shall understand what hath befall'n,
   Which, as I think, you know not. Here is a letter
   Found in the pocket of the slain Roderigo;
   And here another: the one of them imports   310
   The death of Cassio to be undertook
   By Roderigo.
OTH. O villain!
CAS.   Most heathenish and most gross!
LOD. Now here 's another discontented° paper,
   Found in his pocket too; and this, it seems,
   Roderigo meant t' have sent this damned villain;
   But that belike Iago in the interim
   Came in and satisfied him.
OTH.   O thou pernicious caitiff°!—
   How came you, Cassio, by that handkerchief
   That was my wife's?
CAS.   I found it in my chamber: 320
   And he himself confess'd but even now

---

towards his feet i.e., to see if they were cloven like a devil's   **discontented** expressing
dissatisfaction   **caitiff** wretch

That there he dropp'd it for a special purpose
Which wrought to his desire.
OTH.   O fool! O fool! fool!
CAS. There is besides in Roderigo's letter,
How he upbraids Iago, that he made him
Brave° me upon the watch; whereon it came
That I was cast°: and even but now he spake,
After long seeming dead, Iago hurt him,
Iago set him on.
LOD. You must forsake this room, and go with us: 330
Your power and your command is taken off,°
And Cassio rules in Cyprus. For this slave,
If there be any cunning cruelty
That can torment him much and hold him long,
It shall be his. You shall close prisoner rest,
Till that the nature of your fault be known
To the Venetian state. Come, bring him away.
OTH. Soft you; a word or two before you go.
I have done the state some service, and they know 't.
No more of that. I pray you, in your letters,   340
When you shall these unlucky deeds relate,
Speak of me as I am; nothing extenuate,°
Nor set down aught in malice: then must you speak
Of one that lov'd not wisely but too well;
Of one not easily jealous, but being wrought,
Perplex'd° in the extreme; of one whose hand,
Like the base Judean,° threw a pearl away
Richer than all his tribe; of one whose subdu'd eyes,
Albeit unused to the melting mood,
Drop tears as fast as the Arabian trees   350
Their medicinable gum. Set you down this;
And say besides, that in Aleppo° once,
Where a malignant and a turban'd Turk
Beat a Venetian and traduc'd the state,
I took by th' throat the circumcised dog,
And smote him, thus.   [*Stabs himself.*]
LOD. O bloody period°!
GRA.   All that is spoke is marr'd.
OTH. I kiss'd thee ere I kill'd thee: no way but this;
Killing myself, to die upon a kiss.

                                   [*Falls on the bed, and dies.*]
CAS. This did I fear, but thought he had no weapon;   360
For he was great of heart.

Brave defy   **cast** dismissed   **taken off** taken away   **extenuate** diminish, depreciate;
the idea is contrasted with the thought of *malice* in the following line   **Perplex'd** confounded, distracted   **Judean** infidel or disbeliever   **Aleppo** a Turkish city where the
Venetians had special trading privileges. It is stated that it was immediate death for a Christian
to strike a Turk in Aleppo; Othello risked his life for the honor of Venice.   **period** termination, conclusion

LOD.   [*To* IAGO] O Spartan dog,°
 More fell than anguish, hunger, or the sea!
 Look on the tragic loading of this bed;
 This is thy work: the object poisons sight;
 Let it be hid. Gratiano, keep the house,
 And seize upon the fortunes of the Moor,
 For they succeed on you. To you, lord governor,
 Remains the censure of this hellish villain;
 The time, the place, the torture: O, enforce it!
 Myself will straight abroad; and to the state   370
 This heavy act with heavy heart relate.   [*Exeunt.*]

                   (1604)

Spartan dog Spartan dogs were noted for their savagery.

Anton Chekhov *1860–1904*

THE MARRIAGE PROPOSAL

Translated by Ronald Hingley

CHARACTERS

STEPHEN CHUBUKOV, a land-owner
NATASHA, his daughter, aged 25

IVAN LOMOV, a landowning neighbor of Chubukov's, hefty and well-nourished, but a hypochondriac

The action takes place in the drawing-room of CHUBUKOV's *country-house*

SCENE I

[CHUBUKOV *and* LOMOV; *the latter comes in wearing evening dress and white gloves.*]

CHUBUKOV [*going to meet him*]. Why, it's Ivan Lomov—or do my eyes deceive me, old boy? Delighted. [*Shakes hands.*] I say, old bean, this is a surprise! How *are* you?

LOMOV. All right, thanks, And how might you be?

CHUBUKOV. Not so bad, dear boy. Good of you to ask and so on. Now, you simply must sit down. Never neglect the neighbours, old bean—what? But why so formal, old boy—the tails, the gloves and so on? Not going anywhere, are you, dear man?

LOMOV. Only coming here, my dear Chubukov.

CHUBUKOV. Then why the tails, my dear fellow? Why make such a great thing of it?

LOMOV. Well, look, the point is—. [*Takes his arm.*] I came to ask a favour, my dear Chubukov, if it's not too much bother. I have had the privilege of enlisting your help more than once, and you've always, as it were—but I'm so nervous, sorry. I'll drink some water, my dear Chubukov. [*Drinks water.*]

CHUBUKOV [*aside*]. He's come to borrow money. Well, there's nothing doing! [*To him.*] What's the matter, my dear fellow?

LOMOV. Well, you see, my chear Dubukov—my dear Chubukov, I mean, sorry—that's to say, I'm terribly jumpy, as you see. In fact only you can help me, though I don't deserve it, of course and, er, have no claims on you either.

CHUBUKOV. Now don't muck about with it, old bean. Let's have it. Well?

LOMOV. Certainly, this instant. The fact is, I'm here to ask for the hand of your daughter Natasha.

CHUBUKOV [*delightedly*]. My dear Lomov! Say that again, old horse, I didn't quite catch it.

LOMOV. I have the honour to ask——

CHUBUKOV [*interrupting him*]. My dear old boy! I'm delighted and so on, er, and so forth—what? [*Embraces and kisses him.*] I've long wanted it, it's always been my wish. [*Sheds a tear.*] I've always loved you as a son, dear boy. May you both live happily ever after and so on. As for me, I've always wanted—. But why do I stand around like a blithering idiot? I'm tickled pink, I really am! Oh, I most cordially—. I'll go and call Natasha and so forth.

LOMOV [*very touched*]. My dear Chubukov, what do you think—can I count on a favourable response?

CHUBUKOV. What—her turn down a good-looking young fellow like you! Not likely! I bet she's crazy about you and so on. One moment. [*Goes out.*]

SCENE II

[LOMOV, *alone.*]

LOMOV. I feel cold, I'm shaking like a leaf. Make up your mind, that's the great thing. If you keep chewing things over, dithering on the brink, arguing the toss and waiting for your ideal woman or true love to come along, you'll never get hitched up. Brrr! I'm cold. Natasha's a good housewife. She's not bad-looking and she's an educated girl—what more can you ask? But I'm so jumpy, my ears have started buzzing. [*Drinks water.*] And get married I must. In the first place, I'm thirty-five years old—a critical age, so to speak. Secondly, I should lead a proper, regular life. I've heart trouble and constant palpitations, I'm irritable and nervous ás a kitten. See how my lips are trembling now? See my right eyelid twitch? But my nights are the worst thing. No sooner do I get in bed and start dozing off than I have a sort of shooting pain in my left side. It goes right through my shoulder and head. Out I leap like a lunatic, walk about a bit, then lie down again—but the moment I start dropping off I get this pain in my side again. And it happens twenty times over.

SCENE III

[NATASHA *and* LOMOV.]

NATASHA [*comes in*]. Oh, it's you. That's funny, Father said it was a dealer collecting some goods or something. Good morning, Mr. Lomov.

LOMOV. And good morning to you, my dear Miss Chubukov.

NATASHA. Excuse my apron, I'm not dressed for visitors. We've been shelling peas—we're going to dry them. Why haven't you been over for so long? Do sit down. [*They sit.*] Will you have lunch?

LOMOV. Thanks, I've already had some.

NATASHA. Or a smoke? Here are some matches. It's lovely weather, but it rained so hard yesterday—the men were idle all day. How much hay have you cut? I've been rather greedy, you know—I mowed all mine, and now I'm none too happy in case it rots. I should have hung on. But what's this I see? Evening dress, it seems. That *is* a surprise!

Going dancing or something? You're looking well, by the way—but why on earth go round in that get-up?

LOMOV [*agitated*]. Well, you see, my dear Miss Chubukov. The fact is, I've decided to ask you to—er, lend me your ears. You're bound to be surprised—angry, even. But I—. [*Aside.*] I feel terribly cold.

NATASHA. What's up then? [*Pause.*] Well?

LOMOV. I'll try to cut it short. Miss Chubukov, you are aware that I have long been privileged to know your family—since I was a boy, in fact. My dear departed aunt and her husband—from whom, as you are cognizant, I inherited the estate—always entertained the deepest respect for your father and dear departed mother. We Lomovs and Chubukovs have always been on the friendliest terms—you might say we've been pretty thick. And what's more, as you are also aware, we own closely adjoining properties. You may recall that my land at Oxpen Field is right next to your birch copse.

NATASHA. Sorry to butt in, but you refer to Oxpen Field as 'yours'? Surely you're not serious!

LOMOV. I am, madam.

NATASHA. Well, I like that! Oxpen Field is ours, it isn't yours.

LOMOV. You're wrong, my dear Miss Chubukov, that's my land.

NATASHA. This is news to me. How can it be yours?

LOMOV. How? What do you mean? I'm talking about Oxpen Field, that wedge of land between your birch copse and Burnt Swamp.

NATASHA. That's right. It's our land.

LOMOV. No, you're mistaken, my dear Miss Chubukov. It's mine.

NATASHA. Oh, come off it, Mr. Lomov. How long has it been yours?

LOMOV. How long? As long as I can remember—it's always been ours.

NATASHA. I say, this really is a bit steep!

LOMOV. But you have only to look at the deeds, my dear Miss Chubukov. Oxpen Field once *was* in dispute, I grant you, but it's mine now—that's common knowledge, and no argument about it. If I may explain, my aunt's grandmother made over that field rent free to your father's grandfather's labourers for their indefinite use in return for firing her bricks. Now, your great-grandfather's people used the place rent free for forty years or so, and came to look on it as their own. Then when the government land settlement was brought out——

NATASHA. No, that's all wrong. My grandfather and great-grandfather both claimed the land up to Burnt Swamp as theirs. So Oxpen Field was ours. Why argue? That's what I can't see. This is really rather aggravating.

LOMOV. I'll show you the deeds, Miss Chubukov.

NATASHA. Oh, you must be joking or having me on. This *is* a nice surprise! You own land for nearly three hundred years, then someone ups and tells you it's not yours! Mr. Lomov, I'm sorry, but I simply can't believe my ears. I don't mind about the field—it's only the odd twelve acres, worth the odd three hundred roubles. But it's so unfair—that's what infuriates me. I can't stand unfairness, I don't care what you say.

LOMOV. Do you hear me out, please! With due respect, your great-grandfather's people baked bricks for my aunt's grandmother, as I've al-

ready told you. Now, my aunt's grandmother wanted to do them a
favour——

NATASHA. Grandfather, grandmother, aunt—it makes no sense to me. The
field's ours, and that's that.

LOMOV. It's mine.

NATASHA. It's ours! Argue till the cows come home, put on tailcoats by
the dozen for all I care—it'll still be ours, ours, ours! I'm not after
your property, but I don't propose losing mine either, and I don't care
what you think!

LOMOV. My dear Miss Chubukov, it's not that I need that field—it's the
principle of the thing. If you want it, have it. Take it as a gift.

NATASHA. But it's mine to give *you* if I want—it's my property. This is
odd, to put it mildly. We always thought you such a good neighbour
and friend, Mr. Lomov. We lent you our threshing-machine last year,
and couldn't get our own threshing done till November in consequence.
We might be gipsies, the way you treat us. Making me a present of
my own property! I'm sorry, but that's not exactly neighbourly of you.
In fact, if you ask me, it's sheer howling cheek.

LOMOV. So I'm trying to pinch your land now, am I? It's not my habit,
madam, to grab land that isn't mine, and I won't have anyone say it
is! [*Quickly goes to the carafe and drinks some water.*] Oxpen Field belongs
to me.

NATASHA. That's a lie, it's ours.

LOMOV. It's mine.

NATASHA. That's a lie and I'll nail it! I'll send my men to cut that field
this very day.

LOMOV. What do you say?

NATASHA. My men will be out on that field today!

LOMOV. Too right, they'll be out! Out on their ear!

NATASHA. You'd never dare.

LOMOV [*clutches his heart*]. Oxpen Field belongs to me, do you hear? It's
mine!

NATASHA. Kindly stop shouting. By all means yell yourself blue in the
face when you're in your own home, but I'll thank you to keep a civil
tongue in your head in this house.

LOMOV. Madam, if I hadn't got these awful, agonizing palpitations and
this throbbing in my temples, I'd give you a piece of my mind! [*Shouts.*]
Oxpen Field belongs to me.

NATASHA. To us, you mean!

LOMOV. It's mine!

NATASHA. It's ours!

LOMOV. Mine!

SCENE IV

[*The above and* CHUBUKOV]

CHUBUKOV [*coming in*]. What's going on, what's all the row in aid of?

NATASHA. Father, who owns Oxpen Field? Would you mind telling this
gentleman? Is it his or ours?

CHUBUKOV [*to* LOMOV]. That field's ours, old cock!

LOMOV. Now look here, Chubukov, how can it be? You at least might show some sense! My aunt's grandmother made over that field to your grandfather's farm-labourers rent free on a temporary basis. Those villagers had the use of the land for forty years and came to think of it as theirs, but when the settlement came out——

CHUBUKOV. Now hang on, dear man, you forget one thing. That field was in dispute and so forth even in those days—and that's why the villagers paid your grandmother no rent and so on. But now it belongs to us, every dog in the district knows that, what? You can't have seen the plans.

LOMOV. It's mine and I'll prove it.

CHUBUKOV. Oh no you won't, my dear good boy.

LOMOV. Oh yes, I will.

CHUBUKOV. No need to shout, old bean. Shouting won't prove anything, what? I'm not after your property, but I don't propose losing mine, either. Why on earth should I? If it comes to that, old sausage, if you're set on disputing the field and so on, I'd rather give it to the villagers than you. So there.

LOMOV. This makes no sense to me. What right have you to give other people's property away?

CHUBUKOV. Permit me to be the best judge of that. Now, look here, young feller-me-lad—I'm not used to being spoken to like this, what? I'm twice your age, boy, and I'll thank you to talk to me without getting hot under the collar and so forth.

LOMOV. Oh, really, you must take me for a fool. You're pulling my leg. You say my land's yours, then you expect me to keep my temper and talk things over amicably. I call this downright unneighbourly, Chubukov. You're not a neighbour, you're a thoroughgoing shark!

CHUBUKOV. I *beg* your pardon! What did you say?

NATASHA. Father, send the men out to mow that field this very instant!

CHUBUKOV [*to* LOMOV]. What was it you said, sir?

NATASHA. Oxpen Field's ours and I won't let it go, I won't, I won't!

LOMOV. We'll see about that! I'll have the law on you!

CHUBUKOV. You will, will you? Then go right ahead, sir, and so forth, go ahead and sue, sir! Oh, I know your sort! Just what you're angling for and so on, isn't it—a court case, what? Quite the legal eagle, aren't you? Your whole family's always been litigation-mad, every last one of 'em!

LOMOV. I'll thank you not to insult my family. We Lomovs have always been honest, we've none of us been had up for embezzlement like your precious uncle.

CHUBUKOV. The Lomovs have always been mad as hatters!

NATASHA. Yes! All of you! Mad!

CHUBUKOV. Your grandfather drank like a fish, and your younger Aunt What's-her-name—Nastasya—ran off with an architect and so on.

LOMOV. And your mother was a cripple. [*Clutches his heart.*] There's that shooting pain in my side, and a sort of blow on the head. Heavens alive! Water!

CHUBUKOV. Your father gambled and ate like a pig!

NATASHA. Your aunt was a most frightful busybody!

LOMOV. My left leg's gone to sleep. And you're a very slippery customer.

Oh my heart! And it's common knowledge that at election time you
bri—. I'm seeing stars. Where's my hat?

NATASHA. What a rotten, beastly, filthy thing to say.

CHUBUKOV. You're a thoroughly nasty, cantankerous, hypocritical piece
of work, what? Yes, sir!

LOMOV. Ah, there's my hat. My heart—. Which way do I go? Where's
the door? Oh, I think I'm dying. I can hardly drag one foot after another.
[*Moves to the door.*]

CHUBUKOV [*after him*]. You need never set either of those feet in my house
again, sir.

NATASHA. Go ahead and sue, we'll see what happens.

[LOMOV *goes out staggering*]

SCENE V

[CHUBUKOV *and* NATASHA.]

CHUBUKOV. Oh, blast it! [*Walks up and down in agitation.*]

NATASHA. The rotten cad! So much for trusting the dear neighbours!

CHUBUKOV. Scruffy swine!

NATASHA. He's an out-and-out monster! Pinches your land and then has
the cheek to swear at you!

CHUBUKOV. And this monstrosity, this blundering oaf, has the immortal
rind to come here with his proposal and so on, what? A proposal! I
ask you!

NATASHA. A proposal, did you say?

CHUBUKOV. Not half I did! He came here to propose to you!

NATASHA. Propose? To me? Then why didn't you say so before?

CHUBUKOV. That's why he dolled himself up in tails. Damn popinjay!
Twerp!

NATASHA. Me? Propose to me? Oh! [*Falls in an armchair and groans.*] Bring
him back! Bring him back! Bring him back, I tell you!

CHUBUKOV. Bring who back?

NATASHA. Hurry up, be quick, I feel faint. Bring him back. [*Has hysterics.*]

CHUBUKOV. What's this? What do you want? [*Clutches his head.*] Oh, misery!
I might as well go and boil my head! I'm fed up with them!

NATASHA. I'm dying. Bring him back!

CHUBUKOV. Phew! All right then. No need to howl. [*Runs out.*]

NATASHA [*alone, groans*]. What have we done! Bring him, bring him back!

CHUBUKOV [*runs in*]. He'll be here in a moment and so on, damn him!
Phew! You talk to him—I don't feel like it, what?

NATASHA [*groans*]. Bring him back!

CHUBUKOV [*shouts*]. He's coming, I tell you
       'My fate, ye gods, is just too bad—
       To be a grown-up daughter's dad!'
I'll cut my throat, I'll make a point of it. We've sworn at the man,
insulted him and kicked him out of the house. And it was all your
doing.

NATASHA. It was *not*, it was yours!

CHUBUKOV. So now it's my fault, what?

[LOMOV *appears in the doorway.*]

CHUBUKOV. All right, now you talk to him. [*Goes out.*]

SCENE VI

[NATASHA *and* LOMOV.]

LOMOV [*comes in, exhausted*]. My heart's fairly thumping away, my leg's gone to sleep and there's this pain in my side——

NATASHA. I'm sorry we got a bit excited, Mr. Lomov. I've just remembered—Oxpen Field really does belong to you.

LOMOV. My heart's fairly thumping away. That field's mine. I've a nervous tic in both eyes.

NATASHA. The field *is* yours, certainly. Do sit down. [*They sit.*] We were mistaken.

LOMOV. This is a question of principle. It's not the land I mind about, it's the principle of the thing.

NATASHA. Just so, the principle. Now let's change the subject.

LOMOV. Especially as I can prove it. My aunt's grandmother gave your father's grandfather's villagers——

NATASHA. All right, that'll do. [*Aside.*] I don't know how to start. [*To him.*] Thinking of going shooting soon?

LOMOV. Yes, I'm thinking of starting on the woodcock after the harvest, my dear Miss Chubukov. I say, have you heard? What awful bad luck! You know my dog Tracker? He's gone lame.

NATASHA. Oh, I am sorry. How did it happen?

LOMOV. I don't know. Either it must be a sprain, or the other dogs bit him. [*Sighs.*] My best dog, to say nothing of what he set me back! Do you know, I gave Mironov a hundred and twenty-five roubles for him?

NATASHA. Then you were had, Mr. Lomov.

LOMOV. He came very cheap if you ask me—he's a splendid dog.

NATASHA. Father only gave eighty-five roubles for Rover. And Rover's a jolly sight better dog than Tracker, you'll agree.

LOMOV. Rover better than Tracker! Oh, come off it! [*Laughs.*] Rover a better dog than Tracker!

NATASHA. Of course he is. Rover's young, it's true, and not yet in his prime. But you could search the best kennels in the county without finding a nippier animal, or one with better points.

LOMOV. I am sorry, Miss Chubukov, but you forget he has a short lower jaw, and a dog like that can't grip.

NATASHA. Oh, can't he! That's news to me!

LOMOV. He has a weak chin, you can take that from me.

NATASHA. Why, have you measured it?

LOMOV. Yes, I have. Naturally he'll do for coursing, but when it comes to retrieving, that's another story.

NATASHA. In the first place, Rover has a good honest coat on him, and a pedigree as long as your arm. As for that mud-coloured, piebald animal of yours, his antecedents are anyone's guess, quite apart from him being ugly as a broken-down old cart-horse.

LOMOV. Old he may be, but I wouldn't swap him for a half dozen Rovers—not on your life! Tracker's a real dog, and Rover—why, it's absurd to argue. The kennels are lousy with Rovers, he'd be dear at twenty-five roubles.

NATASHA. You *are* in an awkward mood today, Mr. Lomov. First you decide our field is yours, now you say Tracker's better than Rover. I dislike people who won't speak their mind. Now, you know perfectly well that Rover's umpteen times better than that—yes, that stupid Tracker. So why say the opposite?

LOMOV. I see you don't credit me with eyes or brains, Miss Chubukov. Well, get it in your head that Rover has a weak chin.

NATASHA. That's not true.

LOMOV. Oh yes it is!

NATASHA [*shouts*]. Oh no it isn't!

LOMOV. Don't you raise your voice at me, madam.

NATASHA. Then don't you talk such utter balderdash! Oh, this is infuriating! It's time that measly Tracker was put out of his misery—and you compare him with Rover!

LOMOV. I can't go on arguing, sorry—it's my heart.

NATASHA. Men who argue most about sport, I've noticed, are always the worst sportsmen.

LOMOV. Will you kindly hold your trap, madam—my heart's breaking in two. [*Shouts.*] You shut up!

NATASHA. I'll do nothing of the sort till you admit Rover's a hundred times better than Tracker.

LOMOV. A hundred times worse, more like! I hope Rover drops dead! Oh, my head, my eye, my shoulder——

NATASHA. That half-wit Tracker doesn't need to drop dead—he's pretty well a walking corpse already.

LOMOV [*weeps*]. Shut up! I'm having a heart attack!

NATASHA. I will *not* shut up!

SCENE VII

[*The above and* CHUBUKOV.]

CHUBUKOV [*comes in*]. What is it this time?

NATASHA. Father, I want an honest answer: which is the better dog, Rover or Tracker?

LOMOV. Will you kindly tell us just one thing, Chubukov: has Rover got a weak chin or hasn't he? Yes or no?

CHUBUKOV. What if he has? As if that mattered! Seeing he's only the best dog in the county and so on.

LOMOV. Tracker's better, and you know it! Be honest!

CHUBUKOV. Keep your shirt on, dear man. Now look here. Tracker has got some good qualities, what? He's a pedigree dog, has firm paws, steep haunches and so forth. But that dog has two serious faults if you want to know, old bean: he's old and he's pug-nosed.

LOMOV. I'm sorry—it's my heart! Let's just look at the facts. You may recall that Tracker was neck and neck with the Count's Swinger on Maruskino Green when Rover was a good half-mile behind.

CHUBUKOV. He dropped back because the Count's huntsman fetched him a crack with his whip.

LOMOV. Serve him right. Hounds are all chasing the fox and Rover has to start worrying a sheep!

CHUBUKOV. That's not true, sir. I've got a bad temper, old boy, and the fact is—let's please stop arguing, what? He hit him because everyone hates the sight of another man's dog. Oh yes they do. Loathe 'em, they do. And you're no one to talk either, sir! The moment you spot a better dog than the wretched Tracker, you always try to start something and, er, so forth—what? I don't forget, you see.

LOMOV. Nor do I sir.

CHUBUKOV [*mimics him*]. 'Nor do, I sir.' What is it you don't forget then?

LOMOV. My heart! My leg's gone to sleep. I can't go on.

NATASHA [*mimics him*]. 'My heart!' Call yourself a sportsman! You should be lying on the kitchen stove squashing black-beetles, not fox-hunting. His heart!

CHUBUKOV. Some sportsman, I must say! With that heart you should stay at home, not bob around in the saddle, what? I wouldn't mind if you hunted properly, but you only turn out to pick quarrels and annoy the hounds and so on. I have a bad temper, so let's change the subject. You're no sportsman, sir—what?

LOMOV. What about you then? You only turn out so you can get in the Count's good books and intrigue against people. Oh, my heart! You're a slippery customer, sir!

CHUBUKOV. What's that, sir? Oh, I am, am I? [*Shouts.*] Hold your tongue!

LOMOV. You artful old dodger!

CHUBUKOV. Why, you young puppy!

LOMOV. Nasty old fogy! Canting hypocrite!

CHUBUKOV. Shut up, or I'll pot you like a ruddy partridge. And I'll use a dirty gun too, you idle gasbag!

LOMOV. And it's common knowledge that—oh, my heart—your wife used to beat you. Oh, my leg! My head! I can see stars! I can't stand up!

CHUBUKOV. And your housekeeper has you eating out of her hand!

LOMOV. Oh, oh! My heart's bursting. My shoulder seems to have come off—where is the thing? I'm dying. [*Falls into an armchair.*] Fetch a doctor. [*Faints.*]

CHUBUKOV. Why, you young booby! Hot air merchant! I think I'm going to faint. [*Drinks water.*] I feel unwell.

NATASHA. Calls himself a sportsman and can't even sit on a horse! [*To her father.*] Father, what's the matter with him? Father, have a look. [*Screeches.*] Mr. Lomov! He's dead!

CHUBUKOV. I feel faint. I can't breathe! Give me air!

NATASHA. He's dead. [*Tugs* LOMOV's *sleeve.*] Mr. Lomov, Mr. Lomov! What have we done? He's dead. [*Falls into an armchair.*] Fetch a doctor, a doctor! [*Has hysterics.*]

CHUBUKOV. Oh! What's happened? What's the matter?

NATASHA [*groans*]. He's dead! Dead!

CHUBUKOV. Who's dead? [*Glancing at* LOMOV.] My God, you're right! Water! A doctor! [*Holds a glass to* LOMOV's *mouth.*] Drink! No, he's not drinking. He must be dead, and so forth. Oh, misery, misery! Why don't I put a bullet in my brain? Why did I never get round to cutting my throat? What am I waiting for? Give me a knife! A pistol! [LOMOV *makes a movement.*] I think he's coming round. Drink some water! That's right.

LOMOV. I can see stars! There's a sort of mist. Where am I?

CHUBUKOV. Hurry up and get married and—oh, to hell with you! She says yes. [*Joins their hands.*] She says yes, and so forth. You have my blessing, and so on. Just leave me in peace, that's all.

LOMOV. Eh? What? [*Raising himself.*] Who?

CHUBUKOV. She says yes. Well, what about it? Kiss each other and—oh, go to hell!

NATASHA [*groans*]. He's alive. Yes, yes, yes! I agree.

CHUBUKOV. Come on, kiss.

LOMOV. Eh? Who? [*Kisses* NATASHA.] Very nice too. I say, what's all this about? Oh, I see—. My heart! I'm seeing stars! Miss Chubukov, I'm so happy. [*Kisses her hand.*] My leg's gone to sleep.

NATASHA. I, er, I'm happy too.

CHUBUKOV. Oh, what a weight off my mind! Phew!

NATASHA. Still, you must admit now that Tracker's not a patch on Rover.

LOMOV. Oh yes he is!

NATASHA. Oh no he isn't!

CHUBUKOV. You can see those two are going to live happily ever after! Champagne!

LOMOV. He's better.

NATASHA. He's worse, worse, worse.

CHUBUKOV [*trying to shout them down*]. Champagne, champagne, champagne!

CURTAIN

(1888–89)

Henrik Ibsen   *1828–1906*

HEDDA GABLER

Translated by William Archer and Sir Edmund Gosse

CHARACTERS

GEORGE TESMAN   JUDGE BRACK
HEDDA TESMAN   *his wife*   EILERT LÖVBORG
MISS JULIANA TESMAN *his*   BERTA   *servant at the Tes-*
  aunt   *mans'*
MRS. ELVSTED

SCENE
Tesman's villa, in the west end of Christiania.

ACT I

[*A spacious, handsome and tastefully furnished drawing-room, decorated in dark colors. In the back, a wide doorway with curtains drawn back, leading into a smaller room decorated in the same style as the drawing-room. In the right-hand wall of the front room, a folding door leading out to the hall. In the opposite wall, on the left, a glass door, also with curtains drawn back. Through the panes can be seen part of a verandah outside, and trees covered with autumn foliage. An oval table, with a cover on it, and surrounded by chairs, stands well forward. In front, by the wall on the right, a wide stove of dark porcelain, a high-backed arm-chair, a cushioned foot-rest, and two foot-stools. A settee, with a small round table in front of it, fills the upper right-hand corner. In front, on the left, a little way from the wall, a sofa. Farther back than the glass door, a piano. On either side of the doorway at the back a whatnot with terra-cotta and majolica ornaments.— Against the back wall of the inner room a sofa, with a table, and one or two chairs. Over the sofa hangs the portrait of a handsome elderly man in a General's uniform. Over the table a hanging lamp, with an opal glass shade.—A number of bouquets are arranged about the drawing-room, in vases and glasses. Others lie upon the tables. The floors in both rooms are covered with thick carpets.—Morning light. The sun shines in through the glass door.*

MISS JULIANA TESMAN, *with her bonnet on and carrying a parasol, comes in from the hall, followed by* BERTA, *who carries a bouquet wrapped in paper.* MISS TESMAN *is a comely and pleasant-looking lady of about sixty-five. She is nicely but simply*

> *dressed in a gray walking-costume.* BERTA *is a middle-aged woman of plain and rather countrified appearance.*]

MISS TESMAN [*stops close to the door, listens, and says softly*]. Upon my word, I don't believe they are stirring yet!

BERTA [*also softly*]. I told you so, Miss. Remember how late the steamboat got in last night. And then, when they got home!—good Lord, what a lot the young mistress had to unpack before she could get to bed.

MISS TESMAN. Well, well—let them have their sleep out. But let us see that they get a good breath of the fresh morning air when they do appear. [*She goes to the glass door and throws it open.*]

BERTA [*beside the table, at a loss what to do with the bouquet in her hand*]. I declare there isn't a bit of room left. I think I'll put it down here, Miss. [*She places it on the piano.*]

MISS TESMAN. So you've got a new mistress now, my dear Berta. Heaven knows it was a wrench to me to part with you.

BERTA [*on the point of weeping*]. And do you think it wasn't hard for me too, Miss? After all the blessed years I've been with you and Miss Rina.

MISS TESMAN. We must make the best of it, Berta. There was nothing else to be done. George can't do without you, you see—he absolutely can't. He has had you to look after him ever since he was a little boy.

BERTA. Ah, but, Miss Julia, I can't help thinking of Miss Rina lying helpless at home there, poor thing. And with only that new girl, too! She'll never learn to take proper care of an invalid.

MISS TESMAN. Oh, I shall manage to train her. And of course, you know, I shall take most of it upon myself. You needn't be uneasy about my poor sister, my dear Berta.

BERTA. Well, but there's another thing, Miss. I'm so mortally afraid I shan't be able to suit the young mistress.

MISS TESMAN. Oh, well—just at first there may be one or two things—

BERTA. Most like she'll be terrible grand in her ways.

MISS TESMAN. Well, you can't wonder at that—General Gabler's daughter! Think of the sort of life she was accustomed to in her father's time. Don't you remember how we used to see her riding down the road along with the General? In that long black habit—and with feathers in her hat?

BERTA. Yes, indeed—I remember well enough—! But good Lord, I should never have dreamt in those days that she and Master George would make a match of it.

MISS TESMAN. Nor I.—But, by-the-bye, Berta—while I think of it: in future you mustn't say Master George. You must say Dr. Tesman.

BERTA. Yes, the young mistress spoke of that too—last night—the moment they set foot in the house. Is it true, then, Miss?

MISS TESMAN. Yes, indeed it is. Only think, Berta—some foreign university has made him a doctor—while he has been abroad, you understand. I hadn't heard a word about it, until he told me himself upon the pier.

BERTA. Well, well, he's clever enough for anything, he is. But I didn't think he'd have gone in for doctoring people too.

MISS TESMAN. No, no, it's not that sort of doctor he is. [*Nods significantly.*] But let me tell you, we may have to call him something still grander before long.

BERTA. You don't say so! What can that be, Miss?

MISS TESMAN [*smiling*]. H'm—wouldn't you like to know! [*With emotion.*] Ah, dear, dear—if my poor brother could only look up from his grave now, and see what his little boy has grown into! [*Looks around.*] But bless me, Berta—why have you done this? Taken the chintz covers off all the furniture?

BERTA. The mistress told me to. She can't abide covers on the chairs, she says.

MISS TESMAN. Are they going to make this their everyday sitting-room then?

BERTA. Yes, that's what I understood—from the mistress. Master George— the doctor—he said nothing. [GEORGE TESMAN *comes from the right into the inner room, humming to himself, and carrying an unstrapped empty portmanteau. He is a middle-sized, young-looking man of thirty-three, rather stout, with a round, open, cheerful face, fair hair and beard. He wears spectacles, and is somewhat carelessly dressed in comfortable indoor clothes.*]

MISS TESMAN. Good morning, good morning, George.

TESMAN [*in the doorway between the rooms*]. Aunt Julia! Dear Aunt Julia! [*Goes up to her and shakes hands warmly.*] Come all this way—so early! Eh?

MISS TESMAN. Why of course I had to come and see how you were getting on.

TESMAN. In spite of your having had no proper night's rest?

MISS TESMAN. Oh, that makes no difference to me.

TESMAN. Well, I suppose you got home all right from the pier? Eh?

MISS TESMAN. Yes, quite safely, thank goodness. Judge Brack was good enough to see me right to my door.

TESMAN. We were so sorry we couldn't give you a seat in the carriage. But you saw what a pile of boxes Hedda had to bring with her.

MISS TESMAN. Yes, she had certainly plenty of boxes.

BERTA [*to* TESMAN]. Shall I go in and see if there's anything I can do for the mistress?

TESMAN. No thank you, Berta—you needn't. She said she would ring if she wanted anything.

BERTA [*going towards the right*]. Very well.

TESMAN. But look here—take this portmanteau with you.

BERTA [*taking it*]. I'll put it in the attic. [*She goes out by the hall door.*]

TESMAN. Fancy, Auntie—I had the whole of that portmanteau chock full of copies of documents. You wouldn't believe how much I have picked up from all the archives I have been examining—curious old details that no one has had any idea of—

MISS TESMAN. Yes, you don't seem to have wasted your time on your wedding trip, George.

TESMAN. No, that I haven't. But do take off your bonnet, Auntie. Look here! Let me untie the strings—eh?

MISS TESMAN [*while he does so*]. Well, well—this is just as if you were still at home with us.

TESMAN [*with the bonnet in his hand, looks at it from all sides.*]. Why, what a gorgeous bonnet you've been investing in!

MISS TESMAN. I bought it on Hedda's account.

TESMAN. On Hedda's account? Eh?

MISS TESMAN. Yes, so that Hedda needn't be ashamed of me if we happened to go out together.

TESMAN [*patting her cheek*]. You always think of everything, Aunt Julia. [*Lays the bonnet on a chair beside the table.*] And now, look here—suppose we sit comfortably on the sofa and have a little chat, till Hedda comes. [*They seat themselves. She places her parasol in the corner of the sofa.*]

MISS TESMAN [*takes both his hands and looks at him*]. What a delight it is to have you again, as large as life, before my very eyes, George! My George—my poor brother's own boy!

TESMAN. And it's a delight for me, too, to see you again, Aunt Julia! You, who have been father and mother in one to me.

MISS TESMAN. Oh, yes, I know you will always keep a place in your heart for your old aunts.

TESMAN. And what about Aunt Rina? No improvement—eh?

MISS TESMAN. Oh, no—we can scarcely look for any improvement in her case, poor thing. There she lies, helpless, as she has lain for all these years. But heaven grant I may not lose her yet awhile! For if I did, I don't know what I should make of my life, George—especially now that I haven't you to look after any more.

TESMAN [*patting her back*]. There, there, there—!

MISS TESMAN [*suddenly changing her tone*]. And to think that here you are a married man, George!—And that you should be the one to carry off Hedda Gabler, the beautiful Hedda Gabler! Only think of it—she, that was so beset with admirers!

TESMAN [*hums a little and smiles complacently*]. Yes, I fancy I have several good friends about town who would like to stand in my shoes—eh?

MISS TESMAN. And then this fine long wedding-tour you have had! More than five—nearly six months—

TESMAN. Well, for me it has been a sort of tour of research as well. I have had to do so much grubbing among old records—and to read no end of books too, Auntie.

MISS TESMAN. Oh, yes, I suppose so. [*More confidentially, and lowering her voice a little.*] But listen now, George—have you nothing—nothing special to tell me?

TESMAN. As to our journey?

MISS TESMAN. Yes.

TESMAN. No, I don't know of anything except what I have told you in my letters. I had a doctor's degree conferred on me—but that I told you yesterday.

MISS TESMAN. Yes, yes, you did. But what I mean is—haven't you any—any—expectations—?

TESMAN. Expectations?

MISS TESMAN. Why, you know, George—I'm your old auntie!

TESMAN. Why, of course I have expectations.

MISS TESMAN. Ah!

TESMAN. I have every expectation of being a professor one of these days.

MISS TESMAN. Oh, yes, a professor—

TESMAN. Indeed, I may say I am certain of it. But my dear Auntie—you know all about that already!

MISS TESMAN [*laughing to herself*]. Yes, of course I do. You are quite right there. [*Changing the subject.*] But we were talking about your journey. It must have cost a great deal of money, George?

TESMAN. Well, you see—my handsome traveling-scholarship went a good way.

MISS TESMAN. But I can't understand how you can have made it go far enough for two.

TESMAN. No, that's not so easy to understand—eh?

MISS TESMAN. And especially traveling with a lady—they tell me that makes it ever so much more expensive.

TESMAN. Yes, of course—it makes it a little more expensive. But Hedda had to have this trip, Auntie! She really had to. Nothing else would have done.

MISS TESMAN. No, no, I suppose not. A wedding-tour seems to be quite indispensable nowadays.—But tell me now—have you gone thoroughly over the house yet?

TESMAN. Yes, you may be sure I have. I have been afoot ever since daylight.

MISS TESMAN. And what do you think of it all?

TESMAN. I'm delighted! Quite delighted! Only I can't think what we are to do with the two empty rooms between this inner parlor and Hedda's bedroom.

MISS TESMAN [*laughing*]. Oh, my dear George, I dare say you may find some use for them—in the course of time.

TESMAN. Why of course you are quite right, Aunt Julia! You mean as my library increases—eh?

MISS TESMAN. Yes, quite so, my dear boy. It was your library I was thinking of.

TESMAN. I am specially pleased on Hedda's account. Often and often, before we were engaged, she said that she would never care to live anywhere but in Secretary Falk's villa.

MISS TESMAN. Yes, it was lucky that this very house should come into the market, just after you had started.

TESMAN. Yes, Aunt Julia, the luck was on our side, wasn't it—eh?

MISS TESMAN. But the expense, my dear George! You will find it very expensive, all this.

TESMAN [*looks at her, a little cast down*]. Yes, I suppose I shall, Aunt!

MISS TESMAN. Oh, frightfully!

TESMAN. How much do you think? In round numbers?—Eh?

MISS TESMAN. Oh, I can't even guess until all the accounts come in.

TESMAN. Well, fortunately, Judge Brack has secured the most favourable terms for me,—so he said in a letter to Hedda.

MISS TESMAN. Yes, don't be uneasy, my dear boy.—Besides, I have given security for the furniture and all the carpets.

TESMAN. Security? You? My dear Aunt Julia—what sort of security could you give?

MISS TESMAN. I have given a mortgage on our annuity.

TESMAN [*jumps up*]. What! On your—and Aunt Rina's annuity!

MISS TESMAN. Yes, I knew of no other plan, you see.

TESMAN [*placing himself before her*]. Have you gone out of your senses, Auntie! Your annuity—it's all that you and Aunt Rina have to live upon.

Miss Tesman. Well, well, don't get so excited about it. It's only a matter of form you know—Judge Brack assured me of that. It was he that was kind enough to arrange the whole affair for me. A mere matter of form, he said.

Tesman. Yes, that may be all very well. But nevertheless—

Miss Tesman. You will have your own salary to depend upon now. And, good heavens, even if we did have to pay up a little—! To eke things out a bit at the start—! Why, it would be nothing but a pleasure to us.

Tesman. Oh, Auntie—will you never be tired of making sacrifices for me!

Miss Tesman [*rises and lays her hands on his shoulders*]. Have I had any other happiness in this world except to smooth your way for you, my dear boy? You, who have had neither father nor mother to depend on. And now we have reached the goal, George! Things have looked black enough for us, sometimes; but, thank heaven, now you have nothing to fear.

Tesman. Yes, it is really marvelous how everything has turned out for the best.

Miss Tesman. And the people who opposed you—who wanted to bar the way for you—now you have them at your feet. They have fallen, George. Your most dangerous rival—his fall was the worst.—And now he has to lie on the bed he has made for himself—poor misguided creature.

Tesman. Have you heard anything of Eilert? Since I went away, I mean.

Miss Tesman. Only that he is said to have published a new book.

Tesman. What! Eilert Lövborg! Recently—eh?

Miss Tesman. Yes, so they say. Heaven knows whether it can be worth anything! Ah, when your new book appears—that will be another story, George! What is it to be about?

Tesman. It will deal with the domestic industries of Brabant during the Middle Ages.

Miss Tesman. Fancy—to be able to write on such a subject as that!

Tesman. However, it may be some time before the book is ready. I have all these collections to arrange first, you see.

Miss Tesman. Yes, collecting and arranging—no one can beat you at that. There you are my poor brother's own son.

Tesman. I am looking forward eagerly to setting to work at it; especially now that I have my own delightful home to work in.

Miss Tesman. And, most of all, now that you have got the wife of your heart, my dear George.

Tesman [*embracing her*]. Oh, yes, yes, Aunt Julia. Hedda—she is the best part of all! [*Looks towards the doorway.*] I believe I hear her coming— eh? [Hedda *enters from the left through the inner room. She is a woman of nine-and-twenty. Her face and figure show refinement and distinction. Her complexion is pale and opaque. Her steel-gray eyes express a cold, unruffled repose. Her hair is of an agreeable medium brown, but not particularly abundant. She is dressed in a tasteful, somewhat loose-fitting morning-gown.*]

Miss Tesman [*going to meet* Hedda]. Good morning, my dear Hedda! Good morning, and a hearty welcome.

Hedda [*holds out her hand*]. Good morning, dear Miss Tesman! So early a call! This is kind of you.

MISS TESMAN [*with some embarrassment*]. Well—has the bride slept well in her new home?

HEDDA. Oh, yes, thanks. Passably.

TESMAN [*laughing*]. Passably! Come, that's good, Hedda! You were sleeping like a stone when I got up.

HEDDA. Fortunately. Of course one has always to accustom one's self to new surroundings, Miss Tesman—little by little. [*Looking towards the left.*] Oh—there the servant has gone and opened the verandah door, and let in a whole flood of sunshine.

MISS TESMAN [*going towards the door*]. Well, then, we will shut it.

HEDDA. No, no, not that! Tesman, please draw the curtains. That will give a softer light.

TESMAN [*at the door*]. All right—all right. There now, Hedda, now you have both shade and fresh air.

HEDDA. Yes, fresh air we certainly must have, with all these stacks of flowers—But—won't you sit down, Miss Tesman?

MISS TESMAN. No, thank you. Now that I have seen that everything is all right here—thank heaven!—I must be getting home again. My sister is lying longing for me, poor thing.

TESMAN. Give her my very best love, Auntie; and say I shall look in and see her later in the day.

MISS TESMAN. Yes, yes, I'll be sure to tell her. But by-the-bye, George— [*feeling in her dress pocket*]—I have almost forgotten—I have something for you here.

TESMAN. What is it, Auntie? Eh?

MISS TESMAN [*produces a flat parcel wrapped in newspaper and hands it to him*]. Look here, my dear boy.

TESMAN [*opening the parcel*]. Well, I declare! Have you really saved them for me, Aunt Julia! Hedda, isn't this touching—eh?

HEDDA [*beside the whatnot on the right*]. Well, what is it?

TESMAN. My old morning-shoes! My slippers.

HEDDA. Indeed. I remember you often spoke of them while we were abroad.

TESMAN. Yes, I missed them terribly. [*Goes up to her.*] Now you shall see them, Hedda!

HEDDA [*going towards the stove*]. Thanks, I really don't care about it.

TESMAN [*following her*]. Only think—ill as she was, Aunt Rina embroidered these for me. Oh you can't think how many associations cling to them.

HEDDA [*at the table*]. Scarcely for me.

MISS TESMAN. Of course not for Hedda, George.

TESMAN. Well, but now that she belongs to the family, I thought—

HEDDA [*interrupting*]. We shall never get on with this servant, Tesman.

MISS TESMAN. Not get on with Berta?

TESMAN. Why, dear, what puts that in your head? Eh?

HEDDA [*pointing*]. Look there! She has left her old bonnet lying about on a chair.

TESMAN [*in consternation, drops the slippers on the floor*]. Why, Hedda—

HEDDA. Just fancy, if any one should come in and see it.

TESMAN. But Hedda—that's Aunt Julia's bonnet.

HEDDA. Is it!

MISS TESMAN [*taking up the bonnet*]. Yes, indeed it's mine. And what's more, it's not old, Madame Hedda.

HEDDA. I really did not look closely at it, Miss Tesman.

MISS TESMAN [*trying on the bonnet*]. Let me tell you it's the first time I have worn it—the very first time.

TESMAN. And a very nice bonnet it is too—quite a beauty!

MISS TESMAN. Oh, it's no such great thing, George. [*Looks around her.*] My parasol—? Ah, here. [*Takes it.*] For this is mine too— [*mutters*]—not Berta's.

TESMAN. A new bonnet and a new parasol! Only think, Hedda!

HEDDA. Very handsome indeed.

TESMAN. Yes, isn't it? But Auntie, take a good look at Hedda before you go! See how handsome she is!

MISS TESMAN. Oh, my dear boy, there's nothing new in that. Hedda was always lovely. [*She nods and goes towards the right.*]

TESMAN [*following*]. Yes, but have you noticed what splendid condition she is in? How she has filled out on the journey?

HEDDA. [*crossing the room*]. Oh, do be quiet—!

MISS TESMAN [*who has stopped and turned*]. Filled out?

TESMAN. Of course you don't notice it so much now that she has that dress on. But I, who can see—

HEDDA [*at the glass door, impatiently*]. Oh, you can't see anything.

TESMAN. It must be the mountain air in the Tyrol—

HEDDA [*curtly, interrupting*]. I am exactly as I was when I started.

TESMAN. So you insist; but I'm quite certain you are not. Don't you agree with me, Auntie?

MISS TESMAN [*who has been gazing at her with folded hands*]. Hedda is lovely—lovely—lovely. [*Goes up to her, takes her head between both hands, draws it downwards, and kisses her hair*]. God bless and preserve Hedda Tesman—for George's sake.

HEDDA [*gently freeing herself*]. Oh—! Let me go.

MISS TESMAN [*in quiet emotion*]. I shall not let a day pass without coming to see you.

TESMAN. No you won't, will you, Auntie? Eh?

MISS TESMAN. Good-bye—good-bye! [*She goes out by the hall door. TESMAN accompanies her. The door remains half open. TESMAN can be heard repeating his message to Aunt Rina and his thanks for the slippers. In the meantime, HEDDA walks about the room raising her arms and clenching her hands as if in desperation. Then she flings back the curtains from the glass door, and stands there looking out. Presently TESMAN returns and closes the door behind him.*]

TESMAN [*picks up the slippers from the floor*]. What are you looking at, Hedda?

HEDDA [*once more calm and mistress of herself*]. I am looking at the leaves. They are so yellow—so withered.

TESMAN [*wraps up the slippers and lays them on the table*]. Well you see, we are well into September now.

HEDDA [*again restless*]. Yes, to think of it!—Already in—in September.

TESMAN. Don't you think Aunt Julia's manner was strange, dear? Almost solemn? Can you imagine what was the matter with her? Eh?

HEDDA. I scarcely know her, you see. Is she often like that?

TESMAN. No, not as she was today.

HEDDA [*leaving the glass door*]. Do you think she was annoyed about the bonnet?

TESMAN. Oh, scarcely at all. Perhaps a little just at the moment—

HEDDA. But what an idea, to pitch her bonnet about in the drawing-room! No one does that sort of thing.

TESMAN. Well you may be sure Aunt Julia won't do it again.

HEDDA. In any case, I shall manage to make my peace with her.

TESMAN. Yes, my dear, good Hedda, if you only would.

HEDDA. When you call this afternoon, you might invite her to spend the evening here.

TESMAN. Yes, that I will. And there's one thing more you could do that would delight her heart.

HEDDA. What is it?

TESMAN. If you could only prevail on yourself to say *du*[1] to her. For my sake, Hedda? Eh?

HEDDA. No, no, Tesman—you really mustn't ask that of me. I have told you so already. I shall try to call her "Aunt"; and you must be satisfied with that.

TESMAN. Well, well. Only I think now that you belong to the family, you—

HEDDA. H'm—I can't in the least see why— [*She goes up towards the middle doorway.*]

TESMAN [*after a pause*]. Is there anything the matter with you, Hedda? Eh?

HEDDA. I'm only looking at my old piano. It doesn't go at all well with all the other things.

TESMAN. The first time I draw my salary, we'll see about exchanging it.

HEDDA. No, no—no exchanging. I don't want to part with it. Suppose we put it there in the inner room, and then get another here in its place. When it's convenient, I mean.

TESMAN [*a little taken aback*]. Yes—of course we could do that.

HEDDA [*takes up the bouquet from the piano*]. These flowers were not here last night when we arrived.

TESMAN. Aunt Julia must have brought them for you.

HEDDA [*examining the bouquet*]. A visiting-card. [*Takes it out and reads.*] "Shall return later in the day." Can you guess whose card it is?

TESMAN. No. Whose? Eh?

HEDDA. The name is "Mrs. Elvsted."

TESMAN. Is it really? Sheriff Elvsted's wife? Miss Rysing that was.

HEDDA. Exactly. The girl with the irritating hair, that she was always showing off. An old flame of yours, I've been told.

TESMAN [*laughing*]. Oh, that didn't last long; and it was before I knew you, Hedda. But fancy her being in town!

HEDDA. It's odd that she should call upon us. I have scarcely seen her since we left school.

TESMAN. I haven't seen her either for—heaven knows how long. I wonder how she can endure to live in such an out-of-the-way hole—eh?

HEDDA [*after a moment's thought says suddenly*]. Tell me, Tesman—isn't it somewhere near there that he—that—Eilert Lövborg is living?

[1] Thou, the familiar form of the second-person pronoun.

TESMAN. Yes, he is somewhere in that part of the country. [BERTA *enters by the hall door.*]

BERTA. That lady, ma'am, that brought some flowers a little while ago, is here again. [*Pointing.*] The flowers you have in your hand, ma'am.

HEDDA. Ah, is she? Well, please show her in. [BERTA *opens the door for* MRS. ELVSTED, *and goes out herself.—*MRS. ELVSTED *is a woman of fragile figure, with pretty, soft features. Her eyes are light blue, large, round, and somewhat prominent, with a startled, inquiring expression. Her hair is remarkably light, almost flaxen, and unusually abundant and wavy. She is a couple of years younger than* HEDDA. *She wears a dark visiting dress, tasteful, but not quite in the latest fashion.*]

HEDDA [*receives her warmly*]. How do you do, my dear Mrs. Elvsted? It's delightful to see you again.

MRS. ELVSTED [*nervously, struggling for self-control*]. Yes, it's a very long time since we met.

TESMAN [*gives her his hand*]. And we too—eh?

HEDDA. Thanks for your lovely flowers—

MRS. ELVSTED. Oh, not at all—I would have come straight here yesterday afternoon; but I heard that you were away—

TESMAN. Have you just come to town? Eh?

MRS. ELVSTED. I arrived yesterday, about midday. Oh, I was quite in despair when I heard that you were not at home.

HEDDA. In despair! How so?

TESMAN. Why, my dear Mrs. Rysing—I mean Mrs. Elvsted—

HEDDA. I hope that you are not in any trouble?

MRS. ELVSTED. Yes, I am. And I don't know another living creature here that I can turn to.

HEDDA [*laying the bouquet on the table*]. Come—let's sit here on the sofa—

MRS. ELVSTED. Oh, I am too restless to sit down.

HEDDA. Oh, no, you're not. Come here. [*She draws* MRS. ELVSTED *down upon the sofa and sits at her side.*]

TESMAN. Well? What is it, Mrs. Elvsted?

HEDDA. Has anything particular happened to you at home?

MRS. ELVSTED. Yes—and no. Oh—I am so anxious you should not misunderstand me—

HEDDA. Then your best plan is to tell us the whole story, Mrs. Elvsted.

TESMAN. I suppose that's what you have come for—eh?

MRS. ELVSTED. Yes, yes—of course it is. Well then, I must tell you—if you don't already know—that Eilert Lövborg is in town, too.

HEDDA. Lövborg—!

TESMAN. What! Has Eilert Lövborg come back? Fancy that, Hedda!

HEDDA. Well, well—I hear it.

MRS. ELVSTED. He has been here a week already. Just fancy—a whole week! In this terrible town, alone! With so many temptations on all sides.

HEDDA. But my dear Mrs. Elvsted—how does he concern you so much?

MRS. ELVSTED [*looks at her with a startled air, and says rapidly*]. He was the children's tutor.

HEDDA. Your children's?

MRS. ELVSTED. My husband's. I have none.

HEDDA. Your step-children's, then?

Mrs. Elvsted. Yes.

Tesman [*somewhat hesitatingly*]. Then was he—I don't know how to express it—was he—regular enough in his habits to be fit for the post? Eh?

Mrs. Elvsted. For the last two years his conduct has been irreproachable.

Tesman. Has it indeed? Fancy that, Hedda!

Hedda. I hear it.

Mrs. Elvsted. Perfectly irreproachable, I assure you! In every respect. But all the same—now that I know he is here—in this great town— and with a large sum of money in his hands—I can't help being in mortal fear for him.

Tesman. Why did he not remain where he was? With you and your husband? Eh?

Mrs. Elvsted. After his book was published he was too restless and unsettled to remain with us.

Tesman. Yes, by-the-bye, Aunt Julia told me he had published a new book.

Mrs. Elvsted. Yes, a big book, dealing with the march of civilization— in broad outline, as it were. It came out about a fortnight ago. And since it has sold so well, and been so much read—and made such a sensation—

Tesman. Has it indeed? It must be something he has had lying by since his better days.

Mrs. Elvsted. Long ago, you mean?

Tesman. Yes.

Mrs. Elvsted. No, he has written it all since he has been with us—within the last year.

Tesman. Isn't that good news, Hedda? Think of that.

Mrs. Elvsted. Ah, yes, if only it would last!

Hedda. Have you seen him here in town?

Mrs. Elvsted. No, not yet. I have had the greatest difficulty in finding out his address. But this morning I discovered it at last.

Hedda [*looks searchingly at her*]. Do you know, it seems to me a little odd of your husband—h'm—

Mrs. Elvsted [*starting nervously*]. Of my husband! What?

Hedda. That he should send you to town on such an errand—that he does not come himself and look after his friend.

Mrs. Elvsted. Oh, no, no—my husband has no time. And besides, I— had some shopping to do.

Hedda [*with a slight smile*]. Ah, that is a different matter.

Mrs. Elvsted [*rising quickly and uneasily*]. And now I beg and implore you, Mr. Tesman—receive Eilert Lövborg kindly if he comes to you! And that he is sure to do. You see you were such great friends in the old days. And then you are interested in the same studies—the same branch of science—so far as I can understand.

Tesman. We used to be, at any rate.

Mrs. Elvsted. That is why I beg so earnestly that you—you too—will keep a sharp eye upon him. Oh, you will promise me that, Mr. Tesman— won't you?

Tesman. With the greatest of pleasure, Mrs. Rysing—

Hedda. Elvsted.

TESMAN. I assure you I shall do all I possibly can for Eilert. You may rely upon me.

MRS. ELVSTED. Oh, how very, very kind of you! [*Presses his hands.*] Thanks, thanks, thanks! [*Frightened.*] You see, my husband is very fond of him!

HEDDA [*rising*]. You ought to write to him, Tesman. Perhaps he may not care to come to you of his own accord.

TESMAN. Well, perhaps it would be the right thing to do, Hedda? Eh?

HEDDA. And the sooner the better. Why not at once?

MRS. ELVSTED [*imploringly*]. Oh, if you only would!

TESMAN. I'll write this moment. Have you his address, Mrs.—Mrs. Elvsted?

MRS. ELVSTED. Yes. [*Takes a slip of paper from her pocket, and hands it to him.*] Here it is.

TESMAN. Good, good. Then I'll go in— [*Looks about him.*] By-the-bye,— my slippers? Oh, here. [*Takes the packet, and is about to go.*]

HEDDA. Be sure you write him a cordial, friendly letter. And a good long one too.

TESMAN. Yes, I will.

MRS. ELVSTED. But please, please don't say a word to show that I have suggested it.

TESMAN. No, how could you think I would? Eh? [*He goes out to the right, through the inner room.*]

HEDDA [*goes up to* MRS. ELVSTED, *smiles, and says in a low voice*]. There. We have killed two birds with one stone.

MRS. ELVSTED. What do you mean?

HEDDA. Could you not see that I wanted him to go?

MRS. ELVSTED. Yes, to write the letter—

HEDDA. And that I might speak to you alone.

MRS. ELVSTED [*confused*]. About the same thing?

HEDDA. Precisely.

MRS. ELVSTED [*apprehensively*]. But there is nothing more, Mrs. Tesman! Absolutely nothing!

HEDDA. Oh, yes, but there is. There is a great deal more—I can see that. Sit here—and we'll have a cosy, confidential chat. [*She forces* MRS. ELVSTED *to sit in the easy-chair beside the stove, and seats herself on one of the footstools.*]

MRS. ELVSTED [*anxiously, looking at her watch*]. But, my dear Mrs. Tesman— I was really on the point of going.

HEDDA. Oh, you can't be in such a hurry.—Well? Now tell me something about your life at home.

MRS. ELVSTED. Oh, that is just what I care least to speak about.

HEDDA. But to me, dear—? Why, weren't we school-fellows?

MRS. ELVSTED. Yes, but you were in the class above me. Oh, how dreadfully afraid of you I was then!

HEDDA. Afraid of me?

MRS. ELVSTED. *Yes,* dreadfully. For when we met on the stairs you used always to pull my hair.

HEDDA. Did I, really?

MRS. ELVSTED. Yes, and once you said you would burn it off my head.

HEDDA. Oh, that was all nonsense, of course.

MRS. ELVSTED. Yes, but I was so silly in those days.—And since then, too—we have drifted so far—far apart from each other. Our circles have been so entirely different.

HEDDA. Well then, we must try to drift together again. Now listen! At school we said *du* to each other; and we called each other by our Christian names—

MRS. ELVSTED. No, I am sure you must be mistaken.

HEDDA. No, not at all! I can remember quite distinctly. So now we are going to renew our old friendship. [*Draws the foot-stool closer to* MRS. ELVSTED.] There now! [*Kisses her cheek.*] You must say *du* to me and call me Hedda.

MRS. ELVSTED [*presses and pats her hands*]. Oh, how good and kind you are! I am not used to such kindness.

HEDDA. There, there, there! And I shall say *du* to you, as in the old days, and call you my dear Thora.

MRS. ELVSTED. My name is Thea.

HEDDA. Why, of course! I meant Thea. [*Looks at her compassionately.*] So you are not accustomed to goodness and kindness, Thea? Not in your own home?

MRS. ELVSTED. Oh, if I only had a home! But I haven't any; I have never had a home.

HEDDA [*looks at her for a moment*]. I almost suspected as much.

MRS. ELVSTED [*gazing helplessly before her*]. Yes—yes—yes.

HEDDA. I don't quite remember—was it not as housekeeper that you first went to Mr. Elvsted's?

MRS. ELVSTED. I really went as governess. But his wife—his late wife—was an invalid,—and rarely left her room. So I had to look after the housekeeping as well.

HEDDA. And then—at last—you became mistress of the house.

MRS. ELVSTED [*sadly*]. Yes, I did.

HEDDA. Let me see—about how long ago was that?

MRS. ELVSTED. My marriage?

HEDDA. Yes.

MRS. ELVSTED. Five years ago.

HEDDA. To be sure; it must be that.

MRS. ELVSTED. Oh, those five years—! Or at all events the last two or three of them! Oh, if you could only imagine—

HEDDA [*giving her a little slap on the hand*]. De? Fie, Thea!

MRS. ELVSTED. Yes, yes, I will try—Well if—you could only imagine and understand—

HEDDA [*lightly*]. Eilert Lövborg has been in your neighborhood about three years, hasn't he?

MRS. ELVSTED [*looks at her doubtfully*]. Eilert Lövborg? Yes—he has.

HEDDA. Had you known him before, in town here?

MRS. ELVSTED. Scarcely at all. I mean—I knew him by name of course.

HEDDA. But you saw a good deal of him in the country?

MRS. ELVSTED. Yes, he came to us every day. You see, he gave the children lessons; for in the long run I couldn't manage it all myself.

HEDDA. No, that's clear.—And your husband—? I suppose he is often away from home?

MRS. ELVSTED. Yes. Being Sheriff, you know, he has to travel about a good deal in his district.

HEDDA [*leaning against the arm of the chair*]. Thea—my poor, sweet Thea—now you must tell me everything—exactly as it stands.

MRS. ELVSTED. Well then, you must question me.

HEDDA. What sort of a man is your husband, Thea? I mean—you know—in everyday life. Is he kind to you?

MRS. ELVSTED [*evasively*]. I am sure he means well in everything.

HEDDA. I should think he must be altogether too old for you. There is at least twenty years' difference between you, is there not?

MRS. ELVSTED [*irritably*]. Yes, that is true, too. Everything about him is repellent to me! We have not a thought in common. We have no single point of sympathy—he and I.

HEDDA. But is he not fond of you all the same? In his own way?

MRS. ELVSTED. Oh, I really don't know. I think he regards me simply as a useful property. And then it doesn't cost much to keep me. I am not expensive.

HEDDA. That is stupid of you.

MRS. ELVSTED [*shakes her head*]. It cannot be otherwise—not with him. I don't think he really cares for any one but himself—and perhaps a little for the children.

HEDDA. And for Eilert Lövborg, Thea.

MRS. ELVSTED [*looking at her*]. For Eilert Lövborg? What puts that into your head?

HEDDA. Well, my dear—I should say, when he sends you after him all the way to town—[*smiling almost imperceptibly*]. And besides, you said so yourself, to Tesman.

MRS. ELVSTED [*with a little nervous twitch*]. Did I? Yes, I suppose I did. [*Vehemently, but not loudly.*] No—I may just as well make a clean breast of it at once! For it must all come out in any case.

HEDDA. Why, my dear Thea—?

MRS. ELVSTED. Well, to make a long story short: My husband did not know that I was coming.

HEDDA. What! Your husband didn't know it!

MRS. ELVSTED. No, of course not. For that matter, he was away from home himself—he was traveling. Oh, I could bear it no longer, Hedda! I couldn't indeed—so utterly alone as I should have been in future.

HEDDA. Well? And then?

MRS. ELVSTED. So I put together some of my things—what I needed most—as quietly as possible. And then I left the house.

HEDDA. Without a word?

MRS. ELVSTED. Yes—and took the train straight to town.

HEDDA. Why, my dear, good Thea—to think of you daring to do it?

MRS. ELVSTED [*rises and moves about the room*]. What else could I possibly do?

HEDDA. But what do you think your husband will say when you go home again?

MRS. ELVSTED [*at the table, looks at her*]. Back to him?

HEDDA. Of course.

MRS. ELVSTED. I shall never go back to him again.

HEDDA [*rising and going towards her*]. Then you have left your home—for good and all?

MRS. ELVSTED. Yes. There was nothing else to be done.

HEDDA. But then—to take flight so openly.

MRS. ELVSTED. Oh, it's impossible to keep things of that sort secret.

HEDDA. But what do you think people will say of you, Thea?

MRS. ELVSTED. They may say what they like for aught *I* care. [*Seats herself wearily and sadly on the sofa.*] I have done nothing but what I had to do.

HEDDA [*after a short silence*]. And what are your plans now? What do you think of doing?

MRS. ELVSTED. I don't know yet. I only know this, that I must live here, where Eilert Lövborg is—if I am to live at all.

HEDDA [*takes a chair from the table, seats herself beside her, and strokes her hands*]. My dear Thea—how did this—this friendship—between you and Eilert Lövborg come about?

MRS. ELVSTED. Oh, it grew up gradually. I gained a sort of influence over him.

HEDDA. Indeed?

MRS. ELVSTED. He gave up his old habits. Not because I asked him to, for I never dared do that. But of course he saw how repulsive they were to me; and so he dropped them.

HEDDA [*concealing an involuntary smile of scorn*]. Then you have reclaimed him—as the saying goes—my little Thea.

MRS. ELVSTED. So he says himself, at any rate. And he, on his side, has made a real human being of me—taught me to think, and to understand so many things.

HEDDA. Did he give you lessons too, then?

MRS. ELVSTED. No, not exactly lessons. But he talked to me—talked about such an infinity of things. And then came the lovely, happy time when I began to share in his work—when he allowed me to help him!

HEDDA. Oh, he did, did he?

MRS. ELVSTED. Yes! He never wrote anything without my assistance.

HEDDA. You were two good comrades, in fact?

MRS. ELVSTED [*eagerly*]. Comrades! Yes, fancy, Hedda—that is the very word he used!—Oh, I ought to feel perfectly happy; and yet I cannot; for I don't know how long it will last.

HEDDA. Are you no surer of him than that?

MRS. ELVSTED [*gloomily*]. A woman's shadow stands between Eilert Lövborg and me.

HEDDA [*looks at her anxiously*]. Who can that be?

MRS. ELVSTED. I don't know. Some one he knew in his—in his past. Some one he has never been able wholly to forget.

HEDDA. What has he told you—about this?

MRS. ELVSTED. He has only once—quite vaguely—alluded to it.

HEDDA. Well! And what did he say?

MRS. ELVSTED. He said that when they parted, she threatened to shoot him with a pistol.

HEDDA [*with cold composure*]. Oh, nonsense! No one does that sort of thing here.

MRS. ELVSTED. No. And that is why I think it must have been that red-haired singing woman whom he once—

HEDDA. Yes, very likely.

MRS. ELVSTED. For I remember they used to say of her that she carried loaded firearms.

HEDDA. Oh—then of course it must have been her.

MRS. ELVSTED [*wringing her hands*]. And now just fancy, Hedda—I hear that this singing-woman—that she is in town again! Oh, I don't know what to do—

HEDDA [*glancing towards the inner room*]. Hush! Here comes Tesman. [*Rises and whispers.*] Thea—all this must remain between you and me.

MRS. ELVSTED [*springing up*]. Oh, yes, yes! for heaven's sake—! [GEORGE TESMAN, *with a letter in his hand, comes from the right through the inner room.*]

TESMAN. There now—the epistle is finished.

HEDDA. That's right. And now Mrs. Elvsted is just going. Wait a moment—I'll go with you to the garden gate.

TESMAN. Do you think Berta could post the letter, Hedda dear?

HEDDA [*takes it*]. I will tell her to. [BERTA *enters from the hall.*]

BERTA. Judge Brack wishes to know if Mrs. Tesman will receive him.

HEDDA. Yes, ask Judge Brack to come in. And look here—put this letter in the post.

BERTA [*taking the letter*]. Yes, ma'am. [*She opens the door for* JUDGE BRACK *and goes out herself.* BRACK *is a man of forty-five; thick-set, but well-built and elastic in his movements. His face is roundish with an aristocratic profile. His hair is short, still almost black, and carefully dressed. His eyes are lively and sparkling. His eyebrows thick. His moustaches are also thick, with short-cut ends. He wears a well-cut walking-suit, a little too youthful for his age. He uses an eye-glass, which he now and then lets drop.*]

JUDGE BRACK [*with his hat in his hand, bowing*]. May one venture to call so early in the day?

HEDDA. Of course one may.

TESMAN [*presses his hand*]. You are welcome at any time. [*Introducing him.*] Judge Brack—Miss Rysing—

HEDDA. Oh—!

BRACK [*bowing*]. Ah—delighted—

HEDDA [*looks at him and laughs*]. It's nice to have a look at you by daylight, Judge!

BRACK. Do you find me—altered?

HEDDA. A little younger, I think.

BRACK. Thank you so much.

TESMAN. But what do you think of Hedda—eh? Doesn't she look flourishing? She has actually—

HEDDA. Oh, do leave me alone. You haven't thanked Judge Brack for all the trouble he has taken—

BRACK. Oh, nonsense—it was a pleasure to me—

HEDDA. Yes, you are a friend indeed. But here stands Thea all impatience to be off—so *au revoir*, Judge. I shall be back again presently. [*Mutual salutations.* MRS. ELVSTED *and* HEDDA *go out by the hall door.*]

BRACK. Well,—is your wife tolerably satisfied—

TESMAN. Yes, we can't thank you sufficiently. Of course she talks of a little re-arrangement here and there; and one or two things are still wanting. We shall have to buy some additional trifles.

BRACK. Indeed!

TESMAN. But we won't trouble you about these things. Hedda says she herself will look after what is wanting.—Shan't we sit down? Eh?

BRACK. Thanks, for a moment. [*Seats himself beside the table.*] There is something I wanted to speak to you about, my dear Tesman.

TESMAN. Indeed? Ah, I understand! [*Seating himself.*] I suppose it's the serious part of the frolic that is coming now. Eh?

BRACK. Oh, the money question is not so very pressing; though, for that matter, I wish we had gone a little more economically to work.

TESMAN. But that would never have done, you know! Think of Hedda, my dear fellow! You, who know her so well—. I couldn't possibly ask her to put up with a shabby style of living!

BRACK. No, no—that is just the difficulty.

TESMAN. And then—fortunately—it can't be long before I receive my appointment.

BRACK. Well, you see—such things are often apt to hang fire for a time.

TESMAN. Have you heard anything definite? Eh?

BRACK. Nothing exactly definite—[*interrupting himself*]. But, by-the-bye—I have one piece of news for you.

TESMAN. Well?

BRACK. Your old friend, Eilert Lövborg, has returned to town.

TESMAN. I know that already.

BRACK. Indeed! How did you learn it?

TESMAN. From that lady who went out with Hedda.

BRACK. Really? What was her name? I didn't quite catch it.

TESMAN. Mrs. Elvsted.

BRACK. Aha—Sheriff Elvsted's wife? Of course—he has been living up in their regions.

TESMAN. And fancy—I'm delighted to hear that he is quite a reformed character!

BRACK. So they say.

TESMAN. And then he has published a new book—eh?

BRACK. Yes, indeed he has.

TESMAN. And I hear it has made some sensation!

BRACK. Quite an unusual sensation.

TESMAN. Fancy—isn't that good news! A man of such extraordinary talents—I felt so grieved to think that he had gone irretrievably to ruin.

BRACK. That was what everybody thought.

TESMAN. But I cannot imagine what he will take to now! How in the world will he be able to make his living? Eh? [*During the last words,* HEDDA *has entered by the hall door.*]

HEDDA [*to* BRACK, *laughing with a touch of scorn*]. Tesman is forever worrying about how people are to make their living.

TESMAN. Well, you see, dear—we were talking about poor Eilert Lövborg.

HEDDA [*glancing at him rapidly*]. Oh, indeed? [*Seats herself in the arm-chair beside the stove and asks indifferently.*] What is the matter with him?

TESMAN. Well—no doubt he has run through all his property long ago; and he can scarcely write a new book every year—eh? So I really can't see what is to become of him.

BRACK. Perhaps I can give you some information on that point.

TESMAN. Indeed!

BRACK. You must remember that his relations have a good deal of influence.

TESMAN. Oh, his relations, unfortunately have entirely washed their hands of him.

BRACK. At one time they called him the hope of the family.

TESMAN. At one time, yes! But he has put an end to all that.

HEDDA. Who knows? [*With a slight smile.*] I hear they have reclaimed him up at Sheriff Elvsted's—

BRACK. And then this book that he has published—

TESMAN. Well, well, I hope to goodness they may find something for him to do. I have just written to him. I asked him to come and see us this evening, Hedda dear.

BRACK. But, my dear fellow, you are booked for my bachelors' party this evening. You promised on the pier last night.

HEDDA. Had you forgotten, Tesman?

TESMAN. Yes, I had utterly forgotten.

BRACK. But it doesn't matter, for you may be sure he won't come.

TESMAN. What makes you think that? Eh?

BRACK [*with a little hesitation, rising and resting his hands on the back of his chair*]. My dear Tesman—and you too, Mrs. Tesman—I think I ought not to keep you in the dark about something that—that—

TESMAN. That concerns Eilert—?

BRACK. Both you and him.

TESMAN. Well, my dear Judge, out with it.

BRACK. You must be prepared to find your appointment deferred longer than you desired or expected.

TESMAN [*jumping up uneasily*]. Is there some hitch about it? Eh?

BRACK. The nomination may perhaps be made conditional on the result of a competition—

TESMAN. Competition! Think of that, Hedda!

HEDDA [*leans farther back in the chair*]. Aha—aha!

TESMAN. But who can my competitor be? Surely not—?

BRACK. Yes, precisely—Eilert Lövborg.

TESMAN [*clasping his hands*]. No, no—it's quite inconceivable! Quite impossible! Eh?

BRACK. H'm—that is what it may come to, all the same.

TESMAN. Well but, Judge Brack—it would show the most incredible lack of consideration for me. [*Gesticulates with his arms*]. For—just think— I'm a married man. We have been married on the strength of these prospects, Hedda and I; and run deep into debt; and borrowed money from Aunt Julia too. Good heavens, they had as good as promised me the appointment. Eh?

BRACK. Well, well, well—no doubt you will get it in the end; only after a contest.

HEDDA [*immovable in her arm-chair*]. Fancy, Tesman, there will be a sort of sporting interest in that.

TESMAN. Why, my dearest Hedda, how can you be so indifferent about it?

HEDDA [*as before*]. I am not at all indifferent. I am most eager to see who wins.

BRACK. In any case, Mrs. Tesman, it is best that you should know how matters stand. I mean—before you set about the little purchases I hear you are threatening.

HEDDA. This can make no difference.

BRACK. Indeed! Then I have no more to say. Good-bye! [*To* TESMAN.]. I shall look in on my way back from my afternoon walk, and take you home with me.

TESMAN. Oh, yes, yes—your news has quite upset me.

HEDDA [*reclining, holds out her hand*]. Good-bye, Judge; and be sure you call in the afternoon.

BRACK. Many thanks. Good-bye, good-bye!

TESMAN [*accompanying him to the door*]. Good-bye, my dear Judge! You must really excuse me—[JUDGE BRACK *goes out by the hall door*].

TESMAN [*crosses the room*]. Oh, Hedda—one should never rush into adventures. Eh?

HEDDA [*looks at him, smiling*]. Do you do that?

TESMAN. Yes, dear—there is no denying—it was adventurous to go and marry and set up house upon mere expectations.

HEDDA. Perhaps you are right there.

TESMAN. Well—at all events, we have our delightful home, Hedda! Fancy, the home we both dreamed of—the home we were in love with, I may almost say. Eh?

HEDDA [*rising slowly and wearily*]. It was part of our compact that we were to go into society—to keep open house.

TESMAN. Yes, if you only knew how I had been looking forward to it! Fancy—to see you as hostess—in a select circle? Eh? Well, well, well— for the present we shall have to get on without society, Hedda—only to invite Aunt Julia now and then.—Oh, I intended you to lead such an utterly different life, dear—!

HEDDA. Of course I cannot have my man in livery just yet.

TESMAN. Oh no, unfortunately. It would be out of the question for us to keep a footman, you know.

HEDDA. And the saddle-horse I was to have had—

TESMAN [*aghast*]. The saddle-horse!

HEDDA. —I suppose I must not think of that now.

TESMAN. Good heavens, no!—that's as clear as daylight.

HEDDA [*goes up the room*]. Well, I shall have one thing at least to kill time with in the meanwhile.

TESMAN [*beaming*]. Oh, thank heaven for that! What is it, Hedda? Eh?

HEDDA [*in the middle doorway, looks at him with covert scorn*]. My pistols, George.

TESMAN [*in alarm*]. Your pistols!

HEDDA [*with cold eyes.*]. General Gabler's pistols. [*She goes out through the inner room, to the left.*]

TESMAN [*rushes up to the middle doorway and calls after her*]. No, for heaven's sake, Hedda darling—don't touch those dangerous things! For my sake, Hedda! Eh?

ACT II

[*The room at the* TESMANS' *as in the first act, except that the piano has been removed, and an elegant little writing-table with bookshelves put in its place. A smaller table stands near the sofa at the left. Most of the bouquets have been taken away.* MRS. ELVSTED'S *bouquet is upon the large table in front.—It is afternoon.* HEDDA, *dressed to receive callers, is alone in the room. She stands by the open glass door, loading a revolver. The fellow to it lies in an open pistol-case on the writing-table.*]

HEDDA [*looks down the garden, and calls*]. So you are here again, Judge!

BRACK [*is heard calling from a distance*]. As you see, Mrs. Tesman!

HEDDA [*raises the pistol and points*]. Now I'll shoot you, Judge Brack!

BRACK [*calling unseen*]. No, no, no! Don't stand aiming at me!

HEDDA. This is what comes of sneaking in by the back way. [*She fires.*]

BRACK [*nearer*]. Are you out of your senses—!

HEDDA. Dear me—did I happen to hit you?

BRACK [*still outside*]. I wish you would let these pranks alone!

HEDDA. Come in then, Judge. [JUDGE BRACK, *dressed as though for a men's party, enters by the glass door. He carries a light overcoat over his arm.*]

BRACK. What the deuce—haven't you tired of that sport, yet? What are you shooting at?

HEDDA. Oh, I am only firing in the air.

BRACK [*gently takes the pistol out of her hand*]. Allow me, madam! [*Looks at it.*] Ah—I know this pistol well! [*Looks around.*] Where is the case? Ah, here it is. [*Lays the pistol in it, and shuts it.*] Now we won't play at that game any more today.

HEDDA. Then what in heaven's name would you have me do with myself?

BRACK. Have you had no visitors?

HEDDA [*closing the glass door*]. Not one. I suppose all our set are still out of town.

BRACK. And is Tesman not at home either?

HEDDA [*at the writing-table, putting the pistol-case in a drawer which she shuts*]. No. He rushed off to his aunt's directly after lunch; he didn't expect you so early.

BRACK. H'm—how stupid of me not to have thought of that!

HEDDA [*turning her head to look at him*]. Why stupid?

BRACK. Because if I had thought of it I should have come a little—earlier.

HEDDA [*crossing the room*]. Then you would have found no one to receive you; for I have been in my room changing my dress ever since lunch.

BRACK. And is there no sort of little chink that we could hold a parley through?

HEDDA. You have forgotten to arrange one.

BRACK. That was another piece of stupidity.

HEDDA. Well, we must just settle down here—and wait. Tesman is not likely to be back for some time yet.

BRACK. Never mind; I shall not be impatient. [HEDDA *seats herself in the corner of the sofa.* BRACK *lays his overcoat over the back of the nearest chair, and sits down, but keeps his hat in his hand. A short silence. They look at each other.*]

HEDDA. Well?

BRACK [*in the same tone*]. Well?

HEDDA. I spoke first.

BRACK [*bending a little forward*]. Come, let us have a cosy little chat, Mrs. Hedda.

HEDDA [*leaning further back in the sofa*]. Does it not seem like a whole eternity since our last talk? Of course I don't count those few words yesterday evening and this morning.

BRACK. You mean since our last confidential talk? Our last *tête-à-tête?*

HEDDA. Well, yes—since you put it so.

BRACK. Not a day has passed but I have wished that you were home again.

HEDDA. And I have done nothing but wish the same thing.

BRACK. You? Really, Mrs. Hedda? And I thought you had been enjoying your tour so much!

HEDDA. Oh, yes, you may be sure of that!

BRACK. But Tesman's letters spoke of nothing but happiness.

HEDDA. Oh, Tesman! You see, he thinks nothing so delightful as grubbing in libraries and making copies of old parchments, or whatever you call them.

BRACK [*with a spice of malice*]. Well, that is his vocation in life—or part of it at any rate.

HEDDA. Yes, of course; and no doubt when it's your vocation—But *I!* Oh, my dear Mr. Brack, how mortally bored I have been.

BRACK [*sympathetically*]. Do you really say so? In downright earnest?

HEDDA. Yes, you can surely understand it—! To go for six whole months without meeting a soul that knew anything of our circle, or could talk about the things we are interested in.

BRACK. Yes, yes—I too should feel that a deprivation.

HEDDA. And then, what I found most intolerable of all—

BRACK. Well?

HEDDA. —was being everlastingly in the company of—one and the same person—

BRACK [*with a nod of assent*]. Morning, noon, and night, yes—at all possible times and seasons.

HEDDA. I said "everlastingly."

BRACK. Just so. But I should have thought, with our excellent Tesman, one could—

HEDDA. Tesman is—a specialist, my dear Judge.

BRACK. Undeniably.

HEDDA. And specialists are not at all amusing to travel with. Not in the long run at any rate.

BRACK. Not even—the specialist one happens to love?

HEDDA. Faugh—don't use that sickening word!

BRACK [*taken aback*]. What do you say, Mrs. Hedda?

HEDDA [*half laughing, half irritated*]. You should just try it! To hear of nothing but the history of civilization, morning, noon, and night—

BRACK. Everlastingly.

HEDDA. Yes, yes, yes! And then all this about the domestic industry of the middle ages—! That's the most disgusting part of it!

BRACK [*looks searchingly at her*]. But tell me—in that case, how am I to understand your—? H'm—

HEDDA. My accepting George Tesman, you mean?

BRACK. Well, let us put it so.

HEDDA. Good heavens, do you see anything so wonderful in that?

BRACK. Yes and no—Mrs. Hedda.

HEDDA. I had positively danced myself tired, my dear Judge. My day was done— [*With a slight shudder.*] Oh, no—I won't say that; nor think it either!

BRACK. You have assuredly no reason to.

HEDDA. Oh, reasons— [*Watching him closely.*] And George Tesman—after all, you must admit that he is correctness itself.

BRACK. His correctness and respectability are beyond all question.

HEDDA. And I don't see anything absolutely ridiculous about him.—Do you?

BRACK. Ridiculous? N—no—I shouldn't exactly say so—

HEDDA. Well—and his powers of research, at all events, are untiring.—I see no reason why he should not one day come to the front, after all.

BRACK [*looks at her hesitatingly*]. I thought that you, like every one else, expected him to attain the highest distinction.

HEDDA [*with an expression of fatigue*]. Yes, so I did.—And then, since he was bent, at all hazards, on being allowed to provide for me—I really don't know why I should not have accepted his offer?

BRACK. No—if you look at it in that light—

HEDDA. It was more than my other adorers were prepared to do for me, my dear Judge.

BRACK [*laughing*]. Well, I can't answer for all the rest; but as for myself, you know quite well that I have always entertained a—a certain respect for the marriage tie—for marriage as an institution, Mrs. Hedda.

HEDDA [*jestingly*]. Oh, I assure you I have never cherished any hopes with respect to you.

BRACK. All I require is a pleasant and intimate interior, where I can make myself useful in every way, and am free to come and go as—a trusted friend—

HEDDA. Of the master of the house, do you mean?

BRACK [*bowing*]. Frankly—of the mistress first of all; but of course of the master, too, in the second place. Such a triangular friendship—if I may call it so—is really a great convenience for all parties, let me tell you.

HEDDA. Yes, I have many a time longed for some one to make a third on our travels. Oh—those railway-carriage *tête-à-têtes*—!

BRACK. Fortunately your wedding journey is over now.

HEDDA [*shaking her head*]. Not by a long—long way. I have only arrived at a station on the line.

BRACK. Well, then the passengers jump out and move about a little, Mrs. Hedda.

HEDDA. I never jump out.

BRACK. Really?

HEDDA. No—because there is always some one standing by to—

BRACK [*laughing*]. To look at your ankles, do you mean?

HEDDA. Precisely.

BRACK. Well but, dear me—

HEDDA [*with a gesture of repulsion*]. I won't have it. I would rather keep my seat where I happen to be—and continue the *tête-à-tête*.

BRACK. But suppose a third person were to jump in and join the couple.

HEDDA. Ah—that is quite another matter!

BRACK. A trusted, sympathetic friend—

HEDDA. —with a fund of conversation on all sorts of lively topics—

BRACK. —and not the least bit of a specialist!

HEDDA [*with an audible sigh*]. Yes, that would be a relief indeed.

BRACK [*hears the front door open, and glances in that direction*]. The triangle is completed.

HEDDA [*half aloud*]. And on goes the train. [GEORGE TESMAN, *in a gray walking-suit, with a soft felt hat, enters from the hall. He has a number of unbound books under his arm and in his pockets.*]

TESMAN [*goes up to the table beside the corner settee*]. Ouf—what a load for a warm day—all these books. [*Lays them on the table.*] I'm positively perspiring, Hedda. Hallo—are you there already, my dear Judge? Eh? Berta didn't tell me.

BRACK [*rising*]. I came in through the garden.

HEDDA. What books have you got there?

TESMAN [*stands looking them through*]. Some new books on my special subjects—quite indispensable to me.

HEDDA. Your special subjects?

BRACK. Yes, books on his special subjects, Mrs. Tesman. [BRACK *and* HEDDA *exchange a confidential smile.*]

HEDDA. Do you need still more books on your special subjects?

TESMAN. Yes, my dear Hedda, one can never have too many of them. Of course one must keep up with all that is written and published.

HEDDA. Yes, I suppose one must.

TESMAN [*searching among his books*]. And look here—I have got hold of Eilert Lövborg's new book too. [*Offering it to her.*] Perhaps you would like to glance through it, Hedda? Eh?

HEDDA. No, thank you. Or rather—afterwards perhaps.

TESMAN. I looked into it a little on the way home.

BRACK. Well, what do you think of it—as a specialist?

TESMAN. I think it shows quite remarkable soundness of judgment. He never wrote like that before. [*Putting the books together.*] Now I shall take all these into my study. I'm longing to cut the leaves—! And then I must change my clothes. [*To* BRACK.] I suppose we needn't start just yet? Eh?

BRACK. Oh, dear no—there is not the slightest hurry.

TESMAN. Well then, I will take my time. [*Is going with his books, but stops in the doorway and turns.*] By-the-bye, Hedda—Aunt Julia is not coming this evening.

HEDDA. Not coming? Is it that affair of the bonnet that keeps her away?

TESMAN. Oh, not at all. How could you think such a thing of Aunt Julia? Just fancy—! The fact is, Aunt Rina is very ill.

HEDDA. She always is.

TESMAN. Yes, but today she is much worse than usual, poor dear.

HEDDA. Oh, then it's only natural that her sister should remain with her. I must bear my disappointment.

TESMAN. And you can't imagine, dear, how delighted Aunt Julia seemed to be—because you had come home looking so flourishing!

HEDDA [*half aloud, rising*]. Oh, those everlasting aunts!

TESMAN. What?

HEDDA [*going to the glass door*]. Nothing.

TESMAN. Oh, all right. [*He goes through the inner room, out to the right.*]

BRACK. What bonnet were you talking about?

HEDDA. Oh, it was a little episode with Miss Tesman this morning. She had laid down her bonnet on the chair there—[*looks at him and smiles*]—And I pretended to think it was the servant's.

BRACK [*shaking his head*]. Now my dear Mrs. Hedda, how could you do such a thing? To that excellent old lady, too!

HEDDA [*nervously crossing the room*]. Well, you see—these impulses come over me all of a sudden; and I cannot resist them. [*Throws herself down in the easy-chair by the stove.*] Oh, I don't know how to explain it.

BRACK [*behind the easy-chair*]. You are not really happy—that is at the bottom of it.

HEDDA [*looking straight before her*]. I know of no reason why I should be—happy. Perhaps you can give me one?

BRACK. Well—amongst other things, because you have got exactly the home you had set your heart on.

HEDDA [*looks up at him and laughs*]. Do you too believe in that legend?

BRACK. Is there nothing in it, then?

HEDDA Oh, yes, there is something in it.

BRACK. Well?

HEDDA. There is this in it, that I made use of Tesman to see me home from evening parties last summer—

BRACK. I, unfortunately, had to go quite a different way.

HEDDA. That's true. I know you were going a different way last summer.

BRACK [*laughing*]. Oh, fie, Mrs. Hedda! Well, then—you and Tesman—?

HEDDA. Well, we happened to pass here one evening; Tesman, poor fellow, was writhing in the agony of having to find conversation; so I took pity on the learned man—

BRACK [*smiles doubtfully*]. You took pity? H'm—

HEDDA. Yes, I really did. And so—to help him out of his torment—I happened to say, in pure thoughtlessness, that I should like to live in this villa.

BRACK. No more than that?

HEDDA. Not that evening.

BRACK. But afterwards?

HEDDA. Yes, my thoughtlessness had consequences, my dear Judge.

BRACK. Unfortunately that too often happens, Mrs. Hedda.

HEDDA. Thanks! So you see it was this enthusiasm for Secretary Falk's villa that first constituted a bond of sympathy between George Tesman and me. From that came our engagement and our marriage, and our wedding journey, and all the rest of it. Well, well, my dear Judge—as you make your bed so you must lie, I could almost say.

BRACK. This is exquisite! And you really cared not a rap about it all the time?

HEDDA. No, heaven knows I didn't.

BRACK. But now? Now that we have made it so homelike for you?

HEDDA. Uh—the rooms all seem to smell of lavender and dried rose-leaves.—But perhaps it's Aunt Julia that has brought that scent with her.

BRACK [*laughing*]. No, I think it must be a legacy from the late Mrs. Secretary Falk.

HEDDA. Yes, there is an odor of mortality about it. It reminds me of a bouquet—the day after the ball. [*Clasps her hands behind her head, leans back in her chair and looks at him.*] Oh, my dear Judge—you cannot imagine how horribly I shall bore myself here.

BRACK. Why should not you, too, find some sort of vocation in life, Mrs. Hedda?

HEDDA. A vocation—that should attract me?

BRACK. If possible, of course.

HEDDA. Heaven knows what sort of a vocation that could be. I often wonder whether— [*breaking off*]. But that would never do either.

BRACK. Who can tell? Let me hear what it is.

HEDDA. Whether I might not get Tesman to go into politics, I mean.

BRACK [*laughing*]. Tesman? No, really now, political life is not the thing for him—not at all in his line.

HEDDA. No, I daresay not.—But if I could get him into it all the same?

BRACK. Why—what satisfaction could you find in that? If he is not fitted for that sort of thing, why should you want to drive him into it?

HEDDA. Because I am bored, I tell you! [*After a pause.*] So you think it quite out of the question that Tesman should ever get into the ministry?

BRACK. H'm—you see, my dear Mrs. Hedda—to get into the ministry, he would have to be a tolerably rich man.

HEDDA [*rising impatiently*]. Yes, there we have it! It is this genteel poverty I have managed to drop into—! [*Crosses the room.*] That is what makes life so pitiable! So utterly ludicrous!—For that's what it is.

BRACK. Now *I* should say the fault lay elsewhere.

HEDDA. Where, then?

BRACK. You have never gone through any really stimulating experience.

HEDDA. Anything serious, you mean?

BRACK. Yes, you may call it so. But now you may perhaps have one in store.

HEDDA [*tossing her head*]. Oh, you're thinking of the annoyances about this wretched professorship! But that must be Tesman's own affair. I assure you I shall not waste a thought upon it.

BRACK. No, no. I daresay not. But suppose now that what people call—in elegant language—a solemn responsibility were to come upon you? [*Smiling.*] A new responsibility, Mrs. Hedda?

HEDDA [*angrily*]. Be quiet! Nothing of that sort will ever happen!

BRACK [*warily*]. We will speak of this again a year hence—at the very outside.

HEDDA [*curtly*]. I have no turn for anything of the sort, Judge Brack. No responsibilities for me!

BRACK. Are you so unlike the generality of women as to have no turn for duties which—?

HEDDA [*beside the glass door*]. Oh, be quiet, I tell you!—I often think there is only one thing in the world I have any turn for.

BRACK [*drawing near to her*]. And what is that, if I may ask?

HEDDA [*stands looking out*]. Boring myself to death. Now you know it. [*Turns, looks towards the inner room, and laughs.*] Yes, as I thought! Here comes the Professor.

BRACK [*softly, in a tone of warning*]. Come, come, come, Mrs. Hedda! [GEORGE TESMAN, *dressed for the party, with his gloves and hat in his hand, enters from the right through the inner room.*]

TESMAN. Hedda, has no message come from Eilert Lövborg? Eh?

HEDDA. No.

TESMAN. Then you'll see he'll be here presently.

BRACK. Do you really think he will come?

TESMAN. Yes, I am almost sure of it. For what you were telling us this morning must have been a mere floating rumor.

BRACK. You think so?

TESMAN. At any rate, Aunt Julia said she did not believe for a moment that he would ever stand in my way again. Fancy that!

BRACK. Well then, that's all right.

TESMAN [*placing his hat and gloves on a chair on the right*]. Yes, but you must really let me wait for him as long as possible.

BRACK. We have plenty of time yet. None of my guests will arrive before seven or half-past.

TESMAN. Then meanwhile we can keep Hedda company, and see what happens. Eh?

HEDDA [*placing* BRACK's *hat and overcoat upon the corner settee*]. And at the worst Mr. Lövborg can remain here with me.

BRACK [*offering to take his things*]. Oh, allow me, Mrs. Tesman!—What do you mean by "At the worst"?

HEDDA. If he won't go with you and Tesman.

TESMAN [*looks dubiously at her*]. But, Hedda dear—do you think it would quite do for him to remain with you? Eh? Remember, Aunt Julia can't come.

HEDDA. No, but Mrs. Elvsted is coming. We three can have a cup of tea together.

TESMAN. Oh, yes, that will be all right.

BRACK [*smiling*]. And that would perhaps be the safest plan for him.

HEDDA. Why so?

BRACK. Well, you know, Mrs. Tesman, how you used to gird at my little bachelor parties. You declared they were adapted only for men of the strictest principles.

HEDDA. But no doubt Mr. Lövborg's principles are strict enough now. A converted sinner— [BERTA *appears at the hall door.*]

BERTA. There's a gentleman asking if you are at home, ma'am—

HEDDA. Well, show him in.

TESMAN [*softly*]. I'm sure it is he! Fancy that! [EILERT LÖVBORG *enters from the hall. He is slim and lean; of the same age as* TESMAN, *but looks older and somewhat worn-out. His hair and beard are of a blackish brown, his face long and pale, but with patches of color on the cheek-bones. He is dressed in a well-cut black visiting suit, quite new. He has dark gloves and a silk hat. He stops near the door, and makes a rapid bow, seeming somewhat embarrassed.*]

TESMAN [*goes up to him and shakes him warmly by the hand*]. Well, my dear Eilert—so at last we meet again!

EILERT LÖVBORG [*speaks in a subdued voice*]. Thanks for your letter, Tesman. [*Approaching* HEDDA.] Will you too shake hands with me, Mrs. Tesman?

HEDDA [*taking his hand*]. I am glad to see you, Mr. Lövborg. [*With a motion of her hand.*] I don't know whether you two gentlemen—?

LÖVBORG [*bowing slightly*]. Judge Brack, I think.

BRACK [*doing likewise*]. Oh, yes,—in the old days—

TESMAN [*to* LÖVBORG, *with his hands on his shoulders*]. And now you must make yourself entirely at home, Eilert! Mustn't he, Hedda?—For I hear you are going to settle in town again? Eh?

LÖVBORG. Yes, I am.

TESMAN. Quite right, quite right. Let me tell you, I have got hold of your new book; but I haven't had time to read it yet.

LÖVBORG. You may spare yourself the trouble.

TESMAN. Why so?

LÖVBORG. Because there is very little in it.

TESMAN. Just fancy—how can you say so?

BRACK. But it has been very much praised, I hear.

LÖVBORG. That was what I wanted; so I put nothing into the book but what every one would agree with.

BRACK. Very wise of you.

TESMAN. Well but, my dear Eilert—!

LÖVBORG. For now I mean to win myself a position again—to make a fresh start.

TESMAN [*a little embarrassed*]. Ah, that is what you wish to do? Eh?

LÖVBORG [*smiling, lays down his hat, and draws a packet, wrapped in paper, from his coat pocket*]. But when this one appears, George Tesman, you will have to read it. For this is the real book—the book I have put my true self into.

TESMAN. Indeed? And what is it?

LÖVBORG. It is the continuation.

TESMAN. The continuation? Of what?

LÖVBORG. Of the book.

TESMAN. Of the new book?

LÖVBORG. Of course.

TESMAN. Why, my dear Eilert—does it not come down to our own days?

LÖVBORG. Yes, it does; and this one deals with the future.

TESMAN. With the future! But, good heavens, we know nothing of the future!

LÖVBORG. No; but there is a thing or two to be said about it all the same. [*Opens the packet.*] Look here—

TESMAN. Why, that's not your handwriting.

LÖVBORG. I dictated it. [*Turning over the pages.*] It falls into two sections. The first deals with the civilizing forces of the future. And here is the second—[*running through the pages towards the end*]—forecasting the probable line of development.

TESMAN. How odd now! I should never have thought of writing anything of that sort.

HEDDA [*at the glass door, drumming on the pane*]. H'm—I daresay not.

LÖVBORG [*replacing the manuscript in its paper and laying the packet on the table*]. I brought it, thinking I might read you a little of it this evening.

TESMAN. That was very good of you, Eilert. But this evening—? [*Looking at* BRACK.] I don't quite see how we can manage it—

LÖVBORG. Well, then, some other time. There is no hurry.

BRACK. I must tell you, Mr. Lövborg—there is a little gathering at my house this evening—mainly in honor of Tesman, you know—

LÖVBORG [*looking for his hat*]. Oh—then I won't detain you—

BRACK. No, but listen—will you not do me the favor of joining us?

LÖVBORG [*curtly and decidedly*]. No, I can't—thank you very much.

BRACK. Oh, nonsense—do! We shall be quite a select little circle. And I assure you we shall have a "lively time," as Mrs. Hed—as Mrs. Tesman says.

LÖVBORG. I have no doubt of it. But nevertheless—

BRACK. And then you might bring your manuscript with you, and read it to Tesman at my house. I could give you a room to yourselves.

TESMAN. Yes, think of that, Eilert,—why shouldn't you? Eh?

HEDDA [*interposing*]. But, Tesman, if Mr. Lövborg would really rather not! I am sure Mr. Lövborg is much more inclined to remain here and have supper with me.

LÖVBORG [*looking at her*]. With you, Mrs. Tesman?

HEDDA. And with Mrs. Elvsted.

LÖVBORG. Ah—[*Lightly.*] I saw her for a moment this morning.

HEDDA. Did you? Well, she is coming this evening. So you see you are almost bound to remain, Mr. Lövborg, or she will have no one to see her home.

LÖVBORG. That's true. Many thanks, Mrs. Tesman—in that case I will remain.

HEDDA. Then I have one or two orders to give the servant— [*She goes to the hall door and rings.* BERTA *enters.* HEDDA *talks to her in a whisper, and points towards the inner room.* BERTA *nods and goes out again.*]

TESMAN [*at the same time, to* LÖVBORG]. Tell me, Eilert—is it this new subject—the future—that you are going to lecture about?

LÖVBORG. Yes.

TESMAN. They told me at the bookseller's, that you are going to deliver a course of lectures this autumn.

LÖVBORG. That is my intention. I hope you won't take it ill, Tesman.

TESMAN. Oh no, not in the least! But—?

LÖVBORG. I can quite understand that it must be disagreeable to you.

TESMAN [*cast down*]. Oh, I can't expect you, out of consideration for me, to—

LÖVBORG. But I shall wait till you have received your appointment.

TESMAN. Will you wait? Yes, but—yes, but—are you not going to compete with me? Eh?

LÖVBORG. No; it is only the moral victory I care for.

TESMAN. Why, bless me—then Aunt Julia was right after all! Oh yes—I knew it! Hedda! Just fancy—Eilert Lövborg is not going to stand in our way!

HEDDA [*curtly*]. Our way? Pray leave me out of the question. [*She goes up towards the inner room, where* BERTA *is placing a tray with decanters and glasses on the table.* HEDDA *nods approval, and comes forward again.* BERTA *goes out.*]

TESMAN [*at the same time*]. And you, Judge Brack—what do you say to this? Eh?

BRACK. Well, I say that a moral victory—h'm—may be all very fine—

TESMAN. Yes, certainly. But all the same—

HEDDA [*looking at* TESMAN *with a cold smile*]. You stand there looking as if you were thunderstruck—

TESMAN. Yes—so I am—I almost think—

BRACK. Don't you see, Mrs. Tesman, a thunderstorm has just passed over?

HEDDA [*pointing towards the inner room*]. Will you not take a glass of cold punch, gentlemen?

BRACK [*looking at his watch*]. A stirrup-cup? Yes, it wouldn't come amiss.

TESMAN. A capital idea, Hedda! Just the thing! Now that the weight has been taken off my mind—

HEDDA. Will you not join them, Mr. Lövborg?

LÖVBORG [*with a gesture of refusal*]. No, thank you. Nothing for me.

BRACK. Why, bless me—cold punch is surely not poison.

LÖVBORG. Perhaps not for every one.

HEDDA. I will keep Mr. Lövborg company in the meantime.

TESMAN. Yes, yes, Hedda dear, do. [*He and* BRACK *go into the inner room, seat themselves, drink punch, smoke cigarettes, and carry on a lively conversation during what follows.* EILERT LÖVBORG *remains beside the stove.* HEDDA *goes to the writing-table.*]

HEDDA [*raising her voice a little*]. Do you care to look at some photographs, Mr. Lövborg? You know Tesman and I made a tour in the Tyrol on our way home? [*She takes up an album, and places it on the table beside the sofa, in the further corner of which she seats herself.* EILERT LÖVBORG *approaches, stops, and looks at her. Then he takes a chair and seats himself at her left, with his back towards the inner room.*]

HEDDA [*opening the album*]. Do you see this range of mountains, Mr. Lövborg? It's the Ortler group. Tesman has written the name underneath. Here it is: "The Ortler group near Meran."

LÖVBORG [*who has never taken his eyes off her, says softly and slowly*]. Hedda—Gabler!

HEDDA. [*glancing hastily at him*]. Ah! Hush!

LÖVBORG [*repeats softly*]. Hedda Gabler!

HEDDA [*looking at the album*]. That was my name in the old days—when we two knew each other.

LÖVBORG. And I must teach myself never to say Hedda Gabler again—never, as long as I live.

HEDDA [*still turning over the pages*]. Yes, you must. And I think you ought to practice in time. The sooner the better, I should say.

LÖVBORG [*in a tone of indignation*]. Hedda Gabler married? And married to—George Tesman!

HEDDA. Yes—so the world goes.

LÖVBORG Oh, Hedda, Hedda—how could you[1] throw yourself away!

HEDDA [*looks sharply at him*]. What? I can't allow this!

LÖVBORG. What do you mean? [TESMAN *comes into the room and goes towards the sofa.*]

HEDDA [*hears him coming and says in an indifferent tone*]. And this is a view from the Val d'Ampezzo, Mr. Lövborg. Just look at these peaks! [*Looks affectionately up at* TESMAN.] What's the name of these curious peaks, dear?

TESMAN. Let me see? Oh, those are the Dolomites.

HEDDA. Yes, that's it!—Those are the Dolomites, Mr. Lövborg.

TESMAN. Hedda dear,—I only wanted to ask whether I shouldn't bring you a little punch after all? For yourself at any rate—eh?

HEDDA. Yes, do, please; and perhaps a few biscuits.

TESMAN. No cigarettes?

HEDDA. No.

TESMAN. Very well. [*He goes into the inner room and out to the right.* BRACK *sits in the inner room, and keeps an eye from time to time on* HEDDA *and* LÖVBORG.]

LÖVBORG [*softly, as before*]. Answer me, Hedda—how could you go and do this?

HEDDA [*apparently absorbed in the album*]. If you continue to say *du* to me I won't talk to you.

LÖVBORG. May I not say *du* when we are alone?

HEDDA. No. You may think it; but you mustn't say it.

LÖVBORG. Ah, I understand. It is an offense against George Tesman, whom you[2] love.

HEDDA [*glances at him and smiles*]. Love? What an idea!

LÖVBORG. You don't love him then!

HEDDA. But I won't hear of any sort of unfaithfulness! Remember that.

LÖVBORG. Hedda—answer me one thing—

HEDDA. Hush! [TESMAN *enters with a small tray from the inner room.*]

TESMAN. Here you are! Isn't this tempting? [*He puts the tray on the table.*]

HEDDA. Why do you bring it yourself?

TESMAN [*filling the glasses*]. Because I think it's such fun to wait upon you, Hedda.

HEDDA. But you have poured out two glasses. Mr. Lövborg said he wouldn't have any—

TESMAN. No, but Mrs. Elvsted will soon be here, won't she?

HEDDA. Yes, by-the-bye—Mrs. Elvsted—

TESMAN. Had you forgotten her? Eh?

HEDDA. We were so absorbed in these photographs. [*Shows him a picture.*] Do you remember this little village?

---

[1] He uses the familiar form.
[2] He uses the formal form.

TESMAN. Oh, it's that one just below the Brenner Pass. It was there we passed the night—

HEDDA. —and met that lively party of tourists.

TESMAN. Yes, that was the place. Fancy—if we could only have had you with us, Eilert! Eh? [*He returns to the inner room and sits beside* BRACK.]

LÖVBORG. Answer me this one thing, Hedda—

HEDDA. Well?

LÖVBORG. Was there no love in your friendship for me either? Not a spark—not a tinge of love in it?

HEDDA. I wonder if there was? To me it seems as though we were two good comrades—two thoroughly intimate friends. [*Smilingly.*] You especially were frankness itself.

LÖVBORG. It was you that made me so.

HEDDA. As I look back upon it all, I think there was really something beautiful, something fascinating—something daring—in—in that secret intimacy—that comradeship which no living creature so much as dreamed of.

LÖVBORG. Yes, yes, Hedda! Was there not?—When I used to come to your father's in the afternoon—and the General sat over at the window reading his papers—with his back towards us—

HEDDA. And we two on the corner sofa—

LÖVBORG. Always with the same illustrated paper before us—

HEDDA. For want of an album, yes.

LÖVBORG. Yes, Hedda, and when I made my confessions to you—told you about myself, things that at that time no one else knew! There I would sit and tell you of my escapades—my days and nights of devilment. Oh, Hedda—what was the power in you that forced me to confess these things?

HEDDA. Do you think it was any power in me?

LÖVBORG. How else can I explain it? And all those—those roundabout questions you used to put to me—

HEDDA. Which you understood so particularly well—

LÖVBORG. How could you sit and question me like that? Question me quite frankly—

HEDDA. In roundabout terms, please observe.

LÖVBORG. Yes, but frankly nevertheless. Cross-question me about—all that sort of thing?

HEDDA. And how could you answer, Mr. Lövborg?

LÖVBORG. Yes, that is just what I can't understand—in looking back upon it. But tell me now, Hedda—was there not love at the bottom of our friendship? On your side, did you not feel as though you might purge my stains away if I made you my confessor? Was it not so?

HEDDA. No, not quite.

LÖVBORG. What was your motive, then?

HEDDA. Do you think it quite incomprehensible that a young girl—when it can be done—without any one knowing—

LÖVBORG. Well?

HEDDA. —should be glad to have a peep, now and then, into a world which—

LÖVBORG. Which—?

HEDDA. —which she is forbidden to know anything about?

LÖVBORG. So that was it?

HEDDA. Partly. Partly—I almost think.

LÖVBORG. Comradeship in the thirst for life. But why should not that, at any rate, have continued?

HEDDA. The fault was yours.

LÖVBORG. It was you that broke with me.

HEDDA. Yes, when our friendship threatened to develop into something more serious. Shame upon you, Eilert Lövborg! How could you think of wronging your—your frank comrade?

LÖVBORG [*clenching his hands*]. Oh, why did you not carry out your threat? Why did you not shoot me down?

HEDDA. Because I have such a dread of scandal.

LÖVBORG. Yes, Hedda, you are a coward at heart.

HEDDA. A terrible coward. [*Changing her tone.*] But it was a lucky thing for you. And now you have found ample consolation at the Elvsteds'.

LÖVBORG. I know what Thea has confided to you.

HEDDA. And perhaps you have confided to her something about us?

LÖVBORG. Not a word. She is too stupid to understand anything of that sort.

HEDDA. Stupid?

LÖVBORG. She is stupid about matters of that sort.

HEDDA. And I am cowardly. [*Bends over towards him, without looking him in the face, and says more softly—*] But now I will confide something to you.

LÖVBORG [*eagerly*]. Well?

HEDDA. The fact that I dared not shoot you down—

LÖVBORG. Yes!

HEDDA. —that was not my most arrant cowardice—that evening.

LÖVBORG [*looks at her a moment, understands, and whispers passionately*]. Oh, Hedda! Hedda Gabler! Now I begin to see a hidden reason beneath our comradeship! You[3] and I—! After all, then, it was your craving for life—

HEDDA [*softly, with a sharp glance*]. Take care! Believe nothing of the sort! [*Twilight has began to fall. The hall door is opened from without by* BERTA.]

HEDDA [*closes the album with a bang and calls smilingly*]. Ah, at last! My darling Thea,—come along! [MRS. ELVSTED *enters from the hall. She is in evening dress. The door is closed behind her.*]

HEDDA [*on the sofa, stretches out her arms towards her*]. My sweet Thea—you can't think how I have been longing for you! [MRS. ELVSTED, *in passing, exchanges slight salutations with the gentlemen in the inner room, then goes up to the table and gives* HEDDA *her hands.* EILERT LÖVBORG *has risen. He and* MRS. ELVSTED *greet each other with a silent nod.*]

MRS. ELVSTED. Ought I to go in and talk to your husband for a moment?

HEDDA. Oh, not at all. Leave those two alone. They will soon be going.

MRS. ELVSTED. Are they going out?

HEDDA. Yes, to a supper-party.

MRS. ELVSTED [*quickly, to* LÖVBORG]. Not you?

[3] He returns to the familiar form.

Lövborg. No.

Hedda. Mr. Lövborg remains with us.

Mrs. Elvsted [*takes a chair and is about to seat herself at his side*]. Oh, how nice it is here!

Hedda. No, thank you, my little Thea! Not there! You'll be good enough to come over here to me. I will sit between you.

Mrs. Elvsted. Yes, just as you please. [*She goes round the table and seats herself on the sofa on* Hedda's *right.* Lövborg *re-seats himself on his chair.*]

Lövborg [*after a short pause, to* Hedda]. Is not she lovely to look at?

Hedda [*lightly stroking her hair*]. Only to look at?

Lövborg. Yes. For we two—she and I—we are two real comrades. We have absolute faith in each other; so we can sit and talk with perfect frankness—

Hedda. Not round about, Mr. Lövborg?

Lövborg. Well—

Mrs. Elvsted [*softly, clinging close to* Hedda]. Oh, how happy I am, Hedda; for, only think, he says I have inspired him too.

Hedda [*looks at her with a smile*]. Ah! Does he say that, dear?

Lövborg. And then she is so brave, Mrs. Tesman!

Mrs. Elvsted. Good heavens—am I brave?

Lövborg. Exceedingly—where your comrade is concerned.

Hedda. Ah, yes—courage! If one only had that!

Lövborg. What then? What do you mean?

Hedda. Then life would perhaps be liveable, after all. [*With a sudden change of tone.*] But now, my dearest Thea, you really must have a glass of cold punch.

Mrs. Elvsted. No, thanks—I never take anything of that kind.

Hedda. Well then, you, Mr. Lövborg.

Lövborg. Nor I, thank you.

Mrs. Elvsted. No, he doesn't either.

Hedda [*looks fixedly at him*]. But if I say you shall?

Lövborg. It would be no use.

Hedda [*laughing*]. Then I, poor creature, have no sort of power over you?

Lövborg. Not in that respect.

Hedda. But seriously, I think you ought to—for your own sake.

Mrs. Elvsted. Why, Hedda—!

Lövborg. How so?

Hedda. Or rather on account of other people.

Lövborg. Indeed?

Hedda. Otherwise people might be apt to suspect that—in your heart of hearts—you did not feel quite secure—quite confident of yourself.

Mrs. Elvsted [*softly*]. Oh please, Hedda—

Lövborg. People may suspect what they like—for the present.

Mrs. Elvsted [*joyfully*]. Yes, let them!

Hedda. I saw it plainly in Judge Brack's face a moment ago.

Lövborg. What did you see?

Hedda. His contemptuous smile, when you dared not go with them into the inner room.

Lövborg. Dared not? Of course I preferred to stop here and talk to you.

Mrs. Elvsted. What could be more natural, Hedda?

HEDDA. But the Judge could not guess that. And I saw, too, the way he smiled and glanced at Tesman when you dared not accept his invitation to this wretched little supper-party of his.

LÖVBORG. Dared not! Do you say I dared not?

HEDDA. *I* don't say so. But that was how Judge Brack understood it.

LÖVBORG. Well, let him.

HEDDA. Then you are not going with them?

LÖVBORG. I will stay here with you and Thea.

MRS. ELVSTED. Yes, Hedda—how can you doubt that?

HEDDA [*smiles and nods approvingly to* LÖVBORG]. Firm as a rock! Faithful to your principles, now and forever! Ah, that is how a man should be! [*Turns to* MRS. ELVSTED *and caresses her*]. Well now, what did I tell you, when you came to us this morning in such a state of distraction—

LÖVBORG [*surprised*]. Distraction!

MRS. ELVSTED [*terrified*]. Hedda—oh Hedda—!

HEDDA. You can see for yourself; you haven't the slightest reason to be in such mortal terror—[*interrupting herself*]. There! Now we can all three enjoy ourselves!

LÖVBORG [*who has given a start*]. Ah—what is all this, Mrs. Tesman?

MRS. ELVSTED. Oh my God, Hedda! What are you saying? What are you doing?

HEDDA. Don't get excited! That horrid Judge Brack is sitting watching you.

LÖVBORG. So she was in mortal terror! On my account!

MRS. ELVSTED [*softly and piteously*]. Oh, Hedda—now you have ruined everything!

LÖVBORG [*looks fixedly at her for a moment. His face is distorted*]. So that was my comrade's frank confidence in me?

MRS. ELVSTED [*imploringly*]. Oh, my dearest friend—only let me tell you—

LÖVBORG [*takes one of the glasses of punch, raises it to his lips, and says in a low, husky voice*]. Your health, Thea! [*He empties the glass, puts it down, and takes the second.*]

MRS. ELVSTED [*softly*]. Oh, Hedda, Hedda—how could you do this?

HEDDA. *I* do it? *I?* Are you crazy?

LÖVBORG. Here's your health, too, Mrs. Tesman. Thanks for the truth. Hurrah for the truth! [*He empties the glass and is about to re-fill it.*]

HEDDA [*lays her hand on his arm*]. Come, come—no more for the present. Remember you are going out to supper.

MRS. ELVSTED. No, no, no!

HEDDA. Hush! They are sitting watching you.

LÖVBORG [*putting down the glass*]. Now. Thea—tell me the truth—

MRS. ELVSTED. Yes.

LÖVBORG. Did your husband know that you had come after me?

MRS. ELVSTED [*wringing her hands*]. Oh, Hedda—do you hear what he is asking?

LÖVBORG. Was it arranged between you and him that you were to come to town and look after me? Perhaps it was the Sheriff himself that urged you to come? Aha, my dear—no doubt he wanted my help in his office! Or was it at the card-table that he missed me?

MRS. ELVSTED [*softly, in agony*]. Oh, Lövborg, Lövborg—!

LÖVBORG [*seizes a glass and is on the point of filling it*]. Here's a glass for the old Sheriff too!

HEDDA [*preventing him*]. No more just now. Remember, you have to read your manuscript to Tesman.

LÖVBORG [*calmly, putting down the glass*]. It was stupid of me all this, Thea—to take it in this way, I mean. Don't be angry with me, my dear, dear comrade. You shall see—both of you and the others—that if I was fallen once—now I have risen again! Thanks to you, Thea.

MRS. ELVSTED [*radiant with joy*]. Oh, heaven be praised—! [BRACK *has in the meantime looked at his watch. He and* TESMAN *rise and come into the drawing-room.*]

BRACK [*takes his hat and overcoat*]. Well, Mrs. Tesman, our time has come.

HEDDA. I suppose it has.

LÖVBORG [*rising*]. Mine too, Judge Brack.

MRS. ELVSTED [*softly and imploringly*]. Oh, Lövborg, don't do it!

HEDDA [*pinching her arm*]. They can hear you!

MRS. ELVSTED [*with a suppressed shriek*]. Ow!

LÖVBORG [*to* BRACK]. You were good enough to invite me.

BRACK. Well, are you coming after all?

LÖVBORG. Yes, many thanks.

BRACK. I'm delighted—

LÖVBORG [*to* TESMAN, *putting the parcel of MS. in his pocket*]. I should like to show you one or two things before I send it to the printer's.

TESMAN. Fancy—that will be delightful. But, Hedda dear, how is Mrs. Elvsted to get home? Eh?

HEDDA. Oh, that can be managed somehow.

LÖVBORG [*looking towards the ladies*]. Mrs. Elvsted? Of course, I'll come again and fetch her. [*Approaching.*] At ten or thereabouts, Mrs. Tesman? Will that do?

HEDDA. Certainly. That will do capitally.

TESMAN. Well, then, that's all right. But you must not expect me so early, Hedda.

HEDDA. Oh, you may stop as long—as long as ever you please.

MRS. ELVSTED [*trying to conceal her anxiety*]. Well then, Mr. Lövborg—I shall remain here until you come.

LÖVBORG [*with his hat in his hand*]. Pray do, Mrs. Elvsted.

BRACK. And now off goes the excursion train, gentlemen! I hope we shall have a lively time, as a certain fair lady puts it.

HEDDA. Ah, if only the fair lady could be present unseen—!

BRACK. Why unseen?

HEDDA. In order to hear a little of your liveliness at first hand, Judge Brack.

BRACK [*laughing*]. I should not advise the fair lady to try it.

TESMAN [*also laughing*]. Come, you're a nice one, Hedda! Fancy that!

BRACK. Well, good-bye, good-bye, ladies.

LÖVBORG [*bowing*]. About ten o'clock, then. [BRACK, LÖVBORG, *and* TESMAN *go out by the hall door. At the same time* BERTA *enters from the inner room with a lighted lamp, which she places on the dining-room table; she goes out by the way she came.*]

MRS. ELVSTED [*who has risen and is wandering restlessly about the room*]. Hedda—Hedda—what will come of all this?

HEDDA. At ten o'clock—he will be here. I can see him already—with vine-leaves[4] in his hair—flushed and fearless—

MRS. ELVSTED. Oh, I hope he may.

HEDDA. And then, you see—then he will have regained control over himself. Then he will be a free man for all his days.

MRS. ELVSTED. Oh God!—if he would only come as you see him now!

HEDDA. He will come as I see him—so, and not otherwise! [*Rises and approaches* THEA.] You may doubt him as long as you please; I believe in him. And now we will try—

MRS. ELVSTED. You have some hidden motive in this, Hedda!

HEDDA. Yes, I have. I want for once in my life to have power to mold a human destiny.

MRS. ELVSTED. Have you not the power?

HEDDA. I have not—and have never had it.

MRS. ELVSTED. Not your husband's?

HEDDA. Do you think that is worth the trouble? Oh, if you could only understand how poor I am. And fate has made you so rich! [*Clasps her passionately in her arms.*] I think I must burn your hair off, after all.

MRS. ELVSTED. Let me go! Let me go! I am afraid of you, Hedda!

BERTA [*in the middle doorway*]. Tea is laid in the dining-room, ma'am.

HEDDA. Very well. We are coming.

MRS. ELVSTED. No, no, no! I would rather go home alone! At once.

HEDDA. Nonsense! First you shall have a cup of tea, you little stupid. And then—at ten o'clock—Eilert Lövborg will be here—with vine-leaves in his hair. [*She drags* MRS. ELVSTED *almost by force towards the middle doorway.*]

ACT III

[*The room at the* TESMANS'. *The curtains are drawn over the middle doorway, and also over the glass door. The lamp, half turned down, and with a shade over it, is burning on the table. In the stove, the door of which stands open, there has been a fire, which is now nearly burnt out.* MRS. ELVSTED, *wrapped in a large shawl, and with her feet upon a foot-rest, sits close to the stove, sunk back in the arm-chair.* HEDDA, *fully dressed, lies sleeping upon the sofa, with a sofa-blanket over her.*]

MRS. ELVSTED [*after a pause, suddenly sits up in her chair, and listens eagerly. Then she sinks back again wearily, moaning to herself*]. Not yet!—Oh God—oh God—not yet! [BERTA *slips in by the hall door. She has a letter in her hand.*]

MRS. ELVSTED [*turns and whispers eagerly*]. Well—has any one come?

BERTA [*softly*]. Yes, a girl has brought this letter.

MRS. ELVSTED [*quickly, holding out her hand*]. A letter! Give it to me!

BERTA. No, it's for Dr. Tesman, ma'am.

MRS. ELVSTED. Oh, indeed.

---

[4] Worn by Dionysus, god of wine and revelry.

BERTA. It was Miss Tesman's servant that brought it. I'll lay it here on the table.

MRS. ELVSTED. Yes, do.

BERTA [*laying down the letter*]. I think I had better put out the lamp. It's smoking.

MRS. ELVSTED. Yes, put it out. It must soon be daylight now.

BERTA [*putting out the lamp*]. It is daylight already, ma'am.

MRS. ELVSTED. Yes, broad day! And no one come back yet—!

BERTA. Lord bless you, ma'am! I guessed how it would be.

MRS. ELVSTED. You guessed?

BERTA. Yes, when I saw that a certain person had come back to town—and that he went off with them. For we've heard enough about that gentleman before now.

MRS. ELVSTED. Don't speak so loud. You will waken Mrs. Tesman.

BERTA [*looks towards the sofa and sighs*]. No, no—let her sleep, poor thing. Shan't I put some wood on the fire?

MRS. ELVSTED. Thanks, not for me.

BERTA. Oh, very well. [*She goes softly out by the hall door.*]

HEDDA [*is awakened by the shutting of the door, and looks up*]. What's that—?

MRS. ELVSTED. It was only the servant—

HEDDA [*looking about her*]. Oh, we're here—! Yes, now I remember. [*Sits erect upon the sofa, stretches herself, and rubs her eyes.*] What o'clock is it, Thea?

MRS. ELVSTED [*looks at her watch*]. It's past seven.

HEDDA. When did Tesman come home?

MRS. ELVSTED. He has not come.

HEDDA. Not come home yet?

MRS. ELVSTED [*rising*]. No one has come.

HEDDA. Think of our watching and waiting here till four in the morning—

MRS. ELVSTED [*wringing her hands*]. And how I watched and waited for him!

HEDDA [*yawns, and says with her hand before her mouth*]. Well, well—we might have spared ourselves the trouble.

MRS. ELVSTED. Did you get a little sleep?

HEDDA. Oh yes; I believe I have slept pretty well. Have you not?

MRS. ELVSTED. Not for a moment. I couldn't, Hedda!—not to save my life.

HEDDA [*rises and goes towards her*]. There, there, there! There's nothing to be so alarmed about. I understand quite well what has happened.

MRS. ELVSTED. Well, what do you think? Won't you tell me?

HEDDA. Why, of course it has been a very late affair at Judge Brack's—

MRS. ELVSTED. Yes, yes, that is clear enough. But all the same—

HEDDA. And then, you see, Tesman hasn't cared to come home and ring us up in the middle of the night. [*Laughing.*] Perhaps he wasn't inclined to show himself either—immediately after a jollification.

MRS. ELVSTED. But in that case—where can he have gone?

HEDDA. Of course he has gone to his aunts' and slept there. They have his old room ready for him.

MRS. ELVSTED. No, he can't be with them; for a letter has just come for him from Miss Tesman. There it lies.

HEDDA. Indeed? [*Looks at the address.*] Why yes, it's addressed in Aunt Julia's own hand. Well then, he has remained at Judge Brack's. And as for Eilert Lövborg—he is sitting, with vine-leaves in his hair, reading his manuscript.

MRS. ELVSTED. Oh Hedda, you are just saying things you don't believe a bit.

HEDDA. You really are a little blockhead, Thea.

MRS. ELVSTED. Oh, yes, I suppose I am.

HEDDA. And how mortally tired you look.

MRS. ELVSTED. Yes, I am mortally tired.

HEDDA. Well then, you must do as I tell you. You must go into my room and lie down for a little while.

MRS. ELVSTED. Oh no, no—I shouldn't be able to sleep.

HEDDA. I am sure you would.

MRS. ELVSTED. Well, but your husband is certain to come soon now; and then I want to know at once—

HEDDA. I shall take care to let you know when he comes.

MRS. ELVSTED. Do you promise me, Hedda?

HEDDA. Yes, rely upon me. Just you go in and have a sleep in the meantime.

MRS. ELVSTED. Thanks; then I'll try to. [*She goes off through the inner room.* HEDDA *goes up to the glass door and draws back the curtains. The broad daylight streams into the room. Then she takes a little hand-glass from the writing-table, looks at herself in it, and arranges her hair. Next she goes to the hall door and presses the bell-button.* BERTA *presently appears at the hall door.*]

BERTA. Did you want anything, ma'am?

HEDDA. Yes; you must put some more wood in the stove. I am shivering.

BERTA. Bless me—I'll make up the fire at once. [*She rakes the embers together and lays a piece of wood upon them; then stops and listens.*] That was a ring at the front door, ma'am.

HEDDA. Then go to the door. I will look after the fire.

BERTA. It'll soon burn up. [*She goes out by the hall door.* HEDDA *kneels on the foot-rest and lays some more pieces of wood in the stove. After a short pause,* GEORGE TESMAN *enters from the hall. He looks tired and rather serious. He steals on tiptoe towards the middle doorway and is about to slip through the curtains.*]

HEDDA [*at the stove, without looking up.*] Good morning.

TESMAN [*turns*]. Hedda! [*Approaching her.*] Good heavens—are you up so early? Eh?

HEDDA. Yes, I am up very early this morning.

TESMAN. And I never doubted you were still sound asleep! Fancy that, Hedda!

HEDDA. Don't speak so loud. Mrs. Elvsted is resting in my room.

TESMAN. Has Mrs. Elvsted been here all night?

HEDDA. Yes, since no one came to fetch her.

TESMAN. Ah, to be sure.

HEDDA [*closes the door of the stove and rises*]. Well, did you enjoy yourself at Judge Brack's?

TESMAN. Have you been anxious about me? Eh?

HEDDA. No, I should never think of being anxious. But I asked if you had enjoyed yourself.

TESMAN. Oh yes,—for once in a way. Especially the beginning of the evening; for then Eilert read me part of his book. We arrived more than an hour too early—fancy that! And Brack had all sorts of arrangements to make—so Eilert read to me.

HEDDA [*seating herself by the table on the right*]. Well? Tell me, then—

TESMAN [*sitting on a foot-stool near the stove*]. Oh Hedda, you can't conceive what a book that is going to be! I believe it is one of the most remarkable things that have ever been written. Fancy that!

HEDDA. Yes, yes; I don't care about that—

TESMAN. I must make a confession to you, Hedda. When he had finished reading—a horrid feeling came over me.

HEDDA. A horrid feeling?

TESMAN. I felt jealous of Eilert for having had it in him to write such a book. Only think, Hedda!

HEDDA. Yes, yes, I am thinking!

TESMAN. And then how pitiful to think that he—with all his gifts—should be irreclaimable after all.

HEDDA. I suppose you mean that he has more courage than the rest?

TESMAN. No, not at all—I mean that he is incapable of taking his pleasures in moderation.

HEDDA. And what came of it all—in the end?

TESMAN. Well, to tell the truth, I think it might best be described as an orgy, Hedda.

HEDDA. Had he vine-leaves in his hair?

TESMAN. Vine-leaves? No, I saw nothing of the sort. But he made a long, rambling speech in honor of the woman who had inspired him in his work—that was the phrase he used.

HEDDA. Did he name her?

TESMAN. No, he didn't; but I can't help thinking he meant Mrs. Elvsted. You may be sure he did.

HEDDA. Well—where did you part from him?

TESMAN. On the way to town. We broke up—the last of us at any rate— all together; and Brack came with us to get a breath of fresh air. And then, you see, we agreed to take Eilert home; for he had had far more than was good for him.

HEDDA. I daresay.

TESMAN. But now comes the strange part of it, Hedda; or, I should rather say, the melancholy part of it. I declare I am almost ashamed—on Eilert's account—to tell you—

HEDDA. Oh, go on—!

TESMAN. Well, as we were getting near town, you see, I happened to drop a little behind the others. Only for a minute or two—fancy that!

HEDDA. Yes, yes, yes, but—?

TESMAN. And then, as I hurried after them—what do you think I found by the wayside? Eh?

HEDDA. Oh, how should I know!

TESMAN. You mustn't speak of it to a soul, Hedda! Do you hear! Promise me, for Eilert's sake. [*Draws a parcel, wrapped in paper, from his coat pocket.*] Fancy, dear—I found this.

HEDDA. Is not that the parcel he had with him yesterday?

TESMAN. Yes, it is the whole of his precious, irreplaceable manuscript! And he had gone and lost it, and knew nothing about it. Only fancy, Hedda! So deplorably—

HEDDA. But why did you not give him back the parcel at once?

TESMAN. I didn't dare to—in the state he was then in—

HEDDA. Did you not tell any of the others that you had found it?

TESMAN. Oh, far from it! You can surely understand that, for Eilert's sake, I wouldn't do that.

HEDDA. So no one knows that Eilert Lövborg's manuscript is in your possession?

TESMAN. No. And no one must know it.

HEDDA. Then what did you say to him afterwards?

TESMAN. I didn't talk to him again at all; for when we got in among the streets, he and two or three of the others gave us the slip and disappeared. Fancy that!

HEDDA. Indeed! They must have taken him home then.

TESMAN. Yes, so it would appear. And Brack, too, left us.

HEDDA. And what have you been doing with yourself since?

TESMAN. Well, I and some of the others went home with one of the party, a jolly fellow, and took our morning coffee with him; or perhaps I should rather call it our night coffee—eh? But now, when I have rested a little, and given Eilert, poor fellow, time to have his sleep out, I must take this back to him.

HEDDA [*holds out her hand for the packet*]. No—don't give it to him! Not in such a hurry, I mean. Let me read it first.

TESMAN. No, my dearest Hedda, I mustn't, I really mustn't.

HEDDA. You must not?

TESMAN. No—for you can imagine what a state of despair he will be in when he awakens and misses the manuscript. He has no copy of it, you must know! He told me so.

HEDDA [*looking searchingly at him*]. Can such a thing not be reproduced? Written over again?

TESMAN. No, I don't think that would be possible. For the inspiration, you see—

HEDDA. Yes, yes—I suppose it depends on that. [*Lightly.*] But, by-the-bye— here is a letter for you.

TESMAN. Fancy—!

HEDDA [*handing it to him*]. It came early this morning.

TESMAN. It's from Aunt Julia! What can it be? [*He lays the packet on the other foot-stool, opens the letter, runs his eye through it, and jumps up.*] Oh, Hedda—she says that poor Aunt Rina is dying!

HEDDA. Well, we were prepared for that.

TESMAN. And that if I want to see her again, I must make haste. I'll run in to them at once.

HEDDA [*suppressing a smile*]. Will you run?

TESMAN. Oh, dearest Hedda—if you could only make up your mind to come with me! Just think!

HEDDA [*rises and says wearily, repelling the idea*]. No, no, don't ask me.

I will not look upon sickness and death. I loathe all sorts of ugliness.

TESMAN. Well, well, then—! [*Bustling around.*] My hat—My overcoat—? Oh, in the hall—I do hope I mayn't come too late, Hedda! Eh?

HEDDA. Oh, if you run— [BERTA *appears at the hall door.*]

BERTA. Judge Brack is at the door, and wishes to know if he may come in.

TESMAN. At this time! No, I can't possibly see him.

HEDDA. But I can. [*To* BERTA.] Ask Judge Brack to come in. [BERTA *goes out.*]

HEDDA [*quickly whispering*]. The parcel, Tesman! [*She snatches it up from the stool.*]

TESMAN. Yes, give it to me!

HEDDA. No, no, I will keep it till you come back. [*She goes to the writing-table and places it in the book-case.* TESMAN *stands in a flurry of haste, and cannot get his gloves on.* JUDGE BRACK *enters from the hall.*]

HEDDA [*nodding to him*]. You are an early bird, I must say.

BRACK. Yes, don't you think so? [*To* TESMAN.] Are you on the move, too?

TESMAN. Yes, I must rush off to my aunts'. Fancy—the invalid one is lying at death's door, poor creature.

BRACK. Dear me, is she indeed? Then on no account let me detain you. At such a critical moment—

TESMAN. Yes, I must really rush—Good-bye! Good-bye! [*He hastens out by the hall door.*]

HEDDA [*approaching.*] You seem to have made a particularly lively night of it at your rooms, Judge Brack.

BRACK. I assure you I have not had my clothes off, Mrs. Hedda.

HEDDA. Not you, either?

BRACK. No, as you may see. But what has Tesman been telling you of the night's adventures?

HEDDA. Oh, some tiresome story. Only that they went and had coffee some-where or other.

BRACK. I have heard about that coffee-party already. Eilert Lövborg was not with them, I fancy?

HEDDA. No, they had taken him home before that.

BRACK. Tesman, too?

HEDDA. No, but some of the others, he said.

BRACK [*smiling*]. George Tesman is really an ingenuous creature, Mrs. Hedda.

HEDDA. Yes, heaven knows he is. Then is there something behind all this?

BRACK. Yes, perhaps there may be.

HEDDA. Well then, sit down, my dear Judge, and tell your story in comfort. [*She seats herself to the left of the table.* BRACK *sits near her, at the long side of the table.*]

HEDDA. Now then?

BRACK. I had special reasons for keeping track of my guests—or rather of some of my guests—last night.

HEDDA. Of Eilert Lövborg among the rest, perhaps?

BRACK. Frankly, yes.

HEDDA. Now you make me really curious—

BRACK. Do you know where he and one or two of the others finished the night, Mrs. Hedda?

HEDDA. If it is not quite unmentionable, tell me.

BRACK. Oh no, it's not at all unmentionable. Well, they put in an appearance at a particularly animated soirée.

HEDDA. Of the lively kind?

BRACK. Of the very liveliest—

HEDDA. Tell me more of this, Judge Brack—

BRACK. Lövborg, as well as the others, had been invited in advance. I knew all about it. But he had declined the invitation; for now, as you know, he has become a new man.

HEDDA. Up at the Elvsteds', yes. But he went after all, then?

BRACK. Well, you see, Mrs. Hedda—unhappily the spirit moved him at my rooms last evening—

HEDDA. Yes, I hear he found inspiration.

BRACK. Pretty violent inspiration. Well, I fancy, that altered his purpose; for we men folk are unfortunately not always so firm in our principles as we ought to be.

HEDDA. Oh, I am sure you are an exception, Judge Brack. But as to Lövborg—?

BRACK. To make a long story short—he landed at last in Mademoiselle Diana's rooms.

HEDDA. Mademoiselle Diana's?

BRACK. It was Mademoiselle Diana that was giving the soirée, to a select circle of her admirers and her lady friends.

HEDDA. Is she a red-haired woman?

BRACK. Precisely.

HEDDA. A sort of a—singer?

BRACK. Oh yes—in her leisure moments. And moreover a mighty huntress—of men—Mrs. Hedda. You have no doubt heard of her. Eilert Lövborg was one of her most enthusiastic protectors—in the days of his glory.

HEDDA. And how did all this end?

BRACK. Far from amicably, it appears. After a most tender meeting, they seem to have come to blows—

HEDDA. Lövborg and she?

BRACK. Yes. He accused her or her friends of having robbed him. He declared that his pocket-book had disappeared—and other things as well. In short, he seems to have made a furious disturbance.

HEDDA. And what came of it all?

BRACK. It came to a general scrimmage, in which the ladies as well as the gentlemen took part. Fortunately the police at last appeared on the scene.

HEDDA. The police too?

BRACK. Yes. I fancy it will prove a costly frolic for Eilert Lövborg, crazy being that he is.

HEDDA. How so?

BRACK. He seems to have made a violent resistance—to have hit one of the constables on the head and torn the coat off his back. So they had to march him off to the police-station with the rest.

HEDDA. How have you learnt all this?

BRACK. From the police themselves.

HEDDA [*gazing straight before her*]. So that is what happened. Then he had no vine-leaves in his hair.

BRACK. Vine-leaves, Mrs. Hedda?

HEDDA [*changing her tone*]. But tell me now, Judge—what is your real reason for tracking out Eilert Lövborg's movements so carefully?

BRACK. In the first place, it could not be entirely indifferent to me if it should appear in the police-court that he came straight from my house.

HEDDA. Will the matter come into court, then?

BRACK. Of course. However, I should scarcely have troubled so much about that. But I thought that, as a friend of the family, it was my duty to supply you and Tesman with a full account of his nocturnal exploits.

HEDDA. Why so, Judge Brack?

BRACK. Why, because I have a shrewd suspicion that he intends to use you as a sort of blind.

HEDDA. Oh, how can you think such a thing!

BRACK. Good heavens, Mrs. Hedda—we have eyes in our head. Mark my words! This Mrs. Elvsted will be in no hurry to leave town again.

HEDDA. Well, even if there should be anything between them, I suppose there are plenty of other places where they could meet.

BRACK. Not a single home. Henceforth, as before, every respectable house will be closed against Eilert Lövborg.

HEDDA. And so ought mine to be, you mean?

BRACK. Yes. I confess it would be more than painful to me if this personage were to be made free of your house. How superfluous, how intrusive, he would be, if he were to force his way into—

HEDDA. —into the triangle?

BRACK. Precisely. It would simply mean that I should find myself homeless.

HEDDA [*looks at him with a smile*]. So you want to be the one cock in the basket—that is your aim.

BRACK [*nods slowly and lowers his voice*]. Yes, that is my aim. And for that I will fight—with every weapon I can command.

HEDDA [*her smile vanishing*]. I see you are a dangerous person—when it comes to the point.

BRACK. Do you think so?

HEDDA. I am beginning to think so. And I am exceedingly glad to think—that you have no sort of hold over me.

BRACK [*laughing equivocally*]. Well, well, Mrs. Hedda—perhaps you are right there. If I had, who knows what I might be capable of?

HEDDA. Come, come now, Judge Brack. That sounds almost like a threat.

BRACK [*rising*]. Oh, not at all! The triangle, you know, ought, if possible, to be spontaneously constructed.

HEDDA. There I agree with you.

BRACK. Well, now I have said all I had to say; and I had better be getting back to town. Good-bye, Mrs. Hedda. [*He goes towards the glass door.*]

HEDDA [*rising*]. Are you going through the garden?

BRACK. Yes, it's a short cut for me.

HEDDA. And then it is the back way, too.

BRACK. Quite so. I have no objection to back ways. They may be piquant enough at times.

HEDDA. When there is ball practice going on, you mean?

BRACK [*in the doorway, laughing to her*]. Oh, people don't shoot their tame poultry, I fancy.

HEDDA [*also laughing*]. Oh, no, when there is only one cock in the basket— [*They exchange laughing nods of farewell. He goes. She closes the door behind him.* HEDDA, *who has become quite serious, stands for a moment looking out. Presently she goes and peeps through the curtain over the middle doorway. Then she goes to the writing-table, takes* LÖVBORG's *packet out of the book-case, and is on the point of looking through its contents.* BERTA *is heard speaking loudly in the hall.* HEDDA *turns and listens. Then she hastily locks up the packet in the drawer, and lays the key on the inkstand.* EILERT LÖVBORG, *with his great coat on and his hat in his hand, tears open the hall door. He looks somewhat confused and irritated.*]

LÖVBORG [*looking towards the hall*]. And I tell you I must and will come in! There! [*He closes the door, turns and sees* HEDDA, *at once regains his self-control, and bows.*]

HEDDA [*at the writing-table*]. Well, Mr. Lövborg, this is rather a late hour to call for Thea.

LÖVBORG. You mean rather an early hour to call on you. Pray pardon me.

HEDDA. How do you know that she is still here?

LÖVBORG. They told me at her lodgings that she had been out all night.

HEDDA [*going to the oval table*]. Did you notice anything about the people of the house when they said that?

LÖVBORG [*looks inquiringly at her*]. Notice anything about them?

HEDDA. I mean, did they seem to think it odd?

LÖVBORG [*suddenly understanding*]. Oh yes, of course! I am dragging her down with me! However, I didn't notice anything.—I suppose Tesman is not up yet?

HEDDA. No—I think not—

LÖVBORG. When did he come home?

HEDDA. Very late.

LÖVBORG. Did he tell you anything?

HEDDA. Yes, I gathered that you had had an exceedingly jolly evening at Judge Brack's.

LÖVBORG. Nothing more?

HEDDA. I don't think so. However, I was so dreadfully sleepy— [MRS. ELVSTED *enters through the curtains of the middle doorway.*]

MRS. ELVSTED [*going towards him*]. Ah, Lövborg! At last—!

LÖVBORG. Yes, at last. And too late!

MRS. ELVSTED [*looks anxiously at him*]. What is too late?

LÖVBORG. Everything is too late now. It is all over with me.

MRS. ELVSTED. Oh no, no—don't say that!

LÖVBORG. You will say the same when you hear—

MRS. ELVSTED. I won't hear anything!

HEDDA. Perhaps you would prefer to talk to her alone! If so, I will leave you.

LÖVBORG. No, stay—you too. I beg you to stay.

MRS. ELVSTED. Yes, but I won't hear anything, I tell you.

LÖVBORG. It is not last night's adventures that I want to talk about.

MRS. ELVSTED. What is it then—?

LÖVBORG. I want to say that now our ways must part.

MRS. ELVSTED. Part!

HEDDA [*involuntarily*]. I knew it!

LÖVBORG. You can be of no more service to me, Thea.

MRS. ELVSTED. How can you stand there and say that! No more service to you! Am I not to help you now, as before? Are we not to go on working together?

LÖVBORG. Henceforward I shall do no work.

MRS. ELVSTED [*despairingly*]. Then what am I to do with my life?

LÖVBORG. You must try to live your life as if you had never known me.

MRS. ELVSTED. But you know I cannot do that!

LÖVBORG. Try if you cannot, Thea. You must go home again—

MRS. ELVSTED [*in vehement protest*]. Never in this world! Where you are, there will I be also! I will not let myself be driven away like this! I will remain here! I will be with you when the book appears.

HEDDA [*half aloud, in suspense*]. Ah, yes—the book!

LÖVBORG [*looks at her*]. My book and Thea's; for that is what it is.

MRS. ELVSTED. Yes, I feel that it is. And that is why I have a right to be with you when it appears! I will see with my own eyes how respect and honor pour in upon you afresh. And the happiness—the happiness— oh, I must share it with you!

LÖVBORG. Thea—our book will never appear.

HEDDA. Ah!

MRS. ELVSTED. Never appear!

LÖVBORG. Can never appear.

MRS. ELVSTED [*in agonized foreboding*]. Lövborg—what have you done with the manuscript?

HEDDA [*looks anxiously at him*]. Yes, the manuscript—?

MRS. ELVSTED. Where is it?

LÖVBORG. Oh Thea—don't ask me about it!

MRS. ELVSTED. Yes, yes, I will know. I demand to be told at once.

LÖVBORG. The manuscript—Well then—I have torn the manuscript into a thousand pieces.

MRS. ELVSTED [*shrieks*]. Oh no, no—!

HEDDA [*involuntarily*]. But that's not—

LÖVBORG [*looks at her*]. Not true, you think?

HEDDA [*collecting herself*]. Oh well, of course—since you say so. But it sounded so improbable—

LÖVBORG. It is true, all the same.

MRS. ELVSTED [*wringing her hands*]. Oh God—oh God, Hedda—torn his own work to pieces!

LÖVBORG. I have torn my own life to pieces. So why should I not tear my life-work too—?

MRS. ELVSTED. And you did this last night?

LÖVBORG. Yes, I tell you! Tore it into a thousand pieces and scattered them on the fiord—far out. There there is cool sea-water at any rate—let them drift upon it—drift with the current and the wind.

And then presently they will sink—deeper and deeper—as I shall, Thea.

Mrs. Elvsted. Do you know, Lövborg, that what you have done with the book—I shall think of it to my dying day as though you had killed a little child.

Lövborg. Yes, you are right. It is a sort of child-murder.

Mrs. Elvsted. How could you, then—! Did not the child belong to me too?

Hedda [*almost inaudibly*]. Ah, the child—

Mrs. Elvsted [*breathing heavily*]. It is all over then. Well, well, now I will go, Hedda.

Hedda. But you are not going away from town?

Mrs. Elvsted. Oh, I don't know what I shall do. I see nothing but darkness before me. [*She goes out by the hall door.*]

Hedda [*stands waiting for a moment*]. So you are not going to see her home, Mr. Lövborg?

Lövborg. I? Through the streets? Would you have people see her walking with me?

Hedda. Of course I don't know what else may have happened last night. But is it so utterly irretrievable?

Lövborg. It will not end with last night—I know that perfectly well. And the thing is that now I have no taste for that sort of life either. I won't begin it anew. She has broken my courage and my power of braving life out.

Hedda [*looking straight before her*]. So that pretty little fool has had her fingers in a man's destiny. [*Looks at him.*] But all the same, how could you treat her so heartlessly?

Lövborg. Oh, don't say that it was heartless!

Hedda. To go and destroy what has filled her whole soul for months and years. You do not call that heartless!

Lövborg. To you I can tell the truth, Hedda.

Hedda. The truth?

Lövborg. First promise me—give me your word—that what I now confide to you Thea shall never know.

Hedda. I give you my word.

Lövborg. Good. Then let me tell you that what I said just now was untrue.

Hedda. About the manuscript?

Lövborg. Yes. I have not torn it to pieces—nor thrown it into the fiord.

Hedda. No, no—But—where is it then?

Lövborg. I have destroyed it none the less—utterly destroyed it, Hedda!

Hedda. I don't understand.

Lövborg. Thea said that what I had done seemed to her like a child-murder.

Hedda. Yes, so she said.

Lövborg. But to kill his child—that is not the worst thing a father can do to it.

Hedda. Not the worst?

Lövborg. No. I wanted to spare Thea from hearing the worst.

Hedda. Then what is the worst?

Lövborg. Suppose now, Hedda, that a man—in the small hours of the morning—came home to his child's mother after a night of riot and debauchery, and said: "Listen—I have been here and there—in this place and in that. And I have taken our child with me—to this place and to that. And I have lost the child—utterly lost it. The devil knows into what hands it may have fallen—who may have had their clutches on it."

HEDDA. Well—but when all is said and done, you know—that was only a book—

LÖVBORG. Thea's pure soul was in that book.

HEDDA. Yes, so I understand.

LÖVBORG. And you can understand, too, that for her and me together no future is possible.

HEDDA. What path do you mean to take then?

LÖVBORG. None. I will only try to make an end of it all—the sooner the better.

HEDDA [*a step nearer to him*]. Eilert Lövborg—listen to me. Will you not try to—to do it beautifully?

LÖVBORG. Beautifully? [*Smiling.*] With vine-leaves in my hair, as you used to dream in the old days—?

HEDDA. No, no. I have lost my faith in the vine-leaves. But beautifully, nevertheless! For once in a way!—Good-bye! You must go now—and do not come here any more.

LÖVBORG. Good-bye, Mrs. Tesman. And give George Tesman my love. [*He is on the point of going.*]

HEDDA. No, wait! I must give you a memento to take with you. [*She goes to the writing-table and opens the drawer and the pistol-case; then returns to* LÖVBORG *with one of the pistols.*]

LÖVBORG [*looks at her*]. This? Is this the memento?

HEDDA [*nodding slowly*]. Do you recognize it? It was aimed at you once.

LÖVBORG. You should have used it then.

HEDDA. Take it—and do you use it now.

LÖVBORG [*puts the pistol in his breast pocket*]. Thanks!

HEDDA. And beautifully, Eilert Lövborg. Promise me that!

LÖVBORG. Good-bye, Hedda Gabler. [*He goes out by the hall door.* HEDDA *listens for a moment at the door. Then she goes up to the writing-table, takes out the packet of manuscript, peeps under the cover, draws a few of the sheets half out, and looks at them. Next she goes over and seats herself in the arm-chair beside the stove, with the packet in her lap. Presently she opens the stove door, and then the packet.*]

HEDDA [*throws one of the quires*[1] *into the fire and whispers to herself.*] Now I am burning your child, Thea!—Burning it, curly-locks! [*Throwing one or two more quires into the stove.*] Your child and Eilert Lövborg's. [*Throws the rest in.*] I am burning—I am burning your child.

ACT IV

[*The same rooms at the* TESMANS'. *It is evening. The drawing-room is in darkness. The back room is lighted by the hanging lamp over the table. The curtains over the glass door are drawn*

---

[1] Twenty-five sheets of paper.

close. HEDDA *dressed in black, walks to and fro in the dark room. Then she goes into the back room and disappears for a moment to the left. She is heard to strike a few chords on the piano. Presently she comes in sight again, and returns to the drawing-room.* BERTA *enters from the right, through the inner room, with a lighted lamp, which she places on the table in front of the corner settee in the drawing-room. Her eyes are red with weeping, and she has black ribbons in her cap. She goes quietly and circumspectly out to the right.* HEDDA *goes up to the glass door, lifts the curtain a little aside, and looks out into the darkness. Shortly afterwards,* MISS TESMAN, *in mourning, with a bonnet and veil on, comes in from the hall.* HEDDA *goes towards her and holds out her hand.*]

MISS TESMAN. Yes, Hedda, here I am, in mourning and forlorn; for now my poor sister has at last found peace.

HEDDA. I have heard the news already, as you see. Tesman sent me a card.

MISS TESMAN. Yes, he promised me he would. But nevertheless I thought that to Hedda—here in the house of life—I ought myself to bring the tidings of death.

HEDDA. That was very kind of you.

MISS TESMAN. Ah, Rina ought not to have left us just now. This is not the time for Hedda's house to be a house of mourning.

HEDDA [*changing the subject*]. She died quite peacefully, did she not, Miss Tesman?

MISS TESMAN. Oh, her end was so calm, so beautiful. And then she had the unspeakable happiness of seeing George once more—and bidding him good-bye.—Has he come home yet?

HEDDA. No. He wrote that he might be detained. But won't you sit down?

MISS TESMAN. No thank you, my dear, dear Hedda. I should like to, but I have so much to do. I must prepare my dear one for her rest as well as I can. She shall go to her grave looking her best.

HEDDA. Can I help you in any way?

MISS TESMAN. Oh, you must not think of it! Hedda Tesman must have no hand in such mournful work. Nor let her thoughts dwell on it either—not at this time.

HEDDA. One is not always mistress of one's thoughts—

MISS TESMAN [*continuing*]. Ah yes, it is the way of the world. At home we shall be sewing a shroud; and here there will soon be sewing too, I suppose—but of another sort, thank God! [GEORGE TESMAN *enters by the hall door.*]

HEDDA. Ah, you have come at last!

TESMAN. You here, Aunt Julia? With Hedda? Fancy that!

MISS TESMAN. I was just going, my dear boy. Well, have you done all you promised?

TESMAN. No; I'm really afraid I have forgotten half of it. I must come to you again tomorrow. Today my brain is all in a whirl. I can't keep my thoughts together.

MISS TESMAN. Why, my dear George, you mustn't take it this way.

TESMAN. Mustn't—? How do you mean?

MISS TESMAN. Even in your sorrow you must rejoice, as I do—rejoice that she is at rest.

TESMAN. Oh yes, yes—you are thinking of Aunt Rina.

HEDDA. You will feel lonely now, Miss Tesman.

MISS TESMAN. Just at first, yes. But that will not last very long, I hope. I daresay I shall soon find an occupant for poor Rina's little room.

TESMAN. Indeed? Who do you think will take it? Eh?

MISS TESMAN. Oh, there's always some poor invalid or other in want of nursing, unfortunately.

HEDDA. Would you really take such a burden upon you again?

MISS TESMAN. A burden! Heaven forgive you, child—it has been no burden to me.

HEDDA. But suppose you had a total stranger on your hands—

MISS TESMAN. Oh, one soon makes friends with sick folk; and it's such an absolute necessity for me to have some one to live for. Well, heaven be praised, there may soon be something in this house, too, to keep an old aunt busy.

HEDDA. Oh, don't trouble about anything here.

TESMAN. Yes, just fancy what a nice time we three might have together, if—?

HEDDA. If—?

TESMAN [*uneasily*]. Oh, nothing. It will all come right. Let us hope so—eh?

MISS TESMAN. Well, well, I daresay you two want to talk to each other. [*Smiling.*] And perhaps Hedda may have something to tell you too, George. Good-bye! I must go home to Rina. [*Turning at the door.*] How strange it is to think that now Rina is with me and with my poor brother as well!

TESMAN. Yes, fancy that, Aunt Julia! Eh? [MISS TESMAN *goes out by the hall door.*]

HEDDA [*follows* TESMAN *coldly and searchingly with her eyes*]. I almost believe your Aunt Rina's death affects you more than it does your Aunt Julia.

TESMAN. Oh, it's not that alone. It's Eilert I am so terribly uneasy about.

HEDDA [*quickly*]. Is there anything new about him!

TESMAN. I looked in at his rooms this afternoon, intending to tell him the manuscript was in safe keeping.

HEDDA. Well, did you not find him?

TESMAN. No. He wasn't at home. But afterwards I met Mrs. Elvsted, and she told me he had been here early this morning.

HEDDA. Yes, directly after you had gone.

TESMAN. And he said that he had torn his manuscript to pieces—eh?

HEDDA. Yes, so he declared.

TESMAN. Why, good heavens, he must have been completely out of his mind! And I suppose you thought it best not to give it back to him, Hedda?

HEDDA. No, he did not get it.

TESMAN. But of course you told him that we had it?

HEDDA. No. [*Quickly.*] Did you tell Mrs. Elvsted?

TESMAN. No; I thought I had better not. But you ought to have told him. Fancy, if, in desperation, he should go and do himself some injury!

Let me have the manuscript, Hedda! I will take it to him at once. Where
is it?

HEDDA [*cold and immovable, leaning on the arm-chair*]. I have not got it.

TESMAN. Have not got it? What in the world do you mean?

HEDDA. I have burnt it—every line of it.

TESMAN [*with a violent movement of terror*]. Burnt! Burnt Eilert's manuscript!

HEDDA. Don't scream so. The servant might hear you.

TESMAN. Burnt! Why, good God—! No, no, no! It's impossible!

HEDDA. It is so, nevertheless.

TESMAN. Do you know what you have done, Hedda? It's unlawful appropri-
ation of lost property. Fancy that! Just ask Judge Brack, and he'll tell
you what it is.

HEDDA. I advise you not to speak of it—either to Judge Brack, or to any
one else.

TESMAN. But how could you do anything so unheard-of? What put it into
your head? What possessed you? Answer me that—eh?

HEDDA [*suppressing an almost imperceptible smile*]. I did it for your sake,
George.

TESMAN. For my sake!

HEDDA. This morning, when you told me about what he had read to you—

TESMAN. Yes, yes—what then?

HEDDA. You acknowledged that you envied his work.

TESMAN. Oh, of course I didn't mean that literally.

HEDDA. No matter—I could not bear the idea that any one should throw
you into the shade.

TESMAN [*in an outburst of mingled doubt and joy*]. Hedda! Oh, is this true?
But—but—I never knew you to show your love like that before. Fancy
that!

HEDDA. Well, I may as well tell you that—just at this time—[*impatiently,
breaking off*]. No, no; you can ask Aunt Julia. She will tell you, fast
enough.

TESMAN. Oh, I almost think I understand you, Hedda! [*Clasps his hands
together.*] Great heavens! do you really mean it! Eh?

HEDDA. Don't shout so. The servant might hear.

TESMAN [*laughing in irrepressible glee*]. The servant! Why, how absurd you
are, Hedda. It's only my old Berta! Why, I'll tell Berta myself.

HEDDA [*clenching her hands together in desperation*]. Oh, it is killing me,—it
is killing me, all this!

TESMAN. What is, Hedda? Eh?

HEDDA [*coldly controlling herself*]. All this—absurdity—George.

TESMAN. Absurdity! Do you see anything absurd in my being overjoyed
at the news! But after all perhaps I had better not say anything to
Berta.

HEDDA. Oh—why not that too?

TESMAN. No, no, not yet! But I must certainly tell Aunt Julia. And then
that you have begun to call me George too! Fancy that! Oh, Aunt Julia
will be so happy—so happy.

HEDDA. When she hears that I have burnt Eilert Lövborg's manuscript—
for your sake?

TESMAN. No, by-the-bye—that affair of the manuscript—of course nobody must know about that. But that you love me so much, Hedda—Aunt Julia must really share my joy in that! I wonder, now, whether this sort of thing is usual in young wives? Eh?

HEDDA. I think you had better ask Aunt Julia that question too.

TESMAN. I will indeed, some time or other. [*Looks uneasy and downcast again.*] And yet the manuscript—the manuscript! Good God! it is terrible to think what will become of poor Eilert now. [MRS. ELVSTED, *dressed as in the first act, with hat and cloak, enters by the hall door.*]

MRS. ELVSTED [*greets them hurriedly, and says in evident agitation*]. Oh, dear Hedda, forgive my coming again.

HEDDA. What is the matter with you, Thea?

TESMAN. Something about Eilert Lövborg again—eh?

MRS. ELVSTED. Yes! I am dreadfully afraid some misfortune has happened to him.

HEDDA [*seizes her arm*]. Ah,—do you think so?

TESMAN. Why, good Lord—what makes you think that, Mrs. Elvsted?

MRS. ELVSTED. I heard them talking of him at my boarding-house—just as I came in. Oh, the most incredible rumors are afloat about him today.

TESMAN. Yes, fancy, so I heard too! And I can bear witness that he went straight home to bed last night. Fancy that!

HEDDA. Well, what did they say at the boarding-house?

MRS. ELVSTED. Oh, I couldn't make out anything clearly. Either they knew nothing definite, or else— They stopped talking when they saw me; and I did not dare to ask.

TESMAN [*moving about uneasily*]. We must hope—we must hope that you misunderstood them, Mrs. Elvsted.

MRS. ELVSTED. No, no; I am sure it was of him they were talking. And I heard something about the hospital or—

TESMAN. The hospital?

HEDDA. No—surely that cannot be!

MRS. ELVSTED. Oh, I was in such mortal terror! I went to his lodgings and asked for him there.

HEDDA. You could make up your mind to that, Thea!

MRS. ELVSTED. What else could I do? I really could bear the suspense no longer.

TESMAN. But you didn't find him either—eh?

MRS. ELVSTED. No. And the people knew nothing about him. He hadn't been home since yesterday afternoon, they said.

TESMAN. Yesterday! Fancy, how could they say that?

MRS. ELVSTED. Oh, I am sure something terrible must have happened to him.

TESMAN. Hedda dear—how would it be if I were to go and make inquiries—?

HEDDA. No, no—don't you mix yourself up in this affair.

[JUDGE BRACK, *with his hat in his hand, enters by the hall door, which* BERTA *opens, and closes behind him. He looks grave and bows in silence.*]

TESMAN. Oh, is that you, my dear Judge? Eh?

BRACK. Yes. It was imperative I should see you this evening.

TESMAN. I can see you have heard the news about Aunt Rina.

BRACK. Yes, that among other things.

TESMAN. Isn't it sad—eh?

BRACK. Well, my dear Tesman, that depends on how you look at it.

TESMAN [*looks doubtfully at him*]. Has anything else happened?

BRACK. Yes.

HEDDA [*in suspense*]. Anything sad, Judge Brack?

BRACK. That, too, depends on how you look at it, Mrs. Tesman.

MRS. ELVSTED [*unable to restrain her anxiety*]. Oh! it is something about Eilert Lövborg!

BRACK [*with a glance at her*]. What makes you think that, Madam? Perhaps you have already heard something—?

MRS. ELVSTED [*in confusion*]. No, nothing at all, but—

TESMAN. Oh, for heaven's sake, tell us!

BRACK [*shrugging his shoulders*]. Well, I regret to say Eilert Lövborg has been taken to the hospital. He is lying at the point of death.

MRS. ELVSTED [*shrieks*]. Oh God! Oh God—

TESMAN. To the hospital! And at the point of death.

HEDDA [*involuntarily*]. So soon then—

MRS. ELVSTED [*wailing*]. And we parted in anger, Hedda!

HEDDA [*whispers*]. Thea—Thea—be careful!

MRS. ELVSTED [*not heeding her*]. I must go to him! I must see him alive!

BRACK. It is useless, Madam. No one will be admitted.

MRS. ELVSTED. Oh, at least tell me what has happened to him? What is it?

TESMAN. You don't mean to say that he has himself—Eh?

HEDDA. Yes, I am sure he has.

TESMAN. Hedda, how can you—?

BRACK [*keeping his eyes fixed upon her*]. Unfortunately you have guessed quite correctly, Mrs. Tesman.

MRS. ELVSTED. Oh, how horrible!

TESMAN. Himself, then! Fancy that!

HEDDA. Shot himself!

BRACK. Rightly guessed again, Mrs. Tesman.

MRS. ELVSTED [*with an effort at self-control*]. When did it happen, Mr. Brack?

BRACK. This afternoon—between three and four.

TESMAN. But, good Lord, where did he do it? Eh?

BRACK [*with some hesitation*]. Where? Well—I suppose at his lodgings.

MRS. ELVSTED. No, that cannot be; for I was there between six and seven.

BRACK. Well, then, somewhere else. I don't know exactly. I only know that he was found—. He had shot himself—in the breast.

MRS. ELVSTED. Oh, how terrible! That he should die like that!

HEDDA [*to* BRACK]. Was it in the breast?

BRACK. Yes—as I told you.

HEDDA. Not in the temple?

BRACK. In the breast, Mrs. Tesman.

HEDDA. Well, well—the breast is a good place, too.

BRACK. How do you mean, Mrs. Tesman?

HEDDA [*evasively*]. Oh, nothing—nothing.

TESMAN. And the wound is dangerous, you say—eh?

BRACK. Absolutely mortal. The end has probably come by this time.

MRS. ELVSTED. Yes, yes, I feel it. The end! The end! Oh, Hedda—!

TESMAN. But tell me, how have you learnt all this?

BRACK [*curtly*]. Through one of the police. A man I had some business with.

HEDDA [*in a clear voice*]. At last a deed worth doing!

TESMAN [*terrified*]. Good heavens, Hedda! what are you saying?

HEDDA. I say there is beauty in this.

BRACK. H'm, Mrs. Tesman—

TESMAN. Beauty! Fancy that!

MRS. ELVSTED. Oh, Hedda, how can you talk of beauty in such an act!

HEDDA. Eilert Lövborg has himself made up his account with life. He has had the courage to do—the one right thing.

MRS. ELVSTED. No, you must never think that was how it happened! It must have been in delirium that he did it.

TESMAN. In despair!

HEDDA. That he did not. I am certain of that.

MRS. ELVSTED. Yes, yes! In delirium! Just as when he tore up our manuscript.

BRACK [*starting*]. The manuscript? Has he torn that up?

MRS. ELVSTED. Yes, last night.

TESMAN [*whispers softly*]. Oh, Hedda, we shall never get over this.

BRACK. H'm, very extraordinary.

TESMAN [*moving about the room*]. To think of Eilert going out of the world in this way! And not leaving behind him the book that would have immortalized his name—

MRS. ELVSTED. Oh, if only it could be put together again!

TESMAN. Yes, if it only could! I don't know what I would not give—

MRS. ELVSTED. Perhaps it can, Mr. Tesman.

TESMAN. What do you mean?

MRS. ELVSTED [*searches in the pocket of her dress*]. Look here. I have kept all the loose notes he used to dictate from.

HEDDA [*a step forward*]. Ah—!

TESMAN. You have kept them, Mrs. Elvsted! Eh?

MRS. ELVSTED. Yes, I have them here. I put them in my pocket when I left home. Here they still are—

TESMAN. Oh, do let me see them!

MRS. ELVSTED [*hands him a bundle of papers*]. But they are in such disorder—all mixed up.

TESMAN. Fancy, if we could make something out of them, after all! Perhaps if we two put our heads together—

MRS. ELVSTED. Oh, yes, at least let us try—

TESMAN. We will manage it! We must! I will dedicate my life to this task.

HEDDA. You, George? Your life?

TESMAN. Yes, or rather all the time I can spare. My own collections must wait in the meantime. Hedda—you understand, eh? I owe this to Eilert's memory.

HEDDA. Perhaps.

TESMAN. And so, my dear Mrs. Elvsted, we will give our whole minds to it. There is no use in brooding over what can't be undone—eh? We must try to control our grief as much as possible, and—

MRS. ELVSTED. Yes, yes, Mr. Tesman, I will do the best I can.

TESMAN. Well then, come here. I can't rest until we have looked through
the notes. Where shall we sit? Here? No, in there, in the back room.
Excuse me, my dear Judge. Come with me, Mrs. Elvsted.

MRS. ELVSTED. Oh, if only it were possible! [TESMAN *and* MRS. ELVSTED
*go into the back room. She takes off her hat and cloak. They both sit at the
table under the hanging lamp, and are soon deep in an eager examination of
the papers.* HEDDA *crosses to the stove and sits in the arm-chair. Presently* BRACK
goes up to her.]

HEDDA [*in a low voice*]. Oh, what a sense of freedom it gives one, this act
of Eilert Lövborg's.

BRACK. Freedom, Mrs. Hedda? Well, of course, it is a release for him—

HEDDA. I mean for me. It gives me a sense of freedom to know that a
deed of deliberate courage is still possible in this world,—a deed of
spontaneous beauty.

BRACK [*smiling*]. H'm—my dear Mrs. Hedda—

HEDDA. Oh, I know what you are going to say. For you are a kind of a
specialist too, like—you know!

BRACK [*looking hard at her*]. Eilert Lövborg was more to you than perhaps
you are willing to admit to yourself. Am I wrong?

HEDDA. I don't answer such questions. I only know Eilert Lövborg has
had the courage to live his life after his own fashion. And then—the
last great act, with its beauty! Ah! that he should have the will and
the strength to turn away from the banquet of life—so early.

BRACK. I am sorry, Mrs. Hedda,—but I fear I must dispel an amiable illusion.

HEDDA. Illusion?

BRACK. Which could not have lasted long in any case.

HEDDA. What do you mean?

BRACK. Eilert Lövborg did not shoot himself voluntarily.

HEDDA. Not voluntarily?

BRACK. No. The thing did not happen exactly as I told it.

HEDDA [*in suspense*]. Have you concealed something? What is it?

BRACK. For poor Mrs. Elvsted's sake I idealized the facts a little.

HEDDA. What are the facts?

BRACK. First, that he is already dead.

HEDDA. At the hospital?

BRACK. Yes—without regaining consciousness.

HEDDA. What more have you concealed?

BRACK. This—the event did not happen at his lodgings.

HEDDA. Oh, that can make no difference.

BRACK. Perhaps it may. For I must tell you—Eilert Lövborg was found
shot in—in Mademoiselle Diana's boudoir.

HEDDA [*makes a motion as if to rise, but sinks back again*]. That is impossible,
Judge Brack! He cannot have been there again today.

BRACK. He was there this afternoon. He went there, he said, to demand
the return of something which they had taken from him. Talked wildly
about a lost child—

HEDDA. Ah—so that was why—

BRACK. I thought probably he meant his manuscript; but now I hear he
destroyed that himself. So I suppose it must have been his pocket-book.

HEDDA. Yes, no doubt. And there—there he was found?

BRACK. Yes, there. With a pistol in his breast-pocket, discharged. The ball had lodged in a vital part.

HEDDA. In the breast—yes.

BRACK. No—in the bowels.

HEDDA [*looks up at him with an expression of loathing*]. That too! Oh, what curse is it that makes everything I touch turn ludicrous and mean?

BRACK. There is one point more, Mrs. Hedda—another disagreeable feature in the affair.

HEDDA. And what is that?

BRACK. The pistol he carried—

HEDDA [*breathless*]. Well? What of it?

BRACK. He must have stolen it.

HEDDA [*leaps up*]. Stolen it! That is not true! He did not steal it!

BRACK. No other explanation is possible. He must have stolen it—Hush! [TESMAN *and* MRS. ELVSTED *have risen from the table in the back room, and come into the drawing-room.*]

TESMAN [*with the papers in both his hands*]. Hedda dear, it is almost impossible to see under that lamp. Think of that!

HEDDA. Yes, I am thinking.

TESMAN. Would you mind our sitting at your writing-table—eh?

HEDDA. If you like. [*Quickly.*] No, wait! Let me clear it first!

TESMAN. Oh, you needn't trouble, Hedda. There is plenty of room.

HEDDA. No, no; let me clear it, I say! I will take these things in and put them on the piano. There! [*She has drawn out an object, covered with sheet music, from under the book-case, places several other pieces of music upon it, and carries the whole into the inner room, to the left.* TESMAN *lays the scraps of paper on the writing-table, and moves the lamp there from the corner table.* HEDDA *returns.*]

HEDDA [*behind* MRS. ELVSTED's *chair, gently ruffling her hair*]. Well, my sweet Thea,—how goes it with Eilert Lövborg's monument?

MRS. ELVSTED [*looks dispiritedly up at her*]. Oh, it will be terribly hard to put in order.

TESMAN. We must manage it. I am determined. And arranging other people's papers is just the work for me. [HEDDA *goes over to the stove, and seats herself on one of the foot-stools.* BRACK *stands over her, leaning on the arm-chair.*]

HEDDA [*whispers*]. What did you say about the pistol?

BRACK [*softly*]. That he must have stolen it.

HEDDA. Why stolen it?

BRACK. Because every other explanation ought to be impossible, Mrs. Hedda.

HEDDA. Indeed?

BRACK [*glances at her*]. Of course Eilert Lövborg was here this morning. Was he not?

HEDDA. Yes.

BRACK. Were you alone with him?

HEDDA. Part of the time.

BRACK. Did you not leave the room whilst he was here?

HEDDA. No.

BRACK. Try to recollect. Were you not out of the room a moment?

HEDDA. Yes, perhaps just a moment—out in the hall.

BRACK. And where was your pistol-case during that time?

HEDDA. I had it locked up in—

BRACK. Well, Mrs. Hedda?

HEDDA. The case stood there on the writing-table.

BRACK. Have you looked since, to see whether both the pistols are there?

HEDDA. No.

BRACK. Well, you need not. I saw the pistol found in Lövborg's pocket, and I knew it at once as the one I had seen yesterday—and before, too.

HEDDA. Have you it with you?

BRACK. No; the police have it.

HEDDA. What will the police do with it?

BRACK. Search till they find the owner.

HEDDA. Do you think they will succeed?

BRACK [*bends over her and whispers*]. No, Hedda Gabler—not so long as I say nothing.

HEDDA [*looks frightened at him*]. And if you do not say nothing,—what then?

BRACK [*shrugs his shoulders*]. There is always the possibility that the pistol was stolen.

HEDDA [*firmly*]. Death rather than that.

BRACK [*smiling*]. People say such things—but they don't do them.

HEDDA [*without replying*]. And supposing the pistol was stolen, and the owner is discovered? What then?

BRACK. Well, Hedda—then comes the scandal.

HEDDA. The scandal!

BRACK. Yes, the scandal—of which you are mortally afraid. You will, of course, be brought before the court—both you and Mademoiselle Diana. She will have to explain how the thing happened—whether it was an accidental shot or murder. Did the pistol go off as he was trying to take it out of his pocket, to threaten her with? Or did she tear the pistol out of his hand, shoot him, and push it back into his pocket? That would be quite like her; for she is an able-bodied young person, this same Mademoiselle Diana.

HEDDA. But *I* have nothing to do with all this repulsive business.

BRACK. No. But you will have to answer the question: Why did you give Eilert Lövborg the pistol? And what conclusions will people draw from the fact that you did give it to him?

HEDDA [*lets her head sink*]. That is true. I did not think of that.

BRACK. Well, fortunately, there is no danger, so long as I say nothing.

HEDDA [*looks up at him*]. So I am in your power, Judge Brack. You have me at your beck and call, from this time forward.

BRACK [*whispers softly*]. Dearest Hedda—believe me—I shall not abuse my advantage.

HEDDA. I am in your power none the less. Subject to your will and your demands. A slave, a slave then! [*Rises impetuously.*] No, I cannot endure the thought of that! Never!

BRACK [*looks half-mockingly at her*]. People generally get used to the inevitable.

HEDDA [*returns his look*]. Yes, perhaps. [*She crosses to the writing-table. Suppressing an involuntary smile, she imitates* TESMAN's *intonations.*] Well? Are you getting on, George? Eh?

TESMAN. Heaven knows, dear. In any case it will be the work of months.

HEDDA [*as before*]. Fancy that! [*Passes her hands softly through* MRS. ELVSTED's *hair.*] Doesn't it seem strange to you, Thea? Here are you sitting with Tesman—just as you used to sit with Eilert Lövborg?

MRS. ELVSTED. Ah, if I could only inspire your husband in the same way.

HEDDA. Oh, that will come too—in time.

TESMAN. Yes, do you know, Hedda—I really think I begin to feel something of the sort. But won't you go and sit with Brack again?

HEDDA. Is there nothing I can do to help you two?

TESMAN. No, nothing in the world. [*Turning his head.*] I trust to you to keep Hedda company, my dear Brack.

BRACK [*with a glance at* HEDDA]. With the very greatest of pleasure.

HEDDA. Thanks. But I am tired this evening. I will go in and lie down a little on the sofa.

TESMAN. Yes, do dear—eh? [HEDDA *goes into the back room and draws the curtains. A short pause. Suddenly she is heard playing a wild dance on the piano.*]

MRS. ELVSTED [*starts from her chair*]. Oh—what is that?

TESMAN [*runs to the doorway*]. Why, my dearest Hedda—don't play dance music tonight! Just think of Aunt Rina! And of Eilert too!

HEDDA [*puts her head out between the curtains*]. And of Aunt Julia. And of all the rest of them.—After this, I will be quiet. [*Closes the curtains again.*]

TESMAN [*at the writing-table*]. It's not good for her to see us at this distressing work. I'll tell you what, Mrs. Elvsted,—you shall take the empty room at Aunt Julia's, and then I will come over in the evenings, and we can sit and work there—eh?

HEDDA [*in the inner room*]. I hear what you are saying, Tesman. But how am *I* to get through the evenings out here?

TESMAN [*turning over the papers*]. Oh, I daresay Judge Brack will be so kind as to look in now and then, even though I am out.

BRACK [*in the arm-chair, calls out gaily*]. Every blessed evening, with all the pleasure in life, Mrs. Tesman! We shall get on capitally together, we two!

HEDDA [*speaking loud and clear*]. Yes, don't you flatter yourself we will, Judge Brack? Now that you are the one cock in the basket— [*A shot is heard within.* TESMAN, MRS. ELVSTED, *and* BRACK *leap to their feet.*]

TESMAN. Oh, now she is playing with those pistols again. [*He throws back the curtains and runs in, followed by* MRS. ELVSTED. HEDDA *lies stretched on the sofa, lifeless. Confusion and cries.* BERTA *enters in alarm from the right.*]

TESMAN [*shrieks to* BRACK]. Shot herself! Shot herself in the temple! Fancy that!

BRACK [*half-fainting in the arm-chair*]. Good God!—people don't do such things.

(1890)

Oscar Wilde *1854–1900*

THE IMPORTANCE OF BEING EARNEST

CHARACTERS

JOHN WORTHING, J. P.	LANE, *Manservant.*
ALGERNON MONCRIEFF.	LADY BRACKNELL.
REV. CANON CHASUBLE, D. D.	HON. GWENDOLEN FAIRFAX.
MERRIMAN, *Butler.*	CECILY CARDEW.
	MISS PRISM, *Governess.*

THE SCENES OF THE PLAY.

ACT I.

Algernon Moncrieff's Flat in Half-Moon Street, W.

ACT II.

The Garden at the Manor House, Woolton.

ACT III.

Drawing-Room of the Manor House, Woolton.

TIME—The Present.   PLACE—London.

ACT I

SCENE

Morning-room in ALGERNON'S *flat in Half-Moon Street. The room is luxuriously and artistically furnished. The sound of a piano is heard in the adjoining room.*

[LANE *is arranging afternoon tea on the table, and after the music has ceased,* ALGERNON *enters.*]

ALGERNON. Did you hear what I was playing, Lane?

LANE. I didn't think it polite to listen, sir.

ALGERNON. I'm sorry for that, for your sake. I don't play accurately—anyone can play accurately—but I play with wonderful expression. As far as the piano is concerned, sentiment is my forte. I keep science for Life.

LANE. Yes, sir.

ALGERNON. And, speaking of the science of Life, have you got the cucumber sandwiches cut for Lady Bracknell?

LANE. Yes, sir. [*Hands them on a salver.*]

ALGERNON [*inspects them, takes two, and sits down on the sofa*]. Oh! . . . by the way, Lane, I see from your book that on Thursday night, when Lord Shoreman and Mr. Worthing were dining with me, eight bottles of champagne are entered as having been consumed.

LANE. Yes, sir; eight bottles and a pint.

ALGERNON. Why is it that in a bachelor's establishment the servants invariably drink the champagne? I ask merely for information.

LANE. I attribute it to the superior quality of the wine, sir. I have often observed that in married households the champagne is rarely of a first-rate brand.

ALGERNON. Good Heavens! Is marriage so demoralizing as that?

LANE. I believe it *is* a very pleasant state, sir. I have had very little experience of it myself up to the present. I have only been married once. That was in consequence of a misunderstanding between myself and a young woman.

ALGERNON [*languidly*]. I don't know that I am much interested in your family life, Lane.

LANE. No, sir; it is not a very interesting subject. I never think of it myself.

ALGERNON. Very natural, I am sure. That will do, Lane, thank you.

LANE. Thank you, sir. [LANE *goes out.*]

ALGERNON. Lane's views on marriage seem somewhat lax. Really, if the lower orders don't set us a good example, what on earth is the use of them? They seem, as a class, to have absolutely no sense of moral responsibility. [*Enter* LANE.]

LANE. Mr. Ernest Worthing. [*Enter* JACK. LANE *goes out.*]

ALGERNON. How are you, my dear Ernest? What brings you up to town?

JACK. Oh, pleasure, pleasure! What else should bring one anywhere? Eating as usual, I see, Algy!

ALGERNON [*stiffly*]. I believe it is customary in good society to take some slight refreshment at five o'clock. Where have you been since last Thursday?

JACK [*sitting down on the sofa*]. In the country.

ALGERNON. What on earth do you do there?

JACK [*pulling off his gloves*]. When one is in town one amuses oneself. When one is in the country one amuses other people. It is excessively boring.

ALGERNON. And who are the people you amuse?

JACK [*airily*]. Oh, neighbors, neighbors.

ALGERNON. Got nice neighbors in your part of Shropshire?

JACK. Perfectly horrid! Never speak to one of them.

ALGERNON. How immensely you must amuse them! [*Goes over and takes sandwich.*] By the way, Shropshire is your country, is it not?

JACK. Eh? Shropshire? Yes, of course. Hallo! Why all these cups? Why cucumber sandwiches? Why such reckless extravagance in one so young? Who is coming to tea?

ALGERNON. Oh! merely Aunt Augusta and Gwendolen.

JACK. How perfectly delightful!

ALGERNON. Yes, that is all very well; but I am afraid Aunt Augusta won't quite approve of your being here.

JACK. May I ask why?

ALGERNON. My dear fellow, the way you flirt with Gwendolen is perfectly disgraceful. It is almost as bad as the way Gwendolen flirts with you.

JACK. I am in love with Gwendolen. I have come up to town expressly to propose to her.

ALGERNON. I thought you had come for pleasure? . . . I call that business.

JACK. How utterly unromantic you are!

ALGERNON. I really don't see anything romantic in proposing. It is very romantic to be in love. But there is nothing romantic about a definite proposal. Why, one may be accepted. One usually is, I believe. Then the excitement is all over. The very essence of romance is uncertainty. If ever I get married, I'll certainly try to forget the fact.

JACK. I have no doubt about that, dear Algy. The Divorce Court was specially invented for people whose memories are so curiously constituted.

ALGERNON. Oh! there is no use speculating on that subject. Divorces are made in Heaven—[JACK *puts out his hand to take a sandwich.* ALGERNON *at once interferes.*] Please don't touch the cucumber sandwiches. They are ordered specially for Aunt Augusta. [*Takes one and eats it.*]

JACK. Well, you have been eating them all the time.

ALGERNON. That is quite a different matter. She is my aunt. [*Takes plate from below.*] Have some bread and butter. The bread and butter is for Gwendolen. Gwendolen is devoted to bread and butter.

JACK [*advancing to table and helping himself*]. And very good bread and butter it is, too.

ALGERNON. Well, my dear fellow, you need not eat as if you were going to eat it all. You behave as if you were married to her already. You are not married to her already, and I don't think you will ever be.

JACK. Why on earth do you say that?

ALGERNON. Well, in the first place girls never marry the men they flirt with. Girls don't think it right.

JACK. Oh, that is nonsense!

ALGERNON. It isn't. It is a great truth. It accounts for the extraordinary number of bachelors that one sees all over the place. In the second place, I don't give my consent.

JACK. Your consent!

ALGERNON. My dear fellow, Gwendolen is my first cousin. And before I allow you to marry her, you will have to clear up the whole question of Cecily. [*Rings bell.*]

JACK. Cecily! What on earth do you mean? What do you mean, Algy, by Cecily? I don't know anyone of the name of Cecily. [*Enter* LANE.]

ALGERNON. Bring me that cigarette case Mr. Worthing left in the smoking-room the last time he dined here.

LANE. Yes, sir. [LANE *goes out.*]

JACK. Do you mean to say you have had my cigarette case all this time? I wish to goodness you had let me know. I have been writing frantic letters to Scotland Yard about it. I was very nearly offering a large reward.

ALGERNON. Well, I wish you would offer one. I happen to be more than usually hard up.

JACK. There is no good offering a large reward now that the thing is found. [*Enter* LANE *with the cigarette case on a salver.* ALGERNON *takes it at once.* LANE *goes out.*]

ALGERNON. I think that is rather mean of you, Ernest, I must say. [*Opens case and examines it.*] However, it makes no matter, for, now that I look at the inscription, I find that the thing isn't yours after all.

JACK. Of course it's mine. [*Moving to him.*] You have seen me with it a hundred times, and you have no right whatsoever to read what is written inside. It is a very ungentlemanly thing to read a private cigarette case.

ALGERNON. Oh! it is absurd to have a hard-and-fast rule about what one should read and what one shouldn't. More than half of modern culture depends on what one shouldn't read.

JACK. I am quite aware of the fact, and I don't propose to discuss modern culture. It isn't the sort of thing one should talk of in private. I simply want my cigarette case back.

ALGERNON. Yes; but this isn't your cigarette case. This cigarette case is a present from someone of the name of Cecily, and you said you didn't know anyone of that name.

JACK. Well, if you want to know, Cecily happens to be my aunt.

ALGERNON. Your aunt!

JACK. Yes. Charming old lady she is, too. Lives at Tunbridge Wells. Just give it back to me, Algy.

ALGERNON [*retreating to back of sofa*]. But why does she call herself little Cecily if she is your aunt and lives at Tunbridge Wells? [*Reading.*] "From little Cecily with her fondest love."

JACK [*moving to sofa and kneeling upon it*]. My dear fellow, what on earth is there in that? Some aunts are tall, some aunts are not tall. That is a matter that surely an aunt may be allowed to decide for herself. You seem to think that every aunt should be exactly like your aunt! That is absurd! For Heaven's sake give me back my cigarette case. [*Follows* ALGERNON *round the room.*]

ALGERNON. Yes. But why does your aunt call you her uncle? "From little Cecily, with her fondest love to her dear Uncle Jack." There is no objection, I admit, to an aunt being a small aunt, but why an aunt, no matter what her size may be, should call her own nephew her uncle, I can't quite make out. Besides, your name isn't Jack at all; it's Ernest.

JACK. It isn't Ernest; it's Jack.

ALGERNON. You have always told me it was Ernest. I have introduced you to everyone as Ernest. You answer to the name of Ernest. You look as if your name was Ernest. You are the most earnest-looking person I ever saw in my life. It is perfectly absurd your saying that your name isn't Ernest. It's on your cards. Here is one of them. [*Taking it from case.*] "Mr. Ernest Worthing, B 4, The Albany." I'll keep this as a proof your name is Ernest if ever you attempt to deny it to me, or to Gwendolen, or to anyone else. [*Puts the card in his pocket.*]

JACK. Well, my name is Ernest in town and Jack in the country, and the cigarette case was given to me in the country.

ALGERNON. Yes, but that does not account for the fact that your small Aunt Cecily, who lives at Tunbridge Wells, calls you her dear uncle. Come, old boy, you had much better have the thing out at once.

JACK. My dear Algy, you talk exactly as if you were a dentist. It is very vulgar to talk like a dentist when one isn't a dentist. It produces a false impression.

ALGERNON. Well, that is exactly what dentists always do. Now, go on! Tell me the whole thing. I may mention that I have always suspected you of being a confirmed and secret Bunburyist; and I am quite sure of it now.

JACK. Bunburyist? What on earth do you mean by a Bunburyist?

ALGERNON. I'll reveal to you the meaning of that incomparable expression as soon as you are kind enough to inform me why you are Ernest in town and Jack in the country.

JACK. Well, produce my cigarette case first.

ALGERNON. Here it is. [*Hands cigarette case.*] Now produce your explanation, and pray make it improbable. [*Sits on sofa.*]

JACK. My dear fellow, there is nothing improbable about my explanation at all. In fact it's perfectly ordinary. Old Mr. Thomas Cardew, who adopted me when I was a little boy, made me in his will guardian to his grand-daughter, Miss Cecily Cardew. Cecily, who addresses me as her uncle from motives of respect that you could not possibly appreciate, lives at my place in the country under the charge of her admirable governess, Miss Prism.

ALGERNON. Where is that place in the country, by the way?

JACK. That is nothing to you, dear boy. You are not going to be invited. . . . I may tell you candidly that the place is not in Shropshire.

ALGERNON. I suspected that, my dear fellow! I have Bunburyed all over Shropshire on two separate occasions. Now, go on. Why are you Ernest in town and Jack in the country?

JACK. My dear Algy, I don't know whether you will be able to understand my real motives. You are hardly serious enough. When one is placed in the position of guardian, one has to adopt a very high moral tone on all subjects. It's one's duty to do so. And as a high moral tone can hardly be said to conduce very much to either one's health or one's happiness, in order to get up to town I have always pretended to have a younger brother of the name of Ernest, who lives in the Albany, and gets into the most dreadful scrapes. That, my dear Algy, is the whole truth pure and simple.

ALGERNON. The truth is rarely pure and never simple. Modern life would be very tedious if it were either, and modern literature a complete impossibility!

JACK. That wouldn't be at all a bad thing.

ALGERNON. Literary criticism is not your forte, my dear fellow. Don't try it. You should leave that to people who haven't been at a University. They do it so well in the daily papers. What you really are is a Bunburyist. I was quite right in saying you were a Bunburyist. You are one of the most advanced Bunburyists I know.

JACK. What on earth do you mean?

ALGERNON. You have invented a very useful younger brother called Ernest, in order that you may be able to come up to town as often as you like. I have invented an invaluable permanent invalid called Bunbury, in order that I may be able to go down into the country whenever I choose. Bunbury is perfectly invaluable. If it wasn't for Bunbury's extraordinary bad health, for instance, I wouldn't be able to dine with you at Willis' tonight, for I have been really engaged to Aunt Augusta for more than a week.

JACK. I haven't asked you to dine with me anywhere tonight.

ALGERNON. I know. You are absolutely careless about sending out invitations. It is very foolish of you. Nothing annoys people so much as not receiving invitations.

JACK. You had much better dine with your Aunt Augusta.

ALGERNON. I haven't the smallest intention of doing anything of the kind. To begin with, I dined there on Monday, and once a week is quite enough to dine with one's own relatives. In the second place, whenever I do dine there I am always treated as a member of the family, and sent down with either no woman at all, or two. In the third place, I know perfectly well whom she will place me next, tonight. She will place me next Mary Farquhar, who always flirts with her own husband across the dinnertable. That is not very pleasant. Indeed, it is not even decent . . . and that sort of thing is enormously on the increase. The amount of women in London who flirt with their own husbands is perfectly scandalous. It looks so bad. It is simply washing one's clean linen in public. Besides, now that I know you to be a confirmed Bunbury ist I naturally want to talk to you about Bunburying. I want to tell you the rules.

JACK. I'm not a Bunburyist at all. If Gwendolen accepts me, I am going to kill my brother, indeed I think I'll kill him in any case. Cecily is a little too much interested in him. It is rather a bore. So I am going to get rid of Ernest. And I strongly advise you to do the same with Mr. . . . with your invalid friend who has the absurd name.

ALGERNON. Nothing will induce me to part with Bunbury, and if you ever get married, which seems to me extremely problematic, you will be very glad to know Bunbury. A man who marries without knowing Bunbury has a very tedious time of it.

JACK. That is nonsense. If I marry a charming girl like Gwendolen, and she is the only girl I ever saw in my life that I would marry, I certainly won't want to know Bunbury.

ALGERNON. Then your wife will. You don't seem to realize, that in married life three is company and two is none.

JACK [*sententiously*]. That, my dear young friend, is the theory that the corrupt French Drama has been propounding for the last fifty years.

ALGERNON. Yes; and that the happy English home has proved in half the time.

JACK. For heaven's sake, don't try to be cynical. It's perfectly easy to be cynical.

ALGERNON. My dear fellow, it isn't easy to be anything now-a-days. There's such a lot of beastly competition about. [*The sound of an electric bell is heard.*] Ah! that must be Aunt Augusta. Only relatives, or creditors, ever ring in that Wagnerian manner. Now, if I get her out of the way for ten minutes, so that you can have an opportunity for proposing to Gwendolen, may I dine with you tonight at Willis'?

JACK. I suppose so, if you want to.

ALGERNON. Yes, but you must be serious about it. I hate people who are not serious about meals. It is so shallow of them. [*Enter* LANE.]

LANE. Lady Bracknell and Miss Fairfax. [ALGERNON *goes forward to meet them. Enter* LADY BRACKNELL *and* GWENDOLEN.]

LADY BRACKNELL. Good afternoon, dear Algernon, I hope you are behaving very well.

ALGERNON. I'm feeling very well, Aunt Augusta.

LADY BRACKNELL. That's not quite the same thing. In fact the two things rarely go together. [*Sees* JACK *and bows to him with icy coldness.*]

ALGERNON [*to* GWENDOLEN]. Dear me, you are smart!

GWENDOLEN. I am always smart! Aren't I, Mr. Worthing?

JACK. You're quite perfect, Miss Fairfax.

GWENDOLEN. Oh! I hope I am not that. It would leave no room for developments, and I intend to develop in *many directions.* [GWENDOLEN *and* JACK *sit down together in the corner.*]

LADY BRACKNELL. I'm sorry if we are a little late, Algernon, but I was obliged to call on dear Lady Harbury. I hadn't been there since her poor husband's death. I never saw a woman so altered; she looks quite twenty years younger. And now I'll have a cup of tea, and one of those nice cucumber sandwiches you promised me.

ALGERNON. Certainly, Aunt Augusta. [*Goes over to tea-table.*]

LADY BRACKNELL. Won't you come and sit here, Gwendolen?

GWENDOLEN. Thanks, mamma, I'm quite comfortable where I am.

ALGERNON [*picking up empty plate in horror*]. Good heavens! Lane! Why are there no cucumber sandwiches? I ordered them specially.

LANE [*gravely*]. There were no cucumbers in the market this morning, sir. I went down twice.

ALGERNON. No cucumbers!

LANE. No, sir. Not even for ready money.

ALGERNON. That will do, Lane, thank you.

LANE. Thank you, sir. [*Goes out.*]

ALGERNON. I am greatly distressed, Aunt Augusta, about there being no cucumbers, not even for ready money.

LADY BRACKNELL. It really makes no matter, Algernon. I had some crumpets with Lady Harbury, who seems to me to be living entirely for pleasure now.

ALGERNON. I hear her hair has turned quite gold from grief.

LADY BRACKNELL. It certainly has changed its color. From what cause I, of course, cannot say. [ALGERNON *crosses and hands tea.*] Thank you. I've quite a treat for you tonight, Algernon. I am going to send you down with Mary Farquhar. She is such a nice woman, and so attentive to her husband. It's delightful to watch them.

ALGERNON. I am afraid, Aunt Augusta, I shall have to give up the pleasure of dining with you tonight after all.

LADY BRACKNELL [*frowning*]. I hope not, Algernon. It would put my table completely out. Your uncle would have to dine upstairs. Fortunately he is accustomed to that.

ALGERNON. It is a great bore, and, I need hardly say, a terrible disappointment to me, but the fact is I have just had a telegram to say that my poor friend Bunbury is very ill again. [*Exchanges glances with* JACK.] They seem to think I should be with him.

LADY BRACKNELL. It is very strange. This Mr. Bunbury seems to suffer from curiously bad health.

ALGERNON. Yes; poor Bunbury is a dreadful invalid.

LADY BRACKNELL. Well, I must say, Algernon, that I think it is high time that Mr. Bunbury made up his mind whether he was going to live or to die. This shilly-shallying with the question is absurd. Nor do I in any way approve of the modern sympathy with invalids. I consider it morbid. Illness of any kind is hardly a thing to be encouraged in others. Health is the primary duty of life. I am always telling that to your poor uncle, but he never seems to take much notice . . . as far as any improvement in his ailment goes. I should be much obliged if you would ask Mr. Bunbury, from me, to be kind enough not to have a relapse on Saturday, for I rely on you to arrange my music for me. It is my last reception and one wants something that will encourage conversation, particularly at the end of the season when everyone has practically said whatever they had to say, which, in most cases, was probably not much.

ALGERNON. I'll speak to Bunbury, Aunt Augusta, if he is still conscious, and I think I can promise you he'll be all right by Saturday. You see, if one plays good music, people don't listen, and if one plays bad music people don't talk. But I'll run over the program I've drawn out, if you will kindly come into the next room for a moment.

LADY BRACKNELL. Thank you, Algernon. It is very thoughtful of you. [*Rising, and following* ALGERNON.] I'm sure the program will be delightful, after a few expurgations. French songs I cannot possibly allow. People always seem to think that they are improper, and either look shocked, which is vulgar, or laugh, which is worse. But German sounds a thoroughly respectable language, and indeed, I believe is so. Gwendolen, you will accompany me.

GWENDOLEN. Certainly, mamma. [LADY BRACKNELL *and* ALGERNON *go into the music-room,* GWENDOLEN *remains behind.*]

JACK. Charming day it has been, Miss Fairfax.

GWENDOLEN. Pray don't talk to me about the weather, Mr. Worthing. Whenever people talk to me about the weather, I always feel quite certain that they mean something else. And that makes me so nervous.

JACK. I do mean something else.

GWENDOLEN. I thought so. In fact, I am never wrong.

JACK. And I would like to be allowed to take advantage of Lady Bracknell's temporary absence . . .

GWENDOLEN. I would certainly advise you to do so. Mamma has a way of coming back suddenly into a room that I have often had to speak to her about.

JACK [*nervously*]. Miss Fairfax, ever since I met you I have admired you more than any girl . . . I have ever met since . . . I met you.

GWENDOLEN. Yes, I am quite aware of the fact. And I often wish that in public, at any rate, you had been more demonstrative. For me you have always had an irresistible fascination. Even before I met you I was far from indifferent to you. [JACK *looks at her in amazement.*] We live, as I hope you know, Mr. Worthing, in an age of ideals. The fact is constantly mentioned in the more expensive monthly magazines, and has reached the provincial pulpits I am told: and my ideal has always been to love some one of the name of Ernest. There is something in that name that inspires absolute confidence. The moment Algernon first mentioned to me that he had a friend called Ernest, I knew I was destined to love you.

JACK. You really love me, Gwendolen?

GWENDOLEN. Passionately!

JACK. Darling! You don't know how happy you've made me.

GWENDOLEN. My own Ernest!

JACK. But you don't really mean to say that you couldn't love me if my name wasn't Ernest?

GWENDOLEN. But your name is Ernest.

JACK. Yes, I know it is. But supposing it was something else? Do you mean to say you couldn't love me then?

GWENDOLEN [glibly]. Ah! that is clearly a metaphysical speculation, and like most metaphysical speculations has very little reference at all to the actual facts of real life, as we know them.

JACK. Personally, darling, to speak quite candidly, I don't much care about the name of Ernest . . . I don't think that name suits me at all.

GWENDOLEN. It suits you perfectly. It is a divine name. It has a music of its own. It produces vibrations.

JACK. Well, really, Gwendolen, I must say that I think there are lots of other much nicer names. I think, Jack, for instance, a charming name.

GWENDOLEN. Jack? . . . No, there is very little music in the name Jack, if any at all, indeed. It does not thrill. It produces absolutely no vibrations. . . . I have known several Jacks, and they all, without exception, were more than usually plain. Besides, Jack is a notorious domesticity for John! And I pity any woman who is married to a man called John. She would probably never be allowed to know the entrancing pleasure of a single moment's solitude. The only really safe name is Ernest.

JACK. Gwendolen, I must get christened at once—I mean we must get married at once. There is no time to be lost.

GWENDOLEN. Married, Mr. Worthing?

JACK [astounded]. Well . . . surely. You know that I love you, and you led me to believe, Miss Fairfax, that you were not absolutely indifferent to me.

GWENDOLEN. I adore you. But you haven't proposed to me yet. Nothing has been said at all about marriage. The subject has not even been touched on.

JACK. Well . . . may I propose to you now?

GWENDOLEN. I think it would be an admirable opportunity. And to spare you any possible disappointment, Mr. Worthing, I think it only fair to tell you quite frankly beforehand that I am fully determined to accept you.

JACK. Gwendolen!

GWENDOLEN. Yes, Mr. Worthing, what have you got to say to me?

JACK. You know what I have got to say to you.

GWENDOLEN. Yes, but you don't say it.

JACK. Gwendolen, will you marry me? [Goes on his knees.]

GWENDOLEN. Of course I will, darling. How long you have been about it! I am afraid you have had very little experience in how to propose.

JACK. My own one, I have never loved anyone in the world but you.

GWENDOLEN. Yes, but men often propose for practice. I know my brother Gerald does. All my girl-friends tell me so. What wonderfully blue eyes you have, Ernest! They are quite, quite blue. I hope you will always look at me just like that, especially when there are other people present. [Enter LADY BRACKNELL.]

LADY BRACKNELL. Mr. Worthing! Rise, sir, from this semi-recumbent posture. It is most indecorous.

GWENDOLEN. Mamma! [*He tries to rise; she restrains him.*] I must beg you to retire. This is no place for you. Besides, Mr. Worthing has not quite finished yet.

LADY BRACKNELL. Finished what, may I ask?

GWENDOLEN. I am engaged to Mr. Worthing, mamma. [*They rise together.*]

LADY BRACKNELL. Pardon me, you are not engaged to anyone. When you do become engaged to some one, I, or your father, should his health permit him, will inform you of the fact. An engagement should come on a young girl as a surprise, pleasant or unpleasant, as the case may be. It is hardly a matter that she could be allowed to arrange for herself. . . . And now I have a few questions to put to you, Mr. Worthing. While I am making these inquiries, you, Gwendolen, will wait for me below in the carriage.

GWENDOLEN [*reproachfully*]. Mamma!

LADY BRACKNELL. In the carriage, Gwendolen! [GWENDOLEN *goes to the door. She and* JACK *blow kisses to each other behind* LADY BRACKNELL'S *back.* LADY BRACKNELL *looks vaguely about as if she could not understand what the noise was. Finally turns round.*] Gwendolen, the carriage!

GWENDOLEN. Yes, mamma. [*Goes out, looking back at* JACK.]

LADY BRACKNELL [*sitting down*]. You can take a seat, Mr. Worthing. [*Looks in her pocket for note-book and pencil.*]

JACK. Thank you, Lady Bracknell, I prefer standing.

LADY BRACKNELL [*pencil and note-book in hand*]. I feel bound to tell you that you are not down on my list of eligible young men, although I have the same list as the dear Duchess of Bolton has. We work together, in fact. However, I am quite ready to enter your name, should your answers be what a really affectionate mother requires. Do you smoke?

JACK. Well, yes, I must admit I smoke.

LADY BRACKNELL. I am glad to hear it. A man should always have an occupation of some kind. There are far too many idle men in London as it is. How old are you?

JACK. Twenty-nine.

LADY BRACKNELL. A very good age to be married at. I have always been of opinion that a man who desires to get married should know either everything or nothing. Which do you know?

JACK [*after some hesitation*]. I know nothing, Lady Bracknell.

LADY BRACKNELL. I am pleased to hear it. I do not approve of anything that tampers with natural ignorance. Ignorance is like a delicate exotic fruit; touch it and the bloom is gone. The whole theory of modern education is radically unsound. Fortunately in England, at any rate, education produces no effect whatsoever. If it did, it would prove a serious danger to the upper classes, and probably lead to acts of violence in Grosvenor Square. What is your income?

JACK. Between seven and eight thousand a year.

LADY BRACKNELL [*makes a note in her book*]. In land, or in investments?

JACK. In investments, chiefly.

LADY BRACKNELL. That is satisfactory. What between the duties expected of one during one's life-time, and the duties exacted from one after one's death, land has ceased to be either a profit or a pleasure. It gives one position, and prevents one from keeping it up. That's all that can be said about land.

JACK. I have a country house with some land, of course, attached to it, about fifteen hundred acres, I believe; but I don't depend on that for my real income. In fact, as far as I can make out, the poachers are the only people who make anything out of it.

LADY BRACKNELL. A country house! How many bedrooms? Well, that point can be cleared up afterwards. You have a town house, I hope? A girl with a simple, unspoiled nature, like Gwendolen, could hardly be expected to reside in the country.

JACK. Well, I own a house in Belgrave Square, but it is let by the year to Lady Bloxham. Of course, I can get it back whenever I like, at six months' notice.

LADY BRACKNELL. Lady Bloxham? I don't know her.

JACK. Oh, she goes about very little. She is a lady considerably advanced in years.

LADY BRACKNELL. Ah, now-a-days that is no guarantee of respectability of character. What number in Belgrave Square?

JACK. 149.

LADY BRACKNELL [*shaking her head*]. The unfashionable side. I thought there was something. However, that could easily be altered.

JACK. Do you mean the fashion, or the side?

LADY BRACKNELL [*sternly*]. Both, if necessary, I presume. What are your politics?

JACK. Well, I am afraid I really have none. I am a Liberal Unionist.

LADY BRACKNELL. Oh, they count as Tories. They dine with us. Or come in the evening, at any rate. Now to minor matters. Are your parents living?

JACK. I have lost both my parents.

LADY BRACKNELL. Both? . . . That seems like carelessness. Who was your father? He was evidently a man of some wealth. Was he born in what the Radical papers call the purple of commerce, or did he rise from the ranks of the aristocracy?

JACK. I am afraid I really don't know. The fact is, Lady Bracknell, I said I had lost my parents. It would be nearer the truth to say that my parents seem to have lost me . . . I don't actually know who I am by birth. I was . . . well, I was found.

LADY BRACKNELL. Found!

JACK. The late Mr. Thomas Cardew, an old gentleman of a very charitable and kindly disposition, found me, and gave me the name of Worthing, because he happened to have a first-class ticket for Worthing in his pocket at the time. Worthing is a place in Sussex. It is a seaside resort.

LADY BRACKNELL. Where did the charitable gentleman who had a first-class ticket for this seaside resort find you?

JACK [*gravely*]. In a hand-bag.

LADY BRACKNELL. A hand-bag?

JACK [*very seriously*]. Yes, Lady Bracknell. I was in a hand-bag—a somewhat large, black leather hand-bag, with handles to it—an ordinary hand-bag in fact.

LADY BRACKNELL. In what locality did this Mr. James, or Thomas, Cardew come across this ordinary hand-bag?

JACK. In the cloak-room at Victoria Station. It was given to him in mistake for his own.

LADY BRACKNELL. The cloak-room at Victoria Station?

JACK. Yes. The Brighton line.

LADY BRACKNELL. The line is immaterial. Mr. Worthing, I confess I feel somewhat bewildered by what you have just told me. To be born, or at any rate bred, in a hand-bag, whether it had handles or not, seems to me to display a contempt for the ordinary decencies of family life that remind one of the worst excesses of the French Revolution. And I presume you know what that unfortunate movement led to? As for the particular locality in which the hand–bag was found, a cloak-room at a railway station might serve to conceal a social indiscretion—has probably, indeed, been used for that purpose before now—but it could hardly be regarded as an assured basis for a recognized position in good society.

JACK. May I ask you then what you would advise me to do? I need hardly say I would do anything in the world to ensure Gwendolen's happiness.

LADY BRACKNELL. I would strongly advise you, Mr. Worthing, to try and acquire some relations as soon as possible, and to make a definite effort to produce at any rate one parent, of either sex, before the season is quite over.

JACK. Well, I don't see how I could possibly manage to do that. I can produce the hand-bag at any moment. It is in my dressing-room at home. I really think that should satisfy you, Lady Bracknell.

LADY BRACKNELL. Me, sir! What has it to do with me? You can hardly imagine that I and Lord Bracknell would dream of allowing our only daughter—a girl brought up with the utmost care—to marry into a cloak–room, and form an alliance with a parcel? Good morning, Mr. Worthing! [LADY BRACKNELL *sweeps out in majestic indignation.*]

JACK. Good morning! [ALGERNON, *from the other room, strikes up the Wedding March.* JACK *looks perfectly furious, and goes to the door.*] For goodness' sake don't play that ghastly tune, Algy! How idiotic you are! [*The music stops, and* ALGERNON *enters cheerily.*]

ALGERNON. Didn't it go off all right, old boy? You don't mean to say Gwendolen refused you? I know it is a way she has. She is always refusing people. I think it is most ill-natured of her.

JACK. Oh, Gwendolen is as right as a trivet. As far as she is concerned, we are engaged. Her mother is perfectly unbearable. Never met such a Gorgon . . . I don't really know what a Gorgon is like, but I am quite sure that Lady Bracknell is one. In any case, she is a monster, without being a myth, which is rather unfair. . . . I beg your pardon, Algy, I suppose I shouldn't talk about your own aunt in that way before you.

ALGERNON. My dear boy, I love hearing my relations abused. It is the only thing that makes me put up with them at all. Relations are simply a tedious pack of people, who haven't got the remotest knowledge of how to live, nor the smallest instinct about when to die.

JACK. Oh, that is nonsense!

ALGERNON. It isn't!

JACK. Well, I won't argue about the matter. You always want to argue about things.

ALGERNON. That is exactly what things were originally made for.

JACK. Upon my word, if I thought that, I'd shoot myself. . . . [*A pause.*] You don't think there is any chance of Gwendolen becoming like her mother in about a hundred and fifty years, do you, Algy?

ALGERNON. All women become like their mothers. That is their tragedy. No man does. That's his.

JACK. Is that clever?

ALGERNON. It is perfectly phrased! and quite as true as any observation in civilized life should be.

JACK. I am sick to death of cleverness. Everybody is clever now-a-days. You can't go anywhere without meeting clever people. The thing has become an absolute public nuisance. I wish to goodness we had a few fools left.

ALGERNON. We have.

JACK. I should extremely like to meet them. What do they talk about?

ALGERNON. The fools? Oh! about the clever people, of course.

JACK. What fools!

ALGERNON. By the way, did you tell Gwendolen the truth about your being Ernest in town, and Jack in the country?

JACK [*in a very patronizing manner*]. My dear fellow, the truth isn't quite the sort of thing one tells to a nice, sweet, refined girl. What extraordinary ideas you have about the way to behave to a woman!

ALGERNON. The only way to behave to a woman is to make love to her, if she is pretty, and to someone else if she is plain.

JACK. Oh, that is nonsense.

ALGERNON. What about your brother? What about the profligate Ernest?

JACK. Oh, before the end of the week I shall have got rid of him. I'll say he died in Paris of apoplexy. Lots of people die of apoplexy, quite suddenly, don't they?

ALGERNON. Yes, but it's hereditary, my dear fellow. It's a sort of thing that runs in families. You had much better say a severe chill.

JACK. You are sure a severe chill isn't hereditary, or anything of that kind?

ALGERNON. Of course it isn't!

JACK. Very well, then. My poor brother Ernest is carried off suddenly in Paris, by a severe chill. That gets rid of him.

ALGERNON. But I thought you said that . . . Miss Cardew was a little too much interested in your poor brother Ernest? Won't she feel his loss a good deal?

JACK. Oh, that is all right. Cecily is not a silly, romantic girl, I am glad to say. She has got a capital appetite, goes for long walks, and pays no attention at all to her lessons.

ALGERNON. I would rather like to see Cecily.

JACK. I will take very good care you never do. She is excessively pretty, and she is only just eighteen.

ALGERNON. Have you told Gwendolen yet that you have an excessively pretty ward who is only just eighteen?

JACK. Oh! one doesn't blurt these things out to people. Cecily and Gwendo-

len are perfectly certain to be extremely great friends. I'll bet you anything you like that half an hour after they have met, they will be calling
each other sister.

ALGERNON. Women only do that when they have called each other a lot
of other things first. Now, my dear boy, if we want to get a good table
at Willis', we really must go and dress. Do you know it is nearly seven?

JACK [*irritably*]. Oh! it always is nearly seven.

ALGERNON. Well, I'm hungry.

JACK. I never knew you when you weren't. . . .

ALGERNON. What shall we do after dinner? Go to a theater?

JACK. Oh, no! I loathe listening.

ALGERNON. Well, let us go to the Club?

JACK. Oh, no! I hate talking.

ALGERNON. Well, we might trot round to the Empire at ten?

JACK. Oh, no! I can't bear looking at things. It is so silly.

ALGERNON. Well, what shall we do?

JACK. Nothing!

ALGERNON. It is awfully hard work doing nothing. However, I don't mind
hard work where there is no definite object of any kind. [*Enter* LANE.]

LANE. Miss Fairfax. [*Enter* GWENDOLEN. LANE *goes out.*]

ALGERNON. Gwendolen, upon my word!

GWENDOLEN. Algy, kindly turn your back. I have something very particular
to say to Mr. Worthing.

ALGERNON. Really, Gwendolen, I don't think I can allow this at all.

GWENDOLEN. Algy, you always adopt a strictly immoral attitude towards
life. You are not quite old enough to do that. [ALGERNON *retires to the
fireplace.*]

JACK. My own darling!

GWENDOLEN. Ernest, we may never be married. From the expression on
mamma's face I fear we never shall. Few parents now-a-days pay any
regard to what their children say to them. The old-fashioned respect
for the young is fast dying out. Whatever influence I ever had over
mamma, I lost at the age of three. But although she may prevent us
from becoming man and wife, and I may marry someone else, and marry
often, nothing that she can possibly do can alter my eternal devotion
to you.

JACK. Dear Gwendolen.

GWENDOLEN. The story of your romantic origin, as related to me by
mamma, with unpleasing comments, has naturally stirred the deeper
fibers of my nature. Your Christian name has an irresistible fascination.
The simplicity of your character makes you exquisitely incomprehensible to me. Your town address at the Albany I have. What is your address
in the country?

JACK. The Manor House, Woolton, Hertfordshire. [ALGERNON, *who has been
carefully listening, smiles to himself, and writes the address on his shirt-cuff.
Then picks up the Railway Guide.*]

GWENDOLEN. There is a good postal service, I suppose? It may be necessary
to do something desperate. That, of course, will require serious consideration. I will communicate with you daily.

JACK. My own one!

GWENDOLEN. How long do you remain in town?

JACK. Till Monday.

GWENDOLEN. Good! Algy, you may turn round now.

ALGERNON. Thanks, I've turned round already.

GWENDOLEN. You may also ring the bell.

JACK. You will let me see you to your carriage, my own darling?

GWENDOLEN. Certainly.

JACK [*to* LANE, *who now enters*]. I will see Miss Fairfax out.

LANE. Yes, sir. [JACK *and* GWENDOLEN *go off.* LANE *presents several letters on a salver to* ALGERNON. *It is to be surmised that they are bills, as* ALGERNON, *after looking at the envelopes, tears them up.*]

ALGERNON. A glass of sherry, Lane.

LANE. Yes, sir.

ALGERNON. Tomorrow, Lane, I'm going Bunburying.

LANE. Yes, sir.

ALGERNON. I shall probably not be back till Monday. You can put up my dress clothes, my smoking jacket, and all the Bunbury suits . . .

LANE. Yes, sir. [*Handing sherry.*]

ALGERNON. I hope tomorrow will be a fine day, Lane.

LANE. It never is, sir.

ALGERNON. Lane, you're a perfect pessimist.

LANE. I do my best to give satisfaction, sir. [*Enter* JACK. LANE *goes off.*]

JACK. There's a sensible, intellectual girl! the only girl I ever cared for in my life. [ALGERNON *is laughing immoderately.*] What on earth are you so amused at?

ALGERNON. Oh, I'm a little anxious about poor Bunbury, that's all.

JACK. If you don't take care, your friend Bunbury will get you into a serious scrape some day.

ALGERNON. I love scrapes. They are the only things that are never serious.

JACK. Oh, that's nonsense, Algy. You never talk anything but nonsense.

ALGERNON. Nobody ever does. [JACK *looks indignantly at him, and leaves the room.* ALGERNON *lights a cigarette, reads his shirt-cuff, and smiles.*]

ACT DROP

ACT II

SCENE

Garden at the Manor House. A flight of gray stone steps leads up to the house. The garden, an old-fashioned one, full of roses. Time of year, July. Basket chairs, and a table covered with books, are set under a large yew tree.

[MISS PRISM *discovered seated at the table.* CECILY *is at the back watering flowers.*]

MISS PRISM [*calling*]. Cecily, Cecily! Surely such a utilitarian occupation as the watering of flowers is rather Moulton's duty than yours? Especially at a moment when intellectual pleasures await you. Your German grammar is on the table. Pray open it at page fifteen. We will repeat yesterday's lesson.

CECILY [*coming over very slowly*]. But I don't like German. It isn't at all a becoming language. I know perfectly well that I look quite plain after my German lesson.

MISS PRISM. Child, you know how anxious your guardian is that you should improve yourself in every way. He laid particular stress on your German, as he was leaving for town yesterday. Indeed, he always lays stress on your German when he is leaving for town.

CECILY. Dear Uncle Jack is so very serious! Sometimes he is so serious that I think he cannot be quite well.

MISS PRISM [*drawing herself up*]. Your guardian enjoys the best of health, and his gravity of demeanor is especially to be commended in one so comparatively young as he is. I know no one who has a higher sense of duty and responsibility.

CECILY. I suppose that is why he often looks a little bored when we three are together.

MISS PRISM. Cecily! I am surprised at you. Mr. Worthing has many troubles in his life. Idle merriment and triviality would be out of place in his conversation. You must remember his constant anxiety about that unfortunate young man, his brother.

CECILY. I wish Uncle Jack would allow that unfortunate young man, his brother, to come down here sometimes. We might have a good influence over him, Miss Prism. I am sure you certainly would. You know German, and geology, and things of that kind influence a man very much. [CECILY *begins to write in her diary.*]

MISS PRISM [*shaking her head*]. I do not think that even I could produce any effect on a character that, according to his own brother's admission, is irretrievably weak and vacillating. Indeed, I am not sure that I would desire to reclaim him. I am not in favor of this modern mania for turning bad people into good people at a moment's notice. As a man sows so let him reap. You must put away your diary, Cecily. I really don't see why you should keep a diary at all.

CECILY. I keep a diary in order to enter the wonderful secrets of my life. If I didn't write them down I should probably forget all about them.

MISS PRISM. Memory, my dear Cecily, is the diary that we all carry about with us.

CECILY. Yes, but it usually chronicles the things that have never happened, and couldn't possibly have happened. I believe that Memory is responsible for nearly all the three-volume novels that Mudie[1] sends us.

MISS PRISM. Do not speak slightingly of the three-volume novel, Cecily. I wrote one myself in earlier days.

CECILY. Did you really, Miss Prism? How wonderfully clever you are! I hope it did not end happily? I don't like novels that end happily. They depress me so much.

MISS PRISM. The good ended happily, and the bad unhappily. That is what Fiction means.

CECILY. I suppose so. But it seems very unfair. And was your novel ever published?

MISS PRISM. Alas! no. The manuscript unfortunately was abandoned. I

---

[1] Mudie's Lending Library.

use the word in the sense of lost or mislaid. To your work, child, these speculations are profitless.

CECILY [*smiling*]. But I see dear Dr. Chasuble coming up through the garden.

MISS PRISM [*rising and advancing*]. Dr. Chasuble! This is indeed a pleasure. [*Enter* CANON CHASUBLE.]

CHASUBLE. And how are we this morning? Miss Prism, you are, I trust, well?

CECILY. Miss Prism has just been complaining of a slight headache. I think it would do her so much good to have a short stroll with you in the park, Dr. Chasuble.

MISS PRISM. Cecily, I have not mentioned anything about a headache.

CECILY. No, dear Miss Prism, I know that, but I felt instinctively that you had a headache. Indeed I was thinking about that, and not about my German lesson when the Rector came in.

CHASUBLE. I hope, Cecily, you are not inattentive.

CECILY. Oh, I am afraid I am.

CHASUBLE. That is strange. Were I fortunate enough to be Miss Prism's pupil, I would hang upon her lips. [MISS PRISM *glares.*] I spoke metaphorically.—My metaphor was drawn from bees. Ahem! Mr. Worthing, I suppose, has not returned from town yet?

MISS PRISM. We do not expect him till Monday afternoon.

CHASUBLE. Ah yes, he usually likes to spend his Sunday in London. He is not one of those whose sole aim is enjoyment, as, by all accounts, that unfortunate young man, his brother, seems to be. But I must not disturb Egeria[2] and her pupil any longer.

MISS PRISM. Egeria? My name is Laetitia, Doctor.

CHASUBLE [*bowing*]. A classical allusion merely, drawn from the Pagan authors. I shall see you both no doubt at Evensong.

MISS PRISM. I think, dear Doctor, I will have a stroll with you. I find I have a headache after all, and a walk might do it good.

CHASUBLE. With pleasure, Miss Prism, with pleasure. We might go as far as the schools and back.

MISS PRISM. That would be delightful. Cecily, you will read your Political Economy in my absence. The chapter on the Fall of the Rupee you may omit. It is somewhat too sensational. Even these metallic problems have their melodramatic side. [*Goes down the garden with* DR. CHASUBLE.]

CECILY [*picks up books and throws them back on table*]. Horrid Political Economy! Horrid Geography! Horrid, horrid German! [*Enter* MERRIMAN *with a card on a salver.*]

MERRIMAN. Mr. Ernest Worthing has just driven over from the station. He has brought his luggage with him.

CECILY [*takes the card and reads it*]. "Mr. Ernest Worthing, B 4, The Albany, W." Uncle Jack's brother! Did you tell him Mr. Worthing was in town?

MERRIMAN. Yes, Miss. He seemed very much disappointed. I mentioned that you and Miss Prism were in the garden. He said he was anxious to speak to you privately for a moment.

CECILY. Ask Mr. Ernest Worthing to come here. I suppose you had better talk to the housekeeper about a room for him.

---

[2] A Roman nymph noted for wisdom.

MERRIMAN. Yes, Miss. [MERRIMAN *goes off.*]

CECILY. I have never met any really wicked person before. I feel rather frightened. I am so afraid he will look just like everyone else. [*Enter* ALGERNON, *very gay and debonair.*] He does!

ALGERNON [*raising his hat*]. You are my little Cousin Cecily, I'm sure.

CECILY. You are under some strange mistake. I am not little. In fact, I am more than usually tall for my age. [ALGERNON *is rather taken aback.*] But I am your Cousin Cecily. You, I see from your card, are Uncle Jack's brother, my Cousin Ernest, my wicked Cousin Ernest.

ALGERNON. Oh! I am not really wicked at all, Cousin Cecily. You mustn't think that I am wicked.

CECILY. If you are not, then you have certainly been deceiving us all in a very inexcusable manner. I hope you have not been leading a double life, pretending to be wicked and being really good all the time. That would be hypocrisy.

ALGERNON [*looks at her in amazement*]. Oh! of course I have been rather reckless.

CECILY. I am glad to hear it.

ALGERNON. In fact, now you mention the subject, I have been very bad in my own small way.

CECILY. I don't think you should be so proud of that, though I am sure it must have been very pleasant.

ALGERNON. It is much pleasanter being here with you.

CECILY. I can't understand how you are here at all. Uncle Jack won't be back till Monday afternoon.

ALGERNON. That is a great disappointment. I am obliged to go up by the first train on Monday morning. I have a business appointment that I am anxious . . . to miss.

CECILY. Couldn't you miss it anywhere but in London?

ALGERNON. No; the appointment is in London.

CECILY. Well, I know, of course, how important it is not to keep a business engagement, if one wants to retain any sense of the beauty of life, but still I think you had better wait till Uncle Jack arrives. I know he wants to speak to you about your emigrating.

ALGERNON. About my what?

CECILY. Your emigrating. He has gone up to buy your outfit.

ALGERNON. I certainly wouldn't let Jack buy my outfit. He has no taste in neckties at all.

CECILY. I don't think you will require neckties. Uncle Jack is sending you to Australia.

ALGERNON. Australia! I'd sooner die.

CECILY. Well, he said at dinner on Wednesday night, that you would have to choose between this world, the next world, and Australia.

ALGERNON. Oh, well! The accounts I have received of Australia and the next world, are not particularly encouraging. This world is good enough for me, Cousin Cecily.

CECILY. Yes, but are you good enough for it?

ALGERNON. I'm afraid I'm not that. That is why I want you to reform me. You might make that your mission, if you don't mind, Cousin Cecily.

CECILY. I'm afraid I've not time, this afternoon.

ALGERNON. Well, would you mind reforming myself this afternoon?

CECILY. That is rather Quixotic of you. But I think you should try.

ALGERNON. I will. I feel better already.

CECILY. You are looking a little worse.

ALGERNON. That is because I am hungry.

CECILY. How thoughtless of me. I should have remembered that when one is going to lead an entirely new life, one requires regular and wholesome meals. Won't you come in?

ALGERNON. Thank you. Might I have a button-hole first? I never have any appetite unless I have a button-hole first.

CECILY. A Maréchal Niel? [*Picks up scissors.*]

ALGERNON. No, I'd sooner have a pink rose.

CECILY. Why? [*Cuts a flower.*]

ALGERNON. Because you are like a pink rose, Cousin Cecily.

CECILY. I don't think it can be right for you to talk to me like that. Miss Prism never says such things to me.

ALGERNON. Then Miss Prism is a short-sighted old lady. [CECILY *puts the rose in his button-hole.*] You are the prettiest girl I ever saw.

CECILY. Miss Prism says that all good looks are a snare.

ALGERNON. They are a snare that every sensible man would like to be caught in.

CECILY. Oh! I don't think I would care to catch a sensible man. I shouldn't know what to talk to him about. [*They pass into the house.* MISS PRISM *and* DR. CHASUBLE *return.*]

MISS PRISM. You are too much alone, dear Dr. Chasuble. You should get married. A misanthrope I can understand—a womanthrope, never!

CHASUBLE [*with a scholar's shudder*]. Believe me, I do not deserve so neologistic a phrase. The precept as well as the practice of the Primitive Church was distinctly against matrimony.

MISS PRISM [*sententiously*]. That is obviously the reason why the Primitive Church has not lasted up to the present day. And you do not seem to realize, dear Doctor, that by persistently remaining single, a man converts himself into a permanent public temptation. Men should be careful; this very celibacy leads weaker vessels astray.

CHASUBLE. But is a man not equally attractive when married?

MISS PRISM. No married man is ever attractive except to his wife.

CHASUBLE. And often, I've been told, not even to her.

MISS PRISM. That depends on the intellectual sympathies of the woman. Maturity can always be depended on. Ripeness can be trusted. Young women are green. [DR. CHASUBLE *starts.*] I spoke horticulturally. My metaphor was drawn from fruits. But where is Cecily?

CHASUBLE. Perhaps she followed us to the schools. [*Enter* JACK *slowly from the back of the garden. He is dressed in the deepest mourning, with crape hatband and black gloves.*]

MISS PRISM. Mr. Worthing!

CHASUBLE. Mr. Worthing?

MISS PRISM. This is indeed a surprise. We did not look for you till Monday afternoon.

JACK [*shakes* MISS PRISM's *hand in a tragic manner*]. I have returned sooner than I expected. Dr. Chasuble, I hope you are well?

CHASUBLE. Dear Mr. Worthing, I trust this garb of woe does not betoken some terrible calamity?

JACK. My brother.

MISS PRISM. More shameful debts and extravagance?

CHASUBLE. Still leading his life of pleasure?

JACK [*shaking his head*]. Dead.

CHASUBLE. Your brother Ernest dead?

JACK. Quite dead.

MISS PRISM. What a lesson for him! I trust he will profit by it.

CHASUBLE. Mr. Worthing, I offer you my sincere condolence. You have at least the consolation of knowing that you were always the most generous and forgiving of brothers.

JACK. Poor Ernest! He had many faults, but it is a sad, sad blow.

CHASUBLE. Very sad indeed. Were you with him at the end?

JACK. No. He died abroad; in Paris, in fact. I had a telegram last night from the manager of the Grand Hotel.

CHASUBLE. Was the cause of death mentioned?

JACK. A severe chill, it seems.

MISS PRISM. As a man sows, so shall he reap.

CHASUBLE [*raising his hand*]. Charity, dear Miss Prism, charity! None of us are perfect. I myself am peculiarly susceptible to drafts. Will the interment take place here?

JACK. No. He seems to have expressed a desire to be buried in Paris.

CHASUBLE. In Paris! [*Shakes his head.*] I fear that hardly points to any very serious state of mind at the last. You would no doubt wish me to make some slight allusion to this tragic domestic affliction next Sunday. [JACK *presses his hand convulsively.*] My sermon on the meaning of the manna in the wilderness can be adapted to almost any occasion, joyful, or, as in the present case, distressing. [*All sigh.*] I have preached it at harvest celebrations, christenings, confirmations, on days of humiliation and festal days. The last time I delivered it was in the Cathedral, as a charity sermon on behalf of the Society for the Prevention of Discontentment among the Upper Orders. The Bishop, who was present, was much struck by some of the analogies I drew.

JACK. Ah, that reminds me, you mentioned christenings I think, Dr. Chasuble? I suppose you know how to christen all right? [DR. CHASUBLE *looks astounded.*] I mean, of course, you are continually christening, aren't you?

MISS PRISM. It is, I regret to say, one of the Rector's most constant duties in this parish. I have often spoken to the poorer classes on the subject. But they don't seem to know what thrift is.

CHASUBLE. But is there any particular infant in whom you are interested, Mr. Worthing? Your brother was, I believe, unmarried, was he not?

JACK. Oh, yes.

MISS PRISM [*bitterly*]. People who live entirely for pleasure usually are.

JACK. But it is not for any child, dear Doctor. I am very fond of children. No! the fact is, I would like to be christened myself, this afternoon, if you have nothing better to do.

CHASUBLE. But surely, Mr. Worthing, you have been christened already?

JACK. I don't remember anything about it.

CHASUBLE. But have you any grave doubts on the subject?

JACK. I certainly intend to have. Of course, I don't know if the thing would bother you in any way, or if you think I am a little too old now.

CHASUBLE. Not at all. The sprinkling, and, indeed, the immersion of adults is a perfectly canonical practice.

JACK. Immersion!

CHASUBLE. You need have no apprehensions. Sprinkling is all that is necessary, or indeed I think advisable. Our weather is so changeable. At what hour would you wish the ceremony performed?

JACK. Oh, I might trot around about five if that would suit you.

CHASUBLE. Perfectly, perfectly! In fact I have two similar ceremonies to perform at that time. A case of twins that occurred recently in one of the outlying cottages on your own estate. Poor Jenkins the carter, a most hard-working man.

JACK. Oh! I don't see much fun in being christened along with other babies. It would be childish. Would half-past five do?

CHASUBLE. Admirably! Admirably! Admirably! [*Takes out watch.*] And now, dear Mr. Worthing, I will not intrude any longer into a house of sorrow. I would merely beg you not to be too much bowed down by grief. What seem to us bitter trials at the moment are often blessings in disguise.

MISS PRISM. This seems to me a blessing of an extremely obvious kind. [*Enter* CECILY *from the house.*]

CECILY. Uncle Jack! Oh, I am pleased to see you back. But what horrid clothes you have on! Do go and change them.

MISS PRISM. Cecily!

CHASUBLE. My child! my child! [CECILY *goes towards* JACK; *he kisses her brow in a melancholy manner.*]

CECILY. What is the matter, Uncle Jack? Do look happy! You look as if you had a toothache and I have a surprise for you. Who do you think is in the dining-room? Your brother!

JACK. Who?

CECILY. Your brother Ernest. He arrived about half an hour ago.

JACK. What nonsense! I haven't got a brother.

CECILY. Oh, don't say that. However badly he may have behaved to you in the past he is still your brother. You couldn't be so heartless as to disown him. I'll tell him to come out. And you will shake hands with him, won't you, Uncle Jack? [*Runs back into the house.*]

CHASUBLE. These are very joyful tidings.

MISS PRISM. After we had all been resigned to his loss, his sudden return seems to me peculiarly distressing.

JACK. My brother is in the dining-room? I don't know what it all means. I think it is perfectly absurd. [*Enter* ALGERNON *and* CECILY *hand in hand. They come slowly up to* JACK.]

JACK. Good heavens! [*Motions* ALGERNON *away.*]

ALGERNON. Brother John, I have come down from town to tell you that I am very sorry for all the trouble I have given you, and that I intend to lead a better life in the future. [JACK *glares at him and does not take his hand.*]

CECILY. Uncle Jack, you are not going to refuse your own brother's hand?

JACK. Nothing will induce me to take his hand. I think his coming down here disgraceful. He knows perfectly well why.

CECILY. Uncle Jack, do be nice. There is some good in everyone. Ernest has just been telling me about his poor invalid friend, Mr. Bunbury, whom he goes to visit so often. And surely there must be much good in one who is kind to an invalid, and leaves the pleasures of London to sit by a bed of pain.

JACK. Oh, he has been talking about Bunbury, has he?

CECILY. Yes, he has told me all about poor Mr. Bunbury, and his terrible state of health.

JACK. Bunbury! Well, I won't have him talk to you about Bunbury or about anything else. It is enough to drive one perfectly frantic.

ALGERNON. Of course I admit that the faults were all on my side. But I must say that I think that Brother John's coldness to me is peculiarly painful. I expected a more enthusiastic welcome, especially considering it is the first time I have come here.

CECILY. Uncle Jack, if you don't shake hands with Ernest I will never forgive you.

JACK. Never forgive me?

CECILY. Never, never, never!

JACK. Well, this is the last time I shall ever do it. [*Shakes hands with* ALGERNON *and glares.*]

CHASUBLE. It's pleasant, is it not, to see so perfect a reconciliation? I think we might leave the two brothers together.

MISS PRISM. Cecily, you will come with us.

CECILY. Certainly, Miss Prism. My little task of reconciliation is over.

CHASUBLE. You have done a beautiful action today, dear child.

MISS PRISM. We must not be premature in our judgments.

CECILY. I feel very happy. [*They all go off.*]

JACK. You young scoundrel, Algy, you must get out of this place as soon as possible. I don't allow any Bunburying here. [*Enter* MERRIMAN.]

MERRIMAN. I have put Mr. Ernest's things in the room next to yours, sir. I suppose that is all right?

JACK. What?

MERRIMAN. Mr. Ernest's luggage, sir. I have unpacked it and put it in the room next to your own.

JACK. His luggage?

MERRIMAN. Yes, sir. Three portmanteaus, a dressing-case, two hat-boxes, and a large luncheon-basket.

ALGERNON. I am afraid I can't stay more than a week this time.

JACK. Merriman, order the dog-cart at once. Mr. Ernest has been suddenly called back to town.

MERRIMAN. Yes, sir. [*Goes back into the house.*]

ALGERNON. What a fearful liar you are, Jack. I have not been called back to town at all.

JACK. Yes, you have.

ALGERNON. I haven't heard anyone call me.

JACK. Your duty as a gentleman calls you back.

ALGERNON. My duty as a gentleman has never interfered with my pleasures in the smallest degree.

Jack. I can quite understand that.

Algernon. Well, Cecily is a darling.

Jack. You are not to talk of Miss Cardew like that. I don't like it.

Algernon. Well, I don't like your clothes. You look perfectly ridiculous in them. Why on earth don't you go up and change? It is perfectly childish to be in deep mourning for a man who is actually staying for a whole week with you in your house as a guest. I call it grotesque.

Jack. You are certainly not staying with me for a whole week as a guest or anything else. You have got to leave . . . by the four-five train.

Algernon. I certainly won't leave you so long as you are in mourning. It would be most unfriendly. If I were in mourning you would stay with me, I suppose. I should think it very unkind if you didn't.

Jack. Well, will you go if I change my clothes?

Algernon. Yes, if you are not too long. I never saw anybody take so long to dress, and with such little result.

Jack. Well, at any rate, that is better than being always over-dressed as you are.

Algernon. If I am occasionally a little over-dressed, I make up for it by being always immensely over-educated.

Jack. Your vanity is ridiculous, your conduct an outrage, and your presence in my garden utterly absurd. However, you have got to catch the four-five, and I hope you will have a pleasant journey back to town. This Bunburying, as you call it, has not been a great success for you. [*Goes into the house.*]

Algernon. I think it has been a great success. I'm in love with Cecily, and that is everything. [*Enter* Cecily *at the back of the garden. She picks up the can and begins to water the flowers.*] But I must see her before I go, and make arrangements for another Bunbury. Ah, there she is.

Cecily. Oh, I merely came back to water the roses. I thought you were with Uncle Jack.

Algernon. He's gone to order the dog-cart for me.

Cecily. Oh, is he going to take you for a nice drive?

Algernon. He's going to send me away.

Cecily. Then have we got to part?

Algernon. I am afraid so. It's a very painful parting.

Cecily. It is always painful to part from people whom one has known for a very brief space of time. The absence of old friends one can endure with equanimity. But even a momentary separation from anyone to whom one has just been introduced is almost unbearable.

Algernon. Thank you. [*Enter* Merriman.]

Merriman. The dog-cart is at the door, sir. [Algernon *looks appealingly at* Cecily.]

Cecily. It can wait, Merriman . . . for . . . five minutes.

Merriman. Yes, Miss. [*Exit* Merriman.]

Algernon. I hope, Cecily, I shall not offend you if I state quite frankly and openly that you seem to me to be in every way the visible personification of absolute perfection.

Cecily. I think your frankness does you great credit, Ernest. If you will allow me I will copy your remarks into my diary. [*Goes over to table and begins writing in diary.*]

ALGERNON. Do you really keep a diary? I'd give anything to look at it. May I?

CECILY. Oh, no. [*Puts her hand over it.*] You see, it is simply a very young girl's record of her own thoughts and impressions, and consequently meant for publication. When it appears in volume form I hope you will order a copy. But pray, Ernest, don't stop. I delight in taking down from dictation. I have reached "absolute perfection." You can go on. I am quite ready for more.

ALGERNON [*somewhat taken aback*]. Ahem! Ahem!

CECILY. Oh, don't cough, Ernest. When one is dictating one should speak fluently and not cough. Besides, I don't know how to spell a cough. [*Writes as* ALGERNON *speaks.*]

ALGERNON [*speaking very rapidly*]. Cecily, ever since I first looked upon your wonderful and incomparable beauty, I have dared to love you wildly, passionately, devotedly, hopelessly.

CECILY. I don't think that you should tell me that you love me wildly, passionately, devotedly, hopelessly. Hopelessly doesn't seem to make much sense, does it?

ALGERNON. Cecily! [*Enter* MERRIMAN.]

MERRIMAN. The dog-cart is waiting, sir.

ALGERNON. Tell it to come round next week, at the same hour.

MERRIMAN [*looks at* CECILY, *who makes no sign*]. Yes, sir. [MERRIMAN *retires.*]

CECILY. Uncle Jack would be very much annoyed if he knew you were staying on till next week, at the same hour.

ALGERNON. Oh, I don't care about Jack. I don't care for anybody in the whole world but you. I love you, Cecily. You will marry me, won't you?

CECILY. You silly you! Of course. Why, we have been engaged for the last three months.

ALGERNON. For the last three months?

CECILY. Yes, it will be exactly three months on Thursday.

ALGERNON. But how did we become engaged?

CECILY. Well, ever since dear Uncle Jack first confessed to us that he had a younger brother who was very wicked and bad, you of course have formed the chief topic of conversation between myself and Miss Prism. And of course a man who is much talked about is always very attractive. One feels there must be something in him after all. I daresay it was foolish of me, but I fell in love with you, Ernest.

ALGERNON. Darling! And when was the engagement actually settled?

CECILY. On the 4th of February last. Worn out by your entire ignorance of my existence, I determined to end the matter one way or the other, and after a long struggle with myself I accepted you under this dear old tree here. The next day I bought this little ring in your name, and this is the little bangle with the true lovers' knot I promised you always to wear.

ALGERNON. Did I give you this? It's very pretty, isn't it?

CECILY. Yes, you've wonderfully good taste, Ernest. It's the excuse I've always given for your leading such a bad life. And this is the box in which I keep all your dear letters. [*Kneels at table, opens box, and produces letters tied up with blue ribbon.*]

ALGERNON. My letters! But my own sweet Cecily, I have never written you any letters.

CECILY. You need hardly remind me of that, Ernest. I remember only too well that I was forced to write your letters for you. I wrote always three times a week, and sometimes oftener.

ALGERNON. Oh, do let me read them, Cecily?

CECILY. Oh, I couldn't possibly. They would make you far too conceited. [*Replaces box.*] The three you wrote me after I had broken off the engagement are so beautiful, and so badly spelled, that even now I can hardly read them without crying a little.

ALGERNON. But was our engagement ever broken off?

CECILY. Of course it was. On the 22nd of last March. You can see the entry if you like. [*Shows diary.*] "Today I broke off my engagement with Ernest. I feel it is better to do so. The weather still continues charming."

ALGERNON. But why on earth did you break it off? What had I done? I had done nothing at all. Cecily, I am very much hurt indeed to hear you broke it off. Particularly when the weather was so charming.

CECILY. It would hardly have been a really serious engagement if it hadn't been broken off at least once. But I forgave you before the week was out.

ALGERNON [*crossing to her, and kneeling*]. What a perfect angel you are, Cecily.

CECILY. You dear romantic boy. [*He kisses her, she puts her fingers through his hair.*] I hope your hair curls naturally, does it?

ALGERNON. Yes, darling, with a little help from others.

CECILY. I am so glad.

ALGERNON. You'll never break off our engagement again, Cecily?

CECILY. I don't think I could break it off now that I have actually met you. Besides, of course, there is the question of your name.

ALGERNON. Yes, of course. [*Nervously.*]

CECILY. You must not laugh at me, darling, but it had always been a girlish dream of mine to love some one whose name was Ernest. [ALGERNON *rises*, CECILY *also.*] There is something in that name that seems to inspire absolute confidence. I pity any poor married woman whose husband is not called Ernest.

ALGERNON. But, my dear child, do you mean to say you could not love me if I had some other name?

CECILY. But what name?

ALGERNON. Oh, any name you like—Algernon, for instance. . . .

CECILY. But I don't like the name of Algernon.

ALGERNON. Well, my own dear, sweet, loving little darling, I really can't see why you should object to the name Algernon. It is not at all a bad name. In fact, it is rather an aristocratic name. Half of the chaps who get into the Bankruptcy Court are called Algernon. But seriously, Cecily . . . [*moving to her*] . . . if my name was Algy, couldn't you love me?

CECILY [*rising*]. I might respect you, Ernest, I might admire your character, but I fear that I should not be able to give you my undivided attention.

ALGERNON. Ahem! Cecily! [*Picking up hat.*] Your Rector here is, I suppose, thoroughly experienced in the practice of all the rites and ceremonials of the church?

CECILY. Oh, yes. Dr. Chasuble is a most learned man. He has never written a single book, so you can imagine how much he knows.

ALGERNON. I must see him at once on a most important christening—I mean on most important business.

CECILY. Oh!

ALGERNON. I sha'n't be away more than half an hour.

CECILY. Considering that we have been engaged since February the 14th, and that I only met you to-day for the first time, I think it is rather hard that you should leave me for so long a period as half an hour. Couldn't you make it twenty minutes?

ALGERNON. I'll be back in no time. [*Kisses her and rushes down the garden.*]

CECILY. What an impetuous boy he is. I like his hair so much. I must enter his proposal in my diary. [*Enter* MERRIMAN.]

MERRIMAN. A Miss Fairfax has just called to see Mr. Worthing. On very important business, Miss Fairfax states.

CECILY. Isn't Mr. Worthing in his library?

MERRIMAN. Mr. Worthing went over in the direction of the Rectory some time ago.

CECILY. Pray ask the lady to come out here; Mr. Worthing is sure to be back soon. And you can bring tea.

MERRIMAN. Yes, miss. [*Goes out.*]

CECILY. Miss Fairfax! I suppose one of the many good elderly women who are associated with Uncle Jack in some of his philanthropic work in London. I don't quite like women who are interested in philanthropic work. I think it is so forward of them. [*Enter* MERRIMAN.]

MERRIMAN. Miss Fairfax. [*Enter* GWENDOLEN. *Exit* MERRIMAN.]

CECILY [*advancing to meet her*]. Pray let me introduce myself to you. My name is Cecily Cardew.

GWENDOLEN. Cecily Cardew? [*Moving to her and shaking hands.*] What a very sweet name! Something tells me that we are going to be great friends. I like you already more than I can say. My first impressions of people are never wrong.

CECILY. How nice of you to like me so much after we have known each other such a comparatively short time. Pray sit down.

GWENDOLEN [*still standing up*]. I may call you Cecily, may I not?

CECILY. With pleasure!

GWENDOLEN. And you will always call me Gwendolen, won't you?

CECILY. If you wish.

GWENDOLEN. Then that is all quite settled, is it not?

CECILY. I hope so. [*A pause. They both sit down together.*]

GWENDOLEN. Perhaps this might be a favorable opportunity for my mentioning who I am. My father is Lord Bracknell. You have never heard of papa, I suppose?

CECILY. I don't think so.

GWENDOLEN. Outside the family circle, papa, I am glad to say, is entirely unknown. I think that is quite as it should be. The home seems to me to be the proper sphere for the man. And certainly once a man begins to neglect his domestic duties he becomes painfully effeminate, does he not? And I don't like that. It makes men so very attractive. Cecily, mamma, whose views on education are remarkably strict, has brought me up to be extremely short-sighted; it is part of her system; so do you mind my looking at you through my glasses?

CECILY. Oh, not at all, Gwendolen. I am very fond of being looked at.

GWENDOLEN [*after examining* CECILY *carefully through a lorgnette*]. You are here on a short visit, I suppose.

CECILY. Oh, no, I live here.

GWENDOLEN [*severely*]. Really? Your mother, no doubt, or some female relative of advanced years, resides here also?

CECILY. Oh, no. I have no mother, nor, in fact, any relations.

GWENDOLEN. Indeed?

CECILY. My dear guardian, with the assistance of Miss Prism, has the arduous task of looking after me.

GWENDOLEN. Your guardian?

CECILY. Yes, I am Mr. Worthing's ward.

GWENDOLEN. Oh! It is strange he never mentioned to me that he had a ward. How secretive of him! He grows more interesting hourly. I am not sure, however, that the news inspires me with feelings of unmixed delight. [*Rising and going to her.*] I am very fond of you, Cecily. I have liked you ever since I met you. But I am bound to state that now that I know that you are Mr. Worthing's ward, I cannot help expressing a wish you were—well, just a little older than you seem to be—and not quite so very alluring in appearance. In fact, if I may speak candidly——

CECILY. Pray do! I think that whenever one has anything unpleasant to say, one should always be quite candid.

GWENDOLEN. Well, to speak with perfect candor, Cecily, I wish that you were fully forty-two, and more than usually plain for your age. Ernest has a strong upright nature. He is the very soul of truth and honor. Disloyalty would be as impossible to him as deception. But even men of the noblest possible moral character are extremely susceptible to the influence of the physical charms of others. Modern, no less than Ancient History, supplies us with many most painful examples of what I refer to. If it were not so, indeed, History would be quite unreadable.

CECILY. I beg your pardon, Gwendolen, did you say Ernest?

GWENDOLEN. Yes.

CECILY. Oh, but it is not Mr. Ernest Worthing who is my guardian. It is his brother—his elder brother.

GWENDOLEN [*sitting down again*]. Ernest never mentioned to me that he had a brother.

CECILY. I am sorry to say they have not been on good terms for a long time.

GWENDOLEN. Ah! that accounts for it. And now that I think of it I have never heard any man mention his brother. The subject seems distasteful to most men. Cecily, you have lifted a load from my mind. I was growing almost anxious. It would have been terrible if any cloud had come across a friendship like ours, would it not? Of course you are quite, quite sure that it is not Mr. Ernest Worthing who is your guardian?

CECILY. Quite sure. [*A pause.*] In fact, I am going to be his.

GWENDOLEN [*enquiringly*]. I beg your pardon?

CECILY [*rather shy and confidingly*]. Dearest Gwendolen, there is no reason why I should make a secret of it to you. Our little county newspaper is sure to chronicle the fact next week. Mr. Ernest Worthing and I are engaged to be married.

GWENDOLEN [*quite politely, rising*]. My darling Cecily, I think there must be some slight error. Mr. Ernest Worthing is engaged to me. The announcement will appear in the *Morning Post* on Saturday at the latest.

CECILY [*very politely, rising*]. I am afraid you must be under some misconception. Ernest proposed to me exactly ten minutes ago. [*Shows diary.*]

GWENDOLEN [*examines diary through her lorgnette carefully*]. It is certainly very curious, for he asked me to be his wife yesterday afternoon at 5:30. If you would care to verify the incident, pray do so. [*Produces diary of her own.*] I never travel without my diary. One should always have something sensational to read in the train. I am so sorry, dear Cecily, if it is any disappointment to you, but I am afraid *I* have the prior claim.

CECILY. It would distress me more than I can tell you, dear Gwendolen, if it caused you any mental or physical anguish, but I feel bound to point out that since Ernest proposed to you he clearly has changed his mind.

GWENDOLEN [*meditatively*]. If the poor fellow has been entrapped into any foolish promise I shall consider it my duty to rescue him at once, and with a firm hand.

CECILY [*thoughtfully and sadly*]. Whatever unfortunate entanglement my dear boy may have got into, I will never reproach him with it after we are married.

GWENDOLEN. Do you allude to me, Miss Cardew, as an entanglement? You are presumptuous. On an occasion of this kind it becomes more than a moral duty to speak one's mind. It becomes a pleasure.

CECILY. Do you suggest, Miss Fairfax, that I entrapped Ernest into an engagement? How dare you? This is no time for wearing the shallow mask of manners. When I see a spade I call it a spade.

GWENDOLEN [*satirically*]. I am glad to say that I have never seen a spade. It is obvious that our social spheres have been widely different. [*Enter* MERRIMAN, *followed by the footman. He carries a salver, tablecloth, and plate-stand.* CECILY *is about to retort. The presence of the servants exercises a restraining influence, under which both girls chafe.*]

MERRIMAN. Shall I lay tea here as usual, miss?

CECILY [*sternly, in a calm voice*]. Yes, as usual. [MERRIMAN *begins to clear and lay cloth. A long pause.* CECILY *and* GWENDOLEN *glare at each other.*]

GWENDOLEN. Are there many interesting walks in the vicinity, Miss Cardew?

CECILY. Oh, yes, a great many. From the top of one of the hills quite close one can see five counties.

GWENDOLEN. Five counties! I don't think I should like that. I hate crowds.

CECILY [*sweetly*]. I suppose that is why you live in town? [GWENDOLEN *bites her lip, and beats her foot nervously with her parasol.*]

GWENDOLEN [*looking round*]. Quite a well-kept garden this is, Miss Cardew.

CECILY. So glad you like it, Miss Fairfax.

GWENDOLEN. I had no idea there were any flowers in the country.

CECILY. Oh, flowers are as common here, Miss Fairfax, as people are in London.

GWENDOLEN. Personally I cannot understand how anybody manages to exist in the country, if anybody who is anybody does. The country always bores me to death.

CECILY. Ah! This is what the newspapers call agricultural depression, is it not? I believe the aristocracy are suffering very much from it just at present. It is almost an epidemic amongst them, I have been told. May I offer you some tea, Miss Fairfax?

GWENDOLEN [*with elaborate politeness*]. Thank you. [*Aside.*] Detestable girl! But I require tea!

CECILY [*sweetly*]. Sugar?

GWENDOLEN [*superciliously*]. No, thank you. Sugar is not fashionable any more. [CECILY *looks angrily at her, takes up the tongs and puts four lumps of sugar into the cup.*]

CECILY [*severely*]. Cake or bread and butter?

GWENDOLEN [*in a bored manner*]. Bread and butter, please. Cake is rarely seen at the best houses nowadays.

CECILY [*cuts a very large slice of cake, and puts it on the tray*]. Hand that to Miss Fairfax. [MERRIMAN *does so, and goes out with footman.* GWENdolen *drinks the tea and makes a grimace. Puts down cup at once, reaches out her hand to the bread and butter, looks at it, and finds it is cake. Rises in indignation.*]

GWENDOLEN. You have filled my tea with lumps of sugar, and though I asked most distinctly for bread and butter, you have given me cake. I am known for the gentleness of my disposition, and the extraordinary sweetness of my nature, but I warn you, Miss Cardew, you may go too far.

CECILY [*rising*]. To save my poor, innocent, trusting boy from the machinations of any other girl there are no lengths to which I would not go.

GWENDOLEN. From the moment I saw you I distrusted you. I felt that you were false and deceitful. I am never deceived in such matters. My first impressions of people are invariably right.

CECILY. It seems to me, Miss Fairfax, that I am trespassing on your valuable time. No doubt you have many other calls of a similar character to make in the neighborhood. [*Enter* JACK.]

GWENDOLEN [*catching sight of him*]. Ernest! My own Ernest!

JACK. Gwendolen! Darling! [*Offers to kiss her.*]

GWENDOLEN [*drawing back*]. A moment! May I ask if you are engaged to be married to this young lady? [*Points to* CECILY.]

JACK [*laughing*]. To dear little Cecily! Of course not! What could have put such an idea into your pretty little head?

GWENDOLEN. Thank you. You may. [*Offers her cheek.*]

CECILY [*very sweetly*]. I knew there must be some misunderstanding, Miss Fairfax. The gentleman whose arm is at present around your waist is my dear guardian, Mr. John Worthing.

GWENDOLEN. I beg your pardon?

CECILY. This is Uncle Jack.

GWENDOLEN [*receding*]. Jack! Oh! [*Enter* ALGERNON.]

CECILY. Here is Ernest.

ALGERNON [*goes straight over to* CECILY *without noticing anyone else*]. My own love! [*Offers to kiss her.*]

CECILY [*drawing back*]. A moment, Ernest! May I ask you—are you engaged to be married to this young lady?

ALGERNON [*looking round*]. To what young lady? Good heavens! Gwendolen!

CECILY. Yes, to good heavens, Gwendolen, I mean to Gwendolen.

ALGERNON [*laughing*]. Of course not! What could have put such an idea into your pretty little head?

CECILY. Thank you. [*Presenting her cheek to be kissed.*] You may. [ALGERNON *kisses her.*]

GWENDOLEN. I felt there was some slight error, Miss Cardew. The gentleman who is now embracing you is my cousin, Mr. Algernon Moncrieff.

CECILY [*breaking away from* ALGERNON]. Algernon Moncrieff! Oh! [*The two girls move towards each other and put their arms round each other's waists as if for protection.*]

CECILY. Are you called Algernon?

ALGERNON. I cannot deny it.

CECILY. Oh!

GWENDOLEN. Is your name really John?

JACK [*standing rather proudly*]. I could deny it if I liked. I could deny anything if I liked. But my name certainly is John. It has been John for years.

CECILY [*to* GWENDOLEN]. A gross deception has been practised on both of us.

GWENDOLEN. My poor wounded Cecily!

CECILY. My sweet, wronged Gwendolen!

GWENDOLEN [*slowly and seriously*]. You will call me sister, will you not? [*They embrace.* JACK *and* ALGERNON *groan and walk up and down.*]

CECILY [*rather brightly*]. There is just one question I would like to be allowed to ask my guardian.

GWENDOLEN. An admirable idea! Mr. Worthing, there is just one question I would like to be permitted to put to you. Where is your brother Ernest? We are both engaged to be married to your brother Ernest, so it is a matter of some importance to us to know where your brother Ernest is at present.

JACK [*slowly and hesitatingly*]. Gwendolen—Cecily—it is very painful for me to be forced to speak the truth. It is the first time in my life that I have ever been reduced to such a painful position, and I am really quite inexperienced in doing anything of the kind. However I will tell you quite frankly that I have no brother Ernest. I have no brother at all. I never had a brother in my life, and I certainly have not the smallest intention of ever having one in the future.

CECILY [*surprised*]. No brother at all?

JACK [*cheerily*]. None!

GWENDOLEN [*severely*]. Had you never a brother of any kind?

JACK [*pleasantly*]. Never. Not even of any kind.

GWENDOLEN. I am afraid it is quite clear, Cecily, that neither of us is engaged to be married to anyone.

CECILY. It is not a very pleasant position for a young girl suddenly to find herself in. Is it?

GWENDOLEN. Let us go into the house. They will hardly venture to come after us there.

CECILY. No, men are so cowardly, aren't they? [*They retire into the house with scornful looks.*]

JACK. This ghastly state of things is what you call Bunburying, I suppose?

ALGERNON. Yes, and a perfectly wonderful Bunbury it is. The most wonderful Bunbury I have ever had in my life.

JACK. Well, you've no right whatsoever to Bunbury here.

ALGERNON. That is absurd. One has a right to Bunbury anywhere one chooses. Every serious Bunburyist knows that.

JACK. Serious Bunburyist! Good heavens!

ALGERNON. Well, one must be serious about something, if one wants to have any amusement in life. I happen to be serious about Bunburying. What on earth you are serious about I haven't got the remotest idea. About everything, I should fancy. You have such an absolutely trivial nature.

JACK. Well, the only small satisfaction I have in the whole of this wretched business is that your friend Bunbury is quite exploded. You won't be able to run down to the country quite so often as you used to do, dear Algy. And a very good thing, too.

ALGERNON. Your brother is a little off color, isn't he, dear Jack? You won't be able to disappear to London quite so frequently as your wicked custom was. And not a bad thing, either.

JACK. As for your conduct towards Miss Cardew, I must say that your taking in a sweet, simple, innocent girl like that is quite inexcusable. To say nothing of the fact that she is my ward.

ALGERNON. I can see no possible defense at all for your deceiving a brilliant, clever, thoroughly experienced young lady like Miss Fairfax. To say nothing of the fact that she is my cousin.

JACK. I wanted to be engaged to Gwendolen, that is all. I love her.

ALGERNON. Well, I simply wanted to be engaged to Cecily. I adore her.

JACK. There is certainly no chance of your marrying Miss Cardew.

ALGERNON. I don't think there is much likelihood, Jack, of you and Miss Fairfax being united.

JACK. Well, that is no business of yours.

ALGERNON. If it was my business, I wouldn't talk about it. [*Begins to eat muffins.*] It is very vulgar to talk about one's business. Only people like stockbrokers do that, and then merely at dinner parties.

JACK. How you can sit there, calmly eating muffins, when we are in this horrible trouble, I can't make out. You seem to me to be perfectly heartless.

ALGERNON. Well, I can't eat muffins in an agitated manner. The butter would probably get on my cuffs. One should always eat muffins quite calmly. It is the only way to eat them.

JACK. I say it's perfectly heartless your eating muffins at all, under the circumstances.

ALGERNON. When I am in trouble, eating is the only thing that consoles me. Indeed, when I am in really great trouble, as anyone who knows me intimately will tell you, I refuse everything except food and drink. At the present moment I am eating muffins because I am unhappy. Besides, I am particularly fond of muffins. [*Rising.*]

JACK [*rising*]. Well, that is no reason why you should eat them all in that greedy way. [*Takes muffins from* ALGERNON.]

ALGERNON [*offering tea-cake*]. I wish you would have tea-cake instead. I don't like tea-cake.

JACK. Good heavens! I suppose a man may eat his own muffins in his own garden.

ALGERNON. But you have just said it was perfectly heartless to eat muffins.

JACK. I said it was perfectly heartless of you, under the circumstances. That is a very different thing.

ALGERNON. That may be. But the muffins are the same. [*He seizes the muffin-dish from* JACK.]

JACK. Algy, I wish to goodness you would go.

ALGERNON. You can't possibly ask me to go without having some dinner. It's absurd. I never go without my dinner. No one ever does, except vegetarians and people like that. Besides I have just made arrangements with Dr. Chasuble to be christened at a quarter to six under the name of Ernest.

JACK. My dear fellow, the sooner you give up that nonsense the better. I made arrangements this morning with Dr. Chasuble to be christened myself at 5:30, and I naturally will take the name of Ernest. Gwendolen would wish it. We can't both be christened Ernest. It's absurd. Besides, I have a perfect right to be christened if I like. There is no evidence at all that I ever have been christened by anybody. I should think it extremely probable I never was, and so does Dr. Chasuble. It is entirely different in your case. You have been christened already.

ALGERNON. Yes, but I have not been christened for years.

JACK. Yes, but you have been christened. That is the important thing.

ALGERNON. Quite so. So I know my constitution can stand it. If you are not quite sure about your ever having been christened, I must say I think it rather dangerous your venturing on it now. It might make you very unwell. You can hardly have forgotten that someone very closely connected with you was very nearly carried off this week in Paris by a severe chill.

JACK. Yes, but you said yourself that a severe chill was not hereditary.

ALGERNON. It usedn't to be, I know—but I daresay it is now. Science is always making wonderful improvements in things.

JACK [*picking up the muffin-dish*]. Oh, that is nonsense; you are always talking nonsense.

ALGERNON. Jack, you are at the muffins again! I wish you wouldn't. There are only two left. [*Takes them.*] I told you I was particularly fond of muffins.

JACK. But I hate tea-cake.

ALGERNON. Why on earth then do you allow tea-cake to be served up for your guests? What ideas you have of hospitality!

JACK. Algernon! I have already told you to go. I don't want you here. Why don't you go?

ALGERNON. I haven't quite finished my tea yet, and there is still one muffin left. [JACK *groans, and sinks into a chair.* ALGERNON *stills continues eating.*]

ACT DROP

ACT III

SCENE

Morning-room at the Manor House.

[GWENDOLEN *and* CECILY *are at the window, looking out into the garden.*]

GWENDOLEN. The fact that they did not follow us at once into the house, as anyone else would have done, seems to me to show that they have some sense of shame left.

CECILY. They have been eating muffins. That looks like repentance.

GWENDOLEN [*after a pause*]. They don't seem to notice us at all. Couldn't you cough?

CECILY. But I haven't a cough.

GWENDOLEN. They're looking at us. What effrontery!

CECILY. They're approaching. That's very forward of them.

GWENDOLEN. Let us preserve a dignified silence.

CECILY. Certainly. It's the only thing to do now. [*Enter* JACK, *followed by* ALGERNON. *They whistle some dreadful popular air from a British opera.*]

GWENDOLEN. This dignified silence seems to produce an unpleasant effect.

CECILY. A most distasteful one.

GWENDOLEN. But we will not be the first to speak.

CECILY. Certainly not.

GWENDOLEN. Mr. Worthing, I have something very particular to ask you. Much depends on your reply.

CECILY. Gwendolen, your common sense is invaluable. Mr. Moncrieff, kindly answer me the following question. Why did you pretend to be my guardian's brother?

ALGERNON. In order that I might have an opportunity of meeting you.

CECILY [*to* GWENDOLEN]. That certainly seems a satisfactory explanation, does it not?

GWENDOLEN. Yes, dear, if you can believe him.

CECILY. I don't. But that does not affect the wonderful beauty of his answer.

GWENDOLEN. True. In matters of grave importance, style, not sincerity, is the vital thing. Mr. Worthing, what explanation can you offer to me for pretending to have a brother? Was it in order that you might have an opportunity of coming up to town to see me as often as possible?

JACK. Can you doubt it, Miss Fairfax?

GWENDOLEN. I have the gravest doubts upon the subject. But I intend to crush them. This is not the moment for German scepticism. [*Moving to* CECILY.] Their explanations appear to be quite satisfactory, especially Mr. Worthing's. That seems to me to have the stamp of truth upon it.

CECILY. I am more than content with what Mr. Moncrieff said. His voice alone inspires one with absolute credulity.

GWENDOLEN. Then you think we should forgive them?

CECILY. Yes. I mean no.

GWENDOLEN. True! I had forgotten. There are principles at stake that one cannot surrender. Which of us should tell them? The task is not a pleasant one.

CECILY. Could we not both speak at the same time?

GWENDOLEN. An excellent idea! I nearly always speak at the same time as other people. Will you take the time from me?

CECILY. Certainly. [GWENDOLEN *beats time with uplifted finger.*]

GWENDOLEN AND CECILY [*speaking together*]. Your Christian names are still an insuperable barrier. That is all!

JACK AND ALGERNON [*speaking together*]. Our Christian names! Is that all? But we are going to be christened this afternoon.

GWENDOLEN [*to* JACK]. For my sake you are prepared to do this terrible thing?

JACK. I am.

CECILY [*to* ALGERNON]. To please me you are ready to face this fearful ordeal?

ALGERNON. I am!

GWENDOLEN. How absurd to talk of the equality of the sexes! Where questions of self-sacrifice are concerned, men are infinitely beyond us.

JACK. We are. [*Clasps hands with* ALGERNON.]

CECILY. They have moments of physical courage of which we women know absolutely nothing.

GWENDOLEN [*to* JACK]. Darling!

ALGERNON [*to* CECILY]. Darling! [*They fall into each other's arms. Enter* MERRIMAN. *When he enters he coughs loudly, seeing the situation.*]

MERRIMAN. Ahem! Ahem! Lady Bracknell!

JACK. Good heavens! [*Enter* LADY BRACKNELL. *The couples separate in alarm. Exit* MERRIMAN.]

LADY BRACKNELL. Gwendolen! What does this mean?

GWENDOLEN. Merely that I am engaged to be married to Mr. Worthing, mamma.

LADY BRACKNELL. Come here. Sit down. Sit down immediately. Hesitation of any kind is a sign of mental decay in the young, of physical weakness in the old. [*Turns to* JACK.] Apprised, sir, of my daughter's sudden flight by her trusty maid, whose confidence I purchased by means of a small coin, I followed her at once by a luggage train. Her unhappy father is, I am glad to say, under the impression that she is attending a more than usually lengthy lecture by the University Extension Scheme on the Influence of a Permanent Income Tax on Thought. I do not propose to undeceive him. Indeed I have never undeceived him on any question. I would consider it wrong. But of course, you will clearly understand that all communication between yourself and my daughter must cease immediately from this moment. On this point, as indeed on all points, I am firm.

JACK. I am engaged to be married to Gwendolen, Lady Bracknell!

LADY BRACKNELL. You are nothing of the kind, sir. And now, as regards Algernon! . . . Algernon!

ALGERNON. Yes, Aunt Augusta.

LADY BRACKNELL. May I ask if it is in this house that your invalid friend Mr. Bunbury resides?

ALGERNON [*stammering*]. Oh, no! Bunbury doesn't live here. Bunbury is somewhere else at present. In fact, Bunbury is dead.

LADY BRACKNELL. Dead! When did Mr. Bunbury die? His death must have been extremely sudden.

ALGERNON [*airily*]. Oh, I killed Bunbury this afternoon. I mean poor Bunbury died this afternoon.

LADY BRACKNELL. What did he die of?

ALGERNON. Bunbury? Oh, he was quite exploded.

LADY BRACKNELL. Exploded! Was he the victim of a revolutionary outrage? I was not aware that Mr. Bunbury was interested in social legislation. If so, he is well punished for his morbidity.

ALGERNON. My dear Aunt Augusta, I mean he was found out! The doctors found out that Bunbury could not live, that is what I mean—so Bunbury died.

LADY BRACKNELL. He seems to have had great confidence in the opinion of his physicians. I am glad, however, that he made up his mind at the last to some definite course of action, and acted under proper medical advice. And now that we have finally got rid of this Mr. Bunbury, may I ask, Mr. Worthing, who is that young person whose hand my nephew Algernon is now holding in what seems to me a peculiarly unnecessary manner?

JACK. That lady is Miss Cecily Cardew, my ward. [LADY BRACKNELL *bows coldly to* CECILY.]

ALGERNON. I am engaged to be married to Cecily, Aunt Augusta.

LADY BRACKNELL. I beg your pardon?

CECILY. Mr. Moncrieff and I are engaged to be married, Lady Bracknell.

LADY BRACKNELL [*with a shiver, crossing to the sofa and sitting down*]. I do not know whether there is anything peculiarly exciting in the air in this particular part of Hertfordshire, but the number of engagements that go on seems to me considerably above the proper average that statistics have laid down for our guidance. I think some preliminary enquiry on my part would not be out of place. Mr. Worthing, is Miss Cardew at all connected with any of the larger railway stations in London? I merely desire information. Until yesterday I had no idea that there were any families or persons whose origin was a Terminus. [JACK *looks perfectly furious, but restrains himself.*]

JACK [*in a clear, cold voice*]. Miss Cardew is the granddaughter of the late Mr. Thomas Cardew of 149, Belgrave Square, S.W.; Gervase Park, Dorking, Surrey; and the Sporran, Fifeshire, N.B.

LADY BRACKNELL. That sounds not unsatisfactory. Three addresses always inspire confidence, even in tradesmen. But what proof have I of their authenticity?

JACK. I have carefully preserved the Court Guide of the period. They are open to your inspection, Lady Bracknell.

LADY BRACKNELL [*grimly*]. I have known strange errors in that publication.

JACK. Miss Cardew's family solicitors are Messrs. Markby, Markby, and Markby.

LADY BRACKNELL. Markby, Markby and Markby? A firm of the very highest position in their profession. Indeed I am told that one of the Markbys is occasionally to be seen at dinner parties. So far I am satisfied.

JACK [*very irritably*]. How extremely kind of you, Lady Bracknell! I have also in my possession, you will be pleased to hear, certificates of Miss Cardew's birth, baptism, whooping cough registration, vaccination, confirmation, and the measles—both the German and the English variety.

LADY BRACKNELL. Ah! A life crowded with incident, I see; though perhaps somewhat too exciting for a young girl. I am not myself in favor of premature experiences. [*Rises, looks at her watch.*] Gwendolen! the time approaches for our departure. We have not a moment to lose. As a matter of form, Mr. Worthing, I had better ask you if Miss Cardew has any little fortune?

JACK. Oh, about a hundred and thirty thousand pounds in the Funds. That is all. Good-bye, Lady Bracknell. So pleased to have seen you.

LADY BRACKNELL [*sitting down again*]. A moment, Mr. Worthing. A hundred and thirty thousand pounds! And in the Funds! Miss Cardew seems to me a most attractive young lady, now that I look at her. Few girls of the present day have any really solid qualities, any of the qualities that last, and improve with time. We live, I regret to say, in an age of surfaces. [*To* CECILY.] Come over here, dear. [CECILY *goes across.*] Pretty child! your dress is sadly simple, and your hair seems almost as Nature might have left it. But we can soon alter all that. A thoroughly experienced French maid produces a really marvelous result in a very brief space of time. I remember recommending one to young Lady Lancing, and after three months her own husband did not know her.

JACK [*aside*]. And after six months nobody knew her.

LADY BRACKNELL [*glares at* JACK *for a few moments. Then bends, with a practised smile, to* CECILY]. Kindly turn round, sweet child. [CECILY *turns completely round.*] No, the side view is what I want. [CECILY *presents her profile.*] Yes, quite as I expected. There are distinct social possibilities in your profile. The two weak points in our age are its want of principle and its want of profile. The chin a little higher, dear. Style largely depends on the way the chin is worn. They are worn very high, just at present. Algernon!

ALGERNON. Yes, Aunt Augusta!

LADY BRACKNELL. There are distinct social possibilities in Miss Cardew's profile.

ALGERNON. Cecily is the sweetest, dearest, prettiest girl in the whole world. And I don't care twopence about social possibilities.

LADY BRACKNELL. Never speak disrespectfully of society, Algernon. Only people who can't get into it do that. [*To* CECILY.] Dear child, of course you know that Algernon has nothing but his debts to depend upon. But I do not approve of mercenary marriages. When I married Lord Bracknell I had no fortune of any kind. But I never dreamed for a moment of allowing that to stand in my way. Well, I suppose I must give my consent.

ALGERNON. Thank you, Aunt Augusta.

LADY BRACKNELL. Cecily, you may kiss me!

CECILY [*kisses her*]. Thank you, Lady Bracknell.

LADY BRACKNELL. You may also address me as Aunt Augusta for the future.

CECILY. Thank you, Aunt Augusta.

LADY BRACKNELL. The marriage, I think, had better take place quite soon.

ALGERNON. Thank you, Aunt Augusta.

CECILY. Thank you, Aunt Augusta.

LADY BRACKNELL. To speak frankly, I am not in favor of long engagements. They give people the opportunity of finding out each other's character before marriage, which I think is never advisable.

JACK. I beg your pardon for interrupting you, Lady Bracknell, but this engagement is quite out of the question. I am Miss Cardew's guardian, and she cannot marry without my consent until she comes of age. That consent I absolutely decline to give.

LADY BRACKNELL. Upon what grounds, may I ask? Algernon is an extremely, I may almost say an ostentatiously, eligible young man. He has nothing, but he looks everything. What more can one desire?

JACK. It pains me very much to have to speak frankly to you, Lady Bracknell, about your nephew, but the fact is that I do not approve at all of his moral character. I suspect him of being untruthful. [ALGERNON *and* CECILY *look at him in indignant amazement.*]

LADY BRACKNELL. Untruthful! My nephew Algernon? Impossible! He is an Oxonian.

JACK. I fear there can be no possible doubt about the matter. This afternoon, during my temporary absence in London on an important question of romance, he obtained admission to my house by means of the false pretense of being my brother. Under an assumed name he drank, I've just been informed by my butler, an entire pint bottle of my Perrier-Jouet, Brut, '89, a wine I was specially reserving for myself. Continuing his disgraceful deception, he succeeded in the course of the afternoon in alienating the affections of my only ward. He subsequently stayed to tea, and devoured every single muffin. And what makes his conduct all the more heartless is, that he was perfectly well aware from the first that I have no brother, that I never had a brother, and that I don't intend to have a brother, not even of any kind. I distinctly told him so myself yesterday afternoon.

LADY BRACKNELL. Ahem! Mr. Worthing, after careful consideration I have decided entirely to overlook my nephew's conduct to you.

JACK. That is very generous of you, Lady Bracknell. My own decision, however, is unalterable. I decline to give my consent.

LADY BRACKNELL [*to* CECILY]. Come here, sweet child. [CECILY *goes over.*] How old are you, dear?

CECILY. Well, I am really only eighteen, but I always admit to twenty when I go to evening parties.

LADY BRACKNELL. You are perfectly right in making some slight alteration. Indeed, no woman should ever be quite accurate about her age. It looks so calculating. . . . [*In a meditative manner.*] Eighteen, but admitting to twenty at evening parties. Well, it will not be very long before you are of age and free from the restraints of tutelage. So I don't think your guardian's consent is, after all, a matter of any importance.

JACK. Pray excuse me, Lady Bracknell, for interrupting you again, but it is only fair to tell you that according to the terms of her grandfather's will Miss Cardew does not come legally of age till she is thirty-five.

LADY BRACKNELL. That does not seem to me to be a grave objection. Thirty-five is a very attractive age. London society is full of women of the very highest birth who have, of their own free choice, remained thirty-five for years. Lady Dumbleton is an instance in point. To my own knowledge she has been thirty-five ever since she arrived at the age of forty, which was many years ago now. I see no reason why our dear Cecily should not be even still more attractive at the age you mention than she is at present. There will be a large accumulation of property.

CECILY. Algy, could you wait for me till I was thirty-five?

ALGERNON. Of course I could, Cecily. You know I could.

CECILY. Yes, I felt it instinctively, but I couldn't wait all that time. I hate waiting even five minutes for anybody. It always makes me rather cross. I am not punctual myself, I know, but I do like punctuality in others, and waiting, even to be married, is quite out of the question.

ALGERNON. Then what is to be done, Cecily?

CECILY. I don't know, Mr. Moncrieff.

LADY BRACKNELL. My dear Mr. Worthing, as Miss Cardew states positively that she cannot wait till she is thirty-five—a remark which I am bound to say seems to me to show a somewhat impatient nature—I would beg of you to reconsider your decision.

JACK. But my dear Lady Bracknell, the matter is entirely in your own hands. The moment you consent to my marriage with Gwendolen, I will most gladly allow your nephew to form an alliance with my ward.

LADY BRACKNELL [*rising and drawing herself up*]. You must be quite aware that what you propose is out of the question.

JACK. Then a passionate celibacy is all that any of us can look forward to.

LADY BRACKNELL. This is not the destiny I propose for Gwendolen. Algernon, of course, can choose for himself. [*Pulls out her watch.*] Come, dear, [GWENDOLEN *rises.*] we have already missed five, if not six, trains. To miss any more might expose us to comment on the platform. [*Enter* DR. CHASUBLE.]

CHASUBLE. Everything is quite ready for the christenings.

LADY BRACKNELL. The christenings, sir! Is not that somewhat premature?

CHASUBLE [*looking rather puzzled, and pointing to* JACK *and* ALGERNON]. Both these gentlemen have expressed a desire for immediate baptism.

LADY BRACKNELL. At their age? The idea is grotesque and irreligious! Algernon, I forbid you to be baptized. I will not hear of such excesses. Lord Bracknell would be highly displeased if he learned that that was the way in which you wasted your time and money.

CHASUBLE. Am I to understand then that there are to be no christenings at all this afternoon?

JACK. I don't think that, as things are now, it would be of much practical value to either of us, Dr. Chasuble.

CHASUBLE. I am grieved to hear such sentiments from you, Mr. Worthing. They savor of the heretical views of the Anabaptists, views that I have completely refuted in four of my unpublished sermons. However, as your present mood seems to be one peculiarly secular, I will return to the church at once. Indeed, I have just been informed by the pew-opener that for the last hour and a half Miss Prism has been waiting for me in the vestry.

LADY BRACKNELL [*starting*]. Miss Prism! Did I hear you mention a Miss Prism?

CHASUBLE. Yes, Lady Bracknell. I am on my way to join her.

LADY BRACKNELL. Pray allow me to detain you for a moment. This matter may prove to be one of vital importance to Lord Bracknell and myself. Is this Miss Prism a female of repellent aspect, remotely connected with education?

CHASUBLE [*somewhat indignantly*]. She is the most cultivated of ladies, and the very picture of respectability.

LADY BRACKNELL. It is obviously the same person. May I ask what position she holds in your household?

CHASUBLE [*severely*]. I am a celibate, madam.

JACK [*interposing*]. Miss Prism, Lady Bracknell, has been for the last three years Miss Cardew's esteemed governess and valued companion.

LADY BRACKNELL. In spite of what I hear of her, I must see her at once. Let her be sent for.

CHASUBLE [*looking off*]. She approaches; she is nigh. [*Enter* MISS PRISM *hurriedly.*]

MISS PRISM. I was told you expected me in the vestry, dear Canon. I have been waiting for you there for an hour and three-quarters. [*Catches sight of* LADY BRACKNELL, *who has fixed her with a stony glare.* MISS PRISM *grows pale and quails. She looks anxiously round as if desirous to escape.*]

LADY BRACKNELL [*in a severe, judicial voice*]. Prism! [MISS PRISM *bows her head in shame.*] Come here, Prism! [MISS PRISM *approaches in a humble manner.*] Prism! Where is that baby? [*General consternation. The* CANON *starts back in horror.* ALGERNON *and* JACK *pretend to be anxious to shield* CECILY *and* GWENDOLEN *from hearing the details of a terrible public scandal.*] Twenty-eight years ago, Prism, you left Lord Bracknell's house, Number 104, Upper Grosvenor Street, in charge of a perambulator that contained a baby, of the male sex. You never returned. A few weeks later, through the elaborate investigations of the Metropolitan police, the perambulator was discovered at midnight, standing by itself in a remote corner of Bayswater. It contained the manuscript of a three-volume novel of more than usually revolting sentimentality. [MISS PRISM *starts in involuntary indignation.*] But the baby was not there! [*Everyone looks at* MISS PRISM.] Prism, where is that baby? [*A pause.*]

MISS PRISM. Lady Bracknell, I admit with shame that I do not know. I only wish I did. The plain facts of the case are these. On the morning of the day you mention, a day that is forever branded on my memory, I prepared as usual to take the baby out in its perambulator. I had also with me a somewhat old but capacious hand–bag in which I had intended to place the manuscript of a work of fiction that I had written during my few unoccupied hours. In a moment of mental abstraction, for which I never can forgive myself, I deposited the manuscript in the bassinette, and placed the baby in the hand–bag.

JACK [*who has been listening attentively*]. But where did you deposit the hand-bag?

MISS PRISM. Do not ask me, Mr. Worthing.

Jack. Miss Prism, this is a matter of no small importance to me. I insist on knowing where you deposited the hand–bag that contained that infant.

MISS PRISM. I left it in the cloak-room of one of the larger railway stations in London.

JACK. What railway station?

MISS PRISM [*quite crushed*]. Victoria. The Brighton line. [*Sinks into a chair.*]

JACK. I must retire to my room for a moment. Gwendolen, wait here for me.

GWENDOLEN. If you are not too long, I will wait here for you all my life. [*Exit* JACK *in great excitement.*]

CHASUBLE. What do you think this means, Lady Bracknell?

LADY BRACKNELL. I dare not even suspect, Dr. Chasuble. I need hardly tell you that in families of high position strange coincidences are not supposed to occur. They are hardly considered the thing. [*Noises heard overhead as if someone was throwing trunks about. Everybody looks up.*]

CECILY. Uncle Jack seems strangely agitated.

CHASUBLE. Your guardian has a very emotional nature.

LADY BRACKNELL. This noise is extremely unpleasant. It sounds as if he was having an argument. I dislike arguments of any kind. They are always vulgar, and often convincing.

CHASUBLE [*looking up*]. It has stopped now. [*The noise is redoubled.*]

LADY BRACKNELL. I wish he would arrive at some conclusion.

GWENDOLEN. This suspense is terrible. I hope it will last. [*Enter* JACK *with a hand–bag of black leather in his hand.*]

JACK [*rushing over to* MISS PRISM]. Is this the hand–bag, Miss Prism? Examine it carefully before you speak. The happiness of more than one life depends on your answer.

MISS PRISM [*calmly*]. It seems to be mine. Yes, here is the injury it received through the upsetting of a Gower Street omnibus in younger and happier days. Here is the stain on the lining caused by the explosion of a temperance beverage, an incident that occurred at Leamington. And here, on the lock, are my initials. I had forgotten that in an extravagant mood I had had them placed there. The bag is undoubtedly mine. I am delighted to have it so unexpectedly restored to me. It has been a great inconvenience being without it all these years.

JACK [*in a pathetic voice*]. Miss Prism, more is restored to you than this hand–bag. I was the baby you placed in it.

MISS PRISM [*amazed*]. You?

JACK [*embracing her*]. Yes . . . mother!

MISS PRISM [*recoiling in indignant astonishment*]. Mr. Worthing! I am unmarried!

JACK. Unmarried! I do not deny that is a serious blow. But after all, who has the right to cast a stone against one who has suffered? Cannot repentance wipe out an act of folly? Why should there be one law for men and another for women? Mother, I forgive you. [*Tries to embrace her again.*]

MISS PRISM [*still more indignant*]. Mr. Worthing, there is some error. [*Pointing to* LADY BRACKNELL.] There is the lady who can tell you who you really are.

JACK [*after a pause*]. Lady Bracknell, I hate to seem inquisitive, but would you kindly inform me who I am?

LADY BRACKNELL. I am afraid that the news I have to give you will not altogether please you. You are the son of my poor sister, Mrs. Moncrieff, and consequently Algernon's elder brother.

JACK. Algy's elder brother! Then I have a brother after all. I knew I had a brother! I always said I had a brother! Cecily—how could you have ever doubted that I had a brother? [*Seizes hold of* ALGERNON.] Dr. Chasuble, my unfortunate brother. Miss Prism, my unfortunate brother. Gwendolen, my unfortunate brother. Algy, you young scoundrel, you will have to treat me with more respect in the future. You have never behaved to me like a brother in all your life.

ALGERNON. Well, not till today, old boy, I admit. I did my best, however, though I was out of practice. [*Shakes hands.*]

GWENDOLEN [*to* JACK]. My own! But what own are you? What is your Christian name, now that you have become someone else?

JACK. Good heavens! . . . I had quite forgotten that point. Your decision on the subject of my name is irrevocable, I suppose?

GWENDOLEN. I never change, except in my affections.

CECILY. What a noble nature you have, Gwendolen!

JACK. Then the question had better be cleared up at once. Aunt Augusta, a moment. At the time when Miss Prism left me in the hand–bag, had I been christened already?

LADY BRACKNELL. Every luxury that money could buy, including christening, had been lavished on you by your fond and doting parents.

JACK. Then I was christened! That is settled. Now, what name was I given? Let me know the worst.

LADY BRACKNELL. Being the eldest son you were naturally christened after your father.

JACK [*irritably*]. Yes, but what was my father's Christian name?

LADY BRACKNELL [*meditatively*]. I cannot at the present moment recall what the General's Christian name was. But I have no doubt he had one. He was eccentric, I admit. But only in later years. And that was the result of the Indian climate, and marriage, and indigestion, and other things of that kind.

JACK. Algy! Can't you recollect what our father's Christian name was?

ALGERNON. My dear boy, we were never even on speaking terms. He died before I was a year old.

JACK. His name would appear in the Army Lists of the period, I suppose, Aunt Augusta?

LADY BRACKNELL. The General was essentially a man of peace, except in his domestic life. But I have no doubt his name would appear in any military directory.

JACK. The Army Lists of the last forty years are here. These delightful records should have been my constant study. [*Rushes to bookcase and tears the books out.*] M. Generals . . . Mallam, Maxbohm, Magley, what ghastly names they have—Marksby, Migsby, Mobbs, Moncrieff! Lieutenant 1840, Captain, Lieutenant-Colonel, Colonel, General 1869, Christian names, Ernest John. [*Puts book very quietly down and speaks quite calmly.*] I always told you, Gwendolen, my name was Ernest, didn't I? Well, it is Ernest after all. I mean it naturally is Ernest.

LADY BRACKNELL. Yes, I remember that the General was called Ernest. I knew I had some particular reason for disliking the name.

GWENDOLEN. Ernest! My own Ernest! I felt from the first that you could have no other name!

JACK. Gwendolen, it is a terrible thing for a man to find out suddenly that all his life he has been speaking nothing but the truth. Can you forgive me?

GWENDOLEN. I can. For I feel that you are sure to change.

JACK. My own one!

CHASUBLE [*to* MISS PRISM]. Laetitia! [*Embraces her.*]

MISS PRISM [*enthusiastically*]. Frederick! At last!

ALGERNON. Cecily! [*Embraces her.*] At last!

JACK. Gwendolen! [*Embraces her.*] At last!

LADY BRACKNELL. My nephew, you seem to be displaying signs of triviality.

JACK. On the contrary, Aunt Augusta, I've now realized for the first time in my life the vital Importance of Being Ernest.

TABLEAU
CURTAIN

(1895)

Arthur Miller *1915–*

DEATH OF A SALESMAN
CERTAIN PRIVATE CONVERSATIONS IN TWO ACTS
AND A REQUIEM

CAST
[In order of appearance]

WILLY LOMAN.	CHARLEY.
LINDA.	UNCLE BEN.
BIFF.	HOWARD WAGNER.
HAPPY.	JENNY.
BERNARD.	STANLEY.
THE WOMAN (MISS	MISS FORSYTHE.
FRANCIS).	LETTA.

The action takes place in Willy Loman's house and yard and in various places he visits in the New York and Boston of today.

Throughout the play, in the stage directions, left and right mean stage left and stage right.

ACT ONE

A melody is heard, played upon a flute. It is small and fine, telling of grass and trees and the horizon. The curtain rises.

Before us is the Salesman's house. We are aware of towering, angular shapes behind it, surrounding it on all sides. Only the blue light of the sky falls upon the house and forestage; the surrounding area shows an angry glow of orange. As more light appears, we see a solid vault of apartment houses around the small, fragile-seeming home. An air of the dream clings to the place, a dream rising out of reality. The kitchen at center seems actual enough, for there is a kitchen table with three chairs, and a refrigerator. But no other fixtures are seen. At the back of the kitchen there is a draped entrance, which leads to the living-room. To the right of the kitchen, on a level raised two feet, is a bedroom furnished only with a brass bedstead and a straight chair. On a shelf over the bed a silver athletic trophy stands. A window opens onto the apartment house at the side.

Behind the kitchen, on a level raised six and a half feet, is the boys' bedroom, at present barely visible. Two beds are dimly seen, and at the back of the room a dormer window. (This bedroom is above the unseen living-room.) At the left a stairway curves up to it from the kitchen.

The entire setting is wholly or, in some places, partially transparent. The roof-line of the house is one-dimensional; under and over it we see the apartment buildings. Before the house lies an apron, curving beyond the forestage into the orchestra. This forward area serves as the back yard as well as the locale of all WILLY's *imaginings and of his city scenes. Whenever the action is in the present the actors observe the imaginary wall-lines, entering the house only through its door at the left. But in the scenes of the past these boundaries are broken, and characters enter or leave a room by stepping "through" a wall onto the forestage.*

From the right, WILLY LOMAN, *the Salesman, enters, carrying two large sample cases. The flute plays on. He hears but is not aware of it. He is past sixty years of age, dressed quietly. Even as he crosses the stage to the doorway of the house, his exhaustion is apparent. He unlocks the door, comes into the kitchen, and thankfully lets his burden down, feeling the soreness of his palms. A word-sigh escapes his lips—it might be "Oh, boy, oh, boy." He closes the door, then carries his cases out into the living-room, through the draped kitchen doorway.*

LINDA, his wife, has stirred in her bed at the right. She gets out and puts on a robe, listening. Most often jovial, she has developed an iron repression of her exceptions to WILLY's *behavior—she more than loves him, she admires him, as though his mercurial nature, his temper, his massive dreams and little cruelties, served her only as sharp reminders of the turbulent longings within him, longings which she shares but lacks the temperament to utter and follow to their end.*

LINDA [*hearing* WILLY *outside the bedroom, calls with some trepidation*]. Willy!
WILLY. It's all right. I came back.
LINDA. Why? What happened? [*Slight pause.*] Did something happen, Willy?
WILLY. No, nothing happened.
LINDA. You didn't smash the car, did you?
WILLY [*with casual irritation*]. I said nothing happened. Didn't you hear me?
LINDA. Don't you feel well?
WILLY. I'm tired to the death. [*The flute has faded away. He sits on the bed beside her, a little numb.*] I couldn't make it. I just couldn't make it, Linda.
LINDA [*very carefully, delicately*]. Where were you all day? You look terrible.
WILLY. I got as far as a little above Yonkers. I stopped for a cup of coffee. Maybe it was the coffee.
LINDA. What?
WILLY [*after a pause*]. I suddenly couldn't drive any more. The car kept going off onto the shoulder, y'know?
LINDA [*helpfully*]. Oh. Maybe it was the steering again. I don't think Angelo knows the Studebaker.
WILLY. No, it's me, it's me. Suddenly I realize I'm goin' sixty miles an hour and I don't remember the last five minutes. I'm—I can't seem to—keep my mind to it.

LINDA. Maybe it's your glasses. You never went for your new glasses.

WILLY. No, I see everything. I came back ten miles an hour. It took me nearly four hours from Yonkers.

LINDA [*resigned*]. Well, you'll just have to take a rest, Willy, you can't continue this way.

WILLY. I just got back from Florida.

LINDA. But you didn't rest your mind. Your mind is over-active, and the mind is what counts, dear.

WILLY. I'll start out in the morning. Maybe I'll feel better in the morning. [*She is taking off his shoes.*] These goddam arch supports are killing me.

LINDA. Take an aspirin. Should I get you an aspirin? It'll soothe you.

WILLY [*with wonder*]. I was driving along, you understand? And I was fine. I was even observing the scenery. You can imagine, me looking at scenery, on the road every week of my life. But it's so beautiful there, Linda, the trees are so thick, and the sun is warm. I opened the windshield and just let the warm air bathe over me. And then all of a sudden I'm goin' off the road! I'm tellin' ya, I absolutely forgot I was driving. If I'd've gone the other way over the white line I might've killed somebody. So I went on again—and five minutes later I'm dreamin' again, and I nearly—[*He presses two fingers against his eyes.*] I have such thoughts. I have such strange thoughts.

LINDA. Willy, dear. Talk to them again. There's no reason why you can't work in New York.

WILLY. They don't need me in New York. I'm the New England man. I'm vital in New England.

LINDA. But you're sixty years old. They can't expect you to keep traveling every week.

WILLY. I'll have to send a wire to Portland. I'm supposed to see Brown and Morrison tomorrow morning at ten o'clock to show the line. Goddammit, I could sell them! [*He starts putting on his jacket.*]

LINDA [*taking the jacket from him*]. Why don't you go down to the place tomorrow and tell Howard you've simply got to work in New York? You're too accommodating, dear.

WILLY. If old man Wagner was alive I'd a been in charge of New York now! That man was a prince, he was a masterful man. But that boy of his, that Howard, he don't appreciate. When I went north the first time, the Wagner Company didn't know where New England was!

LINDA. Why don't you tell those things to Howard, dear?

WILLY [*encouraged*]. I will, I definitely will. Is there any cheese?

LINDA. I'll make you a sandwich.

WILLY. No, go to sleep. I'll take some milk. I'll be up right away. The boys in?

LINDA. They're sleeping. Happy took Biff on a date tonight.

WILLY [*interested*]. That so?

LINDA. It was so nice to see them shaving together, one behind the other, in the bathroom. And going out together. You notice? The whole house smells of shaving lotion.

WILLY. Figure it out. Work a lifetime to pay off a house. You finally own it, and there's nobody to live in it.

LINDA. Well, dear, life is a casting off. It's always that way.

WILLY. No, no, some people—some people accomplish something. Did Biff say anything after I went this morning?

LINDA. You shouldn't have criticized him, Willy, especially after he just got off the train. You mustn't lose your temper with him.

WILLY. When the hell did I lose my temper? I simply asked him if he was making any money. Is that a criticism?

LINDA. But, dear, how could he make any money?

WILLY [*worried and angered*]. There's such an undercurrent in him. He became a moody man. Did he apologize when I left this morning?

LINDA. He was crestfallen, Willy. You know how he admires you. I think if he finds himself, then you'll both be happier and not fight any more.

WILLY. How can he find himself on a farm? Is that a life? A farmhand? In the beginning, when he was young, I thought, well, a young man, it's good for him to tramp around, take a lot of different jobs. But it's more than ten years now and he has yet to make thirty-five dollars a week!

LINDA. He's finding himself, Willy.

WILLY. Not finding yourself at the age of thirty-four is a disgrace!

LINDA. Shh!

WILLY. The trouble is he's lazy, goddammit!

WILLY. Willy, please!

WILLY. Biff is a lazy bum!

LINDA. They're sleeping. Get something to eat. Go on down.

WILLY. Why did he come home? I would like to know what brought him home.

LINDA. I don't know. I think he's still lost, Willy. I think he's very lost.

WILLY. Biff Loman is lost. In the greatest country in the world a young man with such—personal attractiveness, gets lost. And such a hard worker. There's one thing about Biff—he's not lazy.

LINDA. Never.

WILLY [*with pity and resolve*]. I'll see him in the morning; I'll have a nice talk with him. I'll get him a job selling. He could be big in no time. My God! Remember how they used to follow him around in high school? When he smiled at one of them their faces lit up. When he walked down the street . . . [*He loses himself in reminiscences.*]

LINDA [*trying to bring him out of it*]. Willy, dear, I got a new kind of American-type cheese today. It's whipped.

WILLY. Why do you get American when I like Swiss?

LINDA. I just thought you'd like a change—

WILLY. I don't want a change! I want Swiss cheese. Why am I always being contradicted?

LINDA [*with a covering laugh*]. I thought it would be a surprise.

WILLY. Why don't you open a window in here, for god's sake?

LINDA [*with infinite patience*]. They're all open, dear.

WILLY. The way they boxed us in here. Bricks and windows, windows and bricks.

LINDA. We should've bought the land next door.

WILLY. The street is lined with cars. There's not a breath of fresh air in the neighborhood. The grass don't grow any more, you can't raise a carrot in the back yard. They should've had a law against apartment houses. Remember those two beautiful elm trees out there? When I and Biff hung the swing between them?

LINDA. Yeah, like being a million miles from the city.

WILLY. They should've arrested the builder for cutting those down. They massacred the neighborhood. [*Lost.*] More and more I think of those days, Linda. This time of year it was lilac and wisteria. And then the peonies would come out, and the daffodils. What fragrance in this room!

LINDA. Well, after all, people had to move somewhere.

WILLY. No, there's more people now.

LINDA. I don't think there's more people. I think—

WILLY. There's more people! That's what's ruining this country! Population is getting out of control. The competition is maddening! Smell the stink from that apartment house! And another one on the other side . . . How can they whip cheese? [*On* WILLY's *last line,* BIFF *and* HAPPY *raise themselves up in their beds, listening.*]

LINDA. Go down, try it. And be quiet.

WILLY [*turning to* LINDA, *guiltily*]. You're not worried about me, are you, sweetheart?

BIFF. What's the matter?

HAPPY. Listen!

LINDA. You've got too much on the ball to worry about.

WILLY. You're my foundation and my support, Linda.

LINDA. Just try to relax, dear. You make mountains out of molehills.

WILLY. I won't fight with him any more. If he wants to go back to Texas, let him go.

LINDA. He'll find his way.

WILLY. Sure. Certain men just don't get started till later in life. Like Thomas Edison, I think. Or B. F. Goodrich. One of them was deaf. [*He starts for the bedroom doorway.*] I'll put my money on Biff.

LINDA. And Willy—if it's warm Sunday, we'll drive in the country. And we'll open the windshield, and take lunch.

WILLY. No, the windshields don't open on the new cars.

LINDA. But you opened it today.

WILLY. Me? I didn't. [*He stops.*] Now isn't that peculiar! Isn't that a remarkable— [*He breaks off in amazement and fright as the flute is heard distantly.*]

LINDA. What, darling?

WILLY. That is the most remarkable thing.

LINDA. What, dear?

WILLY. I was thinking of the Chevvy. [*Slight pause.*] Nineteen twenty-eight . . . when I had that red Chevvy—[*Breaks off.*] That funny? I coulda sworn I was driving that Chevvy today.

LINDA. Well, that's nothing. Something must've reminded you.

WILLY. Remarkable. Ts. Remember those days? The way Biff used to simonize that car? The dealer refused to believe there was eighty thousand miles on it. [*He shakes his head.*] Heh! [*To* LINDA.] Close your eyes, I'll be right up. [*He walks out of the bedroom.*]

HAPPY [*to* BIFF]. Jesus, maybe he smashed up the car again!

LINDA [*calling after* WILLY]. Be careful on the stairs, dear! The cheese is on the middle shelf! [*She turns, goes over to the bed, takes his jacket, and goes out of the bedroom. Light has risen on the boys' room. Unseen,* WILLY *is heard talking to himself, "Eighty thousand miles," and a little laugh.* BIFF *gets out of bed, comes downstage a bit, and stands attentively.* BIFF *is two years older than his brother* HAPPY, *well built, but in these days bears a worn air and seems less self-assured. He has succeeded less, and his dreams are stronger and less acceptable than* HAPPY's. HAPPY *is tall, powerfully made. Sexuality is like a visible color on him, or a scent that many women have discovered. He, like his brother, is lost, but in a different way, for he has never allowed himself to turn his face toward defeat and is thus more confused and hard-skinned, although seemingly more content.*]

HAPPY [*getting out of bed*]. He's going to get his license taken away if he keeps that up. I'm getting nervous about him, y'know, Biff?

BIFF. His eyes are going.

HAPPY. No, I've driven with him. He sees all right. He just doesn't keep his mind on it. I drove into the city with him last week. He stops at a green light and then it turns red and he goes. [*He laughs.*]

BIFF. Maybe he's color-blind.

HAPPY. Pop? Why he's got the finest eye for color in the business. You know that.

BIFF [*sitting down on his bed*]. I'm going to sleep.

HAPPY. You're not still sour on Dad, are you, Biff?

BIFF. He's all right, I guess.

WILLY [*underneath them, in the living-room*]. Yes, sir, eighty thousand miles—eighty-two thousand!

BIFF. You smoking?

HAPPY [*holding out a pack of cigarettes*]. Want one?

BIFF [*taking a cigarette*]. I can never sleep when I smell it.

WILLY. What a simonizing job, heh!

HAPPY [*with deep sentiment*]. Funny, Biff, y'know? Us sleeping in here again? The old beds. [*He pats his bed affectionately.*] All the talk that went across those two beds, huh? Our whole lives.

BIFF. Yeah. Lotta dreams and plans.

HAPPY [*with a deep and masculine laugh*]. About five hundred women would like to know what was said in this room. [*They share a soft laugh.*]

BIFF. Remember that big Betsy something—what the hell was her name—over on Bushwick Avenue?

HAPPY [*combing his hair*]. With the collie dog!

BIFF. That's the one. I got you in there, remember?

HAPPY. Yeah, that was my first time—I think. Boy, there was a pig! [*They laugh, almost crudely.*] You taught me everything I know about women. Don't forget that.

BIFF. I bet you forgot how bashful you used to be. Especially with girls.

HAPPY. Oh, I still am, Biff.

BIFF. Oh, go on.

HAPPY. I just control it, that's all. I think I got less bashful and you got more so. What happened, Biff? Where's the old humor, the old confidence? [*He shakes* BIFF's *knee.* BIFF *gets up and moves restlessly about the room.*] What's the matter?

BIFF. Why does Dad mock me all the time?

HAPPY. He's not mocking you, he—

BIFF. Everything I say there's a twist of mockery on his face. I can't get near him.

HAPPY. He just wants you to make good, that's all. I wanted to talk to you about Dad for a long time, Biff. Something's—happening to him. He—talks to himself.

BIFF. I noticed that this morning. But he always mumbled.

HAPPY. But not so noticeable. It got so embarrassing I sent him to Florida. And you know something? Most of the time he's talking to you.

BIFF. What's he say about me?

HAPPY. I can't make it out.

BIFF. What's he say about me?

HAPPY. I think the fact that you're not settled, that you're still kind of up in the air . . .

BIFF. There's one or two other things depressing him, Happy.

HAPPY. What do you mean?

BIFF. Never mind. Just don't lay it all to me.

HAPPY. But I think if you just got started—I mean—is there any future for you out there?

BIFF. I tell ya, Hap, I don't know what the future is. I don't know—what I'm supposed to want.

HAPPY. What do you mean?

BIFF. Well, I spent six or seven years after high school trying to work myself up. Shipping clerk, salesman, business of one kind or another. And it's a measly manner of existence. To get on that subway on the hot mornings in summer. To devote your whole life to keeping stock, or making phone calls, or selling or buying. To suffer fifty weeks of the year for the sake of a two-week vacation, when all you really desire is to be outdoors, with your shirt off. And always to have to get ahead of the next fella. And still—that's how you build a future.

HAPPY. Well, you really enjoy it on a farm? Are you content out there?

BIFF [*with rising agitation*]. Hap, I've had twenty or thirty different kinds of jobs since I left home before the war, and it always turns out the same. I just realized it lately. In Nebraska when I herded cattle, and the Dakotas, and Arizona, and now in Texas. It's why I came home now, I guess, because I realized it. This farm I work on, it's spring there now, see? And they've got about fifteen new colts. There's nothing more inspiring or—beautiful than the sight of a mare and a new colt. And it's cool there now, see? Texas is cool now, and it's spring. And whenever spring comes to where I am, I suddenly get the feeling, my God, I'm not gettin' anywhere! What the hell am I doing, playing around with horses, twenty-eight dollars a week! I'm thirty-four years old, I oughta be makin' my future. That's when I come running home. And now, I get here, and I don't know what to do with myself. [*After a pause.*] I've always made a point of not wasting my life, and every time I come back here I know that all I've done is to waste my life.

HAPPY. You're a poet, you know that, Biff? You're a—you're an idealist!

BIFF. No, I'm mixed up very bad. Maybe I oughta get married. Maybe I

oughta get stuck into something. Maybe that's my trouble. I'm like a
boy. I'm not married, I'm not in business, I just—I'm like a boy. Are
you content, Hap? You're a success, aren't you? Are you content?

HAPPY. Hell, no!

BIFF. Why? You're making money, aren't you?

HAPPY [*moving about with energy, expressiveness*]. All I can do now is wait
for the merchandise manager to die. And suppose I get to be merchandise
manager? He's a good friend of mine, and he's just built a terrific estate
on Long Island. And he lived there about two months and sold it, and
now he's building another one. He can't enjoy it once it's finished. And
I know that's just what I would do. I don't know what the hell I'm
workin' for. Sometimes I sit in my apartment—all alone. And I think
of the rent I'm paying. And it's crazy. But then, it's what I always
wanted. My own apartment, a car, and plenty of women. And still,
goddammit, I'm lonely.

BIFF [*with enthusiasm*]. Listen, why don't you come out West with me?

HAPPY. You and I, heh?

BIFF. Sure, maybe we could buy a ranch. Raise cattle, use our muscles.
Men built like we are should be working out in the open.

HAPPY [*avidly*]. The Loman Brothers, heh?

BIFF [*with vast affection*]. Sure, we'd be known all over the counties!

HAPPY [*enthralled*]. That's what I dream about, Biff. Sometimes I want to
just rip my clothes off in the middle of the store and outbox that goddam
merchandise manager. I mean I can outbox, outrun, and outlift anybody
in that store, and I have to take orders from those common, petty sons-
of-bitches till I can't stand it any more.

BIFF. I'm tellin' you, kid, if you were with me I'd be happy out there.

HAPPY [*enthused*]. See, Biff, everybody around me is so false that I'm constantly lowering my ideals . . .

BIFF. Baby, together we'd stand up for one another, we'd have someone
to trust.

HAPPY. If I were around you—

BIFF. Hap, the trouble is we weren't brought up to grub for money. I
don't know how to do it.

HAPPY. Neither can I!

BIFF. Then let's go!

HAPPY. The only thing is—what can you make out there?

BIFF. But look at your friend. Builds an estate and then hasn't the peace
of mind to live in it.

HAPPY. Yeah, but when he walks into the store the waves part in front
of him. That's fifty-two thousand dollars a year coming through the
revolving door, and I got more in my pinky finger than he's got in
his head.

BIFF. Yeah, but you just said—

HAPPY. I gotta show some of those pompous, self-important executives
over there that Hap Loman can make the grade. I want to walk into
the store the way he walks in. Then I'll go with you, Biff. We'll be
together yet, I swear. But take those two we had tonight. Now weren't
they gorgeous creatures?

BIFF. Yeah, yeah, most gorgeous I've had in years.

HAPPY. I get that any time I want, Biff. Whenever I fell disgusted. The only trouble is, it gets like bowling or something. I just keep knockin' them over and it doesn't mean anything. You still run around a lot?

BIFF. Naa. I'd like to find a girl—steady, somebody with substance.

HAPPY. That's what I long for.

BIFF. Go on! You'd never come home.

HAPPY. I would! Somebody with character, with resistance! Like Mom, y'know? You're gonna call me a bastard when I tell you this. That girl Charlotte I was with tonight is engaged to be married in five weeks. [*He tries on his new hat.*]

BIFF. No kiddin'!

HAPPY. Sure, the guy's in line for the vice-presidency of the store. I don't know what gets into me, maybe I just have an overdeveloped sense of competition or something, but I went and ruined her, and furthermore I can't get rid of her. And he's the third executive I've done that to. Isn't that a crummy characteristic? And to top it all, I go to their weddings! [*Indignantly, but laughing.*] Like I'm not supposed to take bribes. Manufacturers offer me a hundred-dollar bill now and then to throw an order their way. You know how honest I am, but it's like this girl, see. I hate myself for it. Because I don't want the girl, and, still, I take it and—I love it!

BIFF. Let's go to sleep.

HAPPY. I guess we didn't settle anything, heh?

BIFF. I just got one idea that I think I'm going to try.

HAPPY. What's that?

BIFF. Remember Bill Oliver?

HAPPY. Sure, Oliver is very big now. You want to work for him again?

BIFF. No, but when I quit he said something to me. He put his arm on my shoulder, and he said, "Biff, if you ever need anything, come to me."

HAPPY. I remember that. That sounds good.

BIFF. I think I'll go to see him. If I could get ten thousand or even seven or eight thousand dollars I could buy a beautiful ranch.

HAPPY. I bet he'd back you. 'Cause he thought highly of you, Biff. I mean, they all do. You're well liked, Biff. That's why I say to come back here, and we both have the apartment. And I'm tellin' you, Biff, any babe you want . . .

BIFF. No, with a ranch I could do the work I like and still be something. I just wonder, though. I wonder if Oliver still thinks I stole that carton of basketballs.

HAPPY. Oh, he probably forgot that long ago. It's almost ten years. You're too sensitive. Anyway, he didn't really fire you.

BIFF. Well, I think he was going to. I think that's why I quit. I was never sure whether he knew or not. I know he thought the world of me, though. I was the only one he'd let lock up the place.

WILLY [*below*]. You gonna wash the engine, Biff?

HAPPY. Shh! [BIFF *looks at* HAPPY, *who is gazing down, listening.* WILLY *is mumbling in the parlor.*]

HAPPY. You hear that? [*They listen.* WILLY *laughs warmly.*]

BIFF [*growing angry*]. Doesn't he know Mom can hear that?

WILLY. Don't get your sweater dirty, Biff! [*A look of pain crosses* BIFF's *face.*]

HAPPY. Isn't that terrible? Don't leave again, will you? You'll find a job here. You gotta stick around. I don't know what to do about him, it's getting embarrassing.

WILLY. What a simonizing job!

BIFF. Mom's hearing that!

WILLY. No kiddin', Biff, you got a date? Wonderful!

HAPPY. Go on to sleep. But talk to him in the morning, will you?

BIFF [*reluctantly getting into bed*]. With her in the house. Brother!

HAPPY [*getting into bed*]. I wish you'd have a good talk with him. [*The light on their room begins to fade.*]

BIFF [*To himself in bed*]. That selfish, stupid . . .

HAPPY. Sh . . . Sleep, Biff. [*Their light is out. Well before they have finished speaking,* WILLY's *form is dimly seen below in the darkened kitchen. He opens the refrigerator, searches in there, and takes out a bottle of milk. The apartment houses are fading out, and the entire house and surroundings become covered with leaves. Music insinuates itself as the leaves appear.*]

WILLY. Just wanna be careful with those girls, Biff, that's all. Don't make any promises. No promises of any kind. Because a girl, y'know, they always believe what you tell 'em, and you're very young, Biff, you're too young to be talking seriously to girls. [*Light rises on the kitchen.* WILLY, *talking, shuts the refrigerator door and comes downstage to the kitchen table. He pours milk into a glass. He is totally immersed in himself, smiling faintly.*]

WILLY. Too young entirely, Biff. You want to watch your schooling first. Then when you're all set, there'll be plenty of girls for a boy like you. [*He smiles broadly at a kitchen chair.*] That so? The girls pay for you? [*He laughs.*] Boy, you must really be makin' a hit. [WILLY *is gradually addressing—physically—a point offstage, speaking through the wall of the kitchen, and his voice has been rising in volume to that of a normal conversation.*]

WILLY. I been wondering why you polish the car so careful. Ha! Don't leave the hubcaps, boys. Get the chamois to the hubcaps. Happy, use newspaper on the windows, it's the easiest thing. Show him how to do it, Biff! You see, Happy? Pad it up, use it like a pad. That's it, that's it, good work. You're doin' all right, Hap. [*He pauses, then nods in approbation for a few seconds, then looks upward.*] Biff, first thing we gotta do when we get time is clip that big branch over the house. Afraid it's gonna fall in a storm and hit the roof. Tell you what. We get a rope and sling her around, and then we climb up there with a couple of saws and take her down. Soon as you finish the car, boys, I wanna see ya. I got a surprise for you, boys.

BIFF [*offstage*]. Whatta ya got, Dad?

WILLY. No, you finish first. Never leave a job till you're finished—remember that. [*Looking toward the "big trees"*] Biff, up in Albany I saw a beautiful hammock. I think I'll buy it next trip, and we'll hang it right between those two elms. Wouldn't that be something? Just swingin' there under those branches. Boy, that would be . . . [YOUNG BIFF *and* YOUNG HAPPY *appear from the direction* WILLY *was addressing.* HAPPY *carries rags and a pail of water.* BIFF, *wearing a sweater with a block "S," carries a football.*]

BIFF [*pointing in the direction of the car offstage*]. How's that, Pop, professional?
WILLY. Terrific. Terrific job, boys. Good work, Biff.
HAPPY. Where's the surprise, Pop?
WILLY. In the back seat of the car.
HAPPY. Boy! [*He runs off.*]
BIFF. What is it, Dad? Tell me, what'd you buy?
WILLY [*laughing, cuffs him*]. Never mind, something I want you to have.
BIFF [*turns and starts off*].What is it, Hap?
HAPPY [*offstage*]. It's a punching bag!
BIFF. Oh, Pop!
WILLY. It's got Gene Tunney's signature on it! [HAPPY *runs onstage with a punching bag.*]
BIFF. Gee, how'd you know we wanted a punching bag?
WILLY. Well, it's the finest thing for the timing.
HAPPY [*lies down on his back and pedals with his feet*]. I'm losing weight, you notice, Pop?
WILLY [*to* HAPPY]. Jumping rope is good too.
BIFF. Did you see the new football I got?
WILLY [*examining the ball*]. Where'd you get a new ball?
BIFF. The coach told me to practice my passing.
WILLY. That so? And he gave you the ball, heh?
BIFF. Well, I borrowed it from the locker room. [*He laughs confidentially.*]
WILLY [*laughing with him at the theft*]. I want you to return that.
HAPPY. I told you he wouldn't like it!
BIFF [*angrily*]. Well, I'm bringing it back!
WILLY [*stopping the incipient argument, to* HAPPY]. Sure, he's gotta practice with a regulation ball, doesn't he? [*To* BIFF] Coach'll probably congratulate you on your initiative!
BIFF. Oh, he keeps congratulating my initiative all the time, Pop.
WILLY. That's because he likes you. If somebody else took that ball there'd be an uproar. So what's the report, boys, what's the report?
BIFF. Where'd you go this time, Dad? Gee we were lonesome for you.
WILLY [*pleased, puts an arm around each boy and they come down to the apron*]. Lonesome, heh?
BIFF. Missed you every minute.
WILLY. Don't say? Tell you a secret, boys. Don't breathe it to a soul. Someday I'll have my own business, and I'll never have to leave home any more.
HAPPY. Like Uncle Charley, heh?
WILLY. Bigger than Uncle Charley! Because Charley is not—liked. He's liked, but he's not—well liked.
BIFF. Where'd you go this time, Dad?
WILLY. Well, I got on the road, and I went north to Providence. Met the Mayor.
BIFF. The Mayor of Providence!
WILLY. He was sitting in the hotel lobby.
BIFF. What'd he say?
WILLY. He said, "Morning!" And I said, "You got a fine city here, Mayor." And then he had coffee with me. And then I went to Waterbury. Water-

bury is a fine city. Big clock city, the famous Waterbury clock. Sold a
nice bill there. And then Boston—Boston is the cradle of the Revolution.
A fine city. And a couple of other towns in Mass., and on to Portland
and Bangor and straight home!

BIFF. Gee, I'd love to go with you sometime, Dad.

WILLY. Soon as summer comes.

HAPPY. Promise?

WILLY. You and Hap and I, and I'll show you all the towns. America is
full of beautiful towns and fine, upstanding people. And they know
me, boys, they know me up and down New England. The finest people.
And when I bring you fellas up, there'll be open sesame for all of us,
'cause one thing, boys: I have friends. I can park my car in any street
in New England, and the cops protect it like their own. This summer,
heh?

BIFF *and* HAPPY, *together.* Yeah! You bet!

WILLY. We'll take our bathing suits.

HAPPY. We'll carry your bags, Pop!

WILLY. Oh, won't that be something! Me comin' into the Boston stores
with you boys carryin' my bags. What a sensation! [BIFF *is prancing
around, practicing passing the ball.*]

WILLY. You nervous, Biff, about the game?

BIFF. Not if you're gonna be there.

WILLY. What do they say about you in school, now that they made you
captain?

HAPPY. There's a crowd of girls behind him every time the classes change.

BIFF [*taking* WILLY'S *hand*]. This Saturday, Pop, this Saturday—just for
you, I'm going to break through for a touchdown.

HAPPY. You're supposed to pass.

BIFF. I'm takin' one play for Pop. You watch me, Pop, and when I take
off my helmet, that means I'm breakin' out. Then you watch me crash
through that line!

WILLY [*kisses* BIFF]. Oh, wait'll I tell this in Boston! [BERNARD *enters in
knickers. He is younger than* BIFF, *earnest and loyal, a worried boy.*]

BERNARD. Biff, where are you? You're supposed to study with me today.

WILLY. Hey, looka Bernard. What're you lookin' so anemic about, Bernard?

BERNARD. He's gotta study, Uncle Willy. He's got Regents next week.

HAPPY [*tauntingly, spinning* BERNARD *around*]. Let's box, Bernard!

BERNARD. Biff! [*He gets away from* HAPPY].Listen, Biff, I heard Mr. Birnbaum
say that if you don't start studyin' math he's gonna flunk you, and
you won't graduate. I heard him!

WILLY. You better study with him, Biff. Go ahead now.

BERNARD. I heard him!

BIFF. Oh, Pop, you didn't see my sneakers! [*He holds up a foot for* WILLY
to look at.]

WILLY. Hey, that's a beautiful job of printing!

BERNARD [*wiping his glasses*]. Just because he printed University of Virginia
on his sneakers doesn't mean they've got to graduate him, Uncle Willy!

WILLY [*angrily*]. What're you talking about? With scholarships to three
universities they're gonna flunk him?

BERNARD. But I heard Mr. Birnbaum say—

WILLY. Don't be a pest, Bernard! [*To his boys*] What an anemic!

BERNARD. Okay, I'm waiting for you in my house, Biff. [BERNARD *goes off. The* LOMANS *laugh.*]

WILLY. Bernard is not well liked, is he?

BIFF. He's liked, but he's not well liked.

HAPPY. That's right, Pop.

WILLY. That's just what I mean. Bernard can get the best marks in school, y'understand, but when he gets out in the business world, y'understand, you are going to be five times ahead of him. That's why I thank Almighty God you're both built like Adonises. Because the man who makes an appearance in the business world, the man who creates personal interest, is the man who gets ahead. Be liked and you will never want. You take me, for instance. I never have to wait in line to see a buyer. "Willy Loman is here!" That's all they have to know, and I go right through.

BIFF. Did you knock them dead, Pop?

WILLY. Knocked 'em cold in Providence, slaughtered 'em in Boston.

HAPPY [*on his back, peddling again*]. I'm losing weight, you notice, Pop? [LINDA *enters, as of old, a ribbon in her hair, carrying a basket of washing.*]

LINDA [*with youthful energy*]. Hello, dear!

WILLY. Sweetheart!

LINDA. How'd the Chevvy run?

WILLY. Chevrolet, Linda, is the greatest car ever built. [*To the boys*] Since when do you let your mother carry wash up the stairs?

BIFF. Grab hold there, boy!

HAPPY. Where to, Mom?

LINDA. Hang them up on the line. And you better go down to your friends, Biff. The cellar is full of boys. They don't know what to do with themselves.

BIFF. Ah, when Pop comes home they can wait!

WILLY [*laughs appreciatively*]. You better go down and tell them what to do, Biff.

BIFF. I think I'll have them sweep out the furnace room.

WILLY. Good work, Biff.

BIFF [*goes through wall-line of kitchen to doorway at back and calls down*]. Fellas! Everybody sweep out the furnace room! I'll be right down!

VOICES. All right! Okay, Biff.

BIFF. George and Sam and Frank, come out back! We're hangin' up the wash! Come on, Hap, on the double! [*He and* HAPPY *carry out the basket.*]

LINDA. The way they obey him!

WILLY. Well, that's training, the training. I'm tellin' you, I was sellin' thousands and thousands, but I had to come home.

LINDA. Oh, the whole block'll be at that game. Did you sell anything?

WILLY. I did five hundred gross in Providence and seven hundred gross in Boston.

LINDA. No! Wait a minute, I've got a pencil. [*She pulls pencil and paper out of her apron pocket.*] That makes your commission . . . two hundred— my God! Two hundred and twelve dollars!

WILLY. Well, I didn't figure it yet, but . . .

LINDA. How much did you do?

WILLY. Well, I—I did—about a hundred and eighty gross in Providence. Well, no—it came to—roughly two hundred gross on the whole trip.

LINDA [*without hesitation*]. Two hundred gross. That's . . . [*She figures.*]

WILLY. The trouble was that three of the stores were half closed for inventory in Boston. Otherwise I woulda broke records.

LINDA. Well, it makes seventy dollars and some pennies. That's very good.

WILLY. What do we owe?

LINDA. Well, on the first there's sixteen dollars on the refrigerator—

WILLY. Why sixteen?

LINDA. Well, the fan belt broke, so it was a dollar eighty.

WILLY. But it's brand new.

LINDA. Well, the man said that's the way it is. Till they work themselves in, y'know. [*They move through the wall-line into the kitchen.*]

WILLY. I hope we didn't get stuck on that machine.

LINDA. They got the biggest ads of any of them!

WILLY. I know, it's a fine machine. What else?

LINDA. Well, there's nine-sixty for the washing machine. And for the vacuum cleaner there's three and a half due on the fifteenth. Then the roof, you got twenty-one dollars remaining.

WILLY. It don't leak, does it?

LINDA. No, they did a wonderful job. Then you owe Frank for the carburetor.

WILLY. I'm not going to pay that man! That goddam Chevrolet, they ought to prohibit the manufacture of that car!

LINDA. Well, you owe him three and a half. And odds and ends, comes to around a hundred and twenty dollars by the fifteenth.

WILLY. A hundred and twenty dollars! My God, if business don't pick up I don't know what I'm gonna do!

LINDA. Well, next week you'll do better.

WILLY. Oh, I'll knock 'em dead next week. I'll go to Hartford. I'm very well liked in Hartford. [*Pause*] You know, the trouble is, Linda, people don't seem to take to me. [*They move onto the forestage.*]

LINDA. Oh, don't be foolish.

WILLY. I know it when I walk in. They seem to laugh at me.

LINDA. Why? Why would they laugh at you? Don't talk that way, Willy. [WILLY *moves to the edge of the stage.* LINDA *goes into the kitchen and starts to darn stockings.*]

WILLY. I don't know the reason for it, but they just pass me by. I'm not noticed.

LINDA. But you're doing wonderful, dear. You're making seventy to a hundred dollars a week.

WILLY. But I gotta be at it ten, twelve hours a day. Other men—I don't know—they do it easier. I don't know why—I can't stop myself—I talk too much. A man oughta come in with a few words. One thing about Charley. He's a man of few words, and they respect him.

LINDA. You don't talk too much, you're just lively.

WILLY [*smiling*]. Well, I figure, what the hell, life is short, a couple of jokes. [*To himself*] I joke too much! [*The smile goes.*]

LINDA. Why? You're—

WILLY. I'm fat. I'm very—foolish to look at, Linda. I didn't tell you, but Christmas time I happened to be calling on F. H. Stewarts, and a salesman I know, as I was going in to see the buyer, I heard him say something about—walrus. And I—I cracked him right across the face. I won't take that. I simply will not take that. But they do laugh at me. I know that.

LINDA. Darling . . .

WILLY. I gotta overcome it. I know I gotta overcome it. I'm not dressing to advantage, maybe.

LINDA. Willy, darling, you're the handsomest man in the world—

WILLY. Oh, no, Linda.

LINDA. To me you are. [*Slight pause*] The handsomest. [*From the darkness is heard the laughter of a woman.* WILLY *doesn't turn to it, but it continues through* LINDA's *lines.*]

LINDA. And the boys, Willy. Few men are idolized by their children the way you are. [*Music is heard as behind a scrim, to the left of the house.* THE WOMAN, *dimly seen, is dressing.*]

WILLY [*with great feeling*]. You're the best there is, Linda, you're a pal, you know that? On the road—on the road I want to grab you sometimes and just kiss the life outa you. [*The laughter is loud now, and he moves into a brightening area at the left, where* THE WOMAN *has come from behind the scrim and is standing, putting on her hat, looking into a "mirror" and laughing.*]

WILLY. 'Cause I get so lonely—especially when business is bad and there's nobody to talk to. I get the feeling that I'll never sell anything again, that I won't make a living for you, or a business, a business for the boys. [*He talks through* THE WOMAN's *subsiding laughter;* THE WOMAN *primps at the "mirror."*] There's so much I want to make for—

THE WOMAN. Me? You didn't make me, Willy. I picked you.

WILLY [*pleased*]. You picked me?

THE WOMAN [*who is quite proper-looking,* WILLY's *age*]. I did. I've been sitting at that desk watching all the salesmen go by, day in, day out. But you've got such a sense of humor, and we do have such a good time together, don't we?

WILLY. Sure, sure. [*He takes her in his arms.*] Why do you have to go now?

THE WOMAN. It's two o'clock . . .

WILLY. No, come on in! [*He pulls her.*]

THE WOMAN. . . . . . my sisters'll be scandalized. When'll you be back?

WILLY. Oh, two weeks about. Will you come up again?

THE WOMAN. Sure thing. You do make me laugh. It's good for me. [*She squeezes his arm, kisses him.*] And I think you're a wonderful man.

WILLY. You picked me, heh?

THE WOMAN. Sure. Because you're so sweet. And such a kidder.

WILLY. Well, I'll see you next time I'm in Boston.

THE WOMAN. I'll put you right through to the buyers.

WILLY [*slapping her bottom*]. Right. Well, bottoms up!

THE WOMAN [*slaps him gently and laughs*]. You just kill me, Willy. [*He suddenly grabs her and kisses her roughly.*] You kill me. And thanks for the stockings. I love a lot of stockings. Well, good night.

WILLY. Good night. And keep your pores open!

THE WOMAN. Oh, Willy! [THE WOMAN *bursts out laughing, and* LINDA's *laugh-*

ter blends in. THE WOMAN *disappears into the dark. Now the area at the kitchen table brightens.* LINDA *is sitting where she was at the kitchen table, but now is mending a pair of her silk stockings.*]

LINDA. You are, Willy. The handsomest man. You've got no reason to feel that—

WILLY [*coming out of* THE WOMAN's *dimming area and going over to* LINDA]. I'll make it all up to you, Linda, I'll—

LINDA. There's nothing to make up, dear. You're doing fine, better than—

WILLY [*noticing her mending*]. What's that?

LINDA. Just mending my stockings. They're so expensive—

WILLY [*angrily, taking them from her*]. I won't have you mending stockings in this house! Now throw them out! [LINDA *puts the stockings in her pocket.*]

BERNARD [*entering on the run*]. Where is he? If he doesn't study!

WILLY [*moving to the forestage, with great agitation*]. You'll give him the answers!

BERNARD. I do, but I can't on a Regents! That's a state exam! They're liable to arrest me!

WILLY. Where is he? I'll whip him, I'll whip him!

LINDA. And he'd better give back that football, Willy, it's not nice.

WILLY. Biff! Where is he? Why is he taking everything?

LINDA. He's too rough with the girls, Willy. All the mothers are afraid of him!

WILLY. I'll whip him!

BERNARD. He's driving the car without a license! [THE WOMAN's *laugh is heard.*]

WILLY. Shut up!

LINDA. All the mothers—

WILLY. Shut up!

BERNARD [*backing quietly away and out*]. Mr. Birnbaum says he's stuck up.

WILLY. Get outa here!

BERNARD. If he doesn't buckle down he'll flunk math! [*He goes off.*]

LINDA. He's right, Willy, you've gotta—

WILLY [*exploding at her*]. There's nothing the matter with him! You want him to be a worm like Bernard? He's got spirit, personality . . . [*As he speaks,* LINDA *almost in tears, exits into the living-room.* WILLY *is alone in the kitchen, wilting and staring. The leaves are gone. It is night again, and the apartment houses look down from behind.*]

WILLY. Loaded with it. Loaded! What is he stealing? He's giving it back, isn't he? Why is he stealing? What did I tell him? I never in my life told him anything but decent things. [HAPPY *in pajamas has come down the stairs;* WILLY *suddenly becomes aware of* HAPPY's *presence.*]

HAPPY. Let's go now, come on.

WILLY [*sitting down at the kitchen table*]. Huh! Why did she have to wax the floors herself? Every time she waxes the floors she keels over. She knows that!

HAPPY. Shh! Take it easy. What brought you back tonight?

WILLY. I got an awful scare. Nearly hit a kid in Yonkers. God! Why didn't I go to Alaska with my brother Ben that time! Ben! That man was a genius, that man was success incarnate! What a mistake! He begged me to go.

HAPPY. Well, there's no use in—

WILLY. You guys! There was a man started with the clothes on his back and ended up with diamond mines!

HAPPY. Boy, someday I'd like to know how he did it.

WILLY. What's the mystery? The man knew what he wanted and went out and got it! Walked into a jungle, and comes out, the age of twenty-one, and he's rich! The world is an oyster, but you don't crack it open on a mattress!

HAPPY. Pop, I told you I'm gonna retire you for life.

WILLY. You'll retire me for life on seventy goddam dollars a week? And your women and your car and your apartment, and you'll retire me for life? Christ's sake, I couldn't get past Yonkers today! Where are you guys, where are you? The woods are burning! I can't drive a car! [CHARLEY *has appeared in the doorway. He is a large man, slow of speech, laconic, immovable. In all he says, despite what he says, there is pity, and, now, trepidation. He has a robe over pajamas, slippers on his feet. He enters the kitchen.*]

CHARLEY. Everything all right?

HAPPY. Yeah, Charley, everything's . . .

WILLY. What's the matter?

CHARLEY. I heard some noise. I thought something happened. Can't we do something about the walls? You sneeze in here, and in my house hats blow off.

HAPPY. Let's go to bed, Dad. Come on. [CHARLEY *signals to* HAPPY *to go.*]

WILLY. You go ahead, I'm not tired at the moment.

HAPPY [*to* WILLY]. Take it easy, huh? [*He exits.*]

WILLY. What're you doin' up?

CHARLEY [*sitting down at the kitchen table opposite* WILLY]. Couldn't sleep good. I had a heartburn.

WILLY. Well, you don't know how to eat.

CHARLEY. I eat with my mouth.

WILLY. No, you're ignorant. You gotta know about vitamins and things like that.

CHARLEY. Come on, let's shoot. Tire you out a little.

WILLY [*hesitantly*]. All right. You got cards?

CHARLEY [*taking a deck from his pocket*]. Yeah, I got them. Someplace. What is it with those vitamins?

WILLY [*dealing*]. They build up your bones. Chemistry.

CHARLEY. Yeah, but there's no bones in a heartburn.

WILLY. What are you talkin' about? Do you know the first thing about it?

CHARLEY. Don't get insulted.

WILLY. Don't talk about something you don't know anything about. [*They are playing. Pause.*]

CHARLEY. What're you doin' home?

WILLY. A little trouble with the car.

CHARLEY. Oh. [*Pause*] I'd like to take a trip to California.

WILLY. Don't say.

CHARLEY. You want a job?

WILLY. I got a job, I told you that. [*After a slight pause*] What the hell are you offering me a job for?

CHARLEY. Don't get insulted.

WILLY. Don't insult me.

CHARLEY. I don't see no sense in it. You don't have to go on this way.

WILLY. I got a good job. [*Slight pause*] What do you keep comin' in here for?

CHARLEY. You want me to go?

WILLY [*after a pause, withering*]. I can't understand it. He's going back to Texas again. What the hell is that?

CHARLEY. Let him go.

WILLY. I got nothin' to give him, Charley, I'm clean, I'm clean.

CHARLEY. He won't starve. None a them starve. Forget about him.

WILLY. Then what have I got to remember?

CHARLEY. You take it too hard. To hell with it. When a deposit bottle is broken you don't get your nickel back.

WILLY. That's easy enough for you to say.

CHARLEY. That ain't easy for me to say.

WILLY. Did you see the ceiling I put up in the living-room?

CHARLEY. Yeah, that's a piece of work. To put up a ceiling is a mystery to me. How do you do it?

WILLY. What's the difference?

CHARLEY. Well, talk about it.

WILLY. You gonna put up a ceiling?

CHARLEY. How could I put up a ceiling?

WILLY. Then what the hell are you bothering me for?

CHARLEY. You're insulted again.

WILLY. A man who can't handle tools is not a man. You're disgusting.

CHARLEY. Don't call me disgusting, Willy. [UNCLE BEN, *carrying a valise and an umbrella, enters the forestage from around the right corner of the house. He is a stolid man, in his sixties, with a mustache and an authoritative air. He is utterly certain of his destiny, and there is an aura of far places about him. He enters exactly as* WILLY *speaks.*]

WILLY. I'm getting awfully tired, Ben. [BEN'S *music is heard.* BEN *looks around at everything.*]

CHARLEY. Good, keep playing; you'll sleep better. Did you call me Ben? [BEN *looks at his watch.*]

WILLY. That's funny. For a second there you reminded me of my brother Ben.

BEN. I only have a few minutes. [*He strolls, inspecting the place.* WILLY *and* CHARLEY *continue playing.*]

CHARLEY. You never heard from him again, heh? Since that time?

WILLY. Didn't Linda tell you? Couple of weeks ago we got a letter from his wife in Africa. He died.

CHARLEY. That so.

BEN [*chuckling*]. So this is Brooklyn, eh?

CHARLEY. Maybe you're in for some of his money.

WILLY. Naa, he had seven sons. There's just one opportunity I had with that man . . .

BEN. I must make a train, William. There are several properties I'm looking at in Alaska.

WILLY. Sure, sure! If I'd gone with him to Alaska that time, everything would've been totally different.

CHARLEY. Go on, you'd froze to death up there.

WILLY. What're you talking about?

BEN. Opportunity is tremendous in Alaska, William. Surprised you're not up there.

WILLY. Sure, tremendous.

CHARLEY. Heh?

WILLY. There was the only man I ever met who knew the answers.

CHARLEY. Who?

BEN. How are you all?

WILLY [*taking a pot, smiling*]. Fine, fine.

CHARLEY. Pretty sharp tonight.

BEN. Is Mother living with you?

WILLY. No, she died a long time ago.

CHARLEY. Who?

BEN. That's too bad. Fine specimen of a lady, Mother.

WILLY [*to* CHARLEY]. Heh?

BEN. I'd hoped to see the old girl.

CHARLEY. Who died?

BEN. Heard anything from Father, have you?

WILLY [*unnerved*]. What do you mean, who died?

CHARLEY [*taking a pot*]. What're you talkin' about?

BEN [*looking at his watch*]. William, it's half-past eight!

WILLY [*as though to dispel his confusion he angrily stops* CHARLEY's *hand*]. That's my build!

CHARLEY. I put the ace—

WILLY. If you don't know how to play the game I'm not gonna throw my money away on you!

CHARLEY [*rising*]. It was my ace, for God's sake!

WILLY. I'm through, I'm through!

BEN. When did Mother die?

WILLY. Long ago. Since the beginning you never knew how to play cards.

CHARLEY [*picks up the cards and goes to the door*]. All right! Next time I'll bring a deck with five aces.

WILLY. I don't play that kind of game!

CHARLEY [*turning to him*]. You ought to be ashamed of yourself!

WILLY. Yeah?

CHARLEY. Yeah! [*He goes out.*]

WILLY [*slamming the door after him*]. Ignoramus!

BEN [*as* WILLY *comes toward him through the wall-line of the kitchen*]. So you're William.

WILLY [*shaking* BEN's *hand*]. Ben! I've been waiting for you so long! What's the answer? How did you do it?

BEN. Oh, there's a story in that. [LINDA *enters the forestage, as of old, carrying the wash basket.*]

LINDA. Is this Ben?

BEN [*gallantly*]. How do you do, my dear.

LINDA. Where've you been all these years? Willy's always wondered why you—

WILLY [*pulling* BEN *away from her impatiently*]. Where is Dad? Didn't you follow him? How did you get started?

BEN. Well, I don't know how much you remember.

WILLY. Well, I was just a baby, of course, only three or four years old—

BEN. Three years and eleven months.

WILLY. What a memory, Ben!

BEN. I have many enterprises, William, and I have never kept books.

WILLY. I remember I was sitting under the wagon in—was it Nebraska?

BEN. It was South Dakota, and I gave you a bunch of wild flowers.

WILLY. I remember you walking away down some open road.

BEN [*laughing*]. I was going to find Father in Alaska.

WILLY. Where is he?

BEN. At that age I had a very faulty view of geography, William. I discovered after a few days that I was heading due south, so instead of Alaska, I ended up in Africa.

LINDA. Africa!

WILLY. The Gold Coast!

BEN. Principally diamond mines.

LINDA. Diamond mines!

BEN. Yes, my dear. But I've only a few minutes—

WILLY. No! Boys! Boys! [YOUNG BIFF *and* HAPPY *appear.*] Listen to this. This is your Uncle Ben, a great man! Tell my boys, Ben!

BEN. Why, boys, when I was seventeen I walked into the jungle, and when I was twenty-one I walked out. [*He laughs.*] And by God I was rich.

WILLY [*to the boys*]. You see what I been talking about? The greatest things can happen!

BEN [*glancing at his watch*]. I have an appointment in Ketchikan Tuesday week.

WILLY. No, Ben! Please tell about Dad. I want my boys to hear. I want them to know the kind of stock they spring from. All I remember is a man with a big beard, and I was in Mamma's lap, sitting around a fire, and some kind of high music.

BEN. His flute. He played the flute.

WILLY. Sure, the flute, that's right! [*New music is heard, a high, rollicking tune.*]

BEN. Father was a very great and a very wild-hearted man. We would start in Boston, and he'd toss the whole family into the wagon, and then he'd drive the team right across the country; through Ohio, and Indiana, Michigan, Illinois, and all the Western states. And we'd stop in the towns and sell the flutes that he'd made on the way. Great inventor, Father. With one gadget he made more in a week than a man like you could make in a lifetime.

WILLY. That's just the way I'm bringing them up, Ben—rugged, well liked, all-around.

BEN. Yeah? [*To* BIFF.] Hit that, boy—hard as you can. [*He pounds his stomach.*]

BIFF. Oh, no, sir!

BEN [*taking boxing stance*]. Come on, get to me! [*He laughs.*]

WILLY. Go to it, Biff! Go ahead, show him!

BIFF. Okay! [*He cocks his fists and starts in.*]

LINDA [*to* WILLY]. Why must he fight, dear?

BEN [*sparring with* BIFF]. Good boy! Good boy!

WILLY. How's that, Ben, heh?

HAPPY. Give him the left, Biff!

LINDA. Why are you fighting?

BEN. Good boy! [*Suddenly comes in, trips* BIFF, *and stands over him, the point of his umbrella poised over* BIFF's *eye.*]

LINDA. Look out, Biff!

BIFF. Gee!

BEN [*patting* BIFF's *knee*]. Never fight fair with a stranger, boy. You'll never get out of the jungle that way. [*Taking* LINDA's *hand and bowing.*] It was an honor and a pleasure to meet you, Linda.

LINDA [*withdrawing her hand coldly, frightened*]. Have a nice—trip.

BEN [*to* WILLY]. And good luck with your—what do you do?

WILLY. Selling.

BEN. Yes. well . . . [*He raises his hand in farewell to all.*]

WILLY. No, Ben, I don't want you to think . . . [*He takes* BEN's *arm to show him.*] It's Brooklyn, I know, but we hunt too.

BEN. Really, now.

WILLY. Oh, sure, there's snakes and rabbits and—that's why I moved out here. Why, Biff can fell any one of these trees in no time! Boys! Go right over to where they're building the apartment house and get some sand. We're gonna rebuild the entire front stoop right now! Watch this, Ben!

BIFF. Yes, sir! On the double, Hap!

HAPPY [*as he and* BIFF *run off*]. I lost weight, Pop, you notice? [CHARLEY *enters in knickers, even before the boys are gone.*]

CHARLEY. Listen, if they steal any more from that building the watchman'll put the cops on them!

LINDA [*to* WILLY]. Don't let Biff . . . [BEN *laughs lustily.*]

WILLY. You shoulda seen the lumber they brought home last week. At least a dozen six-by-tens worth all kinds a money.

CHARLEY. Listen, if that watchman—

WILLY. I gave them hell, understand. But I got a couple of fearless characters there.

CHARLEY. Willy, the jails are full of fearless characters.

BEN [*clapping* WILLY *on the back, with a laugh at* CHARLEY]. And the stock exchange, friend!

WILLY [*joining in* BEN's *laughter*]. Where are the rest of your pants?

CHARLEY. My wife bought them.

WILLY. Now all you need is a golf club and you can go upstairs and go to sleep. [*To* BEN] Great athlete! Between him and his son Bernard they can't hammer a nail!

BERNARD [*rushing in*]. The watchman's chasing Biff!

WILLY [*angrily*]. Shut up! He's not stealing anything!

LINDA [*alarmed, hurrying off left*]. Where is he? Biff, dear! [*She exits.*]

WILLY [*moving toward the left, away from* BEN]. There's nothing wrong. What's the matter with you?

BEN. Nervy boy. Good!

WILLY [*laughing*]. Oh, nerves of iron, that Biff!

CHARLEY. Don't know what it is. My New England man comes back and he's bleedin', they murdered him up there.

WILLY. It's contacts, Charley, I got important contacts!

CHARLEY [*sarcastically*]. Glad to hear it, Willy. Come in later, we'll shoot a little casino. I'll take some of your Portland money. [*He laughs at* WILLY *and exits.*]

WILLY [*turning to* BEN]. Business is bad, it's murderous. But not for me, of course.

BEN. I'll stop by on my way back to Africa.

WILLY [*longingly*]. Can't you stay a few days? You're just what I need, Ben, because I—I have a fine position here, but I—well, Dad left when I was such a baby and I never had a chance to talk to him and I still feel—kind of temporary about myself.

BEN. I'll be late for my train. [*They are at opposite ends of the stage.*]

WILLY. Ben, my boys—can't we talk? They'd go into the jaws of hell for me, see, but I—

BEN. William, you're being first-rate with your boys. Outstanding, manly chaps!

WILLY [*hanging on to his words*]. Oh, Ben, that's good to hear! Because sometimes I'm afraid that I'm not teaching them the right kind of—Ben, how should I teach them?

BEN [*giving great weight to each word, and with a certain vicious audacity*]. William, when I walked into the jungle, I was seventeen. When I walked out I was twenty-one. And, by God, I was rich! [*He goes off into darkness around the right corner of the house.*]

WILLY. . . . . was rich! That's just the spirit I want to imbue them with! To walk into a jungle! I was right! I was right! I was right! [BEN *is gone, but* WILLY *is still speaking to him as* LINDA, *in nightgown and robe, enters the kitchen, glances around for* WILLY, *then goes to the door of the house, looks out and sees him. Comes down to his left. He looks at her.*]

LINDA. Willy, dear? Willy?

WILLY. I was right!

LINDA. Did you have some cheese? [*He can't answer.*] It's very late, darling. Come to bed, heh?

WILLY [*looking straight up*]. Gotta break your neck to see a star in this yard.

LINDA. You coming in?

WILLY. Whatever happened to that diamond watch fob? Remember? When Ben came from Africa that time? Didn't he give me a watch fob with a diamond in it?

LINDA. You pawned it, dear. Twelve, thirteen years ago. For Biff's radio correspondence course.

WILLY. Gee, that was a beautiful thing. I'll take a walk.

LINDA. But you're in your slippers.

WILLY [*starting to go around the house at the left*]. I was right! I was! [*Half to* LINDA, *as he goes, shaking his head*] What a man! There was a man worth talking to. I was right!

LINDA [*calling after* WILLY]. But in your slippers, Willy! [WILLY *is almost gone when* BIFF, *in his pajamas, comes down the stairs and enters the kitchen.*]

BIFF. What is he doing out there?

LINDA. Sh!

BIFF. God almighty, Mom, how long has he been doing this?

LINDA. Don't, he'll hear you.

BIFF. What the hell is the matter with him?

LINDA. It'll pass by morning.

BIFF. Shouldn't we do anything?

LINDA. Oh, my dear, you should do a lot of things, but there's nothing to do, so go to sleep. [HAPPY *comes down the stairs and sits on the steps.*]

HAPPY. I never heard him so loud, Mom.

LINDA. Well, come around more often; you'll hear him. [*She sits down at the table and mends the lining of* WILLY'S *jacket.*]

BIFF. Why didn't you ever write me about this, Mom?

LINDA. How would I write to you? For over three months you had no address.

BIFF. I was on the move. But you know I thought of you all the time. You know that, don't you, pal?

LINDA. I know, dear, I know. But he likes to have a letter. Just to know that there's still a possibility for better things.

BIFF. He's not like this all the time, is he?

LINDA. It's when you come home he's always the worst.

BIFF. When I come home?

LINDA. When you write you're coming, he's all smiles, and talks about the future, and—he's just wonderful. And then the closer you seem to come, the more shaky he gets, and then, by the time you get here, he's arguing, and he seems angry at you. I think it's just that maybe he can't bring himself to—to open up to you. Why are you so hateful to each other? Why is that?

BIFF [*evasively*]. I'm not hateful, Mom.

LINDA. But you no sooner come in the door than you're fighting!

BIFF. I don't know why. I mean to change. I'm tryin', Mom, you understand?

LINDA. Are you home to stay now?

BIFF. I don't know. I want to look around, see what's doin'.

LINDA. Biff, you can't look around all your life, can you?

BIFF. I just can't take hold, Mom. I can't take hold of some kind of a life.

LINDA. Biff, a man is not a bird, to come and go with the springtime.

BIFF. Your hair . . . [*He touches her hair.*] Your hair got so gray.

LINDA. Oh, it's been gray since you were in high school. I just stopped dyeing it, that's all.

BIFF. Dye it again, will ya? I don't want my pal looking old. [*He smiles.*]

LINDA. You're such a boy! You think you can go away for a year and . . . You've got to get it into your head now that one day you'll knock on this door and there'll be strange people here—

BIFF. What are you talking about? You're not even sixty, Mom.

LINDA. But what about your father?

BIFF [*lamely*]. Well, I meant him too.

HAPPY. He admires Pop.

LINDA. Biff, dear, if you don't have any feeling for him, then you can't have any feeling for me.

BIFF. Sure I can, Mom.

LINDA. No. You can't just come to see me, because I love him. [*With a threat, but only a threat, of tears*] He's the dearest man in the world to me, and I won't have anyone making him feel unwanted and low and blue. You've got to make up your mind now, darling, there's no leeway any more. Either he's your father and you pay him that respect, or else you're not to come here. I know he's not easy to get along with—nobody knows better than me—but . . .

WILLY [*from the left, with a laugh*]. Hey, hey, Biffo!

BIFF [*starting to go out after* WILLY]. What the hell is the matter with him? [HAPPY *stops him.*]

LINDA. Don't—don't go near him!

BIFF. Stop making excuses for him! He always, always wiped the floor with you. Never had an ounce of respect for you.

HAPPY. He's always had respect for—

BIFF. What the hell do you know about it?

HAPPY [*surlily*]. Just don't call him crazy!

BIFF. He's got no character—Charley wouldn't do this. Not in his own house—spewing out that vomit from his mind.

HAPPY. Charley never had to cope with what he's got to.

BIFF. People are worse off than Willy Loman. Believe me, I've seen them!

LINDA. Then make Charley your father, Biff. You can't do that, can you? I don't say he's a great man. Willy Loman never made a lot of money. His name was never in the paper. He's not the finest character that ever lived. But he's a human being, and a terrible thing is happening to him. So attention must be paid. He's not to be allowed to fall into his grave like an old dog. Attention, attention must be finally paid to such a person. You called him crazy—

BIFF. I didn't mean—

LINDA. No, a lot of people think he's lost his—balance. But you don't have to be very smart to know what his trouble is. The man is exhausted.

HAPPY. Sure!

LINDA. A small man can be just as exhausted as a great man. He works for a company thirty-six years this March, opens up unheard-of-territories to their trademark, and now in his old age they take his salary away.

HAPPY [*indignantly*]. I didn't know that, Mom.

LINDA. You never asked, my dear! Now that you get your spending money someplace else you don't trouble your mind with him.

HAPPY. But I gave you money last—

LINDA. Christmas time, fifty dollars! To fix the hot water it cost ninety-seven fifty! For five weeks he's been on straight commission, like a beginner, an unknown!

BIFF. Those ungrateful bastards!

LINDA. Are they any worse than his sons? When he brought them business, when he was young, they were glad to see him. But now his old friends, the old buyers that loved him so and always found some order to hand him in a pinch—they're all dead, retired. He used to be able to make six, seven calls a day in Boston. Now he takes his valises out of the car and puts them back and takes them out again and he's exhausted. Instead of walking he talks now. He drives seven hundred miles, and when he gets there no one knows him any more, no one welcomes him. And what goes through a man's mind, driving seven hundred miles home without having earned a cent? Why shouldn't he talk to himself? Why? When he has to go to Charley and borrow fifty dollars a week and pretend to me that it's his pay? How long can that go on? How long? You see what I'm sitting here and waiting for? And you tell me he has no character? The man who never worked a day but for your benefit? When does he get the medal for that? Is this his reward—to turn around at the age of sixty-three and find his sons, who he loved better than his life, one a philandering bum—

HAPPY. Mom!

LINDA. That's all you are, my baby! [*To* BIFF] And you! What happened to the love you had for him? You were such pals! How you used to talk to him on the phone every night! How lonely he was till he could come home to you!

BIFF. All right, Mom. I'll live here in my room, and I'll get a job. I'll keep away from him, that's all.

LINDA. No, Biff. You can't stay here and fight all the time.

BIFF. He threw me out of this house, remember that.

LINDA. Why did he do that? I never knew why.

BIFF. Because I know he's a fake and he doesn't like anybody around who knows!

LINDA. Why a fake? In what way? What do you mean?

BIFF. Just don't lay it all at my feet. It's between me and him—that's all I have to say. I'll chip in from now on. He'll settle for half my pay check. He'll be all right. I'm going to bed. [*He starts for the stairs.*]

LINDA. He won't be all right.

BIFF [*turning on the stairs, furiously*]. I hate this city and I'll stay here. Now what do you want?

LINDA. He's dying, Biff. [HAPPY *turns quickly to her, shocked.*]

BIFF [*after a pause*]. Why is he dying?

LINDA. He's been trying to kill himself.

BIFF [*with great horror*]. How?

LINDA. I live from day to day.

BIFF. What're you talking about?

LINDA. Remember I wrote you that he smashed up the car again? In February?

BIFF. Well?

LINDA. The insurance inspector came. He said that they have evidence. That all these accidents in the last year—weren't—weren't—accidents.

HAPPY. How can they tell that? That's a lie.

LINDA. It seems there's a woman . . . [*She takes a breath as . . .*

⎡BIFF [*sharply but contained*]. What woman?
⎣LINDA [*simultaneously*]. . . . and this woman . . .

LINDA. What?

BIFF. Nothing. Go ahead.

LINDA. What did you say?

BIFF. Nothing. I just said what woman?

HAPPY. What about her?

LINDA. Well, it seems she was walking down the road and saw his car. She says that he wasn't driving fast at all, and that he didn't skid. She says he came to that little bridge, and then deliberately smashed into the railing, and it was only the shallowness of the water that saved him.

BIFF. Oh, no, he probably just fell asleep again.

LINDA. I don't think he fell asleep.

BIFF. Why not?

LINDA. Last month . . . [*With great difficulty*] Oh, boys, it's so hard to say a thing like this! He's just a big stupid man to you, but I tell you there's more good in him than in many other people. [*She chokes, wipes her eyes.*] I was looking for a fuse. The lights blew out, and I went down the cellar. And behind the fuse box—it happened to fall out—was a length of rubber pipe—just short.

HAPPY. No kidding?

LINDA. There's a little attachment on the end of it. I knew right away. And sure enough, on the bottom of the water heater there's a new little nipple on the gas pipe.

HAPPY [*angrily*]. That—jerk.

BIFF. Did you have it taken off?

LINDA. I'm—I'm ashamed to. How can I mention it to him? Every day I go down and take away that little rubber pipe. But, when he comes home, I put it back where it was. How can I insult him that way? I don't know what to do. I live from day to day, boys. I tell you, I know every thought in his mind. It sounds so old-fashioned and silly, but I tell you he put his whole life into you and you've turned your backs on him. [*She is bent over in the chair, weeping, her face in her hands.*] Biff, I swear to God! Biff, his life is in your hands!

HAPPY [*to* BIFF]. How do you like that damned fool!

BIFF [*kissing her*]. All right, pal, all right. It's all settled now. I've been remiss. I know that, Mom. But now I'll stay, and I swear to you, I'll apply myself. [*Kneeling in front of her, in a fever of self-reproach*] It's just— you see, Mom, I don't fit in business. Not that I won't try. I'll try, and I'll make good.

HAPPY. Sure you will. The trouble with you in business was you never tried to please people.

BIFF. I know, I—

HAPPY. Like when you worked for Harrison's. Bob Harrison said you were tops, and then you go and do some damn fool thing like whistling whole songs in the elevator like a comedian.

BIFF [*against* HAPPY]. So what? I like to whistle in the elevator.

LINDA. Well, don't argue about it now.

HAPPY. Like when you'd go off and swim in the middle of the day instead of taking the line around.

BIFF [*his resentment rising*]. Well, don't you run off? You take off sometimes, don't you? On a nice summer day?

HAPPY. Yeah, but I cover myself!

LINDA. Boys!

HAPPY. If I'm going to take a fade the boss can call any number where I'm supposed to be and they'll swear to him that I just left. I'll tell you something that I hate to say, Biff, but in the business world some of them think you're crazy.

BIFF [*angered*]. Screw the business world!

HAPPY. All right, screw it! Great, but cover yourself!

LINDA. Hap, Hap!

BIFF. I don't care what they think! They've laughed at Dad for years, and you know why? Because we don't belong in this nuthouse of a city! We should be mixing cement on some open plain, or—or carpenters. A carpenter is allowed to whistle! [*Willy walks in from the entrance of the house, at left.*]

WILLY. Even your grandfather was better than a carpenter. [*Pause. They watch him.*] You never grew up. Bernard does not whistle in the elevator, I assure you.

BIFF [*as though to laugh WILLY out of it*]. Yeah, but you do, Pop.

WILLY. I never in my life whistled in an elevator! And who in the business world thinks I'm crazy?

BIFF. I didn't mean it like that, Pop. Now don't make a whole thing out of it, will ya?

WILLY. Go back to the West! Be a carpenter, a cowboy, enjoy yourself!

LINDA. Willy, he was just saying—

WILLY. I heard what he said!

HAPPY [*trying to quiet WILLY*]. Hey, Pop, come on now . . .

WILLY [*continuing over HAPPY's line*]. They laugh at me, heh? Go to Filene's, go to the Hub, go to Slattery's,[1] Boston. Call out the name Willy Loman and see what happens! Big shot!

BIFF. All right, Pop.

WILLY. Big!

BIFF. All right!

WILLY. Why do you always insult me?

BIFF. I didn't say a word. [*To* LINDA.] Did I say a word?

LINDA. He didn't say anything, Willy.

WILLY [*going to the doorway of the living-room*]. All right, good night, good night.

LINDA. Willy, dear, he just decided . . .

WILLY [*to BIFF*]. If you get tired hanging around tomorrow, paint the ceiling I put up in the living-room.

BIFF. I'm leaving early tomorrow.

HAPPY. He's going to see Bill Oliver, Pop.

WILLY [*interestedly*]. Oliver? For what?

BIFF [*with reserve, but trying, trying*]. He always said he'd stake me. I'd like to go into business, so maybe I can take him up on it.

LINDA. Isn't that wonderful?

WILLY. Don't interrupt. What's wonderful about it? There's fifty men in the City of New York who'd stake him. [*To* BIFF] Sporting goods?

BIFF. I guess so, I know something about it and—

---

[1] Boston department stores.

WILLY. He knows something about it! You know sporting goods better than Spalding, for God's sake! How much is he giving you?

BIFF. I don't know, I didn't even see him yet, but—

WILLY. Then what're you talkin' about?

BIFF [*getting angry*]. Well, all I said was I'm gonna see him, that's all!

WILLY [*turning away*]. Ah, you're counting your chickens again.

BIFF [*starting left for the stairs*]. Oh, Jesus, I'm going to sleep!

WILLY [*calling after him*]. Don't curse in this house!

BIFF [*turning*]. Since when did you get so clean?

HAPPY [*trying to stop them*]. Wait a . . .

WILLY. Don't use that language to me! I won't have it!

HAPPY [*grabbing* BIFF, *shouts*]. Wait a minute! I got an idea. I got a feasible idea. Come here, Biff, let's talk this over now, let's talk some sense here. When I was down in Florida last time, I thought of a great idea to sell sporting goods. It just came back to me. You and I, Biff—we have a line, the Loman Line. We train a couple of weeks, and put on a couple of exhibitions, see?

WILLY. That's an idea!

HAPPY. Wait! We form two basketball teams, see? Two waterpolo teams. We play each other. It's a million dollars' worth of publicity. Two brothers, see? The Loman Brothers. Displays in the Royal Palms—all the hotels. And banners over the ring and the basketball court: "Loman Brothers." Baby, we could sell sporting goods!

WILLY. That is a one-million-dollar idea!

LINDA. Marvelous!

BIFF. I'm in great shape as far as that's concerned.

HAPPY. And the beauty of it is, Biff, it wouldn't be like a business. We'd be out playin' ball again . . .

BIFF [*enthused*]. Yeah, that's . . .

WILLY. Million-dollar . . .

HAPPY. And you wouldn't get fed up with it, Biff. It'd be the family again. There'd be the old honor, and comradeship, and if you wanted to go off for a swim or somethin'—well, you'd do it! Without some smart cooky gettin' up ahead of you!

WILLY. Lick the world! You guys together could absolutely lick the civilized world.

BIFF. I'll see Oliver tomorrow. Hap, if we could work that out . . .

LINDA. Maybe things are beginning to—

WILLY [*wildly enthused, to* LINDA]. Stop interrupting! [*To* BIFF] But don't wear sport jacket and slacks when you see Oliver.

BIFF. No, I'll—

WILLY. A business suit, and talk as little as possible, and don't crack any jokes.

BIFF. He did like me. Always liked me.

LINDA. He loved you!

WILLY [*to* LINDA]. Will you stop! [*To* BIFF] Walk in very serious. You are not applying for a boy's job. Money is to pass. Be quiet, fine, and serious. Everybody likes a kidder, but nobody lends him money.

HAPPY. I'll try to get some myself, Biff. I'm sure I can.

WILLY. I see great things for you kids, I think your troubles are over. But remember, start big and you'll end big. Ask for fifteen. How much you gonna ask for?

BIFF. Gee, I don't know—

WILLY. And don't say "Gee." "Gee" is a boy's word. A man walking in for fifteen thousand dollars does not say "Gee!"

BIFF. Ten, I think, would be top though.

WILLY. Don't be so modest. You always started too low. Walk in with a big laugh. Don't look worried. Start off with a couple of your good stories to lighten things up. It's not what you say, it's how you say it—because personality always wins the day.

LINDA. Oliver always thought the highest of him—

WILLY. Will you let me talk?

BIFF. Don't yell at her, Pop, will ya?

WILLY [*angrily*]. I was talking, wasn't I?

BIFF. I don't like you yelling at her all the time, and I'm tellin' you, that's all.

WILLY. What're you, takin' over this house?

LINDA. Willy—

WILLY [*turning on her*]. Don't take his side all the time, goddammit!

BIFF [*furiously*]. Stop yelling at her!

WILLY [*suddenly pulling on his cheek, beaten down, guilt-ridden*]. Give my best to Bill Oliver—he may remember me. [*He exits through the living-room doorway.*]

LINDA [*her voice subdued*]. What'd you have to start that for? [BIFF *turns away.*] You see how sweet he was as soon as you talked hopefully? [*She goes over to* BIFF.] Come up and say good night to him. Don't let him go to bed that way.

HAPPY. Come on, Biff, let's buck him up.

LINDA. Please, dear. Just say good night. It takes so little to make him happy. Come. [*She goes through the living-room doorway, calling upstairs from within the living-room.*] Your pajamas are hanging in the bathroom, Willy!

HAPPY [*looking toward where* LINDA *went out*]. What a woman! They broke the mold when they made her. You know that, Biff?

BIFF. He's off salary. My God, working on commission!

HAPPY. Well, let's face it: he's no hot-shot selling man. Except that sometimes, you have to admit, he's a sweet personality.

BIFF [*deciding*]. Lend me ten bucks, will ya? I want to buy some new ties.

HAPPY. I'll take you to a place I know. Beautiful stuff. Wear one of my striped shirts tomorrow.

BIFF. She got gray. Mom got awful old. Gee, I'm gonna go in to Oliver tomorrow and knock him for a—

HAPPY. Come on up. Tell that to Dad. Let's give him a whirl. Come on.

BIFF [*steamed up*]. You know, with ten thousand bucks, boy!

HAPPY [*as they go into the living-room*]. That's the talk, Biff, that's the first time I've heard the old confidence out of you! [*From within the living-room, fading off*] You're gonna live with me, kid, and any babe you want just say the word . . . [*The last lines are hardly heard. They are mounting the stairs to their parents' bedroom.*]

LINDA [*entering her bedroom and addressing* WILLY, *who is in the bathroom. She is straightening the bed for him*]. Can you do anything about the shower? It drips.

WILLY [*from the bathroom*]. All of a sudden everything falls to pieces! Goddam plumbing, oughta be sued, those people. I hardly finished putting it in and the thing . . . [*His words rumble off.*]

LINDA. I'm just wondering if Oliver will remember him. You think he might?

WILLY [*coming out of the bathroom in his pajamas*]. Remember him? What's the matter with you, you crazy? If he'd've stayed with Oliver he'd be on top by now! Wait'll Oliver gets a look at him. You don't know the average caliber any more. The average young man today— [*He is getting into bed.*]—is got a caliber of zero. Greatest thing in the world for him was to bum around. [BIFF *and* HAPPY *enter the bedroom. Slight pause.*]

WILLY [*stops short, looking at* BIFF]. Glad to hear it, boy.

HAPPY. He wanted to say good night to you, sport.

WILLY [*to* BIFF]. Yeah. Knock him dead, boy. What'd you want to tell me?

BIFF. Just take it easy, Pop. Good night. [*He turns to go.*]

WILLY [*unable to resist*]. And if anything falls off the desk while you're talking to him—like a package or something—don't you pick it up. They have office boys for that.

LINDA. I'll make a big breakfast—

WILLY. Will you let me finish? [*To* BIFF] Tell him you were in the business in the West. Not farm work.

BIFF. All right, Dad.

LINDA. I think everything—

WILLY [*going right through her speech*]. And don't undersell yourself. No less than fifteen thousand dollars.

BIFF [*unable to bear him*]. Okay. Good night, Mom. [*He starts moving.*]

WILLY. Because you got a greatness in you, Biff, remember that. You got all kinds a greatness . . . [*He lies back, exhausted.* BIFF *walks out.*]

LINDA [*calling after* BIFF]. Sleep well, darling!

HAPPY. I'm gonna get married, Mom. I wanted to tell you.

LINDA. Go to sleep, dear.

HAPPY [*going*]. I just wanted to tell you.

WILLY. Keep up the good work. [HAPPY *exits.*] God . . . remember that Ebbets Field game? The championship of the city?

LINDA. Just rest. Should I sing to you?

WILLY. Yeah. Sing to me. [LINDA *hums a soft lullaby.*] When that team came out—he was the tallest, remember?

LINDA. Oh, yes. And in gold. [BIFF *enters the darkened kitchen, takes a cigarette, and leaves the house. He comes downstage into a golden pool of light. He smokes, staring at the night.*]

WILLY. Like a young god. Hercules—something like that. And the sun, the sun all around him. Remember how he waved to me? Right up from the field, with the representatives of three colleges standing by? And the buyers I brought, and the cheers when he came out—Loman, Loman, Loman! God Almighty, he'll be great yet. A star like that, magnificent, can never really fade away! [*The light on* Willy *is fading. The gas heater begins to glow through the kitchen wall, near the stairs, a blue flame beneath red coils.*]

Linda [*timidly*]. Willy dear, what has he got against you?

Willy. I'm so tired. Don't talk any more. [Biff *slowly returns to the kitchen. He stops, stares toward the heater.*]

Linda. Will you ask Howard to let you work in New York?

Willy. First thing in the morning. Everything'll be all right. [Biff *reaches behind the heater and draws out a length of rubber tubing. He is horrified and turns his head toward* Willy's *room, still dimly lit, from which the strains of* Linda's *desperate but monotonous humming rise.*]

Willy [*staring through the window into the moonlight*]. Gee, look at the moon moving between the buildings! [Biff *wraps the tubing around his hand and quickly goes up the stairs.*]

Curtain

ACT TWO

Music is heard, gay and bright. The curtain rises as the music fades away. Willy, *in shirt sleeves, is sitting at the kitchen table, sipping coffee, his hat in his lap.* Linda *is filling his cup when she can.*

Willy. Wonderful coffee. Meal in itself.

Linda. Can I make you some eggs?

Willy. No. Take a breath.

Linda. You look so rested, dear.

Willy. I slept like a dead one. First time in months. Imagine, sleeping till ten on a Tuesday morning. Boys left nice and early, heh?

Linda. They were out of here by eight o'clock.

Willy. Good work!

Linda. It was so thrilling to see them leaving together. I can't get over the shaving lotion in this house!

Willy [*smiling*]. Mmm—

Linda. Biff was very changed this morning. His whole attitude seemed to be hopeful. He couldn't wait to get downtown to see Oliver.

Willy. He's heading for a change. There's no question, there simply are certain men that take longer to get—solidified. How did he dress?

Linda. His blue suit. He's handsome in that suit. He could be a—anything in that suit! [Willy *gets up from the table.* Linda *holds his jacket for him.*]

Willy. There's no question, no question at all. Gee, on the way home tonight I'd like to buy some seeds.

Linda [*laughing*]. That'd be wonderful. But not enough sun gets back there. Nothing'll grow any more.

Willy. You wait, kid, before it's all over we're gonna get a little place out in the country, and I'll raise some vegetables, a couple of chickens . . .

Linda. You'll do it yet, dear. [Willy *walks out of his jacket.* Linda *follows him.*]

WILLY. And they'll get married, and come for a week-end. I'd build a little guest house. 'Cause I got so many fine tools, all I'd need would be a little lumber and some peace of mind.

LINDA [*joyfully*]. I sewed the lining . . .

WILLY. I could build two guest houses, so they'd both come. Did he decide how much he's going to ask Oliver for?

LINDA [*getting him into the jacket*]. He didn't mention it, but I imagine ten or fifteen thousand. You going to talk to Howard today?

WILLY. Yeah. I'll put it to him straight and simple. He'll just have to take me off the road.

LINDA. And Willy, don't forget to ask for a little advance, because we've got the insurance premium. It's the grace period now.

WILLY. That's a hundred . . . ?

LINDA. A hundred and eight, sixty-eight. Because we're a little short again.

WILLY. Why are we short?

LINDA. Well, you had the motor job on the car . . .

WILLY. That goddam Studebaker!

LINDA. And you got one more payment on the refrigerator . . .

WILLY. But it just broke again!

LINDA. Well, it's old, dear.

WILLY. I told you we should've bought a well-advertised machine. Charley bought a General Electric and it's twenty years old and it's still good, that son-of-a-bitch.

LINDA. But, Willy—

WILLY. Whoever heard of a Hastings refrigerator? Once in my life I would like to own something outright before it's broken! I'm always in a race with the junkyard! I just finished paying for the car and it's on its last legs. The refrigerator consumes belts like a goddam maniac. They time those things. They time them so when you finally paid for them, they're used up.

LINDA [*buttoning up his jacket as he unbuttons it*]. All told, about two hundred dollars would carry us, dear. But that includes the last payment on the mortgage. After this payment, Willy, the house belongs to us.

WILLY. It's twenty-five years!

LINDA. Biff was nine years old when we bought it.

WILLY. Well, that's a great thing. To weather a twenty-five year mortgage is—

LINDA. It's an accomplishment.

WILLY. All the cement, the lumber, the reconstruction I put in this house! There ain't a crack to be found in it any more.

LINDA. Well, it served its purpose.

WILLY. What purpose? Some stranger'll come along, move in, and that's that. If only Biff would take this house, and raise a family . . . [*He starts to go.*] Good-by, I'm late.

LINDA [*suddenly remembering*]. Oh, I forgot! You're supposed to meet them for dinner.

WILLY. Me?

LINDA. At Frank's Chop House on Forty-eighth near Sixth Avenue.

WILLY. Is that so! How about you?

LINDA. No, just the three of you. They're gonna blow you to a big meal!

WILLY. Don't say! Who thought of that?

LINDA. Biff came to me this morning, Willy, and he said, "Tell Dad, we want to blow him to a big meal." Be there six o'clock. You and your two boys are going to have dinner.

WILLY. Gee whiz! That's really somethin'. I'm gonna knock Howard for a loop, kid. I'll get an advance, and I'll come home with a New York job. Goddammit, now I'm gonna do it!

LINDA. Oh, that's the spirit, Willy!

WILLY. I will never get behind a wheel the rest of my life!

LINDA. It's changing, Willy, I can feel it changing!

WILLY. Beyond a question. G'by, I'm late. [*He starts to go again.*]

LINDA [*calling after him as she runs to the kitchen table for a handkerchief*]. You got your glasses?

WILLY [*feels for them, then comes back in*]. Yeah, yeah, got my glasses.

LINDA [*giving him the handkerchief*]. And a handkerchief.

WILLY. Yeah, handkerchief.

LINDA. And your saccharine?

WILLY. Yeah, my saccharine.

LINDA. Be careful on the subway stairs. [*She kisses him, and a silk stocking is seen hanging from her hand.* WILLY *notices it.*]

WILLY. Will you stop mending stockings? At least while I'm in the house. It gets me nervous. I can't tell you. Please. [LINDA *hides the stocking in her hand as she follows* WILLY *across the forestage in front of the house.*]

LINDA. Remember, Frank's Chop House.

WILLY [*passing the apron*]. Maybe beets would grow out there.

LINDA [*laughing*]. But you tried so many times.

WILLY. Yeah. Well, don't work hard today. [*He disappears around the right corner of the house.*]

LINDA. Be careful! [*As* WILLY *vanishes,* LINDA *waves to him. Suddenly the phone rings. She runs across the stage and into the kitchen and lifts it.*]

LINDA. Hello? Oh, Biff! I'm so glad you called, I just . . . Yes, sure, I told him. Yes, he'll be there for dinner at six o'clock, I didn't forget. Listen, I was just dying to tell you. You know that little rubber pipe I told you about? That he connected to the gas heater? I finally decided to go down the cellar this morning and take it away and destroy it. But it's gone! Imagine? He took it away himself, it isn't there! [*She listens.*] When? Oh, then you took it. Oh—nothing, it's just that I'd hoped he'd taken it away himself. Oh, I'm not worried, darling, because this morning he left in such high spirits, it was like the old days! I'm not afraid any more. Did Mr. Oliver see you? . . . Well, you wait there then. And make a nice impression on him, darling. Just don't perspire too much before you see him. And have a nice time with Dad. He may have big news too! . . . . That's right, a New York job. And be sweet to him tonight, dear. Be loving to him. Because he's only a little boat looking for a harbor. [*She is trembling with sorrow and joy.*] Oh, that's wonderful, Biff, you'll save his life. Thanks, darling. Just put your arm around him when he comes into the restaurant. Give him a smile. That's the boy . . . Good-by, dear. . . . You got your comb? . . . . That's fine. Good-by, Biff dear. [*In the middle of her speech,* HOWARD WAGNER, *thirty-six, wheels on a small typewriter table on which is a wire-recording machine*

and proceeds to plug it in. This is on the left forestage. Light slowly fades on
LINDA *as it rises on* HOWARD. HOWARD *is intent on threading the machine
and only glances over his shoulder as* WILLY *appears.*]

WILLY. Pst! Pst!

HOWARD. Hello, Willy, come in.

WILLY. Like to have a little talk with you, Howard.

HOWARD. Sorry to keep you waiting. I'll be with you in a minute.

WILLY. What's that, Howard?

HOWARD. Didn't you ever see one of these? Wire recorder.

WILLY. Oh. Can we talk a minute?

HOWARD. Records things. Just got delivery yesterday. Been driving me
crazy, the most terrific machine I ever saw in my life. I was up all
night with it.

WILLY. What do you do with it?

HOWARD. I bought it for dictation, but you can do anything with it. Listen
to this. I had it home last night. Listen to what I picked up. The first
one is my daughter. Get this. [*He flicks the switch and "Roll out the Barrel"
is heard being whistled.*] Listen to that kid whistle.

WILLY. That is lifelike, isn't it?

HOWARD. Seven years old. Get that tone.

WILLY. Ts, ts. Like to ask a little favor of you . . . [*The whistling breaks
off, and the voice of* HOWARD's *daughter is heard.*]

HIS DAUGHTER. "Now you, Daddy."

HOWARD. She's crazy for me! [*Again the same song is whistled.*] That's me!
Ha! [*He winks.*]

WILLY. You're very good! [*The whistling breaks off again. The machine runs
silent for a moment.*]

HOWARD. Sh! Get this now, this is my son.

HIS SON. "The capital of Alabama is Montgomery; the capital of Arizona
is Phoenix; the capital of Arkansas is Little Rock; the capital of California
is Sacramento . . ." [*And on, and on.*]

HOWARD [*holding up five fingers*]. Five years old, Willy!

WILLY. He'll make an announcer some day!

HIS SON [*continuing*]. "The capital . . ."

HOWARD. Get that—alphabetical order! [*The machine breaks off suddenly.*]
Wait a minute. The maid kicked the plug out.

WILLY. It certainly is a—

HOWARD. Sh, for God's sake!

HIS SON. "It's nine o'clock, Bulova watch time. So I have to go to sleep."

WILLY. That really is—

HOWARD. Wait a minute! The next is my wife. [*They wait.*]

HOWARD's VOICE. "Go on, say something." [*Pause.*] "Well, you gonna talk?"

HIS WIFE. "I can't think of anything."

HOWARD's VOICE. "Well, talk—it's turning."

HIS WIFE [*shyly, beaten*]. "Hello." [*Silence.*] "Oh, Howard, I can't talk into
this . . ."

HOWARD [*snapping the machine off*]. That was my wife.

WILLY. That is a wonderful machine. Can we—

HOWARD. I tell you, Willy, I'm gonna take my camera, and my bandsaw, and all my hobbies, and out they go. This is the most fascinating relaxation I ever found.

WILLY. I think I'll get one myself.

HOWARD. Sure, they're only a hundred and a half. You can't do without it. Supposing you wanna hear Jack Benny, see? But you can't be at home at that hour. So you tell the maid to turn the radio on when Jack Benny comes on, and this automatically goes on with the radio . . .

WILLY. And when you come home you . . .

HOWARD. You can come home twelve o'clock, one o'clock, any time you like, and you get yourself a Coke and sit yourself down, throw the switch, and there's Jack Benny's program in the middle of the night!

WILLY. I'm definitely going to get one. Because lots of time I'm on the road, and I think to myself, what I must be missing on the radio!

HOWARD. Don't you have a radio in the car?

WILLY. Well, yeah, but whoever thinks of turning it on?

HOWARD. Say, aren't you supposed to be in Boston?

WILLY. That's what I want to talk to you about, Howard. You got a minute? [*He draws a chair in from the wing.*]

HOWARD. What happened? What're you doing here?

WILLY. Well . . .

HOWARD. You didn't crack up again, did you?

WILLY. Oh, no. No . . .

HOWARD. Geez, you had me worried there for a minute. What's the trouble?

WILLY. Well, tell you the truth, Howard. I've come to the decision that I'd rather not travel any more.

HOWARD. Not travel! Well, what'll you do?

WILLY. Remember, Christmas time, when you had the party here? You said you'd try to think of some spot for me here in town.

HOWARD. With us?

WILLY. Well, sure.

HOWARD. Oh, yeah, yeah. I remember. Well, I couldn't think of anything for you, Willy.

WILLY. I tell ya, Howard. The kids are all grown up, y'know. I don't need much any more. If I could take home—well, sixty-five dollars a week, I could swing it.

HOWARD. Yeah, but Willy, see I—

WILLY. I tell ya why, Howard. Speaking frankly and between the two of us, y'know—I'm just a little tired.

HOWARD. Oh, I could understand that, Willy. But you're a road man, Willy, and we do a road business. We've only got a half-dozen salesmen on the floor here.

WILLY. God knows, Howard, I never asked a favor of any man. But I was with the firm when your father used to carry you in here in his arms.

HOWARD. I know that, Willy, but—

WILLY. Your father came to me the day you were born and asked me what I thought of the name of Howard, may he rest in peace.

HOWARD. I appreciate that, Willy, but there just is no spot here for you. If I had a spot I'd slam you right in, but I just don't have a single solitary spot. [*He looks for his lighter.* WILLY *has picked it up and gives it to him. Pause.*]

WILLY [*with increasing anger*]. Howard, all I need to set my table is fifty dollars a week.

HOWARD. But where am I going to put you, kid?

WILLY. Look, it isn't a question of whether I can sell merchandise, is it?

HOWARD. No, but it's business, kid, and everybody's gotta pull his own weight.

WILLY [*desperately*]. Just let me tell you a story, Howard—

HOWARD. 'Cause you gotta admit, business is business.

WILLY [*angrily*]. Business is definitely business, but just listen for a minute. You don't understand this. When I was a boy—eighteen, nineteen—I was already on the road. And there was a question in my mind as to whether selling had a future for me. Because in those days I had a yearning to go to Alaska. See, there were three gold strikes in one month in Alaska, and I felt like going out. Just for the ride, you might say.

HOWARD [*barely interested*]. Don't say.

WILLY. Oh, yeah, my father lived many years in Alaska. He was an adventurous man. We've got quite a little streak of self-reliance in our family. I thought I'd go out with my older brother and try to locate him, and maybe settle in the North with the old man. And I was almost decided to go, when I met a salesman in the Parker House. His name was Dave Singleman. And he was eighty-four years old, and he'd drummed merchandise in thirty-one states. And old Dave, he'd go up to his room, y'understand, put on his green velvet slippers—I'll never forget—and pick up his phone and call the buyers, and without ever leaving his room, at the age of eighty-four, he made his living. And when I saw that, I realized that selling was the greatest career a man could want. 'Cause what could be more satisfying than to be able to go, at the age of eighty-four, into twenty or thirty different cities, and pick up a phone, and be remembered and loved and helped by so many different people? Do you know? when he died—and by the way he died the death of a salesman, in his green velvet slippers in the smoker of the New York, New Haven and Hartford, going into Boston—when he died, hundreds of salesmen and buyers were at his funeral. Things were sad on a lotta trains for months after that. [*He stands up.* HOWARD *has not looked at him.*] In those days there was personality in it, Howard. There was respect, and comradeship, and gratitude in it. Today, it's all cut and dried, and there's no chance for bringing friendship to bear—or personality. You see what I mean? They don't know me any more.

HOWARD [*moving away, to the right*]. That's just the thing, Willy.

WILLY. If I had forty dollars a week—that's all I'd need. Forty dollars, Howard.

HOWARD. Kid, I can't take blood from a stone, I—

WILLY [*desperation is on him now*]. Howard, the year Al Smith was nominated, your father came to me and—

HOWARD [*starting to go off*]. I've got to see some people, kid.

WILLY [*stopping him*]. I'm talking about your father! There were promises made across this desk! You mustn't tell me you've got people to see— I put thirty-four years into this firm, Howard, and now I can't pay my insurance! You can't eat the orange and throw the peel away—a man is not a piece of fruit! [*After a pause*] Now pay attention. Your father—in 1928 I had a big year. I averaged a hundred and seventy dollars a week in commissions.

Howard [*impatiently*]. Now, Willy, you never averaged—

Willy [*banging his hand on the desk*]. I averaged a hundred and seventy dollars a week in the year of 1928! And your father came to me—or rather, I was in the office here—it was right over his desk—and he put his hand on my shoulder—

Howard [*getting up*]. You'll have to excuse me, Willy, I gotta see some people. Pull yourself together. [*Going out.*] I'll be back in a little while. [*On* Howard's *exit, the light on his chair grows very bright and strange.*]

Willy. Pull myself together! What the hell did I say to him? My God, I was yelling at him! How could I! [Willy *breaks off, staring at the light, which occupies the chair, animating it. He approaches this chair, standing across the desk from it.*] Frank, Frank, don't you remember what you told me that time? How you put your hand on my shoulder, and Frank . . . [*He leans on the desk and as he speaks the dead man's name he accidentally switches on the recorder, and instantly—*]

Howard's Son. ". . . of New York is Albany. The capital of Ohio is Cincinnati, the capital of Rhode Island is . . ." [*The recitation continues.*]

Willy [*leaping away with fright, shouting*]. Ha! Howard! Howard! Howard!

Howard [*rushing in*]. What happened?

Willy [*pointing at the machine, which continues nasally, childishly, with the capital cities*]. Shut if off! Shut it off!

Howard [*pulling the plug out*]. Look, Willy . . .

Willy [*pressing his hands to his eyes*]. I gotta get myself some coffee. I'll get some coffee . . . [Willy *starts to walk out.* Howard *stops him.*]

Howard [*rolling up the cord*]. Willy, look . . .

Willy. I'll go to Boston.

Howard. Willy, you can't go to Boston for us.

Willy. Why can't I go?

Howard. I don't want you to represent us. I've been meaning to tell you for a long time now.

Willy. Howard, are you firing me?

Howard. I think you need a good long rest, Willy.

Willy. Howard—

Howard. And when you feel better, come back, and we'll see if we can work something out.

Willy. But I gotta earn money, Howard. I'm in no position to—

Howard. Where are your sons? Why don't your sons give you a hand?

Willy. They're working on a very big deal.

Howard. This is no time for false pride, Willy. You go to your sons and you tell them that you're tired. You've got two great boys, haven't you?

Willy. Oh, no question, no question, but in the meantime . . .

Howard. Then that's that, heh?

Willy. All right, I'll go to Boston tomorrow.

Howard. No, no.

Willy. I can't throw myself on my sons. I'm not a cripple!

Howard. Look, kid, I'm busy this morning.

WILLY [*grasping* HOWARD's *arm*]. Howard, you've got to let me go to Boston!

HOWARD [*hard, keeping himself under control*]. I've got a line of people to see this morning. Sit down, take five minutes, and pull yourself together, and then go home, will ya? I need the office, Willy. [*He starts to go, turns, remembering the recorder, starts to push off the table holding the recorder.*] Oh, yeah. Whenever you can this week, stop by and drop off the samples. You'll feel better, Willy, and then come back and we'll talk. Pull yourself together, kid, there's people outside. [HOWARD *exits, pushing the table off left.* WILLY *stares into space, exhausted. Now the music is heard—*BEN's *music—first distantly, then closer, closer. As* WILLY *speaks,* BEN *enters from the right. He carries valise and umbrella.*]

WILLY. Oh, Ben, how did you do it? What is the answer? Did you wind up the Alaska deal already?

BEN. Doesn't take much time if you know what you're doing. Just a short business trip. Boarding ship in an hour. Wanted to say good-by.

WILLY. Ben, I've got to talk to you.

BEN [*glancing at his watch*]. Haven't the time, William.

WILLY [*crossing the apron to* BEN]. Ben, nothing's working out. I don't know what to do.

BEN. Now, look here, William. I've bought timberland in Alaska and I need a man to look after things for me.

WILLY. God, timberland! Me and my boys in those grand outdoors!

BEN. You've a new continent at your doorstep, William. Get out of these cities, they're full of talk and time payments and courts of law. Screw on your fists and you can fight for a fortune up there.

WILLY. Yes, yes! Linda, Linda! [LINDA *enters as of old, with the wash.*]

LINDA. Oh, you're back?

BEN. I haven't much time.

WILLY. No, wait! Linda, he's got a proposition for me in Alaska.

LINDA. But you've got— [*To* BEN] He's got a beautiful job here.

WILLY. But in Alaska, kid, I could—

LINDA. You're doing well enough, Willy!

BEN [*to* LINDA]. Enough for what, my dear?

LINDA [*frightened of* BEN *and angry at him*]. Don't say those things to him! Enough to be happy right here, right now. [*To* WILLY, *while* BEN *laughs*] Why must everybody conquer the world? You're well liked, and the boys love you, and someday— [*To* BEN]—why, old man Wagner told him just the other day that if he keeps it up he'll be a member of the firm, didn't he, Willy?

WILLY. Sure, sure. I am building something with this firm, Ben, and if a man is building something he must be on the right track, mustn't he?

BEN. What are you building? Lay your hand on it. Where is it?

WILLY [*hesitantly*]. That's true, Linda, there's nothing.

LINDA. Why? [*To* BEN] There's a man eighty-four years old—

WILLY. That's right, Ben, that's right. When I look at that man I say, what is there to worry about?

BEN. Bah!

WILLY. It's true, Ben. All he has to do is go into any city, pick up the phone, and he's making his living and you know why?

BEN [*picking up his valise*]. I've got to go.

WILLY [*holding* BEN *back*]. Look at this boy! [BIFF, *in his high school sweater, enters carrying suitcase.* HAPPY *carries* BIFF's *shoulder guards, gold helmet, and football pants.*]

WILLY. Without a penny to his name, three great universities are begging for him, and from there the sky's the limit, because it's not what you do, Ben. It's who you know and the smile on your face! It's contacts, Ben, contacts! The whole wealth of Alaska passes over the lunch table at the Commodore Hotel, and that's the wonder, the wonder of this country, that a man can end with diamonds here on the basis of being liked! [*He turns to* BIFF.] And that's why when you get out on that field today it's important. Because thousands of people will be rooting for you and loving you. [*To* BEN, *who has again begun to leave*] And Ben! when he walks into a business office his name will sound out like a bell and all the doors will open to him! I've seen it, Ben, I've seen it a thousand times! You can't feel it with your hand like timber, but it's there!

BEN. Good-by, William.

WILLY. Ben, am I right? Don't you think I'm right? I value your advice.

BEN. There's a new continent at your doorstep, William. You could walk out rich. Rich! [*He is gone.*]

WILLY. We'll do it here, Ben! You hear me? We're gonna do it here! [*Young* BERNARD *rushes in. The gay music of the* BOYS *is heard.*]

BERNARD. Oh, gee, I was afraid you left already!

WILLY. Why? What time is it?

BERNARD. It's half-past one!

WILLY. Well, come on, everybody! Ebbets Field next stop! Where's the pennants? [*He rushes through the wall-line of the kitchen and out into the living-room.*]

LINDA [*to* BIFF]. Did you pack fresh underwear?

BIFF [*who has been limbering up*]. I want to go!

BERNARD. Biff, I'm carrying your helmet, ain't I?

HAPPY. No, I'm carrying the helmet.

BERNARD. Oh, Biff, you promised me.

HAPPY. I'm carrying the helmet.

BERNARD. How am I going to get in the locker room?

LINDA. Let him carry the shoulder guards. [*She puts her coat and hat on in the kitchen.*]

BERNARD. Can I, Biff? 'Cause I told everybody I'm going to be in the locker room.

HAPPY. In Ebbets Field it's the clubhouse.

BERNARD. I meant the clubhouse. Biff!

HAPPY. Biff!

BIFF [*grandly, after a slight pause*]. Let him carry the shoulder guards.

HAPPY [*as he gives* BERNARD *the shoulder guards*]. Stay close to us now. [WILLY *rushes in with the pennants.*]

WILLY [*handing them out*]. Everybody wave when Biff comes out on the field. [HAPPY *and* BERNARD *run off.*] You set now, boy? [*The music has died away.*]

BIFF. Ready to go, Pop. Every muscle is ready.

WILLY [*at the edge of the apron*]. You realize what this means?

BIFF. That's right, Pop.

WILLY [*feeling* BIFF's *muscles*]. You're comin' home this afternoon captain of the All-Scholastic Championship Team of the City of New York.

BIFF. I got it, Pop. And remember, pal, when I take off my helmet, that touchdown is for you.

WILLY. Let's go! [*He is starting out, with his arm around* BIFF, *when* CHARLEY *enters, as of old, in knickers.*] I got no room for you, Charley.

CHARLEY. Room? For what?

WILLY. In the car.

CHARLEY. You goin' for a ride? I wanted to shoot some casino.

WILLY [*furiously*]. Casino! [*Incredulously.*] Don't you realize what today is?

LINDA. Oh, he knows, Willy. He's just kidding you.

WILLY. That's nothing to kid about!

CHARLEY. No, Linda, what's goin' on?

LINDA. He's playing in Ebbets Field.

CHARLEY. Baseball in this weather?

WILLY. Don't talk to him. Come on, come on! [*He is pushing them out.*]

CHARLEY. Wait a minute, didn't you hear the news?

WILLY. What?

CHARLEY. Don't you listen to the radio? Ebbets Field just blew up.

WILLY. You go to hell! [CHARLEY *laughs. Pushing them out.*] Come on, come on! We're late.

CHARLEY [*as they go*]. Knock a homer, Biff, knock a homer!

WILLY [*the last to leave, turning to* CHARLEY]. I don't think that was funny, Charley. This is the greatest day of his life.

CHARLEY. Willy, when are you going to grow up?

WILLY. Yeah, heh? When this game is over, Charley, you'll be laughing out of the other side of your face. They'll be calling him another Red Grange. Twenty-five thousand a year.

CHARLEY [*kidding*]. Is that so?

WILLY. Yeah, that's so.

CHARLEY. Well, then, I'm sorry, Willy. But tell me something.

WILLY. What?

CHARLEY. Who is Red Grange?

WILLY. Put up your hands. Goddam you, put up your hands! [CHARLEY, *chuckling, shakes his head and walks away, around the left corner of the stage.* WILLY *follows him. The music rises to a mocking frenzy.*]

WILLY. Who the hell do you think you are, better than everybody else? You don't know everything, you big, ignorant, stupid . . Put up your hands! [*Light rises, on the right side of the forestage, on a small table in the reception room of* CHARLEY's *office. Traffic sounds are heard.* BERNARD, *now mature, sits whistling to himself. A pair of tennis rackets and an overnight bag are on the floor beside him.*]

WILLY [*offstage*]. What are you walking away for? Don't walk away! If you're going to say something say it to my face! I know you laugh at me behind my back. You'll laugh out of the other side of your goddam face after this game. Touchdown! Touchdown! Eighty thousand people! Touchdown! Right between the goal posts. [BERNARD *is a quiet, earnest, but self-assured young man.* WILLY's *voice is coming from right upstage now.*

BERNARD *lowers his feet off the table and listens.* JENNY, *his father's secretary, enters.*]

JENNY [*distressed*]. Say, Bernard, will you go out in the hall?

BERNARD. What is that noise? Who is it?

JENNY. Mr. Loman. He just got off the elevator.

BERNARD [*getting up*]. Who's he arguing with?

JENNY. Nobody. There's nobody with him. I can't deal with him any more, and your father gets all upset every time he comes. I've got a lot of typing to do, and your father's waiting to sign it. Will you see him?

WILLY [*entering*]. Touchdown! Touch— [*He sees* JENNY.] Jenny, Jenny, good to see you. How're ya? Workin'? Or still honest?

JENNY. Fine. How've you been feeling?

WILLY. Not much any more, Jenny. Ha, Ha! [*He is surprised to see the rackets.*]

BERNARD. Hello, Uncle Willy.

WILLY [*almost shocked*]. Bernard! Well, look who's here! [*He comes quickly, guiltily, to* BERNARD *and warmly shakes his hand.*]

BERNARD. How are you? Good to see you.

WILLY. What are you doing here?

BERNARD. Oh, just stopped by to see Pop. Get off my feet till my train leaves. I'm going to Washington in a few minutes.

WILLY. Is he in?

BERNARD. Yes, he's in his office with the accountant. Sit down.

WILLY [*sitting down*]. What're you going to do in Washington?

BERNARD. Oh, just a case I've got there, Willy.

WILLY. That so? [*Indicating the rackets*] You going to play tennis there?

BERNARD. I'm staying with a friend who's got a court.

WILLY. Don't say. His own tennis court. Must be fine people, I bet.

BERNARD. They are, very nice. Dad tells me Biff's in town.

WILLY [*with a big smile*]. Yeah, Biff's in. Working on a very big deal, Bernard.

BERNARD. What's Biff doing?

WILLY. Well, he's been doing very big things in the West. But he decided to establish himself here. Very big. We're having dinner. Did I hear your wife had a boy?

BERNARD. That's right. Our second.

WILLY. Two boys! What do you know!

BERNARD. What kind of a deal has Biff got?

WILLY. Well, Bill Oliver—very big sporting-goods man—he wants Biff very badly. Called him in from the West. Long distance, carte blanche, special deliveries. Your friends have their own private tennis court?

BERNARD. You still with the old firm, Willy?

WILLY [*after a pause*]. I'm—I'm overjoyed to see how you made the grade, Bernard, overjoyed. It's an encouraging thing to see a young man really—really—Looks very good for Biff—very—[*He breaks off, then*] Bernard— [*He is so full of emotion, he breaks off again.*]

BERNARD. What is it, Willy?

WILLY [*small and alone*]. What—what's the secret?

BERNARD. What secret?

WILLY. How—how did you? Why didn't he ever catch on?

BERNARD. I wouldn't know that, Willy.

WILLY [*confidentially, desperately*]. You were his friend, his boyhood friend. There's something I don't understand about it. His life ended after that Ebbets Field game. From the age of seventeen nothing good ever happened to him.

BERNARD. He never trained himself for anything.

WILLY. But he did, he did. After high school he took so many correspondence courses. Radio mechanics; television; God knows what, and never made the slightest mark.

BERNARD [*taking off his glasses*]. Willy, do you want to talk candidly?

WILLY [*rising, faces* BERNARD]. I regard you as a very brilliant man, Bernard. I value your advice.

BERNARD. Oh, the hell with the advice, Willy. I couldn't advise you. There's just one thing I've always wanted to ask you. When he was supposed to graduate, and the math teacher flunked him—

WILLY. Oh, that son-of-a-bitch ruined his life.

BERNARD. Yeah, but, Willy, all he had to do was go to summer school and make up that subject.

WILLY. That's right, that's right.

BERNARD. Did you tell him not to go to summer school?

WILLY. Me? I begged him to go. I ordered him to go!

BERNARD. Then why wouldn't he go?

WILLY. Why? Why! Bernard, that question has been trailing me like a ghost for the last fifteen years. He flunked the subject, and laid down and died like a hammer hit him!

BERNARD. Take it easy, kid.

WILLY. Let me talk to you—I got nobody to talk to. Bernard, Bernard, was it my fault? Y'see? It keeps going around in my mind, maybe I did something to him. I got nothing to give him.

BERNARD. Don't take it so hard.

WILLY. Why did he lay down? What is the story there? You were his friend!

BERNARD. Willy, I remember, it was June, and our grades came out. And he'd flunked math.

WILLY. That son-of-a-bitch!

BERNARD. No, it wasn't right then. Biff just got very angry, I remember, and he was ready to enroll in summer school.

WILLY [*surprised*]. He was?

BERNARD. He wasn't beaten by it at all. But then, Willy, he disappeared from the block for almost a month. And I got the idea that he'd gone up to New England to see you. Did he have a talk with you then? [WILLY *stares in silence.*]

BERNARD. Willy?

WILLY [*with a strong edge of resentment in his voice*]. Yeah, he came to Boston. What about it?

BERNARD. Well, just that when he came back—I'll never forget this, it always mystifies me. Because I'd thought so well of Biff, even though he'd always taken advantage of me. I loved him, Willy, y'know? And he came back after that month and took his sneakers—remember those sneakers with "University of Virginia" printed on them? He was so proud of those, wore them every day. And he took them down in the cellar, and burned them up in the furnace. We had a fist fight. It lasted at least half an hour. Just the two of us, punching each other down the cellar, and crying right through it. I've often thought of how strange it was that I knew he'd given up his life. What happened in Boston, Willy? [WILLY *looks at him as at an intruder.*]

BERNARD. I just bring it up because you asked me.

WILLY [*angrily*]. Nothing. What do you mean, "What happened?" What's that got to do with anything?

BERNARD. Well, don't get sore.

WILLY. What are you trying to do, blame it on me? If a boy lays down is that my fault?

BERNARD. Now, Willy, don't get—

WILLY. Well, don't—talk to me that way! What does that mean, "What happened?" [CHARLEY *enters. He is in his vest, and he carries a bottle of bourbon.*]

CHARLEY. Hey, you're going to miss that train. [*He waves the bottle.*]

BERNARD. Yeah, I'm going. [*He takes the bottle.*] Thanks, Pop. [*He picks up his rackets and bag.*] Good-by, Willy, and don't worry about it. You know, "If at first you don't succeed . . ."

WILLY. Yes, I believe in that.

Bernard. But sometimes, Willy, it's better for a man just to walk away.

WILLY. Walk away?

BERNARD. That's right.

WILLY. But if you can't walk away?

BERNARD [*after a slight pause*]. I guess that's when it's tough. [*Extending his hand*] Good-by, Willy.

WILLY [*shaking BERNARD's hand*]. Good-by, boy.

CHARLEY [*an arm on BERNARD's shoulder*]. How do you like this kid? Gonna argue a case in front of the Supreme Court.

BERNARD [*protesting*]. Pop!

WILLY [*genuinely shocked, pained, and happy*]. No! The Supreme Court!

BERNARD. I gotta run. 'By, Dad!

CHARLEY. Knock 'em dead, Bernard! [BERNARD *goes off.*]

WILLY [*as CHARLEY takes out his wallet*].The Supreme Court! And he didn't even mention it!

CHARLEY [*counting out money on the desk*]. He don't have to—he's gonna do it.

WILLY. And you never told him what to do, did you? You never took any interest in him.

CHARLEY. My salvation is that I never took any interest in anything. There's some money—fifty dollars. I got an accountant inside.

WILLY. Charley, look . . . [*With difficulty*] I got my insurance to pay. If you can manage it—I need a hundred and ten dollars. [CHARLEY *doesn't reply for a moment; merely stops moving.*]

WILLY. I'd draw it from my bank but Linda would know, and I . . .

CHARLEY. Sit down, Willy.

WILLY [*moving toward the chair*]. I'm keeping an account of everything, remember. I'll pay every penny back. [*He sits.*]

CHARLEY. Now listen to me, Willy.

WILLY. I want you to know I appreciate . . .

CHARLEY [*sitting down on the table*]. Willy, what're you doin'? What the hell is goin' on in your head?

WILLY. Why? I'm simply . . .

CHARLEY. I offered you a job. You can make fifty dollars a week. And I won't send you on the road.

WILLY. I've got a job.

CHARLEY. Without pay? What kind of a job is a job without pay? [*He rises.*] Now, look, kid, enough is enough. I'm no genius but I know when I'm being insulted.

WILLY. Insulted!

CHARLEY. Why don't you want to work for me?

WILLY. What's the matter with you? I've got a job.

CHARLEY. Then what're you walkin' in here every week for?

WILLY [*getting up*]. Well, if you don't want me to walk in here—

CHARLEY. I am offering you a job.

WILLY. I don't want your goddam job!

CHARLEY. When the hell are you going to grow up?

WILLY [*furiously*]. You big ignoramus, if you say that to me again I'll rap you one! I don't care how big you are! [*He's ready to fight. Pause.*]

CHARLEY [*kindly, going to him*]. How much do you need, Willy?

WILLY. Charley, I'm strapped, I'm strapped. I don't know what to do. I was just fired.

CHARLEY. Howard fired you?

WILLY. That snotnose. Imagine that? I named him. I named him Howard.

CHARLEY. Willy, when're you gonna realize that them things don't mean anything? You named him Howard, but you can't sell that. The only thing you got in this world is what you can sell. And the funny thing is that you're a salesman, and you don't know that.

WILLY. I've always tried to think otherwise, I guess. I always felt that if a man was impressive, and well liked, that nothing—

CHARLEY. Why must everybody like you? Who liked J. P. Morgan? Was he impressive? In a turkish bath he'd look like a butcher. But with his pockets on he was very well liked. Now listen, Willy, I know you don't like me, and nobody can say I'm in love with you, but I'll give you a job because—just for the hell of it, put it that way. Now what do you say?

WILLY. I—I just can't work for you, Charley.

CHARLEY. What're you, jealous of me?

WILLY. I can't work for you, that's all, don't ask me why.

CHARLEY [*angered, takes out more bills*]. You been jealous of me all your life, you damned fool! Here, pay your insurance. [*He puts the money in* WILLY's *hand.*]

WILLY. I'm keeping strict accounts.

CHARLEY. I've got some work to do. Take care of yourself. And pay your insurance.

WILLY [*moving to the right*]. Funny, y'know? After all the highways, and the trains, and the appointments, and the years, you end up worth more dead than alive.

CHARLEY. Willy, nobody's worth nothin' dead. [*After a slight pause*] Did you hear what I said? [*Willy stands still, dreaming.*]

CHARLEY. Willy!

WILLY. Apologize to Bernard for me when you see him. I didn't mean to argue with him. He's a fine boy. They're all fine boys, and they'll end up big—all of them. Someday they'll all play tennis together. Wish me luck, Charley. He saw Bill Oliver today.

CHARLEY. Good luck.

WILLY [*on the verge of tears*]. Charley, you're the only friend I got. Isn't that a remarkable thing? [*He goes out.*]

CHARLEY. Jesus! [CHARLEY *stares after him a moment and follows. All light blacks out. Suddenly raucous music is heard, and a red glow rises behind the screen at right.* STANLEY, *a young waiter, appears, carrying a table, followed by* HAPPY, *who is carrying two chairs.*]

STANLEY [*putting the table down*]. That's all right, Mr. Loman, I can handle it myself. [*He turns and takes the chairs from* HAPPY *and places them at the table.*]

HAPPY [*glancing around*]. Oh, this is better.

STANLEY. Sure, in the front there you're in the middle of all kinds a noise. Whenever you got a party, Mr. Loman, you just tell me and I'll put you back here. Y'know, there's a lotta people they don't like it private, because when they go out they like to see a lotta action around them because they're sick and tired to stay in the house by theirself. But I know you, you ain't from Hackensack. You know what I mean?

HAPPY [*sitting down*]. So how's it coming, Stanley?

STANLEY. Ah, it's a dog's life. I only wish during the war they'd a took me in the Army. I coulda been dead by now.

HAPPY. My brother's back, Stanley.

STANLEY. Oh, he come back, heh? From the Far West.

HAPPY. Yeah, big cattle man, my brother, so treat him right. And my father's coming too.

STANLEY. Oh, your father too!

HAPPY. You got a couple of nice lobsters?

STANLEY. Hundred per cent, big.

HAPPY. I want them with the claws.

STANLEY. Don't worry, I don't give you no mice. [HAPPY *laughs.*] How about some wine? It'll put a head on the meal.

HAPPY. No. You remember, Stanley, that recipe I brought you from overseas? With the champagne in it?

STANLEY. Oh, yeah, sure. I still got it tacked up yet in the kitchen. But that'll have to cost a buck apiece anyways.

HAPPY. That's all right.

STANLEY. What'd you, hit a number or somethin'?

HAPPY. No, it's a little celebration. My brother is—I think he pulled off a big deal today. I think we're going into business together.

STANLEY. Great! That's the best for you. Because a family business, you know what I mean?—that's the best.

HAPPY. That's what I think.

STANLEY. 'Cause what's the difference? Somebody steals? It's in the family. Know what I mean? [*Sotto voce*] Like this bartender here. The boss is goin' crazy what kinda leak he's got in the cash register. You put it in but it don't come out.

HAPPY [*raising his head*]. Sh!

STANLEY. What?

HAPPY. You notice I wasn't lookin' right or left, was I?

STANLEY. No.

HAPPY. And my eyes are closed.

STANLEY. So what's the—?

HAPPY. Strudel's comin'.

STANLEY [*catching on, looks around*]. Ah, no, there's no— [*He breaks off as a furred, lavishly dressed girl enters and sits at the next table. Both follow her with their eyes.*]

STANLEY. Geez, how'd ya know?

HAPPY. I got radar or something. [*Staring directly at her profile*] Oooooooo . . . Stanley.

STANLEY. I think that's for you, Mr. Loman.

HAPPY. Look at that mouth. Oh, God. And the binoculars.

STANLEY. Geez, you got a life, Mr. Loman.

HAPPY. Wait on her.

STANLEY [*going to the* GIRL's *table*]. Would you like a menu, ma'am?

GIRL. I'm expecting someone, but I'd like a—

HAPPY. Why don't you bring her—excuse me, miss, do you mind? I sell champagne, and I'll like you to try my brand. Bring her a champagne, Stanley.

GIRL. That's awfully nice of you.

HAPPY. Don't mention it. It's all company money. [*He laughs.*]

GIRL. That's a charming product to be selling isn't it?

HAPPY. Oh, gets to be like everything else. Selling is selling, y'know.

GIRL. I suppose.

HAPPY. You don't happen to sell, do you?

GIRL. No, I don't sell.

HAPPY. Would you object to a compliment from a stranger? You ought to be on a magazine cover.

GIRL [*looking at him a little archly*]. I have been. [STANLEY *comes in with a glass of champagne.*]

HAPPY. What'd I say before, Stanley? You see? She's a cover girl.

STANLEY. Oh, I could see. I could see.

HAPPY [*to the* GIRL]. What magazine?

GIRL. Oh, a lot of them. [*She takes the drink.*] Thank you.

HAPPY. You know what they say in France, don't you? "Champagne is the drink of the complexion"—Hya, Biff! [BIFF *has entered and sits with* HAPPY.]

BIFF. Hello, kid. Sorry I'm late.

HAPPY. I just got here. Uh, Miss—?

GIRL. Forsythe.

HAPPY. Miss Forsythe, this is my brother.

BIFF. Is Dad here?

HAPPY. His name is Biff. You might've heard of him. Great football player.

GIRL. Really? What team?

HAPPY. Are you familiar with football?

GIRL. No, I'm afraid I'm not.

HAPPY. Biff is quarterback with the New York Giants.

GIRL. Well, that is nice, isn't it? [*She drinks.*]

HAPPY. Good health.

GIRL. I'm happy to meet you.

HAPPY. That's my name. Hap. It's really Harold, but at West Point they call me Happy.

GIRL [*now really impressed*]. Oh, I see. How do you do? [*She turns her profile.*]

BIFF. Isn't Dad coming?

HAPPY. You want her?

BIFF. Oh, I could never make that.

HAPPY. I remember the time that idea would never come into your head. Where's the old confidence, Biff?

BIFF. I just saw Oliver—

HAPPY. Wait a minute. I've got to see that old confidence again. Do you want her? She's on call.

BIFF. Oh, no. [*He turns to look at the* GIRL.]

HAPPY. I'm telling you. Watch this. [*Turning to the* GIRL.] Honey? [*She turns to him.*] Are you busy?

GIRL. Well, I am . . . but I could make a phone call.

HAPPY. Do that, will you, honey? And see if you can get a friend. We'll be here for a while. Biff is one of the greatest football players in the country.

GIRL [*standing up*]. Well, I'm certainly happy to meet you.

HAPPY. Come back soon.

GIRL. I'll try.

HAPPY. Don't try, honey, try hard. [*The* GIRL *exits.* STANLEY *follows, shaking his head in bewildered admiration.*]

HAPPY. Isn't that a shame now? A beautiful girl like that? That's why I can't get married. There's not a good woman in a thousand. New York is loaded with them, kid!

BIFF. Hap, look—

HAPPY. I told you she was on call!

BIFF [*strangely unnerved*]. Cut it out, will ya? I want to say something to you.

HAPPY. Did you see Oliver?

BIFF. I saw him all right. Now look, I want to tell Dad a couple of things and I want you to help me.

HAPPY. What? Is he going to back you?

BIFF. Are you crazy? You're out of your goddam head, you know that?

HAPPY. Why? What happened?

BIFF [*breathlessly*]. I did a terrible thing today, Hap. It's been the strangest day I ever went through. I'm all numb, I swear.

HAPPY. You mean he wouldn't see you?

HAPPY. Well, I waited six hours for him, see? All day. Kept sending my name in. Even tried to date his secretary so she'd get me to him, but no soap.

HAPPY. Because you're not showin' the old confidence, Biff. He remembered you, didn't he?

BIFF [*stopping* HAPPY *with a gesture*]. Finally, about five o'clock, he comes out. Didn't remember who I was or anything. I felt like such an idiot, Hap.

HAPPY. Did you tell him my Florida idea?

BIFF. He walked away. I saw him for one minute. I got so mad I could've torn the walls down! How the hell did I ever get the idea I was a salesman there? I even believed myself that I'd been a salesman for him! And then he gave me one look and—I realized what a ridiculous lie my whole life has been! We've been talking in a dream for fifteen years. I was a shipping clerk.

HAPPY. What'd you do?

BIFF [*with great tension and wonder*]. Well, he left, see. And the secretary went out. I was all alone in the waiting-room. I don't know what came over me, Hap. The next thing I know I'm in his office—paneled walls, everything. I can't explain it. I—Hap, I took his fountain pen.

HAPPY. Geez, did he catch you?

BIFF. I ran out. I ran down all eleven flights. I ran and ran and ran.

HAPPY. That was an awful dumb—what'd you do that for?

BIFF [*agonized*]. I don't know, I just—wanted to take something, I don't know. You gotta help me, Hap, I'm gonna tell Pop.

HAPPY. You crazy? What for?

BIFF. Hap, he's got to understand that I'm not the man somebody lends that kind of money to. He thinks I've been spiting him all these years and it's eating him up.

HAPPY. That's just it. You tell him something nice.

BIFF. I can't.

HAPPY. Say you got a lunch date with Oliver tomorrow.

BIFF. So what do I do tomorrow?

HAPPY. You leave the house tomorrow and come back at night and say Oliver is thinking it over. And he thinks it over for a couple of weeks, and gradually it fades away and nobody's the worse.

BIFF. But it'll go on forever!

HAPPY. Dad is never so happy as when he's looking forward to something! [WILLY *enters.*]

HAPPY. Hello, scout!

WILLY. Gee, I haven't been here in years! [STANLEY *has followed* WILLY *in and sets a chair for him.* STANLEY *starts off but* HAPPY *stops him.*]

HAPPY. Stanley! [STANLEY *stands by, waiting for an order.*]

BIFF [*going to* WILLY *with guilt, as to an invalid*]. Sit down, Pop. You want a drink?

WILLY. Sure, I don't mind.

BIFF. Let's get a load on.

WILLY. You look worried.

BIFF. N-no. [*To* STANLEY] Scotch all around. Make it doubles.

STANLEY. Doubles, right. [*He goes.*]

WILLY. You had a couple already, didn't you?

BIFF. Just a couple, yeah.

WILLY. Well, what happened, boy? [*Nodding affirmatively, with a smile.*] Everything go all right?

BIFF [*takes a breath, then reaches out and grasps* WILLY's *hand*]. Pal . . . [*He is smiling bravely, and* WILLY *is smiling too.*] I had an experience today.

HAPPY. Terrific, Pop.

WILLY. That so? What happened?

BIFF [*high, slightly alcoholic, above the earth*]. I'm going to tell you everything from first to last. It's been a strange day. [*Silence. He looks around, composes himself as best he can, but his breath keeps breaking the rhythm of his voice.*] I had to wait quite a while for him, and—

WILLY. Oliver?

BIFF. Yeah, Oliver. All day, as a matter of cold fact. And a lot of—instances—facts, Pop, facts about my life came back to me. Who was it, Pop? Who ever said I was a salesman with Oliver?

WILLY. Well, you were.

BIFF. No, Dad, I was a shipping clerk.

WILLY. But you were practically—

BIFF [*with determination*]. Dad, I don't know who said it first, but I was never a salesman for Bill Oliver.

WILLY. What're you talking about?

BIFF. Let's hold on to the facts tonight, Pop. We're not going to get anywhere bullin' around. I was a shipping clerk.

WILLY [*angrily*]. All right, now listen to me—

BIFF. Why don't you let me finish?

WILLY. I'm not interested in stories about the past or any crap of that kind because the woods are burning, boys, you understand? There's a big blaze going on all around. I was fired today.

BIFF [*shocked*]. How could you be?

WILLY. I was fired, and I'm looking for a little good news to tell your mother, because the woman has waited and the woman has suffered. The gist of it is that I haven't got a story left in my head, Biff. So don't give me a lecture about facts and aspects. I am not interested. Now what've you got to say to me? [STANLEY *enters with three drinks. They wait until he leaves.*]

WILLY. Did you see Oliver?

BIFF. Jesus, Dad!

WILLY. You mean you didn't go up there?

HAPPY. Sure he went up there.

BIFF. I did. I—saw him. How could they fire you?

WILLY [*on the edge of his chair*]. What kind of a welcome did he give you?

BIFF. He won't even let you work on commission?

WILLY. I'm out. [*Driving*] So tell me, he gave you a warm welcome?

HAPPY. Sure, Pop, sure!

BIFF [*driven*]. Well, it was kind of—

WILLY. I was wondering if he'd remember you. [*To* HAPPY] Imagine, man doesn't see him for ten, twelve years and gives him that kind of a welcome!

HAPPY. Damn right!

BIFF [*trying to return to the offensive*]. Pop, look—

WILLY. You know why he remembered you, don't you? Because you impressed him in those days.

BIFF. Let's talk quietly and get this down to the facts, huh?

WILLY [*as though* BIFF *had been interrupting*]. Well, what happened? It's great news, Biff. Did he take you into his office or'd you talk in the waiting-room?

BIFF. Well, he came in, see, and—

WILLY [*with a big smile*]. What'd he say? Betcha he threw his arm around
   you.
BIFF. Well, he kinda—
WILLY. He's a fine man. [*To* HAPPY] Very hard man to see, y'know.
HAPPY [*agreeing*]. Oh, I know.
WILLY [*to* BIFF]. Is that where you had the drinks?
BIFF. Yeah, he gave me a couple of—no, no!
HAPPY [*cutting in*]. He told him my Florida idea.
WILLY. Don't interrupt. [*To* BIFF] How'd he react to the Florida idea?
BIFF. Dad, will you give me a minute to explain?
WILLY. I've been waiting for you to explain since I sat down here! What
   happened? He took you into his office and what?
BIFF. Well—I talked. And—and he listened, see.
WILLY. Famous for the way he listens, y'know. What was his answer?
BIFF. His answer was—[*He breaks off, suddenly angry.*] Dad, you're not letting
   me tell you what I want to tell you!
WILLY [*accusing, angered*]. You didn't see him, did you?
BIFF. I did see him!
WILLY. What'd you insult him or something? You insulted him, didn't
   you?
BIFF. Listen, will you let me out of it, will you just let me out of it!
HAPPY. What the hell!
WILLY. Tell me what happened!
BIFF [*to* HAPPY]. I can't talk to him! [*A single trumpet note jars the ear. The
   light of green leaves stains the house, which holds the air of night and a dream.
   YOUNG BERNARD enters and knocks on the door of the house.*]
YOUNG BERNARD [*frantically*]. Mrs. Loman, Mrs. Loman!
HAPPY. Tell him what happened!
BIFF [*to* HAPPY]. Shut up and leave me alone!
WILLY. No, no! You had to go and flunk math!
BIFF. What math? What're you talking about?
YOUNG BERNARD. Mrs. Loman, Mrs. Loman! [LINDA *appears in the house, as
   of old.*]
WILLY [*wildly*]. Math, math, math!
BIFF. Take it easy, Pop!
YOUNG BERNARD. Mrs. Loman!
WILLY [*furiously*]. If you hadn't flunked you'd've been set by now!
BIFF. Now, look, I'm gonna tell you what happened, and you're going
   to listen to me.
YOUNG BERNARD. Mrs. Loman!
BIFF. I waited six hours—
HAPPY. What the hell are you saying?
BIFF. I kept sending in my name but he wouldn't see me. So finally he
   . . . [*He continues unheard as light fades low on the restaurant.*]
YOUNG BERNARD. Biff flunked math!
LINDA. No!
YOUNG BERNARD. Birnbaum flunked him! They won't graduate him!
LINDA. But they have to. He's gotta go to the university. Where is he?
   Biff! Biff!
YOUNG BERNARD. No, he left. He went to Grand Central.

LINDA. Grand—You mean he went to Boston!

YOUNG BERNARD. Is Uncle Willy in Boston?

LINDA. Oh, maybe Willy can talk to the teacher. Oh, the poor, poor boy!
[*Light on house area snaps out.*]

BIFF [*at the table, now audible, holding up a gold fountain pen*]. . . . so I'm
washed up with Oliver, you understand? Are you listening to me?

WILLY [*at a loss*]. Yeah, sure. If you hadn't flunked—

BIFF. Flunked what? What're you talking about?

WILLY. Don't blame everything on me! I didn't flunk math—you did! What
pen?

HAPPY. That was awful dumb, Biff, a pen like that is worth—

WILLY [*seeing the pen for the first time*]. You took Oliver's pen?

BIFF [*weakening*]. Dad, I just explained it to you.

WILLY. You stole Bill Oliver's fountain pen!

BIFF. I didn't exactly steal it! That's just what I've been explaining to
you!

HAPPY. He had it in his hand and just then Oliver walked in, so he got
nervous and stuck it in his pocket!

WILLY. My God, Biff!

BIFF. I never intended to do it, Dad!

OPERATOR'S VOICE. Standish Arms, good evening!

WILLY [*shouting*]. I'm not in my room!

BIFF [*frightened*]. Dad, what's the matter? [*He and* HAPPY *stand up.*]

OPERATOR. Ringing Mr. Loman for you!

WILLY. I'm not there, stop it!

BIFF [*horrified, gets down on one knee before* WILLY]. Dad, I'll make good,
I'll make good. [WILLY *tries to get to his feet.* BIFF *holds him down.*] Sit
down now.

WILLY. No, you're no good, you're no good for anything.

BIFF. I am, Dad, I'll find something else, you understand? Now don't worry
about anything. [*He holds up* WILLY'S *face.*] Talk to me, Dad.

OPERATOR. Mr. Loman does not answer. Shall I page him?

WILLY [*attempting to stand, as though to rush and silence the* OPERATOR]. No,
no, no!

HAPPY. He'll strike something, Pop.

WILLY. No, no . . .

BIFF [*desperately, standing over* WILLY]. Pop, listen! Listen to me! I'm telling
you something good. Oliver talked to his partner about the Florida idea.
You listening? He—he talked to his partner, and he came to me . . .
I'm going to be all right, you hear? Dad, listen to me, he said it was
just a question of the amount!

WILLY. Then you . . . got it?

HAPPY. He's gonna be terrific, Pop!

WILLY [*trying to stand*]. Then you got it, haven't you? You got it! You
got it!

BIFF [*agonized, holds* WILLY *down*]. No, no. Look, Pop. I'm supposed to
have lunch with them tomorrow. I'm just telling you this so you'll know
that I can still make an impression, Pop. And I'll make good somewhere,
but I can't go tomorrow, see?

WILLY. Why not? You simply—

BIFF. But the pen, Pop!

WILLY. You give it to him and tell him it was an oversight!

HAPPY. Sure, have lunch tomorrow!

BIFF. I can't say that—

WILLY. You were doing a crossword puzzle and accidentally used his pen!

BIFF. Listen, kid, I took those balls years ago, now I walk in with his fountain pen? That clinches it, don't you see? I can't face him like that! I'll try elsewhere.

PAGE'S VOICE. Paging Mr. Loman!

WILLY. Don't you want to be anything?

BIFF. Pop, how can I go back?

WILLY. You don't want to be anything, is that what's behind it?

BIFF [*now angry at* WILLY *for not crediting his sympathy*]. Don't take it that way! You think it was easy walking into that office after what I'd done to him? A team of horses couldn't have dragged me back to Bill Oliver!

WILLY. Then why'd you go?

BIFF. Why did I go? Why did I go! Look at you! Look at what's become of you! [*Off left,* THE WOMAN *laughs.*]

WILLY. Biff, you're going to go to that lunch tomorrow, or—

BIFF. I can't go. I've got no appointment!

HAPPY. Biff, for . . . !

WILLY. Are you spiting me?

BIFF. Don't take it that way! Goddammit!

WILLY [*strikes* BIFF *and falters away from the table*]. You rotten little louse! Are you spiting me?

THE WOMAN. Someone's at the door, Willy!

BIFF. I'm no good, can't you see what I am?

HAPPY [*separating them*]. Hey, you're in a restaurant! Now cut it out, both of you! [*The girls enter.*] Hello, girls, sit down. [THE WOMAN *laughs, off left.*]

MISS FORSYTHE. I guess we might as well. This is Letta.

THE WOMAN. Willy, are you going to wake up?

BIFF [*ignoring* WILLY]. How're ya, miss, sit down. What do you drink?

MISS FORSYTHE. Letta might not be able to stay long.

LETTA. I gotta get up very early tomorrow. I got jury duty. I'm so excited! Were you fellows ever on a jury?

BIFF. No, but I been in front of them! [*The girls laugh.*] This is my father.

LETTA. Isn't he cute? Sit down with us, Pop.

HAPPY. Sit him down, Biff!

BIFF [*going to him*]. Come on, slugger, drink us under the table. To hell with it! Come on, sit down, pal. [*On* BIFF's *last insistence,* WILLY *is about to sit.*]

THE WOMAN [*now urgently*]. Willy, are you going to answer the door! [THE WOMAN's *call pulls* WILLY *back. He starts right, befuddled.*]

BIFF. Hey, where are you going?

WILLY. Open the door.

BIFF. The door?

WILLY. The washroom . . . the door . . . where's the door?

BIFF [*leading* WILLY *to the left.*] Just go straight down. [WILLY *moves left.*]

THE WOMAN. Willy, Willy, are you going to get up, get up, get up, get up? [WILLY *exits left.*]

LETTA. I think it's sweet you bring your daddy along.

MISS FORSYTHE. Oh, he isn't really your father!

BIFF [*at left, turning to her resentfully*]. Miss Forsythe, you've just seen a prince walk by. A fine, troubled prince. A hard-working unappreciated prince. A pal, you understand? A good companion. Always for his boys.

LETTA. That's so sweet.

HAPPY. Well, girls, what's the program? We're wasting time. Come on, Biff. Gather round. Where would you like to go?

BIFF. Why don't you do something for him?

HAPPY. Me!

BIFF. Don't you give a damn for him, Hap?

HAPPY. What're you talking about? I'm the one who—

BIFF. I sense it, you don't give a good goddam about him. [*He takes the rolled-up hose from his pocket and puts it on the table in front of* HAPPY.] Look what I found in the cellar, for Christ's sake. How can you bear to let it go on?

HAPPY. Me? Who goes away? Who runs off and—

BIFF. Yeah, but he doesn't mean anything to you. You could help him— I can't! Don't you understand what I'm talking about? He's going to kill himself, don't you know that?

HAPPY. Don't I know it! Me!

BIFF. Hap, help him! Jesus . . . help him . . . Help me, help me, I can't bear to look at his face! [*Ready to weep he hurries out, up right.*]

HAPPY [*starting after him*]. Where are you going?

MISS FORSYTHE. What's he so mad about?

HAPPY. Come on, girls, we'll catch up with him.

MISS FORSYTHE [*as* HAPPY *pushes her out*]. Say, I don't like that temper of his!

HAPPY. He's just a little overstrung, he'll be all right!

WILLY [*off left, as* THE WOMAN *laughs*]. Don't answer! Don't answer!

LETTA. Don't you want to tell your father—

HAPPY. No, that's not my father. He's just a guy. Come on, we'll catch Biff, and, honey, we're going to paint this town! Stanley, where's the check! Hey, Stanley! [*They exit,* STANLEY *looks toward left.*]

STANLEY [*calling to* HAPPY *indignantly*]. Mr. Loman! Mr. Loman! [STANLEY *picks up a chair and follows them off. Knocking is heard off left.* THE WOMAN *enters, laughing,* WILLY *follows her. She is in a black slip; he is buttoning his shirt. Raw, sensuous music accompanies their speech.*]

WILLY. Will you stop laughing? Will you stop?

THE WOMAN. Aren't you going to answer the door? He'll wake the whole hotel.

WILLY. I'm not expecting anybody.

THE WOMAN. Whyn't you have another drink, honey, and stop being so damn self-centered?

WILLY. I'm so lonely.

THE WOMAN. You know you ruined me. Willy? From now on, whenever you come to the office, I'll see that you go right through to the buyers. No waiting at my desk any more, Willy. You ruined me.

WILLY. That's nice of you to say that.

THE WOMAN. Gee, you are self-centered! Why so sad? You are the saddest, self-centeredest soul I ever did see-saw. [*She laughs. He kisses her.*] Come on inside, drummer boy. It's silly to be dressing in the middle of the night. [*As knocking is heard.*] Aren't you going to answer the door?

WILLY. They're knocking on the wrong door.

THE WOMAN. But I felt the knocking. And he heard us talking in here. Maybe the hotel's on fire!

WILLY [*his terror rising*]. It's a mistake.

THE WOMAN. Then tell him to go away!

WILLY. There's nobody there.

THE WOMAN. It's getting on my nerves, Willy. There's somebody standing out there and it's getting on my nerves!

WILLY [*pushing her away from him*]. All right, stay in the bathroom here, and don't come out. I think there's a law in Massachusetts about it, so don't come out. It may be that new room clerk. He looked very mean. So don't come out. It's a mistake, there's no fire. [*The knocking is heard again. He takes a few steps away from her, and she vanishes into the wing. The light follows him, and now he is facing* YOUNG BIFF, *who carries a suitcase.* BIFF *steps toward him. The music is gone.*]

BIFF. Why didn't you answer?

WILLY. Biff! What are you doing in Boston?

BIFF. Why didn't you answer? I've been knocking for five minutes, I called you on the phone—

WILLY. I just heard you. I was in the bathroom and had the door shut. Did anything happen home?

BIFF. Dad—I let you down.

WILLY. What do you mean?

BIFF. Dad . . .

WILLY. Biffo, what's this about? [*Putting his arm around* BIFF.] Come on, let's go downstairs and get you a malted.

BIFF. Dad, I flunked math.

WILLY. Not for the term?

BIFF. The term. I haven't got enough credits to graduate.

WILLY. You mean to say Bernard wouldn't give you the answers?

BIFF. He did, he tried, but I only got a sixty-one.

WILLY. And they wouldn't give you four points?

BIFF. Birnbaum refused absolutely. I begged him, Pop, but he won't give me those points. You gotta talk to him before they close the school. Because if he saw the kind of man you are, and you just talked to him in your way, I'm sure he'd come through for me. The class came right before practice, see, and I didn't go enough. Would you talk to him? He'd like you, Pop. You know the way you could talk.

WILLY. You're on. We'll drive right back.

BIFF. Oh, Dad, good work! I'm sure he'll change it for you!

WILLY. Go downstairs and tell the clerk I'm checkin' out. Go right down.

BIFF. Yes, sir! See, the reason he hates me, Pop—one day he was late for class so I got up at the blackboard and imitated him. I crossed my eyes and talked with a lithp.

WILLY [*laughing*]. You did? The kids like it?

BIFF. They nearly died laughing!

WILLY. Yeah! What'd you do?

BIFF. The thquare root of thixthy twee is . . . [WILLY *bursts out laughing;* BIFF *joins him.*] And in the middle of it he walked in! [WILLY *laughs and* THE WOMAN *joins in offstage.*]

WILLY [*without hesitation*]. Hurry downstairs and—

BIFF. Somebody in there?

WILLY. No, that was next door. [THE WOMAN *laughs offstage.*]

BIFF. Somebody got in your bathroom!

WILLY. No, it's the next room, there's a party—

THE WOMAN [*enters, laughing. She lisps this*]. Can I come in? There's something in the bathtub, Willy, and it's moving! [WILLY *looks at* BIFF, *who is staring open-mouthed and horrified at* THE WOMAN.]

WILLY. Ah—you better go back to your room. They must be finished painting by now. They're painting her room so I let her take a shower here. Go back, go back . . . [*He pushes her.*]

THE WOMAN [*resisting*]. But I've got to get dressed, Willy, I can't—

WILLY. Get out of here! Go back, go back . . . [*Suddenly striving for the ordinary.*] This is Miss Francis, Biff, she's a buyer. They're painting her room. Go back, Miss Francis, go back . . .

THE WOMAN. But my clothes, I can't go out naked in the hall!

WILLY [*pushing her offstage*]. Get outa here! Go back, go back! [BIFF *slowly sits down on his suitcase as the argument continues offstage.*]

THE WOMAN. Where's my stockings? You promised me stockings, Willy!

WILLY. I have no stockings here!

THE WOMAN. You have two boxes of size nine sheers for me, and I want them!

WILLY. Here, for God's sake, will you get outa here!

THE WOMAN [*enters holding a box of stockings*]. I just hope there's nobody in the hall. That's all I hope. [*To* BIFF.] Are you football or baseball?

BIFF. Football.

THE WOMAN [*angry, humiliated*]. That's me too. G'night. [*She snatches her clothes from* WILLY, *and walks out.*]

WILLY [*after a pause*]. Well, better get going. I want to get to the school first thing in the morning. Get my suits out of the closet. I'll get my valise. [BIFF *doesn't move.*] What's the matter? [BIFF *remains motionless, tears falling.*] She's a buyer. Buys for J. H. Simmons. She lives down the hall—they're painting. You don't imagine—[*He breaks off. After a pause.*] Now listen, pal, she's just a buyer. She sees merchandise in her room and they have to keep it looking just so . . . [*Pause. Assuming command.*] All right, get my suits. [BIFF *doesn't move.*] Now stop crying and do as I say. I gave you an order. Biff, I gave you an order! Is that what you do when I give you an order? How dare you cry! [*Putting his arm around* BIFF.] Now look, Biff, when you grow up you'll understand about these things. You mustn't—you mustn't overemphasize a thing like this. I'll see Birnbaum first thing in the morning.

BIFF. Never mind.

WILLY [*getting down beside* BIFF]. Never mind! He's going to give you those points. I'll see to it.

BIFF. He wouldn't listen to you.

WILLY. He certainly will listen to me. You need those points for the U.
of Virginia.

BIFF. I'm not going there.

WILLY. Heh? If I can't get him to change that mark you'll make it up in
summer school. You've got all summer to—

BIFF [*his weeping breaking from him*]. Dad . . .

WILLY [*infected by it*]. Oh, my boy . . .

BIFF. Dad . . .

WILLY. She's nothing to me, Biff. I was lonely, I was terribly lonely.

BIFF. You—you gave her Mama's stockings! [*His tears break through and he
rises to go.*]

WILLY [*grabbing for* BIFF]. I gave you an order!

BIFF. Don't touch me, you—liar!

WILLY. Apologize for that!

BIFF. You fake! You phony little fake! You fake! [*Overcome, he turns quickly
and weeping fully goes out with his suitcase.* WILLY *is left on the floor on his
knees.*]

WILLY. I gave you an order! Biff, come back here or I'll beat you! Come
back here! I'll whip you! [STANLEY *comes quickly in from the right and
stands in front of* WILLY.]

WILLY [*shouts at* STANLEY]. I gave you an order . . .

STANLEY. Hey, let's pick it up, pick it up, Mr. Loman. [*He helps* WILLY *to
his feet.*] Your boys left with the chippies. They said they'll see you at
home. [*A second waiter watches some distance away.*]

WILLY. But we were supposed to have dinner together. [*Music is heard,*
WILLY'S *theme.*]

STANLEY. Can you make it?

WILLY. I'll—sure, I can make it. [*Suddenly concerned about his clothes.*] Do
I—I look all right?

STANLEY. Sure, you look all right. [*He flicks a speck off* WILLY'S *lapel.*]

WILLY. Here—here's a dollar.

STANLEY. Oh, your son paid me. It's all right.

WILLY [*putting it in* STANLEY'S *hand*]. No, take it. You're a good boy.

STANLEY. Oh, no, you don't have to . . .

WILLY. Here—here's some more, I don't need it any more. [*After a slight
pause.*] Tell me—is there a seed store in the neighborhood?

STANLEY. Seeds? You mean like to plant? [*As* WILLY *turns,* STANLEY *slips
the money back into his jacket pocket.*]

WILLY. Yes. Carrots, peas . . .

STANLEY. Well, there's hardware stores on Sixth Avenue, but it may be
too late now.

WILLY [*anxiously*]. Oh, I'd better hurry. I've got to get some seeds. [*He
starts off to the right.*] I've got to get some seeds, right away. Nothing's
planted. I don't have a thing in the ground. [WILLY *hurries out as the
light goes down.* STANLEY *moves over to the right after him, watches him off.
The other waiter has been staring at* WILLY.]

STANLEY [*to the waiter*]. Well, whatta you looking at? [*The waiter picks up
the chairs and moves off right.* STANLEY *takes the table and follows him. The
light fades on this area. There is a long pause, the sound of the flute coming
over. The light gradually rises on the kitchen, which is empty.* HAPPY *appears*

at the door of the house, followed by BIFF. HAPPY *is carrying a large bunch of long-stemmed roses. He enters the kitchen, looks around for* LINDA. *Not seeing her, he turns to* BIFF, *who is just outside the house door, and makes a gesture with his hands, indicating "Not here, I guess." He looks into the living-room and freezes. Inside,* LINDA, *unseen, is seated,* WILLY'S *coat on her lap. She rises ominously and quietly and moves toward* HAPPY, *who backs up into the kitchen, afraid.*]

HAPPY. Hey, what're you doing up? [LINDA *says nothing but moves toward him implacably.*] Where's Pop? [*He keeps backing to the right, and now* LINDA *is in full view in the doorway to the living-room.*] Is he sleeping?

LINDA. Where were you?

HAPPY [*trying to laugh it off.*]. We met two girls, Mom, very fine types. Here, we brought you some flowers. [*Offering them to her.*] Put them in your room, Ma. [*She knocks them to the floor at* BIFF'S *feet. He has now come inside and closed the door behind him. She stares at* BIFF, *silent.*]

HAPPY. Now what'd you do that for? Mom, I want you to have some flowers—

LINDA [*cutting* HAPPY *off, violently to* BIFF]. Don't you care whether he lives or dies?

HAPPY [*going to the stairs*]. Come upstairs, Biff.

BIFF [*with a flare of disgust, to* HAPPY]. Go way from me! [*To* LINDA.] What do you mean, lives or dies? Nobody's dying around here, pal.

LINDA. Get out of my sight! Get out of here!

BIFF. I wanna see the boss.

LINDA. You're not going near him!

BIFF. Where is he? [*He moves into the living-room and* LINDA *follows.*]

LINDA [*shouting after* BIFF]. You invite him for dinner. He looks forward to it all day—[BIFF *appears in his parents' bedroom, looks around, and exits.*] —and then you desert him there. There's no stranger you'd do that to!

HAPPY. Why? He had a swell time with us. Listen, when I—[LINDA *comes back into the kitchen.*]—desert him I hope I don't outlive the day!

LINDA. Get out of here!

HAPPY. Now look, Mom . . .

LINDA. Did you have to go to women tonight? You and your lousy rotten whores! [BIFF *re-enters the kitchen.*]

HAPPY. Mom, all we did was follow Biff around trying to cheer him up! [*To* BIFF] Boy, what a night you gave me!

LINDA. Get out of here, both of you, and don't come back! I don't want you tormenting him any more. Go on now, get your things together! [*To* BIFF] You can sleep in his apartment. [*She starts to pick up the flowers and stops herself.*] Pick up this stuff, I'm not your maid any more. Pick it up, you bum, you! [HAPPY *turns his back to her in refusal.* BIFF *slowly moves over and gets down on his knees, picking up the flowers.*]

LINDA. You're a pair of animals! Not one, not another living soul would have had the cruelty to walk out on that man in a restaurant!

BIFF [*not looking at her*]. Is that what he said?

LINDA. He didn't have to say anything. He was so humiliated he nearly limped when he came in.

HAPPY. But, Mom, he had a great time with us—

BIFF [*cutting him off violently*]. Shut up! [*Without another word,* HAPPY *goes upstairs.*]

LINDA. You! You didn't even go in to see if he was all right!

BIFF [*still on the floor in front of* LINDA, *the flowers in his hand; with self-loathing*]. No. Didn't. Didn't do a damned thing. How do you like that, heh? Left him babbling in a toilet.

LINDA. You louse. You . . .

BIFF. Now you hit it on the nose! [*He gets up, throws the flowers in the waste-basket.*] The scum of the earth, and you're looking at him!

LINDA. Get out of here!

BIFF. I gotta talk to the boss, Mom. Where is he?

LINDA. You're not going near him. Get out of this house!

BIFF [*with absolute assurance, determination*]. No. We're gonna have an abrupt conversation, him and me.

LINDA. You're not talking to him! [*Hammering is heard from outside the house, off right.* BIFF *turns toward the noise.*]

LINDA [*suddenly pleading*]. Will you please leave him alone?

BIFF. What's he doing out there?

LINDA. He's planting the garden!

BIFF [*quietly*]. Now? Oh, my God! [BIFF *moves outside,* LINDA *following. The light dies down on them and comes up on the center of the apron as* WILLY *walks into it. He is carrying a flashlight, a hoe, and a handful of seed packets. He raps the top of the hoe sharply to fix it firmly, and then moves to the left, measuring off the distance with his foot. He holds the flashlight to look at the seed packets, reading off the instructions. He is in the blue of night.*]

WILLY. Carrots . . . quarter-inch apart. Rows . . . one-foot rows. [*He measures it off.*] One foot. [*He puts down a package and measures off.*] Beets. [*He puts down another package and measures again.*] Lettuce. [*He reads the package, puts it down.*] One foot—[*He breaks off as* BEN *appears at the right and moves slowly down to him.*] What a proposition, ts, ts. Terrific, terrific. 'Cause she's suffered, Ben, the woman has suffered. You understand me? A man can't go out the way he came in, Ben, a man has got to add up to something. You can't, you can't—[BEN *moves toward him as though to interrupt.*] You gotta consider, now. Don't answer so quick. Remember, it's a guaranteed twenty-thousand-dollar proposition. Now look, Ben, I want you to go through the ins and outs of this thing with me. I've got nobody to talk to, Ben, and the woman has suffered, you hear me?

BEN [*standing still, considering*]. What's the proposition?

WILLY. It's twenty thousand dollars on the barrelhead. Guaranteed, gilt-edged, you understand?

BEN. You don't want to make a fool of yourself. They might not honor the policy.

WILLY. How can they dare refuse? Didn't I work like a coolie to meet every premium on the nose? And now they don't pay off? Impossible!

BEN. It's called a cowardly thing, William.

WILLY. Why? Does it take more guts to stand here the rest of my life ringing up a zero?

BEN [*yielding*]. That's a point, William. [*He moves, thinking, turns.*] And twenty thousand—that *is* something one can feel with the hand, it is there.

WILLY [*now assured, with rising power*]. Oh, Ben, that's the whole beauty of it! I see it like a diamond, shining in the dark, hard and rough, that I can pick up and touch in my hand. Not like—like an appointment! This would not be another damned-fool appointment, Ben, and it changes all the aspects. Because he thinks I'm nothing, see, and so he spites me. But the funeral—[*Straightening up.*] Ben, that funeral will be massive! They'll come from Maine, Massachusetts, Vermont, New Hampshire! All the oldtimers with the strange license plates—that boy will be thunder-struck, Ben, because he never realized—I am known! Rhode Island, New York, New Jersey—I am known, Ben, and he'll see it with his eyes once and for all. He'll see what I am, Ben! He's in for a shock, that boy!

BEN [*coming down to the edge of the garden*]. He'll call you a coward.

WILLY [*suddenly fearful*]. No, that would be terrible.

BEN. Yes, and a damned fool.

WILLY. No, no, he mustn't, I won't have that! [*He is broken and desperate.*]

BEN. He'll hate you, William. [*The gay music of the* BOYS *is heard.*]

WILLY. Oh, Ben, how do we get back to all the great times? Used to be so full of light, and comradeship, the sleigh-riding in winter, and the ruddiness on his cheeks. And always some kind of good news coming up, always something nice coming up ahead. And never even let me carry the valises in the house, and simonizing, simonizing that little red car! Why, why can't I give him something and not have him hate me?

BEN. Let me think about it. [*He glances at his watch.*] I still have a little time. Remarkable proposition, but you've got to be sure you're not making a fool of yourself. [BEN *drifts off upstage and goes out of sight.* BIFF *comes down from the left.*]

WILLY [*suddenly conscious of* BIFF, *turns and looks up at him, then begins picking up the packages of seeds in confusion.*] Where the hell is that seed? [*Indignantly.*] You can't see nothing out here! They boxed in the whole goddam neighborhood!

BIFF. There are people all around here. Don't you realize that?

WILLY. I'm busy. Don't bother me.

BIFF [*taking the hoe from* WILLY]. I'm saying good-by to you, Pop. [WILLY *looks at him, silent, unable to move.*] I'm not coming back any more.

WILLY. You're not going to see Oliver tomorrow?

BIFF. I've got no appointment, Dad.

WILLY. He put his arm around you, and you've got no appointment?

BIFF. Pop, get this now, will you? Every time I've left it's been a fight that sent me out of here. Today I realized something about myself and I tried to explain it to you and I—I think I'm just not smart enough to make any sense out of it for you. To hell with whose fault it is or anything like that. [*He takes* WILLY's *arm.*] Let's just wrap it up, heh? Come on in, we'll tell Mom. [*He gently tries to pull* WILLY *to left.*]

WILLY [*frozen, immobile, with guilt in his voice*]. No, I don't want to see her.

BIFF. Come on! [*He pulls again, and* WILLY *tries to pull away.*]

WILLY [*highly nervous*]. No, no, I don't want to see her.

BIFF [*tries to look into* WILLY'S *face, as if to find the answer there*]. Why don't you want to see her?

WILLY [*more harshly now*]. Don't bother me, will you?

BIFF. What do you mean, you don't want to see her? You don't want them calling you yellow, do you? This isn't your fault; it's me, I'm a bum. Now come inside! [WILLY *strains to get away.*] Did you hear what I said to you? [WILLY *pulls away and quickly goes by himself into the house.* BIFF *follows.*]

LINDA [*to* WILLY]. Did you plant, dear?

BIFF [*at the door, to* LINDA]. All right, we had it out. I'm going and I'm not writing any more.

LINDA [*going to* WILLY *in the kitchen*]. I think that's the best way, dear. 'Cause there's no use drawing it out, you'll just never get along. [WILLY *doesn't respond.*]

BIFF. People ask where I am and what I'm doing, you don't know, and you don't care. That way it'll be off your mind and you can start brightening up again. All right? That clears it, doesn't it? [WILLY *is silent, and* BIFF *goes to him.*] You gonna wish me luck, scout? [*He extends his hand.*] What do you say?

LINDA. Shake his hand, Willy.

WILLY [*turning to her, seething with hurt*]. There's no necessity to mention the pen at all, y'know.

BIFF [*gently*]. I've got no appointment, Dad.

WILLY [*erupting fiercely*]. He put his arm around . . . ?

BIFF. Dad, you're never going to see what I am, so what's the use of arguing? If I strike oil I'll send you a check. Meantime forget I'm alive.

WILLY [*to* LINDA]. Spite, see?

BIFF. Shake hands, Dad.

WILLY. Not my hand.

BIFF. I was hoping not to go this way.

WILLY. Well, this is the way you're going. Good-by. [BIFF *looks at him a moment, then turns sharply and goes to the stairs.*]

WILLY [*stops him with*]. May you rot in hell if you leave this house!

BIFF [*turning*]. Exactly what is it that you want from me?

WILLY. I want you to know, on the train, in the mountains, in the valleys, wherever you go, that you cut down your life for spite!

BIFF. No, no.

WILLY. Spite, spite, is the word of your undoing! And when you're down and out, remember what did it. When you're rotting somewhere beside the railroad tracks, remember, and don't you dare blame it on me!

BIFF. I'm not blaming it on you!

WILLY. I won't take the rap for this, you hear? [HAPPY *comes down the stairs and stands on the bottom step, watching.*]

BIFF. That's just what I'm telling you!

WILLY [*sinking into a chair at the table, with full accusation*]. You're trying to put a knife in me—don't think I don't know what you're doing!

BIFF. All right, phony! Then let's lay it on the line. [*He whips the rubber tube out of his pocket and puts it on the table.*]

HAPPY. You crazy—

LINDA. Biff! [*She moves to grab the hose, but* BIFF *holds it down with his hand.*]

BIFF. Leave it there! Don't move it!

WILLY [*not looking at it*]. What is that?

BIFF. You know goddam well what that is.

WILLY [*caged, wanting to escape*]. I never saw that.

BIFF. You saw it. The mice didn't bring it into the cellar! What is this supposed to do, make a hero out of you? This supposed to make me sorry for you?

WILLY. Never heard of it.

BIFF. There'll be no pity for you, you hear it? No pity!

WILLY [*to* LINDA]. You hear the spite!

BIFF. No, you're going to hear the truth—what you are and what I am!

LINDA. Stop it!

WILLY. Spite!

HAPPY [*coming down toward* BIFF]. You cut it now!

BIFF [*to* HAPPY]. The man don't know who we are! The man is gonna know! [*To* WILLY.] We never told the truth for ten minutes in this house!

HAPPY. We always told the truth!

BIFF [*turning on him*]. You big blow, are you the assistant buyer? You're one of the two assistants to the assistant, aren't you?

HAPPY. Well, I'm practically—

BIFF. You're practically full of it! We all are! And I'm through with it. [*To* WILLY.] Now hear this, Willy, this is me.

WILLY. I know you!

BIFF. You know why I had no address for three months? I stole a suit in Kansas City and I was in jail. [*To* LINDA, *who is sobbing.*] Stop crying. I'm through with it. [LINDA *turns away from them, her hands covering her face.*]

WILLY. I suppose that's my fault!

BIFF. I stole myself out of every good job since high school!

WILLY. And whose fault is that?

BIFF. And I never got anywhere because you blew me so full of hot air I could never stand taking orders from anybody! That's whose fault it is!

WILLY. I hear that!

LINDA. Don't, Biff!

BIFF. It's goddam time you heard that! I had to be boss big shot in two weeks, and I'm through with it!

WILLY. Then hang yourself! For spite, hang yourself!

BIFF. No! Nobody's hanging himself, Willy! I ran down eleven flights with a pen in my hand today. And suddenly I stopped, you hear me? And in the middle of that office building, do you hear this? I stopped in the middle of that building and I saw—the sky. I saw the things that I love in this world. The work and the food and time to sit and smoke. And I looked at the pen and said to myself, what the hell am I grabbing this for? Why am I trying to become what I don't want to be? What am I doing in an office, making a contemptuous, begging fool of myself,

when all I want is out there, waiting for me the minute I say I know
who I am! Why can't I say that, Willy? [*He tries to make* WILLY *face
him, but* WILLY *pulls away and moves to the left.*]

WILLY [*with hatred, threateningly*]. The door of your life is wide open!

BIFF. Pop! I'm a dime a dozen, and so are you!

WILLY [*turning on him now in an uncontrolled outburst*]. I am not a dime a
dozen! I am Willy Loman, and you are Biff Loman! [BIFF *starts for* WILLY,
but is blocked by HAPPY. *In his fury,* BIFF *seems on the verge of attacking
his father.*]

BIFF. I am not a leader of men, Willy, and neither are you. You were
never anything but a hard-working drummer who landed in the ash
can like all the rest of them! I'm one dollar an hour, Willy! I tried
seven states and couldn't raise it. A buck an hour! Do you gather my
meaning? I'm not bringing home any prizes any more, and you're going
to stop waiting for me to bring them home!

WILLY [*directly to* BIFF]. You vengeful, spiteful mutt! [BIFF *breaks from*
HAPPY. WILLY, *in fright, starts up the stairs.* BIFF *grabs him.*]

BIFF [*at the peak of his fury*]. Pop, I'm nothing! I'm nothing, Pop. Can't
you understand that? There's no spite in it any more. I'm just what I
am, that's all. [BIFF's *fury has spent itself, and he breaks down, sobbing, holding
on to* WILLY, *who dumbly fumbles for* BIFF's *face.*]

WILLY [*astonished*]. What're you doing? What're you doing? [*To* LINDA.]
Why is he crying?

BIFF [*crying, broken*]. Will you let me go, for Christ's sake? Will you
take that phony dream and burn it before something happens? [*Struggling to contain himself, he pulls away and moves to the stairs.*] I'll go in
the morning. Put him—put him to bed. [*Exhausted,* BIFF *moves up the
stairs to his room.*]

WILLY [*after a long pause, astonished, elevated*]. Isn't that—isn't that remarkable? Biff—he likes me!

LINDA. He loves you, Willy!

HAPPY [*deeply moved*]. Always did, Pop.

WILLY. Oh, Biff! [*Staring wildly.*] He cried! Cried to me. [*He is choking with
his love, and now cries out his promise.*] That boy—that boy is going to
be magnificent! [BEN *appears in the light just outside the kitchen.*]

BEN. Yes, outstanding, with twenty thousand behind him.

LINDA [*sensing the racing of his mind, fearfully, carefully*]. Now come to bed,
Willy. It's all settled now.

WILLY [*finding it difficult not to rush out of the house*]. Yes, we'll sleep. Come
on. Go on to sleep, Hap.

BEN. And it does take a great kind of a man to crack the jungle. [*In accents
of dread,* BEN's *idyllic music starts up.*]

HAPPY [*his arm around* LINDA]. I'm getting married, Pop, don't forget it.
I'm changing everything. I'm gonna run that department before the
year is up. You'll see, Mom. [*He kisses her.*]

BEN. The jungle is dark but full of diamonds, Willy. [WILLY *turns, moves,
listening to* BEN.]

LINDA. Be good. You're both good boys, just act that way, that's all.

HAPPY. 'Night, Pop. [*He goes upstairs.*]

LINDA [*to* WILLY]. Come, dear.

BEN [*with greater force*]. One must go in to fetch a diamond out.

WILLY [*to* LINDA, *as he moves slowly along the edge of the kitchen, toward the door*]. I just want to get settled down, Linda. Let me sit alone for a little.

LINDA [*almost uttering her fear*]. I want you upstairs.

WILLY [*taking her in his arms*]. In a few minutes, Linda. I couldn't sleep right now. Go on, you look awful tired. [*He kisses her.*]

BEN. Not like an appointment at all. A diamond is rough and hard to the touch.

WILLY. Go on now. I'll be right up.

LINDA. I think this is the only way, Willy.

WILLY. Sure, it's the best thing.

BEN. Best thing!

WILLY. The only way. Everything is gonna be—go on, kid, get to bed. You look so tired.

LINDA. Come right up.

WILLY. Two minutes. [LINDA *goes into the living-room, then reappears in her bedroom.* WILLY *moves just outside the kitchen door.*]

WILLY. Loves me. [*Wonderingly.*] Always loved me. Isn't that a remarkable thing? Ben, he'll worship me for it!

BEN [*with promise*]. It's dark there, but full of diamonds.

WILLY. Can you imagine that magnificence with twenty thousand dollars in his pocket?

LINDA [*calling from her room*]. Willy! Come up!

WILLY [*calling into the kitchen*]. Yes! Yes. Coming! It's very smart, you realize that, don't you, sweetheart? Even Ben sees it. I gotta go, baby. 'By! 'By! [*Going over to* BEN, *almost dancing.*] Imagine? When the mail comes he'll be ahead of Bernard again!

BEN. A perfect proposition all around.

WILLY. Did you see how he cried to me? Oh, if I could kiss him, Ben!

BEN. Time, William, time!

WILLY. Oh, Ben, I always knew one way or another we were gonna make it, Biff and I!

BEN [*looking at his watch*]. The boat. We'll be late. [*He moves slowly off into the darkness.*]

WILLY [*elegiacally, turning to the house*]. Now when you kick off, boy, I want a seventy-yard boot, and get right down the field under the ball, and when you hit, hit low and hit hard, because it's important, boy. [*He swings around and faces the audience.*] There's all kinds of important people in the stands, and the first thing you know . . . [*Suddenly realizing he is alone.*] Ben! Ben, where do I . . . ? [*He makes a sudden movement of search.*] Ben, how do I . . . ?

LINDA [*calling*]. Willy, you coming up?

WILLY [*uttering a gasp of fear, whirling about as if to quiet her*]. Sh! [*He turns around as if to find his way; sounds, faces, voices, seem to be swarming in upon him and he flicks at them, crying.*] Sh! Sh! [*Suddenly music, faint and high, stops him. It rises in intensity, almost to an unbearable scream. He goes up and down on his toes, and rushes off around the house.*] Shhh!

LINDA. Willy? [*There is no answer.* LINDA *waits.* BIFF *gets up off his bed. He is still in his clothes.* HAPPY *sits up.* BIFF *stands listening.*]

LINDA [*with real fear*]. Willy, answer me! Willy! [*There is the sound of a car starting and moving away at full speed.*]

LINDA. No!

BIFF [*rushing down the stairs*]. Pop! [*As the car speeds off, the music crashes down in a frenzy of sound, which becomes the soft pulsation of a single cello string. BIFF slowly returns to his bedroom. He and HAPPY gravely don their jackets. LINDA slowly walks out of her room. The music has developed into a dead march. The leaves of day are appearing over everything. CHARLEY and BERNARD, somberly dressed, appear and knock on the kitchen door. BIFF and HAPPY slowly descend the stairs to the kitchen as CHARLEY and BERNARD enter. All stop a moment when LINDA, in clothes of mourning, bearing a little bunch of roses, comes through the draped doorway into the kitchen. She goes to CHARLEY and takes his arm. Now all move toward the audience, through the wall-line of the kitchen. At the limit of the Apron, LINDA lays down the flowers, kneels, and sits back on her heels. All stare down at the grave.*]

REQUIEM

CHARLEY. It's getting dark, Linda. [LINDA *doesn't react. She stares at the grave.*]

BIFF. How about it, Mom? Better get some rest, heh? They'll be closing the gate soon. [LINDA *makes no move. Pause.*]

HAPPY [*deeply angered*]. He had no right to do that. There was no necessity for it. We would've helped him.

CHARLEY [*grunting*]. Hmmm.

BIFF. Come along, Mom.

LINDA. Why didn't anybody come?

CHARLEY. It was a very nice funeral.

LINDA. But where are all the people he knew? Maybe they blame him.

CHARLEY. Naa. It's a rough world, Linda. They wouldn't blame him.

LINDA. I can't understand it. At this time especially. First time in thirty-five years we were just about free and clear. He only needed a little salary. He was even finished with the dentist.

CHARLEY. No man only needs a little salary.

LINDA. I can't understand it.

BIFF. There were a lot of nice days. When he'd come home from a trip; or on Sundays, making the stoop; finishing the cellar; putting on the new porch; when he built the extra bedroom; and put up the garage. You know something, Charley, there's more of him in that front stoop than in all the sales he ever made.

CHARLEY. Yeah. He was a happy man with a batch of cement.

LINDA. He was so wonderful with his hands.

BIFF. He had the wrong dreams. All, all, wrong.

HAPPY [*almost ready to fight BIFF*]. Don't say that!

BIFF. He never knew who he was.

CHARLEY [*stopping HAPPY's movement and reply. To BIFF*]. Nobody dast blame this man. You don't understand: Willy was a salesman. And for a salesman, there is no rock bottom to the life. He don't put a bolt to a nut, he don't tell you the law or give you medicine. He's a man way out there in the blue, riding on a smile and a shoeshine. And when they start not smiling back—that's an earthquake. And then you get yourself a couple of spots on your hat, and you're finished. Nobody dast blame this man. A salesman is got to dream, boy. It comes with the territory.

BIFF. Charley, the man didn't know who he was.

HAPPY [*infuriated*]. Don't say that!

BIFF. Why don't you come with me, Happy?

HAPPY. I'm not licked that easily. I'm staying right in this city, and I'm gonna beat this racket! [*He looks at* BIFF, *his chin set.*] The Loman Brothers!

BIFF. I know who I am, kid.

HAPPY. All right, boy. I'm gonna show you and everybody else that Willy Loman did not die in vain. He had a good dream. It's the only dream you can have—to come out number-one man. He fought it out here, and this is where I'm gonna win it for him.

BIFF [*with a hopeless glance at* HAPPY, *bends toward his mother*]. Let's go, Mom.

LINDA. I'll be with you in a minute. Go on, Charley. [*He hesitates.*] I want to, just for a minute. I never had a chance to say good-by. [CHARLEY *moves away, followed by* HAPPY. BIFF *remains a slight distance up and left of* LINDA. *She sits there, summoning herself. The flute begins, not far away, playing behind her speech.*]

LINDA. Forgive me, dear. I can't cry. I don't know what it is, but I can't cry. I don't understand it. Why did you ever do that? Help me, Willy, I can't cry. It seems to me that you're just on another trip. I keep expecting you. Willy, dear, I can't cry. Why did you do it? I search and search and I search, and I can't understand it, Willy. I made the last payment on the house today. Today, dear. And there'll be nobody home. [*A sob rises in her throat.*] We're free and clear. [*Sobbing more fully, released.*] We're free. [BIFF *comes slowly toward her.*] We're free . . . We're free . . . [BIFF *lifts her to her feet and moves out up right with her in his arms.* LINDA *sobs quietly.* BERNARD *and* CHARLEY *come together and follow them, followed by* HAPPY. *Only the music of the flute is left on the darkening stage as over the house the hard towers of the apartment buildings rise into sharp focus, and The Curtain Falls.*]

(1949)

Harold Pinter *1930–*

THE DUMB WAITER

SCENE: *A basement room. Two beds, flat against the back wall. A serving hatch, closed, between the beds. A door to the kitchen and lavatory, left. A door to a passage, right.*

BEN *is lying on a bed, left, reading a paper.* GUS *is sitting on a bed, right, tying his shoelaces, with difficulty. Both are dressed in shirts, trousers and braces.* Silence.

GUS *ties his laces, rises, yawns and begins to walk slowly to the door, left. He stops, looks down, and shakes his foot.*

BEN *lowers his paper and watches him.* GUS *kneels and unties his shoe-lace and slowly takes off the shoe. He looks inside it and brings out a flattened matchbox. He shakes it and examines it. Their eyes meet.* BEN *rattles his paper and reads.* GUS *puts the matchbox in his pocket and bends down to put on his shoe. He ties his lace, with difficulty.* BEN *lowers his paper and watches him.* GUS *walks to the door, left, stops, and shakes the other foot. He kneels, unties his shoe-lace, and slowly takes off the shoe. He looks inside it and brings out a flattened cigarette packet. He shakes it and examines it. Their eyes meet.* BEN *rattles his paper and reads.*

GUS *puts the packet in his pocket, bends down, puts on his shoe and ties the lace. He wanders off, left.*

BEN *slams the paper down on the bed and glares after him. He picks up the paper and lies on his back, reading.*

Silence.

A lavatory chain is pulled twice off left, but the lavatory does not flush.

Silence.

GUS *re-enters, left, and halts at the door, scratching his head.*

BEN *slams down the paper.*

BEN. Kaw!

[*He picks up the paper.*]

What about this? Listen to this!

[*He refers to the paper.*]

A man of eighty-seven wanted to cross the road. But there was a lot of traffic, see? He couldn't see how he was going to squeeze through. So he crawled under a lorry.

GUS. He what?

BEN. He crawled under a lorry. A stationary lorry.

GUS. No?

BEN. The lorry started and ran over him.

GUS. Go on!

BEN. That's what it says here.

GUS. Get away.

BEN. It's enough to make you want to puke, isn't it?

GUS. Who advised him to do a thing like that?

BEN. A man of eighty-seven crawling under a lorry!

GUS. It's unbelievable.

BEN. It's down here in black and white.

GUS. Incredible.

[*Silence.*

GUS *shakes his head and exits.* BEN *lies back and reads.*

The lavatory chain is pulled once off left, but the lavatory does not flush.

BEN *whistles at an item in the paper.*

GUS *re-enters.*]

I want to ask you something.

BEN. What are you doing out there?

GUS. Well, I was just—

BEN. What about the tea?

GUS. I'm just going to make it.

BEN. Well, go on, make it.

GUS. Yes, I will. [*He sits in a chair. Ruminatively.*] He's laid on some very nice crockery this time, I'll say that. It's sort of striped. There's a white stripe.

[BEN *reads.*]

It's very nice. I'll say that.

[BEN *turns the page.*]

You know, sort of round the cup. Round the rim. All the rest of it's black, you see. Then the saucer's black, except for right in the middle, where the cup goes, where it's white.

[BEN *reads.*]

Then the plates are the same, you see. Only they've got a black stripe— the plates—right across the middle. Yes, I'm quite taken with the crockery.

BEN [*still reading*]. What do you want plates for? You're not going to eat.

GUS. I've brought a few biscuits.

BEN. Well, you'd better eat them quick.

GUS. I always bring a few biscuits. Or a pie. You know I can't drink tea without anything to eat.

BEN. Well, make the tea then, will you? Time's getting on.

[GUS *brings out the flattened cigarette packet and examines it.*]

GUS. You got any cigarettes? I think I've run out.

[*He throws the packet high up and leans forward to catch it.*]

I hope it won't be a long job, this one.

[*Aiming carefully, he flips the packet under his bed.*]

Oh, I wanted to ask you something.

BEN [*slamming his paper down*]. Kaw!

GUS. What's that?

BEN. A child of eight killed a cat!

GUS. Get away.

BEN. It's a fact. What about that, eh? A child of eight killing a cat!

GUS. How did he do it?

BEN. It was a girl.

GUS. How did she do it?

BEN. She—

[*He picks up the paper and studies it.*]

It doesn't say.

GUS. Why not?

BEN. Wait a minute. It just says—Her brother, aged eleven, viewed the incident from the toolshed.

GUS. Go on!

BEN. That's bloody ridiculous.

[*Pause.*]

GUS. I bet he did it.

BEN. Who?

GUS. The brother.

BEN. I think you're right.

[*Pause.*]

[*Slamming down the paper.*] What about that, eh? A kid of eleven killing a cat and blaming it on his little sister of eight! It's enough to—

[*He breaks off in disgust and seizes the paper.* GUS *rises.*]

GUS. What time is he getting in touch?

[BEN *reads.*]

What time is he getting in touch?

BEN. What's the matter with you? It could be any time. Any time.

GUS [*moves to the foot of* BEN's *bed*]. Well, I was going to ask you something.

BEN. What?

GUS. Have you noticed the time that tank takes to fill?

BEN. What tank?

GUS. In the lavatory.

BEN. No. Does it?

GUS. Terrible.

BEN. Well, what about it?

GUS. What do you think's the matter with it?

BEN. Nothing.

GUS. Nothing?

BEN. It's got a deficient ballcock, that's all.

GUS. A deficient what?

BEN. Ballcock.

GUS. No? Really?

BEN. That's what I should say.

GUS. Go on! That didn't occur to me.

[GUS *wanders to his bed and presses the mattress.*]

I didn't have a very restful sleep today, did you? It's not much of a bed. I could have done with another blanket too. [*He catches sight of a picture on the wall.*] Hello, what's this? [*Peering at it.*] "The First Eleven." Cricketers. You seen this, Ben?

BEN [*reading*]. What?

GUS. The first eleven.

BEN. What?

GUS. There's a photo here of the first eleven.

BEN. What first eleven?

GUS [*studying the photo*]. It doesn't say.

BEN. What about that tea?

GUS. They all look a bit old to me.

[GUS *wanders downstage, looks out front, then all about the room.*]

I wouldn't like to live in this dump. I wouldn't mind if you had a window, you could see what it looked like outside.

BEN. What do you want a window for?

GUS. Well, I like to have a bit of a view, Ben. It whiles away the time. [*He walks about the room.*]

I mean, you come into a place when it's still dark, you come into a room you've never seen before, you sleep all day, you do your job, and then you go away in the night again.

[*Pause.*]

I like to get a look at the scenery. You never get the chance in this job.

BEN. You get your holidays, don't you?

GUS. Only a fortnight.

BEN [*lowering the paper*]. You kill me. Anyone would think you're working every day. How often do we do a job? Once a week? What are you complaining about?

GUS. Yes, but we've got to be on tap though, haven't we? You can't move out of the house in case a call comes.

BEN. You know what your trouble is?

GUS. What?

BEN. You haven't got any interests.

GUS. I've got interests.

BEN. What? Tell me one of your interests.

[*Pause.*]

GUS. I've got interests.

BEN. Look at me. What have I got?

GUS. I don't know. What?

BEN. I've got my woodwork. I've got my model boats. Have you ever seen me idle? I'm never idle. I know how to occupy my time, to its best advantage. Then when a call comes, I'm ready.

GUS. Don't you ever get a bit fed up?

BEN. Fed up? What with?

[*Silence.*]

[BEN *reads.* GUS *feels in the pocket of his jacket, which hangs on the bed.*]

GUS. You got any cigarettes? I've run out.

[*The lavatory flushes off left.*]

There she goes.

[GUS *sits on his bed.*]

No, I mean, I say the crockery's good. It is. It's very nice. But that's about all I can say for this place. It's worse than the last one. Remember that last place we were in? Last time, where was it? At least there was a wireless there. No, honest. He doesn't seem to bother much about our comfort these days.

BEN. When are you going to stop jabbering?

GUS. You'd get rheumatism in a place like this, if you stay long.

BEN. We're not staying long. Make the tea, will you? We'll be on the job in a minute.

[GUS *picks up a small bag by his bed and brings out a packet of tea. He examines it and looks up.*]

GUS. Eh, I've been meaning to ask you.

BEN. What the hell is it now?

GUS. Why did you stop the car this morning, in the middle of that road?

BEN [*lowering the paper*]. I thought you were asleep.

GUS. I was, but I woke up when you stopped. You did stop, didn't you? [*Pause.*]

    In the middle of that road. It was still dark, don't you remember? I looked out. It was all misty. I thought perhaps you wanted to kip, but you were sitting up dead straight, like you were waiting for something.

BEN. I wasn't waiting for anything.

GUS. I must have fallen asleep again. What was all that about then? Why did you stop?

BEN [*picking up the paper*]. We were too early.

GUS. Early? [*He rises.*] What do you mean? We got the call, didn't we, saying we were to start right away. We did. We shoved out on the dot. So how could we be too early?

BEN [*quietly*]. Who took the call, me or you?

GUS. You.

BEN. We were too early.

GUS. Too early for what?

[*Pause.*]

    You mean someone had to get out before we got in?

[*He examines the bedclothes.*]

    I thought these sheets didn't look too bright. I thought they ponged a bit. I was too tired to notice when I got in this morning. Eh, that's taking a bit of a liberty, isn't it? I don't want to share my bed-sheets. I told you things were going down the drain. I mean, we've always had clean sheets laid on up till now. I've noticed it.

BEN. How do you know those sheets weren't clean?

GUS. What do you mean?

BEN. How do you know they weren't clean? You've spent the whole day in them, haven't you?

GUS. What, you mean it might be my pong? [*He sniffs sheets.*] Yes. [*He sits slowly on bed.*] It could be my pong, I suppose. It's difficult to tell. I don't really know what I pong like, that's the trouble.

BEN [*referring to the paper*]. Kaw!

GUS. Eh, Ben.

BEN. Kaw!

GUS. Ben.

BEN. What?

GUS. What town are we in? I've forgotten.

BEN. I've told you. Birmingham.

GUS. Go on!

[*He looks with interest about the room.*]

    That's in the Midlands. The second biggest city in Great Britain. I'd never have guessed.

[*He snaps his fingers.*]

    Eh, it's Friday today, isn't it? It'll be Saturday tomorrow.

BEN. What about it?

GUS [*excited*]. We could go and watch the Villa.

BEN. They're playing away.

GUS. No, are they? Caarr! What a pity.

BEN. Anyway, there's no time. We've got to get straight back.

GUS. Well, we have done in the past, haven't we? Stayed over and watched a game, haven't we? For a bit of relaxation.

BEN. Things have tightened up, mate. They've tightened up.

[GUS *chuckles to himself.*]

GUS. I saw the Villa get beat in a cup tie once. Who was it against now? White shirts. It was one-all at half-time. I'll never forget it. Their opponents won by a penalty. Talk about drama. Yes, it was a disputed penalty. Disputed. They got beat two–one, anyway, because of it. You were there yourself.

BEN. Not me.

GUS. Yes, you were there. Don't you remember that disputed penalty?

BEN. No.

GUS. He went down just inside the area. Then they said he was just acting. I didn't think the other bloke touched him myself. But the referee had the ball on the spot.

BEN. Didn't touch him! What are you talking about? He laid him out flat!

GUS. Not the Villa. The Villa don't play that sort of game.

BEN. Get out of it.

[*Pause.*]

GUS. Eh, that must have been here, in Birmingham.

BEN. What must?

GUS. The Villa. That must have been here.

BEN. They were playing away.

GUS. Because you know who the other team was? It was the Spurs. It was Tottenham Hotspur.

BEN. Well, what about it?

GUS. We've never done a job in Tottenham.

BEN. How do you know?

GUS. I'd remember Tottenham.

[BEN *turns on his bed to look at him.*]

BEN. Don't make me laugh, will you?

[BEN *turns back and reads.* GUS *yawns and speaks through his yawn.*]

GUS. When's he going to get in touch?

[*Pause.*]

Yes, I'd like to see another football match. I've always been an ardent football fan. Here, what about coming to see the Spurs tomorrow?

BEN [*tonelessly*]. They're playing away.

GUS. Who are?

BEN. The Spurs.

GUS. Then they might be playing here.

BEN. Don't be silly.

GUS. If they're playing away they might be playing here. They might be playing the Villa.

BEN [*tonelessly*]. But the Villa are playing away.

[*Pause. An envelope slides under the door, right.* GUS *sees it. He stands, looking at it.*]

Gus. Ben.
Ben. Away. They're all playing away.
Gus. Ben, look here.
Ben. What?
Gus. Look.
[Ben *turns his head and sees the envelope. He stands.*]
Ben. What's that?
Gus. I don't know.
Ben. Where did it come from?
Gus. Under the door.
Ben. Well, what is it?
Gus. I don't know.
[*They stare at it.*]
Ben. Pick it up.
Gus. What do you mean?
Ben. Pick it up!
[Gus *slowly moves towards it, bends and picks it up.*]
    What is it?
Gus. An envelope.
Ben. Is there anything on it?
Gus. No.
Ben. Is it sealed?
Gus. Yes.
Ben. Open it.
Gus. What?
Ben. Open it!
[Gus *opens it and looks inside.*]
    What's in it?
[Gus *empties twelve matches into his hand.*]
Gus. Matches.
Ben. Matches?
Gus. Yes.
Ben. Show it to me.
[Gus *passes the envelope.* Ben *examines it.*]
    Nothing on it. Not a word.
Gus. That's funny, isn't it?
Ben. It came under the door?
Gus. Must have done.
Ben. Well, go on.
Gus. Go on where?
Ben. Open the door and see if you can catch anyone outside.
Gus. Who, me?
Ben. Go on!
[Gus *stares at him, puts the matches in his pocket, goes to his bed and brings a revolver from under the pillow. He goes to the door, opens it, looks out and shuts it.*]
Gus. No one.
[*He replaces the revolver.*]
Ben. What did you see?
Gus. Nothing.

BEN. They must have been pretty quick.

[GUS *takes the matches from pocket and looks at them.*]

GUS. Well, they'll come in handy.

BEN. Yes.

GUS. Won't they?

BEN. Yes, you're always running out, aren't you?

GUS. All the time.

BEN. Well, they'll come in handy then.

GUS. Yes.

BEN. Won't they?

GUS. Yes, I could do with them. I could do with them too.

BEN. You could, eh?

GUS. Yes.

BEN. Why?

GUS. We haven't got any.

BEN. Well, you've got some now, haven't you?

GUS. I can light the kettle now.

BEN. Yes, you're always cadging matches. How many have you got there?

GUS. About a dozen.

BEN. Well, don't lose them. Red too. You don't even need a box.

[GUS *probes his ear with a match.*]

[*Slapping his hand.*] Don't waste them! Go on, go and light it.

GUS. Eh?

BEN. Go and light it.

GUS. Light what?

BEN. The kettle.

GUS. You mean the gas.

BEN. Who does?

GUS. You do.

BEN [*his eyes narrowing*]. What do you mean, I mean the gas?

GUS. Well, that's what you mean, don't you? The gas.

BEN [*powerfully*]. If I say go and light the kettle I mean go and light the kettle.

GUS. How can you light a kettle?

BEN. It's a figure of speech! Light the kettle. It's a figure of speech!

GUS. I've never heard it.

BEN. Light the kettle! It's common usage!

GUS. I think you've got it wrong.

BEN [*menacing*]. What do you mean?

GUS. They say put on the kettle.

BEN [*taut*]. Who says?

[*They stare at each other, breathing hard.*]

[*Deliberately.*] I have never in all my life heard anyone say put on the kettle.

GUS. I bet my mother used to say it.

BEN. Your mother? When did you last see your mother?

GUS. I don't know, about—

BEN. Well, what are you talking about your mother for?

[*They stare.*]

Gus, I'm not trying to be unreasonable. I'm just trying to point out something to you.

GUS. Yes, but—

BEN. Who's the senior partner here, me or you?

GUS. You.

BEN. I'm only looking after your interests, Gus. You've got to learn, mate.

GUS. Yes, but I've never heard—

BEN [*vehemently*]. Nobody says light the gas! What does the gas light?

GUS. What does the gas—?

BEN [*grabbing him with two hands by the throat, at arm's length*]. THE KETTLE, YOU FOOL!

[GUS *takes the hands from his throat.*]

GUS. All right, all right.

[*Pause.*]

BEN. Well, what are you waiting for?

GUS. I want to see if they light.

BEN. What?

GUS. The matches.

[*He takes out the flattened box and tries to strike.*]

No.

[*He throws the box under the bed.*

BEN *stares at him.*

GUS *raises his foot.*]

Shall I try it on here?

[BEN *stares.* GUS *strikes a match on his shoe. It lights.*]

Here we are.

BEN [*wearily*]. Put on the bloody kettle, for Christ's sake.

[BEN *goes to his bed, but, realizing what he has said, stops and half turns. They look at each other.* GUS *slowly exits, left.* BEN *slams his paper down on the bed and sits on it, head in hands.*]

GUS [*entering*]. It's going.

BEN. What?

GUS. The stove.

[GUS *goes to his bed and sits.*]

I wonder who it'll be tonight.

[*Silence.*]

Eh, I've been wanting to ask you something.

BEN [*putting his legs on the bed*]. Oh, for Christ's sake.

GUS. No. I was going to ask you something.

[*He rises and sits on* BEN's *bed.*]

BEN. What are you sitting on my bed for?

[GUS *sits.*]

What's the matter with you? You're always asking me questions. What's the matter with you?

GUS. Nothing.

BEN. You never used to ask me so many damn questions. What's come over you?

GUS. No, I was just wondering.

BEN. Stop wondering. You've got a job to do. Why don't you just do it and shut up?

GUS. That's what I was wondering about.

BEN. What?

GUS. The job.

BEN. What job?

GUS [*tentatively*]. I thought perhaps you might know something.

[BEN *looks at him.*]

I thought perhaps you—I mean—have you got any idea—who it's going to be tonight?

BEN. Who what's going to be?

[*They look at each other.*]

GUS [*at length*]. Who it's going to be.

[*Silence.*]

BEN. Are you feeling all right?

GUS. Sure.

BEN. Go and make the tea.

GUS. Yes, sure.

[GUS *exits, left,* BEN *looks after him. He then takes his revolver from under the pillow and checks it for ammunition.* GUS *re-enters.*]

The gas has gone out.

BEN. Well, what about it?

GUS. There's a meter.

BEN. I haven't got any money.

GUS. Nor have I.

BEN. You'll have to wait.

GUS. What for?

BEN. For Wilson.

GUS. He might not come. He might just send a message. He doesn't always come.

BEN. Well, you'll have to do without it, won't you?

GUS. Blimey.

BEN. You'll have a cup of tea afterwards. What's the matter with you?

GUS. I like to have one before.

[BEN *holds the revolver up to the light and polishes it.*]

BEN. You'd better get ready anyway.

GUS. Well, I don't know, that's a bit much, you know, for my money.

[*He picks up a packet of tea from the bed and throws it into the bag.*]

I hope he's got a shilling, anyway, if he comes. He's entitled to have. After all, it's his place, he could have seen there was enough gas for a cup of tea.

BEN. What do you mean, it's his place?

GUS. Well, isn't it?

BEN. He's probably only rented it. It doesn't have to be his place.

GUS. I know it's his place. I bet the whole house is. He's not even laying on any gas now either.

[GUS *sits on his bed.*]

It's his place all right. Look at all the other places. You go to this address, there's a key there, there's a teapot, there's never a soul in sight—[*He pauses.*] Eh, nobody ever hears a thing, have you ever thought of that? We never get any complaints, do we, too much noise or anything like that? You never see a soul, do you?—except the bloke who comes. You

ever noticed that? I wonder if the walls are sound-proof. [*He touches
the wall above his bed.*] Can't tell. All you do is wait, eh? Half the time
he doesn't even bother to put in an appearance, Wilson.
BEN. Why should he? He's a busy man.
GUS [*thoughtfully*]. I find him hard to talk to, Wilson. Do you know that,
Ben?
BEN. Scrub round it, will you?
[*Pause.*]
GUS. There are a number of things I want to ask him. But I can never
get round to it, when I see him.
[*Pause.*]
I've been thinking about the last one.
BEN. What last one?
GUS. That girl.
[BEN *grabs the paper, which he reads.*]
[*Rising, looking down at* BEN]. How many times have you read that paper?
[BEN *slams the paper down and rises.*]
BEN [*angrily*]. What do you mean?
GUS. I was just wondering how many times you'd—
BEN. What are you doing, criticizing me?
GUS. No, I was just—
BEN. You'll get a swipe round your earhole if you don't watch your step.
GUS. Now look here, Ben—
BEN. I'm not looking anywhere! [*He addresses the room.*] How many times
have I—! A bloody liberty!
GUS. I didn't mean that.
BEN. You just get on with it, mate. Get on with it, that's all.
[BEN *gets back on the bed.*]
GUS. I was just thinking about that girl, that's all.
[GUS *sits on his bed.*]
She wasn't much to look at, I know, but still. It was a mess though,
wasn't it? What a mess. Honest, I can't remember a mess like that one.
They don't seem to hold together like men, women. A looser texture,
like. Didn't she spread, eh? She didn't half spread. Kaw! But I've been
meaning to ask you.
[BEN *sits up and clenches his eyes.*]
Who clears up after we've gone? I'm curious about that. Who does the
clearing up? Maybe they don't clear up. Maybe they just leave them
there, eh? What do you think? How many jobs have we done? Blimey,
I can't count them. What if they never clear anything up after we've
gone.
BEN [*pityingly*]. You mutt. Do you think we're the only branch of this
organization? Have a bit of common. They got departments for everything.
GUS. What, cleaners and all?
BEN. You birk!
GUS. No, it was that girl made me start to think—
[*There is a loud clatter and racket in the bulge of wall between the beds, of something
descending. They grab their revolvers, jump up and face the wall. The noise
comes to a stop. Silence. They look at each other.* BEN *gestures sharply towards*

the wall. GUS *approaches the wall slowly. He bangs it with his revolver. It is hollow.* BEN *moves to the head of his bed, his revolver cocked.* GUS *puts his revolver on his bed and pats along the bottom of the centre panel. He finds a rim. He lifts the panel. Disclosed is a serving-hatch, a "dumb waiter." A wide box is held by pulleys.* GUS *peers into the box. He brings out a piece of paper.*]

BEN. What is it?

GUS. You have a look at it.

BEN. Read it.

GUS [*reading*]. Two braised steak and chips. Two sago puddings. Two teas without sugar.

BEN. Let me see that. [*He takes the paper.*]

GUS [*to himself*]. Two teas without sugar.

BEN. Mmnn.

GUS. What do you think of that?

BEN. Well—

[*The box goes up.* BEN *levels his revolver.*]

GUS. Give us a chance! They're in a hurry, aren't they?

[BEN *re-reads the note.* GUS *looks over his shoulder.*]

That's a bit—that's a bit funny, isn't it?

BEN [*quickly*]. No. It's not funny. It probably used to be a café here, that's all. Upstairs. These places change hands very quickly.

GUS. A café?

BEN. Yes.

GUS. What, you mean this was the kitchen, down here?

BEN. Yes, they change hands overnight, these places. Go into liquidation. The people who run it, you know, they don't find it a going concern, they move out.

GUS. You mean the people who ran this place didn't find it a going concern and moved out?

BEN. Sure.

GUS. WELL, WHO'S GOT IT NOW?

[*Silence.*]

BEN. What do you mean, who's got it now?

GUS. Who's got it now? If they moved out, who moved in?

BEN. Well, that all depends—

[*The box descends with a clatter and bang.* BEN *levels his revolver.* GUS *goes to the box and brings out a piece of paper.*]

GUS [*reading*]. Soup of the day. Liver and onions. Jam tart.

[*A pause.* GUS *looks at* BEN. BEN *takes the note and reads it. He walks slowly to the hatch.* GUS *follows.* BEN *looks into the hatch but not up it.* GUS *puts his hand on* BEN's *shoulder.* BEN *throws if off.* GUS *puts his finger to his mouth. He leans on the hatch and swiftly looks up it.* BEN *flings him away in alarm.* BEN *looks at the note. He throws his revolver on the bed and speaks with decision.*]

BEN. We'd better send something up.

GUS. Eh?

BEN. We'd better send something up.

GUS. Oh! Yes. Yes. Maybe you're right.

[*They are both relieved at the decision.*]

BEN [*purposefully*]. Quick! What have you got in that bag?

GUS. Not much.

[GUS *goes to the hatch and shouts up it.*]

Wait a minute!

BEN. Don't do that!

[GUS *examines the contents of the bag and brings them out, one by one.*]

GUS. Biscuits. A bar of chocolate. Half a pint of milk.

BEN. That all?

GUS. Packet of tea.

BEN. Good.

GUS. We can't send the tea. That's all the tea we've got.

BEN. Well, there's no gas. You can't do anything with it, can you?

GUS. Maybe they can send us down a bob.

BEN. What else is there?

GUS [*reaching into bag*]. One Eccles cake.

BEN. One Eccles cake?

GUS. Yes.

BEN. You never told me you had an Eccles cake.

GUS. Didn't I?

BEN. Why only one? Didn't you bring one for me?

GUS. I didn't think you'd be keen.

BEN. Well, you can't send up one Eccles cake, anyway.

GUS. Why not?

BEN. Fetch one of those plates.

GUS. All right.

[GUS *goes towards the door, left, and stops.*]

Do you mean I can keep the Eccles cake then?

BEN. Keep it?

GUS. Well, they don't know we've got it, do they?

BEN. That's not the point.

GUS. Can't I keep it?

BEN. No, you can't. Get the plate.

[GUS *exits, left.* BEN *looks in the bag. He brings out a packet of crisps. Enter*
GUS *with a plate.*]

[*Accusingly, holding up the crisps*] Where did these come from?

GUS. What?

BEN. Where did these crisps come from?

GUS. Where did you find them?

BEN [*hitting him on the shoulder*]. You're playing a dirty game, my lad!

GUS. I only eat those with beer!

BEN. Well, where were you going to get the beer?

GUS. I was saving them till I did.

BEN. I'll remember this. Put everything on the plate.

[*They pile everything on to the plate. The box goes up without the plate.*]

Wait a minute!

[*They stand.*]

GUS. It's gone up.

BEN. It's all your stupid fault, playing about!

GUS. What do we do now?

BEN. We'll have to wait till it comes down.

[BEN *puts the plate on the bed, puts on his shoulder holster, and starts to put on his tie.*]

    You'd better get ready.

[GUS *goes to his bed, puts on his tie, and starts to fix his holster.*]

GUS. Hey, Ben.

BEN. What?

GUS. What's going on here?

[*Pause.*]

BEN. What do you mean?

GUS. How can this be a café?

BEN. It used to be a café.

GUS. Have you seen the gas stove?

BEN. What about it?

GUS. It's only got three rings.

BEN. So what?

GUS. Well, you couldn't cook much on three rings, not for a busy place like this.

BEN [*irritably*]. That's why the service is slow!

[BEN *puts on his waistcoat.*]

GUS. Yes, but what happens when we're not here? What do they do then? All these menus coming down and nothing going up. It might have been going on like this for years.

[BEN *brushes his jacket.*]

    What happens when we go?

[BEN *puts on his jacket.*]

    They can't do much business.

[*The box descends. They turn about.* GUS *goes to the hatch and brings out a note.*]

GUS [*reading*]. Macaroni Pastitsio. Ormitha Macarounada.

BEN. What was that?

GUS. Macaroni Pastitsio. Ormitha Macarounada.

BEN. Greek dishes.

GUS. No.

BEN. That's right.

GUS. That's pretty high class.

BEN. Quick before it goes up.

[GUS *puts the plate in the box.*]

GUS [*calling up the hatch*]. Three McVitie and Price! One Lyons Red Label! One Smith's Crisps! One Eccles cake! One Fruit and Nut!

BEN. Cadbury's.

GUS [*up the hatch*]. Cadbury's!

BEN [*handing the milk*]. One bottle of milk.

GUS [*up the hatch*]. One bottle of milk! Half a pint! [*He looks at the label.*] Express Dairy! [*He puts the bottle in the box.*]

[*The box goes up.*]

    Just did it.

BEN. You shouldn't shout like that.

GUS. Why not?

BEN. It isn't done.

[BEN *goes to his bed.*]

Well, that should be all right, anyway, for the time being.

GUS. You think so, eh?

BEN. Get dressed, will you? It'll be any minute now.

[GUS *puts on his waistcoat.* BEN *lies down and looks up at the ceiling.*]

GUS. This is some place. No tea and no biscuits.

BEN. Eating makes you lazy, mate. You're getting lazy, you know that? You don't want to get slack on your job.

GUS. Who me?

BEN. Slack, mate, slack.

GUS. Who me? Slack?

BEN. Have you checked your gun? You haven't even checked your gun. It looks disgraceful, anyway. Why don't you ever polish it?

[GUS *rubs his revolver on the sheet.* BEN *takes out a pocket mirror and straightens his tie.*]

GUS. I wonder where the cook is. They must have had a few, to cope with that. Maybe they had a few more gas stoves. Eh! Maybe there's another kitchen along the passage.

BEN. Of course there is! Do you know what it takes to make an Ormitha Macarounada?

GUS. No, what?

BEN. An Ormitha—! Buck your ideas up, will you?

GUS. Takes a few cooks, eh?

[GUS *puts his revolver in its holster.*]

The sooner we're out of this place the better.

[*He puts on his jacket.*]

Why doesn't he get in touch? I feel like I've been here years. [*He takes his revolver out of its holster to check the ammunition.*] We've never let him down though, have we? We've never let him down. I was thinking only the other day, Ben. We're reliable, aren't we?

[*He puts his revolver back in its holster.*]

Still, I'll be glad when it's over tonight.

[*He brushes his jacket.*]

I hope the bloke's not going to get excited tonight, or anything. I'm feeling a bit off. I've got a splitting headache.

[*Silence.*

The box descends. BEN *jumps up.*

GUS *collects the note.*]

[*Reading.*] One Bamboo Shoots, Water Chestnuts and Chicken. One Char Siu and Beansprouts.

BEN. Beansprouts?

GUS. Yes.

BEN. Blimey.

GUS. I wouldn't know where to begin.

[*He looks back at the box. The packet of tea is inside it. He picks it up.*]

They've sent back the tea.

BEN [*anxious*]. What'd they do that for?

GUS. Maybe it isn't tea-time.

[*The box goes up. Silence.*]

BEN [*throwing the tea on the bed, and speaking urgently*]. Look here. We'd better tell them.

GUS. Tell them what?

BEN. That we can't do it, we haven't got it.

GUS. All right then.

BEN. Lend us your pencil. We'll write a note.

[GUS, *turning for a pencil, suddenly discovers the speaking-tube, which hangs on the right wall of the hatch facing his bed.*]

GUS. What's this?

BEN. What?

GUS. This.

BEN [*examining it*]. This? It's a speaking-tube.

GUS. How long has that been there?

BEN. Just the job. We should have used it before, instead of shouting up there.

GUS. Funny I never noticed it before.

BEN. Well, come on.

GUS. What do you do?

BEN. See that? That's a whistle.

GUS. What, this?

BEN. Yes, take it out. Pull it out.

[GUS *does so.*]

That's it.

GUS. What do we do now?

BEN. Blow into it.

GUS. Blow?

BEN. It whistles up there if you blow. Then they know you want to speak. Blow.

[GUS *blows. Silence.*]

GUS [*tube at mouth*]. I can't hear a thing.

BEN. Now you speak! Speak into it!

[GUS *looks at* BEN, *then speaks into the tube.*]

GUS. The larder's bare!

BEN. Give me that!

[*He grabs the tube and puts it to his mouth.*]

[*Speaking with great deference.*] Good evening. I'm sorry to—bother you, but we just thought we'd better let you know that we haven't got anything left. We sent up all we had. There's no more food down here.

[*He brings the tube slowly to his ear.*]

What?

[*To mouth.*]

What?

[*To ear. He listens. To mouth.*]

No, all we had we sent up.

[*To ear. He listens. To mouth.*]

Oh, I'm very sorry to hear that.

[*To ear. He listens. To* GUS.]

The Eccles cake was stale.

[*He listens. To* GUS.]

The chocolate was melted.

[*He listens. To* GUS.]

The milk was sour.

Gus. What about the crisps?

Ben [*listening*]. The biscuits were mouldy.

[*He glares at* Gus. *Tube to mouth.*]

Well, we're very sorry about that.

[*Tube to ear.*]

What?

[*To mouth.*]

What?

[*To ear.*]

Yes, yes.

[*To mouth.*]

Yes certainly. Certainly. Right away.

[*To ear. The voice has ceased. He hangs up the tube.*]

[*Excitedly*]. Did you hear that?

Gus. What?

Ben. You know what he said? Light the kettle! Not put on the kettle! Not light the gas! But light the kettle!

Gus. How can we light the kettle?

Ben. What do you mean?

Gus. There's no gas.

Ben [*clapping hand to head*]. Now what do we do?

Gus. What did he want us to light the kettle for?

Ben. For tea. He wanted a cup of tea.

Gus. *He* wanted a cup of tea! What about me? I've been wanting a cup of tea all night!

Ben [*despairingly*]. What do we do now?

Gus. What are we supposed to drink?

[Ben *sits on his bed, staring.*]

What about us?

[Ben *sits.*]

I'm thirsty too. I'm starving. And he wants a cup of tea. That beats the band, that does.

[Ben *lets his head sink on to his chest.*]

I could do with a bit of sustenance myself. What about you? You look as if you could do with something too.

[Gus *sits on his bed.*]

We send him up all we've got and he's not satisfied. No, honest, it's enough to make the cat laugh. Why did you send him up all that stuff? [*Thoughtfully.*] Why did I send it up?

[*Pause.*]

Who knows what he's got upstairs? He's probably got a salad bowl. They must have something up there. They won't get much from down here. You notice they didn't ask for any salads? They've probably got a salad bowl up there. Cold meat, radishes, cucumbers. Watercress. Roll mops.

[*Pause.*]

Hardboiled eggs.

[*Pause.*]

The lot. They've probably got a crate of beer too. Probably eating my crisps with a pint of beer now. Didn't have anything to say about those crisps, did he? They do all right, don't worry about that. You don't think they're just going to sit there and wait for stuff to come up from down here, do you? That'll get them nowhere.

[*Pause.*]

They do all right.

[*Pause.*]

And he wants a cup of tea.

[*Pause.*]

That's past a joke, in my opinion.

[*He looks over at* BEN, *rises, and goes to him.*]

What's the matter with you? You don't look too bright. I feel like an Alka-Seltzer myself.

[BEN *sits up.*]

BEN [*in a low voice*]. Time's getting on.

GUS. I know. I don't like doing a job on an empty stomach.

BEN [*wearily*]. Be quiet a minute. Let me give you your instructions.

GUS. What for? We always do it the same way, don't we?

BEN. Let me give you your instructions.

[GUS *sighs and sits next to Ben on the bed. The instructions are stated and repeated automatically.*]

When we get the call, you go over and stand behind the door.

GUS. Stand behind the door.

BEN. If there's a knock on the door you don't answer it.

GUS. If there's a knock on the door I don't answer it.

BEN. But there won't be a knock on the door.

GUS. So I won't answer it.

BEN. When the bloke comes in—

GUS. When the bloke comes in—

BEN. Shut the door behind him.

GUS. Shut the door behind him.

BEN. Without divulging your presence.

GUS. Without divulging my presence.

BEN. He'll see me and come towards me.

GUS. He'll see you and come towards you.

BEN. He won't see you.

GUS [*absently*]. Eh?

BEN. He won't see you.

GUS. He won't see me.

BEN. But he'll see me.

GUS. He'll see you.

BEN. He won't know you're there.

GUS. He won't know you're there.

BEN. He won't know *you're* there.

GUS. He won't know I'm there.

BEN. I take out my gun.

GUS. You take out your gun.

BEN. He stops in his tracks.

GUS. He stops in his tracks.

BEN. If he turns round—

GUS. If he turns round—

BEN. You're there.

GUS. I'm here.

[BEN *frowns and presses his forehead.*]

   You've missed something out.

BEN. I know. What?

GUS. I haven't taken my gun out, according to you.

BEN. You take your gun out—

GUS. After I've closed the door.

BEN. After you've closed the door.

GUS. You've never missed that out before, you know that?

BEN. When he sees you behind him—

GUS. Me behind him—

BEN. And me in front of him—

GUS. And you in front of him—

BEN. He'll feel uncertain—

GUS. Uneasy.

BEN. He won't know what to do.

GUS. So what will he do?

BEN. He'll look at me and he'll look at you.

GUS. We won't say a word.

BEN. We'll look at him.

GUS. He won't say a word.

BEN. He'll look at us.

GUS. And we'll look at him.

BEN. Nobody says a word.

[*Pause.*]

GUS. What do we do if it's a girl?

BEN. We do the same.

GUS. Exactly the same?

BEN. Exactly.

[*Pause.*]

GUS. We don't do anything different?

BEN. We do exactly the same.

GUS. Oh.

[GUS *rises, and shivers.*]

   Excuse me.

[*He exits through the door on the left.* BEN *remains sitting on the bed, still. The
   lavatory chain is pulled once off left, but the lavatory does not flush. Silence.*
GUS *re-enters and stops inside the door, deep in thought. He looks at* BEN, *then
   walks slowly across to his own bed. He is troubled. He stands, thinking. He
   turns and looks at* BEN. *He moves a few paces towards him.*]
   [*Slowly in a low, tense voice.*] Why did he send us matches if he knew
   there was no gas?

[*Silence.*]

[BEN *stares in front of him.* GUS *crosses to the left side of* BEN, *to the foot of
   his bed, to get to his other ear.*]

   Ben. Why did he send us matches if he knew there was no gas?

[BEN *looks up.*]

   Why did he do that?

BEN. Who?

Gus. Who sent us those matches?

Ben. What are you talking about?

[Gus *stares down at him.*]

Gus [*thickly*]. Who is it upstairs?

Ben [*nervously*]. What's one thing to do with another?

Gus. Who is it, though?

Ben. What's one thing to do with another?

[Ben *fumbles for his paper on the bed.*]

Gus. I asked you a question.

Ben. Enough!

Gus [*with growing agitation*]. I asked you before. Who moved in? I asked you. You said the people who had it before moved out. Well, who moved in?

Ben [*hunched*]. Shut up.

Gus. I told you, didn't I?

Ben [*standing*]. Shut up!

Gus [*feverishly*]. I told you before who owned this place, didn't I? I told you.

[Ben *hits him viciously on the shoulder.*]

I told you who ran this place, didn't I?

[Ben *hits him viciously on the shoulder.*]

[*Violently.*] Well, what's he playing all these games for? That's what I want to know. What's he doing it for?

Ben. What games?

Gus [*passionately, advancing*]. What's he doing it for? We've been through our tests, haven't we? We got right through our tests, years ago, didn't we? We took them together, don't you remember, didn't we? We've proved ourselves before now, haven't we? We've always done our job. What's he doing all this for? What's the idea? What's he playing these games for?

[*The box in the shaft comes down behind them. The noise is this time accompanied by a shrill whistle, as it falls.* Gus *rushes to the hatch and seizes the note.*]

[*Reading.*] Scampi!

[*He crumples the note, picks up the tube, takes out the whistle, blows and speaks.*]

WE'VE GOT NOTHING LEFT! NOTHING! DO YOU UNDERSTAND?

[Ben *seizes the tube and flings* Gus *away. He follows* Gus *and slaps him hard, back-handed, across the chest.*]

Ben. Stop it! You maniac!

Gus. But you heard!

Ben [*savagely*]. That's enough! I'm warning you!

[*Silence.*

Ben *hangs the tube. He goes to his bed and lies down. He picks up his paper and reads.*

Silence.

The box goes up.

They turn quickly, their eyes meet. Ben *turns to his paper.*

Slowly Gus *goes back to his bed, and sits.*

Silence.

The hatch falls back into place.

They turn quickly, their eyes meet. Ben *turns back to his paper.*

Silence.
BEN *throws his paper down.*]
BEN. Kaw!
[*He picks up the paper and looks at it.*]
    Listen to this!
[*Pause.*]
    What about that, eh?
[*Pause.*]
    Kaw!
[*Pause.*]
    Have you ever heard such a thing?
GUS [*dully*]. Go on!
BEN. It's true.
GUS. Get away.
BEN. It's down here in black and white.
GUS [*very low*]. Is that a fact?
BEN. Can you imagine it.
GUS. It's unbelievable.
BEN. It's enough to make you want to puke, isn't it?
GUS [*almost inaudible*]. Incredible.
[BEN *shakes his head. He puts the paper down and rises. He fixes the revolver in his holster.*
GUS *stands up. He goes towards the door on the left.*]
BEN. Where are you going?
GUS. I'm going to have a glass of water.
[*He exits.* BEN *brushes dust off his clothes and shoes. The whistle in the speaking-tube blows. He goes to it, takes the whistle out and puts the tube to his ear. He listens. He puts it to his mouth.*]
BEN. Yes.
[*To ear. He listens. To mouth.*]
    Straight away. Right.
[*To ear. He listens. To mouth.*]
    Sure we're ready.
[*To ear. He listens. To mouth.*]
    Understood. Repeat. He has arrived and will be coming in straight away.
    The normal method to be employed. Understood.
[*To ear. He listens. To mouth.*]
    Sure we're ready.
[*To ear. He listens. To mouth.*]
    Right.
[*He hangs the tube up.*]
    Gus!
[*He takes out a comb and combs his hair, adjusts his jacket to diminish the bulge of the revolver. The lavatory flushes off left.* BEN *goes quickly to the door, left.*]
    Gus!
The door right opens sharply. BEN *turns, his revolver levelled at the door.*
    GUS *stumbles in.*
    He is stripped of his jacket, waistcoat, tie, holster and revolver.

He stops, body stooping, his arms at his sides.
He raises his head and looks at BEN.
A long silence.
They stare at each other.

CURTAIN

(1957)

PART FIVE

The Editing Process

The following material provides a concise Handbook for Correcting Errors *and a handy* Glossary of Rhetorical and Literary Terms.

A Handbook for Correcting Errors

Once you have become a good editor and proofreader, you will find editing the easiest part of the writing process. But just because locating and correcting errors is less taxing than composing the paper, do not consider it unimportant. Correcting errors is crucial. Errors will lower your grades in college and undermine the confidence of your readers in any writing that you do.

Proofreading

As we suggested in Chapter 3 (pp. 39–41), you will need to proofread at least twice, concentrating on catching different types of errors each time. Here are some general rules to follow:

1. Read sentence by sentence from the bottom of the page to the top (to keep your attention focused on finding errors).
2. Read again, looking for any particular errors that you know you tend to make: fragments, comma splices, typical misspellings etc.
3. Go over each page using an index card with a small rectangle cut in the middle. This will force you to look at only a few words at a time to catch typographical errors and misspellings.
4. When in doubt about either spelling or meaning, use your dictionary.
5. If the piece of writing is of cardinal importance, find a literate friend to read it over for mistakes after you have completed all of the above.

Correcting Sentence Boundary Errors

Probably the most serious errors you need to check for are those that involve faulty sentence punctuation: fragments, comma splices, and run-on sentences. These errors reflect uncertainty or carelessness about the acceptable boundaries for written sentences.

PHRASES AND CLAUSES

To punctuate correctly, you need to know the difference between phrases and clauses. The following charts will help you remember.

CHART A. **Examples of Phrases and Clauses**

PHRASES

to the lighthouse
having been converted
a still, eerie, deserted beach

Phrases do not have subject and verb combinations.

CLAUSES

Independent:
Clarissa finished.
She completed her essay.
John gave her the assignment.

Dependent (incomplete sentences):
after Clarissa finished
which completed the essay
because John gave her the assignment

All clauses have subject and verb combinations.

CHART B. **Kinds of Phrases**

PHRASE: a string of related words that does not contain a subject and verb combination

1. *Noun phrase:* a noun plus modifiers
      an old yellowed photograph

2. *Prepositional phrase:* a preposition plus its object and modifiers of the object
      against the dusty curtains

3. *Verbal phrase:* a verbal (word derived from a verb) plus modifiers and objects or completers
   A. *Infinitive* (verb with *to* before it)
         to leave her father
   B. *Gerund* (-*ing* word used as a noun)
         leaving her father
   C. *Participle* (-*ing* or -*ed* word used as an adjective)
         leaning against the curtains
         frightened by her father

4. *Verb phrase:* an action or being verb plus its auxiliary verbs
      have been
      might be leaving
      will go

CHART C. **Kinds of Clauses**

CLAUSE: a group of related words containing a subject and verb combination

1. *Independent (main) clause:*
> subject + verb: Her hands trembled.
> subject + verb + completer: Her hands gripped the railing.

2. *Dependent (subordinate) clause:* incomplete sentence that depends on an independent clause to complete its meaning

> A. *Noun clause:* used as a noun
>> She could not believe *what Frank told her.*
>>> (direct object)
>> *Whoever called her* did not identify himself.
>> (subject)

> B. *Adjective clause:* modifies a noun or pronoun
>> The promise *that Eveline made to her mother* weighed heavily on her conscience.
>> She loved her younger brother, *who had died some years ago.*

An adjective clause is introduced by a relative pronoun: *who, which, that, whose, whom.*

> C. *Adverb clause:* modifies a verb, adjective, or adverb
>> *After Eveline wrote the letters,* she held them in her lap.
>> She could not leave with Frank *because she was afraid.*

An adverb clause is introduced by a subordinating conjunction: *after, although, as, as if, because, before, if, only, since, so as, as far as, so that, than, though, till, unless, until, when, whenever, while, whereas.*

FRAGMENTS

As the term suggests, a sentence *fragment* is an incomplete group of words punctuated as a complete sentence. Fragments occur frequently in speech and are often used by professional writers for emphasis and convenience. But a fragmentary sentence may also represent a fragmentary idea that would be more effective if it were completed or connected to another idea.

The following are examples of typical sentence fragments that need to be revised:

1. **Phrases that can be joined to the preceding sentence:**

(*Questionable fragment*)   Eveline gripped the iron railing and stared ahead. With no glimmer of "love or recognition in her eyes." [The fragment is a prepositional phrase without a subject or verb; see Chart A]

(*Revision*)   Eveline gripped the iron railing and stared ahead with no glimmer of "love or recognition" in her eyes.

2. **Explanatory phrases that begin with such expressions as *for example*, *that is*, and *such as* and belong in the sentence with the material they are explaining:**

(*Questionable fragment*)   As Eveline looked around the room, she noticed familiar objects that she might never see again. For instance, the yellowing photograph of the priest and the broken harmonium.

(*Revision*)   As Eveline looked around the room, she noticed familiar objects that she might never see again—for instance, the yellowing photograph of the priest and the broken harmonium.

3. **Dependent (or subordinate) clauses that can be added to another sentence or rewritten as complete sentences:**

(*Questionable fragment*)   Eveline decided to stay with her family. Even though she felt she could forget her worries and be happy forever with Frank. [adverb clause, beginning with *even though*; see Chart C]

(*Revision*)   Even though she felt she could forget her worries and be happy forever with Frank, Eveline decided to stay with her family.

(*Questionable fragment*)   Frank had told Eveline numerous stories about his adventures on the high seas. Many of which seemed suspiciously vague and predictably romantic. [adjective clause, indicated by *which*; see Chart C]

(*Revision*)   Frank had told Eveline numerous stories about his adventures on the high seas. Many of his tales seemed suspiciously vague and predictably romantic.

Note: In English we typically begin sentences with adverbial clauses. But if you often write fragments, you may not be attaching those dependent clauses to independent clauses.

Remember that a group of words beginning with a subordinating word like *although, if, because, since, unless, when, which,* or *who* will be a fragment unless connected to an independent clause. If you typically have problems with fragments, put a bookmark at page 962 and consult Chart B and Chart C.

4. **Verbal phrases that do not contain a complete verb:**

(*Questionable fragment*)   Eveline sat by the window and thought about her home and family. Leaning her head against the dusty curtains. [The second group of words is a participle phrase; *leaning* is not a complete verb. See Chart B.]

(*Revision*)   Leaning her head against the dusty curtains, Eveline sat by the window and thought about her home and family.

Note: Words ending in *-ing* or *-ed* sound like verbs, but often they are *verbals* (verb forms used as adjectives or nouns) and do not function as full verbs for a sentence.

5. **Semicolon fragments:**

(*Questionable fragment*)   Eveline was fearful of her father and helplessly trapped; feeling immobile, like the dust on the curtains. [The words which follow the semicolon do not constitute a full sentence. See Chart B.]

(*Revision*)   Eveline was fearful of her father and helplessly trapped; she felt immobile, like the dust on the curtains.

Note: A semicolon is often used as a weak period to separate independent clauses that are closely related. Be sure you have written an independent clause before and after a semicolon (unless the semicolon separates items in a series which themselves contain commas).

COMMA SPLICES

A comma splice (or comma fault or comma blunder) occurs when a writer places two independent clauses together with only a comma between them. Because the result appears to be a single sentence, it can momentarily confuse the reader:

Frank has become the Prince Charming in Eveline's fairy tale world, the other man in her life is much more real. [comma splice]

Because the two clauses joined here are independent (i.e., each could stand alone as a sentence), the two clauses should be linked by a stronger mark than a comma. Here are some options:

A. **Punctuate both clauses as complete sentences:**

> Frank has become the Prince Charming in Eveline's fairy tale world. The other man in her life is much more real.

B. **Use a semicolon:**

> Frank has become the Prince Charming in Eveline's fairy tale world; the other man in her life is much more real.

C. **Keep the comma and add a coordinating conjunction** (*and, but, or, not, for, yet, so*)

> Frank has become the Prince Charming in Eveline's fairy tale world, but the other man in her life is much more real.

D. **Subordinate one of the independent clauses:**

> Although Frank has become the Prince Charming in Eveline's fairy tale world, the other man in her life is much more real.

To avoid comma splices, follow this general advice:

1. Be Careful with Commas.
   If you understand sentence structure, your writing probably won't contain many comma splices. But if you are not paying attention to sentence boundaries, you may be joining independent clauses without realizing it and separating them with commas.

2. Check Your Conjunctive Adverbs.
   Transitional expressions like *indeed, however, thus, therefore, nevertheless, furthermore,* and *consequently* may lead you to use just a comma when connecting two independent clauses with these words. Do not do it. These words are called *conjunctive adverbs;* they do not serve to join clauses the way coordinating conjunctions do. Their main force is adverbial. Thus, you still need a semicolon (or a period and a capital letter) when you use these connectives:

> (*Comma splice*)   Eveline's father is violent and overbearing, however, he is the man who really loves her.

> (*Correct*)   Eveline's father is violent and overbearing; however, he is the man who really loves her.

3. Use Commas with Short Clauses.
   Although we advise you not to use commas to join independent clauses, many professional writers intentionally violate this advice if the clauses are short, if they are parallel in structure, if they are antithetical, or if there is no chance of misunderstanding:

He's not brave, he's crazy.
She felt one way, she acted another.
It was sunny, it was crisp, it was a perfect day.

EXERCISE

If any of the following sentences contain commas splices, correct these flawed sentences twice: once by adding a suitable coordinating conjunction (*and, but, or, for, nor, yet, so*) and once by changing the comma to a semicolon.

1. Clyde is constantly revising his essays, thus he turns in fine finished papers.
2. Your analysis is flawed in several ways, because you need to rewrite it, let's discuss your problems.
3. You have written an excellent analysis, Bertha, you should read it to the class.
4. Monroe complains that he never understands the stories, yet he only reads them through once, hastily.
5. Plot is the main element in this story, as far as one can tell, characterization is scarcely important at all.

RUN-ON SENTENCES

A run-on sentence (also called a fused sentence) is similar to a comma splice, except that there is no punctuation at all to separate the independent clauses:

> Eveline realizes that she leads a dull and unhappy home life she is also safely and securely encircled in her own little world.

Few writers ignore sentence boundaries so completely. Most people at least put a comma in (and thus produce a comma splice). When you edit, make sure that you have not run any sentences together. Run-ons will confuse and annoy your readers.

Clearing up Confused Sentences

Sometimes you can get careless and lose track of the way a sentence is developing. The result is called a confused sentence or a mixed construction. Repunctuating will not correct this kind of error. You will have to rewrite the garbled passage into readable prose:

> (*Confused*) One reason to conclude Eveline's hopeless situation would have to be related to her indecisive and timid lifestyle.
> (*Revised*) One reason for Eveline's hopeless situation is her indecisive and timid personality.

Sentences can go astray in many ways. The only sure defense against sentence confusion is to understand the basic principles of sentence structure. Checking your writing carefully and reading your sentences aloud will also help.

Solving Faulty Predication Problems

Another kind of sentence confusion occurs when you carelessly complete a linking verb (*is, am, are, was, were, will be, has been, becomes, appears,* etc.) with a predicate noun or predicate adjective that does not match the subject of the sentence. This error is called *faulty predication.* In this kind of sentence the linking verb acts as an equal sign and sets up a verbal equation: the subject = the predicate noun (or predicate adjective).

> (*Logical*)   Eveline is a passive, sheltered young woman.
> (*Logical*)   At least at home Eveline would be secure.

In the first sentence, Eveline = young woman; and in the second, "secure" (predicate adjective) logically modifies "Eveline" (the subject). Here are some faulty predications followed by logical revisions:

> (*Faulty*)   The importance of religion in the story is important to Eveline's decision.
> (*Logical*)   Religion is important to Eveline's decision.
>
> (*Faulty*)   They walk with their shoulders back, and the expression on their faces is usually pride.
> (*Logical*)   They walk with their shoulders back, and the expression on their faces is usually a look of pride. (expression = look)
>
> (*Faulty*)   The setting for the advertisement is a man and a woman walking through a jungle in Safari suits.
> (*Logical*)   The setting for the advertisement includes a man and a woman walking through the jungle in Safari suits.

Note: The most common linking verb is *be* in its various forms: *is, are, was, were, has been, will be, might be.* Other linking verbs include *seem* and *appear* and, in some instances, *feel, grow, act, look, smell, taste,* and *sound.*

EXERCISE

Revise the following sentences to eliminate faulty predications and confused constructions.

1. The changes of tone are used in a way where the characters singing the jingle dance.
2. Lyrics to country music are broken hearts and forgotten dreams.
3. By using a psychological approach to the modern novel can provide significant insights.

4. The fact that Chicano poets reflect their Aztec heritage describes the culture they depict in their works.

5. The reason Wharton's fiction is becoming more respected is a result of the woman's movement.

Fixing Subject-Verb Agreement Errors

1. **Verbs agree with their subjects in number** (that is, being either singular or plural).

> Victorian *novels are* usually long.
> A Victorian *novel is* often moral.
> A Victorian *novel* and a post-modernist *novel are* radically different.

2. **Be sure to find the grammatical subject.**

> A. *Sometimes a clause or phrase comes between the subject and verb to confuse you, like this:*

> (*Wrong*)   The good movies that come out in the fall makes up for the summer's trash.

The clause—*that come out in the fall*—intervenes between the subject *movies* and the verb, which should be *make* (plural to agree with *movies*):

> (*Right*)   The good movies that come out in the fall make up for the summer's trash.

Note: The plural form of the verb drops the *s*, unlike nouns, which add an *s* to form the plural (one villain lies, two villains lie).

> B. *Sometimes—especially in questions—the subject will come after the verb, like this:*

> (*Right*)   Why *are Romeo* and *Juliet* so impetuous?
> (*Right*)   From boredom, restlessness, and ignorance *comes* an otherwise senseless *crime*.

> C. *If you begin a sentence with* here, there, what, where, when, *or* why, *these words can never be subjects. Find the real subject (or subjects) and make the verb agree.*

> (*Wrong*)   Where is the climax and the denouement?
> (*Wrong*)   There is suspense and tension in DuMaurier's novel.

The subjects in both of those examples are compound, requiring a plural verb:

> (*Right*)   Where *are* the *climax* and the *denouement*?
> (*Right*)   There *are suspense* and *tension* in DuMaurier's novel.

3. **Compound singular subjects connected by correlative conjunctions** (either. . .or, not only. . .but also, neither. . .nor, not. . .but, etc.) **require a singular verb.**

> (*Right*)   Either *Antigone* or *Creon* is going to prevail.
> (*Right*)   Not a *beau* but a *husband* is what Amanda wants for Laura.

If both subjects are plural, make the verb plural:

> (*Right*)   Either *poems* or *stories are* fine with me.

If one subject is singular and the other one plural, make the verb agree with the subject closer to it:

> (*Right*)   Either *poems* or a *story* is a good choice.
> (*Right*)   Either a *story* or some *poems are* fine.

4. **Some prepositions sound like conjunctions**—with, like, along with, as well as, no less than, including, besides—**and may appear to connect compound subjects, but they do not; the subject, if singular, remains singular.**

> (*Right*)   My *career*, as well as my reputation, *is* lost.
> (*Right*)   *Alcohol*, together with my passion for filmy underthings, *is* responsible.
> (*Right*)   My *mother*, like my aunt Chloe, my uncle Zeke, and my cousin Zelda, *is* not speaking to me.

5. **Collective nouns** (like *jury, family, company, staff, group, committee*) **take either singular or plural verbs, depending upon your meaning.**

If the group is acting in unison, use the singular:

> (*Right*)   The *jury has* agreed upon a verdict.

If the group is behaving like separate individuals, use the plural:

> (*Right*)   The *jury* still *are* not in agreement.

Or avoid the problem this way:

> (*Right*)   The *members* of the jury still *are* not in agreement.

Fixing Pronoun Errors

1. **Avoid ambiguous or unclear pronoun reference.**

> (*Ambiguous*)   Marvin gave Tom *his* pen back, but *he* swore it wasn't *his*.
> (*Clear*)   Marvin gave Tom's pen back, but Tom swore it wasn't his.

Sometimes it is necessary to replace an inexact pronoun with a noun:

(*Unclear*)   She did not know how to make quiche until I wrote *it* out for her.
(*Clear*)   She did not know how to make quiche until I wrote out *the recipe* for her.

2. **Use *this* and *which* with care.**
These pronouns often refer to whole ideas or situations, and the reference is sometimes not clear:

(*Unclear*)   Renaldo runs three miles a day and works out with weights twice a week. He says *this* controls his high blood pressure and prevents heart attacks.
(*Clear*)   Renaldo runs three miles a day and works out with weights twice a week. He says *this exercise program* controls his high blood pressure and prevents heart attacks.

Avoid using *this* without a noun following it. Get in the habit of writing *this idea, this point,* or *this remark,* instead of having a pronoun that means nothing in particular.

The pronoun *which* can cause similar problems:

(*Unclear*)   Craig told me that he didn't like the movie, *which* upset me.
(*Clear*)   Craig told me that he didn't like the movie. His opinion upset me.
(*Clear*)   Craig told me that he didn't like the movie. The film upset me too.

3. **Be sure your pronouns agree with their antecedents in number (singular or plural).**
Agreement errors occur when the pronoun is separated from its antecedent (the preceding noun which the pronoun replaces):

(*Incorrect*)   Although the average *American* believes in the ideal of justice for all, *they* do not always practice it.
(*Correct*)   Although most *Americans* believe in the ideal of justice for all, *they* do not always practice it.

4. **Take care with indefinite pronouns.**
Many indefinite pronouns sound plural but are considered grammatically singular: *anybody, anyone, everyone, everybody, someone, none, no one, neither, either.* If you follow this grammatical guideline in all cases, you may produce an illogical sentence:

Everybody applauded my speech, and I was glad *he* did.

It is now acceptable to use plural pronouns when referring to indefinite words:

Everyone should have *their* own pinking shears.
None of the students would admit *they* were cheating.

Some readers still question this practice and will insist that you refer to *everyone* and *none* with singular pronouns. This dilemma can sometimes be avoided by recasting your sentence or by writing in the plural:

> (*Recast*)   None of the students would admit to cheating.

> (*Questionable*)   *Each* of the contestants must supply *their* own water skis.
> (*No question*)   *All contestants* must supply *their* own water skis.

If you prefer to write in the singular, you may have to revise sentences with indefinite pronouns or stick to the old rule of referring to such words as *anyone, somebody, everyone, none,* and *neither* with singular pronouns:

> (*Singular agreement*)   *Neither* of the drivers escaped the crash with *his* life.

That sentence is all right if both drivers were indeed males. But if one was a woman or if you are not sure of the gender of both drivers, you may want to use *his or her* to make your statement completely accurate. Or you can revise and avoid the problem altogether:

> (*Revised*)   Neither driver survived the crash.

5. **Choose the proper case.**
   Except for possessives and plurals, nouns do not change form when used in different ways in a sentence. You can write "Ernie was watching the new kitten" or "The new kitten was watching Ernie" and neither noun (Ernie, kitten) changes. But pronouns do change with their function:

> *He* watched the kitten.
> The kitten watched *him*.

In the first sentence the subjective form (he) is used because the pronoun acts as the subject. In the second sentence the pronoun is the direct object of *watched,* so the objective form (him) is used. (The objective form is used for any objects—of prepositions, indirect objects, and direct objects.) The forms vary according to the *case* of the pronoun; in English there are three cases of pronouns:

Subjective	*Objective*	*Possessive*
I	me	mine
he	him	his
she	her	hers
you	your	yours
it	it	its

Subjective	*Objective*	*Possessive*
we	us	ours
they	them	theirs
who	whom	whose
whoever	whomever	whosever

You probably select the correct case for most of the pronouns you use, but you may need to keep the following warnings in mind:

A. Do not confuse the possessive *its* with the contraction *it's*.

If you look at the list of case forms above, you will notice that possessive pronouns do *not* include an apostrophe. This information may confuse you because the possessives of nouns and indefinite words *do* contain an apostrophe:

my mother's jewels
the students' books
everyone's appetite

Remember that *it's* is a contraction of *it is* and that *its* is a possessive like *his*, *her*, and *ours*.

B. Be careful of pronouns in compound subjects and objects:

(*Faulty*)	Nanouchka and *me* went to the movies.
(*Preferred*)	Nanouchka and *I* went to the movies.
(*Faulty*)	Shelly went with Nan and *I*.
(*Preferred*)	Shelly went with Nan and *me*.

If you are uncertain about which pronoun to use, drop the first part of the compound and see how the pronoun sounds alone:

I went? or *me* went?
with *I*? or with *me*?

You will recognize at once that "me went" and "with I" are not standard constructions.

C. Watch out for pronouns used with appositives. The pronoun should be in the same case as the word it is in apposition with:

(*Faulty*)	*Us* video game addicts are slaves to our hobby.
(*Preferred*)	*We* video game addicts are slaves to our hobby.
(*Faulty*)	Video games are serious business to *we* addicts.
(*Preferred*)	Video games are serious business to *us* addicts.

Again, you can test this construction by dropping the noun and letting the sound guide you: "us are slaves" and "to we" should sound unacceptable to you.

D. Take care with pronouns in comparisons:

(*Faulty*)	Ernie is a lot stronger than *me*.
(*Preferred*)	Ernie is a lot stronger than *I*.

This comparison is not complete. There is an implied (or understood) verb after *than:* "stronger than I am." If you complete such comparative constructions in your mind, you will be able to choose the appropriate case for the pronoun.

E. Choose carefully between *who* and *whom:*

My ex-roommate was a con artist *whom* we all trusted too much. (Preferred)

Although informal usage would allow you to use *who* in this sentence, the objective case form (*whom*) is preferred in some writing because the pronoun is the direct object in the clause it introduces: "we all trusted *him* too much." You can get around the choice between *who* and *whom* in this instance by using *that:*

My ex-roommate was a con artist *that* we all trusted too much. (Acceptable)

Some people will still insist that you use *whom* in this sentence, even though the use of *that* is now considered standard. But you should not substitute *which* for *who* or *whom,* because standard usage does not permit *which* to refer to people:

(*Preferred*)   the taxidermist *whom* I often dated
(*Acceptable*)   the taxidermist *that* I often dated
(*Faulty*)   the taxidermist *which* I often dated

EXERCISE

Rewrite the following sentences to avoid vague pronoun reference.

1. The policeman yelled at Walter Mitty. This irritated him very much.
2. A good dramatist always respects the intelligence of his audience.
3. A perfectly clear story can be made obscure by a literary critic. They use abstract words and vague terms.
4. You should reread the story and underline key words, which will help you analyze it better.
5. An optimist and a pessimist will always be able to find examples of poetry to support their point of view.

Correcting Shifts in Person

1. **Decide before you begin writing whether to use first, second, or third person, and then be consistent.**

   A. *Formal usage requires third person:*

   The reader senses foreboding in Poe's opening lines.
   One senses forboding in Poe's opening lines.

or first person plural:

We sense foreboding in Poe's opening lines.

B. *Informal usage allows first person singular:*

I find his characters too one-dimensional.

and many readers accept second person (*as long as* you *means* you, the reader):

If you examine his plots, you discover that the success of his tales lies elsewhere.

C. *Do not switch person carelessly once you have begun:*

(*Wrong*)   The *reader* feels the tension mount as *you* wait for the beast to spring.
(*Right*)   *We* feel the tension mount as *we* wait for the beast to spring.

EXERCISE

We have added shifts in person to this paragraph (which was originally written correctly by one of our students). Edit the passage to correct the unwarranted shifts in person.

In Willa Cather's short story, "Neighbor Rosicky," we see a comparison between the debilitating life of the city and the harsh life of the country. Yet you notice a difference in the quality of these lifestyles. Through Rosicky, Cather shows us the stagnant, draining effects of urban life, which serve to enhance the birth-death-rebirth theme of the story. Rosicky, one can easily observe, is a gentle, loving, and tender person. Through the trials of city living and country living, he has, you know, gained knowledge about the meaning of true happiness. We see him, in his gentle, unobtrusive manner, try to share his enlightenment with those around him. If one observes closely, you notice that even a minor character, Dr. Ed, is affected by Rosicky's example. By examining this relationship, we see Cather put forth a plea for tasting the simple pleasures your life has to offer. Education, wealth, and career cannot guarantee you happiness. Cather wants us to realize that the enjoyment of one's life makes living worthwhile.

Correcting Shifts in Tense

1. **Stay in the same tense unless you have cause to change.**

   A. *Sometimes you need to switch tenses because you are discussing events that happened* (or will happen) *at different times* (past, present, or future), *like this:*

(*Right*)   Although I *saw* the Split Banana in concert last week, I *am going* to hear them again tonight when they *perform* in Chicago.

B. *Do not change tense, though, without a reason:*

(*Wrong*)   The group *appears* on stage, obviously drunk; the drummer *dropped* his sticks, the lead singer *trips* over the microphone cord, and the bass player *had* his back to the audience during the entire show.

C. *When writing about literature, use the historical present tense even when discussing authors long dead:*

(*Right*)   Hawthorne, in the opening scene of *The Scarlet Letter*, creates a somber setting relieved only by the flowers on a single rosebush.

Or you may write in the past tense:

(*Right*)   Hawthorne, in the opening scene of *The Scarlet Letter*, created a somber setting.

But do not switch carelessly back and forth:

(*Wrong*)   Hawthorne *creates* a somber setting into which Hester *stepped* with Pearl in her arms.

EXERCISE

Make the tense consistent wherever appropriate in the following sentences.

1. Dudley Randall's shocking images included "a stub, a stump, a butt, a scab, a knob" as he describes the possible victim of mercy killing.

2. When Dickinson writes, "To ache is human—not polite," she made a statement about the nature of politeness as well as humanity.

3. The relationship between the ideal lovers in Donne's poem is illuminated by a comparison between the two legs of a compass, whose interdependence was emphasized.

4. In "Design," Frost pondered the possible meanings of a chance meeting of a spider, a flower, and a moth and makes the apparent coincidence seem ominous.

5. The first line of Donald Hall's poem sets up the paradox the persona expressed: he finds his own mortality brought home to him by his new baby, an "instrument of immortality."

Finding Modifier Mistakes

A modifier is a word, phrase, or clause that describes, limits, or qualifies something else in the sentence. Be sure that every modifier has only one thing to refer to and that the relationship is clear.

1. **Avoid dangling modifiers.**
   An introductory adjective phrase that does not modify the subject of the sentence is called a *dangling modifier:*

   (*Dangling*) Wheezing and shivering from the cold, the warm fire slowly revived Orville.
   (*Improved*) Wheezing and shivering from the cold, Orville slowly revived in front of the warm fire.

   Sometimes you need to add a subject, making the phrase into a clause:

   (*Dangling*) While asleep in class, the instructor called on Jocasta to recite.
   (*Improved*) While Jocasta was asleep in class, the instructor called on her to recite.

2. **Avoid misplaced modifiers.**
   Do not allow modifiers to stray too far from the thing they modify or you may produce confusing (and sometimes unintentionally amusing) sentences:

   (*Misplaced*) I can jog to the grocery store; then we can have lox and bagels for breakfast in just three minutes.
   (*Improved*) In just three minutes I can jog to the grocery store; then we can have lox and bagels for breakfast.

   (*Dangling*) Seymour was caught taking a nap in the restroom where he works.
   (*Improved*) While supposedly working, Seymour was caught taking a nap in the restroom.

3. **Avoid squinting modifiers.**
   Be sure your modifiers have only one possible word to modify, or you may puzzle your readers:

   (*Squinting*) Arvilla suspects privately Agnes reads Harlequin romances.
   (*Improved*) Arvilla privately suspects that Agnes reads Harlequin romances.
   (*Improved*) Arvilla suspects that Agnes privately reads Harlequin romances.

EXERCISE

In the following sentences, move any misplaced modifier so that the statements make better sense. You may have to rewrite the sentences that have dangling or squinting modifiers.

1. Antigone's faith without doubt sustained her in her struggle with Creon.
2. After attempting to kill his father, Haimon's sword becomes the instrument of his own death.
3. Ismene feels in her heart Antigone is right.
4. Creon has no illusions about the stupidity of the populace, thinking the edict is good enough for them.
5. Antigone wants to bury her brother Polyneices in the opening scene.
6. Championing unwritten universal laws, the burial of Polyneices turns Antigone into an enemy of the state in Creon's eyes.

Coping with Irregular Verbs

Some verbs are irregular; their principal parts must be memorized. Here is a list of the most common ones:

Present	*Past*	*Past participle*
begin	began	begun
break	broke	broken
burst	burst	burst (not busted)
choose	chose	chosen
come	came	come
do	did	done
drag	dragged	dragged (not drug)
drink	drank	drunk
forget	forgot	forgotten (or forgot)
get	got	got (or gotten)
lay	laid	laid (meaning "placed")
lead	led	led
lie	lay	lain (meaning "reclined")
ride	rode	ridden
rise	rose	risen
run	ran	run
see	saw	seen
swim	swam	swum
take	took	taken
wake	waked (or woke)	waked (or woke)

If you find yourself wondering whether someone's heart was *broke* or *broken*, whether the sun has *rose* or *risen*, your dictionary can clear up your difficulty. Each dictionary has a guide to itself in the front, explaining how to use it and how the entries are arranged. You need to look up *inflected forms* and *principal parts of verbs* in this guide. Those sections will tell you how your dictionary lists irregular verb forms. Usually, the past and past participle are given in boldface type within the entry for the present tense verb.

EXERCISE

Fill in the proper forms of the verbs in the following sentences.

1. None of the characters in *The Glass Menagerie* seems to be living lives they have [choose] themselves.
2. Amanda had [begin] to worry about Laura's becoming an old maid.
3. Tom was [wake] from a sound sleep by the resounding "Rise and shine!" of Amanda's voice.
4. Laura had [lay] the glass unicorn on a small table.
5. Once when Tom had [drink] too much, he lost his apartment keys.

Setting Verbs Right

Even regular verbs sometimes cause trouble for two reasons.

1. The third person *singular* adds an -s (or -es), whereas with nouns, the plural adds an -s or -es:

(*Plural nouns*)	two aardvarks, ten kisses
(*Singular verbs*)	cream rises, a horse gallops, a goose hisses

2. The regular -ed ending that forms the past tense often is not heard in speech:

   talked deliberately
   used to go
   supposed to come
   locked the gate

Solving Punctuation Problems

The most direct approach to punctuating your writing involves two questions:

1. What kinds of word groups are concerned?
2. What pieces of punctuation are standard and appropriate for this situation?

To answer question one, you need to remember the terms *phrase, dependent clause,* and *independent clause.* See charts A, B, and C on pages 962–63 for a refresher. Using these terms, you can probably identify any group of words you are trying to punctuate and classify it into one of the four writing situations we describe in the following section. Under each situation, we list guidelines for deciding what punctuation to use.

1. **Punctuation between two independent clauses:**
   A *period,* usually:

   > I enjoy a strong plot in a novel. Allen cares about style more than plot.

   A *comma,* only if the two independent clauses are connected by *and, or, for, but, nor, yet,* and *so:*

   > I enjoy a strong plot in a novel, so I liked *The Skull Beneath the Skin.*

   A *semicolon,* to show a close relationship in meaning between the two:

   > I enjoy a strong plot in a novel; however, Allen cares more about style.

   A *colon,* if the second independent clause restates or exemplifies the first:

   > I enjoy a strong plot in a novel: I read *The Skull Beneath the Skin* in just three days.

2. **Punctuation between a phrase or dependent clause and an independent clause:**
   A *comma,* if the phrase or dependent clause comes first and is long or transitional:

   > When we were discussing epidemics this morning, Helen provided some new information. In fact, she had researched the subject recently. As a result, her knowledge was up-to-date.

   No punctuation, usually, if the independent clause comes first:

   > Helen described recent research when we were discussing epidemics this morning.

   A *comma,* if the independent clause comes first and is followed by a transitional phrase or a tacked-on thought:

   > She had researched the subject recently, in fact. She told us what she had found out, at least the main points.

3. **Punctuation in an independent clause interrupted by a phrase or dependent clause:**
No punctuation if the interrupter (italicized in the example) limits the meaning of the word before it:

> Students *who are living alone for the first time* make several mistakes. Mistakes *that make them feel foolish* include accidentally dyeing all their underwear blue. Mistakes *that are more serious* include not budgeting their time and money.

Commas on both ends of the interrupter (italicized) if it simply adds information or detail about the word before it:

> Students, *who usually lead hectic lives,* must learn to budget their time and money. A night of cramming, *no matter how thorough,* cannot substitute for seven weeks of steady studying. And snacks at fast food restaurants, *which seem cheap,* can be expensive if they are a nightly habit.

Parentheses to play down the interrupter:

> Sue went to the concert with Pam (her friend from Denver) to hear the all-female rock 'n' roll band.

Dashes to emphasize the interrupter:

> The music—though some might call it noise—made Sue and Pam get up and dance.

4. **Punctuation in a list or series of words, phrases, or clauses:**
A *comma* between all parallel items:

> Pam planned to trim Sue's hair, do some paperwork, make dinner for seven, and take her granddaughter shopping all in the same day.

A *semicolon* to separate each of the items when one of them already has a comma in it:

> To me, the ideal novel has a strong plot; is intelligent, touching, and funny; and involves characters I would like to know personally.

A *colon* after an independent clause followed by a list:

> I usually read three kinds of fiction for pleasure: detective stories, feminist science fiction, and long nineteenth-century novels.

Using Apostrophes

1. **Use an apostrophe to indicate the possessive form of nouns.**
   A. Use an apostrophe followed by *s* to form the possessive of a singular noun or a plural noun not ending in *s:*

a child's toy
the boss's tie
the children's toys
Tom's parents

B. Use an apostrophe without *s* to form the possessive of a plural noun that ends in *s*:

the boys' locker room
my parents' house

C. Use an apostrophe with *s* or use the apostrophe alone to form the possessive of proper nouns ending in *s*:

James's hat or James' hat
the Jones's car or the Jones' car

D. Use an apostrophe with *s* to indicate the possessive of indefinite pronouns:

everybody's business
someone's book

E. Do NOT use an apostrophe for possessive pronouns:

his   its   yours   whose
hers   ours   theirs

2. **Use an apostrophe to indicate that some letters or figures have been omitted in contractions:**

isn't   o'clock   it's   I'll
the best film of '68   class of '82

3. **An apostrophe is optional in forming the plural of letters, figures, and words referred to as words:**

Your 2's look like 7's. *or* Your 2s look like 7s.
You use too many *and*'s in your sentences. *or* You use too many *and*s.
Dot your *i*'s and cross your *t*'s.

Punctuating Quoted Material

1. **Put quotation marks around words that you copy from any source.**

A. Quoted complete sentence using a comma:

As Joan Didion points out, "Almost everything can trigger an attack of migraine: stress, allergy, fatigue, an abrupt change in barometric pressure, a contretemps over a parking ticket."

B. Quoted complete sentence introduced by *that* (without a comma):

Didion asserts that "Migraine is something more than the fancy of a neurotic imagination."

C. Quoted partial sentence that readers can clearly tell is a partial sentence:

Didion explains that migraines stem from various causes, even so minor a trauma as "a contretemps over a parking ticket."

Didion is clearly irritated by people who attribute migraine to "the fancy of a neurotic imagination."

D. Quoted partial sentence in which readers *cannot* tell something has been omitted; use ellipsis dots (three spaced periods) to show the omission:

According to Didion, "Once the attack is under way. . . , no drug touches it."
[Original sentence: "Once the attack is under way, however, no drug touches it."]

Didion complains that ". . . nothing so tends to prolong an attack as the accusing eye of someone who has never had a headache."
[Original sentence: "My husband also has migraine, which is unfortunate for him but fortunate for me: perhaps nothing so tends to prolong an attack as the accusing eye of someone who has never had a headache."]

Didion attests that "All of us who have migraine suffer not only from the attacks themselves but from this common conviction that we are perversely refusing to cure ourselves by taking a couple of aspirin. . . ."
[Original sentence: "All of us who have migraine suffer not only from the attacks themselves but from this common conviction that we are perversely refusing to cure ourselves by taking a couple of aspirin, that we are making ourselves sick, that we 'bring it on ourselves.' "]

Note: When the omission occurs at the end of the sentence, use *four* dots, not three. The fourth dot is the period.

2. **When you quote material already containing quotation marks, use single quotation marks or indent the passage.**

A. If quoted material within quotation marks is short, enclose within single quotation marks, using the apostrophe on your typewriter:

Didion observes, "There certainly is what doctors call a 'migraine personality,' and that personality tends to be ambitious, inward, intolerant of error, rather rigidly organized, perfectionist."

B. If quoting extensive conversation, set off the entire passage
by indenting ten spaces and single spacing the quotation:

Howell's attitude toward the sentimental novel is made clear when
the dinner conversation turns to discussion of a current bestseller,
Tears, Idle Tears:

"Ah, that's the secret of its success," said Bromfield Corey.
"It flatters the reader by painting the characters collosal, but
with his limp and stoop, so that he feels himself of their
supernatural proportions. You've read it, Nanny?"
"Yes," said his daughter. "It ought to have been called *Slop,
Silly Slop.*"

This same scorn for sentimentality is reflected in the subplot involving
Lapham's daughters.

C. If quoted conversation is *brief*, use single quotation marks
within double ones:

We soon realize that the characters are hopelessly lost: " 'It's a funny
thing,' said Rabbit ten minutes later, 'how everything looks the same
in a mist. Have you noticed it, Pooh?' "

3. **When quoting poetry, be sure to reproduce capitalization and
punctuation exactly within each line, but adjust punctuation
at the end of your quotation to suit your sentence.**

A. If quoting only a couple of lines, use a slash mark to indicate
the end of each line (except the last):

Blake reminds us of the traditional repression of sexuality by the
church when he observes, "And the gates of this chapel were shut,/
And 'thou shalt not' writ over the door."

B. If quoting several lines of poetry, indent and single-space
without quotation marks:

Blake's persona emphasizes the sexual restrictions imposed by
Christian doctrine as he looks at the ruined Garden of Love:

And I saw it was filled with graves,
And tombstones where flowers should be,
And priests in black gowns were walking their rounds,
And binding with briars my joys & desires.

C. Use ellipsis marks to show omissions when quoting poetry,
just as you would if quoting prose:

When Blake's persona revisits the Garden of Love, he sees "priests
in black gowns . . . walking their rounds" instead of the lush, sensual
flowers he remembers.

4. **Put periods and commas inside quotation marks, except when citing a page or line number in parentheses at the end of a quotation:**

> Kurt Vonnegut advises that "Simplicity of language is not only reputable, but perhaps even sacred."

> "Simplicity of language," advises Kurt Vonnegut, "is not only reputable, but perhaps even sacred."

> As Kurt Vonnegut advises, "Simplicity of language is not only reputable, but perhaps even sacred" (113).

> Iago, in soliloquy, reveals his devious intentions toward Othello early in the play: "Though I do hate him as I do hell-pains,/ Yet, for necessity of present life,/ I must show out a flag and sign of love,/ Which is indeed but sign" (I.i.152–55).

5. **Put question marks and exclamation marks inside the quotation marks if they belong with the quotation; put these marks *outside* if they punctuate the whole sentence:**

> Is this an exact quotation from Twain, "Truth is more of a stranger than fiction"?

> E. M. Forster asks, "How do I know what I think until I see what I say?"

6. **Put colons, semicolons, and dashes outside the quotation marks:**

> Avoid aphorisms like these in stating the theme of a work: "Appearances can be deceiving"; "Do unto others . . ."; "The love of money is the root of all evil."

7. **Put quotation marks (or underline to indicate italics) around words used as words:**

> The term "sentimentality" carries a negative meaning when applied to literature.

8. **Put quotation marks around the titles of works that are short:** essays and articles in magazines, short stories and poems, chapters in books:

> "A Hanging " (essay by George Orwell)
> "Rope" (short story by Katherine Anne Porter)
> "Living in Sin" (poem by Adrienne Rich)
> "Paper Pills" (chapter title in Sherwood Anderson's *Winesburg, Ohio*)

9 **Underline the titles of works that are long:** books, movies, plays, long poems, names of magazines and newspapers:

> *Adventures of Huckleberry Finn*
> *Casablanca*

Death of a Salesman
Paradise Lost
Sports Illustrated
The Detroit *Free Press*

Note: Do not underline or put in quotation marks the title of your own essay.

10. **Put square brackets around words or letters that you add to clarify a quotation or change the verb tense:**

Iago early declares his ill feelings: "Though I do hate [Othello] as I do hell-pains,/ Yet, for necessity of present life,/ I must show out a flag and sign of love. . . ."

The crowd is hushed; then "Mr. Graves open[s] the slip of paper and there [is] a general sigh through the crowd . . . ," as his proves to be blank.

Catching Careless Mistakes

These are errors that you make, even though you know better, because you are paying more attention to your thoughts than to the mechanical act of getting them down properly. In the rough drafts, careless mistakes are no real problem, but in a finished paper, they are an extreme embarrassment. Some of the most common ones are these:

1. **Skipping a word or letter**
   As you race along on an inspired part, your thoughts run ahead of your hand, and you may write sentences like

   Without knowing it, Emilia been an aid to an evil plot.

   leaving the auxiliary verb *has* out before the *been*. Or you could end up with

   Five of the main characters die violently befor the end of the play.

2. **Repeating a word**
   Most people have pens or typewriters that stutter sometimes, producing sentences like

   The characters who survive are are dramatically altered.

   Short words like *the* and *of* seem to invite careless repetition more than long ones do.

3. **Creative capitalization**
   Out of habit or due to the idiosyncracies of your handwriting, you sometimes capitalize or fail to capitalize on impulse rather than by the rules. For example, one student wrote,

Last thursday I took my Final Exam in History.

Though the capitalization surely reflects what the student considers important in the sentence, it should be altered to conform to standard capitalization. These rules are listed in the front of your collegiate dictionary.

4. **Typographical errors**
   In a final draft, there's no such thing as *"just* a typing error." Most readers are irritated, some even offended, by negligent proofreading. Correct typographical errors neatly in ink.

Glossary of Literary and Rhetorical Terms

Allegory A literary work in which characters, events, and often settings combine to convey another complete level of meaning.

Alliteration Repetition of the same consonant sounds, usually at the beginning of words:
> "Should the glee—glaze—
> In Death's—stiff—stare—"
> (Emily Dickinson)

Allusion An indirect reference to some character or event in literature, history, or mythology that enriches the meaning of the passage:
> In Eliot's poem "The Love Song of J. Alfred Prufrock," the persona says, "No! I am not Prince Hamlet, nor was meant to be," suggesting that he lacks Hamlet's nobility.

Ambiguity Something that may be validly interpreted in more than one way; double meaning.

Antagonist The character (or a force such as war or poverty) in a drama, poem, or work of fiction whose actions oppose those of the protagonist (hero or heroine).

Anticlimax A trivial event following immediately after significant events.

Apostrophe A poetic figure of speech in which a personification is addressed:
> "You sea! I resign myself to you also—I guess what you mean."
> (Walt Whitman)

Archetype A recurring character-type, plot, symbol, or theme of universal significance: the blind prophet figure, the journey to the underworld, the sea as source of life, the initiation theme.

Assonance The repetition of similar vowel sounds within syllables:
> "On desperate seas long wont to roam"
> (Edgar Allan Poe)

Atmosphere *See* Mood.

Audience In composition, the readers for whom a piece of writing is intended.

Ballad A narrative poem in four-line stanzas, rhyming *xaxa,* often sung or recited as a folk tale.

Blank Verse Unrhymed iambic pentameter, the line that most closely resembles speech in English:
> "When I see birches bend to left and right
> Across the lines of straighter darker trees,
> I like to think some boy's been swinging them."
>   (Robert Frost)

Carpe Diem Literally, seize the day, a phrase applicable to many lyric poems advocating lustful living:
> "Gather ye rosebuds while ye may,
> Old time is still a-flying:
> And this same flower that smiles today
> Tomorrow will be dying."
>   (Robert Herrick)

Catharsis In classical tragedy, the purging of pity and fear experienced by the audience at the end of the play; a "there but for the grace of the gods go I" sense of relief.

Central Point of View *See* Point of View.

Chorus In Greek drama, a group (often led by an individual) who comment on or interprets the action of the play.

Climax The point toward which the action of a plot builds as the conflicts become increasingly intense or complex; the turning point.

Coherence In good writing, the orderly, logical relationship among the many parts—the smooth moving forward of ideas through clearly related sentences. *Also see* Unity.

Comedy A play, light in tone, designed to amuse and entertain, that usually ends happily, often with a marriage.

Comedy of Manners A risqué play satirizing the conventions of courtship and marriage.

Complication The rising action of a plot during which the conflicts build toward the climax.

Conceit A highly imaginative, often startling, figure of speech drawing an analogy between two unlike things in an ingenious way:
> "In this sad state, God's tender bowels run
> Out streams of grace. . . ."
>   (Edward Taylor)

Concrete That which can be touched, seen, or tasted; not abstract. Concrete illustrations make abstractions easier to understand.

Conflict The struggle between opposing characters or forces that causes tension or suspense in the plot.

Connotation The associations that attach themselves to many words, deeply affecting their literal meanings (i.e., *haze, smog*).

Consonance Close repetition of the same consonant sounds preceded by different vowel sounds (*slip, slap, slop*). At the end of lines of poetry, this pattern produces half-rhyme.

Controlling Idea *See* Thesis.

Controlling Image In a short story, novel, play, or poem, an image that recurs and carries such symbolic significance that it embodies the theme of the work, as the wallpaper does in Gilman's "The Yellow Wall–Paper," as the thunderstorm does in Chopin's "The Storm," as the General's pistols do in Ibsen's *Hedda Gabler*, as the grass does in Whitman's "Leaves of Grass."

Convention An accepted improbability in a literary work, such as the dramatic aside, in which an actor turns from the stage and addresses the audience.

Couplet Two rhymed lines of poetry:
"For thy sweet love remembered such wealth brings
Then I scorn to change my state with kings."
(William Shakespeare)

Crisis *See* Plot.

Denotation The literal meaning of a word.

Denouement Literally, the "untying"; the resolution of the conflicts following the climax (or crisis) of a plot.

Diction Choice of words in writing or speaking.

Double Entendre A double meaning, one of which usually carries sexual suggestions, as in the country-western song about a truck driver who calls his wife long distance to say he is bringing his "big ol' engine" home to her.

Dramatic Monologue A poem consisting of a self-revealing speech delivered by one person to a silent listener; for instance, Robert Browning's "My Last Duchess."

Dramatic Irony *See* Irony.

Dramatic Point of View *See* Point of View.

Elegy A poem commemorating someone's death.

Empathy Literally, "feeling in"; the emotional identification that a reader or an audience feels with a character.

English Sonnet *See* Sonnet.

Epigram A short, witty saying that often conveys a bit of wisdom:
"Heaven for climate; hell for society."
(Mark Twain)

Epigraph A quotation at the beginning of a poem, novel, play, or essay that suggests the theme of the work.

Epilogue The concluding section of a literary work, usually a play, in which loose threads are tied together or a moral is drawn.

Epiphany A moment of insight for a character, in which the light of truth suddenly dawns.

Episode In a narrative, a unified sequence of events; in Greek drama, the action between choruses.

Exposition That part of a plot devoted to supplying background information, explaining events that happened before the current action.

Extended Metaphor *See* Metaphor.

Fable A story, usually using symbolic characters and settings, designed to teach a lesson.

Falling Action In classical dramatic structure, the part of a play after the climax, in which the consequences of the conflict are revealed. *Also see* Denouement.

Figurative Language Words that carry suggestive or symbolic meaning beyond the literal level.

First Person Point of View *See* Point of View.

Flashback Part of a narrative that interrupts the chronological flow by relating events from the past.

Flat Character In contrast to a well-developed round character, a flat one is stereotyped or shallow, not seeming as complex as real people.

Foil A character, usually a minor one, who emphasizes the qualities of another one through implied comparison and contrast between the two.

Foreshadowing Early clues about what will happen later in a narrative or play.

Formal Writing The highest level of usage, in which no contractions, fragments, or slang are used.

Free Verse Poetry that does not have regular rhythm, rhyme, or standard form.

Free Writing Writing without regard to coherence or correctness, intended to relax the writer and produce ideas for further writing.

Genre A classification of literature: drama, novel, short story, poem.

Hero/Heroine The character intended to engage most fully the audience's or reader's sympathies and admiration. *Also see* Protagonist.

Hubris Unmitigated pride, often the cause of the hero's downfall in Greek tragedy.

Hyperbole A purposeful exaggeration.

Image/Imagery Passages or words that appeal to the senses.

Informal Writing The familiar, everyday level of usage, which includes contractions and perhaps slang but precludes nonstandard grammar and punctuation.

Internal Rhyme The occurrence of similar sounds within the lines of a poem rather than just at the ends of lines.

Invention The process of generating subjects, topics, details, and plans for writing.

Irony Incongruity between expectation and actuality.
> *Verbal irony* involves a discrepancy between the words spoken and the intended meaning, as in sarcasm.
> *Dramatic irony* involves the difference between what a character believes true and what the better-informed reader or audience knows to be true.
> *Situational irony* involves the contrast between characters' hopes and fears and their eventual fate.

Italian Sonnet *See* Sonnet.

Jargon The specialized words and expressions belonging to certain professions, sports, hobbies, or social groups. Sometimes any tangled and incomprehensible prose is called jargon.

Juxtaposition The simultaneous presentation of two conflicting images or ideas, designed to make a point of the contrast: for example, an elaborate and well-kept church surrounded by squalorous slums.

Limited Omniscient Point of View *See* Point of View.

Lyric A poem that primarily expresses emotion.

Metaphor A figure of speech that makes an imaginative comparison between two literally unlike things:
> Lothario is a crumb.

Metaphysical Poetry A style of poetry (usually associated with seventeenth century poet John Donne) that boasts intellectual, complex, and even strained images (called *conceits*) which frequently link the personal and familiar to the cosmic and mysterious. *Also see* Conceit.

Meter *See* Rhythm.

Mood The emotional content of a scene or setting, usually described in terms of feeling: somber, gloomy, joyful, expectant. *Also see* Tone.

Motif A pattern of identical or similar images recurring throughout a passage or entire work.

Myth A traditional story involving deities and heroes, usually expressing and inculcating the established values of a culture.

Narrative A story line in prose or verse.

Narrator The person who tells the story to the audience or reader. *Also see* Unreliable Narrator.

Objective Point of View *See* Point of View.

Ode A long, serious lyric focusing on a stated theme: "Ode to the West Wind," "Ode on Melancholy."

Omniscient Point of View *See* Point of View.

Onomatopoeia A word that sounds like what it names: whoosh, clang, babble.

Oxymoron A single phrase that juxtaposes opposite terms:
the lonely crowd, a roaring silence.

Parable A story designed to demonstrate a principle or lesson using symbolic characters, details, and plot lines.

Paradox An apparently contradictory statement that nonetheless makes sense:
"Time held me green and dying"
(Dylan Thomas, "Fern Hill")

Paraphrase A restatement in different words, usually briefer than the original version.

Parody An imitation of a piece of writing, copying some features such as diction, style, and form, but changing or exaggerating other features for humorous effect.

Peripheral Point of View *See* Point of View.

Persona The person created by the writer to be the speaker of the poem or story. The persona is not usually identical to the writer: for example, a personally optimistic writer could create a cynical persona to narrate a story.

Personification Giving human qualities to nonhuman things:
"Rain come down, give this dirty town a drink of water."
(Dire Straits)

Plagiarism Carelessly or deliberately presenting the words or ideas of another writer as your own.

Plot A series of causally related events or episodes that occur in a narrative or play. *Also see* Climax, Complication, Conflict, Denouement, Falling Action, Resolution, and Rising Action.

Point of View The angle or perspective from which a story is reported and interpreted. An *omniscient* or *shifting* point of view, which may include the author's comments on the action, presents the story through a combination of characters, shifting from one person's thoughts to another's. An *objective* or *dramatic* point of view presents the story directly, as a play does, using only external actions, speech, and gestures. A *central* point of view tells the story through the voice of a central character and is often presented as a first-person account. A *peripheral* point of view uses a minor character to tell the story. Both central and peripheral points of view are considered *limited omniscient* because they give only one character's perceptions. *Also see* Narrator *and* Tone.

Prewriting The process that writers use to gather ideas, consider audience, determine purpose, develop a thesis and tentative structure (plan), and generally prepare for the actual writing stage.

Protagonist The main character in drama or fiction, sometimes called the hero or heroine.

Pun A verbal joke based on the similarity of sound between words that have different meanings:
"They went and *told* the sexton and the sexton *tolled* the bell."
(Thomas Hood)

Quatrain A four-line stanza of poetry, with any number of rhyme schemes.

Resolution The conclusion of the conflict in a fictional or dramatic plot. *Also see* Denouement *and* Falling Action.

Rhyme Similar or identical sounds between words, usually the end sounds in lines of verse (brain/strain; liquor/quicker).

Rhythm The recurrence of stressed and unstressed syllables in a regular pattern; also called *meter*.

Rising Action The complication and development of the conflict leading to the climax in a plot.

Round Character A literary character with sufficient complexity to be convincing, true to life.

Sarcasm A form of *verbal irony* that presents caustic and bitter disapproval in the guise of praise. *Also see* Irony.

Satire Literary expression that uses humor and wit to attack and expose human folly and weakness. *Also see* Parody.

Sentimentality The attempt to produce an emotional response that exceeds the circumstances and to draw from the readers unthinking feeling instead of intellectual judgment.

Setting The time and place in which a story, play, or novel occurs. *Also see* Mood.

Shakespearean Sonnet *See* Sonnet.

Simile A verbal comparison in which a similarity is expressed directly, using *like* or *as* ("houses leaning together like conspirators."—James Joyce). *Also see* Metaphor.

Situational Irony *See* Irony.

Soliloquy A speech in which a dramatic character reveals what is going through her mind by talking aloud to herself. *Also see* Dramatic Monologue.

Sonnet A poem of fourteen ten-syllable lines, arranged in a pattern of rhyme schemes. The *English* or *Shakespearean* sonnet uses seven rhymes that divide the poem into three quatrains and a couplet: abab, cdcd, efef, gg. The *Italian* sonnet usually divides into an octave (eight lines) and a sestet (six lines) by using only five rhymes: abba, abba, cdecde. (The rhyme scheme of the sestet varies widely from sonnet to sonnet.)

Speaker The voice or person presenting a poem.

Standard English The language that is written and spoken by most educated persons.

Stereotype An oversimplified, commonly held image or opinion about a person, a race, an issue.

Stilted Language Words and expressions that are too formal for the writing situation; unnatural, artificial language.

Structure The general plan, framework, or form of a piece of writing.

Style Individuality of expression, achieved in writing through the selection and arrangement of words and punctuation.

Symbol Something that suggests or stands for an idea, quality, or concept larger than itself; the lion is a symbol of courage; a voyage or journey can symbolize life; water suggests spirituality; dryness the lack thereof.

Synesthesia Figurative language in which one sense impression is described in terms of another:

"hot pink" or "blue uncertain stumbling buzz"

Syntax Sentence structure; the relationship between words and among word groups in sentences.

Theme The central or dominating idea conveyed by a literary work.

Thesis The main point or position that a writer develops and supports in a composition.

Tone The attitude a writer conveys toward his or her subject and audience. In poetry this attitude is sometimes called *voice*.

Tragedy A serious drama that relates the events in the life of a protagonist, or *tragic hero*, whose error in judgment, dictated by a *tragic flaw*, results in the hero's downfall and culminates in catastrophe. In less classical terms, any serious drama, novel, or short story which ends with the death or defeat of the main character may be called tragic.

Type character A literary character who embodies a number of traits that are common to a particular group or class of people (a rebellious daughter, a stern father, a jealous lover).

Understatement A form of ironic expression that intentionally minimizes the importance of an idea or fact.

Unity The fitting together or agreement of all elements in a piece of writing. *Also See* coherence.

Unreliable Narrator A viewpoint character who presents a biased or erroneous report that may mislead or distort a reader's judgments about other characters and actions; sometimes the unreliable narrator may be self-deceived.

Usage The actual or expressed way in which a language is used.

Verbal Irony *See* Irony.

Verisimilitude The appearance of truth or actuality in a literary work.

Versification The mechanics of poetic composition, including such elements as rhyme, rhythm, meter, and stanza form.

Index of Authors, Titles, and First Lines of Poems

NOTE: Names of authors are in capitals; first lines of poems are in roman type; all titles are italicized except titles of poems listed under authors' names.

Subject Index